CONVERSATIONS

Readings for Writing

JACK SELZER

The Pennsylvania State University

Longman

New York • San Francisco • Boston
London • Toronto • Sydney • Tokyo • Singapore • Madrid
Mexico City • Munich • Paris • Cape Town • Hong Kong • Montreal

Senior Vice President and Editor-in-Chief: Joseph Opiela
Vice President and Publisher: Eben W. Ludlow
Senior Marketing Manager: Ann Stypuloski
Senior Supplements Editor: Donna Campion
Media Supplements Editor: Nancy Garcia
Production Manager: Douglas Bell
Project Coordination, Text Design, and Electronic Page Makeup:
    The Clarinda Company, Inc.
Cover Design Manager: John Callahan
Cover Designer: Maria Ilardi
Cover Photo: Copyright © Jim Arbogast/Getty Images/PhotoDisc
Photo Researcher: Photosearch, Inc.
Manufacturing Buyer: Al Dorsey
Printer and Binder: R.R. Donnelley & Sons Company,
    Crawfordsville
Cover Printer: Coral Graphic Services, Inc.

For permission to use copyrighted material, grateful
acknowledgment is made to the copyright holders on pp. 930–938,
which are hereby made part of this copyright page.

Library of Congress Cataloging-in-Publication Data

Conversations : readings for writing / [compiled by] Jack Selzer.—
    5th ed. p. cm.
  Includes bibliographical references and index.
  ISBN 0-321-10323-8 (pbk.)
    1. College readers. 2. Report writing—Problems, exercises, etc.
3. English language—Rhetoric—Problems, exercises, etc. I. Selzer,
Jack.
PE1417.C6545 2003
808'.0427—dc21   2002067142

Please visit our website at http://www.ablongman.com/selzer

ISBN 0-321-10323-8

3 4 5 6 7 8 9 10—DOC—05 04 03

For Molly and Maggie:
Still Their Book

"If a physician of high standing, and one's own husband, assures friends and relatives that there is really nothing the matter with one but temporary nervous depression—a slight hysterical tendency—what is one to do?" A feminist and social reformer answers the question, and in the process shows how writing can be an instrument of personal—and public—health.

A student reflects on the difficulties of not using Standard English: "we all carry the contact zone within us."

Mary had a little lamb, its fleece as white as snow. "What happened to all the cute Black lambs?"

An English teacher recalls the frustration and confusion she felt at being caught between two worlds, two languages—it's a story of language use for survival.

"[One day I hope to find] a place where my American ghost and Chinese spirit can live coexist in harmony. One day I will succeed. One day . . . I will know who I am."

Contents

"I wasn't an enemy, in fact or in feeling. I was an ally. If I had known, then, how to tell them so, would they have believed me?"

One of our best-known writers offers her fictional account of an encounter with the men's movement.

AFFIRMATIVE ACTION

An African American college professor details the "Faustian bargain" that is affirmative action.

An expert on education and ethnicity argues the affirmative.

A long-time critic of affirmative action answers Nathan Glazer: "ETS is proposing to send the worst possible message to these kids: If you start out in life with less, we expect less of you—today, tomorrow, maybe forever."

"How, then, can we develop a model of selection that expresses a more inclusive, transparent, and accountable vision of democratic opportunity—an approach to selection that will benefit everyone, and advance racial and gender justice?"

An ironic commentary on "the trouble with you gay people. . . ."

Not only are antipornography feminists harming
the cause of women's rights by promoting a puritanical approach to sexual issues, contends an
ACLU leader, but proposals for censorship are offering aid and comfort to the political right wing.

An international student finds Calvin Klein ads
not to be pornographic.

Stars and the handlers debate together the merits
of Napster: Would an unfettered Napster be death
to artistic creativity?

What does the Dewey Decimal system have to do
with Napster, for crying out loud?

"If people [are] free to copy, print, and exchange
books, instead of buying them, pretty soon authors and publishers would have to find other
lines of work." Right?

"The time has come to straighten out copyright
law," not to straighten out Napster.

Contents

RHETORICAL CONTENTS

Description and Narration

PROCESS

ILLUSTRATION, EXAMPLE

ANALYSIS

CAUSE AND EFFECT

DEFINITION

ARGUMENT: CATEGORICAL PROPOSITION ("X IS IN FACT Y")

ARGUMENT: EVALUATION

ARGUMENT: REFUTATION

IRONY AND SATIRE

WRITING FROM SOURCES

Imagine that you enter a parlor. You come late. When you arrive, others have long preceded you, and they are engaged in a heated discussion, a discussion too heated for them to pause and tell you exactly what it is about. In fact, the discussion had already begun long before any of them got there, so that no one present is qualified to retrace for you all the steps that had gone before. You listen for a while, until you decide that you have caught the tenor of the argument; then you put in your oar. Someone answers; you answer him; another comes to your defense; another aligns himself against you, to either the embarrassment or gratification of your opponent, depending upon the quality of your ally's assistance.

This well-known passage from Kenneth Burke's *Philosophy of Literary Form* explains the basic metaphor and the orientation of this anthology of readings for first-year college composition courses. *Conversations* contains conversations: public discourse on contemporary issues that is calculated to engage students' interests, to encourage and empower their own contributions to contemporary civic discussions, and to represent a broad cross section of the kinds of conversational styles and genres that are available to writers today.

What's Different about *Conversations*?

Conversations encourages student writing on important current civic issues. The premise of this reader is that writing is less a private act of making personal meaning out of thin air than it is a public and social act of making meaning within a specific rhetorical situation—a specific situation that guides and shapes the meaning-making activity. To put the matter more simply, writing emerges from other writing, other discourse. Though nearly every anthology claims to encourage student responses, those anthologies just as often actually intimidate students because they present only one or two authoritative voices on a given issue and because those voices are given little context outside the anthology; the student reads an essay by Orwell or Baldwin or Woolf or some other eloquent writer and says to himself or herself, "Gee, that sure seems right to me. How could I disagree with such an expert?" By contrast, instead of one or two authoritative items on an issue or topic, this reader contains "conversations" on public issues or topics, conversations-with-contexts that will seem less intimidating and therefore invite student responses.

In fact, the book will encourage students to adopt a social and rhetorical model—a "conversation model"—for their own writing. Instead of seeing writing merely as private or as point-counterpoint debate, students should sense from *Conversations* that "people are talking about this issue—and I'd like to get in on the talk somewhere." The conversation metaphor does not mean that students should "write like they talk" (since conversational informality is not always appropriate in public discourse); rather, the metaphor simply implies that students should see writing as a response to other writing or to other forms of discourse, a response that students make after considering the implications and importance of what they have read and heard. Students should be encouraged to cooperate as well as to compete with other writers, to address subissues as well as the main chance, to seek consensus and new syntheses as often as victory.

Thus, *Conversations* is organized around focused, topical, contemporary public issues (e.g., censorship, what to do about public education, affirmative action, legalization of drugs, abortion, gun control), each within seven larger thematic groupings (education, language, race and gender, family matters, civil liberties and civil rights, crime and punishment, and science and society) that lend additional historical and conceptual perspective to those contemporary issues. *Intertextuality* would be the buzzword from contemporary critical theory: The book includes items that "talk to each other" both directly and indirectly. Some pieces speak directly and explicitly to each other (as in the case of the four-way discussion of single parenthood, or Milton Friedman's exchange with William Bennett about the legalization of drugs, or the e-mail discussion of Ebonics). Some pieces refer only indirectly to others, as in the sections on education, gun control, and affirmative action. And still other items comment on selections in other sections of *Conversations:* for example, selections on education comment on those on language and race; the section on pornography is informed by the sections on gender and the causes of crime; the items on gay, lesbian, and bisexual rights are related to the section on AIDS and same-sex marriage. And so forth. There is certainly no reason why the selections in this anthology cannot be read individually as they are in other books, without reference to other selections, especially since the headnotes orient readers to each item. And there is certainly no reason why the selections could not be read in some other order than the order in which they are presented here. Nevertheless, *Conversations* does give students a particular incentive to write because it establishes contexts for writing.

The conversation model should make the book suitable to a range of writing courses. There is plenty of expository prose here: comparisons of all kinds; a careful analysis of the language of men and women by Deborah Tannen; overviews of the cloning issue and the meanings of "wilderness"; cool descriptions of schools and school choice, men and women, the Internet, single parenthood, and a hanging; expositions of the reasons why Napster should be disassembed and why Malcolm X opposed Martin Luther King Jr.; etc.—lots of et cetera. The "modes of exposition" are illustrated by numerous selections, as the rhetorical table of contents makes clear. But *Conversations* will also accommodate courses with an argumentative edge, for this book includes a fair proportion of explicitly or implicitly argumentative writing and tends to encourage a broadly argumentative approach to all discourse. In short, the conversation metaphor implies an inclusive approach to prose, one that subsumes and includes exposition as well as argument, dialogue as well as dialectic. *Conversations* includes not only Jonathan Kozol's prescriptions for the high school classroom, but a debate over school vouchers as well; not only partisan arguments for and against gun control, but also a careful analysis of the issue by Leonard Kriegel; and not only passionate pro and con arguments on capital punishment, abortion, cloning, and same-sex marriage, but also dispassionate analyses of language issues, race and gender, the Internet, the environment—and more.

Consequently—and this is another notable feature of *Conversations*—this anthology includes a very broad range of genres and tries to represent as fully as possible the full spectrum of the "universe of discourse." True, essays are prominent in *Conversations*—familiar and formal essays, academic as well as nonacademic ones—because the essay is a common and important genre and because the form has important correspondences with other genres (e.g., the letter, the sermon, the report, the news story). But essays are not so prominent here as to exclude other genres. Students will find other ways of engaging in public discourse as well: through fiction, poetry, drama, letters of various kinds, Internet postings, public oratory, posters, congressional hearings and reports, cartoons, advertisements, and journals. The occasions for public discourse are many and various. Students and their teachers will find news stories and memoirs, literary narratives and studies of cultural artifacts, parodies and satires, letters to the editor and counter-responses, laws and proposed laws.

And they will hear a range of voices as well. *Conversations* assumes that students are ready, willing, and able to engage in civic, public discourse, but that does not preclude the possibility for personal inventiveness. Indeed, *Conversations* is committed to the proposition that there are many possible rhetorical stances, that there is no one "correct" way to address a reader. This anthology therefore exposes students to as many rhetorical choices as possible—from the studied erudition of John Searle to the semiformal, "objective" voice associated with the academy; from the conversational informality of E. B. White, Frederick Douglas, and Deborah Tannen to satiric invective by Keith Gilyard, Mike Royko, David Horsey, and Lewis Grizzard; from the thrilling oratory of Sojourner Truth to the careful reasoning of Iris Young; from *Rolling Stone, Ms., Mother Jones,* and *The Village Voice* to *Esquire, The New Yorker,* and *The American Scholar;* from Andrew Sullivan and Charlotte Perkins Gilman to George Orwell, bell hooks, Richard Rodriguez, and Andrea Dworkin. Students will encounter mainstream texts and dissenting views, conventional rhetorical maneuvers and startlingly inventive ones. They will hear from famous professional writers and anonymous but eloquent fellow citizens; from public figures and fellow students (a dozen or so contributions by students are included); from women and men, gays and heterosexuals; from majority and minority voices. *Conversations* gives students a better chance to find their own voices because they've experienced a full range of possible voices in their reading.

"A rhetorician," says Kenneth Burke in his essay "Rhetoric—Old and New," "is like one voice in a dialogue. Put several such voices together, with each voicing its own special assertion, let them act upon one another in co-operative competition, and you get a dialectic that, properly developed, can lead to views transcending the limitations of each." Fostering that "co-operative competition" is the aim of *Conversations*.

Editorial Apparatus

Substantial editorial assistance has been provided to the users of *Conversations*. The book's introduction orients students to social motives for writing and domesticates for them the metaphor of conversation. It also introduces students to the notion of critical or rhetorical reading, so that they might have a practical means of approaching every item in *Conversations*—and so that they might better understand how careful reading habits can reinforce effective writing habits. In addition, a headnote is provided for each selection so that students can orient themselves to the rhetoric of each piece. The headnotes provide background on the author (especially when prior knowledge about the author affects one's response to an item), on the topic of the selection (when the matter requires any explanation), and on the specific occasion for the piece (especially on when and where it was originally published). The assumption of most anthologies is that the original context of an essay or story—or whatever—doesn't matter much, or that the anthology itself comprises the context. *Conversations* assumes instead that careful reading must take into account the original circumstances that prompted a given piece of writing. Writing, after all, most often emerges from other writing, so situating each item by means of the headnotes is essential to the concept of *Conversations*. Finally, each of the seven major parts of the book includes an introductory overview of the particular issues under discussion in that part. In sum, the editorial apparatus ensures that the selections in *Conversations* can be used in any order that a teacher or student might wish.

Otherwise, the text of *Conversations* assumes that students are already quite capable readers. On the grounds that students and teachers can handle things on their own and can appropriate readings to their own ends, the book includes no questions after selections, no suggestions for writing assignments or class discussions, no exercises, and limited footnotes. Space that might have been devoted to those matters is given instead to additional selections so that teachers might have as many selections as possible from which to choose.

Instructor's Manual

Teachers who do want additional background on unfamiliar readings or specific suggestions for making the most of *Conversations* will find plenty of help in the detailed Instructor's Manual I compiled with Dominic Delli Carpini of York College of Pennsylvania. The manual contains further information on writers, overviews of the parts and discussions of each selection, some suggestions for further reading, and ideas for discussion and writing. It also offers pointers for teaching each "conversation"—for how particular selections can be used with other selections. Together, the editorial apparatus and the Instructor's Manual are designed to help *Conversations* engage the intelligence and passion of students and teachers, without getting in the way of either.

Companion Website

The Companion Website by Dominic Delli Carpini of York College of Pennsylvania (http://www.ablongman.com/selzer) offers a wealth of resources for both students and instructors. Students can access detailed chapter summaries, prewriting exercises and essay activities related to material in the text, Web explorations, and annotated Web links for further study. Instructors will find a sample syllabus, useful Web links, and the Instructor's Manual available for download.

Acknowledgments

There may be only one name cited on the cover of *Conversations*, but this book too is the product of conversation—many conversations, in fact—with a number of people who collaborated in one way or another on its development and production. My greatest debt is to those who assisted me in finding appropriate selections. Christine Caver, Lester Faigley, Bob Burkholder, Steven Tumino, Dana Anderson, Vincent Lankewish, Dominic Delli Carpini, and Linda Selzer deserve special mention for this edition. Several reviewers of previous editions of the book made excellent suggestions, as did the reviewers of this edition: Jon Burton, North Virginia Community College; Josh Emmons, University of Iowa; Cara Finnegan, University of Illinois; Carrie Leverenz, Texas Christian University; John Prince, Ball State University; and Marcus Slease, Western Washington University. Other colleagues across the country and at Penn State have stimulated my thinking on a daily basis. Sheila Varela worked diligently to secure permissions, and Todd Post, Anneliese Watt, Chris Malone, Andy Alexander, Dana Anderson, and Keith Waddle did research for some of the headnotes.

Thanks too to those on the production end of things. Dana Anderson helped me out of a thousand small scrapes. Another thousand that I don't even know about were taken care of by Cindy Miller and her colleagues at The Clarinda Company. Eben Ludlow has been an ideal editor: full of excellent suggestions, encouraging without ever being overbearing, supportive at every turn. His confidence in this project brought it into being and has sustained it now for over a decade.

Jack Selzer

INTRODUCTION

Why Write?

Why do people write?

For many reasons, of course. Sometimes the impulse to write derives from a personal need. The motive to write can come from within. Everyone needs to sort out feelings at one time or another or to make some personal sense of the world and its parts, and a good way to do such sorting is by writing. If you keep a diary or journal, or if you've shared your most intimate feelings through correspondence with a trusted friend, or if you've written essays—or notes toward an essay—in order to explore possible explanations for things, then you know what it means to write for personal reasons. (A root meaning of the word *essay* is "to try out, to experiment.") People do need a means of expressing powerful feelings and personal insights, and writing seems to provide just the tranquility required for a gathering of thoughts.

Other times the world itself motivates a writer. We seem to have a need to note our observations about the world, especially if those observations are indeed noteworthy—if they seem special or unique in some way. Sometimes this process of "taking note" is relatively formalized, as when a scientist records observations in a log of some kind or when the president at the end of a day records significant details for future reference or when you keep score at a baseball game or when a reporter transcribes "just the facts" into a news article. But just as often it is something less formal—when you take notes for a course, for instance, or when I write something in my journal about the life and times of my two children. The drive "to hold the mirror up to nature," as Hamlet called it, to record our understanding about the way of the world, accounts for much of the prose we encounter and produce each day.

The motive to write can also derive from one's vocation. In other words, some people write because it's their life's work. They are professional writers—poets, news reporters, novelists, technical writers, screenwriters. And they are semiprofessional writers, people who don't think of themselves as writers but who indeed spend a large amount of their time writing—police officers, engineers, college professors, lawyers, physicians, corporate managers, teachers, and so forth. (You'd be surprised at how much time such people spend on the writing required by their jobs.) Professional writers and professionals who write sometimes put words onto paper for the reasons named in the previous paragraphs—to express personal feelings or ideas, or to record their impressions or interpretations of their workaday worlds. But they also often think in terms of a particular kind of writing—a genre—when they compose: Newspaper employees think of themselves as writing news stories or editorials; poets set out to write poems; engineers or police officers think of the reports they have to turn in; lawyers have to produce those legal briefs next week. Their sense of completing a particular genre can sometimes take precedence over other motives.

Of course all these motives to write are legitimate, and seldom do these motives exist in a pure state. It is probably better to think of motives to write, instead of *a* motive, and to think of primary and secondary motives, instead of a single, all-consuming aim. When John Milton wrote *Paradise Lost,* for instance, he was certainly out to record his assessment of the nature of things and to express his most personal thoughts—and to write an epic. When Henry David Thoreau wrote *Walden,* he certainly had personal motives— the book originated in his daily journals—but he wanted "to hold the mirror up to nature" as well. (The very title of *Walden* suggests that Thoreau was attempting to record his close observations of nature.)

But *Walden* and *Paradise Lost* are "public" documents, too—attempts to sway public opinion and public behavior. Thoreau advertised *Walden,* after all, as his attempt to "brag as lustily as Chanticleer [the rooster] in the morning, if only to wake my neighbor up." He wanted to awaken his fellow citizens to nature and to persuade them to renew their own lives after his own example and experience. Milton's stated purpose—"to justify the ways of God to man"—was just as social. He wanted to change how people conceive of their relation to God and to detail his vision of the heroic life to be lived by every wayfaring Christian. Writing to persuade, to have an effect on the thinking of others, does not preclude writing to discover or writing to record or writing in a particular genre. Indeed, writing to persuade nearly always means writing *about something* in a *particular genre* for reasons that are *intensely personal.* But writing to persuade does mean writing something that has designs on the hearts or minds (or both) of particular readers. It is writing that is calculated to have an effect on a real reader. This goes for John Milton and Anna Quindlen, and it goes for you, too.

For though a writer may work in private, a writer is never really alone. A writer out "to wake people up" or "to justify the ways of God" to men and women is obviously anything but working privately, for the writer out to persuade is inherently social. But every other kind of writing is social as well. The engineer who writes a report on a project is out to influence the project's managers. A physician's report on a patient is used by other caregivers in the short run and long run to direct medical attention in a specific way. The lawyer's brief is meant to sway judges. The movie reviewer's account is designed to direct people to (or away from) the film. Even private writing is often quite public in fact. The letters in which you pour out your feelings get read by sympathetic and responsive friends. The essays you write to discover your version of the truth become written attempts to convert readers to that version. Even journal entries that no one but you will read are shaped to an extent by what society considers to be noteworthy and by what a different "you" will want to read a few years from now; and the very words you choose to use reflect a vocabulary you share with others and learn from others. Writing is a social act. It is a primary means for touching others, and reading what others have written is a primary way of being touched in turn. The words you read and write are surrounded and shaped by the words and attitudes and beliefs of the many people who share your society, your "social context." People may write to express themselves, or to complete a particular kind of writing, or to say something about their world—or some combination of these—but in some sense they do so in order to have an effect on someone else.

In fact, usually writing emerges quite specifically in response to other writing. When you write, your reasons for writing are nearly always related to the people around you and what they have said or written themselves. A friend expects a letter or an email; a supervisor at work has asked for a report; a professor assigns a paper; a job is advertised that requires a written application; a story or an editorial is printed in a local paper or national magazine that arouses your ire; an encouraging teacher or a moving story inspires you to write a journal entry or your own story. That is why this book is titled *Conversations*. It assumes that your writing emerges from other writing or from other speech, and that other writing is likely to follow in response to your own. You want to stay in touch, answer a friend's questions, ask your own questions, and maybe gossip or otherwise entertain along the way, so you return a friend's letter; you expect a response in a week or two. You've listened to a controversy or witnessed some expression of confusion in one of your classes, so you write a paper to straighten things out; you anticipate an argument, a counterresponse (or assent and praise), in turn. You want the person who takes your job to have an easier time than you did, so you rewrite the directions on how to do it; you figure the next person will make further revisions next year. Your cousin asks you how you like your school, so you write to encourage her to join you there next year; you end by asking her to let you know if she needs more information. Writing is engaging in a kind of conversation. To get in on it, you have to know what others have said about the matter at hand, and you must be able to anticipate possible responses.

This collection of readings comprises "public conversations"—conversations on public issues that concern American society (in general and within your local community) as we contemplate a new century. Not every burning issue is represented here, of course; that would be impossible. But this book does include conversations—give-and-take discussions—on many matters that concern you and your community today. What do you want to get out of your years in college? What kind of experience should your college or university be providing? What changes ought to be made to improve U.S. secondary schools? Should English be our official or semiofficial national language? What does it (or should it) mean to be a woman or a man these days? Is affirmative action legitimate? Should we be doing something to strengthen the American family? Should pornography and Napster be banned or regulated? Should certain books be kept out of the curriculum? Should abortion remain legal? Should the ownership of handguns be restricted? What are the causes and cures of crime? Is capital punishment ever justified? Should drugs be legalized? Should wilderness areas be protected? How should we fight AIDS? And so forth. This book assumes that you'll want to get in on some of those conversations, that you'll want to contribute to resolving some of those questions either nationally or within your own community.

For while there is plenty of discussion of these matters in the national media, there is plenty of local discussion as well. What you read here about the reform of secondary education or the control of the curriculum probably frames in many ways discussions of particular school matters in your local community. What you read here about race or censorship probably is relevant to what is happening someplace on your own campus. What you read here about gender issues will be relevant to your campus (do many women major in science or engineering at your school?), your community (does your town have adequate child-care facilities?), your job (how are women treated where you work?), even your own family (are family chores apportioned in stereotypical ways?). Sometimes you will want to be involved in a debate over The Larger Issue—for instance, should pornography be banned? Other times you'll want to take up more local concerns or subissues: Should X-rated films be shown on your campus? Does pornography demean women—or men? Is a particular item really pornographic? How might pornography be defined? Democracy can be seen as a sometimes messy but always spirited exchange of ideas on how we should conduct ourselves as a society and as individual communities. The readings here are designed to introduce you to public conversations going on in our democracy, and to encourage you to contribute in some way to those conversations yourself. Even if these particular issues do not always engage you personally, they should provide you with models of how to engage in public discussions when an issue does concern you.

There are plenty of ways to make such contributions. The contents to follow will introduce you to many different genres, many different kinds of writing. Essays are most prominent because the essay is a common genre and because the essay (or article) has important analogs with other forms, like the letter, the sermon, the report, or the editorial. But you will see other ways of engaging in public discourse as well—through fiction, poetry, speeches, plays, interviews, e-mail exchanges, cartoons, and advertisements, for instance. There are news stories and memoirs, reports and literacy narratives, personal letters and letters to the editor and counterresponses, parodies and satires, explanations and analyses and outright arguments. As you think about what to contribute to discussions going on around you, you'll need to think about how to contribute, too—in what form, in what manner.

Indeed, there are as many ways of addressing issues as reasons for doing so. Do you want to be formal, less formal, or downright intimate with your reader? Do you want to present yourself as something of an expert on the matter in question, or as someone on the same level as your readers? Do you want to speak dispassionately, or do you want to let your feelings show? Do you want to be explicit in stating your purpose, or less direct? Do you want to compose sentences that are careful and complex and qualified, or ones that are direct and emphatic? You'll see a broad range of tactics illustrated in the following pages, a broad range that will represent the possible ways of engaging in public discourse. You'll encounter mainstream, classic items—and dissenting views. You'll see conventional presentations and startlingly inventive ones. You'll see how famous professional writers earned their fame, and you'll hear from anonymous but just-as-eloquent fellow citizens and fellow students. You'll hear from women as well as men, from majority as well as minority voices. The idea is to give you a better chance of finding your voice in a given circumstance by exposing you to a full range of possible voices in your reading. The idea is to empower you to engage in civic discourse—now, today—on the issues that concern you and your community.

How to Read This Book—And an Example

As the previous section explains, an answer to the question "Why write?" ultimately depends on several factors: on the writer's personal needs and motives, on the state of the world or issues within our world, on a genre or form of writing that a writer may be drawn or compelled toward, and on a reader or a community of readers that the writer wants to influence. Many times all those factors, in combination, are involved in the decision to write.

All those factors, in combination, are also involved in decisions on *how* to write. Effective writers consider what they want to accomplish (aim), on what subject or issue, in what genre, for which particular readers. A writer's decisions on those matters compose what rhetoricians call a writer's "rhetorical stance"—what *you* decide to say to *someone* on a given *issue* in a particular *genre*. But the matter might be put more simply: Your decisions about how to write at a given time are colored by the *occasion* for that writing and your attitude toward that occasion. A football coach will prepare his team for a game by considering the opponent's strengths and weaknesses (audience), by thinking about his own aims (to win, of course, but also perhaps "to establish our running game" or "to get some experience for our younger players"), by assessing his own team's strengths, and so forth. Writers devise their own game plans as well, based on aim, issue, genre, and audience.

But what does all of that have to do with reading—with reading in general and reading this book in particular? When you read this book, try to distinguish between two kinds of reading that in practice usually go on together whenever you engage yourself with a particular document.

In the first kind of reading, think of yourself as part of each writer's intended audience—as someone who the writer actually hoped would read and respond to his or her message. In other words, in this first kind of reading, read as you normally read the things that are directed to you every day: as you would read a newspaper or an article in your favorite magazine or a personal letter from a friend. Read as if the writer has written just for you, and react accordingly. In most cases this will be quite easy to do, for most of the items in *Conversations* (e.g., the articles on abortion by Sallie Tisdale and Mike Royko, the exchange on pornography between John Irving and Andrea Dworkin) are directed to the public—people like you—and were written quite recently in magazines and newspapers that you read yourself. In some other cases you will feel more remote from an article because it was written some time ago (e.g., John Muir's letter about damming a river in Yosemite National Park or Martin Luther King Jr.'s "Letter from Birmingham Jail") or because it is not on a topic that has interested you, but even then you can behave as a member of the writer's intended audience and react to the selection as if the piece were written directly to you.

In the second kind of reading—let's call it "critical reading" or "rhetorical reading"—you read a document not as the intended reader but as a student of it, as someone studying it to understand and appreciate its tactics. Since you are probably reading this book as part of a writing course, as a critical reader encountering the selections in *Conversations* you should remember your role as student and try to use the readings to advance your sophistication as a writer and an analyst of writing. Although you normally read as a writer's intended audience, when you read critically you try to get some distance on the experience; it's almost as if you are eavesdropping on what someone is saying to someone else, with the purpose of understanding better how—and how well—it is said. When you read critically you not only react to the message, but you also appreciate *how* the writer is conveying that message to his or her intended audience, whether that intended audience includes you or not. For example, as a critical reader you try to consider how Sallie Tisdale's content, arrangement, and style advance her aims, or how Martin Luther King Jr. and Malcolm X adapted their presentations to the particular situations in which they found themselves. Again, let me emphasize that normally in the act of reading you read critically as well as for content, and the two activities aren't really separable. But for the sake of your progress in writing, here in this introduction to *Conversations* it is important to emphasize critical reading.

Critical readers—readers committed to understanding how prose works—must attend to the same matters that writers attend to: shaping an idea to an audience in a particular form for a specific purpose. When you read each item in this book, therefore, read with those matters in mind. Read the headnotes carefully, for the headnotes are designed to orient you to the original situation in which the writers found themselves: You'll hear about the writer's audience in the headnote, you'll learn more about the writer (especially when the writer is well-known enough that prior reputation affects the reading experience), and you'll learn anything else necessary to orient you to the original occasion of each selection. That way, you'll be in a position to read critically. When you do, consider the issue of course; consider what the writer has to offer on a given subject. But also consider the writer's purpose, the limitations (or opportunities) that a given genre exerts, and the way the item is adapted by the writer to specific readers' knowledge, attitudes, and needs. Consider how those matters affect *what* is said (what rhetoricians call "invention"—the art of discovering what information and arguments will affect readers), in what *order* it is said (or arrangement), and *how* it is said (style and tone). Reading, like writing, is a social and rhetorical activity. It involves not simply passively decoding a message but actively understanding the designs the message has for the reader and how it is calculated to achieve its effects.

Let me offer an extended example of critical reading. The first item in this book is E. B. White's short essay, "Education." What is its purpose? (If you haven't read "Education" yet, take five minutes to do so now; that way, you can more easily follow the rest of this introduction.) White wrote this brief essay over half a century ago, but you probably find it to be interesting still, in part at least because it concerns a perennial question in our nation: What should our schools be like? Is education better carried out in large, fully equipped, but relatively impersonal settings, or in smaller but intensely personal, teacher-dominated schools? Which should count for more: the efficiencies of an educational system that is "progressive" (the word comes from paragraph two), or the personal traits of the individual classroom teacher? The essay is a personal one, in that it is the education of his son that White is "worried about"; yet it is a public matter, too. After all, as the headnote indicates, White published it in *Harper's*, a magazine with a readership wide and influential and well educated.

What is White's position on the issue? At first it might seem that the author takes no side, that he simply wants to describe objectively the two alternatives and to record his son's experiences in each circumstance. He gives equal time to each school, he spends the same amount of space on concrete details about each, and he seems in firm control of his personal biases ("I have always rather favored public schools"). Through his light and comic tone White implies that all will be well for his son—and our children—in either circumstance, that the two schools each are to be neither favored nor feared by us. "All one can say is that the situation is different" (paragraph four), not better, in the two places.

Or is it? Many readers—myself among them—contend that "Education" is less an objective, neutral appraisal than it is a calculated argument that subtly favors the country school. To such readers, White's objective pose is only that—a created pose, an attempt to create a genial, sympathetic, and trustworthy speaker. By caring so obviously for his son (final paragraph), by confessing his biases, and by treating both schools with distance and detachment and reliable detail, White creates what rhetoricians call "ethos"— that quality of a piece of writing that persuades through the character of the speaker or writer. By poking gentle humor at just about everything—his son "the scholar"; his wife the prim graduate of Miss Winsor's private schools; himself "the victim of a young ceramist"; and, of course, both schools—White makes himself seem enormously sympathetic and trustworthy: fair-minded and unflappable, balanced and detached.

But is this reliable speaker arguing or describing? Those who see the essay as an argument for the ways of the country school can point to the emotional aspects of the essay—to its pathos, in other words. The image of the one-room schoolhouse, for instance, is imprinted in positive terms on the U.S. psyche, and White exploits that image for his argumentative purposes. The "scholar" walks miles through the snow to get his education; like the schoolhouse itself, he has the self-reliance and weather- resistance to care for himself and to fit into a class with children both younger and older; and he learns a practical curriculum—there is "no time at all for the esoteric"—"just as fast and as hard as he can." It is all Abraham Lincoln, *Little House on the Prairie,* and Ben Franklin arriving in Philadelphia, isn't it? And the teacher who presides over the country school appeals to the reader's emotions as only The Ideal Mother can. This teacher-mother is not only "a guardian of their health, their clothes, their habits . . . and their snowball engagements," but "she has been doing this sort of Augean task for twenty years, and is both kind and wise. She cooks for the children on the stove that heats the room, and she can cool their passions or warm their soup with equal competence."

No such individual Ideal Mother presides over the city school. Instead, that school is presided over by a staff of Educational Professionals—a bus driver, half a dozen anonymous teachers, a nurse, an athletic instructor, dietitians. The school itself is institutional, regimented, professionalized. There the scholar is "worked on," "supervised," "pulled." Like the one-room schoolhouse, the regimented institution is ingrained in the national psyche. But in this case the emotional appeal is negative, for "The System" is something that Americans instinctively resist. True, the city school is no prison, and true, the scholar in this school learns "to read with a gratifying discernment." But the accomplishments remain rather abstract. Faced with such an education, such a school, no wonder the students literally become ill. At least that is the implication of the end of paragraph three, where the account of the city school is concluded with an account of the networks of professional physicians that discuss diseases that never seem to appear in the country schools.

For these reasons many readers see "Education" as an argument against the city school (and its "progressive" education) and an endorsement of the country one (and its "basics"). They see the essay as a comparison with an aim like most comparison essays: to show a preference. The evaluative aim is carried out by reference to specific criteria, namely that schools are better if they are less structured and if they make students want to attend (because motivated students learn better); a structured, supervised curriculum and facilities are inferior to a personalized, unstructured environment that makes students love school. Days at the country school pass "just like lightning"; to attend the country school the boy is willing literally to walk through snowdrifts, while to get to the city school he must be escorted to the bus stop—or be "pulled" there. The country school is full of "surprises" and "individual instruction," while the city school is full of supervision; there are no surprises in the "progressive" school. In a real sense, therefore, White persuades not only by the force of his personality or through emotional appeals but also through hard evidence, what rhetoricians call "logos." "Education" amounts to an argument by example wherein the single case—the boy scholar—stands for many such cases. This case study persuades like other case studies: by being presented as representative. White creates through his unnamed son, who is described as typical in every way, a representative example that stands for the education of Everychild. The particular details provided in the essay become not mere "concrete description" but hard evidence, summoned to support White's implicit thesis. The logic of the piece seems to go something like this: "Country schools are a bit superior to city ones. They make up for what they lack in facilities with a more personal, less authoritarian atmosphere that children respond to."

E. B. White, then, wins his reader's assent by means of ethos, pathos, and logos. But the country-school approach is also reinforced by the essay's arrangement. Notice, for example, that the essay begins and ends with favorable accounts of the country school. In other words, the emphatic first and final positions of the essay are reserved for the virtues of country schools, while the account of the city school is buried in the unemphatic middle of the essay. The article could easily have begun with the second paragraph (wouldn't sentence two of paragraph two have made a successful opener?), but such a strategy would have promoted the value of the city school. By choosing to add the loving vignette of the Ideal Teacher in his opening paragraph, White disposes his readers to favor country schools from the very start. Notice too that the comparison of the two schools in the body of "Education" proceeds from city to country. Again, it didn't have to be so; White could have discussed the country school first, or he could have gone back and forth from city to country more often (adopting what some handbooks call an "alternating" method of comparison as opposed to the "divided" pattern that White actually did use). By choosing to deal first with the city school, all in one lump, and then to present the country school in another lump, White furthered his persuasive aim. After all, most "preference comparisons" move from the inferior item to the superior one. In other words, writers of comparisons usually move from "this one is good" to "but this other one is even better," rather than vice versa. So when White opts to deal first with the city schools, he subtly reinforces his persuasive end through very indirect means. White's arrangement serves his purpose in two ways, then: it permits him to end with the item he wishes to prefer; and it permits him to add an introductory paragraph that places his country school in that favorable spot as well.

Even the arrangement of details within White's individual paragraphs serves his goals. It appears that the central paragraphs (three, four, and five) are arranged chronologically, that details in those paragraphs are arranged according to the rhythm of the school day. But a closer examination shows that paragraph three closes on a note of sickness. That detail could have come earlier in the paragraph, but White places the negative detail in the emphatic final position. Similarly, the two paragraphs on the country school are manipulated for rhetorical ends. Why does White divide the account of the country school into two paragraphs? (After all, he dealt with the city school in one paragraph.) By doing so he is able to give special emphasis to the first sentence of one of his paragraphs, "There is no supervised play," highlighting thereby a key difference between the two schools. (It is also possible that publication in *Harper's* called for shorter paragraphs.)

A critical reading of "Education" must also consider expression, those sentence and word choices that are sometimes equated with the style of a particular essay or author.

Like most rhetoricians, I personally resist the idea that "style is the person"—that style is something inherent in a writer, that it amounts to a sort of genetic code or set of fingerprints that are idiosyncratic to each person, that it is possible to speak generically of Anna Quindlen's style or Martin Luther King's style or E. B. White's style. It has always seemed to me more appropriate to think of style as characteristic of a particular *occasion* for writing, as something that is as appropriate to reader and subject and genre as it is to a particular author. Words and sentences are chosen in response to rhetorical and social circumstances, and those words and sentences change as the occasion changes. If it is possible to characterize E. B. White's style or Hemingway's style in general (and I'm not sure even of that), then it is so only with respect to certain kinds of writing that they did again and again and again. For when those writers found themselves writing outside *Harper's* or *The New Yorker* (in White's case) or outside fiction (in Hemingway's), they did indeed adopt different stylistic choices. It is probably wiser to focus not on the apparent idiosyncrasies associated with a Quindlen or a King or a Hemingway or an E. B. White, but on the particular word and sentence choices at work in a particular rhetorical situation.

Take the case at hand. What stylistic choices are worthy of note in "Education"? How has White chosen particular sentence patterns and words in order to further the aims of his essay?

The sentences of White's essay are certainly appropriate for public discourse. There are roughly a thousand words and fifty sentences in "Education," so average sentence length comes to about twenty words. Many are shorter than twenty words, though (the shortest is five words), and only one forty-three-word sentence seems particularly long. The result is that this essay can probably be readily comprehended by most adults, without its sentences creating the impression of superficiality or childishness. (The sentences in White's book for children *Charlotte's Web*, by contrast, have an average length of about twelve words.)

Moreover, White's sentences are unpretentious. They move in conventional ways—from subjects and verbs to objects and modifiers. There are no sentence inversions (violations of the normal subject/verb/ object order), few distracting interrupters (the parentheses and the "I suspect" in that one long sentence in paragraph two are exceptions), and few lengthy opening sentence modifiers that keep us too long from subjects and verbs. Not only that, the sentences are simple and unpretentious in another sense: White comparatively rarely uses subordinate (or modifying) clauses— clauses containing a subject and verb and beginning with *who* or *although* or *that* or *because* or the like. I count only two such modifying (or dependent) clauses in the first and third paragraphs, for instance, and just five in the second; if you don't think that is a low number, compare it to a six-hundred-word sample of your own prose. When White does add length to a sentence, he does it not by adding complex clauses that modify other clauses, but by adding independent clauses (ones that begin with *and* or *but*) and by adding phrases and modifiers in parallel series. Some examples? The children's teacher is a guardian "of their health, their clothes, their habits, their mothers, and their snowball engagements"; the boy "learned fast, kept well, and we were satisfied"; the bus "would sweep to a halt, open its mouth, suck the boy in, and spring away." And so forth. The *ands* make White's essay informal and conversational, never remote or scholarly or full of disclaimers and qualifiers.

White uses relatively simple sentence patterns in "Education," then, but his prose is still anything but simple. Some of his sentences are beautifully parallel: "she can cool their passions or warm their soup"; "she conceives their costumes, cleans up their noses, and shares their confidences"; "in a cinder court he played games supervised by an athletic instructor, and in a cafeteria he ate lunch worked out by a dietitian"; "when the snow is deep or the motor is dead"; "rose hips in fall, snowballs in winter." These precise, mirror-image parallel structures are known as isocolons to rhetoricians. White delights in them and in the artful informality they create. He uses parallel structures and relentless coordination—*and* after *and* after *and*—to make his prose accessible to a large audience of appreciative readers. And he uses those lists of specific items in parallel series to give his writing its remarkably concrete, remarkably vivid quality.

That brings us to White's word choices. They too contributed to White's purposes. Remember the sense of detachment and generosity in White's narrative voice, the ethos of involvement and detachment apparent in the speaker? In large measure that is the result of White's word choices. For instance, White has the ability to attach mock-heroic terminology to his descriptions so that he comes across as balanced and wise, as someone who doesn't take himself or his world too seriously. The boy is a "scholar" who "sallied forth" on a "journey" to school or to "make Indian weapons of a semi-deadly nature." The gentle hyperbole fits in well with the classical allusion inherent in the word "Augean" (one of Hercules' labors was to clean the Augean stables): there is a sophistication and worldly wisdom in the speaker's voice that qualifies him to speak on this subject. And remember the discussion of whether White's aim was purely descriptive or more argumentative in character? White's metaphors underscore his argumentative aim: the city school bus "was as punctual as death," a sort of macabre monster that "would sweep to a halt, open its mouth, suck the boy in, and spring away with an angry growl"; or it is "like a train picking up a bag of mail." At the country school, by contrast, the day passes "just like lightning." If the metaphors do not provide enough evidence of White's persuasive aim, consider the connotations of words—their emotional charges, that is—that are associated with the city school: *regimented, supervised, worked on, uniforms, fevers.* And then compare these with the connotation of some words White associates with the country school: *surprises, bungalow, weather-resistant, individual instruction, guardian,* and so forth. The diction and sentence choices made by White indeed do reinforce his argumentative purpose.

This analysis by no means exhausts the full measure of rhetorical sophistication that E. B. White brings to the composition of "Education." You may have noticed other tactics at work, or you may disagree with some of the generalizations presented here. But the purpose of this discussion is not to detail the rhetoric of White's "Education." It is merely to illustrate a method of critical reading that you might employ as you read the selections in this book and the public rhetoric that you encounter in your life each day. The point has been to encourage you to read not just for *what* is said—though this is crucial—but for *how* it is said as well. For reading is as "rhetorical" an activity as is writing. It depends on an appreciation of how writer, subject, and reader are all "negotiated" through a particular document.

If you read for "how" as well as "what," the distinction between the two may begin to shorten for you. Appreciation of the rhetoric of public discourse can make you more skeptical of the arguments presented to you and to other citizens. It can make you a reader less likely to be won over on slender grounds, more likely to remain the doubter than the easy victim or trusting soul who accepts all arguments at face value. Therefore, whether or not you decide to take part in any of the particular "conversations" captured in this book, your thinking can be stimulated by critical reading.

Not only that, you'll find yourself growing as a writer; if you read critically, you'll begin to adopt and adapt for your own purposes the best rhetorical maneuvers on display in this book and elsewhere. What is a particular writer's real aim? What evidence is used to win the assent of readers? How does a particular writer establish credibility? What kind of emotional and logical appeals are at work in a given circumstance? How does the arrangement of a presentation influence its reception? How can sentence style and word choices sustain a writer's aim? By asking and answering questions like these, you can gain confidence as reader and writer. By becoming better able to understand and appreciate the conversations going on around you, you'll learn to make more powerful and sophisticated contributions to the discussions that most engage you personally. Critical reading of the selections in this book can make you a better writer, a better citizen.

EDUCATION

Introduction

Americans have always been passionate about issues related to education. Why? For one thing, education issues affect every American in a personal way. True, there is a strong anti-intellectual strain in our national culture; but it is also true that Americans pursue with a passion the ideal of "education for all" both as a means of self-improvement and as the source of the enlightened citizenry required by democratic institutions. For another thing, education issues are decided locally and immediately. The relatively decentralized nature of our educational "system" (U.S. education is hardly as monolithic as the term "system" implies) encourages continuing and passionate public discussion among citizens interested in shaping the policies and practices of local schools. (About 93 percent of the money spent on primary and secondary education in the United States in 1998 came from state and local governments. Incidentally, Americans spend more per capita on education than all but three other Western nations.)

Portions of three current discussions related to education are included in this part of *Conversations*. The first—"What to Do about the Schools"—concerns proposals for improving public education, particularly secondary education. In the past decade, particularly in response to the economic crises of the early 1980s and early 1990s, a number of committees and commissions launched well-publicized reform efforts aimed at everything from teacher education and school governance to classroom climate and the curriculum—at everything from competency testing and conduct codes to the size of schools and the wisdom of "tracking." Presidents Bush and Clinton also promoted reform efforts that they believed would invigorate U.S. education. Those calls for reform can be seen in the selections included here. Should schools be large, centralized, efficient, and comprehensive? Or should they be smaller and more personal—have all the advantages of small size? Is discipline a major problem in the schools, and (if so) how can it be improved? Or does an overemphasis on discipline make schools confining and constricting—places that value order and conformity over independence and freedom of inquiry? What about the curriculum—should it emphasize mastery of bodies of knowledge, "what every educated person needs to know"? Or instead should it emphasize learning skills—

problem-solving ability, flexibility, independent thinking, and resourcefulness? Should the way schools are funded be reconsidered, to even out differences between the "haves" and the "have-nots"? Or would that undermine a cornerstone of our educational tradition, local control? Should schools be "privatized"? Should citizens have more choice over which schools to attend? Could citizens through some sort of voucher system be given more choices over which school to attend? Or would that tend to widen the gap in educational opportunities now available to rich and poor? Does the concept of "charter schools," one that in a handful of states permits private companies or groups of teachers and parents or nonprofit organizations to operate schools— hold promise? And finally, what about the teachers? Should they be given better pay and more responsibility for what goes on in the classroom? Or should we continue to honor top-down administrative mechanisms for ensuring competency and consistency and currency?

The second set of readings addresses the question, "What's College For?" No doubt on your own campus you have listened in on discussions of this topic in one form or another, and no doubt you have given your own educational goals considerable thought. In broad terms, the question can be posed this way: Is college an opportunity for personal growth and general intellectual development? Or is it a means to economic advancement? If college should foster both general education and professional specialization, then in what proportions should it do so? And through what means? Is college designed for the intellectual elite who are sophisticated enough to pursue truly advanced learning, or is it something that ought to be within the reach of most high school graduates? Does college offer a critical perspective on our institutions and habits? Or is it merely a way of socializing students into willing servants of the status quo?

That last question introduces the final group of readings, on the issue of literacy. After all, the matter of socialization relates to how people achieve literacy—how they develop their abilities to read and write in a given culture. The "literacy narratives" collected here typically record people's encounter with other cultures, for that is one of the conventions of this kind of writing; literacy narratives often dramatize a person's attempt to assimilate. Those who write literacy narratives usually mean to tell others about their struggle to accommodate the language structures and conventions associated with a culture that is "alien" in some way. Sometimes that encounter is presented in positive terms: the literacy narrative in that case records a story of positive transformation as the subject of the narrative attains new power and command by virtue of coming to grips with a new community and its language patterns. (That may be the subtext of Benjamin Franklin's literacy narrative, included in his famous *Autobiography*.) But other times the encounter can be less positive. The narrative can disclose the inability of a person to become integrated with a new community and can record the community's efforts to keep aliens outside. Still other literacy narratives can be ambiguous: as in the case of Eliza Doolittle, who becomes "a lady" in George Bernard Shaw's *Pygmalion* (and in the Broadway version of that play, *My Fair Lady*), but at a terrible cost to her own identity and autonomy, the protagonists of literacy narratives sometimes offer stories that are mixed in tone. Whatever the point of the story, literacy narratives nearly always give readers an opportunity to reflect on the profound power of language to shape lives (and in that sense, these narratives offer an ideal transition to the next section of *Conversations*, on Language). The narratives will also invite you to reflect on the record of your own growth as a language user, your own encounters through language with alien cultures of one kind or another, at a time when you are encountering a specific new "culture," that of your college or university. Did you grow from all those encounters? Were the transformations they brought about singularly powerful and useful? Or was something also lost in the transition from one kind of language use to another?

Some of these ideas related to education are developed further in Part Two of *Conversations*, which opens with a sort of literacy narrative, Richard Rodriguez's "Aria." Education issues also will develop in Part Three, in the section on Race and Gender, and in Part Five, which takes up issues of Civil Liberties and Civil Rights. But in this part of *Conversations*, the emphasis is on education in general and college education in particular. The readings you encounter should give you a better understanding of the issues that you and your classmates are grappling with right now. As you read, remember that the perennial nature of debates about education can be frustrating, especially to educational leaders. But the very relentlessness of the debates probably brings out the best feature of a democratic society: the freedom of citizens to shape policy through open and public exchange.

E. B. White

EDUCATION

E. B. White (1899–1985), who contributed regularly to The New Yorker *and whose work has been collected into several books, was perhaps America's most popular essayist. You may also know him as the author of the children's classic* Charlotte's Web *(1952). First published in 1939 in* Harper's *and in White's* One Man's Meat, *the following comparison of two educational philosophies remains relevant over half a century later.*

1   I have an increasing admiration for the teacher in the country school where we have a third-grade scholar in attendance. She not only undertakes to instruct her charges in all the subjects of the first three grades, but she manages to function quietly and effectively as a guardian of their health, their clothes, their habits, their mothers, and their snowball engagements. She has been doing this sort of Augean task for twenty years, and is both kind and wise. She cooks for the children on the stove that heats the room, and she can cool their passions or warm their soup with equal competence. She conceives their costumes, cleans up their messes, and shares their confidences. My boy already regards his teacher as his great friend, and I think tells her a great deal more than he tells us.

2   The shift from city school to country school was something we worried about quietly all last summer. I have always rather favored public school over private school, if only because in public school you meet a greater variety of children. This bias of mine, I suspect, is partly an attempt to justify my own past (I never knew anything but public schools) and partly an involuntary defense against getting kicked in the shins by a young

ceramist on his way to the kiln. My wife was unacquainted with public schools, never having been exposed (in her early life) to anything more public than the washroom of Miss Winsor's. Regardless of our backgrounds, we both knew that the change in schools was something that concerned not us but the scholar himself. We hoped it would work out all right. In New York our son went to a medium-priced private institution with semi-progressive ideas of education, and modern plumbing. He learned fast, kept well, and we were satisfied. It was an electric, colorful, regimented existence with moments of pleasurable pause and giddy incident. The day the Christmas angel fainted and had to be carried out by one of the Wise Men was educational in the highest sense of the term. Our scholar gave imitations of it around the house for weeks afterward, and I doubt if it ever goes completely out of his mind.

His days were rich in formal experience. Wearing overalls   3
and an old sweater (the accepted uniform of the private seminary), he sallied forth at morn accompanied by a nurse or a parent and walked (or was pulled) two blocks to a corner where the school bus made a flag stop. This flashy vehicle was as punctual as death: seeing us waiting at the cold curb, it would sweep to a halt, open its mouth, suck the boy in, and spring away with an angry growl. It was a good deal like a train picking up a bag of mail. At school the scholar was worked on for six or seven hours by half a dozen teachers and a nurse, and was revived on orange juice in mid-morning. In a cinder court he played games supervised by an athletic instructor, and in a cafeteria he ate lunch worked out by a dietitian. He soon learned to read with gratifying facility and discernment and to make Indian weapons of a semi-deadly nature. Whenever one of his classmates fell low of a fever the news was put on the wires and there were breathless phone calls to physicians, discussing periods of incubation and allied magic.

In the country all one can say is that the situation is differ-   4
ent, and somehow more casual. Dressed in corduroys, sweatshirt, and short rubber boots, and carrying a tin dinner pail, our scholar departs at the crack of dawn for the village school, two and a half miles down the road, next to the cemetery. When the road is open and the car will start, he makes the journey by motor, courtesy of his old man. When the snow is deep or the motor is dead or both, he makes it on the hoof. In the afternoons he walks or hitches all or part of the way home in fair weather, gets transported in foul. The schoolhouse is a two-room frame building, bungalow type, shingles stained a burnt brown with weather-resistant stain. It has a chemical toilet in the basement and two teachers above the stairs. One

takes the first three grades, the other the fourth, fifth, and sixth. They have little or no time for individual instruction, and no time at all for the esoteric. They teach what they know themselves, just as fast and as hard as they can manage. The pupils sit still at their desks in class, and do their milling around outdoors during recess.

5   There is no supervised play. They play cops and robbers (only they call it "Jail") and throw things at one another— snowballs in winter, rose hips in fall. It seems to satisfy them. They also construct darts, pinwheels, and "pick-up-sticks" (jackstraws), and the school itself does a brisk trade in penny candy, which is for sale right in the classroom and which contains "surprises." The most highly prized surprise is a fake cigarette, made of cardboard, fiendishly lifelike.

6   The memory of how apprehensive we were at the beginning is still strong. The boy was nervous about the change too. The tension, on that first fair morning in September when we drove him to school, almost blew the windows out of the sedan. And when later we picked him up on the road, wandering along with his little blue lunch-pail, and got his laconic report "All right" in answer to our inquiry about how the day had gone, our relief was vast. Now, after almost a year of it, the only difference we can discover in the two school experiences is that in the country he sleeps better at night—and *that* probably is more the air than the education. When grilled on the subject of school-in-country vs. school-in-city, he replied that the chief difference is that the day seems to go so much quicker in the country. "Just like lightning," he reported.

Paul E. Peterson

A Liberal Case for Vouchers

*A professor of government at Harvard, Paul Peterson has stud-
ied the issue of school choice for a number of years. His research group has attempted to determine the effects of voucher
systems on the education of students in Milwaukee and other
cities. In October 1999, he published the following essay on
vouchers in a special issue of* New Republic *magazine given
over to "the future of education reform."* New Republic,

founded nearly a century ago in order to promote a liberal agenda—hence its title—is now a respected middle-of-the-road forum for discussions of politics, culture, and public policy.

Perhaps you're familiar with the "skimming" argument against 1 school vouchers. As this line of thinking goes, the parents most likely to opt for vouchers will be the ones who are already most involved with their children's education—which, on average, will mean the parents of the most motivated and gifted students. Once the best and the brightest flee to private schools, public schools will only get worse; this debilitating cycle will continue until the best students are skimmed off and the only kids left in public schools are those with the fewest skills and the least-involved parents—in other words, the students most in need of help. "Vouchers are like leeches," says North Carolina Governor Jim Hunt. "They drain the lifeblood—public support—from our schools." Bob Chase, president of the National Education Association, concurs: Establishing a system of vouchers, he says, would be like "bleeding a patient to death."

We liberals are sensitive to this argument because we know 2 that needy students are now getting the short end of the educational stick. Yet, while liberals are right to be concerned about these students, new data from a privately financed voucher program in Texas suggest that we should give vouchers a second, more serious look. Far from aggravating income and racial disparities in education, vouchers may actually help to ameliorate them.

In April 1998, the Children's Educational Opportunity 3 (CEO) Foundation offered vouchers to any low-income child in San Antonio's Edgewood school district. Almost all of the district's 13,490 students were eligible for the program, because Edgewood is among the poorest of the city's twelve school districts—more than 90 percent of its students are economically disadvantaged, and 93 percent are Latino. (Nonetheless, the district, which receives 90 percent of its funding from state and federal aid, spends more than $6,000 per pupil, which exceeds the state average.)

The vouchers were hardly paltry: Providing up to $3,600 a 4 year for elementary school students and $4,000 a year for those in high school, they would cover tuition at most San Antonio private schools, which for voucher students averages less than $2,000 annually. And, once a child's family decided to use vouchers, the CEO Foundation promised to continue providing them until that child graduated from high school, as long as he or she still lived in Edgewood. In addition, students could use the vouchers anywhere in San Antonio, even in public schools outside Edgewood that were willing to accept them. In the program's first year (the 1998–1999 school year), approximately 800 Edgewood students made use of the vouchers.

5 The Texas Federation of Teachers howled that private schools would "cherry pick" the best students and predicted the program would "shorten the honor roll" in public schools. "Right now, I don't have the profile of every child," Edgewood School Superintendent Dolores Muñoz said on PBS's "News Hour with Jim Lehrer," "[but] I guarantee you that at least 80 percent will be the high-achieving students."

6 To make matters worse, stories of private schools shutting out applicants quickly circulated. Edgewood's school board president, Manuel Garza, wrote in the *San Antonio Express News* that he had received a call from "a mother . . . for help because their application to the [Horizon program] had been denied. . . . I asked why she was denied. The mother said she was a single mom, had two jobs, and was told she was unacceptable because she could not dedicate time for extracurricular requirements, like helping out with homework and fundraising." In other words, not only were the voucher students an unusually strong group academically, but the private schools were then allegedly winnowing their ranks even further.

7 But data from a recently completed evaluation (funded by the Packard Foundation) that included results from tests of student achievement and questionnaires filled out by parents during testing sessions yields a more complicated, and more encouraging, picture. (Standard techniques were employed to ensure a representative sample, and Mathematica Policy Research, a well-respected evaluation firm with contracts with the Department of Education and other government agencies, collected the data.)

8 It's true that the private schools had only limited capacity, in part because the program was unveiled in April and went into effect the very next August. Yet there is little evidence that the schools were weeding out all but the best students. For example, on the math component of the Iowa Test of Basic Skills, on which the national median score falls at the fiftieth percentile, the voucher students, upon arriving at their new schools, scored at the thirty-seventh percentile, while the students who stayed in public school scored at the thirty-fifth—a difference that is not statistically significant. In reading, voucher students scored at the thirty-fifth percentile, while public school students scored at the twenty-eighth. This difference is significant but is hardly the gaping disparity voucher opponents predicted. In addition, just 23 percent of the voucher students had

been enrolled in programs for gifted students, while 29 percent of the students who stayed in public school were.

These results are consistent with analyses conducted by the research department at the Edgewood public schools, which compared the test scores of students who later accepted vouchers with the scores of those who remained behind. Never made public, perhaps because it directly contradicted the school superintendent's assertions, the research did not show a significant "skimming" effect. In the authors' technical language: "[F]ew statistically significant differences [in average test scores] are to be found between [the voucher] students . . . and those not . . . identified" as voucher students.

Apparently, families have many reasons for choosing private schools. They may be looking for better schools for children who are doing poorly just as often as they are looking for other schools for bright youngsters. But admission to private school is one thing; keeping one's place in school is another. Since private schools can suspend or expel students more easily than public schools can, critics say, they are able to weed out the worse students. Again, the numbers refute this seemingly logical argument. Suspension rates were equal for the voucher students and the Edgewood public school students—around five percent for both groups. And what about income? Average household income was nearly identical—right around $16,000. The students' ethnic background (96 percent Latino) and their levels of welfare dependency and residential stability were also extremely similar. Quite apart from suspensions, the voucher students were more likely to remain in the same school for the year and were just as likely to return to that school the next year.

This isn't to say that there were no distinctions whatsoever among the students. Eight percent of voucher students were enrolled in some sort of special education, while the figure for public school students was 16 percent. There were also some modest demographic differences between the two groups of parents. The average mother of a voucher student had completed twelve years of education, compared to eleven years for the average public school mother. Half of the voucher-student mothers worked full time, compared to just 37 percent of the mothers who kept their kids in public school. Only 22 percent of voucher-student mothers were on food stamps, but 33 percent of public school mothers were.

But these small distinctions are hardly enough to justify the extreme resistance to vouchers. For one thing, those helped by vouchers were far from well-off—the parents reported making less than $16,000 a year! There are plenty of other government programs, from Pell Grants to the Earned Income Tax Credit,

9

10

11

12

that predominantly benefit the working poor, and nobody (well, almost nobody) protests them on the grounds that they don't benefit people further down the economic ladder. Support for vouchers is particularly strong among minority families, especially those living in cities. According to a recent survey undertaken at Stanford University, 85 percent of the inner-city poor favor a voucher plan, compared with 59 percent of more advantaged parents who live in the suburbs. Asked if they "strongly" favor a voucher plan, 58 percent of poor urbanites agreed, compared to just one-third of upper-middle-class suburbanites.

13   More important, though, vouchers have the potential to improve socioeconomic and racial integration, as long as they are generous enough to cover most of the tuition and as long as schools are prohibited from racial or ethnic discrimination in admissions. Remember, our public school system is *already* plagued by vast inequalities. Because most school funding comes through local property taxes, disparities among affluent suburban schools and city or rural schools are legendary. The story on race is no better: Despite three decades of busing, public schools today are more segregated, not less. In 1997, 69 percent of African Americans attended schools composed predominantly of minority students, up from 64 percent in 1973. For Latinos, the increase is much steeper, from 57 percent to 75 percent over the past 25 years. Today, despite federal interventions ranging from Head Start to compensatory education, we have disturbingly large test-score gaps between cities and suburbs, as well as between blacks and whites. According to one 1994 survey, only 43 percent of urban fourth-graders read at a basic level, compared with 63 percent of students in nonurban areas.

14   Private schools, on the other hand, are already more racially integrated than public ones. University of Texas Professor Jay Greene estimates that private school classrooms are seven percentage points more integrated than public schools. Examining Department of Education data, he also found more interracial friendships in private schools than in public ones (as reported by students) as well as less interracial fighting (as reported by administrators, teachers, and students). And, sure enough, in all the voucher programs for which we have been able to obtain ethnic data, students were less likely—or at least no more likely—to be attending segregated schools than students remaining in public school. This isn't surprising, given that private schools can draw students from across school district boundaries, and religious schools provide a common tie that cuts across racial lines.

Oh, yes, and how about those voucher families in   15
Edgewood—what do they think of their new schools? More
than 60 percent say they are "very satisfied" with the schools'
academic quality, compared to 35 percent of the Edgewood
public school parents. Similar differences in satisfaction levels
are reported by parents regarding school safety, school discipline, and quality of teaching.

There are, of course, many other arguments against voucher   16
programs, from the church-and-state issue to questions about
for-profit schools. I don't happen to buy those arguments, either, but I'm happy to continue letting pilot programs provide a
testing ground. Given the potential of vouchers to achieve
more racial and socioeconomic diversity in education—one of
the great goals of education reformers since the 1960s—you'd
think more liberals would be open to experimenting with them.

Martin Carnoy

DO SCHOOL VOUCHERS IMPROVE SCHOOL PERFORMANCE?

*Martin Carnoy, a professor of education at Stanford
University, has written several books, among them* Sustaining
the New Economy: Work, Family, and Community in the
Information Age. *In January 2001,* The American Prospect
*published the following essay, which is something of a re-
sponse to the previous essay by Paul E. Peterson. The*
American Prospect *publishes (every two months) essays on
politics, public affairs, and contemporary culture. It is a product of the Hudson Institute, a think tank that claims not to advocate an expressed ideology or political position. According to
its website, "the institution's viewpoint embodies skepticism
about conventional wisdom, an appreciation of technology's
role in achieving progress, optimism about solving problems, a
futurist orientation, a commitment to individuality and free
institutions, and a respect for the importance of religion, culture, and values in human affairs."*

1   With George W. Bush's assumption of the presidency, a campaign to provide vouchers for private schooling may gain new life. The idea of public funding of private schools is not new, nor does it belong exclusively to conservative free market reformers.

2   In the 1960s and early 1970s, academics on the left, such as Christopher Jencks of Harvard University's Kennedy School of Government, argued that vast differences between the quality of public schooling for inner-city blacks and suburban whites could not be resolved within the structure of a residentially segregated public-education system. Jencks argued for a policy concept introduced by economist Milton Friedman more than a decade earlier. Friedman proposed to offer public funds to families that could only be used for education, but in any educational institution, public or private. Such "vouchers" would serve to give families increased choice about the kind of education their children received. Friedman saw vouchers as a way to break the "monopoly" of the public sector over education, increase consumer choice, and, hence, promote economic well-being. Jencks saw vouchers as a way of improving educational opportunities for a historically discriminated-against group within American society. Both shared a distrust of the state—Friedman of the bureau-centric state interfering with "democratic" markets, Jencks of the class-centric and race-centric state reproducing inequality through public education.

3   But conditions may have changed in the last 40 years. While there is still a glaring gap between the achievement of black students and that of white students, it has been considerably narrowed. In the last decade, however, the progress seems to have stopped, and it is unclear what the causes of the continued disparity might be. In his latest book (co-edited with Meredith Phillips), *The Black-White Test Score Gap*, Jencks seems to argue that the biggest cause of the persistent gap is differences in family characteristics over which schools, public or private, have very little control. But he does suggest that some school improvements, like smaller classes or better-prepared teachers, might make a difference.

4   With so much attention focused on the problem, voucher advocates have been attempting to prove that private schools supported by public funds actually can do a better job than public schools of educating the children most at risk of school failure—whether because vouchers are a route to smaller classes and better teachers, or because private schools are superior in other respects. Over the last few years, the leading proponent of the idea that private schools are demonstrably more effective at educating low-income African-American students has been Harvard Professor Paul Peterson.

In the most recent salvo in this dispute, Peterson and his col- 5
leagues (David Campbell, also of Harvard; William Howell of
the University of Wisconsin, Madison; and Patrick Wolf of
Georgetown University) announced last August that their
voucher experiments in New York City, Washington, D.C., and
Dayton, Ohio, showed that at least some pupils—African
Americans—achieve better in private than in public schools.
The finding was widely hailed by voucher supporters across the
political spectrum as showing that private schools could solve a
problem public schools apparently could not: that of raising the
lagging achievement of low-income inner-city black children.

"This hard evidence is not what teacher unionists want to
hear," William Safire noted in *The New York Times*. "The 6
Harvard study shows Bush is on the right side of this. He
should embrace the successful voucher students and joyfully
join the controversy."

But soon after the results were presented, another member
of the Peterson team, David Myers, contractor for the New York 7
City part of the research, openly challenged Peterson's interpretation, arguing that the New York results do not show voucher
students—even African Americans—with a statistically significant advantage. Earlier voucher studies in Milwaukee and
Cleveland seemed to support this more skeptical view.

Who is right? How sanguine should we be that black, inner-
city pupils would gain by switching to private schools? 8

The short answer is that the three-city study is not nearly as
reliable as its authors claim. As a basis for educational policy, 9
it should be interpreted cautiously. A more structured private-
school environment with smaller classes and higher-achieving
peers could possibly help African Americans make greater
gains than if they stayed in public schools. It is also possible
that improvements to public schools would yield comparable
improvements. But that said, the Peterson results may misrep-
resent gains that typical low-income African-American students can make by switching to private schools. Using statistical techniques not easily understood by the media or the
public, the studies' methodology is laced with potential biases.
In the context of an intense ideological push for privatizing education, the question to ask is not whether this latest report
overestimates private school effects, but by how much.

In four cities—Dayton, New York, Washington, and
Charlotte, North Carolina (where data was released more re- 10
cently)—the Peterson team built evaluations into the voucher
plans themselves. Evaluating these evaluations is not easy, because the researchers have not publicly released their data.

11   Earlier, in Milwaukee and Cleveland, the Peterson studies were constructed after the fact, in response to research originally carried out by scholars not politically committed to vouchers. The Peterson estimates in those studies have a different character. For one, the data were available to others and thus are subject to re-analysis. More important, "experimental" controls were nonexistent.

The Milwaukee Voucher Experiment

12   The longest-running voucher initiative in the United States is Milwaukee's. It began in 1990–91 on the initiative of Polly Williams, an African-American Wisconsin legislator. The $2,500 vouchers were awarded by lottery to very-low-income families, almost all of them African Americans, to be used only in secular private schools. Five private schools agreed to take 1,500 voucher students.

13   The legislature commissioned John Witte, a professor at the University of Wisconsin, Madison, to study the students who received vouchers and compare their achievement with similar students in public schools. Witte found high levels of satisfaction among families who received vouchers, but no significant differences in math and reading performance between pupils in private schools and socioeconomically similar students who remained in public schools.

14   The initial voucher amount was set at roughly one-half of the annual per-pupil spending in Milwaukee's public schools. This changed quickly, with private schools demanding and getting a higher voucher payment, until it was at least as high as (or even higher than) public costs. Of the five private schools in the initial experiment, one subsequently closed. And of the initial voucher takers, more than a third left the private schools by the end of the fourth year.

15   In 1996 Peterson obtained the Milwaukee data and published his own study, using a "quasi-experimental" design that compared achievement of students who got vouchers in the lottery with those who did not. Results showed the pupils attending private schools making gains in math but not reading. At the same time, Peterson claimed that Witte had misspecified his model by comparing private-school pupils with those who remained in public schools but had not applied for vouchers.

16   Witte countered that students who applied but did not get vouchers included students rejected by the private schools; they displayed falling test scores, unlike most public-school students of similar background.

A third party, Princeton economist Cecilia Rouse, then took 17
the same data, reworked them, and found that students in private schools made small gains in math but none in reading. A second Rouse paper found that in Milwaukee gains for low-income public-school students in smaller classes were higher than gains of voucher students in private schools.

In 1997 the Wisconsin legislature expanded the voucher pro- 18
gram to 15,000 low-income students and included religious schools. The Wisconsin Supreme Court upheld this legislation. By the school year 2001–02, about 10,000 children will use vouchers at more than 100 mostly religious private schools. No one knows whether voucher students are performing better because, unlike public students, they are not required to take state-mandated tests.

The Cleveland Voucher Program

Cleveland's program began in 1995 with a $2,500 voucher. 19
Private schools have since unsuccessfully tried to increase it. Almost all voucher students attend religious schools. On December 11, the Sixth Circuit Court of Appeals upheld a lower court ruling that these vouchers gave unconstitutional aid to religious schools. The U.S. Supreme Court will decide the program's future.

The Peterson group evaluated Cleveland vouchers in 1997. 20
The study found significant test score gains. In 1997 University of Indiana researchers led by Kim Metcalf undertook a separate study and found no significant gains. When the Peterson group re-analyzed Metcalf's data, it found only barely significant gains for private-school students.

The Peterson group's new round of research concerns efforts 21
by well-financed public-school opponents to fund "scholarships" (vouchers) for low-income children to attend private schools. The programs establish lotteries for parents who apply, give applicants a baseline test, award scholarships to applicants at random, and later test children who did and did not receive them. Some families who get vouchers do not actually send their children to private school, because they either cannot come up with the extra tuition or cannot find convenient private schools to accept their children.

Results for Dayton, New York, and Washington show no sig- 22
nificant test score gains for Hispanic and white voucher recipients. Gains for African Americans are found to be statistically significant in New York and Washington, D.C., and marginally

significant in reading (but not math) in Dayton. Reported gains are largest in Washington.

23   If the same methodology is used, the Charlotte gains are found to be about 6 percentile points in reading and about 6 percentile points in math. These are not broken down by ethnic group, but 80 percent of the sample is African American.

Closer Scrutiny

24   Comparing students who are already in public or in private schools has a major disadvantage: private-school students may come from more motivated families and may have survived selection processes. Solving this requires an "experiment": randomly assigning students to private and to public schools. But a truly blind trial, as in medical experiments in which control subjects are given a placebo and do not know whether they are receiving the treatment, is not possible, since families know whether they get a voucher. This makes education experiments subject to the so-called Hawthorne effect, whereby the participants' knowledge that they are involved in a program designed to produce a positive impact can cause them to try harder. The motivation of families whose voucher applications were rejected (that is, the control group) can also be affected.

25   The voucher experiments in various cities call for families to apply for a voucher, give baseline tests to all applicants, and then randomly select some to get vouchers to attend private schools. But the students in these experiments are not necessarily representative of low-income urban students. Families applying for vouchers whose children attend public schools are more motivated to switch their children and more dissatisfied with public schools than are average low-income parents, most of whom do not apply. Not receiving a voucher for parents already dissatisfied with their child's schooling could have an adverse "disappointment" effect on the child's performance.

26   The differential gains recorded in these experiments may therefore be partly attributable to lower gains by discouraged voucher rejectees rather than to greater gains by recipients. For a better comparison, voucher experiments would also need to draw a random sample of pupils from urban public schools whose low-income parents do not apply for vouchers and give the students the initial and follow-up tests. These pupils would come from families who are probably more satisfied with their current situation.

27   Another problem is self-selection of who gets the follow-up evaluation. Voucher researchers measure academic gains by

convincing families to bring children in on a weekend to take follow-up math and reading tests. As in medical trials, high participation rates may require inducements. For those families who received vouchers, the New York inducement was that children would have to take the test to continue getting a voucher. Researchers used only moral suasion in other cities. For those who received but did not use the voucher and for those in the control group (who did not get a voucher), the inducement was typically $20 plus eligibility for a voucher in the future. Participation rates varied: The highest rates occurred in New York (about 66 percent in the second-year follow-up), while D.C. and Dayton both experienced about 50 percent. The participation rate in Charlotte was particularly low—40 percent. All these are considerably lower than in medical trials.

The Peterson group deals with participation problems by estimating the probability that a student with a certain initial test score and set of family characteristics and attitudes would participate in each follow-up test; then the actual scores are weighted according to this probability. Thus, students who came back to take follow-up tests but had characteristics that made them unlikely follow-up participants were counted more heavily, so test scores would be more "representative" of the original group of students. 28

The researchers could not do much more than this to correct for no-shows. But the procedure is hardly free of potential bias. It assumes that follow-up test scores for the many who didn't take the tests would be the same as scores for those who did show up and had similar initial scores and parent characteristics. But we really don't know how follow-up scores of no-shows might be related to their not showing up. The large non-participation rates could easily have affected the relative gains of voucher recipients and nonrecipients. 29

Yet another problem is bias in who accepts the voucher offer. The vouchers, which range in value from $1,200 to $1,700, depending on the city, are not large enough to cover tuition at most of the available private schools. Many families that received vouchers were unable to use them. In New York, 62 percent of families whose children started out in public school used the scholarships for two years; in Dayton and Washington, 53 percent used the voucher in the first year, with an unreported drop-off in the second year. 30

Voucher takers in each city, as would be expected, have higher income than nontakers. Critics have argued that this biases results. But the researchers have made a valid attempt to deal with the problem by comparing the controls with all 31 students who were offered the voucher, not only those who actually used it.

32   In New York, the only students who made significant improvement were African Americans who switched to private schools when they were entering the fifth grade and whose gains were large enough to produce a significant average gain for the entire New York sample of African Americans.

33   Results for African-American students in Dayton also have a strange inconsistency. Certain cohorts—those who entered second, fourth, and sixth grades in the first year of the experiment—had large gains and those in the other grades did not. The D.C. results are more consistent.

34   With gains so variable by cohort, it is fair to ask, as did David Myers, whether one can claim that students in private schools do better than those in public schools. Shouldn't we, instead, wonder what conditions produced such large gains for some cohorts but not for others?

35   A final problem is erratic results. Big differences between first- and second-year gains in Washington, D.C., may relate to which students failed to show up for testing in the second year. Students might have failed to participate in the second-year testing either because of negative first-year experiences in private schools or because of disappointment with the first-year testing result. For such students, the probability is higher that they would do badly again than that they would do well. If they leave the sample, that alone could drive up the second-year result.

What Have We Learned?

36   Voucher evaluators have made a concerted effort to eliminate "selection bias" by offering vouchers to families with low incomes by lottery. In comparing pupils who receive vouchers to those who do not, bias from differential motivation and socioeconomic background is allegedly eliminated.

37   But this strategy does not speak to other issues. The sample of low-income, urban parents seeking vouchers does not represent the average low-income urban parent with children in public school. Parents who file for vouchers are, for one thing, more dissatisfied than other parents. To argue that they are more satisfied with their child's new, private school than parents who never applied for a voucher does not measure whether private schools are better than public, even if the comparison only concerns parental satisfaction.

38   The new studies also suffer from uncorrected potential bias, including "disappointment effects" of families that do

not receive vouchers, low participation rates in follow-up tests, concentration of gains in small, particular cohorts that the researchers do not attempt to explain, and possible non-random declines in participation between the first and second years of testing.

The Peterson group's model has yet another problem. Low-income urban pupils who attend private schools may do better because private schools are able to select their students, so the influence of peers on student achievement is more positive than in a public school. The ability to select students is not a feature of private education that voucher advocates care to stress. And peer effects can run out quickly as private education expands in inner cities.   39

The Peterson group could deal with this problem if they tested a random sample of students already in the private schools attended by voucher recipients, identified them by school, and estimated the peer effect (the average test score of nonvoucher students in each school) on the scores of voucher recipients attending the school. It may not be easy to convince the private schools to allow such testing, simply because they would then be subjecting themselves to evaluation. But without such information, it is difficult to understand the source of private-school advantage—if such advantage even exists.   40

Susan Tarves

ANOTHER KIND OF
SCHOOL CHOICE

Susan Tarves was a student in a first-year composition course at Penn State in 1998 when she wrote the following essay, which was intended as a contribution to a Philadelphia-area newspaper. A product of the (coed) Haverford, Pennsylvania, public schools, near Philadelphia, Tarves is currently undecided about an area of college study. Tarves will be graduating soon with a degree in speech communication.

"School choice": everywhere you go these days, you hear about   1
school choice. Usually the people who advocate (or oppose) school choice are referring to offering students a choice among public schools, or making it easier for parents to choose

among public and private schools. But in fact there is also another school choice that is increasingly being discussed these days: the choice of a single-gender education. Recently many people have been advocating single-gender schools as a means of offering students a better educational experience; at the same time, others have been ridiculing single-gender schools as anachronistic. Do single-gender schools offer something special to their students? Is a gender-segregated environment the best option for your son or daughter? Let me outline the arguments for and against this educational philosophy so that you can make a more informed decision about the matter.

2   Just what is single-gender education? Actually, there are several forms of it, and different approaches to its implementation. Sometimes a coeducational school will offer certain courses to all students, separate students in those courses by gender, and structure the class and teaching method according to different learning styles depending on gender. The Walker School in Marietta, Georgia is an example of this approach. For her first two classes of the day, seventh grader Amanda Xiques does not encounter boys, reports Jeff Archer in *Education Weekly* (April 8, 1998). More commonly, however, an entire school consists of students of only one gender. Indeed, all-female and all-male institutions are widespread in this country. These schools are either private or parochial. Single-gender public elementary and high schools (but not colleges) are considered illegal in the United States because they constitute discrimination based on gender, explains Robert McGinnis of the Family Research Council. Many all-male institutions, such as The Haverford School located outside of Philadelphia, have long and proud histories stretching back over a century. All female schools, including Villa Maria Academy in Malvern, Pennsylvania, have emerged more recently.

3   The Family Research Council offers several reasons why single-gender schools offer a wise choice. Students of both genders enrolled in single-gender schools seem to enjoy higher academic performance: they interact more with faculty and exhibit increased verbal aggressiveness and higher intellectual self-esteem. Women at single-sex schools are more likely than their peers at coed institutions to pursue majors such as science, management, and economics. They also have more opportunities for leadership and aspire to higher academic degrees. Men at single-gender schools are more likely than their peers at coed schools to get good grades, participate in honors programs, graduate with honors, and pursue careers in business, law, or college teaching. Both men and women at single-sex schools are more likely than students at coed institutions to be satisfied with curricular variety, stu-

dent and faculty relations, quality of instruction, and friendships with other students. According to research from the Harvard School of Education and the American Association of University Women (http://dsha.k12.wi.us/single.htm), in a coed classroom, teachers call on the boys four times more often than the girls; the teachers most often direct the "challenging questions" to the boys while the female students receive less difficult questions; the teachers are far more likely to praise and give positive reinforcement to the intellectual contributions of males in the classroom, while making note of the socialization skills of girls; and in general, teachers give more attention to boys than girls. It's little wonder, then, that many young women experience a decline in self-esteem as their voices become silenced.

Researchers confirm that by senior year, students at single-gender schools excel beyond their peers from coed schools in the areas of reading, writing, and science. Overall graduates of women's high schools are more satisfied with their schools and the quality of the teaching, more open-minded about their roles and possibilities, and relieved of some of the social pressures of adolescence (http://dsha.k12.wi.us/single.htm). In her widely praised recent book *Reviving Ophelia: Saving the Selves of Adolescent Girls,* Dr. Mary Pipher explains the extent of gender discrimination in the typical classroom:

> In classes, boys are twice as likely to be seen as role models, five times as likely to receive teachers' attention and twelve times as likely to speak up in class. In textbooks, one-seventh of all illustrations of children are of girls. Teachers choose many more classroom activities that appeal to boys than to girls. Girls are exposed to almost three times as many boy-centered stories as girl-centered stories. Boys tend to be portrayed as clever, brave, creative and resourceful, while girls are depicted as kind, dependent and docile. Girls read six times as many biographies of males as of females. Boys are more likely to be praised for academics and intellectual work, while girls are more likely to be praised for their clothing, behaving properly and obeying rules. Boys are likely to be criticized for their behavior, while girls are criticized for intellectual inadequacy. (62)

Proponents of single-gender schools, therefore, argue that separating girls and boys results in positive effects for both. Chris Mikles, the founder of a successful female-only math class, notes on the Contemporary Women's Issues Database that "Girls learn in different ways than boys, and, up until now, educators have failed to recognize that." "They [girls] are intellectually curious, serious about their studies, and achieve more," adds Robert Johnson (an English teacher in an all girl school) in *Failing at Fairness* by Myra and David Sadker. Many people support the belief that girls and boys respond differently to different learning styles. "Boys tend to compete in class, quickly raising their hands or even blurting out answers; girls more often work well in small groups with other students," reports Jeff Archer. By acknowledging these differences, single-gender schools benefit both boys and girls, many believe.

7   Many people also agree that single-sex education is more comfortable for the students, especially during adolescence, typically an awkward time for teenagers who are beginning to gain interest in the opposite sex and striving to be accepted by their peers. "Sometimes you do feel more comfortable, more inclined to ask questions. . . . Your hand just seems to go up," says thirteen-year-old Amanda (reported by Archer). And it is not just girls who feel more comfortable. Boys at this age respond similarly to the girls. Sixth-grader Casey McDonagh says, "It's easier [in a single-sex environment] because we don't have to worry about being embarrassed in front of the girls," reports Ann O'Hanlon (in the January 24, 1998 *Washington Post*). By eliminating the element of possible embarrassment, girls and boys often find it easier to voice their opinion; therefore, they become more assertive and self-assured.

8   But not everyone feels so positive about single-gender education. A report by The American Association for University Women, summarized by Beth Reinhard in the May/June 1998 issue of *Teacher Magazine,* contends that single-gender education is not necessarily better than coeducation. The group believes that it is "small classes and schools, a focused curriculum, and unbiased teaching are what matters," not gender segregation. In other words, the report indicates other factors besides gender segregation account for the high quality of many such schools. For example, teachers need to address the learning styles of individuals, not genders. Just because children are of the same gender, one cannot assume that they possess the same learning style; learning styles vary more among individuals than between genders.

9   Others contend that there is still far too little research to justify a rush to single-gender education. James Bulter in an article entitled "Counterpoint" speaks for many others:

10   Recently, some public schools have re-instituted single sex education and this raises some serious questions. These schools use statistics from many studies to justify this deci-

sion. They claim that once girls reach the junior high and high school years, they let themselves be ignored in the fields of math and science in order not to show up the boys. If this is happening, then this is something we have to deal with but single sex education is not the answer. . . . If girls are being intimidated in the math and science fields then we need to change this. Somebody is obviously teaching girls this behavior so it should be able to be untaught. (www.ukiahilite. zapcom.net/pcpl.html)

In "Don't Separate the Girls from the Boys," Anne Fuentes (a   11
Prudential Fellow at Columbia Journalism School researching children's issues) agrees: "Single-sex education is worse than a cheap fix masked as educational reform. It's a strategy that depends on stereotyping both boys and girls. Boys learn that they are the problem. Girls learn that they are helpless victims who can't count on the system to create a safe learning environment for all students."

Studies on the subject of single-gender schools are still pre-   12
liminary. Janice Weinman, executive director of American Association of University Women, is "concerned that people are rushing it [single-gender education] without the research to back it up," reports Archer. Critics of gender-segregated schools frequently charge that the students in those schools may be unprepared to interact with the opposite sex in college. "It was definitely an adjustment," Trish Henwood told me. (She is a freshman at Georgetown University who attended an all-girls high school outside of Philadelphia.) "I really wasn't quite sure how to act with guys in my classes. I hope it will just take a little time and I'll get used to it." Many feel that isolating the sexes is doing a social disservice to the students—that sheltering students from the real world makes little sense. When these students graduate from high school and enter college, they will suddenly be exposed to the opposite sex in classroom, work, and social environments. Often their ability to communicate with the opposite sex is weak in comparison with their peers who have been educated in a coed environment. "It's kind of frustrating; sometimes I feel like I'm the only one not used to having guys in my class," offers Trish Henwood. "Girls and boys are going to need to know how to deal with one another before they find themselves in a job situation," claims Bulter; "this would slow production and create higher degrees of stress." Students from gender-segregated schools may not only find themselves at a comparative disadvantage socially, but they may also find it difficult to relate to their peers of the opposite sex, simply because they have never had to do so in

the past. A gender-sheltered environment, many feel, lacks the gender diversity needed to develop lifelong skills in students.

13   Is single-sex education the best choice for your child? Maybe. The argument between proponents and opponents may reflect the fact that research on the question is still preliminary and incomplete. It probably also reflects differences between what people value most about elementary and secondary education. In the end, a decision about which kind of school is best perhaps depends on the individual child.

Marc Fisher

TO EACH ITS OWN

The following essay on charter schools appeared as the cover story for the April 8, 2001 issue of the Washington Post Magazine. *That particular issue focused on education: it included articles on choosing a college, for-profit schools, adult education, and potential curricular reforms for primary grades. Marc Fisher writes a column three times a week for the* Metro *section of the* Post. *Do you think the essay shows Fisher's own opinion about the merits of charter schools?*

1   On paper, in a dream, a charter school—in essence, a privately run public school—is a way out, an answer, an engine for change.

2   On the street, in a kid's life, a charter school is a building with teachers, students, headaches, tragedies and, once in a while, a moment of shining success.

3   Nikole Richardson teaches at a charter school in Washington. She is very good at what she does. She does not feel very good about it:

4   "I hope [charters] are an experiment and they will succeed and go away. To take out a handful of our kids and give them something doesn't improve the lives of most of our kids. Charters have no training, no certification. They may be dedicated to teaching black kids, but that's not enough. The advantage we have has to do with resources that the public schools do not have, and parents who find out about the charter schools and do whatever they need to get their kids in. What about all the kids who don't have a family saying, 'Go here'?"

Paul Vance is superintendent of D.C. Public Schools, chief   5
target of the city's fast-growing charter system—33 schools
with about 10,000 students, or almost 15 percent of the children in the public schools. Charters are an in-your-face rebuke
to him, his teachers, his students. He wishes charters did not
have to exist, but readily concedes their advantages:

"What I've heard about the charters is that they don't have to   6
deal with insensitive bureaucracy. They have supplies and materials. They teach with few, if any, interruptions. They teach
where no one loses sight of the main thing, which is teaching
and learning. They aren't bogged down with conflicting direc-
tives from central administration. The teachers who have gone
from our schools to the charters have found the freedom and
collegiality which they were promised. There's a siphoning off
of our talented and competent teachers and administrators.
They saw an opportunity to do what they had dreamed of doing, to become unshackled."

Washington's first charters opened in 1996, when a devas-   7
tating report on the D.C. public schools prompted the federally appointed financial control board to sack the superintendent and strip authority from the elected school board. D.C.'s
charters are a paradox: They were imposed on the city by
school-choice ideologues—many of them veterans of the
Reagan-era Education Department—who believe that all parents ought to have the same options as rich folks who buy
their way out of lousy public schools. Yet in this heavily
Democratic, mostly black and low-income city, parents who
often know nothing of the conservative charter movement
have embraced the schools as an alternative to a system that
chronically fails its children.

Now, with charter enrollment in the District soaring every fall,   8
the question is no longer Charters Yes or No. The question is,
what's happening in the classroom? And what comes out of the
schools? Are charters a rejection of the governing philosophy of
American education—an admission that the idea of a single system molding useful citizens from all walks of life has failed?

In his inaugural address, President Bush mentioned only a   9
few specific goals—one was improving education, and the words
he used to express his ideal were these: "common schools."

In a world of school choice, is there such a thing as a "com-   10
mon school"?

Charters, as Bates College professor Stacy Smith has writ-   11
ten, "blur the boundary between public and private schools."
Charters are public schools—they take public money, usually
use public buildings, cannot choose their students. But the
schools are free to do as they wish in the classroom.

12   Before regulators approve a charter school, they want to know how it will assess student progress, how it will hire and train teachers, what it will do with learning-disabled kids. But while the city's two school chartering boards say they indeed inquire about what's being taught, school founders say they're really on their own.

13   "The charter board looked seriously at our application only in the broadest sense," says Eric Adler, a founder of the Seed charter school in Northeast. "No one asked what in American history we were going to teach. Now, we obviously care very much about that. Some schools might not."

14   Charter advocates happily embrace the ideals of private education and the idiom of the marketplace; their language is laden with references to parents as consumers and charters as entrepreneurs. But Smith argues that charters are not simply an attempt to privatize the public system. She believes charters can make public education more democratic by educating all students to be effective citizens without forcing every child into a one-size-fits-all system.

15   Vance and other charter critics aren't buying. "There has to be a common body of knowledge," he says. "No one has convinced me that there's a better educational form than the classic and traditional education. In charter schools, there isn't a consistent philosophy. They tend to be finding their way."

16   America's public schools were founded on the notion that for a democracy to work, all children need to be able to read, write and compute, and all children must understand their responsibilities and rights as citizens. For many years, no secondary school subject was more important than history, with its curricular cousins civics and government—here, public schools could inculcate immigrants and natives alike in the American Way, teaching the nation's roots and rationale.

17   But in recent decades, it's become clear that no subject is more ineffectively taught than history. Amid the innumerable studies of the deficiencies of American students, history stands at the apex of Failure Mountain. National surveys repeatedly find that students get less homework in history than in most other subjects, that history is often taught from lifeless textbooks rather than from original documents, and that student interest and success in the subject decline with every year of schooling.

18   History is also a prime battleground in the culture wars of the past 30 years: What should American teens know about their country, their world? Whose history is it, anyway?

19   And what will charter schools do to the ideal of a common foundation? Even if charters find a better way to teach, doesn't their freedom to go their own way mean that each curriculum

will be a world unto itself? Some charters set out to teach one slice of American reality—some are Afrocentric, while others focus on the military, the classics or the world of technology.

Go to a handful of charters and ask how they teach history. 20 Answer: Every which way.

Eleven students, seventh- and eighth-graders all dressed in 21 white shirts and chinos, sit opposite Mr. Lloyd, who is crisp in attire and cadence. The bell sounds in the cramped room—a converted law office—and Lloyd wastes not one second. "Which amendment says American people do not have to house soldiers in their homes?"

Five hands pop up. A boy in the back says, "Third." 22

Swiftly, a check mark goes next to the boy's name on the 23 whiteboard. Even as he's posing the next question, Lloyd moves to the back and gives the boy a two-fingered, mighty cool handshake.

"How many electoral votes does the District of Columbia 24 have?"

"Three," comes the answer, and kids are egging one another 25 on, and the atmosphere is somewhere between "It's Academic" and "Who Wants to Be a Millionaire."

"Name three duties of American citizens." 26

"Appear in court, attend school, obeying the law." 27

The teacher pauses, then slowly: "Absolutely, positively . . . " 28 Long pause. "Correct."

Over the whiteboard at the front of the room, hand-cut pa- 29 per letters spell out, "Move Mountains."

Felix "Brandon" Lloyd is the star of the 122-student Seed 30 school, the city's only all-residential charter school, now in its third year. He's the teacher observers are sent to watch—a charismatic, no-nonsense dynamo who connects with kids in that magical way that students remember for the rest of their lives. Even in the austere surroundings of the eight floor of a 16th Street NW office building—Seed held classes there until it moved this winter to a site in Southeast near the Benning Road Metro station—Lloyd manages to exude warmth and firm expectations at the same time.

Quiz over, Lloyd explains the roots of the constitutional right 31 to bear arms. He works without notes. "We lived far apart in those days. Demond over here, Danielle over there. And between us was cows, yarns, collard greens, corn. And we needed weapons to protect ourselves, and this is how we defended ourselves, and this led to the right to bear arms."

The lessons are parables, the facts infused like tea in hot wa- 32 ter. "Terrible thing happened to me this weekend," Lloyd tells one class. "Mr. Ramirez and I were driving 90 miles per hour down 14th Street. Police stopped us and said, 'We'd like to search the car.' Which amendment protected us from that?"

33   Quizzes and games fly at the kids from all directions, at any moment. There's a five-minute detour to talk about outlining skills, a 99-second break (Lloyd sets the timer) for an impromptu discussion of whether there are limits on the right to petition. Not one head rests on a desk. Not one note gets passed from student to student. The class is highly regimented, yet students are free to check their e-mail if they finish a task early. There's a PC on every second desk.

34   Lloyd tolerates no deviation from the rules—a boy who calls out an answer without being recognized gets no credit for it— yet the teacher has given each child a street tag (Peanut, Y-Not, Kingpin, Shakespeare), and they love him for it. Lloyd requires no disciplinary tools beyond a glance of menace, a lethal shot of glare. The 75 minutes zip by, and suddenly he's asking the kids to "take good care, taaaake *good* care," and more than a handful of students linger to debate constitutional principles.

35   Brandon Lloyd never taught a minute of school before he came to Seed. He's the classic charter school hire, one who would be viewed with suspicion, if at all, by the public schools. (None of Seed's teachers came from the D.C. schools; they came from Sidwell Friends and other private schools, or from public schools in the Midwest, or from Teach for America, a sort of Peace Corps for liberal arts graduates who want to work in urban schools.) He has never taken an education course. He holds no certification in anything. Seed hired him from a city recreation center, where he taught drama and creative writing in an after-school program. He loves teaching, but what he really wants to do is write the Great American Novel. His work in progress is titled "Shades of a Man-child." His favorite movie is "Dead Poets Society," the inspirational Robin Williams flick about the power and majesty of a traditional prep school.

36   Brandon Lloyd is all of 24.

37   His philosophy of teaching is "to do the opposite of the teachers I had" in D.C. public schools. He credits St. John's, the private military school in upper Northwest where he went to high school, with preparing him well for Syracuse University, where he earned degrees in dramatic writing and African American studies. He designed his history and civics courses for Seed by looking at Virginia's Standards of Learning, California's standards and a bunch of textbooks—then discarding most of what he saw because "the standards were just too dense. You'd be amazed at how poor these kids' conception is of where they are. We decided that less is more." Free of the

public schools' obsession with standardized tests, Seed permits Lloyd to teach what he loves and to teach it intensely.

Lloyd lived with the students in their dormitory at Trinity 38 College during Seed's first year, and he still drops by a couple of evenings a week to eat dinner or play ball. "I want to help create thinking people who are responsible citizens," he says. Toward that end, Seed students adhere to a dress code and are prohibited from watching TV. "Their music is increasingly censored" by the school, Lloyd says.

"Cultures form consciously and unconsciously," he explains. 39 "We try to direct them. I want to see these kids entering all different colleges and then being teachers and journalists, daring to be different. I want to expand their world in a way it wouldn't be in public school. If you ask them what percentage of Americans are African American, they'll say 70 percent, which is absurd, but that's their world."

Lloyd, like almost all the school's students, is black. At Seed, 40 the majority of the teaching staff is white, and Lloyd says, "That's important. The D.C. schools don't have this diversity, and the kids grow up apart from the rest of society."

Seconds after one class leaves, the next one arrives. Lloyd 41 sets an egg timer at six minutes and six seconds and starts them off with a high-energy exercise called the Instigator. "Time is wasting," he warns as he hands out questions on the Constitution and U.S. law. "Time is ticking on you, Dominique."

After the exercise, a student raises her hand. "I got a question." 42
"You *have* a question." 43
"Yeah." 44
"You *have* a question." 45
"I *have* a question. It's about the Seventh Amendment . . ." 46

At Cesar Chavez High School for Public Policy on Florida 47 Avenue NW, the focus is on constitutional issues and "what students might do to change the world," says history and government teacher Andrew Touchette. So kids study District neighborhoods—Columbia Heights, Anacostia, Cleveland Park. They paint murals and produce radio shows. But they also study the Bill of Rights and engage in heated debate over how it applies to their own lives.

"What's great about teaching in a charter school is that each 48 teacher designs his own course," says Touchette, whose close-cropped red hair, long sideburns, wire rims and vest make him look like a character out of Henry James. The only restriction he faces is that he must show which standards from the Modern Red Schoolhouse handbook—a favorite curriculum tool among charter schools—each of his units meets. Last year, Touchette taught in the Charles County schools, where, he says, "they just plopped a 200-page curriculum guide in front of us and said, 'Do this.' It was all about what happened on December 7, 1941, as opposed to being able to understand the concepts."

49 In Touchette's 11th-grade politics and citizenship class, the subject is the civil rights amendments. As in most classes at Chavez, blacks and Latinos—the 180-student school is almost evenly divided between the two—sit apart. (A disproportionate number of Hispanics choose charters. Six D.C. charter schools have student bodies that are 20 percent or more Hispanic, more than double the percentage in the public system.)

50 Touchette is trying to get the 15 kids to focus on the idea of equal protection and the reality of life for immigrants and minorities. But first he has to get past the kids' clean slates. To understand where the 14th Amendment came from, you need to know the basics of slavery and the Civil War. These kids don't.

51 "Did you guys ever have an American history class?" he asks after a series of questions go unanswered.

52 "Yeah, eighth grade, too long ago," Larry Peterson replies.

53 "Is there still slavery in the United States?" Touchette asks.

54 After a chorus of "Yeah" sweeps the room, he tries to distinguish between slavery and discrimination. There's a spirited discussion of a TV news broadcast about the difficulties blacks have hailing taxis on city streets. Touchette divides the class into three groups and assigns an instant essay, 15 minutes to write a memo in which you are an Alabama redneck in 1870 and you're figuring out how to sidestep the civil rights amendments, how to make the law work for you.

55 One of the groups is clueless; the concept eludes them entirely. The other two struggle to get something on paper. One parrots back what the teacher has said, but the other makes the leap, reading out an imaginative memo in which craven Klansmen conspire to set up a system of "separate but equal" schools and businesses. "'Cause it says you have to be equal but it doesn't say you have to be together," Peterson notes.

56 This is the kind of moment that gives Irasema Salcido reason to believe. A former D.C. public schools administrator who has emerged as one of the most vibrant principals in the city's charter schools, Salcido is Chavez's founder, and her life is a rushing, jam-packed trainload of moments both frustrating and fantastic.

57 From the start, Salcido got swept up in the high-flying rhetoric of the charter movement. She and her teachers were going to create a new kind of school, focused on involving kids in public policy. Together, they would write a bold new curriculum.

But Chavez's new curriculum exists largely as inchoate piles   58
of paper in Salcido's office. She looks at the stacks of pulp and
she can either laugh or cry. Or she can get back out into the
hallway, corner a kid who hasn't been showing up to class, and
sit him down for a talk. She's out the door.

In theory, charters are free to teach as they wish, to experi-   59
ment boldly or hew to basics. In fact, charters do not brim with
new ideas about how to teach kids. An evaluation of the District's
charters by a George Washington University study team found
that most of them do not emphasize innovation and about half
offer programs barely distinguishable from the public schools'.

Chavez has turned out to be one of the most innovative char-   60
ters, even if its test scores have been unimpressive. Its students
spend weeks working as interns at Washington's think tanks,
policy shops and advocacy groups. The school's project-based
design gets kids out on the streets, exploring architecture, de-
signing solutions to problems in their own neighborhoods.

At Chavez and many of the best charters, principals are up-   61
front about the yawning gap between the theory of charters
and the reality of opening a new school for academically struggling kids from dysfunctional families and violent neighborhoods—not to mention the perils of stop-and-go funding, temporary buildings, hostility from the public system and a
hunger for results from parents and regulators.

"It's not as easy as I thought it was going to be," Salcido says.   62
"We couldn't really implement the curriculum." Salcido, like
several other charter principals, has refused to promote large
numbers of students—holding back as much as half of a class.
"We underestimated the low skills of the students. We have
young people who cannot do long division and have never
written an essay. We want to have a rigorous curriculum, but
there are no shortcuts."

The Washington Math, Science and Technology charter   63
school at Waterside Mall in Southwest now expects to take at
least five years to implement its new curriculum. "The biggest
problem charters face is that the public school system lies to
these kids by telling them that they're ninth-graders when really they read at a fifth-grade level and do math at a sixth-grade
level," says Jack McCarthy, managing director of the Apple
Tree Institute, which launched the school in 1998. "You risk
losing your charter if you don't graduate enough kids, but if
you promote socially instead of promoting mastery, then
you're not doing what we all came here to do."

Families who choose charters clearly are searching for   64
something better for their kids, but they are not necessarily

the kind of parents who are available to help their children navigate adolescence. Salcido and other principals tell of going to great lengths to get parents to attend meetings or student performances. "I do not mail report cards," Salcido says. "You have to come and get them so I can discuss your child."

65 On the main bulletin board in Chavez's lobby, an essay is posted under "Best Student Work of the Month." It is a passionate piece of writing about a student's journey from the District's Duke Ellington high school to Chavez and from her heavy drinking and cocaine use to a no-holds-barred examination of her wayward father and a poisonous family dynamic.

66 "My true, honest, moral belief," says David Domenici, founder of the Maya Angelou School, "is that if anybody understood the level of emotional and academic needs kids come to us with, we would be having a completely different conversation about education." Angelou is a charter school that combines public money and private donations to provide all-day, year-round, nearly one-on-one instruction and counseling for troubled high school-age kids, most of whom have been in the juvenile justice system. "You cannot imagine what urban America has come to. These are kids who have spent 10 years sleeping in classrooms."

67 "We've gone back and forth on this," says Darry Strickland, a humanities teacher at the Angelou School, at Ninth and T streets NW. "What is to be valued out of all these dates, people, places and events? For me as an African American teacher teaching African American students, this is what has to be covered: slavery, the Civil War, the civil rights movement, the Harlem Renaissance. Start with that." In a three-year sequence of courses—African American studies, American studies, world studies—Angelou uses novels and movies as well as straight-ahead history to connect major events with the lives of its almost exclusively black student body.

68 "For example, we'll read *Angela's Ashes* to learn not just about the Irish, but the relationship between Irish and African Americans," Strickland says. "How African American maids were displaced when the Irish came.

69 "Is it fair that we're teaching our own version of history? I think it is."

70 "These are topics more interesting to our students than Benjamin Franklin," adds Nikole Richardson, who also teaches humanities at Angelou. "It's all a way of getting across the skills—writing, primary vs. secondary sources, thinking critically. There's a big gap between what happens on paper

and what happens in the classroom. Four years ago, I would have said I want them to understand their feelings. Now I want them to be equipped with skills, and that's it."

"I'm not sure what comes through," Strickland concedes. 71 "Are we teaching them to despair? I don't think so. But they'll be in their early twenties before they can make sense of what they're reading and doing here."

The Angelou School long ago abandoned the idea of a stan- 72 dard curriculum. With its population—two-thirds of the 65 students are just out of the justice system, many have dropped out of school at least once, most read and compute at an elementary-school level—you do what you can. Which doesn't mean you just pass them along. You push where you can, you teach individually.

The school's first-year humanities course, "Self, Family, 73 Country and Beyond," is "a very intense immersion in yourself, your neighborhood, D.C. and beyond," says founder Domenici, a lawyer and the son of Sen. Pete Domenici of New Mexico. "It's pretty much Afrocentric."

Richardson's humanities class consists of three students, 74 ages 15 and 16. If she can teach them at seventh-grade level, she'll be boosting them to new heights. The kids know it.

"If I was going to public school, I wouldn't be going to class," 75 says Amanda Curry, who came to Angelou from Shaw Junior High School.

A timeline runs along the classroom wall, listing major 76 events in American history, but the class is just as likely to watch a Bill Cosby video and discuss methods of communication as it is to study dates and events.

Richardson is talking about monologue and dialogue, gesture 77 and inflection, the tools of a storyteller. But one student cannot pronounce "exaggeration," and so the class stops to work on that. The student just wants to get on with it, get the focus off himself. But Richardson persists, moving close to him, leaning over, speaking softly. She pushes, prods, backs off, moves in again. Five minutes later, he's got the idea. He's relieved to get the teacher out of his face, but a moment later, he whispers the word to himself, gets it right, and smiles for no one but himself.

Richardson has moved on to definitions of "myth" and "cus- 78 tom."

"What's a custom?" she asks. "We don't have too many cus- 79 toms anymore. What would be a custom about 40 years ago if somebody got married?"

Jose Reyes: "Get an abortion." 80

"That's not a custom. What would be a custom?" 81

Tiara Young: "Get married." 82

83 "Is that a custom anymore?"
84 Jose: "Nope."
85 Tiara: "No."
86 Not in this world.
87 Domenici readily concedes, "There are a lot of D.C. Public Schools standards we are not hitting and will never meet, partly because some of them are inane, and partly because some of them our kids just cannot meet. But we're trying something different. We're spending $20,000 to $25,000 a kid [more than double what public schools spend] and just going at this for five years and we'll see where we end up. And if it works, then we can say to the public and private sectors that here we have kids who you expected to end up marginal or incarcerated, who started out reading at fifth-grade level but can now hold full-time jobs and understand long-term commitments."
88 The Angelou School has graduated eight students in its first two years. All eight went to college; seven are still enrolled.

89 Korey Brown's nine students at Marriott Hospitality charter school are spread around the room on the third floor of a D.C. government office building at Eighth and E streets NW, listening to loudly lilting, ca-chunking West African music.
90 "They're supposed to be working on knowing where every African country is," Brown says. They are not. A few work on other subjects, one dozes, two chat. "We have a lot of students who are here because their mother forced them to come, and a few who were assigned here by the courts. Most are here because their parents say the D.C. schools are wild now."
91 Marriott is anything but wild. The soft colors of the freshly painted walls are calming, and the students here are quiet and polite. With just 145 students in the high school, it's a gentle, even sleepy atmosphere. There's even a bed right next to the principal's office—part of a mock hotel room, ready for practical lessons in bed-changing and customer service. Marriott was created by the hospitality industry in good part to train its future workers.
92 Brown, 24, is the school's only social studies teacher. Fresh out of Vanderbilt, he is in his first year as a teacher. His ninth-grade course in world geography and D.C. history is the closest thing to a history course Marriott offers in the fall. In the spring, 10th- and 11th-graders study world and U.S. history. Brown teaches all of those courses.
93 "I like to deal with popular culture and not just political history," says Brown, who has carte blanche to set up his courses. "In the hospitality industry, you have to know how people deal with one another. In history, you see how people have related to one another in the past."

Brown relies heavily on the D.C. Public Schools curriculum. 94
His students "will learn pretty much the same information as
the D.C. public students, though I will take them more to mu-
seums. I often get up in the morning and decide I want to go to
the Museum of Natural History, and we just walk over at the
drop of a hat."

Administrators at Marriott like Brown, and he is a friendly, 95
energetic teacher. But his superiors don't seem to know exactly
what he's teaching this year, and in the classroom, the students'
attention is elsewhere. It's a loose atmosphere in a school that
has its heart in things nonacademic.

Depending on whom you talk to, Marriott is a training 96
school for the hotels and restaurants that helped to get it going
or a comprehensive high school with a vocational option.
Many students are here because they or their parents see
Marriott—named for the company that is its largest private
donor—as a sure route to a decent hotel job. Students, who
spend half of each year in internships at local hotels and
restaurants, say they want even more hotel training—cooking
and catering classes—in addition to the eight hospitality
courses the school already provides. School leaders are at
pains to say that the school is like any other, with an emphasis
on preparing graduates for college.

"We're trying to prepare people for the world of work," says 97
principal Flossie Johnson. "It's a way for the industry to boost
up their workforce. We're hoping that through internships,
mentoring, job shadowing, enough students will be influenced to go into the hospitality industry," not merely as desk
clerks and housekeepers, but in management, personnel and
marketing.

Hospitality is worked into all academic classes, says assis- 98
tant principal Sheena Reid. And former hospitality industry
workers teach not only the hotel courses, but some academic
classes as well. English teacher Bruce Pennington, for example, was a chef at a Washington restaurant before he came to
Marriott for his first teaching job.

In an introductory hospitality class, students work on simu- 99
lated job interviews, résumé writing and "employability
skills." The problem on the whiteboard reads, "If it costs $100
to take care of a baby, how many hours would you need to
work at $4 an hour?"

The topic in Milton Lane's 12th-grade U.S. government 100
class at the IDEA school is the unitary form of government,
taught straight from the textbook—a standard text adopted
from the D.C. schools curriculum, which IDEA's principal calls
"a good plan."

101   The 15 students take turns reading the text aloud, without expression, without the slightest sign of interest. They are in their chairs, in uniform, on another planet. Several talk to one another, one builds forts with his pencils, one scribbles notes to her friends, two have found solace in slumber.

102   Lane tries to draw their attention by assigning a task on the blackboard. Three students at a time must figure out the correct order of four sentences copied from the textbook and written in slightly jumbled form on the board. The students shuffle up to the board and seem genuinely stuck. Two girls write the same words over and over in chalk, then erase them and start again.

103   Teacher reads from text: "'Unitary governments tend to be inflexible.' They use the word 'inflexible.' What does that mean?"

104   "Not able to be worked around," one girl offers.

105   "Unbendable," a boy calls out.

106   Lane nods. "It can't be changed."

107   The bell rings. "We'll pick up on that point tomorrow."

108   This is Lane's first full year at IDEA (for Integrated Design Electronics Academy) after teaching at the District's Ballou High, which let him go in a downsizing. His style is gentle, low-energy. As the school's sole history teacher, he enjoys the freedom to construct his courses as he wishes. "In the public schools, I was at my wit's end," he says, "not necessarily because of the kids, but the politics. Here, the kids are motivated, or helped to be."

109   IDEA is a military high school with an emphasis on career training—electronics, drafting, construction—and an expectation that all students will graduate and go on to the military, work or college. Teachers put it to the students straight: In computer class, a whirlwind of learning in a converted closet, Brian Davis tells kids they will either master the innards of a PC and become well-paid technicians, or rake in that minimum wage at McDonald's. In electronics shop, Gerald Bell, who came to his first teaching job here after working for the Florida Department of Corrections, trains kids to walk out of IDEA and wire a house—a skill that could earn them $90,000 a year and more. The alternative, he warns, is checking in videos at Blockbuster.

110   The administrators and some teachers are real officers, retired. They are can-do. "A kid will say, 'Well, I'm learning-disabled,'" says Bell. "I say, 'So what? So am I.' They say, 'Well, it's hard for me.' I say, 'Okay, work harder.'"

111   The students—about two-thirds of them male—wear uniforms and take part in military drills. As at many charters, classes are longer than in public schools—85 minutes here, as

long as 100 minutes at other schools. IDEA's day is longer, too, stretching from 8 a.m. to 4:15 p.m.

Some IDEA students chose the school; most were sent by their 112 parents, often over strenuous objections about going to a military school or having to leave their friends and neighborhood—which in many cases was precisely their parents' reason for picking IDEA. "They are resistant, they are angry," says Col. William Dexter, the principal. "They hate that they have to work hard. They hate the fact that there are no D's—we go from C to F. You cannot slide by."

"My father felt that if I stayed in public school, I'd fall to bad 113 influences," says Alycia Walker, 17, a junior in her third year at IDEA. "I thought, 'Oh my God, what did I get myself into?' When I got here, I did a lot of push-ups because I broke rules, chewing gum, talking out. Twenty every time, then it moved to 60 and 80, drop on the spot, right there in the classroom. It made me a different person."

If Alycia can hit 920 on the SAT, she will qualify for an ROTC 114 college scholarship. She wants to be the first in her family to finish college. Her father, who holds two jobs as a banquet worker at two Washington hotels, wants his child to get there. He knew she needed discipline to make it. And despite her initial opposition, Alycia has come around.

"My old friends make negative comments about me. They 115 see me in uniform and they're, 'Why do you have that on? Do you think you're better than I am?' They say I don't pay attention to them. Well, they're going to graduate on a second-grade reading level, and I'm going to go to college, so they can say what they want."

IDEA shares space with another charter school and a day-care 116 center at what was once Carver Elementary, a decrepit, 92-year-old D.C. public school building in far Northeast. The hallways are dark and dank, the exterior looks like it was abandoned long ago. Along the street, more buildings are boarded up than occupied.

IDEA's founders taught together at the public system's JROTC 117 Career Academy, a school-within-a-school at a vocational high school. The program was funded by the Defense Department at first, but when that grant ran out, the city said there was no money to continue. So the leaders converted it into a charter.

The formula is small classes (as few as 10 students), no social 118 promotion (many IDEA students repeat ninth grade) and tough discipline (drill sergeants patrol the halls). Of the school's 171 students, only eight are prepared to take geometry. "Only three students have come in at grade level in math," notes Dexter. "They come in with A's and B's and they cannot add fractions.

We will not just pass them along. I had a parent come in extremely irate. Her daughter had passed algebra in the public schools and I put her in pre-algebra. I showed the mother the test paper: The child may have passed, but she didn't get the answers right."

119   A great school is a benevolent cult, led by a slightly insane visionary with an obsessive devotion to the place and its people. If you buy in—if, as student, parent or teacher, you suspend normal disbelief and adopt your school as a separate and better world than anything outside its walls—the job is halfway done.

120   In that sense, all the mountains of paper, the curricula and the applications, the test scores and evaluations, are beside the point. The GW study found that, based on test results, charter schools "are not achieving higher standards" than the public system. But teachers—about half of whom are refugees from DCPS—and students seem more satisfied at the charters. They boast not about test scores—nothing to boast about there—but about small classes and dedicated teachers, about schools where each child is known and encouraged.

121   What matters, many parents, teachers and students say, is Brian Davis at IDEA, taking kids who've never owned a computer and turning them into fact machines, fluent in the history, innards and functions of every PC ever made. What matters is Irasema Salcido creating an atmosphere at Chavez where 10th-grader Micheal Angelo Daniels can sit me down and explain that he made A's and B's when he was in the D.C. schools, but he's getting C's and D's now, and that's *good* because for the first time, teachers are making him learn, not just passing him through.

122   "Most of us come here and say, 'Oh, yeah, whatever, it's just school,'" says Brittney Morse, a 10th-grader at Chavez. "Then you're here all the time—all day, evenings, weekends, summer—and your attitude changes."

123   "If we want to get something changed, like lunch, we can do it if we sell our position," says Chessie Moquete, 16, a startlingly swift mind who came to Chavez from a Montgomery County school. "Try going to some big old school and saying that. They'll laugh at you." It doesn't particularly matter if that is true; the kids believe it, and so Chavez is, in their hearts, their place.

124   Chessie had zero desire to be torn from her friends and hauled off to an inner-city school in a cruddy building, a place where, she says, "there's no foreign language, no art, no gym." But she, like many students, has found less and less time for old friendships, for hanging out in the neighborhood.

"You live your life at school," says Larry Peterson, who is 125
also 16. "School is your life."

Chavez, like Angelou, Seed and some other charters, has 126
found its edge in longer days, longer school years. "If I can
have the kids most of the time, we can influence more,"
Salcido says. "So yes, mandatory summer school, and mandatory tutoring and the longer day, and Saturday school. And in
summer vacation, I try to get them jobs so that I can pick the
companies. The more I see them, the less the outside world can
take hold of them."

Charter schools were supposed to initiate an intense compe- 127
tition with the public schools; the idea was that both would
benefit from a robust contest of ideas and methods. Neither
side has seen much of a contest; the two worlds operate almost
entirely apart.

And each charter is a world unto itself, teaching its own ver- 128
sion of history. Charter advocates see America's children in tiny,
school-size universes, each with its own flavor of education.
That, they say, will best serve a place like Washington, where an
ill-prepared student body requires specially crafted lessons.

But the content of teaching has remained deep in the back- 129
ground as public and charter schools engage in a different kind
of rivalry—a political wrestling match in which both sides
scramble for funding, facilities and the hearts and minds of
parents. The weapons in this war are TV ads, op-ed pieces, lobbying and the spinning of test results. Every new number is
taken as evidence that either the public schools or the charters
are advancing beyond the enemy.

Public school administrators accuse charters of skimming— 130
stripping talented students from the public system. Charters
respond by cataloguing the dysfunctions of their students.

Impartial studies show most of the sniping between the two 131
systems is much ado about nothing: The populations of the
city schools and the charters are nearly indistinguishable, except that charters attract a higher percentage of Hispanic children, according to the GW study, which was led by Prof.
Jeffrey Henig. In both systems, about 66 percent of students
are low-income. Nor are charter school parents more involved
than DCPS parents.

But the GW study found some important differences be- 132
tween the two populations, notably that those parents who
choose charters have nurtured more stable families and have
higher educational aspirations for their children.

The arguments between the two sets of schools will continue 133
as long as they operate under different rules while fighting
for the same pot of tax money. While some charter advocates

jealously guard their independence, a few are open to putting all public schools—regular and charter—under the superintendent, who would then be judged by his ability to promote success in both systems.

134　　Superintendent Vance would like that. Vance is something new to the D.C. schools—a confident leader who knows education and does not need this job. Vance can and does tell folks to take a hike. But that is not what he's telling the charter schools.

135　　Vance has watched as charters have drained students, teachers and money from his system. He has seen and even admired the TV ads for charters, the ones that show what he calls "salt of the earth, upwardly mobile black Americans—believable people who want something better for their kids." Vance came into office last year intent on reversing his predecessor's antagonistic approach to charters. Former superintendent Arlene Ackerman fought the charters at every turn—over access to facilities, over payments, over bureaucratic matters large and small. Vance has resolved to cooperate with the charters on all that, to do battle with them instead at a completely different level—in the classroom.

136　　He can claim some victories there: D.C. public school test scores are rising, while preliminary numbers from many charters show flat-lining at best and depressing declines in some cases. But the charter movement has not yet peaked: Next fall, Washington will have 41 characters, up from 33. The public system, by comparison, will operate 146 schools.

137　　"You would have thought by now, after two, three years, that the public schools would be asking, 'Why are kids leaving? What should we be doing?'" Salcido says. "But I don't see it. Instead, they just fight with us, and more students leave them."

138　　Vance knows there is a certain romance to charters, and a reality that weighs very much on their side. "What I've seen are excellent examples of teaching and energetic principals who are real leaders," he says, and he vows to break through the public school bureaucracy to allow the same examples to emerge there.

139　　Can charters survive in the long run as separate worlds, as an alternative to Bush's "common schools"? The GW study concludes that charters need more time to show what they can do: "It is simply not yet clear whether charter schools will lead to the revitalization of the traditional public education system or its evisceration."

140　　Vance surveys the city's charters and sees "schools that are as good as our best. I haven't seen any that are extraordinary. I believe based on my 90 years as a professional educator"—he lets slip the slightest of smiles—"that charters, like most changes in public education, will have a life of their own. Their numbers will level off and then decline, and then seek their own level. Those that survive will be those that are really exemplary. And others will not survive. And we in the public schools will need a series of small successes that help us reclaim our schools and make them acceptable again to our citizens."

Jonathan Kozol

A TALE OF TWO SCHOOLS: HOW POOR CHILDREN ARE LOST TO THE WORLD

The following article was published in the Los Angeles Times in October 1991; it amounts to an excerpt from Kozol's polemical book Savage Inequalities: Children in America's Schools, *published in the same year. In 1964, Kozol, a teacher at the time at an inner-city school in Boston, had described in* Death at an Early Age *the terrible conditions that he found in schools in poor neighborhoods.* Savage Inequalities *emerged from his visits twenty-five years later to similar schools in places like Camden, New Jersey; Bronx, New York; East St. Louis, Illinois; and Washington, D.C.—and from his conviction that the gap between schools for the rich and those for the poor in the United States has only been widening, not narrowing.*

New Trier's physical setting might well make the students of Du Sable High School envious. The Chicago suburb school is, says a student, "a maple land of beauty and civility." While Du Sable is sited on one crowded Chicago city block, New Trier students have the use of 27 acres. While Du Sable's science students have to settle for makeshift equipment, New Trier's students have superior labs and up-to-date technology. One wing of the school, a physical-education center that includes three separate gyms, also contains a fencing room, a wrestling room and studios for dance instruction. In all, the school has seven gyms as well as an Olympic pool.

2   "This is a school with a lot of choices," says one student at New Trier; and this hardly seems an overstatement if one studies the curriculum. Courses in music, art and drama are so varied and abundant that students can virtually major in these subjects in addition to their academic programs. The modern and classical language department offers Latin and six other foreign languages. In a senior literature class, students are reading Nietzsche, Darwin, Plato, Freud and Goethe.

3   Average class size is 24 children; classes for slower learners hold 15.

4   The wealth of New Trier's geographical district provides $340,000 worth of taxable property for each child; Chicago's property wealth affords only one-fifth this much. Nonetheless, *Town and Country*, which profiled the school, gives New Trier's parents credit for a "willingness to pay enough . . . in taxes" to make this one of the state's best-funded schools. New Trier, according to the magazine, is "a striking example of what is possible when citizens want to achieve the best for their children." Families move here "seeking the best," and their children "make good use" of what they're given. Both statements may be true, but *Town and Country* flatters the privileged for having privilege but terms it aspiration.

5   "Competition is the lifeblood of New Trier," *Town and Country* writes. But there is one kind of competition that these children will not need to face. They will not compete against the children who attended Du Sable.

6   Conditions at Du Sable High School, which I visited in 1990, seem in certain ways to be improved. Improvement, however, is a relative term. Du Sable is better than it was three or four years ago. It is still a school that would be shunned—or, probably, shut down—if it were serving a white middle-class community. The building, a three-story Tudor structure, is in fairly good repair and, in this respect, contrasts with its immediate surroundings, which are almost indescribably despairing. The school, whose student population is 100% black, has no campus and no schoolyard, but there is at least a full-sized playing field and track. Overcrowding is not a problem. Much to the reverse, it is uncomfortably empty. Built in 1935 and holding some 4,500 students in past years, its student population is now fewer than 1,600. Of these students, according to data provided by the school, 646 are "chronic truants."

7   The graduation rate is 25%. Of those who get to senior year, only 17% are in a college-preparation program. Twenty percent

are in the general curriculum, a stunning 63% in vocational classes.

A vivid sense of loss is felt by standing in the cafeteria in early spring, when students file in to choose their courses for the following year. "These are the ninth graders," says a supervising teacher; but, of the official freshman class of some 600 children, only 350 fill the room. An hour later the 11th graders come to choose their classes: I count at most 170 students.

The faculty includes some excellent teachers, but there are others, says the principal, who don't belong in education. "I can't do anything with them but I'm not allowed to fire them," he says.

In a 12th-grade English class, the students are learning to pronounce a list of words. The words are not derived from any context; they are simply written on a list. A tall boy struggles to read "fastidious," "gregarious," "auspicious," "fatuous." When he struggles to pronounce "egregious," I ask him if he knows its meaning. It turns out that he has no idea. The teacher never asks the children to write the words or use them in a sentence. The lesson baffles me. It may be that these are words that will appear on a required test that states impose now in the name of "raising standards," but it all seems dreamlike and surreal.

After lunch, I talk with a group of students who are hoping to go on to college but do not seem sure of what they'll need to do to make this possible. Only one out of five seniors in the group has filed an application, and it is already April. Pamela, the one who did apply, however, tells me she neglected to submit her grades and college-entrance test results and therefore has to start again. The courses she is taking seem to rule out application to a four-year college. She tells me she is taking Spanish, literature, physical education, Afro-American history and a class she terms "job strategy." When I ask her what this is, she says, "It teaches how to dress and be on time and figure your deductions." She's a bright, articulate student, and it seems quite sad that she has not had any of the richness of curriculum that would have been given to her at a high school like New Trier.

The children in the group seem not just lacking in important, useful information that would help them to achieve their dreams, but, in a far more drastic sense, cut off and disconnected from the outside world. In talking of some recent news events, they speak of Moscow and Berlin, but all but Pamela are unaware that Moscow is the capital of the Soviet Union or that Berlin is in Germany. Several believe that Jesse Jackson is the mayor of New York City. Listening to their guesses and observing their confusion, I am thinking of the students at New Trier High. These children live in truly separate worlds. What do they have in common? Yet the kids before me seem so innocent and spiritually clean and also—most of all—so vulnerable. It's as if they have been stripped of all the armament—the reference points, the facts, the reasoning, the elemental weapons—that suburban children take for granted.

13   "It took an extraordinary combination of greed, racism, political cowardice and public apathy," writes James D. Squires, the former editor of the Chicago Tribune, "to let the public schools in Chicago get so bad." He speaks of the schools as a costly result of "the political orphaning of the urban poor . . . daytime warehouses for inferior students . . . a bottomless pit."

14   The results of these conditions are observed in thousands of low-income children in Chicago, who are virtually disjoined from the worldview, even from the basic reference points, of the American experience. A 16-year-old girl who has dropped out discusses her economic prospects with a TV interviewer.

15   "How much money would you like to make in a year?" asks the reporter.

16   "About $2,000," she replies.

17   The reporter looks bewildered by this answer. This teenage girl, he says, "has no clue that $2,000 a year isn't enough to survive anywhere in America, not even in her world."

Charles Dickens

WHAT IS A HORSE?

Was Charles Dickens (1812–1870) the greatest English novelist? This selection from the opening pages of Hard Times *(1854) illustrates Dickens's satiric edge; designed as a commentary on a "mechanical" system of education devised during the industrial revolution, it may also offer perspective on the schools of today.*

1   Thomas Gradgrind, sir. A man of realities. A man of fact and calculations. A man who proceeds upon the principle that two and two are four, and nothing over, and who is not to be talked into allowing for anything over. Thomas Gradgrind, sir—peremptorily Thomas—Thomas Gradgrind. With a rule and a pair of scales, and the multiplication table always in his pocket, sir, ready to weigh and measure any parcel of human nature, and tell you exactly what it comes to. It is a mere ques-

tion of figures, case of simple arithmetic. You might hope to get some other nonsensical belief into the head of George Gradgrind, or Augustus Gradgrind, or John Gradgrind, or Joseph Gradgrind (all suppositious, nonexistent persons), but into the head of Thomas Gradgrind—no sir!

In such terms Mr. Gradgrind always mentally introduced 2 himself, whether to his private circle of acquaintance, or to the public in general. In such terms, no doubt, substituting the words 'boys and girls', for 'sir', Thomas Gradgrind now presented Thomas Gradgrind to the little pitchers before him, who were to be filled so full of facts.

Indeed, as he eagerly sparkled at them from the cellarage 3 before mentioned, he seemed a kind of cannon loaded to the muzzle with facts, and prepared to blow them clean out of the regions of childhood at one discharge. He seemed a galvanizing apparatus, too, charged with a grim mechanical substitute for the tender young imaginations that were to be stormed away.

'Girl number twenty,' said Mr. Gradgrind, squarely pointing 4 with his square forefinger, 'I don't know that girl. Who is that girl?'

'Sissy Jupe, sir,' explained number twenty, blushing, standing 5 up, and curtseying.

'Sissy is not a name,' said Mr. Gradgrind. 'Don't call yourself 6 Sissy. Call yourself Cecilia.'

'It's father as calls me Sissy, sir,' returned the young girl in a 7 trembling voice, and with another curtsey.

'Then he has no business to do it,' said Mr. Gradgrind. 'Tell 8 him he mustn't. Cecilia Jupe. Let me see. What is your father?'

'He belongs to the horse-riding, if you please, sir.' 9

Mr. Gradgrind frowned, and waved off the objectionable 10 calling with his hand.

'We don't want to know anything about that, here. You 11 mustn't tell us about that, here. Your father breaks horses, don't he?'

'If you please, sir, when they can get any to break, they do 12 break horses in the ring, sir.'

'You mustn't tell us about the ring, here. Very well, then. 13 Describe your father as a horsebreaker. He doctors sick horses, I dare say?'

'Oh yes, sir.' 14

'Very well, then. He is a veterinary surgeon, a farrier and 15 horsebreaker. Give me your definition of a horse.'

(Sissy Jupe thrown into the greatest alarm by this demand.) 16

'Girl number twenty unable to define a horse!' said Mr. 17 Gradgrind, for the general behoof of all the little pitchers. 'Girl number twenty possessed of no facts, in reference to one of the commonest of animals! Some boy's definition of a horse. Bitzer, yours.'

18   The square finger, moving here and there, lighted suddenly on Bitzer, perhaps because he chanced to sit in the same ray of sunlight which, darting in at one of the bare windows of the intensely whitewashed room, irradiated Sissy. For, the boys and girls sat on the face of the inclined plane in two compact bodies, divided up the centre by a narrow interval; and Sissy, being at the corner of a row on the sunny side, came in for the beginning of a sunbeam, of which Bitzer, being at the corner of a row on the other side, a few rows in advance, caught the end. But, whereas the girl was so dark-eyed and dark-haired, that she seemed to receive a deeper and more lustrous colour from the sun when it shone upon her, the boy was so light-eyed and light-haired that the self-same rays appeared to draw out of him what little colour he ever possessed. His cold eyes would hardly have been eyes, but for the short ends of lashes which, by bringing them into immediate contrast with something paler than themselves, expressed their form. His short-cropped hair might have been a mere continuation of the sandy freckles on his forehead and face. His skin was so unwholesomely deficient in the natural tinge, that he looked as though, if he were cut, he would bleed white.

19   'Bitzer,' said Thomas Gradgrind. 'Your definition of a horse.'

20   'Quadruped. Graminivorous. Forty teeth, namely twenty-four grinders, four eye-teeth, and twelve incisive. Sheds coat in the spring; in marshy countries, sheds hoofs, too. Hoofs hard, but requiring to be shod with iron. Age known by marks in mouth.' Thus (and much more) Bitzer.

21   'Now girl number twenty,' said Mr. Gradgrind. 'You know what a horse is.'

Jerome Stern

WHAT THEY LEARN
IN SCHOOL

Jerome Stern taught English at Florida State University for many years until his death in 1996. This "monologue" aired March 17, 1989, on National Public Radio's All Things Considered. *It was later reprinted in* Harper's *magazine.*

In the schools now, they want them to know all about
marijuana, crack, heroin, and amphetamines,
   Because then they won't be interested in marijuana,
crack, heroin, and amphetamines,
   But they don't want to tell them anything about sex
because if the schools tell them about sex, then they will be
interested in sex,
   But if the schools don't tell them anything about sex,
   Then they will have high morals and no one will get   5
pregnant, and everything will be all right,
   And they do want them to know a lot about computers so
they will outcompete the Japanese,
   But they don't want them to know anything about real
science because then they will lose their faith and become
secular humanists,
   And they do want them to know all about this great land
of ours so they will be patriotic,
   But they don't want them to learn about the tragedy and
pain in its real history because then they will be critical
about this great land of ours and we will be passively taken
over by a foreign power,
   And they want them to learn how to think for themselves   10
so they can get good jobs and be successful,
   But they don't want them to have books that confront
them with real ideas because that will confuse their values,
   And they'd like them to be good parents,
   But they can't teach them about families because that
takes them back to how you get to be a family,
   And they want to warn them about how not to get AIDS
   But that would mean telling them how not to get AIDS,   15
   And they'd like them to know the Constitution,
   But they don't like some of those amendments except
when they are invoked by the people they agree with,

And they'd like them to vote,
But they don't want them to discuss current events because
it might be controversial and upset them and make them want
to take drugs, which they already have told them all about,

20   And they want to teach them the importance of morality,
But they also want them to learn that Winning is not
everything—it is the Only Thing,
And they want them to be well-read,
But they don't want them to read Chaucer or Shakespeare
or Aristophanes or Mark Twain or Ernest Hemingway or
John Steinbeck, because that will corrupt them,
And they don't want them to know anything about art
because that will make them weird,

25   But they do want them to know about music so they can
march in the band,
And they mainly want to teach them not to question, not
to challenge, not to imagine, but to be obedient and behave
well so that they can hold them forever as children to their
bosoms as the second millennium lurches toward its
panicky close.

Alice Walker

EVERYDAY USE

FOR YOUR GRANDMAMA

*Alice Walker (born 1944) is an essayist, poet, feminist, and ac-
tivist, but she is best known for her Pulitzer Prize–winning
third novel,* The Color Purple *(1982). Asked why she writes,
she once explained, "I'm really paying homage to people I love,
the people who are thought to be dumb and backward but who
were the ones who first taught me to see beauty." "Everyday
Use" appeared in her acclaimed collection of stories,* In Love
and Trouble, *published in 1973.*

1 I will wait for her in the yard that Maggie and I made so clean
and wavy yesterday afternoon. A yard like this is more comfortable than most people know. It is not just a yard. It is like an extended living room. When the hard clay is swept clean as a
floor and the fine sand around the edges lined with tiny, irregu-
lar grooves anyone can come and sit and look up into the elm
tree and wait for the breezes that never come inside the house.

2 Maggie will be nervous until after her sister goes: she will
stand hopelessly in corners homely and ashamed of the burn
scars down her arms and legs, eyeing her sister with a mixture
of envy and awe. She thinks her sister has held life always in
the palm of one hand, that "no" is a word the world never
learned to say to her.

3 You've no doubt seen those TV shows where the child who
has "made it" is confronted, as a surprise, by her own mother
and father, tottering in weakly from backstage. (A pleasant surprise, of course: What would they do if parent and child came
on the show only to curse out and insult each other?) On TV
mother and child embrace and smile into each other's faces.

Sometimes the mother and father weep, the child wraps them in her arms and leans across the table to tell how she would not have made it without their help. I have seen these programs.

4   Sometimes I dream a dream in which Dee and I are suddenly brought together on a TV program of this sort. Out of a dark and soft-seated limousine I am ushered into a bright room filled with many people. There I meet a smiling, gray, sporty man like Johnny Carson who shakes my hand and tells me what a fine girl I have. Then we are on the stage and Dee is embracing me with tears in her eyes. She pins on my dress a large orchid, even though she has told me once that she thinks orchids are tacky flowers.

5   In real life I am a large, big-boned woman with rough, man-working hands. In the winter I wear flannel nightgowns to bed and overalls during the day. I can kill and clean a hog as mercilessly as a man. My fat keeps me hot in zero weather. I can work outside all day, breaking ice to get water for washing; I can eat pork liver cooked over the open fire minutes after it comes steaming from the hog. One winter I knocked a bull calf straight in the brain between the eyes with a sledge hammer and had the meat hung up to chill before nightfall. But of course all this does not show on television. I am the way my daughter would want me to be: a hundred pounds lighter, my skin like an uncooked barley pancake. My hair glistens in the hot bright lights. Johnny Carson has much to do to keep up with my quick and witty tongue.

6   But that is a mistake. I know even before I wake up. Who ever knew a Johnson with a quick tongue? Who can even imagine me looking a strange white man in the eye? It seems to me I have talked to them always with one foot raised in flight, and my head turned in whichever way is farthest from them. Dee, though. She would always look anyone in the eye. Hesitation was no part of her nature.

7   "How do I look, Mama?" Maggie says, showing just enough of her thin body enveloped in pink skirt and red blouse for me to know she's there, almost hidden by the door.

8   "Come out into the yard," I say.

9   Have you ever seen a lame animal, perhaps a dog run over by some careless person rich enough to own a car, sidle up to someone who is ignorant enough to be kind to him? That is the way my Maggie walks. She has been like this, chin on chest, eyes on ground, feet in shuffle, ever since the fire that burned the other house to the ground.

10   Dee is lighter than Maggie, with nicer hair and a fuller figure. She's a woman now, though sometimes I forget. How long

ago was it that the other house burned? Ten, twelve years? Sometimes I can still hear the flames and feel Maggie's arms sticking to me, her hair smoking and her dress falling off her in little black papery flakes. Her eyes seemed stretched open, blazed open by the flames reflected in them. And Dee. I see her standing off under the sweet gum tree she used to dig gum out of: a look of concentration on her face as she watched the last dingy gray board of the house fall in toward the red-hot brick chimney. Why don't you do a dance around the ashes? I'd wanted to ask her. She hated the house that much.

I used to think she hated Maggie, too. But that was before we raised the money, the church and me, to send her to Augusta to school. She used to read to us without pity; forcing words, lies, other folks' habits, whole lives upon us two, sitting trapped and ignorant underneath her voice. She washed us in a river of make-believe, burned us with a lot of knowledge we didn't necessarily need to know. Pressed us to her with the serious way she read, to shove us away at just the moment, like dimwits, we seemed about to understand.   11

Dee wanted nice things. A yellow organdy dress to wear to her graduation from high school; black pumps to match a green suit she'd made from an old suit somebody gave me. She was determined to stare down any disaster in her efforts. Her eyelids would not flicker for minutes at a time. Often I fought off the temptation to shake her. At sixteen she had a style of her own: and knew what style was.   12

I never had an education myself. After second grade the school was closed down. Don't ask me why: in 1927 colored asked fewer questions than they do now. Sometimes Maggie reads to me. She stumbles along good-naturedly but can't see well. She knows she is not bright. Like good looks and money, quickness passed her by. She will marry John Thomas (who has mossy teeth in an earnest face) and then I'll be free to sit here and I guess just sing church songs to myself. Although I never was a good singer. Never could carry a tune. I was always better at a man's job. I used to love to milk till I was hooked in the side in '49. Cows are soothing and slow and don't bother you, unless you try to milk them the wrong way.   13

I have deliberately turned my back on the house. It is three rooms, just like the one that burned, except the roof is tin; they don't make shingle roofs anymore. There are no real windows, just some holes cut in the sides, like the portholes in a ship, but not round and not square, with rawhide holding the shutters up on the outside. This house is in a pasture, too, like the other one. No doubt when Dee sees it she will want to tear it down.   14

She wrote me once that no matter where we "choose" to live, she will manage to come see us. But she will never bring her friends. Maggie and I thought about this and Maggie asked me, "Mama, when did Dee ever *have* any friends?"

15 She had a few. Furtive boys in pink shirts hanging about on washday after school. Nervous girls who never laughed. Impressed with her they worshiped the well-turned phrase, the cute shape, the scalding humor that erupted like bubbles in lye. She read to them.

16 When she was courting Jimmy T she didn't have much time to pay to us, but turned all her faultfinding power on him. He *flew* to marry a cheap gal from a family of ignorant flashy people. She hardly had time to recompose herself.

17 When she comes I will meet—but there they are!

18 Maggie attempts to make a dash for the house, in her shuffling way, but I stay her with my hand. "Come back here," I say. And she stops and tries to dig a well in the sand with her toe.

19 It is hard to see them clearly through the strong sun. But even the first glimpse of leg out of the car tells me it is Dee. Her feet were always neat-looking, as if God himself had shaped them with a certain style. From the other side of the car comes a short, stocky man. Hair is all over his head a foot long and hanging from his chin like a kinky mule tail. I hear Maggie suck in her breath. "Uhnnnh," is what it sounds like. Like when you see the wriggling end of a snake just in front of your foot on the road. "Uhnnnh."

20 Dee next. A dress down to the ground, in this hot weather. A dress so loud it hurts my eyes. There are yellows and oranges enough to throw back the light of the sun. I feel my whole face warming from the heat waves it throws out. Earrings gold, too, and hanging down to her shoulders. Bracelets dangling and making noises when she moves her arm up to shake the folds of the dress out of her armpits. The dress is loose and flows, and as she walks closer, I like it. I hear Maggie go "Uhnnnh" again. It is her sister's hair. It stands straight up like the wool on a sheep. It is black as night and around the edges are two long pigtails that rope about like small lizards disappearing behind the ears.

21 "Wa-su-zo-Tean-o!" she says, coming on in that gliding way the dress makes her move. The short stocky fellow with the hair to his navel is all grinning and he follows up with "Asalamalakim, my mother and sister!" He moves to hug Maggie but she falls back, right up against the back of my chair. I feel her trembling there and when I look up I see the perspiration falling off her chin.

"Don't get up," says Dee. Since I am stout it takes something 22
of a push. You can see me trying to move a second or two before I make it. She turns, showing white heels through her san-
dals, and goes back to the car. Out she peeks next with a
Polaroid. She stoops down quickly and lines up picture after
picture of me sitting there in front of the house with Maggie
cowering behind me. She never takes a shot without making
sure the house is included. When a cow comes nibbling around
the edge of the yard she snaps it and me and Maggie *and* the
house. Then she puts the Polaroid in the back seat of the car,
and comes up and kisses me on the forehead.

Meanwhile Asalamalakim is going through the motions with 23
Maggie's hand. Maggie's hand is as limp as a fish, and probably
as cold, despite the sweat, and she keeps trying to pull it back.
It looks like Asalamalakim wants to shake hands but wants to
do it fancy. Or maybe he don't know how people shake hands.
Anyhow, he soon gives up on Maggie.

"Well," I say. "Dee." 24

"No, Mama," she says. "Not 'Dee,' Wangero Leewanika 25
Kemanjo!"

"What happened to 'Dee'?" I wanted to know. 26

"She's dead." Wangero said. "I couldn't bear it any longer be- 27
ing named after the people who oppress me."

"You know as well as me you was named after your aunt 28
Dicie," I said. Dicie is my sister. She named Dee. We called her
"Big Dee" after Dee was born.

"But who was *she* named after?" asked Wangero. 29

"I guess after Grandma Dee," I said. 30

"And who was she named after?" asked Wangero. 31

"Her mother," I said, and saw Wangero was getting tired. 32
"That's about as far back as I can trace it," I said. Though, in
fact, I probably could have carried it back beyond the Civil War
through the branches.

"Well," said Asalamalakim, "there you are." 33

"Uhnnnh," I heard Maggie say. 34

"There I was not," I said, "before 'Dicie' cropped up in our 35
family, so why should I try to trace it that far back?"

He just stood there grinning, looking down on me like some- 36
body inspecting a Model A car. Every once in a while he and
Wangero sent eye signals over my head.

"How do you pronounce this name?" I asked. 37

"You don't have to call me by it if you don't want to," said 38
Wangero.

"Why shouldn't I?" I asked. "If that's what you want us to call 39
you, we'll call you."

"I know it might sound awkward at first," said Wangero. 40

41   "I'll get used to it," I said. "Ream it out again."

42   Well, soon we got the name out of the way. Asalamalakim had a name twice as long and three times as hard. After I tripped over it two or three times he told me to just call him Hakim-a-barber. I wanted to ask him was he a barber, but I didn't really think he was, so I didn't ask.

43   "You must belong to those beef-cattle peoples down the road," I said. They said "Asalamalakim" when they met you, too, but they didn't shake hands. Always too busy: feeding the cattle, fixing the fences, putting up salt-lick shelters, throwing down hay. When the white folks poisoned some of the herd the men stayed up all night with rifles in their hands. I walked a mile and a half just to see the sight.

44   Hakim-a-barber said, "I accept some of their doctrines, but farming and raising cattle is not my style." (They didn't tell me, and I didn't ask, whether Wangero [Dee] had really gone and married him.)

45   We sat down to eat and right away he said he didn't eat collards and pork was unclean. Wangero, though, went on through the chitlins and corn bread, the greens and everything else. She talked a blue streak over the sweet potatoes. Everything delighted her. Even the fact that we still used the benches her daddy made for the table when we couldn't afford to buy chairs.

46   "Oh, Mama!" she cried. Then turned to Hakim-a-barber. "I never knew how lovely these benches are. You can feel the rump prints," she said, running her hands underneath her and along the bench. Then she gave a sigh and her hand closed over Grandma Dee's butter dish. "That's it!" she said. "I knew there was something I wanted to ask you if I could have." She jumped up from the table and went over in the corner where the churn stood, the milk in it clabber by now. She looked at the churn and looked at it.

47   "This churn top is what I need," she said. "Didn't Uncle Buddy whittle it out of a tree you all used to have?"

48   "Yes," I said.

49   "Uh huh," she said happily. "And I want the dasher, too."

50   "Uncle Buddy whittle that, too?" asked the barber.

51   Dee (Wangero) looked up at me.

52   "Aunt Dee's first husband whittle the dash," said Maggie so low you almost couldn't hear her. "His name was Henry, but they called him Stash."

53   "Maggie's brain is like an elephant's," Wangero said, laughing. "I can use the churn top as a centerpiece for the alcove table," she said, sliding a plate over the churn, "and I'll think of something artistic to do with the dasher."

When she finished wrapping the dasher the handle stuck 54
out. I took it for a moment in my hands. You didn't even have
to look close to see where hands pushing the dasher up and
down to make butter had left a kind of sink in the wood. In
fact, there were a lot of small sinks; you could see where
thumbs and fingers had sunk into the wood. It was beautiful
light yellow wood, from a tree that grew in the yard where Big
Dee and Stash had lived.

After dinner Dee (Wangero) went to the trunk at the foot of my 55
bed and started rifling through it. Maggie hung back in the
kitchen over the dishpan. Out came Wangero with two quilts.
They had been pieced by Grandma Dee and then Big Dee and me
had hung them on the quilt frames on the front porch and quilted
them. One was in the Lone Star pattern. The other was Walk
Around the Mountain. In both of them were scraps of dresses
Grandma Dee had worn fifty and more years ago. Bits and pieces
of Grandpa Jarrell's Paisley shirts. And one teeny faded blue
piece, about the size of a penny matchbox, that was from Great
Grandpa Ezra's uniform that he wore in the Civil War.

"Mama," Wangero said sweet as a bird. "Can I have these 56
old quilts?"

I heard something fall in the kitchen, and a minute later the 57
kitchen door slammed.

"Why don't you take one or two of the others?" I asked. 58
"These old things was just done by me and Big Dee from some
tops your grandma pieced before she died."

"No," said Wangero. "I don't want those. They are stitched 59
around the borders by machine."

"That'll make them last better," I said. 60

"That's not the point," said Wangero. "These are all pieces of 61
dresses Grandma used to wear. She did all this stitching by
hand. Imagine!" She held the quilts securely in her arms,
stroking them.

"Some of the pieces, like those lavender ones, come from old 62
clothes her mother handed down to her," I said, moving up to
touch the quilts. Dee (Wangero) moved back just enough so
that I couldn't reach the quilts. They already belonged to her.

"Imagine!" she breathed again, clutching them closely to her 63
bosom.

"The truth is," I said, "I promised to give them quilts to 64
Maggie, for when she marries John Thomas."

She gasped like a bee had stung her. 65

"Maggie can't appreciate these quilts!" she said. "She'd prob- 66
ably be backward enough to put them to everyday use."

"I reckon she would," I said. "God knows I been saving 'em 67
for long enough with nobody using 'em. I hope she will!" I

didn't want to bring up how I had offered Dee (Wangero) a quilt when she went away to college. Then she had told me they were old-fashioned, out of style.

68   "But they're *priceless!*" she was saying now, furiously; for she has a temper. "Maggie would put them on the bed and in five years they'd be in rags. Less than that!"

69   "She can always make some more," I said. "Maggie knows how to quilt."

70   Dee (Wangero) looked at me with hatred. "You just will not understand. The point is these quilts, *these* quilts!"

71   "Well," I said, stumped. "What would *you* do with them?"

72   "Hang them," she said. As if that was the only thing you *could* do with quilts.

73   Maggie by now was standing in the door. I could almost hear the sound her feet made as they scraped over each other.

74   "She can have them, Mama," she said, like somebody used to never winning anything, or having anything reserved for her. "I can 'member Grandma Dee without the quilts."

75   I looked at her hard. She had filled her bottom lip with checkerberry snuff and it gave her face a kind of dopey, hang-dog look. It was Grandma Dee and Big Dee who taught her how to quilt herself. She stood there with her scarred hands hidden in the folds of her skirt. She looked at her sister with something like fear but she wasn't mad at her. This was Maggie's portion. This was the way she knew God to work.

76   When I looked at her like that something hit me in the top of my head and ran down to the soles of my feet. Just like when I'm in church and the spirit of God touches me and I get happy and shout. I did something I never had done before: hugged Maggie to me, then dragged her on into the room, snatched the quilts out of Miss Wangero's hands and dumped them into Maggie's lap. Maggie just sat there on my bed with her mouth open.

77   "Take one or two of the others," I said to Dee.

78   But she turned without a word and went out to Hakim-a-barber.

79   "You just don't understand," she said, as Maggie and I came out to the car.

80   "What don't I understand?" I wanted to know.

81   "Your heritage," she said. And then she turned to Maggie, kissed her, and said, "You ought to try to make something of yourself, too, Maggie. It's really a new day for us. But from the way you and Mama still live you'd never know it."

82   She put on some sunglasses that hid everything above the tip of her nose and her chin.

83   Maggie smiled; maybe at the sunglasses. But a real smile, not scared. After we watched the car dust settle I asked Maggie

to bring me a dip of snuff. And then the two of us sat there just enjoying, until it was time to go in the house and go to bed.

Bell Hooks
PEDAGOGY
AND POLITICAL
COMMITMENT:
A COMMENT

Writer, feminist, cultural critic, and teacher, Bell Hooks teaches at City College of New York. You will learn more about her by reading the following essay, which is a chapter in her book Talking Back: Thinking Feminist, Thinking Black *(1989), one of her many books on race, gender, politics, and culture.*

Education is a political issue for exploited and oppressed people. The history of slavery in the United States shows that black people regarded education—book learning, reading, and writing—as a political necessity. Struggle to resist white supremacy and racist attacks informed black attitudes toward education. Without the capacity to read and write, to think critically and analytically, the liberated slave would remain forever bound, dependent on the will of the oppressor. No aspect of black liberation struggle in the United States has been as charged with revolutionary fervor as the effort to gain access to education at all levels.   1

From slavery to the present, education has been revered in black communities, yet it has also been suspect. Education represented a means of radical resistance but it also led to caste/class divisions between the educated and the uneducated, as it meant the learned black person could more easily adopt the values and attitudes of the oppressor. Education could help one assimilate. If one could not become the white oppressor, one could at least speak and think like him or her, and in some cases the educated black person assumed the role of mediator—explaining uneducated black folks to white folks.   2

Given this history, many black parents have encouraged children to acquire an education while simultaneously warning us   3 about the danger of education. One very real danger, as many black parents traditionally perceived it, was that the learned black person might lose touch with the concrete reality of everyday black experience. Books and ideas were important but not important enough to become barriers between the individual and community participation. Education was considered to have the potential to alienate one from community and awareness of our collective circumstance as black people. In my family, it was constantly emphasized that too much book learning could lead to madness. Among everyday black folks, madness was deemed to be any loss of one's ability to communicate effectively with others, one's ability to cope with practical affairs.

4   These ambivalent attitudes toward education have made it difficult for black students to adapt and succeed in educational settings. Many of us have found that to succeed at the very education we had been encouraged to seek would be most easily accomplished if we separated ourselves from the experience of black folk, the underprivileged experience of the black underclass that was our grounding reality. This ambivalent stance toward education has had a tremendous impact on my psyche. Within the working-class black community where I grew up, I learned to be suspicious of education and suspicious of white folks. I went for my formative educational years to all-black schools. In those schools, I learned about the reality of white people but also about the reality of black people, about our history. We were taught in those schools to be proud of ourselves as black people and to work for the uplift of our race.

5   Experiencing as I did an educational environment structured to meet our needs as black people, we were deeply affected when those schools ceased to exist and we were compelled to attend white schools instead. At the white school, we were no longer people with a history, a culture. We did not exist as anything other than primitives and slaves. School was no longer the place where one learned how to use education as a means to resist white-supremacist oppression. Small wonder that I spent my last few years of high school depressed about education, feeling as though we had suffered a grave loss, that the direction had shifted, the goals had changed. We were no longer taught by people who spoke our language, who understood our culture; we were taught by strangers. And further, we were dependent on those strangers for evaluation, for approval. We learned not to challenge their racism since they had power over us. Although we were told at home that we were not to openly challenge whites, we were also told not to learn to think like them.

Within this atmosphere of ambivalence toward education, I,   6
who had been dubbed smart, was uncertain about whether or
not I wanted to go to college. School was an oppressive drag.
Yet the fate of smart black women had already been decided;
we would be schoolteachers. At the private, mostly white
women's college where I spent my first year, I was an outsider.
Determined to stay grounded in the reality of southern black
culture, I kept myself aloof from the social practices of the
white women with whom I lived and studied. They, in their
turn, perceived me as hostile and alien. I, who had always been
a member of a community, was now a loner. One of my white
teachers suggested to me that the alienation I experienced was
caused by being at a school that was not intellectually challenging, that I should go to Stanford where she had gone.

My undergraduate years at Stanford were difficult ones. Not   7
only did I feel myself alienated from the white people who
were my peers and teachers, but I met black people who were
different, who did not think the way I did about black culture
or black life—who seemed in some ways as strange to me as
white people. I had known black people from different classes
in my hometown, but we still experienced much the same reality, shared similar world views. It was different at Stanford. I
was in an environment where black people's class backgrounds
and their values were radically different than my own.

To overcome my feelings of isolation, I bonded with workers,   8
with black women who labored as maids, as secretaries. With
them I felt at home. During holiday break, I would stay in their
homes. Yet being with them was not the same as being home.
In their houses I was an honored guest, someone to be looked
up to, because I was getting a college education. My undergraduate years at Stanford were spent struggling to find meaning and significance in education. I had to succeed. I could not
let my family or the race down. And so I graduated in English.
I had become an English major for the same reason that hundreds of students of all races become English majors: I like to
read. Yet I did not fully understand that the study of literature
in English departments would really mean the study of works
by white males.

It was disheartening for me and other non-white students to   9
face the extent to which education in the university was not the
site of openness and intellectual challenge we had longed for.
We hated the racism, the sexism, the domination. I began to
have grave doubts about the future. Why was I working to be
an academic if I did not see people in that environment who
were opposing domination? Even those very few concerned
professors who endeavored to make courses interesting, to

create a learning atmosphere, rarely acknowledged destructive and oppressive aspects of authoritarian rule in and outside the classroom. Whether one took courses from professors with feminist politics or marxist politics, their presentations of self in the classroom never differed from the norm. This was especially so with marxist professors. I asked one of these professors, a white male, how he could expect students to take his politics seriously as a radical alternative to a capitalist structure if we found marxist professors to be even more oppressively authoritarian than other professors. Everyone seemed reluctant to talk about the fact that professors who advocated radical politics rarely allowed their critique of domination and oppression to influence teaching strategies. The absence of any model of a professor who was combining a radical politic opposing domination with practice of that politic in the classroom made me feel wary about my ability to do differently. When I first began to teach, I tried not to emulate my professors in any way. I devised different strategies and approaches that I felt were more in keeping with my politics. Reading the work of Paulo Freire greatly influenced my sense that much was possible in the classroom setting, that one did not simply need to conform.

10   In the introduction to a conversation with Paulo Freire published in *idac*, emphasis is placed on an educative process that is not based on an authoritarian, dominating model where knowledge is transferred from a powerful professor to a powerless student. Education, it was suggested, could be a space for the development of critical consciousness, where there could be dialogue and mutual growth of both student and professor:

> If we accept education in this richer and more dynamic sense of acquiring a critical capacity and intervention in reality, we immediately know that there is no such thing as neutral education. All education has an intention, a goal, which can only be political. Either it mystifies reality by rendering it impenetrable and obscure—which leads people to a blind march through incomprehensible labyrinths—or it unmasks the economic and social structures which are determining the relationships of exploitation and oppression among persons, knocking down labyrinths and allowing people to walk their own road. So we find ourselves confronted with a clear option: to educate for liberation or to educate for domination.

In retrospect, it seems that my most radical professors were still educating for domination. And I wondered if this was so because we could not imagine how to educate for liberation in the corporate university. In Freire's case, he speaks as a white man of privilege who stands and acts in solidarity with oppressed and exploited groups, especially in their efforts to establish literacy programs that emphasize education for critical consciousness. In my case, as a black woman from a working-class background, I stand and act as a member of an oppressed, exploited group who has managed to acquire a degree of privilege. While I choose to educate for liberation, the site of my work has been within the walls of universities peopled largely by privileged white students and a few non-white students. Within those walls, I have tried to teach literature and Women's Studies courses in a way that does not reinforce structures of domination: imperialism, racism, sexism, and class exploitation.

I do not pretend that my approach is politically neutral, yet this disturbs students who have been led to believe that all education within the university should be "neutral." On the first day of classes, I talk about my approach, about the ways the class may be different from other classes as we work to create strategies of learning to meet our needs—and of course we must discover together what those needs are. Even though I explain that the class will be different, students do not always take it seriously. One central difference is that all students are expected to contribute to class discussion, if not spontaneously, then through the reading of paragraphs and short papers. In this way, every student makes a contribution, every student's voice is heard. Despite the fact that this may be stated at the onset of class, written clearly on the syllabus, students will complain and whine about having to speak. It is only recently that I have begun to see much of the complaining as "change back" behavior. Students and teachers find it hard to shift their paradigms even though they have been longing for a different approach. 11

Struggling to educate for liberation in the corporate university is a process that I have found enormously stressful. Implementing new teaching strategies that aim to subvert the norm, to engage students fully, is really a difficult task. Unlike the oppressed or colonized, who may begin to feel as they engage in education for critical consciousness a newfound sense of power and identity that frees them from colonization of the mind, that liberates, privileged students are often downright unwilling to acknowledge that their minds have been colonized, that they have been learning how to be oppressors, how to dominate, or at least how to passively accept the domination of others. This past teaching year, a student confronted me (a black male student from a middle-class urban experience) in 12 class with the question of what I expected from them (like his tone of voice was: did I have the right to expect anything). Seriously, he wanted to know what I wanted from them. I told him and the class that I thought the most important learning experience that could happen in our classroom was that students would learn to think critically and analytically, not just about the required books, but about the world they live in. Education for critical consciousness that encourages all students—privileged or non-privileged—who are seeking an entry into class privilege rather than providing a sense of freedom and release, invites critique of conventional expectations and desires. They may find such an experience terribly threatening. And even though they may approach the situation with great openness, it may still be difficult, and even painful.

13   This past semester, I taught a course on black women writers in which students were encouraged to think about the social context in which literature emerges, the impact of politics of domination—racism, sexism, class exploitation—on the writing. Students stated quite openly and honestly that reading the literature in the context of class discussion was making them feel pain. They complained that everything was changing for them, that they were seeing the world differently, and seeing things in that world that were painful to face. Never before had a group of students so openly talked about the way in which learning to see the world critically was causing pain. I did not belittle their pain or try to rationalize it. Initially, I was uncertain about how to respond and just asked us all to think about it. Later, we discussed the way in which all their comments implied that to experience pain is bad, an indication that something is wrong. We talked about changing how we perceive pain, about our society's approach to pain, considering the possibility that this pain could be a constructive sign of growth. I shared with them my sense that the experience should not be viewed as static, that at another point the knowledge and new perspectives they had might lead to clarity and a greater sense of well-being.

14   Education for liberation can work in the university setting but it does not lead students to feel they are enjoying class or necessarily feeling positive about me as a teacher. One aspect of radical pedagogy that has been difficult for me is learning to cope with not being seen positively by students. When one provides an experience of learning that is challenging, possibly threatening, it is not entertainment, or necessarily a fun experience, though it can be. If one primary function of such a pedagogy is to prepare students to live and act more fully in the world, then it is usually when they are in that context, outside

the classroom, that they most feel and experience the value of what they have shared and learned. For me, this often means that most positive feedback I receive as a teacher comes after students have left the class and rarely during it.

Recently talking with a group of students and faculty at 15
Duke University, we focussed on the issue of exposure and vulnerability. One white male professor, who felt his politics to be radical, his teaching to be an education for liberation, his teaching strategies subversive, felt it was important that no one in the university's bureaucratic structure know what was happening in the classroom. Fear of exposure may lead teachers with radical visions to suppress insight, to follow set norms. Until I came to teach at Yale, no one outside my classes had paid much attention to what was going on inside them. At Yale, students talked a lot outside about my classes, about what happens in them. This was very difficult for me as I felt both exposed and constantly scrutinized. I was certainly subjected to much critical feedback both from students in my classes and faculty and students who heard about them. Their responses forced recognition of the way in which teaching that is overtly political, especially if it radically challenges the status quo, requires acknowledgement that to choose education as the practice of freedom is to take a political stance that may have serious consequences.

Despite negative feedback or pressures, the most rewarding 16
aspect of such teaching is to influence the way students mature and grow intellectually and spiritually. For those students who wish to try to learn in a new way but who have fears, I try to reassure them that their involvement in different types of learning experiences need not threaten their security in other classes; it will not destroy the backing system of education, so they need not panic. Of course, if all they can do is panic, then that is a sign that the course is not for them. My commitment to education as the practice of freedom is strengthened by the large number of students who take my courses and, by doing so, affirm their longing to learn in a new way. Their testimony confirms that education as the practice of liberation does take place in university settings, that our lives are transformed there, that there we do meaningful radical political work.

The ad for Hofstra University on this page appeared in several magazines and newspapers in 1989 and 1990; the ad for Seton Hall University on the next page appeared in the same places in 2001 and 2002. What does each ad imply about the purpose of a college education? Which is more persuasive?

What does it take to be the best?

Determination and hard work, at any age, can lead to being the best. Hofstra University, just 50 years old, is already among the top ten percent of American colleges and universities in almost all academic criteria and resources.

Professionally accredited programs in such major areas as business, engineering, law, psychology and education.

A library with over 1.1 million volumes *on campus*—a collection larger than that of 95% of American universities.

Record enrollments with students from 31 states and 59 countries— with a student-faculty ratio of only 17 to 1.

The largest, most sophisticated non-commercial television facility in the East. A high technology undergraduate teaching resource with broadcast-quality production capability.

A ranking in *Barron's Guide to the Most Prestigious Colleges*—one of only 262 colleges and universities chosen from almost 4,000.

At Hofstra, determination, inspiration and hard work are qualities our faculty demands in itself and instills in our students. These qualities are what it takes to be the best. In anything.

HOFSTRA UNIVERSITY
WE TEACH SUCCESS.

50th Anniversary
Hempstead, L.I., New York 11550

Garry B. Trudeau
DOONESBURY

Garry B. Trudeau (born 1948) is one of America's most influential (and controversial) political and social commentators. His vehicle is the comic strip "Doonesbury," which appears in more than 850 newspapers and whose audience may top 100 million readers.

W.D. Snodgrass
THE EXAMINATION

W. D. Snodgrass (born 1926), educated at Geneva College and the University of Iowa, taught for years at the University of Delaware. His book of poetry Heart's Needle *won the Pulitzer Prize in 1960.*

Under the thick beams of that swirly smoking light,   1
   The black robes are clustering, huddled in together.
Hunching their shoulders, they spread short, broad sleeves
    like night-
   Black grackles' wings; then they reach bone-yellow

Leathery fingers, each to each. And are prepared. Each turns   5
   His single eye—or since one can't discern their eyes,
That reflective single, moon-pale disc which burns
   Over each brow—to watch this uncouth shape that lies

Strapped to their table. One probes with his ragged nails
   The slate-sharp calf, explores the thigh and the lean thews   10
Of the groin. Others raise, red as piratic sails,
   His wing, stretching, trying the pectoral sinews.

One runs his finger down the whet of that cruel
   Golden beak, lifts back the horny lids from the eyes,
Peers down in one bright eye malign as a jewel,   15
   And steps back suddenly. "He is anaesthetized?"

"He is. He is. Yes. Yes." The tallest of them, bent
   Down by the head, rises: "This drug possesses powers
Sufficient to still all gods in this firmament.
   This is Garuda who was fierce. He's yours for hours.   20

"We shall continue, please." Now, once again, he bends
   To the skull, and its clamped tissues. Into the cran-
ial cavity, he plunges both of his hands
   Like obstetric forceps and lifts out the great brain,

Holds it aloft, then gives it to the next who stands   25
   Beside him. Each, in turn, accepts it, although loath,
Turns it this way, that way, feels it between his hands
   Like a wasp's nest or some sickening outsized growth.

They must decide what thoughts each part of it must think;
30   They tap at, then listen beside, each suspect lobe;
Next, with a crow's quill dipped into India ink,
     Mark on its surface, as if on a map or globe,

Those dangerous areas which need to be excised.
     They rinse it, then apply antiseptics to it;
35   Now silver saws appear which, inch by inch, slice
     Through its ancient folds and ridges, like thick suet.

It's rinsed, dried, and daubed with thick salves. The smoky saws
     Are scrubbed, resterilized, and polished till they gleam.
The brain is repacked in its case. Pinched in their claws,
40   Glimmering needles stitch it up, that leave no seam.

Meantime, one of them has set blinders to the eyes,
     Inserting light packing beneath each of the ears,
And calked the nostrils in. One, with thin twine, ties
     The genitals off. With long wood-handled shears,

45   Another chops pinions out of the scarlet wings.
     It's hoped that with disuse he will forget the sky
Or, at least, in time, learn, among other things,
     To fly no higher than his superiors fly.

Well; that's a beginning. The next time, they can split
50   His tongue and teach him to talk correctly, can give
Him opinions on fine books and choose clothing fit
     For the integrated area where he'll live.

Their candidate may live to give them thanks one day.
     He will recover and may hope for such success.
55   He might return to join their ranks. Bowing away,
     They nod, whispering, "One of ours; one of ours. Yes. Yes."

John Searle
THE CASE FOR A TRADITIONAL LIBERAL ARTS EDUCATION

John Searle, who has been a professor of philosophy at the University of California–Berkeley for many years, is best known for his advocacy of "speech-act theory," a theory of communication which has been both influential and roundly debated in philosophy, linguistics, and rhetoric since it appeared in Searle's Speech Acts: An Essay in the Philosophy of Language *in 1969. Searle has been controversial in other ways too, and the following essay is certainly polemical in many respects. "The Case for a Traditional Liberal Arts Education" was originally published, interestingly enough, in* The Journal of Blacks in Higher Education *(an academically oriented magazine specializing in articles that explore one or another aspect of the African American experience in higher education), in the fall of 1996. Perhaps anticipating that people might wonder why the essay appeared there, the editor's headnote to the article explained its placement in the journal by quoting Nobel prize winner Toni Morrison's statement that "the first gesture of contempt for working-class students is to trivialize and devalue their need for an interest in art, languages, and culture."*

There is supposed to be a major debate—or even a set of debates—going on at present concerning a crisis in the universities, specifically a crisis in the teaching of the humanities. This debate is supposed to be in large part about whether a certain traditional conception of liberal education should be replaced by something sometimes called "multiculturalism." These disputes have even reached the mass media, and several best-selling books are devoted to discussing them and related issues. Though the arguments are ostensibly about Western civilization itself, they are couched in a strange jargon that includes not only "multiculturalism" but also "the canon," "political correctness," "ethnicity," "affirmative action," and even more rebarbative expressions such as "hegemony," "empowerment," "poststructuralism," "deconstruction," and "patriarchalism." 1

Since I do not know of a neutral vocabulary, I will describe the debate as between the "defenders" and the "challengers" of 2 the tradition. I realize that there is a great deal of variety on each side and more than one debate going on, but I am going to try to expose some common core assumptions of each side, assumptions seldom stated explicitly but which form the unstated premises behind the enthymemes that each side tends to use. Let us start by stating naively the traditionalists' view of higher education and, equally naively, the most obvious of the challengers' objections to it. This will, I hope, enable us to get into the deeper features of the debate.

3   Here is the traditionalists' view: There is a certain tradition in American higher education, especially in the teaching of the humanities. The idea behind this tradition is that there is a body of works of philosophy, literature, history, and art that goes from the Greeks right up to the present day, and though it is not a unified tradition, there are certain family resemblances among the leading works in it, and for want of a better name, we call it the Western intellectual tradition. It extends in philosophy from Socrates to Wittgenstein or, if you like, from the pre-Socratics to Quine, in literature from the Greek poets and playwrights right up to, for example, James Joyce and Ernest Hemingway. The idea is that if you are going to be an educated person in the United States, you must have some familiarity with some of the chief works in this tradition because it defines our particular culture. You do not know who you are, in a sense, unless you have some familiarity with these works, because America is a product of this tradition, and the Constitution in particular is a product of a certain philosophical element in this tradition, the European Enlightenment. And then, too, we think that many works in this tradition, some of those by Shakespeare and Plato, for example, are really so good that they are of *universal* human interest.

4   So much for the naive statement of the traditionalist view. There is an objection put by the challengers, and the objection, to put it in its crudest form, is as follows: If you look closely at the reading lists of this "Great Tradition," you will discover that the books are almost all by white males from Europe and North America. There are vast areas of the earth and great civilizations whose achievements are totally unrepresented in this conception of "liberal education." Furthermore, within the population of the United States as it is presently constituted, there are lots of ethnic minorities, as well as the largest minority of all, women, whose special needs, interests, traditions, and achievements are underrepresented or in some cases not represented at all in this tradition.

5   What is the response of the traditionalists to this objection? At this point the debate already begins to get murky, because it

is hard to find traditionalist authors who address the objection directly, so I am going to interject myself and present what I think the traditionalists should say, given their other assumptions. The traditionalist should just accept this objection as a valid criticism and amend the "canon" accordingly. If great works by Asian authors, for example, have been excluded from the "canon" of great works of literature, then by all means let us expand the so-called canon to include them. Closer to home, if great women writers have been excluded, often because they are women, then let us expand membership in the list to include them as well. According to the traditionalist theory, one of the advantages of higher education is that it enables us to see our own civilization and mode of sensibility as one possible form of life among others. And one of the virtues of the tradition is the enormous variety within it. In fact, there never was a "canon." There was a set of constantly revised judgments about which books deserve close study, which deserve to be regarded as "classics." So, based on the traditionalists' own conception, there should be no objection to enlarging the list to include classics from sources outside the Western tradition and from neglected elements within it.

As I have presented it, the challengers are making a commonsense objection, to which the traditionalists have a commonsense answer. So it looks as if we have an obvious solution to an interesting problem and can all go home. What is there left to argue about? But it is at this point that the debate becomes interesting. What I have discovered in reading books and articles about this debate is that the objection to the so-called canon—that it is unrepresentative, that it is too exclusive—cannot be met by opening membership to include works by previously excluded elements of the population, since some people would accept such reform as adequate, but many will not. Why not? In order to answer that question I am going to try to state the usually unstated presuppositions made by both the traditionalists and the challengers. I realize, to repeat, that there is a great deal of variety on both sides, but I believe that each side holds certain assumptions, and it is important to try to make them explicit. In the debates one sees, the fundamental issues often are not coming out into the open, and as a result the debaters are talking past each other, seldom making contact. One side accuses the other of racism, imperialism, sexism, elitism, and of being hegemonic and patriarchal. The other side accuses the first of trying to destroy intellectual standards and of politicizing the university. So what is actually going on? What is in dispute?

Assumptions Behind the Tradition

7   I will try to state the assumptions behind the tradition as a set of propositions, confining myself to half a dozen for the sake of brevity. The first assumption is that the criteria for inclusion in the list of "the classics" is supposed to be a combination of intellectual merit and historical importance. Some authors, Shakespeare for example, are included because of the quality of their work; others, Marx for example, are included because they have been historically so influential. Some, Plato for instance, are both of high quality and historically influential.

8   A second assumption made by the traditionalists is that there are intersubjective standards of rationality, intelligence, truth, validity, and general intellectual merit. In our list of required readings we include Plato but not randomly selected comic strips, because we think there is an important distinction in quality between the two, and *we think we can justify the claim that there is a distinction.* The standards are not algorithmic. Making judgments of quality is not like measuring velocities, but it is not arbitrary either.

9   A third assumption behind the tradition is that one of the things we are to do is to enable our students to overcome the mediocrity, provincialism, or other limitations of whatever background from which they may have come. The idea is that your life is likely to be in large measure a product of a lot of historical accidents: the town you were born in, the community you grew up in, the sort of values you learned in high school. One of the aims of a liberal education is to liberate our students from the contingencies of their backgrounds. We invite the student into the membership of a much larger intellectual community. This third feature of the traditional educational theory, then, is what one might call an invitation to transcendence. The professor asks his or her students to read books that are designed to challenge any complacencies that the students may have brought to the university when they first arrived there.

10   A fourth assumption made by the traditionalists, which is related to the third, is that in the Western tradition, there is a peculiar combination of what one might call extreme universalism and extreme individualism. Again, this tends to be tacit and is seldom made explicit. The idea is that the most precious thing in the universe is the human individual, but that the human individual is precious as part of the universal human civilization. The idea is that one achieves one's maximum intellectual *individual* potential by coming to see oneself as part of a *universal* human species with a universal human culture.

A fifth feature of this tacit theory behind educational tradi- 11
tionalism is that a primary function of liberal education is criticism of oneself and one's community. According to this conception, the unexamined life is not worth living, and the
examined life is life criticized. I do not know of any intellectual
tradition that is as savagely self-critical as the Western tradition. Its hero is Socrates, and of course we all know what happened to him. "I would rather die by the present argument
than live by any other," he said. This is the model we hold up to
our students: the lone individual, standing out against the
hypocrisy, stupidity, and dishonesty of the larger community.
And that tradition goes right through to the nineteenth and
twentieth centuries, through Freud, Nietzsche, Marx, and
Bertrand Russell, to mention just a few. The tradition is that of
the extremely critical intellectual commentator attacking the
pieties and inadequacies, the inconsistencies and hypocrisies
of the surrounding community.

I will mention a sixth and final feature. Objectivity and truth 12
are possible because there is an independently existing reality
to which our true utterances correspond. This view, called realism, has often been challenged by various forms of idealism
and relativism within Western culture but it has remained the
dominant metaphysical view in our culture. Our natural science, for example, is based on it. A persistent topic of debate is:
How far does it extend? Is there, for example, an independently existing set of moral values that we can discover, or are
we, for example, just expressing our subjective feelings and attitudes when we make moral judgments? I am tempted to continue this list but I hope that what I have said so far will give
you a feel for the underlying assumptions of the traditionalist
theory of liberal education.

I am now going to try to do the same for the challengers, but 13
this is harder to do without distortion, simply because there is
more variety among the critics of the tradition than there is in
the tradition itself. Nonetheless, I am going to do my best to try
to state a widely held set of core assumptions made by the
challengers. Perhaps very few people, maybe no one, believe all
of the assumptions I will try to make explicit, but they are
those I have found commonly made in the debates. The first
assumption made by the challengers is that the subgroup into
which you were born—your ethnic, racial, class, and gender
background—matters enormously; it is important for education. In the extreme version of this assumption, you are essentially defined by your ethnic, racial, class, and gender background. That is the most important thing in your life. The dean
of an American state university told me, "The most important

thing in my life is being a woman and advancing the cause of women." Any number of people think that the most important thing in their lives is their blackness or their Hispanic identity, et cetera. This is something new in American higher education. Of course, there have always been people who were defined or who preferred to be defined by their ethnic group or by other such affiliations, but it has not been part of the theory of what the university was trying to do that we should *encourage* self-definition by ethnicity, race, gender, or class. On the contrary, as I noted in my list of the traditionalist assumptions, we were trying to encourage students to rise above the accidents of such features. But to a sizable number of American academics, it has now become acceptable to think that the most important thing in one's life is precisely these features. Notice the contrast between the traditionalists and the challengers on this issue. For the traditionalists, what matters is the individual within the universal. For the challengers, the universal is an illusion, and the individual has an identity only as a member of some subgroup.

14   A second feature of this alternative view is the belief that, to state it crudely, all cultures are equal. Not only are they morally equal, as human beings are morally equal, but all cultures are intellectually equal as well. According to this view, the idea that we have more to learn from the representatives of one race, gender, class, or ethnic group than we do from the representatives of others is simply racism and old-fashioned imperialism. It is simply a residue of Eurocentric imperialism to suppose, as the traditionalists have been supposing, that certain works of European white males are somehow superior to the products of other cultures, classes, genders, and ethnic groups. Belief in the superiority of the Western canon is a priori objectionable because all authors are essentially representatives of their culture, and all cultures are intellectually equal.

15   In this alternative view, a third feature is that when it comes to selecting what you should read, representativeness is obviously crucial. In a multiculturalist educational democracy, every culture must be represented. The difficulty with the prevailing system is that most groups are underrepresented, and certain groups are not represented at all. The proposal of opening up doors just to let a few superstars in is no good, because that still leaves you, in plain and simple terms, with too many dead, white, European males. Even if you include every great woman novelist that you want to include—every Jane Austen, George Eliot, and Virginia Woolf—you are still going to have too many dead, white, European males on your list. It is part of

the elitism, the hegemonism, and the patriarchalism of the existing ideology that it tries to perpetuate the same patterns of repression even while pretending to be opening up. Worse yet, the lack of diversity in the curriculum is matched by an equal lack of *diversity in the faculty*. It's no use getting rid of the hegemony of *dead* white males in the curriculum if the faculty that teaches the multicultural curriculum is still mostly *living* white males. Representativeness is crucial not only in the curriculum but even more so in the composition of the faculty.

I want to pause here to contrast these three assumptions of the challengers with those of the traditionalists. The traditionalists think they are selecting both reading lists and faculty members on grounds of quality and not on grounds of representation. They think they select Plato and Shakespeare, for example, because they produced works of genius, not because they are specimens or representatives of some group. The challengers think this is self-deception at best, oppression at worst. They think that since the canon consists mostly of white European males, the authors must have been selected *because* they are white European males. And they think that because most of the professors are white males, this fact by itself is proof that there is something wrong with the composition of the faculty.   16

You can see the distinction between the challengers and the traditionalists if you imagine a counterfactual situation. Suppose it was discovered by an amazing piece of historical research that the works commonly attributed to Plato and Aristotle were not written by Greek males but by two Chinese women who were cast ashore on the coast of Attica when a Chinese junk shipwrecked off the Pireaus in the late fifth century B.C. What difference would this make to our assessment of the works of Plato and Aristotle? From the traditionalist point of view, none whatever. It would be just an interesting historical fact. From the challengers' point of view, I think it would make a tremendous difference. Ms. Plato and Ms. Aristotle would now acquire a new authenticity as genuine representatives of a previously underrepresented minority, and the most appropriate faculty to teach their work would then be Chinese women. Implicit in the traditionalists' assumptions I stated is the view that the faculty member does not have to exemplify the texts he or she teaches. They assume that the works of Marx can be taught by someone who is not a Marxist, just as Aquinas can be taught by someone who is not a Catholic, and Plato by someone who is not a Platonist. But the challengers assume, for example, that women's studies should be taught by feminist women, Chicano studies by Chicanos committed to a certain set of values, and so on.   17

18   These three points, that you are defined by your culture, that all cultures are created equal, and that representation is the criterion for selection both of the books to be read and the faculty to teach them, are related to a fourth assumption: The primary purpose of education in the humanities is political transformation. I have read any number of authors who claim this, and I have had arguments with several people, some of them in positions of authority in universities, who tell me that the purpose of education, in the humanities at least, is political transformation. For example, another dean at a big state university, herself a former Berkeley radical, has written that her academic life is just an extension of her political activities. In its most extreme version, the claim is not just that the purpose of education in the humanities *ought* to be political, but rather that all education always has been political and always will necessarily be political, so it might as well be beneficially political. The idea that the traditionalists with their "liberal education" are somehow teaching some politically neutral philosophical tradition is entirely a self-deceptive masquerade. According to this view, it is absurd to accuse the challengers of politicizing the university; it already is politicized. Education is political down to the ground. And, so the story goes, the difference between the challengers, as against the traditional approach, is that the traditional approach tries to disguise the fact that it is essentially engaged in the political indoctrination of generations of young people so that they will continue to accept a system of hegemonic, patriarchal imperialism. The challengers, on the other hand, think of themselves as accepting the inevitably political nature of the university, and they want to use it so that they and their students can be liberated into a genuine multicultural democracy. When they say that the purpose of the university is political, this is not some new proposal that they are making. They think of themselves as just facing up to the facts as they always have been.

19   Once you understand that the challengers regard the university as essentially political, then several puzzling features of the present debate become less puzzling. Why has radical politics migrated into academic departments of literature? In my intellectual childhood, there were plenty of radical activists about, but they tended to operate in a public political arena, or, to the extent they tended to be in universities at all, they were usually in departments of political science, sociology, and economics. Now, as far as I can tell, the leading intellectual centers of radical political activity in the United States are departments of English, French, and comparative literature. We are, for example, in the odd situation where America's two "leading

Marxists" are both professors of English. How did this come about? What would Marx think if he knew that his main impact was on literary criticism? Well, part of the reason for the migration of radical politics into literature departments is that Marxism in particular and left-wing radicalism in general have been discredited as theories of politics, society, and historical change. If ever a philosophical theory was refuted by events, it was the Marxist theory of the inevitable collapse of the capitalist economies and their revolutionary overthrow by the working class, to be followed by the rise of a classless society. Instead, it is the Marxist economies that have collapsed and the Marxist governments that have been overthrown. So, having been refuted as theories of society, these views retreated into departments of literature, where to some extent they still flourish as tools of "interpretation."

There is a more important reason, however. During the 20 1960s a fairly sizable number of leftist intellectuals became convinced that the best arena of social change was culture, that high culture in general and university departments of literature in particular could become important weapons in the struggle to overcome racism, imperialism, et cetera. We are now witnessing some of the consequences of this migration. As someone—I think it was Irving Howe—remarked, it is characteristic of this generation of radicals that they don't want to take over the country, they want to take over the English department. But, I would add, they think taking over the English department is the first step toward taking over the country.

So far, then, I have tried to isolate four presuppositions of 21 the challengers: that ethnicity is important; that cultures are intellectually equal; that representativeness is crucial in the curriculum and in faculty composition; and that an important function of the humanities is political and social change. Now let me identify a fifth: There are no such things as objective standards. As one pamphlet published by the American Council of Learned Societies put it, "As the most powerful modern philosophies and theories have been demonstrating, claims of disinterest, objectivity, and universality are not to be trusted, and themselves tend to reflect local historical conditions." According to the ACLS pamphlet, such claims usually involve some power grab on the part of the person who is claiming to be objective. This presupposition, that there are no objective or intersubjective standards to which one can appeal in making judgments of quality, is a natural underpinning of the first four. The idea that there might be some objective standards of what is good and what is bad, that you might be able to show that Shakespeare is better than Mickey Mouse, for example, threatens the concept that all cultures are equal and that representativeness must be the criterion for inclusion in the curriculum. The whole idea of objectivity, truth, rationality, intelligence, as they are traditionally construed, and distinctions of intellectual quality, are all seen as part of the same system of repressive devices.

22   This leads to the sixth presupposition, which is the hardest of all to state, because it is an inchoate attitude rather than a precise thesis. Roughly speaking, it involves a marriage of left-wing politics with certain antirationalist strands derived from recent philosophy. The idea is that we should stop thinking there is an objective reality that exists independently of our representations of it; we should stop thinking that propositions are true when they correspond to that reality; and we should stop thinking of language as a set of devices for conveying meanings from speakers to hearers. In short, the sixth presupposition is a rejection of realism and truth in favor of some version of relativism, the idea that all of reality is ultimately textual. This is a remarkable guise for left-wing views to take, because until recently extreme left-wing views claimed to have a scientific basis. The current challengers are suspicious of science and equally suspicious of the whole apparatus of rationality, objective truth, and metaphysical realism, which go along with the scientific attitude.

23   A seventh presupposition is this: Western civilization is historically oppressive. Domestically, its history is one of oppressing women, slaves, and serfs. Internationally, its history is one of colonialism and imperialism. It is no accident that the works in the Western tradition are by white males, because the tradition is dominated by a caste consisting of white males. In this tradition, white males are the group in power.

24   I have tried to make explicit some of the unstated assumptions of both sides, because I think that otherwise it is impossible to explain why the contestants don't seem to make any contact with each other. They seem to be talking about two different sets of issues. I believe that is because they proceed from different sets of assumptions and objectives. If I have succeeded here in articulating the two sets of assumptions, that should be enough. However, the philosopher in me insists on making a few comments about each side and stating a few assumptions of my own. I think the basic philosophical underpinnings of the challengers are weak. Let us start with the rejection of metaphysical realism. This view is derived from deconstructionist philosophers as well as from an interpreta-

tion of the works of Thomas Kuhn and Richard Rorty. The idea, roughly speaking, is that Kuhn is supposed to have shown that science does not give us an account of an independently existing reality. Rather, scientists are an irrational bunch who run from one paradigm to another, for reasons with no real connection to finding objective truths. What Kuhn did for science, Rorty supposedly also did for philosophy. Philosophers don't provide accounts that mirror how the world is, because the whole idea of language as mirroring or corresponding to reality is flawed from the beginning. (The works of Kuhn and Rorty, by the way, are more admired in academic departments of literature than they are in departments in the sciences and philosophy.) Whether or not this is the correct interpretation of the works of Kuhn, Rorty, and the deconstructionists, the effect of these works has been to introduce into various humanities departments versions of relativism, anti-objectivism, and skepticism about science and the correspondence theory of truth.

Because of the limitation of space, I am going to be rather 25 swift in my refutation of this view. The only defense that one can give of metaphysical realism is a transcendental argument in one of Kant's many senses of that term. We assume that something is the case and show how that metaphysical realism is a condition of possibility of its being the case. If both we and our adversaries share the assumption that something is the case and that which we assume presupposes realism, then the transcendental argument is a refutation of our adversaries' view. It seems to me obvious in this case that we as well as the antirealists assume we are communicating with each other in a public language. When the antirealists present us with an argument they claim to do so in a language that is publicly intelligible. But, I wish to argue, public intelligibility presupposes the existence of a publicly accessible world. Metaphysical realism is not a thesis; rather, it is the condition of the possibility of having theses which are publicly intelligible. Whenever we use a language that purports to have public objects of reference, we commit ourselves to realism. The commitment is not a specific theory as to *how* the world is, but rather that there is a way the world is. Thus, it is self-refuting for someone to claim in a public language that metaphysical realism is false, because a public language presupposes a public world, and that presupposition is metaphysical realism.

Though I will not develop it here, it seems that a similar ar- 26 gument applies to objective standards of rationality. Again, to put it very crudely, one can't make sense out of presenting a thesis, or having a belief, or defending a view without presupposing certain standards of rationality. The very notions of mental and linguistic representation already contain certain logical principles built into them. For those who think that I am exaggerating the extent to which the traditional values are challenged, I suggest they read the ACLS pamphlet from which I quoted earlier.

27   Another fallacious move made by the challengers is to infer, from the fact that the university's educational efforts invariably have political consequences, that therefore the primary objective of the university and the primary criteria for assessing its success or failure should be political. The conclusion does not follow from the premise. Obviously, everything has political consequences, whether it's art, music, literature, sex, or gastronomy. For example, right now you could be campaigning for the next presidential election, and therefore this article has political consequences, because it prevents you from engaging in political activities in which you might otherwise be engaging. In this sense, *everything* is political. But from the fact that everything is political in this sense, it doesn't follow that our academic *objectives* are political, nor does it follow that the criteria for assessing our successes and failures are political. The argument, in short, does not justify the current attempts to use the classroom and the curriculum as tools of political transformation.

28   A further fallacy concerns the notion of empowerment. The most general form of this fallacy is the supposition that power is a property of groups rather than of individuals and organizations. A moment's reflection will reveal that this is not true. Most positions of power in the United States are occupied by middle-aged white males, but it does not follow that power accrues to middle-aged white males as a group. Most white males, middle-aged or otherwise, are as powerless as anyone else. In these discussions, there is a fallacy that goes as follows: People assume because most people in positions of power are white males that therefore most white males are in a position of power. I hope the fallacy is obvious.

29   Finally, in my list of criticisms of the challengers, I want to point out that we should not be embarrassed by the fact that a disproportionately large percentage of the major cultural achievements in our society have been made by white males. This is an interesting historical fact that requires analysis and explanation. But it doesn't in any way discredit the works of, for example, Descartes or Shakespeare that they happen to have been white males, any more than it discredits the work of Newton and Darwin that they were both English. Representativeness as such is not the primary aim in the study of the humanities. Rather, representativeness comes in as a de-

sirable goal when there is a question of articulating the different varieties of human experience. And our aim in seeking works that articulate this variety is always to find works of high quality. The problem with the predominance of white males is not that there is any doubt about the quality of the work, but that we have been excessively provincial, that great works in other cultures may have been neglected, and that, even within Western civilization, there have been groups, most notably women, whose works have been discriminated against.

My criticism of the traditionalists is somewhat different 30 from my criticism of the challengers because I do not, as a matter of fact, find much that is objectionable in the assumptions behind the traditionalist philosophy of education. The difficulty is how those assumptions are being implemented in contemporary American universities.

There are many forms of decay and indeed corruption that 31 have become entrenched in the actual practice of American universities, especially where undergraduate education is concerned. The most obvious sign of decay is that we have simply lost enthusiasm for the traditional philosophy of a liberal education. As our disciplines have become more specialized, as we have lost faith in the ideal of an integrated undergraduate education, we simply provide the student with the familiar cafeteria of courses and hope things turn out for the best. The problem with the traditionalists' ideology is not that it is false but that it has run out of gas. It is somewhat hypocritical to defend a traditional liberal education with a well-rounded reading list that goes from Plato to James Joyce if one is unwilling actually to attempt to educate undergraduates in this tradition. I do not, frankly, think that the challengers have superior ideas. Rather, they have something which may be more important to influencing the way things are actually done. They have more energy and enthusiasm, not to say fanaticism and intolerance. In the long run, these may be more effective in changing universities than rigorous arguments can be.

Benjamin Franklin

FROM

THE AUTOBIOGRAPHY
OF BENJAMIN FRANKLIN

If you have ever visited Philadelphia, you probably know quite a bit about Benjamin Franklin, for Franklin is literally that city's towering figure: Franklin was one of those versatile and energetic polymaths that we associate with the American Revolution (Thomas Jefferson and George Washington were, of course, others): in the course of his long life, he was famous as an inventor, publisher, and statesman, and his pragmatic way of life stamped itself indelibly onto the American character.

Born in Boston in 1706, he arrived in Philadelphia as a teenager to make his fortune. Finding work as a printer, he rose quickly in his profession, took over a newspaper, published Poor Richard's Almanac *(a compendium of information and commonsense advice on every topic that made his name and fortune), and took an interest in civic affairs. After 1750, he was established enough to turn the rest of his life to science—his famous kite experiment related to electricity was conducted in 1752—and to politics. Franklin played a pivotal role in the establishment of the new United States by serving in the Second Continental Congress (which developed the Declaration of Independence), by securing support from France during the war with Britain, and by helping to resolve differences during the Constitutional Convention of 1787.*

Many of the details of Franklin's life are described in his memoir, The Autobiography, *which he began in 1771, abandoned for a time, and then completed just before he died in 1790. The following excerpts, parts of a "letter to his son" that grew into the larger* Autobiography, *concern how Franklin developed his rhetorical skill. (In the passage, the references to* Pilgrim's Progress, *Bunyan's* Works, *Burton's* Historical Collections, *and so forth, all refer to well-known eighteenth-century books; the* Spectator *was an influential literary paper that was put out by Joseph Addison and Richard Steele from 1711–1712.)*

From a Child I was fond of Reading, and all the little Money that came into my Hands was ever laid out in Books. Pleas'd with the Pilgrim's Progress, my first Collection was of John Bunyan's Works, in separate little Volumes. I afterwards sold them to enable me to buy R. Burton's Historical Collections; they were small Chapmen's Books and cheap, 40 or 50 in all. My Father's little Library consisted chiefly of Books in polemic Divinity, most of which I read, and have since often regretted, that at a time when I had such a Thirst for Knowledge, more proper Books had not fallen in my Way, since it was now resolv'd I should not be a Clergyman. Plutarch's Lives there was, in which I read abundantly, and I still think that time spent to great Advantage. There was also a Book of Defoe's, called an Essay on Projects, and another of Dr. Mather's, call'd Essays to do Good which perhaps gave me a Turn of Thinking that had an Influence on some of the principal future Events of my Life. 1

 This Bookish Inclination at length determin'd my Father to make me a Printer, tho' he had already one Son, (James) of that Profession. In 1717 my Brother James return'd from England with a Press and Letters to set up his Business in Boston. I lik'd it much better than that of my Father, but still had a Hankering for the Sea. To prevent the apprehended Effect of such an Inclination, my Father was impatient to have me bound to my Brother. I stood out some time, but at last was persuaded and signed the Indentures, when I was yet but 12 Years old. I was to serve as an Apprentice till I was 21 Years of Age, only I was to be allow'd Journeyman's Wages during the last Year. In a little time I made great Proficiency in the Business, and became a useful Hand to my Brother. I now had Access to better Books. An Acquaintance with the Apprentices of Booksellers, enabled me sometimes to borrow a small one, which I was careful to return soon and clean. Often I sat up in my Room reading the greatest Part of the Night, when the Book was borrow'd in the Evening and to be return'd early in the Morning lest it should be miss'd or wanted. And after some time an ingenious 2

Tradesman Mr. Matthew Adams who had a pretty Collection of Books, and who frequented our Printing House, took Notice of me, invited me to his Library, and very kindly lent me such Books as I chose to read. I now took a Fancy to Poetry, and made some little Pieces. My Brother, thinking it might turn to account encourag'd me, and put me on composing two occasional Ballads. One was called the *Light House Tragedy*, and contain'd an account of the drowning of Capt. Worthilake with his Two Daughters; the other was a Sailor Song on the Taking of *Teach* or Blackbeard the Pirate. They were wretched Stuff, in the Grubstreet Ballad Stile, and when they were printed he sent me about the Town to sell them. The first sold wonderfully, the Event being recent, having made a great Noise. This flatter'd my Vanity. But my Father discourag'd me, by ridiculing my Performances, and telling me Verse-makers were generally Beggars; so I escap'd being a Poet, most probably a very bad one. But, as Prose Writing has been of great Use to me in the Course of my Life, and was a principal Means of my Advancement, I shall tell you how in such a Situation I acquir'd what little Ability I have in that Way.

3   There was another Bookish Lad in the Town, John Collins by Name, with whom I was intimately acquainted. We sometimes disputed, and very fond we were of Argument, and very desirous of confuting one another. Which disputacious Turn, by the way, is apt to become a very bad Habit, making People often extreamly disagreable in Company, by the Contradiction that is necessary to bring it into Practice, and thence, besides souring and spoiling the Conversation, is productive of Disgusts and perhaps Enmities where you may have occasion for Friendship. I had caught it by reading my Father's Books of Dispute about Religion. Persons of good Sense, I have since observ'd, seldom fall into it, except Lawyers, University Men, and Men of all Sorts that have been bred at Edinborough. A Question was once some how or other started between Collins and me, of the Propriety of educating the Female Sex in Learning, and their Abilities for Study. He was of Opinion that it was improper; and that they were naturally unequal to it. I took the contrary Side, perhaps a little for Dispute sake. He was naturally more eloquent, had a ready Plenty of Words, and sometimes as I thought bore me down more by his Fluency than by the Strength of his Reasons. As we parted without settling the Point, and were not to see one another again for some time, I sat down to put my Arguments in Writing, which I copied and sent to him. He answer'd and I reply'd. Three or four Letters of a Side had pass'd, when my Father happen'd to find my Papers, and read them. Without entring into the

Discussion, he took occasion to talk to me about the Manner of my Writing, observ'd that tho' I had the Advantage of my Antagonist in correct Spelling and [punctuation] (which I ow'd to the Printing House) I fell far short in elegance of Expression, in Method and in Perspicuity, of which he convinc'd me by several Instances. I saw the Justice of his Remarks, and thence grew more attentive to the *Manner* in Writing, and determin'd to endeavour at Improvement.

About this time I met with an odd Volume of the Spectator. 4 It was the third. I had never before seen any of them. I bought it, read it over and over, and was much delighted with it. I thought the Writing excellent, and wish'd if possible to imitate it. With that View, I took some of the Papers, and making short Hints of the Sentiment in each Sentence, laid them by a few Days, and then without looking at the Book, try'd to compleat the Papers again, by expressing each hinted Sentiment at length and as fully as it had been express'd before, in any suitable Words, that should come to hand.

Then I compar'd my Spectator with the Original, discover'd 5 some of my Faults and corrected them. But I found I wanted a Stock of Words or a Readiness in recollecting and using them, which I thought I should have acquir'd before that time, if I had gone on making Verses, since the continual Occasion for Words of the same Import but of different Length, to suit the Measure, or of different Sound for the Rhyme, would have laid me under a constant Necessity of searching for Variety, and also have tended to fix that Variety in my Mind, and make me Master of it. Therefore I took some of the Tales and turn'd them into Verse: And after a time, when I had pretty well forgotten the Prose, turn'd them back again. I also sometimes jumbled my Collections of Hints into Confusion, and after some Weeks, endeavour'd to reduce them into the best Order, before I began to form the full Sentences, and compleat the Paper. This was to teach me Method in the Arrangement of Thoughts. By comparing my work afterwards with the original, I discover'd many faults and amended them; but I sometimes had the Pleasure of Fancying that in certain Particulars of small Import, I had been lucky enough to improve the Method or the Language and this encourag'd me to think I might possibly in time come to be a tolerable English Writer, of which I was extreamly ambitious.

Frederick Douglass

FROM

THE NARRATIVE OF THE LIFE OF FREDERICK DOUGLASS

Frederick Douglass's rise from obscurity to prominence was even more astounding than the rise of Benjamin Franklin. Born a slave in 1818 under the name of Frederick Bailey—he never knew his father and seldom saw his mother after he was taken from her as a child—Douglass escaped to the North in 1839 and assumed a new identity. He quickly became active in abolitionist circles and, after a decade of flight, was able to purchase his freedom. Later, he began his own newspaper, The North Star, *in Rochester, New York, as a vehicle for his beliefs and causes. A prominent orator and essayist, during the Civil War he urged President Lincoln to enlist African Americans in the army, and after the war he continued to campaign for freedom, not only by advocating antilynching laws and better conditions for tenant farmers but also by supporting women's suffrage.*

Douglass gives his own account of his early life in his Narrative of the Life of Frederick Douglass, *the most famous of the hundreds of "slave narratives" (i.e., first-hand accounts of slave life) that were published in the years before the Civil War. (You may have read Toni Morrison's recent slave narrative,* Beloved.*) When the book was published in 1845, it established Douglass as a major voice in the antislavery movement and gave rise to images of the self that would affect the way other Americans would forever think of themselves. The following passage from Chapter 7 of the* Narrative *describes how Douglass began to learn to read and write.*

1   I lived in Master Hugh's family about seven years. During this time, I succeeded in learning to read and write. In accomplishing this, I was compelled to resort to various stratagems. I had no regular teacher. My mistress, who had kindly commenced to instruct me, had, in compliance with the advice and direction of her husband, not only ceased to instruct, but had set her face against my being instructed by any one else. It is due, however, to my mistress to say of her, that she did not adopt this course of treatment immediately. She at first lacked the depravity indispensable to shutting me up in mental darkness.

It was at least necessary for her to have some training in the exercise of irresponsible power, to make her equal to the task of treating me as though I were a brute.

My mistress was, as I have said, a kind and tender-hearted woman; and in the simplicity of her soul she commenced, when I first went to live with her, to treat me as she supposed one human being ought to treat another. In entering upon the duties of a slaveholder, she did not seem to perceive that I sustained to her the relation of a mere chattel, and that for her to treat me as a human being was not only wrong, but dangerously so. Slavery proved as injurious to her as it did to me. When I went there, she was a pious, warm, and tender-hearted woman. There was no sorrow or suffering for which she had not a tear. She had bread for the hungry, clothes for the naked, and comfort for every mourner that came within her reach. Slavery soon proved its ability to divest her of these heavenly qualities. Under its influence, the tender heart became stone, and the lamblike disposition gave way to one of tigerlike fierceness. The first step in her downward course was in her ceasing to instruct me. She now commenced to practise her husband's precepts. She finally became even more violent in her opposition than her husband himself. She was not satisfied with simply doing as well as he had commanded; she seemed anxious to do better. Nothing seemed to make her more angry than to see me with a newspaper. She seemed to think that here lay the *danger*. I have had her rush at me with a face made all up of fury, and snatch from me a newspaper, in a manner that fully revealed her apprehension. She was an apt woman; and a little experience soon demonstrated, to her satisfaction, that education and slavery were incompatible with each other. 2

From this time I was most narrowly watched. If I was in a separate room any considerable length of time, I was sure to be suspected of having a book, and was at once called to give an account of myself. All this, however, was too late. The first step had been taken. Mistress, in teaching me the alphabet, had given me the *inch*, and no precaution could prevent me from taking the *ell*. 3

The plan which I adopted, and the one by which I was most successful, was that of making friends of all the little white boys whom I met in the street. As many of these as I could, I converted into teachers. With their kindly aid, obtained at different times and in different places, I finally succeeded in learning to read. When I was sent of errands, I always took my book with me, and by going one part of my errand quickly, I found time to get a lesson before my return. I used also to carry bread with me, enough of which was always in the 4 house, and to which I was always welcome; for I was much better off in this regard than many of the poor white children in our neighborhood. This bread I used to bestow upon the hungry little urchins, who, in return, would give me that more valuable bread of knowledge. I am strongly tempted to give the names of two or three of those little boys, as a testimonial of the gratitude and affection I bear them; but prudence forbids;—not that it would injure me, but it might embarrass them; for it is almost an unpardonable offence to teach slaves to read in this Christian country. It is enough to say of the dear little fellows, that they lived on Philpot Street, very near Durgin and Bailey's ship-yard. I used to talk this matter of slavery over with them. I would sometimes say to them, I wished I could be as free as they would be when they got to be men. "You will be free as soon as you are twenty-one, *but I am a slave for life!* Have not I as good a right to be free as you have?" These words used to trouble them; they would express for me the liveliest sympathy, and console me with the hope that something would occur by which I might be free.

5   I was now about twelve years old, and the thought of being a *slave for life* began to bear heavily upon my heart. Just about this time, I got hold of a book entitled "The Columbian Orator." Every opportunity I got, I used to read this book. Among much of other interesting matter, I found in it a dialogue between a master and his slave. The slave was represented as having run away from his master three times. The dialogue represented the conversation which took place between them, when the slave was retaken the third time. In this dialogue, the whole argument in behalf of slavery was brought forward by the master, all of which was disposed of by the slave. The slave was made to say some very smart as well as impressive things in reply to his master—things which had the desired though unexpected effect; for the conversation resulted in the voluntary emancipation of the slave on the part of the master.

6   In the same book, I met with one of Sheridan's mighty speeches on and in behalf of Catholic emancipation. These were choice documents to me. I read them over and over again with unabated interest. They gave tongue to interesting thoughts of my own soul, which had frequently flashed through my mind, and died away for want of utterance. The moral which I gained from the dialogue was the power of truth over the conscience of even a slaveholder. What I got from Sheridan was a bold denunciation of slavery, and a powerful vindication of human rights. The reading of these documents enabled me to utter my thoughts, and to meet the arguments

brought forward to sustain slavery; but while they relieved me of one difficulty, they brought on another even more painful than the one of which I was relieved. The more I read, the more I was led to abhor and detest my enslavers. I could regard them in no other light than a band of successful robbers, who had left their homes, and gone to Africa, and stolen us from our homes, and in a strange land reduced us to slavery. I loathed them as being the meanest as well as the most wicked of men. As I read and contemplated the subject, behold! that very discontentment which Master Hugh had predicted would follow my learning to read had already come, to torment and sting my soul to unutterable anguish. As I writhed under it, I would at times feel that learning to read had been a curse rather than a blessing. It had given me a view of my wretched condition, without the remedy. It opened my eyes to the horrible pit, but to no ladder upon which to get out. In moments of agony, I envied my fellow-slaves for their stupidity. I have often wished myself a beast. I preferred the condition of the meanest reptile to my own. Any thing, no matter what, to get rid of thinking! It was this everlasting thinking of my condition that tormented me. There was no getting rid of it. It was pressed upon me by every object within sight or hearing, animate or inanimate. The silver trump of freedom had roused my soul to eternal wakefulness. Freedom now appeared, to disappear no more forever. It was heard in every sound, and seen in every thing. It was ever present to torment me with a sense of my wretched condition. I saw nothing without seeing it, I heard nothing without hearing it, and felt nothing without feeling it. It looked from every star, it smiled in every calm, breathed in every wind, and moved in every storm.

I often found myself regretting my own existence, and wishing myself dead; and but for the hope of being free, I have no doubt but that I should have killed myself, or done something for which I should have been killed. While in this state of mind, I was eager to hear any one speak of slavery. I was a ready listener. Every little while, I could hear something about the abolitionists. It was some time before I found what the word meant. It was always used in such connections as to make it an interesting word to me. If a slave ran away and succeeded in getting clear, or if a slave killed his master, set fire to a barn, or did any thing very wrong in the mind of a slave-holder, it was spoken of as the fruit of *abolition*. Hearing the word in this connection very often, I set about learning what it meant. The dictionary afforded me little or no help. I found it was "the act of abolishing;" but then I did not know what was to be abolished. Here I was perplexed. I did not dare to ask any one about its meaning, for I was satisfied that it was something they wanted me to know very little about. After a patient waiting, I got one of our city papers, containing an account of the number of petitions from the north, praying for the abolition of slavery in the District of Columbia, and of the slave trade between the States. From this time I understood the words *abolition* and *abolitionist,* and always drew near when that word was spoken, expecting to hear something of importance to myself and fellow-slaves. The light broke in upon me by degrees. I went one day down on the wharf of Mr. Waters; and seeing two Irishmen unloading a scow of stone, I went, unasked, and helped them. When we had finished, one of them came to me and asked me if I were a slave. I told him I was. He asked, "Are ye a slave for life?" I told him that I was. The good Irishman seemed to be deeply affected by the statement. He said to the other that it was a pity so fine a little fellow as myself should be a slave for life. He said it was a shame to hold me. They both advised me to run away to the north; that I should find friends there, and that I should be free. I pretended not to be interested in what they said, and treated them as if I did not understand them; for I feared they might be treacherous. White men have been known to encourage slaves to escape, and then, to get the reward, catch them and return them to their masters. I was afraid that these seemingly good men might use me so; but I nevertheless remembered their advice, and from that time I resolved to run away. I looked forward to a time at which it would be safe for me to escape. I was too young to think of doing so immediately; besides, I wished to learn how to write, as I might have an occasion to write my own pass. I consoled myself with the hope that I should one day find a good chance. Meanwhile, I would learn to write.

8   The idea as to how I might learn to write was suggested to me by being in Durgin and Bailey's ship-yard, and frequently seeing the ship carpenters, after hewing, and getting a piece of timber ready for use, write on the timber the name of that part of the ship for which it was intended. When a piece of timber was intended for the larboard side, it would be marked thus— "L." When a piece was for the starboard side, it would be marked thus—"S." A piece for the larboard side forward, would be marked thus—"L. F." When a piece was for starboard side forward, it would be marked thus—"S. F." For larboard aft, it would be marked thus—"L. A." For starboard aft, it would be marked thus—"S. A." I soon learned the names of these letters, and for what they were intended when placed upon a piece of timber in the ship-yard. I immediately commenced copying them, and in a short time was able to make

the four letters named. After that, when I met with any boy who I knew could write, I would tell him I could write as well as he. The next word would be, "I don't believe you. Let me see you try it." I would then make the letters which I had been so fortunate as to learn, and ask him to beat that. In this way I got a good many lessons in writing, which it is quite possible I should never have gotten in any other way. During this time, my copy-book was the board fence, brick wall, and pavement; my pen and ink was a lump of chalk. With these, I learned mainly how to write. I then commenced and continued copying the Italics in Webster's Spelling Book, until I could make them all without looking on the book. By this time, my little Master Thomas had gone to school, and learned how to write, and had written over a number of copy-books. These had been brought home, and shown to some of our near neighbors, and then laid aside. My mistress used to go to class meeting at the Wilk Street meeting-house every Monday afternoon, and leave me to take care of the house. When left thus, I used to spend the time in writing in the spaces left in Master Thomas's copy-book, copying what he had written. I continued to do this until I could write a hand similar to that of Master Thomas. Thus, after a long, tedious effort for years, I finally succeeded in learning how to write.

Charlotte Perkins Gilman

THE YELLOW
WALLPAPER

Charlotte Perkins Gilman (1860–1935) crusaded throughout her life against "masculinist" ideas and the cult of female domesticity, and in favor of reforms like day care services and legal changes that would permit women to be more active outside the home. In the 1880s, while living in Connecticut, she published her first newspaper articles, married, gave birth to her daughter Katherine—and was plunged into a depression. She came under the care of a prominent physician, but after three months she fled her husband (they were later divorced) and her physician to pursue her own method of cure, a method that included writing down her experiences. These events are mirrored in "The Yellow Wallpaper," a mixture of autobiography, fantasy, gothic fiction, and clinical record that was published in 1892 in New England Magazine. Later she married George Houghton Gilman. The two enjoyed an egalitarian match, and Charlotte Perkins Gilman wrote fiction and nonfiction in support of progressive ideals for the rest of her life. What role does the activity of writing play in "The Yellow Wallpaper"?

1   It is very seldom that mere ordinary people like John and myself secure ancestral halls for the summer.

2   A colonial mansion, a hereditary estate, I would say a haunted house and reach the height of romantic felicity—but that would be asking too much of fate!

3   Still I will proudly declare that there is something queer about it.

4   Else, why should it be let so cheaply? And why have stood so long untenanted?

5   John laughs at me, of course, but one expects that.

6   John is practical in the extreme. He has no patience with faith, an intense horror of superstition, and he scoffs openly at any talk of things not to be felt and seen and put down in figures.

7   John is a physician, and *perhaps*—(I would not say it to a living soul, of course, but this is dead paper and a great relief to my mind)—*perhaps* that is one reason I do not get well faster.

8   You see, he does not believe I am sick! And what can one do?

9   If a physician of high standing, and one's own husband, assures friends and relatives that there is really nothing the matter with one but temporary nervous depression—a slight hysterical tendency—what is one to do?

10   My brother is also a physician, and also of high standing, and he says the same thing.

11   So I take phosphates or phosphites—whichever it is—and tonico, and air and exercise, and journeys, and am absolutely forbidden to "work" until I am well again.

12   Personally, I disagree with their ideas.

13   Personally, I believe that congenial work, with excitement and change, would do me good.

14   But what is one to do?

15   I did write for a while in spite of them; but it *does* exhaust me a good deal—having to be so sly about it, or else meet with heavy opposition.

16   I sometimes fancy that in my condition, if I had less opposition and more society and stimulus—but John says the very worst thing I can do is to think about my condition, and I confess it always makes me feel bad.

17   So I will let it alone and talk about the house.

The most beautiful place! It is quite alone, standing well 18
back from the road, quite three miles from the village. It makes
me think of English places that you read about, for there are
hedges and walls and gates that lock, and lots of separate little
houses for the gardeners and people.

There is a *delicious* garden! I never saw such a garden—large 19
and shady, full of box-bordered paths, and lined with long
grape-covered arbors with seats under them.

There were greenhouses, but they are all broken now. 20

There was some legal trouble, I believe, something about the 21
heirs and co-heirs; anyhow, the place has been empty for years.

That spoils my ghostliness, I am afraid, but I don't care— 22
there is something strange about the house—I can feel it.

I even said so to John one moonlight evening, but he said 23
what I felt was a draught, and shut the window.

I get unreasonably angry with John sometimes. I'm sure I 24
never used to be so sensitive. I think it is due to this nervous
condition.

But John says if I feel so, I shall neglect proper self-control; 25
so I take pains to control myself—before him, at least, and that
makes me very tired.

I don't like our room a bit. I wanted one downstairs that 26
opened on the piazza and had roses all over the window, and
such pretty old-fashioned chintz hangings! But John would not
hear of it.

He said there was only one window and not room for two 27
beds, and no near room for him if he took another.

He is very careful and loving, and hardly lets me stir without 28
special direction.

I have a schedule prescription for each hour in the day; he 29
takes all care from me, and so I feel basely ungrateful not to
value it more.

He said we came here solely on my account, that I was to 30
have perfect rest and all the air I could get. "Your exercise depends on your strength, my dear," said he, "and your food
somewhat on your appetite; but air you can absorb all the
time." So we took the nursery at the top of the house.

It is a big, airy room, the whole floor nearly, with windows 31
that look all ways, and air and sunshine galore. It was nursery
first and then playroom and gymnasium, I should judge; for
the windows are barred for little children, and there are rings
and things in the walls.

The paint and paper look as if a boys' school had used it. It is 32
stripped off—the paper—in great patches all around the head
of my bed, about as far as I can reach, and in a great place
on the other side of the room low down. I never saw a worse

paper in my life. One of those sprawling flamboyant patterns committing every artistic sin.

33   It is dull enough to confuse the eye in following, pronounced enough to constantly irritate and provoke study, and when you follow the lame uncertain curves for a little distance they suddenly commit suicide—plunge off at outrageous angles, destroy themselves in unheard-of contradictions.

34   The color is repellant, almost revolting; a smouldering unclean yellow, strangely faded by the slow-turning sunlight. It is a dull yet lurid orange in some places, a sickly sulphur tint in others.

35   No wonder the children hated it! I should hate it myself if I had to live in this room long. There comes John, and I must put this away—he hates to have me write a word.

•   •   •   •   •   •

36   We have been here two weeks, and I haven't felt like writing before, since that first day.

37   I am sitting by the window now, up in this atrocious nursery, and there is nothing to hinder my writing as much as I please, save lack of strength.

38   John is away all day, and even some nights when his cases are serious.

39   I am glad my case is not serious!

40   But these nervous troubles are dreadfully depressing.

41   John does not know how much I really suffer. He knows there is no reason to suffer, and that satisfies him.

42   Of course it is only nervousness. It does weigh on me so not to do my duty in any way!

43   I mean to be such a help to John, such a real rest and comfort, and here I am a comparative burden already!

44   Nobody would believe what an effort it is to do what little I am able—to dress and entertain, and order things.

45   It is fortunate Mary is so good with the baby. Such a dear baby!

46   And yet I *cannot* be with him, it makes me so nervous.

47   I suppose John never was nervous in his life. He laughs at me so about this wallpaper!

48   At first he meant to repaper the room, but afterwards he said that I was letting it get the better of me, and that nothing was worse for a nervous patient than to give way to such fancies.

49   He said that after the wallpaper was changed it would be the heavy bedstead, and then the barred windows, and then that gate at the head of the stairs, and so on.

50   "You know the place is doing you good," he said, "and really, dear, I don't care to renovate the house just for a three months' rental."

"Then do let us go downstairs," I said. "There are such pretty rooms there." 51

Then he took me in his arms and called me a blessed little goose, and said he would go down cellar, if I wished, and have it whitewashed into the bargain. 52

But he is right enough about the beds and windows and things. 53

It is as airy and comfortable a room as anyone need wish, and, of course, I would not be so silly as to make him uncomfortable just for a whim. 54

I'm really getting quite fond of this big room, all but that horrid paper. 55

Out of one window I can see the garden—those mysterious deep-shaded arbors, the riotous old-fashioned flowers, and bushes and gnarly trees. 56

Out of another I get a lovely view of the bay and a little private wharf belonging to the estate. There is a beautiful shaded lane that runs down there from the house. I always fancy I see people walking in these numerous paths and arbors, but John has cautioned me not to give way to fancy in the least. He says that with my imaginative power and habit of story-making, a nervous weakness like mine is sure to lead to all manner of excited fancies, and that I ought to use my will and good sense to check the tendency. So I try. 57

I think sometimes that if I were only well enough to write a little it would relieve the press of ideas and rest me. 58

But I find I get pretty tired when I try. 59

It is so discouraging not to have any advice and companionship about my work. When I get really well, John says we will ask Cousin Henry and Julia down for a long visit; but he says he would as soon put fireworks in my pillowcase as to let me have those stimulating people about now. 60

I wish I could get well faster. 61

But I must not think about that. This paper looks to me as if it *knew* what a vicious influence it had! 62

There is a recurrent spot where the pattern lolls like a broken neck and two bulbous eyes stare at you upside down. 63

I get positively angry with the impertinence of it and the everlastingness. Up and down and sideways they crawl, and those absurd unblinking eyes are everywhere. There is one place where two breadths didn't match, and the eyes go all up and down the line, one a little higher than the other. 64

I never saw so much expression in an inanimate thing before, and we all know how much expression they have! I used to lie awake as a child and get more entertainment and terror 65 out of blank walls and plain furniture than most children could find in a toy-store.

66   I remember what a kindly wink the knobs of our big old bureau used to have, and there was one chair that always seemed like a strong friend.

67   I used to feel that if any of the other things looked too fierce I could always hop into that chair and be safe.

68   The furniture in this room is no worse than inharmonious, however, for we had to bring it all from downstairs. I suppose when this was used as a playroom they had to take the nursery things out, and no wonder! I never saw such ravages as the children have made here.

69   The wallpaper, as I said before, is torn off in spots, and it sticketh closer than a brother—they must have had perseverance as well as hatred.

70   Then the floor is scratched and gouged and splintered, the plaster itself is dug out here and there, and this great heavy bed which is all we found in the room, looks as if it had been through the wars.

71   But I don't mind it a bit—only the paper.

72   There comes John's sister. Such a dear girl as she is, and so careful of me! I must not let her find me writing.

73   She is a perfect and enthusiastic housekeeper, and hopes for no better profession. I verily believe she thinks it is the writing which made me sick!

74   But I can write when she is out, and see her a long way off from these windows.

75   There is one that commands the road, a lovely shaded winding road, and one that just looks off over the country. A lovely country, too, full of great elms and velvet meadows.

76   This wallpaper has a kind of sub-pattern in a different shade, a particularly irritating one, for you can only see it in certain lights, and not clearly then.

77   But in the places where it isn't faded and where the sun is just so—I can see a strange, provoking, formless sort of figure that seems to skulk about behind that silly and conspicuous front design.

78   There's sister on the stairs!

•   •   •   •   •   •

79   Well, the Fourth of July is over! The people are all gone, and I am tired out. John thought it might do me good to see a little company, so we just had Mother and Nellie and the children down for a week.

80   Of course I didn't do a thing. Jennie sees to everything now.

81   But it tired me all the same.

John says if I don't pick up faster he shall send me to Weir 82
Mitchell[1] in the fall.

But I don't want to go there at all. I had a friend who was in 83
his hands once, and she says he is just like John and my
brother, only more so!

Besides, it is such an undertaking to go so far. 84

I don't feel as if it was worthwhile to turn my hand over for 85
anything, and I'm getting dreadfully fretful and querulous.

I cry at nothing, and cry most of the time. 86

Of course I don't when John is here, or anybody else, but 87
when I am alone.

And I am alone a good deal just now. John is kept in town 88
very often by serious cases, and Jennie is good and lets me
alone when I want her to.

So I walk a little in the garden or down that lovely lane, sit on 89
the porch under the roses, and lie down up here a good deal.

I'm getting really fond of the room in spite of the wallpaper. 90
Perhaps *because* of the wallpaper.

It dwells in my mind so! 91

I lie here on this great immovable bed—it is nailed down, I 92
believe—and follow that pattern about by the hour. It is as
good as gymnastics. I assure you. I start, we'll say, at the bottom, down in the corner over there where it has not been
touched, and I determine for the thousandth time that I *will*
follow that pointless pattern to some sort of conclusion.

I know a little of the principle of design, and I know this 93
thing was not arranged on any laws of radiation, or alterna-
tion, or repetition, or symmetry, or anything else that I ever
heard of.

It is repeated, of course, by the breadths, but not otherwise. 94

Looked at in one way, each breadth stands alone; the bloated 95
curves and flourishes—a kind of "debased Romanesque" with
delirium tremens—go waddling up and down in isolated
columns of fatuity.

But, on the other hand, they connect diagonally, and the 96
sprawling outlines run off in great slanting waves of optic horror, like a lot of wallowing sea-weeds in full chase.

The whole thing goes horizontally, too, at least it seems so, 97
and I exhaust myself trying to distinguish the order of its going
in that direction.

---

[1]Silas Weir Mitchell (1829–1914) was a prominent Philadelphia physician (he was also a poet and a novelist). He advocated "rest cures" for nervous disorders. Among his medical works are *Fat and Blood* (1877), describing his rest cure, and *Diseases of the Nervous System, Especially of
Women* (1881).

98   They have used a horizontal breadth for a frieze, and that adds wonderfully to the confusion.

99   There is one end of the room where it is almost intact, and there, when the crosslights fade and the low sun shines directly upon it, I can almost fancy radiation after all—the interminable grotesque seems to form around a common center and rush off in headlong plunges of equal distraction.

100   It makes me tired to follow it. I will take a nap, I guess.

•   •   •   •   •   •

101   I don't know why I should write this.

102   I don't want to.

103   I don't feel able.

104   And I know John would think it absurd. But I *must* say what I feel and think in some way—it is such a relief!

105   But the effort is getting to be greater than the relief.

106   Half the time now I am awfully lazy, and lie down ever so much.

107   John says I mustn't lose my strength, and has me take cod liver oil and lots of tonics and things, to say nothing of ale and wine and rare meat.

108   Dear John! He loves me very dearly, and hates to have me sick. I tried to have a real earnest reasonable talk with him the other day, and tell him how I wish he would let me go and make a visit to Cousin Henry and Julia.

109   But he said I wasn't able to go, nor able to stand it after I got there; and I did not make out a very good case for myself, for I was crying before I had finished.

110   It is getting to be a great effort for me to think straight. Just this nervous weakness, I suppose.

111   And dear John gathered me up in his arms, and just carried me upstairs and laid me on the bed, and sat by me and read to me till it tired my head.

112   He said I was his darling and his comfort and all he had, and that I must take care of myself for his sake, and keep well.

113   He says no one but myself can help me out of it, that I must use my will and self-control and not let any silly fancies run away with me.

114   There's one comfort—the baby is well and happy, and does not have to occupy this nursery with the horrid wallpaper.

115   If we had not used it, that blessed child would have! What a fortunate escape! Why, I wouldn't have a child of mine, an impressionable little thing, live in such a room for worlds.

116   I never thought of it before, but it is lucky that John kept me here after all, I can stand it so much easier than a baby, you see.

Of course I never mention it to them any more—I am too   117
wise—but I keep watch for it all the same.

There are things in that paper that nobody knows about but   118
me, or ever will.

Behind that outside pattern the dim shapes get clearer every   119
day.

It is always the same shape, only very numerous.   120

And it is like a woman stooping down and creeping about   121
behind that pattern. I don't like it a bit. I wonder—I begin to
think—I wish John would take me away from here!

•   •   •   •   •   •

It is so hard to talk with John about my case, because he is   122
so wise, and because he loves me so.

But I tried it last night.   123

It was moonlight. The moon shines in all around just as   124
the sun does.

I hate to see it sometimes, it creeps so slowly, and always   125
comes in by one window or another.

John was asleep and I hated to waken him, so I kept still   126
and watched the moonlight on that undulating wallpaper till I
felt creepy.

The faint figure behind seemed to shake the pattern, just as   127
if she wanted to get out.

I got up softly and went to feel and see if the paper *did* move,   128
and when I came back John was awake.

"What is it, little girl?" he said. "Don't go walking about like   129
that—you'll get cold."

I thought it was a good time to talk, so I told him that I really   130
was not gaining here, and that I wished he would take me away.

"Why, darling!" said he. "Our lease will be up in three weeks,   131
and I can't see how to leave before.

"The repairs are not done at home, and I cannot possibly   132
leave town just now. Of course if you were in any danger, I
could and would, but you really are better, dear, whether you
can see it or not. I am a doctor, dear, and I know. You are gaining flesh and color, your appetite is better, I feel really much
easier about you."

"I don't weigh a bit more," said I, "nor as much; and my ap-   133
petite may be better in the evening when you are here but it is
worse in the morning when you are away!"

"Bless her little heart!" said he with a big hug. "She shall be   134
as sick as she pleases! But now let's improve the shining hours
by going to sleep, and talk about it in the morning!"

"And you won't go away?" I asked gloomily.   135

136   "Why, how can I, dear? It is only three weeks more and then we will take a nice little trip of a few days while Jennie is getting the house ready. Really, dear, you are better!"

137   "Better in body perhaps—" I began, and stopped short, for he sat up straight and looked at me with such a stern, reproachful look that I could not say another word.

138   "My darling," said he, "I beg of you, for my sake and for our child's sake, as well as for your own, that you will never for one instant let that idea enter your mind! There is nothing so dangerous, so fascinating, to a temperament like yours. It is a false and foolish fancy. Can you not trust me as a physician when I tell you so?"

139   So of course I said no more on that score, and we went to sleep before long. He thought I was asleep first, but I wasn't, and lay there for hours trying to decide whether that front pattern and the back pattern really did move together or separately.

•   •   •   •   •   •

140   On a pattern like this, by daylight, there is a lack of sequence, a defiance of law, that is a constant irritant to a normal mind.

141   The color is hideous enough, and unreliable enough, and infuriating enough, but the pattern is torturing.

142   You think you have mastered it, but just as you get well under way in following, it turns a back-somersault and there you are. It slaps you in the face, knocks you down, and tramples upon you. It is like a bad dream.

143   The outside pattern is a florid arabesque, reminding one of a fungus. If you can imagine a toadstool in joints, an interminable string of toadstools, budding and sprouting in endless convolutions—why, that is something like it.

144   That is, sometimes!

145   There is one marked peculiarity about this paper, a thing nobody seem to notice but myself, and that is that it changes as the light changes.

146   When the sun shoots in through the east window—I always watch for that first long, straight ray—it changes so quickly that I never can quite believe it.

147   That is why I watch it always.

148   By moonlight—the moon shines in all night when there is a moon—I wouldn't know it was the same paper.

149   At night in any kind of light, in twilight, candlelight, lamplight, and worst of all by moonlight, it becomes bars! The outside pattern, I mean, and the woman behind it is as plain as can be.

150   I didn't realize for a long time what the thing was that showed behind, that dim subpattern, but now I am quite sure it is a woman.

By daylight she is subdued, quiet. I fancy it is the pattern that 151
keeps her so still. It is so puzzling. It keeps me quiet by the hour.

I lie down ever so much now. John says it is good for me, and 152
to sleep all I can.

Indeed he started the habit by making me lie down for an 153
hour after each meal.

It is a very bad habit I am convinced, for you see, I don't sleep. 154

And that cultivates deceit, for I don't tell them I'm awake—O 155
no!

The fact is I am getting a little afraid of John. 156

He seems very queer sometimes, and even Jennie has an in- 157
explicable look.

It strikes me occasionally, just as a scientific hypothesis, that 158
perhaps it is the paper!

I have watched John when he did not know I was look- 159
ing, and come into the room suddenly on the most innocent
excuses, and I've caught him several times *looking at the paper!* And Jennie too. I caught Jennie with her hand on it
once.

She didn't know I was in the room, and when I asked her in a 160
quiet, a very quiet voice, with the most restrained manner possible, what she was doing with the paper—she turned around
as if she had been caught stealing, and looked quite angry—
asked me why I should frighten her so!

Then she said that the paper stained everything it touched, 161
that she had found yellow smooches on all my clothes and
John's, and she wished we would be more careful!

Did not that sound innocent? But I know she was studying 162
that pattern, and I am determined that nobody shall find it out
but myself!

•   •   •   •   •   •

Life is very much more exciting now than it used to be. You 163
see I have something more to expect, to look forward to, to
watch. I really do eat better, and am more quiet than I was.

John is so pleased to see me improve! He laughed a little 164
the other day, and said I seemed to be flourishing in spite of
my wallpaper.

I turned it off with a laugh. I had no intention of telling him 165
it was *because* of the wallpaper—he would make fun of me. He
might even want to take me away.

I don't want to leave now until I have found it out. There is a 166
week more, and I think that will be enough.

•   •   •   •   •   •

I'm feeling so much better! 167

168   I don't sleep much at night, for it is so interesting to watch developments; but I sleep a good deal during the daytime.

169   In the daytime it is tiresome and perplexing.

170   There are always new shoots on the fungus, and new shades of yellow all over it. I cannot keep count of them, though I have tried conscientiously.

171   It is the strangest yellow, that wallpaper! It makes me think of all the yellow things I ever saw—not beautiful ones like buttercups, but old, foul, bad yellow things.

172   But there is something else about that paper—the smell! I noticed it the moment we came into the room, but with so much air and sun it was not bad. Now we have had a week of fog and rain, and whether the windows are open or not, the smell is here.

173   It creeps all over the house.

174   I find it hovering in the dining-room, skulking in the parlor, hiding in the hall, lying in wait for me on the stairs.

175   It gets into my hair.

176   Even when I go to ride, if I turn my head suddenly and surprise it—there is that smell!

177   Such a peculiar odor, too! I have spent hours in trying to analyze it, to find what it smelled like.

178   It is not bad—at first—and very gentle, but quite the subtlest, most enduring odor I ever met.

179   In this damp weather it is awful, I wake up in the night and find it hanging over me.

180   It used to disturb me at first. I thought seriously of burning the house—to reach the smell.

181   But now I am used to it. The only thing I can think of that it is like is the *color* of the paper! A yellow smell.

182   There is a very funny mark on this wall, low down, near the mopboard. A streak that runs round the room. It goes behind every piece of furniture, except the bed, a long, straight, even *smooch*, as if it had been rubbed over and over.

183   I wonder how it was done and who did it, and what they did it for. Round and round and round—round and round and round—it makes me dizzy!

•   •   •   •   •   •

184   I really have discovered something at last.

185   Through watching so much at night, when it changes so, I have finally found out.

186   The front pattern *does* move—and no wonder! The woman behind shakes it!

187   Sometimes I think there are a great many women behind, and sometimes only one, and she crawls around fast, and her crawling shakes it all over.

Then in the very bright spots she keeps still, and in the very 188
shady spots she just takes hold of the bars and shakes them hard.

And she is all the time trying to climb through. But nobody 189
could climb through that pattern—it strangles so; I think that
is why it has so many heads.

They get through, and then the pattern strangles them off 190
and turns them upside down, and makes their eyes white!

If those heads were covered or taken off it would not be 191
half so bad.

• • • • • •

I think that woman gets out in the daytime! 192

And I'll tell you why—privately—I've seen her! 193

I can see her out of every one of my windows! 194

It is the same woman, I know, for she is always creeping, and 195
most women do not creep by daylight.

I see her in that long shaded lane, creeping up and down. I see 196
her in those dark grape arbors, creeping all around the garden.

I see her on that long road under the trees, creeping along, and 197
when a carriage comes she hides under the blackberry vines.

I don't blame her a bit. It must be very humiliating to be 198
caught creeping by daylight!

I always lock the door when I creep by daylight. I can't do it 199
at night, for I know John would suspect something at once.

And John is so queer now that I don't want to irritate him. I 200
wish he would take another room! Besides, I don't want anybody to get that woman out at night but myself.

I often wonder if I could see her out of all the windows at once. 201

But, turn as fast as I can, I can only see out of one at one time. 202

And though I always see her, she *may* be able to creep faster 203
than I can turn! I have watched her sometimes away off in the
open country, creeping as fast as a cloud shadow in a wind.

• • • • • •

If only that top pattern could be gotten off from the under 204
one! I mean to try it, little by little.

I have found out another funny thing, but I shan't tell it this 205
time! It does not do to trust people too much.

There are only two more days to get this paper off, and I be- 206
lieve John is beginning to notice. I don't like the look in his eyes.

And I heard him ask Jennie a lot of professional questions 207
about me. She had a very good report to give.
208
She said I slept a good deal in the daytime.

John knows I don't sleep very well at night, for all I'm so quiet! 209

He asked me all sorts of questions, too, and pretended to be 210
very loving and kind.

As if I couldn't see through him! 211

212   Still, I don't wonder he acts so, sleeping under this paper for three months.

213   It only interests me, but I feel sure John and Jennie are affected by it.

•   •   •   •   •   •

214   Hurrah! This is the last day, but it is enough. John is to stay in town over night, and won't be out until this evening.

215   Jennie wanted to sleep with me—the sly thing; but I told her I should undoubtedly rest better for a night all alone.

216   That was clever, for really I wasn't alone a bit! As soon as it was moonlight and that poor thing began to crawl and shake the pattern, I got up and ran to help her.

217   I pulled and she shook, I shook and she pulled, and before morning we had peeled off yards of that paper.

218   A strip about as high as my head and half around the room.

219   And then when the sun came and that awful pattern began to laugh at me, I declared I would finish it today!

220   We go away tomorrow, and they are moving all my furniture down again to leave things as they were before.

221   Jennie looked at the wall in amazement, but I told her merrily that I did it out of pure spite at the vicious thing.

222   She laughed and said she wouldn't mind doing it herself, but I must not get tired.

223   How she betrayed herself that time!

224   But I am here, and no person touches this paper but Me—not *alive!*

225   She tried to get me out of the room—it was too patent! But I said it was so quiet and empty and clean now that I believed I would lie down again and sleep all I could; and not to wake me even for dinner—I would call when I woke.

226   So now she is gone, and the servants are gone, and the things are gone, and there is nothing left but that great bedstead nailed down, with the canvas mattress we found on it.

227   We shall sleep downstairs tonight, and take the boat home tomorrow.

228   I quite enjoy the room, now it is bare again.

229   How those children did tear about here!

230   This bedstead is fairly gnawed!

231   But I must get to work.

232   I have locked the door and thrown the key down into the front path.

233   I don't want to go out, and I don't want to have anybody come in, till John comes.

234   I want to astonish him.

235   I've got a rope up here that even Jennie did not find. If that woman does get out, and tries to get away, I can tie her!

But I forgot I could not reach far without anything to stand on! 236
This bed will *not* move! 237

I tried to lift and push it until I was lame, and then I got so 238
angry I bit off a little piece at one corner—but it hurt my teeth.

Then I peeled off all the paper I could reach standing on the 239
floor. It sticks horribly and the pattern just enjoys it! All those
strangled heads and bulbous eyes and waddling fungus
growths just shriek with derision!

I am getting angry enough to do something desperate. To 240
jump out of the window would be admirable exercise, but the
bars are too strong even to try.

Besides I wouldn't do it. Of course not. I know well enough 241
that a step like that is improper and might be misconstrued.

I don't like to *look* out of the windows even—there are so 242
many of those creeping women, and they creep so fast.

I wonder if they all come out of that wallpaper as I did? 243

But I am securely fastened now by my well-hidden rope— 244
you don't get *me* out in the road there!

I suppose I shall have to get back behind the pattern when it 245
comes night, and that is hard!

It is so pleasant to be out in this great room and creep 246
around as I please!

I don't want to go outside. I won't, even if Jennie asks me to. 247

For outside you have to creep on the ground, and everything 248
is green instead of yellow.

But here I can creep smoothly on the floor, and my shoul- 249
der just fits in that long smooch around the wall, so I cannot
lose my way.

Why there's John at the door! 250

It is no use, young man, you can't open it! 251

How he does call and pound! 252

Now he's crying to Jennie for an axe. 253

It would be a shame to break down that beautiful door! 254

"John dear!" said I in the gentlest voice. "The key is down by 255
the front steps, under a plantain leaf!"

That silenced him for a few moments. 256

Then he said—very quietly indeed, "Open the door, my dar- 257
ling?"

"I can't," said I. "The key is down by the front door under a 258
plantain leaf!"

And then I said it again, several times, very gently and 259
slowly, and said it so often that he had to go and see, and he
got it of course, and came in. He stopped short by the door.

"What is the matter?" he cried. "For God's sake, what are 260
you doing?"

I kept on creeping just the same, but I looked at him over 261
my shoulder.

262   "I've got out at last," said I, "in spite of you and Jane. And
I've pulled off most of the paper, so you can't put me back!"

263   Now why should that man have fainted? But he did, and
right across my path by the wall, so that I had to creep over
him every time!

Marcus Gilmore

THE HUMAN
CONTACT ZONE

*Born in 1982 in Houston, Marcus Gilmore wrote the following
essay in a first-year writing course at the University of
Texas–San Antonio in 2001. He is majoring in biology in
preparation for a career in medical research.*

1   I don't have a problem admitting that I'm not the best dancer
in the world. I'm not a great basketball player, nor have I ever
had dreams of playing professional basketball. As a matter of
fact, I can't remember the last time I played a game of basketball. I listen to rap music, but I can't say that it's my favorite
genre of music.

2   To the average American, there is nothing unusual about the
previous statement—at least not until they find out that the
statements are from a 5'11" nineteen-year-old African
American male. I've always struggled with "being black" versus
conforming to the norms of the dominant culture. In an essay
titled "Arts of the Contact Zone" by Mary Louise Pratt, the author describes contact zones as "social spaces where cultures
meet, clash, and grapple with each other." There are many examples of contact zones as defined by Pratt, but I believe that
contact zones can also emerge within an individual as a result
of conflicts among cultures. An example of a contact zone
emerging within the individual could be the conflict encountered by members of many minority groups.

3   The behavior of minorities at first tends to be influenced by
their ethnic culture. But then a desire for upward mobility and
the need to function in a society controlled by the dominant
ethnicity sometimes forces minorities to abandon many of the
customs and traditions unique to their ethnicity and adopt the

ways of the dominant ethnicity. In my case, I was raised in a predominantly black, working-class neighborhood in Houston, and until kindergarten, the only people with whom I interacted with any regularity were African Americans. My relatives and the people in my community were in many ways representative of the standardized conception of the African American way of life. Most of them spoke a dialect of English unique to African American communities, most were working class citizens, most maintained close relationships with relatives outside of the immediate family, and many took part in rituals such as preparing soul food dinners on Sunday evenings after church, an institution that has historically served as a social and political center of the African American community. One of the characteristic aspects of the African American community is the dialect of English spoken. This dialect, generally known as Ebonics, is probably the result of the origin and experiences of African Americans and of past policies designed to limit or prevent blacks from having the same educational opportunities as whites, policies going back to slavery when black literacy was illegal and continuing until school desegregation orders in the 1950s and 1960s. As Geneva Smitherman indicates in her essay "White English in Blackface, or Who Do I Be" [included in *Conversations* on page 203], Ebonics derives from the unique communication patterns that black Americans used as slaves, overlaid with the forms of English syntax and lexicon deriving from the oppressor's language, and reinforced by the experience of de facto segregation for many years. The dialect, primarily oral, has been passed on from one generation to the next over the years.

But my parents, the people responsible for my primary language development, spoke a relatively traditional standardized form of English. While neither of my parents possessed a college degree, they both had experience in occupations that required them to adjust the dialect of English spoken in their households to a more socially acceptable, standardized American English dialect. Just as many bilingual Hispanic parents have opted to raise their children speaking only English in hopes that they will have less trouble in being accepted by our Anglo-American society, my parents opted to speak a more socially acceptable dialect of English. My mother was probably the most influential force behind my speech habits. The best way I could describe her when it came to my language usage was as the "grammar nazi." When speaking to her I couldn't complete a sentence until I corrected my grammatical errors to conform to standard English. For example, if I made the statement "me an' Michael just . . . ," my mother would interject

"Michael and I . . . ." I suppose my mother's experience working in occupations that required her to constantly communicate with other people and to revise and type documents as part of her clerical work gave her the ability to quickly recognize and "correct" the grammatical errors I made in my conversations with her. As a result, I grew up speaking relatively standardized English.

5   Problems started once I began to interact with other children from different backgrounds. I communicated well with most of my white friends and many of my Hispanic friends. I really didn't think that there was anything peculiar about the way I spoke until I began to notice how most of my white friends and some of my Hispanic friends interacted with other African Americans. Initially, they tended to keep their distance and were very cautious about what they said in front of other blacks. My explanation for this behavior is that members of all ethnic or cultural groups tend to be a little uncomfortable when first interacting with members of other backgrounds because they are simply unaccustomed to interacting with people who may look different or speak differently. For example, most Americans would initially feel some level of discomfort if placed in an unfamiliar culture in South American or Asia. While I obviously looked like an African American to my peers, I didn't sound like the "typical" African American. After years of observation, it appears as if the dialect similarities I share with most of my white friends and many of my Hispanic and Asian friends gave us some common ground to start with, and so they didn't feel as uncomfortable initiating a conversation with me as they would other African Americans at our school. Some probably also associated the dialect of English spoken by some African Americans with negative stereotypes so in their eyes, I may have subconsciously or consciously been perceived as "one of the good ones."

6   Ironically, it took a while for many of my black friends to get used to me. When they would first hear me speak, they would look at me as if I were a neon platypus riding a unicycle. I have been given this look many times by African Americans throughout my life. Because of the way I speak and carry myself, I have been called "Oreo," "Uncle Tom," and "a sellout that's trying to act white." In an attempt to "fit in" with other black students, I have sometimes found myself trying to speak the same way the kids in my neighborhood do. As I got older, I occasionally encountered the same problem not just with blacks, but with everyone.

7   To the black students, I was an Uncle Tom, and to everyone else, I was a "smart" black person. Both sides have been evalu-

ating me against our society's expectations for a particular segment of the population. The sad reality is that young black males are often categorized as inarticulate aspiring athletes, gangsters, drug dealers, or just lazy slackers with no goals or direction in life. A lot of children in black communities actually choose to identify themselves with one of those images simply because they are the only ones they are exposed to through the media. Those children are socialized into believing that their niche in this world is to play ball, rap, sell drugs, or just "chill" for the rest of their life. Many people outside of the black community make similar assumptions because it's what they see on television and in movies, and it's the closest some will ever come to a minority community. The media images these people are exposed to usually include sassy, finger-snapping African American secretaries engaged in shallow personal conversations over the phone instead of working, and black guys who are portrayed as burglars in affluent neighborhoods inhabited by the characters in "Beverly Hills 90210" and "Melrose Place"—which is actually an upgrade from the past images of African Americans as jive talkin', tap dancin', and watermelon eatin' characters sittin' within old television shows and movies. As a result, since I don't fit the stereotypical image of a young black male, some blacks have a difficult time relating to me.

Many whites perceive me as intelligent or as "one of the good ones" based on my speech, interest, and demeanor. "Oh, he is just so intelligent," sometimes sounds to me like a translation for "this one can use complete sentences and has mastered standard subject and verb agreement." Because I don't normally use urban street slang, I've had white acquaintances laugh in my face when I have told them that I am from a dilapidated, predominantly black, working-class area of Houston. I've had many people make the assumption that I come from a wealthy family, which could not be further from the truth. All of this simply because I am a black male who can put five "standard" sentences together in a row without using "ain't" or "fixin-ta." A lot of people even make inferences about my personality before I even speak based on the stereotypical view of African Americans. By the time they visualize me and realize that they are going to interact with me, they have already planned how they are going to approach and speak to me; but once I open my mouth and begin to speak, they don't know what to do. The little voice in their head is saying "this isn't what we expected, what do we do now?" Well, at that point the reactions vary, but one of the more common responses I have received, from elementary school and even currently in college, is the question, "Where are you from?" or "Are you from some European country or something?"

9   I am just one of thousands of other African Americans who have the same internal struggle. From one angle, many African Americans feel an obligation to "stay true to our culture" or to "keep it real." We maintain our ties to African American culture, in part by using Ebonics. On the other side, in order to function outside of the black community, whether it's through academia, corporate America, or in simple social situations, we must conform to a certain extent—and conforming entails assimilating into the dominant culture. This is an example of how two cultures clash and conflict within individuals. I have personally known of Asian Americans and Hispanic Americans that have encountered similar conflicts. It appears that a population within an ethnic group, such as lower-income blacks, view the more assimilated members of their ethnicity as abandoning their culture and find it difficult to relate to them.

10   Is there any way of resolving this conflict? Not really. We just all have to come to the realization of who we are and try not to let outside views and influences shape our life to the point that we forget who we are. Not an easy solution, but the only one I can think of. As I mentioned earlier, I have attempted to deal with this internal contact zone by acting as a social chameleon. I have simply learned how to blend in with my surroundings. When interacting with friends of other ethnic and cultural backgrounds, I make sure that my speech patterns model theirs and that our discussions usually center on topics that are of interest to them. When interacting with African American friends in my neighborhood, I let my accent slip naturally into the traditional urban African American dialect. Our conversations usually involve discussing topics and events of concern to many young members of the African American community. I have observed this type of behavior on several occasions in other African Americans. It reminds me of stories about toys coming to life in toy stores once all of the people are gone. A similar phenomenon occurs every day in business offices and other places of employment all across America: once the Caucasian co-workers leave the office, ethnic dialects come to life.

11   Some minorities have coped with the internal contact zone by fully assimilating into the mainstream Anglo-American influenced American culture and completely abandoning their ethnic subculture. In the United States, this behavior was seen in German and Irish Americans at the beginning of the twentieth century, and later in Italian Americans, and now it appears that the trend is slowly occurring in black, Asian, and some Hispanic communities. Social conflicts have emerged within

various ethnic groups as the result of large numbers of minorities abandoning the lifestyle and traditions unique to their ethnic background. Today in the United States, many Hispanic parents choose to raise their kids speaking only English as compared to raising them in a bilingual household, and many Hispanic girls are choosing to celebrate a sixteenth birthday by having a "sweet sixteen" party instead of having the traditional *quincienera* on their fifteenth birthday. Some members of the Hispanic community naturally find it difficult to understand why other Hispanics would abandon some of the traditions and rituals so unique to their culture. I've heard Italian Americans speak about how some Italian Americans, especially in the Northeast, insist on embracing the stereotypical Italian American lifestyle. When an audition was held in New York for extras on the television program, "The Sopranos," apparently thousands of people showed up, most of them willing to display the stereotypical image of Italian Americans: guys wearing sweat suits and gold chains; gum-chewing women with "big" hair styles and Long Island accents.

These are just a few examples of the conflicts that emerge 12 within ethnic communities as a result of the way ethnic minorities choose to deal with the internal contact zones caused by conflicting cultures. It is unfortunate that people are driven to mold themselves based on stereotypes. I see it all the time in the African American community; the homogenous way of thinking and acting I see in many young African American men is appalling. Whites can fall into a variety of social groups—hippies, yuppies, rednecks, gothics, etc.—but if you are black, you are just black; regardless of your dress, your hobbies, your interests, or your income, people tend to put you in one category: a black guy. Personally, I no longer really care about what people say or think about the way I carry myself, how I speak, the music I listen to, or my hobbies. I can appreciate and enjoy the hip-hop wizardry of the late Notorious B.I.G. as well as enjoy the music of Beck and the classical masterpieces of the French composer Maurice Ravel. I enjoy basketball but I also enjoy capoeira, a Brazilian martial art. I sometimes go the extra mile to shatter stereotypes by doing things like dancing at a party to prove that not all of us are gifted with the rhythm and coordination of Sammy Davis Jr. On the other end of the spectrum, I no longer routinely try to alter my speech to display my "blackness." If anything, I'm happy to speak to some of my younger relatives back in Houston just to show them that you don't always have to let your environment and society dictate who you become. I always hear statistics state that black males are this or that—so much more likely to go to jail than college, so much less likely to finish high school. At my high school, not only did every black male I know graduate, but almost all of them went to college, to Stanford, to Morehouse, to Vanderbilt. We all refused to become statistics and refused to let society dictate who we are. And we all carry the contact zone within us.

Mary Ann Williams

TURNING TOPSY TURVEY

Before her untimely death in 1991 at the age of 46, Mary Ann Williams was a poet, playwright, actress, and director—as well as chair of the Department of Black Studies at Ohio State University. Williams composed the following poem on the occasion of the dedication of Shepard Library in Columbus, Ohio.

Mary had a little lamb
    Who said so?
Its fleece were white as snow
    What happened to all the cute Black lambs?
5 Little Miss muffet sat on a tuffet
    Say, Man, doesn't Topsy have a leading role?

All the school books that I saw cried jungle savages and lifetime
        primitives
    when it came to my kind
10 But now more books talk about me.
    Phillis Wheatley and Paul Lawrence D
    Paved the way for the writing of Black Like Me

When I scan the packed shelves of Shepard I'm proud to see
    Maya Angelou and good ol' Alex Haley lookin' right back
15   as determined as can be

These polished books have neat pages and the pages, long and
        short words and the words, friendly letters
My Black people shuffled, cried and died to learn those strange
        letters, study those long words, turn the endless

pages and fondle the worn covers of books with   20
trembling but with the steadfast stubbornness of a
mule who will work no more

My strawhatted and bandana covered Black people shined with
quiet folk wisdom in the days when Death was the
grader of all who dared to read   25
Swift Death pranced by with each Black letter committed to
memory and each ragged book that these brave
poets of life hid in the rhythms of their curious
souls

Tender thoughts met Death's whip and hooves with a relentless   30
hope of freeing the mind as well as the body
Death trampled many on the backroad to learning

Unlike the story of Jesus of Nazareth, they did not rise on the
third day
They yet cry from their unmarked graves   35
to all mothers and fathers of would-be literates:
"Teach your children to read and write. You must live
for the answer to ignorance. You must twist each
darkened hollow stare into a glimmer of knowing.
Each little face must feel the joy of unlocking the   40
ageless secrets of the written word."
These impressionable bits of human clay can travel without
leaving your doorstep.
They can unravel the countless mysteries of their sorrow-
filled past and cloudy future.   45
They can rush into the arms of God by understanding the
many voices of the past who leave their marks in the
Holy Book
Teach these young Black children to laugh at themselves
through our tales of long ago.   50
Teach them to love letters, words, pages, books—so that
when they look at you, they will know that you
care.

Min-zhan Lu

FROM SILENCE
TO WORDS:
WRITING AS STRUGGLE

Min-zhan Lu teaches a variety of courses related to composition, rhetoric, and literacy at the University of Wisconsin at Milwaukee. She is active in professional organizations related to those areas, and in 1987, she published the following essay in College English, *which is produced by one of those organizations, the College Section of the National Council of Teachers of English, and which is read mostly by college English teachers. You will learn more about Professor Lu's background when you read her narrative.*

1   My mother withdrew into silence two months before she died. A few nights before she fell silent, she told me she regretted the way she had raised me and my sisters. I knew she was referring to the way we had been brought up in the midst of two conflicting worlds—the world of home, dominated by the ideology of the Western humanistic tradition, and the world of a society dominated by Mao Tse-tung's Marxism. My mother had devoted her life to our education, an education she knew had made us suffer political persecution during the Cultural Revolution. I wanted to find a way to convince her that, in spite of the persecution, I had benefited from the education she had worked so hard to give me. But I was silent. My understanding of my education was so dominated by memories of confusion and frustration that I was unable to reflect on what I could have gained from it.

2   This paper is my attempt to fill up that silence with words, words I didn't have then, words that I have since come to by reflecting on my earlier experience as a student in China and on my recent experience as a composition teacher in the United States. For in spite of the frustration and confusion I experienced growing up caught between two conflicting worlds, the conflict ultimately helped me to grow as a reader and writer. Constantly having to switch back and forth between the discourse of home and that of school made me sensitive and self-conscious about the struggle I experienced every time I tried to read, write, or think in either discourse. Eventually, it led me to search for constructive uses for such struggle.

From early childhood, I had identified the differences be- 3
tween home and the outside world by the different languages I
used in each. My parents had wanted my sister and me to get
the best education they could conceive of—Cambridge. They
had hired a live-in tutor, a Scot, to make us bilingual. I learned
to speak English with my parents, my tutor, and my sisters. I
was allowed to speak Shanghai dialect only with the servants.
When I was four (the year after the Communist revolution of
1949), my parents sent me to a local private school where I
learned to speak, read, and write in a new language—Standard
Chinese, the official written language of New China.

In those days, I moved from home to school, from English to 4
Standard Chinese to Shanghai dialect, with no apparent friction. I spoke each language with those who spoke the language. All seemed quite "natural"—servants spoke only
Shanghai dialect because they were servants; teachers spoke
Standard Chinese because they were teachers; languages had
different words because they were different languages. I
thought of English as my family language, comparable to the
many strange dialects I didn't speak but had often heard some
of my classmates speak with their families. While I was happy
to have a special family language, until second grade I didn't
feel that my family language was any different than some of
my classmates' family dialects.

My second grade homeroom teacher was a young graduate 5
from a missionary school. When she found out I spoke
English, she began to practice her English on me. One day she
used English when asking me to run an errand for her. As I
turned to close the door behind me, I noticed the puzzled faces
of my classmates. I had the same sensation I had often experienced when some stranger in a crowd would turn on hearing
me speak English. I was more intensely pleased on this occasion, however, because suddenly I felt that my family language
had been singled out from the family languages of my classmates. Since we were not allowed to speak any dialect other
than Standard Chinese in the classroom, having my teacher
speak English to me in class made English an official language
of the classroom. I began to take pride in my ability to speak it.

This incident confirmed in my mind what my parents had al- 6
ways told me about the importance of English to one's life.
Time and again, they had told me of how my paternal grandfather, who was well versed in classic Chinese, kept losing good-
paying jobs because he couldn't speak English. My grandmother reminisced constantly about how she had slaved and
saved to send my father to a first-rate missionary school. And
we were made to understand that it was my father's fluent

English that had opened the door to his success. Even though my family had always stressed the importance of English for my future, I used to complain bitterly about the extra English lessons we had to take after school. It was only after my home-room teacher had "sanctified" English that I began to connect English with my education. I became a much more eager student in my tutorials.

7   What I learned from my tutorials seemed to enhance and reinforce what I was learning in my classroom. In those days each word had one meaning. One day I would be making a sentence at school: "The national flag of China is red." The next day I would recite at home, "My love is like a red, red rose." There seemed to be an agreement between the Chinese "red" and the English "red," and both corresponded to the patch of color printed next to the word. "Love" was my love for my mother at home and my love for my "motherland" at school: both "loves" meant how I felt about my mother. Having two loads of homework forced me to develop a quick memory for words and a sensitivity to form and style. What I learned in one language carried over to the other. I made sentences such as, "I saw a red, red rose among the green leaves," with both the English lyric and the classic Chinese lyric—red flower among green leaves—running through my mind, and I was praised by both teacher and tutor for being a good student.

8   Although my elementary schooling took place during the fifties, I was almost oblivious to the great political and social changes happening around me. Years later, I read in my history and political philosophy textbooks that the fifties were a time when "China was making a transition from a semi-feudal, semi-capitalist and semi-colonial country into a socialist country," a period in which "the Proletarians were breaking into the educational territory dominated by Bourgeois Intellectuals." While people all over the country were being officially classified into Proletarians, Petty-bourgeois, National-bourgeois, Poor-peasants, and Intellectuals, and were trying to adjust to their new social identities, my parents were allowed to continue the upper middle-class life they had established before the 1949 Revolution because of my father's affiliation with British firms. I had always felt that my family was different from the families of my classmates, but I didn't perceive society's view of my family until the summer vacation before I entered high school.

9   First, my aunt was caught by her colleagues talking to her husband over the phone in English. Because of it, she was criticized and almost labeled a Rightist. (This was the year of the Anti-Rightist movement, a movement in which the

Intellectuals became the target of the "socialist class-struggle.") I had heard others telling my mother that she was foolish to teach us English when Russian had replaced English as the "official" foreign language. I had also learned at school that the American and British Imperialists were the arch-enemies of New China. Yet I had made no connection between the arch-enemies and the English our family spoke. What happened to my aunt forced the connection on me. I began to see my parents' choice of a family language as an anti-Revolutionary act and was alarmed that I had participated in such an act. From then on, I took care not to use English outside home and to conceal my knowledge of English from my new classmates.

Certain words began to play important roles in my new life   10 at the junior high. On the first day of school, we were handed forms to fill out with our parents' class, job, and income. Being one of the few people not employed by the government, my father had never been officially classified. Since he was a medical doctor, he told me to put him down as an Intellectual. My homeroom teacher called me into the office a couple of days afterward and told me that my father couldn't be an Intellectual if his income far exceeded that of a Capitalist. He also told me that since my father worked for Foreign Imperialists, my father should be classified as an Imperialist Lackey. The teacher looked nonplussed when I told him that my father couldn't be an Imperialist Lackey because he was a medical doctor. But I could tell from the way he took notes on my form that my father's job had put me in an unfavorable position in his eyes.

The Standard Chinese term "class" was not a new word for   11 me. Since first grade, I had been taught sentences such as, "The Working class are the masters of New China." I had always known that it was good to be a worker, but until then, I had never felt threatened for not being one. That fall, "class" began to take on a new meaning for me. I noticed a group of Working-class students and teachers at school. I was made to understand that because of my class background, I was excluded from that group.

Another word that became important was "consciousness."   12 One of the slogans posted in the school building read, "Turn our students into future Proletarians with socialist consciousness and education!" For several weeks we studied this slogan in our political philosophy course, a subject I had never had in elementary school. I still remember the definition of "socialist consciousness" that we were repeatedly tested on through the years: "Socialist consciousness is a person's political soul. It is the consciousness of the Proletarians represented by Marxist

Mao Tse-tung thought. It takes expression in one's action, language, and lifestyle. It is the task of every Chinese student to grow up into a Proletarian with a socialist consciousness so that he can serve the people and the motherland." To make the abstract concept accessible to us, our teacher pointed out that the immediate task for students from Working-class families was to strengthen their socialist consciousnesses. For those of us who were from other class backgrounds, the task was to turn ourselves into Workers with socialist consciousnesses. The teacher never explained exactly how we were supposed to "turn" into Workers. Instead, we were given samples of the ritualistic annual plans we had to write at the beginning of each term. In these plans, we performed "self-criticism" on our consciousnesses and made vows to turn ourselves into Workers with socialist consciousnesses. The teacher's division between those who did and those who didn't have a socialist consciousness led me to reify the notion of "consciousness" into a thing one possesses. I equated this intangible "thing" with a concrete way of dressing, speaking, and writing. For instance, I never doubted that my political philosophy teacher had a socialist consciousness because she was from a steelworker's family (she announced this the first day of class) and was a Party member who wore grey cadre suits and talked like a philosophy textbook. I noticed other things about her. She had beautiful eyes and spoke Standard Chinese with such a pure accent that I thought she should be a film star. But I was embarrassed that I had noticed things that ought not to have been associated with her. I blamed my observation on my Bourgeois consciousness.

13   At the same time, the way reading and writing were taught through memorization and imitation also encouraged me to reduce concepts and ideas to simple definitions. In literature and political philosophy classes, we were taught a large number of quotations from Marx, Lenin, and Mao Tse-tung. Each concept that appeared in these quotations came with a definition. We were required to memorize the definitions of the words along with the quotations. Every time I memorized a definition, I felt I had learned a word: "The national red flag symbolizes the blood shed by Revolutionary ancestors for our socialist cause"; "New China rises like a red sun over the eastern horizon." As I memorized these sentences, I reduced their metaphors to dictionary meanings: "red" meant "Revolution" and "red sun" meant "New China" in the "language" of the Working class. I learned mechanically but eagerly. I soon became quite fluent in this new language.

14   As school began to define me as a political subject, my parents tried to build up my resistance to the "communist poison-

ing" by exposing me to the "great books"—novels by Charles Dickens, Nathaniel Hawthorne, Emily Brontë, Jane Austen, and writers from around the turn of the century. My parents implied that these writers represented how I, their child, should read and write. My parents replaced the word "Bourgeois" with the word "cultured." They reminded me that I was in school only to learn math and science. I needed to pass the other courses to stay in school, but I was not to let the "Red doctrines" corrupt my mind. Gone were the days when I could innocently write, "I saw the red, red rose among the green leaves," collapsing, as I did, English and Chinese cultural traditions. "Red" came to mean Revolution at school, "the Commies" at home, and adultery in *The Scarlet Letter.* Since I took these symbols and metaphors as meanings natural to people of the same class, I abandoned my earlier definitions of English and Standard Chinese as the language of home and the language of school. I now defined English as the language of the Bourgeois and Standard Chinese as the language of the Working class. I thought of the language of the Working class as someone else's language and the language of the Bourgeois as my language. But I also believed that, although the language of the Bourgeois was my real language. I could and would adopt the language of the Working class when I was at school. I began to put on and take off my Working class language in the same way I put on and took off my school clothes to avoid being criticized for wearing Bourgeois clothes.

In my literature classes, I learned the Working-class formula   15
for reading. Each work in the textbook had a short "Author's Biography": "XXX, born in 19– in the province of XXX, is from a Worker's family. He joined the Revolution in 19–. He is a Revolutionary realist with a passionate love for the Party and Chinese Revolution. His work expresses the thought and emotions of the masses and sings praise to the prosperous socialist construction on all fronts of China." The teacher used the "Author's Biography" as a yardstick to measure the texts. We were taught to locate details in the texts that illustrated these summaries, such as words that expressed Workers' thoughts and emotions or events that illustrated the Workers' lives.

I learned a formula for Working-class writing in the compo-   16
sition classes. We were given sample essays and told to imitate them. The theme was always about how the collective taught the individual a lesson. I would write papers about labor-learning experiences or school-cleaning days, depending on the occasion of the collective activity closest to the assignment. To make each paper look different, I dressed it up with details about the date, the weather, the environment, or the

appearance of the Master-worker who had taught me "the lesson." But as I became more and more fluent in the generic voice of the Working-class Student, I also became more and more self-conscious about the language we used at home.

17   For instance in senior high, we began to have English classes ("to study English for the Revolution," as the slogan on the cover of the textbook said), and I was given my first Chinese-English dictionary. There I discovered the English version of the term "class-struggle." (The Chinese characters for a school "class" and for a social "class" are different.) I had often used the English word "class" at home in sentences such as, "So and so has class," but I had not connected this sense of "class" with "class-struggle." Once the connection was made, I heard a second layer of meaning every time someone at home said a person had "class." The expression began to mean the person had the style and sophistication characteristic of the Bourgeoisie. The word lost its innocence. I was uneasy about hearing that second layer of meaning because I was sure my parents did not hear the word that way. I felt that therefore I should not be hearing it that way either. Hearing the second layer of meaning made me wonder if I was losing my English.

18   My suspicion deepened when I noticed myself unconsciously merging and switching between the "reading" of home and the "reading" of school. Once I had to write a report on *The Revolutionary Family,* a book about an illiterate woman's awakening and growth as a Revolutionary through the deaths of her husband and all her children for the cause of the Revolution. In one scene the woman deliberated over whether she should encourage her youngest son to join the Revolution. Her memory of her husband's death made her afraid to encourage her son. Yet she also remembered her earlier married life and the first time her husband tried to explain the meaning of the Revolution to her. These memories made her feel she should encourage her son to continue the cause his father had begun.

19   I was moved by this scene. "Moved" was a word my mother and sisters used a lot when we discussed books. Our favorite moments in novels were moments of what I would now call internal conflict, moments which we said "moved" us. I remember that we were "moved" by Jane Eyre when she was torn between her sense of ethics, which compelled her to leave the man she loved, and her impulse to stay with the only man who had ever loved her. We were also moved by Agnes in *David Copperfield* because of the way she restrained her love for David so that he could live happily with the woman he loved. My standard method of doing a book report was to model it on the review by the Publishing Bureau and to dress it up with

detailed quotations from the book. The review of *The Revolutionary Family* emphasized the woman's Revolutionary spirit. I decided to use the scene that had moved me to illustrate this point. I wrote the report the night before it was due. When I had finished, I realized I couldn't possibly hand it in. Instead of illustrating her Revolutionary spirit, I had dwelled on her internal conflict, which could be seen as a moment of weak sentimentality that I should never have emphasized in a Revolutionary heroine. I wrote another report, taking care to illustrate the grandeur of her Revolutionary spirit by expanding on a quotation in which she decided that if the life of her son could change the lives of millions of sons, she should not begrudge his life for the cause of Revolution. I handed in my second version but kept the first in my desk.

I never showed it to anyone. I could never show it to people   20 outside my family, because it had deviated so much from the reading enacted by the jacket review. Neither could I show it to my mother or sisters, because I was ashamed to have been so moved by such a "Revolutionary" book. My parents would have been shocked to learn that I could like such a book in the same way they liked Dickens. Writing this book report increased my fear that I was losing the command over both the "language of home" and the "language of school" that I had worked so hard to gain. I tried to remind myself that, if I could still tell when my reading or writing sounded incorrect, then I had retained my command over both languages. Yet I could no longer be confident of my command over either language because I had discovered that when I was not careful—or even when I was—my reading and writing often surprised me with its impurity. To prevent such impurity, I became very suspicious of my thoughts when I read or wrote. I was always asking myself why I was using this word, how I was using it, always afraid that I wasn't reading or writing correctly. What confused me and frustrated me most was that I could not figure out why I was no longer able to read or write correctly without such painful deliberation.

I continued to read only because reading allowed me to keep   21 my thoughts and confusion private. I hoped that somehow, if I watched myself carefully, I would figure out from the way I read whether I had really mastered the "languages." But writing became a dreadful chore. When I tried to keep a diary, I was so afraid that the voice of school might slip in that I could only list my daily activities. When I wrote for school, I worried that my Bourgeois sensibilities would betray me.

The more suspicious I became about the way I read and   22 wrote, the more guilty I felt for losing the spontaneity with which I had learned to "use" these "languages." Writing the book report made me feel that my reading and writing in the "language" of either home or school could not be free of the interference of the other. But I was unable to acknowledge, grasp, or grapple with what I was experiencing, for both my parents and my teachers had suggested that, if I were a good student, such interference would and should not take place. I assumed that once I had "acquired" a discourse, I could simply switch it on and off every time I read and wrote as I would some electronic tool. Furthermore, I expected my reading and writings to come out in their correct forms whenever I switched the proper discourse on. I still regarded the discourse of home as natural and the discourse of school alien, but I never had doubted before that I could acquire both and switch them on and off according to the occasion.

23   When my experience in writing conflicted with what I thought should happen when I used each discourse, I rejected my experience because it contradicted what my parents and teachers had taught me. I shied away from writing to avoid what I assumed I should not experience. But trying to avoid what should not happen did not keep it from recurring whenever I had to write. Eventually my confusion and frustration over these recurring experiences compelled me to search for an explanation: how and why had I failed to learn what my parents and teachers had worked so hard to teach me?

24   I now think of the internal scene for my reading and writing about *The Revolutionary Family* as a heated discussion between myself, the voices of home, and those of school. The review on the back of the book, the sample student papers I came across in my composition classes, my philosophy teacher—these I heard as voices of one group. My parents and my home readings were the voices of an opposing group. But the conversation between these opposing voices in the internal scene of my writing was not ... polite and respectful. ... Rather, these voices struggled to dominate the discussion, constantly incorporating, dismissing, or suppressing the arguments of each other, like the battles between the hegemonic and counter-hegemonic forces described in Raymond Williams' *Marxism and Literature*. ...

25   When I read *The Revolutionary Family* and wrote the first version of my report, I began with a quotation from the review. The voices of both home and school answered, clamoring to be heard. I tried to listen to one group and turn a deaf ear to the other. Both persisted. I negotiated my way through these conflicting voices, now agreeing with one, now agreeing with the other. I formed a reading out of my interaction with both. Yet I

was afraid to have done so because both home and school had implied that I should speak in unison with only one of these groups and stand away from the discussion rather than participate in it.

My teachers and parents had persistently called my attention   26
to the intensity of the discussion taking place on the external social scene. The story of my grandfather's failure and my father's success had from my early childhood made me aware of the conflict between Western and traditional Chinese cultures. My political education at school added another dimension to the conflict: the war of Marxist-Maoism against them both. Yet when my parents and teachers called my attention to the conflict, they stressed the anxiety of having to live through China's transformation from a semi-feudal, semi-capitalist, and semi-colonial society to a socialist one. Acquiring the discourse of the dominant group was, to them, a means of seeking alliance with that group and thus of surviving the whirlpool of cultural currents around them. As a result, they modeled their pedagogical practices on this utilitarian view of language. Being the eager student, I adopted this view of language as a tool for survival. It came to dominate my understanding of the discussion on the social and historical scene and to restrict my ability to participate in that discussion.

To begin with, the metaphor of language as a tool for survival   27
led me to be passive in my use of discourse, to be a bystander in the discussion. In Burke's "parlor," everyone is involved in the discussion. As it goes on through history, what we call "communal discourses"—arguments specific to particular political, social, economic, ethnic, sexual, and family groups—form, reform and transform. To use a discourse in such a scene is to participate in the argument and to contribute to the formation of the discourse. But when I was growing up, I could not take on the burden of such an active role in the discussion. For both home and school presented the existent conventions of the discourse each taught me as absolute laws for my action. They turned verbal action into a tool, a set of conventions produced and shaped prior to and outside of my own verbal acts. Because I saw language as a tool, I separated the process of producing the tool from the process of using it. The tool was made by someone else and was then acquired and used by me. How the others made it before I acquired it determined and guaranteed what it produced when I used it. I imagined that the more experienced and powerful members of the community were the ones responsible for making the tool. They were the ones who participated in the discussion and fought with opponents. When I used what they made, their labor

and accomplishments would ensure the quality of my reading and writing. By using it I could survive the heated discussion. When my immediate experience in writing the book report suggested that knowing the conventions of school did not guarantee the form and content of my report, when it suggested that I had to write the report with the work and responsibility I had assigned to those who wrote book reviews in the Publishing Bureau, I thought I had lost the tool I had earlier acquired.

28 Another reason I could not take up an active role in the argument was that my parents and teachers contrived to provide a scene free of conflict for practicing my various languages. It was as if their experience had made them aware of the conflict between their discourse and other discourses and of the struggle involved in reproducing the conventions of any discourse on a scene where more than one discourse exists. They seemed convinced that such conflict and struggle would overwhelm someone still learning the discourse. Home and school each contrived a purified space where only one discourse was spoken and heard. In their choice of textbooks, in the way they spoke, and in the way they required me to speak, each jealously silenced any voice that threatened to break the unison of the scene. The homogeneity of home and of school implied that only one discourse could and should be relevant in each place. It led me to believe I should leave behind, turn a deaf ear to, or forget the discourse of the other when I crossed the boundary dividing them. I expected myself to set down one discourse whenever I took up another just as I would take off or put on a particular set of clothes for school or home.

29 Despite my parents' and teachers' attempts to keep home and school discrete, the internal conflict between the two discourses continued whenever I read or wrote. Although I tried to suppress the voice of one discourse in the name of the other, having to speak aloud in the voice I had just silenced each time I crossed the boundary kept both voices active in my mind. Every "I think . . . " from the voice of home or school brought forth a "However . . . " or a "But . . . " from the voice of the opponents. To identify with the voice of home or school, I had to negotiate through the conflicting voices of both by restating, taking back, qualifying my thoughts. I was unconsciously doing so when I did my book report. But I could not use the interaction comfortably and constructively. Both my parents and my teachers had implied that my job was to prevent that interaction from happening. My sense of having failed to accomplish what they had taught silenced me.

30 To use the interaction between the discourses of home and school constructively, I would have to have seen reading or

writing as a process in which I worked my way toward a stance through a dialectical process of identification and division. To identify with an ally, I would have to have grasped the distance between where he or she stood and where I was positioning myself. In taking a stance against an opponent, I would have to have grasped where my stance identified with the stance of my allies. Teetering along the "wavering line of pressure and counter-pressure" from both allies and opponents, I might have worked my way towards a stance of my own (Burke, *A Rhetoric of Motives* 23). Moreover, I would have to have understood that the voices in my mind, like the participants in the parlor scene, were in constant flux [see the epigraph in the Preface—editor]. As I came into contact with new and different groups of people or read different books, voices entered and left. Each time I read or wrote, the stance I negotiated out of these voices would always be at some distance from the stances I worked out in my previous and my later readings or writings.

I could not conceive such a form of action for myself because I saw reading and writing as an expression of an established stance. In delineating the conventions of a discourse, my parents and teachers had synthesized the stance they saw as typical for a representative member of the community. Burke calls this the stance of a "god" or the "prototype"; Williams calls it the "official" or "possible" stance of the community. Through the metaphor of the survival tool, my parents and teachers had led me to assume I could automatically reproduce the official stance of the discourse I used. Therefore, when I did my book report on *The Revolutionary Family*, I expected my knowledge of the official stance set by the book review to ensure the actual stance of my report. As it happened, I began by trying to take the official stance of the review. Other voices interrupted. I answered back. In the process, I worked out a stance approximate but not identical to the official stance I began with. Yet the experience of having to labor to realize my knowledge of the official stance or to prevent myself from wandering away from it frustrated and confused me. For even though I had been actually reading and writing in a Burkean scene, I was afraid to participate actively in the discussion. I assumed it was my role to survive by staying out of it.

Not long ago, my daughter told me that it bothered her to hear her friend "talk wrong." Having come to the United States from China with little English, my daughter has become sensitive to the way English, as spoken by her teachers, operates. As a result, she has amazed her teachers with her success in picking up the language and in adapting to life at school. Her concern to speak the English taught in the classroom "correctly" makes her uncomfortable when she hears people using "ain't" or double negatives, which her teacher considers "improper." I see in her the me that had eagerly learned and used the discourse of the Working class at school. Yet while I was torn between the two conflicting worlds of school and home, she moves with seeming ease from the conversations she hears over the dinner table to her teacher's words in the classroom. My husband and I are proud of the good work she does at school. We are glad she is spared the kinds of conflict between home and school I experienced at her age. Yet as we watch her becoming more and more fluent in the language of the classroom, we wonder if, by enabling her to "survive" school, her very fluency will silence her when the scene of her reading and writing expands beyond that of the composition classroom.

33   For when I listen to my daughter, to students, and to some composition teachers talking about the teaching and learning of writing, I am often alarmed by the degree to which the metaphor of a survival tool dominates their understanding of language as it once dominated my own. I am especially concerned with the way some composition classes focus on turning the classroom into a monological scene for the students' reading and writing. Most of our students live in a world similar to my daughter's, somewhere between the purified world of the classroom and the complex world of my adolescence. When composition classes encourage these students to ignore those voices that seem irrelevant to the purified world of the classroom, most students are often able to do so without much struggle. Some of them are so adept at doing it that the whole process has for them become automatic.

34   However, beyond the classroom and beyond the limited range of these students' immediate lives lies a much more complex and dynamic social and historical scene. To help these students become actors in such a scene, perhaps we need to call their attention to voices that may seem irrelevant to the discourse we teach rather than encourage them to shut them out. For example, we might intentionally complicate the classroom scene by bringing into it discourses that stand at varying distances from the one we teach. We might encourage students to explore ways of practicing the conventions of the discourse they are learning by negotiating through these conflicting voices. We could also encourage them to see themselves as responsible for forming or transforming as well as preserving the discourse they are learning.

35   As I think about what we might do to complicate the external and internal scenes of our students' writing, I hear my par-

ents and teachers saying: "Not now. Keep them from the wrangle of the marketplace until they have acquired the discourse and are skilled at using it." And I answer: "Don't teach them to 'survive' the whirlpool of crosscurrents by avoiding it. Use the classroom to moderate the currents. Moderate the currents, but teach them from the beginning to struggle." When I think of the ways in which the teaching of reading and writing as classroom activities can frustrate the development of students, I am almost grateful for the overwhelming complexity of the circumstances in which I grew up. For it was this complexity that kept me from losing sight of the effort and choice involved in reading or writing with and through a discourse.

Chi-Fan Jennifer Ku
AN INTERNAL DIVIDE

Chi-Fan Jennifer Ku wrote the following essay in 1997 for a first-year writing course at the University of Arizona. She won an award for her work on the sixteenth anniversary of her arrival in the United States.

During my senior year in high school, despite my being an honors student, the registrar's office accidentally scheduled me for study hall, which I attended for a week until my schedule could be changed. When the study hall teacher was taking attendance, he called out my name, Chi-Fan Ku, and told me that he wanted to see me afterwards. He sat me down and asked slowly, pronouncing each word clearly, "Do you understand English? Do you need a translator?" His questions shocked me. I had lived in the United States for 15 years; I spoke English and Chinese fluently and understood the basics of Spanish. I was almost trilingual, yet I did not know how to answer his questions.

"Yes sir, I understand English. I have been in the United States since I was three years old." The study hall teacher had no way of knowing that I had been a U.S. citizen for over six years or that I had an English name and a legal name, Jennifer and Chi-Fan, because very few Americans could pronounce my birth name correctly. While the study hall teacher probably wanted to help me, he simply assumed from my oriental name and my presence in study hall that I did not understand enough English to take another class.

3   At my high school, the widely accepted, stereotypical image was that all Chinese students were geniuses, the top students in the accelerated classes. The only exception was if a Chinese student had recently arrived from another country. Only then would you find a Chinese student in a non-accelerated class or study hall. Such mistakes and misunderstandings result from conclusions based on a combination of physical features and preconceptions. While such perceptions create misunderstandings between cultures, they also create internal rifts within those who live as individuals straddling those cultures.

4   Due to economic conditions, cultural differences, and their unwillingness to assimilate into the American culture, the Chinese immigrants in the late 1800s endured hostile feelings from American citizens and the government. Many Americans wanted to deport all Chinese immigrants because they believed that the Chinese stole most of their jobs. Yet these Americans never stopped to think that the jobs the Chinese accepted were either jobs Americans refused or dangerous jobs that employers were unwilling to give to American workers. Why endanger American lives, when employers could exploit another group of people that few in the United States considered to be human beings? If they did not use the Chinese, then they would have exploited another group, such as the Japanese, the Mexicans, or the Irish.

5   The majority of Chinese immigrants did not want to stay in the United States. They only wanted to earn enough money to support their families in China. They were willing to risk their health, happiness, and lives for their family because to the Chinese, the family always comes first. If you succeed, the entire family succeeds. If you fail, the entire family is disgraced. This basic ideology is drilled into all Chinese at an early age. If the Americans had seen the terror, heartache, sacrifice, and shattered pride these hard-working Chinese immigrants faced each day, would they have demanded that the government pass the Chinese Exclusion Act? Would they have treated the Chinese like dogs? All the Americans saw were the golden complexion, the black hair, the queue hair style, the small almond-shaped eyes. To the Americans, the Chinese were simply automatons—people unwilling to assimilate, nothing like them.

6   Today, Chinese immigrants try to learn from their ancestors' mistakes. Some Chinese parents believe that only through assimilation can their children survive and succeed in the United States. They encourage their children to immerse themselves in

the American culture; they believe this is the key to allowing their children to be successful in America. They believe assimilation will protect their children from racial bias and the suffering that previous Chinese immigrants have endured. "Learn to speak English without an accent," some parents tell their children. "Become educated about the American culture through music and fashion, accept the dominant religion, have only Americanized friends." Unfortunately, many American-born Chinese, or ABCs, do not hear the one sentence that parents add to their long list of advice: "Do not forget who you are."

Some parents try to tell their children this indirectly by sending them to Chinese language schools. At such schools, Chinese teachers, who are usually other Chinese parents, try to teach us grammar, cultural traditions, and history. However, most Chinese students attend only to socialize with each other. Do they hear anything the teacher says? Do they understand that a proper Chinese student respects the teacher and listens attentively? Sometimes when I was in Chinese language school I wanted to slap my classmates and shake them. My heart screamed, "Have you drunk so much Coke and eaten so many Big Macs that you have forgotten who you are? How could you trade your Chinese heritage for a superficial image?" Most graduate from Chinese school without really knowing a word of Chinese. Sometimes being around them, I felt shame and disgrace; they did not know that their actions reflected upon all of us, just as the early Chinese immigrant represented his family and his nation.

Perhaps my feelings result from my fear that someday I may awaken from a deep sleep and realize that the American ghost that haunts me has stolen my Chinese spirit. In the Chinese culture, Chinese ghosts are dangerous, because they are cunning and can kill you by just looking at you. Only the confident, strong, and brave will be able to overcome and destroy such a terrifying being. The American ghost, according to many of my Chinese elders, is not dreadful and elusive like the Chinese ghost. Rather, the American ghost is just a term that some Chinese people use to describe Americans, because the first American missionaries that arrived in China had complexions that were considerably paler than those of the Chinese, so the Chinese believed they were ghosts. While my relatives do not fear them, I do. As Chinese American author Maxine Hong Kingston wrote in *The Woman Warrior: Memoirs of a Girlhood Among Ghosts*, "we were born among ghosts, were taught by ghosts, and were ourselves half ghosts." I am part American ghost. I cannot hide from it or deny its existence. But I must be careful; otherwise the American ghost will overcome and dominate me. Then my Chinese spirit would be forced to leave. Then I would forget who I am.

9   My American ghost has no manners; it appears suddenly, without an invitation. For example, when I visit my relatives in Taiwan, I do not know the proper titles I should use to address my elders. They laugh when they hear me speak because I do not speak correctly. They excuse me, however. "She is just an American," my relatives tell their friends. One of their friends once asked me if I knew who the American president was. When I responded, "Bill Clinton," she seemed surprised. "I thought that all Chinese children who grow up in America were stupid." Her words sliced through my heart. "I am not completely American!" I wanted to scream back at her. But such behavior would not have been proper. My aunts tell me my shorts need to be longer—they need to cover the knees and would be better if they reached mid-calf. My uncles point out that I am too fat. They suggest that I stop eating American food. My relatives and other Chinese people do not see the black haired, brown eyed, yellow complexioned Chinese girl. Instead, they tell me that I might as well dye my hair blond and wear blue contacts. My relatives and Chinese school teachers call me a banana—a person with a yellow complexion, who is completely white inside. Ironically, my classmates at Chinese school, who want to be the typical American, tell me that I am the stereotypical Chinese. They claim that I have the mentality of the traditional, nonconforming Chinese student—always serious, always studying.

10   I am American. I am not American. I am Chinese. I am not Chinese. How do I explain my situation to others if I am lost and confused? I cannot only accept my American background while ignoring my Chinese heritage. Nor can I live solely by feeding off my Chinese upbringing. I want to cry. I feel scared. I am alone. Yet I can find comfort in other sources, such as the works of some multicultural authors. Mexican American writer Gloria Anzaldúa recommends to those who live between cultures to "live *sin fronteras* / be a crossroads." We must find an existence that allows us to accept both cultures, yet not drown in either, a difficult task requiring all my concentration. Yet, when I find that place, I will not have any borders to prevent me from moving between both cultures—a place where my American ghost and Chinese spirit will coexist in harmony. One day I will succeed. One day I will smile because I will know who I am.

LANGUAGE

Oakland, California, school board members address questions about Ebonics during a press conference on January 12, 1997. Standing behind school superintendent Carolyn Getridge is Sylvester Hodges, chairperson of the committee that brought forward the resolution on Ebonics that is discussed in Part II of Conversations.

Introduction

People used to think of language as being ideologically neutral—as a sort of transparent window through which ideas are conveyed. Now many people agree that language is not transparent but colored by ideological and cultural biases. Far from being neutral, language is a product (as well as a producer) of culture. As such, it inevitably reflects (as well as shapes) that particular culture. The three issues explored in this part of *Conversations*—Should We Have a National Language?; Is There a "Standard" English?; and Is English Sexist?—share the assumption that language is culture-bound, that social issues inevitably mingle with language issues.

The first section includes five items that are generally related to those in the previous part of the book, items that include literacy narratives and that consider language against the backdrop of the ethnic diversity of the United States. (These readings also relate closely to the pieces in the section on Defining Race reprinted elsewhere in *Conversations.*) Should public policies enforce English as our national language and discourage the use of other tongues? For many years federal, state, and local governments, for instance, have supported the policy of giving students schoolwork in their native languages—English for most, but Spanish and Chinese and many other languages as well—so that students with limited proficiency in English would not fall behind in other subjects while they mastered English "as a second language." In 1974, Congress required schools to promote knowledge of students' native languages and cultures as well as to promote growth in English. But in the past decade the policy of bilingual education has come under fire. Some educators have contended that bilingual programs do not work well or that they are too expensive. Other critics, noting the importance of English as a unifying force in our society, contend that bilingual programs—because they interfere with students' mastery of English—prevent non-English-speaking citizens from assuming a central role in life in the United States. As a result, some citizens in over two dozen states have advocated, and in some cases even passed, laws designating English as "the official language" of the United States. They argue partly on the grounds of cost (bilingual education, bilingual ballots, bilingual forms and signs and menus all cost money), partly to promote a more unified nation, and partly to avoid the possibility that states in the Southwest might become Spanish-speaking "American Quebecs." (You probably remember that in 1995, the predominantly French-speaking Canadian province of Quebec nearly approved a resolution to secede from Canada.) Opponents contend that creating English as an official language would foster intolerance and bigotry, would compromise the civil rights of citizens who have not mastered English, and would undermine the richness of our nation's ethnic diversity.

The second section amounts to a conversation about relationships between language and power, particularly about the ideology of standard American English. Is Black English (or Ebonics) a robust dialect that proceeds according to normal conventions of sound and structure? Or is it (especially in its written form) a substandard dialect that impedes communication and clouds thinking? Do Black English and other "nonstandard" dialects empower their users as fully as any other language, or do they undermine literacy, discourage the chances of their users for success in the main streams of American life, and keep their users politically and socially marginalized? Several of the selections in this section comment in particular on a December 1996 resolution by the Oakland (California) school board, which recognized Ebonics as a language and directed the school superintendent to "implement the best possible academic program for imparting instruction to African American students in their primary language."

Power is also at the heart of feminist critiques of the English language. As the three selections and cartoon printed in the section on sexist language disclose, the English language can favor some groups at the expense of others—particularly men at the expense of women. To what extent does English, as the product of a culture dominated by males, demean and delimit women? To what extent does English perpetuate outworn cultural assumptions about women? In other words, to what extent is English itself sexist? And what can be done about it? Those are the questions taken up in this final section.

Most citizens in this country have been proud of the metaphor of the United States as a melting pot—a place where immigrants are assimilated into the sustenance of American life and American language. Recently, another metaphor has been proposed: the United States as salad bowl, as a place where immigrant citizens become American but still retain their unique cultural flavor even as they contribute to the mix. Whatever the metaphor, language will continue to be an area where differences between individuals and their society are negotiated, where conflicts between "American society" and its diverse individuals are adjudicated. In other words, language itself will remain an issue.

Richard Rodriguez

ARIA: A MEMOIR
OF A BILINGUAL
CHILDHOOD

Richard Rodriguez, born in 1944 into a Spanish-speaking, Mexican American family, was educated at Stanford, Columbia, and Berkeley. Many of his eloquent essays—like the ones in his 1992 book Days of Obligation: An Argument with My Mexican Father—*mix memoir and argument, and many measure the gains and losses that result when English replaces Spanish that is spoken at home. This essay, first published in the magazine* The American Scholar *(1981), was incorporated into his acclaimed (and controversial) book* Hunger of Memory *(1982). Read Rodriguez's essay—and then turn to the following one by Victor Villanueva Jr.*

I remember, to start with, that day in Sacramento, in a California now nearly thirty years past, when I first entered a classroom—able to understand about fifty stray English words. The third of four children, I had been preceded by my older brother and sister to a neighborhood Roman Catholic school. But neither of them had revealed very much about their classroom experiences. They left each morning and returned each afternoon, always together, speaking Spanish as they climbed the five steps to the porch. And their mysterious books, wrapped in brown shopping-bag paper, remained on the table next to the door, closed firmly behind them.

An accident of geography sent me to a school where all my classmates were white and many were the children of doctors

1

2

and lawyers and business executives. On that first day of school, my classmates must certainly have been uneasy to find themselves apart from their families, in the first institution of their lives. But I was astonished. I was fated to be the "problem student" in class.

3   The nun said, in a friendly but oddly impersonal voice: "Boys and girls, this is Richard Rodriguez." (I heard her sound it out: *Rich-heard Road-ree-guess.*) It was the first time I had heard anyone say my name in English. "Richard," the nun repeated more slowly, writing my name down in her book. Quickly I turned to see my mother's face dissolve in a watery blur behind the pebbled-glass door.

4   Now, many years later, I hear of something called "bilingual education"—a scheme proposed in the late 1960s by Hispanic-American social activists, later endorsed by a congressional vote. It is a program that seeks to permit non-English-speaking children (many from lower class homes) to use their "family language" as the language of school. Such, at least, is the aim its supporters announce. I hear them, and am forced to say no: It is not possible for a child, any child, ever to use his family's language in school. Not to understand this is to misunderstand the public uses of schooling and to trivialize the nature of intimate life.

5   Memory teaches me what I know of these matters. The boy reminds the adult. I was a bilingual child, but of a certain kind: "socially disadvantaged," the son of working-class parents, both Mexican immigrants.

6   In the early years of my boyhood, my parents coped very well in America. My father had steady work. My mother managed at home. They were nobody's victims. When we moved to a house many blocks from the Mexican-American section of town, they were not intimidated by those two or three neighbors who initially tried to make us unwelcome. ("Keep your brats away from my sidewalk!") But despite all they achieved, or perhaps because they had so much to achieve, they lacked any deep feeling of ease, of belonging in public. They regarded the people at work or in crowds as being very distant from us. Those were the others, *los gringos.* That term was interchangeable in their speech with another, even more telling: *los americanos.*

7   I grew up in a house where the only regular guests were my relations. On a certain day, enormous families of relatives would visit us, and there would be so many people that the noise and the bodies would spill out to the backyard and onto the front porch. Then for weeks no one would come. (If the doorbell rang, it was usually a salesman.) Our house stood apart—gaudy yellow in a row of white bungalows. We were the

people with the noisy dog, the people who raised chickens. We were the foreigners on the block. A few neighbors would smile and wave at us. We waved back. But until I was seven years old, I did not know the name of the old couple living next door or the names of the kids living across the street.

In public, my father and mother spoke a hesitant, accented, and not always grammatical English. And then they would have to strain, their bodies tense, to catch the sense of what was rapidly said by *los gringos*. At home, they returned to Spanish. The language of their Mexican past sounded in counterpoint to the English spoken in public. The words would come quickly, with ease. Conveyed through those sounds was the pleasing, soothing, consoling reminder that one was at home. 8

During those years when I was first learning to speak, my mother and father addressed me only in Spanish; in Spanish I learned to reply. By contrast, English (*inglés*) was the language I came to associate with gringos, rarely heard in the house. I learned my first words of English overhearing my parents speaking to strangers. At six years of age, I knew just enough words for my mother to trust me on errands to stores one block away—but no more. 9

I was then a listening child, careful to hear the very different sounds of Spanish and English. Wide-eyed with hearing, I'd listen to sounds more than to words. First, there were English (gringo) sounds. So many words still were unknown to me that when the butcher or the lady at the drugstore said something, exotic polysyllabic sounds would bloom in the midst of their sentences. Often the speech of people in public seemed to me very loud, booming with confidence. The man behind the counter would literally ask, "What can I do for you?" But by being so firm and clear, the sound of his voice said that he was a gringo; he belonged in public society. There were also the high, nasal notes of middle-class American speech—which I rarely am conscious of hearing today because I hear them so often, but could not stop hearing when I was a boy. Crowds at Safeway or at bus stops were noisy with the birdlike sounds of *los gringos*. I'd move away from them all—all the chirping chatter above me. 10

My own sounds I was unable to hear, but I knew that I spoke English poorly. My words could not extend to form complete thoughts. And the words I did speak I didn't know well enough to make distinct sounds. (Listeners would usually lower their heads to hear better what I was trying to say.) But it was one thing for *me* to speak English with difficulty; it was more troubling to hear my parents speaking in public: their high-whining vowels and guttural consonants; their sentences that got stuck with "eh" and "ah" sounds; the confused syntax; the hesitant 11 rhythm of sounds so different from the way gringos spoke. I'd notice, moreover, that my parents' voices were softer than those of gringos we would meet.

12   I am tempted to say now that none of this mattered. (In adulthood I am embarrassed by childhood fears.) And, in a way, it didn't matter very much that my parents could not speak English with ease. Their linguistic difficulties had no serious consequences. My mother and father made themselves understood at the county hospital clinic and at government offices. And yet, in another way, it mattered very much. It was unsettling to hear my parents struggle with English. Hearing them, I'd grow nervous, and my clutching trust in their protection and power would be weakened.

13   There were many times like the night at a brightly lit gasoline station (a blaring white memory) when I stood uneasily hearing my father talk to a teenage attendant. I do not recall what they were saying, but I cannot forget the sounds my father made as he spoke. At one point his words slid together to form one long word—sounds as confused as the threads of blue and green oil in the puddle next to my shoes. His voice rushed through what he had left to say. Toward the end, he reached falsetto notes, appealing to his listener's understanding. I looked away at the lights of passing automobiles. I tried not to hear any more. But I heard only too well the attendant's reply, his calm, easy tones. Shortly afterward, headed for home, I shivered when my father put his hand on my shoulder. The very first chance that I got, I evaded his grasp and ran on ahead into the dark, skipping with feigned boyish exuberance.

14   But then there was Spanish: *español*, the language rarely heard away from the house; *español*, the language which seemed to me therefore a private language, my family's language. To hear its sounds was to feel myself specially recognized as one of the family, apart from *los otros*. A simple remark, an inconsequential comment could convey that assurance. My parents would say something to me and I would feel embraced by the sounds of their words. Those sounds said: *I am speaking with ease in Spanish. I am addressing you in words I never use with los gringos. I recognize you as someone special, close, like no one outside. You belong with us. In the family. Ricardo.*

15   At the age of six, well past the time when most middle-class children no longer notice the difference between sounds uttered at home and words spoken in public, I had a different experience. I lived in a world compounded of sounds. I was a child longer than most. I lived in a magical world, surrounded by sounds both pleasing and fearful. I shared with my family a

language enchantingly private—different from that used in the city around us.

Just opening or closing the screen door behind me was an im- 16 portant experience. I'd rarely leave home all alone or without feeling reluctance. Walking down the sidewalk, under the canopy of tall trees, I'd warily notice the (suddenly) silent neighborhood kids who stood warily watching me. Nervously, I'd arrive at the grocery store to hear there the sounds of the gringo, reminding me that in this so-big world I was a foreigner. But if leaving home was never routine, neither was coming back. Walking toward our house, climbing the steps from the sidewalk, in summer when the front door was open, I'd hear voices beyond the screen door talking in Spanish. For a second or two I'd stay, linger there listening. Smiling, I'd hear my mother call out, saying in Spanish, "Is that you, Richard?" Those were her words, but all the while her sounds would assure me: *You are home now. Come closer inside. With us.* "Sí," I'd reply.

Once more inside the house, I would resume my place in the 17 family. The sounds would grow harder to hear. Once more at home, I would grow less conscious of them. It required, however, no more than the blurt of the doorbell to alert me all over again to listen to sounds. The house would turn instantly quiet while my mother went to the door. I'd hear her hard English sounds. I'd wait to hear her voice turn to soft-sounding Spanish, which assured me, as surely as did the clicking tongue of the lock on the door, that the stranger was gone.

Plainly it is not healthy to hear such sounds often. It is not 18 healthy to distinguish public from private sounds so easily. I remained cloistered by sounds, timid and shy in public, too dependent on the voices at home. And yet I was a very happy child when I was at home. I remember many nights when my father would come back from work, and I'd hear him call out to my mother in Spanish, sounding relieved. In Spanish, his voice would sound the light and free notes that he never could manage in English. Some nights I'd jump up just hearing his voice. My brother and I would come running into the room where he was with our mother. Our laughing (so deep was the pleasure!) became screaming. Like others who feel the pain of public alienation, we transformed the knowledge of our public separateness into a consoling reminder of our intimacy. Excited, our voices joined in a celebration of sounds. *We are speaking now the way we never speak out in public—we are together,* the sounds told me. Some nights no one seemed willing to loosen the hold that sounds had on us. At dinner we invented new words that sounded Spanish, but made sense only to us. We pieced together new words by taking, say, an English verb and giving it Spanish endings. My mother's instructions at bedtime would be lacquered with mock-urgent tones. Or a word like *sí,* sounded in several notes, would convey added measures of feeling. Tongues lingered around the edges of words, especially fat vowels, and we happily sounded that military drum roll, the twirling roar of the Spanish *r.* Family language, my family's sounds: the voices of my parents and sisters and brother. Their voices insisting: *You belong here. We are family members. Related. Special to one another. Listen!* Voices singing and sighing, rising and straining, then surging, teeming with pleasure which burst syllables into fragments of laughter. At times it seemed there was steady quiet only when, from another room, the rustling whispers of my parents faded and I edged closer to sleep.

19   Supporters of bilingual education imply today that students like me miss a great deal by not being taught in their family's language. What they seem not to recognize is that, as a socially disadvantaged child, I regarded Spanish as a private language. It was a ghetto language that deepened and strengthened my feeling of public separateness. What I needed to learn in school was that I had the right, and the obligation, to speak the public language. The odd truth is that my first-grade classmates could have become bilingual, in the conventional sense of the word, more easily than I. Had they been taught early (as upper middle-class children often are taught) a "second language" like Spanish or French, they could have regarded it simply as another public language. In my case, such bilingualism could not have been so quickly achieved. What I did not believe was that I could speak a single public language.

20   Without question, it would have pleased me to have heard my teachers address me in Spanish when I entered the classroom. I would have felt much less afraid. I would have imagined that my instructors were somehow "related" to me; I would indeed have heard their Spanish as my family's language. I would have trusted them and responded with ease. But I would have delayed—postponed for how long?—having to learn the language of public society. I would have evaded—and for how long?—learning the great lesson of school: that I had a public identity.

21   Fortunately, my teachers were unsentimental about their responsibility. What they understood was that I needed to speak public English. So their voices would search me out, asking me questions. Each time I heard them I'd look up in surprise to see a nun's face frowning at me. I'd mumble, not really meaning to answer. The nun would persist. "Richard, stand up. Don't look at the floor. Speak up. Speak to the entire class, not just to me!"

But I couldn't believe English could be my language to use. (In part, I did not want to believe it.) I continued to mumble. I resisted the teacher's demands. (Did I somehow suspect that once I learned this public language my family life would be changed?) Silent, waiting for the bell to sound, I remained dazed, diffident, afraid.

Because I wrongly imagined that English was intrinsically a 22 public language and Spanish was intrinsically private, I easily noted the difference between classroom language and the language at home. At school, words were directed to a general audience of listeners. ("Boys and girls . . . ") Words were meaningfully ordered. And the point was not self-expression alone, but to make oneself understood by many others. The teacher quizzed: "Boys and girls, why do we use that word in this sentence? Could we think of a better word to use there? Would the sentence change its meaning if the words were differently arranged? Isn't there a better way of saying much the same thing?" (I couldn't say. I wouldn't try to say.)

Three months passed. Five. A half year. Unsmiling, ever 23 watchful, my teachers noted my silence. They began to connect my behavior with the slow progress my brother and sisters were making. Until, one Saturday morning, three nuns arrived at the house to talk to our parents. Stiffly they sat on the blue living-room sofa. From the doorway of another room, spying on the visitors, I noted the incongruity, the clash of two worlds, the faces and voices of school intruding upon the familiar setting of home. I overheard one voice gently wondering, "Do your children speak only Spanish at home, Mrs. Rodriguez?" While another voice added, "That Richard especially seems so timid and shy."

That Rich-heard! 24

With great tact, the visitors continued, "Is it possible for you 25 and your husband to encourage your children to practice their English when they are home?" Of course my parents complied. What would they not do for their children's well-being? And how could they question the Church's authority which those women represented? In an instant they agreed to give up the language (the sounds) which had revealed and accentuated our family's closeness. The moment after the visitors left, the change was observed. *"Ahora,* speak to us only *en inglés,"* my father and mother told us.

At first, it seemed a kind of game. After dinner each night, 26 the family gathered together to practice "our" English. It was still then *inglés,* a language foreign to us, so we felt drawn to it as strangers. Laughing, we would try to define words we could not pronounce. We played with strange English sounds, often overanglicizing our pronunciations. And we filled the smiling gaps of our sentences with familiar Spanish sounds. But that was cheating, somebody shouted, and everyone laughed.

27   In school, meanwhile, like my brother and sisters, I was required to attend a daily tutoring session. I needed a full year of this special work. I also needed my teachers to keep my attention from straying in class by calling out, *"Rich-heard"*—their English voices slowly loosening the ties to my other name, with its three notes, *Ri-car-do.* Most of all, I needed to hear my mother and father speak to me in a moment of seriousness in "broken"—suddenly heartbreaking—English. This scene was inevitable. One Saturday morning I entered the kitchen where my parents were talking, but I did not realize that they were talking in Spanish until, the moment they saw me, their voices changed and they began speaking English. The gringo sounds they uttered startled me. Pushed me away. In that moment of trivial misunderstanding and profound insight, I felt my throat twisted by unsounded grief. I simply turned and left the room. But I had no place to escape to where I could grieve in Spanish. My brother and sisters were speaking English in another part of the house.

28   Again and again in the days following, as I grew increasingly angry, I was obliged to hear my mother and father encouraging me: "Speak to us *en inglés.*" Only then did I determine to learn classroom English. Thus, sometime afterward it happened: one day in school, I raised my hand to volunteer an answer to a question. I spoke out in a loud voice and I did not think it remarkable when the entire class understood. That day I moved very far from being the disadvantaged child I had been only days earlier. Taken hold at last was the belief, the calming assurance, that I *belonged* in public.

29   Shortly after, I stopped hearing the high, troubling sounds of *los gringos.* A more and more confident speaker of English, I didn't listen to how strangers sounded when they talked to me. With so many English-speaking people around me, I no longer heard American accents. Conversations quickened. Listening to persons whose voices sounded eccentrically pitched, I might note their sounds for a few seconds, but then I'd concentrate on what they were saying. Now when I heard someone's tone of voice—angry or questioning or sarcastic or happy or sad—I didn't distinguish it from the words it expressed. Sound and word were thus tightly wedded. At the end of each day I was often bemused, and always relieved, to realize how "soundless," though crowded with words, my day in public had been. An eight-year-old boy, I finally came to accept what had been technically true since my birth: I was an American citizen.

But diminished by then was the special feeling of closeness 30
at home. Gone was the desperate, urgent, intense feeling of being at home among those with whom I felt intimate. Our family
remained a loving family, but one greatly changed. We were no
longer so close, no longer bound tightly together by the knowledge of our separateness from *los gringos*. Neither my older
brother nor my sisters rushed home after school any more. Nor
did I. When I arrived home, often there would be neighborhood
kids in the house. Or the house would be empty of sounds.

Following the dramatic Americanization of their children, 31
even my parents grew more publicly confident—especially my
mother. First she learned the names of all the people on the
block. Then she decided we needed to have a telephone in our
house. My father, for his part, continued to use the word
gringo, but it was no longer charged with bitterness or distrust.
Stripped of any emotional content, the word simply became a
name for those Americans not of Hispanic descent. Hearing
him, sometimes, I wasn't sure if he was pronouncing the
Spanish word *gringo*, or saying gringo in English.

There was a new silence at home. As we children learned 32
more and more English, we shared fewer and fewer words
with our parents. Sentences needed to be spoken slowly when
one of us addressed our mother or father. Often the parent
wouldn't understand. The child would need to repeat himself.
Still the parent misunderstood. The young voice, frustrated,
would end up saying, "Never mind"—the subject was closed.
Dinners would be noisy with the clinking of knives and forks
against dishes. My mother would smile softly between her remarks; my father, at the other end of the table, would chew and
chew his food while he stared over the heads of his children.

My mother! My father! After English became my primary 33
language, I no longer knew what words to use in addressing
my parents. The old Spanish words (those tender accents of
sound) I had earlier used—*mamá* and *papá*—I couldn't use any
more. They would have been all-too-painful reminders of how
much had changed in my life. On the other hand, the words I
heard neighborhood kids call their parents seemed equally unsatisfactory. "Mother" and "father," "ma," "papa," "pa," "dad,"
"pop" (how I hated the all-American sound of that last word)—
all these I felt were unsuitable terms of address for *my* parents.
As a result, I never used them at home. Whenever I'd speak to
my parents, I would try to get their attention by looking at
them. In public conversations, I'd refer to them as my "parents" or my "mother" and "father."

My mother and father, for their part, responded differently, 34
as their children spoke to them less. My mother grew restless,

seemed troubled and anxious at the scarceness of words exchanged in the house. She would question me about my day when I came home from school. She smiled at my small talk. She pried at the edges of my sentences to get me to say something more. ("What . . . ?") She'd join conversations she overheard, but her intrusions often stopped her children's talking. By contrast, my father seemed to grow reconciled to the new quiet. Though his English somewhat improved, he tended more and more to retire into silence. At dinner he spoke very little. One night his children and even his wife helplessly giggled at his garbled English pronunciation of the Catholic "Grace Before Meals." Thereafter he made his wife recite the prayer at the start of each meal, even on formal occasions when there were guests in the house.

35   Hers became the public voice of the family. On official business it was she, not my father, who would usually talk to strangers on the phone or in stores. We children grew so accustomed to his silence that years later we would routinely refer to his "shyness." (My mother often tried to explain: both of his parents died when he was eight. He was raised by an uncle who treated him as little more than a menial servant. He was never encouraged to speak. He grew up alone—a man of few words.) But I realized my father was not shy whenever I'd watch him speaking Spanish with relatives. Using Spanish, he was quickly effusive. Especially when talking with other men, his voice would spark, flicker, flare alive with varied sounds. In Spanish he expressed ideas and feelings he rarely revealed when speaking English. With firm Spanish sounds he conveyed a confidence and authority that English would never allow him.

36   The silence at home, however, was not simply the result of fewer words passing between parents and children. More profound for me was the silence created by inattention to sounds. At about the time I no longer bothered to listen with care to the sounds of English in public, I grew careless about listening to the sounds made by the family when they spoke. Most of the time I would hear someone speaking at home and didn't distinguish his sounds from the words people uttered in public. I didn't even pay much attention to my parents' accented and ungrammatical speech—at least not at home. Only when I was with them in public would I become alert to their accents. But even then their sounds caused me less and less concern. For I was growing increasingly confident of my own public identity.

37   I would have been happier about my public success had I not recalled, sometimes, what it had been like earlier, when my family conveyed its intimacy through a set of conveniently private sounds. Sometimes in public, hearing a stranger, I'd hark back to

my lost past. A Mexican farm worker approached me one day downtown. He wanted directions to some place. *"Hijito, . . . "* he said. And his voice stirred old longings. Another time I was standing beside my mother in the visiting room of a Carmelite convent, before the dense screen which rendered the nuns shadowy figures. I heard several of them speaking Spanish in their busy, singsong, overlapping voices, assuring my mother that yes, yes, we were remembered, all our family was remembered, in their prayers. Those voices echoed faraway family sounds. Another day a dark-faced old woman touched my shoulder lightly to steady herself as she boarded a bus. She murmured something to me I couldn't quite comprehend. Her Spanish voice came near, like the face of a never-before-seen relative in the instant before I was kissed. That voice, like so many of the Spanish voices I'd hear in public, recalled the golden age of my childhood.

Bilingual educators say today that children lose a degree of "individuality" by becoming assimilated into public society. (Bilingual schooling is a program popularized in the seventies, that decade when middle-class "ethnics" began to resist the process of assimilation—the "American melting pot.") But the bilingualists oversimplify when they scorn the value and necessity of assimilation. They do not seem to realize that a person is individualized in two ways. So they do not realize that, while one suffers a diminished sense of *private* individuality by being assimilated into public society, such assimilation makes possible the achievement of *public* individuality.   38

Simplistically again, the bilingualists insist that a student should be reminded of his difference from others in mass society, of his "heritage." But they equate mere separateness with individuality. The fact is that only in private—with intimates— is separateness from the crowd a prerequisite for individuality; an intimate "tells" me that I am unique, unlike all others, apart from the crowd. In public, by contrast, full individuality is achieved, paradoxically, by those who are able to consider themselves members of the crowd. Thus it happened for me. Only when I was able to think of myself as an American, no longer an alien in gringo society, could I seek the rights and opportunities necessary for full public individuality. The social and political advantages I enjoy as a man began on the day I came to believe that my name is indeed *Rich-heard Road-ree-guess.* It is true that my public society today is often impersonal; in fact, my public society is usually mass society. But despite the anonymity of the crowd, and despite the fact that the individuality I achieve in public is often tenuous—because it depends on my being one in a crowd—I celebrate the day I   39 acquired my new name. Those middle-class ethnics who scorn assimilation seem to me filled with decadent self-pity, obsessed by the burden of public life. Dangerously, they romanticize public separateness and trivialize the dilemma of those who are truly socially disadvantaged.

40   If I rehearse here the changes in my private life after my Americanization, it is finally to emphasize a public gain. The loss implies the gain. The house I returned to each afternoon was quiet. Intimate sounds no longer greeted me at the door. Inside there were other noises. The telephone rang. Neighborhood kids ran past the door of the bedroom where I was reading my schoolbooks—covered with brown shopping-bag paper. Once I learned the public language, it would never again be easy for me to hear intimate family voices. More and more of my day was spent hearing words, not sounds. But that may only be a way of saying that on the day I raised my hand in class and spoke loudly to an entire roomful of faces, my childhood started to end.

Victor Villanueva Jr.
WHOSE VOICE IS IT ANYWAY? RODRIGUEZ' SPEECH IN RETROSPECT

Victor Villanueva Jr., on the faculty at Northern Arizona University until 1995, now teaches English at Washington State University. In 1993, he published the award-winning Bootstraps: From an American Academic of Color, *a personal and intellectual narrative of his own encounter with language issues in the United States in general and in the academy in particular. Villanueva also reveals a lot about himself in the following essay, which he wrote in 1987 for* English Journal, *a professional magazine directed to high school and elementary school English teachers.*

1   During the 1986 annual conference of the NCTE (National Council of Teachers of English) I attended a luncheon sponsored by the secondary section. Richard Rodriguez, author of *Hunger of Memory,* was the guest speaker. He spoke of how he

came to be an articulate speaker of this standard dialect, and he spoke of the conclusions concerning language that his experiences had brought him to. He was impressive. I was taken by his quiet eloquence. His stage presence recalled Olivier's Hamlet. He spoke well. But for all his eloquence and his studied stage presence, I was nevertheless surprised by the audience's response, an enthusiastic, uncritical acceptance, marked by a long, loud standing ovation. I was surprised because he had blurred distinctions between language and culture, between his experiences and those more typical of the minority in America, between the history of the immigrant and that of the minority, in a way that I had thought would raise more than a few eyebrows. Yet all he raised was the audience to its feet.

In retrospect, I think I can understand the rave reception. 2 The message he so softly delivered relieved us all of some anxiety. Classroom teachers' shoulders stoop under the weight of the paper load. They take 150 students through writing and grammar, spelling and punctuation. Within those same forty-five-minute spurts they also work on reading: drama, poetry, literature, the great issues in literature. After that, there's the writers' club or the school paper or the yearbook, coaching volleyball or producing the school play. And throughout it all, they are to remain sensitive to the language of the nonstandard or non-English speaker. They are not really told how—just "be sensitive," while parents, the media, sometimes it seems the whole world, shake their fingers at them for not doing something about America's literacy problems. Richard Rodriguez told the teachers to continue to be sensitive but to forget about doing anything special. The old ways may be painful, but they really are best. There is a kind of violence to the melting pot, he said, but it is necessary. He said that this linguistic assimilation is like alchemy, initially destructive perhaps but magical, creating something new and greater than what was. Do as you have always done. And the teachers sighed.

Richard Rodriguez is the authority, after all: a bilingual child 3 of immigrant parents, a graduate of two of the nation's more prestigious schools, Stanford and Berkeley, an English teacher, the well-published author of numerous articles and a well-received, well-anthologized book. He knows. And he says that the teachers who insisted on a particular linguistic form can be credited with his fame. But what is it, really, that has made him famous? He is a fine writer; of that there can be no doubt. But it is his message that has brought him fame, a message that states that the minority is no different than any other immigrant who came to this country not knowing its culture or its language, leaving much of the old country behind to become part of this new one, and in becoming part of America subtly changing what it means to be American. The American who brought his beef and pudding from England became the American of frankfurter, the bologna sandwich, pizza. Typically American foods—like typical Americans—partake of the world.

4   At the luncheon, Richard Rodriguez spoke of a TV ad for Mexican-style Velveeta, "the blandest of American cheeses," he called it, now speckled with peppers. This cultural contrast, said Rodriguez, demonstrated how Mexico—no less than England or Germany—is part of America.

5   But I think it shows how our times face a different kind of assimilation. Let's put aside for the moment questions as to why, if Mexicans really are being assimilated, they have taken so much longer than other groups, especially since Mexicans were already part of the West and Southwest when the West and Southwest became part of America. Let's look, rather, at the hyphen in Mexican-Velveeta. Who speaks of a German-American sausage, for instance? It's a hot dog. Yet tacos remain ethnic, sold under a mock Spanish mission bell or a sombrero. You will find refried beans under "ethnic foods" in the supermarket, not among other canned beans, though items as foreign-sounding as sauerkraut are simply canned vegetables. Mexican foods, even when Americanized as the taco salad or Mexican-Velveeta, remain distinctly Mexican.[1]

6   And like the ethnic food, some ethnic minorities have not been assimilated in the way the Ellis Islanders were. The fires of the melting pot have cooled. No more soup. America's more a stew today. The difference is the difference between the immigrant and the minority, a difference having to do with how each, the immigrant and the minority, came to be Americans, the difference between choice and colonization. Those who emigrated from Europe chose to leave unacceptable conditions in search of better. Choice, I realize, is a tricky word in this context: religious persecution, debtor's prison, potato famine, fascism, foreign takeover, when compared with a chance at prosperity and self-determination, don't seem to make for much of a choice; yet most people apparently remained in their homelands despite the intolerable, while the immigrants did leave, and in leaving chose to sever ties with friends and

[1]Mexican food is not the only ethnic food on the market, of course. Asian and Mediterranean food share the shelves. But this too is telling, since Asians alone had had restricted access to the US before the country ended its Open Door Immigration Policy. When the US closed its doors in 1942, it was to regulate the flow of less desirable "new immigrants"—the Eastern and Southern Europeans who remain "ethnic" to this day. See Oscar Handlin's *Race in American Life*, New York, Anchor, 1957.

families, created a distance between themselves and their histories, cultures, languages. There is something heroic in this. It's a heroism shared by the majority of Americans.

But choice hardly entered into most minorities' decisions to   7
become American. Most of us recognize this when it comes to Blacks or American Indians. Slavery, forcible displacement, and genocide are fairly clear-cut. Yet the circumstances by which most minorities became Americans are no less clear-cut. The minority became an American almost by default, as part of the goods in big-time real estate deals or as some of the spoils of war. What is true for the Native American applies to the Alaska Native, the Pacific Islander (including the Asian), Mexican-Americans, Puerto Ricans. Puerto Rico was part of Christopher Columbus' great discovery, Arawaks and Boriquens among his "Indians," a real-estate coup for the Queen of Spain. Then one day in 1898, the Puerto Ricans who had for nearly four hundred years been made proud to be the offspring of Spain, so much so that their native Arawak and Boricua languages and ways were virtually gone, found themselves the property of the United States, property without the rights and privileges of citizenship until—conveniently—World War I. But citizenship notwithstanding, Puerto Rico remains essentially a colony today.[2]

One day in 1845 and in 1848 other descendants of Spain   8
who had all but lost their Indian identities found themselves Americans. These were the long-time residents and landowners of the Republic of Texas and the California Republic: the area from Texas to New Mexico, Arizona, Utah, and California. Residents in the newly established US territories were given the option to relocate to Mexico or to remain on their native lands, with the understanding that should they remain they would be guaranteed American Constitutional rights. Those who stayed home saw their rights not very scrupulously guarded, falling victim over time to displacement, dislocation, and forced expatriation. There is something tragic in losing a long-established birthright, tragic but not heroic—especially not heroic to those whose ancestors had fled their homelands rather than acknowledge external rule.

The immigrant gave up much in the name of freedom—and   9
for the sake of dignity. For the Spanish-speaking minority in particular, the freedom to be American without once again relinquishing one's ancestry is also a matter of dignity.

[2]Nor is it a simple matter of Puerto Rico's deciding whether it wants to remain a commonwealth, gaining statehood, or independence. The interests of US industry, of the US military, and the social and economic ramifications of Puerto Rico's widespread poverty complicate matters.

10   This is not to say that Richard Rodriguez forfeited his dignity in choosing not to be Ricardo. The Mexican's status includes not only the descendants of the West and Southwest, Spanish-speaking natives to America, but also immigrants and the descendants of immigrants. Richard Rodriguez is more the immigrant than the minority. His father, he told us, had left his native Mexico for Australia. He fell in love along the way, eventually settling with wife and family in Sacramento. America was not his father's first choice for a new home perhaps, but he did choose to leave his homeland in much the same way European immigrants had. The Rodriguezes no doubt felt the immigrants' hardships, the drive to assimilate, a drive compounded perhaps by the association in their and others' minds between them and the undocumented migrant worker or between them and the minority.

11   And it is this confusion of immigrant and minority in Richard Rodriguez with which we must contend. His message rings true to the immigrant heritage of his audience because it happens to be the immigrant's story. It is received as if it were a new story because it is confused with this story of the minority. The complexities of the minority are rendered simple—not easy, but easily understood.

12   Others tell the story of the minority. I think, for instance, of Piri Thomas and Tato Laviera, since theirs are stories of Puerto Ricans. My own parents had immigrated to New York from Puerto Rico, though not in the way of most. My mother, an American, a US citizen like all Puerto Ricans, fair-skinned and proud of her European descent, had been sold into servitude to a wealthy Chicago family. My father, recently discharged from the US Army, followed my mother, rescued his sweetheart, and together they fled to New York. I was born a year later, 1948.

13   My mother believed in the traditional idea of assimilation. She and my father would listen to the radio shows in English and try to read the American newspapers. They spoke to me in two languages from the start. The local parochial school's tuition was a dollar a month, so I was spared PS 168. Rodriguez tells of nuns coming to his home to suggest that the family speak English at home. For Rodriguez this was something of a turning point in his life; intimacy lost, participation in the public domain gained. A public language would dominate, the painful path to his assimilation, the path to his eventual success. A nun spoke to my parents, too, when I was in kindergarten. I spoke with an accent, they were told. They should speak to me in English. My mother could only laugh: my English was as it was *because* they spoke to me in English. The

irony reinforced our intimacy while I continued to learn the "public language."

There is more to assimilating than learning the language. I earned my snacks at the Saturday matinee by reading the credits on the screen. I enjoyed parsing sentences, was good at it too. I was a Merriam-Webster spelling bee champ. I was an "A" student who nevertheless took a special Saturday course on how to do well on the standardized test that would gain me entry to the local Catholic high school. I landed in the public vo-tech high school, slotted for a trade. Jarapolk, whose parents had fled the Ukraine, made the good school; so did Marie Engels, the daughter of German immigrants. Lana Walker, a Black girl whose brains I envied, got as far as the alternate list. I don't recall any of the Black or Puerto Rican kids from my class getting in. I never finished high school, despite my being a bright boy who knew the public language intimately.

I don't like thinking minorities were intentionally excluded from the better school. I would prefer to think minorities didn't do as well because we were less conscious than the immigrants of the cultural distances we had to travel to be truly Americans. We were Americans, after all, not even seeing ourselves as separated by language by the time most of us got to the eighth grade. I spoke Spanglish at home, a hybrid English and Spanish common to New York Puerto Ricans; I spoke the Puerto Rican version of Black English in the streets, and as far as I knew, I spoke something close to the standard dialect in the classroom. We thought ourselves Americans, assimilated. We didn't know about cultural bias in standardized tests. I still don't do well on standardized tests.

A more pointed illustration of the difference between the minority and the immigrant comes by way of a lesson from my father. I was around ten. We went uptown one day, apartment hunting. I don't recall how he chose the place. He asked about an apartment in his best English, the sounds of a Spanish speaker attempting his best English. No vacancies. My father thanked the man, then casually slipped into the customary small talk of the courteous exit. During the talk my father mentioned our coming from Spain. By the end of the chat a unit became available. Maybe my father's pleasing personality had gained us entry. More likely, Puerto Rican stereotypes had kept us out. The immigrant could enter where the minority could not. My father's English hadn't improved in the five minutes it had taken for the situation to change.

Today I sport a doctorate in English from a major university, study and teach rhetoric at another university, do research in and teach composition, continue to enjoy and teach English

14

15

16

17

literature. I live in an all-American city in the heart of America. And I know I am not quite assimilated. In one weekend I was asked if I was Iranian one day and East Indian the next. "No," I said. "You have an accent," I was told. Yet tape recordings and passing comments throughout the years have told me that though there is a "back East" quality to my voice, there isn't much of New York to it anymore, never mind the Black English of my younger years or the Spanish of my youngest. My "accent" was in my not sounding midwestern, which does have a discernible, though not usually a pronounced, regional quality. And my "accent," I would guess, was in my "foreign" features (which pale alongside the brown skin of Richard Rodriguez).

18   Friends think I make too much of such incidents. Minority hypersensitivity, they say. They desensitize me (and display their liberal attitudes) with playful jabs at Puerto Ricans: greasy hair jokes, knife-in-pocket jokes, spicy food jokes (and Puerto Ricans don't even eat hot foods, unless we're eating Mexican or East Indian foods). If language alone were the secret to assimilation, the rate of Puerto Rican and Mexican success would be greater, I would think. So many Mexican-Americans and Puerto Ricans remain in the barrios—even those who are monolingual, who have never known Spanish. If language alone were the secret, wouldn't the secret have gotten out long before Richard Rodriguez recorded his memoirs? In fact, haven't we always worked with the assumption that language learning—oral and written—is the key to parity, even as parity continues to elude so many?

19   I'm not saying the assumption is wrong. I think teachers are right to believe in the potential power of language. We want our students to be empowered. That's why we read professional journals. That's why we try to accommodate the pronouncements of linguists. That's why we listen to the likes of Richard Rodriguez. But he spoke more of the English teacher's power than the empowerment of the student. "Listen to the sound of my voice," he said. He asked the audience to forget his brown skin and listen to his voice, his "unaccented voice." "This is your voice," he told the teachers. Better that we, teachers at all levels, give students the means to find their own voices, voices that don't have to ask that we ignore what we cannot ignore, voices that speak of their brown or yellow or red or black skin with pride and without need for bravado or hostility, voices that can recognize and exploit the conventions we have agreed to as the standards of written discourse—without necessarily accepting the ideology of those for whom the standard dialect is the language of home as well as commerce,

for whom the standard dialect is as private as it is public, to use Rodriguez' terms.

Rodriguez said at the luncheon that he was not speaking of 20 pedagogy as much as of ideology. He was. It is an ideology which grew out of the memoirs of an immigrant boy confronting contrasts, a child accommodating his circumstances. He remembers a brown boy in a white middle-class school and is forced to say no to bilingual education. His classmates were the descendants of other immigrants, the products of assimilation, leading him to accept the traditional American ideology of a multiculturalism that manifests as one new culture and language, a culture and language which encompasses and transcends any one culture. I remember a brown boy among other brown boys and girls, blacks, and olives, and variations on white, and must agree with Richard that bilingualism in the classroom would have been impractical. But my classmates were in the process of assimilation—Polish, German, Ukrainian, and Irish children, the first of their families to enter American schools; my classmates were also Black and Puerto Rican. It seemed to this boy's eyes that the immigrants would move on but the minority would stay, that the colonized do not melt. Today I do not hear of the problems in educating new immigrants, but the problems of Black literacy continue to make the news. And I hear of an eighty per cent dropout rate among Puerto Ricans in Boston, of Mexicans in the Rio Grande Valley where the dropout rate exceeds seventy per cent, of places where English and the education system do not address the majority—Spanish speakers for whom menial labor has been the tradition and is apparently the future. I must ask how *not* bilingual education in such situations. One person's experiences must remain one person's, applicable to many others, perhaps, but not all others. Simple, monolithic, universal solutions simply can't work in a complex society.

When it comes to the nonstandard speaker, for instance, we 21 are torn between the findings of linguists and the demands of the marketplace. Our attempts at preparing students for the marketplace only succeed in alienating nonstandard speakers, we are told. Our attempts at accommodating their nonstandard dialects, we fear, only succeed in their being barred from the marketplace. So we go back to the basics. Or else we try to change their speech without alienating them, in the process perhaps sensing that our relativism might smack of condescension. Limiting the student's language to the playground and home still speaks of who's right and who's wrong, who holds the power. I would rather we left speaking dialects relatively alone (truly demonstrating a belief in the legitimacy of the nonstandard). The relationship between speaking and writing is complex, as the debate sparked by Thomas Farrell has made clear. My own research and studies, as well as my personal experiences, suggest that exposure to writing and reading affects speaking. My accent changes, it seems, with every book I read. We don't have to give voices to students. If we give them pen and paper and have them read the printed page aloud, no matter what their grade, they'll discover their own voices.

22   And if we let the printed page offer a variety of world views, of ideologies, those voices should gather the power we wish them to have. Booker T. Washington, Martin Luther King, Jr., W. E. B. DuBois all wrote with eloquence. Each presents a different world view. Maxine Hong Kingston's "voice" resounds differently from Frank Chin's. Ernesto Galarza saw a different world than Richard Rodriguez. Rodriguez' is only one view, one voice. Yet it's his voice which seems to resound the loudest. Rodriguez himself provided the reason why this is so. He said at the luncheon that the individual's story, the biography or autobiography, has universal appeal because it strikes at experiences we have in common. The immigrant's story has the most in common with the majority.

23   Rodriguez implied that he didn't feel much kinship to minority writers. He said he felt a special bond with D. H. Lawrence. It seems appropriate that Rodriguez, who writes of his alienation from family in becoming part of the mainstream, would turn to Lawrence. Lawrence, too, was a teacher turned writer. Lawrence, too, felt alienated from his working-class background. It was Lawrence who argued, in "Reflections on the Death of the Porcupine," that equality is not achievable; Lawrence who co-opted, left the mastered to join the masters. Is this what we want for our minority students? True, Lawrence's mastery of the English language cannot be gainsaid. I would be proud to have a Lawrence credit me with his voice, would appreciate his accomplishment. But I would rather share credit in a W. B. Yeats, Anglo and Irish, assimilated but with a well-fed memory of his ancestry, master of the English language, its beauty, its traditions—and voice of the colony.

Ron Unz and Gloria Matta Tuchman

THE ENGLISH EDUCATION FOR CHILDREN INITIATIVE

California voters passed the following initiative (a reaction against bilingual education) on June 2, 1998; soon after, the law was challenged in the courts. Dubbed the "English for the Children Initiative" by its advocates, the resolution was designed to encourage immigrants to learn English as quickly as possible by means of "full immersion" into English instruction in the schools and to undermine the bilingual education measures that have prevailed in California schools for many years. Ron Unz, who grew up in a Yiddish-speaking household and who became wealthy after founding a Silicon Valley software firm, was defeated in a run for the California governorship in 1994; he then turned his attention to opposing bilingual education by chairing the English for the Children effort. Gloria Matta Tuchman has taught for many years at Taft Elementary School in Santa Ana, California, and was active in the initiative campaign. In 2001, Unz began working in New York City to end bilingual education, which he has described as "a well intentioned but misguided policy that has resulted in a state-mandated segregation system for Hispanic and immigrant children."

The actual text of the English Education for Children Initiative follows.

SECTION 1. Chapter 3 (commencing with Section 300) is added to Part 1 of the Educational Code, to read: 1

CHAPTER 3. ENGLISH LANGUAGE EDUCATION FOR IMMIGRANT CHILDREN   2

ARTICLE 1. Findings and Declarations   3

300. The People of California find and declare as follows: 4

(a) WHEREAS the English language is the national public language of the United States of America and of the state of California, is spoken by the vast majority of California residents,   5 and is also the leading world language for science, technology, and international business, thereby being the language of economic opportunity; and

6   (b) WHEREAS immigrant parents are eager to have their children acquire a good knowledge of English, thereby allowing them to fully participate in the American Dream of economic and social advancement; and

7   (c) WHEREAS the government and the public schools of California have a moral obligation and a constitutional duty to provide all of California's children, regardless of their ethnicity or national origins, with the skills necessary to become productive members of our society, and of these skills, literacy in the English language is among the most important; and

8   (d) WHEREAS the public schools of California currently do a poor job of educating immigrant children, wasting financial resources on costly experimental language programs whose failure over the past two decades is demonstrated by the current high drop-out rates and low English literacy levels of many immigrant children; and

9   (e) WHEREAS young immigrant children can easily acquire full fluency in a new language, such as English, if they are heavily exposed to that language in the classroom at an early age.

10   (f) THEREFORE it is resolved that: all children in California public schools shall be taught English as rapidly and effectively as possible.

11   ARTICLE 2. English Language Education

12   305. Subject to the exceptions provided in Article 3 (commencing with Section 310), all children in California public schools shall be taught English by being taught in English. In particular, this shall require that all children be placed in English language classrooms. Children who are English learners shall be educated through sheltered English immersion during a temporary transition period not normally intended to exceed one year. Local schools shall be permitted to place in the same classroom English learners of different ages but whose degree of English proficiency is similar. Local schools shall be encouraged to mix together in the same classroom English learners from different native-language groups but with the same degree of English fluency. Once English learners

have acquired a good working knowledge of English, they shall be transferred to English language mainstream classrooms. As much as possible, current supplemental funding for English learners shall be maintained, subject to possible modification under Article 8 (commencing with Section 335) below.

306. The definitions of the terms used in this article and in   13
Article 3 (commencing with Section 310) are as follows:

(a) "English learner" means a child who does not speak   14
English or whose native language is not English and who is not
currently able to perform ordinary classroom work in English,
also known as a Limited English Proficiency or LEP child.

(b) "English language classroom" means a classroom in which   15
the language of instruction used by the teaching personnel is
overwhelmingly the English language, and in which such teaching personnel possess a good knowledge of the English language.

(c) "English language mainstream classroom" means a class-   16
room in which the students either are native English language
speakers or already have acquired reasonable fluency in English.

(d) "Sheltered English immersion" or "structured English   17
immersion" means an English language acquisition process
for young children in which nearly all classroom instruction is
in English but with the curriculum and presentation designed
for children who are learning the language.

(e) "Bilingual education/native language instruction" means   18
a language acquisition process for students in which much or
all instruction, textbooks, and teaching materials are in the
child's native language.

ARTICLE 3. Parental Exceptions   19

310. The requirements of Section 305 may be waived with   20
the prior written informed consent, to be provided annually, of
the child's parents or legal guardian under the circumstances
specified below and in Section 311. Such informed consent
shall require that said parents or legal guardian personally visit
the school to apply for the waiver and that they there be provided a full description of the educational materials to be used
in the different educational program choices and all the educational opportunities available to the child. Under such parental
waiver conditions, children may be transferred to classes

where they are taught English and other subjects through bilingual education techniques or other generally recognized educational methodologies permitted by law. Individual schools in which 20 students or more of a given grade level receive a waiver shall be required to offer such a class; otherwise, they must allow the students to transfer to a public school in which such a class is offered.

21   311. The circumstances in which a parental exception waiver may be granted under Section 310 are as follows:

22   (a) Children who already know English: the child already possesses good English language skills, as measured by standardized tests of English vocabulary comprehension, reading, and writing, in which the child scores at or above the state average for his grade level or at or above the 5th grade average, whichever is lower; or

23   (b) Older children: the child is age 10 years or older, and it is the informed belief of the school principal and educational staff that an alternate course of educational study would be better suited to the child's rapid acquisition of basic English language skills; or

24   (c) Children with special needs: the child already has been placed for a period of not less than thirty days during that school year in an English language classroom and it is subsequently the informed belief of the school principal and educational staff that the child has such special physical, emotional, psychological, or educational needs that an alternate course of educational study would be better suited to the child's overall educational development. A written description of these special needs must be provided and any such decision is to be made subject to the examination and approval of the local school superintendent, under guidelines established by and subject to the review of the local Board of Education and ultimately the State Board of Education. The existence of such special needs shall not compel issuance of a waiver, and the parents shall be fully informed of their right to refuse to agree to a waiver.

25   ARTICLE 4. Community-Based English Tutoring

26   315. In furtherance of its constitutional and legal requirement to offer special language assistance to children coming from backgrounds of limited English proficiency, the state

shall encourage family members and others to provide personal English language tutoring to such children, and support these efforts by raising the general level of English language knowledge in the community. Commencing with the fiscal year in which this initiative is enacted and for each of the nine fiscal years following thereafter, a sum of fifty million dollars ($50,000,000) per year is hereby appropriated from the General Fund for the purpose of providing additional funding for free or subsidized programs of adult English language instruction to parents or other members of the community who pledge to provide personal English language tutoring to California school children with limited English proficiency.

316. Programs funded pursuant to this section shall be provided through schools or community organizations. Funding for these programs shall be administered by the Office of the Superintendent of Public Instruction, and shall be disbursed at the discretion of the local school boards, under reasonable guidelines established by, and subject to the review of, the State Board of Education.   27

ARTICLE 5. Legal Standing and Parental Enforcement   28

320. As detailed in Article 2 (commencing with Section 305) and Article 3 (commencing with Section 310), all California school children have the right to be provided with an English language public education. If a California school child has been denied the option of an English language instructional curriculum in public school, the child's parent or legal guardian shall have legal standing to sue for enforcement of the provisions of this statute, and if successful shall be awarded normal and customary attorney's fees and actual damages, but not punitive or consequential damages. Any school board member or other elected official or public school teacher or administrator who willfully and repeatedly refuses to implement the terms of this statute by providing such an English language educational option at an available public school to a California school child may be held personally liable for fees and actual damages by the child's parents or legal guardian.   29

ARTICLE 6. Severability   30

325. If any part or parts of this statute are found to be in conflict with federal law or the United States or the California State Constitution, the statute shall be implemented to the maximum extent that federal law, and the United States and the California   31

State Constitution permit. Any provision held invalid shall be severed from the remaining portions of this statute.

32   ARTICLE 7. Operative Date

33   330. This initiative shall become operative for all school terms which begin more than sixty days following the date at which it becomes effective.

34   ARTICLE 8. Amendment.

35   335. The provisions of this act may be amended by a statute that becomes effective upon approval by the electorate or by a statute to further the act's purpose passed by a two-thirds vote of each house of the Legislature and signed by the Governor.

36   ARTICLE 9. Interpretation

37   340. Under circumstances in which portions of this statute are subject to conflicting interpretations, Section 300 shall be assumed to contain the governing intent of the statute.

The American Civil Liberties Union

BRIEFING PAPER ON "ENGLISH ONLY"

The American Civil Liberties Union (ACLU), famous for its defense of freedoms protected by the Constitution, has developed a reputation over many decades for taking up liberal causes and positions—sometimes very controversial ones. In 1997, the ACLU developed the following "Briefing Paper" and posted it on the World Wide Web. Note how it takes the form of a "Frequently Asked Questions" (or "FAQ") page—a common Internet genre.

Introduction

1   At the time of the nation's founding, it was commonplace to hear as many as 20 languages spoken in daily life, including Dutch, French, German and numerous Native American lan-

guages. Even the Articles of Confederation were printed in German, as well as English. During the 19th and early 20th centuries, the nation's linguistic diversity grew as successive waves of Europeans immigrated to these shores and U.S. territory expanded to include Puerto Rico, Hawaii and the Philippines.

Just as languages other than English have always been a part   2
of our history and culture, debate over establishing a national language dates back to the country's beginnings. John Adams proposed to the Continental Congress in 1780 that an official academy be created to "purify, develop, and dictate usage of" English. His proposal was rejected as undemocratic and a threat to individual liberty.

Nonetheless, restrictive language laws have been enacted pe-   3
riodically since the late 19th century, usually in response to new waves of immigration. These laws, in practice if not in intent, have punished immigrants for their foreignness and violated their rights.

In the early 1980s, again during a period of concern about   4
new immigration, a movement arose that seeks the establishment of English as the nation's official language. The "English Only" movement promotes the enactment of legislation that restricts or prohibits the use of languages other than English by government agencies and, in some cases, by private businesses. The movement has met with some success, "English Only" laws having been passed in several states. And, for the first time in the nation's history, an English Language Amendment to the Constitution has been proposed.

The ACLU opposes "English Only" laws because they can   5
abridge the rights of individuals who are not proficient in English, and because they perpetuate false stereotypes of immigrants and non-English speakers. We believe, further, that such laws are contrary to the spirit of tolerance and diversity embodied in our Constitution. An English Language Amendment to the Constitution would transform that document from being a charter of liberties and individual freedom into a charter of restrictions that limits, rather than protects, individual rights.

Here are the ACLU's answers to some questions frequently   6
posed by the public about "English Only" issues.

Q. What is an "English Only" law?   7

A. "English Only" laws vary. Some state statutes simply de-   8
clare English as the "official" language of the state. Other state and local edicts limit or bar government's provision of non-English language assistance and services. For example, some restrict bilingual education programs, prohibit multilingual

ballots, or forbid non-English government services in general—including such services as courtroom translation or multilingual emergency police lines.

9 **Q. Where have such laws been enacted?**

10 A. Sixteen states have "English Only" laws, and many others are considering such laws. In some states, the laws were passed decades ago during upsurges of nativism, but most were passed within the last few years. The "English Only" states are Arizona, Arkansas, California, Colorado, Florida, Georgia, Illinois, Indiana, Kentucky, Mississippi, Nebraska, North Carolina, North Dakota, South Carolina, Tennessee and Virginia.

11 **Q. What are the consequences of "English Only" laws?**

12 A. Some versions of the proposed English Language Amendment would void almost all state and federal laws that require the government to provide services in languages other than English. The services affected would include: health, education and social welfare services, job training, translation assistance to crime victims and witnesses in court and administrative proceedings; voting assistance and ballots, drivers' licensing exams, and AIDS-prevention education.

13 Passage of an "English Only" ordinance by Florida's Dade County in 1980, barring public funding of activities that involved the use of languages other than English, resulted in the cancellation of all multicultural events and bilingual services, ranging from directional signs in the public transit system to medical services at the county hospital.

14 Where basic human needs are met by bilingual or multilingual services, the consequences of their elimination could be dire. For example, the Washington Times reported in 1987 that a 911 emergency dispatcher was able to save the life of a Salvadoran woman's baby son, who had stopped breathing, by coaching the mother in Spanish over the telephone to administer mouth-to-mouth and cardio-pulmonary resuscitation until the paramedics arrived.

15 **Q. Do "English Only" laws affect only government services and programs?**

16 A. "English Only" laws apply primarily to government programs. However, such laws can also affect private businesses. For example, several Southern California cities have passed ordinances that forbid or restrict the use of foreign languages on private business signs.

17 Some "English Only" advocates have opposed a telephone company's use of multilingual operators and multilingual directories, Federal Communications Commission licensing of

Spanish-language radio stations, and bilingual menus at fast food restaurants.

Q. Who is affected by "English Only" laws?   18

A. "English Only" campaigns target primarily Latinos and   19
Asians, who make up the majority of recent immigrants.
Most language minority residents are Spanish-speaking, a result of the sharp rise in immigration from Latin America during the mid-1960s.

While the overwhelming majority of U.S. residents—96 per-   20
cent—are fluent, approximately ten million residents are not
fluent in English, according to the most recent census.

Q. How do "English Only" laws deprive people of their   21
rights?

A. The ACLU believes that "English Only" laws are inconsis-   22
tent with the Equal Protection Clause of the Fourteenth
Amendment. For example, laws that have the effect of eliminating courtroom translation severely jeopardize the ability of
people on trial to follow and comprehend the proceedings.
"English Only" laws interfere with the right to vote by banning
bilingual ballots, or with a child's right to education by restricting bilingual instruction. Such laws also interfere with the
right of workers to be free of discrimination in workplaces
where employers have imposed "speak English only" rules.

In 1987, the ACLU adopted a national policy opposing   23
"English Only" laws or laws that would "characterize English
as the official language in the United States . . . to the extent
that [they] would mandate or encourage the erosion" of the
rights of language minority persons.

Q. What kinds of language policies were adopted with   24
regard to past generations of immigrants?

A. Our nation was tolerant of linguistic diversity up until the   25
late 1800s, when an influx of Eastern and Southern Europeans,
as well as Asians, aroused nativist sentiments and prompted
the enactment of restrictive language laws. A 1911 Federal
Immigration Commission report falsely argued that the "old"
Scandinavian and German immigrants had assimilated
quickly, while the "new" Italian and Eastern European immigrants were inferior to their predecessors, less willing to learn
English, and more prone to political subversion.

In order to "Americanize" the immigrants and exclude peo-   26
ple thought to be of the lower classes and undesirable, English
literacy requirements were established for public employment,
naturalization, immigration and suffrage. The New York State
Constitution was amended to disfranchise over one million

Yiddish-speaking citizens. The California Constitution was similarly amended to disfranchise the Chinese, who were seen as a threat to the "purity of the ballot box."

27   Ironically, during the same period, the government sought to "Americanize" Native American Indian children by taking them from their families and forcing them to attend English-language boarding schools, where they were punished for speaking their indigenous languages.

28   The intense anti-German sentiment that accompanied the outbreak of World War I prompted several states, where bilingual schools had been commonplace, to enact extreme language laws. For example, Nebraska passed a law in 1919 prohibiting the use of any other language than English through the eighth grade. The Supreme Court subsequently declared the law an unconstitutional violation of due process.

29   Today, as in the past, "English Only" laws in the U.S. are founded on false stereotypes of immigrant groups. Such laws do not simply disparage the immigrants' native languages but assault the rights of the people who speak the languages.

30   **Q. Why are bilingual ballots needed since citizenship is required to vote, English literacy is required for citizenship, and political campaigns are largely conducted in English?**

31   A. Naturalization for U.S. citizenship does not require English literacy for people over 50, and/or who have been in the U.S. for 20 years or more. Thus, there are many elderly immigrant citizens whose ability to read English is limited, and who cannot exercise their right to vote without bilingual ballots and other voter materials. Moreover, bilingual campaign materials and ballots foster a better informed electorate by increasing the information available to people who lack English proficiency.

32   **Q. Doesn't bilingual education slow immigrant children's learning of English, in contrast to the "sink or swim" method that was used in the past?**

33   A. The primary purpose of bilingual programs in elementary and secondary schools, which use both English and a child's native language to teach all subjects, is to develop proficiency in English and, thus, facilitate the child's transition to all-English instruction. Although debate about this approach continues, the latest studies show that bilingual education definitely enhances a child's ability to acquire the second language. Some studies even show that the more extensive the native language instruction, the better students perform all around, and that the bilingual method engenders a positive

self-image and self-respect by validating the child's native language and culture.

The "sink or swim" experience of past immigrants left more 34 of them underwater than not. In 1911, the U.S. Immigration Service found that 77 percent of Italian, 60 percent of Russian, and 51 percent of German immigrant children were one or more grade levels behind in school compared to 28 percent of American-born white children. Moreover, those immigrants who did manage to "swim" unaided in the past, when agricultural and factory jobs were plentiful, might not do so well in today's "high-tech" economy, with its more rigorous educational requirements.

Q. But won't "English Only" laws speed up the assimila- 35 **tion of today's immigrants into our society and prevent their isolation?**

A. In fact, contrary to what "English Only" advocates as- 36 sume, the vast majority of today's Asian and Latino immigrants are acquiring English proficiency and assimilating as fast as did earlier generations of Italian, Russian and German immigrants. For example, research studies show that over 95 percent of first generation Mexican Americans are English proficient, and that more than 50 percent of second generation Mexican Americans have lost their native tongue entirely.

In addition, census data reveals that nearly 90 percent of 37 Latinos five years old or older speak English in their households. And 98 percent of Latinos surveyed said they felt it is "essential" that their children learn to read and write English "perfectly." Unfortunately, not enough educational resources are available for immigrants—over 40,000 are on the waiting list for over-enrolled adult English classes in Los Angeles. "English Only" laws do not increase resources to meet these needs.

The best insurance against social isolation of those who im- 38 migrate to our nation is acceptance—and celebration—of the differences that exist within our ethnically diverse citizenry. The bond that unites our nation is not linguistic or ethnic homogeneity but a shared commitment to democracy, liberty, and equality.

The advertisement printed here appeared in the National Review, *a staunchly conservative magazine on current affairs, on June 16, 1997.*

Mauro E. Mujica, Architect
Chairman/CEO, U.S.English

Why An Immigrant Heads An Organization Called U.S.English.

His name is Mauro E. Mujica. He immigrated to the United States in 1965 to study architecture at Columbia University. English was not his first language then – but he is perfectly bilingual today. Learning English was never an option. It was required for success. Now he is the Chairman of U.S.ENGLISH, the nation's largest organization fighting to make English the common language of government at all levels. Why? Because English is under assault in our schools, in our courts and by bureaucrats and self-appointed leaders for immigrant groups. The whole notion of a melting pot society is threatened if new immigrants aren't encouraged to adopt the common language of this country. We're not suggesting that people shouldn't hold onto their native languages.

We just don't believe the government should spend money providing services in multiple languages when money could be better used teaching new immigrants English.

Join us. Support us. Fight with us.

Because English is the key to opportunity for all new immigrants.

Speak up for America. Call 1-800-U.S.ENGLISH

1747 Pennsylvania Avenue, NW, Suite 1100
Washington, DC 20006
http://www.us-english.org

IS THERE A
"STANDARD" ENGLISH?

Barbara Mellix
FROM OUTSIDE, IN

*You will learn a lot about Barbara Mellix from reading the fol-
lowing essay, which was published in* The Georgia Review *in
the summer of 1987, just after Mellix completed her master's
degree in creative writing at the University of Pittsburgh. The*
Georgia Review *is a quarterly journal of arts and letters that
includes scholarly articles, fiction, poetry, and book reviews.*

Two years ago, when I started writing this paper, trying to
bring order out of chaos, my ten-year-old daughter was suffering from an acute attack of boredom. She drifted in and out of
the room complaining that she had nothing to do, no one to
"be with" because none of her friends were at home. Patiently I
explained that I was working on something special and needed
peace and quiet, and I suggested that she paint, read, or work
with her computer. None of these interested her. Finally, she
pulled up a chair to my desk and watched me, now and then
heaving long, loud sighs. After two or three minutes (nine or
ten sighs), I lost my patience. "Looka here, Allie," I said, "you
too old for this kinda carryin' on. I done told you this is important. You wronger than dirt to be in here haggin' me like this
and you know it. Now git on outta here and leave me off before
I put my foot all the way down."

I was at home, alone with my family, and my daughter understood that this way of speaking was appropriate in that context. She knew, as a matter of fact, that it was almost inevitable; when I get angry at home, I speak some of my finest,
most cherished black English. Had I been speaking to my
daughter in this manner in certain other environments, she

would have been shocked and probably worried that I had taken leave of my sense of propriety.

3   Like my children, I grew up speaking what I considered two distinctly different languages—black English and standard English (or as I thought of them then, the ordinary everyday speech of "country" coloreds and "proper" English)—and in the process of acquiring these languages, I developed an understanding of when, where, and how to use them. But unlike my children, I grew up in a world that was primarily black. My friends, neighbors, minister, teachers—almost everybody I associated with every day—were black. And we spoke to one another in our own special language: *That sho is a pretty dress you got on. If she don't soon leave me off I'm gon tell her head a mess. I was so mad I could'a pissed a blue nail. He all the time trying to low-rate somebody. Ain't that just about the nastiest thing you ever set ears on?*

4   Then there were the "others," the "proper" blacks, transplanted relatives and one-time friends who came home from the city for weddings, funerals, and vacations. And the whites. To these we spoke standard English. "Ain't?" my mother would yell at me when I used the term in the presence of "others." "You *know* better than that." And I would hang my head in shame and say the "proper" word.

5   I remember one summer sitting in my grandmother's house in Greeleyville, South Carolina, when it was full of the chatter of city relatives who were home on vacation. My parents sat quietly, only now and then volunteering a comment or answering a question. My mother's face took on a strained expression when she spoke. I could see that she was being careful to say just the right words in just the right way. Her voice sounded thick, muffled. And when she finished speaking, she would lapse into silence, her proper smile on her face. My father was more articulate, more aggressive. He spoke quickly, his words sharp and clear. But he held his proud head higher, a signal that he, too, was uncomfortable. My sisters and brothers and I stared at our aunts, uncles, and cousins, speaking only when prompted. Even then, we hesitated, formed our sentences in our minds, then spoke softly, shyly.

6   My parents looked small and anxious during those occasions, and I waited impatiently for leave-taking when we would mock our relatives the moment we were out of their hearing. "Reeely," we would say to one another, flexing our wrists and rolling our eyes, "how dooo you stan' this heat? Chile, it just too hy*ooo*-mid for words." Our relatives had made us feel "country," and this was our way of regaining pride in ourselves

while getting a little revenge in the bargain. The words bubbled in our throats and rolled across our tongues, a balming.

As a child I felt this same doubleness in uptown Greeleyville 7 where the whites lived. "Ain't that a pretty dress you're wearing!" Toby, the town policeman, said to me one day when I was fifteen. "Thank you very much," I replied, my voice barely audible in my own ears. The words felt wrong in my mouth, rigid, foreign. It was not that I had never spoken that phrase before— it was common in black English, too—but I was extremely conscious that this was an occasion for proper English. I had taken out my English and put it on as I did my church clothes, and I felt as if I were wearing my Sunday best in the middle of the week. It did not matter that Toby had not spoken grammatically correct English. He was white and could speak as he wished. I had something to prove. Toby did not.

Speaking standard English to whites was our way of demon- 8 strating that we knew their language and could use it. Speaking it to standard-English-speaking blacks was our way of showing them that we, as well as they, could "put on airs." But when we spoke standard English, we acknowledged (to ourselves and to others—but primarily to ourselves) that our customary way of speaking was inferior. We felt foolish, embarrassed, somehow diminished because we were ashamed to be our real selves. We were reserved, shy in the presence of those who owned and/or spoke *the* language.

My parents never set aside time to drill us in standard 9 English. Their forms of instruction were less formal. When my father was feeling particularly expansive, he would regale us with tales of his exploits in the outside world. In almost flawless English, complete with dialogue and flavored with gestures and embellishment, he told us about his attempt to get a haircut at a white barbershop; his refusal to acknowledge one of the town merchants until the man addressed him as "Mister"; the time he refused to step off the sidewalk uptown to let some whites pass; his airplane trip to New York City (to visit a sick relative) during which the stewardesses and porters— recognizing that he was a "gentleman"—addressed him as "Sir." I did not realize then—nor, I think, did my father—that he was teaching us, among other things, standard English and the relationship between language and power.

My mother's approach was different. Often, when one of us 10 said, "I'm gon wash off my feet," she would say, "And what will you walk on if you wash them off?" Everyone would laugh at the victim of my mother's "proper" mood. But it was different when one of us children was in a proper mood. "You think you are so superior," I said to my oldest sister one day when we were arguing and she was winning. "Superior!" my sister mocked. "You mean I'm acting 'biggidy'?" My sisters and brothers sniggered, then joined in teasing me. Finally, my mother said, "Leave your sister alone. There's nothing wrong with using proper English." There was a half-smile on her face. I had gotten "uppity," had "put on airs" for no good reason. I was at home, alone with the family, and I hadn't been prompted by one of my mother's proper moods. But there was also a proud light in my mother's eyes; her children were learning English very well.

11   Not until years later, as a college student, did I begin to understand our ambivalence toward English, our scorn of it, our need to master it, to own and be owned by it—an ambivalence that extended to the public school classroom. In our school, where there were no whites, my teacher taught standard English but used black English to do it. When my grammar-school teachers wanted us to write, for example, they usually said something like, "I want y'all to write five sentences that make a statement. Anybody git done before the rest can color." It was probably almost those exact words that led me to write these sentences in 1953 when I was in the second grade:

> The white clouds are pretty.
> There are only 15 people in our room.
> We will go to gym.
> We have a new poster.
> We may go out doors.

Second grade came after "Little First" and "Big First," so by then I knew the implied rules that accompanied all writing assignments. Writing was an occasion for proper English. I was not to write in the way we spoke to one another: The white clouds pretty; There ain't but fifteen people in our room; We going to gym; We got a new poster; We can go out in the yard. Rather I was to use the language of "other": clouds *are*, there *are*, we *will*, we *have*, we *may*.

12   My sentences were short, rigid, perfunctory, like the letters my mother wrote to relatives:

Dear Papa,

How are you? How is Mattie? Fine I hope. We are fine. We will come to see you Sunday. Cousin Ned will give us a ride.

>   Love,
>   Daughter

The language was not ours. It was something from outside us, something we used for special occasions.

But my coloring on the other side of that second-grade pa- 13 per is different. I drew three hearts and a sun. The sun has a smiling face that radiates and envelops everything it touches. And although the sun and the world are enclosed in a circle, the colors I used—red, blue, green, purple, orange, yellow, black—indicate that I was less restricted with drawing and coloring than I was with writing standard English. My valentines were not just red. My sun was not just a yellow ball in the sky.

By the time I reached the twelfth grade, speaking and writ- 14 ing standard English had taken on new importance. Each year, about half of the newly graduated seniors of our school moved to large cities—particularly in the North—to live with relatives and find work. Our English teacher constantly corrected our grammar: "Not 'ain't,' but 'isn't.'" We seldom wrote papers, and even those few were usually plot summaries of short stories. When our teacher returned the papers, she usually lectured on the importance of using standard English: "I *am;* you *are;* he, she, or it *is,*" she would say, writing on the chalkboard as she spoke. "How you gon git a job talking about 'I is,' or 'I isn't' or 'I ain't'?"

In Pittsburgh, where I moved after graduation, I watched my 15 aunt and uncle—who had always spoken standard English when in Greeleyville—switch from black English to standard English to a mixture of the two, according to where they were or who they were with. At home and with certain close relatives, friends, and neighbors, they spoke black English. With those less close, they spoke a mixture. In public and with strangers, they generally spoke standard English.

In time, I learned to speak standard English with ease and to 16 switch smoothly from black to standard or a mixture, and back again. But no matter where I was, no matter what the situation or occasion, I continued to write as I had in school:

Dear Mommie,
How are you? How is everybody else? Fine I hope. I am fine. So are Aunt and Uncle. Tell everyone I said hello. I will write again soon.
     Love,
     Barbara

At work, at a health insurance company, I learned to write letters to customers. I studied form letters and letters written by co-workers, memorizing the phrases and the ways in which they were used. I dictated:

> Thank you for your letter of January 5. We have made the changes in your coverage you requested. Your new premium will be $150 every three months. We are pleased to have been of service to you.

In a sense, I was proud of the letters I wrote for the company: they were proof of my ability to survive in the city, the outside world—an indication of my growing mastery of English. But they also indicated that writing was still mechanical for me, something that didn't require much thought.

17   Reading also became a more significant part of my life during those early years in Pittsburgh. I had always liked reading, but now I devoted more and more of my spare time to it. I read romances, mysteries, popular novels. Looking back, I realize that the books I liked best were simple, unambiguous: good versus bad and right versus wrong with right rewarded and wrong punished, mysteries unraveled and all set right in the end. It was how I remembered life in Greeleyville.

18   Of course I was romanticizing. Life in Greeleyville had not become very uncomplicated. Back there I had been—first as a child, then as a young woman with limited experience in the outside world—living in a relatively closed-in society. But there were implicit and explicit principles that guided our way of life and shaped our relationships with one another and the people outside—principles that a newcomer would find elusive and baffling. In Pittsburgh, I had matured, become more experienced. I had worked at three different jobs, associated with a wider range of people, married, had children. This new environment with different prescripts for living required that I speak standard English much of the time and slowly, imperceptibly, I had ceased seeing a sharp distinction between myself and "others." Reading romances and mysteries, characterized by dichotomy, was a way of shying away from change, from the person I was becoming.

19   But that other part of me—that part which took great pride in my ability to hold a job writing business letters—was increasingly drawn to the new developments in my life and the attending possibilities, opportunities for even greater change. If I could write letters for a nationally known business, could I not also do something better, more challenging, more important? Could I not, perhaps, go to college and become a school teacher? For years, afraid and a little embarrassed, I did no more than imagine this different me, this possible me. But six-

teen years after coming north, when my youngest daughter entered kindergarten, I found myself unable—or unwilling—to resist the lure of possibility. I enrolled in my first college course: Basic Writing, at the University of Pittsburgh.

For the first time in my life, I was required to write exten- 20 sively about myself. Using the most formal English at my command, I wrote these sentences near the beginning of the term:

> One of my duties as a homemaker is simply picking up after others. A day seldom passes that I don't search for a mislaid toy, book, or gym shoe, etc. I change the Ty-D-Bol, fight "ring around the collar," and keep our laundry smelling "April fresh." Occasionally, I settle arguments between my children and suggest things to do when they're bored. Taking telephone messages for my oldest daughter is my newest (and sometimes most aggravating) chore. Hanging the toilet paper roll is my most insignificant.

My concern was to use "appropriate" language, to sound as if I belonged in a college classroom. But I felt separate from the language—as if it did not and could not belong to me. I couldn't think and feel genuinely in that language, couldn't make it express what I thought and felt about being a housewife. A part of me resented, among other things, being judged by such things as the appearance of my family's laundry and toilet bowl, but in that language I could only imagine and write about a conventional housewife.

For the most part, the remainder of the term was a period of 21 adjustment, a time of trying to find my bearings as a student in a college composition class, to learn to shut out my black English whenever I composed, and to prevent it from creeping into my formulations; a time for trying to grasp the language of the classroom and reproduce it in my prose; for trying to talk about myself in that language, reach others through it. Each experience of writing was like standing naked and revealing my imperfection, my "otherness." And each new assignment was another chance to make myself over in language, reshape myself, make myself "better" in my rapidly changing image of a student in a college composition class.

But writing became increasingly unmanageable as the term 22 progressed, and by the end of the semester, my sentences sounded like this:

> My excitement was soon dampened, however, by what seemed like a small voice in the back of my head saying that I

should be careful with my long awaited opportunity. I felt
frustrated and this seemed to make it difficult to concentrate.

There is a poverty of language in these sentences. By this point,
I knew that the clichéd language of my Housewife essay was
unacceptable, and I generally recognized trite expressions. At
the same time, I hadn't yet mastered the language of the classroom, hadn't yet come to see it as belonging to me. Most notable is the lifelessness of the prose, the apparent absence of a
person behind the words. I wanted those sentences—and the
rest of the essay—to convey the anguish of yearning to, at
once, become something more and yet remain the same. I had
the sensation of being split in two, part of me going into a future the other part didn't believe possible. As that person, the
student writer at that moment, I was essentially mute. I could
not—in the process of composing—use the language of the old
me, yet I couldn't imagine myself in the language of "others."

23   I found this particularly discouraging because at midsemes-
ter I had been writing in a much different way. Note the language of this introduction to an essay I had written then, near
the middle of the term:

> Pain is a constant companion to the people in "Footwork."
> Their jobs are physically damaging. Employers are insensi-
> tive to their feelings and in many cases add to their problems.
> The general public wounds them further by treating them
> with disgrace because of what they do for a living. Although
> the workers are as diverse as they are similar, there is a defi-
> nite link between them. They suffer a great deal of abuse.

The voice here is stronger, more confident, appropriating
terms like "physically damaging," "wounds them further," "insensitive," "diverse"—terms I couldn't have imagined using
when writing about my own experience—and shaping them
into sentences like, "Although the workers are as diverse as
they are similar, there is a definite link between them." And
there is the sense of a personality behind the prose, someone
who sympathizes with the workers: "The general public
wounds them further by treating them with disgrace because
of what they do for a living."

24   What caused these differences? I was, I believed, explaining
other people's thoughts and feelings, and I was free to move
about in the language of "others" so long as I was speaking *of*
others. I was unaware that I was transforming into my best

classroom language my own thoughts and feelings about people whose experiences and ways of speaking were in many ways similar to mine.

The following year, unable to turn back or let go of what had become something of an obsession with language (and hoping to catch and hold the sense of control that had eluded me in Basic Writing), I enrolled in a research writing course. I spent most of the term learning how to prepare for and write a research paper. I chose sex education as my subject and spent hours in libraries, searching for information, reading, taking notes. Then (not without messiness and often-demoralizing frustration) I organized my information into categories, wrote a thesis statement, and composed my paper—a series of paraphrases and quotations spaced between carefully constructed transitions. The process and results felt artificial, but as I would later come to realize I was passing through a necessary stage. My sentences sounded like this: 25

> This reserve becomes understandable with examination of who the abusers are. In an overwhelming number of cases, they are people the victims know and trust. Family members, relatives, neighbors and close family friends commit seventy-five percent of all reported sex crimes against children, and parents, parent substitutes and relatives are the offenders in thirty to eighty percent of all reported cases. While assault by strangers does occur, it is less common, and is usually a single episode. But abuse by family members, relatives and acquaintances may continue for an extended period of time. In cases of incest, for example, children are abused repeatedly for an average of eight years. In such cases, "the use of physical force is rarely necessary because of the child's trusting, dependent relationship with the offender. The child's cooperation is often facilitated by the adult's position of dominance, an offer of material goods, a threat of physical violence, or a misrepresentation of moral standards."

The completed paper gave me a sense of profound satisfaction, and I read it often after my professor returned it. I know now that what I was pleased with was the language I used and the professional voice it helped me maintain. "Use better words," my teacher had snapped at me one day after reading the notes I'd begun accumulating from my research, and slowly I began taking on the language of my sources. In my next set of notes, I used the word "vacillating"; my professor 26 applauded. And by the time I composed the final draft, I felt at ease with terms like "overwhelming number of cases," "single episode," and "reserve," and I shaped them into sentences similar to those of my "expert" sources.

27   If I were writing the paper today, I would of course do some things differently. Rather than open with an anecdote—as my teacher suggested—I would begin simply with a quotation that caught my interest as I was researching my paper (and which I scribbled, without its source, in the margin of my notebook): "Truth does not do so much good in the world as the semblance of truth does evil." The quotation felt right because it captured what was for me the central idea of my essay—an idea that emerged gradually during the making of my paper— and expressed it in a way I would like to have said it. The anecdote, a hypothetical situation I invented to conform to the information in the paper, felt forced and insincere because it represented—to a great degree—my teacher's understanding of the essay, *her* idea of what in it was most significant. Improving upon my previous experiences with writing, I was beginning to think and feel in the language I used, to find my own voices in it, to sense that how one speaks influences how one means. But I was not yet secure enough, comfortable enough with the language to trust my intuition.

28   Now that I know that to seek knowledge, freedom, and autonomy means always to be in the concentrated process of becoming—always to be venturing into new territory, feeling one's way at first, then getting one's balance, negotiating, accommodating, discovering one's self in ways that previously defined "others"—I sometimes get tired. And I ask myself why I keep on participating in this highbrow form of violence, this slamming against perplexity. But there is no real futility in the question, no hint of that part of the old me who stood outside standard English, hugging to herself a disabling mistrust of a language she thought could not represent a person with her history and experience. Rather, the question represents a person who feels the consequence of her education, the weight of her possibilities as a teacher and writer and human being, a voice in society. And I would not change that person, would not give back the good burden that accompanies my growing expertise, my increasing power to shape myself in language and share that self with "others."

29   "To speak," says Frantz Fanon, "means to be in a position to use a certain syntax, to grasp the morphology of this or that language, but it means above all to assume a culture, to support the

weight of a civilization."* To write means to do the same, but in a more profound sense. However, Fanon also says that to achieve mastery means to "get" to a position of power, to "grasp," to "assume." This, I have learned—both as a student and subsequently as a teacher—can involve tremendous emotional and psychological conflict for those attempting to master academic discourse. Although as a beginning student writer I had a fairly good grasp of ordinary spoken English and was proficient at what Labov calls "code switching" (and what John Baugh in *Black Street Speech* terms "style shifting"), when I came face to face with the demands of academic writing, I grew increasingly self-conscious, constantly aware of my status as a black and a speaker of one of the many black English vernaculars, a traditional outsider. For the first time, I experienced my sense of doubleness as something menacing, a built-in enemy. Whenever I turned inward for salvation, the balm so available during my childhood, I found instead this new fragmentation which spoke to me in many voices. It was the voice of my desire to prosper, but at the same time it spoke of what I had relinquished and could not regain: a safe way of being, a state of powerlessness which exempted me from responsibility for who I was and might be. And it accused me of betrayal, of turning away from blackness. To recover balance, I had to take on the language of the academy, the language of "others." And to do that, I had to learn to imagine myself a part of the culture of that language, and therefore someone free to manage that language, to take liberties with it. Writing and rewriting, practicing, experimenting, I came to comprehend more fully the generative power of language. I discovered—with the help of some especially sensitive teachers—that through writing one can continually bring new selves into being, each with new responsibilities and difficulties, but also with new possibilities. Remarkable power, indeed. I write and continually give birth to myself.

Black Skin, White Masks (1952, rpt. New York: Grove Press, 1967), pp. 17–18.

Amy Tan
MOTHER TONGUE

Amy Tan was born in Oakland, California, in 1952 to parents who had immigrated from China. She is the best-selling author of novels, short fiction, and children's books. In college she became interested in linguistics, eventually earning a master's degree in the subject in 1973. After working as a language development consultant for projects designed to help disabled children, she turned to fiction in the mid-1980s. In 1989 The Joy Luck Club *was published and became a bestseller; in 1994 it was adapted into a feature film. She has since completed* The Kitchen God's Wife, The Hundred Secret Senses, *and* The Bonesetter's Daughter. *Her essay "Mother Tongue," first given as a lecture, was chosen for* Best American Essays *in 1991.*

1   I am not a scholar of English or literature. I cannot give you much more than personal opinions on the English language and its variations in this country or others.

2   I am a writer. And by that definition, I am someone who has always loved language. I am fascinated by language in daily life. I spend a great deal of my time thinking about the power of language—the way it can evoke an emotion, a visual image, a complex idea, or a simple truth. Language is the tool of my trade. And I use them all—all the Englishes I grew up with.

3   Recently, I was made keenly aware of the different Englishes I do use. I was giving a talk to a large group of people, the same talk I had already given to half a dozen other groups. The nature of the talk was about my writing, my life, and my book, *The Joy Luck Club.* The talk was going along well enough, until I remembered one major difference that made the whole talk sound wrong. My mother was in the room. And it was perhaps the first time she had heard me give a lengthy speech, using the kind of English I have never used with her. I was saying things like, "The intersection of memory upon imagination" and "There is an aspect of my fiction that relates to thus-and-thus"—a speech filled with carefully wrought grammatical phrases, burdened, it suddenly seemed to me, with nominalized forms, past perfect tenses, conditional phrases, all the forms of standard English that I had learned in school and through books, the forms of English I did not use at home with my mother.

Just last week, I was walking down the street with my 4
mother, and I again found myself conscious of the English I
was using, the English I do use with her. We were talking about
the price of new and used furniture and I heard myself saying
this: "Not waste money that way." My husband was with us as
well, and he didn't notice any switch in my English. And then I
realized why. It's because over the twenty years we've been together I've often used the same kind of English with him, and
sometimes he even uses it with me. It has become our language of intimacy, a different sort of English that relates to
family talk, the language I grew up with.

So you'll have some idea of what this family talk I heard 5
sounds like, I'll quote what my mother said during a recent
conversation which I videotaped and then transcribed. During
this conversation, my mother was talking about a political
gangster in Shanghai who had the same last name as her family's, Du, and how the gangster in his early years wanted to be
adopted by her family, which was rich by comparison. Later,
the gangster became more powerful, far richer than my
mother's family, and one day showed up at my mother's wedding to pay his respects. Here's what she said in part:

"Du Yusong having business like fruit stand. Like off the 6
street kind. He is Du like Du Zong—but not Tsung-ming
Island people. The local people call putong, the river east side,
he belong to that side local people. That man want to ask Du
Zong father take him in like become own family. Du Zong father wasn't look down on him, but didn't take seriously, until
that man big like become a mafia. Now important person,
very hard to inviting him. Chinese way, came only to show respect, don't stay for dinner. Respect for making big celebration, he shows up. Mean gives lots of respect. Chinese custom.
Chinese social life that way. If too important won't have to
stay too long. He come to my wedding. I didn't see, I heard it.
I gone to boy's side, they have YMCA dinner. Chinese age I
was nineteen."

You should know that my mother's expressive command of 7
English belies how much she actually understands. She reads
the Forbes report, listens to "Wall Street Week," converses
daily with her stockbroker, reads all of Shirley MacLaine's
books with ease—all kinds of things I can't begin to understand. Yet some of my friends tell me they understand 50 percent of what my mother says. Some say they understand 80 to
90 percent. Some say they understand none of it, as if she were
speaking pure Chinese. But to me, my mother's English is
perfectly clear, perfectly natural. It's my mother tongue. Her
language, as I hear it, is vivid, direct, full of observation and

imagery. That was the language that helped shape the way I saw things, expressed things, made sense of the world.

8   Lately, I've been giving more thought to the kind of English my mother speaks. Like others, I have described it to people as "broken" or "fractured" English. But I wince when I say that. It has always bothered me that I can think of no way to describe it other than "broken," as if it were damaged and needed to be fixed, as if it lacked a certain wholeness and soundness. I've heard other terms used, "limited English," for example. But they seem just as bad, as if everything is limited, including people's perceptions of the limited English speaker.

9   I know this for a fact, because when I was growing up, my mother's "limited" English limited my perception of her. I was ashamed of her English. I believed that her English reflected the quality of what she had to say. That is, because she expressed them imperfectly her thoughts were imperfect. And I had plenty of empirical evidence to support me: the fact that people in department stores, at banks, and at restaurants did not take her seriously, did not give her good service, pretended not to understand her, or even acted as if they did not hear her.

10   My mother has long realized the limitations of her English as well. When I was fifteen, she used to have me call people on the phone to pretend I was she. In this guise, I was forced to ask for information or even to complain and yell at people who had been rude to her. One time it was a call to her stockbroker in New York. She had cashed out her small portfolio and it just so happened we were going to go to New York the next week, our very first trip outside California. I had to get on the phone and say in an adolescent voice that was not very convincing, "This is Mrs. Tan."

11   And my mother was standing in the back whispering loudly, "Why he don't send me check, already two weeks late. So mad he lie to me, losing me money."

12   And then I said in perfect English, "Yes, I'm getting rather concerned. You had agreed to send the check two weeks ago, but it hasn't arrived."

13   Then she began to talk more loudly. "What he want, I come to New York tell him front of his boss, you cheating me?" And I was trying to calm her down, make her be quiet, while telling the stockbroker, "I can't tolerate any more excuses. If I don't receive the check immediately, I am going to have to speak to your manager when I'm in New York next week." And sure enough, the following week there we were in front of this astonished stockbroker, and I was sitting there red-faced and quiet, and my mother, the real Mrs. Tan, was shouting at his boss in her impeccable broken English.

We used a similar routine just five days ago, for a situation 14
that was far less humorous. My mother had gone to the hospital for an appointment, to find out about a benign brain tumor
a CAT scan had revealed a month ago. She said she had spoken
very good English, her best English, no mistakes. Still, she said,
the hospital did not apologize when they said they had lost the
CAT scan and she had come for nothing. She said they did not
seem to have any sympathy when she told them she was anxious to know the exact diagnosis, since her husband and son
had both died of brain tumors. She said they would not give her
any more information until the next time and she would have
to make another appointment for that. So she said she would
not leave until the doctor called her daughter. She wouldn't
budge. And when the doctor finally called her daughter, me,
who spoke in perfect English—lo and behold—we had assurances the CAT scan would be found, promises that a conference
call on Monday would be held, and apologies for any suffering
my mother had gone through for a most regrettable mistake.

I think my mother's English almost had an effect on limiting 15
my possibilities in life as well. Sociologists and linguists probably will tell you that a person's developing language skills are
more influenced by peers. But I do think that the language spoken in the family, especially in immigrant families which are
more insular, plays a large role in shaping the language of the
child. And I believe that it affected my results on achievement
tests, IQ tests, and the SAT. While my English skills were never
judged as poor, compared to math, English could not be considered my strong suit. In grade school I did moderately well,
getting perhaps B's, sometimes B-pluses, in English and scoring perhaps in the sixtieth or seventieth percentile on achievement tests. But those scores were not good enough to override
the opinion that my true abilities lay in math and science, because in those areas I achieved A's and scored in the ninetieth
percentile or higher.

This was understandable. Math is precise; there is only one 16
correct answer. Whereas, for me at least, the answers on
English tests were always a judgment call, a matter of opinion
and personal experience. Those tests were constructed around
items like fill-in-the-blank sentence completion, such as, "Even
though Tom was _____ Mary thought he was _____." And the
correct answer always seemed to be the most bland combinations of thoughts, for example, "Even though Tom was shy,
Mary thought he was charming," with the grammatical structure "even though" limiting the correct answer to some sort of
semantic opposites, so you wouldn't get answers like, "Even
though Tom was foolish, Mary thought he was ridiculous."

Well, according to my mother, there were very few limitations as to what Tom could have been and what Mary might have thought of him. So I never did well on tests like that.

17   The same was true with word analogies, pairs of words in which you were supposed to find some sort of logical, semantic relationship—for example, "Sunset is to nightfall as _____ is to _____." And here you would be presented with a list of four possible pairs, one of which showed the same kind of relationship: red is to stoplight, bus is to arrival, chills is to fever, yawn is to boring. Well, I could never think that way. I knew what the tests were asking, but I could not block out of my mind the images already created by the first pair, "sunset is to nightfall"—and I would see a burst of colors against a darkening sky, the moon rising, the lowering of a curtain of stars. And all the other pairs of words—red, bus, stoplight, boring—just threw up a mass of confusing images, making it impossible for me to sort out something as logical as saying: "A sunset precedes nightfall" is the same as "a chill precedes a fever." The only way I would have gotten that answer right would have been to imagine an associative situation, for example, my being disobedient and staying out past sunset, catching a chill at night, which turns into feverish pneumonia as punishment, which indeed did happen to me.

18   I have been thinking about all this lately, about my mother's English, about achievement tests. Because lately I've been asked, as a writer, why there are not more Asian Americans represented in American literature. Why are there few Asian Americans enrolled in creative writing programs? Why do so many Chinese students go into engineering? Well, these are broad sociological questions I can't begin to answer. But I have noticed in surveys—in fact, just last week—that Asian students, as a whole, always do significantly better on math achievement tests than in English. And this makes me think that there are other Asian-American students whose English spoken in the home might also be described as "broken" or "limited." And perhaps they also have teachers who are steering them away from writing and into math and science, which is what happened to me.

19   Fortunately, I happen to be rebellious in nature and enjoy the challenge of disproving assumptions made about me. I became an English major my first year in college, after being enrolled as pre-med. I started writing nonfiction as a freelancer the week after I was told by my former boss that writing was my worst skill and I should hone my talents toward account management.

20   But it wasn't until 1985 that I finally began to write fiction. And at first I wrote using what I thought to be wittily crafted

sentences, sentences that would finally prove I had mastery over the English language. Here's an example from the first draft of a story that later made its way into *The Joy Luck Club*, but without this line: "That was my mental quandary in its nascent state." A terrible line, which I can barely pronounce.

Fortunately, for reasons I won't get into today, I later decided   21
I should envision a reader for the stories I would write. And the reader I decided upon was my mother, because these were stories about mothers. So with this reader in mind—and in fact she did read my early drafts—I began to write stories using all the Englishes I grew up with: the English I spoke to my mother, which for lack of a better term might be described as "simple"; the English she used with me, which for lack of a better term might be described as "broken"; my translation of her Chinese, which could certainly be described as "watered down"; and what I imagined to be her translation of her Chinese if she could speak in perfect English, her internal language, and for that I sought to preserve the essence, but neither an English nor a Chinese structure. I wanted to capture what language ability tests can never reveal: her intent, her passion, her imagery, the rhythms of her speech and the nature of her thoughts.

Apart from what any critic had to say about my writing, I knew   22
I had succeeded where it counted when my mother finished reading my book and gave me her verdict: "So easy to read."

Geneva Smitherman
WHITE ENGLISH
IN BLACKFACE,
OR WHO DO I BE?

Geneva Smitherman is a professor of linguistics at Michigan State University. Her contention, printed here, that Black English (also known as Ebonics) is not slang but an English dialect that follows careful rules first appeared in The Black Scholar *in 1973. Note that two readings that follow this essay comment on it: Eldridge Cleaver's "We Need to Rescue Kids from Ebonics" and Douglas Haneline's "A Comment on Teaching Standard Edited English."*

1   Ain nothin in a long time lit up the English teaching profession like the current hassle over Black English. One finds beaucoup sociolinguistic research studies and language projects for the "disadvantaged" on the scene in nearly every sizable black community in the country.[1] And educators from K-Grad. School bees debating whether: (1) blacks should learn and use only standard white English (hereafter referred to as WE); (2) blacks should command both dialects, i.e., be bidialectal (hereafter BD); (3) blacks should be allowed (??????) to use standard Black English (hereafter BE or BI). The appropriate choice having everything to do with American political reality, which is usually ignored, and nothing to do with the educational process, which is usually claimed. I say without qualification that we cannot talk about the Black Idiom apart from Black Culture and the Black Experience. Nor can we specify educational goals for blacks apart from considerations about the structure of (white) American society.

2   And we black folks is not gon take all that weight, for no one has empirically demonstrated that linguistic/stylistic features of BE impede educational progress in communication skills, or any other area of cognitive learning. Take reading. It's don been charged, but not actually verified, that BE interferes with mastery of reading skills.[2] Yet beyond pointing out the gap between the young brother/sistuh's phonological and syntactical patterns and those of the usually-middle-class-WE-speaking-teacher, this claim has not been validated. The distance between the two systems is, after all, short and is illuminated only by the fact that reading is taught *orally*. (Also get to the fact that preceding generations of BE-speaking folks learned to read, despite the many classrooms in which the teacher spoke a dialect different from that of their students.)

3   For example, a student who reads *den* for *then* probably pronounces initial /th/ as /d/ in most words. Or the one who reads

---

[1]For examples of such programs see *Non-Standard Dialect,* Board of Education of the City of New York (National Council of Teachers of English, 1968); San-Su C. Lin, *Pattern Practices in the Teaching of Standard English with a Non-Standard Dialect* (USOE Project 1339, 1965); Arno Jewett, Joseph Mersand, Doris Gunderson, *Improving English Skills of Culturally Different Youth in Large Cities* (U.S. Department of Health, Education and Welfare, 1964); *Language Programs for the Disadvantaged* (NCTE, 1965).

[2]See, for example, Joan Baratz and Roger Shuy, eds., *Teaching Black Children to Read* (Center for Applied Linguistics, 1969); A. L. Davis, ed., *On the Dialects of Children* (NCTE, 1968); Eldonna L. Evertts, ed., *Dimensions of Dialect* (NCTE, 1967).

doing for *during* probably deletes intervocalic and final /r/ in most words. So it is not that such students can't read, they is simply employing the black phonological system. In the reading classrooms of today, what we bees needin is teachers with the proper attitudinal orientation who thus can distinguish actual reading problems from mere dialect differences. Or take the writing of an essay. The only percentage in writing a paper with WE spelling, punctuation, and usage is in maybe eliciting a positive *attitudinal* response from a prescriptivist middle-class-aspirant-teacher. Dig on the fact that sheer "correctness" does not a good writer make. And is it any point in dealing with the charge of BE speakers being "nonverbal" or "linguistically deficient" in oral communication skills—behind our many Raps who done disproved that in living, vibrant colors?[3]

What linguists and educators need to do at this juncture is to take serious cognizance of the Oral Tradition in Black Culture. The uniqueness of this verbal style requires a language competence/performance model to fit the black scheme of things. Clearly BI speakers possess rich communication skills (i.e., are highly *competent* in using language), but as yet there bees no criteria (evaluative, testing, or other instrument of measurement), based on black communication patterns, wherein BI speakers can demonstrate they competence (i.e., *performance*). Hence brothers and sisters fail on language performance tests in English classrooms. Like, to amplify on what Nikki [Giovanni] said, that's why we always lose, not only cause we don't know the rules, but it ain't even our game.   4

We can devise a performance model only after an analysis of the components of BI. Now there do be linguists who supposedly done did this categorization and definition of BE.[4] But the descriptions are generally confining, limited as they are to discrete linguistic units. One finds simply ten to fifteen patterns cited, as for example, the most frequently listed one, the use of *be* as finite verb, contrasting with its deletion: (a) *The coffee be cold* contrasts with (b) *The coffee cold,* the former statement denoting a continuing state of affairs, the latter applying to the   5

---

[3]For the most racist and glaring of these charges, see Fred Hechinger, ed., *Pre-School Education Today* (Doubleday, 1966); for an excellent rebuttal, see William Labov, *Nonstandard English* (NCTE, 1970); for a complete overview of the controversy and issues involved as well as historical perspective and rebuttal to the non-verbal claim, see my "Black Idiom and White Institutions," *Negro American Literature Forum,* Fall 1971.

[4]The most thorough and scholarly of these, though a bit overly technical, is Walter Wolfram, *Detroit Negro Speech* (Center for Applied Linguistics, 1969).

present moment only. (Like if you the cook, (a) probably get you fired, and (b) only get you talked about.) In WE no comparable grammatical distinction exists and *The coffee is cold* would be used to indicate both meanings. However, rarely does one find an investigation of the total vitality of black expressive style, a style inextricable from the Black Cultural Universe, for after all, BI connects with Black Soul and niggers is more than deleted copulas.[5]

6   The Black Idiom should be viewed from two important perspectives: linguistic and stylistic. The linguistic dimension is comprised of the so-called nonstandard features of phonology and syntax (patterns like *dis heah* and *The coffee be cold*), and a lexicon generally equated with "slang" or hip talk. The stylistic dimension has to do with *rapping, capping, jiving,* etc., and with features such as cadence, rhythm, resonance, gestures, and all those other elusive, difficult-to-objectify elements that make up what is considered a writer or speaker's "style." While I am separating linguistic and stylistic features, I have done so only for the purpose of simplifying the discussion since the BI speaker runs the full gamut of both dimensions in any given speech event.

7   I acknowledge from the bell that we's dealing with a dialect structure which is a subsystem of the English language; thus BE and WE may not appear fundamentally different. Yet, though black folks speak English, it do seem to be an entirely different lingo altogether. But wherein lies the uniqueness? Essentially in language, as in other areas of Black Culture, we have the problem of isolating those elements indigenous to black folks from those cultural aspects shared with white folks. Anthropologist Johnnetta Cole suggests that Black Culture has three dimensions: (1) those elements shared with mainstream America; (2) those elements shared with all oppressed peoples; (3) those elements peculiar to the black condition in America.[6] Applying her concepts to language, I propose the accompanying schematic representation.

8   Referring to the first column, contemporary BE is simply one of the many dialects of contemporary American English,

---

[5]Kochman is one linguist who done gone this route; see for instance his "Rapping in the Black Ghetto," *Trans-action* February 1969. However, he makes some black folks mad because of what one of my students called his "superfluity," and others shame cause of his exposure of our "bad" street elements. Kochman's data: jam up with muthafuckas and pussy-copping raps collected from Southside Chicago.

[6]Johnnetta B. Cole, "Culture: Negro, Black and Nigger," *The Black Scholar,* June 1970.

and it is most likely the case that the linguistic patterns of BE differ from those of WE in surface structure only. There's no essential linguistic difference between *dis heah* and *this here*, and from a strictly linguistic point of view, *God don't never change* can be written *God doesn't ever change* (though definitely not from a socio-cultural/political perspective, as Baraka quite rightly notes).[7] Perhaps we could make a case for deep structure difference in the BE use of *be* as finite verb (refer to *The coffee be cold* example above), but we be hard pressed to find any other examples, and even in this case, we could posit that the copula exists in the deep structure, and is simply deleted by some low-level phonological deletion rule, dig: The coffee is cold . . . The coffee's cold . . . The coffee cold. My conclusion at this point is that despite the claims of some highly respected Creole linguists (with special propers to bad Sistuh Beryl Bailey),[8] the argument for deep structure differences between contemporary BE and WE syntax cannot pass the test of rigorous transformational analysis.

Referring to the second column, we note the psychological 9
tendency of oppressed people to adopt the modes of behavior and expression of their oppressors (also, during the African slave trade, the functional necessity of pidginized forms of European language). Not only does the conqueror force his victims into political subjugation, he also coerces them into adopting his language and doles out special rewards to those among the oppressed who best mimic his language and cultural style. In the initial language contact stage, the victims attempt to assemble the new language into their native linguistic mold, producing a linguistic mixture that is termed *pidgin*. In the next stage, the pidgin may develop into a Creole, a highly systematic, widely used mode of communication among the oppressed, characterized by a substratum of patterns from the victim's language with an overlay of forms from the oppressor's language. As the oppressed people's identification with the victor's culture intensifies, the pidgin/Creole begins to lose its linguistic currency and naturally evolves in the direction of the victor's language. Reconstructing the linguistic history of BE, we theorize that it followed a similar pattern; due to the radically different condition of black oppression in America, the

---

[7]Imamu Baraka, "Expressive Language," *Home*, pp. 166–172.

[8]See her "Toward a New Perspective in Negro English Dialectology," *American Speech* (1965); and "Language and Communicative Styles of Afro-American Children in the United States," *Florida FL Reporter* 7 (Spring-Summer 1969).

FEATURES SHARED WITH MAINSTREAM AMERICA	FEATURES SHARED WITH ALL OPPRESSED PEOPLES	FEATURES UNIQUE TO BLACK AMERICANS
Linguistic	*Linguistic*	*Linguistic*
1. British/ American English lexicon	1. Superimpositions of dominant culture's language on native language, yielding	Unique meanings attributed to certain English lexical items
2. Most aspects of British/ American English phonology and syntax	2. Pidginized form of dominant culture's language, subject to becoming extinct, due to	*Stylistic* Unique communication patterns and rhetorical flourishes
	3. Historical evolution, linguistic leveling out in direction of dominant culture's dialect	

process of *de-creolization* is nearly complete and has been for perhaps over a hundred years.

10   The most important features of BI are, of course, those referred to in column three, for they point us toward the linguistic uniqueness and cultural significance of the Oral Tradition in the Black Experience. It should be clear that all along I been talkin about that Black Experience associated with the grass-roots black folks, the masses, the sho-nuff niggers—in short, all those black folks who do not aspire to white middle-class American standards.

11   Within this tradition, language is used as a teaching/socializing force and as a means of establishing one's reputation via his verbal competence. Black talk is never meaningless cocktail chit-chat but a functional dynamic that is simultaneously a mechanism for acculturation and information-passing and a vehicle for achieving group recognition. Black communication is highly verbal and highly stylized; it is a performance before a black audience who become both observers and participants in the speech event. Whether it be through a slapping of hands ("giving five" or "giving skin"), Amen's, or Right on's, the audience influences the direction of a given rap and at the same time acknowledges or withholds its approval, depending on

the linguistic skill and stylistic ingenuity of the speaker. I mean like a Brother is only as bad as his rap bees.

I. Toward a Black Language Model: Linguistic

While we concede that black people use the vocabulary of the English language, certain words are always selected out of that lexicon and given a special black semantic slant. So though we rappin bout the same language, the reality referents are different. As one linguist has suggested, the proper question is not what do words mean but what do the users of the words mean? These words may be associated with and more frequently used in black street culture but not necessarily. *Muthafucka* has social boundaries, but not *nigger*. 12

Referring to the lexicon of BI, then, the following general principles obtain: 13

1. The words given the special black slant exist in a dynamic state. The terms are discarded when they move into the white mainstream. (Example: One no longer speaks of a "hip" brother; now he is a "togetha" brother.) This was/is necessitated by our need to have a code that was/is undecipherable by foreigners (i.e., whites). 14

2. In BI, the concept of denotation vs. connotation does not apply. 15

3. What does apply is shades of meaning along the connotative spectrum. For example, depending on contextual environment, the word *bad* can mean extraordinary; beautiful; good; versatile; or a host of other terms of positive value. Dig it; after watching a Sammy Davis performance, a BI speaker testified: "Sammy sho did some *bad* stuff," i.e., extraordinary stuff. Or upon observing a beautiful sister: "She sho is *bad*," i.e., beautiful, pretty, or good-looking. Or, noticing how a brother is dressed: "You sho got on some *bad* shit," i.e., *good* shit = attractively dressed. 16

Note that the above examples are all in the category of *approbation*. It is necessary to rap about *denigration* as well, since certain words in the black lexicon can frequently be used both ways. Consider the word *nigger*, for instance. "He's my main nigger" means my best friend (hence, approbation); "The nigger ain't shit," means he's probably lazy, trifling, scheming, wrong-doing, or a host of other *denigrating* terms, depending on the total context of the utterance. 17

4. Approbation and denigration relate to the semantic level; we can add two other possible functions of the same word on the grammatical level: *intensification* and *completion*. Slide 18

back to *nigger* for a minute, and dig that often the word is void of real meaning and simply supplies the sentence with a subject. "Niggers was getting out of there left and right, then the niggers was running, and so the niggers said . . . " etc., etc., my main point being that a steady stream of overuse means neither denigration nor approbation. Some excellent illustrations of this function of the word are to be found in *Manchild in the Promised Land*, where you can observe the word used in larger contexts.

19   To give you a most vivid illustration, consider the use of what WE labels "obscenities." From the streets of Detroit: (a) "That's a bad *muthafucka.*" Referring to a Cadillac Eldorado, obviously indicating approval. (b) "He's a no-good *muthafucka.*" Referring to a person who has just "put some game" on the speaker, obviously indicating disapproval. (c) "You *muthafuckin* right I wasn't gon let him do that." Emphasizing how correct the listener's assessment is, obviously using the term as a grammatical intensifier, modifying "right." (d) "We wasn't doin nothing, just messing round and *shit.*" Though a different "obscenity," the point is nonetheless illustrated, "shit" being used neutrally, as an expletive (filler) to complete the sentence pattern; semantically speaking, it is an empty word in this contextual environment.

20   Where I'm comin from is that the lexicon of BI, consisting of certain specially selected words, requires a unique scheme of analysis to account for the diverse range and multiplicity of meanings attributed to these words. While there do be some dictionaries of Afro-American "slang," they fail to get at the important question: what are the psycho-cultural processes that guide our selection of certain words out of the thousands of possible words in the Anglo-Saxon vocabulary? Like, for instance, Kochman[9] has suggested that we value action in the black community, and so those words that have action implied in them, we take and give positive meanings to, such as *swing, game, hip, hustle,* etc.; whereas words of implied stasis are taken and given negative connotations, such as *lame, square, hung-up, stiffin and jivin,* etc. At any rate, what I've tried to lay here are some suggestions in this particular linguistic dimension; the definitive word on black lexicon is yet to be given.

21   I shall go on to discuss the stylistic dimension of black communication patterns, where I have worked out a more definitive model.

[9]See Thomas Kochman, "The Kinetic Element in Black Idiom," paper read at the American Anthropological Association Convention, Seattle, Washington, 1968; also his *Rappin' and Stylin' Out: Communication in Urban Black America.*

II. Toward a Black Language Model: Stylistic

Black verbal style exists on a sacred-secular continuum, as rep-   22
resented by the accompanying scheme. The model allows us to
account for the many individual variations in black speech,
which can all be located at some point along the continuum.

The sacred style is rural and Southern. It is the style of the   23
black preacher and that associated with the black church tradition. It tends to be more emotive and highly charged than the
secular style. It is also older in time. However, though I've
called it "sacred," it abounds in secularisms. Black church service tends to be highly informal, and it ain't nothin for a
preacher to get up in the pulpit and, say, show off what he's
wearing: "Y'all didn't notice the new suit I got on today, did
y'all? Ain the Lord good to us. . . ."

The secular style is urban and Northern, but since it proba-   24
bly had its beginnings in black folk tales and proverbs, its *roots*
are Southern and rural. This is the street culture; the style
found in barbershops and on street corners in the black ghettos of American cities. It tends to be more cool, more emotionally restrained than sacred style. It is newer and younger in
time and only fully evolved as a distinct style with the massive
wave of black migration to the cities.

Both sacred and secular styles share the following character-   25
istics:

1. *Call and Response.* This is basic black oral tradition. The   26
speaker's solo voice alternates or is intermingled with the audience's response. In the sacred style, the minister is urged by the
congregation's Amen's, That's right, Reverend's, or Preach
Reverend's. One also hears occasional Take your time's when
the preacher is initiating his sermon, the congregation desiring
to savor every little bit of this good message they bout to hear.

SACRED	SECULAR
Political Rap Style	*Political Rap Style*
Examples: Jesse Jackson	*Examples*: Malcolm X
Martin Luther King	Rap Brown
Political Literary Style	*Political Literary Style*
Examples: Barbara Ann Teer's	*Examples*: Don Lee
National Black Theater	Last Poets
Nikki Giovanni's "Truth	
Is on Its Way"	

(In both sacred and secular political rap styles, the "Preach Reverend" is transposed to "Teach Brother.") In the secular style, the response can take the form of a back-and-forth banter between the speaker and various members of the audience. Or the audience might manifest its response in giving skin (fives) when a really down verbal point is scored. Other approval responses include laughter and phrases like "Oh, you mean, nigger," "Get back, nigger," "Git down, baby," etc.

27   2. *Rhythmic Pattern.* I refer to cadence, tone, and musical quality. This is a pattern that is lyrical, sonorous, and generally emphasizing sound apart from sense. It is often established through repetition, either of certain sounds or words. The preacher will get a rhythm going, conveying his message through sound rather than depending on sheer semantic import. "I-I-I-I-I-Oh-I-I-Oh, yeah, Lord-I-I-heard the voice of Jesus saying. . . ." Even though the secular style is characterized by rapidity, as in the toasts (narrative tales of bad niggers and they exploits like Stag-O-Lee, or bad animals and they trickeration, like the Signifying Monkey), the speaker's voice tone still has that rhythmic, musical quality, just with a faster tempo.

28   3. *Spontaneity.* Generally, the speaker's performance is improvisational, with the rich interaction between speaker and audience dictating and/or directing the course and outcome of the speech event. Since the speaker does not prepare a formal document, his delivery is casual, nondeliberate, and uncontrived. He speaks in a lively, conversational tone, and with an ever-present quality of immediacy. All emphasis is on process, movement, and creativity of the moment. The preacher says "Y'all dont wont to hear dat, so I'm gon leave it lone," and his audience shouts, "Naw, tell it Reverend, tell it!," and he does. Or, like, once Malcolm [X] mentioned the fact of his being in prison, and sensing the surprise of his audience, he took advantage of the opportunity to note that all black people were in prison: "That's what American means: prison."

29   4. *Concreteness.* The speaker's imagery and ideas center around the empirical world, the world of reality, and the contemporary Here and Now. Rarely does he drift off into esoteric abstractions; his metaphors and illustrations are commonplace and grounded in everyday experience. Perhaps because of his concreteness, there is a sense of identification with the event being described or narrated, as in the secular style where the toast-teller's identity merges with that of the protagonist of his tale, and he becomes Stag-O-Lee or Shine; or when the preacher assumes the voice of God or the personality of a Biblical character. Even the experience of being saved takes on a presentness and rootedness in everyday life: "I first met God in 1925. . . ."

5. *Signifying.* This is a technique of talking about the entire   30
audience or some member of the audience either to initiate
verbal "war" or to make a point hit home. The interesting
thang bout this rhetorical device is that the audience is not offended and realizes—naw, expects—the speaker to launch this
offensive to achieve this desired effect. "Pimp, punk, prostitute, Ph.D.—all the P's—you still in slavery!" announces the
Reverend Jesse Jackson. Malcolm puts down the nonviolent
movement with: "In a revolution, you swinging, not singing."
(Notice the characteristic rhythmic pattern in the above examples—the alliterative poetic effect of Jackson's statement and
the rhyming device in Malcolm's.)

An analysis of black expressive style, such as presented here,   31
should facilitate the construction of a performance instrument
to measure the degree of command of the style of any given BI
speaker. Linguists and educators sincerely interested in black
education might be about the difficult, complex business of devising such a "test," rather than establishing linguistic remediation programs to correct a nonexistent remediation. Like in
any other area of human activity, some BI rappers are better
than others, and today's most effective black preachers, leaders, politicians, writers are those who rap in the black expressive style, appropriating the ritual framework of the Oral
Tradition as vehicle for the conveyance of they political ideologies. Which brings me back to what I said from Jump Street.
The real heart of this language controversy relates to/is the underlying political nature of the American educational system.
Brother Frantz Fanon is highly instructive at this point. From
his "Negro and Language," in *Black Skin, White Masks:*

> I ascribe a basic importance to the phenomenon of lan-
> guage. . . . To speak means . . . above all to assume a culture,
> to support the weight of a civilization. . . . Every dialect is a
> way of thinking. . . . And the fact that the newly returned
> [i.e., from white schools] Negro adopts a language different
> from that of the group into which he was born is evidence of
> a dislocation, a separation. . . .

In showing why the "Negro adopts such a position . . . with respect to European languages," Fanon continues:

> It is because he wants to emphasize the rupture that has
> now occurred. He is incarnating a new type of man that he
> imposes on his associates and his family. And so his old

mother can no longer understand him when he talks to her about his *duds,* the family's *crummy joint,* the *dump* . . . all of it, of course, tricked out with the appropriate accent.

In every country of the world, there are climbers, "the ones who forget who they are," and in contrast to them, "the ones who remember where they came from." The Antilles Negro who goes home from France expresses himself in the dialect if he wants to make it plain that nothing has changed.

32

As black people go moving on up toward separation and cultural nationalism, the question of the moment is not which dialect, but which culture, not whose vocabulary but whose values, not *I am* vs. *I be,* but WHO DO I BE?

Eldridge Cleaver

WE NEED TO RESCUE
KIDS FROM EBONICS

Born in 1935 in Wabbaseka, Arkansas, Eldridge Cleaver as a young man had numerous run-ins with police, and in the late 1950s he ended up in California prisons—a formative experience for him. He gained fame upon his release from prison when he published Soul on Ice, *a series of essays on racial issues, and in the mid-1960s he was a founder of the Black Panthers, a radical black nationalist group that operated social programs in the African American community. Wounded in 1968 in a shootout with police, he fled to Algeria to escape criminal charges. On his return to the United States in 1975, Cleaver renounced the Black Panthers, had criminal charges against him dropped, and was "born again" yet again as a Christian and a Republican. During the mid-1980s, he became addicted to cocaine and had further brushes with the law, but he remained committed to evangelical Christianity. Eighteen months before he died in May 1998, Cleaver published the following comment on the Ebonics controversy in the* Los Angeles Times.

There are children who go around biting other children. 1
Should our response be to legalize and institutionalize canni-
balism and hand out bottles of ketchup?

I am one of the most liberal people in the world. And I am all 2
for black pride. I am not just a freedom talker; I am a freedom
fighter. But I say no to Ebonics.

When I was growing up, what is now being euphemistically 3
called Ebonics was accurately called bad English. I have the
greatest respect for linguistic diversity. I speak English,
Spanish and French. If I hadn't learned Spanish growing up in
Los Angeles, I would not have survived my sojourn in Cuba.
And I survived Algeria and France because I speak French. At
the same time, I insist that as U.S. citizens, we must put
English first and uphold a standard of excellence. I understand
and applaud cultural and linguistic diversity, but I reject all arguments that carry political correctness to the extreme of promoting anything other than English as our official language.

I believe that schoolchildren should be required to study for- 4
eign languages, particularly Spanish, but not to the detriment
of their mastery and excelling in English.

The thirst for exclusivity and recognition is often misguided, 5
as it is in this instance. It is like Jesse Jackson running down
the street naked, screaming "I am a man! I am somebody!"
Thanks for telling us. We never would have noticed.

The only place for Ebonics is the streets. We don't need it in 6
the classroom; we need to rescue kids from Ebonics, the illegitimate offspring of the shotgun wedding of ebony and phonics.
African Americans are linguistically creative and have en-
riched the English language. But Ebonics is the opposite of
creative. It is a pathetic attempt to institutionalize dysfunction
and to establish an idol.

Begone, you poots. And you teachers of Ebonics, get a real 7
job teaching something with a redeeming social value. Stop
flaunting your ignorance.

Douglas Haneline
A COMMENT ON TEACHING STANDARD EDITED ENGLISH

Although it in some ways seems like a response to Geneva Smitherman's essay on Black English, the following short essay by Douglas Haneline was actually published in May 2001 in College English, *a professional magazine for English teachers. Douglas Haneline teaches at Ferris State University in Michigan.*

1   I teach edited American English as a vehicle of expository expression and think that it is important to do so, whether I am teaching writing or literature, at any level; in fact, English teachers who fail to do so are not doing their jobs. Why do I say this?

2   *English is not a "white" language anymore:* It is used throughout the world by those in every race and culture. Its widespread use is not simply the result of past colonialism and current business and technological dominance by English-speaking countries. Compared to many other languages, English is easy to learn, is relatively uninflected, has a large vocabulary, and has a history of welcoming foreign terms, perhaps because of the fact that before English became an imperial language, it was for many centuries the language of the conquered and marginalized. Its alphabetic base gives it additional accessibility and utility in a technological age. Millions of people learn it for the same reason that they use the Gregorian calendar—practicality and convenience. Identifying the year as "2001" does not mean that one is affirming the divinity of Christ, and mastering edited American English does not mean that one is affirming "white" hegemony.

3   *English is the new international language:* If the Internet and the presence of students from all over the world in today's American college English classrooms are not sufficiently convincing on this score, then skeptics should look at Burton Bollag's "The New Latin: English Dominates in Academe" in the 8 September 2000 issue of the *Chronicle of Higher Education.* All over the world, English is becoming the dominant vehicle of expression for research and international meetings. For this reason, we in the profession need to avoid thinking of English language issues as being solely the concern of Americans, or of blacks and whites.

English and teachers of English: It is also important to re- 4
member our true relationship to the language: as an association, a profession, or individuals, we do not own it, and we
cannot change it; that privilege belongs to its users. But, regarding our students, we do have one unique power—denial of
opportunity. In our time education confers an unparalleled socioeconomic privilege on those who possess it, a power that ri-
vals race, ethnicity, and nationality. We can, as a profession,
keep poorly educated Americans of any racial and ethnic
group off or in the back of the bus simply by failing in our duty
to teach them edited American English.

I would agree that the process by which English became the 5
dominant world language bears inspection. That it has been
not only the vehicle of knowledge and liberty but also of oppression and racism cannot be denied. But our students are
taking English writing and literature courses because English
expression is needed for the careers and future they want. In
edited American English we have a versatile tool we can give
them, one whose mastery will contribute to their well-being.
Our hesitating to do so will not change the global shift toward
English, nor will it benefit our students—of any race, ethnic
group, or nationality.

On Ebonics:
A Discussion
of Black English

*In December 1996 the school board in Oakland, California,
where 53 percent of the students are black, decided to recognize Black English (Ebonics) as a second language in the district and told its teachers to respect its use in the classroom.
The board took steps to ensure that teachers would be able to
understand Black English and able to translate Black English
into standard English—and vice versa—when necessary.*

*The action of the school board inspired a nationwide debate
about the wisdom, practicality, and fairness of incorporating
Black English into the educational system. Magazine and newspaper editorial pages were filled with discussions about the issue. (Elridge Cleaver's piece on page 214–215 is an example.) In
the midst of the discussion, the leaders of the Internet group*
Interracial Voice *decided to encourage an Internet discussion
of the matter. In the following months a great many people*

responded; here are some of the contributions that were made over the next sixteen months.

Date: Mon, 30 Dec 1996
From: "Alton E. Paris" XXXXX@airmail.net
Organization: Quinn Chapel AME Church
Subject: Ebonics

1   How far have we fallen. Ebonics is just "bad" grammar. We are afraid to say a person can be wrong. It is not disrespectful to tell a child that he/she must learn to speak correct English. The main purpose of school is to teach children to read, write, speak, and calculate. Let me give you an example:

2   In the late sixties I was stationed in France. One of my sons reached kindergarten age and we were living in a small French village near Metz, France. A friend suggested we send him to French kindergarten. I had concerns because he could not speak French. We went to see the school to see the principal, a priest, and expressed my concerns to him. His response was, "That's OK. The French children do not speak French either." Rodney learned French along with the little French kids and was at their level in about six months. He was also bi-lingual because we spoke English at home.
        Regards, Al Paris

From: n.hayes1@XXXXX.geis.com
Date: Mon, 6 Jan 97
Subject: Ebonics

3   The various registers of English should be given due respect. For too long, white America has devalued Black English, working to make it the symbol of stupidity. Nevertheless, many Black linguistic patterns/words/phrases have come into general use. They then are admitted (drum roll) into "Standard English" and Psychological destruction. People with African ancestry are generally aware of the scorn reserved for Black English. Some blacks are negatively affected by this, using Black English only when they are expressing negative ideas and attitudes.

4   Too many times in school, Black English is seen by teachers as a fault to be corrected. I don't agree with the contention of some that black patterns of speech are genetically determined. Some phrases are antique forms of English, used during the 1700s, 1800s, that have since been dropped by the white population. Many people are bilingual, trilingual (especially abroad). Learning to differentiate between Standard English and Black

English has been done by blacks for generations. The Oakland School District has publicly announced their respect for Black English; this is their revolutionary act.

Sincerely, Nancy Hayes

Date: Thu, 09 Jan 1997
From: Sharon Teuben-Rowe XXXXX@wam.umd.edu
Subject: Ebonics (BEV)—a linguist's view

The Oakland Unified Schools District and the general media 5 haven't done an effective job of informing the public. The Oakland schools ARE NOT AND NEVER PLANNED TO TEACH EBONICS.

Once the school board passed its resolution regarding recog- 6 nition, they would petition the Federal government for Bilingual Education funds for teacher training in linguistics and ESL and bilingual education teaching methodologies. This is about teacher education. OAKLAND IS NOT TEACHING EBONICS to anyone's children.

BEV has a regular grammar . . . a descriptive grammar . . . 7 which utilizes tree diagrams and discusses morphological changes, syntax, semantics, and its lexicon among other linguistic science based features. Prescriptive grammar, the grammar rules we learn in school (subject-verb agreement, adjectives modifying nouns and the sins of splitting infinitives) are not the grammar rules referred to when BEV is said to have a grammar. Linguistic research focuses on descriptive grammar. School teachers teach prescriptive grammar . . . so OAKLAND TEACHERS ARE NOT TEACHING EBONICS since the corpus of research data on BEV is on its descriptive grammar.

BEV is a dialect of American English, not a slang, improper 8 English, street English, gutter English, sign of stubbornness, poverty, ignorance, intellectual capacity, evil conspiracy, bad upbringing, parental neglect, teenage parenthood, hip-hop culture or any other uninformed pejorative. Dialects are communicative systems borne out of parent languages. They incorporate and systematically abbreviate forms, thus creating new ones. BEV uses an American English lexicon (words/vocabulary) and English and various West African descriptive grammar rules. It's not hokum, malevolent or goofy, it's linguistics. All modern languages began as dialects.

No one speaks BEV/Ebonics exclusively. Millions and mil- 9 lions of African Americans are bi-dialectal and engage in code-switching. These speakers recognize the appropriateness of their communicative codes and act accordingly.

10   Examples of BEV are usually given in linguistic shorthand, using the IPA (International Phonetic Alphabet) complete with diacritics. Most so-called examples of BEV in the media have been hideously erroneous . . . examples of contemporary slang which is a separate linguistic feature.

11   Courtland Milloy's example works well.

/JʌuwicôĵˆElo/ which ~sounds like Dju-weet-yo-jello?

There are several things going on here but a descriptive grammar observation is the noun-consonant-noun pattern . . . a morphological rule.

12   So, what do I think . . . after all that? Oakland was grossly inarticulate in stating their intent and has published some weakly written documents. A visit to their local linguist would have helped. Nonetheless, this is not a silver bullet. Training teachers is fine, but all children need to attend school regularly, have a place to study at home, have stability and consistency in the home which is conducive and supportive of their academics and the children themselves must be motivated. No amount of funding and teacher training will influence these aspects of their lives.

　　　　Sharon

From: "Susanne Heine" XXXXX@mailbox.calypso.net
Subject: Ebonics: Or what are certain self-serving ignoramuses trying to wreak?
Date: Fri, 13 Feb 1998

13   When I was a little girl in P.S. 116, Jamaica, Long Island, I was mobbed for years by the other kids. "Long-haired yalla bitch, always talkin white!" . . . and no, I didn't talk like them. My mother, a woman from an educated creole (on her father's side) South Carolina family didn't talk like them, either. Mom and I read a lot, she often quoted poetry (everything from James Weldon Johnson to Shakespeare), and she encouraged me to write. Blessed with a rich lyric soprano voice (trained), she often practised arias in the afternoon when we children came home from school. She sang spirituals, Mozart, Bach, art songs and airs while we did our homework. She loved language, and instilled in me the very same passion. In 1957, when I took the SAT at age 16, I finished in the top 5% of the United States on the English section.

14   Since 1964, I have lived in Sweden. I have worked here, raised a family (2 children) with my ex, a German manufacturer, and I make a quite good living as a translator and editor

of English, a highly sought-after commodity in the powerful cultural sphere that the European Union has become.

Last year when I read about the Ebonics nonsense in the international papers, I couldn't believe my eyes. It was as if I had been violently thrust back again into the schoolyard at P.S. 116: "Why you talkin white, bitch? Whussamatta wich-too? You's uppity! C'mon, git huh yella butt!" But I couldn't react with the icy paralysed fear of the mobbed child any longer, all I could feel was a towering fury, the righteous rage, of an American once more watching her country's ideals betrayed. (Vietnam is a story all by itself; we needn't touch on it here.) Jefferson wrote of "life, liberty and the pursuit of happiness," and I believe that every American, regardless of color, is born to enjoy—at the very least—these entitlements.

My point is this: Are studies such as the Arts and Humanities, Physics, Mathematics, Economics, Linguistics, Psychology, Medicine, the Law etc., taught in Ebonics? Is there an extensive literature written in Ebonics? Have the laws, the Constitution, the history of the United States of America been translated into Ebonics for every black schoolchild to take part of and become enlightened by? Where are the universities that offer baccalaureates and doctorates to honor research that is performed in that language, using its references and sources? Which are the multinational companies crying out for expertise and trained professionals who have mastered Ebonics?

In fact, what is Ebonics at all, if not an atavistic manifestation of a slaveyard patois, which—if not for the intellectually, culturally and morally debilitating effects of a botched post-integration politics—would probably have weakened in importance of its own accord, made obsolescent by its own irrelevance? The Jewish and Italian kids I went to school with when I was eleven (the Russians had detonated an A-bomb, so the government snatched all us kids with IQs over 130 and sent us to special schools) all knew words (exotic), phrases (colorful) and expressions (usually downright rude) in their parents' languages, but that stuff was "inside" stuff; you didn't talk that way to your teachers, or to non-Jews and non-Italians. The patois stayed at home, because these kids were preparing to switch tracks into the mainstream of American life, just as their parents willingly—and albeit with some pain—wanted them to do. Dominic, Murray, Sofia, Barbara, all of them were on the threshold of what their parents wanted for them. I was privileged to be among them and to catch the spark of their ambition. We weren't "ethnic," we were just damned smart.

18   In My Fair Lady, Higgins makes an observation on catching sight of Eliza:

HIGGINS: Look at her, a prisoner of the gutter,
            Condemned by every syllable she utters—
            By right, she should be taken out and hung
            For the cold-blooded murder of the English tongue!

ELIZA: Aaoouww!

HIGGINS: Chickens cackling in a barn,
            Just like this one—

ELIZA: Garn!

HIGGINS: It's "Aaoouww" and "Garn!" that keep her in her place,
            Not her wretched clothes and dirty face . . .

That, of course, is the premise of Shaw's "Pygmalion." At a completely different level, it is also the key to the plight of the black underprivileged classes in America (and please, let's confine ourselves to class now; race is a tad too sticky and requires other parameters).

19   By 1981, I was tired of Europe in general and Sweden in particular, so I went to live in California for a couple of years. Tuned into the old culture as only a former expatriate could be, I noticed how many new immigrants there were from all the Asian countries, as well as from Mexico, Latin America, the Middle East, the Horn of Africa and the Caribbean. As an American, I felt proud seeing how many of them had caught a foothold in society, were making a living, getting ahead and moving upwards. But at the same time, it galled me to see so many of my own people living as if they were still outsiders in their own country. At the checkout counter in the local supermarket in Hollywood, the clerks were mostly Asian, young kids whose names—judging from their name-tags—were "Scott" and "Kimberly" and "Sue-Ann," and who spoke clear, mainstream American. And I thought: If any one of these kids calls up looking for a new job somewhere, the person they get on the line will hear someone who speaks like he does himself, someone whose voice, intonation and vocabulary are in tune with what the customers want to hear, someone who in no way threatens him with some kind of cultural "otherness" that— sooner or later—will have to be dealt with. Out in the parking lot, the black kids were always hanging out, talking their slave patois (Oh God forgive me, I meant "Ebonics"!), too proud, and

manifestly too ignorant, to take a job at a checkout counter, and looking at a future in which—hopefully!—Scott and Kimberly and Sue-Ann will be helping to pay their welfare checks.

Furthermore, I maintain that black people in America will 20 never attain their rightful place in American society and business, will never be able to transcend the pain and backwardness of slavery or the intellectual squalor of the slave mentality, until they make the mainstream language their own. "In the Beginning was the Word, and the Word was God."

Calling the slaveyard patois that keeps black people in 21 chains "Ebonics" is just another huckster's attempt to gold-plate slave shackles. I'll be damned if I'll buy it.

    With all due respect, Susanne

From: "William Javier Nelson" XXXXX@aol.com
Subject: Ebonics—English as a second language
Date: Fri, 24 Apr 1998

Dear Susanne:
In addition to being a Ph.D. in Sociology, I am a licensed (state 22 of Minnesota) E.S.L. instructor. What you said in your letter . . . is the basis for much of my philosophy when teaching English to Latinos.

I am also a Dominican and speak Spanish with a decided 23 Dominican accent of the lower middle class (dropping the letter "s" from the ends of many words, etc.). When I am around other lower-middle class Dominicans of my ilk (mainly from the cities of Santo Domingo and Santiago, Dominican Republic) I can let my hair down and go to town. However, I still regularly do (and complete) the English language New York Times crossword (in ink).

    Respectfully, William Javier Nelson

From: "Susanne Heine" XXXXX@mailbox.calypso.net
Subject: Re: Ebonics—English as a second language
Date: Fri, 25 Apr 1998

Dear William,
How nice hearing from you! And how encouraging it is to re- 24 alise that there are people out there who have eyes to see and the brains to fathom what I meant . . . I feel that all of us, whatever we want to call ourselves—black, brown, African-American, mixed-race, mulatto or whatever—have been short-changed by the way the US has progressed in the last 30 years or so. We've lost sight of so many things that were important to

an older, and I dare say wiser, generation than ours. They were wiser because anything they ever had, they had to earn, and dearly too. There were no quick-fixes for them. They couldn't turn millionaire overnight on the strength of some foul-mouthed rap-jingle, or make heads turn on the street by getting themselves up like outlaws and giving society the finger. Or fascinate the entire nation by giving the cops a run for their money in a white Bronco . . .

25   As a fellow academic who works with language, you of course understand how our use of it affects our destinies, and I'm sure you know that this knowledge is not widespread enough. I recognise what you mean when you say that, privately, you can "get down" with the folks who speak Spanish the way you speak it: you feel idiomatically comfortable and therefore in complete control socially. However, the fact that this in no way threatens or is in conflict with your sense of belonging in a public context, is a testimony to your sophistication, as well as to your complete grasp of the problem, such as it is. . . .

26   The point is this: the more we seek to disassociate ourselves from America, the more justified she feels in turning her back on us. We are probably the most genuine "Americans" of all; there is not a race, not a national group, not a tribe that has ever set foot on American soil that is not amply represented among us. But how can we define ourselves as "Americans" if we, of our own doing, abrogate our contract with what America has—in its finest moments—always believed itself to be? Some people, black as well as white and for equally dubious reasons, have been telling us for a long time that the one central and absolutely defining paradigm in our lives is our race. Now the amazing thing is, WE HAVE ACCEPTED THAT! WE HONESTLY BELIEVE THAT! We have made it part and parcel of our identity, we have allowed that choice piece of nonsense to shape and pattern our lives, to influence our attitudes to ourselves as well as to the world at large, and we spend—if only subconsciously—every minute of our lives thinking about our colour as if it were a REAL factor in the world, like unemployment, or pollution or the price of butter, for God's sake! One thing that I have learnt in 34 years abroad is this: the colour of your skin has no more bearing on anything REAL than the colour of your eyes, or, for that matter, the colour of the tie you have on.

27   What does have meaning, on the other hand, is how you conduct yourself. How you act and move, how you relate to people physically as well as mentally. And most important, how you SPEAK. I'm sure that when you watch your students progress,

you feel you are giving them a tool that they will be able to shape their world with, and William, you are so right.

Keep on believing! 28

　　　All the best, Susanne

　　P.S. Yeah, I know what you mean. I still do the Times cross- 29 word in ink, though I can no longer boast of doing it in 15 minutes flat the way I could when I was twenty and living in New York. Boy, did that ever annoy my fellow commuters! Especially the chubby guy with his pencil and eraser!

Keith Gilyard

IT AIN'T HARD TO TELL: DISTINGUISHING FACT FROM FALLACY IN THE EBONICS CONTROVERSY

Keith Gilyard teaches rhetoric and composition at Penn State. His books include Voices of the Self: A Study of Language Competence *(1991) and* Let's Flip the Script: An African American Discourse on Language, Literature, and Learning *(1996). A poet and critic as well as a student of language and culture, especially African American language and culture, he wrote the following essay for a collection entitled* Ebonics and Language Education, *edited by Clinton Crawford in 2001.*

One of the things I am sure about as the debate over Ebonics 1 continues to unfold is that not much of it is taking place in libraries. Despite voluminous books on linguistics and education housed in many institutions, much of the general conversation, including the overwhelmingly negative discussion still taking place in the media, is disconnected from the decades of language scholarship represented by books and journals. My major purpose here, therefore, is to bring essential insights from serious language study to bear on public debate. By doing so, I hope to improve the quality of the overall discourse on

Ebonics. I acknowledge that some of my own political biases will become evident as I suggest what might be done about some of the facts of language, but I at least aim to get the facts straight, a phenomenon occurring too infrequently in newspapers and on electronic outlets.

2   Let us examine the most frequently stated criticisms of Ebonics, or Black English Vernacular, or African American Vernacular English (the term I usually prefer) and of the Oakland school board, which has served as the flash point for this particular phase of what has been an ongoing language controversy. First let us consider the popular claim that Ebonics is a substandard, incorrect, or broken variety of English.

3   The former mayor of New York City, Edward Koch, who apparently verges on cardiac arrest every time he hears an African American pronounce "asked" as "axed," wrote an article debasing Ebonics in the *New York Post*, January 10, 1997. He termed Ebonics a series of linguistic violations and made reference to a letter he wrote in 1985 to the *New York Times*, a paper that had been critical of Koch's seeming obsession with pronunciation. In that 1985 letter, Koch purposely, and unsystematically, misspelled a few words. He was supposedly representing African American speech. Now he claims, with characteristic arrogance and ridicule, that he was speaking and writing Ebonics before it was even named. Because the term Ebonics has been in use since 1973, Koch himself proves that he doesn't know what he is talking about. You know he's not in the knowledge loop on this issue. But, nonetheless, he is given considerable print space, and airtime as well, to pretend to be an expert on language. Shelby Steele, in a particularly convoluted essay in the *New York Times* (January 10, 1997), stated: "Ebonics makes broken English the equivalent of standard English" and argued that there is no evidence that Ebonics derives from Africa. Shelby Steele has screwed up his verbs. The truth is that Ebonics *is* something. It is a language variety. It doesn't *make* another language variety anything. And of course there is irrefutable evidence, which Steele obviously has not consulted, but which linguists at least as far back as Lorenzo Turner (1949) have presented, to establish the African origins of African American varieties of speech. As one reads Steele, who in his article called for academic rigor in schools, one can start to wonder why academic rigor is not required at the Hoover Institution, where he is employed as a research fellow. Even Jesse Jackson, who reversed his initial criticism of the Oakland school board, persists in referring to the patterned speech of Black children as "jive talk." Nobody jive talks better than Jesse, the undisputed rhyme laureate of African American

speech. But because he can also put standard semantics on display, as well as standard syntax—he never gets there phonologically; he be soundin' totally Black—he cannot see his way clear to view Ebonics as anything other than incorrect English.

Linguistics teaches us that African American Vernacular   4
English (AAVE) is a legitimate language variety in its own right. It is not a broken version of any other verbal system and has the same standing among linguists as any other variety of language, be it an English version or otherwise. Like spoken languages worldwide, AAVE is fully conceptual, is composed of between ten to seventy meaningful sounds; has consonants and the requisite number of vowels; has noun and verb elements; has rules of syntax; and contains statements, commands, questions, and exclamations. No linguist would talk about AAVE or Ebonics the way Koch, Steele, and Jackson do.

It is important to note, especially for the benefit of those   5
Black folk who get all uptight about their own speech and identity whenever Black English or anything that sounds like it is mentioned, that when linguists speak of African American Vernacular English, they are speaking about a set, or even sets, of linguistic features. They are not talking about people *per se.* They are talking about social practice, about performance, not innate capacity. In other words, anyone can speak this language variety, at least potentially, and no adult ever has to. And although there is a range of AAVE from lower prestige forms (basilect) to higher prestige forms (acrolect), and although most African Americans speak some version of AAVE, some do not, though this number is not as great as the number of speakers who would claim such status. I became sure about this last point as I heard AAVE speakers phone talk shows to argue that Ebonics should be discouraged.

Some of the people who do recognize the systematic nature   6
of Ebonics insist that it is at best a dialect and should not be described as a language. *They really trippin' on this one.* Nor, they argue, should the fact that Black children speak Ebonics lead to a claim on federal funds designated for bilingual education. However, linguistics does not back them on this score. Nor does all legal precedent.

Linguists shy away from making the superior-inferior sorts   7
of distinctions that the general public makes between languages and dialects because such distinctions are impossible to defend on strictly linguistic grounds. The problematic cases often cited by linguists, as you may have noticed in recent accounts, are that the major dialects of Chinese are mutually unintelligible while Norwegian and Swedish are mutually intelligible. So we can have two speakers in China who cannot

understand one another while they are said to be speaking the same language. And we can have two speakers in Scandinavia who can hold a conversation while each is said to be speaking a different language. Why does this situation exist? The answer is simple. Power. All the dialects of Chinese are under one state rule. If the heads of state want to call them all Chinese, then that's what they are called. Norway and Sweden are sovereign. If one nation wants to call its language Norwegian and the other wants to call a very similar language variety Swedish, then that's the way it is. But these are facts of politics, not linguistics. Norwegian is no more a language to linguists than any of the dialects of Chinese. Similarly, if some folks founded a nation, say, Ebonyland, and ensured that the official language of Ebonyland was Ebonics, then that's the way it would be. Ebonyland would be like Norway.

8   Two traditional ways of distinguishing dialects from languages are size and prestige. In other words, a language is said to be larger than any dialect of the language. If this definition were employed, however, then African American Vernacular English would have to be considered the linguistic equivalent of Standard English. Both forms would have to be considered dialects, among many others, of the total English language. AAVE is no more a dialect than Standard English is a dialect. It is no less a language than Standard English is a language. As for prestige, that is obviously a social, not linguistic, call. For a dialect to become a language in the prestige sense, it has to be selected over other language varieties, codified (usually with dictionaries and grammar books), employed in official functions, and accepted, even if by coercion, as the norm by a general populace. This is what occurred in the case of Standard English. If you insist that Standard English is a language and then label nonstandard varieties dialects, then you are merely affirming that Standard English has the juice. It is the dialect with the Army and Navy, to paraphrase an old phrase, and has the Air Force, Marines, Language Police, and Most Powerful Media Hitmen too!

9   One of the leading linguists in the country, MIT professor Steven Pinker, uses the terms "dialect" and "language" interchangeably when referring to African American Vernacular English. As he writes in his best-selling book, *The Language Instinct*, a passage which more or less captures how I be feelin about the whole thing as well, "the most linguistically interesting thing about the dialect is how linguistically uninteresting it is: if Labov did not have to call attention to it to debunk the claim that ghetto children lack true linguistic competence, it would have been filed away as just another

language" (pp. 29–30). Such filing away would be an acknowledgment that programs involving Ebonics should be eligible for federal funding under bilingual education initiatives. However, Secretary of Education Richard Riley has taken a strong stance against such a proposal, and many agree with him, a position that runs counter to several major legal decisions. In 1974, the decision in favor of the plaintiffs in the landmark *Lau* vs. *Nichols* lawsuit, filed on behalf of non-English-speaking Chinese students against the San Francisco Unified School District, helped to usher in the era of federal involvement in bilingual education. The same year, Congress reinforced the spirit of the *Lau* vs. *Nichols* decision by passing the Equal Educational Opportunities Act, which required schools to act to overcome language barriers that block full academic participation by students. This act was the basis for Judge Joiner's 1979 ruling in the celebrated King case. Joiner ruled that Black English had to become part of a preparation program for teachers at Ann Arbor's Martin Luther King, Jr. Elementary School. Viewed in the context of the legal history concerning language rights, the idea of seeking federal funding for Ebonics programs, although the Oakland school board says it is not going to do so, is not an outlandish idea at all.

Although evidence from linguistics shows clearly that noth- 10
ing in African American Vernacular English makes it *a priori* unsuitable for teaching and learning, proposals like the one made by the Oakland school board still will be attacked, even by those who concede to linguists the arguments made above, on the basis that any use of AAVE in formal educational settings is disabling to African American children. These critics contend that using it in school implies that Black children cannot learn Standard English; they assert that it lowers educational standards and perpetuates ghetto culture; they admonish that it holds kids back from success in the mainstream. I call these the "upward mobility criticisms." Unfortunately, these critics ignore the first principle of sociolinguistics, which is the study of language in relation to society. That principle is this: language use is inextricably connected to other social variables. Sociolinguistics does not tell us how important or determining any of those variables are in any given situation. This is why we have to study each situation on its own merits. But we can definitely say that language alone is not powerful enough to reject, fail, and exclude African Americans. Nor will language alone empower them. As Dell Hymes once noted, "everything depends, not on the presence of variation in speech—there is always that—but on whether, and to what extent, difference is invested with social meaning" (p. xxv).

Obviously, many young speakers of Ebonics invest their language use with a great deal of meaning. In many instances they are exhibiting hostility and resistance toward institutions they don't perceive to be operating in their best interests. Teachers, too, invest African American difference with meaning; difference is often a signal for them to fail students. So although there is no magic in a teacher preparation program that features attention to Ebonics, nor is there any harm, and there are potential benefits worth the venture. Recognition on the part of teachers that African American Vernacular English is a legitimate form of language certainly *could* spur students to embrace formal education and to expand their verbal repertoires. Such repertoire expansion is a complex and sophisticated feat to expect of students. The message contained therein is not that they cannot learn Standard English, but quite the opposite.

11 A curriculum will be successful to the extent that students subscribe to it. It's not that hard to figure out. If a fellow comes along and bellows, "march," some folks will merely ask how fast and others will defiantly ask why. Some will comply reluctantly and others will refuse altogether. Where I grew up, that fellow may get knocked upside his head and told to take them marching orders somewhere else. Language use involves similar choices. With respect to Standard English, I marched quite a bit myself. I often perceived it to be to my advantage to do so. I learned how to juggle standard and vernacular varieties to my communicative benefit, a juggling that linguists refer to as code-switching. I juggled several sub-identities into one big, complicated, code-switching identity. Even while running the streets, and running them pretty well from a street point of view, I always desired to be a player in the public arena, in respectable forums. I had my eye on the Civil Rights and Black Power movements as well as on school. At the beginning of my fifth grade James Meredith was shot while trying to attend the University of Mississippi. The murder of Medgar Wiley Evers occurred at the end of my fifth grade. "Freedom Summer" and the killing of Chaney, Schwerner, and Goodman marked my summer vacation after the sixth grade, the end of elementary school. During my junior high school days Malcolm X was assassinated. King's assassination and the growing popularity of the Black Panthers were memorable events during high school. I always wanted to voice opinions about the American social order and knew I had to acquire as much language power as I could to do so effectively. Along the way, and because of my goals, I excelled at reading and writing. Now the trip was not the smoothest one and in psychic terms it was expensive. But I

paid. This does not, however, mean that I could or should get anyone else to make the exact same payments. If I truly want to teach African American children to attain the language power I have, then I have to find a way to motivate them to achieve it. *Them,* not the assimilation-minded East European immigrants that are often held up as role models. *Them,* not the alienated African Americans who often put down these children and their communities.

Standard English may be cultural capital, so of course students should accumulate as much of it as they can. But such acquisition is not likely to be facilitated by programs that emphasize the eradication of AAVE or, frankly, by programs that merely focus on getting students to translate from AAVE to Standard English. If African American children perceived that social circumstances were in their favor, then learning another dialect would be viewed as favorable. In fact, it would be hard to *prevent* them from learning Standard English. Merely turning classrooms into translation seminars avoids the education in critical perspectives, especially about issues such as language, that African American children need to become the most insightful, and for my money most activist, members of society they can be. Merely pushing a doctrine of "translation for success in the mainstream" ignores some of the realities of American racism. James Sledd said years ago that "in job-hunting in America, pigmentation is more important than pronunciation." Top executives at Texaco have been proving him right. Remember, they were not taped saying, "keep those Ebonics-speaking jelly beans at the bottom of the jar." They said, "keep those *black* jelly beans at the bottom of the jar." Remember, too, that African American college graduates, among the best speakers of Standard English we have, earn a fraction of what white college graduates earn. What you look like, what you speak about, and whom you speak for can cancel out the so-called benefits of an uncritical verbal conformity to the dominant mode of expression.

The last major criticism I will address here is the notion that Ebonics is just a hustle by Afrocentrists. Brent Staples, for example (*New York Times,* January 4, 1997), actually uses more wordage slamming Kwanzaa, knocking Leonard Jeffries, speculating that Europeans would have fared quite badly under African slaveholders, and disparaging Afrocentricity in general than he does discussing Ebonics, a discussion he mishandles anyway with his talk about "broken English" and "poor speech." But despite this sort of uninformed posturing, programs involving Ebonics are justified in paradigms beyond Afrocentricity. Mainstream linguistics and solid ideas by an ethnically and ideologically diverse array of scholars could lead any intelligent person to recommend some use of Ebonics in a curriculum for some African American students. It was Basil Bernstein of the University of London Institute of Education, not some Afrocentrist, who wrote that "if the culture of the teacher is to become part of the consciousness of the child, then the culture of the child must first be in the consciousness of the teacher." Fundamentally, this is what the Oakland school board was arguing. Opposing such fundamentally sound reasoning don't never make no kind of sense to me.

Gary Larson
THE FAR SIDE

*Gary Larson grew up in Tacoma, Washington, and
from Washington State University. Though Larson
publishes new cartoons, "The Far Side" continues to b
America's most popular (and offbeat) cartoons.*

"Ha! The idiots spelled 'surrender' with only one 'r'!"

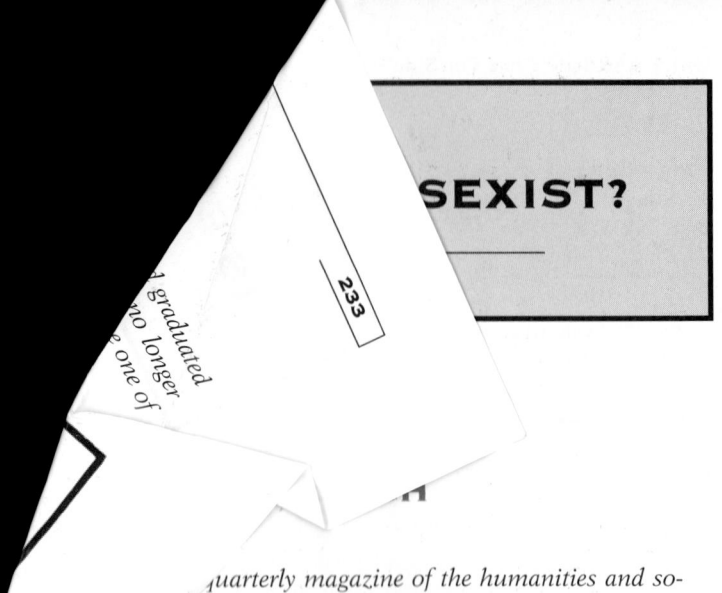

...quarterly magazine of the humanities and so-
...at is produced at Skidmore College, carries po-
...critical essays, and social analyses on a variety of
...the summer of 1994, it published the following med-
...on language by Beverly Gross, a professor of English at
...niversity of New York.

...were discussing Mary McCarthy's *The Group* in a course
...led Women Writers and Literary Tradition. McCarthy's biog-
...apher Carol Gelderman, I told the class, had been intrigued by
how often critics called Mary McCarthy a bitch. I read a few citations. "Her novels are crammed with cerebration and bitchiness" (John Aldridge). "Her approach to writing [is] reflective of
the modern American bitch" (Paul Schlueter). Why McCarthy?
a student asked. Her unrelenting standards, I ventured, her
tough-minded critical estimates—there was no self-censoring,
appeasing Angel in the House of Mary McCarthy's brain. Her
combativeness (her marital battles with Edmund Wilson became the stuff of academic legend). Maybe there were other factors. But the discussion opened up to the more inclusive issue
of the word bitch itself. What effect does that appellation have
on women? What effect might it have had on McCarthy? No one
ever called Edmund Wilson a bitch. Do we excuse, even pay respect when a man is critical, combative, assertive? What is the
male equivalent of the word bitch, I asked the class.

2   "Boss," said Sabrina Sims.

3   This was an evening class at a branch of the City University
of New York. Most of the students are older adults trying to fit
a college education into otherwise busy lives. Most of them
have fulltime jobs during the day. Sabrina Sims works on Wall

Street, is a single mother raising a ten year old daughter, is black, and had to take an Incomplete in the course because she underwent a kidney transplant in December.

Her answer gave us all a good laugh. I haven't been able to 4 get it out of my mind. I've been thinking about bitch, watching how it is used by writers and in conversation, and have explored its lexical history. "A name of reproach for a woman" is how Doctor Johnson's Dictionary dealt with the word in the eighteenth century, as though anticipating the great adaptability of this particular execration, a class of words that tends toward early obsolescence. Not bitch, however, which has been around for a millennium, outlasting a succession of definitions. Its longevity is perhaps attributable to its satisfying misogyny. Its meaning matters less than its power to denounce and subjugate. Francis Grose in *A Classical Dictionary of the Vulgar Tongue* (1785) considered bitch "the most offensive appellation that can be given to an English woman, even more provoking than that of whore." He offered as evidence "a low London woman's reply on being called a bitch" in the late eighteenth century: "I may be a whore but can't be a bitch!" The meaning of bitch has changed over the centuries but it remains the word that comes immediately to the tongue, still "the most offensive appellation" the English language provides to hurl at a woman.

The *Oxford English Dictionary* records two main meanings 5 for the noun bitch up through the nineteenth century:

1. The female of the dog
2. Applied opprobriously to a woman; strictly a lewd or sensual woman. Not now in decent use.

It was not until the twentieth century that bitch acquired its 6 opprobrious application in realms irrespective of sensuality. The Supplement to the *OED* (1972) adds:

2a: "In mod. use, esp. a malicious or treacherous woman."

Every current desk dictionary supplies some such meaning:

A spiteful, ill-tempered woman [*World Book Dictionary*]

A malicious, unpleasant, selfish woman, esp. one who stops at nothing to reach her goal. [*Random House Dictionary*]

But malice and treachery only begin to tell the story. The informal questionnaire that I administered to my students and a number of acquaintances elicited ample demonstration of the slippery adaptability of bitch as it might be used these days:

a conceited person, a snob
a self-absorbed woman
a complainer
a competitive woman
a woman who is annoying, pushy, possibly underhanded (in
    short, a man in a woman's body)
someone rich, thin and free!

7   "A word used by men who are threatened by women" was one astute response. Threat lurks everywhere: for women the threat is in being called a bitch. "Someone whiny, threatening, crabby, pestering" is what one woman offered as her definition. "Everything I try hard not to be," she added, "though it seeps through." I offer as a preliminary conclusion that bitch means to men whatever they find threatening in a woman and it means to women whatever they particularly dislike about themselves. In either case the word functions as a misogynistic club. I will add that the woman who defined bitch as everything she tries hard not to be when asked to free associate about the word came up immediately with "mother." That woman happens to be my sister. We share the same mother, who was often whiny and crabby, though I would never have applied the word bitch to her, but then again, I don't consider whiny, crabby and pestering to be prominent among my own numerous flaws.

8   Dictionaries of slang are informative sources, in touch as they are with nascent language and the emotive coloration of words, especially words of abuse. A relatively restrained definition is offered by the only female lexicographer I consulted for whom bitch is "a nasty woman" or "a difficult task" (Anita Pearl, *Dictionary of Popular Slang*). The delineations of bitch by the male lexicographers abound with such cascading hostility that the compilers sometimes seem to be reveling in their task. For example, Howard Wentworth and Stuart Berg Flexner in *Dictionary of American Slang*:

A woman, usu., but not necessarily, a mean, selfish, malicious, deceiving, cruel, or promiscuous woman.

Eugene E. Landy's *The Underground Dictionary* (1971) offers:

1. Female who is mean, selfish, cruel, malicious, deceiving. a.k.a. cunt.
2. Female. See Female.

I looked up the entry for "Female" (Landy, by the way, provides 9
no parallel entry for "Male"):

> beaver, bird, bitch, broad, bush, cat, chick, crack, cunt,
> douche, fish, fox, frail, garbage can, heffer, pussy, quail,
> ruca, scag, snatch, stallion, slave, sweet meat, tail, trick,
> tuna. See GIRLFRIEND; WIFE.

Richard A. Spear's *Slang and Euphemism* comments on the derivative adjective:

> bitchy 1. pertaining to a mood wherein one complains inces-
> santly about anything. Although this applies to men or
> women, it is usually associated with women, especially when
> they are menstruating. Cf. DOG DAYS

Robert L. Chapman's definition in *Thesaurus of American* 10
Slang starts off like a feminist analysis:

> bitch. 1 n. A woman one dislikes or disapproves of.

Followed, however, by a sobering string of synonyms:
"broad, cunt, witch."

And then this most interesting note:

> Female equivalents of the contemptuous terms for men,
> listed in this book under "asshole," are relatively rare.
> Contempt for females, in slang, stresses their putative sexual
> promiscuity and weakness rather than their moral vile-
> ness and general odiousness. Some terms under "asshole,"
> though, are increasingly used of women.

"See ball-buster." Chapman suggests under his second defin- 11
ition for bitch ("anything arduous or very disagreeable"). I
looked up "ball-buster":

> n. Someone who saps or destroys masculinity.
> ball-whacker
> bitch
> nut-cruncher.

Some*thing* has become some*one*. The ball-buster is not a dis- 12
agreeable thing but a disagreeable (disagreeing?) person. A female person. "A woman one dislikes or disapproves of." For
someone so sensitive to the nuances of hostility and verbal put-
down, Chapman certainly takes a circuitous route to get to the

underlying idea that no other dictionary even touches: Bitch means ball-buster.

13   What one learns from the dictionaries: there is no classifiable thing as a bitch, only a label produced by the act of name-calling. The person named is almost always a female. The name-calling refers to alleged faults of ill-temper, selfishness, malice, cruelty, spite, all of them faults in the realm of interpersonal relating—women's faults: it is hard to think of a put-down word encompassing these faults in a man. "Bastard" and even "son of a bitch" have bigger fish to fry. And an asshole is an asshole in and of himself. A bitch is a woman who makes the name-caller feel uncomfortable. Presumably that name-caller is a man whose ideas about how a woman should behave toward him are being violated.

14   "Women," wrote Virginia Woolf, "have served all these centuries as looking-glasses possessing the magic and delicious power of reflecting the figure of man at twice its natural size." The woman who withholds that mirror is a bitch. Bitchiness is the perversion of womanly sweetness, compliance, pleasantness, ego-building. (Male ego-building, of course, though that is a virtual tautology; women have egos but who builds them?) If a woman is not building ego she is busting balls.

15   Ball-buster? The word is a nice synecdoche (like asshole) with great powers of revelation. A ball-buster, one gathers, is a demanding bitch who insists on overexertion from a man to satisfy her sexual or material voraciousness. "The bitch is probably his wife." But balls also bust when a disagreeable woman undermines a guy's ego and "saps or destroys masculinity." The bitch could be his wife, but also his boss, Gloria Steinem, the woman at the post office, the woman who spurns his advances. The familiar Freudian delineation of the male-female nexus depicts male sexuality as requiring the admiration, submission and subordination of the female. The ultimate threat of (and to) the back-talking woman is male impotence.

16   Bitch, the curse and concept, exists to insure male potency and female submissiveness. Men have deployed it to defend their power by attacking and neutralizing the upstart. "Bitch" is admonitory, like "whore," like "dyke." Borrowing something from both words, "bitch" is one of those verbal missiles with the power of shackling women's actions and impulses.

17   The metamorphosis of bitch from the context of sexuality (a carnal woman, a promiscuous woman) to temperament (an angry woman, a malicious woman) to power (a domineering woman, a competitive woman) is a touchstone to the changing position of women through this century. As women have become more liberated, individually and collectively, the word

has taken on connotations of aggressive, hostile, selfish. In the old days a bitch was a harlot; nowadays she is likely to be a woman who won't put out. Female sensuality, even carnality, even infidelity, have been supplanted as what men primarily fear and despise in women. Judging by the contemporary colorations of the word bitch, what men primarily fear and despise in women is power.

Some anecdotes: 18
1) Barbara Bush's name-calling of Geraldine Ferraro during the 1984 presidential election: "I can't say it but it rhymes with 'rich.'"

How ladylike of the future First Lady to avoid uttering the 19
unmentionable. The slur did its dirty work, particularly among those voters disturbed by the sudden elevation of a woman to such unprecedented political heights. In what possible sense did Barbara Bush mean that Geraldine Ferraro is a bitch? A loose woman? Hardly. A nasty woman? Not likely. A pushy woman? Almost certainly. The unspoken syllable was offered as a response to Ferraro's lofty ambitions, potential power, possibly her widespread support among feminists. Imagine a woman seeking to be vice-president instead of vice-husband.

The ascription of bitchery seems to have nothing to do with 20
Ferraro's bearing and behavior. Certainly not the Ferraro who wrote about the event in her autobiography:

Barbara Bush realized what a gaffe she had made. . .

"I just want to apologize to you for what I said," she told me over the phone while I was in the middle of another debate rehearsal. "I certainly didn't mean anything by it."

"Don't worry about it," I said to her. "We all say things at times we don't mean. It's all right."

"Oh," she said breathlessly. "You're such a lady."

All I could think of when I hung up was: Thank God for my convent school training.

2) Lady Ashley at the end of *The Sun Also Rises:* "It makes one 21
feel rather good, deciding not to be a bitch." The context here is something like this: a bitch is a woman who ruins young heroic bullfighters. A woman who is propelled by her sexual drive, desires and vanity. The fascination of Brett Ashley is that she lives and loves like a man: her sexuality is unrepressed and she doesn't care much for monogamy. (Literary critics until the 1960s commonly called her a nymphomaniac.) She turns her male admirers into women—Mike becomes a self-destructive

alcoholic, Robert a moony romantic, Pedro a sacrificial virgin, and Jake a frustrated eunuch. At her entrance in the novel she is surrounded by an entourage of twittering fairies. Lady Ashley is a bitch not because she is nasty, bossy or ill-tempered (she has lovely manners and a terrific personality). And perhaps not even because of her freewheeling, strident sexuality. She is a bitch because she overturns the male/female nexus. What could be a more threatening infraction in a Hemingway novel?

22   2a) Speaking of Hemingway: After his falling out with Gertrude Stein who had made unflattering comments about his writing in *The Autobiography of Alice B. Toklas,* Hemingway dropped her off a copy of his newly published *Death in the Afternoon* with the handwritten inscription, "A bitch is a bitch is a bitch."
      [Q.] Why was Gertrude Stein a bitch?
      [A.] For no longer admiring Hemingway. A bitch is a woman who criticizes.

23   3) "Ladies and gentlemen. I don't believe Mrs. Helmsley is charged in the indictment with being a tough bitch" is how her defense lawyer Gerald A. Feffer addressed the jury in Leona Helmsley's trial for tax fraud and extortion. He acknowledged that she was "sometimes rude and abrasive," and that she "may have overcompensated for being a woman in a hard-edged men's business world." Recognizing the difficulty of defending what the New York *Post* called "the woman that everyone loves to hate," his tactic was to preempt the prosecution by getting there first with "tough bitch." He lost.

24   4) *Esquire* awarded a Dubious Achievement of 1990 to Victor Kiam, owner of the New England Patriots football team, for saying "he could never have called Boston *Herald* reporter Lisa Olson 'a classic bitch' because he doesn't use the word classic." Some background on what had been one of that year's most discussed controversies: Olson aroused the ire of the Patriots for showing up in their locker room with the male reporters after a game. Members of the Patriots, as *Esquire* states, surrounded her, "thrusting their genitals in her face and daring her to touch them."

25   Why is Lisa Olson a bitch? For invading the male domain of sports reportage and the male territory of the locker room? For telling the world, instead of swallowing her degradation, pain and anger? The club owner's use of "bitch" seems meant to conjure up the lurking idea of castrating female. Seen in that

light the Patriots' act of "thrusting their genitals in her face" transforms an act of loutishness into a position of innocent vulnerability.

5) Bumper sticker observed on back of pickup truck: 26

> Impeach Jane Fonda, American Traitor Bitch

The bumper sticker seemed relatively new and fresh. I observed it a full two decades after Jane Fonda's journey to North Vietnam which is the event that surely inspired this call to impeachment (from what? aerobics class?). Bitch here is an expletive. It originates in and sustains anger. Calling Jane Fonda a "traitor" sounds a bit dated in the 1990s, but adding "bitch" gives the accusation timelessness and does the job of rekindling old indignation.

6) Claude Brown's account in *Manchild in the Promised Land* of   27
how he learned about women from a street-smart older friend:

> Johnny was always telling us about bitches. To Johnny, every chick was a bitch. Even mothers were bitches. Of course there were some nice bitches, but they were still bitches. And a man had to be a dog in order to handle a bitch.
>
> Johnny said once, "If a bitch ever tells you she's only got a penny to buy the baby some milk, take it. You take it, 'cause she's gon git some more. Bitches can always git some money." He really knew about bitches. Cats would say, "I saw your sister today, and she is a fine bitch." Nobody was offended by it. That's just the way things were. It was easy to see all women as bitches.

Bitch in black male street parlance seems closer to its origi-   28
nal meaning of a female breeder—not a nasty woman and not a powerful woman, but the biological bearer of litters. The word is likely to be used in courting as well as in anger by males seeking the sexual favor of a female, and a black female addressed as bitch by an admirer is expected to feel not insulted but honored by the attention. (Bitch signifies something different when black women use it competitively about other black women.) But even as an endearment, from male to female, there is no mistaking the lurking contempt.

A Dictionary of Afro-American Slang compiled by Clarence   29
Major (under the imprint of the leftist International Publishers) provides only that bitch in black parlance is "a

mean, flaunting homosexual," entirely omitting any reference to its rampant use in black street language as the substitute word for woman. A puzzling omission. Perhaps the word is so taken for granted that its primary meaning is not even recognized as black vernacular.

30   Bitch, mama, motherfucker—how frequently motherhood figures in street language. Mothers are the object of insults when playing the dozens. The ubiquitous motherfucker simultaneously strikes out at one's immediate foe as well as the sanctity of motherhood. Mama, which Clarence Major defines as "a pretty black girl," is an endearment that a man might address to a sexy contemporary. "Hey mama" is tinged with a certain sweetness. "Hey bitch" has more of an edge, more likely to be addressed to a woman the man no longer needs to sweet-talk. It is hard to think of white males coming on by evoking motherhood or of white women going for it. A white male addressing a woman as bitch is not likely to be expecting a sexual reward. She will be a bitch behind her back and after the relationship is over or didn't happen.

31   The widespread use of bitch by black men talking to black women, its currency in courting, and its routine acceptance by women are suggestive of some powerful alienation in male-female relations and in black self-identity. Although there may be the possibility of ironic inversion, as in calling a loved one nigger, a black man calling a loved one bitch is expressing contempt for the object of his desire with the gratuitous fillip of associative contempt for the woman who gave him life. Bitch, like motherfucker, bespeaks something threatening to the male sense of himself, a furious counter to emasculation in a world where, as the young Claude Brown figured out, mothers have all the power. It is not hard to see that the problem of black men is much more with white racism than it is with black women. Whatever the cause, however, the language sure doesn't benefit the women. Here is still one more saddening instance of the victim finding someone even more hapless to take things out on. (Does this process explain why Clarence Major's only reference for bitch is to the "mean, flaunting homosexual"?)

32   7) "Do you enjoy playing that role of castrating bitch" is a question put to Madonna by an interviewer for *The Advocate*. Madonna's answer: "I enjoy expressing myself. . . ."

33   A response to another question about the public's reaction to her movie *Truth or Dare:* "They already think I'm a cunt bitch, they already think I'm Attila the Hun. They already compare me to Adolf Hitler and Saddam Hussein."

Bitch has lost its power to muzzle Madonna. Unlike other fe- 34
male celebrities who have cringed from accusations of bitchiness (Joan Rivers, Imelda Marcos, Margaret Thatcher, Nancy
Reagan), Madonna has made her fortune by exploiting criticism. Her career has skyrocketed with the media's charges of
obscenity and sacrilege; she seems to embrace the bitch label
with the same eager opportunism.

"I enjoy expressing myself" is not merely the explanation for 35
why Madonna gets called bitch; "I enjoy expressing myself" is
the key to defusing the power of bitch to fetter and subdue.
Madonna has appropriated the word and turned the intended
insult to her advantage. This act of appropriation, I predict,
will embolden others with what consequences and effects it is
impossible to foresee.

David F. Sally

GENDERATOR I.I:
A MODISH PROPOSAL

*David Sally (born 1960) teaches courses in management at the
business school at Cornell University. He is especially interested in how language functions within organizations. In 1999
he published the following spoof in* Georgia Review, *a quarterly magazine of the arts and culture that publishes fiction,
poetry, reviews, and scholarly articles.*

Dear *person*⊗[1] or *individual*⊗[6],

Remember the last time you were writing and somehow, despite all your best attempts to keep your analysis structural
and your text within bounds, you found yourself describing a
given categorical, individual human being? Then, after following a single phrase down this path, you faced a second that, for
efficiency's sake, demanded a personal pronoun? Take, for example, this sentence from a recent issue of the *American
Journal of Politics:* "The death of the American voter paradoxically implies that in a Chicagonian fashion, [_____] will be
able to vote twice." What do you put in the blank? How do you

refer to the prototypical voter? Is *he* a *he* or *not a he*♂[8]?*You are confronted with the need to put on what we here at the Neuter Corporation refer to as the GENDERATION CAP™. When you wear this cap you are not just picking a personal pronoun, you are making a political statement.

God knows, using language is getting harder all the time. Let's look at the current options you have in the sentence above. If you use *he*, then every reader can only guess where on the right wing you are positioned: are you a fascist Neanderthal willing to promulgate the continued oppression of women through the biased use of language, or an uncaring conservative who ignores the deleterious effects of conventional personal pronouns in favor of preserving tradition? On the other hand, if you use *she*, then you imperfectly signal to the reader that you are located on the left somewhere between a sensitive, caring liberal capable of achieving even more enlightenment than you already have, and a rabid communist who names a daughter Karla and a dog Barx.

If you are a political independent, you are even more out of luck. *It* is unavailable. The constructions, *he or she* or *she/he* or *she or he* or *he or she*, require that one gender take spatial/temporal precedence. A footnote attached to your first use of a personal pronoun explaining your deep concern about this issue and your numerous reasons for choosing either *he* or *she* will be ignored by many readers in light of your apparent political bias; random selection of a pronoun cannot be verified by the reader and hence can never be trusted.

Everyone loses! Those who wish to be unlabeled cannot be, and those who wish to wear their ideological hearts on their rhetorical sleeves may be mislabeled. And it's not just pronouns: other words—verbs, adjectives, and even prepositions—are suffused with meanings that you have a hard time controlling.

Now, the Neuter Corporation is proud to introduce a word processing tool/utensil that will make all your gender worries vanish in the night—GENDERATOR 1.1®!

GENDERATOR 1.1 is fully compatible with Windows 98, works seamlessly with all major word processing and desktop publishing programs, and uses only 50k of EWE♀[10]. GENDERATOR 1.1 will almost certainly be approved shortly by all the major journals in literary criticism and sociology, and by many in political science, art history, psychology, and history.*

*This question has been genderated. As you read further here you will notice how much more meaningful it is and how much more you learn about the author!

You will never find another syntactic program this easy to use. Once you are done typing a document, you simply click on the Genderator icon ☿, specify a particular set of options based either on provided labels or on custom menus, and then let the powerful and sensitive search-and-replace engine do its work in the blink of an eye. Each and every nominal change initiated by the program is italicized and marked with an appropriate icon (♀ and ♂ for left and right, respectfully respectively; ⊗ for neutrality). The icon is then given a specific numerical exponent to indicate fervor and seriousness (you can find examples throughout this brochure). We like to say, "Be a proponent—use the exponent!"

For professional publication we suggest that you use one of the packaged options that allows your editors and readers to be fully informed with regard to your ideological preferences. The program will automatically print, either within the title/author footnote or within the author's *acknowledgmynts* ♀^{5}, the phrase "Genderated @ _____ and guaranteed by the Neuter Corporation," with the blank being filled by one of the preset package names such as "really random," "revolutionary red," "burning Burke," or "flaming Foucault." To learn more about specific features of GENDERATOR I.I, find your category in the ideological spectrum that follows:

Liberal. No longer will you have to be tormented by the thought of your reader not appreciating just how sensitive and enlightened you are. If confusion about your own reality, identity, and gender has led you to refer to yourself only through third person pronouns, then think how the female side of (what might be) you will be comforted, knowing that the "wicked Woolf" level of GENDERATOR I.I is doing all the expressing. At sensitivity levels of ♀^{7} and above, this program is capable of spotting crossword, anagrammatic, and homonymic insensitivity: "Wilbur's pen is home to a variety of animals" would become "The enclosure of Wilbur is..."; Dorothy's quest would take her to the "Efemerald City"; and the automatic replacement of "penal code" by "the set of statutes dealing with crimes and punishments" will finally unfetter the field of feminist criminal studies.

Among the Liberal preset packages offered is "mocking MacKinnon," an option designed especially for humorous pieces. Watch as "mocking MacKinnon" works wonders in

---

*We are hopeful that within the next few months the *American Economic Review* and the *Journal of Theoretical Biology* will become new clients. There are unresolved problems in chemistry and zoology due to such proper nouns as *maleate, hymenopteron,* and *myna.*

combining the magic of power, gender, and laughter in this passage from Jonathan Swift's infamous essay:

> I, *being the oppressive male that I am* ♀^{3}, think it is agreed by all parties that this prodigious number of children in the arms, or on the backs, or at the heels of their mothers, *i.e., postsocietally transmuted womyn* ♀^{8}, and frequently of their fathers, *i.e., postsocietally transmuted worms* ♀^{8}, is in the present deplorable state of the kingdom a very great additional grievance; and, therefore, whoever could find out a fair, cheap, and easy method of making these children sound, useful members of the commonwealth, would deserve so well of the public as to have his statue set up for a preserver of the nation, *as if I even need to comment on the obvious connections among patriarchy, statuary, and phony phalluses* ♀^{7}.

Just think: if GENDERATOR 1.1 can cut this decrepit Brobdingnagian down to size, obviously it can help you turn the rest of the so-called Literary Canon into mere fodder!

Unrepentant Conservative. You are tired of all the games people play with the English language, and you want those people to know it. If *he* was good enough for the Greeks and the Romans and the Bible, it is good enough for you and for everybody else. Why waste any time even thinking about this issue? GENDERATOR 1.1 gives you this freedom from thought. Just use the simple, pull-down windows to reveal "Doctor Johnson," for example, or some other conservative guardian of English, and rest assured that your document will boldly satisfy every convention. At levels of rigidity of ♂^{7} and above, this program will even suggest ways in which your prose can be altered to transform third-person-plural phrases to singular ones, to utilize phallic metaphors and symbols, and to employ telling anagrams such as "spineless."

The only socially constructed roles you believe in are the ones from Pillsbury that your wife pops in the oven for dinner. Imagine the pleasure of improving Shakespeare by combining the "full-well Falwell" content option with the "Quayle quality" grammatical option, as in this dramatic monologue:

> *Oh* Romeo, Romeo, are *you therefor* Romeo?
> Deny *your* father, *who works so hard to provide for you and
> your mother* ♂^{6}, and refuse *your* name;
> swear, *but not with the Lord's name* ♂^{4}, to   Or, if *you* will not,
> be my love,
> And I'll no longer be a Capulet,
> *But a Montague, since I will take your last name as all good
> wives should* ♂^{8}.

Moreover, you can count your blessings that after the plot is genderated at "full-well Falwell," Romeo never lays his hands on Juliet's balcony until after they are married!

Modern language, orthodox pronouns, and good old-fashioned family values . . . GENDERATOR I.I lets you have it all!

Independent. It used to be that if you didn't want to get involved, you could just say so. But times have changed. Uninvolvement requires its own language of meaning and a new passion. Think of GENDERATOR I.I as the soap and water that allow you to wash your hands of the controversy over biased language, your neutrality expressible in two ways: first, there is a special icon, ⟨♂⟩, the Spinning Randogenderator©, that will randomly produce either masculine or feminine pronominal forms. The reputation of the Neuter Corporation stands behind the stochasticity of this function, and assures the reader that you had no idea what you were writing.

Second, depending on the level of neutrality you specify, common nouns such as *human being, person,* and *individual* will fill the role of personal pronouns. These substitutes appear on a pop-up menu and change as your need for impartiality increases: at $\otimes^2$, *humyn* is a possible selection; at $\otimes^4$, *per offspring* may be chosen; at the maximal level of uninvolvement, the only term available is *individual*, which receives a subscript, e.g., "The tension within Henry Fielding between licentious convention and conventional license is revealed in *Tom Jones:* '*Individual$_1$'s* intentions were strictly honourable, as the phrase is; that is, to rob an *individual$_2$ of individuals$_2$'s* fortune by way of marriage $\otimes^{10}$.'"* With GENDERATOR I.I, your honorable intent to stay well out of the fray can finally be recognized!

Best of all, no matter what your position on objective reality, GENDERATOR I.I is now available at a special low price for all academic users. Don't let the new standard in language processing pass you by. Depending on how you employ it, GENDERATOR I.I can allow you to spend a lot more time on substance and a lot less on form or, a lot more on form and a lot less on substance. It's up to the individual, and the way *she* wants to use *his* time ⟨♂⟩.

---

*Yoon, S. H. 1996. "Fielding's *Tom Jones:* Woe, woe, woe, is he a lady?" *Critical Review of Canonical Literature*, v. 2:235–48. Note that this journal was one of the first to make GENDERATOR I.I obligatory.

Our guarantee to you, our valued customer, is to keep you fully *achest* ⊗[5] of the latest refinements in social language. As more labels are attached to more words, we promise to *mail* ♂[1] to your *residential postal location* ♀[3] frequent updates of GEN-DERATOR software, including special offers on future versions that *speak directly to* ♀[3] such areas as:

Race
Generational Conflict
Ethnicity
Sexual Orientation.

Please call 1-800-NEUTRAL to reserve your new trial copy of GENDERATOR I.I. We guarantee your satisfaction, and we hope that you will continue to look to the Neuter Corporation for all your sensitive, social, syntactic software needs.

This cartoon appeared in The New Yorker, *famous for its very funny and rather sophisticated cartoons. Is the cartoon just for fun, or does it make a serious point?*

"You'll just love the way he handles."

Drawing by Bernard Schoenbaum; © 1991 The New Yorker Magazine, Inc.

Deborah Tannen
CROSSTALK

Deborah Tannen, a professor of linguistics at Georgetown University in Washington, D.C., published You Just Don't Understand: Women and Men in Conversation *in 1990. This exploration of the complexities of communication between men and women became a national best-seller. The following selection from the book has been printed elsewhere as a self-contained piece.*

A woman who owns a bookstore needed to have a talk with the store manager. She had told him to help the bookkeeper with billing, he had agreed, and now, days later, he still hadn't done it. Thinking how much she disliked this part of her work, she sat down with the manager to clear things up. They traced the problem to a breakdown in communication.

She had said, "Sarah needs help with the bills. What do you think about helping her out?" He had responded, "OK," by which he meant, "OK, I'll think about whether or not I want to help her." During the next day, he thought about it and concluded that he'd rather not.

This wasn't just an ordinary communication breakdown that could happen between any two people. It was a particular sort of breakdown that tends to occur between women and men.

Most women avoid giving orders. More comfortable with decision-making by consensus, they tend to phrase requests as questions, to give others the feeling they have some say in the matter and are not being bossed around. But this doesn't mean they aren't making their wishes clear. Most women would have understood the bookstore owner's question, "What do you think about helping her out?" as assigning a task in a considerate way.

The manager, however, took the owner's words literally. She had asked him what he thought; she hadn't told him to *do* anything. So he felt within his rights when he took her at her word, thought about it and decided not to help Sarah.

Women in positions of authority are likely to regard such responses as insubordination: "He knows I am in charge, and he knows what I want; if he doesn't do it, he is resisting my authority."

There may be a kernel of truth in this view—most men are inclined to resist authority if they can because being in a subordinate position makes them intensely uncomfortable. But indirect requests that are transparent to women may be genuinely opaque to men. They assume that people in authority will give orders if they really want something done.

8 These differences in management styles are one of many manifestations of gender differences in how we talk to one another. Women use language to create connection and rapport; men use it to negotiate their status in a hierarchical order. It isn't that women are unaware of status or that men don't build rapport, but that *the genders tend to focus on different goals.*

The Source of Gender Differences

9 These differences stem from the way boys and girls learn to use language while growing up. Girls tend to play indoors, either in small groups or with one other girl. The center of a girl's social life is her best friend, with whom she spends a great deal of time sitting, talking and exchanging secrets. It is the telling of secrets that makes them best friends. Boys tend to play outdoors, in larger groups, usually in competitive games. It's doing things together that makes them friends.

10 Anthropologist Marjorie Harness Goodwin compared boys and girls at play in a black innercity neighborhood in Philadelphia. Her findings, which have been supported by researchers in other settings, show that the boys' groups are hierarchical: high-status boys give orders, and low-status boys have to follow them, so they end up being told what to do. Girls' groups tend to be egalitarian: girls who appeared "better" than others or gave orders were not countenanced and in some cases were ostracized.

11 So while boys are learning to fear being "put down" and pushed around, girls are learning to fear being "locked out." Whereas high-status boys establish and reinforce their authority by giving orders and resisting doing what others want, girls tend to make suggestions, which are likely to be taken up by the group.

Cross-Gender Communication in the Workplace

12 The implications of these different conversational habits and concerns in terms of office interactions are staggering. Men are inclined to continue to jockey for position, trying to resist following orders as much as possible within the constraints of their jobs.

Women, on the other hand, are inclined to do what they 13
sense their bosses want, whether or not they are ordered to.
By the same token, women in positions of authority are inclined to phrase their requests as suggestions and to assume
they will be respected because of their authority. These assumptions are likely to hold up as long as both parties are
women, but they may well break down in cross-gender communication.

When a woman is in the position of authority, such as the 14
bookstore owner, she may find her requests are systematically
misunderstood by men. And when a woman is working for a
male boss, she may find that her boss gives bald commands
that seem unnecessarily imperious because most women
would prefer to be asked rather than ordered. One woman who
worked at an all-male radio station commented that the way
the men she worked for told her what to do made her feel as if
she should salute and say, "Yes, boss."

Many men complain that a woman who is indirect in mak- 15
ing requests is manipulative: she's trying to get them to do
what she wants without telling them to do it. Another common accusation is that she is insecure: she doesn't know
what she wants. But if a woman gives direct orders, the same
men might complain that she is aggressive, unfeminine or
worse.

Women are in a double bind: *If we talk like women, we are* 16
not respected. If we talk like men, we are not liked.

We have to walk a fine line, finding ways to be more direct 17
without appearing bossy. The bookstore owner may never be
comfortable by directly saying, "Help Sarah with the billing today," but she might find some compromise such as, "Sarah
needs help with the billing. I'd appreciate it if you would make
some time to help her out in the next day or two." This request
is clear, while still reflecting women's preferences for giving
reasons and options.

What if you're the subordinate and your boss is a man who's 18
offending you daily by giving you orders? If you know him well
enough, one potential solution is "metacommunication"—that
is, talk about communication. Point out the differences between women and men, and discuss how you could accommodate to each other's styles. (You may want to give him a copy of
this article or my book.)

But if you don't have the kind of relationship that makes 19
metacommunication possible, you could casually, even jok-
ingly, suggest he give orders another way. Or just try to remind
yourself it's a cross-cultural difference and try not to take his
curtness personally.

How to Handle a Meeting

20   There are other aspects of women's styles that can work against us in a work setting. Because women are most comfortable using language to create rapport with someone they feel close to, and men are used to talking in a group where they have to prove themselves and display what they know, a formal meeting can be a natural for men and a hard nut to crack for women. Many women find it difficult to speak up at meetings; if they do, they may find their comments ignored, perhaps later to be resuscitated by a man who gets credit for the idea. Part of this is simply due to the expectation that men will have more important things to contribute.

21   But the way women and men tend to present themselves can aggravate this inequity. At meetings, men are more likely to speak often, at length and in a declamatory manner. They may state their opinions as fact and leave it to others to challenge them.

22   Women, on the other hand, are often worried about appearing to talk too much—a fear that is justified by research showing that when they talk equally, women are perceived as talking more than men. As a result, many women are hesitant to speak at a meeting and inclined to be succinct and tentative when they do.

Developing Options

23   Working on changing your presentational style is one option; another is to make your opinions known in private conversation with the key people before a meeting. And if you are the key person, it would be wise to talk personally to the women on your staff rather than assuming all participants have had a chance to express themselves at the meeting.

24   Many women's reticence about displaying their knowledge at a meeting is related to their reluctance to boast. They find it more humble to keep quiet about their accomplishments and wait for someone else to notice them. But most men learn early on to display their accomplishments and skills. And women often find that no one bothers to ferret out their achievements if they don't put them on display. Again, a woman risks criticism if she talks about her achievements, but this may be a risk she needs to take, to make sure she gets credit for her work.

I would never want to be heard as telling women to adopt   25
men's styles across the board. For one thing, there are many
situations in which women's styles are more successful. For example, the inclination to make decisions by consensus can be a
boon to a woman in a managerial position. Many people, men
as well as women, would rather feel they have influence in decision-making than be given orders.

Moreover, recommending that women adopt men's styles   26
would be offensive, as well as impractical, because women are
judged by the norms for women's behavior, and doing the same
thing as men has a very different, often negative, effect.

A Starting Point

Simply knowing about gender differences in conversational   27
style provides a starting point for improving relations with the
women and men who are above and below you in a hierarchy.

The key is *flexibility;* a way of talking that works beautifully   28
with one person may be a disaster with another. If one way of
talking isn't working, try another, rather than trying harder to
do more of the same.

Once you know what the parameters are, you can become an   29
observer of your own interactions, and a style-switcher when
you choose.

RACE AND GENDER

Introduction

One of the stunning social developments of the twentieth century has been the economic and political and cultural emergence of women and people of color. Beginning with the success of the women's suffrage movement early in the century and continuing through the civil rights movement and a series of legal and legislative victories in the past forty years, the women's movement and the movement for civil rights for nonwhite Americans have largely achieved the goal of political equality in the United States—at least on paper. But that has not closed discussion of women's concerns and of the means of combating racism, of course, because social, economic, and political parity between women and men and between African Americans and European Americans remains incomplete and because the specific terms of social and economic liberation have not yet been agreed on. In fact, discussion of racial issues and gender issues has intensified in the past decade as race and gender concerns continue to be negotiated through public discourse. This part of *Conversations* barely begins to capture the range of issues currently under debate, but it does present discussions of three general issues: How do you define race? How do you define gender? And should affirmative action policies continue? (In addition, issues of race and gender are taken up elsewhere in this book, most notably—but not only—in Part Two, Language, in Part Four, Family Matters, and the sections in Part Five on pornography, civil disobedience, and abortion.)

In the midst of all the discussions related to race in the United States, it is inevitable that the question of the nature of race itself would be raised as an issue. Is race something that is biologically determined? If so, what features distinguish one race from another—skin color? The shape of one's eyes or nose? Or what? What happens to the concept of race when people of different "races" intermarry and have children? Is it reasonable to consider someone "black" if only one of that person's grandparents was African American, or does that merely perpetuate the outdated thinking of antimiscegenation laws? How and why do people think of themselves in one or another racial or ethnic category? Although people in the past assumed that racial designations corresponded to particular physical traits, now many argue that racial identities derive from social and historical forces, that those designations can vary over time—and that such designations are now being reconsidered in the United States. In the past decade, since multicultural and multiethnic considerations have been pressed, since immigration from Latin America and Asia has created new citizens less easily categorized than in the past, since interracial marriage has become more common, and since some vestiges of segregation have become less virulent, it seems that racial categories are particularly being reconsidered. To many people, Americans have taken a too "binary" approach to race; while other nations (rightly or wrongly) often recognize gradations of color in their citizens, Americans often persist in thinking of race as an either-or proposition. While in one sense, black-white antagonisms have persisted in the face of challenges to affirmative action and the continuation of social inequities in our society, in another sense those antagonisms seem somehow anachronistic as Americans shift their views of race in the face of a social interrogation of the concept of race itself. Consequently, the first section of this part considers definitions of race—especially the question of whether inherited notions of race benefit our national community.

The concept of race is not the only thing that is being redefined right now. Until very recently it was men who defined women, mostly in a misogynist (women-hating) tradition that is deeply seated in Western cultures. But the fact that women are now involved in defining gender roles has not effaced that tradition of misogyny, nor has it ended discussion of the nature of those roles. Just what form will the feminist revolution take? Just what is it that defines the essential natures of women and men? Beyond reproductive differences, are there inevitable distinctions between the sexes in terms of emotions, sexuality, physiology, morals, values, and so forth? Or are all such distinctions the result of social conditioning—social conditioning that might be altered? That is the basic issue under discussion in the second section of this part. A half dozen or so selections of various kinds describe, explain, dramatize, or argue for various positions on the question of the "essential natures" of women and men and the extent to which history and culture and environment determine those natures. The selections also illustrate the range of voices that can be summoned in support of a discussion of gender roles. While most of the selections address women's concerns directly, each one has direct and indirect implications for men as well.

Gender issues and race issues have been emphasized in a central document of the civil rights movement, the Civil Rights Act of 1964, which attempted to eradicate discrimination from a range of public institutions in the United States. Part of Title VII of that act prohibited discrimination on the job because of race, color, religion, sex, or national origin:

> It shall be an unlawful employment practice for an employer... to fail or refuse to hire or to discharge any individual, or otherwise to discriminate against any individual with respect to his compensation, terms, conditions, or privileges of employment, because of such individual's race, color, religion, sex, or national origin.... It shall be an unlawful employment practice for any employer, labor organization, or joint labor-management committee controlling apprenticeship or other training or retraining, including on-the-job training programs, to discriminate against any individual because of his race, color, religion, sex, or national origin in admission to, or employment in, any program established to provide apprenticeship or other training.... If the court finds that the respondent has intentionally engaged in an unlawful employment practice... the court may enjoin the respondent from engaging in such unlawful employment practice, and order such affirmative action as may be appropriate.

Title VII thus initiated a period of "affirmative action" to redress past injustices and to establish for everyone the possibility of equal opportunity.

But just what should affirmative action mean? Should it be a means of ensuring that everyone has a chance to compete on equal terms for jobs and education? Or should it denote a more active process of ensuring equal results, especially for people who arrive at jobs and schools with disadvantages that arise from past inequality? For some people, affirmative action means the former; in the words of the late Hubert Humphrey, nothing in Title VII should "give any power to the [Civil Rights] Commission or any court to require hiring, firing, or promotion of employees in order to meet a racial quota." For others, however, affirmative action means action: active measures (at least in the short run) such as goals, timetables, guidelines, and quotas designed to promote balanced results.

Are such actions fair? Is affirmative action a legitimate, short-term measure for breaking up a rigid caste system and for ameliorating the long-term effects of Jim Crow laws, sexist traditions, and inequitable education policies? Or is it inherently unfair? Has the "short-term" expired by now? Can we now justify passing over someone or favoring someone else because of the group that person is born into? Is the goal of affirmative action the reduction of social injustice or proportional representation of all races and both sexes? Is affirmative action inefficient, in that it favors racial and gender factors over job performance? Or is it more efficient, in that it speeds the progress of women and minorities and therefore allows those people a chance, at last, to show their right stuff? Does affirmative action damage self-esteem or promote it? Should colleges and universities eliminate racial and gender preferences in admissions decisions? Finally, would affirmative action make better sense if it were administered on a class-wide basis instead of on the basis of race or gender? Those sensitive questions are discussed in the selections reprinted here on affirmative action.

So where do you stand on these questions of race and gender? The selections in this part are designed to provoke further discussion, not to close it off. In fact, a premise of this part on race and gender is that by engaging in open, public discourse on these complex questions, writers can hasten the day when the effects of racial and sexual polarization—perhaps racial and sexual polarization itself— might be minimized and when codes of personal behavior might be more freely chosen, to the benefit of everyone.

DEFINING RACE

▪

Sharon Begley
THREE IS NOT ENOUGH

The following essay was published as a Newsweek *magazine story on February 13, 1995. Since the cover of* Newsweek *that day posed the question, "What Color Is Black?" this was one of several essays in the magazine that discussed one or another aspect of the issue of defining race: one considered biracial children and interracial marriage; another looked at affirmative action; still another was a historical analysis of definitions of race in the United States. Sharon Begley is a senior writer for* Newsweek, *where her work often appears.*

1   To most Americans race is as plain as the color of the nose on your face. Sure, some light-skinned blacks, in some neighborhoods, are taken for Italians, and some Turks are confused with Argentines. But even in the children of biracial couples, racial ancestry is writ large—in the hue of the skin and the shape of the lips, the size of the brow and the bridge of the nose. It is no harder to trace than it is to judge which basic colors in a box of Crayolas were combined to make tangerine or burnt umber. Even with racial mixing, the existence of primary races is as obvious as the existence of primary colors.

2   Or is it? C. Loring Brace has his own ideas about where race resides, and it isn't in skin color. If our eyes could perceive more than the superficial, we might find race in chromosome 11: there lies the gene for hemoglobin. If you divide humankind by which of two forms of the gene each person has, then equatorial Africans, Italians and Greeks fall into the "sickle-cell race"; Swedes and South Africa's Xhosas (Nelson Mandela's ethnic group) are in the healthy-hemoglobin race. Or do you prefer to group people by whether they have epicanthic eye folds, which produce the "Asian" eye? Then the !Kung

San (Bushmen) belong with the Japanese and Chinese. Depending on which trait you choose to demarcate races, "you won't get anything that remotely tracks conventional [race] categories," says anthropologist Alan Goodman, dean of natural science at Hampshire College.

The notion of race is under withering attack for political and cultural reasons—not to mention practical ones like what to label the child of a Ghanaian and a Norwegian. But scientists got there first. Their doubts about the conventional racial categories—black, white, Asian—have nothing to do with a sappy "we are all the same" ideology. Just the reverse. "Human variation is very, very real," says Goodman. "But race, as a way of organizing [what we know about that variation], is incredibly simplified and bastardized." Worse, it does not come close to explaining the astounding diversity of humankind—not its origins, not its extent, not its meaning. "There is no organizing principle by which you could put 5 billion people into so few categories in a way that would tell you anything important about humankind's diversity," says Michigan's Brace, who will lay out the case against race at the annual meeting of the American Association for the Advancement of Science.   3

About 70 percent of cultural anthropologists, and half of physical anthropologists, reject race as a biological category, according to a 1989 survey by Central Michigan University anthropologist Leonard Liebermnan and colleagues. The truths of science are not decided by majority vote, of course. Empirical evidence, woven into a theoretical whole, is what matters. The threads of the argument against the standard racial categories: 4

• **Genes:** In 1972, population biologist Richard Lewontin of Harvard University laid out the genetic case against race. Analyzing 17 genetic markers in 168 populations such as Austrians, Thais and Apaches, he found that there is more genetic difference within one race than there is between that race and another. Only 6.3 percent of the genetic differences could be explained by the individuals' belonging to different races. That is, if you pick at random any two "blacks" walking along the street, and analyze their 23 pairs of chromosomes, you will probably find that their genes have less in common than do the genes of one of them with that of a random "white" person. Last year the Human Genome Diversity Project used 1990s genetics to extend Lewontin's analysis. Its conclusion: genetic variation from one individual to another of the same "race" swamps the average differences between racial groupings. The more we learn about humankind's genetic differences, says   5 geneticist Luca Cavalli-Sforza of Stanford University, who chairs the committee that directs the biodiversity project, the more we see that they have almost nothing to do with what we call race.

6 • **Traits:** As sickle-cell "races" and epicanthic-fold "races" show, there are as many ways to group people as there are traits. That is because "racial" traits are what statisticians call non-concordant. Lack of concordance means that sorting people according to *these* traits produces different groupings than you get in sorting them by *those* (equally valid) traits. When biologist Jared Diamond of UCLA surveyed half a dozen traits for a recent issue of *Discover* magazine, he found that, depending on which traits you pick, you can form very surprising "races." Take the scooped-out shape of the back of the front teeth, a standard "Asian" trait. Native Americans and Swedes have these shovel-shaped incisors, too, and so would fall in the same race. Is biochemistry better? Norwegians, Arabians, north Indians and the Fulani of northern Nigeria, notes Diamond, fall into the "lactase race" (the lactase enzyme digests milk sugar). Everyone else—other Africans, Japanese, Native Americans—forms the "lactase-deprived race" (their ancestors did not drink milk from cows or goats and hence never evolved the lactase gene). How about blood types, the familiar A, B and O groups? Then Germans and New Guineans, populations that have the same percentages of each type, are in one race; Estonians and Japanese comprise a separate one for the same reason, notes anthropologist Jonathan Marks of Yale University. Depending on which traits are chosen, "we could place Swedes in the same race as either Xhosas, Fulani, the Ainu of Japan or Italians," writes Diamond.

7 • **Subjectivity:** If race is a valid biological concept, anyone in any culture should be able to look at any individual and say, Aha, you are a . . . It should not be the case, as French tennis star Yannick Noah said a few years ago, that "in Africa I am white, and in France I am black" (his mother is French and his father is from Cameroon). "While biological traits give the impression that race is a biological unit of nature," says anthropologist George Armelagos of Emory University, "it remains a cultural construct. The boundaries between races depend on the classifier's own cultural norms."

8 • **Evolution:** Scholars who believe in the biological validity of race argue that the groupings reflect human pre-history. That is, populations that evolved together, and separately from others, constitute a race. This school of thought holds that blacks should all be in one race because they are descended from people who stayed on the continent where humanity be-

gan. Asians, epitomized by the Chinese, should be another race because they are the children of groups who walked north and east until they reached the Pacific. Whites of the pale, blond variety should be another because their ancestors filled Europe. Because of their appearance, these populations represent the extremes, the archetypes, of human diversity—the reds, blues and yellows from which you can make every other hue. "But if you use these archetypes as your groups you have classified only a very tiny proportion of the world's people, which is not very useful," says Marks, whose incisive new book "Human Biodiversity" deconstructs race. "Also, as people walked out of Africa, they were differentiating along the way. Equating 'extreme' with 'primordial' is not supported by history."

Often, shared traits are a sign of shared heritage—racial heritage. "Shared traits are not random," says Alice Brues, an anthropologist at the University of Colorado. "Within a continent, you of course have a number of variants [on basic traits], but some are characteristic of the larger area, too. So it's natural to look for these major divisions. It simplifies your thinking." A wide distribution of traits, however, makes them suspect as evidence of a shared heritage. The dark skin of Somalis and Ghanaians, for instance, indicates that they evolved under the same selective force (a sunny climate). But that's all it shows. It does *not* show that they are any more closely related, in the sense of sharing more genes, than either is to Greeks. Calling Somalis and Ghanaians "black" therefore sheds no further light on their evolutionary history and implies—wrongly—that they are more closely related to each other than either is to someone of a different "race." Similarly, the long noses of North Africans and northern Europeans reveal that they evolved in dry or cold climates (the nose moistens air before the air reaches the lungs, and longer noses moisten more air). The tall, thin bodies of Kenya's Masai evolved to dissipate heat; Eskimos evolved short, squat bodies to retain it. Calling these peoples "different races" adds nothing to that understanding.

Where did the three standard racial divisions come from? They entered the social, and scientific, consciousness during the Age of Exploration. Loring Brace doesn't think it's a coincidence that the standard races represent peoples who, as he puts it, "lived at the end of the Europeans' trade routes"— in Africa and China—in the days after Prince Henry the Navigator set sail. Before Europeans took to the seas, there was little perception of races. If villagers began to look different to an Englishman riding a horse from France to Italy and on to Greece, the change was too subtle to inspire notions of races. But if the English sailor left Lisbon Harbor and dropped anchor off the Kingdom of Niger, people looked so different he felt compelled to invent a scheme to explain the world—and, perhaps, distance himself from the Africans.

11   This habit of sorting the world's peoples into a small number of groups got its first scientific gloss from Swedish taxonomist Carolus Linnaeus. (Linnaeus is best known for his system of classifying living things by genus and species—*Escherichia coli, Homo sapiens* and the rest.) In 1758 he declared that humanity falls into four races: white (Europeans), red (Native Americans), dark (Asians) and black (Africans). Linnaeus said that Native Americans (who in the 1940s got grouped with Asians) were ruled by custom. Africans were indolent and negligent, and Europeans were inventive and gentle, said Linnaeus. Leave aside the racist undertones (not to mention the oddity of ascribing gentleness to the group that perpetrated the Crusades and Inquisition): that alone should not undermine its validity. More worrisome is that the notion and the specifics of race predate genetics, evolutionary biology and the science of human origins. With the revolutions in those fields, how is it that the 18th-century scheme of race retains its powerful hold? Consider these arguments:

12   • **If I parachute into Nairobi, I know I'm not in Oslo:** Colorado's Alice Brues uses this image to argue that denying the reality of race flies in the face of common sense. But the parachutists, if they were familiar with the great range of human diversity, could also tell that they were in Nairobi rather than Abidjan—east Africans don't look much like west Africans. They could also tell they were in Istanbul rather than Oslo, even though Turks and Norwegians are both called Caucasian.

13   • **DOA, male, 5'11".. . black:** When U.S. police call in a forensic anthropologist to identify the race of a skeleton, the scientist comes through 80 to 85 percent of the time. If race has no biological validity, how can the sleuths get it right so often? The forensic anthropologist could, with enough information about bone structure and genetic markers, identify the region from which the corpse came—south and west Africa, Southeast Asia and China, Northern and Western Europe. It just so happens that the police would call corpses from the first two countries black, from the middle two Asian, and the last pair white. But lumping these six distinct populations into three groups of two serves no biological purpose, only a social convention. The larger grouping may reflect how society views humankind's diversity, but does not explain it.

14   • **African-Americans have more hypertension:** If race is not real, how can researchers say that blacks have higher rates of infant mortality, lower rates of osteoporosis and a higher in-

cidence of hypertension? Because a social construct can have biological effects, says epidemiologist Robert Hahn of the U.S. Centers for Disease Control and Prevention. Consider hypertension among African-Americans. Roughly 34 percent have high blood pressure, compared with about 16 percent of whites. But William Dressler finds the greatest incidence of hypertension among blacks who are upwardly mobile achievers. "That's probably because in mundane interactions, from the bank to the grocery store, they are treated in ways that do not coincide with their self-image as respectable achievers," says Dressler, an anthropologist at the University of Alabama. "And the upwardly mobile are more likely to encounter discriminatory white culture." Lab studies show that stressful situations—like being followed in grocery stores as if you were a shoplifter—elevate blood pressure and lead to vascular changes that cause hypertension. "In this case, race captures social factors such as the experience of discrimination," says sociologist David Williams of the University of Michigan. Further evidence that hypertension has more to do with society than with biology: black Africans have among the lowest rates of hypertension in the world.

If race is not a biological explanation of hypertension, can it 15 offer a biological explanation of something as complex as intelligence? Psychologists are among the strongest proponents of retaining the three conventional racial categories. It organizes and explains their data in the most parsimonious way, as Charles Murray and Richard Herrnstein argue in "The Bell Curve." But anthropologists say that such conclusions are built on a foundation of sand. If nothing else, argues Brace, every ethnic group evolved under conditions where intelligence was a requirement for survival. If there are intelligence "genes," they must be in all ethnic groups equally: differences in intelligence must be a cultural and social artifact.

Scientists who doubt the biological meaningfulness of race 16 are not nihilists. They just prefer another way of capturing, and explaining, the great diversity of humankind. Even today most of the world's peoples marry within their own group. Intramarriage preserves features—fleshy lips, small ears, wideset eyes—that arose by a chance genetic mutation long ago. Grouping people by geographic origins—better known as ethnicity—"is more correct both in a statistical sense and in understanding the history of human variation," says Hampshire's Goodman. Ethnicity also serves as a proxy for differences—from diet to a history of discrimination—that can have real biological and behavioral effects.

17   In a 1942 book, anthropologist Ashley Montagu called race "Man's Most Dangerous Myth." If it is, then our most ingenuous myth must be that we sort humankind into groups in order to understand the meaning and origin of humankind's diversity. That isn't the reason at all; a greater number of smaller groupings, like ethnicities, does a better job. The obsession with broad categories is so powerful as to seem a neurological imperative. Changing our thinking about race will require a revolution in thought as profound, and profoundly unsettling, as anything science has ever demanded. What these researchers are talking about is changing the way in which we see the world—and each other. But before that can happen, we must do more than understand the biologist's suspicions about race. We must ask science, also, why it is that we are so intent on sorting humanity into so few groups—us and Other—in the first place.

Karla Brundage

PASSING

Karla Brundage, a graduate of Vassar College, teaches now in Hawaii. She offers more information about herself in the following essay, which was published in Multi-America, *a collection of several dozen essays exploring multiculturalism that was edited by the well-known writer and multiculturalist Ishmael Reed and published in 1997.*

1   It happens all the time. . . I am walking down the street and a complete stranger stops me, maybe even interrupting my conversation, and urgently asks, "What are you?"

2   Or I am minding my own business, living on my street, when I notice that the Black woman who lives next door to me, who has a child the same age as my child, blatantly ignores my "hellos" and my "we should have tea sometimes." Then one day I find that we have a friend in common. From this friend I learn the reason for her standoffishness. My neighbor does not know I am Black, but I live with a very Black man. She finds such a relationship repulsive. I make her sick.

3   What about my other neighbor, a Black woman of forty-plus with a grown child, who speaks only to my partner, and won't even wave to me from the car?

Or what about my sister-in-law who warned me, serious and   4
superstitious, "Don't cut that hair, girl. You know your man
won't like it; you got good hair."

I can't forget my partner's teacher and spiritual leader, who   5
said offhand to him after meeting me, "Shit, man, you already
got yourself a white girl."

"White girl! White girl! How dare he," came my response.   6

My partner looked at me almost innocently and said, "Karla,   7
he didn't mean what you think he meant. What he meant was . . . "

"Don't even try to explain. I know what he meant . . . "   8

"But. . . "   9

"I said, I know what he meant. I certainly don't need you to   10
try and explain it. End of conversation."

He was talking about passing. He was talking about all of   11
those instances I just listed. He was trying to explain my life to
me. Do I think I am white? Many people want to know. Do I
think I can pass as Black? I cannot give a definitive answer.
That is the problem. People are always trying to define me,
while at the same time limiting my answer. I have had people
ask me what I am, and then refuse to believe me. Others never
ask; they just hate me for not fitting into their little box.
Meanwhile, I have been teaching myself all my life to define
myself in uncertainties, in abstractions, in illusions. I am not
who you think I am. Even you, reader, may have a fixed opinion from generalizations that are easy to make. My vital statistics make stereotyping even easier.

I was born in Berkeley in 1967. My parents were flower chil-   12
dren. According to my father, they thought they could save the
world through love. The story is shaky. I think they really got
married for two totally different reasons. My mother, who was
born and raised in Tuskegee, Alabama, had gone to all-white
boarding schools much of her life. I don't think she planned to
marry white, but it happened. My father, who was from
Pleasantville, New York, came from a dysfunctional alcoholic
family. He was being educated at a liberal arts college, and he
really felt that there was no better way to live out his newfound
beliefs than by marrying this Black woman he met on a college
exchange and with whom he fell head over heels in love. He believed—and still believes—that by having an interracial child,
along with others in their generation they would be one step
closer to ending racism.

So I was born with a cross to carry, so to speak. I say this be-   13
cause I have always known of my father's expectations as well
as his bitterness that the sexual revolution did not save the
world, and especially at the failure of his marriage, which
could not overcome racism. But that's another story.

14   This is who I am and where I came from: conservative, middle class, educated, on both sides, Black and white. My parents were the rebels. They were married until I was three. During this time, my mother's first cousin, who was involved with SNCC, was killed for using a white bathroom. It is my opinion that my mother could never really love my father in the same way after that incident. After all, his family is very racist. I have some relatives who still refuse to meet me. After her cousin Sammy's death, my mother became involved with the Black Panthers, and my father became resentful that she could exclude him from her life when, in his mind, he had sacrificed his, having been disowned as a result of the marriage. So they moved to Hawaii to try to escape the racism that they had once been willing to fight. This is the beginning of my memory.

15   I lived with my mother. I had a happy childhood, most of which was spent outdoors, playing. However, although my mother is a professor in African American studies at the University of Hawaii, she could not provide for me what did not exist. I knew of racism, I knew I was Black, but I did not grow up knowing what it is to be Black. I had no Black culture or community. In Hawaii, there are many brown people. I was brown, so I fit right in. I basically grew up as a local girl. If people asked, I would tell them I was Black, but people rarely asked. In a weird way, I have been passing for something or another all my life.

16   I remember at seven and eight wishing to be Hawaiian. I wanted nothing more than to really be what people thought I was. I wanted to go to Kamehameha School, which is a school for people who have traceable Hawaiian blood in them. I can remember using my spare time, when I wasn't swimming in the ocean or running relay races in our huge yard, trying to think up ways to get into that school. In the bathtub was one of my favorite places to dream. I would stand in front of the mirror wet and with a towel on, pretending it was native Hawaiian garb, and that I was really Hawaiian. I don't remember when I accepted the fact that it would not happen.

17   In seventh grade, my mother told me that we were going to move to the mainland for a couple of years. My fantasy changed, although not so abruptly. I remember now at age twelve lying in bed and praying to God: "God, please let California be fun. Let me have a boyfriend, and God, if there is any way, can you please take the time to look at my eyes? See God, they are brown. And God, my dad has blue eyes. I know that people in California have blue eyes and light skin. I mean, they are white. I don't have to be white, but maybe while I am

there I will be a little lighter, and then I'll be tan, and if my eyes were blue. . . It would be perfect, not to mention my hair, which if it were just a little lighter. My dad has blond hair; if only I could just look more like my dad. I am not asking for much, just to look more like my dad than my mom. Please, God, just let me be more beautiful."

This is not a lie or even an exaggeration. I prayed this prayer all the way up until the night we left. Many years later when I read Toni Morrison's *The Bluest Eye*, I broke down crying from relief. My secret was out, and it wasn't just me. *The Bluest Eye* connected me to other Black women in a way I had never been able to connect, in that I am always told that, because of my near-white attributes, I somehow think I am better than others. That story is one of the truest tales I know. 18

So I moved, but not to California. Instead, I moved with my father to upstate New York; Hope, to be exact. I lived in Hope for one year. I hoped that no one would find out that I was black. I often wonder what it was that made me think I needed to pass in order to survive up there in the land where my father was raised and the KKK thrives. Was it my mother, who cried every day before I left, telling me that people are racist, especially when they see a brown girl with a white man? Or was it my father, who did not give me the strength to stand up for who I was. I remember telling him that I told my new friends I was Hawaiian, but I don't remember him giving me any helpful advice. I didn't even have to lie; it was easier than that. When they asked where I was from, I said, "Hawaii." And they said, "Oh, so you're Hawaiian, then." And I just smiled, my killer Hawaiian smile. All the people in Hope were thrilled, because they had a real Hawaiian living in their town. My wish had come true. 19

The only problem was my mother. She ruined my plan. She called almost every other night from California, and cried. "Karla, don't deny me," she would say, "please, don't deny me. Don't lie about who you are." But I was thirteen, I had never been Black before, and I wanted to have friends. I was in a new place completely foreign to me. It was too hard. I chose to tell only one person who I really was. She was my best friend, her name was Squeaker. And Squeak she did. It wound up that eventually everybody found out that I was really Black. Some people resented that. Some were just bummed that I was not a "real" Hawaiian. But I really think that misleading them to think I was Hawaiian first softened the blow. I mean, I was already a cheerleader by the time the word got out. This was what I think was the beginning of a long series of events in which I learned how to objectify myself in order to survive. I 20 was making myself more and more invisible, in order to escape the lasso of definition.

21   In ninth grade, I finally did move to Oakland, California. In Oakland, I was for the first time immersed in Black culture. And for the first time, I had a boyfriend who told me I was beautiful for who I was, a Black girl with a white father. Of course, this was my first love, and he was also mixed. What I did not know about was the deadly lines drawn between dark and light within the Black community itself. Since I did not know, I existed happily. Loving myself for perhaps the first time. I had Black and white friends. I declared myself a rebel from the traditional cliques of high school, the "stoners," who were white; the Chicanos; and the soul or disco lovers, who were Black. I declared myself a peacemaker between the three sides, neutral by virtue of my skin. After all, I looked more Chicano than anything. For a time it was my father's dream of racelessness come true.

22   When I finally went to college, passing became an issue again. Once again I found myself on a plane bound for upstate New York—Poughkeepsie, to be exact. Vassar College was like no place I had been before. Looking back on it, I see that I spent most of my college career in culture shock. I was not only adapting to race but to class differences. I entered Vassar with the same attitude that I had when I left Oakland. I was Black and white, and therefore part of both groups.

23   What I found at Vassar was that I could never be a part of the elite white world, and worse, the Blacks there resented me for even trying. I remember walking into the cafeteria on the first day of school with my new roommate, who happened to be white. I walked past a table where all ten of the Black freshmen were eating dinner and said hello. They barely looked at me, and when I walked away I heard someone comment that I must think I am white. From the first day, I was never accepted by the African Americans at Vassar; it was a very small, very tight group. Those who were mixed were forced to choose sides, and most of us chose white. The animosity between lighter- and darker-skinned Blacks, especially women, was a part of Black culture that I did not yet understand. I did not get why they would hate me or why they would think I thought I was white.

24   I was so hurt. I figured if they did not like me, then I would just hang out with the whites. This was a big mistake. During my entire college career, I was never invited to anyone's house for Thanksgiving, I was never asked to a ball. What I could not see was that with the whites, I was accepted as an object, an exotic. I existed on the periphery.

To lessen the pain, I drank excessively and found myself sink- 25
ing deeper and deeper into a hole of self-hatred. Yet I refused to
see my rejection as racially motivated, until one night when I was
at the school bar, drunk as usual. A man I had slept with grabbed
me and locked me in a phone booth. While in the phone booth,
we began to argue about what had happened between us. I accused him and many of his friends of using me. To this he replied,
"Don't you see, Karla, it's your fault! You are beautiful, so beautiful and exotic, and don't you know what that does to men?"

That night I cut off all my hair. That night I also began to see 26
that I had been trying to be white most of the time I was at college, and that in reality, I did not know who I was. By the time
I graduated, I was an alcoholic, and I knew that I had to go
back to Oakland to be around Black people.

I don't know if I thought it would be better to be in the Black 27
community, but I knew that I was missing something. I have
lived in Oakland for five years now, and one thing I have
learned is that as a people, we as Blacks have been truly indoc-
trinated into racist ways. When I first arrived, I obtained a position as a teacher's aide at a home for emotionally disturbed
teens, many of whom were Black. These youths had nothing to
hide in their evaluations of me. I began to notice by their reactions to me the confusion we feel as a people about our skin.
Most did not believe I was Black. I found myself in a position
again where I felt forced to disguise my real identity. Instead of
answering that I was part Black, mixed, *hapa*, half, or mulatto—all terms that I had used my entire life—I found myself
saying I was Black. I wanted so desperately to be accepted as
Black, but still no one would believe me. Whenever I said,
"Black," in response to the question, "What are you?", the person attacking me would say, "Black and what. . . ?"

So, I began to denounce my whiteness. I was angry at my fa- 28
ther for cursing me. I was angry at all white people for being
racists and for promoting racism everywhere. Once again I
looked for acceptance of my new identify in men. I chose Black
men who were "revolutionary" in their beliefs, men who had
forsaken the system completely. Over and over I found myself
in the same predicament. I was not Black enough for them. Yet
to this day almost all the men in that group are living with (off)
white women. Naturally, I began to hate white women. All the
anger I had felt at Vassar surfaced and I was able to bond with
Black women for the first time, as well as justify my hypocrisy,
until I began to realize that many Black women hated me, too,
for the same reasons. They thought I was white.

This was my latest disillusion. It was really all too much for 29
me. I opened my eyes and began to look at my life. Many of my

friends are mixed. Not deliberately, but maybe out of some common pool of experience. I realized that it was not only hypocritical but impossible to hate my father, a part of myself. At the age of twenty-five, I finally realized that I am mixed. Not definable, not in any box, and probably not all that new a phenomenon. But certainly an enigma.

30   Still, people are constantly trying to define me—all people, white and Black. For a while I wanted to wear a sign around my neck that said, "I am Black." But slowly I began to realize, I am not just Black. I certainly am not white. I am mixed. What does it mean to be a mixed-race, Black/white woman in America in the nineties? Recently, my mother told me that we are actually one-eighth Cherokee. This is another part of me that I never even explored, let alone identified with. I am still trying to figure it all out, but I think right now it's about defining myself, taking that step to say, Hey, I am mixed. I am not going to pretend anymore. I am not going to go to Castlemont, a predominantly Black high school in East Oakland, and argue with teenagers about my race. I am not going to drive myself to the point of suicide trying to be white, either. I am just going to be me.

Linda Hogan

Linda Hogan, a Chickasaw, was born in Denver in 1947 and grew up in Oklahoma. A poet, novelist, essayist, and playwright, she now teaches creative writing at the University of Colorado. Hogan's work has won wide acclaim and many awards, including a Guggenheim Fellowship. Her poems often touch on environmental concerns, and she is active in the antinuclear movement. Her poem "The History of Red" comes from her 1993 collection The Book of Medicines, *and the one following it, "Heritage," appeared in* Red Clay, *a 1991 book of stories and poems.*

THE HISTORY OF RED

First
there was some other order of things
never spoken
but in dreams of darkest creation.

Then there was black earth,   5
lake, the face of light on water.
Then the thick forest all around
that light,
and then the human clay
whose blood we still carry   10
rose up in us
who remember caves with red bison
painted in their own blood,
after their kind.

A wildness   15
swam inside our mothers,
desire through closed eyes,
a new child
wearing the red, wet mask of birth,
delivered into this land   20
already wounded,
stolen and burned
beyond reckoning.

Red is this yielding land
turned inside out   25
by a country of hunters
with iron, flint and fire.
Red is the fear
that turns a knife back
against men, holds it at their throats,   30
and they cannot see the claw on the handle,
the animal hand
that haunts them
from some place inside their blood.

So that is hunting, birth,   35
and one kind of death.
Then there was medicine, the healing of wounds.
Red was the infinite fruit
of stolen bodies.
The doctors wanted to know   40
what invented disease
how wounds healed
from inside themselves
how life stands up in skin,
if not by magic.   45

They divined the red shadow of leeches
that swam in white bowls of water;
they believed stars
in the cup of sky,
50   They cut the wall of skin
to let
what was bad escape
but they were reading the story of fire
gone out
55   and that was a science.

As for the animal hand on death's knife,
knives have as many sides
as the red father of war
who signs his name
60   in the blood of other men.

And red was the soldier
who crawled
through a ditch
of human blood in order to live.
65   It was the canal of his deliverance.

It is his son who lives near me.
Red is the thunder in our ears
when we meet.
Love, like creation,
70   is some other order of things.

Red is the share of fire
I have stolen
from root, hoof, fallen fruit.
And this was hunger.

75   Red is the human house
I come back to at night
swimming inside the cave of skin
that remembers bison.
In that round nation
80   of blood
we are all burning,
red, inseparable fires
the living have crawled
and climbed through
85   in order to live
so nothing will be left
for death at the end.

This life in the fire, I love it,
I want it,
this life.   90

HERITAGE

From my mother, the antique mirror
where I watch my face take on her lines.
She left me the smell of baking bread
to warm fine hairs in my nostrils,
she left the large white breasts that weigh down   5
my body.

From my father I take his brown eyes,
the plague of locusts that leveled our crops,
they flew in formation like buzzards.

From my uncle the whittled wood   10
that rattles like bones
and is white
and smells like all our old houses
that are no longer there. He was the man
who sang old chants to me, the words   15
my father was told not to remember.

From my grandfather who never spoke
I learned to fear silence.
I learned to kill a snake
when begging for rain.   20

And grandmother, blue-eyed woman
whose skin was brown,
she used snuff.
When her coffee can full of black saliva
spilled on me   25
it was like the brown cloud of grasshoppers
that leveled her fields.
It was the brown stain
that covered my white shirt.
That sweet black liquid like the food   30
she chewed up and spit into my father's mouth
when he was an infant.

It was the brown earth of Oklahoma
stained with oil.
She said tobacco would purge your body of poisons. 35

It has more medicine than stones and knives
against your enemies.
That tobacco is the dark night that covers me.

She said it is wise to eat the flesh of deer
40   so you will be swift and travel over many miles.
She told me how our tribe has always followed a stick
that pointed west
that pointed east.
From my family I have learned the secrets
45   of never having a home.

Demian Hess
BUT YOU DON'T
LOOK CHINESE!

*Demian Hess first published the following account of his expe-
riences in 1995 in the* Journal of the Asian American
Renaissance. *Since then the article has been reprinted on the
Internet by the organization known as Interracial Voice, which
promotes understanding of interracial issues.*

1   I've never felt particularly "oppressed." Or outraged. Or angry
or upset or downtrodden or victimized. Well, maybe not "never."
But I've never carried a grudge about it. I've never had an ax to
grind. I've never felt I had a statement to make about the
RACISM in our SOCIETY or the OPPRESSION by the DOMI-
NANT CULTURE. Capital letters give me a headache, I guess.
And I guess my friends would be surprised if I did make a fuss.
2   "But, what have you got to complain about?" they say to me.
"You're not a minority." And when I point out to them that, in
fact, I am a minority: "Oh, well, yeah, your mom's Chinese, but
you're not. I mean, you don't look Chinese."
3   Yeah, I don't look Chinese. I've heard that before.
4   I remember this one time when I lived in Rhode Island. I was
taking the bus home from the beach when this old woman got
on board. The bus was half empty, but she chose to sit down
right next to me.
5   "You're Jewish, aren't you?" she said, just like that, right after she sat down. I stared at her for a second and then admitted

that, yes, I was Jewish. I have no idea how she knew. Maybe it was the nose. I had this tiny little bean-shaped nose until I was about twelve, and then a huge mass exploded out of my face. The family nose. The Jewish stigma.

"You can always tell," the old woman said, and patted my knee. "It's so nice to have someone to talk to, I hardly ever see anyone. My children, they never call, they never visit. It's so hard when you're old. You'll see." 6

Then she stopped and squinted at me. "But you're not all Jewish, are you?" she said. I shook my head and explained that my mother was Chinese. "Oh," she said, and paused. "Well, don't worry. It doesn't show." 7

She was right, it doesn't show. And I guess that I'm lucky it doesn't show. But I wasn't born lucky. I was born looking Chinese and I grew up looking Chinese. When I was six, I had straight black hair, this tiny little bean nose, almond-shaped eyes and yellow skin. I was very slight, not stocky-tending-to-fat like other kids. I seemed to speak differently, too, although I'm not sure whether that's actually a Chinese trait or not. Did it have something to do with the size and shape of my Asiatic larynx and nasal passages? I don't know, but to my ear I had a strange pitch to my voice, a sort of high, lilting, whistling quality that made me cringe to hear it on tape. I'm probably crazy to think there's anything Chinese about this part of myself. 8

Whether or not my voice was really different, my appearance certainly was, and none of the other kids in school ever let me forget it. When I was five, my folks had moved to a little farm in the Born Again Bible Belt of Minnesota. That's Hickesville, the Boonies, Red Neck City. Everyone was white. Germanic or Scandinavian, maybe a little English, but white. And Christian. My family wasn't any of those things. My parents were hippies, atheists, graduate students. And not white. Well, OK, so my father was white, but my mother definitely wasn't. The neighbors didn't know exactly what she was. Chinese? Indian? It didn't matter. She was brown. And so were her kids. 9

"Chin Chan, China man, get his meals from a garbage can." I heard that nearly every week from the other kids, as they danced around me during recess, making slanty eyes with their fingers. Actually, this came from the more enlightened bigots. The ones who had taken the time to study the issue and determine which racial category I belonged to and which slur was appropriate. Most didn't bother with such distinctions. 10

"You see this?" a student asked me one day, pointing to a small, green country on the globe. I peered at it. It was Nigeria. "See that? That says 'nigger.' That's where you're from, 'cause you're a nigger." Not only bigoted, but illiterate as well. 11

12   But the Chinese thing was only a phase. I grew out of it. One of those unpleasant things you need to get out of your system, like gawkiness, or acne, or a breaking voice. You know, growing pains. Sometime around the age of twelve, my nose exploded, my eyes grew round, my hair lightened and took on a bit of a wave. *Voilà,* instant white.

13   Well, not quite white. Maybe Mediterranean—anathema at one point in history as well, but pretty much accepted, nowadays, in polite society.

14   It seemed natural that I should turn white. My parents had never encouraged me to be Chinese. Well, I should say that my mom never did. That was her job, right? To teach me to be Chinese? My father was more than willing to spread his Jewishness around. He wasn't religious himself, but he loved the idea of being Jewish. The history, the culture, the jokes. "Oy, the goyim," he'd say. "They got no chutzpah."

15   But my mom was silent about her heritage. It was the family secret. Although she'd been raised in New York in Chinatown speaking Chinese, she never uttered a word of it in the house. She said she couldn't remember any. And she let us kids bust up her family heirlooms, like the dowry swords made from old coins that came from her grandparents' wedding. My sister and I smacked them together in sword fights, the coins tinkling down around us like a metallic rainshower with each thrust and parry.

16   The only hint of her past came from food. We ate a lot of Chinese food. Stirfry for dinner. Soy sauce-braised carp, or grouse, or pheasant, whenever we caught any. And chopsticks. But she cooked and served it up without comment, whereas my father went through this big, Jewish routine whenever he opened a box of matzo. "Bar-ruch a-ta Adonai eh-lo-hei-nu," he'd intone, ripping off the cellophane.

17   After I started looking white, I never thought much about being Chinese. It was out of sight, so I pretty much pushed it out of mind. This lasted until I started applying to colleges. I had to fill out all these forms and check boxes specifying which race I was. All of the schools took pride in touting the "diversity" of their students, so I immediately identified myself as Chinese American. I thought it was an advantage—a unique feature that made me stand out from an anonymous sea of applicants. I checked those boxes for "Asian/Pacific Islander" proudly. It was my most Chinese moment.

18   But when I got into school, being Chinese didn't seem like a good idea after all. On the one hand, believe it or not, there was guilt. Guilt for not looking Chinese. This came up right away. During orientation week my freshman year, the minority

students' center held a big get-together for its "community." I
felt like I should go, having checked all those boxes on my admissions forms. I felt sort of like I'd used the organization.
Already the guilt was setting in.

As soon as I walked into the students' center, I knew I'd gone   19
to the wrong place. Just about everyone there looked really ethnic—African American, Asian, Native American, Latino. And
there I was, this white-looking guy. A few other students looked
kind of white, too, but at least their name tags made up for it:
last names like "Chan" or "Lee" or "Wong." What's my last
name? Jewish. Great.

I stood around feeling really out of place until this other stu-   20
dent began talking to me. He was African American. "So what
are you?" he asked me, right away. I was relieved to tell him my
mom was Chinese, like I was explaining myself. "Oh, OK, yeah,
you can sort of see it," he said, after eyeing me carefully. "But
would you look at some of the guys here? I don't know what
they're supposed to be." I left a little later and never went back.

It was just as well that I wasn't welcome at the minority cen-   21
ter, because I found out that the other students on my freshman hall frowned on minorities. It wasn't a matter of racism.
They weren't racist. Everyone on my hall welcomed diversity.
Everyone went to rallies on the Green to protest the university's investment in South Africa. It was a question of style, of
fitting in, of dressing like everyone else, being laid back, socia-
ble, and cool. Foreign students, the ones straight from China
and Korea, weren't bad because they were Chinese or Korean.
African American students had every right to eat by themselves
in the dining hall and have their own frats. But those students
just weren't that cool. They didn't fit in with what was normal.
You never saw that kind of behavior in the "Breakfast Club"—a
film all the students on my hall tried to emulate. Well, OK,
maybe you saw it in "Sixteen Candles"—from that weird,
geeky, Chinese guy.

Don't misunderstand. I didn't pretend that I was white. I still   22
admitted that I was half Chinese to everyone. But I avoided doing anything that would make me stand out and get labeled
"Asian American." There were a few close calls all the same. I
remember the worst incident.

The summer before my junior year I was working in   23
Pennsylvania. Every now and then I had a long weekend and
went up to Providence to hang out with a house full of friends.
Quite often, I'd get there to find that all my friends had ditched
me to take off for New York or Boston or Maine. So it would be
me alone in the house with this Taiwanese student who was
subletting a room. He didn't fit in too well. He had a bad hair

cut and wore sneakers with black socks all the time. He spoke with an accent and studied engineering and economics. I talked to him a little, and we went to some movies. One time his mother came up from New York, and I took the two of them to the beach in my beat-up VW bug. She cooked us dinner later. She seemed really happy that her son had such a good American friend.

24   One thing that really drove me crazy was that this Chinese guy was sleeping in a lawn chair because he hadn't realized that his sublet would be unfurnished. I knew that an old roommate had left her bed in the last apartment I'd lived in, and I still had a key. It turns out that she had arranged to sell the damn thing to the next people moving in, but I didn't care. I hated her guts. So I went over there, got the bed, tied it down to my Volkswagen, and drove it back to the Chinese guy. He was really grateful.

25   I didn't see him much after I gave him the bed. I went back down to Pennsylvania and didn't return to the start of school. I ran into him halfway through the first semester in the dining hall. He was still wearing those awful clothes and was with a big group of foreign students. He came up to me in the middle of the dining room, grinning like an idiot. He was still thanking me for the damn bed. He turned to the foreign students. "This is my friend," he said, really loudly. I smiled nervously, conscious of everyone watching and listening. "He's Chinese, too," he exclaimed. The foreign students all gave me an odd look—I couldn't read it. Surprise? Confusion? I thought it was admiration. I went crimson from head to foot. I didn't see him after that, although he gave me his phone number in Providence, and New York.

26   Whenever I think about the incident, I still blush. I'm embarrassed by the way I acted, embarrassed for even thinking they admired me because they couldn't tell I was Chinese. I guess, even though I don't look Chinese, I can't escape it. It keeps coming back in the way I worry and in the way I treat other people. You know, sometimes the problem isn't what others do to you, it's what you do to yourself.

27   On the whole, though, I feel pretty lucky that I don't have to look Chinese and deal with all that other crap as well. I know what the alternative would be. I only need to look at my uncle. That's my mother's brother. He lives in the Northeast, has a professional job, and drives a Porsche. He's always rushing around, going to the club, the office, the gym. He got married my last year in college and I went out for the wedding. I didn't know his wife, I'd only met her once: vague impression of blonde hair and blue eyes, the type my uncle always goes for.

As soon as my uncle sees me, it starts. "God, you're lucky," he   28
says. "I wish I looked like you." My uncle, he's always going on
about being Chinese, like it's the worst thing in the world. I
guess he's really just like me. He only wants to feel sure of himself and to fit in. But in addition to the normal human burden
of insecurity is added the extra weight of being Chinese. This
does not help his self image. It's not that society is "oppressing"
him or that he's being turned down for jobs or that he's being
snubbed at parties or anything really important. It's just that
he's not white, so he's not quite "normal."

Whenever he goes to a bar, he's never that "guy standing over   29
there," or the "guy in the expensive suit," or the "guy with the
black hair," or the "good-looking guy" to any of the women.
He's always "that Asian guy." As in: "Yeah, look over there at
that Asian guy looking at you." It drives him crazy.

My uncle's telling me all this while we're whipping down the   30
highway in his Porsche. We're going to get something to eat.
We're heading for this Yuppie bar and restaurant he goes to a
lot when suddenly he hits the brakes.

"Shit," he says. "We can't go there, I'm not dressed.   31
Whenever I go there I try to look really nice. Good suit, tie. I
can't go looking like this." So he screeches down the next exit
and heads the Porsche the other way.

"Maybe we'll go to Wong's, this Chinese place," he says to   32
me. "Yeah, that'd be good. It's open late, service is fast, it doesn't
matter how I'm dressed. Yeah, maybe Wong's'd be good."

But then he hits the brakes again. No, no, no. Not Wong's.   33
Not tonight. He's getting married tomorrow (my God, why is
he getting married?), he can't deal with Wong's tonight. Can't
deal, I guess, with the Chinese ambiance. Can't deal with the
fact that he blends in there, that it looks like he belongs. Can't
deal with it because he doesn't want to belong. That's Chinese,
it's not white, it's just not normal.

So we're off at the next exit and heading back in the direc-   34
tion we were first going. Yeah, we'll go to the other place. It'll
be OK. We'll sit at the bar. You don't have to dress up at the bar.

"You're lucky," he says to me. "Really lucky."   35

Ranier Spencer
RACE AND MIXED RACE

Ranier Spencer contributed the following article—which he subtitles "a personal tour"—to a book entitled As We Are Now: Mixed Blood Essays on Race and Identity, *edited by William S. Penn and published in 1997. Since the book was published by the University of California Press, it certainly has an academic audience in mind, but the subject and presentation of the book indicate that it sought a wide readership.*

The truth is that there are no races; there is nothing in the world that can do all we ask race to do for us.
—Kwame Anthony Appiah In My Father's House

The Dream

1   999 Afro-Americans arranged in a line—not by height or age—but chromatically, from darkest to lightest, lightest to darkest. Colors blending slowly, imperceptibly, into one another. Not just colors, but lips, noses, and types of hair too. . . light people with thick lips and wide noses, dark people with thin noses and straight hair. Enter a white person to take her place in line. Does she go to the end? No, for she isn't the palest one there—not by far. After much searching she finally finds one who looks similar to herself, so much so that they could be sisters. The only difference between them is that the black woman's eyes are blue, while her own are brown. Meanwhile, the color line has begun to curve in on itself—enveloping her, pushing her up against her near-twin—until it finally engulfs itself as well and simply dissolves. . . .

2   Race is our historical curse, our great confusion. Race is what future generations will look back on with incredulity and pity, just as present-day third-graders look back with amazed disbelief on the cosmology of learned medieval Europeans: "How could they have been so stupid?" My personal engagement with race and racial identity is a consequence of my own lived experience as a so-called mixed-race person. That experience has revolved around what we in this country refer to as the One-Drop Rule, the idea that any trace of African ancestry—one drop of black blood, so to speak—is enough to make a person wholly and unalterably black. My personal journey has

taken me from unconscious acceptance of the One-Drop Rule, to what I thought was considered agreement with it, to, finally, a critical rejection of the rule and the racial categories on which it is based.

Questioning a concept so embedded and so naturalized as race always involves the breaking up of foundations and the toppling of superstructures that appear unassailable. In my case it involved appraising and ultimately rejecting everything I'd thought previously about identity. However, this is not to say that I feel myself a tragic mulatto—an overused and exaggerated term—for there is a vast difference between wondering whether one is black or white and questioning whether anyone really is.[1] It is the transition between these two modes of thought, the transition from being trapped within the constraints of an entrenched system of thought to challenging that system and ultimately transcending it that is the essence of my personal racial journey. 3

News Flash

Grouped by the sickle cell gene, Yemenites, Greeks, New Guineans, Thais, and Dinkas all belong in one race, Norwegians and several black African peoples in another. Grouped by lactase retention, northern and central Europeans, Arabians, and certain west Africans share the same race, while other African blacks, east Asians, American Indians, southern Europeans, and Australian Aborigines all make up another race. Grouped by finger print patterns. . . .[2]

If there were a blood test that could determine definitively whether a person had any sub-Saharan African ancestors within the past 2,000 years, I doubt many white people would take it. Disruptions, disjunctions—it's so important that skeletons stay in their closets. Indeed, if there were a test to show the precise extent of European ancestry in individual Afro-Americans—just how much Irish and just how much English, for instance—I don't think many would really want to know, for it would be just the kind of interesting information that would complicate the very simple view most Americans have of race and identity.[3] 4

The scientific jury is in and has been for some time. Biological races don't exist, never have. Everyone is always already mixed. The Mediterranean slave trade of the ancient world moved sub-Saharan Africans into North Africa and Southern Europe, and moved Black Sea Europeans into North 5 and sub-Saharan Africa. The later trans-Atlantic slave trade ensured contact between southern and northern Europeans, sub-Saharan West Africans, and the indigenous peoples of North and South America. Additionally, the still more recent phenomenon of passing has served especially well as a vehicle for the injection of African genetic material into unsuspecting white American families. Easily over a hundred thousand blacks have passed into white society, easily.[4] Keeping in mind that a successful act of passing is one that goes undetected, what white person can know that there is no African branch (or root) on her family tree? So many different people today carry so many different genetic heritages that in all likelihood when two white Americans mate they are transferring African genetic material without even being aware of it. If only they knew. . .

Into the Mix: Beginnings

6   Mixed-race identity, or *mestizaje,* can be experienced in a variety of ways. It can be ignored, put in context, glorified, denied, and, as with race, reified. *Mestizaje* has, for me, always been just below the surface. As far back as I can remember, I've known I was mixed. That was the word my mother used— *mixed.* I don't remember my father talking about it at all. His work at sea took him away much of the year, so it's fair to say I grew up in a white household, albeit an immigrant one, specifically a German one. Psychologists and sociologists tell us that placing a child in this type of situation is a sure-fire recipe for identity confusion, but when I was young you could have fooled me. I was simply who I was. I knew I was unique the same way my friends all knew that they were themselves unique. All this business of either conforming to rigid identity types or being labeled confused is a pipe dream of psychologists desperately in search of a theory. . . but more on that later.

7   Though it didn't start out that way, our neighborhood of post–World War II attached houses in Queens, New York, eventually became a black neighborhood, so nearly all my friends outside of school were black. I don't recall this confusing me either, however; and in no sense was I torn by loyalties between my friends and home. In fact, I don't understand how such a loyalty dichotomy could even be possible. I was a little colored boy—*mixed,* if that level of precision was called for, and it usually wasn't. My nonblack school friends saw my mother from time to time, yet I was still a little colored boy to them. Racial issues certainly didn't complicate my life or cause me to hate who I was. Being called *yellow* by someone marginally darker than me was hardly a major psychological event.

Indeed, when I was growing up in the early 1960s, having very dark skin color was what brought one the most insults and criticisms. From my own point of view, the two things I hated most about myself are still clear as a bell to me: (1) having an irredeemably strange name and (2) having a head that was flat in the back. These two things brought me more teasing than any child deserves. I'd gladly have traded anything for a normal head and a regular name.

As I recall, nearly all my friends had some aspect of identity that was in conflict with some imagined standard and therefore subject to teasing. Some were adopted, some were fostered; some were very poor, others were rather well-off; some were unhip, some had physical deformities, some were retarded mentally; some were ugly, some were gay, while some had seemingly nothing *wrong* with them and were teased precisely because of it.[5] I had an entire neighborhood of friends who treated me as well and as poorly as any other kid we knew. If one of them called me an Oreo or Frankenstein, I likely responded by insulting his mother, and then we'd probably go over to my house or his to play Monopoly, chess, Sorry, or slot cars.[6] Sticks and stones and all that.

Psychobabble and the Sociology of Reification

That the Earth is flat is as easy to prove as driving a car. You never turn upside-down no matter how far you travel.

Too few people know the difference between racism (which does exist) and race (which doesn't). The reality of the former implies nothing about the latter. Unfortunately, though, it is much safer and much less complicated to believe that racism somehow proves race, even though racism no more validates race than did medieval European belief in a flat Earth actually make the Earth flat. Racism acts to support and perpetuate racist systems of categorization and social evil, much like Christianity supported and perpetuated the arrogant notion that the Earth was the center of the Universe while in no sense proving that false claim. The same goes for calling race a social reality, and treating it as if it existed simply because so many people think it does. It might seem reasonable on the surface to suggest that we ought to consider race to be real if people's belief in it affects their lives and others', for I could then say that race is de facto real under such conditions. But this would be to confuse the pathology with its (nonexistent) object.

Take the case of witchcraft, for instance. There have been sorry times in this world when people have believed so strongly in witches that in their paranoia they've put innocent persons to death. Yet the fervor of that belief is no reason to look back and agree with the unenlightened of those days that witches indeed existed among them. There is an important conceptual difference between recognizing that other people's mistaken belief in witchcraft may affect the way you express yourself publicly and acquiescing in the same belief merely because many other people do.[7] To accept the notion that other persons' beliefs can make race or witchcraft a reality is to believe that the Earth actually was flat during medieval times in Europe.

12   So the claim that race is a social reality is a mystification that takes us nowhere. When sociologists tell us that race is a social reality (their caveats notwithstanding), they perpetuate the myth of race and thereby become part of the problem, helping to ensure that the unreal is reified and that the truth becomes heresy. The analogy with flat-Earth thinking is perfect.

13   Even before elementary school I had a clear conception of the racial dynamics in my environment. My mother was white, my father was black, and my older brother and I were mixed. On another level I also knew that I was black and my brother was white. It was a fact of life, nothing at all confusing about it.[8] Nine years my senior, his looks, his hair texture, and the fact that the first seven years of his life were spent in Germany as a German all worked to channel his identity choices in certain directions, while my looks and my environment led me elsewhere. He never announced it (did he need to?), but there was no doubt he considered himself white. From his own phenotype to that of his various girlfriends to his musical tastes— and, I might add, his disparaging remarks about mine—it was both plain to see and utterly sensible, especially to someone who grew up as part of it. And this was in no way an identity crisis, for *he* certainly wasn't confused, and he's never to my knowledge been taken to be black by anyone who didn't know his background. It would be silly to even call it passing, which is a psychological phenomenon more than a physical one anyway. So, who, if not the individual, decides mixed-race identity? Do we really want to leave it up to color-struck psychologists and professional organizations such as the National Association of Black Social Workers?[9] Those of us who consider it vitally important to dismantle the racial categories put in place by racists long ago are frustrated, especially when so-called black intellectuals uphold the same illogical, racist categories and presume to dictate *healthy* identity choices for people other than themselves.

14   Psychologists inform us, on the one hand, that there are races and that there are stages of racial development (analogous perhaps to the cosmological formation of flat planets?).

They assure us of the importance of telling mixed-race children in no uncertain terms that they are black, so that they will develop positive racial identities. Otherwise such children will grow to be confused individuals, marginal people, Oreos. On the other hand, people who question black and white racial categories are said by many black psychologists to be classic examples of confused identity development. People who question the racial categories that fly in the face of their own personal histories and everyday experiences are *diagnosed* by the psychologist ideologues as paranoid, schizophrenic, and in denial of their true identities. Conveniently then, disagreement with such prescribed racial identity is proof of faulty psychological development.

But the simplistic notion of possessing a distinct racial identity is, like the pompous idea that the Sun revolves around the Earth, a farce. There is no identity; there are identities, various and fluid. Depending on the situation and my mood I can identify as an American, German-American, Afro-American, Afro-German, male, New Yorker, Texan, Georgian, antiracialist, antisexist, academic, human, straight-ahead jazz loving, baby boomer. I can deploy these identities separately or in combination with full consistency. No one of them necessarily defines me more than any other; all of them come into play to constitute my whole personality. Moreover, some of my identities will be with me for life, while others will fall away, as my child identity became a past identity at adulthood.   15

Yet, many psychologists persist in declaring that there are such things as monoracial identities, that they are the primary category of personal identification, that they are crucial to our psychological well-being, and that each mentally healthy American has one and only one. I can't help wondering, though, why the uncritical acceptance of racial identity (like the one-time dogmatic belief in geocentrism and flat-Earth theory) is taken to be a sign of mature reasoning, while the questioning of imposed racial categories marks one as *confused*, which sounds ominously less like objective sociology or psychology than like the double-speak of religious dogmatists excommunicating those members of the flock who dare inconveniently to think for themselves. Consider the absurdity of the racial analysis: if the mixed-race person has difficulty identifying with the so-called black group, she is confused, fractured, and therefore sick; if she is well-adjusted and happy in identifying as neither black nor white but mixed, she is diagnosed is being utterly sick since the test of healthy identity for mixed-race persons is that they identify as black. And all the while the prospect of American blacks—with their centuries of   16

European admixture—identifying as black only is taken to be a sign of robust psychological development, as if the healthiest person is the one who never, ever questions the identity imposed on her.

17   I prefer to see an unwillingness to accept racial categories as the *beginning* of mature identity development. Far from being confused about who I am, I'm certain it's the psychologists who haven't a clue about their own identities, much less about the identities of others. Simple reflection on the impossibility of racial categories turns the dogma of such identities upside-down by asking questions no psychologist or sociologist can answer. What is a race? How many races are there? Are any of them pure? Why can blacks be mixed but not whites? Why is a single drop of blood enough to make a person black but far from enough to make one a U.S. government-recognized Indian? Aren't racial purity and mixed-race incompatible ideas? It is a curious phenomenon that Americans, black and white alike, are perfectly willing to accept the so-called racial passer as white until the $\frac{1}{2}$, $\frac{1}{4}$, or $\frac{1}{256}$ of African ancestry is uncovered. In what way, though, has the person herself changed on the basis of that new knowledge? If what we truly are concerned about are positive identities, then being positive about the various identities one *has* is the issue, not being positive about whatever mythical racial identity a racist society says one ought to have. And so I fantasize: a racist white politician suddenly discovers he is $\frac{1}{256}$ black, which makes him therefore, according his own rules, all and only black. I can always hope.

Mixture, Unmixture, Dissolution

18   I grew through childhood and into adulthood without incident. There were no stares that I noticed when walking with my mother, no insults from passing cars when my brother would occasionally fetch me home for dinner, no social ostracism of which I was aware when the entire family went out to eat.[10] The dreaded racial identity crisis predicted by today's psychologists missed me somehow.[11] No longer a little colored boy, I was a full-fledged Afro-American, a presumably well-adjusted black male who (like most Afro-Americans) happened to be mixed in some degree.[12] It wasn't until I was in my thirties, teaching philosophy at a small northeastern college, that *mestizaje* began to surface and affect me. Initially, it was just a feeling that logically it made no sense to categorize myself as black or half-black when I was clearly half-white as well. And if

some rule said I couldn't be white, then surely I couldn't be black either. It seemed to me strange and inconsistent that racially mixed people could be black or mixed but not white. What was the secret?

At about this time my identity development received a boost 19 from my being exposed to two theories that shared as a central theme the idea that race is real and that blacks are superior to whites. The first of these, Afrocentricity, in addition to agreeing with the racist notion of the One-Drop Rule, claimed also that the one drop takes you all the way back to Africa. According to Afrocentrism, American blacks are in a proper relation to themselves only when they have placed Africa at the center of their being. Simply put, Afrocentrism is said to be natural for blacks, and Eurocentrism for whites. Of course, both *centrisms* are erroneous. Europe is no more at the center of all things for white Americans than Africa is for Afro-Americans. Afrocentrism is a tit-for-tat response to Eurocentrism and as such is every bit as flawed and racist as the fractured theory it proposes to displace.

The Afrocentrists stated that the Afro-American had a circu- 20 lar pattern of thought, was community-oriented, antimaterial, and had non-exploitive relations with nature (unless, of course, he suffered from confused racial-identity development); the white American was by nature individualistic, material, and had a linear thought pattern. I wondered, though, what was supposed to be natural for mixed-race persons?[13] Perhaps I had an oval thought pattern, or did it alternate between linear and circular depending on the day of the week? Even more difficult to understand was how I was to be material and antimaterial both at the same time. Afrocentric writers did not offer much in the way of clarification, the following analysis being a case in point:

> Africanity is a comprehensive theme shared by all types of Black families, a commonality tied to the African cultural heritage. The basis of that African cultural heritage is described as a oneness of being (everyone and everything is a part of the Supreme being) and the interconnectedness of all things.[14]

Given the crude, binary structuring of Afrocentric theory, 21 even the most basic of questions concerning the extensive mixture of European and African genetic material in Afro-Americans, and why this should result in Africanity but not Eurocanity for Afro-American families are questions left unaddressed, presumably because they would only complicate the ideology at work.

22   The other theory I came across, the Sun People/Ice People hypothesis, said that the skin pigment melanin made blacks friendly and cooperative; while a corresponding lack thereof made whites hateful and evil by nature. The reason given had to do with the ancestors of black Americans living peaceful, communal lives under the friendly sun in Africa, while Europeans huddled barbarously in caves during the Ice Ages. Molefi Asante writes that "it is again the strong inherent desire in European man growing out of the nomadic, hunting context of Europe that makes him seek conquest of nature."[15] According to this theory, which along with Afrocentrism enjoys a sad but understandable currency among those it is meant to uplift, I was destined by nature at the very least to be friendly and evil at the same time. As an American of European *and* African descent it was unclear what I was to do.

23   What these two simplistic, essentialist, and thoroughly racist theories did for me was to make me see that there were some very deep and very serious inconsistencies involved in accepting racial categories—inconsistencies that were brought out especially by *mestizaje*. Slowly, what I'd taken for granted for more than three decades became a nagging philosophical problem. What was it about blackness that allowed it to be mixed with whiteness and yet stay black? And conversely, what was it about whiteness that caused it to be corrupted irretrievably by one drop of black blood, one black sperm, one black egg?

24   If there is such a thing as racial-identity development, then this is where mine began—with the first stirrings of skepticism toward the idea of race. For me, it was more than wanting to acknowledge both sides of my heritage, much more. Simply arguing that I was both black *and* white was not to the point, was not going far enough, for it was only an intermediate step on the path to rejecting race altogether. *Mestizaje* opened my eyes to the tyranny of the One-Drop Rule and forced me to question its meaning. I began to understand mixture that valued one component over the other for the racist hegemony it was. More than that, though, I found *mestizaje* capable of negating race altogether. *Mestizaje* is a contingent concept, its existence depending entirely on a prior notion of race. If you take race to be real, then either *mestizaje* is impossible or it is not. If *mestizaje* is impossible people are born either black or white only and not in-between. But it is precisely because American society recognizes some people to be born in-between that we have the One-Drop Rule.

25   We know that American society accepts the idea of *mestizaje* if by no other evidence than the mounds of laws and regulations generated in the past 370-odd years that govern the deter-

mination of racial identity in our society. We know because of words such as *mulatto, quadroon,* and *octoroon;* we know because of court cases; and we know because of blood quanta. We are all mixed—not just the visible mulattos—but everyone else as well. One does not walk down the streets of any town or city in this country and mistake the black inhabitants for West Africans. That has been impossible since the end of the African slave trade.

So, as long as people take race to be real, they also take   26
mestizaje to be real; but this reality signals the impossibility of race, for race is nothing if not a rigid categorization. Race thought is safe thought, uncomplicated and familiar, while mestizaje is a disruptive, subversive threat to turn the whole universe upside down. Race, if you take it seriously, is pure stability and fixity. It depends on the words *white* and *black* having concrete and unchanging meanings. Race cannot allow ambiguity, fluidity, or mixture, for it then ceases to refer to something pure, something distinct. The absolute strength of *mestizaje* is the power it has—by its even being able to be thought—of dissolving race and everything associated with it, ultimately dissolving even itself.

It was, finally, with more than a bit of shock and disappoint-   27
ment that I came to realize that all my life I had—by accepting that I was black and by accepting that I was mixed—bought fully into a doctrine of white supremacy, had accepted that whiteness was purity and perfection, had accepted that blackness was something much less. How else to explain acceptance of the One-Drop Rule? By accepting the idea that because one of my parents was black and one white I was therefore mixed or black but not white, I was endorsing the most subtle and pervasive form of white supremacy ever to exist. The perfect hegemony is the one you never notice.

No, I'm not white, and I don't want to be. Nor am I mixed or   28
black either, for the words are meaningless as predicates in the real world. Like the terms *unicorn* and *flat Earth* they describe fantasies, unrealities, wishes. My journey has taken me past constructions of race, past constructions of mixed-race, and into an understanding of human difference that does not include race as a meaningful category. Despite the psychologists' predictions, I survived my formative years as a mixed-race/black child in a so-called white household. I wasn't confused then about my identity when I thought I was mixed and when I thought I was black, but I was certainly wrong. Likewise, while the psychologists today may not be confused about who they think they are, they too are as wrong as they can be. Who is in denial of true identity? Is it the person who

accepts and endorses a racist system of classification that has no scientific or logical reality, or the person who rejects the categorizations of others in favor of self-definition as a complex, genetically mixed, multi-identified human being? Who indeed?

Notes

1. It is a special difficulty of engaging the topic of race that one often must utilize terms that have no meaning, such as *black* and *white*, if only in order to demonstrate that they have no meaning. Throughout this essay, the words *black* and *white* should be read as if they were contained in quotation marks and should be understood as if they read *so-called black* and *so-called white*. Nor is this inconsistent, or somehow an admission that race exists. That people indeed think they are white or black or Asian no more makes them so than thinking one stands on a flat Earth makes it so.

2. Jared Diamond, "Race without Color," *Discover*, November 1994, 84–88.

3. References to *America* and *Americans* are meant to be national, not continental, in character.

4. F. James Davis, in *Who Is Black?: One Nation's Definition* (University Park: Pennsylvania State University Press, 1991), calculates that "passing probably reached an all-time peak between 1880 and 1925" (56). Estimates of the number of black persons passing over into white society range from 2,000 per year to 12,000 per year during this time period. Even using only the lower rate, at least 90,000 blacks began passing as white during those forty-five years alone.

5. Lest the sarcasm slip by unnoticed, there is of course nothing wrong with any of these traits.

6. The Oreo reference would have been to being brown on the outside and white on the inside like the popular cookies, and the Frankenstein reference would have been to my head. Being teased about my head hurt me so much, while being called an Oreo didn't hurt at all. There is a difference that children can easily discern between insults and teasing that have some measure of truth to them and those that are just plain silly. Children are tougher than many psychologists are willing to give them credit for.

7. It's one thing to acknowledge that many people believe in a thing, whether race or witchcraft, but quite another to accept the thing as real on the basis of people's belief in it. The latter is what the social-reality concept entails.

8. I can only shake my head at all the psychologists and sociologists running around like Chicken Little, spreading alarms about imminent identity crises in the fragile lives of mixed-race and transracially adopted black children. It's a wonder

any of us older ones survived at all without the benefit of these professionals' intervention.

9. The National Association of Black Social Workers is a premier evangelizer of racial religion. This organization has gone on record as opposing the adoption of black children by white parents on the grounds that such transracially adopted children would suffer racial identity crises, despite study after longitudinal study demonstrating precisely the opposite. The position of the National Association of Black Social Workers is that such children should remain institutionalized and in foster care rather than be adopted by willing white parents. The even more ominous side of this ideology is the group's assertion that transracial adoptions are tantamount to cultural genocide, as if the children in question are some sort of renewable resource whose fleeting chance to have a loving adoptive family is less important than their sacrifice on the altar of pseudoscientific, pseudopsychological, and pseudosociological racial mythology.

10. This is not to say that no such incidents ever occurred. Whether or not such things happened, I never noticed any and therefore was not subjected to the inevitable identity crises promised by the psychologists.

11. It's interesting to note, too, that other predictions of dire consequences made by today's psychologists were not borne out by my generation. For instance, between kindergarten and the start of my Ph.D. program I had exactly one black teacher, yet, by all accounts, the lack of racial role models as teachers was of little, if any, consequence in my academic development. The same is true for my childhood contemporaries, many of whom are now successful doctors, lawyers, and entrepreneurs. There are good reasons for stamping out racial discrimination in teaching, but the role-model argument is a wrong-headed attempt at pseudopsychology. Why not make specific demands for light- and dark-skinned black teachers? Why not insist on visibly and invisibly mixed teachers as well? Why should *black* alone be enough of a predicate, as if all Afro-Americans are exactly the same?

12. Afro-Americans are always already mixed; they are Euro-Americans as much as they are Afro-Americans. But it's a curious thing that in the United States even those blacks who are recognized specifically as mixed-race lose their mixed status when they have children and simply become black parents. A child with two white and two black grandparents is mixed if the maternal and paternal grandparents are of the same race respectively, but black if they are not. In what sense is the one child mixed and the other black? In what sense is neither of them white? The One-Drop Rule acts continuously to erase mixture and to perpetuate the mythology of distinct races.

13. Putting aside again the fact that most, if not all, American blacks are part European anyway.
14. Terry Kershaw, "Toward a Black Studies Paradigm: An Assessment and Some Directions," *Journal of Black Studies* 22, no. 4 (June 1992): 482.
15. Molefi K. Asante, *Afrocentricity* (Trenton, N.J.: Africa World Press, 1988), 81.

Works Cited

Appiah, Anthony Kwame. *In My Father's House: Africa in the Philosophy of Culture*. Oxford: Oxford University Press, 1992.

Asante, Molefi K. *Afrocentricity*. Trenton, N.J.: Africa World Press, 1988.

Davis, F. James. *Who Is Black?: One Nation's Definition*. University Park: Pennsylvania State University Press, 1991.

Diamond, Jared. "Race without Color." *Discover*, November 1994, 82–89.

Kershaw, Terry. "Toward a Black Studies Paradigm: An Assessment and Some Directions." *Journal of Black Studies* 22, no. 4 (June 1992): 477–493.

DEFINING GENDER

—————●—————

John Adams and Abigail Adams
LETTERS

Here are two letters and part of a third written by John Adams of Massachusetts, one of the Founding Fathers, and later the second president, of the United States, and his wife Abigail Adams (a formidable person as well) in the spring of 1776— while the nation was considering declaring its freedom from British rule. Abigail sent the first letter to John while he was in Philadelphia debating with his colleagues the merits of a declaration of independence: Note how Abigail uses the occasion to press her husband to "remember the ladies" in his discussions about freedom from tyranny. She was probably thinking not of suffrage—too radical an idea—but of fairer laws regarding inheritance, wifebeating, and so forth. John's response to that letter follows. The third letter, from John Adams to James Sullivan (who had proposed that one's power at the ballot box should be proportional to one's financial worth), indicates that John Adams understood all too well the probable long-term implications of what was being written in the Declaration.

Letter from Abigail Adams to John Adams, March 31, 1776

I long to hear that you have declared an independancy—and by   1
the way in the new Code of Laws which I suppose it will be
necessary for you to make I desire you would Remember the
Ladies, and be more generous and favourable to them than
your ancestors. Do not put such unlimited power into the
hands of the Husbands. Remember all Men would be tyrants if
they could. If perticuliar care and attention is not paid to the
Laidies we are determined to foment a Rebelion, and will not

hold ourselves bound by any Laws in which we have no voice, or Representation.

2   That your Sex are Naturally Tyrannical is a Truth so thoroughly established as to admit of no dispute, but such of you as wish to be happy willingly give up the harsh title of Master for the more tender and endearing one of Friend. Why then, not put it out of the power of the vicious and the Lawless to use us with cruelty and indignity with impunity. Men of Sense in all Ages abhor those customs which treat us only as the vassals of your Sex. Regard us then as Beings placed by providence under your protection and in immitation of the Supreem Being make use of that power only for our happiness.

Letter from John Adams to Abigail Adams, April 14, 1776

3   As to Declarations of Independency, be patient. Read our Privateering Laws, and our Commercial Laws. What signifies a Word.

4   As to your extraordinary Code of Laws, I cannot but laugh. We have been told that our Struggle has loosened the bands of Government every where. That Children and Apprentices were disobedient—that schools and Colledges were grown turbulent—that Indians slighted their Guardians and Negroes grew insolent to their Masters. But your Letter was the first Intimation that another Tribe more numerous and powerfull than all the rest were grown discontented.—This is rather too coarse a Compliment but you are so saucy, I wont blot it out.

5   Depend upon it, We know better than to repeal our Masculine systems. Altho they are in full Force, you know they are little more than Theory. We dare not exert our Power in its full Latitude. We are obliged to go fair, and softly, and in Practice you know We are the subjects. We have only the Name of Masters, and rather than give up this, which would compleatly subject Us to the Despotism of the Peticoat, I hope General Washington, and all our brave Heroes would fight. I am sure every good Politician would plot, as long as he would against Despotism, Empire, Monarchy, Aristocracy, Oligarchy, or Ochlocracy.—A fine Story indeed. I begin to think the Ministry as deep as they are wicked. After stirring up Tories, Landjobbers, Trimmers, Bigots, Canadians, Indians, Negroes, Hanoverians, Hessians, Russians, Irish Roman Catholicks, Scotch Renegadoes, at last they have stimulated the[m] to demand new Priviledges and threaten to rebell.

Letter from John Adams to James Sullivan, May 26, 1776

. . . The same reasoning which will induce you to admit all men 6
who have no property, to vote, with those who have, for those
laws which affect the person, will prove that you ought to admit women and children; for, generally speaking, women and
children have as good judgments, and as independent minds,
as those men who are wholly destitute of property; these last
being to all intents and purposes as much dependent upon others, who will please to feed, clothe, and employ them, as
women are upon their husbands, or children on their parents.

As to your idea of proportioning the votes of men, in money 7
matters, to the property they hold, it is utterly impracticable.
There is no possible way of ascertaining, at any one time, how
much every man in a community is worth; and if there was, so
fluctuating is trade and property, that this state of it would
change in half an hour. . . .

Depend upon it, Sir, it is dangerous to open so fruitful a 8
source of controversy and altercation as would be opened by
attempting to alter the qualifications of voters; there will be no
end of it. New claims will arise; women will demand a vote;
lads from twelve to twenty-one will think their rights not
enough attended to; and every man who has not a farthing,
will demand an equal voice with any other, in all acts of state.
It tends to confound all distinctions, and prostrate all ranks to
one common level.

Sojourner Truth
AIN'T I A WOMAN?

*Sojourner Truth's story is fascinating and moving. Born into
slavery in Ulster County, New York, around 1797 and given the
name Isabella, she was sold three times before she turned
twelve. Perhaps sexually abused by one of her owners, she fled
to freedom in 1827, a year before slavery was outlawed in New
York. In New York City she worked as a domestic and fell in
with an evangelical preacher who encouraged her efforts to
convert prostitutes. Though illiterate, she managed to negate*

the sale of her son Peter to the South when her former "owner" tried to accomplish the sale. In 1843, inspired by mystical visions, she took the name Sojourner Truth and set off alone and undeterred by her illiteracy to preach and sing about religion and the abolition of slavery. By 1850, huge crowds were coming to witness the oratory of the ex-slave with the resounding voice and message. During the Civil War she was presented to President Lincoln at the White House. After the war she spoke out for women's suffrage, but she never gave up her spiritual and racial themes—or her humor and exuberance. She continued to lecture until near her death in Battle Creek, Michigan, in 1883.

Sojourner Truth accepted neither the physical inferiority of women nor the idea that they should be placed on pedestals; nor did she subordinate women's rights to the pursuit of racial equality. At a women's rights convention in May 1851, Sojourner Truth rose extemporaneously to rebut speakers who had impugned the rights and capabilities of women. According to an eyewitness who recorded the scene in his diary, this is what she said:

1 Well, children, where there is so much racket there must be something out of kilter. I think that 'twixt the negroes of the South and the women at the North, all talking about rights, the white men will be in a fix pretty soon. But what's all this here talking about?

2 That man over there says that women need to be helped into carriages, and lifted over ditches, and to have the best place everywhere. Nobody ever helps me into carriages, or over mud-puddles, or gives me any best place! And ain't I a woman? Look at me! Look at my arm! I have ploughed and planted, and gathered into barns, and no man could head me! And ain't I a woman? I could work as much and eat as much as a man— when I could get it—and bear the lash as well! And ain't I a woman? I have borne thirteen children, and seen them most all sold off to slavery, and when I cried out with my mother's grief, none but Jesus heard me! And ain't I a woman?

3 Then they talk about this thing in the head; what's this they call it? [Intellect, someone whispers.] That's it, honey. What's that got to do with women's rights or negro's rights? If my cup won't hold but a pint, and yours holds a quart, wouldn't you be mean not to let me have my little half-measure full?

4 Then that little man in black there, he says women can't have as much rights as men, 'cause Christ wasn't a woman! Where did your Christ come from? Where did your Christ come from? From God and a woman! Man had nothing to do with Him.

If the first woman God ever made was strong enough to turn 5
the world upside down all alone, these women together ought
to be able to turn it back, and get it right side up again! And
now they is asking to do it, the men better let them.

Obliged to you for hearing on me, and now old Sojourner 6
ain't got nothing more to say.

Susan Glaspell

TRIFLES

*Susan Glaspell (1882–1948), an Iowan by birth and educa-
tion, moved east in 1911. A Pulitzer Prize–winning dramatist
and a prolific fiction writer, she cofounded the Provincetown
Playhouse on Cape Cod in 1915, which became a center for experimental and innovative drama. In 1916, she wrote* Trifles,
*the one-act play reprinted here; then she adapted it a few
months later into the story "A Jury of Her Peers."*

Characters

GEORGE HENDERSON, *County Attorney*
HENRY PETERS, *Sheriff*
LEWIS HALE, *A Neighboring Farmer*
MRS. PETERS,
MRS. HALE

SCENE

The kitchen in the now abandoned farmhouse of JOHN WRIGHT, *a* 1
*gloomy kitchen, and left without having been put in order—un-
washed pans under the sink, a loaf of bread outside the breadbox, a dish towel on the table—other signs of incompleted work.
At the rear the outer door opens and the* SHERIFF *comes in followed by the* COUNTY ATTORNEY *and* HALE. *The* SHERIFF *and* HALE
are men in middle life, the COUNTY ATTORNEY *is a young man; all
are much bundled up and go at once to the stove. They are followed by two women—the* SHERIFF'S *wife first; she is a slight wiry
woman, a thin nervous face.* MRS. HALE *is larger and would ordinarily be called more comfortable looking, but she is disturbed
now and looks fearfully about as she enters. The women have
come in slowly, and stand close together near the door.*

2 COUNTY ATTORNEY. [*Rubbing his hands.*] This feels good. Come up to the fire, ladies.

3 MRS. PETERS. [*After taking a step forward.*] I'm not—cold.

4 SHERIFF. [*Unbuttoning his overcoat and stepping away from the stove as if to mark the beginning of official business.*] Now, Mr. Hale, before we move things about, you explain to Mr. Henderson just what you saw when you came here yesterday morning.

5 COUNTY ATTORNEY. By the way, has anything been moved? Are things just as you left them yesterday?

6 SHERIFF. [*Looking about.*] It's just the same. When it dropped below zero last night I thought I'd better send Frank out this morning to make a fire for us—no use getting pneumonia with a big case on, but I told him not to touch anything except the stove—and you know Frank.

7 COUNTY ATTORNEY. Somebody should have been left here yesterday.

8 SHERIFF. Oh—yesterday. When I had to send Frank to Morris Center for that man who went crazy—I want you to know I had my hands full yesterday. I knew you could get back from Omaha by today and as long as I went over everything here myself—

9 COUNTY ATTORNEY. Well, Mr. Hale, tell just what happened when you came here yesterday morning.

10 HALE. Harry and I had started to town with a load of potatoes. We came along the road from my place and as I got here I said, "I'm going to see if I can't get John Wright to go in with me on a party telephone." I spoke to Wright about it once before and he put me off, saying folks talked too much anyway, and all he asked was peace and quiet—I guess you know about how much he talked himself; but I thought maybe if I went to the house and talked about it before his wife, though I said to Harry that I didn't know as what his wife wanted made much difference to John—

11 COUNTY ATTORNEY. Let's talk about that later, Mr. Hale. I do want to talk about that, but tell now just what happened when you got to the house.

12 HALE. I didn't hear or see anything; I knocked at the door, and still it was all quiet inside. I knew they must be up, it was past eight o'clock. So I knocked again, and I thought I heard somebody say, "Come in." I wasn't sure, I'm not sure yet, but I opened the door—this door [*Indicating the door by which the two women are still standing*] and there in that rocker—[*Pointing to it.*] sat Mrs. Wright. [*They all look at the rocker.*]

13 COUNTY ATTORNEY. What—was she doing?

HALE. She was rockin' back and forth. She had her apron in her   14
hand and was kind of—pleating it.
COUNTY ATTORNEY. And how did she—look?   15
HALE. Well, she looked queer.   16
COUNTY ATTORNEY. How do you mean—queer?   17
HALE. Well, as if she didn't know what she was going to do next.   18
And kind of done up.
COUNTY ATTORNEY. How did she seem to feel about your com-   19
ing?
HALE. Why, I don't think she minded—one way or other. She   20
didn't pay much attention. I said, "How do, Mrs. Wright, it's
cold, ain't it?" And she said, "Is it?"—and went on kind of
pleating at her apron. Well, I was surprised; she didn't ask
me to come up to the stove, or to set down, but just sat
there, not even looking at me, so I said, "I want to see John."
And then she—laughed. I guess you would call it a laugh. I
thought of Harry and the team outside, so I said a little
sharp: "Can't I see John?" "No," she says, kind o' dull like.
"Ain't he home?" says I. "Yes," says she, "he's home." "Then
why can't I see him?" I asked her, out of patience. "'Cause
he's dead," says she. "*Dead?*" says I. She just nodded her
head, not getting a bit excited, but rockin' back and forth.
"Why—where is he?" says I, not knowing what to say. She
just pointed upstairs—like that [*Himself pointing to the
room above.*] I got up, with the idea of going up there. I
walked from there to here—then I says, "Why, what did he
die of?" "He died of a rope round his neck," says she, and
just went on pleatin' at her apron. Well, I went out and
called Harry. I thought I might—need help. We went upstairs and there he was lyin'—
COUNTY ATTORNEY. I think I'd rather have you go into that up-   21
stairs, where you can point it all out. Just go on now with
the rest of the story.
HALE. Well, my first thought was to get that rope off. It   22
looked ... [*Stops, his face twitches.*] ... but Harry, he went
up to him, and he said, "No, he's dead all right, and we'd
better not touch anything." So we went back down stairs.
She was still sitting that same way. "Has anybody been no-
tified?" I asked. "No," says she, unconcerned. "Who did
this, Mrs. Wright?" said Harry. He said it businesslike—
and she stopped pleatin' of her apron. "I don't know," she
says. "You don't *know?*" says Harry. "No," says she.
"Weren't you sleepin' in bed with him?" says Harry. "Yes,"
says she, "but I was on the inside." "Somebody slipped a
rope round his neck and strangled him and you didn't
wake up?" says Harry. "I didn't wake up," she said after

him. We must 'a looked as if we didn't see how that could be, for after a minute she said, "I sleep sound." Harry was going to ask her more questions but I said maybe we ought to let her tell her story first to the coroner, or the sheriff, so Harry went fast as he could to Rivers' place, where there's a telephone.

23 COUNTY ATTORNEY. And what did Mrs. Wright do when she knew that you had gone for the coroner?

24 HALE. She moved from that chair to this one over here [*Pointing to a small chair in the corner.*] and just sat there with her hands held together and looking down. I got a feeling that I ought to make some conversation, so I said I had come in to see if John wanted to put in a telephone, and at that she started to laugh, and then she stopped and looked at me—scared. [*The* COUNTY ATTORNEY, *who has had his notebook out, makes a note.*] I dunno, maybe it wasn't scared. I wouldn't like to say it was. Soon Harry got back, and then Dr. Lloyd came, and you, Mr. Peters, and so I guess that's all I know that you don't.

25 COUNTY ATTORNEY. [*Looking around.*] I guess we'll go upstairs first—and then out to the barn and around there. [*To the* SHERIFF] You're convinced that there was nothing important here—nothing that would point to any motive.

26 SHERIFF. Nothing here but kitchen things. [*The* COUNTY ATTORNEY, *after again looking around the kitchen, opens the door of a cupboard closet. He gets up on a chair and looks on a shelf. Pulls his hand away, sticky.*]

27 COUNTY ATTORNEY. Here's a nice mess.
[*The women draw nearer.*]

28 MRS. PETERS. [*To the other woman.*] Oh, her fruit; it did freeze. [*To the* COUNTY ATTORNEY.] She worried about that when it turned so cold. She said the fire'd go out and her jars would break.

29 SHERIFF. Well, can you beat the women! Held for murder and worryin' about her preserves.

30 COUNTY ATTORNEY. I guess before we're through she may have something more serious than preserves to worry about.

31 HALE. Well, women are used to worrying over trifles. [*The two women move a little closer together.*]

32 COUNTY ATTORNEY. [*With the gallantry of a young politician.*] And yet, for all their worries, what would we do without the ladies? [*The women do not unbend. He goes to the sink, takes a dipperful of water from the pail and pouring it into a basin, washes his hands. Starts to wipe them on the roller towel, turns it for a cleaner place.*] Dirty towels! [*Kicks his foot*

against the pans under the sink.] Not much of a housekeeper, would you say, ladies?

MRS. HALE. [*Stiffly.*] There's a great deal of work to be done on a 33 farm.

COUNTY ATTORNEY. To be sure. And yet [*With a little bow to her.*] I 34 know there are some Dickson county farmhouses which do not have such roller towels.

[*He gives it a pull to expose its full length again.*]

MRS. HALE. Those towels get dirty awful quick. Men's hands 35 aren't always as clean as they might be.

COUNTY ATTORNEY. Ah, loyal to your sex, I see. But you and Mrs. 36 Wright were neighbors. I suppose you were friends, too.

MRS. HALE. [*Shaking her head.*] I've not seen much of her of late 37 years. I've not been in this house—it's more than a year.

COUNTY ATTORNEY. And why was that? You didn't like her? 38

MRS. HALE. I liked her all well enough. Farmers' wives have 39 their hands full, Mr. Henderson. And then—

COUNTY ATTORNEY. Yes—? 40

MRS. HALE. [*Looking about.*] It never seemed a very cheerful 41 place.

COUNTY ATTORNEY. No—it's not cheerful. I shouldn't say she had 42 the homemaking instinct.

MRS. HALE. Well, I don't know as Wright had, either. 43

COUNTY ATTORNEY. You mean that they didn't get on very well? 44

MRS. HALE. No, I don't mean anything. But I don't think a 45 place'd be any cheerfuller for John Wright's being in it.

COUNTY ATTORNEY. I'd like to talk more of that a little later. I 46 want to get the lay of things upstairs now.

[*He goes to the left, where three steps lead to a stair door.*]

SHERIFF. I suppose anything Mrs. Peters does'll be all right. She 47 was to take in some clothes for her, you know, and a few little things. We left in such a hurry yesterday.

COUNTY ATTORNEY. Yes, but I would like to see what you take, 48 Mrs. Peters, and keep an eye out for anything that might be of use to us.

MRS. PETERS. Yes, Mr. Henderson. 49

[*The women listen to the men's steps on the stairs, then look about the kitchen.*]

MRS. HALE. I'd hate to have men coming into my kitchen, 50 snooping around and criticising.

[*She arranges the pans under sink which the* COUNTY ATTORNEY *had shoved out of place.*]

MRS. PETERS. Of course it's no more than their duty. 51

MRS. HALE. Duty's all right, but I guess that deputy sheriff that 52 came out to make the fire might have got a little of this on.

[*Gives the roller towel a pull.*] Wish I'd thought of that sooner. Seems mean to talk about her for not having things slicked up when she had to come away in such a hurry.

53   MRS. PETERS. [*Who has gone to a small table in the left rear corner of the room, and lifted one end of a towel that covers a pan.*] She had bread set.
[*Stands still.*]

54   MRS. HALE. [*Eyes fixed on a loaf of bread beside the breadbox, which is on a low shelf at the other side of the room. Moves slowly toward it.*] She was going to put this in there. [*Picks up loaf, then abruptly drops it. In a manner of returning to familiar things.*] It's a shame about her fruit. I wonder if it's all gone. [*Gets up on the chair and looks.*] I think there's some here that's all right, Mrs. Peters. Yes—here; [*Holding it toward the window.*] this is cherries too. [*Looking again.*] I declare I believe that's the only one. [*Gets down, bottle in her hand. Goes to the sink and wipes it off on the outside.*] She'll feel awful bad after all her hard work in the hot weather. I remember the afternoon I put up my cherries last summer. [*She puts the bottle on the big kitchen table, center of the room. With a sigh, is about to sit down in the rocking-chair. Before she is seated realizes what chair it is; with a slow look at it, steps back. The chair which she has touched rocks back and forth.*]

55   MRS. PETERS. Well, I must get those things from the front room closet. [*She goes to the door at the right, but after looking into the other room, steps back.*] You coming with me, Mrs. Hale? You could help me carry them.
[*They go in the other room; reappear, MRS. PETERS carrying a dress and skirt, MRS. HALE following with a pair of shoes.*]

56   MRS. PETERS. My, it's cold in there.
[*She puts the clothes on the big table, and hurries to the stove.*]

57   MRS. HALE. [*Examining her skirt.*] Wright was close. I think maybe that's why she kept so much to herself. She didn't even belong to the Ladies Aid. I suppose she felt she couldn't do her part, and then you don't enjoy things when you feel shabby. She used to wear pretty clothes and be lively, when she was Minnie Foster, one of the town girls singing in the choir. But that—oh, that was thirty years ago. This all you was to take in?

58   MRS. PETERS. She said she wanted an apron. Funny thing to want, for there isn't much to get you dirty in jail, goodness knows. But I suppose just to make her feel more natural. She said they was in the top drawer in this cupboard. Yes, here. And then her little shawl that always hung behind the door. [*Opens stair door and looks.*] Yes, here it is.
[*Quickly shuts door leading upstairs.*]

MRS. HALE. [*Abruptly moving toward her.*] Mrs. Peters?   59
MRS. PETERS. Yes, Mrs. Hale?   60
MRS. HALE. Do you think she did it?   61
MRS. PETERS. [*In a frightened voice.*] Oh, I don't know.   62
MRS. HALE. Well, I don't think she did. Asking for an apron and   63
her little shawl. Worrying about her fruit.
MRS. PETERS. [*Starts to speak, glances up, where footsteps are*   64
heard in the room above. In a low voice.] Mr. Peters says it
looks bad for her. Mr. Henderson is awful sarcastic in a
speech and he'll make fun of her sayin' she didn't wake up.
MRS. HALE. Well, I guess John Wright didn't wake when they   65
was slipping that rope under his neck.
MRS. PETERS. No, it's strange. It must have been done awful   66
crafty and still. They say it was such a—funny way to kill a
man, rigging it all up like that.
MRS. HALE. That's just what Mr. Hale said. There was a gun in   67
the house. He says that's what he can't understand.
MRS. PETERS. Mr. Henderson said coming out that what was   68
needed for the case was a motive; something to show anger,
or—sudden feeling.
MRS. HALE. [*Who is standing by the table.*] Well, I don't see   69
any signs of anger around here. [*She puts her hand on the*
dish towel which lies on the table, stands looking down at
table, one half of which is clean, the other half messy.] It's
wiped to here. [*Makes a move as if to finish work, then*
turns and looks at loaf of bread outside the breadbox. Drops
towel. In that voice of coming back to familiar things.]
Wonder how they are finding things upstairs. I hope she
had it a little more red-up up there. You know, it seems
kind of *sneaking.* Locking her up in town and then coming out here and trying to get her own house to turn
against her!
MRS. PETERS. But Mrs. Hale, the law is the law.   70
MRS. HALE. I s'pose 'tis. [*Unbuttoning her coat.*] Better loosen up   71
your things, Mrs. Peters. You won't feel them when you go
out.
[MRS. PETERS *takes off her fur tippet, goes to hang it on hook at*
back of room, stands looking at the under part of the small
corner table.]
MRS. PETERS. She was piecing a quilt.   72
[*She brings the large sewing basket and they look at the bright*
pieces.]
MRS. HALE. It's log cabin pattern. Pretty, isn't it? I wonder if she   73
was goin' to quilt it or just knot it?
[*Footsteps have been heard coming down the stairs. The*
SHERIFF *enters followed by* HALE *and the* COUNTY ATTORNEY.]

74 SHERIFF. They wonder if she was going to quilt it or just knot it!
    [*The men laugh; the women look abashed.*]
75 COUNTY ATTORNEY. [*Rubbing his hands over the stove.*] Frank's
    fire didn't do much up there, did it? Well, let's go out to the
    barn and get that cleared up.
    [*The men go outside.*]
76 MRS. HALE. [*Resentfully.*] I don't know as there's anything so
    strange, our takin' up our time with little things while we're
    waiting for them to get the evidence. [*She sits down at the
    big table smoothing out a block with decision.*] I don't see as
    it's anything to laugh about.
77 MRS. PETERS. [*Apologetically.*] Of course they've got awful im-
    portant things on their minds.
    [*Pulls up a chair and joins* MRS. HALE *at the table.*]
78 MRS. HALE. [*Examining another block.*] Mrs. Peters, look at this
    one. Here, this is the one she was working on, and look at
    the sewing! All the rest of it has been so nice and even. And
    look at this! It's all over the place! Why, it looks as if she
    didn't know what she was about!
    [*After she has said this they look at each other, then start to
    glance back at the door. After an instant* MRS. HALE *has pulled
    at a knot and ripped the sewing.*]
79 MRS. PETERS. Oh, what are you doing, Mrs. Hale?
80 MRS. HALE. [*Mildly.*] Just pulling out a stitch or two that's not
    sewed very good. [*Threading a needle.*] Bad sewing always
    made me fidgety.
81 MRS. PETERS. [*Nervously.*] I don't think we ought to touch
    things.
82 MRS. HALE. I'll just finish up this end. [*Suddenly stopping and
    leaning forward.*] Mrs. Peters?
83 MRS. PETERS. Yes, Mrs. Hale?
84 MRS. HALE. What do you suppose she was so nervous about?
85 MRS. PETERS. Oh—I don't know. I don't know as she was ner-
    vous. I sometimes sew awful queer when I'm just tired.
    [MRS. HALE *starts to say something, looks at* MRS. PETERS, *then
    goes on sewing.*] Well, I must get these things wrapped up.
    They may be through sooner than we think. [*Putting apron
    and other things together.*] I wonder where I can find a piece
    of paper, and string.
86 MRS. HALE. In that cupboard, maybe.
87 MRS. PETERS. [*Looking in cupboard.*] Why, here's a birdcage.
    [*Holds it up.*] Did she have a bird, Mrs. Hale?
88 MRS. HALE. Why, I don't know whether she did or not—I've not
    been here for so long. There was a man around last year
    selling canaries cheap, but I don't know as she took one;
    maybe she did. She used to sing real pretty herself.

MRS. PETERS. [*Glancing around.*] Seems funny to think of a bird   89
here. But she must have had one, or why would she have a
cage? I wonder what happened to it.

MRS. HALE. I s'pose maybe the cat got it.   90

MRS. PETERS. No, she didn't have a cat. She's got that feeling   91
some people have about cats—being afraid of them. My cat
got in her room and she was real upset and asked me to take
it out.

MRS. HALE. My sister Bessie was like that. Queer, ain't it?   92

MRS. PETERS. [*Examining the cage.*] Why, look at this door. It's   93
broke. One hinge is pulled apart.

MRS. HALE. [*Looking too.*] Looks as if someone must have been   94
rough with it.

MRS. PETERS. Why, yes.   95
[*She brings the cage forward and puts it on the table.*]

MRS. HALE. I wish if they're going to find any evidence they'd be   96
about it. I don't like this place.

MRS. PETERS. But I'm awful glad you came with me, Mrs. Hale.   97
It would be lonesome for me sitting here alone.

MRS. HALE. It would, wouldn't it? [*Dropping her sewing.*] But I   98
tell you what I do wish, Mrs. Peters. I wish I had come over
sometimes when *she* was here. I—[*Looking around the
room.*]—wish I had.

MRS. PETERS. But of course you were awful busy, Mrs. Hale—   99
your house and your children.

MRS. HALE. I could've come. I stayed away because it weren't   100
cheerful—and that's why I ought to have come. I—I've never
liked this place. Maybe because it's down in a hollow and
you don't see the road. I dunno what it is but it's a lonesome
place and always was. I wish I had come over to see Minnie
Foster sometimes. I can see now—[*Shakes her head.*]

MRS. PETERS. Well, you mustn't reproach yourself, Mrs. Hale.   101
Somehow we just don't see how it is with other folks until—
something comes up.

MRS. HALE. Not having children makes less work—but it makes   102
a quiet house, and Wright out to work all day, and no company when he did come in. Did you know John Wright, Mrs.
Peters?

MRS. PETERS. Not to know him; I've seen him in town. They say   103
he was a good man.

MRS. HALE. Yes—good; he didn't drink, and kept his word as   104
well as most, I guess, and paid his debts. But he was a hard
man, Mrs. Peters. Just to pass the time of day with him—
[*Shivers.*] Like a raw wind that gets to the bone. [*Pauses, her
eye falling on the cage.*] I should think she would'a wanted a
bird. But what do you suppose went with it?

105 MRS. PETERS. I don't know, unless it got sick and died. [*She reaches over and swings the broken door, swings it again. Both women watch it.*]

106 MRS. HALE. You weren't raised round here, were you? [MRS. PETERS *shakes her head.*] You didn't know—her?

107 MRS. PETERS. Not till they brought her yesterday.

108 MRS. HALE. She—come to think of it, she was kind of like a bird herself—real sweet and pretty, but kind of timid and—fluttery. How—she—did—change. [*Silence; then as if struck by a happy thought and relieved to get back to every day things.*] Tell you what, Mrs. Peters, why don't you take the quilt in with you? It might take up her mind.

109 MRS. PETERS. Why, I think that's a real nice idea, Mrs. Hale. There couldn't possibly be any objection to it, could there? Now, just what would I take? I wonder if her patches are in here—and her things. [*They look in the sewing basket.*]

110 MRS. HALE. Here's some red. I expect this has got sewing things in it. [*Brings out a fancy box.*] What a pretty box. Looks like something somebody would give you. Maybe her scissors are in here. [*Opens box. Suddenly puts her hand to her nose.*] Why—[MRS. PETERS *bends nearer, then turns her face away.*] There's something wrapped up in this piece of silk.

111 MRS. PETERS. Why, this isn't her scissors.

112 MRS. HALE. [*Lifting the silk.*] Oh, Mrs. Peters—its—[MRS. PETERS *bends closer.*]

113 MRS. PETERS. It's the bird.

114 MRS. HALE. [*Jumping up.*] But, Mrs. Peters—look at it! Its neck! Look at its neck! It's all—other side *to.*

115 MRS. PETERS. Somebody—wrung—its—neck. [*Their eyes meet. A look of growing comprehension, of horror. Steps are heard outside.* MRS. HALE *slips box under quilt pieces, and sinks into her chair. Enter* SHERIFF *and* COUNTY ATTORNEY. MRS. PETERS *rises.*]

116 COUNTY ATTORNEY. [*As one turning from serious things to little pleasantries.*] Well, ladies, have you decided whether she was going to quilt it or knot it?

117 MRS. PETERS. We think she was going to—knot it.

118 COUNTY ATTORNEY. Well, that's interesting, I'm sure. [*Seeing the birdcage.*] Has the bird flown?

119 MRS. HALE. [*Putting more quilt pieces over the box.*] We think the—cat got it.

120 COUNTY ATTORNEY. [*Preoccupied.*] Is there a cat? [MRS. HALE *glances in a quick covert way at* MRS. PETERS.]

MRS. PETERS. Well, not *now*. They're superstitious, you know.   121
They leave.

COUNTY ATTORNEY. [*To* SHERIFF PETERS, *continuing an interrupted*   122
conversation.] No sign at all of anyone having come from
the outside. Their own rope. Now let's go up again and go
over it piece by piece. [*They start upstairs.*] It would have to
have been someone who knew just the—[MRS. PETERS *sits
down. The two women sit there not looking at one another,
but as if peering into something and at the same time holding
back. When they talk now it is in the manner of feeling their
way over strange ground, as if afraid of what they are saying,
but as if they can not help saying it.*]

MRS. HALE. She liked the bird. She was going to bury it in that   123
pretty box.

MRS. PETERS. [*In a whisper.*] When I was a girl—my kitten—   124
there was a boy took a hatchet, and before my eyes—and before I could get there—[*Covers her face an instant.*] If they
hadn't held me back I would have—[*Catches herself, looks
upstairs where steps are heard, falters weakly.*]—hurt him.

MRS. HALE. [*With a slow look around her.*] I wonder how it   125
would seem never to have had any children around. [*Pause.*]
No, Wright wouldn't like the bird—a thing that sang. She
used to sing. He killed that, too.

MRS. PETERS. [*Moving uneasily.*] We don't know who killed the   126
bird.

MRS. HALE. I knew John Wright.   127

MRS. PETERS. It was an awful thing was done in this house that   128
night, Mrs. Hale. Killing a man while he slept, slipping a
rope around his neck that choked the life out of him.

MRS. HALE. His neck. Choked the life out of him.   129
[*Her hand goes out and rests on the birdcage.*]

MRS. PETERS. [*With rising voice.*] We don't know who killed him.   130
We don't know.

MRS. HALE. [*Her own feeling not interrupted.*] If there'd been   131
years and years of nothing, then a bird to sing to you, it
would be awful—still, after the bird was still.

MRS. PETERS. [*Something within her speaking.*] I know what still-   132
ness is. When we homesteaded in Dakota, and my first baby
died—after he was two years old, and me with no other then—

MRS. HALE. [*Moving.*] How soon do you suppose they'll be   133
through, looking for the evidence?

MRS. PETERS. I know what stillness is. [*Pulling herself back.*] The   134
law has got to punish crime, Mrs. Hale.

MRS. HALE. [*Not as if answering that.*] I wish you'd seen Minnie   135
Foster when she wore a white dress with blue ribbons and

stood up there in the choir and sang. [*A look around the room.*] Oh, I *wish* I'd come over here once in a while! That was a crime! That was a crime! Who's going to punish that?

136 MRS. PETERS. [*Looking upstairs.*] We mustn't—take on.

137 MRS. HALE. I might have known she needed help! I know how things can be—for women. I tell you, it's queer, Mrs. Peters. We live close together and we live far apart. We all go through the same things—it's all just a different kind of the same thing. [*Brushes her eyes; noticing the bottle of fruit, reaches out for it.*] If I was you I wouldn't tell her her fruit was gone. Tell her it *ain't*. Tell her it's all right. Take this in to prove it to her. She—she may never know whether it was broke or not.

138 MRS. PETERS. [*Takes the bottle, looks about for something to wrap it in; takes petticoat from the clothes brought from the other room, very nervously begins winding this around the bottle. In a false voice.*] My, it's a good thing the men couldn't hear us. Wouldn't they just laugh! Getting all stirred up over a little thing like a—dead canary. As if that could have anything to do with—with—wouldn't they *laugh!*
[*The men are heard coming down stairs..*]

139 MRS. HALE. [*Under her breath.*] Maybe they would—maybe they wouldn't.

140 COUNTY ATTORNEY. No, Peters, it's all perfectly clear except a reason for doing it. But you know juries when it comes to women. If there was some definite thing. Something to show—something to make a story about—a thing that would connect up with this strange way of doing it—[*The women's eyes meet for an instant. Enter* HALE *from outer door.*]

141 HALE. Well, I've got the team around. Pretty cold out there.

142 COUNTY ATTORNEY. I'm going to stay here a while by myself. [*To the* SHERIFF.] You can send Frank out for me, can't you? I want to go over everything. I'm not satisfied that we can't do better.

143 SHERIFF. Do you want to see what Mrs. Peters is going to take in? [*The* COUNTY ATTORNEY *goes to the table, picks up the apron, laughs.*]

144 COUNTY ATTORNEY. Oh, I guess they're not very dangerous things the ladies have picked out. [*Moves a few things about, disturbing the quilt pieces which cover the box. Steps back.*] No, Mrs. Peters doesn't need supervising. For that matter, a sheriff's wife is married to the law. Ever think of it that way, Mrs. Peters?

145 MRS. PETERS. Not—just that way.

SHERIFF. [*Chuckling.*] Married to the law. [*Moves toward the other room.*] I just want you to come in here a minute, George. We ought to take a look at these windows.   146

COUNTY ATTORNEY. [*Scoffingly.*] Oh, windows!   147

SHERIFF. We'll be right out, Mr. Hale.   148

[HALE *goes outside. The* SHERIFF *follows the* COUNTY ATTORNEY *into the other room. Then* MRS. HALE *rises, hands tight together, looking intensely at* MRS. PETERS, *whose eyes make a slow turn, finally meeting* MRS. HALE'S. *A moment* MRS. HALE *holds her, then her own eyes point the way to where the box is concealed. Suddenly* MRS. PETERS *throws back quilt pieces and tries to put the box in the bag she is wearing. It is too big. She opens box, starts to take bird out, cannot touch it, goes to pieces, stands there helpless. Sound of a knob turning in the other room.* MRS.HALE *snatches the box and puts it in the pocket of her big coat. Enter* COUNTY ATTORNEY *and* SHERIFF.]

COUNTY ATTORNEY. [*Facetiously.*] Well, Henry, at least we found out that she was not going to quilt it. She was going to— what is it you call it, ladies?   149

MRS. HALE. [*Her hand against her pocket.*] We call it—knot it, Mr. Henderson.   150

CURTAIN

Marge Piercy

BARBIE DOLL

Marge Piercy (born 1936 in Detroit) is an essayist, novelist, and poet who enjoys a wide following among feminist readers. "Barbie Doll" was published in her book Circles on the Water, *a collection of poems that she wrote between 1963 and 1982.*

This girlchild was born as usual
and presented dolls that did pee-pee
and miniature GE stoves and irons
and wee lipsticks the color of cherry candy.
Then in the magic of puberty, a classmate said: 5
You have a great big nose and fat legs.

The Barbie doll was introduced in 1959 by Ruth Handler, the founder of Mattel, Incorporated. Ms. Handler always contended that Barbie represented that a young girl had choices (for Barbie had some outfits and accessories with a career orientation), but many people have contended that Barbie's amazing shape gave young girls exactly the wrong message about their bodies.

She was healthy, tested intelligent,
possessed strong arms and back,
abundant sexual drive and manual dexterity.
She went to and fro apologizing.   10
Everyone saw a fat nose on thick legs.

She was advised to play coy,
exhorted to come on hearty,
exercise, diet, smile and wheedle.
Her good nature wore out   15
like a fan belt.

So she cut off her nose and her legs
and offered them up.

In the casket displayed on satin she lay
with the undertaker's cosmetics painted on,   20
a turned-up putty nose,
dressed in a pink and white nightie.
Doesn't she look pretty? everyone said.
Consummation at last.

To every woman a happy ending.   25

Sharon Olds

RITES OF PASSAGE

*Sharon Olds was born in 1942 in San Francisco. Educated at
Stanford and Columbia, she published her first book of poems
in 1980. The following poem appeared in her second book
(published in 1983),* The Dead and the Living. *She now lives,
writes, and teaches in New York City.*

As the guests arrive at my son's party
they gather in the living room—
short men, men in first grade
with smooth jaws and chins.
Hands in pockets, they stand around   5
jostling, jockeying for place, small fights
breaking out and calming. One says to another

How old are you? Six. I'm seven. So?
They eye each other, seeing themselves
10   tiny in the other's pupils. They clear their
throats a lot, a room of small bankers,
they fold their arms and frown. I could beat you
up, a seven says to a six,
the dark cake, round and heavy as a
15   turret, behind them on the table. My son,
freckles like specks of nutmeg on his cheeks,
chest narrow as the balsa keel of a
model boat, long hands
cool and thin as the day they guided him
20   out of me, speaks up as a host
for the sake of the group.
We could easily kill a two-year-old,
he says in his clear voice. The other
men agree, they clear their throats
25   like Generals, they relax and get down to
playing war, celebrating my son's life.

Scott Russell Sanders

THE MEN WE CARRY IN OUR MINDS

Scott Russell Sanders (born 1945 in Memphis) grew up in rural Ohio and Tennessee. Active in the environmental movement through organizations such as the Nature Conservancy, the Audubon Society, and the Wilderness Society, he has the ability to cross between the so-called two cultures (science and the humanities) in his fiction, science fiction, and essays. A member of the faculty at Indiana University and the author of many books, he recently told the editors of Contemporary Authors *that "a writer should be a servant of language, community, and nature."*

1   "This must be a hard time for women," I say to my friend Anneke. "They have so many paths to choose from, and so many voices calling them."

"I think it's a lot harder for men," she replies. 2

"How do you figure that?" 3

"The women I know feel excited, innocent, like crusaders in 4
a just cause. The men I know are eaten up with guilt."

"Women feel such pressure to be everything, do everything," 5
I say. "Career, kids, art, politics. Have their babies and get back
to the office a week later. It's as if they're trying to overcome a
million years' worth of evolution in one lifetime."

"But we help one another. And we have this deep-down sense 6
that we're in the *right*—we've been held back, passed over,
used—while men feel they're in the wrong. Men are the ones
who've been discredited, who have to search their souls."

I search my soul. I discover guilty feelings aplenty—toward 7
the poor, the Vietnamese, Native Americans, the whales, an
endless list of debts. But toward women I feel something more
confused, a snarl of shame, envy, wary, tenderness, and amazement. This muddle troubles me. To hide my unease I say,
"You're right, it's tough being a man these days."

"Don't laugh," Anneke frowns at me. "I wouldn't be a man for 8
anything. It's much easier being the victim. All the victim has
to do is break free. The persecutor has to live with his past."

How deep is that past? I find myself wondering. How much 9
of an inheritance do I have to throw off?

When I was a boy growing up on the back roads of 10
Tennessee and Ohio, the men I knew labored with their bodies.
They were marginal farmers, just scraping by, or welders, steel-
workers, carpenters; they swept floors, dug ditches, mined
coal, or drove trucks, their forearms ropy with muscle; they
trained horses, stoked furnaces, made tires, stood on assembly
lines wrestling parts onto cars and refrigerators. They got up
before light, worked all day long whatever the weather, and
when they came home at night they looked as though somebody had been whipping them. In the evenings and on weekends they worked on their own places, tilling gardens that were
lumpy with clay, fixing broken-down cars, hammering on
houses that were always too drafty, too leaky, too small.

The bodies of the men I knew were twisted and maimed in 11
ways visible and invisible. The nails of their hands were black
and split, the hands tattooed with scars. Some had lost fingers.
Heavy lifting had given many of them finicky backs and guts
weak from hernias. Racing against conveyor belts had given
them ulcers. Their ankles and knees ached from years of standing on concrete. Anyone who had worked for long around machines was hard of hearing. They squinted, and the skin of
their faces was creased like the leather of old work gloves.
There were times, studying them, when I dreaded growing up.

Most of them coughed, from dust or cigarettes, and most of them drank cheap wine or whiskey, so their eyes looked blood-shot and bruised. The fathers of my friends always seemed older than the mothers. Men wore out sooner. Only women lived into old age.

12   As a boy I also knew another sort of men, who did not sweat and break down like mules. They were soldiers, and so far as I could tell they scarcely worked at all. But when the shooting started, many of them would die. This was what soldiers were *for*, just as a hammer was for driving nails.

13   Warriors and toilers: those seemed, in my boyhood vision, to be the chief destinies for men. They weren't the only destinies, as I learned from having a few male teachers, from reading books, and from watching television. But the men on televi-sion—the politicians, the astronauts, the generals, the savvy lawyers, the philosophical doctors, the bosses who gave orders to both soldiers and laborers—seemed as remote and unreal to me as the figures in Renaissance tapestries. I could no more imagine growing up to become one of these cool, potent crea-tures than I could imagine becoming a prince.

14   A nearer and more hopeful example was that of my father, who had escaped from a red-dirt farm to a tire factory, and from the assembly line to the front office. Eventually he dressed in a white shirt and tie. He carried himself as if he had been born to work with his mind. But his body, remembering the earlier years of slogging work, began to give out on him in his fifties, and it quit on him entirely before he turned 65.

15   A scholarship enabled me not only to attend college, a rare enough feat in my circle, but even to study in a university meant for the children of the rich. Here I met for the first time young men who had assumed from birth that they would lead lives of comfort and power. And for the first time I met women who told me that men were guilty of having kept all the joys and privileges of the earth for themselves. I was baffled. What privileges? What joys? I thought about the maimed, dismal lives of most of the men back home. What had they stolen from their wives and daughters? The right to go five days a week, 12 months a year, for 30 or 40 years to a steel mill or a coal mine? The right to drop bombs and die in war? The right to feel every leak in the roof, every gap in the fence, every cough in the en-gine as a wound they must mend? The right to feel, when the layoff comes or the plant shuts down, not only afraid but ashamed?

16   I was slow to understand the deep grievances of women. This was because, as a boy, I had envied them. Before college, the only people I had ever known who were interested in art or

music or literature, the only ones who read books, the only ones who ever seemed to enjoy a sense of ease and grace were the mothers and daughters. Like the menfolk, they fretted about money, they scrimped and made do. But, when the pay stopped coming in, they were not the ones who had failed. Nor did they have to go to war, and that seemed to me a blessed fact. By comparison with the narrow, ironclad days of fathers, there was an expansiveness, I thought, in the days of mothers. They went to see neighbors, to shop in town, to run errands at school, at the library, at church. No doubt, had I looked harder at their lives, I would have envied them less. It was not my fate to become a woman, so it was easier for me to see the graces. I didn't see, then, what a prison a house could be, since houses seemed to me brighter, handsomer places than any factory. I did not realize—because such things were never spoken of— how often women suffered from men's bullying. Even then I could see how exhausting it was for a mother to cater all day to the needs of young children. But if I had been asked, as a boy, to choose between tending a baby and tending a machine, I think I would have chosen the baby. (Having now tended both, I know I would choose the baby.)

So I was baffled when the women at college accused me and my sex of having cornered the world's pleasures. I think something like my bafflement has been felt by other boys (and by girls as well) who grew up in dirt-poor farm country, in mining country, in black ghettos, in Hispanic barrios, in the shadows of factories, in Third World nations—any place where the fate of men is just as grim and bleak as the fate of women.

When the women I met a college thought about the joys and privileges of men, they did not carry in their minds the sort of men I had known in my childhood. They thought of their fathers, who were bankers, physicians, architects, stockbrokers, the big wheels of the big cities. They were never laid off, never short of cash at month's end, never lined up for welfare. These fathers made decisions that mattered. They ran the world.

The daughters of such men wanted to share in this power, this glory. So did I. They yearned for a say over their future, for jobs worthy of their abilities, for the right to live at peace, unmolested, whole. Yes, I thought, yes yes. The difference between me and these daughters was that they saw me, because of my sex, as destined from birth to become like their fathers, and therefore as an enemy to their desires. But I knew better. I wasn't an enemy, in fact or in feeling. I was an ally. If I had known, then, how to tell them so, would they have believed me? Would they now?

Ursula K. Le Guin
LIMBERLOST

Ursula K. Le Guin (born 1929) is one of the most respected science fiction and fantasy writers in America: perhaps you have read her children's books or poetry or short fiction or one of her many novels—maybe The Left Hand of Darkness *(1969) or* The Dispossessed *(1974) or one of the pieces of her* Earthsea Trilogy. *A resident of Portland, Oregon, a conservationist, and a passionate devotee of the western United States, she has received a National Book Award and a host of other prizes for her work. In 1992, she contributed her story "Limberlost" to a book of readings called* Women Respond to the Men's Movement *edited by Kay Leigh Hagan and containing contributions by many prominent feminists. In an afterword, Le Guin notes that although the story is presented as fiction, nothing except its title is invented: the events depicted actually took place in 1985. Le Guin had been invited to a conference on "The Great Mother" in order to read from her novel* Always Coming Home, *which celebrates a society where gender issues have been resolved, when she experienced something akin to the events fictionalized here.*

1   The poet revolved slowly counterclockwise in the small, dark, not very deep pool. The novelist sat on the alder log that dammed the creek to make the pool. Also on the log were the poet's clothes, except his underpants. Coming upstream to the swimming hole, they had passed a naked nut-brown maid, beached and frontal to the sun; but she was young and they were not; and the poet was not Californian. "You don't mind if I'm old-fashioned about modesty?" he had asked, disarmingly. The novelist, although a Californian, did not mind. The poet's massive body was impressive enough as it was. Age, slacking here and tightening there what had been all smooth evenness in youth, gave pathos and dignity to that strong beast turning in the dark water. Among roots and the dark shadows of the banks, the hands and arms shone white. The novelist's bare feet, though tanned, also gleamed pallid under the water, as she sat rather less than comfortably on the log, wondering whether she should have pulled off shirt and jeans and joined the poet in his pool. She had been at his conference less than an hour and did not know the rules. Did he want a companion, or a spectator? Did it matter? She splashed the water with her

feet and deplored her inability to do, to know, what she wanted herself—fifty-five years old and sitting in adolescent paralysis, a bump on a log. Should I swim? I don't want to. I want to. Should I? Which underpants am I wearing? This is like the first day of summer camp. I want to go home. I ought to swim. Ought I? Now?

The poet spared her further debate by hauling out on the far   2 end of the log. He was shivering. The log was in sunlight, but the air was cool. Discovering that he would not soon get dry in wet boxer shorts, he did then remove them, but very modestly, back turned, sitting down again quickly. He spread his under-pants out on the log to dry, and conversed with his guest.

An expansive gesture as he described the events of the first   3 week of the conference swept his socks into the water. He caught one, but the current took the other out of reach. It sank slowly. He mourned; the novelist commiserated. He dismissed the sock.

"The Men have raised a Great Phallus farther up the river,"   4 he said, smiling. "It was their own idea. I'd show you, but it's off limits to the Women. A temenos. Very interesting, some of the ritual that has developed this week! I am hearing men talk—not sports scores and business, but talk—"

Impressed and interested, the novelist listened, trying to ig-   5 nore a lesser fascination: the sock. It had reemerged, all the way across the sun-flecked water, under a muddy, rooty bank. It was now moving very slowly but apparently—yes—definitely clockwise in a circle that would bring it back toward the log. The novelist sought and found a broken branch and held it ready, idly teasing the water with it. Housewife, she thought, ashamed. Fixated on socks. Prose writer!

The poet, sensitive and alert even when talking of his con-   6 cerns, observed, and asked what she was fishing for.

"Your sock is coming back," she said.   7

In a silence of complete fellow feeling, they both watched the   8 stately progress of the floating sock coming round unhurried in the fullness of time, astronomically certain, till the current brought it within branch reach. It was lifted dripping on the forked end. In quiet triumph the novelist turned the branch to the poet, presenting the sock to its owner, who removed it from the branch and squeezed it thoughtfully.

Soon after this he dressed, and they returned downstream to   9 the conference center and the scattered cabins under the red-woods.

The food was marvelous. Infinitely imaginatively vegetarian,   10 eclectic but not hodgepodge: the chilis hot, the salads delicate, the curries fragrant. The kitchen staff who produced these wonders were unlike the other people at the conference, though in fact several of them were members of the conference working out their fees. When they came out front and listened to the lecture on the Hero, they disappeared into the others and she could not recognize them; but in the crowded, hot, flashing kitchen, each of them seemed almost formidably individual, laughing more than anyone else here, talking differently, moving with deft purpose, so that the onlooker felt superfluous and inferior, not because the cooks meant to impress or to exclude but only because, being busy with the work in hand, they were quite unconscious of doing so.

11   After dinner on the second day, in honey-colored evening sunlight, crossing the broad wooden bridge across the creek between the main hall and her set of cabins, the novelist stopped and set her hands on the rough railing. I have been here before! I know this creek, this bridge, that trail going up into the trees—Such moments were a familiar accompaniment to tension and self-consciousness. She had felt them waiting to be asked to dance in dancing class at twelve, and at fifty in a hotel room in a city she had never seen before. Sometimes they justified themselves as a foresight remembered, bringing with them a queer double-exposure effect of that place where she had foreseen being in this place. But this time the experience was one of pure recognition, unexplainable but not uncanny, though solemnized by the extraordinary grandeur of the setting.

12   For the creek ran and the path led from fog-softened golden light into a darkness under incredible trees. It was always dark under them, and silent, and bare, for their huge community admitted little on a smaller scale. In the open clearings weeds and brambles and birds and bugs made the usual lively mess and tangle; under the big trees the flash of a scrub jay's wing startled as it would in the austere reaches of a Romanesque church. To come under the trees was as definite a transition as entering a building, but a building the size of a county.

13   Yet in among those immense living trunks there were also some black, buttressed objects that confused the sense of scale still further, for though squat, they were bigger than the cabins—much bigger. In bulk and girth, they were bigger than the trees. They were ruins. Tree ruins, the logged and burned-over stumps of the original forest. With effort, the novelist comprehended that the sequoias so majestically towering their taper bulk and gracile limbs all around here were second growth, not even a century old, mere saplings, shoots, scions of the great presences that had grown here in a length of silence now altogether and forever lost.

All the same, it was very quiet under the trees, and still qui- 14
eter at night. There were refinements of the absence of sound,
which the novelist had never before had the opportunity to observe. The cabins of her group straggled along, one every ten or
twenty yards, unlighted, above the creek, which ran shallow
but almost soundless, as if obeying the authority of the red-
woods, their counsel of silence. There was no wind. Fog would
mosey in over the hills from the sea before dawn to hush what
was hushed already. Far away one small owl called once. Later,
one mosquito shrilled hopelessly for a moment at the screen.

The novelist lay in darkness on her narrow board bunk in 15
her sleeping bag listening to nothing and wondering if this was
the bag her daughter had been using when she got the flu
camping last summer and how long flu germs might live in the
dark, warm, moist medium of a zippered sleeping bag. Her
thoughts ran on such matters because she was acutely uncomfortable. Sometimes she thought it was diarrhea, sometimes a
bladder infection, sometimes a coward spirit. Whatever it was,
would it force her yet again to leave the germy warmth of the
sleeping bag and take her flashlight and try to find the evasive
path up that ominous hiss to the all too communal, doorless,
wet-floored toilets, praying that nobody would join her in her
misery? Yes. No, maybe not. She heard a screen door creak, a
cabin or two downstream, and almost immediately after, a
soft, rushing noise: a man pissing off his cabin porch onto the
dark, soft, absorbent ground of redwood leaf and twig and
bark. O lucky Men, who need not crouch and straddle! Her
bladder twinged, remorseless. "I do not have to go pee," she
told herself, unconvinced. "I am not sick." She listened to the
terrific silence. Nothing lived. But there, deep in the hollow
darkness, a soft, lively sound: a little fart. And, now that she
was all ears, presently another fart, louder, from a cabin on
higher ground. The beans with chilis would probably explain
it. Or did it need explanation, did people like cattle add nightly
to the methane in the atmosphere, had those who had slept in
longhouses by this creek been accustomed to this soft concert?
For it was pleasing, almost melodious, this sparse pattern of a
snore here—a long efflatus there—a little sigh—against the
black and utter stillness.

When she was nearly asleep, she heard voices far up-stream, 16
male voices, chanting, as if from the dawn of history. Deep,
primeval. The Men were performing the rituals of manhood.
But the little farts in the night were nearer and dearer.

17

The Women sat in a circle on the sand, about thirty of them.
Nearby the shallow river widened to the sea. Soft, fog-paled

sunshine of the north coast lay beautifully on low breakers and dunes. The Women passed an ornamented wooden wand from hand to hand; who held the wand, spoke; the others listened. It did not seem quite right to the novelist. A good thing, but not the right one. Men wanted wands, women did not, she thought. These women had dutifully accepted the wand, but left to themselves they might have preferred some handwork and sat talking round and about like a flock of sparrows. Sparrows are disorderly, don't take turns, don't shut up to listen to the one with the wand, peck and talk at the same time. The wind blew softly, the wand passed. A woman in her twenties who wore an emblem of carved wood and feathers on a chain round her neck read a manuscript poem in a trembling voice half lost in the distant sound of the breakers. "My arms are those wings," she read, her voice shaken by fear and passion till it broke. The wand passed. A blond, fine-boned woman in her forties spoke of the White Goddess, but the novelist had ceased to listen, nervously rehearsing what she would say, should she say it? should she not? The wand passed to her. "It seems to me, coming in from outside, into the middle of this, you know, just for a couple of days, but perhaps just because of that I can be useful, anyhow it seems to me that to some extent some of the women here are sort of looking for a, for something actually to sort of *do*. Instead of kind of talking mostly in a sort of derivative way," she said in a harsh, chirping voice like a sparrow's. Shaking, she passed the wand. After the circle broke up, several women told her with enthusiasm about the masked dancing last Wednesday night, when the Women had acted out the female archetype of their choice. "It got wild," one said cheerfully. Another woman told her that this leader of the Women had quarreled with that one and personalities were destroying harmony. Several of them started making a large dragon out of wet sand, and while doing so told her that this year was different from earlier years, before the Men and the Women were separated, and that the East Coast meetings were always more spiritual than the West Coast meetings, or vice versa. They all chattered till the Men came back from their part of the beach, some with faces marked splendidly with charcoal.

18   The fine-boned blond whom the novelist had not listened to rode beside her in the car going back inland, a long, rough road through the logged-out coast range. "I've been coming to this place all my life," she said with a laugh. "It was a summer camp. I started coming when I was ten. Oh, it was wonderful then! I still meet people who came to Limberlost."

19   "Limberlost!" said the novelist.

"It was Camp Limberlost," said the other woman, and 20
laughed again, affectionately.

"But I went there," said the novelist. "I went to Camp 21
Limberlost. You mean this is it? Where the conference is? But I
was wondering, earlier this year, I realized I had no idea where
it was, or how to find out. I didn't know where it was when I
went there. It was in the redwoods, that's literally all I knew.
We all got into a bus downtown, and talked for six hours, you
know, and then we were there—you know how kids are, they
don't *notice*—but it was a Girl Reserve camp then. The YW ran
it. I had to join the Girl Reserves to come."

"The city took it over after the war," the other woman said, 22
her eyes merry and knowing. "This really is it. This is
Limberlost."

"But I don't remember it," the novelist said in distress. 23

"The conference is in the old Boys Camp. The Girls Camp 24
was upstream about a mile. Maybe you never came down
here."

Yes. The novelist remembered that Jan and Dorothy had cut 25
Camp Fire one evening and sneaked out of camp and down the
creek to Boys Camp. They had hidden across the creek behind
stumps and shrubs in the twilight, they had hooted and bleated
and meowed until the Boys began coming out of their cabins,
and then a counselor had come out, and Jan and Dorothy had
run away, and got back after dark, muddy and triumphant,
madly giggling in the jammed cabin after Lights Out, reciting
their adventure, counting coup. . . .

But she had not gone with them. There was no way she 26
could have remembered that bridge across the creek, the trail
going up out of the evening light.

Still, how could she not have recognized the place as a 27
whole—the forest, the cabins? Two weeks of three summers
she had lived here, at twelve and thirteen and fourteen, and
had she never noticed the silence? the size of the redwoods?
the black, appalling, giant stumps?

It was forty years; the trees might have grown a good deal— 28
and now as she thought it did seem that she and Jan had actually
climbed one of the stumps one day, to sit and talk, cutting Crafts,
probably. But they hadn't thought anything about the stump but
that it was climbable, a place to talk in privacy. No sense of what
that huge wreck meant, except (like those who had cut the tree)
to their own convenience; no notion of what it was in relation to
anything else, or where it was, or where they were. They were
here. Despairingly homesick the first night, thereafter settled in.
At home in the world, as cheekily indifferent to cause and effect

as sparrows, as ignorant of death and geography as the red-woods.

29   She had envied Jan and Dorothy their exploit, knowing them to be a good deal braver than she was. They had agreed to take her back to Boys Camp with them, and hoot and meow, or just hide and watch, but they never got around to it. They all went to Camp Fire and sang lonesome cowboy songs instead. So she had never seen Boys Camp until she came here and sat on the log and watched the poet circle slowly in the pool, and what would she and Jan and Dorothy, fourteen, merciless, have thought of *that?* "Oh, Lord!" she said involuntarily.

30   The woman beside her in the car laughed, as if in sympathy. "It's such a beautiful place," she said. "It's wonderful to be able to come back. What do you think of the conference?"

31   "I like the drumming," the novelist replied, after a pause, with fervor. "The drumming is wonderful. I never did that before." Indeed she had found that she wanted to do nothing else. If only there weren't a lecture tonight and they could drum again after dinner, thirty or forty people each with a drum on or between their knees, the rhythm set and led by a couple of drummers who knew what they were doing and kept the easy yet complex beat and pattern going, going, going till there was nothing in consciousness but that and nothing else needed, no words at all.

32   The lecture was on the Wild Man. That night she woke up in the pitch dark and went out without using her flashlight and pissed beside her cabin, almost noiselessly. She heard no local breaking of wind, but guessed that many of the cabins were still empty; the Men had all gone off upstream, off limits, after the lecture, and now she heard them not chanting but yelling and roaring, a wild noise, but so far away that it didn't make much of a dent on the silence here. Here at Limberlost.

33   In the low, cold mist of morning, the poet came from cabin to cabin. The novelist heard him coming, chanting and making animal sounds, banging the screen doors of the cabins. He wore a dramatic animal mask, a gray, snarling, hairy snout. "Up! Up! Daybreak! The old wolf's at the door! The wolf, the wolf!" he chanted entering a cabin in a predatory crouch. Sleepy voices protested laughingly. The novelist was already up and dressed and had performed t'ai chi. She had stayed inside the screened cabin instead of going out on its spacious porch, because she was self-conscious, because doing t'ai chi was just too damn much the kind of thing you did here and yet didn't fit at all with what they were doing here and anyhow she was going home today and would damn well do t'ai chi in the broom closet if that's where she felt like doing it.

The poet approached her cabin and paused. "Good morn- 34
ing!" he said politely and incongruously through his staring,
hairy muzzle. "Good morning," said the novelist from behind
her screens, feeling a surge of snobbish irritation at the silly
poet parading his power to wake everybody up, but *she* was up
already!—and at the same time yearning to be able to go out
and pat the wolf, to call him brave, to play the game he wanted
so much to play, or at least to offer him something better than
a wet sock on a stick.

AFFIRMATIVE ACTION

Shelby Steele

A NEGATIVE VOTE
ON AFFIRMATIVE ACTION

An English professor by trade, Shelby Steele (born 1946) is currently on leave from San Jose State University and serving as a Hoover Fellow at Stanford University. His essays, which frequently reflect on one or another aspect of race in the United States, especially on the causes of friction between African Americans and white Americans, have appeared in many respected magazines and newspapers, including The American Scholar, The Washington Post, *and* The New Republic. *He collected many of those essays, including the one reprinted here, in his 1990 book* The Content of Our Character: A New Vision of Race in America. *The article first appeared in* The New York Times Magazine *in 1990.*

1   In a few short years, when my two children will be applying to college, the affirmative-action policies by which most universities offer black students some form of preferential treatment will present me with a dilemma. I am a middle-class black, a college professor, far from wealthy, but also well removed from the kind of deprivation that would qualify my children for the label "disadvantaged." Both of them have endured racial insensitivity from whites. They have been called names, have suffered slights and have experienced first hand the peculiar malevolence that racism brings out of people. Yet they have never experienced racial discrimination, have never been stopped by their race on any path they have chosen to follow. Still, their society now tells them that if they will only designate themselves as black on their college applications, they will probably do better in the college lottery than if they conceal this fact. I think there is something of a Faustian bargain in this.

Of course many blacks and a considerable number of whites 2
would say that I was sanctimoniously making affirmative action into a test of character. They would say that this small
preference is the meagerest recompense for centuries of unre-
lieved oppression. And to these arguments other very obvious
facts must be added. In America, many marginally competent
or flatly incompetent whites are hired every day—some because their white skin suits the conscious or unconscious racial
preference of their employers. The white children of alumni
are often grandfathered into elite universities in what can only
be seen as a residual benefit of historic white privilege. Worse,
white incompetence is always an individual matter, but for
blacks it is often confirmation of ugly stereotypes. Given that
unfairness cuts both ways, doesn't it only balance the scales of
history, doesn't this repair, in a small way, the systematic denial
under which my children's grandfather lived out his days?

In theory, affirmative action certainly has all the moral sym- 3
metry that fairness requires. It is reformist and corrective,
even repentent and redemptive. And I would never sneer at
these good intentions. Born in the late 1940's in Chicago, I
started my education (a charitable term, in this case) in a segregated school, and suffered all the indignities that come to
blacks in a segregated society. My father, born in the South,
made it only to the third grade before the white man's fields
took permanent priority over his formal education. And
though he educated himself into an advanced reader with an
almost professorial authority, he could only drive a truck for a
living, and never earned more than $90 a week in his entire
life. So yes, it is crucial to my sense of citizenship, to my ability
to identify with the spirit and the interests of America, to know
that this country, however imperfectly, recognizes its past sins
and wishes to correct them.

Yet good intentions can blind us to the effects they generate 4
when implemented. In our society affirmative action is, among
other things, a testament to white good will and to black
power, and in the midst of these heavy investments its effects
can be hard to see. But after 20 years of implementation I
think that affirmative action has shown itself to be more bad
than good and that blacks—whom I will focus on in this essay—now stand to lose more from it than they gain.

In talking with affirmative-action administrators and with 5
blacks and whites in general, I found that supporters of affirmative action focus on its good intentions and detractors emphasize its negative effects. It was virtually impossible to find
people outside either camp. The closest I came was a white
male manager at a large computer company who said, "I think

it amounts to reverse discrimination, but I'll put up with a little of that for a little more diversity." But this only makes him a half-hearted supporter of affirmative action. I think many people who don't really like affirmative action support it to one degree or another anyway.

6   I believe they do this because of what happened to white and black Americans in the crucible of the 1960's, when whites were confronted with their racial guilt and blacks tasted their first real power. In that stormy time white absolution and black power coalesced into virtual mandates for society. Affirmative action became a meeting ground for those mandates in the law. At first, this meant insuring equal opportunity. The 1964 civil-rights bill was passed on the understanding that equal opportunity would not mean racial preference. But in the late 60's and early 70's, affirmative action underwent a remarkable escalation of its mission from simple anti-discrimination enforcement to social engineering by means of quotas, goals, timetables, set-asides and other forms of preferential treatment.

7   Legally, this was achieved through a series of executive orders and Equal Employment Opportunity Commission guidelines that allowed racial imbalances in the workplace to stand as proof of racial discrimination. Once it could be assumed that discrimination explained racial imbalances, it became easy to justify group remedies to presumed discrimination rather than the normal case-by-case redress.

8   Even though blacks had made great advances during the 60's without quotas, the white mandate to achieve a new racial innocence and the black mandate to gain power, which came to a head in the very late 60's, could no longer be satisfied by anything less than racial preferences. I don't think these mandates, in themselves, were wrong, because whites clearly needed to do better by blacks and blacks needed more real power in society. But as they came together in affirmative action, their effect was to distort our understanding of racial discrimination. By making black the color of preference, these mandates have re-burdened society with the very marriage of color and preference (in reverse) that we set out to eradicate.

9   When affirmative action grew into social engineering, diversity became a golden word. Diversity is a term that applies democratic principles to races and cultures rather than to citizens, despite the fact that there is nothing to indicate that real diversity is the same thing as proportionate representation. Too often the result of this, on campuses for example, has been a democracy of colors rather than of people, an artificial diversity that gives the appearance of an educational parity between black and white students that has not yet been achieved in re-

ality. Here again, racial preferences allow society to leapfrog over the difficult problem of developing blacks to parity with whites and into a cosmetic diversity that covers the blemish of disparity—a full six years after admission, only 26 to 28 percent of blacks graduate from college.

Racial representation is not the same thing as racial development. Representation can be manufactured; development is always hard earned. But it is the music of innocence and power that we hear in affirmative action that causes us to cling to it and to its distracting emphasis on representation. The fact is that after 20 years of racial preferences the gap between median incomes of black and white families is greater than it was in the 1970's. None of this is to say that blacks don't need policies that insure our right to equal opportunity, but what we need more of is the development that will let us take advantage of society's efforts to include us.

I think one of the most troubling effects of racial preferences for blacks is a kind of demoralization. Under affirmative action, the quality that earns us preferential treatment is an implied inferiority. However this inferiority is explained—and it is easily enough explained by the myriad deprivations that grew out of our oppression—it is still inferiority. There are explanations and then there is the fact. And the fact must be borne by the individual as a condition apart from the explanation, apart even from the fact that others like himself also bear this condition. In integrated situations in which blacks must compete with whites who may be better prepared, these explanations may quickly wear thin and expose the individual to racial as well as personal self-doubt. (Of course whites also feel doubt, but only personally, not racially.)

What this means in practical terms is that when blacks deliver themselves into integrated situations they encounter a nasty little reflex in whites, a mindless, atavistic reflex that responds to the color black with negative stereotypes, such as intellectual ineptness. I think this reflex embarrasses most whites today and thus it is usually quickly repressed. On an equally atavistic level, the black will be aware of the reflex his color triggers and will feel a stab of horror at seeing himself reflected in this way. He, too, will do a quick repression, but a lifetime of such stabbings is what constitutes his inner realm of racial doubt. Even when the black sees no implication of inferiority in racial preferences, he knows that whites do, so that—consciously or unconsciously—the result is virtually the same. The effect of preferential treatment—the lowering of normal standards to increase black representation—puts blacks at war with an expanded realm of debilitating doubt, so that the doubt itself becomes an unrecognized preoccupation that undermines their ability to perform, especially in integrated situations.

13 I believe another liability of affirmative action comes from the fact that it indirectly encourages blacks to exploit their own past victimization. Like implied inferiority, victimization is what justifies preference, so that to receive the benefits of preferential treatment one must, to some extent, become invested in the view of one's self as a victim. In this way, affirmative action nurtures a victim-focused identity in blacks and sends us the message that there is more power in our past suffering than in our present achievements.

14 When power itself grows out of suffering, blacks are encouraged to expand the boundaries of what qualifies as racial oppression, a situation that can lead us to paint our victimization in vivid colors even as we receive the benefits of preference. The same corporations and institutions that give us preference are also seen as our oppressors. At Stanford University, minority group students—who receive at least the same financial aid as whites with the same need—recently took over the president's office demanding, among other things, more financial aid.

15 But I think one of the worst prices that blacks pay for preference has to do with an illusion. I saw this illusion at work recently in the mother of a middle-class black student who was going off to his first semester of college: "They owe us this, so don't think for a minute that you don't belong there." This is the logic by which many blacks, and some whites, justify affirmative action—it is something "owed," a form of reparation. But this logic overlooks a much harder and less digestible reality, that it is impossible to repay blacks living today for the historic suffering of the race. If all blacks were given a million dollars tomorrow it would not amount to a dime on the dollar for three centuries of oppression, nor would it dissolve the residues of that oppression that we still carry today. The concept of historic reparation grows out of man's need to impose on the world a degree of justice that simply does not exist. Suffering can be endured and overcome, it cannot be repaid. To think otherwise is to prolong the suffering.

16 Several blacks I spoke with said they were still in favor of affirmative action because of the "subtle" discrimination blacks were subject to once they were on the job. One photojournalist said, "They have ways of ignoring you." A black female television producer said: "You can't file a lawsuit when your boss doesn't invite you to the insider meetings without ruining your career. So we still need affirmative action." Others mentioned the infamous "glass ceiling" through which blacks can see the

top positions of authority but never reach them. But I don't think racial preferences are a protection against this subtle discrimination; I think they contribute to it.

In any workplace, racial preferences will always create two-   17
tiered populations composed of preferreds and unpreferred. In the case of blacks and whites, for instance, racial preferences imply that whites are superior just as they imply that blacks are inferior. They not only reinforce America's oldest racial myth but, for blacks, they have the effect of stigmatizing the already stigmatized.

I think that much of the "subtle" discrimination that blacks   18
talk about is often (not always) discrimination against the stigma of questionable competence that affirmative action marks blacks with. In this sense, preferences make scapegoats of the very people they seek to help. And it may be that at a certain level employers impose a glass ceiling, but this may not be against the race so much as against the race's reputation for having advanced by color as much as by competence. This ceiling is the point at which corporations shift the emphasis from color to competency and stop playing the affirmative-action game. Here preference backfires for blacks and becomes a taint that holds them back. Of course one could argue that this taint, which is after all in the minds of whites, becomes nothing more than an excuse to discriminate against blacks. And certainly the result is the same in either case—blacks don't get past the glass ceiling. But this argument does not get around the fact that racial preferences now taint this color with a new theme of suspicion that makes blacks even more vulnerable to discrimination. In this crucial yet gray area of perceived competence, preferences make whites look better than they are and blacks worse, while doing nothing whatever to stop the very real discrimination that blacks may encounter. I don't wish to justify the glass ceiling here, but only suggest the very subtle ways that affirmative action revives rather than extinguishes the old rationalizations for racial discrimination.

I believe affirmative action is problematic in our society be-   19
cause we have demanded that it create parity between the races rather than insure equal opportunity. Preferential treatment does not teach skills, or educate, or instill motivation. It only passes out entitlement, by color, a situation that in my profession has created an unrealistically high demand for black professors. The social engineer's assumption is that this high demand will inspire more blacks to earn Ph.D's and join the profession. In fact, the number of blacks earning Ph.D's has declined in recent years. Ph.D's must be developed from preschool on. They require family and community support.

They must acquire an entire system of values that enables them to work hard while delaying gratification.

20   It now seems clear that the Supreme Court, in a series of recent decisions, is moving away from racial preferences. It has disallowed preferences except in instances of "identified discrimination," eroded the precedent that statistical racial imbalances are prima facie evidence of discrimination, and, in effect, granted white males the right to challenge consent decrees that use preference to achieve racial balances in the workplace. Referring to this and other Supreme Court decisions, one civil-rights leader said, "Night has fallen . . . as far as civil rights are concerned." But I am not so sure. The effect of these decisions is to protect the constitutional rights of everyone rather than to take rights away from blacks. Night has fallen on racial preferences, not on the fundamental rights of black Americans. The reason for this shift, I believe, is that the white mandate for absolution from past racial sins has weakened considerably in the 1980's. Whites are now less willing to endure unfairness to themselves in order to grant special entitlements to blacks, even when those entitlements are justified in the name of past suffering. Yet the black mandate for more power in society has remained unchanged. And I think part of the anxiety many blacks feel over these decisions has to do with the loss of black power that they may signal.

21   But the power we've lost by these decisions is really only the power that grows out of our victimization. This is not a very substantial or reliable power, and it is important that we know this so we can focus more exclusively on the kind of development that will bring enduring power. There is talk now that Congress may pass new legislation to compensate for these new limits on affirmative action. If this happens, I hope the focus will be on development and antidiscrimination, rather than entitlement, on achieving racial parity rather than jerry-building racial diversity.

22   But if not preferences, what? The impulse to discriminate *is* subtle and cannot be ferreted out unless its many guises are made clear to people. I think we need social policies that are committed to two goals: the educational and economic development of disadvantaged people regardless of race and the eradication from our society—through close monitoring and severe sanctions—of racial, ethnic or gender discrimination. Preferences will not get us to either of these goals, because they tend to benefit those who are not disadvantaged—middle-class white women and middle-class blacks—and attack one form of discrimination with another. Preferences are inexpensive and carry the glamour of good intentions—change the

NATHAN GLAZER, Should the SAT Account for Race? Yes

333

numbers and the good deed is done. To be against them is to be unkind. But I think the unkindest cut is to bestow on children like my own an undeserved advantage while neglecting the development of those disadvantaged children in the poorer sections of my city who will most likely never be in a position to benefit from a preference. Give my children fairness; give disadvantaged children a better shot at development—better elementary and secondary schools, job training, safer neighborhoods, better financial assistance for college and so on. A smaller percentage of black high school graduates go to college today than 15 years ago; more black males are in prison, jail or in some other way under the control of the criminal-justice system than in college. This despite racial preferences.

The mandates of black power and white absolution out of   23
which preferences emerged were not wrong in themselves. What was wrong was that both races focused more on the goals of those mandates than on the means to the goals. Blacks can have no real power without taking responsibility for their own educational and economic development. Whites can have no racial innocence without earning it by eradicating discrimination and helping the disadvantaged to develop. Because we ignored the means, the goals have not been reached and the real work remains to be done.

Nathan Glazer

SHOULD THE SAT ACCOUNT FOR RACE? YES

Nathan Glazer (born 1932) has been interested in education for many years. Professor of education and sociology at Harvard, he writes about many aspects of American education, especially as they involve ethnicity—see for examples his books Beyond the Melting Pot *and* Ethnic Dilemmas. *The following essay originally appeared along with the following one by Abigail Thernstrom in* New Republic *(a middle-of-the-road publication on public affairs and contemporary culture) in September 1999.*

1   This month, the Educational Testing Service (ETS), creator and marketer of the SAT—the most widely used test of academic ability and the key measure that colleges and universities take into account when making admissions decisions—announced that it is developing a "Strivers" score, an adjustment of the SAT score to take into account a student's socioeconomic background and race, increasing the scores of those whose socioeconomic background or race is considered to put them at a disadvantage. Colleges and universities will be able to use the new Strivers score, if they wish, in making their admissions decisions. The ETS will offer institutions both a "race-blind" model, which includes only social, economic, and educational factors, and a model that also takes into account race—that is, whether the applicant is black, Hispanic, or Native American. ETS's chief competitor, the American College Testing Program, which produces a test used by many institutions instead of the SAT, will be developing a similar model.

2   Clearly, these developments are a response to the crumbling of the legal support that colleges and universities have relied upon to justify the almost universal practice among selective institutions of giving some kind of preference to black and Hispanic students. And, just as surely, critics of racial preference in college admissions will not be mollified by the new Strivers score and other, similar new strategies. If the formula using race is factored into admissions decisions, the new procedure will be just as legally vulnerable as the existing formal or informal preferences for race that have been struck down by a federal appeals court ruling in a University of Texas case and are now being challenged in an important University of Michigan case. Nor, one would think, would the new approach survive in the courts of the states—California and Washington—where popular referenda have forbidden the states and their agencies, including colleges and universities, to take race into account when making admissions decisions.

3   And, if the Strivers score without the race factor is used, present statistical patterns show that it will be less effective in identifying black students who may qualify for admission than the score that includes race as part of the formula. For race is indeed a factor in reducing test scores, independent of family wealth, education, and the other socioeconomic factors. It has a particularly strong independent effect in reducing scores for blacks, and, for most institutions, increasing the number of black students is a higher priority than increasing the number of Hispanic students.

4   What is most striking about the development of the Strivers score is the evidence it gives us of the strength of the commit-

NATHAN GLAZER, Should the SAT Account for Race? Yes

335

ment to maintaining a higher number of black and Hispanic
students in selective institutions than would qualify on the basis of academic promise alone. It is not only the testing agencies that show this commitment. They are, after all, responding to their customers, the educational institutions, whose
presidents and administrations universally support racial preference in admissions. They may call it "diversity," a softer and
more benign term, but what diversity in practice means is
more blacks than they would admit under admissions procedures that didn't take race into account. Writing in *National
Review*, Stephan Thernstrom, a strong critic of racial preferences, informs us with disapproval that "[William] Bowen and
[Derek] Bok argue [in their study of racial preference *The
Shape of the River*] that administrators barred from using
racial double-standards in admissions will elect to lower standards for all applicants so as to secure enough non-Asian minorities in the student body."

While this is not quite their position—it is, rather, that ad- 5
ministrators will do what they can to maintain the number of
black students even when legal bans on taking race into account exist—the fact is that it is not administrators alone who
will do this in the effort to evade the clear effect of the elimination of race preference. The Texas legislature voted that the
state university should consider the top ten percent of the graduating class of every Texas high school eligible for the state university, a far more radical lowering of the standards for eligibil-
ity than any university administrator would have proposed.

Even more remarkably, the Regents of the University of 6
California, who had earlier voted that race could not be taken
into account in admissions decisions, have voted that the top
four percent of the graduates of every California high school
should be eligible for admission to the state university system!
The Texas and California actions both radically expand the
number of black and Hispanic students eligible for the state
universities, for in both states there are many high schools almost exclusively Hispanic and black in composition that
would not be capable of producing students eligible for the top
branches of the state university without the new policies.

The faculties of colleges and universities have not played 7
much of a role in all this. Faculty members critical of racial
preferences berate their colleagues for not speaking up—
indeed, faculty members rarely speak up when a controversial
issue does not affect them directly. But recent surveys show
that the critics of racial preference will not get much support
from university faculties. Although a recent survey of 34,000
faculty members conducted by the Higher Education Research

Institute of the University of California at Los Angeles does not ask the racial preference question directly, it does ask whether "promoting diversity leads to the admission of too many under-prepared students." Only 28 percent of respondents agreed. And 90.5 percent of respondents agreed with the following statement, admittedly not much more controversial than arguing the virtues of motherhood: "A racially/ethnically diverse student body enhances the educational experience of all students."

8   Thus college and university faculty and administrators, state legislatures, and the ruling political bodies in charge of public universities all seem to have a commitment to maintaining the number of black and Hispanic students receiving higher education, and, bluntly, are willing to take evasive action to do it. They will use substitutes for race—and, if one substitute does not work, they will look for others. If focusing on applicants who live in a poor neighborhood doesn't help—perhaps there are too many Asians in one poor California neighborhood or another—they will try focusing on applicants who live in housing projects. One way or another, the commitment to enrolling more blacks than would qualify based on academic criteria alone will be pursued.

9   I believe this commitment, however cloaked in subterfuge it may be, is a valid one. True, it has been clear from the beginning of affirmative action that the majority of the American population—and even a very substantial part of the black population—does not like the idea of making an individual's fate dependent on his or her race or ethnic background. We are all, in principle, in favor of a race-blind society, and clearly that is an important principle, one that we all hope to realize in time. But it has turned out that the use of strict race-blind admissions procedures will radically reduce the number of black students, and in lesser measure the number of Hispanic students, in the selective institutions of higher education—key institutions of our society. This can only serve to further divide non-Asian minorities and whites and to further postpone the day when we can achieve a truly race-blind, fully integrated society. And this is simply too high a price to pay for adhering to the principle of race-blind admissions today.

10   IF, THEN, ONE accepts that admitting more non-Asian minorities than would make the cut through academic criteria alone is a legitimate goal, the Strivers score is not such a terrible way to achieve it. The new score, which is simply an adjustment of the actual SAT score, is based on the common observation that students from wealthier and more educated families, from well-to-do suburbs, from high schools with better students, and the like, will on average do better on the SAT than students

NATHAN GLAZER, Should the SAT Account for Race? Yes

337

from poorer and less-educated families and from worse high schools—the circumstances of a disproportionate number of minorities. It stands to reason that a student from a materially and educationally impoverished environment who does fairly well on the SAT and better than other students who come from a similar environment is probably stronger than the unadjusted score indicates. In the past, those colleges and universities whose admissions staffs and procedures permitted individual evaluation of applications took such factors into account informally. With the new Strivers score, they will have a statistical tool that includes no fewer than 14 characteristics that are expected to affect SAT scores. It will, of course, be up to individual institutions to decide whether they want to make use of the Strivers adjustment, just as individual institutions now determine how much weight the SAT score should have in the admissions decision. Still, the Strivers score may make what was essentially an intuitive system more rational.

Of course, there's a strong possibility that it may not survive 11 the inevitable legal challenges. It also remains to be seen just how effective the new approach will be at maintaining or increasing the number of blacks and Hispanic students in our colleges and universities. For instance, it's possible that the main effect may be instead to increase the number of Asians, in which case the effectiveness of the Strivers adjustment would undoubtedly be reviewed.

But even if the Strivers score approach does not succeed, its 12 introduction has highlighted the need for institutions under legal attack to improve the informal and messy procedures that they have been using to raise their enrollment of minority students. Perhaps we can bury the overt emphasis on race while trying to reach the same objective; perhaps race can become the dirty little secret we are trying to take account of without directly saying so. Hypocrisy in the matter may be no minor gain. But it is clear that, for some time, if we are to maintain the appearance of being one nation when by many measures we are, in fact, two, a pure race-blind policy will be so strongly resisted that racial preference will by some means prevail.

Abigail Thernstrom

SHOULD THE SAT
ACCOUNT FOR RACE?
NO

Abigail Thernstrom's essay reprinted here is a companion piece to the preceding essay by Nathan Glazer; both of them appeared in New Republic *in September 1999. Thernstrom, the coauthor of* America in Black and White: One Nation, Indivisible *(1999), has been outspoken about issues related to affirmative action.*

1   THE EDUCATIONAL TESTING SERVICE (ETS) calls them "strivers." They could just as well be called the "but for" kids: kids who would have done better on their SATs *but for* . . . their racial or ethnic identities, their families' income, the quality of their schools, and so forth. Or so ETS believes. These and other circumstances call for college admissions officers to treat these students' scores differently than they otherwise would, the company suggests. Never mind that selective colleges already take such factors into account when weighing student applications. That inevitably subjective process is inadequate, ETS apparently believes. Schools with high admissions standards need further instruction and a tool to help read scores properly. "A combined score of 1000 on the SATs is not always a 1000," Anthony Carnevale, an ETS vice president who heads the Strivers project, has said. "When you look at a striver who gets a 1000, you're looking at someone who really performs at a 1200."

2   The students ETS has in mind are those who have done better than their demographic profile would predict. Carnevale suggests the low score is, in effect, a false negative, but ETS has evidently decided to leave the actual process of readjusting scores up to the schools themselves. It will provide the unadjusted score and a statistical formula that colleges can use to convert it to the Strivers number, should they so choose.

3   Or so it seems. In the wake of negative press, the company released an obfuscating memo denying any current "program or service based upon the Strivers research." But it did not rule out offering a "program or service" once its final report is completed—in about two months. "Researchers" have been "studying the effect of considering additional background information" in order to "provide a richer context for candidates'

ABIGAIL THERNSTROM, Should the SAT Account for Race? No

339

scores," the memo explained. "ETS is committed to continuing a dialogue about fairness and equity in higher education."

That ongoing "dialogue" has largely been prompted, of 4 course, by the end of the use of racial preferences in admissions decisions in public higher education in Texas, California, and Washington state. Although University of Michigan President Lee Bollinger recently declared diversity to be "as vital as teaching Shakespeare or mathematics," the University of Michigan's own race-based admissions processes will soon be on trial in a federal district court. Suits against other elite colleges (all of which sort students on the basis of race and ethnicity) are sure to follow. But ETS may be riding to the schools' partial rescue with a formula that gives a pseudoscientific imprimatur to setting lower SAT standards for "disadvantaged" students.

ETS broadens the definition of disadvantage beyond race 5 and ethnicity and is said to be working on two formulas. One will factor in race. The other will reportedly focus on only such variables as the employment status of the student's mother and the kinds of electrical appliances and number of books in the student's home, as reported—accurately or inaccurately—by the student. Thus, the University of California and the handful of other schools that are no longer allowed to make race-based admissions decisions will be able to use it. A formal acknowledgment that disadvantage comes in all colors and many forms would certainly be a step forward. But not a very big one. Expanding the universe of preferential admits does not solve the basic problem. ETS is simply adding more variables to a victimology index and reinforcing the already-too-widespread belief that demography is destiny. And once you start factoring in variables that lead to disadvantage, where do you stop? Should you take into account an applicant's birth order? Her relationship with her parents? The psychologists haven't even gotten into the act yet.

Of course, literally no one believes that SAT scores alone 6 should determine who gets into which schools. And, in fact, no college entirely ignores the "context" that ETS wants to stress. But does ETS really want high schools telling a black kid in the Bronx that no one expects him to do as well as the Vietnamese immigrant in his class? Should a teacher say to a white student from a low-income family, "I'll count your C in math as an A? You come to the test with a disadvantage; I understand."

Across the nation, states are getting serious about promoting 7 high academic standards in their elementary and secondary schools. But, in Massachusetts and elsewhere, anti-testing voices have argued that it is simply unfair to expect suburban skills in urban schools with high concentrations of non-Asian minority kids. Teachers, critics say, are being asked to achieve the impossible. Moreover, the Office of Civil Rights in the U.S. Department of Education has recently weighed in with an attack on all high-stakes testing as potentially discriminatory.

8   Without doubt, school is easier for children who grow up in affluent and educated households. And yet, without tough tests and uniformly high expectations, the academic performance of black and Hispanic children—which, on average, is woefully behind that of whites and Asians—is unlikely to improve. ETS is proposing to send the worst possible message to these kids: If you start out in life with less, we expect less of you—today, tomorrow, maybe forever. The die has been cast. The fix is in.

9   The students who meet high academic expectations in the kindergarten-through-twelfth-grade years are likely to do well on the SATs, and for most students those tests are excellent predictors of how they will fare in college. As a consequence (as Carnevale surely knows), a score of 1000 is simply not the same as 1200; the lower-scoring student is less academically prepared. Even a score of 1200 means a rough academic ride for students at universities such as Princeton and Stanford, where the median SAT score exceeds 1400.

10   If elite schools want to become nonselective, or if they want to choose their matriculants randomly from the pool of applicants with scores over, say, 1000, who could object on grounds of principle? Needless to say, their fancy professors and devoted alumni might not like the idea. The physics professor who is a Nobel laureate generally wants to teach high-powered students, and the alumni like the prestige that accompanies highly selective admissions. A more random system would let in plenty of strivers, but the schools themselves would change. Students who were less prepared would require less rigorous courses—unless the colleges suddenly became willing to flunk them out.

11   ETS is obviously trying to suggest otherwise. Strivers (by definition) have tried harder and thus can do as well as the kid with the much higher SAT, the testing service implies. The disadvantaged student with a score of 1000 will do just as well as the privileged one who got 1200.

12   Well, maybe, in some cases. But the notion rests on a questionable assumption—namely that a score of 1000, when it beats a racial or other group norm, represents extraordinary effort. That may not be the case. Perhaps the student from an impoverished family who seems to have beaten the SAT odds is simply good at taking standardized tests. Or perhaps her par-

ABIGAIL THERNSTROM, Should the SAT Account for Race? No

341

ents have intangible qualities that the ETS formula has failed to capture. It is even possible that she didn't try hard enough—that she is underperforming relative to her intellectual gifts. Her score may reflect academic talent, not hard work. In fact, if ETS is serious about finding the kids who really "strive," it might make much more sense to look at grade point averages, adjusted for the difficulty of the courses taken. Arguably, it is the student with a low SAT score but a high GPA who has demonstrated dedication and perseverance—true grit.

In addition, there is no evidence that students who outscore 13
peers with the same demographic characteristics will experience exceptional intellectual growth in college. In general, for unknown reasons, black students, for instance, earn substantially lower grades in college than their SATs would lead us to predict. (This is one of the buried but depressing facts contained in William Bowen and Derek Bok's pro-affirmative-action book, *The Shape of the River.*) Another recent study, which focused on University of San Diego undergraduates, looked not only at blacks and Hispanics but also at the records of students who attended impoverished high schools, came from low-income families, or lived in neighborhoods with few college graduates. These disadvantaged youths also underperformed, by the measure of their SAT scores.

Most important, why should the measure of achievement be 14
a group norm? Asians do better than whites on math SATs; should whites who outperform the white group norm be given special preference? Should a high-scoring Asian be rejected from MIT if she beats the non-Asian competition but scores lower than Asians in general? In fact, both Asians and Jews will suffer under any leveling scheme that penalizes applicants who come from more prosperous and better-educated homes. These two groups are strikingly overrepresented on elite campuses today, precisely because they score so high on the SATs. Asians constitute only four percent of the population, but they represent almost a quarter of all students scoring above 750 on the math SATs, with the result that they make up nearly one-fifth of the student body at Harvard and a quarter or more at MIT and Cal Tech. It appears that the end of racial preferences in California has primarily benefited Asians.

ETS is perfectly right, of course, to say that race, ethnicity, 15
and socioeconomic status correlate with SAT scores. And SAT scores, the company should add, correlate with college performance. Instead of trafficking in group stereotypes, endlessly tinkering with scores, giving extra points for this or that sort of disadvantage, and pretending lower-scoring students are competitive when they are not, why not just educate the kids? Does

ETS believe good schools are an impossible dream? Shame on it, if it does.

Susan Sturm and Lani Guinier
THE FUTURE
OF AFFIRMATIVE ACTION

Susan Sturm is professor of law at Columbia University; she has committed her career to issues related to social justice. Lani Guinier, professor of law at Harvard University, has written Tyranny of the Majority *and* Lift Every Voice. *She was President Clinton's choice to serve as U. S. Attorney General until her nomination was withdrawn on account of reactions to her controversial legal opinions. Sturm and Guinier wrote the following essay for a legal journal called* Boston Review. *Responses to this essay, as well as the essays themselves, are printed in a book entitled* The Future of Affirmative Action, *published by Beacon Press in 2001.*

1 For more than two decades, affirmative action has been under sustained assault. In courts, legislatures, and the media, opponents have condemned it as an unprincipled program of racial and gender preferences that threatens fundamental American values of fairness, equality, and democratic opportunity. Such preferences, they say, are extraordinary departures from prevailing "meritocratic" modes of selection, which they present as both fair and functional: fair, because they treat all candidates as equals; functional, because they are well suited to picking the best candidates.

2 This challenge to affirmative action has met with concerted response. Defenders argue that affirmative action is still needed to rectify continued exclusion and marginalization. And they marshal considerable evidence showing that conventional standards of selection exclude women and people of color, and that people who were excluded in the past do not yet operate on a level playing field. But this response has largely been reactive. Proponents typically treat affirmative action as a crucial but peripheral supplement to an essentially sound framework of selection for jobs and schools.

We think it is time to shift the terrain of debate. We need to   3
situate the conversation about race, gender, and affirmative action in a wider account of democratic opportunity by refocus-
ing attention from the contested periphery of the system of selection to its settled core. The present system measures merit
through scores on paper-and-pencil tests. But this measure is
fundamentally unfair. In the educational setting, it restricts opportunities for many poor and working-class Americans of all
colors and genders who could otherwise obtain a better education. In the employment setting, it restricts access based on inadequate predictors of job performance. In short, it is neither
fair nor functional in its distribution of opportunities for admission to higher education, entry-level hiring, and job promotion.

To be sure, the exclusion experienced by women and people   4
of color is especially revealing of larger patterns. The race- and
gender-based exclusions that are the target of current affirmative action policies remain the most visible examples of bias
in ostensibly neutral selection processes. Objectionable in
themselves, these exclusions also signal the inadequacy of traditional methods of selection for everyone, and the need to rethink how we allocate educational and employment opportunities. And that re-thinking is crucial to our capacity to develop
productive, fair, and efficient institutions that can meet the
challenges of a rapidly changing and increasingly complex
marketplace. By using the experience of those on the margin to
rethink the whole, we may forge a new, progressive vision of
cross-racial collaboration, functional diversity, and genuinely
democratic opportunity.

Affirmative Action Narratives

Competing narratives drive the affirmative action debate. The   5
stock story told by critics in the context of employment concerns the white civil servant—say a police officer or firefighter—
John Doe. (Similar stories abound in the educational setting.)
Doe scores several points higher on the civil service exam and
interview rating process, but loses out to a woman or person of
color who did not score as high on those selection criteria.[1]

Doe and others in similar circumstances advance two basic   6
claims: first, that they have more merit than beneficiaries of affirmative action; and second, that as a matter of fairness they
are entitled to the position for which they applied. Consider
these claims in turn.

The idea of merit can be interpreted in a variety of ways: for   7
example, as a matter of desert (because they were next in line,

based on established criteria of selection, they deserve the position), or as earned recognition ("when an individual has worked hard and succeeded, she deserves recognition, praise and/or reward"[2]). But, most fundamentally, arguments about merit are functional: a person merits a job if he or she has, to an especially high degree, the qualities needed to perform well in that job. Many critics of affirmative action equate merit, functionally understood, with a numerical ranking on standard paper-and-pencil tests. Those with higher scores are presumed to be most qualified, and therefore most deserving.

8 Fairness, like merit, is a concept with varying definitions. The stock story defines fairness formally. Fairness, it assumes, requires treating everyone the same: allowing everyone to enter the competition for a position, and evaluating each person's results the same way. If everyone takes the same test, and every applicant's test is evaluated in the same manner, then the assessment is fair. So affirmative action is unfair because it takes race and gender into account, and thus evaluates some test results differently. A crucial premise of this fairness challenge to affirmative action is the assumption that tests afford equal opportunity to demonstrate individual merit, and therefore are not biased.

9 Underlying the standard claims about merit and fairness, then, is the idea that we have an objective yardstick for measuring qualification. Institutions are assumed to know what they are looking for (to continue the yardstick analogy, length), how to measure it (yards, meters), how to replicate the measurement process (using the ruler), and how to rank people accordingly (by height). Both critics and proponents of affirmative action typically assume that objective tests for particular attributes of merit—perhaps supplemented by subjective methods such as unstructured interviews and reference checks —can be justified as predictive of performance, and as the most efficient method of selection.

Merit, Fairness, and Testocracy

10 The basic premise of the stock narrative is that the selection criteria and processes used to rank applicants for jobs and admission to schools are fair and valid tests of merit. This premise is flawed. The conventional system of selection does not give everyone an equal opportunity to compete. Not everyone who could do the job, or could bring new insights about how to do the job even better, is given an opportunity

to perform or succeed. The yardstick metaphor simply does not withstand scrutiny.

Fictive Merit   For present purposes, we accept the idea that   11
capacity to perform—functional merit—is a legitimate consideration in distributing jobs and educational opportunities. But we dispute the notion that merit is identical to performance on standardized tests. Such tests do not fulfill their stated function. They do not reliably identify those applicants who will succeed in college or later in life, nor do they consistently predict those who are most likely to perform well in the jobs they will occupy. Particularly when used alone or to rank-order candidates, timed paper-and-pencil tests screen out applicants who could nevertheless do the job.

Those who use standardized tests need to be able to identify   12
and measure successful performance in the job or at school. In both contexts, however, those who use tests lack meaningful measures of successful performance. In the employment area, many employers have not attempted to correlate test performance with worker productivity or pay. In the educational context, researchers have attempted to correlate standardized tests with first-year performance in college or post-graduate education.[3] But this measure does not reflect successful overall academic achievement or performance in other areas valued by the educational institution.

Moreover, "successful performance" needs to be interpreted   13
broadly. A study of three classes of Harvard alumni over three decades, for example, found a high correlation between "success"—defined by income, community involvement, and professional satisfaction—and two criteria that might not ordinarily be associated with Harvard freshmen: low SAT scores and a blue-collar background.[4] When asked what predicts *life success*, college admissions officers at elite universities report that, above a minimum level of competence, "initiative" or "drive" are the best predictors.[5]

By contrast, the conventional measures attempt to predict   14
successful performance, narrowly defined, in the short-run. They focus on immediate success in school and a short timeframe between taking the test and demonstrating success. Those who excel based on those short-term measures, however, may not in fact excel over the long-run in areas that are equally or more important. For example, a study of graduates of the University of Michigan Law School found a negative relationship between high LSAT scores and subsequent community leadership or community service.[6]

15 Those with higher LSAT scores are less likely, as a general matter, to serve their community or do pro bono service as a lawyer. In addition, the study found that admission indexes—including the LSAT—fail to correlate with other accomplishments after law school, including income levels and career satisfaction.

16 Standardized tests may thus compromise an institution's capacity to search for what it really values in selection. Privileging the aspects of performance measured by standardized tests may well screen out the contributions of people who would bring important and different skills to the workplace or educational institution. It may reward passive learning styles that mimic established strategies rather than creative, critical, or innovative thinking.

17 Finally, individuals often perform better in both workplace and school when challenged by competing perspectives or when given the opportunity to develop in conjunction with the different approaches or skills of others.

18 The problem of using standardized tests to predict performance is particularly acute in the context of employment. Standardized tests may reward qualities such as willingness to guess, conformity, and docility. If they do, then test performance may not relate significantly to the capacity to function well in jobs that require creativity, judgment, and leadership. In a service economy, creativity and interpersonal skills are important, though hard to measure. In the stock scenario of civil service exams for police and fire departments, traits such as honesty, perseverance, courage, and ability to manage anger are left out. In other words, people who rely heavily on numbers to make employment decisions may be looking in the wrong place. While John Doe scored higher on the civil service exam, he may not perform better as a police officer.

19 *Fictive Fairness* Scores on standardized tests are, then, inadequate measures of merit. But are the conventional methods of selecting candidates for high-stakes positions fair? The stock affirmative action narrative implicitly embraces the idea that fairness consists in sameness of treatment. But this conception of fairness assumes a level playing field—that if everyone plays by the same rules, the game does not favor or disadvantage anyone.

20 An alternative conception of fairness—we call it "fairness as equal access and opportunity"—rejects the automatic equation of sameness with fairness. It focuses on providing members of various races and genders with opportunities to demonstrate their capacities and recognizes that formal sameness can camouflage actual difference and apparently neutral screening de-

vices can be exclusionary. The central idea is that the standards governing the process must not *arbitrarily advantage* members of one group over another. It is not "fair," in this sense, to use entry-level credentials that appear to treat everyone the same, but in effect deny women and people of color a genuine opportunity to demonstrate their capacities.

On this conception, the "testocracy" fails to provide a fair 21 playing field for candidates. Many standardized tests assume that there is a single way to complete a job, and assess applicants solely on the basis of this uniform style. In this way, the testing process arbitrarily excludes individuals who may perform equally effectively, but with different approaches.

For example, in many police departments, strength, military 22 experience, and speed weigh heavily in the decision to hire police officers. These characteristics relate to a particular mode of policing focusing on "command presence" and control through authority and force.[7]

If the job of policing is defined as subduing dangerous sus- 23 pects, then it makes sense to favor the strongest, fastest, and most disciplined candidates. But not every situation calls for quick reaction time. Indeed, in some situations, responding quickly gets police officers and whole departments in trouble.

This speed-and-strength standard normalizes a particular 24 type of officer: tough, brawny, and macho. But other modes of policing—dispute resolution, persuasion, counseling, and community involvement—are also critical, and sometimes superior, approaches to policing. One study of the Los Angeles Police Department, conducted in the wake of the Rodney King trials, recommended that the department increase the number of women on the police force as part of a strategy to reduce police brutality and improve community relations. The study found that women often display a more interactive and engaged approach to policing.[8]

Similarly, an informal survey of police work in some New 25 York City Housing Authority projects found that many women housing authority officers, because they could not rely on their brawn to intimidate potential offenders, developed a mentoring style with young adolescent males.[9] The women, many of whom came from the community they were patrolling, increased public safety because they did not approach the young men in a confrontational way. Their authority was respected because they offered respect.

The retention and success of new entrants to institutions of- 26 ten depend on expanding measures of successful performance. But because conventional measures camouflage their bias, one-size-fits-all testocracies invite people to believe that they have earned their status because of a test score, and invite beneficiaries of affirmative action to believe exactly the opposite—that they did not earn their opportunity. By allowing partial and underinclusive selection standards to proceed without criticism, affirmative action perpetuates an asymmetrical approach to evaluation.

27   In addition to arbitrarily favoring certain standards of performance, conventional selection methods advantage candidates from higher socioeconomic backgrounds and disproportionately screen out women and people of color, as well as those in lower income brackets. When combined with other unstructured screening practices, such as personal connections and alumni preferences, standardized testing creates an arbitrary barrier for many otherwise-qualified candidates.

28   The evidence that the testocracy is skewed in favor of wealthy contestants is consistent and striking. Consider the linkage between test performance and parental income. Average family income rises with each 100-point increase in SAT scores, except for the highest SAT category, where the number of cases is small. Within each racial and ethnic group, SAT scores increase with income.

29   Reliance on high school rank alone excludes fewer people from lower socioeconomic backgrounds. When the SAT is used in conjunction with high school rank to select college applicants, the number of applicants admitted from lower-income families decreases. This is because the SAT is more strongly correlated with every measure of socioeconomic background than is high school rank.[10]

30   Existing methods of selection, both objective and subjective, also exclude people based on their race and gender. For example, although women as a group perform worse than males on the SAT, they equal or outperform men in grade point average during the first year of college, the most common measure of successful performance. Similar patterns have been detected in the results of the ACT and other standardized college selection tests.[11]

31   Supplementing class rank with the SAT also decreases black acceptances and black enrollments.[12] Studies show that the group of black applicants rejected based on their SAT scores includes both those who would likely have failed and those who would likely have succeeded, and that these groups offset each other. Consequently, the rejection of more blacks as a result of using SAT scores "does not translate into improved admissions outcomes. The SAT does not improve colleges' ability to admit successful blacks and reject potentially unsuccessful ones."[13]

Thus, it is incontestable that the existing meritocracy dispro-   32
portionately includes wealthy white men. Is this highly unequal outcome fair? Even if the "meritocracy" screens out
women, people of color, and those of lower socioeconomic status, it could be argued that those screens are fair if they serve
an important function. But the testocracy fails even on this
measure; it does not reliably distinguish successful future per-
formers from unsuccessful ones, even when supplemented by
additional subjective criteria. Therefore, racial, gender, and socioeconomic exclusion cannot legitimately be justified in the
name of a flawed system of selection.

A New Approach

We have seen how the stock affirmative action narrative nor-   33
malizes and legitimates selection practices that are neither
functional nor fair. Now it is time to use these criticisms as an
occasion to move from affirmative action as an add-on to affirmative action as an occasion to rethink the organizing framework for selection generally.

Such rethinking should begin by reconsidering the connec-   34
tion between predetermined qualifications and future performance. The standard approach proceeds as if selection were a
fine-tuned matching process that measures the capacity to perform according to some predetermined criteria of performance. This assumes that the capacity to perform—functional
merit—exists in people apart from their opportunity to work
on the job. It further assumes that institutions know in advance
what they are looking for, and that these functions will remain
constant across a wide range of work sites and over time.

But neither candidates nor positions remain fixed. Often   35
people who have been given an opportunity to do a job perform well because they learn the job by doing it. Moreover, on-
the-job learning has assumed even greater significance in the
current economy, in which unstable markets, technological advances, and shorter product cycles have created pressures for
businesses to increase the flexibility and problem-solving capacity of workers. Under these circumstances, access to on-
the-job training opportunities will contribute to functional
merit—the opportunity to perform will precede the capacity.

The concept of selection as a matching process also pre-   36
sumes that institutions have a clear idea of what they value,
and of the relationship of particular jobs to their institutional
goals. Even in a relatively stable economic and technological

environment, institutions rarely attempt to articulate goals, much less develop a basis for measuring successful achievement of those goals. But without a definition of successful performance, it is difficult to develop fair and valid selection criteria and processes.

37   Defining successful performance has also become more complicated in the current economic and political environment. Traditional measures of success, such as short-term profitability, do not fully define success, and may in fact distort the capacity to evaluate and monitor employee performance. In addition, standards must increasingly change to adapt to technological developments and shifting consumer demand. Students of economic organization and human resources now emphasize the importance of developing complex, interactive, and holistic approaches to measuring both institutional and individual performance.[14] Conventional matching approaches to selection do not easily accommodate this move toward more dynamic and interrelated assessments of successful performance.

38   Current selection approaches also focus on the decontextualized individual, who is assumed to possess merit in the abstract and to demonstrate it through a test or interview. Social science evidence shows that the testing environment can selectively depress the test performance of highly qualified individuals.[15] And individual performance does not take into account how an applicant functions as part of a group. Increasingly, work requires the capacity to interact effectively with others, and the demands of the economy are moving in the direction of more interactive, team-oriented production. The capacity to adapt to rapid changes in technology, shifts in consumer preferences, and fluid markets for goods requires greater collaboration at every level.[16] Paper-and-pencil tests do not measure or predict an individual's capacity for creativity and collaboration.

39   Assessment through opportunity to perform often works better than testing for performance. Various studies have shown that "experts often fail on 'formal' measures of their calculating or reasoning capacities but can be shown to exhibit precisely those same skills in the course of their ordinary work."[17] Those who assess individuals in situations that more closely resemble actual working conditions make better predictions about those individuals' ultimate performance. Particularly when those assessments are integrated into day-to-day work over a period of time, they have the potential to produce better information about workers and better workers.

40   Moreover, many of those who are given an opportunity to perform, even when their basic preparation is weaker, catch up if they are motivated to achieve. Indeed, a recent study of a 25-

year policy of open admissions at the City University of New York found that the school was one of the largest sources in the United States of undergraduate students going on to earn doctorates, even though many of its undergraduates come from relatively poor backgrounds and take twice as long to complete their bachelor's degree.[18]

Reclaiming Merit and Fairness

Critics of affirmative action defend prevailing selection practices in the name of meritocracy and democracy. We have argued that those practices put democratic opportunity fundamentally at risk. Even when they are modified by a commitment to affirmative action, current modes of selection jeopardize democratic values of inclusiveness (no one is arbitrarily shut out or excluded); transparency (the processes employed are open and are functionally linked to the public character or public mission of the institution); and accountability (the choice of beneficiaries is directly linked to a public good). The failure of existing practice to achieve inclusiveness is perhaps the most telling. Although some people will lose as a result of any sorting and ranking, a democratic system needs to give those losers a sense of hope in the future, not divide us into classes of permanent losers and permanent winners. But that is precisely what happens when we make opportunity dependent on past success.   41

How, then, can we develop a model of selection that expresses a more inclusive, transparent, and accountable vision of democratic opportunity—an approach to selection that will benefit everyone, and advance racial and gender justice?   42

An Emerging Model   Because of the importance in a democracy of ensuring opportunities to perform, we can start by shifting the model of selection from prediction to performance. This model builds on the insight that the opportunity to participate helps to create the capacity to perform, and that actual performance offers the best evidence of capacity to perform. So instead of making opportunity depend on a strong prior showing of qualification, we should expand opportunities as a way of building the relevant qualifications.   43

To follow this model, organizations need to build assessment into their activities, integrate considerations of inclusion and diversity into the process of selection, and develop mechanisms of evaluation that are accountable to those considerations. The result would be a dynamic process of selection, with feedback   44 integrated into productivity. At the level of individual performance assessment, it would mean less reliance on one-shot predictive tests and more on performance-based evaluation.

45 One fundamental change resulting from our framework would be a shift away from reliance on tests as a means of distinguishing among candidates. Tests would be limited to screening out individuals who could not learn to perform competently with adequate training and mentoring, or be simply discontinued as a part of the selection process. Of course, decreasing reliance on tests to rank candidates would create the need to develop other ways of distinguishing among applicants. There is no single, uniform solution to this problem. One approach would be a lottery system that would distribute opportunity to participate among relatively indistinguishable candidates by chance. Concerns about a lottery's insensitivity to particular institutional needs or values could be addressed by increasing the selection prospects of applicants with skills, abilities, or backgrounds that are particularly valued by the institution. A weighted lottery may be the fairest and most functional approach for some institutions. Particularly in the education arena, where opportunity lies at the core of the institution's mission, a lottery may be an important advance. Above that test-determined floor, applicants could be chosen by several alternatives, including portfolio-based assessment or a more structured and participatory decision-making process.[19]

46 A more institutionally grounded approach might work in non-educational contexts. In some jobs, for example, decision-makers would assume responsibility for constructing a dynamic and interactive process of selection that is integrated into the day-to-day functioning of the organization. Recent developments in the assessment area, such as portfolio-based and authentic assessment, move in this direction. These might build on the tradition and virtues of apprenticeship, and indeed might "more closely resemble traditional apprenticeship measures than formal testing."[20] They would build from and acknowledge the effects of context on performance and the importance of measuring performance in relation to context.

47 To take the next step in developing an experience-based approach to opportunity and assessment, it would be necessary to consider the needs, interests, and possibilities of the particular institutional setting. The central challenge is to develop systems of accountable decision-making that minimize the expression of bias, and structure judgment around identified, although not static, norms. For each assessment, decision-makers would articulate criteria of successful performance, document activities and tasks relevant to the judgment, assess

candidates in relation to those criteria, and offer sufficient information about the candidates' performance to enable others to exercise independent judgment.

For this model to work, institutions would also need to change the relationship between race, gender, and other categories of exclusion to the overall decision-making process. Institutions would continue to assess the impact of various selection processes on traditionally excluded groups. But institutions would use that information in different ways. Rather than operating as an add-on, after-the-fact response to failures of the overall process, race and gender would serve as both a signal of organizational failure and a catalyst of organizational innovation. We will return to this issue later, but let's first try to imagine what this more integrated approach would look like. [48]

Consider the case of Bernice, now the general counsel of a major financial institution. Initially, she was hired as local general counsel to a bank, after having previously been partner in a prestigious law firm. (She left the firm after reaching the glass ceiling, unable to bring in enough new clients to progress further.) [49]

Bernice ultimately became general counsel to a major national corporation that previously had no women in high-level management positions. Her promotion resulted from the opportunities presented in an interactive and extended selection process. Her local bank merged with a larger company. In part to create the appearance of including women, she was permitted to compete for the job of general counsel for the new entity. Three lawyers shared the position for nine months. She initially did not view herself as in the running for the final cut. [50]

During this time period, Bernice had a series of contacts with high-level corporate officials, contacts she never would have had without this probationary team approach. As it turned out, Bernice was able to deal unusually well with a series of crises. If standard criteria, such as recommendations and interpersonal contacts, had been used to select a candidate, it is doubtful Bernice would have been picked. But teamwork, decentralized management, and collaborative and flexible working relationships allowed her to develop the contacts and experiences that trained her. The opportunity to interact over a period of time allowed her to demonstrate her strengths to those who made promotion decisions. Bernice did not know she had those strengths until she took the job.[21] [51]

Now, as general counsel, she is positioned to expand opportunities for women, and corporate culture in general. She can structure the same kind of collaborative decision-making in selection that provided her the opportunity to work her way into the job. She determines who is promoted within the legal [52] department, and who is hired as outside counsel. She is also in a position to influence how women are assessed as managers within the company.

53   This story illustrates the potential for integrating concerns about diversity into the process of recruitment and selection. It also shows the value of using performance to assess performance. At the core of this integrative move is a functional theory of diversity animated both by principles of justice and fairness (the inclusion of marginalized groups and the minimization of bias) and by strategic concerns (improving productivity). It is crucial to this integration that decision-makers and advocates understand and embrace a conception of diversity that comprises normative and instrumental elements. In public discourse, diversity has become a catchall phrase or cliché used to substitute for a variety of goals, or a numerical concept that is equated with proportional representation.[22] Too often, the different strands of diversity remain separate, with those concerned about justice emphasizing racial and gender diversity as a project of remediation, and those concerned about productivity emphasizing differences in background and skills. Without an articulated theory that links diversity to the goals of particular enterprises and to the project of racial justice, public discussion and public policy-making around race and gender issues is more complicated.

54   *Selection and Productivity*   One argument for more closely integrating selection and performance is that doing so has the potential to improve institutions' capacity to select productive workers, pursue innovative performance, and adapt quickly to the demands of a changing economic environment. The conventional top-down approach short-circuits the capacity of selection to serve as a mechanism for feedback about an institution's performance and its need to adapt to changing conditions. It also keeps institutions from developing more responsive, integrated, and dynamically efficient selection processes.

55   Instead of relying on standardized tests, the system of performance-based selection would focus decision-makers' attention on creating suitable scenarios for making informed judgments about performance. This would improve the capacity of institutions to find people who are creative, adaptive, reliable, and committed, rather than just good test-takers. In some instances, these structured opportunities could directly contribute to the productivity of the organization.

56   A more interactive process of selection also provides an ongoing opportunity to assess and monitor organizational performance and to perceive and react to the changing character and

needs of clients and employees. It provides information learned through the process of selection to the rest of the organization. In the process of redefining the standards for recruitment, the organization also redefines how those already in the institution should function. Selection operates at the boundaries of the organization. It exposes decision-makers to the environment they operate in, provides access to information about the world in which the organization operates, and forces choices about its relationship with that environment. The process of defining the standards for positions also reflects and reinscribes the organization's priorities and direction. Emphasizing one set of skills over another in the selection process communicates to employees and students how the organization defines good work. Thus, the selection process provides the opportunity and challenge of continually redefining standards in relation to stakeholders, both inside and outside of the organization.

The Benefits of Diversity   More open-ended processes of selection also embrace and harness difference. And the resulting diversity—in particular, an interactive dynamic among individuals with different vantage points, skills, or values—appears to help generate creative solutions to problems.   57

Studies have shown that work-team heterogeneity promotes more critical strategic analysis, creativity, innovation, and high-quality decisions. Analyses of group decision-making suggest that participation of groups with different prior beliefs or predispositions in decision making improves the quality of the decision for everyone. Studies of jury deliberations support the contention that diversity of participants contributes to improved deliberation. A jury consisting of people from diverse backgrounds has more accurate recall and "more nuanced understanding of the behavior of the parties than [a more homogeneous jury]."[23]   58

Diversity in culture, style, and background also enhances the knowledge base and repertoire of skills and responses available to a particular group or institution, which can enhance institutions' capacity to perform and innovate. Again, the example of the Los Angeles Police Department illustrates this theory. The benefits of racial and gender diversity may be most obvious in the educational and human services areas, where customers, clients, and perspectives may themselves be identified by race and gender.   59

Racial and cultural diversity in a workforce can also provide opportunities for companies marketing products that serve racially and culturally diverse client groups. As David Thomas   60 and Robin Ely have documented, customers and clients from different racial, ethnic, and cultural communities constitute distinctive market niches that companies have sought to address by diversifying their workforces.

61   Inside an organization, the experience of those who have been excluded or marginalized often signals more general or systemic problems that affect a much larger group and may hurt the organization's overall productivity. Race and gender complaints may be symptomatic of more general management problems, such as poor organization or arbitrary treatment of workers. For example, recent studies documenting that many women find law school silencing and exclusionary reveal patterns of problems that many men experience as well.[24]

62   Similarly, sexual harassment of graduate students sometimes reveals a more general institutional inadequacy that would otherwise remain hidden. Faculty and students frequently lack shared understandings about fair, respectful, nonexploitative supervisory relationships between students and their faculty advisors. Addressing sexual harassment—a problem ordinarily associated with women—can prompt a conversation on ways to promote productive and successful working relationships in general.

63   These observations answer a large question about the status of affirmative action in the performance-based model: Once we use the lens of the margins to rethink the whole, why do group status and performance continue to be crucial in assessing the adequacy of selection criteria? If we are successful in transforming the discourse and practice of merit and selection for everyone, why are race, gender, and other categories of exclusion still relevant to the discussion?

64   In responding to this question, we take the world as it currently exists. The workforce is becoming increasingly diverse: almost two-thirds of entrants to the civilian workforce in the period between 1992 and 2005 are projected to be women and racial minorities. Women and people of color have long been excluded and marginalized, and continue to experience exclusion in many institutional settings. Race continues to be a divisive issue for many Americans, one that prompts skepticism and mistrust. Our continued focus on race and gender moves forward from the current legal and organizational landscape. In many institutions, particularly those that are private and non-union, categories such as race and gender offer the only avenue for challenging decisions and practices.

65   Under these conditions, race- and gender-based inquiries continue to form the cornerstone of an integrated approach to a progressive economic agenda. Many members of marginal-

ized groups predicate their willingness to participate in collaborative conversation on the majority's recognition of the ongoing significance of group-based exclusion. For members of historically excluded groups, a meaningful program of inclusion is a prerequisite to participating in ventures that benefit the whole community. Affirmative action has become a symbol of society's recognition of its responsibility for its history of legal disenfranchisement, and of the equal citizenship and respect of those who have historically been excluded. History shapes the perception and experience of those who have experienced formal exclusion, and this historic pattern of racial inequality will continue to be experienced unless it is affirmatively acknowledged and altered.

Without the cooperation of those concerned with race and 66 gender justice in building this new progressive agenda, the dialogue will continue to be polarized, divisive, and adversarial. Unless we can build the concerns of racial and gender inclusion into the process of collaboration, these issues will continue to be addressed in settings that undermine the capacity of institutions to adapt to changing conditions.

In addition, research consistently shows that ignoring patterns of racial and gender exclusion causes these patterns to recur. A proven method of minimizing the expression of bias in decision-making consists of reminding decision-makers of the risk of bias or exclusion and requiring them be fair and unbiased. Unless we continue to pay attention to the impact of our decisions on members of groups that are the target of subtle bias and exclusion, those group members will continue to be marginalized.

Fairness Using the margins to rethink the whole—by using 68 performance to develop opportunity—will help with fairness as well as functionality. The functional approach to selection reduces the importance of criteria that have excluded women and people of color and favored wealthier applicants. It enables previously excluded people to "show their stuff." Moreover, by rethinking the standards of selection for everyone, this approach destabilizes the idea that the existing meritocracy is fair. Embedding the role of diversity enables other people to see how benefiting women and people of color benefits them. In addition, the functional approach has the potential to create a participatory and accountable selection process, which can enhance individuals' autonomy and institutions' legitimacy.

Finally, conditions for sustained contact, genuine collabora- 69 tion, and fair assessment provide outsiders with a meaningful opportunity to learn, perform, and succeed. Studies of multi-racial teamwork suggest that the opportunity to work as relative co-equals in interdependent, cooperative teams may also reduce bias.[25] Indeed, carefully structured, accountable, and participatory work groups may replicate the conditions most likely to reduce bias and permit genuine participation by women and people of color.

70   To be sure, these more interactive and informal forms of selection and management rely explicitly on discretion and subjectivity. Preconceptions and biases will likely affect evaluations of performance in ways that often exclude women and people of color. And unstructured discretion exercised without accountability or participation by diverse decision-makers will likely reproduce biased and exclusionary results. But these biases have not been eliminated by formal selection practices and paper-and-pencil tests. More importantly, the model of formal fairness that is outcome-driven, rule-bound, and centralized will not reach many of the places where women and people of color seek to enter.[26] If the economy is moving in the direction of creating and restructuring work along more team-oriented, participatory lines, we need approaches to selection and performance that permit women and people of color to participate fairly and to succeed in this changing environment. Otherwise, women and people of color will remain on the margins of the new economy. Moreover, as business entities become more fluid and rely more on subcontracting and temporary work, we must devise new and more interactive strategies for inclusion and empowerment that embrace a workforce existing in the margins of traditional legal categories. The exercise of discretion cannot and should not be eliminated. Instead, discretionary decision making must become the subject and site of participation, accountability, and creative problem-solving.

A Democratic Imperative

71   Access to work and education is a fundamental attribute of modern citizenship. Work provides an identity that is valued by others. Work organizes and shapes the citizen's sense of self. Virtually every aspect of citizenship is channeled through participation in the workplace. For most people, medical care, pensions, and social insurance are linked to workplace participation. In these ways, work has become a proxy for citizenship.

72   Increasingly, the opportunity to work in a non-contingent, full-time position that provides these benefits of citizenship depends on access to higher education. People who are not edu-

cated do not get jobs, and thus cannot participate in the responsibilities and benefits of citizenship. Moreover, those without the benefits of higher education increasingly work in shifting, temporary, and task-centered jobs. Such individuals may fail to develop a sense of personal worth, institutional or communal loyalty, or positive agency, all attributes essential to functioning as citizens.

In addition, voting—the process that has traditionally served 73 to permit participation and influence public decision making—does not afford individuals the capacity to deliberate and exercise much influence over the conditions of day-to-day life. Without the opportunity to participate in intermediate institutions, such as places of work and schools, many citizens have no sense that their voices are being heard.[27]

If, as we believe, work and education are basic components 74 of citizenship, screens or barriers to participation should be drawn in the least exclusive manner consistent with the institution's mission. Access and opportunity to participate is critical to equipping citizens to fulfill their responsibilities, to respecting their status and autonomy as individuals, and to legitimating society's decisions as reflecting the participation of the community. People who feel they have a voice in the decision-making process are more likely to accept the ultimate decision as legitimate, even if it is different from the one they initially supported.

Through the first two centuries of our nation's history, re- 75 strictions on voting based on race, gender, and wealth were gradually lifted "only after wide public debate" about "the very nature of the type of society in which Americans wished to live."[28] These barriers were invalidated because they came to be seen as unduly burdening access to this fundamental aspect of citizenship. Courts also recognized that these burdens, through the exercise of selective discretion by local officials, fell disproportionately on disempowered groups such as African Americans.[29]

We believe a national debate on the terms of participation in 76 equivalent forms of citizenship is long overdue. Just as "history has seen a continuing expansion of the scope of the right of suffrage in this country,"[30] so we would argue that 21st-century democracy will depend on a commensurate expansion of the scope of access to higher education and opportunities for on-the-job training. Even if there are justifications for requirements relating to the capacity to exercise citizenship responsibilities effectively, these requirements must be drawn in the most narrow way possible because of the importance of assuring democratic access and legitimacy in the distribution of citizenship opportunities and responsibilities. A performance-based framework of selection is the equivalent, in employment and education, to the elimination of poll taxes and restrictive registration laws in the arena of voting.

77   We seek to open up a conversation about issues that many people treat as resolved. Our institutions do not currently function as fair and functional meritocracies. Only by rethinking our assumptions about the current system and future possibilities can we move toward the ideals that so many Americans share. This enterprise offers the possibility of bringing together many who are adversaries in the current affirmative action debate but share an interest in forging fairer, more inclusive, and more democratic institutions. It reconnects affirmative action to the innovative ideal. In this way, affirmative action can reclaim the historic relationship between racial justice and the revitalization of institutions to the benefit of everyone.

Notes

1. See *Johnson v. Transportation Agency*, 480 US 616 (1987); *Wygant v. Jackson Board of Education*, 476 US 267 (1986). The most politicized version of the anti-affirmative action narrative is typified by the campaign strategy used by Sen. Jesse Helms, the white incumbent, against Harvey Gantt, his black challenger in 1990. The Helms campaign commercial displayed a white working class man tearing up a rejection letter while the voice-over said, "You needed that job, and you were the best qualified. . . . But it had to go to a minority because of a racial quota." See Andrew Hacker, *Two Nations: Black and White, Separate, Hostile, Unequal* (New York: Scribner, 1992), p. 202.

2. Laura K. Bass, "Affirmative Action: Reframing the Discourse" (unpublished manuscript, December 4, 1995).

3. No tester claims that the LSAT or SAT, which is designed to predict academic performance, has ever been validated to predict job performance or pay. One study by Christopher Jencks finds that people who had higher paying jobs also had higher test scores. One problem with this conclusion is that higher test scores were used to screen out applicants from earlier, formative opportunities. Another study, by David Chambers, et al., of graduates of the University of Michigan Law School finds no correlation between LSAT and either job satisfaction or pay.

4. See David K. Shipler, "My Equal Opportunity, Your Free Lunch," *New York Times*, 5 March 1995.

5. As Walter Willingham, an industrial psychologist who consults with the Educational Testing Service (the organization that prepares and administers the SAT), points out, leadership in an extracurricular activity for two or more years is also a good proxy for academic performance, future leadership, and professional satisfaction.

6. "In all decades, those with higher index scores tend to make fewer social contributions ... than those with lower index scores." See Richard O. Lempert, David L. Chambers, and Terry K. Adams, "The River Runs Through Law School," *Journal of Law and Social Inquiry* 25 (2000): 468. See also, William G. Bowen and Derek Bok, *The Shape of the River: Long-Term Consequences of Considering Race in College and University Admissions* (Princeton, N.J.: Princeton University Press, 1998).

7. See Mary Anne C. Case, "Disaggregating Gender from Sex and Sexual Orientation: The Effeminate Man in the Law and Feminist Jurisprudence," *Yale Law Journal* 105 (1995): 88–89.

8. See the *Report of the Independent Commission on the Los Angeles Police Department*, pp. 83–84. "Female LAPD officers are involved in excessive use of force at rates substantially below those of male officers.... The statistics indicate that female officers are not reluctant to use force, but they are not nearly as likely to be involved in use of excessive force," due to female officers' perceived ability to be "more communicative, more skillful at deescalating potentially violent situations and less confrontational."

9. J. Phillip Thompson, director of management and operations for the New York City Housing Authority from 1992–93, told us that an internal evaluation conducted by the Housing Authority revealed that women housing authority officers were policing in a different, but successful, way. As a result of this evaluation, the authority sought to recruit new cops based on their ability to relate to young people, their knowledge of the community, their willingness to live in the housing projects, and their interest in police work. They also offered free housing to any successful recruit willing to live in the projects.

10. See James Crouse and Dale Trusheim, *The Case Against the SAT* (Chicago: University of Chicago Press, 1988), p. 128.

11. See Phyllis Rosser, *The SAT Gender Grap: Identifying the Causes* (Washington, D.C.: Center for Women's Policy Studies, 1989), p. 4. Also, "ETS Developing 'New' GRE," *FairTest Examiner,* Fall/Winter 1995–96, p.11. "Research ... shows the GRE under-predicts the success of minority students. And an ETS Study concluded the GRE particularly under-predicts for women over 25, who represent more than half of female test-takers."

12. Crouse and Trusheim, p. 103.

13. Crouse and Trusheim, pp. 107–08.

14. See John G. Belcher, "Gainsharing and Variable Pay: The State of the Art," *Compensation & Benefits Review* 26 (May-June 1994): 50–51. Belcher advocates the use of a family of measures approach, which "utilizes multiple, independent measures to quantify performance improvement."

15. See, for example, Claude M. Steele and Joshua Aronson, "Stereotype Threat and the Intellectual Test Performance of

African Americans," *Journal of Personality and Social Psychology* 69 (1995); 797–811.

16. Although there is debate about the degree of fundamental change in approaches to management, a significant portion of private businesses have adopted some form of collaborative or team-oriented production. See Edward E. Lawler III et al., *Employee Involvement and Total Quality Management: Practices and Results in Fortune 1000 Companies* (1992), which analyzes the employee-involvement programs many corporations have adopted; Paul Osterman, "How Common is Workplace Transformation and Who Adopts It?" *Industrial & Labor Relations Review* 47 (1994): 173, 176–78, which finds that over 50 percent of firms surveyed had introduced at least one innovation such as quality circles and work teams, and that 36.6 percent have at least two practices in place with at least 50 percent of employees involved in each.

17. Howard Gardner, *Multiple Intelligences: The Theory in Practice* (New York: Basic Books, 1993), p. 172.

18. See Karen W. Arenson, "Study Details Success Stories in Open Admissions at CUNY," *New York Times,* 7 May 1996. A study of open-admissions policy at City University of New York (CUNY) found more than half of the students eventually graduated, even though it took many as long as ten years to do so. Many of these students had to work full time while they attended college. According to Professor David Lavin, one of the co-authors of the CUNY study, open admissions "provided opportunities that students used well, and that translated into direct benefits in the job market and clearly augmented the economic base." Similarly, at Haverford College, professors of biology, chemistry, and mathematics told one of us in interviews that many students of color with weak preparation in the natural sciences took two years to catch up with their better prepared peers. However, by junior year, those same students managed to excel, having overcome their initial disadvantages.

19. When one of us was on the admissions committee in the early 1990s at the University of Pennsylvania Law School, the process of admitting people who had some "special" quality to be considered—which included being a poor, white chicken farmer from Alabama—was an openly deliberative process. It included students who knew more about the specific localities in which many of the applicants resided. The applications were redacted to eliminate personal identifying information but were otherwise available to the entire committee. The recommendations were read and considered (by contrast to the 50 percent of the class who were admitted solely on a mathematical equation based on their LSAT scores, their college rank, and the "quality" of their college as determined by the median LSAT score of its graduating class). In this process, the committee of both faculty, students and admissions per-

sonnel had a sense we were admitting a "class" of students, not just random individuals. Thus, we might give weight to some factors over others, depending upon the "needs" of the institution to have racial and demographic diversity, but also upon our commitment to fulfilling the needs of the profession to serve the entire public and to train private and public problem-solvers who would become the next generation of leaders. Thus, not all students were admitted primarily because of their academic talents. We considered those who might be better oral advocates and eventual litigators. Others were already accomplished negotiators or future practitioners of alternative dispute-resolution practices. None of these students were admitted if we felt they were unqualified to do the work demanded of them at the institution.

20. Gardner, *Multiple Intelligences*, pp. 171–73.
21. She learned that she was proficient in skills that she did not previously identify as related to lawyering: problem solving, thinking about the public-relations management of crises, strategic planning, and dealing with internal disruption stemming from crisis and change.
22. For example, the court in *Hopwood* v. *Texas* rejected the concept of diversity as a basis for using affirmative action. The opinion lacked almost any reflection on the functional role diversity plays in higher education. It simply asserted that "the use of race, in and of itself, to choose students simply achieves a student body that looks different." 78 F.3d 932, 945 (Fifth Circuit, 1996), cert. denied, 116 S. Ct. 2582 (1996).
23. Jonathan D. Casper, "Restructuring the Traditional Civil Jury: The Effects of Changes in Composition and Procedures," in *Verdict: Assessing the Civil Jury System*, ed. Robert E. Litan (Washington, D.C.: Brookings Institution Press, 1993), p. 420.
24. See Susan P. Sturm, "From Gladiators to Problem Solvers: Women the Academy, and the Legal Profession," *Duke Journal of Gender Law & Policy* (1996).
25. See Samuel L. Gaertner et al., "The Contact Hypothesis: The Role of a Common Ingroup Identity on Reducing Intergroup Bias," *Small Group Research* 25 (1994): 224, 226; Samuel L. Gaertner et al., "How Does Cooperation Reduce Intergroup Bias?" *Journal of Personality & Social Psychology* 59 (1990): 692.
26. See Elizabeth Bartholet, "Application of Title VII to Jobs in High Places," *Harvard Law Review* 95 (1982): 947, 967–78, which discusses courts' reluctance to scrutinize high-level employment decisions; Deborah L. Rhode, "Perspectives on Professional Women," *Stanford Law Review* 40 (1988): 1163, 1193–94 notes courts' deference to employers' judgments.
27. This is a complex argument that requires more elaboration than the limits of this article permit. Suffice it to state the obvious: we are experiencing a retreat from public life on many levels, evidenced by, among other factors, declining voter

turnout. See also Lani Guinier, "More Democracy," *University of Chicago Legal Forum* (1995): 16–22.
28. *Harper* v. *Virginia Board of Elections,* 383 US 684 (1966) (Harlan, J., dissenting).
29. See *United States* v. *Louisiana,* 225 F. Supp. 353, 355–56 (E.E. La. 1963). The decision found that the interpretation test as a prerequisite for registration "has been the highest, best-guarded, most effective barrier to Negro voting in Louisiana," and that the test "has no rational relation to measuring the ability of an elector to read and write," aff'd., 380 US 145 (1965).
30. *Reynolds* v. *Sims,* 377 US 533, 544 (1964).

Kurt Vonnegut Jr.

HARRISON BERGERON

After graduating from Cornell University, Kurt Vonnegut Jr. (born in 1922 in Indianapolis) worked in journalism and public relations. Then he started publishing best-selling novels that often feature imaginary (yet all too real) settings, a satiric edge, and his characteristic narrative voice. Among them are Cat's Cradle, Slaughterhouse-Five, Breakfast of Champions, *and* Jailbird. *"Harrison Bergeron" was published as part of his collection of stories titled* Welcome to the Monkey House *(1961).*

1   The year was 2081, and everybody was finally equal. They weren't only equal before God and the law. They were equal every which way. Nobody was smarter than anybody else. Nobody was better looking than anybody else. Nobody was stronger or quicker than anybody else. All this equality was due to the 211th, 212th, and 213th Amendments to the Constitution, and to the unceasing vigilance of agents of the United States Handicapper General.

2   Some things about living still weren't quite right, though. April, for instance, still drove people crazy by not being springtime. And it was in that clammy month that the H-G men took George and Hazel Bergeron's fourteen-year-old son, Harrison, away.

3   It was tragic, all right, but George and Hazel couldn't think about it very hard. Hazel had a perfectly average intelligence, which meant she couldn't think about anything except in short bursts. And George, while his intelligence was way

above normal, had a little mental handicap radio in his ear. He was required by law to wear it at all times. It was tuned to a government transmitter. Every twenty seconds or so, the transmitter would send out some sharp noise to keep people like George from taking unfair advantage of their brains.

George and Hazel were watching television. There were tears on Hazel's cheeks, but she'd forgotten for the moment what they were about.   4

On the television screen were ballerinas.   5

A buzzer sounded in George's head. His thoughts fled in panic, like bandits from a burglar alarm.   6

"That was a real pretty dance, that dance they just did," said Hazel.   7

"Huh?" said George.   8

"That dance—it was nice," said Hazel.   9

"Yup," said George. He tried to think a little about the ballerinas. They weren't really very good—no better than anybody else would have been, anyway. They were burdened with sash-weights and bags of birdshot, and their faces were masked, so that no one, seeing a free and graceful gesture or a pretty face, would feel like something the cat drug in. George was toying with the vague notion that maybe dancers shouldn't be handicapped. But he didn't get very far with it before another noise in his ear radio scattered his thoughts.   10

George winced. So did two out of the eight ballerinas.   11

Hazel saw him wince. Having no mental handicap herself, she had to ask George what the latest sound had been.   12

"Sounded like somebody hitting a milk bottle with a ball peen hammer," said George.   13

"I'd think it would be real interesting, hearing all the different sounds," said Hazel, a little envious. "All the things they think up."   14

"Um," said George.   15

"Only, if I was Handicapper General, you know what I would do?" said Hazel. Hazel, as a matter of fact, bore a strong resemblance to the Handicapper General, a woman named Diana Moon Glampers. "If I was Diana Moon Glampers," said Hazel, "I'd have chimes on Sunday—just chimes. Kind of in honor of religion."   16

"I could think, if it was just chimes," said George.   17

"Well—maybe make 'em real loud," said Hazel. "I think I'd make a good Handicapper General."   18

"Good as anybody else," said George.   19

"Who knows better'n I do what normal is?" said Hazel.   20

"Right," said George. He began to think glimmeringly about his abnormal son who was now in jail, about Harrison, but a twenty-one-gun salute in his head stopped that.   21

22   "Boy!" said Hazel, "that was a doozy, wasn't it?"

23   It was such a doozy that George was white and trembling, and tears stood on the rims of his red eyes. Two of the eight ballerinas had collapsed to the studio floor, [and] were holding their temples.

24   "All of a sudden you look so tired," said Hazel. "Why don't you stretch out on the sofa, so's you can rest your handicap bag on the pillows, honeybunch." She was referring to the forty-seven pounds of birdshot in a canvas bag, which was padlocked around George's neck. "Go on and rest the bag for a little while," she said. "I don't care if you're not equal to me for a while."

25   George weighed the bag with his hands. "I don't mind it," he said. "I don't notice it any more. It's just a part of me."

26   "You been so tired lately—kind of wore out," said Hazel. "If there was just some way we could make a little hole in the bottom of the bag, and just take out a few of them lead balls. Just a few."

27   "Two years in prison and two thousand dollars fine for every ball I took out," said George. "I don't call that a bargain."

28   "If you could just take a few out when you came home from work," said Hazel. "I mean—you don't compete with anybody around here. You just set around."

29   "If I tried to get away with it," said George, "then other people'd get away with it—and pretty soon we'd be right back to the dark ages again, with everybody competing against everybody else. You wouldn't like that, would you?"

30   "I'd hate it," said Hazel.

31   "There you are," said George. "The minute people start cheating on laws, what do you think happens to society?"

32   If Hazel hadn't been able to come up with an answer to this question George couldn't have supplied one. A siren was going off in his head.

33   "Reckon it'd fall all apart," said Hazel.

34   "What would?" said George blankly.

35   "Society," said Hazel uncertainly. "Wasn't that what you just said?"

36   "Who knows?" said George.

37   The television program was suddenly interrupted for a news bulletin. It wasn't clear at first as to what the bulletin was about, since the announcer, like all announcers, had a serious speech impediment. For about half a minute, and in a state of high excitement, the announcer tried to say, "Ladies and gentlemen—"

38   He finally gave up, handed the bulletin to a ballerina to read.

39   "That's all right—" Hazel said of the announcer, "he tried. That's the big thing. He tried to do the best he could with what God gave him. He should get a nice raise for trying so hard."

"Ladies and gentlemen—" said the ballerina, reading the bul- 40
letin. She must have been extraordinarily beautiful, because
the mask she wore was hideous. And it was easy to see that she
was the strongest and most graceful of all the dancers, for her
handicap bags were as big as those worn by two-hundred-
pound men.

And she had to apologize at once for her voice, which was a 41
very unfair voice for a woman to use. Her voice was a warm,
luminous, timeless melody. "Excuse me—" she said, and she
began again, making her voice absolutely uncompetitive.

"Harrison Bergeron, age fourteen," she said in a grackle 42
squawk, "has just escaped from jail, where he was held on suspicion of plotting to overthrow the government. He is a genius
and an athlete, is under-handicapped, and should be regarded
as extremely dangerous."

A police photograph of Harrison Bergeron was flashed on 43
the screen upside down, then sideways, upside down again,
then right side up. The picture showed the full length of
Harrison against a background calibrated in feet and inches.
He was exactly seven feet tall.

The rest of Harrison's appearance was Halloween and hard- 44
ware. Nobody had ever borne heavier handicaps. He had outgrown hindrances faster than the H-G men could think them
up. Instead of a little ear radio for a mental handicap, he wore
a tremendous pair of earphones, and spectacles with thick
wavy lenses. The spectacles were intended to make him not
only half blind, but to give him whanging headaches besides.

Scrap metal was hung all over him. Ordinarily, there was a 45
certain symmetry, a military neatness to the handicaps issued
to strong people, but Harrison looked like a walking junkyard.
In the race of life, Harrison carried three hundred pounds.

And to offset his good looks, the H-G men required that he 46
wear at all times a red rubber ball for a nose, keep his eyebrows shaved off, and cover his even white teeth with black
caps at snaggle-tooth random.

"If you see this boy," said the ballerina, "do not—I repeat, do 47
not—try to reason with him."

There was the shriek of a door being torn from its hinges. 48

Screams and barking cries of consternation came from the 49
television set. The photograph of Harrison Bergeron on the
screen jumped again and again, as though dancing to the tune
of an earthquake.

George Bergeron correctly identified the earthquake, and 50
well he might have—for many was the time his own home had
danced to the same crashing tune. "My God—" said George,
"that must be Harrison!"

Tom Toles
CUT THE GORDIAN KNOT

You probably recognize Tom Toles's political cartoons from their distinctive style and sharp wit. The cartoons appear in many newspapers and magazines, including the conservative newsweekly U.S. News & World Report, *which carried the following cartoon in June 1995. What exactly is the object of this particular satire—or does it cut in several ways?*

IV

FAMILY MATTERS

Introduction

During the 1996 presidential campaign, both Bob Dole and Bill Clinton promised to sustain vigorous efforts to protect the American family—one indication of just how broad concern about the family has become in the United States during the past decade. That concern emerged again during the 2000 election campaign, as candidates from both major parties offered one after another solution to The Family Problem—whatever that may be. No doubt you have heard the general concerns mentioned again and again—concerns about the state of the family during a time of increasing divorce and out-of-wedlock births; concerns about child support that ought to be honored by absent spouses, but isn't; concerns about teenage crime, suicide, pregnancy, substance abuse, and truancy that seem to be associated with broken homes; concerns about the effectiveness of day care, education, and children's health; concerns about child abuse. Moreover, you have probably also heard discussions in the media about new family matters that have come about as a result of new social customs and developments in reproductive technology—about who should have custody of children in cases of divorce, about whether or not single-sex couples should share in the benefits and responsibilities of marriage, about controversial adoption cases of one kind or another. Consequently, Part Four of *Conversations* takes up several topics related to the family, most of which are related to each other in some way.

The first section offers several readings on broad questions about the current condition of the American family. Is the family indeed in trouble in our country? Does it require some sort of repair—or is our society simply experiencing understandable and temporary pains associated with a transition from the traditional, two-parent home to less monolithic, less misogynist, more varied, and ultimately healthier versions of the family? Are children in our society being routinely damaged by broken homes, absent fathers, and general neglect of the family, or are those problems the result of other social factors, mostly associated with poverty? Would tougher child support laws help to amend the family? Should we make it more difficult to divorce in our society? More difficult to reproduce outside marriage? More difficult to retain children born out of wedlock or living in abusive households? Do we need more stringent laws to discourage deadbeat fathers and mothers?

Those questions also lead to the next section, which takes up the specific issue of single parenthood. As you may know, during the past two decades the number of single-parent households in the United States has increased dramatically, as divorce and illegitimacy rates have increased. Since 1950, the number of children living in mother-only families has quadrupled, from about 5 million to about 20 million, and since 1970, the number of single parents has tripled, from about 4 million to about 12 million. Ten percent of all live births in the United States are to mothers under eighteen. In 2000, more than 30 percent of all U.S. children under eighteen lived with one parent, compared to 12 percent in 1970. As a result, former Senator Daniel Patrick Moynihan (a Democrat) and former Vice President Dan Quayle (a Republican) have made well-publicized attempts to draw attention to the problem of single parenthood: Moynihan through congressional hearings and reports, Quayle through his much-publicized charges that television's Murphy Brown was glamorizing unwed motherhood. And of course radio's Dr. Laura has been railing against single parenthood for years now.

But is single parenthood a problem? Is it the cause of social ills? Or are single parents, especially if they work, themselves the victims of difficult circumstances and unrealistic expectations, particularly if their spouses offer insufficient child support? And if single parenthood is a problem, what should be done about it? Can and should the federal government play a role in this matter at a time when many Americans are suspicious about the federal government's role in their lives? In 1995, Newt Gingrich introduced the Personal Responsibility Act, which would have eliminated welfare benefits for children born to unwed mothers under the age of eighteen and would have required mothers to establish paternity as a condition for receiving welfare: Is such an act a good idea? *Conversations* presents a spirited exchange among five women concerning all these questions.

Part Four of *Conversations* closes with a discussion of same-sex marriage at a time when many states are considering legislation that would permit it. Should such matches be sanctioned by our laws so that same-sex couples can enjoy the civic benefits associated with marriage—that is, health benefits tied to family membership, tax benefits, the right to adopt children, the right to inherit money, and so forth? Would recognizing same-sex partners as lawfully married somehow undermine the family? Or would it put unwelcome pressure on same-sex couples to conform to an institution that many people find ill-suited to same-sex couples?

If this introduction has focused more on questions than on answers, that is because the discussion of family matters in the United States is so problematic right now. The selections in this part will give you the opportunity to confront some of the most vexing questions in our culture—and an opportunity to have your own say during a time when people are particularly interested in reading about these questions.

CAN THE FAMILY
BE SAVED?

———————————■———————————

Roger Rosenblatt

THE SOCIETY THAT
PRETENDS TO LOVE
CHILDREN

Roger Rosenblatt (born 1940) is a writer and editor at Time
magazine; he is also a frequent contributor to the New York
Times Magazine, *a publication on current events that is enclosed with every Sunday* Times. *The following essay appeared
in a special issue of the* New York Times Magazine *(October
8, 1995) on childhood in the United States.*

Henry will not face me. We sit close together on small plastic   1
chairs in a classroom at P.S. 314, an elementary school in the
Sunset Park area of Brooklyn, where he works with small children in a summer camp. Our knees, drawn high because we
are sitting on the low chairs, almost touch. Still, Henry angles
his body so that he shows me only his profile. If he turns toward me briefly and catches my eye, he immediately turns
away again and gazes out the large schoolroom window at kids
on a stoop across the street.

His neighborhood, Sunset Park, consists of approximately   2
110,000 people, most of them poor, with a per capita income of
$11,115. A quarter of the residents have incomes below the
poverty line. They represent a variety of backgrounds—Puerto
Rican, African-American, Dominican, Mexican, Jordanian,
Pakistani, Chinese, Korean and Vietnamese. These groups are
the latest to populate Sunset Park. They follow the Irish, Finns,
Swedes, Norwegians, Poles and Italians of the late 19th century, and the Greeks, Russians and Jews of the early 20th. The

first area residents were the Dutch and the English, who established farms where the Canarsie Indians had lived.

3   A little over a mile wide and 2.6 miles long, the area lies between middle-class Bay Ridge to the south and gentrified Park Slope to the north. The rectangle of the neighborhood slopes down from the high ridge at Eighth Avenue to the east to Upper New York Bay, where the Statue of Liberty rises. At the top of the ridge is Sunset Park itself—an 18-acre public park with old trees and a W.P.A. swimming pool. On the grid of narrow streets and wide avenues between the ridge and the bay lie two- and three-story brownstones with attractive cornices; brick-and-masonry houses with little gardens in the front, where corn is sometimes grown, and many rows of drab no-color tenements. Henry lives in one of these. His home is near Third Avenue, which is close to the water, and is shadowed by the Gowanus Expressway, one of the highways built by Robert Moses to carry white people away from places like Sunset Park.

4   Henry is 16, tall for his age at about 6 foot 1. His skin is a dull dark brown; antiperspirant under his arms foams white against it. His hair is spun into curlicues. He rarely smiles, though when he does, he looks warm and welcoming—in contrast to his usual self-concealing blankness. He is sleepy this morning. He yawns frequently, and fully, his mouth wide open like a baby's.

5   "What else have you seen?" I ask him. He is talking about life on the streets.

6   "I saw a man throw a telephone out the window," he says. "It hit a baby in a carriage. It nearly killed her. So her father ran up the stairs, and he grabbed the man who threw the phone, and he cut him." He traces a line across his throat with his index finger. "He lived, but he's got this necklace now."

7   "Did you know the men involved?" I ask him.

8   "I knew the man who threw the phone," he says. "He's my mother's boyfriend."

9   "Why did he do that?"

10   "He was drunk, crazy." He shrugs to indicate that the behavior is normal for his mother's boyfriend.

11   "What did you do when the baby's father slit his throat?" I ask.

12   "I was happy," Henry says. "I laughed when he did it. I even testified against the boyfriend in court. My mother was mad. She's always mad at me." He gives me a glance, then turns his head to the side. "That was when things really blew up at home. So I went to the Center for Family Life and told Jennifer. She's been everything to me." He says this without emotion. "She makes me think about what I do."

13   "What about your mother?"

"She screams. Says I'm the Devil. Calls me stupid and re- 14
tarded. She says I'm bad. I *am* bad." He holds his head down.
"I hang out. I write up—you know?—do graffiti. I fight, maybe
less now, but I used to fight all the time. When I start fighting,
it's like seek and destroy. You start with me and you're the enemy. Nobody else in sight. You my spotlight, my way out. You
the exit door."

"The exit door from what?" He does not answer. "Are other 15
grown-ups in your life good to you? Teachers?"

"Some are O.K.," he says. "I had a teacher tell me: 'I don't 16
care if you come to class or not. I get paid anyway.'"

"Police?" 17

"When I got arrested for writing up, a woman cop told me 18
she hopes they send me to jail."

"Ministers? Priests?" I ask. 19

He shakes his head. "I don't have religion." 20

"The Mayor? The Governor? The President?" I am speaking 21
a foreign language. "Are there any grown-ups who help you?"

"Jennifer," he says softly. "People at the center." 22

I ask him: "Henry, do you think that your mother loves you?" 23

"She pretends to love me," he says. 24

The fact that Henry is poor and black, and that he lives in vi- 25
olent circumstances, makes him an unusually dramatic and
sadly familiar example of the mistreatment of American children. But, for what he represents, he could be any child, anywhere in the country. I could have the wrong Henry. Henry is
not a kid from Sunset Park, Brooklyn. He is a rich, white, 16-
year-old senior at Groton, who has just cheated on his Greek
exam because his father, a true-blue Yalie, yells at him constantly for being stupid and retarded and for not being good
enough to get into Yale.

No, that isn't Henry, either. Henry is a 12-year-old girl from 26
Corpus Christi, Tex., who is trying to get pregnant "to have love
in my life." Or the boy whose father set him on fire to strike
back at his wife in a custody case. Or those teen-agers who
made a suicide pact in New Jersey. Henry is a 14-year-old girl
from Aspen, Colo., who wears all that oversize clothing and
who heads for the ladies' room immediately after meals. He is
the toddler in Los Angeles whose grandmother punished him
by holding a pillow over his head and squeezing him between a
table and a sofa. His last words were "Me no breathe."

Here's Henry now. That's his key in the door. His folks are 27
both at work and will be out till midnight. He has the house to
himself. He pours himself a Coors, calls his girlfriend to come
over and plunks down in front of the TV to watch the Jenny
Jones show bring him a picture of America.

28   Actually, the Henry of Sunset Park is a bit luckier than the tens of millions of American children, of all economic classes, races and regions, whom the country pretends to love. At least this Henry has an effective local social service agency—the Center for Family Life to which he has been referred—that is devoted to his well-being.

29   In 1993, according to several child interest groups like the Children's Defense Fund, an estimated three million children were reported to public social service agencies to be suffering from abuse or neglect. Some 1,300 of them died. Approximately half a million children are in foster care or similar substitute homes, an increase of 250,000 since 1986. About 14 million live in poverty. About 100,000 children are homeless. The welfare bill passed overwhelmingly by the Senate last month, ending guaranteed assistance to poor families, should add significantly to the number of children in need.

30   The American Humane Association reports that since 1988 American teen-age boys are more likely to die from gunshot wounds than from all natural causes combined. Studies of teen-age pregnancy in Seattle and Chicago show that two-thirds of teen-age mothers reported having been sexually abused. Figures on sexual abuse have been disputed as being too high, but even if the true figures are only half of those reported, they are still considerable.

31   While poor children, black and white, suffer a disproportionate share of ills, the increasing affliction of the American child occurs in rural regions as well as in the cities, and among the middle and upper classes, too. Responses to a survey of girls in grades 6 through 12 in mainly Midwestern states, in 111 communities with populations under 100,000, indicated that by grade nine, one in five girls had been sexually abused. By grade 10, the number was still one in five, but one in three girls had been abused physically, sexually or both. The survey defined physical abuse as an adult causing a scar, bruises, welts, bleeding or a broken bone and sexual abuse as a family member or "someone else" imposing sexual behavior on the child. In 1993, there were 19,466 incidents of child abuse reported to the Iowa Department of Human Services. The advocacy organization, Girls Inc. in Omaha, states that sexual abuse of girls reported in Nebraska (3 in a class of 25) is that of the national average. The abuse of boys is more rarely reported, so the numbers are probably comparable.

32   Statistics on poor families, like Henry's, are more available than those on better-off families; welfare agencies rarely invade the homes of the rich. But the mistreatment of children is also a middle-class problem. A random sampling of adoles-

cents in Minnesota found that 6 percent of middle- or middle-to-high-income families had at least one child in alcohol or drug treatment programs by ages 14 to 17. Adolescents in an additional 5 percent of families were using as much alcohol and drugs as the kids who were in treatment.

Middle-class whites like to think that kids with guns are a 33 black or Latino inner-city menace exclusively. But William C. Haynes, juvenile justice director of the Tennessee Commission on Children and Youth, reports that groups of middle-class white kids in Antioch had a gunfight armed with 9-millimeter semiautomatic pistols. Richard Louv, the author of "Childhood's Future," notes that the shooting programs of the 4-H Clubs drew at least 100,000 kids at the end of the 1980's, a tenfold increase since the mid-1980's.

Two middle-class parents who work full time will, naturally, 34 spend less time with their children. In 1976, according to the economist Sylvia Ann Hewlett, author of "When the Bough Breaks," 11 percent of children under the age of 1 year had mothers in the work force. By 1994, the number had risen to 54.5 percent. Another economist, Victor Fuchs, contends that children have lost 10 to 12 hours a week of parental time since 1960 because of the added number of hours that both parents work. The Bureau of Labor Statistics reports that the average work week was 43.3 hours in 1994, with professional people working an average of 43.8.

At an exhibit of children's artwork at Christie's in New York 35 City last year, paintings were displayed depicting "Images of Mothers and Fathers." One, showing a man with his hands held up in surrender and surrounded by clocks, carried the caption: "This is my father." A ninth grader drew a picture of her mother *as* a clock.

Neglect is a varied form of abuse and is difficult to pin down. 36 Martha Farrell Erickson of the Children, Youth and Family Consortium at the University of Minnesota reports that 45 percent of child-abuse cases are officially cited as neglect, but "it seems likely that the actual incidence is much higher." Erickson also notes that many neglected children are infants: "Given that neglect is often chronic rather than episodic, these children may grow up thinking this is the way life is."

Violent and destructive behavior by middle-class and upper- 37 middle-class kids—generally considered to be a consequence of neglect—is a daily news story. In the placid seaport town of Dartmouth, Mass., in 1993, three teen-agers burst into a high-school classroom, beat a freshman over the head with a base-ball bat and stabbed him to death. In Williamson County, Tenn., the richest county in the state, a boy driving the new car that his parents had just bought him shot and killed a horse in a field—for the fun of it. High-school kids go on destructive binges in Montana and Vermont. In 1989, ABC's television news program, "20/20," ran a piece on high-living teenagers in wealthy Pacific Palisades, Calif., who were lost to drugs and drink. Last year, the network news shows broadcast a video of middle-class teenagers in Florida on a rampage. They tore apart elegant homes, tortured a dog and cooked a goldfish in the microwave. The teenagers made the video themselves.

38   Divorce is not always a destructive event in a child's life, but it is more often so than the divorcing parents care to admit. Fully 40 percent of children living with their mothers do not see their fathers after the breakup. Of the 58 percent of divorced fathers ordered to pay child support, less than two-thirds actually pay in full. One father explained that he could not pay child support because he needed the money to board his two Doberman pinschers. Even when both parents maintain contact with the children, the children can pay penalties. The headmaster of one of New York's distinguished private schools tells of an afternoon when he was summoned to the school lobby, where two parents were shouting and fighting. Each had thought that the coming weekend was the one in which he or she was to take their child. When the headmaster arrived on the scene, the parents were yanking at the child's arms, stretching him between them.

39   If some wealthier parents are not looking out for their children, they are looking out for themselves. Many young couples simply do not have children, even if they are able to, because a child will cut into their income and their time for self-interested pursuits. Many who do have kids did not really want the responsibility of rearing a human being; they wanted another witty, charming, urbane adult in the house. So neglect was built into their vision of the child in the first place. And, of course, when the child turned out not to be the delightful companion the parents originally had in mind, they abandoned it to "independence."

40   In "Habits of the Heart," Robert Bellah points out that since 1965, Americans have been hooked on the therapeutic mentality. The social critic Christopher Lasch also concluded that therapy has replaced religion in American adult lives. A guidance counselor in Alabama tells me that a reason many parents do not come home at night to their children is that they are taking therapy classes to help them be better parents.

41   The neglect and abuse of children is hardly new in American history. One may go back through the 350 years represented by the different inhabitants of Sunset Park alone, starting with the

Puritans, and discover an unbroken pattern of beating children, psychologically tormenting children, imposing one or another form of miseducation on them, forcing them into labor, giving them too little freedom, or giving them too much. Every major intellectual influence on American children, from Locke to Spock, has wound up distorting their lives. In 1646, "stubborn child laws" were enacted (though never enforced) in Massachusetts, which provided the death penalty for a rebellious son. In the 1850's, the Rev. Samuel Arnold of Ossipee, N.H., nearly beat his adopted son to death because the boy failed to pronounce the words "utter" and "gutter" to the reverend's satisfaction. In 1985, a Sunset Park father, who wanted to show off how smart his 6-year-old son was, forced him to stand and read aloud from a book. When the boy mispronounced the word "bite" as "bit," his father slammed his fist on the kitchen table and made him read the book from the beginning.

The difference between past and present abuses is that to- 42 day's children are not assaulted by one or two destructive forces. They are assaulted by everything, all at once. Individual parents may love their kids, but the society seems to wish the children disappeared. It is as if children are seen as interfering with life, rather than as contributing to it or perpetuating it. Modern living is too difficult, too much to handle or to bear. Children get in the way of one's pleasure or of one's survival. They compete for one's money, resources and affections. Worse, like Henry, they remind adults of their incapacity to love them.

"What is to be done?" I ask Mary Paul and Geraldine, the 43 two Sisters of the Good Shepherd who founded the Center for Family Life 17 years ago. The center, which is a lay institution, addresses all sources of difficulty for children, works with the family members involved, and embraces every facet of life in the neighborhood. Besides counseling, it provides an employment agency, an emergency food program, advocacy and legal services, a theater program, a literacy program, summer camps like the one in which Henry works, day care for school-age children and a neighborhood foster-care program. The foster families are selected within the community of the original family, so that the children do not lose touch with their homes.

"Better ask what is *not* to be done," Mary Paul says. "People 44 do have positive goals in regard to children. But somehow these goals become subverted because, paradoxically, they become overcommitted to whatever they are doing. Life ceases to be an adaptation and an exchange with an outside environment. We become mere doers. We do and we do and we do, and we grow to be more narrowly focused and more narrowly driven. Soon we lose energy and we fail. It's the law of entropy."

45   "Does that happen in education?" I ask.

46   "Absolutely," she says. "A few years ago, schools in places like New York started out being attentive to the needs of children in a multicultural environment. Perfectly sensible, given all the new immigrant groups who were coming in. Then people became overcommitted to that one goal of multiculturalism. They forgot about what else was worthwhile in education. They thought that education was about self-esteem. They came up with the idea of teaching bilingualism, which serves no useful purpose at all for children trying to make it in American society. In Sunset Park, bilingualism is promoted solely to get patronage jobs for Spanish teachers."

47   "The reason we instituted neighborhood foster care," says Geraldine, "is that child welfare in this country—the Child Welfare Administration in particular—focuses only on the well-being of the child."

48   "The aim is to remove the child from the original family as far away as possible," Mary Paul says. "Often the taking of children is done abruptly. The C.W.A. will take a child from school because it's easier than confronting the mother. Sometimes children are removed in the middle of the night, with the police in attendance. They'll use even more coercive methods. I cannot stand the violence of it."

49   Geraldine breaks in. "This is why we began neighborhood foster care in Sunset Park. We've been doing this seven years now, and sometimes we succeed and sometimes not. But even the failures can be a partial success. A child whom we placed in foster care here has a mother who is seriously mentally ill. The woman will stand in the street and scream up at the windows of the little girl's foster parents' house. She will sit in the hallway and bang on the door with her fists all night. And she will not go for treatment. And still the little girl—because she has been allowed to remain close to her mother—sees the disease for what it is. She understands. It doesn't make the mother well but it helps the *girl.*"

50   "Everyone suffers from tunnel vision," says Mary Paul. "We are in an economic depression right now. All one reads is how strapped city, state and Federal budgets are. Politicians win points by coming up with ways to save the country money. 'We have to reduce the deficit. We have to reduce the national debt.' For whose benefit should we rescue the economy? It is always the children and the grandchildren. Yet how should we save the economy?"

51   "Take money away from children," Geraldine offers, and laughs.

"Exactly," says Mary Paul. "Take the money from the chil-   52
dren even though you are focusing on the children as the reason for rescuing the economy. By this logic, you will amass a
fortune as a legacy and, at the same time, kill off the legatees."

"When parents fail their children," says Geraldine, "it is al-   53
most always because of an excessive commitment to one or another pursuit. Henry's mother yells at him and degrades him
because she thinks that's how to make him toe the mark. And
naturally, Henry is angry at her. He's in a constant rage. And he
takes out his rage in street fights."

"This is a poor neighborhood," says Mary Paul. "Money dri-   54
ves much of people's behavior. The rage of parents who have
sacrificed so much and invested so much and then nothing
works . . . they begin to see the child as a repudiation of their
capacity for giving."

"What happens when a parent assaults or kills a child?" I ask.   55

"You know," Mary Paul says, "the feeling that one has to love   56
a child can be overwhelming, especially for those—and there
are many—who do not. And then the child reminds you every
day of your inability to build a world for it. It calls forth something that the parent cannot give.

"A Mexican mother in this neighborhood killed her child by   57
repeated beatings. It said in the papers that the family 'somehow made its way from Mexico to Sunset Park.' Somehow
made its way! Can you imagine what commitment it took to
get from Mexico to here, what ambitions for a new life they
had? They wind up in a situation where all forms of love and
rationality are abandoned to that dream, which had at its center the children, after all. And then one day the child becomes
a noise. And the noise has to be stilled.

"We have to remind the child that it belongs to a community.   58
We have to do that for adults, too. Adults are yesterday's children."

"A client of ours killed her daughter," says Geraldine. "The   59
girl was about 3½. She had diabetes and she was always
thirsty. So she would go to the refrigerator again and again for
juice. The mother, who was unaware that the child had diabetes, was very poor. She had so little food. She told the girl
not to keep going to the refrigerator, but the girl kept going
anyway. So the mother hit her in the head, the child went into
a coma and eventually died. The mother did not want to kill
her little girl, of course. She was thinking about the juice."

Jennifer, the social worker who has been counseling Henry,   60
says: "We spend so much time protecting ourselves from the
realities because we can't bear to see what we are doing to our

kids. How could we live with ourselves if we really knew what we are creating?"

61 She started working with Henry after the incident involving his mother's boyfriend. She had seen him around the center but had no idea of the trouble in his life until he approached her the day he testified against the boyfriend in court. His mother was shutting him out. "'I need to talk to you,' he told me." Then he burst into tears.

62 "The situation was terrible in the beginning. It is getting a bit better now. But with his mother at that time, my God! She did not speak to him for three whole months. The afternoon that Geraldine and I first went over to their house, the mother pulled a kitchen knife on Henry. He stood there helplessly, repeating, 'I don't want to hurt you.' And she kept screaming at him.

63 "Henry has a very tender heart. He is struggling with the question of whether it is possible to feel something without being hurt. Once he came to me and said. 'I saw something in the park today that almost made me tear. A mother and her daughter were sitting on a bench. The mother said, I love you. And the daughter said, I love *you*. I thought: Can people really be that way? And then I thought: Nah.'

64 "He is very gentle. He's wonderful with little kids in the summer camp. He would never harm a smaller child. But if an older person attacks or offends him, he is livid beyond control. He is so deeply hurt that the slightest thing sets him off. Fighting is a power issue for him. He tells me, 'When I'm in a fight, I think of my mother and it gives me the energy.'

65 "This graffiti business, this 'writing up.' I've said to him so many times: 'Please. Explain it to me. I want to understand.' Because he keeps getting arrested for these petty offenses, and they're building up to a point where a prosecutor will want to put him away. One time he was arrested for writing up two days in a row. I get a call and I go down to the 68th Precinct, and there he is—no shoes on, handcuffed to the bench. The cop was awful. She said: 'I hope you go to jail because that's where you deserve to be.' So I wind up being on Henry's side, even though I want to confront him for doing the wrong thing.

66 "And the third day, there is Henry *again*, down at the station house, handcuffed to the bench. I said to him: 'Look. If you want to spend time with me, just say so. We'll go do something. You don't need to get arrested to get my attention.' He said, in that glum way of his, 'Very funny, Jennifer.' But on the way out, he leans down and tells me: 'You shouldn't help me. You should help someone else. It's past my time already.' He was 15."

67 Sitting with Henry in the P.S. 314 classroom, I ask him what he thinks about when he's alone.

"I think about the future, about getting out of here. I'd like to 68
live somewhere else, upstate maybe. I wouldn't want to grow up
and have a kid and live in this neighborhood. It's too dangerous.

"A man held a gun to my head one time, 'cause he wanted 69
my fronts." Fronts are gold caps that kids wear on their teeth
for show. I said, 'I won't take 'em off for you or anybody.'"

"Why not give him the fronts?" I ask. 70

"It's the way I am." 71

"Did you think he would shoot you?" He shrugs. "How 72
would you treat a kid of your own?"

"I wouldn't hit him. I'd never hit him. If you hit a kid, he 73
cries at first. Then he stops crying after a while and he doesn't
care. You can hit him forever and it won't matter."

"Have people hit you?" He nods. "What for?" 74

"Writing up." 75

"Why do you keep doing it?" 76

"I don't know," he says. "I know it gets me into trouble, but I 77
just can't stop."

"What do you write?" 78

"TM1," he says. "Everywhere I see some open space I write 79
it. TM1. In the hallways, on the buildings, I just have to see it."

"What does TM1 mean?" 80

He looks me in the eye for the first time. "The Magnificent 81
One," he says.

Steven L. Nock

THE PROBLEM
WITH MARRIAGE

*Steven L. Nock teaches sociology at the University of Virginia.
His special area of interest is the family, and he has written
widely on the subject—as for example in his recent book*
Marriage in Men's Lives. *The following essay by Nock appeared in 1999 in* Society, *a magazine devoted to social issues
(broadly considered), along with several other articles that describe a "moral crisis" in America associated with the decline
of the family. Together the contributors represented The
Council on Civil Society (CCS), a nonpartisan group of social*

scientists jointly sponsored by the Institute for American Values and the University of Chicago Divinity School. CCS is committed to the health of America's civic institutions and concerned about challenges to the health of the family. In 1999 the group (which includes Jean Bethke Elshtain, Cornel West, and Senator Joseph Lieberman) issued a formal Call to Civil Society, which called attention to a range of social ills related to families and children.

1   *A Call to Civil Society* warns that the institutions most critical to democratic society are in decline. "What ails our democracy is not simply the loss of certain organizational forms, but also the loss of certain organizing ideals—moral ideals that authorize our civic creed, but do not derive from it. At the end of this century, our most important challenge is to strengthen the moral habits and ways of living that make democracy possible." I suggest that American institutions have traditionally been organized around gender and that the loss of this organizing principle explains many of the trends discussed in the report. Specifically, the continued centrality of gender in marriage—and its growing irrelevance everywhere else—helps explain many contemporary family problems. The solution is to restore marriage to a privileged status from which both spouses gain regardless of gender.

2   The family trends we are now seeing reflect a conflict between the ideals central to marriage and those that define almost all other institutions. Growing numbers of Americans reject the idea that adults should be treated differently based on their gender. But it is difficult to create a new model of marriage based on such a premise. For many people, assumptions about gender equality conflict with the reality of their marriages. It may hardly matter if one is male or female in college, on the job, at church, in the voting booth, or almost anywhere else in public. But it surely matters in marriage. The family, in short, is still organized around gender while virtually nothing else is. Alternatively, marriage has not been redefined to accommodate the changes in male-female relations that have occurred elsewhere. This, I believe, is the driving force behind many of the problematic trends identified in *A Call to Civil Society.*

3   Stable marriages are forged of extensive dependencies. Yet trends toward gender equality and independence have made the traditional basis of economic dependency in marriage increasingly problematic. The challenge is to reinvent marriage as an institution based on dependency that is not automatically related

issues. Institutions like the family are bigger than any individual. So when large numbers of people create new patterns of family life, we should consider the collective forces behind such novel arrangements. And if some of those innovations are harmful to adults or children, fixing them will require more than a call for stronger moral habits (though there is certainly nothing wrong with such advice). Fixing them will require restructuring some basic social arrangements.

Since *A Call to Civil Society* focuses on *institutional* decline, I 10 want to consider the meaning of an institution. A society is a cluster of social institutions, and institutions are clusters of *shared* ideals. Only when people agree about how some core dimension of life should be organized is there a social institution. The family is a good example.

Although individual families differ in detail, collectively they 11 share common features as a result of common problems and tested solutions. In resolving and coping with the routine challenges of family life such as child care, the division of household labor, or relations with relatives, individuals draw on conventional (i.e., shared) ideals. As disparate individuals rely on shared answers to questions about family life, typical patterns emerge that are understood and recognized—mother, father, son, daughter, husband, and wife. To the extent that such ideals are widely shared, the family is a social institution. Were individuals left completely on their own to resolve the recurring problems of domestic life, there would be much less similarity among families. Alternatively, were there no conventional values and beliefs to rely on, the family would not be an institution. The family, as an institution, differs in *form* from one culture to another. Yet everywhere, it consists of patterned (i.e., shared and accepted) solutions to the problems of dependency (of partners, children, and the elderly).

The problem today is that an assumption that was once central to all social institutions is no longer so compelling. Beliefs 12 about gender have long been an organizing template that guided behaviors in both public and private. Yet while gender has become increasingly unimportant in public, neither women nor men have fully adjusted to these changes in their private married lives. If men and women are supposed to be indistinguishable at work or school, does the same standard apply in marriage? Americans have not yet agreed about the answer. As a result, the institution of the family (the assumptions about how married life should be organized) no longer complements other social arrangements. Increasingly, the family is viewed as a problem for people because the assumptions about domestic life no longer agree with those in other settings.

When husbands and wives return home from work, school, church, or synagogue, they often struggle with traditional ideals about marriage that do not apply in these other areas. No matter what her responsibilities at work, the married mother will probably be responsible for almost all child care at home, for instance. Responsibilities at work are unlikely to be dictated by whether the person is male or female. But responsibilities at home are. This contradiction helps explain the trends identified in *A Call to Civil Society*.

13   High rates of divorce, cohabitation, and unmarried child-bearing are documented facts, and all have clearly increased this century. Do such trends suggest that the family is losing its institutional anchor? In fact, the traditional arrangements that constitute the family are less compelling today than in the past. In this respect, the institution of the family is weaker. To understand why, I now consider the traditional basis of the family, legal marriage.

Legal Marriage and the Institution of the Family

14   The extent to which the family *based on legal marriage* is an institution becomes obvious when one considers an alternative way that adult couples arrange their intimate lives. Certainly there is no reason to believe that two people cannot enjoy a harmonious and happy life without the benefit of legal marriage. In fact, growing numbers of Americans appear to believe that unmarried *cohabitation* offers something that marriage does not. One thing that cohabitation offers is freedom from the rules of marriage because there are no widely accepted and approved boundaries around cohabitation. Unmarried partners have tremendous freedom to decide how they will arrange their legal and other relationships. Each partner must decide how to deal with the other's parents, for example. Parents, in turn, may define a cohabiting child's relationship as different from a married child's. Couples must decide whether vacations will be taken together or separately. Money may be pooled or held in separate accounts. If children are born, cohabiting parents must decide about the appropriate (non-legal) obligations each incurred as a result. In such small ways, cohabiting couples and their associates must *create* a relationship. Married couples may also face decisions about some of these matters. However, married spouses have a pattern to follow. For most matters of domestic life, marriage supplies a template. This is what cohabiting couples lack. They are exempt from the vast range of marriage norms and laws in our society.

A man can say to his wife: "I am your husband. You are my 15
wife. I am expected to do certain things for you, and you likewise. We have pledged our faithfulness. We have promised to
care for one another in times of sickness. We have sworn to
forego others. We have made a commitment to our children.
We have a responsibility and obligation to our close relatives,
as they have to us." These statements are not simply personal
pledges. They are also enforceable. Others will expect these
things of the couple. Laws, religion, and customs bolster this
contract. When this man says to someone, "I would like you to
meet my wife," this simple declaration says a great deal.

Compare this to an unmarried couple living happily to- 16
gether. What, if any, are the conventional assumptions that can
be made? What are the limits to behavior? To whom is each
obligated? Who can this couple count on for help in times of
need? And how do you complete this introduction of one's cohabiting partner: "I would like you to meet my . . . "? The lack
of a word for such a partner is a clear indication of how little
such relationships are governed by convention. Alternatively,
we may say that such a relationship is *not* an institution, marriage is. I believe this helps explain why cohabiting couples are
less happy, and less satisfied with their relationships than married couples.

Almost all worrisome social trends in regard to the *family* are 17
actually problems related to *marriage:* declining rates of marriage, non-marital fertility, unmarried cohabitation, and divorce. Any understanding of the family must begin with a consideration of marriage. I now offer a *normative definition of
marriage;* a statement of what Americans agree it *should* be, the
assumptions and taken-for-granted notions involved. In so doing, I will lay the foundation for an explanation of family decline.

In *Marriage in Men's Lives,* I developed the details of norma- 18
tive marriage by consulting three diverse sources. First, I examined large national surveys conducted repeatedly over the
past two decades. Second, I read domestic relations law, including state and federal appellate decisions. Finally, I consulted sources of religious doctrine, especially the Bible.
Throughout, my goal was to identify all aspects of marriage
that are widely shared, accepted as legitimate, and broadly
viewed as compelling.

A normative definition of marriage draws attention to the 19
central idea that marriage is more than the sum of two
spouses. As an institution, marriage includes rules that origi-
nate outside the particular union that establish boundaries
around the relationship. Those boundaries are the understood
limits of behavior that distinguish marriage from all other

relationships. Married couples have something that all other couples lack; they are heirs to a system of shared principles that help organize their lives. If we want to assess changes in the family, the starting point is an examination of the institutional foundation of marriage. Six ideals define legal marriage in America.

20   1) *Individual Free Choice.* Mate selection is based on romantic love. In the course of a century, parents have come to play a smaller and smaller role in the choice of married partners. Dating supplanted courtship as compatibility, attractiveness, and love replaced other bases for matrimony. National surveys show that "falling in love" is the most frequently cited reason for marrying one's spouse, and that the most important traits in successful marriages are thought to be "satisfying one another's needs" and "being deeply in love." Western religious ceremonies admonish partners to love one another until death, and every state permits a legal divorce when love fails ('incompatibility', 'irreconcilable differences' or similar justifications). Love is associated with feelings of security, comfort, companionship, erotic attraction, overlooking faults, and persistence. Since love and marriage are so closely related, people expect all such feelings from their marriages.

21   2) *Maturity.* Domestic relations law defines an age at which persons may marry. Throughout the U.S., the minimum is 18, though marriage may be permitted with approval by parents or the court at earlier ages. Parental responsibilities for children end with legal *emancipation* at age 18. Thus, marriage may occur once parents are released from their legal obligations to children, when children are legally assumed to be mature enough to enter binding contracts, and once children are assumed able to become self-sufficient and able to provide for offspring. Traditional religious wedding ceremonies celebrate a new form of maturity as Genesis states: "A man leaves his father and mother and cleaves to his wife and they become one flesh."

22   3) *Heterosexuality.* Traditionally, and legally, the only acceptable form of sex has been with one's spouse. Sex outside of marriage (fornication or adultery) is still illegal in half of U.S. states. And sexual expression within marriage has traditionally been legally restricted to vaginal intercourse (sodomy laws). Though such laws are rarely enforced even where they exist, they remind us of the very close association of marriage and conventional forms of heterosexual sexuality. Recent efforts to legalize homosexual marriage have been strenuously resisted. Since the full-faith-and-credit clause of the Constitution requires that marriages conducted legally in one state be recognized as legal in others, the possibility of legal homosexual

marriage in Hawaii prompted an unprecedented federal "Defense of Marriage Act" in September 1996. This law will allow states to declare homosexual Hawaiian marriages void in their jurisdiction. Despite growing acceptance of homosexuality, there is very little support for homosexual marriages. The 1990 General Social Survey showed that only 12 percent of Americans believe homosexuals should be allowed to marry.

4) *Husband as Head.* Though Americans generally endorse 23
equality between the sexes, men and women still occupy different roles in their marriages. Even if more and more couples are interested in egalitarian marriages, large numbers of people aren't. The 1994 General Social Survey shows that adults are almost evenly divided about whether both spouses should contribute to family income (57 percent approve of wives working, and in fact, 61 percent of wives are employed). Four in ten adults endorse a very traditional division of roles, where the wife takes care of the home and family, and the husband earns all the income. Traditional religious wedding ceremonies ask women to "honor and obey" their husbands. In reality, most husbands have more authority than their wives do. The spouse who is primarily responsible for income enjoys more authority, and in the overwhelming majority of American marriages, that is the husband. Demands made of husbands at work are translated into legitimate demands made on the family. So most husbands have more authority than their wives do, regardless of professed beliefs.

5) *Fidelity and Monogamy.* In law, sexual exclusivity is the 24
symbolic core of marriage, defining it in more obvious ways than any other. Husbands and wives have a legal right to engage in (consensual) sex with one another. Other people may not have a legal right to engage in sex with either married partner. Adultery is viewed as sufficiently threatening to marriages that homicides provoked by the discovery of it may be treated as manslaughter. Extramarital sex is viewed as more reprehensible than any other form, including sex between young teenagers, premarital sex, and homosexual sex. Eight in ten adults in the 1994 General Social Survey described extramarital sex as "always wrong." Adultery, in fact, is rare. Recent research reported by Laumann and his colleagues in *The Social Organization of Sexuality* revealed that only 15 percent of married men and 5 percent of married women have ever had extramarital sex. Among divorced people these percentages are only slightly higher, 25 percent for men and 10 percent for women. Monogamy is closely related to fidelity because it restricts all sexual expression to one married partner. With the exception of Utah where some Mormons practice polygamy (against the

canons of the Mormon Church), monogamy has gone largely unchallenged in the United States since 1878 when the U.S. Supreme Court upheld the conviction of a Mormon who practiced polygamy.

25   6) *Parenthood*. With rare exceptions, married people become parents. Despite high rates of unmarried fertility, there is little to suggest that married couples are less likely to have, or desire to have children today than they were several decades ago. Only 13 percent of ever-married women aged 34 to 45 are childless today. Two decades ago, the comparable figure was 7 percent. The six-point difference, however, is due to delayed fertility, rather than higher childlessness. Overall completed cohort fertility (i.e., the total number of children born to women in their lifetime) has remained stable since the end of the Baby Boom. And while the legal disabilities once suffered by illegitimate children have been declared unconstitutional, marital and nonmarital fertility differ in important respects. Unmarried fathers may, through legal means, obtain the custody of their children, although few do. Indeed, a vast legal apparatus exists to enforce the parental obligations of men who do not voluntarily assume them. On the other hand, married men are automatically presumed to be the legal father of their wife's children, and nothing (except the absence of "unfitness") is required of them to establish custody.

Challenges to Normative Marriage

26   This ensemble of behaviors and beliefs describes how most Americans understand marriage. Even if particular marriages depart in some ways from this model, this should be the starting point when attempting to assess family change. If "the family" has declined, then such change will be obvious in one or more of the foregoing dimensions. Widespread attempts to change normative marriage, or wholesale departures from it, are evidence that Americans do not agree about the institution. I now briefly review three obvious challenges to the normative model of marriage just outlined. High divorce rates, late ages at marriage, and declining rates of remarriage are a reflection of an underlying theme in such challenges. That theme is the importance of gender in marriage

27   The increasingly common practice of unmarried *cohabitation* is an example of a challenge to normative marriage. In 1997, 4.1 million opposite-sex cohabiting couples were counted by the U.S. Bureau of the Census, the majority of whom (58 percent) have never married, and one in five of

whom (22 percent) is under 25 years old. Research on cohabiting partners has identified a central theme in such relationships. Cohabiting individuals are more focused on gender equality in economic and other matters than married spouses. They are also less likely to have a gender-based division of tasks in most forms of household labor except the care of infants.

Yet another challenge to normative marriage is unmarried childbearing. One in three children in America is born to an unmarried woman; six in ten of those children were conceived outside of marriage (the balance were conceived prior to a divorce or separation). The historical connection between sexual intercourse and marriage weakened once effective contraception and abortion became available. Without contraception, married women became pregnant if fecund. There was no reason to ask a married woman why, or when she would have a child. Parenthood in an era of universal contraception, however, is a choice. It is now possible to ask *why* someone had a child. Since childbearing is thought to be a choice, it is viewed as a decision made chiefly by women. And the type of woman who chooses to have children differs from the childless woman because motherhood now competes with many other legitimate roles in a woman's life. Research has shown that women who choose motherhood give occupational and income considerations lower priority than childless women. [28]

By the late 1960s, feminists who argued that wives should not be completely dependent on husbands joined this critique of the exclusive breadwinner role of husbands. Just as the exclusive breadwinner role for men was criticized, the exclusive homemaker-mother role for married women was identified as oppressive. And, of course, such women are the statistical exception today. Maternity must be balanced with many other adult roles in women's lives, and traditional marriage is faulted as creating a "second shift" for women who return home from work only to assume responsibility for their households with little help from their husbands. [29]

All significant challenges to marriage focus on various aspects of gender. The traditional assignment of marital roles based on sex (i.e., husband as head of household) is the core problem in marriage. Other dimensions of normative marriage are less troublesome. There is little evidence of widespread disagreement about the ideas of free choice of spouses, fidelity, monogamy, heterosexual marriage, maturity, or parenthood. [30]

Whether Americans are now less committed to common moral beliefs than in the past is an empirical question. Values (i.e., moral beliefs) are researchable issues, and it would be possible to investigate their role in matters of family life. [31]

Increases in divorce, cohabitation, illegitimacy, or premarital sex are certainly evidence that some beliefs are changing. However, social scientists have yet to identify all the various causes of these family trends. Undoubtedly there are many, including demographic (e.g., longer life, lower fertility), technological (e.g., contraception, public health) and cultural (e.g., shifting patterns of immigration). Changing values about gender are but one cause of family change. Still, I suspect they are the most important. When something as basic and fundamental as what it means to be a man or woman changes, virtually everything else must change accordingly. Now we must incorporate such new ideas into the institution of marriage.

New Families

32   It is easy to imagine how a new model of marriage would look. None of the basic elements of normative marriage are likely to change except the gender assumptions about who heads the family. Husbands and wives are already familiar with this new model of marriage, even if we have yet to acknowledge it. In 1995, virtually all (95 percent) of married men with children in the household were employed. Two-thirds (65 percent) of wives in such families were employed. Husbands are still breadwinners, but so are wives. While employment does not typically eliminate a wife's dependency on her husband, it does mean that husbands are also dependent on wives. Most American marriages now involve a pooling of incomes. The resulting lifestyle, therefore, is produced jointly by wives and husbands. Income pooling has increasingly replaced the breadwinner/ homemaker pattern.

33   These new economic realities of married life have not been fully incorporated into the institution of normative marriage— the way we think about marriage. Husbands and wives have yet to reconcile their joint economic dependency with the routine of married life. Even if most married couples today depend on one another's earnings, traditional patterns of domestic responsibilities persist. Such gendered marriages are a problem because they do not fit with the assumptions about men and women in all other spheres of their lives.

34   The trends in the family that worry us might better be viewed as a consequence of redefining the institution. We are now struggling to resolve ideas about what is proper in our marriages with ideas about what is proper outside of them. Repeated studies have shown that conflicts over gender (Should the wife work? Who should do what?) are leading causes of di-

vorce. Growing numbers of women find it difficult to live in marriages that appear to devalue their roles as breadwinners. On the other hand, full-time housewives feel that housework is devalued. Growing numbers of couples opt for "informal" marriage, or cohabitation, as a way to live without strict gender assumptions. Large numbers of women decide to pursue parenthood without the limitations and restrictions that would be imposed by marriage. It is easy to see why people make these choices. But though understandable, they are costly. Adults and children thrive in stable, nuclear families, even if they are not always happy. No feasible alternative comes close in its economic or emotional benefits for children or adults.

But the solution is not complete independence in marriage. 35 Cohabitation has taught us that two soloists do not make a very good duet. Such equal partnerships do not last very long, and cohabiting couples report low levels of happiness and satisfaction. That is probably because nothing binds cohabiting couples together except love and affection. As desirable as those emotions are, they are a flimsy basis for an enduring relationship without alternative bonds. Stable, enduring marriages must be forged of extensive dependencies. Each person must depend on the other for many things. But such dependencies need not be inequitable or unfair.

What is the problem with marriage? The problem is the role 36 of gender in the institution. More accurately, the problem is how to deal with widespread social change in matters of gender. But there is good reason to believe that we will come to terms with such challenges. Few boys today will grow up with mothers who are not employed. Young men are unlikely to inherit their fathers' or grandfathers' traditional views about marriage or women. Fewer men work with colleagues who openly view women and wives in traditional restricted roles. More and more of the youthful life course is spent in nontraditional families or outside of families altogether. Children, especially boys, who experience such childhoods (employed mothers, divorce, non-family living) are more accepting of women's new roles and options and are willing to perform more housework. It is not, therefore, a dramatic change in the basic institution of normative marriage that we need. Rather, it is a recognition and accommodation to the changes in women's lives and patience for intergenerational (cohort) change to catch up with current expectations. And men must become a part of the gender revolution. Even if this is not a fundamental redefinition of marriage, it will have profound consequences for how marriage is experienced because the tension between public and private lives will be reduced.

Marriage and Public Policy

37   Social institutions can be changed intentionally, but not easily, not quickly, and not without widespread discussion and debate. I have been studying covenant marriage in Louisiana for the past year. In that state (and in Arizona) couples may elect one of two marriage regimes; the traditional one based on no-fault divorce rules, and covenant marriage which requires premarital counseling, and is governed by traditional fault-grounds for divorce. Covenant marriage laws are the first in over 200 years in America designed explicitly to make *marriage more permanent and divorce more restrictive*. Not surprisingly therefore, they are extremely controversial. It is much too early to know if this legal innovation will affect divorce rates. But one thing is clear. The passage of more restrictive divorce laws, even if optional, has provoked intense debate and discussion about the meaning of marriage and the role of the state in family affairs. Covenant marriage is discussed and debated almost weekly in the Louisiana media. A public discussion about marriage has begun in that state. Only through such *megalogues*, as Etzioni calls them, will institutions change. Social change is not being legislated. It is simply being encouraged, debated, and discussed.

38   Proposals that marriage be recognized, promoted, and protected by revisions in federal tax codes, increased use of premarital counseling, and revisions in divorce laws are a good start. I believe we must go further, however, to create and reinforce dependencies in marriage. Dependency based automatically on gender will eventually be purged from marriage, as it is now being purged from work, school, and other public realms. The transition is clearly difficult and painful as we now can see. But what will bind couples to such new families? The answer is that bases of dependency other than gender must be created. Significant benefits must flow from the marriage, and significant exit costs must exist for both partners.

39   The most sensible, though controversial way to achieve these goals is for states to establish a preference for married couples in the distribution of discretionary benefits. My research on covenant marriage has convinced me that any attempt to privilege marriage over other statuses will be controversial and resisted, especially by those who see traditional marriage as unfair to women. Since the inequities in marriage are being resolved, I would focus on ways to privileged marriage by granting significant economic benefits to couples willing to commit to a restrictive regime. The purpose would be to create a new distinction between married and unmarried persons,

though not one automatically based on gender. If marriage is to thrive, significant benefits *other than emotional ones* must flow from the status. And men and women alike must benefit from the status of marriage.

Marriage has traditionally been founded on dependencies of many types. But unequal (i.e. women's) economic dependencies are the most obvious (and often the source of inequity). In a world where men and women may each be economically independent, the benefits of pooled incomes may not suffice to sustain couples during those inevitable times when love fades. What the authors of *A Call to Civil Society* refer to as "the philosophy of expressive individualism—a belief in the "sovereignty of the self" is fostered by gender equality and individual economic independence. In the absence of unequal economic dependencies, marriage must become a privileged status again, or else divorce rates will remain high, and marriage rates will continue to fall. To make it a privileged status, we should establish significant economic incentives. To the extent that people benefit economically in obvious and large ways by virtue of their marriages, (and to the extent that such benefits are not available to unmarried people) each spouse is dependent on *the union, per se* (dependency is typically measured by the costs of exiting a relationship).

The state has an enormous economic interest in promoting stable marriages. Strangely, the *macroeconomic* costs of divorce are rarely discussed in deliberations about public policy. Yet the *microeconomic* consequences are well known. Divorce and single-parenthood take a toll on earnings, educational attainment, labor-force attachment, subsequent marital stability, and the likelihood of poverty for the adults and the children involved. The aggregate consequences of all such individual losses are vast, even if unknown. Promoting marriage makes very good economic sense, beyond any other benefits to children or adults.

There are many ways we might promote marriage. Here I offer one example. We should consider significant tax credits for some married couples to create an economic interest in the marital union and significant exit costs for both partners. Americans will not tolerate mandatory family policy, so states should follow the lead of Louisiana in offering couples the option of two marriage regimes. Any couple could elect to be married under the customary no-fault divorce system without requirements for pre-marital and marital counseling. The more restrictive marriage regime would require premarital and marital counseling (as a prerequisite for a divorce), and would apply prevailing "best interests of the child" custody standards in granting a divorce. Divorce would be denied if the court determined that it was not in the best interest of the child (or children) involved. ("Best interests of the child" divorce proposals have been considered in several states, though never enacted.)

43   Couples who marry under the more restrictive marriage regime would qualify for very significant tax credits. Such credits must be quite large—$2,500 or $3,500 a year—sufficient to offset the costs of a college education for the children of married parents, or to underwrite the costs of a home, for example. Such tax credits would create a financial interest in the marriage *per se*, a benefit that flows to married couples by virtue of their marital status and nothing else. It also creates a significant exit cost at divorce. Both partners benefit so long as they remain married, both lose at divorce. How will we pay for such generous benefits? In fact, it is not certain that there would be net costs. A more appropriate question is how we will continue to pay for single parenthood and divorce.

44   Such a proposal seeks to restore marriage to a privileged status. It also addresses the need for a new basis of dependency in modern marriages where both spouses are likely to be breadwinners. It is intended to foster higher rates of marriage, lower rates of unmarried childbearing, and delays in divorce. Were any policy to be partially successful in having these consequences, the long-term economic ledgers (i.e., costs and benefits) may balance. Even if they didn't, such proposals would surely provoke discussion and debate about the importance of marriage in America. *A Call to Civil Society* asks us to begin such a debate about the loss of organizing ideals. Let's start with a consideration of the centrality of gender to the problem with marriage.

Shere Hite

BRINGING DEMOCRACY
HOME

In the spring of 1995, Ms. *magazine carried the following excerpt from Shere Hite's book* The Hite Report on the Family: Growing Up under Patriarchy *(1995), the product of her study of several thousand families. Hite has made a reputation not only on this report but also on her books* The Hite Report: A Nationwide Study of Female Sexuality *(1976) and* The Hite Report: A Study of Male Sexuality *(1981)-both controversial, widely discussed titles.*

Love and anger, love and obedience, love and power, love and hate. These are all present in family relationships. It's easy to say that they are inevitable, that stresses and strains are unavoidable, given "human nature." To some extent this is true, but these stresses and strains are exaggerated by a tense and difficult family system that is imposed upon our emotions and our lives, structuring them to fit its own specified goals. 1

Is the family as we have known it for so long the only way to create safe, loving, and caring environments for people? The best way? To understand the family in Western tradition, we must remember that much of what we see, say, and think about it is based on the archetypal family that is so pervasive in our society—Jesus, Mary, and Joseph. There is no daughter icon. This is the "holy family" model that we are expected, in one way or another, to live up to. But is this model really the right one for people who believe in equality and justice? Does it teach a good understanding of love and the way to make relationships work when we become adults? 2

One constantly hears that the family is in trouble, that it doesn't work anymore, that we must find ways to help it. If the family doesn't work, maybe there is something wrong with its structure. People must have reasons for fleeing the nuclear family: human rights abuses and the battering of women are well documented in many governments' statistics. 3

The family is changing because only in recent decades has the process of democratization, which began in Western political life more than two centuries ago, reached private life. Although John Stuart Mill wrote in favor of women's rights in the egalitarian democratic theory he helped develop, the family and women's role in the world were left out of most discussions of 4 democracy, left in the "sacred" religious domain. Women and nonproperty owners, as well as "minorities," did not have the vote when democracy first began. Men made a fatal mistake. The democracy they thought they could make work in the public sphere would not really work without democracy in private life.

5   Some people, of course, are alarmed by changes in the family. Reactionary fundamentalist groups have gone on the offensive to try to stop this process. Yet most people are happier with their personal lives today than people were 50 years ago. Women especially have more choices and freedom than they did in the past. There is a positive new diversity springing up in families and relationships today in Western society. This pluralism should be valued and encouraged: far from signaling a breakdown of society, it is a sign of a new, more open and tolerant society springing up, a new world being born out of the clutter of the old.

6   Democracy could work even better if we changed the aggressive personality that is being created by the patriarchal family system. Children brought up with choice about whether to accept their parents' power are more likely to be confident about believing in themselves and their own ideas, less docile or habituated to bending to power. Such a population would create and participate in public debate very differently. And there are many more advances we are on the threshold of achieving: naming and eliminating emotional violence, redefining love and friendship, progressing in the areas of children's rights and in men's questioning of their own lives.

7   My work salutes the gentler and more diverse families that seem to be arising. They are part of a system that does not keep its members in terror: fathers in terror lest they not be "manly" and able to support it all; mothers in terror lest they be beaten in their own bedrooms and ridiculed by their children; children in terror of being forced to do things against their will and having absolutely no recourse, no door open to them for exit.

8   What I am offering is a new interpretation of relationships between parents and children, a new theory of the family. My interpretation of the data from my questionnaires takes into account not only the individual's unique experiences, as is done in psychology, but also the cultural backdrop—the canvas of social "approval" or "disapproval" against which children's lives are lived. This interdisciplinary theory also takes into account the historical ideology of the family; those who took part in my research are living in a world where perception of "family" is filtered through the Christian model of the "holy family"

with its reproductive icons of Jesus, Mary, and Joseph. But no matter how beautiful it appears (especially in its promise of "true love"), this family model is an essentially repressive one, teaching authoritarian psychological patterns, meekness in women, and a belief in the unchanging rightness of male power. In this hierarchical family, love and power are inextricably linked, a pattern that has damaging effects not only on all family members but on the politics of the wider society. How can there be successful democracy in public life if there is an authoritarian model in private life?

So used have we become to these symbols that we continue 9 to believe—no matter what statistics we see in the newspapers about divorce, violence in the home, mental breakdown—that the icons and the system they represent are right, fair, and just. We assume without thinking that this model is the only "natural" form of family, and that if there are problems it must be the individual who is at fault, not the institution.

We need a new interpretation of what is going on. We may 10 be at one of the most important turning points of the Western world, the creation of a new social base that will engender an advanced and improved democratic political structure.

What Is the Family All About?

Creating new, more democratic families means taking a clear 11 and rational look at our institutions. We tend to forget that the family was created in its current form in early patriarchy for political, not religious, reasons. The new political order had to solve a specific problem: How could lineage or inheritance flow through men (and not women as it had previously) if men do not bear children?

The modern patriarchal family was created so that each man 12 would "own" a woman who would reproduce for him. He then had to control the sexuality of "his" woman, for how else could he be sure that "his" child was really his? Restrictions were placed on women's lives and bodies by men; women's imprisonment in marriage was made a virtue, for example, through the later archetype of the self-sacrificing Mary, who was happy to be of service, never standing up for herself or her own rights. Mary, it is important to note, is a later version of a much earlier Creation Mother goddess. In her earlier form, she had many more aspects, more like the Indian goddess Kali than the "mother" whom the Christian patriarchal system devised.

Fortunately, the family is a human institution: humans made 13 it and humans can change it. My research indicates that the extreme aggression we see in society is not a characteristic of biological "human nature" (as Freud concluded), nor a result of hormones. "Human nature" is a psychological structure that is carefully implanted in our minds—for life—as we learn the love and power equations of the family. Power and love are combined in the family structure: in order to receive love, most children have to humiliate themselves, over and over again, before power.

14   In our society, parents have the complete legal, economic, and social "right" to control children's lives. Parents' exclusive power over children creates obedience. Children are likely to take on authoritarian emotional, psychological, and sexual patterns, and to see power as one of the central categories of existence.

15   Love is at the heart—so to speak—of our belief in the importance of the family. The desire for love is what keeps us returning to the icons. Even when they don't seem to work in our lives, we try and try again. We are told that we will never find love if we don't participate in the family. We hear repeatedly that the only place we will ever be able to get security, true acceptance, and understanding is in the family; that we are only "half a family" or a "pretend family" if we create any other human group; that without being a member of the family we will be forever "left out," lonely, or useless. No one would want to deny the importance of love, or of lasting relationships with other people. But the violent, distorted definitions of love created by the patriarchal family make it difficult for love to last, and to be as profound as it could be.

16   How confusing it is for children, the idea of being loved! They are so often told by their parents, "Of course we love you, why do you even ask?" It is easy for children to believe that the emotion they feel when faced with a powerful person is "love"—or that the inscrutable ways of a person who is sometimes caring and friendly, and other times punitive and angry, are loving. The problem then is that, since the parents are still the providers and "trainers" of the children, legally and economically the "owners" of the children, they exercise incredible power over the children—the very power of survival itself.

17   Children must feel gratitude, and so, in their minds, this gratitude is mixed with love. How much of the love they feel is really supplication before the power of the parents? How will they define love later in life? Won't they be highly confused by passion (either emotional or physical) and what it means, unable to connect it with other feelings of liking and concern? Of course, long-term caring for others is something positive that can also be learned in families, but it can be learned in other kinds of families, not just the nuclear model.

Does "Love" Include Sex? The Body?

And what definition of love do children learn from the way   18
their parents relate physically? Isn't it strange to think of your
parents having sex? Finding parents in any kind of physical
embrace comes as a fascinating shock to most children: 83 percent of children in my research say their parents seem completely asexual.

It would be logical if children drew the conclusion that "real   19
love" is never sexual, or even physically affectionate. But isn't
affection a great part of what love is? If parents don't hug and
kiss each other, is the definition of adult "love" different? And
if so, what is it? Why do parents feel that they shouldn't touch
each other in front of the children? Because the children
would be jealous? Because it would give the children sexual
feelings and ideas? Or, do many parents really not want to
touch each other? Children wonder, if the parents don't want to
be affectionate, why exactly are they together? If they are only
together "for the sake of the children," this puts an awfully big
burden on the children to be "worth it" or to "make their parents happy," thus confusing the definitions of love even further.

Another way children learn that power and domination are   20
part of love is through observing the relationship of their parents. Gender tension and especially second-class treatment of
the mother by the father is reported by the majority of people
from two-parent families in this study. Girls in particular find
this gender inequality mixed with "love" confusing, even psychologically violent and terrifying. Why? Because for girls it
means coming to terms with what this power relationship will
mean for them: Will they inherit this gender inequality? Can
they avoid being considered lesser beings when they become
women? How can they love a father who represents this system? Or a mother who lets herself participate in it?

Are Single-Parent Families Bad for Children?

There are very few carefully controlled studies of the effects of   21
single-parent families on children. Today, much popular journalism assumes that the two-parent family is better for children. My data show that there are beneficial effects for the majority of children living in single-parent families. It is more
positive for children not to grow up in an atmosphere poisoned
by gender inequality.

Do girls who grow up with "only" their mother have a better   22
relationship with her? According to my study, 49 percent of

such girls felt that it was a positive experience; 20 percent did not like it; and the rest had mixed feelings. Mothers in one-parent families are more likely to feel freer to confide in daughters because no "disloyalty to the spouse" is implied. Daughters in such families are less likely to see the mother as a "wimp"—she is an independent person.

23 Boys who grow up with "only" their mother experience less pressure to demonstrate contempt for things "feminine" and for nonaggressive parts of themselves. In *The Hite Report on Men and Male Sexuality,* I was surprised to find that boys who grew up with their mother alone were much more likely to have good relationships with women in their adult lives: 80 percent of men from such families had formed strong, lasting ties with women (in marriage or long-term relationships), as opposed to only 40 percent from two-parent families. This does not mean that the two-parent family cannot be reformed so that it provides a peaceful environment for children—indeed this is part of the ongoing revolution in the family in which so many people today are engaged.

24 Single-parent families are mostly headed by mothers, yet there is an increasing number of single-father families. Many single fathers don't take much part in child care but instead hire female nannies or ask their mothers, sisters, or girlfriends to take care of the children. Men could change the style of families by taking more part domestically, and by opening up emotionally and having closer contact with children. My research highlights men's traumatizing and enforced split from women at puberty. . . .

25 Healing this is the single most important thing we as a society could do to bridge the distance men feel from "family."

Democracy of the Heart: A New Politics

26 If you listen to people talk about their families, it becomes clear that we must give up on the outdated notion that the only acceptable families are nuclear families. We should not see the new society that has evolved over the last 40 years as a disaster simply because it is not like the past.

27 The new diversity of families is part of a positive pluralism, part of a fundamental transition in the organization of society that calls for open-minded brainstorming by all of us: What do we believe "love" and "family" are? Can we accept that the many people fleeing the nuclear family are doing so for valid reasons? If reproduction is no longer the urgent priority that it was when societies were smaller, before industrialization took

hold, then the revolt against the family is not surprising. Perhaps it was even historically inevitable. It is not that people don't want to build loving, family-style relationships, it is that they do not want to be forced to build them within one rigid, hierarchical, heterosexist, reproductive framework. Diversity in family forms can bring joy and enrichment to a society: new kinds of families can be the basis for a renaissance of spiritual dignity and creativity in political as well as personal life.

Continuing this process of bringing private life into an ethi-   28
cal and egalitarian frame of reference will give us the energy and moral will to maintain democracy in the larger political sphere. We can create a society with a new spirit and will—but politics will have to be transformed. We can use the interactive frame of reference most often found today in friendships between women. Diversity in families can form the basic infrastructure for a new and advanced type of political democracy to be created, imagined, developed—a system that suits the massive societies that communications technology today has made into one "global village."

One cannot exaggerate the importance of the current debate: 29
there has been fascism in societies before; it could certainly emerge again, alongside fascism in the family. If we believe in the democratic, humanist ideals of the last 200 years, we have the right, almost the duty, to make our family system a more just one; to follow our democratic ideals and make a new, more inclusive network of private life that will reflect not a preordained patriarchal structure, but our belief in justice and equality for all—women, men, and children. Let's continue the transformation, believe in ourselves, and go forward with love instead of fear. In our private lives and in our public world, let's hail the future and make history.

Stephanie Coontz
HOW IGNORING
HISTORICAL AND
SOCIETAL CHANGE CAN
PUT KIDS AT RISK

Stephanie Coontz is a professional sociologist who teaches at Evergreen State College. In 1992, she published The Way We Never Were: American Families and the Nostalgia Trip, *a historical study of the American family that cut through many myths. In the wake of that book, she appeared on a number of talk shows—everything from* Oprah *to* Crossfire—*and began to work on a second book,* The Way We Really Are *(1997), which investigates current issues related to the family. The following is Chapter 8 of* The Way We Really Are. *(Notice that it contains references to Barbara Dafoe Whitehead and to Iris Marion Young, whose work is included in the next section of* Conversations.*)*

1   Even before recent economic setbacks, long-term historical processes had already undermined the ability of families to raise the next generation without outside assistance. Children used to be economic assets to a family, and the costs of raising them to an age where they could contribute to family subsistence were quite small. Industrialization gradually increased the expense of raising, educating, or training children and decreased their returns to the family, whether nuclear or extended. The cost of caring for all family dependencies rose as it became more difficult to integrate caregiving with the locations and rhythms of modern workplaces.[1]

2   After the turn of the century, the abolition of child labor, positive though it was, further increased the costs of raising children. Marital desertion became a growing problem, since fathers were less likely to seek child custody or maintain contact once the economic benefits of children had fallen. At the same time, more and more elderly Americans were ending up in almshouses. States passed laws requiring adult children to support their parents and absent fathers to support their children but found them hard to enforce. Private charities were unable to come anywhere near meeting the needs of children or the elderly, and local institutions could no longer cope with the concentrations of poverty that occurred in urban areas.[2]

As early as the mid-nineteenth century, new public institu-   3
tions, such as schools, had become essential supplements to
family child rearing in all classes, and government had begun
to recognize its responsibility to invest in programs to ensure
safe and adequate supplies of food, clean air, water, housing,
and sanitation facilities. In the early twentieth century, the federal government gradually took over many other functions that
had formerly been provided by extended families and voluntary societies, establishing pensions, disability funds, insurance programs, and supplemental cash assistance for families.
Government also performed a number of new functions, such
as helping to protect family members from abuse. Some of the
services government provided were inadequate, while others
were unnecessarily intrusive. But I know of no serious historian who doesn't believe that children of all classes were better
off as a result of government's expanded role.[3]

The growth of public schooling and government assistance   4
programs for families reflected society's recognition that the
rising cost of children made it essential for the task of raising
and educating future workers to be shared by all members of
society, not just dumped onto parents. The Federal government
expanded the education system and instituted maternity and
child nutrition programs in the early 1900s. During the 1930s,
the Civilian Conservation Corps and the National Youth
Administration were formed to meet what was agreed to be a
societal, not just a parental, responsibility to find work for
youths. In the 1940s, the government organized child care centers for women war-production workers. In the 1950s and
1960s, state and federal governments expanded their housing
subsidies for families and began providing much more extensive higher education and job programs for young people.

Passing the Buck on Child Support

But in the economic and social climate that has prevailed since   5
the mid-1970s, the long historical expansion of support systems for child raising has been reversed. Governments and
corporations have transferred more and more of the costs of
raising, educating, and training children back onto parents. As
politicians and employers have demonstrated growing indifference to the needs of the next generation, these attitudes have
spread throughout society, with nonparents pushing the costs
of the next generation onto parents and many parents engaging in their own cost-shifting behaviors.[4]

Spending on education, child and maternal health, and in-   6
frastructure for the future generations has not kept up with

needs for the past twenty years. Government has developed, economist Sylvia Hewlett observes, "a mindset . . . that is extraordinarily careless of children." As public policy analyst Iris Marion Young argues, "American society has been severely damaged by three decades of private and public disinvestment in basic manufacturing, new and rehabilitated housing, bridges and rail lines, public education, adult retraining, and social services such as preventative health care and libraries." Yet parents are increasingly expected, on their own, "to fill these gaping holes in the American dream."[5]

7   The extent to which America has shifted the cost of raising children back onto parents can be seen in the extraordinary retreat from the expansion of public education—a child-centered reform in which the United States once led the world. A 1989 study by the Educational Writers Association found that a quarter of the country's school buildings were inadequate, obsolete, or downright dangerous. A 1994 survey found that the conditions had continued to deteriorate, and the 1997 budget does not provide enough money to make a dent in the problem. Researchers report a direct correlation between poor physical conditions in schools and poor test scores.[6]

8   Teachers' salaries, expenditures per pupil, and other indicators of school quality (including the physical plant) significantly affect the employment prospects and wages of high school graduates. Yet unlike other nations, American schools are financed at the local rather than the federal level. If parents do not live in affluent communities with a high enough proportion of neighbors willing to vote for school bonds, they have few ways of assuring a quality education other than to enroll their children in private schools. And voters, many of them parents who believe they already "did their bit" by raising their own children, are becoming less and less willing to subsidize schools for "other" people's kids. School bond failures are way up in comparison with earlier decades. At the same time, the property tax cuts of the 1970s and 1980s greatly decreased the resources available to schools.

9   Child advocate and educational researcher Jonathan Kozol reports that New York City spends half as much per student as surrounding suburbs. In 1992, the country's forty-seven largest urban school districts spent nearly *$900 less on each student* than did their suburban counterparts—even though the urban schools were far more likely to have students needing special services. There are also substantial variations *within* school districts. Poorer neighborhoods, which often contain more children, receive much lower public subsidies than affluent ones.[7]

International comparisons reveal that education is simply   10
not a national priority in the United States the way it is in
many countries. We have a piecemeal, incoherent system that
fails to train teachers thoroughly, keep track of student
progress in a consistent way, or ensure equality of access.
Things are no better in the work world. Only 1 percent of the
funding employers devote to training goes towards raising basic skills, those most needed by young entry-level workers.
Both publicly and privately funded education is heavily skewed
against the apprenticeship programs and vocational training
needed by youngsters whose parents cannot afford to send
them to college. Government spending on employment and
training programs, in inflation-adjusted dollars, is today only
one-third of what it was in 1980. At the same time, the cost of
higher education has soared, while loans and scholarships
have been cut back.[8]

Housing policies provide another example of government   11
disinvestment in future generations. In the 1970s, government
was financing about 400,000 new apartments a year. In 1996,
Congress cut the number of new families who can expect rent
subsidies or vouchers to zero.[9]

Economists and political scientists debate where this disin-   12
vestment in the next generation began and why it has spread
so widely in the United States. Part of the problem is that the
economic and political changes of the past few decades have
increasingly put families with children at a disadvantage. The
pressures of a fast-paced, winner-take-all economy handicap
parents in comparison to nonparents, because parents have
less time to produce income and more demands on them for
redistribution than nonparents.

Under a system such as Social Security, furthermore, econo-   13
mist Nancy Folbre argues, nonparents can actually become
"free riders" on parents. By now, most people realize that retirees get much more from Social Security than they actually
put in. It is future workers, raised by parents at their personal
expense, who create the Social Security funds on which all aging workers will later draw, even if they did not invest in rearing any of those future workers. Thus nonparents can benefit
from other people's children without contributing to the costs
of raising them.[10]

These trends have been exacerbated by what economist   14
Robert Reich calls the "secession of the successful."
Increasingly, affluent parents as well as nonparents have withdrawn funding from "public institutions shared by all and dedicated their savings to their own private services"—from exclusive schools and recreational facilities to private security for

their walled-off neighborhoods. Government disinvestment widens the cycle, leaving middle-class families scrambling to buy privately what they can no longer count on receiving from public institutions, and needing to cut other expenses to make ends meet. In a tax system where voters have no say about whether expensive bombers get built, but plenty of chances to take out their frustrations in local school levies, children increasingly lose out in the contest for resources.[11]

15   In other words, long-term economic processes have gradually undermined Americans' consciousness of intergenerational obligations, while short-term economic setbacks have encouraged them to seize on quick-fix ways to keep more of their shrinking paychecks. Politicians have opportunistically encouraged people to rob the next generation. In confrontations over scarce resources or contested priorities, children, after all, are not an organized lobbying group.

16   The historical rise in the private costs of rearing children, combined with the recent public disinvestment in social capital, forms the background to what economist Joan Acker calls "a growing crisis of distribution" in modern industrial societies. In this crisis, it is not only children in single-parent families who have lost ground. There has been a decline in the economic and social resources available to children of *all* families except those in the top 20 percent of the income hierarchy.[12]

The Impact of Economic Inequality on Families

17   Cutbacks in social support systems, economic decline for working families, growing poverty for the unemployed or marginally employed, and highly visible affluence for the top 20 percent, along with the dazzling increase in consumer goods and services, all combine to make family life more difficult and social solidarity more elusive for everyone. The main countertrend to the job and wage setbacks in the United States since the mid-1970s has been a tremendous expansion of the consumer economy in fields that compete with family life and social ties, providing youth of all classes with fleeting and sometimes dangerous compensation for their exclusion from meaningful participation in work, civic life, and public space.

18   I spoke a year or so ago near Lakewood, California, a town made famous by the Spur Posse, a group of high school athletes who developed a point system for sexual conquests. One of the women at my talk had a son who attended the same school as the Spur Posse youths, and she made a memorable

comment about the life that faces so many young people in this city of middle-class homes but increasingly lower-class jobs. "A lot of these kids," she said, "have way too little future, but way too much *now*."[13]

For many families, of course, the *now* is already bleak, and it   19 is naive to think that parents can always protect their children from the impact of economic loss. Researchers find that the risk of violent behavior is nearly six times higher among people who are laid off from their jobs than among their employed counterparts, regardless of whether or not the individuals had a prior history of psychiatric disorder or alcohol abuse. A study of 350 white families in rural Iowa found that declining income, unstable work, or family debt in 1989 were linked to significantly higher levels of aggression in middle-school children two years later. These youths were more likely to beat someone up, deface property, set fires, and use weapons against others than youths who had not experienced economic stress.[14]

One of the main ways that children are hurt by unemploy-   20 ment and income loss, in middle- and upper- income families as well as low-income ones, is through the increase in stress and depression that their parents experience. When parents are distracted or irritated with each other because of financial or job worries, they tend to be less supportive of their children. Too preoccupied to reinforce—or even notice—their children's considerate behavior, parents become overly sensitive to disruptive behavior because it adds to their feelings of stress. Their attempts to nip "bad" behavior in the bud increase hostile exchanges with their children. With their own emotional resources overtaxed, parents find it hard to summon the patience for negotiation, tact, and complex reasoning. Instead, they issue orders, followed by physical punishment when immediate obedience is not forthcoming. Parents may see children's resistance as yet another challenge to their authority and self-esteem, which are already threatened by economic setbacks having nothing to do with the kids.[15]

Often, parents are not aware that they have fallen into these   21 patterns. When researchers ask parents who have been laid off about the effects on their families, few report problems. Some even tell researchers it's great to have the extra time with their kids. Children's accounts, however, almost invariably mention increased conflict and tension with parents. Observers' comparisons of interactions between employed and unemployed parents and their children suggests the kids' perceptions are more accurate than the parents'. Without other adult mentors or social support systems in the community, kids often bear the brunt of their parents' economic stress.[16]

22   Most of the effect of economic loss on children is channeled through changes in parenting practices, but economic insecurity also reduces kids' confidence in their parents and thereby increases their vulnerability to peer pressure. They become depressed and less motivated, and their lowered aspirations often have long-range consequences for their future.[17]

23   I got a vivid illustration of this a year or so ago when, after we had read studies of these family processes in class, one of my male students broke down crying. Embarrassed, he came to my office later and told me that he had transferred to the state college where I teach after two years at a community college and a year of full-time work. He had been raised to think he would go directly to a major university from high school. But his father had lost a well-paying job in the early 1980s, and by the time he found another, the family had gone through most of its savings.

24   My student told me how much he had resented his parents' inability to send him to the college of his choice. He had begun hanging out with a crowd that reinforced his growing contempt for his parents and their seemingly ineffectual response to the family crisis. During his last two years of high school he had defied rules, frequently staying out all night, binging on alcohol, and letting his grades slip. There were shouting matches with his father, tearful recriminations from his mother.

25   Recently he and his parents had begun to mend their fences, but this was the first time, he said, he had really thought about how much pain his contempt had added to their lives. "I couldn't get past my father yelling at me and insulting me," he said. "I couldn't see how he must have been hurting. And when my mom cried, it just made me feel more like going out and getting stoned."

26   The effects of economic loss on children seem to be more pronounced for boys than for girls. In contrast to the cycles of anger and disrespect between sons and fathers triggered by economic hardship, mothers in deprived families often gain regard for their daughters' opinions, allowing them to participate more in family decisions. There are also gender differences in the ways that economic loss affects parenting. Both fathers and mothers are likely to respond to economic stress with inconsistent and harsh parenting, but men are more likely to explode at their children.[18]

27   When marital conflict is part of the equation, things get even worse. Fathers tend to react to children in an increasingly hostile, arbitrary manner, while children tend "to question the father's authority and form coalitions with the mother against the father." A strong marital relationship can temper these re-

actions, but economic loss has been found to produce dramatic declines in marital quality and supportiveness. Furthermore, whereas support from husbands lessens the impact of economic hardship on women's parenting practices, support from wives does not always have the same effect on fathers. Even with highly supportive wives, men under economic stress are far more likely to be explosive, inconsistent parents.[19]

Individuals with exceptionally good interpersonal skills can   28
and do survive economic stress without such severe reactions, but those from less than ideal backgrounds, who in better conditions often overcome their personal weaknesses, may find the gains they have made over the years wiped away. For example, the Iowa study found that parents who had grown up in troubled families had fewer people skills and less self-confidence as adults. They were therefore "less capable of eliciting social support from others" to help them "withstand the psychological onslaught of economic disadvantage." As the social safety net has unraveled, such individuals and their children increasingly fall by the wayside.[20]

The Effects of Poverty on Families and Children

Here's what Robert Rector of the Heritage Foundation has to   29
say about the relationship between economic trends and family issues: "Is poverty harmful for children? I think not. Your bank account does not indicate the type of home you have."[21]

Do Rector and his counterparts have any idea of the terrible   30
binds faced by unemployed or impoverished Americans, or of the havoc that poverty wreaks on families? I think not. Consider the fact that the number of underweight infants seen at hospitals rises sharply in the three months after the coldest snap of winter, in what Dr. Deborah Frank calls the "heat-or-eat" choice that many families have to make.[22]

Actually, the size of people's bank accounts has a lot to do   31
with what type of home they can provide, which in turn has a tremendous impact on children's health and well-being. For example, poor children are especially likely to live in older homes where drinking water still flows through lead pipes and where there hasn't been a new paint job since 1978—the last year lead-based paint was used. It's estimated that 64 million homes contain lead-based paint. More than 1.7 million American children suffer from lead poisoning, the Environmental Protection Agency reported in 1996.[23]

Children who have been exposed to lead are seven times less   32
likely to graduate from high school, six times more likely to

have a reading disability, and six times more likely to engage in violence than other children, regardless of their family background. A four-year study of more than 800 boys in Pittsburgh, released February 7, 1996, showed that boys with higher lead levels were more likely than other boys to engage in antisocial acts, regardless of their parents' marital status or intelligence, and aside from any differences in income, medical problems, race, or ethnicity. Another study that followed 987 African-American children from birth to age 22 found that a history of lead poisoning was "the strongest predictor of disciplinary problems in junior high school boys and the third strongest predictor of both juvenile and adult offenses."[24]

33   Rector also claims that "the biggest dietary problem of people living in poverty is obesity, not hunger." Many poor adults *are* obese, since empty calories cost less than fruits or fish, but for kids, this is simply false. Children in poverty are not more overweight than other children, but they are two to three times more likely to suffer from stunted growth. Columnist George Will says of the urban poor, "theirs is a poverty of inner resources." Yes, indeed—like nutrients. In 1992, an estimated 12 million American children had diets whose nutrient levels were significantly below the recommended allowances established by the National Academy of Sciences. Iron deficiency anemia affects nearly a quarter of America's impoverished children, and this condition is associated with long-term intellectual impairment. An article in the *American Journal of Epidemiology* concludes that "differences in nutritional status between poor and nonpoor children remain large even when controls for other characteristics associated with poverty, such as low maternal educational attainment, single-parent family structure, young maternal age, low maternal academic ability, and minority racial identification, are included."[25]

34   Poverty exerts direct effects on children's health and mental functioning even in the most solid families, with completely devoted and competent parents. But poverty, like job and income loss in general, also strains marital relationships and parent-child interactions. With nowhere to turn, increasingly cut off from social support or hope for help from public agencies, desperate parents sometimes behave in desperate ways.

35   Contrary to much of the discussion in the family values camp, most of the parenting problems in impoverished families have to do with harsh, punitive discipline rather than permissiveness. But poverty can distract parents from effective follow-through on discipline. A study of children raised during the Great Depression of the 1930s found that poverty interfered with parental control over youths, making delinquency

more likely "regardless of children's initial temperament, the parents' own tendencies toward crime or deviance or mental instability, marital status and other factors." It's interesting to note that the two peaks in murder rates in the twentieth century occurred in 1933 and 1993. Yet whereas researchers easily recognize the social roots of violence in the Great Depression, many persist in denying the social and economic causes of today's troubled family and neighborhood relationships.[26]

Exceptionally competent parents, of course, can protect   36
their children from many risks. Considering how many children from deprived backgrounds manage to get through school, avoid criminal involvement, and find jobs, it's clear that there are some very competent and caring parents in poverty-stricken communities. Indeed, when you look at the effort it takes in such communities to keep children fed and physically safe, not to mention finding them warm clothes to wear and a quiet place to study, you have to admire the heroism that so many parents show. But if we made heroism a requirement for raising children, how many of us would have been issued the children with which we've been blessed? And even heroes can lose a child to lead poisoning, asthma, violence, or the bad breaks that occur so much more often in impoverished neighborhoods than in affluent communities.[27]

Impoverished families in urban areas are especially vulnerable   37
today because changes in the nature and location of jobs over the past two decades mean that urban poverty has come to play an unprecedented role in society. Once urban poverty was a harsh but temporary way of forcing rural migrants to accept the demands and rhythms of industrial work in the city, as well as providing a cheap labor pool to hold down wages. Today, however, it permanently channels people out of the labor market—and, increasingly, out of any claim to common humanity with those who venture into the city to eat, shop, or work downtown and then retreat to their suburban homes at night.[28]

The proportion of poor people who live in areas where at   38
least 40 percent of the other residents are also poor has more than doubled since the mid-1970s. And the chance of escaping poverty has declined. "In the 1970s, 37 out of 100 people who were poor moved out of poverty within a year; by the 1980s that figure was only 23 out of 100."[29]

The length of time spent in poverty has a powerful impact on   39
children's well-being. Simple annual comparisons of income levels do not adequately measure the degree of disadvantage experienced by children who live for years at a time in areas of concentrated poverty. Persistent poverty during the first five years of life, for example, leaves children with an IQ deficit of

more than nine points, regardless of family structure, race, ethnic group, or maternal education. Several studies have shown that the corrosive effect of chronic poverty outweighs the impact of individual life events and family histories on peo-
40   ple's depression levels and coping skills.[30]

It is no wonder, then, that the odds of extreme behavioral problems are more than twice as high for poor children as for nonpoor ones. The most careful studies suggest that poverty, economic insecurity, and the effects of neglected neighbor-hoods pose stronger risks to children than growing up in single-parent families, and are better predictors of low educational achievement or serious difficulties with the law. A child's chance of experiencing a poor home environment goes up in associa-tion with a number of different factors, including single parent-hood, large numbers of siblings, and low maternal education, but the largest effects are almost invariably found to be family and neighborhood poverty rather than family structure.[31]

41   Poor children are twice as likely to drop out of high school as other children. Mothers in one-parent families that are poor are no more likely to be abusive than mothers in two-parent families that are poor, but poor mothers—single or married—are significantly more likely to be abusive than mothers with incomes above the poverty line. For men, single fatherhood by itself does have an independent effect on abuse rates, but poverty has a stronger impact. Poor single fathers are three times as likely as nonpoor single fathers to abuse their chil-dren, and four times as likely as nonpoor fathers in a two-parent family.[32]

Poverty, Family Form, and Crime: What Sociological Studies Can and Cannot Tell Us

42   You've undoubtedly heard studies quoted that contradict the findings presented here, especially when it comes to explaining antisocial behavior. Many researchers claim that even after controlling for income, single parenthood is the major cause of crime and violence. Barbara Dafoe Whitehead of the Institute for American Values, who wrote the "Dan Quayle Was Right" article in 1993, is often cited on this point. According to Whitehead, "more than 70 percent of all juveniles in state re-form institutions come from fatherless homes." Mayors, po-lice, and social workers, she claims, "consistently point to fam-ily breakup as the most important source of rising rates of crime." In the eight months after Whitehead's article appeared, I almost never gave a lecture without being drawn aside at the

end by a single mother, often with the article in hand and the quote circled, asking me fearfully if I thought that her situation would really cause her child to end up in trouble with the law. Whitehead had clearly reached a mass audience and touched a raw nerve.[33]

But the studies are not nearly so unanimous as Whitehead   43
suggests. According to a 1993 report of the National Academy of Sciences, for example, "personal and neighborhood income are the strongest predictors of violent crime." A recent summary of research on gangs, issued by the U.S. Department of Justice, concluded that single-parent families do not on their own predict gang membership. Martin Sanchez Janowski spent ten years hanging out with gangs to write an ethnographic account of their activities. He found that there were "as many gang members from homes where the nuclear family was intact as there were from families where the father was absent" and "as many members who claim close relationships with their families as those who denied them." Of course, many gangs are concentrated in neighborhoods that have high rates of single-parent families, so they will have a higher than average number of kids from one-parent families, but not necessarily disproportionate for their community.[34]

Cause and effect in human behavior are seldom simple. If   44
single parenthood "caused" crime and violence, then Sweden and Denmark ought to have higher rates than the United States, instead of rates that are dramatically lower. Indeed, research in other countries does not find the same association between single-parent families and adolescent risk-taking behaviors that so much American research notes, which suggests that something more complicated is going on.[35]

Even in American studies, there is good reason to doubt how   45
powerful the reported "associations" really are. Researchers who say they have "controlled" for other variables often overlook the dynamics of class. Controlling for income, for example, does not take into account the broader patterns of a person's life. College students frequently have very low incomes, but their social status and future prospects are generally greater than someone who pulls down a higher wage working at a low-skill, dead-end job. An African-American family with the same income as a white family is likely to have less than half as many total assets. Nor are all poverty incomes alike. The deeper and more long-lasting poverty is, the worse its effects. Yet many studies do not distinguish between current income and long-term economic status.[36]

A few years ago, there was a short-lived fad for public offi-   46
cials or reporters to try living on a welfare mother's budget or a

poverty-level income for a month. The conclusion was usually: "It's very hard, but it can be done." Every time I glanced at such a magazine article or heard a news story about such an experiment on the radio, I knew I could expect a visit from an African-American friend of mine who had spent her first twenty-two years in a housing project in the San Francisco Bay Area. As the only professor she had access to, it was my job to brew the coffee and let her vent.

47   "Did they have their teeth unstraightened or their grammar undone, so everyone would know they were bottom of the barrel?" she would demand. "Did they first wear their car down to its last legs so that a tire or part would be sure to go and they'd have to choose between paying the rent and making it to a job interview? Did they throw out all the staples in their kitchen before they started cooking on a food-stamp allotment? Did they let their kids get mugged a couple of times and then, just to teach them that life is hard, make sure that they also got shoved up against a nearby building by the cops every few days?"

48   My friend's outbursts were sometimes emotionally draining for us both, but they certainly reinforced in me a healthy skepticism about what you can and can't capture in a study of the separate "factors" affecting youthful behavior. Most statistics also do not control for bias in police and court records or reports of outside observers. When researchers have asked young people themselves how much delinquency they engage in, "family structure was unrelated to the seriousness of the offense." But school officials, juvenile authorities, and police are more likely to record behaviors committed by children from single-parent families and more likely to take measures against those kids.[37]

49   Youths from single-parent families are certainly overrepresented among the prison population. Part of the reason is that the majority of people in prison come from impoverished, desperate neighborhoods where there are high proportions of single-parent families that generally are a result, not a cause, of the community's problems. Another part of the story is legal bias. "When a white middle-class youth is arrested for a nonviolent offense," writes former Judge Lois Forer, "the juvenile court usually 'adjusts' the offense. The boy has no record. In the inner city, youths are routinely adjudicated delinquent. Later this record counts heavily against them." Public defenders consistently tell me that they have a much slimmer chance of getting a youngster off with probation if the child has one parent than if he has two, regardless of the nature of the crime committed.[38]

Criminologist William Chambliss has spent several years, 50
along with his students, riding with the Rapid Deployment
Unit of the Washington, D.C., Metropolitan Police. He points
out that "the intensive surveillance of black neighborhoods"
leads to arrest and sentencing disparities that actually help
create the single-parent families that "pro-family" spokespeople tell us are the source of crime.[39]

To deny that one-parent families are the cause of crime and 51
violence is not to say there aren't some potentially dangerous
interactions that occur between family structure, economic
stress, parenting behaviors, and child outcomes. This is especially true in neighborhoods whose men have been marginalized by economic change. But crime and violence generally result only from the interaction and mutual reinforcement of
several different factors, not from family factors alone.

One study found that on its own a high concentration of 52
poverty in a neighborhood is not always linked to predelinquent childhood behaviors. Nor is a high level of residential
turnover. But if the two factors exist together they do produce
significant antisocial behavior. Similarly, "economic deprivation combined with a lack of social support creates an especially dangerous situation for children." The more risk factors
at play, the more likely children are to get into trouble. One
study found that more than half of adolescent delinquents
"grew up with five or more separate risk factors."[40]

Children in inner-city African-American communities, for 53
example, have risk factors piled on top of each other. Chronic
joblessness, extreme segregation, economic and political abandonment of the cities, and the resultant discouragement, researcher Philip Bowman argues, have made the transition
from adolescence to adulthood an acute challenge for impoverished African Americans.[41]

Columnist George Will has a simple formula to explain their 54
problems: "What is called the race crisis is a class problem
arising from dysfunctional families and destructive behaviors."
He's got it partly right. Many family forms and behaviors that
are commonly attributed to race are in fact responses to class
position. But race and racism help explain why African
Americans and Latinos are concentrated in the industries and
regions where economic setbacks have been the most devastating, and why minorities have accumulated so few assets over
the years, leaving them especially vulnerable to unemployment
and income loss. And the evidence suggests that the rest of
Will's statement is almost exactly backward. America's class
problem is a major *cause* of dysfunctional families and destructive behaviors, especially among impoverished racial

groups on whom government and society have turned their backs.[42]

55   In many inner-city communities, long-term poverty combines with lack of social support, dilapidated schools, overcrowded classrooms, and the sense that the rest of society doesn't care to create chronic despair in children, punctuated by bouts of rage. Herb Schreier, chief of psychiatry at Children's Hospital in Oakland, California, described to me how some of the kids in an African-American and Asian high school went on a rampage after the fire that swept through Berkeley and Oakland in 1991. When the teachers talked with the students later, it turned out that they were infuriated by the outpouring of public sympathy and aid that victims of the fire had received. How could they have reacted so disgracefully to such a heartwarming response? Almost exactly two years earlier the Cypress Expressway had collapsed in the great Bay Area earthquake. The rubble was still sitting in their neighborhood, and this devastated community had received no such aid and sympathy. "No one cares about *us*," the kids said. "No one ever does anything about us."

56   No wonder such youths become alienated. They have watched their parents get fired after diligently trudging off to a menial job for twenty years. They have seen building after building on their block abandoned. And when some kids have the perfectly normal response of throwing stones at a vacant building, the broken windows and boards stay unrepaired. Everything in their environment is ugly except for the images on TV. And don't think they don't notice: One of the first proposals the notorious Bloods and Crips gangs made to the city of L.A. after the riots in 1992 was that the city place flowerboxes on their street corners. It hasn't happened yet. Meanwhile, mired in poverty but surrounded by images of affluence, is it any wonder that young people look for some other way to get a piece of the American dream?[43]

57   Joe Marshall, cofounder of the Omega Boys Club, works with youth in an impoverished San Francisco neighborhood very similar to that in which he grew up. He remarks that there are not more hard-core "bad guys" today, but there are fewer alternatives to throwing in your lot with them. In his youth, he recalls, poverty was widespread, but at least there were jobs that gave young people work experience, spending money, and a sense of dignity. Even with high unemployment rates and low wages, the hope that these jobs provided kept most people working or looking for work. Kids who fell for the lure of easy money or the street life used to see it as a bad choice they had made. "Don't turn out like me," they would tell younger boys.

"Run on home now." Today, with fewer and fewer alternatives almost every year, the "bad guys" play a different role.[44]

Not every social ill in America, of course, is caused by eco- 58 nomic deprivation. Conservatives are quite right to say that poverty alone does not explain the alienation and fragmentation so prevalent today, or the terrible turmoil in so many families. But the shattering of older social expectations, along with the evolution of rich and poor into two separate universes, explains much of it. And the abandonment of the social safety net explains even more. As Jerome Skolnick put it in his 1994 presidential address to the American Society of Criminology, "Unemployment is a risk factor for crime. Patterned unemployment through time, and across racial and ethnic divisions, is a cause." Especially, criminologist Gilbert Geiss points out, when unemployment and poverty rub shoulders with "a society of affluence, in which your self-esteem is tied to failure to achieve that affluence."[45]

It is time to abandon denial, self-righteousness, and scape- 59 goating and to deal directly with the moral issues raised by these economic changes and by the last few decades of disinvestment in the younger generation. The question that gets lost in the debate over marital stability, parental responsibility, and personal character is whether we as a nation are willing to foster long-term commitments in economic and social life, whether we as a people have the character to defer immediate gratification in order to invest in the future of our communities. At heart, this is not a family crisis but a social crisis.

The worst effect of today's family values crusade is that by 60 blaming our problems on the breakdown of the traditional family it fails to recognize the strengths of today's diverse families—strengths we can mobilize to help *solve* our social problems. We need to reject the false notion that there is one perfect family form that automatically protects its members from outside forces, while other family forms or values automatically put them at risk. *All* families are at risk when they're left to face new challenges on their own. All families have the potential to rise above their weaknesses when they get support and encouragement from others.

When you read life histories of children from impoverished 61 neighborhoods, the first point that strikes you is the stunning number of obstacles they face, the hundreds of tiny curves where it's possible to fall off a path much narrower and higher than any that more privileged children have to tread. But the second point is how eager most parents are to do right by their children.

Similarly, when I talk with families undergoing major 62 changes in their marital roles, family norms, or work relations, I am constantly amazed by their resilience and creativity. What they need is social and moral support to meet their challenges and hone their strengths. What they don't need is to be subjected to a family values exam on which they are graded on the basis of some standardized form that was codified a century ago.

Notes

1. Nancy Folbre, *Who Pays for the Kids? Gender and the Structures of Constraint* (New York: Routledge, 1994), pp. 112–119; James Coleman, "The Rational Reconstruction of Society," *American Sociological Review* 58 (1993), p. 12.

2. John Coatsworth, "Presidential Address," *American Historical Review* 101 (1996), p. 9; P. Lindsay Chase-Landsdale and Maris A. Vinovskis, "Whose Responsibility? An Historical Analysis of the Changing Roles of Mothers, Fathers, and Society," in P. Lindsay Chase-Lansdale and J. Brooks-Gunn, eds., *Escape from Poverty: What Makes a Difference for Children?* (New York: Cambridge University Press, 1995); Linda Gordon, *Heroes of Their Own Lives: The Politics and History of Family Violence, Boston 1880–1960* (New York: Viking, 1988), p. 42.

3. Michael Katz, *Improving Poor People: The Welfare State, the "Underclass," and Urban Schools as History* (Princeton, N.J.: Princeton University Press, 1995); Gordon, *Heroes of Their Own Lives*, p. 42; Brian Gratton and Frances Rotundo, "Industrialization, the Family Economy, and the Economic Status of the American Elderly," *Social Science History* 15 (1991), p. 356; Walter Trattner, *From Poor Law to Welfare State: A History of Social Welfare in America* (New York: Free Press, 1984); Seth Koven and Sonya Michel, eds., *Mothers of a New World: Maternalist Politics and the Origins of Welfare States* (New York: Routledge, 1993); Gwendolyn Mink, *The Wages of Motherhood: Inequality in the Welfare State, 1917–1942* (Ithaca, N.Y.: Cornell University Press, 1995); Julius B. Richmond, "The Hull House Era: Vintage Years for Children," *American Journal of Orthopsychiatry* 65 (1995).

4. Judith Bruce, Cynthia Lloyd, and Ann Leonard, with Patrice Engle and Niev Duffy, *Families in Focus: New Perspectives on Mothers, Fathers, and Children* (New York: The Population Council, 1995), p. 14; Geoffrey Holtz, *Welcome to the Jungle: The Why Behind "Generation X"* (New York: St. Martin's Press, 1995), p. 50; Mike Males, *The Scapegoat Generation: America's War on Adolescents* (Monroe, Me.: Common Courage Press, 1996), p. 10; Sylvia Hewlett, *When the Bough Breaks: The Costs of Neglecting Our Children* (New York: Basic Books, 1991), p. 211; Lynn Curtis, *The State of Families* (Milwaukee, Wisc.: Family Service America, 1995), p. 25; *Welfare Myths: Fact or Fiction? Exploring the Truth About Welfare* (New York: Center

on Social Welfare Policy and Law, 1996), p. 36; Steven Rendall, Jim Naurekas, and Jeff Cohen, *The Way Things Aren't: Rush Limbaugh's Reign of Error* (New York: The New Press, 1995), p. 25.

5. Hewlett, *When the Bough Breaks*, p. 211; Iris Marion Young, "Reply to Jean Elshtain and Margaret Steinfels," *Dissent* (Spring 1994), p. 272; Joan Smith, "Transforming Households: Working-Class Women and Economic Crisis," *Social Problems* 34 (1987), p. 436.

6. *Olympian*, December 13, 1989, p. A8; Betsy Wagner and Stephen Hedges, "Education in Decay," *U.S. News & World Report*, September 12, 1994, p. 79; Joseph Altonji and Thomas Dunn, "Using Siblings to Estimate the Effect of School Quality on Wages," *Center for Urban Affairs and Policy Research Working Paper 96–10* (Evanston, Ill.: Northwestern University, 1996); Shazia Rufiullah Miller and James Rosenbaum, "The Missing Link: Social Infrastructure and Employers' Use of Information," *Center for Urban Affairs and Policy Research Working Paper 96–15* (Evanston, Ill.: Northwestern University, 1996).

7. Jonathan Kozol, *Savage Inequalities: Children in America's Schools* (New York: Crown, 1991), p. 237; "Hard Data," *Washington Post Weekly* Edition, September 28–October 4, 1992, p. 37.

8. David Whitman, "The Forgotten Half," *U.S. News & World Report*, June 26, 1989; Randy Abelda, Nancy Folbre, and the Center for Popular Economies, *The War Against the Poor: A Defense Manual* (New York: The New Press, 1996), p. 68; Peter Applebome, "U.S. Gets 'Average' Grade in Math and Science Studies," *New York Times*, November 21, 1996.

9. Jason De Parle, "Slamming the Door," *New York Times*, October 20, 1996, p. 52.

10. Folbre, *Who Pays for the Kids?* pp. 112–119, 208–210.

11. Bruce et al., *Families in Focus*, p. 14; Folbre, *Who Pays for the Kids?*; Holly Sklar, *Chaos or Community? Seeking Solutions, Not Scapegoats for Bad Economics* (Boston: South End Press, 1995), p. 145.

12. Folbre, *Who Pays for the Kids?*; Pamela Smock, "Gender and the Short-Run Economic Consequences of Marital Disruption," *Social Forces* 73 (1994), p. 259; Joan Acker, "Class, Gender, and the Relations of Distribution," *Signs* 13 (1988), p. 496.

13. For an insightful analysis of the class, cultural, and sexual tensions behind the Spur Posse story, see Joan Didion, "Trouble in Lakewood," *The New Yorker*, July 26, 1993.

14. Vonnie McCloyd, "The Impact of Economic Hardship on Black Families and Children: Psychological Distress, Parenting, and Socioemotional Development," *Child Development* 61 (1990), pp. 324–325; Richard Gelles, "Though

a Sociological Lens: Social Structure and Family Violence," in Richard Gelles and Donileen Loseke, eds., *Current Controversies on Family Violence* (Newbury Park, Calif.: Sage, 1993), p. 33; Ralph Catalano et al., "Using ECA Data to Examine the Effect of Job Layoffs on Violent Behavior," *Hospital and Community Psychiatry* 44 (1993), pp. 874, 878; Rand D. Conger, Xiaojia Ge, Glen H. Elder, Jr., Frederick O. Lorenz, and Ronald L. Simons, "Economic Stress, Coercive Family Process, and Developmental Problems of Adolescents," *Child Development* 65 (1994).

15. Robert Solow, *Wasting America's Future* (Boston: Beacon Press, 1994), pp. 30–32; Gene H. Brody, Zolinda Stoneman, and Douglas Flor, "Linking Family Process and Academic Competence among Rural African American Youths," *Journal of Marriage and the Family* 57 (1995), p. 567; Ralph Catalano, "The Health Effects of Economic Insecurity," *American Journal of Public Health* 81 (1991), p. 1149; Conger et al., "Economic Stress, Coercive Family Process"; McLoyd, "Impact of Economic Hardship," pp. 330–331; P. Lindsay Chase-Lansdale and Jeanne Brooks-Gunn, "Introduction," in Chase-Lansdale and Brooks-Gunn, eds., *Escape from Poverty*, p. 3; Gerald Patterson, John Reid, and Thomas Dishion, *Antisocial Boys* (Eugene, Ore.: Castalia, 1992); Craig Mason, Ana Mari Cauce, Nancy Gonzales, Yumi Hiraga, and Kwai Grove, "An Ecological Model of Externalizing Behaviors in African-American Adolescents: No Family Is an Island," *Journal of Research on Adolescence* 4, no. 4 (1994), p. 651; Rand D. Conger and Glen H. Elder, Jr., in collaboration with Frederick O. Lorenz, Ronald L. Simons, and Les B. Whitbeck, *Families in Troubled Times: Adapting to Change in Rural America* (New York: Aldine de Gruyter, 1994), pp. 219–220.

16. McLoyd, "Impact of Economic Hardship," p. 324; Vonnie McLoyd and Constance Flanagan, eds., *Economic Stress: Effects on Family Life and Child Development* (San Francisco: Jossey-Bass, 1991).

17. Conger and Elder et al., *Families in Troubled Times*, p. 261; Constance Flanagan, "Families and Schools in Hard Times," and Rainier Silberstien, Sabine Walper, and Helfried Albrecht, "Family Income Loss and Economic Hardship: Antecedents of Adolescents' Problem Behavior," in McLoyd and Flanagan, eds., *Economic Stress*.

18 Flanagan, "Families and Schools in Hard Times," p. 19; McLoyd, "Impact of Economic Hardship," p. 319; Jeffrey K. Liker and Glen H. Elder, Jr., "Economic Hardship and Marital Relations in the 1930s," *American Sociological Review* 48 (June 1983), p. 356.

19. McLoyd, "Impact of Economic Hardship," pp. 330, 336; Ann Crouter and Beth Manke, "The Changing American Workplace: Implications for Individuals and Families," *Family*

Relations 43 (1994), p. 119; Liker and Elder, "Economic Hardship and Marital Relations in the 1930s," p. 343; Conger and Elder et al., *Families in Troubled Times*, p. 219–221.

20. Conger and Elder et al., *Families in Troubled Times*, p. 259.

21. Rector quoted in *Washington Post National Weekly Edition,* September 11–17, 1995, p. 8.

22. Perri Klass, "Tackling Problems We Thought We Solved," *New York Times Magazine*, December 13, 1992, p. 62; Robert A. Hahn, Elaine Eaker, Nancy D. Barker, Steven M. Teutsch, Waldemar Sosniak, and Nancy Krieger, "Poverty and Death in the United States—1973 and 1991," *Epidemiology* 6 (1995), p. 490. My thanks to Carole Oshinsky of the New York-based National Center for Children in Poverty for supplying additional references and fact sheets.

23. "Tough Lead-Paint Rule Issued," *Olympian*, March 7, 1996, p. A4; Geoffrey Cowley, "Children in Peril," *Newsweek Special Issue*, Summer 1991, p. 20; James Sargent, Mary Jean Brown, Jean Freeman, Adrian Bailey, David Goodman, and Daniel H. Freeman, Jr., "Childhood Lead Poisoning in Massachusetts Communities: Its Association with Sociodemographic and Housing Characteristics," *American Journal of Public Health* 85 (1995), p. 531; Jane Brody, "Aggressiveness and Delinquency in Boys Is Linked to Lead in Bones," *New York Times*, February 7, 1996, p. B6.

24. Harold Hodgkinson, "Reform Versus Reality," *Phi Delta Kappan*, September, 1991, p. 14; Herbert Needleman, "Childhood Exposure to Lead: A Common Cause of School Failure," *Phi Delta Kappan*, September 1992, p. 36; Brody, "Aggressiveness Linked to Lead."

25. Rector quoted in Albeda and Folbre, *The War Against the Poor,* p. 34. See also Solow, *Wasting America's Future*, p. 15; J. Larry Brown and Ernesto Pollitt, "Malnutrition, Poverty and Intellectual Development," *Scientific American*, February 1996, p. 38; Rendall, Naurekas, and Cohen, *The Way Things Aren't*, p. 22; Jane E. Miller and Sanders Korenman, "Poverty and Children's Nutritional Status in the United States," *American Journal of Epidemiology* 140 (1994), p. 233. Estimates of the prevalence of hunger are currently being revised, with researchers beginning to talk about "food insecurity" rather than hunger and malnutrition alone. The Food Security Study, directed by Dr. John T. Cook, should be available in 1997. For further information, contact the Center on Hunger, Poverty and Nutrition Policy, Tufts University, Medford, Massachusetts 02155. The George Will quote appeared in Will, "Soft Voice in a Deadly Crisis," *Washington Post*, June 19, 1994.

26. Solow, *Wasting America's Future*, pp. 29–36, 88; Mason et al., "An Ecological Model of Externalizing Behaviors in African-American Adolescents"; Robert Sampson and John Laub,

"Urban Poverty and the Family Context of Delinquency: A New Look at Structure and Process in a Classic Study," *Child Development* 65 (1994); Males, *The Scapegoat Generation,* p. 109.

27. Katherine Brown Rosier and William A. Corsaro, "Competent Parents, Complex Lives: Managing Parenthood in Poverty," *Journal of Contemporary Ethnography* 22 (1993); Patricia Garrett, Nicholas Ng'andu, and John Ferron, "Poverty Experiences of Young Children and the Quality of Their Home Environments," *Child Development* 65 (1994); Bonnie Leadbeater and Sandra Bishop, "Predictors of Behavior Problems in Preschool Children of Inner-City Afro-American and Puerto Rican Adolescent Mothers," *Child Development* 65 (1994).

28. Michael Katz, ed., *The "Underclass" Debate: Views from History* (Princeton, N.J.: Princeton University Press, 1993); Douglas Massey and Nancy Denton, *American Apartheid: Segregation and the Making of the Underclass* (Cambridge, Mass.: Harvard University Press, 1993).

29. Katz, *The "Underclass" Debate;* James Gabarino and Kathleen Kolstelny, "Neighborhood and Community Influences on Parenting," in Tom Luster and Lynn Okagaki, eds., *Parenting: An Ecological Perspective* (Hillsdale, N.J.: Lawrence Erlbaum, 1993), p. 205.

30. Jane McLeod and Michael Shanahan, "Poverty, Parenting, and Children's Mental Health," *American Sociological Review* 58 (1993), p. 351; Spencer Rich, "Study: Poverty in First 5 Years Lowers Kids' IQs," *Morning News Tribune,* March 28, 1993; Greg J. Duncan et al., "Economic Deprivation and Early-Childhood Development," *Child Development* 65 (1994), pp. 296–318; McLoyd "Impact of Economic Hardship," p. 318; Gabarino and Kostelny, "Neighborhood and Community Influences on Parenting," p. 205.

31. Solow, *Wasting America's Future,* pp. 82, 90; Greg J. Duncan, Jeanne Brooks-Gunn, and Pamela Kato Klebanov, "Economic Deprivation and Early Childhood Development," *Child Development* 65 (1994), p. 296; Pamela Kato Klebanov, Jeanne Brooks-Gunn, and Greg J. Duncan, "Does Neighborhood and Family Poverty Affect Mothers' Parenting, Mental Health, and Social Support?" *Journal of Marriage and the Family* 56 (May 1994), p. 441; Sanders Korenman, Jane Miller, and John Sjaastad, "Long-Term Poverty and Child Development in the United States: Results from the NLSY" (National Longitudinal Study of Youth), *Children and Youth Services Review* 17 (1995); Carolyn Smith and Marvin Krohn, "Delinquency and Family Life Among Male Adolescents," *Journal of Youth and Adolescence* 24 (1995).

32. Albeda and Folbre, *War against the Poor,* p. 27; James Garbarino, "The Meaning of Poverty in the World of

Children," *American Behavioral Scientist* 35 (1992), p. 228; Solow, *Wasting America's Future,* p. 82.

33. Barbara Dafoe Whitehead, "Dan Quayle Was Right," *Atlantic Monthly,* April 1993, p. 77.

34. Solow, *Wasting America's Future,* pp. 82–91; Irving Spergel et al., *Gang Suppression and Intervention: Problem and Response* (Washington, D.C.: U.S. Department of Justice, 1994), p. 4; Martin Sanchez Jankowski, *Islands in the Street: Gangs and American Urban Society* (Berkeley: University of California, 1991), p. 39. For an insight into the socioeconomic and cultural context of gangs, see the disturbing memoir of gang life by Luis Rodriguez, *Always Running: La Vida Loca: Gang Days in L.A.* (New York: Simon and Schuster, 1993). Rodriguez came from a two-parent family that tried continually to escape the poverty of L.A.'s barrios and to provide an education for their kids. What turned Rodriguez around was not his family life but the sense of pride and social solidarity he began to feel when he was exposed to the Chicano power movement.

35. Marvin Free, Jr., "Clarifying the Relationship Between the Broken Home and Juvenile Delinquency: A Critique of the Current Literature," *Deviant Behavior: An Interdisciplinary Journal* 12 (1991), p. 130.

36. Melvin Oliver and Thomas Shapiro, *Black Wealth/White Wealth: A New Perspective on Racial Inequality* (New York: Routledge, 1995), p. 119; Korenman, Miller, and Sjaastad, "Long-Term Poverty," pp. 147–148; Greg Duncan, Wei-Jun Yeung, and Jeanne Brooks-Gunn, *Does Childhood Poverty Affect the Life Chances of Children?* Working Paper 96–2, Center for Urban Affairs and Policy Research, Northwestern University, April 24, 1996; Solow, *Wasting America's Future,* p. 91; Jeanne Brooks-Gunn, "Strategies for Altering the Outcomes of Poor Children and Their Families," in Chase-Lansdale and Brooks-Gunn, eds., *Escape from Poverty,* pp. 88–89.

37. Free, "Clarifying the Relationship Between the Broken Home and Juvenile Delinquency," pp. 144, 158.

38. Free, "Clarifying the Relationship Between the Broken Home and Juvenile Delinquency," p. 158; Sklar, *Chaos or Community?* pp. 128–129.

39. Sklar, *Chaos or Community?* p. 128; William Chambliss, "Policing the Ghetto Underclass: The Politics of Law and Law Enforcement," *Social Problems* 41 (1994).

40. Karole Kumpfer, *Strengthening America's Families: Promising Parenting Strategies for Delinquency Prevention* (Washington, D.C.: Office of Juvenile Justice and Delinquency Prevention, 1993), p. 9; Solow, *Wasting America's Future,* pp. 53–55; Robert Angel and Jacqueline Angel, *Painful Inheritance: Health and the New Generation of Fatherless Families* (Madison: University of Wisconsin Press, 1993), pp. 22, xix; Patricia

Hashima and Paul Amato, "Poverty, Social Support, and Parental Behavior," *Child Development* 65 (1994), p. 400.

41. Sam Roberts, *Who We Are: A Portrait of America Based on the Latest U.S. Census* (New York: Times Books, 1995), p. 181; Reynolds Farley and Walter Allen, *The Color Line and the Quality of Life in America* (New York: Russell Sage, 1987); Maxine Baca Zinn, "Minority Families in Crisis: The Public Discussion" (Memphis, Tenn.: Center for Research on Women, 1985); "Still Far from the Dream: Recent Developments in Black Income, Employment and Poverty," Washington, D.C.: Center on Budget and Policy Priorities, October 1988; Phillip Bowman, "The Adolescent-to-Adult Transition: Discouragement Among Jobless Black Youth," in McLoyd and Flanagan, eds., *Economic Stress.*

42. George Will, "Powell's Candidacy in Question," *Olympian,* April 16, 1995, p. A9; John Mirowsky and Catherine E. Ross, *Social Causes of Psychological Distress* (New York: Aldine de Gruyter, 1989), p. 17.

43. To see the odds such children and their families face, even when they try their best, watch the documentary *Hoop Dreams,* or read Alex Kotlowitz, *There Are No Children Here: The Story of Two Boys Growing Up in the Other America* (New York: Doubleday, 1991).

44. For more on Marshall's work, see his book, *Street Soldier: One Man's Struggle to Save a Generation—One Life at a Time* (New York: Delacorte, 1996).

45. Jerome Skolnick, "What Not to Do About Crime," *Criminology* 33 (1995), p. 2; Geiss quoted in Mike Males and Faye Docuyanan, "Crack-down on Kids," *The Progressive,* February 1996, p. 24.

IS SINGLE PARENTHOOD A PROBLEM?

■

Barbara Dafoe Whitehead

DAN QUAYLE
WAS RIGHT

The Atlantic Monthly, *a respected left-of-center magazine of current affairs and opinion, received more letters in response to the following excerpted essay by Barbara Dafoe Whitehead than it has ever received in response to an article. When it was published in April 1993, its title was alluding to former Vice President Dan Quayle's controversial opposition to the family arrangements of TV character Murphy Brown. Whitehead, a native of Wisconsin (born 1944) and a research associate at the Institute for American Values, a nonpartisan New York City organization devoted to issues of the family, in part defends a position that she expressed in an earlier article in the* Washington Post, *which helped motivate the vice president to make family issues central to the 1992 presidential campaign.*

Divorce and out-of-wedlock childbirth are transforming the   1
lives of American children. In the postwar generation more
than 80 percent of children grew up in a family with two biological parents who were married to each other. By 1980 only 50
percent could expect to spend their entire childhood in an intact
family. If current trends continue, less than half of all children
born today will live continuously with their own mother and father throughout childhood. Most American children will spend
several years in a single-mother family. Some will eventually
live in stepparent families, but because stepfamilies are more

likely to break up than intact (by which I mean two-biological-parent) families, an increasing number of children will experience family breakup two or even three times during childhood.

2   According to a growing body of social-scientific evidence, children in families disrupted by divorce and out-of-wedlock birth do worse than children in intact families on several measures of well-being. Children in single-parent families are six times as likely to be poor. They are also likely to stay poor longer. Twenty-two percent of children in one-parent families will experience poverty during childhood for seven years or more, as compared with only two percent of children in two-parent families. A 1988 survey by the National Center for Health Statistics found that children in single-parent families are two to three times as likely as children in two-parent families to have emotional and behavioral problems. They are also more likely to drop out of high school, to get pregnant as teenagers, to abuse drugs, and to be in trouble with the law. Compared with children in intact families, children from disrupted families are at a much higher risk for physical or sexual abuse.

3   Contrary to popular belief, many children do not "bounce back" after divorce or remarriage. Difficulties that are associated with family breakup often persist into adulthood. Children who grow up in single-parent or stepparent families are less successful as adults, particularly in the two domains of life—love and work—that are most essential to happiness. Needless to say, not all children experience such negative effects. However, research shows that many children from disrupted families have a harder time achieving intimacy in a relationship, forming a stable marriage, or even holding a steady job.

4   Despite this growing body of evidence, it is nearly impossible to discuss changes in family structure without provoking angry protest. Many people see the discussion as no more than an attack on struggling single mothers and their children: Why blame single mothers when they are doing the very best they can? After all, the decision to end a marriage or a relationship is wrenching, and few parents are indifferent to the painful burden this decision imposes on their children. Many take the perilous step toward single parenthood as a last resort, after their best efforts to hold a marriage together have failed. Consequently, it can seem particularly cruel and unfeeling to remind parents of the hardships their children might suffer as a result of family breakup. Other people believe that the dramatic changes in family structure, though regrettable, are impossible to reverse. Family breakup is an inevitable feature of American life, and anyone who thinks otherwise is indulging in nostalgia or trying to turn back the clock. Since these new

family forms are here to stay, the reasoning goes, we must accord respect to single parents, not criticize them. Typical is the view expressed by a Brooklyn woman in a recent letter to *The New York Times:* "Let's stop moralizing or blaming single parents and unwed mothers, and give them the respect they have earned and the support they deserve."

Such views are not to be dismissed. Indeed, they help to explain why family structure is such an explosive issue for Americans. The debate about it is not simply about the social-scientific evidence, although that is surely an important part of the discussion. It is also a debate over deeply held and often conflicting values. How do we begin to reconcile our long-standing belief in equality and diversity with an impressive body of evidence that suggests that not all family structures produce equal outcomes for children? How can we square traditional notions of public support for dependent women and children with a belief in women's right to pursue autonomy and independence in childbearing and child-rearing? How do we uphold the freedom of adults to pursue individual happiness in their private relationships and at the same time respond to the needs of children for stability, security, and permanence in their family lives? What do we do when the interests of adults and children conflict? These are the difficult issues at stake in the debate over family structure. 5

In the past these issues have turned out to be too difficult and too politically risky for debate. In the mid-1960s Daniel Patrick Moynihan, then an assistant secretary of labor, was denounced as a racist for calling attention to the relationship between the prevalence of black single-mother families and the lower socioeconomic standing of black children. For nearly twenty years the policy and research communities backed away from the entire issue. In 1980 the Carter Administration convened a historic White House Conference on Families, designed to address the growing problems of children and families in America. The result was a prolonged, publicly subsidized quarrel over the definition of "family." No President since has tried to hold a national family conference. Last year, at a time when the rate of out-of-wedlock births had reached a historic high, Vice President Dan Quayle was ridiculed for criticizing Murphy Brown. In short, every time the issue of family structure has been raised, the response has been first controversy, then retreat, and finally silence. 6

Yet it is also risky to ignore the issue of changing family structure. In recent years the problems associated with family disruption have grown. Overall child well-being has declined, despite a decrease in the number of children per family, an in- 7 crease in the educational level of parents, and historically high levels of public spending. After dropping in the 1960s and 1970s, the proportion of children in poverty has increased dramatically, from 15 percent in 1970 to 20 percent in 1990, while the percentage of adult Americans in poverty has remained roughly constant. The teen suicide rate has more than tripled. Juvenile crime has increased and become more violent. School performance has continued to decline. There are no signs that these trends are about to reverse themselves.

8   If we fail to come to terms with the relationship between family structure and declining child well-being, then it will be increasingly difficult to improve children's life prospects, no matter how many new programs the federal government funds. Nor will we be able to make progress in bettering school performance or reducing crime or improving the quality of the nation's future work force—all domestic problems closely connected to family breakup. Worse, we may contribute to the problem by pursuing policies that actually increase family instability and breakup.

From Death to Divorce

9   Across time and across cultures, family disruption has been regarded as an event that threatens a child's well-being and even survival. This view is rooted in a fundamental biological fact: unlike the young of almost any other species, the human child is born in an abjectly helpless and immature state. Years of nurture and protection are needed before the child can achieve physical independence. Similarly, it takes years of interaction with at least one but ideally two or more adults for a child to develop into a socially competent adult. Children raised in virtual isolation from human beings, though physically intact, display few recognizably human behaviors. The social arrangement that has proved most successful in ensuring the physical survival and promoting the social development of the child is the family unit of the biological mother and father. Consequently, any event that permanently denies a child the presence and protection of a parent jeopardizes the life of the child.

10   The classic form of family disruption is the death of a parent. Throughout history this has been one of the risks of childhood. Mothers frequently died in childbirth, and it was not unusual for both parents to die before the child was grown. As recently as the early decades of this century children commonly suffered the death of at least one parent. Almost a quarter of the children born in this country in 1900 lost one parent by the

time they were fifteen years old. Many of these children lived with their widowed parent, often in a household with other close relatives. Others grew up in orphanages and foster homes.

The meaning of parental death, as it has been transmitted 11 over time and faithfully recorded in world literature and lore, is unambiguous and essentially unchanging. It is universally regarded as an untimely and tragic event. Death permanently severs the parent-child bond, disrupting forever one of the child's earliest and deepest human attachments. It also deprives a child of the presence and protection of an adult who has a biological stake in, as well as an emotional commitment to, the child's survival and well-being. In short, the death of a parent is the most extreme and severe loss a child can suffer.

Because a child is so vulnerable in a parent's absence, there 12 has been a common cultural response to the death of a parent: an outpouring of support from family, friends, and strangers alike. The surviving parent and child are united in their grief as well as their loss. Relatives and friends share in the loss and provide valuable emotional and financial assistance to the bereaved family. Other members of the community show sympathy for the child, and public assistance is available for those who need it. This cultural understanding of parental death has formed the basis for a tradition of public support to widows and their children. Indeed, as recently as the beginning of this century widows were the only mothers eligible for pensions in many states, and today widows with children receive more generous welfare benefits from Survivors Insurance than do other single mothers with children who depend on Aid to Families With Dependent Children.

It has taken thousands upon thousands of years to reduce the 13 threat of parental death. Not until the middle of the twentieth century did parental death cease to be a commonplace event for children in the United States. By then advances in medicine had dramatically reduced mortality rates for men and women.

At the same time, other forms of family disruption—separa- 14 tion, divorce, out-of-wedlock birth—were held in check by powerful religious, social, and legal sanctions. Divorce was widely regarded both as a deviant behavior, especially threatening to mothers and children, and as a personal lapse: "Divorce is the public acknowledgment of failure," a 1940s sociology textbook noted. Out-of-wedlock birth was stigmatized, and stigmatization is a powerful means of regulating behavior, as any smoker or overeater will testify. Sanctions against nonmarital childbirth discouraged behavior that hurt children and exacted compensatory behavior that helped them. Shotgun marriages and adoption, two common responses to nonmarital birth, carried a strong message about the risks of premarital sex and created an intact family for the child.

15 Consequently, children did not have to worry much about losing a parent through divorce or never having had one because of nonmarital birth. After a surge in divorces following the Second World War, the rate leveled off. Only 11 percent of children born in the 1950s would by the time they turned eighteen see their parents separate or divorce. Out-of-wedlock childbirth barely figured as a cause of family disruption. In the 1950s and early 1960s, five percent of the nation's births were out of wedlock. Blacks were more likely than whites to bear children outside marriage, but the majority of black children born in the twenty years after the Second World War were born to married couples. The rate of family disruption reached a historic low point during those years.

16 A new standard of family security and stability was established in postwar America. For the first time in history the vast majority of the nation's children could expect to live with married biological parents throughout childhood. Children might still suffer other forms of adversity—poverty, racial discrimination, lack of educational opportunity—but only a few would be deprived of the nurture and protection of a mother and a father. No longer did children have to be haunted by the classic fears vividly dramatized in folklore and fable—that their parents would die, that they would have to live with a stepparent and stepsiblings, or that they would be abandoned. These were the years when the nation confidently boarded up orphanages and closed foundling hospitals, certain that such institutions would never again be needed. In movie theaters across the country parents and children could watch the drama of parental separation and death in the great Disney classics, secure in the knowledge that such nightmare visions as the death of Bambi's mother and the wrenching separation of Dumbo from his mother were only make-believe.

17 In the 1960s the rate of family disruption suddenly began to rise. After inching up over the course of a century, the divorce rate soared. Throughout the 1950s and early 1960s the divorce rate held steady at fewer than ten divorces a year per 1,000 married couples. Then, beginning in about 1965, the rate increased sharply, peaking at twenty-three divorces per 1,000 marriages by 1979. (In 1974 divorce passed death as the leading cause of family breakup.) The rate has leveled off at about twenty-one divorces per 1,000 marriages—the figure for 1991. The out-of-wedlock birth rate also jumped. It went from five percent in 1960 to 27 percent in 1990. In 1990 close to 57 percent of births among black mothers were non-

marital, and about 17 percent among white mothers. Altogether, about one out of every four women who had a child in 1990 was not married. With rates of divorce and nonmarital birth so high, family disruption is at its peak. Never before have so many children experienced family breakup caused by events other than death. Each year a million children go through divorce or separation and almost as many more are born out of wedlock.

Half of all marriages now end in divorce. Following divorce, many people enter new relationships. Some begin living together. Nearly half of all cohabiting couples have children in the household. Fifteen percent have new children together. Many cohabiting couples eventually get married. However, both cohabiting and remarried couples are more likely to break up than couples in first marriages. Even social scientists find it hard to keep pace with the complexity and velocity of such patterns. In the revised edition (1992) of his book *Marriage, Divorce, Remarriage,* the sociologist Andrew Cherlin ruefully comments: "If there were a truth-in-labeling law for books, the title of this edition should be something long and unwieldy like *Cohabitation, Marriage, Divorce, More Cohabitation, and Probably Remarriage.*"

Under such conditions growing up can be a turbulent experience. In many single-parent families children must come to terms with the parent's love life and romantic partners. Some children live with cohabiting couples, either their own unmarried parents or a biological parent and a live-in partner. Some children born to cohabiting parents see their parents break up. Others see their parents marry, but 56 percent of them (as compared with 31 percent of the children born to married parents) later see their parents' marriages fall apart. All told, about three quarters of children born to cohabiting couples will live in a single-parent home at least briefly. One of every four children growing up in the 1990s will eventually enter a stepfamily. According to one survey, nearly half of all children in stepparent families will see their parents divorce again by the time they reach their late teens. Since 80 percent of divorced fathers remarry, things get even more complicated when the romantic or marital history of the noncustodial parent, usually the father, is taken into account. Consequently, as it affects a significant number of children, family disruption is best understood not as a single event but as a string of disruptive events: separation, divorce, life in a single-parent family, life with a parent and live-in lover, the remarriage of one or both parents, life in one stepparent family combined with visits to another stepparent family; the breakup of one or both stepparent families. And so on. This is one reason why public schools have a hard time knowing whom to call in an emergency.

20 Given its dramatic impact on children's lives, one might reasonably expect that this historic level of family disruption would be viewed with alarm, even regarded as a national crisis. Yet this has not been the case. In recent years some people have argued that these trends pose a serious threat to children and to the nation as a whole, but they are dismissed as declinists, pessimists, or nostalgists, unwilling or unable to accept the new facts of life. The dominant view is that the changes in family structure are, on balance, positive.

A Shift in the Social Metric

21 There are several reasons why this is so, but the fundamental reason is that at some point in the 1970s Americans changed their minds about the meaning of these disruptive behaviors. What had once been regarded as hostile to children's best interests was now considered essential to adults' happiness. In the 1950s most Americans believed that parents should stay in an unhappy marriage for the sake of the children. The assumption was that a divorce would damage the children, and the prospect of such damage gave divorce its meaning. By the mid-1970s a majority of Americans rejected that view. Popular advice literature reflected the shift. A book on divorce published in the mid-1940s tersely asserted: "Children are entitled to the affection and *association* of two parents, not one." Thirty years later another popular divorce book proclaimed just the opposite: "A two-parent home is not the only emotional structure within which a child can be happy and healthy. . . . The parents who take care of themselves will be best able to take care of their children." At about the same time, the long-standing taboo against out-of-wedlock childbirth also collapsed. By the mid-1970s three fourths of Americans said that it was not morally wrong for a woman to have a child outside marriage.

22 Once the social metric shifts from child well-being to adult well-being, it is hard to see divorce and nonmarital birth in anything but a positive light. However distressing and difficult they may be, both of these behaviors can hold out the promise of greater adult choice, freedom, and happiness. For unhappy spouses, divorce offers a way to escape a troubled or even abusive relationship and make a fresh start. For single parents, remarriage is a second try at marital happiness as well as a chance for relief from the stress, loneliness, and economic hardship of raising a child alone. For some unmarried women, nonmarital birth is a way to beat the biological clock, avoid

marrying the wrong man, and experience the pleasures of motherhood. Moreover, divorce and out-of-wedlock birth involve a measure of agency and choice; they are man- and woman-made events. To be sure, not everyone exercises choice in divorce or nonmarital birth. Men leave wives for younger women, teenage girls get pregnant accidentally—yet even these unhappy events reflect the expansion of the boundaries of freedom and choice.

This cultural shift helps explain what otherwise would be inexplicable: the failure to see the rise in family disruption as a severe and troubling national problem. It explains why there is virtually no widespread public sentiment for restigmatizing either of these classically disruptive behaviors and no sense—no public consensus—that they can or should be avoided in the future. . . .   23

Dinosaurs Divorce

It is true that many adults benefit from divorce or remarriage. According to one study, nearly 80 percent of divorced women and 50 percent of divorced men say they are better off out of the marriage. Half of divorced adults in the same study report greater happiness. A competent self-help book called *Divorce and New Beginnings* notes the advantages of single parenthood: single parents can "develop their own interests, fulfill their own needs, choose their own friends and engage in social activities of their choice. Money, even if limited, can be spent as they see fit." Apparently, some women appreciate the opportunity to have children out of wedlock. "The real world, however, does not always allow women who are dedicated to their careers to devote the time and energy it takes to find—or be found by—the perfect husband and father wannabe," one woman said in a letter to *The Washington Post*. A mother and chiropractor from Avon, Connecticut, explained her unwed maternity to an interviewer this way: "It is selfish, but this was something I needed to do for me."   24

There is very little in contemporary popular culture to contradict this optimistic view. But in a few small places another perspective may be found. Several racks down from its divorce cards, Hallmark offers a line of cards for children—To Kids With Love. These cards come six to a pack. Each card in the pack has a slightly different message. According to the package, the "thinking of you" messages will let a special kid "know how much you care." Though Hallmark doesn't quite say so, it's clear these cards are aimed at divorced parents. "I'm sorry I'm not always there when you need me but I hope you know   25

I'm always just a phone call away." Another card reads: "Even though your dad and I don't live together anymore, I know he's still a very special part of your life. And as much as I miss you when you're not with me, I'm still happy that you two can spend time together."

26   Hallmark's messages are grounded in a substantial body of well-funded market research. Therefore it is worth reflecting on the divergence in sentiment between the divorce cards for adults and the divorce cards for kids. For grown-ups, divorce heralds new beginnings (A HOT NEW SINGLE). For children, divorce brings separation and loss ("I'm sorry I'm not always there when you need me").

27   An even more telling glimpse into the meaning of family disruption can be found in the growing children's literature on family dissolution. Take, for example, the popular children's book *Dinosaurs Divorce: A Guide for Changing Families* (1986), by Laurene Krasny Brown and Marc Brown. This is a picture book, written for very young children. The book begins with a short glossary of "divorce words" and encourages children to "see if you can find them" in the story. The words include "family counselor," "separation agreement," "alimony," and "child custody." The book is illustrated with cartoonish drawings of green dinosaur parents who fight, drink too much, and break up. One panel shows the father dinosaur, suitcase in hand, getting into a yellow car.

28   The dinosaur children are offered simple, straightforward advice on what to do about the divorce. *On custody decisions:* "When parents can't agree, lawyers and judges decide. Try to be honest if they ask you questions; it will help them make better decisions." *On selling the house:* "If you move, you may have to say good-bye to friends and familiar places. But soon your new home will feel like the place you really belong." *On the economic impact of divorce:* "Living with one parent almost always means there will be less money. Be prepared to give up some things." *On holidays:* "Divorce may mean twice as much celebrating at holiday times, but you may feel pulled apart." *On parents' new lovers:* "You may sometimes feel jealous and want your parent to yourself. Be polite to your parents' new friends, even if you don't like them at first." *On parents' remarriage:* "Not everyone loves his or her stepparents, but showing them respect is important."

29   These cards and books point to an uncomfortable and generally unacknowledged fact: what contributes to a parent's happiness may detract from a child's happiness. All too often the adult quest for freedom, independence, and choice in family relationships conflicts with a child's developmental needs for stability, constancy, harmony, and permanence in family life.

In short, family disruption creates a deep division between parents' interests and the interests of children.

One of the worst consequences of these divided interests is a withdrawal of parental investment in children's well-being. As the Stanford economist Victor Fuchs has pointed out, the main source of social investment in children is private. The investment comes from the children's parents. But parents in disrupted families have less time, attention, and money to devote to their children. The single most important source of disinvestment has been the widespread withdrawal of financial support and involvement by fathers. Maternal investment, too, has declined, as women try to raise families on their own and work outside the home. Moreover, both mothers and fathers commonly respond to family breakup by investing more heavily in themselves and in their own personal and romantic lives.

Sometimes the tables are completely turned. Children are called upon to invest in the emotional well-being of their parents. Indeed, this seems to be the larger message of many of the children's books on divorce and remarriage. *Dinosaurs Divorce* asks children to be sympathetic, understanding, respectful, and polite to confused, unhappy parents. The sacrifice comes from the children: "Be prepared to give up some things." In the world of divorcing dinosaurs, the children rather than the grown-ups are the exemplars of patience, restraint, and good sense.

Three Seventies Assumptions

As it first took shape in the 1970s, the optimistic view of family change rested on three bold new assumptions. At that time, because the emergence of the changes in family life was so recent, there was little hard evidence to confirm or dispute these assumptions. But this was an expansive moment in American life.

The first assumption was an economic one: that a woman could now afford to be a mother without also being a wife. There were ample grounds for believing this. Women's work-force participation had been gradually increasing in the postwar period, and by the beginning of the 1970s women were a strong presence in the workplace. What's more, even though there was still a substantial wage gap between men and women, women had made considerable progress in a relatively short time toward better-paying jobs and greater employment opportunities. More women than ever before could aspire to serious careers as business executives, doctors, lawyers, airline pilots, and politicians. This circumstance, combined with the increased availability of child care, meant that women could take on the responsibilities of a breadwinner, perhaps even a sole breadwinner. This was particularly true for middle-class women. According to a highly regarded 1977 study by the Carnegie Council on Children, "The greater availability of jobs for women means that more middle-class children today survive their parents' divorce without a catastrophic plunge into poverty."

34 Feminists, who had long argued that the path to greater equality for women lay in the world of work outside the home, endorsed this assumption. In fact, for many, economic independence was a stepping-stone toward freedom from both men and marriage. As women began to earn their own money, they were less dependent on men or marriage, and marriage diminished in importance. In Gloria Steinem's memorable words, "A woman without a man is like a fish without a bicycle."

35 This assumption also gained momentum as the meaning of work changed for women. Increasingly, work had an expressive as well as an economic dimension: being a working mother not only gave you an income but also made you more interesting and fulfilled than a stay-at-home mother. Consequently, the optimistic economic scenario was driven by a cultural imperative. Women would achieve financial independence because, culturally as well as economically, it was the right thing to do.

36 The second assumption was that family disruption would not cause lasting harm to children and could actually enrich their lives. *Creative Divorce: A New Opportunity for Personal Growth,* a popular book of the seventies, spoke confidently to this point: "Children can survive any family crisis without permanent damage—and grow as human beings in the process. . . ." Moreover, single-parent and stepparent families created a more extensive kinship network than the nuclear family. This network would envelop children in a web of warm and supportive relationships. "Belonging to a stepfamily means there are more people in your life," a children's book published in 1982 notes. "More sisters and brothers, including the step ones. More people you think of as grandparents and aunts and uncles. More cousins. More neighbors and friends. . . . Getting to know and like so many people (and having them like you) is one of the best parts of what being in a stepfamily . . . is all about."

37 The third assumption was that the new diversity in family structure would make America a better place. Just as the nation has been strengthened by the diversity of its ethnic and racial groups, so it would be strengthened by diverse family forms. The emergence of these brave new families was but the latest chapter in the saga of American pluralism.

Another version of the diversity argument stated that the 38
real problem was not family disruption itself but the stigma
still attached to these emergent family forms. This lingering
stigma placed children at psychological risk, making them feel
ashamed or different; as the ranks of single-parent and stepparent families grew, children would feel normal and good
about themselves.

These assumptions continue to be appealing, because they 39
accord with strongly held American beliefs in social progress.
Americans see progress in the expansion of individual opportunities for choice, freedom, and self-expression. Moreover,
Americans identify progress with growing tolerance of diversity. Over the past half century, the pollster Daniel Yankelovich
writes, the United States has steadily grown more open-
minded and accepting of groups that were previously perceived as alien, untrustworthy, or unsuitable for public leadership or social esteem. One such group is the burgeoning
number of single-parent and stepparent families.

The Education of Sara McLanahan

In 1981 Sara McLanahan, now a sociologist at Princeton 40
University's Woodrow Wilson School, read a three-part series
by Ken Auletta in *The New Yorker.* Later published as a book titled *The Underclass,* the series presented a vivid portrait of the
drug addicts, welfare mothers, and school dropouts who took
part in an education-and-training program in New York City.
Many were the children of single mothers, and it was Auletta's
clear implication that single-mother families were contributing to the growth of an underclass. McLanahan was taken
aback by this notion. "It struck me as strange that he would be
viewing single mothers at that level of pathology."

"I'd gone to graduate school in the days when the politically 41
correct argument was that single-parent families were just another alternative family form, and it was fine," McLanahan explains, as she recalls the state of social-scientific thinking in
the 1970s. Several empirical studies that were then current
supported an optimistic view of family change. (They used tiny
samples, however, and did not track the well-being of children
over time.)

One, *All Our Kin,* by Carol Stack, was required reading for 42
thousands of university students. It said that single mothers
had strengths that had gone undetected and unappreciated by
earlier researchers. The single-mother family, it suggested, is
an economically resourceful and socially embedded institu-

tion. In the late 1970s McLanahan wrote a similar study that looked at a small sample of white single mothers and how they coped. "So I was very much of that tradition."

43   By the early 1980s, however, nearly two decades had passed since the changes in family life had begun. During the intervening years a fuller body of empirical research had emerged: studies that used large samples, or followed families through time, or did both. Moreover, several of the studies offered a child's-eye view of family disruption. The National Survey on Children, conducted by the psychologist Nicholas Zill, had set out in 1976 to track a large sample of children aged seven to eleven. It also interviewed the children's parents and teachers. It surveyed its subjects again in 1981 and 1987. By the time of its third round of interviews the eleven-year-olds of 1976 were the twenty-two-year-olds of 1987. The California Children of Divorce Study, directed by Judith Wallerstein, a clinical psychologist, had also been going on for a decade. E. Mavis Hetherington, of the University of Virginia, was conducting a similar study of children from both intact and divorced families. For the first time it was possible to test the optimistic view against a large and longitudinal body of evidence.

44   It was to this body of evidence that Sara McLanahan turned. When she did, she found little to support the optimistic view of single motherhood. On the contrary. When she published her findings with Irwin Garfinkel in a 1986 book, *Single Mothers and Their Children,* her portrait of single motherhood proved to be as troubling in its own way as Auletta's.

45   One of the leading assumptions of the time was that single motherhood was economically viable. Even if single mothers did face economic trials, they wouldn't face them for long, it was argued, because they wouldn't remain single for long: single motherhood would be a brief phase of three to five years, followed by marriage. Single mothers would be economically resilient: if they experienced setbacks, they would recover quickly. It was also said that single mothers would be supported by informal networks of family, friends, neighbors, and other single mothers. As McLanahan shows in her study, the evidence demolishes all these claims.

46   For the vast majority of single mothers, the economic spectrum turns out to be narrow, running between precarious and desperate. Half the single mothers in the United States live below the poverty line. (Currently, one out of ten married couples with children is poor.) Many others live on the edge of poverty. Even single mothers who are far from poor are likely to experience persistent economic insecurity. Divorce almost always brings a decline in the standard of living for the mother and children.

Moreover, the poverty experienced by single mothers is no 47
more brief than it is mild. A significant number of all single
mothers never marry or remarry. Those who do, do so only after spending roughly six years, on average, as single parents.
For black mothers the duration is much longer. Only 33 percent of African-American mothers had remarried within ten
years of separation. Consequently, single motherhood is hardly
a fleeting event for the mother, and it is likely to occupy a third
of the child's childhood. Even the notion that single mothers
are knit together in economically supportive networks is not
borne out by the evidence. On the contrary, single parenthood
forces many women to be on the move, in search of cheaper
housing and better jobs. This need-driven restless mobility
makes it more difficult for them to sustain supportive ties to
family and friends, let alone other single mothers.

Single-mother families are vulnerable not just to poverty but 48
to a particularly debilitating form of poverty: welfare dependency. The dependency takes two forms: First, single mothers,
particularly unwed mothers, stay on welfare longer than other
welfare recipients. Of those never-married mothers who receive
welfare benefits, almost 40 percent remain on the rolls for ten
years or longer. Second, welfare dependency tends to be passed
on from one generation to the next. McLanahan says,
"Evidence on intergenerational poverty indicates that, indeed,
offspring from [single-mother] families are far more likely to be
poor and to form mother-only families than are offspring who
live with two parents most of their pre-adult life." Nor is the intergenerational impact of single motherhood limited to
African-Americans, as many people seem to believe. Among
white families, daughters of single parents are 53 percent more
likely to marry as teenagers, 111 percent more likely to have
children as teenagers, 164 percent more likely to have a premarital birth, and 92 percent more likely to dissolve their own marriages. All these intergenerational consequences of single motherhood increase the likelihood of chronic welfare dependency.

McLanahan cites three reasons why single-mother families 49
are so vulnerable economically. For one thing, their earnings
are low. Second, unless the mothers are widowed, they don't receive public subsidies large enough to lift them out of poverty.
And finally, they do not get much support from family members—especially the fathers of their children. In 1982 single
white mothers received an average of $1,246 in alimony and
child support, black mothers an average of $322. Such pay-
ments accounted for about 10 percent of the income of single
white mothers and for about 3.5 percent of the income of single black mothers. These amounts were dramatically smaller

than the income of the father in a two-parent family and also smaller than the income from a second earner in a two-parent family. Roughly 60 percent of single white mothers and 80 percent of single black mothers received no support at all.

50   Until the mid-1980s, when stricter standards were put in place, child-support awards were only about half to two-thirds what the current guidelines require. Accordingly, there is often a big difference in the living standards of divorced fathers and of divorced mothers with children. After divorce the average annual income of mothers and children is $13,500 for whites and $9,000 for nonwhites, as compared with $25,000 for white nonresident fathers and $13,600 for non-white nonresident fathers. Moreover, since child-support awards account for a smaller portion of the income of a high-earning father, the drop in living standards can be especially sharp for mothers who were married to upper-level managers and professionals.

51   Unwed mothers are unlikely to be awarded any child support at all, partly because the paternity of their children may not have been established. According to one recent study, only 20 percent of unmarried mothers receive child support.

52   Even if single mothers escape poverty, economic uncertainty remains a condition of life. Divorce brings a reduction in income and standard of living for the vast majority of single mothers. One study, for example, found that income for mothers and children declines on average about 30 percent, while fathers experience a 10 to 15 percent increase in income in the year following a separation. Things get even more difficult when fathers fail to meet their child-support obligations. As a result, many divorced mothers experience a wearing uncertainty about the family budget: whether the check will come in or not; whether new sneakers can be bought this month or not; whether the electric bill will be paid on time or not. Uncertainty about money triggers other kinds of uncertainty. Mothers and children often have to move to cheaper housing after a divorce. One study shows that about 38 percent of divorced mothers and their children move during the first year after a divorce. Even several years later the rate of moves for single mothers is about a third higher than the rate for two-parent families. It is also common for a mother to change her job or increase her working hours or both following a divorce. Even the composition of the household is likely to change, with other adults, such as boyfriends or babysitters, moving in and out.

53   All this uncertainty can be devastating to children. Anyone who knows children knows that they are deeply conservative creatures. They like things to stay the same. So pronounced is this tendency that certain children have been known to request

the same peanut-butter-and-jelly sandwich for lunch for years on end. Children are particularly set in their ways when it comes to family, friends, neighborhoods, and schools. Yet when a family breaks up, all these things may change. The novelist Pat Conroy has observed that "each divorce is the death of a small civilization." No one feels this more acutely than children.

Sara McLanahan's investigation and others like it have 54 helped to establish a broad consensus on the economic impact of family disruption on children. Most social scientists now agree that single motherhood is an important and growing cause of poverty, and that children suffer as a result. (They continue to argue, however, about the relationship between family structure and such economic factors as income inequality, the loss of jobs in the inner city, and the growth of low-wage jobs.) By the mid-1980s, however, it was clear that the problem of family disruption was not confined to the urban underclass, nor was its sole impact economic. Divorce and out-of-wedlock childbirth were affecting middle- and upper-class children, and these more privileged children were suffering negative consequences as well. It appeared that the problems associated with family breakup were far deeper and far more widespread than anyone had previously imagined.

The Missing Father

Judith Wallerstein is one of the pioneers in research on the 55 long-term psychological impact of family disruption on children. The California Children of Divorce Study, which she directs, remains the most enduring study of the long-term effects of divorce on children and their parents. Moreover, it represents the best-known effort to look at the impact of divorce on middle-class children. The California children entered the study without pathological family histories. Before divorce they lived in stable, protected homes. And although some of the children did experience economic insecurity as the result of divorce, they were generally free from the most severe forms of poverty associated with family breakup. Thus the study and the resulting book (which Wallerstein wrote with Sandra Blakeslee), *Second Chances: Men, Women, and Children a Decade After Divorce* (1989), provide new insight into the consequences of divorce which are not associated with extreme forms of economic or emotional deprivation.

When, in 1971, Wallerstein and her colleagues set out to 56 conduct clinical interviews with 131 children from the San

Francisco area, they thought they were embarking on a short-term study. Most experts believed that divorce was like a bad cold. There was a phase of acute discomfort, and then a short recovery phase. According to the conventional wisdom, kids would be back on their feet in no time at all. Yet when Wallerstein met these children for a second interview more than a year later, she was amazed to discover that there had been no miraculous recovery. In fact, the children seemed to be doing worse.

57   The news that children did not "get over" divorce was not particularly welcome at the time. Wallerstein recalls, "We got angry letters from therapists, parents, and lawyers saying we were undoubtedly wrong. They said children are really much better off being released from an unhappy marriage. Divorce, they said, is a liberating experience." One of the main results of the California study was to overturn this optimistic view. In Wallerstein's cautionary words, "Divorce is deceptive. Legally it is a single event, but psychologically it is a chain—sometimes a never-ending chain—of events, relocations, and radically shifting relationships strung through time, a process that forever changes the lives of the people involved."

58   Five years after divorce more than a third of the children experienced moderate or severe depression. At ten years a significant number of the now young men and women appeared to be troubled, drifting, and underachieving. At fifteen years many of the thirtyish adults were struggling to establish strong love relationships of their own. In short, far from recovering from their parents' divorce, a significant percentage of these grownups were still suffering from its effects. In fact, according to Wallerstein, the long-term effects of divorce emerge at a time when young adults are trying to make their own decisions about love, marriage, and family. Not all children in the study suffered negative consequences. But Wallerstein's research presents a sobering picture of divorce. "The child of divorce faces many additional psychological burdens in addition to the normative tasks of growing up," she says.

59   Divorce not only makes it more difficult for young adults to establish new relationships. It also weakens the oldest primary relationship: that between parent and child. According to Wallerstein, "Parent-child relationships are permanently altered by divorce in ways that our society has not anticipated." Not only do children experience a loss of parental attention at the onset of divorce, but they soon find that at every stage of their development their parents are not available in the same way they once were. "In a reasonably happy intact family," Wallerstein observes, "the child gravitates first to one parent and then to the other, using skills and attributes from each in

climbing the developmental ladder." In a divorced family, children find it "harder to find the needed parent at needed times." This may help explain why very young children suffer the most as the result of family disruption. Their opportunities to engage in this kind of ongoing process are the most truncated and compromised.

The father-child bond is severely, often irreparably, damaged 60 in disrupted families. In a situation without historical precedent, an astonishing and disheartening number of American fathers are failing to provide financial support to their children. Often, more than the father's support check is missing. Increasingly, children are bereft of any contact with their fathers. According to the National Survey of Children, in disrupted families only one child in six, on average, saw his or her father as often as once a week in the past year. Close to half did not see their father at all in the past year. As time goes on, contact becomes even more infrequent. Ten years after a marriage breaks up, more than two thirds of children report not having seen their father for a year. Not surprisingly, when asked to name the "adults you look up to and admire," only 20 percent of children in single-parent families named their father, as compared with 52 percent of children in two-parent families. A favorite complaint among Baby Boom Americans is that their fathers were emotionally remote guys who worked hard, came home at night to eat supper, and didn't have much to say to or do with the kids. But the current generation has a far worse father problem: many of their fathers are vanishing entirely.

Even for fathers who maintain regular contact, the pattern 61 of father-child relationships changes. The sociologists Andrew Cherlin and Frank Furstenberg, who have studied broken families, write that the fathers behave more like other relatives than like parents. Rather than helping with homework or carrying out a project with their children, nonresidential fathers are likely to take the kids shopping, to the movies, or out to dinner. Instead of providing steady advice and guidance, divorced fathers become "treat" dads.

Apparently—and paradoxically—it is the visiting relation- 62 ship itself, rather than the frequency of visits, that is the real source of the problem. According to Wallerstein, the few children in the California study who reported visiting with their fathers once or twice a week over a ten-year period still felt rejected. The need to schedule a special time to be with the child, the repeated leave-takings, and the lack of connection to the child's regular, daily schedule leaves many fathers adrift, frustrated, and confused. Wallerstein calls the visiting father a parent without portfolio.

63   The deterioration in father-child bonds is most severe among children who experience divorce at an early age, according to a recent study. Nearly three quarters of the respondents, now young men and women, report having poor relationships with their fathers. Close to half have received psychological help, nearly a third have dropped out of high school, and about a quarter report having experienced high levels of problem behavior or emotional distress by the time they became young adults.

Long-Term Effects

64   Since most children live with their mothers after divorce, one might expect that the mother-child bond would remain unaltered and might even be strengthened. Yet research shows that the mother-child bond is also weakened as the result of divorce. Only half of the children who were close to their mothers before a divorce remained equally close after the divorce. Boys, particularly, had difficulties with their mothers. Moreover, mother-child relationships deteriorated over time. Whereas teenagers in disrupted families were no more likely than teenagers in intact families to report poor relationships with their mothers, 30 percent of young adults from disrupted families have poor relationships with their mothers, as compared with 16 percent of young adults from intact families. Mother-daughter relationships often deteriorate as the daughter reaches young adulthood. The only group in society that derives any benefit from these weakened parent-child ties is the therapeutic community. Young adults from disrupted families are nearly twice as likely as those from intact families to receive psychological help.

65   Some social scientists have criticized Judith Wallerstein's research because her study is based on a small clinical sample and does not include a control group of children from intact families. However, other studies generally support and strengthen her findings. Nicholas Zill has found similar long-term effects on children of divorce, reporting that "effects of marital discord and family disruption are visible twelve to twenty-two years later in poor relationships with parents, high levels of problem behavior, and an increased likelihood of dropping out of high school and receiving psychological help." Moreover, Zill's research also found signs of distress in young women who seemed relatively well adjusted in middle childhood and adolescence. Girls in single-parent families are also at much greater risk for precocious sexuality, teenage mar-

riage, teenage pregnancy, nonmarital birth, and divorce than are girls in two-parent families.

Zill's research shows that family disruption strongly affects school achievement as well. Children in disrupted families are nearly twice as likely as those in intact families to drop out of high school; among children who do drop out, those from disrupted families are less likely eventually to earn a diploma or a GED. Boys are at greater risk for dropping out than girls, and are also more likely to exhibit aggressive, acting-out behaviors. Other research confirms these findings. According to a study by the National Association of Elementary School Principals, 33 percent of two-parent elementary school students are ranked as high achievers, as compared with 17 percent of single-parent students. The children in single-parent families are also more likely to be truant or late or to have disciplinary action taken against them. Even after controlling for race, income, and religion, scholars find significant differences in educational attainment between children who grow up in intact families and children who do not. In his 1992 study *America's Smallest School: The Family,* Paul Barton shows that the proportion of two-parent families varies widely from state to state and is related to variations in academic achievement. North Dakota, for example, scores highest on the math-proficiency test and second highest on the two-parent-family scale. The District of Columbia is second lowest on the math test and lowest in the nation on the two-parent-family scale. 66

Zill notes that "while coming from a disrupted family significantly increases a young adult's risks of experiencing social, emotional or academic difficulties, it does not foreordain such difficulties. The majority of young people from disrupted families have successfully completed high school, do *not* currently display high levels of emotional distress or problem behavior, and enjoy reasonable relationships with their mothers." Nevertheless, a majority of these young adults do show maladjustment in their relationships with their fathers. 67

These findings underscore the importance of both a mother and a father in fostering the emotional well-being of children. Obviously, not all children in two-parent families are free from emotional turmoil, but few are burdened with the troubles that accompany family breakup. Moreover, as the sociologist Amitai Etzioni explains in a new book, *The Spirit of Community,* two parents in an intact family make up what might be called a mutually supportive education coalition. When both parents are present, they can play different, even contradictory, roles. One parent may goad the child to achieve, while the other may encourage the child to take time out to 68 daydream or toss a football around. One may emphasize taking intellectual risks, while the other may insist on following the teacher's guidelines. At the same time, the parents regularly exchange information about the child's school problems and achievements, and have a sense of the overall educational mission. However, Etzioni writes,

> The sequence of divorce followed by a succession of boy or girlfriends, a second marriage, and frequently another divorce and another turnover of partners often means a repeatedly disrupted educational coalition. Each change in participants involves a change in the educational agenda for the child. Each new partner cannot be expected to pick up the previous one's educational post and program. . . . As a result, changes in parenting partners mean, at best, a deep disruption in a child's education, though of course several disruptions cut deeper into the effectiveness of the educational coalition than just one. . . .

Poverty, Crime, Education

69   Family disruption would be a serious problem even if it affected only individual children and families. But its impact is far broader. Indeed, it is not an exaggeration to characterize it as a central cause of many of our most vexing social problems. Consider three problems that most Americans believe rank among the nation's pressing concerns: poverty, crime, and declining school performance.

70   More than half of the increase in child poverty in the 1980s is attributable to changes in family structure, according to David Eggebeen and Daniel Lichter, of Pennsylvania State University. In fact, if family structure in the United States had remained relatively constant since 1960, the rate of child poverty would be a third lower than it is today. This does not bode well for the future. With more than half of today's children likely to live in single-parent families, poverty and associated welfare costs threaten to become even heavier burdens on the nation.

71   Crime in American cities has increased dramatically and grown more violent over recent decades. Much of this can be attributed to the rise in disrupted families. Nationally, more than 70 percent of all juveniles in state reform institutions come from fatherless homes. A number of scholarly studies find that even after the groups of subjects are controlled for in-

come, boys from single-mother homes are significantly more likely than others to commit crimes and to wind up in the juvenile justice, court, and penitentiary systems. One such study summarizes the relationship between crime and one-parent families in this way: "The relationship is so strong that controlling for family configuration erases the relationship between race and crime and between low income and crime. This conclusion shows up time and again in the literature." The nation's mayors, as well as police officers, social workers, probation officers, and court officials, consistently point to family breakup as the most important source of rising rates of crime.

Terrible as poverty and crime are, they tend to be concentrated in inner cities and isolated from the everyday experience of many Americans. The same cannot be said of the problem of declining school performance. Nowhere has the impact of family breakup been more profound or widespread than in the nation's public schools. There is a strong consensus that the schools are failing in their historic mission to prepare every American child to be a good worker and a good citizen. And nearly everyone agrees that the schools must undergo dramatic reform in order to reach that goal. In pursuit of that goal, moreover, we have suffered no shortage of bright ideas or pilot projects or bold experiments in school reform. But there is little evidence that measures such as curricular reform, school-based management, and school choice will address, let alone solve, the biggest problem schools face: the rising number of children who come from disrupted families. 72

The great educational tragedy of our time is that many American children are failing in school not because they are intellectually or physically impaired but because they are emotionally incapacitated. In schools across the nation principals report a dramatic rise in the aggressive, acting-out behavior characteristic of children, especially boys, who are living in single-parent families. The discipline problems in today's suburban schools—assaults on teachers, unprovoked attacks on other students, screaming outbursts in class—outstrip the problems that were evident in the toughest city schools a generation ago. Moreover, teachers find many children emotionally distracted, so upset and preoccupied by the explosive drama of their own family lives that they are unable to concentrate on such mundane matters as multiplication tables. 73

In response, many schools have turned to therapeutic remediation. A growing proportion of many school budgets is devoted to counseling and other psychological services. The curriculum is becoming more therapeutic: children are taking courses in self-esteem, conflict resolution, and aggression 74 management. Parental advisory groups are conscientiously debating alternative approaches to traditional school discipline, ranging from teacher training in mediation to the introduction of metal detectors and security guards in the schools. Schools are increasingly becoming emergency rooms of the emotions, devoted not only to developing minds but also to repairing hearts. As a result, the mission of the school, along with the culture of the classroom, is slowly changing. What we are seeing, largely as a result of the new burdens of family disruption, is the psychologization of American education.

75   Taken together, the research presents a powerful challenge to the prevailing view of family change as social progress. Not a single one of the assumptions underlying that view can be sustained against the empirical evidence. Single-parent families are not able to do well economically on a mother's income. In fact, most teeter on the economic brink, and many fall into poverty and welfare dependency. Growing up in a disrupted family does not enrich a child's life or expand the number of adults committed to the child's well-being. In fact, disrupted families threaten the psychological well-being of children and diminish the investment of adult time and money in them. Family diversity in the form of increasing numbers of single-parent and stepparent families does not strengthen the social fabric. It dramatically weakens and undermines society, placing new burdens on schools, courts, prisons, and the welfare system. These new families are not an improvement on the nuclear family, nor are they even just as good, whether you look at outcomes for children or outcomes for society as a whole. In short, far from representing social progress, family change represents a stunning example of social regress.

The Two-Parent Advantage

76   All this evidence gives rise to an obvious conclusion: growing up in an intact two-parent family is an important source of advantage for American children. Though far from perfect as a social institution, the intact family offers children greater security and better outcomes than its fast-growing alternatives: single-parent and stepparent families. Not only does the intact family protect the child from poverty and economic insecurity; it also provides greater noneconomic investments of parental time, attention, and emotional support over the entire life course. This does not mean that all two-parent families are better for children than all single-parent families. But in the face

of the evidence it becomes increasingly difficult to sustain the proposition that all family structures produce equally good outcomes for children.

Curiously, many in the research community are hesitant to 77 say that two-parent families generally promote better outcomes for children than single-parent families. Some argue that we need finer measures of the extent of the family-structure effect. As one scholar has noted, it is possible, by disaggregating the data in certain ways, to make family structure "go away" as an independent variable. Other researchers point to studies that show that children suffer psychological effects as a result of family conflict preceding family breakup. Consequently, they reason, it is the conflict rather than the structure of the family that is responsible for many of the problems associated with family disruption. Others, including Judith Wallerstein, caution against treating children in divorced families and children in intact families as separate populations, because doing so tends to exaggerate the differences between the two groups. "We have to take this family by family," Wallerstein says.

Some of the caution among researchers can also be attrib- 78 uted to ideological pressures. Privately, social scientists worry that their research may serve ideological causes that they themselves do not support, or that their work may be misinterpreted as an attempt to "tell people what to do." Some are fearful that they will be attacked by feminist colleagues, or, more generally, that their comments will be regarded as an effort to turn back the clock to the 1950s—a goal that has almost no constituency in the academy. Even more fundamental, it has become risky for anyone—scholar, politician, religious leader—to make normative statements today. This reflects not only the persistent drive toward "value neutrality" in the professions but also a deep confusion about the purposes of public discourse. The dominant view appears to be that social criticism, like criticism of individuals, is psychologically damaging. The worst thing you can do is to make people feel guilty or bad about themselves.

When one sets aside these constraints, however, the case 79 against the two-parent family is remarkably weak. It is true that disaggregating data can make family structure less significant as a factor, just as disaggregating Hurricane Andrew into wind, rain, and tides can make it disappear as a meteorological phenomenon. Nonetheless, research opinion as well as common sense suggests that the effects of changes in family structure are great enough to cause concern. Nicholas Zill argues that many of the risk factors for children are doubled or more than doubled as the result of family disruption. "In epidemiological terms," he writes, "the doubling of a hazard is a substantial increase. . . . the increase in risk that dietary cholesterol poses for cardiovascular disease, for example, is far less than double, yet millions of Americans have altered their diets because of the perceived hazard."

80   The argument that family conflict, rather than the breakup of parents, is the cause of children's psychological distress is persuasive on its face. Children who grow up in high-conflict families, whether the families stay together or eventually split up, are undoubtedly at great psychological risk. And surely no one would dispute that there must be societal measures available, including divorce, to remove children from families where they are in danger. Yet only a minority of divorces grow out of pathological situations; much more common are divorces in families unscarred by physical assault. Moreover, an equally compelling hypothesis is that family breakup generates its own conflict. Certainly, many families exhibit more conflictual and even violent behavior as a consequence of divorce than they did before divorce.

81   Finally, it is important to note that clinical insights are different from sociological findings. Clinicians work with individual families, who cannot and should not be defined by statistical aggregates. Appropriate to a clinical approach, moreover, is a focus on the internal dynamics of family functioning and on the immense variability in human behavior. Nevertheless, there is enough empirical evidence to justify sociological statements about the causes of declining child well-being and to demonstrate that despite the plasticity of human response, there are some useful rules of thumb to guide our thinking about and policies affecting the family.

82   For example, Sara McLanahan says, three structural constants are commonly associated with intact families, even intact families who would not win any "Family of the Year" awards. The first is economic. In intact families, children share in the income of two adults. Indeed, as a number of analysts have pointed out, the two-parent family is becoming more rather than less necessary, because more and more families need two incomes to sustain a middle-class standard of living.

83   McLanahan believes that most intact families also provide a stable authority structure. Family breakup commonly upsets the established boundaries of authority in a family. Children are often required to make decisions or accept responsibilities once considered the province of parents. Moreover, children, even very young children, are often expected to behave like

mature adults, so that the grown-ups in the family can be free to deal with the emotional fallout of the failed relationship. In some instances family disruption creates a complete vacuum in authority; everyone invents his or her own rules. With lines of authority disrupted or absent, children find it much more difficult to engage in the normal kinds of testing behavior, the trial and error, the failing and succeeding, that define the developmental pathway toward character and competence. McLanahan says, "Children need to be the ones to challenge the rules. The parents need to set the boundaries and let the kids push the boundaries. The children shouldn't have to walk the straight and narrow at all times."

Finally, McLanahan holds that children in intact families 84 benefit from stability in what she neutrally terms "household personnel." Family disruption frequently brings new adults into the family, including stepparents, live-in boyfriends or girlfriends, and casual sexual partners. Like stepfathers, boyfriends can present a real threat to children's, particularly to daughters', security and well-being. But physical or sexual abuse represents only the most extreme such threat. Even the very best of boyfriends can disrupt and undermine a child's sense of peace and security, McLanahan says. "It's not as though you're going from an unhappy marriage to peacefulness. There can be a constant changing until the mother finds a suitable partner."

McLanahan's argument helps explain why children of wid- 85 ows tend to do better than children of divorced or unmarried mothers. Widows differ from other single mothers in all three respects. They are economically more secure, because they receive more public assistance through Survivors Insurance, and possibly private insurance or other kinds of support from family members. Thus widows are less likely to leave the neighborhood in search of a new or better job and a cheaper house or apartment. Moreover, the death of a father is not likely to disrupt the authority structure radically. When a father dies, he is no longer physically present, but his death does not dethrone him as an authority figure in the child's life. On the contrary, his authority may be magnified through death. The mother can draw on the powerful memory of the departed father as a way of intensifying her parental authority: "Your father would have wanted it this way." Finally, since widows tend to be older than divorced mothers, their love life may be less distracting.

Regarding the two-parent family, the sociologist David 86 Popenoe, who has devoted much of his career to the study of families, both in the United States and in Scandinavia, makes this straightforward assertion:

> Social science research is almost never conclusive. There are always methodological difficulties and stones left unturned. Yet in three decades of work as a social scientist, I know of few other bodies of data in which the weight of evidence is so decisively on one side of the issue: on the whole, for children, two-parent families are preferable to single-parent and stepfamilies.

The Regime Effect

87   The rise in family disruption is not unique to American society. It is evident in virtually all advanced nations, including Japan, where it is also shaped by the growing participation of women in the work force. Yet the United States has made divorce easier and quicker than in any other Western nation with the sole exception of Sweden—and the trend toward solo motherhood has also been more pronounced in America. (Sweden has an equally high rate of out-of-wedlock birth, but the majority of such births are to cohabiting couples, a long-established pattern in Swedish society.) More to the point, nowhere has family breakup been greeted by a more triumphant rhetoric of renewal than in America.

88   What is striking about this rhetoric is how deeply it reflects classic themes in American public life. It draws its language and imagery from the nation's founding myth. It depicts family breakup as a drama of revolution and rebirth. The nuclear family represents the corrupt past, an institution guilty of the abuse of power and the suppression of individual freedom. Breaking up the family is like breaking away from Old World tyranny. Liberated from the bonds of the family, the individual can achieve independence and experience a new beginning, a fresh start, a new birth of freedom. In short, family breakup recapitulates the American experience.

89   This rhetoric is an example of what the University of Maryland political philosopher William Galston has called the "regime effect." The founding of the United States set in motion a new political order based to an unprecedented degree on individual rights, personal choice, and egalitarian relationships. Since then these values have spread beyond their original domain of political relationships to define social relationships as well. During the past twenty-five years these values have had a particularly profound impact on the family.

Increasingly, political principles of individual rights and 90
choice shape our understanding of family commitment and
solidarity. Family relationships are viewed not as permanent or
binding but as voluntary and easily terminable. Moreover, under the sway of the regime effect the family loses its central importance as an institution in the civil society, accomplishing
certain social goals such as raising children and caring for its
members, and becomes a means to achieving greater individual happiness—a lifestyle choice. Thus, Galston says, what is
happening to the American family reflects the "unfolding logic
of authoritative, deeply American moral-political principles."

One benefit of the regime effect is to create greater equality 91
in adult family relationships. Husbands and wives, mothers
and fathers, enjoy relationships far more egalitarian than past
relationships were, and most Americans prefer it that way. But
the political principles of the regime effect can threaten another kind of family relationship—that between parent and
child. Owing to their biological and developmental immaturity,
children are needy dependents. They are not able to express
their choices according to limited, easily terminable, voluntary
agreements. They are not able to act as negotiators in family
decisions, even those that most affect their own interests. As
one writer has put it, "a newborn does not make a good 'partner.'" Correspondingly, the parental role is antithetical to the
spirit of the regime. Parental investment in children involves a
diminished investment in self, a willing deference to the needs
and claims of the dependent child. Perhaps more than any
other family relationship, the parent-child relationship—
shaped as it is by patterns of dependency and deference—can
be undermined and weakened by the principles of the regime.

More than a century and a half ago Alexis de Tocqueville 92
made the striking observation that an individualistic society
depends on a communitarian institution like the family for its
continued existence. The family cannot be constituted like the
liberal state, nor can it be governed entirely by that state's principles. Yet the family serves as the seedbed for the virtues required by a liberal state. The family is responsible for teaching
lessons of independence, self-restraint, responsibility, and right
conduct, which are essential to a free, democratic society. If
the family fails in these tasks, then the entire experiment in
democratic self-rule is jeopardized.

To take one example: independence is basic to successful 93
functioning in American life. We assume that most people in
America will be able to work, care for themselves and their
families, think for themselves, and inculcate the same traits of
independence and initiative in their children. We depend on

families to teach people to do these things. The erosion of the two-parent family undermines the capacity of families to impart this knowledge; children of long-term welfare-dependent single parents are far more likely than others to be dependent themselves. Similarly, the children in disrupted families have a harder time forging bonds of trust with others and giving and getting help across the generations. This, too, may lead to greater dependency on the resources of the state.

94   Over the past two and a half decades Americans have been conducting what is tantamount to a vast natural experiment in family life. Many would argue that this experiment was necessary, worthwhile, and long overdue. The results of the experiment are coming in, and they are clear. Adults have benefited from the changes in family life in important ways, but the same cannot be said for children. Indeed, this is the first generation in the nation's history to do worse psychologically, socially, and economically than its parents. Most poignantly, in survey after survey the children of broken families confess deep longings for an intact family.

95   Nonetheless, as Galston is quick to point out, the regime effect is not an irresistible undertow that will carry away the family. It is more like a swift current, against which it is possible to swim. People learn; societies can change, particularly when it becomes apparent that certain behaviors damage the social ecology, threaten the public order, and impose new burdens on core institutions. Whether Americans will act to overcome the legacy of family disruption is a crucial but as yet unanswered question.

Ellen Willis
WHY I'M NOT "PRO-FAMILY"

Ellen Willis, author of No More Nice Girls: Countercultural Essays *(1992), teaches journalism at NYU. The article published here originally appeared in* Glamour *(October 1994), a national magazine devoted to fashions, cultural matters, careers, nutrition, and civic issues interesting to women.*

1   In 1992, "Family Values" bombed in Houston. Right-wingers at the Republican convention, sneering at career women and

single mothers, turned voters off. Now the Democrats are in power—yet ironically, the family issue has reemerged, more strongly than ever. Last year New York's influential Democratic senator, Daniel Patrick Moynihan, suggested that in relaxing the stigma against unmarried childbearing, we had laid the groundwork for the burgeoning crime rate. Then *The Atlantic* published a cover story provocatively titled: "Dan Quayle Was Right." Its author, social historian Barbara Dafoe Whitehead, invoked recent research to argue that high rates of divorce and single parenthood hurt children and underlie "many of our most vexing social problems."

The article hit a nerve. It provoked an outpouring of mail,   2 was condensed for *Reader's Digest* and won an award from the National Women's Political Caucus. Commentators both conservative and liberal praised it in newspapers across the country. Together, Moynihan's and Whitehead's salvos launched a national obsession with "the decline of the family." President Clinton joined the bandwagon: "For 30 years," he declared in his State of the Union message, "family life in America has been breaking down."

The new advocates of the family seem more sympathetic to   3 women than their right-wing precursors. They know women are in the workforce to stay; they are careful to talk about the time pressures faced by "parents"—not "mothers"—with jobs, and they put an unaccustomed emphasis on men's family obligations, such as contributing their fair share of child support. Some advocate liberal reforms ranging from antipoverty programs to federally funded child care to abortion rights, arguing that such measures are pro-family because they help existing families. (A recent Planned Parenthood fund-raising letter proclaims, "Pro-choice is pro-family.")

I'm all for reforms that make it easier to give children the   4 care they need, and I'm certainly in favor of men's equal participation in childrearing. My quarrel is with the underlying terms of the discussion, especially the assumption that anyone who cares about children must be "pro-family." I grew up in the fifties, in a family with two committed parents—the kind of home the pro-familists idealize. I had security; I had love. Yet like many of my peers, especially women, I saw conventional family life as far from ideal and had no desire to replicate it. It wasn't only that I didn't want to be a housewife like my mother; I felt that family life promoted self-abnegation and social conformity while stifling eroticism and spontaneity. I thought the nuclear family structure was isolating, and that within it, combining childrearing with other work would be exhausting, even if both parents shared the load—impressions I can now confirm from experience.

5   To me the alternative that made the most sense was not single parenthood—we needed *more* parents, not fewer, to share the daily responsibilities of childrearing and homemaking. In the seventies, a number of people I knew were bringing up children in communal households, and I imagined someday doing the same. But by the time my companion and I had a child ten years ago, those experiments and the counterculture that supported them were long gone.

6   From my perspective, the new champions of the family are much like the old. They never consider whether the current instability of families might signal that an age-old institution is failing to meet modern needs and ought to be reexamined. The idea that there could be other possible structures for domestic life and childrearing has been excluded from the conversation—so much so that cranks like me who persist in broaching the subject are used to getting the sort of tactful and embarrassed reaction accorded, say, people who claim to have been kidnapped by aliens. And the assumption that marriage is the self-evident solution to single parents' problems leads to impatience and hostility toward anyone who can't or won't get with the nuclear-family program.

7   Consider the hottest topic on the pro-family agenda: the prevalence of unwed motherhood in poor black communities. For Moynihan and other welfare reformers, the central cause of inner-city poverty and crime is not urban economic collapse, unemployment or racism, but fatherless households. Which means the solution is to bring back the stigma of "illegitimacy" and restrict or eliminate welfare for single mothers. Clinton has proposed requiring welfare recipients to leave the rolls after two years and look for work, with temporary government jobs as a backup (where the permanent jobs are supposed to come from, in an economy where massive layoffs and corporate shrinkage are the order of the day, is not explained).

8   As the reformers profess their concern for poor children (while proposing to make them even poorer), the work ethic (as jobs for the unskilled get even scarcer) and the overburdened taxpayer, it's easy to miss their underlying message— that women have gotten out of hand. They may pay lip service to the idea that men too should be held responsible for the babies they father. But in practice there is no way to force poor, unemployed men to support their children or to stigmatize men as well as women for having babies out of wedlock. This is, after all, still a culture that regards pregnancy as the woman's problem and childrearing as the woman's job. And so, predictably, women are the chief targets of the reformers' punitive policies and rhetoric. It's women who will lose benefits;

women who stand accused of deliberately having babies as a meal ticket; women who are (as usual) charged with the social failures of their sons. Given the paucity of decently paying jobs available to poor women or the men they're likely to be involved with, demanding that they not have children unless they have jobs or husbands to support them is tantamount to demanding that they not have children at all. (Note the logic: Motherhood is honorable work if supported by a man but parasitic self-indulgence if supported by the public.) Put that demand together with laws restricting abortion for poor women and teenagers, and the clear suggestion is that they shouldn't have sex either.

While this brand of misogyny is specifically aimed at poor   9
black women, it would be a mistake to think the rest of us are off the hook. For one thing (as Whitehead and other pro-familists are quick to remind us), it's all too easy in this age of high divorce and unemployment rates for a woman who imagined herself securely middle-class to unexpectedly become an impoverished single mother. Anyway, there is a thin line between fear and loathing of welfare mothers and moral distaste for unmarried mothers per se. Secretary of Health and Human Services Donna Shalala, a feminist and one of the more liberal members of the Clinton cabinet, has said, "I don't like to put this in moral terms, but I do believe that having children out of wedlock is just wrong." The language the welfare reformers use—the vocabulary of *stigma* and *illegitimacy*—unnervingly recalls the repressive moral climate of my own teenage years.

I can't listen to harangues about illegitimacy without getting   10
posttraumatic flashbacks. Let's be clear about what the old stigma meant: a vicious double standard of sexual morality for men and women; the hobbling of female sexuality with shame, guilt and inhibition; panic over dislodged diaphragms and late periods; couples trapped into marriages one or both never wanted; pregnant girls barred from school and hidden in homes for unwed mothers; enormous pressure on women to get married early and not be too picky about it.

Is it silly to worry that in the post-*Roe* v. *Wade*, post-Pill   11
nineties some version of fifties morality could reassert itself? I don't think so. Activists with a moral cause can be very persuasive. Who would have imagined a few years ago that there would be a public debate about restricting cigarettes as an addictive drug? Abortion may still be legal, but its opponents have done a good job of bringing back its stigma (ironically, this is one reason a lot of pregnant teenagers decide to give birth).

Many pro-familists, above all those who call themselves   12
communitarians, are openly nostalgic for a sterner moral or-

needs the family once fulfilled. This means, first of all, making a collective commitment to the adequate support of every child. Beyond that, it means opening our minds to the possibility of new forms of community, in which children have close ties with a *number* of adults and therefore a stable home base that does not totally depend either on one vulnerable parent or on one couple's emotional and sexual bond.

21   Of course, no social structure can guarantee permanence: In earlier eras, families were regularly broken up by death, war and abandonment. Yet a group that forms for the specific purpose of cooperative child-rearing might actually inspire more long-term loyalty than marriage, which is supposed to provide emotional and sexual fulfillment but often does not. The practical support and help parents would gain from such an arrangement—together with the greater freedom to pursue their own personal lives—would be a strong incentive for staying in it, and the inevitable conflicts and incompatibilities among the group members would be easier to tolerate than the intense deprivation of an unhappy marriage.

22   It's time, in other words, to think about what has so long been unthinkable, to replace reflexive dismissiveness with questions. What, for instance, can we learn from the kibbutz—how might some of its principles be adapted to Americans' very different circumstances? What worked and didn't work about the communal experiments of the sixties and seventies? What about more recent projects, like groups of old people moving in together to avoid going to nursing homes? Or the "co-housing" movement of people who are buying land in the suburbs or city apartment buildings and dividing the space between private dwellings and communal facilities such as dining rooms and child-care centers?

23   I'm not suggesting that there's anything like an immediate practical solution to our present family crisis. What we can do, though, is stop insisting on false solutions that scapegoat women and oversimplify the issues. Perhaps then a real discussion—worthy of Americans' inventiveness and enduring attraction to frontiers—will have a chance to begin.

Iris Marion Young
MAKING SINGLE
MOTHERHOOD NORMAL

Iris Marion Young, a philosopher by trade and a leading feminist who now teaches at the University of Pittsburgh, has written Throwing Like a Girl and Other Essays in Feminist Philosophy and Social Theory *(1990) and* Justice and the Politics of Difference *(1990). She contributed the following essay in the winter of 1994 to* Dissent, *a very progressive bimonthly journal of public affairs. A few months later her essay was answered in* Dissent *by Jean Bethke Elshtain, a prominent political scientist from the University of Chicago who has a particular interest in family issues. Margaret O'Brien Steinfels, the editor of* Commonweal *magazine (a liberal publication on public affairs loosely associated with Catholicism— and another place where Elshtain places some of her work), also responded in the same issue of* Dissent *to Young's essay, right after Elshtain's piece. Iris Young then responded to both Elshtain and Steinfels. Their entire exchange is reprinted here.*

When Dan Quayle denounced Murphy Brown for having a   1
baby without a husband in May 1992, most liberals and leftists
recognized it for the ploy it was: a Republican attempt to win
an election by an irrational appeal to "tradition" and "order."
To their credit, American voters did not take the bait. The
Clinton campaign successfully turned the family values
rhetoric against the GOP by pointing to George Bush's veto of
the Family and Medical Leave Act and by linking family well-
being to economic prosperity.

Nonetheless, family values rhetoric has survived the elec-   2
tion. Particularly disturbing is the fact that the refrain has
been joined by people who, by most measures, should be called
liberals, but who can accept only the two-parent heterosexual
family. Communitarians are leading the liberal chorus de-
nouncing divorce and single motherhood. In *The Spirit of
Community,* Amitai Etzioni calls for social measures to privilege two-parent families and encourage parents to take care of
young children at home. Etzioni is joined by political theorist
William Galston—currently White House adviser on domestic
policy—in supporting policies that will make divorce more difficult. Jean Bethke Elshtain is another example of a social
liberal—that is, someone who believes in state regulation of

business, redistributive economic policies, religious toleration and broad principles of free speech—who argues that not all kinds of families should be considered equal from the point of view of social policy or moral education. William Julius Wilson, another academic who has been close to Democratic party policy makers, considers out-of-wedlock birth to be a symptom of social pathology and promotes marriage as one solution to problems of urban black poverty.

3   Although those using family values rhetoric rarely mention gays and lesbians, this celebration of stable marriage is hardly good news for gay and lesbian efforts to win legitimacy for their lives and relationships. But I am concerned here with the implications of family values rhetoric for another despised and discriminated-against group: single mothers. Celebrating marriage brings a renewed stigmatization of these women, and makes them scapegoats for social ills of which they are often the most serious victims. The only antidote to this injustice is for public policy to regard single mothers as normal, and to give them the social supports they need to overcome disadvantage.

4   Most people have forgotten another explicit aim of Dan Quayle's appeal to family values: to "explain" the disorders in Los Angeles in May 1992. Unmarried women with children lie at the source of the "lawless social anarchy" that sends youths into the streets with torches and guns. Their "welfare ethos" impedes individual efforts to move ahead in society.

5   Liberal family values rhetoric also finds the "breakdown" of "the family" to be a primary cause of all our social ills. "It is not an exaggeration," says Barbara Dafoe Whitehead in the *Atlantic* (April 1993) "to characterize [family disruption] as a central cause of many of our most vexing social problems, including poverty, crime, and declining school performance." Etzioni lays our worst social problems at the door of self-indulgent divorced or never-married parents. "Gang warfare in the streets, massive drug abuse, a poorly committed workforce, and a strong sense of entitlement and a weak sense of responsibility are, to a large extent, the product of poor parenting." Similarly, Galston attributed fearsome social consequences to divorce and single parenthood. "The consequences of family failure affect society at large. We all pay for systems of welfare, criminal justice, and incarceration, as well as for physical and mental disability; we are all made poorer by the inability or unwillingness of young adults to become contributing members of society; we all suffer if our society is unsafe and divided."

6   Reductionism in the physical sciences has faced such devastating criticism that few serious physicists would endorse a

theory that traced a one-way causal relationship between the behavior of a particular sort of atom and, say, an earthquake. Real-world physical phenomena are understood to have many mutually conditioning forces. Yet here we have otherwise subtle and intelligent people putting forward the most absurd social reductionism. In this simplistic model of society, the family is the most basic unit, the first cause that is itself uncaused. Through that magical process called socialization, families cause the attitudes, dispositions, and capacities of individual children who in turn as adults cause political and economic institutions to work or not work.

The great and dangerous fallacy in this imagery, of course, is 7 its implicit assumption that non-familial social processes do not cause family conditions. How do single-mother families "cause" poverty, for example? Any sensible look at some of these families shows us that poverty is a cause of their difficulties and failures. Doesn't it make sense to trace some of the conflicts that motivate divorce to the structure of work or to the lack of work? And what about all the causal influences on families and children over which parents have very little control— peer groups, dilapidated and understaffed schools, consumer culture, television and movie imagery, lack of investment in neighborhoods, cutbacks in public services? Families unprotected by wide networks of supportive institutions and economic resources are bound to suffer. Ignoring the myriad social conditions that affect families only enables the government and the public to escape responsibility for investing in the ghettos, building new houses and schools, and creating the millions of decent jobs that we need to restore millions of people to dignity.

Family-values reductionism scapegoats parents, and especially single parents, and proposes a low-cost answer to crime, poverty, and unemployment: get married and stay married.

Whitehead, Galston, Etzioni, and others claim that there is 9 enough impressive evidence that divorce harms children emotionally to justify policies that discourage parents from divorcing. A closer look at the data, however, yields a much more ambiguous picture. One meta-analysis of ninety-two studies of the effects of divorce on American children, for example, finds statistically insignificant differences between children of divorced parents and children from intact families in various measures of well-being. Many studies of children of divorce fail to compare them to children from "intact" families, or fail to rule out predivorce conditions as causes. A ten-year longitudinal study released in Australia last June found that conflict between parents—whether divorced or not—is a frequent cause of emotional distress in children. This stress is mitigated, however, if the child has a close supportive relationship with at least one of the parents. Results also suggest that Australia's stronger welfare state and less adversarial divorce process may partly account for differences with U.S. findings.

10   Thus the evidence that divorce produces lasting damage to children is ambiguous at best, and I do not see how the ambiguities can be definitively resolved one way or the other. Complex and multiple social causation makes it naive to think we can conclusively test for a clear causal relationship between divorce and children's well-being. Without such certainty, however, it is wrong to suggest that the liberty of adults in their personal lives should be restricted. Galston and Etzioni endorse proposals that would impose a waiting period between the time a couple applied for divorce and the beginning of divorce proceedings. Divorce today already often drags on in prolonged acrimony. Children would likely benefit more from making it easier and less adversarial.

11   Although many Americans agree with me about divorce, they also agree with Quayle, Wilson, Galston, and others that single motherhood is undesirable for children, a deviant social condition that policy ought to try to correct. Etzioni claims that children of single parents receive less parental supervision and support than do children in two-parent families. It is certainly plausible that parenting is easier and more effective if two or more adults discuss the children's needs and provide different kinds of interactions for them. It does not follow, however, that the second adult must be a live-in husband. Some studies have found that the addition of any adult to a single-mother household, whether a relative, lover, or friend, tends to offset the tendency of single parents to relinquish decision making too early. Stephanie Coontz suggests that fine-tuned research on single-parent families would probably find that they are better for children in some respects and worse in others. For example, although adults in single-parent families spend less time supervising homework, single parents are less likely to pressure their children into social conformity and more likely to praise good grades.

12   Much less controversial is the claim that children in single-parent families are more often poor than those in two-parent families. One should be careful not to correlate poverty with single-parenthood, however; according to Coontz, a greater part of the increase in family poverty since 1979 has occurred in families with both spouses present, with only 38 percent concentrated in single-parent families. As many as 50 percent of single-parent families are likely to be poor, which is a shock-

ing fact, but intact two-parent families are also increasingly likely to be poor, especially if the parents are in their twenties or younger.

It is harder to raise children alone than with at least one 13 other adult, and the stresses of doing so can take their toll on children. I do not question that children in families that depend primarily on a woman's wage-earning ability are often disadvantaged. I do question the conclusion that getting single mothers married is the answer to childhood disadvantage.

Conservatives have always stated a preference for two-par- 14 ent families. Having liberals join this chorus is disturbing because it makes such preference much more mainstream, thus legitimizing discrimination against single mothers. Single mothers commonly experience credit and employment discrimination. Discrimination against single mothers in renting apartments was legal until 1988, and continues to be routine in most cities. In a study of housing fairness in Pittsburgh in which I participated, most people questioned said that rental housing discrimination is normal in the area. Single mothers and their children also face biases in schools.

There is no hope that discrimination of this sort will ever 15 end unless public discourse and government policy recognize that female-headed families are a viable, normal, and permanent family form, rather than something broken and deviant that policy should eradicate. Around one-third of families in the United States are headed by a woman alone; this proportion is about the same world-wide. The single-mother family is not going to fade away. Many women raise children alone because their husbands left them or because lack of access to contraception and abortion forced them to bear unwanted children. But many women are single mothers by choice. Women increasingly initiate divorces, and many single mothers report being happier after divorce and uninterested in remarriage, even when they are poorer.

Women who give birth out of wedlock, moreover, often 16 have chosen to do so. Discussion of the "problem" of "illegitimate" births commonly assumes the image of the irresponsible and uneducated teenager (of color) as the unwed mother. When citing statistics about rising rates of out-of-wedlock birth, journalists and scholars rarely break them down by the mother's age, occupation, and so on. Although the majority of these births continue to be to young mothers, a rising proportion are to mid-life women with steady jobs who choose to have children. Women persist in such choices despite the fact that they are stigmatized and sometimes punished for them.

17   In a world where it can be argued that there are already too many people, it may sometimes be wrong for people to have babies. The planned birth of a third child in a stable two-parent family may be morally questionable from this point of view. But principles of equality and reproductive freedom must hold that there is nothing *more* wrong with a woman in her thirties with a stable job and income having a baby than with a similar married couple.

18   If teen pregnancy is a social problem, this is not because the mothers are unmarried, but because they are young. They are inexperienced in the ways of the world and lack the skills necessary to get a job to support their children; once they become parents, their opportunities to develop those skills usually decrease. But these remain problems even when the women marry the young men with whom they have conceived children. Young inexperienced men today are just as ill prepared for parenting and just as unlikely to find decent jobs.

19   Although many young unmarried women who bear children do so because they are effectively denied access to abortions, many of these mothers want their babies. Today the prospects for meaningful work and a decent income appear dim to many youth, and especially to poor youth. Having a baby can give a young woman's life meaning, earn her respectful attention, make her feel grown up, and give her an excuse to exit the "wild" teenager scene that has begun to make her uncomfortable. Constructing an education and employment system that took girls as seriously as boys, that trained girls and boys for meaningful and available work would be a far more effective antidote to teen birth than reprimanding, stigmatizing, and punishing these girls.

20   Just as we should examine the assumption that something is wrong with a mid-life woman having a child without a husband, so we ought to ask a more radical question: just what *in principle* is *more* wrong in a young woman's bearing a child without a husband than in an older woman's doing so? When making their reproductive decisions, everyone ought to ask whether there are too many people in the world. Beyond that, I submit that we should affirm an unmarried young woman's right to bear a child as much as any other person's right.

21   There is reason to think that much of the world, including the United States, has plural childbearing cultures. Recently I heard a radio interview with an eighteen-year-old African American woman in Washington, D.C. who had recently given birth to her second child. She affirmed wanting both children, and said that she planned to have no more. She lives in a subsidized apartment and participates in a job training program as

a condition for receiving AFDC. She resisted the interviewer's suggestion that there was something morally wrong or at least unfortunate with her choices and her life. She does not like being poor, and does not like having uncertain child care arrangements when she is away from her children. But she believes that in ten years, with hard work, social support, and good luck, she will have a community college degree and a decent job doing something she likes, as does her mother, now thirty-four.

There is nothing in principle wrong with such a pattern of 22
having children first and getting education and job training later. Indeed, millions of white professional women currently in their fifties followed a similar pattern. Most of them, of course, were supported by husbands, and not state subsidy, when they stayed home to take care of their young children. Our racism, sexism, and classism are only thinly concealed when we praise stay-at-home mothers who are married, white, and middle class, and propose a limit of two years on welfare to unmarried, mostly non-white, and poor women who do the same thing. From a moral point of view, is there an important difference between the two kinds of dependence? If there is any serious commitment to equality in the United States, it must include an equal respect for people's reproductive choices. In order for children to have equal opportunities, moreover, equal respect for parents, and especially mothers, requires state policies that give greater support to some than others.

If we assume that there is nothing morally wrong with single- 23
mother families, but that they are often disadvantaged by lack of child care and by economic discrimination and social stigma, then what follows for public policy? Some of the answers to this question are obvious, some not so obvious, but in the current climate promoting a stingy and punitive welfare state, all bear discussion. I will close by sketching a few proposals.

1. *There is nothing in principle any more wrong with a* 24
teenage woman's choice to have a child than with anyone else's.
Still, there is something wrong with a society that gives her few alternatives to a mothering vocation and little opportunity for meaningful job training. If we want to reduce the number of teenage women who want to have babies, then education and employment policies have to take girls and women much more seriously.

2. *Whether poor mothers are single because they are divorced* 25
or because they never married, it is wrong for a society to allow
mothers to raise children in poverty and then tell them that it's
their fault when their children have deprived lives. Only if the

economy offered women decent-paying jobs, moreover, would forcing welfare women to get jobs lift them out of poverty. Of course, with good job opportunities most of them would not need to be forced off welfare. But job training and employment programs for girls and women must be based on the assumption that a large proportion of them will support children alone. Needless to say, there is a need for massive increases in state support for child care if these women are to hold jobs. Public policy should, however, also acknowledge that taking care of children at home is work, and then support this work with unstigmatized subsidy where necessary to give children a decent life.

26   3. *The programs of schools, colleges, and vocational and professional training institutions ought to accommodate a plurality of women's life plans, combining childbearing and child-rearing with other activities.* They should not assume that there is a single appropriate time to bear and rear children. No woman should be disadvantaged in her education and employment opportunities because she has children at age fifteen, twenty-five, thirty-five, or forty-five (for the most part, education and job structures are currently such that each of these ages is the "wrong time").

27   4. *Public policy should take positive steps to dispel the assumption that the two-parent heterosexual nuclear family is normal and all other family forms deviant.* For example, the state should assist single-parent support systems, such as the "mothers' houses" in some European countries that provide spaces for shared child minding and cooking while at the same time preserving family privacy.

28   5. *Some people might object that my call for recognizing single motherhood as normal lets men off the hook when it comes to children.* Too many men are running out on pregnant women and on the mothers of their children with whom they have lived. They are free to seek adventure, sleep around, or start new families, while single mothers languish in poverty with their children. This objection voices a very important concern, but there are ways to address it other than forcing men to get or stay married to the mothers of their children.

29   First, the state should force men who are not poor themselves to pay child support for children they have recognized as theirs. I see nothing wrong with attaching paychecks and bank accounts to promote this end. But the objection above requires more than child support. Relating to children is a good thing in itself. Citizens who love and are committed to some particular children are more apt than others to think of the world in the long term, and to see it from the perspective of the more vulnerable people. Assuming that around one-third of households will

continue to be headed by women alone, men should be encouraged to involve themselves in close relationships with children,
not necessarily their biological offspring.

6. *More broadly, the American public must cease assuming that*   30
support and care for children are the responsibility of their parents
alone, and that parents who require social support have somehow
failed. Most parents require social support, some more than others. According to Coontz, for a good part of American history
this fact was assumed. I am not invoking a Platonic vision of
communal childrearing; children need particular significant
others. But non-parents ought to take substantial economic and
social responsibility for the welfare of children.

After health care, Clinton's next big reform effort is likely to   31
be aimed at welfare. Condemning single mothers will legitimate harsh welfare reforms that will make the lives of some of
them harder. The left should press instead for the sorts of principles and policies that treat single mothers as equal citizens.

Jean Bethke Elshtain
SINGLE MOTHERHOOD
A RESPONSE TO IRIS YOUNG

What I found most surprising in Iris Young's analysis ("Making   1
Single Motherhood Normal," Winter 1994) is the radical dis-
connection between her policy proposals and the constraints
and possibilities of our current situation. She calls for "massive
increases in state support for child care" when state budgets are
strapped, cutbacks are being ordered across the board, and new
initiatives in health care will gobble up whatever additional revenues are available. (Presumably she supports universal health
care and favors moves in that direction.) She calls for "public
policy" to dispel any notion of "normality" in family structure.
But, surely, we have already conducted that experiment and it
has failed. It has failed for the very people it was designed to
help—single mothers and their children. I will offer up evidence on this score—evidence Young systematically overlooks.

She calls for states to "force men" to "pay child support for   2
children they have recognized as theirs." She claims men
shouldn't be let off the hook where their responsibilities are
concerned. But her formulation continues to put the onus for
child-rearing and child "recognition," if you will, on women. In
fact, startlingly, her argument is a call for a return to a particularly rigid form of "separate spheres," something I thought

feminists had a strong stake in criticizing and reforming. Once again we are in a world of "women and children only," where a woman can do it all by herself, thank you. A man could easily bypass Young's requirement by refusing to recognize a child as "his." Who is to compel this recognition if the institutional framework within which it has taken place historically—the two-parent family—has been entirely dismantled as a "norm" or "ideal" of any sort? There are no "fathers" or "daddies" in Young's universe with direct, daily responsibility for child care and family sustenance, something not reducible to a paycheck. Still, Young would "encourage" men to "involve themselves in close relationships with children, not necessarily their biological offspring." How? Why? What institutional forms will nurture and sustain such relationships? Are we to see forlorn bands of disconnected men roaming neighborhoods, knocking on doors, and asking if there is a baby inside they can "bond" with for a few hours? Young's rhetorical demolition of what she takes to be onerous tradition combined with her wholly abstract, vague pleas for connection and responsibility shows us again that politics of denunciation and sentimentalism that undermined much of 1960s radicalism. (I know: I was there.)

3   Let's enter the real world. For Young misses altogether what is at stake in the travail of the present moment. She reverts to the claim that "poverty" is the cause of all other troubles. This is curious because Young thrashes reductionism before rapidly moving to her own reductionist formula, namely, that any "sensible look" at the plight of poor families reveals that "poverty" is the cause of, well, being poor. Here she reproduces the very "one-way" causal claims she attacked just a few sentences earlier. The problem, of course, is that matters are far more complex than this. The mountain of evidence now available from reputable scholars tells us that cultural changes—alterations in norms and values—are not mere epiphenomenal foam on the causal sea but are themselves vectors of economic trouble. We know that poverty is associated with single parents. This means mothers, often very young mothers (those "babies having babies" Jesse Jackson talks about) in a father-absent situation. We also know, from the National Commission on Children, the Center for the Study of Social Policy, the U.S. Department of Health and Human Services, and dozens of other reliable sources that children growing up in single-parent households are at greater risk on every index of well-being (crime, violence, substance abuse, mental illness, dropping out of school, and so on).

4   But mark this: there is no compelling evidence that a decline in government spending accounts for the past several decades'

burgeoning litany of risks to children. Economists Victor Fuchs and Diane Reklis have shown that the well-being of children worsened in a period when "purchases of goods and services for children by government rose very rapidly, as did real household income per child, and the poverty rate of children plummeted. Thus, we must seek explanations for the rising problems of that period in the cultural realm." The period to which Fuchs and Reklis refer is the 1960–1970 decade. If you continue to track direct government expenditures per child up to the present moment you find no compelling correlation between government support and child well-being per se. Indeed, we are spending more for children today in the public sphere than ever before. The sad truth is that our public investment in children is being outstripped by "private disinvestment," in other words, the breakup of the two-parent home. If you control for all other factors, *including* economic status, you learn that father absence is the single most important risk factor for children, whether one is talking about poor health or poverty or behavioral problems (the latter being a euphemistic way of gesturing toward drug addiction, being the victim or perpetrator of violence, adolescent out-of-wedlock birth, and so on). Do we change all of this by making a one-parent family suddenly "normal"? That won't stop children from suffering. That won't help a child find security and trust and safety. Of course, we should do our best for all children. But that means doing our best to create situations that do best for children, not continuing to try to patch things up when we *know*, because the evidence is in, that some familial arrangements are better for children than others.

The *Kids Count Data Book*, published by the liberal Center   5
for the Study of Social Policy, one of the most widely accepted scholarly sources in this area, offers up annual "Profiles of Child Well-Being." The most recent profile included the following startling information. Researchers looked at two groups and compared them: couples who completed high school, married, and waited until age twenty to have their first child against couples who did none of the above—they neither married nor finished school, and in which the girl gave birth before age twenty. In the first group, the number of children who fell below the poverty line was 8 percent. In the second group, the number of children who fell below the poverty line was a startling 79 percent. What this suggests is that marriage, somewhat delayed child-bearing, and high school completion—cultural and educational factors—fuel economic outcomes. It is high time we set aside economic reductionism of the sort Young oddly endorses and looked to the dissolution of the

fabric of families and communities, a tragedy entangled with the repudiation of those "norms" for male and female responsibility for children that Young finds oppressive because they "stigmatize" single mothers. The stigma attached to single motherhood has virtually disappeared, if we trust the survey data, but the problems associated with the children of single parents do not go away so readily.

6   If we are to see investment "in the ghettos," the building of new houses and schools, the creation of "millions of decent jobs," no less, we need people capable of holding jobs; we need secure social institutions; we need children who are compelled by parents to stay in school; we need all the things Young blithely ignores. The most successful organizing for change over the past fifty years has come from poor and working-class communities who form broad-based coalitions to work for housing, jobs, schools, in the most devastated urban areas— from Brownsville to San Antonio. I have in mind, for example, the activities of the Industrial Areas Foundation. If Young wants to see revitalization of communities in action she should check out the work of the East Brooklyn Congregations (EBC) and their Nehemiah Homes project or Baltimoreans United in Leadership Development (BUILD), a group that has made significant strides in school reform in the inner city. There are dozens and dozens of such examples. The organizing base is families and churches—the remnants of intact institutions— for you cannot make lasting, meaningful change of any kind outside institutions.

7   Civic philosophy dies when academics, in the name of radicalism, in the name, heaven help us, of that democratic socialism for which this journal has traditionally stood, endorse values that erode the only possible bases for creating and sustaining community institutions over time—calling for more individualism (hence Young's celebration of an individual woman's "choice" to have a baby whether she is thirteen years old or fifty, as if that choice and not any consideration of the child's well-being were the only value at stake); more vast government projects, hence more clientage; normlessness as a norm; and on and on. It is depressing to see these old nostrums refurbished as radical or reformist when they could scarcely be more conformist—to the naively anti-institutionalist, hyper-individualist tendencies of our time, with a heavy dollop of "separate spheres with a feminist face" thrown in for good measure.

Margaret O'Brien Steinfels
RIGHTS AND
RESPONSIBILITIES
A RESPONSE TO IRIS YOUNG

Fully achieved, Iris Young's proposals would be a disaster for 1
women and children, probably for men too, and certainly for
liberal and left politics.

She is wrong on three points, at least: single mothers are *not* 2
despised; liberals don't view single mothers as the sole source
of our social ills; liberalism has *not* abandoned its heritage by
rallying to the two-parent family.

If only *Time* magazine had made Marla Maples—an unwed 3
mother—the woman of the year, we would fully realize that a
mother's unwedded state is no bar to celebrity or social lioniz-
ing—and a kiss on the cheek from (former) Mayor David
Dinkins. The press and television treat single motherhood as a
variant of the American family. I suspect that teachers, principals, social workers, acquaintances, and neighbors don't ask
and don't care. That changes when the individual choice of single motherhood becomes a collective responsibility. It is
women who have children that they can't support or get fathers
to support that exercise tax-paying Americans, at least some of
whom are single-mother families themselves! Plain and simple, the problem is not single mothers but single mothers who
depend on the rest of us to support them and their children.

The Reagan administration and accompanying pundits con- 4
vinced the American electorate that the welfare system now
functions as a dowry system for adolescent girls, who, becoming pregnant, are launched into motherhood and adulthood
with food stamps, child support, housing allowances, and
Medicaid long before they are ready to be good mothers. And it
doesn't end there, the critics go on: rather than supporting
people in need until they can get back on their feet, the system
is failing children and undermining young men's sense of responsibility for their children. Conservatives think that welfare
is hurting poor people. Among others, a lot of poor people
agree with them.

This analysis has penetrated the thinking of Democrats and 5
other liberals. Some speak of job training, of community service in return for welfare. Some speak of two-year limits; others of withholding aid for infants born when a woman is already on welfare; all stand behind that once unthinkable policy
of dunning delinquent dads for court-ordered child support.

Even Wisconsin, with its tradition of progressive politics, is bailing out of the federal welfare system in order to limit and control in its own expenditures.

6   Should these be counted traitors to the liberal cause?

7   Those old enough to remember will recall that liberals created the welfare system to keep families together, to help tide over those in temporary trouble, and to help widows maintain a household. Aid to Families with Dependent Children (AFDC) and other welfare measures were never meant to support teenage moms or help their boyfriends elude the responsibilities of fatherhood; nor were they intended to make up for missing child-support payments. The system has been adapted to meet these needs on the assumption that women with children often have no other recourse. Often they do not. When, however, the system itself seems to encourage unwed motherhood or male abandonment and to contribute to family breakdown, reasonable people ask their politicians why. To their credit some liberals are reconsidering the merits of the two-parent family. Were two-parent families to come back into vogue, our social ills would not disappear. But there is reason to expect that children would have saner, more secure, and—boys especially—more disciplined upbringings. These would be a good in themselves.

8   Iris Young wants us to assume that "there is nothing morally wrong with single-mother families." What does she mean? Women of any age, educational attainment, income level, or marital status should be able to bear and raise a child. I agree. At least I agree that no one else—the state, the father, the woman's relatives—has a right to force a woman to get an abortion if she is pregnant. Or force her to use contraception. Or, barring abusive or seriously neglectful behavior, take her child from her. In that sense the mother-child relationship is sacrosanct; the right to conceive and bear a child is basic.

9   But not every exercise of a "right" adds up to a moral good. Nations have a right to protect their sovereignty; not every act in pursuit of that right is moral. Individuals in our society have a right to free speech; not every sentence uttered in exercising that right constitutes a moral good. The analogy applies to childbearing decisions: it may be a right, but that does not make it a moral good. Single motherhood—though not wrong in and of itself—can undermine the well-being of others.

10   First, there is the child and his or her need for care, comfort, and stability—constant attention as an infant and consistent attention as a child and adolescent. Even with two (or more)

adults, this is an arduous undertaking spanning more than two decades. Can single-mother families really meet this responsibility? Many do; many others do not.

Then, consider alternative child-care support systems. There   11 is the woman's own family, which may be her surest recourse. But what if this, too, is a single-mother family? or siblings need attention? or husband and wife both work? A single mother's need may be great, but families have limits. Other child-caring facilities—day-care centers, schools, camps—are available, but they may be overwhelmed with the needs of materially and emotionally deprived children. Young believes more money and more personnel are the answer. But can a single mother (or father) act on the assumption that they are? And from where do these additional and abundant new resources come?

This brings us to the question of the common good and the   12 implicit social contract on which it rests. Young refers to the "state" and the "welfare state" as if these were entities capable of delivering goods and services at will. The United States is a democracy that eventually comes to reflect—if only imperfectly—the views of its citizens. Underlying at least some of the critical views of welfare—which Young thinks stingy—is a sense of quid pro quo: Social responsibility ought to encourage individual responsibility, not undermine or replace it. Is that unreasonable? The reservoirs of social responsibility that Young wants to draw upon will be swiftly depleted in a society whose citizens, women and men alike, do not habitually feel and exercise responsibility for themselves and their families.

Our social experiment in single motherhood over the last   13 twenty-five years is failing great numbers of women and children while corroding the bonds that tie men to familial responsibilities. In the name of reform, we should not take from them the admittedly meager resources provided by the current system. But neither can opinion makers, academics, or intellectual elites, feminist and otherwise, go on arguing that this situation is normal, and will be made even "more normal" by increased welfare payments and better support systems.

The communitarians have a slogan that we might all take to   14 heart: strong rights entail strong responsibilities—that goes for the right to bear and raise children.

Iris Marion Young

RESPONSE TO ELSHTAIN
AND STEINFELS

1   Jean Elshtain and Margaret Steinfels and I agree at least on one thing: too many children are poor, badly educated, at risk of being un- or underemployed, becoming substance dependent, criminal, or dead. What we disagree on are the solutions to these problems. Indeed, for all their strong language, I find neither offering any action. Calls for "secure institutions," restoring the "fabric of families," and living up to "strong responsibilities" are empty exhortations unless we specify just who should take responsibility to do what. The form of the rhetoric, moreover, leaves the impression that it's "they" and not "we" who have shirked responsibilities. This vague rhetoric seems to function as an excuse not only for doing nothing, but for not even thinking about what to do.

2   Elshtain and Steinfels both claim that "we" have undertaken a "social experiment" in single motherhood that has "failed." What odd phrasing! Who are "we" who designed such a cruel "experiment"? But, of course, no one designed the patchwork of plural family living arrangements in the United States today. In some respects, it has always been with us. There is no question, however, that the last two decades have seen more divorce and less marriage, though the rate of teenage pregnancy has not in fact increased.

3   What do Elshtain and Steinfels propose that we do about the lives of children? We should, in the words of Elshtain, "create situations that do best for children," that is, promote intact two-parent families. But how shall we do that? It is hard to believe that Elshtain and Steinfels would forbid divorce. Perhaps they favor making divorce more difficult, as some recommend, with a waiting period. This assumes that couples now rush into divorce without thinking, which is for the most part not so. Since divorce in the United States is already painful and costly, especially when there are children, making divorce more difficult is not likely to reduce appreciably the number of divorces.

4   And what shall we do about women who give birth without being married? Again, Elshtain and Steinfels would not force abortions, and I suspect that they would not force men to marry and live with the women they have impregnated. Would they recommend punishing women who give birth out of wedlock as a deterrent to others, or punishing fathers who do not marry them? This alternative is frighteningly close to the minds

of some people in the current debate, but it doesn't sound like Elshtain or Steinfels. Perhaps the carrot is a better idea: cash awards and medals for couples who get and stay married.

The most that Elshtain's and Steinfels's calls for restoration 5 of family values and responsibilities can mean practically is that public discussion promote the idea that intact two-parent families are better than other families; churches, schools, community groups, perhaps occasional television ad campaigns should send out this message. If such a society-wide educational campaign were implemented, it might indeed have some measurable impact on marriage and divorce rates, but I submit not very much. Thus I find Elshtain and Steinfels recommending virtually no social action to improve the lives of children.

Their insistence that although women have a "right" to par- 6 ent alone, their family lives are less valuable, moreover, is an affront to the worth and dignity of women who have tried marriage and found it wanting, are out on their own with their children, and are not interested in a new husband. Is a liberal society really to condemn these women, and if it does can it claim it is respecting them as equal citizens?

With the communitarian refrain, "strong rights entail strong 7 responsibilities," Steinfels suggests that it's about time the parents of those children did something, instead of sitting around waiting for handouts from the state. Elshtain, too, suggests a kind of quid pro quo: if we are to see investment in dilapidated neighborhoods, building of new schools and houses, we need secure social institutions and children who are compelled by their parents to stay in school. Once parents get off their duffs and build these institutions and discipline their children, then maybe we can talk about social support.

Are Elshtain and Steinfels really suggesting that single 8 mothers (not all of whom are poor) or poor people (not all of whom are in families with one parent) are, as a group, more irresponsible than other people? When middle-class, married couples refuse to support the local school system through a tax increase, complain about the quality of the schools, and enroll their kids in private school, are they behaving responsibly? When bank executives refuse to make loans to homeowners and businesses in poor neighborhoods and invest instead in risky tourism ventures on the other side of the country, are they behaving responsibly? I submit that irresponsibility is randomly distributed across race, class, gender, and family form, and I agree that there is far too much of it. But I also submit that most people most of the time are trying to meet their responsibilities to their families, friends, and coworkers. Less often, perhaps, do people think about and meet their responsibilities to distant strangers, but here responsibility increases with social privilege. We live in a time of a "responsibility deficit," some say, but I don't know the measure of responsibility levels. If the measure for single mothers is the income level of their children and the state of the schools, health clinics, and parks in the neighborhoods where they live, then this is a most unforgivable example of blaming the victims.

9   I completely agree with Elshtain that a vigorous and just society depends on the active participation of citizens in civic institutions of their own making, either not connected or only loosely connected to the state—neighborhood cleanup crews, parent councils in schools, volunteer social services, community arts and culture centers, cooperatives, political advocacy organizations. Despite communitarian complaints, I find no evidence that this sort of volunteer community organizing and service provision has waned in the United States in the last two decades. The heroic activities of organizations like the Industrial Areas Foundation or the Cabrini Green Tenants Association, which Elshtain applauds, are very often led by single mothers. Other such volunteer civic activities are led by the "forlorn bands of disconnected men" Elshtain imagines "roaming neighborhoods." Many men run athletic and cultural programs for children, or volunteer in tutoring centers, drug-prevention, and skills-building workshops. Despite what I regard as a healthy level of civic activity in the United States among people of both genders and all races and classes, there is certainly need for more. Public expenditures on street lighting and better transportation, along with private corporate decisions to reduce working hours without reducing pay, might enable more people to engage in more self-defined civic activities to improve their lives and their neighborhoods.

10   It is Elshtain and Steinfels who have their heads in the sand if they think that "private disinvestment" in the two-parent family has destroyed our schools and taken jobs away from the neighborhoods. American society has been severely damaged by three decades of private and public disinvestment in basic manufacturing, new and rehabilitated housing, bridges and rail lines, public education, adult retraining, and social services such as preventive health care and libraries. Volunteers can only barely begin to fill these gaping holes in the American dream.

11   Elshtain and Steinfels write as though I have called for more of the same tired old welfare policies in order to respond to the stresses of single motherhood and the economic disadvantage many children suffer. But my policy principles call for social *investment* (this word that Elshtain seems to find so hyper-

bolic), not draining handouts. Private industry should bear as much responsibility for this investment, moreover, as government does. Elshtain suggests that a condition for the creation of decent jobs is that children be motivated to stay in school. Only a little reflection should suggest that precisely the reverse is true. She accuses me of resuscitating a separate spheres ideology that would keep women at home caring for children, yet scoffs at my call for the massive increases in state support for child care that would enable more mothers—and fathers—to work outside the home and volunteer, knowing that their children were cared for. Steinfels suggests that parents cannot assume that more money and personnel will make quality child care more available and affordable. I do not understand why we cannot assume that it would help a great deal.

Neither Elshtain nor Steinfels mentions the single most important cause of the economic disadvantage in which children of many single mothers live: low wages for women's work. Coupled with the scarcity or expense of child care, low wages make it rational for many women to stay on welfare. Millions of single mothers nevertheless take jobs that enable them and their children only barely to escape poverty, if that. We do not have to accept as given the sex segregation of women's work that helps keep those wages low. It is simple sexism to decide that the only way to pull the children of single mothers out of poverty is to get them live-in fathers; it is also an unrealistic expectation, since male unemployment rates have been steadily rising in the last decade, and male wage rates have been falling. Public and private programs should be devoted to training women for higher wage jobs and raising the wages of traditionally female jobs. This is not a wasteful handout; it is justice. 12

Decent schools, housing, infrastructure, decent jobs for all able to work, wage equalization, and affordable child care can come about only through significant levels of public spending combined with both coerced and voluntary efforts of private capital. Elshtain and Steinfels throw up their hands at the absurdity of such a statement in these days "when state budgets are strapped, cutbacks are being ordered across the board." Are these facts of nature? If caring progressives treat them as such, then we are certainly doomed. Americans must engage in a serious and prolonged discussion of public and private spending and taxation, with the aim of shifting resources from waste and quick profits to investment in people and neighborhoods. 13

Topping the agenda for such discussion must be the fat public larder where we still see very little in the way of cutbacks: military spending. According to the Center for Defense Information, Clinton's 1994 budget contains $340 billion in 14 military spending, only $10 billion lower than Bush's 1993 budget. Compare this to $54 billion for education and social services, or $11 billion for community and regional development. In his State of the Union Address, Clinton vowed not to cut another dime from military spending. Surely this is madness. I wouldn't say that we should leave ourselves defenseless, or even unable to fight one imperialist war at a time; let's just take *half* of that $340 billion over the next five years and rechannel it into job-creating schools, day-care centers, new houses and apartments, steel, clean trains, parks, libraries, bridges and roads, and, yes, community organizing clearinghouses.

Andrew Sullivan
HERE COMES
THE GROOM

Andrew Sullivan (born 1963) is one of the leading commentators on gay, lesbian, and bisexual issues in the nation. Openly gay, devotedly Catholic, critical of certain aspects of the gay community, and outspokenly iconoclastic, he advocates the full intergration of gays, lesbians, and bisexuals into American life. In 1996, Sullivan disclosed that he was receiving treatment for AIDS. He entered graduate school at Harvard to study government and resigned from his position as an associate editor at New Republic, *which had published the argument that follows in 1989. In addition to many articles, he is the author of* Virtually Normal: An Argument about Homosexuality *(1995) and* Love Undetectable: Notes on Friendship, Sex, and Survival *(1999).*

Last month in New York, a court ruled that a gay lover had the   1
right to stay in his deceased partner's rent-control apartment
because the lover qualified as a member of the deceased's family. The ruling deftly annoyed almost everybody. Conservatives
saw judicial activism in favor of gay rent control: three reasons
to be appalled. Chastened liberals (such as the *New York Times*
editorial page), while endorsing the recognition of gay relationships, also worried about the abuse of already stretched
entitlements that the ruling threatened. What neither side
quite contemplated is that they both might be right, and that
the way to tackle the issue of unconventional relationships in

conventional society is to try something both more radical and more conservative than putting courts in the business of deciding what is and is not a family. That alternative is the legalization of civil gay marriage.

2   The New York rent-control case did not go anywhere near that far, which is the problem. The rent-control regulations merely stipulated that a "family" member had the right to remain in the apartment. The judge ruled that to all intents and purposes a gay lover is part of his lover's family, inasmuch as a "family" merely means an interwoven social life, emotional commitment, and some level of financial interdependence.

3   It's a principle now well established around the country. Several cities have "domestic partnership" laws, which allow relationships that do not fit into the category of heterosexual marriage to be registered with the city and qualify for benefits that up till now have been reserved for straight married couples. San Francisco, Berkeley, Madison, and Los Angeles all have legislation, as does the politically correct Washington, D.C., suburb, Takoma Park. In these cities, a variety of interpersonal arrangements qualify for health insurance, bereavement leave, insurance, annuity and pension rights, housing rights (such as rent-control apartments), adoption and inheritance rights. Eventually, according to gay lobby groups, the aim is to include federal income tax and veterans' benefits as well. A recent case even involved the right to use a family member's accumulated frequent-flier points. Gays are not the only beneficiaries; heterosexual "live-togethers" also qualify.

4   There's an argument, of course, that the current legal advantages extended to married people unfairly discriminate against people who've shaped their lives in less conventional arrangements. But it doesn't take a genius to see that enshrining in the law a vague principle like "domestic partnership" [DP] is an invitation to qualify at little personal cost for a vast array of entitlements otherwise kept crudely under control.

5   To be sure, potential DPs have to prove financial interdependence, shared living arrangements, and a commitment to mutual caring. But they don't need to have a sexual relationship or even closely mirror old-style marriage. In principle, an elderly woman and her live-in nurse could qualify. A couple of uneuphemistically confirmed bachelors could be DPs. So could two close college students, a pair of seminarians, or a couple of frat buddies. Left as it is, the concept of domestic partnership could open a Pandora's box of litigation and subjective judicial decision-making about who qualifies. You either are or are not married; it's not a complex question. Whether you are in a "domestic partnership" is not so clear.

More important, the concept of domestic partnership chips 6
away at the prestige of traditional relationships and undermines the priority we give them. This priority is not necessarily
a product of heterosexism. Consider heterosexual couples.
Society has good reason to extend legal advantages to heterosexuals who choose the formal sanction of marriage over simply living together. They make a deeper commitment to one another and to society; in exchange, society extends certain
benefits to them. Marriage provides an anchor, if an arbitrary
and weak one, in the chaos of sex and relationships to which
we are all prone. It provides a mechanism for emotional stability, economic security, and the healthy rearing of the next generation. We rig the law in its favor not because we disparage all
forms of relationship other than the nuclear family, but because we recognize that not to promote marriage would be to
ask too much of human virtue. In the context of the weakened
family's effect upon the poor, it might also invite social disintegration. One of the worst products of the New Right's "family
values" campaign is that its extremism and hatred of diversity
has disguised this more measured and more convincing case
for the importance of the marital bond.

The concept of domestic partnership ignores these concerns, 7
indeed directly attacks them. This is a pity, since one of its
most important objectives—providing some civil recognition
for gay relationships—is a noble cause and one completely
compatible with the defense of the family. But the decision to
go about it is not to undermine straight marriage; it is to legalize old-style marriage for gays.

The gay movement has ducked this issue primarily out of 8
fear of division. Much of the gay leadership clings to notions
of gay life as essentially outsider, antibourgeois, radical.
Marriage, for them, is co-optation into straight society. For the
Stonewall generation, it is hard to see how this vision of conflict will ever fundamentally change. But for many other
gays—my guess, a majority—while they don't deny the importance of rebellion 20 years ago and are grateful for what was
done, there's now the sense of a new opportunity. A need to
rebel has quietly ceded to a desire to belong. To be gay and to
be bourgeois no longer seems such an absurd proposition.
Certainly, since AIDS, to be gay and to be responsible has become a necessity.

Gay marriage squares several circles at the heart of the do- 9
mestic partnership debate. Unlike domestic partnership, it allows for recognition of gay relationships, while casting no as-
persions on traditional marriage. It merely asks that gays be

allowed to join in. Unlike domestic partnership, it doesn't open up avenues for heterosexuals to get benefits without the responsibilities of marriage, or a nightmare of definitional litigation. And unlike domestic partnership, it harnesses to an already established social convention the yearnings for stability and acceptance among a fast-maturing gay community.

10   Gay marriage also places more responsibilities upon gays: it says for the first time that gay relationships are not better or worse than straight relationships, and that the same is expected of them. And it's clear and dignified. There's a legal benefit to a clear, common symbol of commitment. There's also a personal benefit. One of the ironies of domestic partnership is that it's not only more complicated than marriage, it's more demanding, requiring an elaborate statement of intent to qualify. It amounts to a substantial invasion of privacy. Why, after all, should gays be required to prove commitment before they get married in a way we would never dream of asking of straights?

11   Legalizing gay marriage would offer homosexuals the same deal society now offers heterosexuals: general social approval and specific legal advantages in exchange for a deeper and harder-to-extract-yourself-from commitment to another human being. Like straight marriage, it would foster social cohesion, emotional security, and economic prudence. Since there's no reason gays should not be allowed to adopt or be foster parents, it could also help nurture children. And its introduction would not be some sort of radical break with social custom. As it has become more acceptable for gay people to acknowledge their loves publicly, more and more have committed themselves to one another for life in full view of their families and their friends. A law institutionalizing gay marriage would merely reinforce a healthy social trend. It would also, in the wake of AIDS, qualify as a genuine public health measure. Those conservatives who deplore promiscuity among some homosexuals should be among the first to support it. Burke could have written a powerful case for it.

12   The argument that gay marriage would subtly undermine the unique legitimacy of straight marriage is based upon a fallacy. For heterosexuals, straight marriage would remain the most significant—and only legal—social bond. Gay marriage could only delegitimize straight marriage if it were a real alternative to it, and this is clearly not true. To put it bluntly, there's precious little evidence that straights could be persuaded by any law to have sex with—let alone marry—someone of their own sex. The only possible effect of this sort would be to persuade gay men and women who force themselves into heterosexual marriage (often at appalling cost to themselves and

their families) to find a focus for their family instincts in a more personally positive environment. But this is clearly a plus, not a minus: gay marriage could both avoid a lot of tortured families and create the possibility for many happier ones. It is not, in short, a denial of family values. It's an extension of them.

Of course, some would claim that any legal recognition of homosexuality is a de facto attack upon heterosexuality. But even the most hardened conservatives recognize that gays are a permanent minority and aren't likely to go away. Since persecution is not an option in a civilized society, why not coax gays into traditional values rather than rail incoherently against them? 13

There's a less elaborate argument for gay marriage: it's good for gays. It provides role models for young gay people who, after the exhilaration of coming out, can easily lapse into short-term relationships and insecurity with no tangible goal in sight. My own guess is that most gays would embrace such a goal with as much (if not more) commitment as straights. Even in our society as it is, many lesbian relationships are virtual textbook cases of monogamous commitment. Legal gay marriage could also help bridge the gulf often found between gays and their parents. It could bring the essence of gay life—a gay couple—into the heart of the traditional straight family in a way the family can most understand and the gay offspring can most easily acknowledge. It could do as much to heal the gay-straight rift as any amount of gay rights legislation. 14

If these arguments sound socially conservative, that's no accident. It's one of the richest ironies of our society's blind spot toward gays that essentially conservative social goals should have the appearance of being so radical. But gay marriage is not a radical step. It avoids the mess of domestic partnership; it is humane; it is conservative in the best sense of the word. It's also practical. Given the fact that we already allow legal gay relationships, what possible social goal is advanced by framing the law to encourage those relationships to be unfaithful, undeveloped, and insecure? 15

Hadley Arkes
THE CLOSET STRAIGHT

Hadley Arkes (born 1944) is a professor of law at Amherst College in Massachusetts. His response (following) to the arguments of Andrew Sullivan originally appeared in 1993 in the National Review, *which maintains a conservative editorial stance. Arkes's essay counters not the previous essay in* Conversations *by Sullivan but a similar one, entitled "The Politics of Homosexuality," that Sullivan wrote in 1993.*

1   John Courtney Murray once observed that the atheist and the theist essentially agree in their understanding of the problem: The atheist does not mean to reject the existence of God only in Staten Island; he means to reject God universally, as a necessary truth. He accepts the same framework of reference, and he makes the same move to a transcendent standard of judgment. In a thoughtful, extended essay, Andrew Sullivan, the young, gay editor of *The New Republic,* has made a comparable concession for the advocate of "gay rights." For Sullivan has put into place, as the very ground and framework of his argument, a structure of understanding that must call into question any claims for the homosexual life as a rival good.

2   "The Politics of Homosexuality" confirms, at length, what anyone who has been with Andrew Sullivan can grasp within five minutes: he regards his erotic life as the center of his being, but he also conveys the most powerful need to seek that erotic fulfillment within a framework of domesticity, of the normal and the *natural.* The most persisting thread of anguish in the essay is the pain of awareness and reconciliation in his own family, with the recurring memory of his father weeping when Andrew declared, as he says, his sexuality. Sullivan reserves some of his most stinging words for the producers of a "queer" politics, aimed at "cultural subversion." That brand of politics would simply confirm the strangeness of homosexuals, and deepen the separation from their families. Ironically, says Sullivan, "queer" politics "broke off dialogue with the heterosexual families whose cooperation is needed in every generation, if gay children are to be accorded a modicum of dignity and hope."

3   The delicacy barely conceals that "cooperation is needed in every generation" precisely because "homosexual families" cannot produce "gay children." Gay children must come into being through the only kind of family that nature knows. Those who wish to preserve, say, a Jewish people, know that

Jews need to reproduce and raise their children as Jews. But what would be the comparable path of obligation for the person who is committed to the preservation of a "gay community"? Sullivan is convinced that there is something in our biology or chemistry that "determines" our sexuality, and in that case, the tendency to gay sex may be passed along to the next generation, as readily as temperament and allergies. The person who wishes to preserve, for the next generation, a gay community may be tempted then to render the ultimate service: For the good of the cause, he may cross the line and enter another domain of sex. But in crossing that line, he makes a decisive concession: implicitly, but unmistakably, he is compelled to acknowledge that homosexuality cannot even pretend to stand on the same plane as the way of life it would displace. We do not really find two kinds of "families" carrying out transactions with one another. But rather, we come to recognize again the primacy of "sexuality" in the strictest sense, the only sexuality that can produce "another generation."

It is evidently important to Sullivan to insist that homosexu- 4 ality is rooted in "nature," that it is determined for many people by something in their makeup quite beyond their control. He would wish to draw to his side a certain strand of natural law to suggest that anything so rooted in nature cannot be wrong. And yet, he falls there into an ancient mistake. As the great expounders of natural law explained, we do not make our way to the "natural" simply by generalizing upon the mixed record of our species: by that reckoning, incest and genocide would be in accord with natural law, since they seem to form an intractable part of the human experience. And even if we could show, say, that some of us carried a gene for "arson," that would not settle the moral question on arson. We might not be as quick to blame the bearers of these genes, but we would expect them to exert more self-control, and we would hardly waive our moral reservations about arson.

In a passage of searing candor, Sullivan acknowledges that 5 discrimination has not affected gays with the same kinds of deprivations that have been visited upon blacks. "[Gay] men and lesbians suffer no discernible communal economic deprivations and already operate at the highest levels of society." But when they call to their aid the levers of the law, they cultivate the sense of themselves as vulnerable and weak, in need of protection, and they perpetuate, among gays, the tendencies to self-doubt. They suggest that the things most needful to gays are in the hands of other people to confer. In the sweep of his own conviction, Sullivan would soar past those demands altogether. He would stop demanding laws, which confer, upon straight people, the franchise of confirming, or discounting, the worth of gays.

Love and Marriage

6 Except for one, notable thing. What Andrew Sullivan wants, most of all, is marriage. And he wants it for reasons that could not have been stated more powerfully by any heterosexual who had been raised, as Sullivan was, in the Catholic tradition and schooled in political philosophy. "[T]he apex of emotional life," says Sullivan, "is found in the marital bond." The erotic interest may seek out copulation, but the fulfillment of eros depends on the integrity of a bond woven of sentiment and confirmed by law. Marriage is more than a private contract; it is "the highest public recognition of our personal integrity." Its equivalent will not be supplied by a string of sensual nights, accumulated over many years of "living together." The very existence of marriage "premises the core of our emotional development. It is the architectonic institution that frames our emotional life."

7 No one could doubt for a moment: as much as any of the "guys" in the Damon Runyon stories, the man who wrote those lines is headed, irresistibly, for marriage. What he craves—homosexual marriage—would indeed require the approval conferred by law. It would also require a benediction conferred by straight people, who would have to consent to that vast, new modeling of our laws. That project will not be undertaken readily, and it may not be undertaken at all. Still, there is something, rooted in the nature of Andrew Sullivan, that must need marriage.

8 But as Mona Charen pointed out, in an encounter with Sullivan at the National Review Institute conference this winter, it is not marriage that domesticates men; it is women. Left to themselves, these forked creatures follow a way of life that George Gilder once recounted in its precise, chilling measures: bachelors were 22 times more likely than married men to be committed to hospitals for mental disease (and 10 times more likely to suffer chronic diseases of all kinds). Single men had nearly double the mortality rate of married men and 3 times the mortality rate of single women. Divorced men were 3 times more likely than divorced women to commit suicide or die by murder, and they were 6 times more likely to die of heart disease.

9 We have ample reason by now to doubt that the bipeds described in these figures are likely to be tamed to a sudden civility

if they are merely arranged, in sets of two or three, in the same house. I had the chance to see my own younger son, settled with three of his closest friends in a townhouse in Georgetown during his college years. The labors of the kitchen and the household were divided with a concern for domestic order, and the abrasions of living together were softened by the ties of friendship. And yet, no one, entering that house, could doubt for a moment that he was in a camp occupied for a while by young males, with their hormones flowing.

This is not to deny, of course, that men may truly love men,   10 or commit themselves to a life of steady friendship. But many of us have continued to wonder just why any of these relations would be enhanced in any way by adding to them the ingredients of penetration—or marriage. The purpose of this alliance, after all, could not be the generation of children, and a marriage would not be needed then as the stable framework for welcoming and sheltering children. For gays, the ceremony of marriage could have the function of proclaiming to the world an exclusive love, a special dedication, which comes along with a solemn promise to forgo all other, competing loves. In short, it would draw its power from the romance of monogamy. But is that the vision that drives the movement for "gay rights"? An excruciating yearning for monogamy?

That may indeed be Andrew Sullivan's own yearning, but his   11 position is already marking him as a curious figure in the camp of gay activists. When Sullivan commends the ideal of marriage for gays, he would seem to be pleading merely for the inclusion of gay "couples" in an institution that is indeed confined to pairs, of *adults,* in monogamous unions. But that is not exactly the vision of gay sex.

For many activists and connoisseurs, Sullivan would repre-   12 sent a rather wimpish, constricted view of the world they would open to themselves through sexual liberation. After all, the permissions for this new sexual freedom have been cast to that amorphous formula of "sexual orientation": the demand of gay rights is that we should recede from casting moral judgments on the way that people find their pleasure in engagements they regard as "sexual." In its strange abstraction, "sexual orientation" could take in sex with animals or the steamier versions of sado-masochism. The devotees of S&M were much in evidence during the recent march in Washington, but we may put aside for a moment these interests, to consider others which are even more exotic yet. There is, for example, the North American Man-Boy Love Association, a contingent of gay activists who identify themselves, unashamedly, as pedophiles. They insist that nothing in their "sexual orientation" should disqualify them to work as professional counselors, say, in the schools of New York, and to counsel young boys. And since they respect themselves, they will not hold back from commending their own way of life to their young charges. If there is to be gay marriage, would it be confined then only to adults? And if men are inclined to a life of multiple partners, why should marriage be confined to two persons? Why indeed should the notion of gay marriage be scaled down to fit the notions held by Andrew Sullivan?

Sullivan's Dilemma

13 The sources of anguish run even deeper here than Sullivan may suspect, for his dilemma may be crystallized in this way: If he would preserve the traditional understanding of marriage and monogamy, he would not speak for much of a constituency among gays. But if the notion of "marriage" were enlarged and redefined—if it could take in a plurality of people and shifting combinations—it could hardly be the kind of marriage that Sullivan devoutly wishes as "the apex of emotional life" and "the highest public recognition of our personal integrity."

14 In traditional marriage, the understanding of monogamy was originally tied to the "natural teleology" of the body—to the recognition that only two people, no more and no fewer, can generate children. To that understanding of a union, or a "marriage," the alliance of two men would offer such an implausible want of resemblance that it would appear almost as a mocking burlesque. It would be rather like confounding, as Lincoln used to say, a "horse chestnut" and a "chestnut horse." The mockery would be avoided if the notion of marriage could be opened, or broadened, to accommodate the varieties of sexual experience. The most notable accommodation would be the acceptance of several partners, and the change could be readily reckoned precisely because it would hardly be novel: the proposal for gay marriage would compel us to look again— to look anew with eyes unclouded by prejudice—to the ancient appeal of polygamy. After all, there would be an Equal Protection problem now: we could scarcely confine this new "marital" arrangement only to members of one gender. But then, once the arrangement is opened simply to "consenting adults," on what ground would we object to the mature couplings of aunts and nephews, or even fathers and daughters— couplings that show a remarkable persistence in our own age, even against the barriers of law and sentiment that have been cast up over centuries? All kinds of questions, once placed in a

merciful repose, may reasonably be opened again. They become live issues once we are willing to ponder that simple question, Why should marriage be confined, after all, to couples, and to pairs drawn from different sexes?

That question, if it comes to be treated as open and problematic, will not readily be closed, or not at least on the terms that Andrew Sullivan seeks. The melancholy news then is this: We cannot deliver to him what he wants without introducing, into our laws, notions that must surely undercut the rationale and the justification for marriage. The marriage that he wants, he cannot practicably have; but in seeking it, he runs the risk of weakening even further the opinion that sustains marriage as "the architectonic institution that frames our emotional life."   15

But for marriage so understood, Sullivan does not seem to command a large following, or even a substantial interest, among gays. New York City must surely contain one of the largest concentrations of accomplished, successful gay men. Since March, New York has allowed the registering of "domestic partners," and by the first of June, 822 couples had come forth to register. By the unofficial estimate of people in the bureau, those couples have been just about evenly distributed between gays and lesbians. Four hundred gay couples would not be a trivial number, but in a city like New York, it does rather suggest that the craving for this public recognition may not be widely diffused. If all of the couples registered under the new law were collected in Yankee Stadium, they would hardly be noticeable in the crowd. Their numbers would not exactly suggest that there is a strong political constituency out there for gay marriage.   16

Unintended Consequence

In making then his own, heartfelt case for marriage, Andrew Sullivan is swept well past the interests and enthusiasms that mark most other people who now make up the "gay community." And he may earnestly put this question to himself: In the sweep of his own convictions, in the sentiment that draws him, powerfully, to marriage, has he not in fact swept past, and discarded, the rationales that sustain the homosexual life?   17

What comes through the writing, finally, is a man who finds his eros in domesticity, who will find pleasure in driving his own children to their soccer games on Saturday mornings. He will explain again to his friends that we must "cooperate" with heterosexual families; that if we would protect gay children we must raise them, and even produce them. There may be winks all around, and the sense that he is doing something for "the   18 cause." But as Andrew Sullivan appreciates, "queer" politics always seeks to take "shame-abandonment to a thrilling conclusion." And what could be more exquisite and subtle than this reversal upon a reversal?: A man lives a highly visible public life as a homosexual, but he enters a marriage, which is taken as a kind of charade, and he is content to abet the jest with knowing glances. But the secret that dare not speak its name is that he really is, after all, a domesticated man, settled in his marriage. As a writer and a man, Andrew Sullivan is committed to an understanding of political life that finds its ground in nature. And he takes, as the core of our civic life, marriage and the laws that sustain marriage. For all of that, we here, composed, as we are, of eros and of dust, love him.

Ralph Pomeroy

A TARDY EPITHALAMIUM
FOR E. AND N.

New Yorker Ralph Pomeroy (1926–1998) wrote the following poem in 1969, about the time of the famous Stonewall riot that jumpstarted the gay rights movement. It was later collected in The Penguin Book of Homosexual Verse *(1983). An epithalamium is a wedding poem, so Pomeroy is remembering an evening that he once spent with a committed gay couple. Do you think the speaker in the poem is endorsing or rejecting the idea of gay marriage? Or is he ambivalent about it?*

1   You are proof that it can happen
    and that it should.
    There is as little hysteria
    attached to your household
5   as to that of the most 'normal' couple.

    Because you are outlaw lovers though
    I must salute you only with initials.
    I hate this.

    After eight years you still seem examples of clarity:
10   clear about looking at one another,
    clear about getting up in the morning,
    clear about people in relation to you,

clear about me when I arrive for dinner,
drink,
end up drunk.   15

All three writers, whenever we get together
we carp about careers and such.
We do this for some time, eating delicious
meals meanwhile, 'keeping it down' because of
the nosey neighbors (who express their   20
contempt by making love or fighting
with their shades up).

At regular intervals we seem—like deer
perked-up to the sense of something—
to stop and see the joke of it all,   25
and laughter comes barging in and takes over.

I, sooner or later, grow jealous of you
and begin to realize that I have to get up and go,
alone,
while you get to stay with each other.   30

This makes me blue and close to tearful
and defiant even. So I kiss you both gingerly
and head resolutely for the subway,
or resolutely for the bars.

Grateful for you   35
all the same.

Anna Quindlen

EVAN'S TWO MOMS

Anna Quindlen (born 1955) for a number of years wrote a widely praised, syndicated column for the New York Times *and many other newspapers. She won a Pulitzer Prize for commentary in 1992 and she now contributes an essay to* Newsweek *every other week. Her work has been collected in several books, including* Thinking Out Loud: On the Personal, the Political, the Public, and the Private *(1993). The following essay comes from that collection. (For another essay by Quindlen, see page 627.)*

1   Evan has two moms. This is no big thing. Evan has always had two moms—in his school file, on his emergency forms, with his friends. "Ooooh, Evan, you're lucky," they sometimes say. "You have two moms." It sounds like a sitcom, but until last week it was emotional truth without legal bulwark. That was when a judge in New York approved the adoption of a six-year-old boy by his biological mother's lesbian partner. Evan. Evan's mom. Evan's other mom. A kid, a psychologist, a pediatrician. A family.

2   The matter of Evan's two moms is one in a series of events over the last year that lead to certain conclusions. A Minnesota appeals court granted guardianship of a woman left a quadriplegic in a car accident to her lesbian lover, the culmination of a seven-year battle in which the injured woman's parents did everything possible to negate the partnership between the two. A lawyer in Georgia had her job offer withdrawn after the state attorney general found out that she and her lesbian lover were planning a marriage ceremony; she's brought suit. The computer company Lotus announced that the gay partners of employees would be eligible for the same benefits as spouses.

3   Add to these public events the private struggles, the couples who go from lawyer to lawyer to approximate legal protections their straight counterparts take for granted, the AIDS survivors who find themselves shut out of their partners' dying days by biological family members and shut out of their apartments by leases with a single name on the dotted line, and one solution is obvious.

4   Gay marriage is a radical notion for straight people and a conservative notion for gay ones. After years of being sledgehammered by society, some gay men and lesbian women are deeply suspicious of participating in an institution that seems to have "straight world" written all over it.

5   But the rads of twenty years ago, straight and gay alike, have other things on their minds today. Family is one, and the linchpin of family has commonly been a loving commitment between two adults. When same-sex couples set out to make that commitment, they discover that they are at a disadvantage: No joint tax returns. No health insurance coverage for an uninsured partner. No survivor's benefits from Social Security. None of the automatic rights, privileges, and responsibilities society attaches to a marriage contract. In Madison, Wisconsin, a couple who applied at the Y with their kids for a family membership were turned down because both were women. It's one of those small things that can make you feel small.

6   Some took marriage statutes that refer to "two persons" at their word and applied for a license. The results were court decisions that quoted the Bible and embraced circular argument:

marriage is by definition the union of a man and a woman because that is how we've defined it.

No religion should be forced to marry anyone in violation of 7
its tenets, although ironically it is now only in religious ceremonies that gay people can marry, performed by clergy who find the blessing of two who love each other no sin. But there is no secular reason that we should take a patchwork approach of corporate, governmental, and legal steps to guarantee what can be done simply, economically, conclusively, and inclusively with the words "I do."

"Fran and I chose to get married for the same reasons that any 8
two people do," said the lawyer who was fired in Georgia. "We fell in love; we wanted to spend our lives together." Pretty simple.

Consider the case of *Loving* v. *Virginia,* aptly named. At the 9
time, sixteen states had laws that barred interracial marriage, relying on natural law, that amorphous grab bag for justifying prejudice. Sounding a little like God throwing Adam and Eve out of paradise, the trial judge suspended the one-year sentence of Richard Loving, who was white, and his wife, Mildred, who was black, provided they got out of the State of Virginia.

In 1967 the Supreme Court found such laws to be unconsti- 10
tutional. Only twenty-five years ago and it was a crime for a black woman to marry a white man. Perhaps twenty-five years from now we will find it just as incredible that two people of the same sex were not entitled to legally commit themselves to each other. Love and commitment are rare enough; it seems absurd to thwart them in any guise.

Barbara Findlen

IS MARRIAGE THE ANSWER?

Barbara Findlen is the former executive editor of Ms. *magazine, the famous feminist publication that carried the following article in the May/June 1995 issue.*

In December 1990, Ninia Baehr and Genora Dancel applied for 1
a marriage license at their local health department office in Honolulu. When the license was denied because they are both women, they—along with two other same-sex couples who

applied for marriage licenses on the same day—sued the state of Hawaii on the grounds of discrimination. The three couples—two lesbian and one gay male—were well prepared: before applying for the licenses, they'd already determined that they might have a shot at changing Hawaii's marriage laws.

2   And indeed, by May 1993, the Hawaii Supreme Court ruled that prohibiting members of the same sex from marrying constitutes sex discrimination and is therefore a violation of the state constitution, which includes an equal rights amendment. The supreme court then proceeded to send the case back to a lower court, ordering the state to show a "compelling interest" in maintaining the discrimination. Remarkably, most observers believe that, barring a change in the makeup of the court or some other extreme circumstance, the couples will triumph when the case is finally decided sometime within the next 18 months.

3   The case is significant, not just for the future of gay marriage, but also for the fate of domestic partnership agreements, which give benefits such as health insurance coverage to unmarried couples. Some activists are wondering, for example, what will become of the dozens of domestic partnership policies that have sprung up over the last decade, many of which also benefit unmarried heterosexual couples. If gay marriage were to become legal, entities that currently offer these policies might decide that since anyone can marry, benefits should be offered only to spouses. Domestic partnership policies would therefore be seen as unnecessary. Many of those who favor domestic partnership policies over marriage espouse the arguably radical notion that *no* rights or benefits should be based on marriage. Other critics would even prefer to see marriage, with its patriarchal trappings, abolished altogether.

4   While some people might view lesbian and gay marriage as a radical development because it would at last put homosexual relationships on a par with heterosexual ones, domestic partnership advocates view it as conservative because it upholds the basic primacy of marriage as the foundation of the family and marginalizes people who are outside that unit. Notes Paula L. Ettelbrick, a legislative counsel at New York's Empire State Pride Agenda: "The marriage campaign has moved our community to a more conservative, middle-of-the-road political perspective. It has taken people out of the broader, social justice view of family."

5   But there are different agendas among those who advocate domestic partnership, acknowledges Matt Coles, the director of the ACLU Lesbian and Gay Rights Project and coauthor of one of the first domestic partnership policies ever proposed in

the U.S. (for the city of San Francisco in 1980). Some view domestic partnership as a straightforward equal-pay-for-equal-work issue: employment benefits that are offered to employees' legal spouses should be offered to partners of unmarried employees. For others, it's a way station en route to lesbian and gay marriage. Still others see it as a way to begin to fundamentally redefine the legal meaning of "family," thus undermining the power of the patriarchal nuclear family.

Melinda Paras, executive director of the National Gay and   6
Lesbian Task Force (NGLTF), is aiming for the latter. "Part of our struggle," she says, "is to fight for a broader definition of families. Domestic partners shouldn't have to be gay or lesbian. They shouldn't have to be having sex. They can be two adults sharing a home and sharing commitment, responsible to each other."

Currently, about 35 municipalities and scores of private   7
companies, educational institutions, and nonprofit organizations offer some kind of policy that bestows benefits on unmarried cohabiting couples—gay *and* straight. There are two kinds of domestic partnership policies—those offered by the private sector, which generally do not provide benefits to unmarried heterosexuals, and municipal policies created by city governments, which cover both same-sex and opposite-sex partners. A typical municipal policy might well define domestic partners in terms similar to those of Paras. In Madison, Wisconsin, for example, they can be any two unrelated adults "in a relationship of mutual support, caring, and commitment." In Seattle, the partners must "have a close and personal relationship" and share "basic living expenses." In many cities, more straight couples than gay couples register as domestic partners. Municipalities establish a registry, and city employees who file are usually given a certificate that validates their domestic partnership and often provides access to spousal equivalent benefits (health insurance, bereavement leave, and other benefits granted to married employees). People who don't work for the city may also receive a certificate. Though organizations in the private sector, such as auto clubs or health clubs, may honor this municipal certificate as a basis for providing benefits, it's strictly optional, and the benefits offered by the city to nonemployees are limited—perhaps access to family memberships at a museum or a gym, or the right to hospital or jail visitation.

Private sector policies tend to be much narrower than mu-   8
nicipal policies. Most apply only to same-sex partners. The major benefit is usually health insurance, and some policies even stop short of that, offering only bereavement or family care

leave, use of recreational facilities, access to married faculty or student housing—benefits that cost the institution little.

9   The rationale behind most private sector plans is: lesbian and gay employees can't marry, so as a matter of workplace equity, they should have access to benefits they would have if they could marry. Nancy Polikoff, a law professor whose work has focused on lesbian and gay families, cites the policy at her own institution, American University, which applies only to same-sex domestic partners. "What happens when there's gay and lesbian marriage?" she says. "That's the end of domestic partnership benefits. We will be told, 'Get married.' What does that say about the notion that we can choose not to get married?"

10   What about a corporation like Levi Strauss & Co., which offers benefits to unmarried heterosexual partners? It's hard to predict whether policies like that will disappear, but it seems likely that the possibility of same-sex marriage would remove a lot of the impetus behind the domestic partnership movement. Although the policies often benefit straight people, the initiative has mostly come from lesbians and gay men, who don't have access to marriage rights.

11   "My big fear," says Ettelbrick, "is that if gay people were allowed to marry tomorrow, I know that we would lose a substantial part of our community that is working on domestic partner benefits. The point is that neither straight people nor gay people should have to get married in order to have some very basic protections for the families that they've chosen. I don't think we have a unified sense of social reform anymore. We have a piece-by-piece approach—we'll make change where we can. We no longer have bigger picture items on our agendas."

12   Domestic partnership, like many other issues that now concern this country, is curiously tied to health care. The word "benefit," after all, is often synonymous with health insurance. And why, many ask, is health insurance coverage tied to marital, couple, *or* employment status? "If universal health care were available, no one would be forced to say, 'I want to be able to get married to take advantage of my partner's health insurance benefits,'" says Polikoff. "What we ought to do is let every employee designate a person to receive co-benefits. That person could be your sexual partner, best friend, aunt, or sister. Why are we making people's sexual partners more important than others with whom they share their lives? This kind of arrangement would be my way station to uncoupling all of these benefits from marriage and creating a world in which the things that are now considered components of marriage become social entitlements or can be designated by individuals."

Adds Robin Kane, NGLTF's communications director: "We   13
could wait for universal health care coverage to be enacted by
Congress. We could wait for the Hawaii marriage ruling to
come down and then for every state to battle out whether or
not they'll recognize it. But in the meantime, there are people
who are actually getting health insurance for their partners
through domestic partner benefits."

But domestic partnership policies don't hold a candle to the   14
entitlements that come with marriage. It is already possible to
approximate some of the rights granted automatically to married people—inheritance can be addressed through wills, the
right to make health care decisions through durable powers of
attorney. Compare these with the rights that come with a marriage license and cannot be exercised by unmarried couples,
no matter where they live or what agreements they have made:
the right to joint parenting, through birth or adoption; the
right to file joint income tax returns; legal immigration and
residency for partners from other countries; benefits such as
annuities, pensions, and Social Security for surviving spouses;
wrongful death benefits for surviving partners; immunity from
having to testify in court against a spouse.

Jane, a health club manager, and Beth, a teacher in subur-   15
ban New York (not their real names), know the consequences
of not having those rights. Five years ago, Jane gave birth to a
daughter conceived via insemination by an anonymous donor.
When a married couple have a baby in this way, the husband is
automatically declared the father. Beth's application to legally
adopt their daughter was denied on the grounds that the couple, who have been together for 18 years, were not married.
"I'm considered her mother by our community, day care,
school, and families," says Beth, "but I have no legal rights as
her mother."

Whether or not lesbians and gay men should fight for the   16
right to marry has been a subject of debate in the gay community for years. In 1989, the lesbian and gay magazine *Outlook*
published opposing articles, "Since When Is Marriage a Path
to Liberation?" by Paula Ettelbrick, and "Why Gay People
Should Seek the Right To Marry," by Thomas B. Stoddard.
Both authors are lawyers who were working for the Lambda
Legal Defense and Education Fund at the time. "Marriage runs
contrary to two of the primary goals of the lesbian and gay
movement: the affirmation of gay identity and culture, and the
validation of many forms of relationships," argued Ettelbrick.
Answered Stoddard: "The issue is not the desirability of marriage, but rather the desirability of the right to marry."

17   Even Beth and Jane aren't sure they would exercise that right. "It's for heterosexuals," says Jane. "Our union doesn't need that ceremony. We would only do it for legal protection."

18   Feminists have long criticized the institution of marriage as a place of oppression, danger, and drudgery for women. Nineteenth-century feminists protested that a woman's legal identity literally disappeared upon marriage. Even in 1969, a New York City organization called the Feminists declared: "All the discriminatory practices against women are patterned and rationalized by this slavery-like practice. We can't destroy the inequities between men and women until we destroy marriage." These days the uneasiness is due to marriage's power as the singular definer of family, a reinforcer of sex roles, and an institution of heterosexual privilege. Karen Lindsey has been thinking about different forms of family for more than 15 years. Her 1981 book, *Friends as Family*, begins, "The traditional family isn't working," and goes on to explore workplace families, "honorary kin," and chosen families. "In my ideal world, there would be no such thing as marriage," she says today. "What there would be is individuals choosing to live together on whatever terms meet their needs, and then appropriate legal connections to address those needs."

19   "People say that there are all these goodies that go with being married and why shouldn't gay people get to have them," agrees Polikoff. "My vision is one in which the goodies are not tied to marriage."

20   As feminists, Ninia Baehr and Genora Dancel, two of the Hawaii plaintiffs, are well aware of these arguments. But for them, the decision to marry was an emotional, not a political, one. Baehr, who was the codirector of the women's center at the University of Hawaii when the suit was filed, says: "If I had sat down and planned my career as a feminist years ago, I would never have said, 'The most important thing I can do is legalize marriage for lesbian and gay people.' But the reality is that when I met Genora, I thought, 'My God, she's the one that I've been dreaming about.' I wanted to get married. I wanted to be able to say at the end of my life that I had loved someone really well for a long time."

21   Hawaii state legislators meanwhile are doing whatever they can to keep Baehr and Dancel and the other two couples from legally tying the knot. Alarmed at the prospect of their state being the first to allow gay marriage, they passed a law last year that explicitly defines marriage as being between a man and a woman. However, this legislation will presumably be subject to the same "compelling interest" requirement as the previous policy, so it's unlikely that the law will change the outcome of the

case. A few legislators have proposed amending the state constitution to exclude same-sex marriage—the one sure way around
the state supreme court—but these proposals have failed.

Although the Hawaii court ruling would apply only to mar-   22
riages performed in that state, the decision could spark legal
chaos all over the country. Lesbian and gay couples will likely
flock to Hawaii to marry, then return to their home states and
try to file joint tax returns, sign up for spousal health insurance coverage, or adopt children together. Currently every
state recognizes marriages performed in other states. Couples
who are denied recognition of their legal same-sex marriages
granted in Hawaii will have grounds to sue their home states.

"There will be litigation in many states for years to come,"   23
says Evan Wolfson, cocounsel for the three Hawaii couples
and director of the Lambda Legal Defense and Education
Fund's Marriage Project. The dozens of expected cases could
implicate even the federal government, which relies on the
states to determine who is married for purposes of taxes,
Social Security benefits, immigration, and other matters. And
though all marriage laws are state laws, the question potentially could be settled by the U.S. Supreme Court. If that happened, lawyers for the couples would likely base their arguments on the provision of the U.S. Constitution that requires
states to give "full faith and credit" to the lawful marriages of
other states.

And these other states are keeping an anxious eye on   24
Hawaii. The state legislature of Utah has passed legislation
that would refuse recognition of any same-sex marriage performed in another state. South Dakota also tried, but failed, to
pass such a law.

The ACLU's Matt Coles thinks one significant result of the   25
pending Hawaii ruling will be a proliferation of domestic partnership protections for lesbians and gay men as states try—by
offering spousal equivalent benefits—to avoid the need to recognize gay marriage.

NGLTF's Paras says: "I think we will end up with marriage   26
and domestic partnership as simultaneously existing legal con-
structs. Marriage will be a huge battle that will mostly be lost
for a long time. In the meantime, domestic partnership practices are expanding and will become a much larger body of law
and policy. By the time equality finally gets won universally,
we'll be in a whole other place about the definition of family,
and gay marriage may become almost irrelevant."

Tom Toles
THE TROUBLE
WITH GAYS

Tom Toles's sharpwitted cartoons regularly appear in the con-servative U.S. News & World Report *as well as in many news-papers. He created this one in June 2000. (For another Toles cartoon, see page 370.)*

V

CIVIL LIBERTIES AND CIVIL RIGHTS

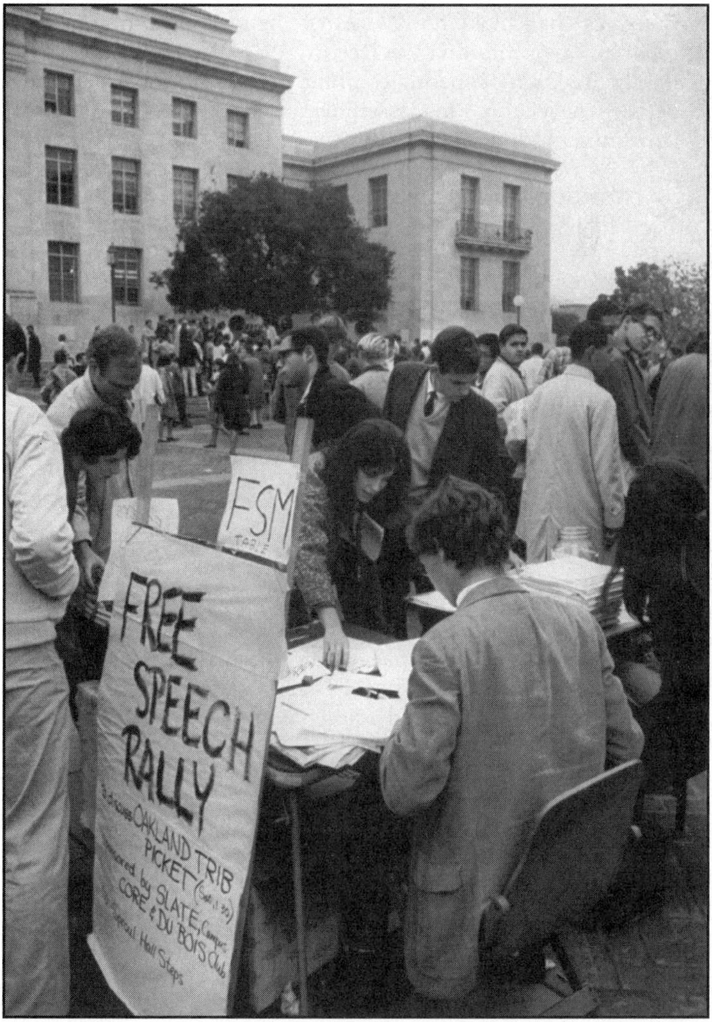

Introduction

A basic premise of *Conversations* is that writing typically emerges from other writing. As a demonstration of that premise, consider the very large body of writing that has emerged from some very basic texts in our political history. Consider, for instance, the words of the First Amendment to the Constitution:

> Congress shall make no law respecting an establishment of religion, or prohibiting the free exercise thereof; or abridging the freedom of speech, or of the press; or the right of the people peaceably to assemble, and to petition the Government for a redress of grievances.

Or consider section one of the Fourteenth Amendment, ratified in 1868:

> All persons born or naturalized in the United States, and subject to the jurisdiction thereof, are citizens of the United States and of the State wherein they reside. No State shall make or enforce any law which shall abridge the privileges or immunities of citizens of the United States; nor shall any State deprive any person of life, liberty, or property, without due process of law; nor deny to any person within its jurisdiction the equal protection of the laws.

Or this fragment from the Declaration of Independence:

> We hold these Truths to be self-evident, that all Men are created equal, that they are endowed by their Creator with certain inalienable Rights, that among these are Life, Liberty, and the Pursuit of Happiness. That to secure these rights, Governments are instituted among Men. . . .

The readings in Part Five explore some of the implications of these seminal passages.

Two sets of readings on the issue of censorship are included: one (on pornography) that picks up gender and language concerns from Part Two; and another (the Napster case) that looks forward to Internet issues that are discussed in Part Seven of this book.

Is pornography harmful? Should it be censored or restricted according to the guidelines of the so-called

Brandenburg test (named for a late-1960s court case, *Brandenburg* v. *Ohio*), which permits restrictions on expression "if speech will result in lawless action"? Speaking for the affirmative, many women (as well as men) contend that pornography does indeed have harmful effects, that pornography provides a dangerous "theory" on how to treat women and rape or other forms of misogyny, the "practice." But other people see pornography as neutral in its effects or contend that the First Amendment protects all varieties of speech and writing from censorship. Did the framers of the Constitution intend to protect free speech and a free press in an absolute sense (as Hugo Black and William Douglas argued in a 1957 Supreme Court decision)? Or were the framers speaking only of political speech and writing (as the seven other Supreme Court justices agreed in that same 1957 case)? Is it indeed constitutional to restrict pornography? (After all, we do restrict libel, and we ban cigarette ads on TV and ads aimed at minors, on the grounds of their harmful effects and apolitical content.) And just what is pornography, anyway? Can it be defined in a way that makes restrictions practical, or would such definitions and restrictions undermine artistic and political freedom? The issue of pornography makes for strange bedfellows; it is an issue about which liberals and conservatives disagree among themselves, and it is an issue that has divided feminists. In fact, the argument among feminists is represented in this section by Susan Brownmiller and Andrea Dworkin, who find themselves arguing with Nadine Strossen.

Liberals and conservatives also break ranks over whether it would be wise to restrict Napster, the technology developed by Shawn Fanning that enables people to download music through the Internet. Is Napster (and its imitators) a form of piracy that threatens artistic freedom and expression? Will it bankrupt recording companies? Is Napster (and its imitators) guilty of copyright infringement? If everyone is free to copy, will booksellers, authors, and newspapers be ruined? Or is Napster an expression of democracy, no more illegal than a photocopying machine? This section of *Conversations* considers questions like these, particuarly through a literal conversation from the pages of *Yahoo-Life*. While Napster is gone, the controversy about it continues as other companies here and abroad keep testing the legality of on-line music sharing.

The conflict between the individual and society, so apparent in discussions of censorship, is central to culture in the United States because we value both the dignity of the private individual and the importance of public institutions sanctioned through the democratic process. Faced with the dilemma of paying taxes to support a popular war, which he disagreed with, Henry David Thoreau proposed civil disobedience—a private act of personal conscience against "the tyranny of the majority." Later in history, Mahatma Gandhi and Martin Luther King Jr. refined civil disobedience into an effective tactic for achieving public justice and political equality. Were they right to do so? What is civil disobedience anyway? Is it a legitimate political tool or an invitation to anarchy that would destroy the principle of democratic rule? What should people do when "higher laws" put them in conflict with majority rule? What else can a democratic society do except be ruled by a majority? Can such a majority be a "tyranny," or is it the resistance to legitimate, democratic authority that is arrogant and tyrannical? Could civil disobedience even exist in a truly tyrannical society, one without a free press and trial by jury, one in which political minorities disappear in the middle of the night? The selections in this civil disobedience section articulate and debate the question of the legitimacy of civil disobedience, and they also offer a critical context for understanding a central document of civil disobedience and the U.S. civil rights movement: King's "Letter from Birmingham Jail."

Civil disobedience has been a common tactic since the mid-1950s, especially in connection with campaigns to expand the civil rights of African Americans and women. Civil disobedience has also been employed at times by pro-life groups eager to see the practice of abortion restricted in the United States; that is only one indication that the recognition of the right to abortion is still inspiring heated discussion in our society. Since the Supreme Court in the *Roe* v. *Wade* decision of 1973 legalized abortions performed in the first three months of a pregnancy, a pitched battle has been fought between those absolutely committed to upholding the Supreme Court position and those just as absolutely committed to overturning it. One camp, which sees the developing fetus as only a potential human being, is protective of women's right to privacy and personal freedom; the other camp, which sees the fetus as a human being with the rights of a human being, supports various restrictions on the right to abortion, if not an outright reversal of *Roe v. Wade.* In both camps, many people are convinced that only one side or the other can prevail in the abortion debate— that "victory" without substantial compromise can be achieved through the ballot box, rallies, and Supreme Court appointments. Those who seek absolute victory on either side are often so committed to their positions that they are unwilling to participate in reasoned discussions. They often produce more heat than light on the subject.

But other people are convinced that a resolution of the issue of abortion is not just possible but essential. Some pro-choice advocates understand abortion as a morally cloudy act and recognize that the Supreme Court has already placed some restrictions on abortion (i.e., abortion is restricted to the first months of pregnancy). On the other side, many pro-life advocates are confronting the apparent fact that our Constitution permits abortion, whether they like it or not, and are pursuing efforts to persuade people to avoid abortion not because it is illegal but because better contraceptive choices are usually available, if people would only seek them out. Members of both camps, in short, are seeking continuing discussion, reasoned exchange, and mutual respect; and they tend to hold out a hope for negotiated consensus on the matter—incremental progress toward national agreement. When does a fetus become a person? What circumstances justify abortion? Are there ways of reducing abortions and at the same time protecting women's right to privacy (e.g., through improved methods of contraception)? Are any additional restrictions on abortions (*Roe v. Wade* restricts abortions to the first three months of pregnancy) sensible? Can those restrictions protect the rights of everyone involved, even as those rights are also somewhat compromised? These matters are confronted in the readings in the section on abortion.

Five other readings (and a cartoon) follow on another matter of civil rights. In the past decade, members of another minority group—homosexuals—have clamored for additional civil rights, often quite publicly through marches and protests and other highly publicized tactics marshaled by organizations such as Act Up and Queer Nation. Should homosexuals be permitted to serve openly in the military? Should they be protected by fair housing and fair employment practices? Should gay couples be permitted to claim the rights enjoyed by married couples, such as the right to adopt children or share health benefits? For that matter, should they be permitted to marry? Does the AIDS epidemic have implications for civil rights in this country? Those last two questions are taken up in greater detail in the section on same-sex marriage in Part Four, Family Matters, and in the section on combating AIDS in Part Seven, Science and Society (for AIDS is an issue that is certainly not limited to the gay community).

No doubt questions like the ones posed in the preceding paragraphs are being discussed on every campus in the United States this year.

I. Non-Legislative Recommendation

The Commission believes that much of the "problem" regard- 5
ing materials which depict explicit sexual activity stems from
the inability or reluctance of people in our society to be open
and direct in dealing with sexual matters. . . .

The Commission believes that accurate, appropriate sex in- 6
formation provided openly and directly through legitimate
channels and from reliable sources in healthy contexts can
compete successfully with potentially distorted, warped, inac-
curate, and unreliable information about clandestine, illegitimate sources; and it believes that the attitudes and orientations toward sex produced by the open communication of
appropriate sex information from reliable sources through legitimate channels will be normal and healthy, providing a solid
foundation for the basic institutions of our society.

The Commission, therefore, . . . *recommends that a massive* 7
sex education effort be launched. . . . The Commission feels that
such a sex education program would provide a powerful positive approach to the problems of obscenity and pornography.
By providing accurate and reliable sex information through legitimate sources, it would reduce interest in and dependence
upon clandestine and less legitimate sources. By providing
healthy attitudes and orientations toward sexual relationships,
it would provide better protection for the individual against
distorted and warped ideas he may encounter regarding sex.
By providing greater ease in talking about sexual matters in
appropriate contexts, the shock and offensiveness of encounters with sex would be reduced. . . .

II. Legislative Recommendation

The Commission recommends that federal, state, and local legis- 8
lation prohibiting the sale, exhibition, or distribution of sexual
materials to consenting adults should be repealed. . . .

Our conclusion is based upon the following considerations:

1. Extensive empirical investigation, both by the Commission 9
and by others, provides no evidence that exposure to or use of
explicit sexual materials plays a significant role in causation of
social or individual harms such as crime, delinquency, sexual
or nonsexual deviancy or severe emotional disturbances. . . .
Empirical investigation thus supports the opinion of a substantial majority of persons professionally engaged in the

treatment of deviancy, delinquency and antisocial behavior, that exposure to sexually explicit materials has no harmful causal role in these areas. Studies show that a number of factors, such as disorganized family relationships and unfavorable peer influences, are intimately related to harmful sexual behavior or adverse character development. Exposure to sexually explicit materials, however, cannot be counted as among these determinative factors.

10   2. On the positive side, explicit sexual materials are sought as a source of entertainment and information by substantial numbers of American adults. At times, these materials also appear to serve to increase and facilitate constructive communication about sexual matters within marriage. The most frequent purchaser of explicit sexual materials is a college-educated, married male, in his thirties or forties, who is of above average socio-economic status. Even where materials are legally available to them, young adults and older adolescents do not constitute an important portion of the purchasers of such materials.

11   3. Society's attempts to legislate for adults in the area of obscenity have not been successful. Present laws prohibiting the consensual sale or distribution of explicit sexual materials to adults are extremely unsatisfactory in their practical application. The Constitution permits material to be deemed "obscene" for adults only if, as a whole, it appeals to the "prurient" interest of the average person, is "patently offensive" in light of "community standards," and lacks "redeeming social value." These vague and highly subjective aesthetic, psychological and moral tests do not provide meaningful guidance for law enforcement officials, juries or courts. As a result, law is inconsistently and sometimes erroneously applied and the distinctions made by courts between prohibited and permissible materials often appear indefensible. Errors in the application of the law and uncertainty about its scope also cause interference with the communication of constitutionally protected materials.

12   4. Public opinion in America does not support the imposition of legal prohibitions upon the right of adults to read or see explicit sexual materials. While a minority of Americans favors such prohibitions, a majority of the American people presently are of the view that adults should be legally able to read or see explicit sexual materials if they wish to do so.

13   5. The lack of consensus among Americans concerning whether explicit sexual materials should be available to adults in our society, and the significant number of adults who wish to have access to such materials, pose serious problems regarding the enforcement of legal prohibitions upon adults, even aside from the vagueness and subjectivity of present law.

Consistent enforcement of even the clearest prohibitions upon consensual adult exposure to explicit sexual materials would require the expenditure of considerable law enforcement resources. In the absence of a persuasive demonstration of damage flowing from consensual exposure to such materials, there seems no justification for thus adding to the overwhelming tasks already placed upon the law enforcement system. Inconsistent enforcement of prohibitions, on the other hand, invites discriminatory action based upon considerations not directly relevant to the policy of the law. The latter alternative also breeds public disrespect for the legal process.

6. The foregoing considerations take on an added signifi- 14
cance because of the fact that adult obscenity laws deal in the realm of speech and communication. Americans deeply value the right of each individual to determine for himself what books he wishes to read and what pictures or films he wishes to see. Our traditions of free speech and press also value and protect the right of writers, publishers, and booksellers to serve the diverse interests of the public. The spirit and letter of our Constitution tell us that government should not seek to interfere with these rights unless a clear threat of harm makes that course imperative. Moreover, the possibility of the misuse of general obscenity statutes prohibiting distributions of books and films to adults constitutes a continuing threat to the free communication of ideas among Americans—one of the most important foundations of our liberties.

7. In reaching its recommendation that government should 15
not seek to prohibit consensual distributions of sexual materials to adults, the Commission discussed several arguments which are often advanced in support of such legislation. The Commission carefully considered the view that adult legislation should be retained in order to aid in the protection of young persons from exposure to explicit sexual materials. We do not believe that the objective of protecting youth may justifiably be achieved at the expense of denying adults materials of their choice. It seems to us wholly inappropriate to adjust the level of adult communication to that considered suitable for children. Indeed, the Supreme Court has unanimously held that adult legislation premised on this basis is a clearly unconstitutional interference with liberty. . . .

8. The Commission has also taken cognizance of the concern 16
of many people that the lawful distribution of explicit sexual materials to adults may have a deleterious effect upon the individual morality of American citizens and upon the moral climate in America as a whole. This concern appears to flow from a belief that exposure to explicit materials may cause moral

confusion which, in turn, may induce antisocial or criminal behavior. As noted above, the Commission has found no evidence
to support such a contention. Nor is there evidence that exposure to explicit sexual materials adversely affects character or
moral attitudes regarding sex and sexual conduct. . . .

President's Commission on Obscenity and Pornography
MINORITY REPORT

Overview

1   The Commission's majority report is a Magna Carta for the
pornographer. . . . The fundamental "finding" on which the entire report is based is: that "empirical research" has come up
with "no reliable evidence to indicate that exposure to explicit
sexual materials plays a significant role in the causation of
delinquent or criminal behavior among youth or adults." The
inference from this statement, i.e., pornography is harmless, is
not only insupportable on the slanted evidence presented; it is
preposterous. How isolate one factor and say it causes or does
not cause criminal behavior? How determine that one book or
one film caused one man to commit rape or murder? A man's
entire life goes into one criminal act. No one factor can be said
to have caused that act.

2   The Commission has deliberately and carefully avoided
coming to grips with the basic underlying issue. The government interest in regulating pornography has always related
primarily to the prevention of moral corruption and *not* to prevention of overt criminal acts and conduct, or the protection of
persons from being shocked and/or offended. The basic question is whether and to what extent society may establish and
maintain certain moral standards. If it is conceded that society
has a legitimate concern in maintaining moral standards, it
follows logically that government has a legitimate interest in at
least attempting to protect such standards against any source
which threatens them. . . .

3   Sex education, recommended so strongly by the majority, is
the panacea for those who advocate license in media. The report suggests sex education, with a plaint for the dearth of instructors and materials. It notes that three schools have used

"hard-core pornography" in training potential instructors. The report does not answer the question that comes to mind immediately: Will these instructors not bring the hard-core pornography into the grammar schools? Many other questions are left unanswered: How assure that the instructor's moral or ethical code (or lack of same) will not be communicated to children? Shouldn't parents, not children, be the recipients of sex education courses?

Children cannot grow in love if they are trained with pornog- 4 raphy. Pornography is loveless; it degrades the human being, reduces him to the level of animal. And if this Commission majority's recommendations are heeded, there will be a glut of pornography for teachers and children.

In contrast to the Commission report's amazing statement 5 that public opinion in America does not support the imposition of legal prohibitions upon the consensual distribution of pornography to adults, we find, as a result of public hearings conducted by two of the undersigned in eight cities throughout the country, that the majority of the American people favor tighter controls. Twenty-six out of twenty-seven witnesses at the hearing in New York City expressed concern and asked for remedial measures. Witnesses were a cross section of the community, ranging from members of the judiciary to members of women's clubs. This pattern was repeated in the cities of New Orleans, Indianapolis, Chicago, Salt Lake City, San Francisco, Washington, D.C., and Buffalo. . . . Additionally, law enforcement officers testifying at the Hill-Link hearings were unanimous in declaring that the problem of obscenity and pornography is a serious one. . . . We point also to the results of a Gallup poll, published in the summer of 1969. Eighty-five out of every 100 adults interviewed said they favored stricter state and local laws dealing with pornography sent through the mails, and 76 of every 100 wanted stricter laws on the sort of magazines and newspapers available on newsstands. . . .

Some have argued that because sex crimes have apparently 6 declined in Denmark while the volume of pornography has increased, we need not be concerned about the potential effect in our country of this kind of material (because, essentially, of Denmark's benign experience). However two considerations must be noted. First we are a different culture with a greater commitment to the Judeo-Christian tradition; and secondly, we are actually only a year or so behind Denmark in the distribution and sale of pornography. Hardcore written pornography can be purchased anywhere in the U.S. now. Hardcore still pictures and movies can now be purchased over the counter in some cities. Anything can be purchased through the mails. And in a few cities people can attend hard-core pornographic movies. About the only thing we don't have, which Denmark has, are live sex shows. What is most relevant are sex crime statistics in this country, not Denmark. . . :

Reported Rapes (verified)
    Up 116% 1960–69 (absolute increase)
    Up 93% 1960–69 (controlled for Pop. Growth)

Rape Arrests
    Up 56.6% all ages 1960–69
    Up 85.9% males under 18 1960–69

7   However, it should be stated that conclusively proving causal relationships among social science type variables is extremely difficult if not impossible. Among adults whose life histories have included much exposure to pornography it is nearly impossible to disentangle the literally hundreds of causal threads or chains that contributed to their later adjustment or maladjustment. Because of the extreme complexity of the problem and the uniqueness of the human experience it is doubtful that we will ever have absolutely convincing scientific proof that pornography is or isn't harmful. And the issue isn't restricted to, "Does pornography cause or contribute to sex crimes?" The issue has to do with how pornography affects or influences the individual in his total relationship to members of the same as well as opposite sex, children and adults, with all of its ramifications.

Susan Brownmiller

LET'S PUT PORNOGRAPHY BACK IN THE CLOSET

Susan Brownmiller is a journalist, novelist, women's rights activist, and a founder of Women against Pornography. Her book Against Our Will: Men, Women, and Rape, *published in 1975, articulates a position on pornography that has been developed by later feminists. The following essay originally appeared in* Newsday, *a Long Island newspaper, in 1979 and a year later in* Take Back the Night, *a collection of essays against pornography.*

Free speech is one of the great foundations on which our democracy rests. I am old enough to remember the Hollywood Ten, the screenwriters who went to jail in the late 1940s because they refused to testify before a congressional committee about their political affiliations. They tried to use the First Amendment as a defense, but they went to jail because in those days there were few civil liberties lawyers around who cared to champion the First Amendment right to free speech, when the speech concerned the Communist Party.   1

The Hollywood Ten were correct in claiming the First Amendment. Its high purpose is the protection of unpopular ideas and political dissent. In the dark, cold days of the 1950s, few civil libertarians were willing to declare themselves First Amendment absolutists. But in the brighter, though frantic, days of the 1960s, the principle of protecting unpopular political speech was gradually strengthened.   2

It is fair to say now that the battle has largely been won. Even the American Nazi Party has found itself the beneficiary of the dedicated, tireless work of the American Civil Liberties Union. But—and please notice the quotation marks coming up—"To equate the free and robust exchange of ideas and political debate with commercial exploitation of obscene material demeans the grand conception of the First Amendment and its high purposes in the historic struggle for freedom. It is a misuse of the great guarantees of free speech and free press."   3

I didn't say that, although I wish I had, for I think the words are thrilling. Chief Justice Warren Burger said it in 1973, in the United States Supreme Court's majority opinion in *Miller* v. *California.* During the same decades that the right to political free speech was being strengthened in the courts, the nation's obscenity laws also were undergoing extensive revision.   4

It's amazing to recall that in 1934 the question of whether James Joyce's *Ulysses* should be banned as pornographic actually went before the Court. The battle to protect *Ulysses* as a work of literature with redeeming social value was won. In later decades, Henry Miller's *Tropic* books, *Lady Chatterley's Lover* and the *Memoirs of Fanny Hill* also were adjudged not obscene. These decisions have been important to me. As the author of *Against Our Will,* a study of the history of rape that does contain explicit sexual material, I shudder to think how my book would have fared if James Joyce, D. H. Lawrence and Henry Miller hadn't gone before me.   5

6   I am not a fan of *Chatterley* or the *Tropic* books, I should quickly mention. They are not to my literary taste, nor do I think they represent female sexuality with any degree of accuracy. But I would hardly suggest that we ban them. Such a suggestion wouldn't get very far anyway. The battle to protect these books is ancient history. Time does march on, quite methodically. What, then, is unlawfully obscene, and what does the First Amendment have to do with it?

7   In the Miller case of 1973 (not Henry Miller, by the way, but a porn distributor who sent unsolicited stuff through the mails), the Court came up with new guidelines that it hoped would strengthen obscenity laws by giving more power to the states. What it did in actuality was throw everything into confusion. It set up a three-part test by which materials can be adjudged obscene. The materials are obscene if they depict patently offensive, hard-core sexual conduct; lack serious scientific, literary, artistic or political value; and appeal to the prurient interest of an average person—as measured by contemporary community standards.

8   "Patently offensive," "prurient interest" and "hard-core" are indeed words to conjure with. "Contemporary community standards" are what we're trying to redefine. The feminist objection to pornography is not based on prurience, which the dictionary defines as lustful, itching desire. We are not opposed to sex and desire, with or without the itch, and we certainly believe that explicit sexual material has its place in literature, art, science and education. Here we part company rather swiftly with old-line conservatives who don't want sex education in the high schools, for example.

9   No, the feminist objection to pornography is based on our belief that pornography represents hatred of women, that pornography's intent is to humiliate, degrade and dehumanize the female body for the purpose of erotic stimulation and pleasure. We are unalterably opposed to the presentation of the female body being stripped, bound, raped, tortured, mutilated and murdered in the name of commercial entertainment and free speech.

10   These images, which are standard pornographic fare, have nothing to do with the hallowed right of political dissent. They have everything to do with the creation of a cultural climate in which a rapist feels he is merely giving in to a normal urge and a woman is encouraged to believe that sexual masochism is healthy, liberated fun. Justice Potter Stewart once said about hard-core pornography, "You know it when you see it," and that certainly used to be true. In the good old days, pornography

looked awful. It was cheap and sleazy, and there was no mistaking it for art.

Nowadays, since the porn industry has become a multimillion dollar business, visual technology has been employed in its service. Pornographic movies are skillfully filmed and edited, pornographic still shots using the newest tenets of good design artfully grace the covers of *Hustler, Penthouse* and *Playboy,* and the public—and the courts—are sadly confused. 11

The Supreme Court neglected to define "hard-core" in the Miller decision. This was a mistake. If "hard-core" refers only to explicit sexual intercourse, then that isn't good enough. When women or children or men—no matter how artfully— are shown tortured or terrorized in the service of sex, that's obscene. And "patently offensive," I would hope, to our "contemporary community standards." 12

Justice William O. Douglas wrote in his dissent to the Miller case that no one is "compelled to look." This is hardly true. To buy a paper at the corner newsstand is to subject oneself to a forcible immersion in pornography, to be demeaned by an array of dehumanized, chopped-up parts of the female anatomy, packaged like cuts of meat at the supermarket. I happen to like my body and I work hard at the gym to keep it in good shape, but I am embarrassed for my body and for the bodies of all women when I see the fragmented parts of us so frivolously, and so flagrantly, displayed. 13

Some constitutional theorists (Justice Douglas was one) have maintained that any obscenity law is a serious abridgement of free speech. Others (and Justice Earl Warren was one) have maintained that the First Amendment was never intended to protect obscenity. We live quite compatibly with a host of free-speech abridgements. There are restraints against false and misleading advertising or statements—shouting "fire" without cause in a crowded movie theater, etc.—that do not threaten, but strengthen, our societal values. Restrictions on the public display of pornography belong in this category. 14

The distinction between permission to publish and permission to display publicly is an essential one and one which I think consonant with First Amendment principles. Justice Burger's words which I quoted above support this without question. We are not saying "Smash the presses" or "Ban the bad ones," but simply "Get the stuff out of our sight." Let the legislatures decide—using realistic and humane contemporary community standards—what can be displayed and what cannot. The courts, after all, will be the final arbiters. 15

John Irving

PORNOGRAPHY
AND THE NEW PURITANS

If you saw the films The World According to Garp *or* The Cider
House Rules, *you have had some experience with the work of
John Irving (born 1942), for he is the author of the novels on
which both films were based as well as seven other novels. He
contributed the following essay to the* New York Times Book
Review *in March 1992. Notice that a response to the article,
also printed in the* Times Book Review, *is reprinted right after it.*

1   These are censorial times. I refer to the pornography victims'
compensation bill, now under consideration by the Senate
Judiciary Committee—that same bunch of wise men who dis-
patched such clearheaded, objective jurisprudence in the
Clarence Thomas hearings. I can't wait to see what they're going to do with this maladroit proposal. The bill would encourage victims of sexual crimes to bring civil suits against publishers and distributors of material that is "obscene or constitutes
child pornography"—*if* they can prove that the material was "a
substantial cause of the offense," *and if* the publisher or distributor should have "foreseen" that such material created an
"unreasonable risk of such a crime." If this bill passes, it will
be the first piece of legislation to give credence to the un-
proven theory that sexually explicit material actually *causes*
sexual crimes.

2   At the risk of sounding old-fashioned, I'm still pretty sure
that rape and child molestation predate erotic books and
pornographic magazines and X-rated videocassettes. I also remember the report of the two-year, $2 million President's
Commission on Obscenity and Pornography (1970), which
concluded there was "no reliable evidence . . . that exposure to
explicit sexual material plays a significant role in the causation
of delinquent or criminal sexual behavior." In 1986, not satisfied with that conclusion, the Meese commission on pornography and the Surgeon General's conference on pornography
also failed to establish such a link. Now, here they go again.

3   This time, it's Republican Senators Mitch McConnell of
Kentucky, Charles Grassley of Iowa and Strom Thurmond of
South Carolina; I can't help wondering if they read much.
Their charmless bill is a grave mistake for several reasons; for
starters, it's morally reprehensible to shift the responsibility for

any sexual crime onto a third party—namely, *away* from the actual perpetrator.

And then, of course, there's the matter of the bill running 4
counter to the spirit of the First Amendment of the United States Constitution; this bill is a piece of back-door censorship, plain and simple. Moreover, since the laws on obscenity differ from state to state, and no elucidation of the meaning of obscenity is presented in the bill, how are the publishers or distributors to know in advance if their material is actionable or not? It is my understanding, therefore, that the true intent of the bill is to make the actual creators of this material think very conservatively—that is, when their imaginations turn to sex and violence.

I recall that I received a lot of unfriendly mail in connection 5
with a somewhat explicit scene in my novel *The World According to Garp*, wherein a selfish young man loses part of his anatomy while enjoying oral sex in a car. (I suppose I've always had a fear of rear-end collisions.) But thinking back about that particular hate mail, I don't recall a single letter from a young woman saying that she intended to rush out and *do* this to someone; and in the 14 years since that novel's publication, in more than 35 foreign languages, no one who actually *has done* this to someone has written to thank me for giving her the idea. Boy, am I lucky!

In a brilliant article on the Op-Ed page of *The New York* 6
Times, Teller, of those marvelous magicians Penn & Teller, had this to say about the pornography victims' compensation bill: "The advocates of this bill seem to think that if we stop showing rape in movies people will stop committing it in real life. Anthropologists call this 'magical thinking.' It's the same impulse that makes people stick pins in voodoo dolls, hoping to cripple an enemy. It feels logical, but it does not work." (For those of you who've seen these two magicians and are wondering which is Penn and which is Teller, Teller is the one who never talks. He *writes* very well, however.) "It's a death knell for creativity, too," Teller writes. "Start punishing make-believe, and those gifted with imagination will stop sharing it." He adds, "We will enter an intellectual era even more insipid than the one we live in."

Now *there's* a scary idea! I remember when the film version 7
of Günter Grass's novel *The Tin Drum* was banned in Canada. I always assumed it was the eel scene that offended the censors, but I don't know. In those days, a little naked sex—in the conventional position—was permissible, but unpleasant suggestiveness with eels was clearly going too far. But now, in the light of this proposed pornography victims' compensation bill,

is there any evidence to suggest that there have been *fewer* hellish incidents of women being force-fed eels in Canada than in those countries where the film was available? Somehow, I doubt it. I know that they're out there—those guys who want to force-feed eels to women—but I suspect they're going to do what they're going to do, unaided by books or films. The point is: let's do something about *them,* instead of trying to control what they read or see.

8   It dismays me how some of my feminist friends are hot to ban pornography. I'm sorry that they have such short memories. It wasn't very long ago when a book as innocent and valuable as *Our Bodies, Ourselves* was being banned by school boards and public libraries across the country. The idea of this good book was that women should have access to detailed information about their bodies and their health, yet the so-called feminist ideology behind the book was thought to be subversive; indeed, it was (at that time) deplored. But many writers and writers' organizations (like PEN) wrote letters to those school boards and those public libraries. I can't speak to the overall effectiveness of these letters in regard to reinstating the book, but I'm aware that some of the letters worked; I wrote several of those letters. Now here are some of my old friends, telling me that attitudes toward rape and child molestation can be changed only if we remove the offensive *ideas.* Once again, it's ideology that's being banned. And although the movement to ban pornography is especially self-righteous, it looks like blacklisting to me.

9   Fascism has enjoyed many name changes, but it usually amounts to banning something you dislike and can't control. Take abortion, for example. I think groups should have to apply for names; if the Right to Life people had asked me, I'd have told them to find a more fitting label for themselves. It's morally inconsistent to manifest such concern for the poor fetus in a society that shows absolutely no pity for the poor child after it's born.

10   I'm also not so sure that these so-called Right to Lifers are as fired up about those fetuses as they say. I suspect what really makes them sore is the idea of women having sex and somehow not having to *pay* for it—pay in the sense of suffering all the way through an unwanted pregnancy. I believe this is part of the loathing for promiscuity that has always fueled those Americans who feel that a life of common decency is slipping from their controlling grasp. This notion is reflected in the unrealistic hope of those wishful thinkers who tell us that sexual abstinence is an alternative to wearing a condom. But I say how about *carrying* a condom, just in case you're moved to *not* abstain?

No one is coercing women into having abortions, but the   11
Right to Lifers want to coerce women into having babies; that's
why the pro-choice people are well named. It's unfortunate,
however, that a few of my pro-choice friends think that the
pornography victims' compensation bill is a good idea. I guess
that they're really not entirely pro-choice. They want the
choice to reproduce or not, but they *don't* want too broad a
choice of things to read and see; they know what *they* want to
read and see, and they expect other people to be content with
what they want. This sounds like a Right to Life idea to me.

Most feminist groups, despite their vital advocacy of full en-   12
forcement of laws against violence to women and children,
seem opposed to Senate Bill 1521. As of this writing, both the
National Organization for Women in New York State and in
California have written to the Senate Judiciary Committee in
opposition to the bill, although the Los Angeles chapter of
NOW states that it has "no position." I admit it is perverse of
me even to imagine what Tammy Bruce thinks about the
pornography victims' compensation bill; I hope Ms. Bruce is
not such a loose cannon as she appears, but she has me worried. Ms. Bruce is president of L.A. NOW, and she has lately
distinguished herself with two counts of knee-jerk overreac-
tion. Most recently, she found the Academy of Motion Picture
Arts and Sciences to be guilty of an "obvious exhibition of sexism" in not nominating Barbra Streisand for an Oscar for best
director. Well, maybe. Ms. Streisand's other talents have not
been entirely overlooked; I meekly submit that the academy
might have found *The Prince of Tides* lacking in directorial
merit—it wouldn't be the first I've heard of such criticism. (Ms.
Bruce says the L.A. chapter received "unrelenting calls" from
NOW members who were riled up at the perceived sexism.)

Most readers will remember Tammy Bruce for jumping all   13
over that nasty novel by Bret Easton Ellis. To refresh our memories: Simon & Schuster decided at the 11th hour not to publish *American Psycho* after concluding that its grisly content
was in "questionable taste." Now please don't get excited and
think I'm going to call that censorship; that was merely a
breach of contract. And besides, Simon & Schuster has a right
to its own opinion of what questionable taste is. *People* magazine tells us that Judith Regan, a vice president and senior editor at Simon & Schuster, recently had a book idea, which she
pitched to Madonna. "My idea was for her to write a book of
her sexual fantasies, her thoughts, the meanderings of her
erotic mind," Ms. Regan said. The pity is, Madonna hasn't delivered. And according to Mitchell Fink, author of the Insider
column for *People*, "Warner Books confirmed it is talking about

a book—no word on what kind—with Madonna." I don't know Madonna, but maybe she thought the Simon & Schuster book idea was in questionable taste. Simon & Schuster, clearly, subscribes to more than one opinion of what questionable taste *is*.

14   But only two days after Mr. Ellis's book was dropped by Simon & Schuster, Sonny Mehta, president of Alfred A. Knopf and Vintage Books, bought *American Psycho*, which was published in March 1991. Prior to the novel's publication, Ms. Bruce called for a boycott of all Knopf and Vintage titles—except for books by feminist authors, naturally—until *American Psycho* was withdrawn from publication (it wasn't), or until the end of 1991. To the charge of censorship, Ms. Bruce declared that she was *not* engaged in it; she sure fooled me.

15   But Ms. Bruce wasn't alone in declaring what *wasn't* censorship, nor was she alone in her passion; she not only condemned Mr. Ellis's novel—she condemned its availability. And not only the book itself *but its availability* were severely taken to task in the very pages in which I now write. In December 1990—three months *before American Psycho* was published, and at the urging of *The Book Review*—Roger Rosenblatt settled Mr. Ellis's moral hash in a piece of writing prissy enough to please Jesse Helms. According to Mr. Rosenblatt, Jesse Helms has never engaged in censorship, either. For those of us who remain improperly educated in regard to what censorship actually *is*, Mr. Rosenblatt offers a blanket definition. "Censorship is when a government burns your manuscript, smashes your presses and throws you in jail," he says.

16   Well, as much as I may identify with Mr. Rosenblatt's literary taste, I'm of the opinion that there are a few forms of censorship more subtle than that, and Mr. Rosenblatt has engaged in one of them. If you slam a book when it's published, that's called book reviewing, but if you write about a book three months in advance of its publication and your conclusion is "don't buy it," your intentions are more censorial than critical.

17   And it *is* censorship when the writer of such perceived trash is not held *as* accountable as the book's publisher; the pressure that was brought to bear on Mr. Mehta was totally censorial. *The Book Review* is at its most righteous in abusing Mr. Mehta, who is described as "clearly as hungry for a killing as Patrick Bateman." (For those of you who don't know Mr. Ellis's book, Patrick Bateman is the main character and a serial killer.) Even as reliable a fellow as the editorial director of *Publisher's Weekly*, John F. Baker, described *American Psycho* as a book that "does transcend the boundaries of what is acceptable in mainstream publishing."

It's the very idea of making or keeping publishing "acceptable" that gives *me* the shivers, because that's the same idea that lurks behind the pornography victims' compensation bill—making the *publisher* (not the perpetrator of the crime or the writer of the pornography) responsible for what's "acceptable." If you want to bash Bret Easton Ellis for what he's written, go ahead and bash him. But when you presume to tell Sonny Mehta, or any other publisher, what he can or can't—or should or shouldn't—*publish*, that's when you've stepped into dangerous territory. In fact, that's when you're knee-deep in blacklisting, and you ought to know better—all of you.

18

Mr. Rosenblatt himself actually says, "No one argues that a publishing house hasn't the right to print what it wants. We fight for that right. But not everything is a right. At some point, someone in authority somewhere has to look at Mr. Ellis's rat and call the exterminator." Now this is interesting, and perhaps worse than telling Sonny Mehta what he should or shouldn't publish—because that's exactly what Mr. Rosenblatt *is* doing while he's *saying* that he isn't.

19

Do we remember that tangent of the McCarran-Walter Act of 1952, that finally defunct business about ideological exclusion? That was when we kept someone from coming into our country because we perceived that the person had *ideas* that were in conflict with the "acceptable" ideas of our country. Under this act of exclusion, writers as distinguished as Graham Greene and Gabriel Garcia Márquez were kept out of the United States. Well, when we attack what a publisher has the right to publish, we are simply applying the old ideological exclusion act at home. Of all people, those of us in the idea business should know better than that.

20

As for the pornography victims' compensation bill, the vote in the Senate Judiciary Committee will be close. As of this writing, seven senators have publicly indicated their support of the bill; they need only one more vote to pass the bill out of committee. Friends at PEN tell me that the committee has received a lot of letters from women saying that support of the bill would in some way "make up for" the committee's mishandling of the Clarence Thomas hearings. Some women are putting the decision to support Justice Thomas alongside the decision to find William Kennedy Smith innocent of rape; these women think that a really strong antipornography bill will make up for what they perceive to be the miscarriage of justice in both cases.

21

The logic of this thinking is more than a little staggering. What would these women think if lots of men were to write the committee and say that because Mike Tyson has been found

22

guilty of rape, what we need is *more* pornography to make up for what's happened to Iron Mike? This would make a lot of sense, wouldn't it?

23   I conclude that these are not only censorial times; these are stupid times. However, there is some hope that opposition to Senate Bill 1521 is mounting. The committee met on March 12 but the members didn't vote on the bill. Discussion was brief, yet encouraging. Colorado Senator Hank Brown told his colleagues that there are serious problems with the legislation; he should be congratulated for his courageous decision to oppose the other Republicans on the committee, but he should also be encouraged not to accept any compromise proposal. Ohio Senator Howard Metzenbaum suggested that imposing third-party liability on producers and distributors of books, magazines, movies and recordings raises the question of whether the bill shouldn't be amended to cover the firearms and liquor industries as well.

24   It remains to be seen if the committee members will resist the temptation to *fix* the troubled bill. I hope they will understand that the bill cannot be fixed because it is based on an erroneous premise—namely, that publishers or distributors should be held liable for the acts of criminals. But what is important for us to recognize, even if this lame bill is amended out of existence or flat-out defeated, is that *new* antipornography legislation will be proposed.

25   Do we remember Nancy Reagan's advice to would-be drug users? ("Just say no.") As applied to drug use, Mrs. Reagan's advice is feeble in the extreme. But writers and other members of the literary community *should* just say no to censorship in any and every form. Of course, it will always be the most grotesque example of child pornography that will be waved in front of our eyes by the Good Taste Police. If we're opposed to censorship, they will say, are we in favor of filth like this?

26   No; we are not in favor of child pornography if we say no to censorship. If we disapprove of reinstating public hangings, that doesn't mean that we want all the murderers to be set free. No writer or publisher or *reader* should accept censorship in any form; fundamental to our freedom of expression is that each of us has a right to decide what is obscene and what isn't.

27   But lest you think I'm being paranoid about the iniquities and viciousness of our times, I'd like you to read a description of Puritan times. It was written in 1837—more than 150 years ago—and it describes a scene in a Puritan community in Massachusetts that you must imagine taking place more than 350 years ago. This is from a short story by Nathaniel Hawthorne called "Endicott and the Red Cross," which itself

was written more than 10 years before Hawthorne wrote *The Scarlet Letter*. This little story contains the germ of the idea for that famous novel about a woman condemned by Puritan justice to wear the letter A on her breast. But Hawthorne, obviously, had been thinking about the iniquities and viciousness of early New England morality for many years.

Please remember, as you read what Nathaniel Hawthorne 28 thought of the Puritans, that the Puritans are not dead and gone. We have many new Puritans in our country today; they are as dangerous to freedom of expression as the old Puritans ever were. An especially sad thing is, a few of these new Puritans are formerly liberal-thinking feminists.

"In close vicinity to the sacred edifice [the meeting-house] 29 appeared that important engine of Puritanic authority, the whipping-post—with the soil around it well trodden by the feet of evil doers, who had there been disciplined. At one corner of the meeting-house was the pillory, and at the other the stocks; ... the head of an Episcopalian and suspected Catholic was grotesquely incased in the former machine; while a fellow-criminal, who had boisterously quaffed a health to the king, was confined by the legs in the latter. Side by side, on the meeting-house steps, stood a male and a female figure. The man was a tall, lean, haggard personification of fanaticism, bearing on his breast this label,—A WANTON GOSPELLER,— which betokened that he had dared to give interpretations of Holy Writ unsanctioned by the infallible judgment of the civil and religious rulers. His aspect showed no lack of zeal ... even at the stake. The woman wore a cleft stick on her tongue, in appropriate retribution for having wagged that unruly member against the elders of the church; and her countenance and gestures gave much cause to apprehend that, the moment the stick should be removed, a repetition of the offence would demand new ingenuity in chastising it.

"The above-mentioned individuals had been sentenced to 30 undergo their various modes of ignominy, for the space of one hour at noonday. But among the crowd were several whose punishment would be life-long; some, whose ears had been cropped, like those of puppy dogs; others, whose cheeks had been branded with the initials of their misdemeanors; one, with his nostrils slit and seared; and another, with a halter about his neck, which he was forbidden ever to take off, or to conceal beneath his garments. Methinks he must have been grievously tempted to affix the other end of the rope to some convenient beam or bough. There was likewise a young woman, with no mean share of beauty, whose doom was to wear the letter A on the breast of her gown, in the eyes of all the world and her own children. And even her own children knew what that initial signified. Sporting with her infamy, the lost and desperate creature had embroidered the fatal token in scarlet cloth, with golden thread and the nicest art of needlework; so that the capital A might have been thought to mean Admirable, or anything rather than Adulteress.

31   "Let not the reader argue, from any of these evidences of iniquity, that the times of the Puritans were more vicious than our own."

32   In my old-fashioned opinion, Mr. Hawthorne sure got that right.

Andrea Dworkin
REPLY TO JOHN IRVING

As she notes in the following reply, Andrea Dworkin (born 1947) has written (with University of Michigan law professor Catherine MacKinnon) antipornography ordinances for Minneapolis, Indianapolis, and other cities. (The ordinances later were overturned by the courts.) A successful and controversial essayist and fiction writer, she has also written Pornography: Men Possessing Women *(1988) and* Pornography and Civil Rights *(1988), both of which argue in favor of the kinds of laws that she advocates.*

To the Editor:

1   As a woman determined to destroy the pornography industry, a writer of 10 published books and someone who reads, perhaps I should be the one to tell John Irving ("Pornography and the New Puritans," March 29) who the new Puritan is. The old Puritans wouldn't like her very much; but then, neither does Mr. Irving.

2   I am 45 years old now. When I was a teen-ager, I baby-sat. In any middle-class home one could always find the dirty books— on the highest shelf, climbing toward God, usually behind a parched potted plant. The books themselves were usually "Ulysses," "Tropic of Cancer" or "Lady Chatterley's Lover." They always had as a preface or afterword the text of an obscenity decision in which the book was exonerated and art extolled. Or a lawyer would stand in for the court to tell us that through his mighty efforts law had finally vindicated a persecuted genius.

Even at 15 and 16, I noticed something strange about the 3
special intersection of art, law and sex under the obscenity
rubric: some men punished other men for producing or publishing writing that caused arousal in (presumably) still other
men. Although Mrs. Grundy got the blame, women didn't make
these laws or enforce them or sit on juries to deliberate guilt or
innocence. This was a fight among men—but about what?

Meanwhile, my life as a woman in prefeminist times went 4
on. This means that I thought I was a human being with rights.
But before I was much over 18, I had been sexually assaulted
three times. Did I report these assaults (patriarchy's first question, because surely the girl must be lying)?

When I was 9, I told my parents. To protect me, for better or 5
worse, they did not call the police.

The second time, beaten as well as raped, I told no one. I was 6
working for a peace group, and I heard jokes about rape day in
and day out. What do you tell the draft board when they ask
you if you would kill a Nazi who was going to rape your sister?
"I'd tell my sister to have a good time" was the answer of choice.

The third time, I was 18, a freshman in college, and I had 7
been arrested for taking part in a sit-in outside the United
Nations to protest the Vietnam War. It was February of 1965.
This time, my experience was reported in *The New York Times,*
newspapers all around the world and on television: girl in
prison—New York's notorious Women's House of Detention—
says she was brutalized by two prison doctors. Forced entry
with a speculum—for 15 days I had vaginal bleeding, a vagina
so bruised and ripped that my stone-cold family doctor burst
into tears when he examined me.

I came out of the Women's House of Detention mute. Speech 8
depends on believing you can make yourself understood: a
community of people will recognize the experience in the
words you use and they will care. You also have to be able to
understand what happened to you enough to convey it to others. I lost speech. I was hurt past what I had words for. I lived
out on the streets for several days, not having a bed of my own,
still bleeding; and finally spoke because Grace Paley convinced
me that she would understand and care. Then I spoke a lot. A
grand jury investigated. Columnists indicted the prison. But
neither of the prison doctors was charged with sexual assault
or sexual battery. In fact, no one ever mentioned sexual assault.
The grand jury concluded that the prison was fine. In despair, I
left the country—to be a writer, my human dream.

A year later I came back. I have since discovered that what 9
happened to me is common: homeless, poor, still sexually trau-
matized, I learned to trade sex for money. I spent a lot of years
out on the street, living hand to mouth, these New York streets

and other streets in other hard cities. I thought I was a real tough woman, and I was: tough-calloused; tough-numb; tough-desperate; tough-scared; tough-hungry; tough-beaten by men often; tough-done it every which way including up. All of my colleagues who fight pornography with me know about this. I know about the lives of women in pornography because I lived the life. So have many feminists who fight pornography. Freedom looks different when you are the one it is being practiced on. It's his, not yours. Speech is different, too. Those sexy expletives are the hate words he uses on you while he is using you. Your speech is an inchoate protest never voiced.

10   In my work, fiction and nonfiction, I've tried to voice the protest against a power that is dead weight on you, fist and penis organized to keep you quiet. I would do virtually anything to get women out of prostitution and pornography, which is mass-produced, technologized prostitution. With pornography, a woman can still be sold after the beatings, the rapes, the pain, the humiliation have killed her. I write for her, on behalf of her. I know her. I have come close to being her.

11   I read a lot of books. None of them ever told me the truth about what happens to women until feminists started writing and publishing in this wave, over these last 22 years. Over and over, male writers consider prostituted women "speech"—their speech, their right. Without this exploitation, published for profit, the male writer feels censored. The woman lynched naked on a tree, or restrained with ropes and a ball gag in her mouth, has what? Freedom of what?

12   I lost my ability to speak—became mute—a second time in my life. I've written about being a battered wife: I was beaten and tortured over a period of a few years. Amnesty International never showed up. Toward the end, I lost all speech. Words were useless to the likes of me. I had run away and asked for help—from friends, neighbors, the police—and had been turned away many times. My words didn't seem to mean anything, or it was O.K. to torture me.

13   Taken once by my husband to a doctor when hurt, I risked asking for help. The doctor said he could write me a prescription for Valium or have me committed. The neighbors heard the screaming, but no one did anything. So what are words? I have always been good with them, but never good enough to be believed or helped. No, there were no shelters then.

14   But I am talking about speech: it isn't easy for me. I come to speech from under a man, tortured and tormented. What he did to me took away everything; he was the owner of everything. He hurt all the words out of me, and no one would listen anyway. I come to speech from under the brutalities of thou-

sands of men. For me, the violence of marriage was worse than the violence of prostitution; but this is no choice. Men act out pornography. They have acted it out on me. Women's lives become pornography. Mine did. And so for 20 years now I have been looking for the words to say what I know.

But maybe liberal men—so open-minded and intellectually 15 curious—can't find the books that would teach them about women's real lives. Maybe, while John Irving and PEN are defending *Hustler*, snuff films and *Deep Throat*, the direct product of the coercion of Linda Marchiano, political dissidents like myself are anathema—especially to the free-speech fetishists— not because the publishing industry punishes prudes but because dissenters who mean it, who stand against male power over women, are pariahs.

Maybe Mr. Irving and others do not know that in the world 16 of women, pornography is the real geography of how men use us and torment us and hate us. *Def*

With Catharine A. MacKinnon, I drafted the first civil law 17 against pornography. It held pornographers accountable for what they do: they traffic women (contravening the United Nations Universal Declaration of Human Rights and the Convention on the Elimination of All Forms of Discrimination Against Women); they eroticize inequality in a way that materially promotes rape, battery, maiming and bondage; they make a product that they know dehumanizes, degrades and exploits women; they hurt women to make the pornography, and then consumers use the pornography in assaults both verbal and physical.

Mr. Irving refers to a scene in *The World According to Garp* in 18 which a woman bites off a man's penis in a car when the car is accidentally rammed from behind. This, he says, did not cause women to bite off men's penises in cars. I have written (in my novels, *Ice and Fire* and *Mercy*, and in the story "The New Woman's Broken Heart") about a woman raped by two men sequentially, the first aggressor routed by the second one, to whom the woman, near dead, submits; he bites viciously and repeatedly into her genitals. When I wrote it, someone had already done it—to me. Mr. Irving uses his imagination for violent farce. My imagination can barely grasp my real life. The violence, as Mr. Irving must know, goes from men to women.

Women write to me because of our shared experiences. In 19 my books they find their lives—until now beyond the reach of language. A letter to me dated March 11 says in part: "The abuse was quite sadistic—it involved bestiality, torture, the making of pornography. Sometimes, when I think about my life, I'm not sure why I'm alive, but I'm always sure about why

I do what I do, the feminist theory and the antipornography activism." Another letter, dated March 13, says: "It was only when I was almost [raped] to pieces that I broke down and learned to hate. . . . I have never stopped resenting the loss of innocence that occurred the day I learned to hate."

20   Male liberals seem to think we fight pornography to protect sexual innocence, but we have none to protect. The innocence we want is the innocence that lets us love. People need dignity to love.

21   Mr. Irving quoted Hawthorne's condemnation of Puritan orthodoxy in the short story "Endicott and the Red Cross"—a graphic description of public punishments of women: bondage, branding, maiming, lynching. Today pornographers do these things to women, and the public square is a big place—every newsstand and video store. A photograph shields rape and torture for profit. In defending pornography as if it were speech, liberals defend the new slavers. The only fiction in pornography is the smile on the woman's face.

Nadine Strossen

THE PERILS
OF PORNOPHOBIA

Nadine Strossen's essay on pornography appeared in The Humanist *in the spring of 1995. Strossen, a member of the faculty at New York Law School, is president of the American Civil Liberties Union, an organization famous for defending the constitutional rights of U.S. citizens. Her essay was adapted from her 1995 book* Defending Pornography: Free Speech, Sex, and the Fight for Women's Rights.

1   In 1992, in response to a complaint, officials at Pennsylvania State University unceremoniously removed Francisco de Goya's masterpiece, *The Nude Maja*, from a classroom wall. The complaint had not been lodged by Jesse Helms or some irate member of the Christian Coalition. Instead, the complainant was a feminist English professor who protested that the eighteenth-century painting of a recumbent nude woman made her and her female students "uncomfortable."

2   This was not an isolated incident. At the University of Arizona at Tucson, feminist students physically attacked a

graduate student's exhibit of photographic self-portraits. Why? The artist had photographed *herself* in her *underwear*. And at the University of Michigan Law School feminist students who had organized a conference on "Prostitution: From Academia to Activism" removed a feminist-curated art exhibition held in conjunction with the conference. Their reason? Conference speakers had complained that a composite videotape containing interviews of working prostitutes was "pornographic" and therefore unacceptable.

What is wrong with this picture? Where have they come   3 from—these feminists who behave like religious conservatives, who censor works of art because they deal with sexual themes? Have not feminists long known that censorship is a dangerous weapon which, if permitted, would inevitably be turned against them? Certainly that was the irrefutable lesson of the early women's rights movement, when Margaret Sanger, Mary Ware Dennett, and other activists were arrested, charged with "obscenity" and prosecuted for distributing educational pamphlets about sex and birth control. Theirs was a struggle for freedom of sexual expression and full gender equality, which they understood to be mutually reinforcing.

Theirs was also a lesson well understood by the second wave   4 of feminism in the 1970s, when writers such as Germaine Greer, Betty Friedan, and Betty Dodson boldly asserted that women had the right to be free from discrimination not only in the workplace and in the classroom but in the bedroom as well. Freedom from limiting, conventional stereotypes concerning female sexuality was an essential aspect of what we then called "women's liberation." Women should not be seen as victims in their sexual relations with men but as equally assertive partners, just as capable of experiencing sexual pleasure.

But it is a lesson that, alas, many feminists have now forgot-   5 ten. Today, an increasingly influential feminist pro-censorship movement threatens to impair the very women's rights movement it professes to serve. Led by law professor Catharine MacKinnon and writer Andrea Dworkin, this faction of the feminist movement maintains that sexually oriented *expression*—not sex-segregated labor markets, sexist concepts of marriage and family, or pent-up rage—is the preeminent cause of discrimination and violence against women. Their solution is seemingly simple: suppress all "pornography."

Censorship, however, is never a simple matter. First, the of-   6 fense must be described. And how does one define something so infinitely variable, so deeply personal, so uniquely individualized as the image, the word, and the fantasy that cause sexual arousal? For decades, the U.S. Supreme Court has engaged in a Sisyphean struggle to craft a definition of *obscenity* that the lower courts can apply with some fairness and consistency. Their dilemma was best summed up in former Justice Potter Stewart's now famous statement: "I shall not today attempt further to define [obscenity]; and perhaps I could never succeed in intelligibly doing so. But I know it when I see it."

The censorious feminists are not so modest as Justice Stewart. They have fashioned an elaborate definition of *pornography* that encompasses vastly more material than does the currently recognized law of *obscenity*. As set out in their model law (which has been considered in more than a dozen jurisdictions in the United States and overseas, and which has been substantially adopted in Canada), pornography is "the sexually explicit subordination of women through pictures and/or words." The model law lists eight different criteria that attempt to illustrate their concept of "subordination," such as depictions in which "women are presented in postures or positions of sexual submission, servility, or display" or "women are presented in scenarios of degradation, humiliation, injury, torture . . . in a context that makes these conditions sexual." This linguistic driftnet can ensnare anything from religious imagery and documentary footage about the mass rapes in the Balkans to self-help books about women's health. Indeed, the Boston Women's Health Book Collective, publisher of the now-classic book on women's health and sexuality, *Our Bodies, Ourselves,* actively campaigned against the MacKinnon-Dworkin model law when it was proposed in Cambridge, Massachusetts, in 1985, recognizing that the book's explicit text and pictures could be targeted as pornographic under the law.

8   Although the "MacDworkinite" approach to pornography has an intuitive appeal to many feminists, it is *itself* based on subordinating and demeaning stereotypes about women. Central to the pornophobic feminists—and to many traditional conservatives and right-wing fundamentalists, as well—is the notion that *sex* is inherently degrading to women (although not to men). Not just sexual expression but sex itself—even consensual, nonviolent sex—is an evil from which women, like children, must be protected.

9   MacKinnon puts it this way: "Compare victims' reports of rape with women's reports of sex. They look a lot alike. . . . The major distinction between intercourse (normal) and rape (abnormal) is that the normal happens so often that one cannot get anyone to see anything wrong with it." And from Dworkin: "Intercourse remains a means or the means of physiologically making a woman inferior." Given society's pervasive sexism, she believes, women cannot freely consent to sexual relations

with men; those who do consent are, in Dworkin's words, "collaborators ... experiencing pleasure in their own inferiority."

These ideas are hardly radical. Rather, they are a reincarna- 10
tion of disempowering puritanical, Victorian notions that feminists have long tried to consign to the dustbin of history: woman as sexual victim; man as voracious satyr. The MacDworkinite approach to sexual expression is a throwback to the archaic stereotypes that formed the basis for nineteenth-century laws which prohibited "vulgar" or sexually suggestive language from being used in the presence of women and girls.

In those days, women were barred from practicing law and 11
serving as jurors lest they be exposed to such language. Such "protective" laws have historically functioned to bar women from full legal equality. Paternalism always leads to exclusion, discrimination, and the loss of freedom and autonomy. And in its most extreme form, it leads to purdah, in which women are completely shrouded from public view.

The pro-censorship feminists are not fighting alone. Although 12
they try to distance themselves from such traditional "family-values" conservatives as Jesse Helms, Phyllis Schlafly, and Donald Wildmon, who are less interested in protecting women than in preserving male dominance a common hatred of sexual expression and fondness for censorship unite the two camps. For example, the Indianapolis City Council adopted the MacKinnon-Dworkin model law in 1984 thanks to the hard work of former council member Beulah Coughenour, a leader of the Indiana Stop ERA movement. (Federal courts later declared the law unconstitutional.) And when Phyllis Schlafly's Eagle Forum and Beverly LaHaye's Concerned Women for America launched their "Enough Is Enough" anti-pornography campaign, they trumpeted the words of Andrea Dworkin in promotional materials.

This mutually reinforcing relationship does a serious disser- 13
vice to the fight for women's equality. It lends credibility to and strengthens the right wing and its anti-feminist, anti-choice, homophobic agenda. This is particularly damaging in light of the growing influence of the religious right in the Republican Party and the recent Republican sweep of both Congress and many state governments. If anyone doubts that the newly empowered GOP intends to forge ahead with anti-woman agendas, they need only read the party's "Contract with America" which, among other things, reintroduces the recently repealed "gag rule" forbidding government-funded family-planning clinics from even discussing abortion with their patients.

The pro-censorship feminists base their efforts on the largely 14
unexamined assumption that ridding society of pornography

would reduce sexism and violence against women. If there were any evidence that this were true, anti-censorship feminists—myself included—would be compelled at least to reexamine our opposition to censorship. But there is no such evidence to be found.

15   A causal connection between exposure to pornography and the commission of sexual violence has never been established. The National Research Council's Panel on Understanding and Preventing Violence concluded in a 1993 survey of laboratory studies that "demonstrated empirical links between pornography and sex crimes in general are weak or absent." Even according to another research literature survey that former U.S. Surgeon General C. Everett Koop conducted at the behest of the staunchly anti-pornography Meese Commission, only two reliable generalizations could be made about the impact of "degrading" sexual material on its viewers: it caused them to think that a variety of sexual practices was more common than they had previously believed, and to more accurately estimate the prevalence of varied sexual practices.

16   Correlational studies are similarly unsupportive of the pro-censorship cause. There are no consistent correlations between the availability of pornography in various communities, states, and countries and their rates of sexual offenses. If anything, studies suggest an inverse relationship: a greater availability of sexually explicit material seems to correlate not with higher rates of sexual violence but, rather, with higher indices of gender equality. For example, Singapore, with its tight restrictions on pornography, has experienced a much greater increase in rape rates than has Sweden, with its liberalized obscenity laws.

17   There *is* mounting evidence, however, that MacDworkinite-type laws will be used against the very people they are supposed to protect—namely, women. In 1992, for example, the Canadian Supreme Court incorporated the MacKinnon-Dworkin concept of pornography into Canadian obscenity law. Since that ruling, in *Butler* v. *The Queen*—which MacKinnon enthusiastically hailed as "a stunning victory for women"— well over half of all feminist bookstores in Canada have had materials confiscated or detained by customs. According to the *Feminist Bookstore News*, a Canadian publication, "The *Butler* decision has been used . . . only to seize lesbian, gay, and feminist material."

18   Ironically but predictably, one of the victims of Canada's new law is Andrea Dworkin herself. Two of her books, *Pornography: Men Possessing Women* and *Women Hating*, were seized, customs officials said, because they "illegally eroticized pain and

bondage." Like the MacKinnon-Dworkin model law, the *Butler* decision makes no exceptions for material that is part of a feminist critique of pornography or other feminist presentation. And this inevitably overbroad sweep is precisely why censorship is antithetical to the fight for women's rights.

The pornophobia that grips MacKinnon, Dworkin, and their followers has had further counterproductive impacts on the fight for women's rights. Censorship factionalism within the feminist movement has led to an enormously wasteful diversion of energy from the real cause of and solutions to the ongoing problems of discrimination and violence against women. Moreover, the "porn-made-me-do-it", defense, whereby convicted rapists cite MacKinnon and Dworkin in seeking to reduce their sentences, actually impedes the aggressive enforcement of criminal laws against sexual violence.

A return to the basic principles of women's liberation would put the feminist movement back on course. We women are entitled to freedom of expression—to read, think, speak, sing, write, paint, dance, dream, photograph, film, and fantasize as we wish. We are also entitled to our dignity, autonomy, and equality. Fortunately, we can—and will—have both.

Maria Soto

IS IT PORNOGRAPHY?

Maria Soto was a student at the University of Kentucky when she wrote the following essay in a first-year writing course. Born in Panama, raised in Nicaragua, and a resident for a time in Brazil, she speaks a number of languages fluently; but English is of course not her first language. Just after this essay was completed, Calvin Klein responded to public pressure and removed the ads that Soto discusses.

During September of 1995 a major controversy arose about the printed ads of Calvin Klein that were exposed, publicly, on buses in New York City, as well as in advertisements in various magazines. Many people considered the ads to be child pornography because the pictures in the ads showed adolescents (apparently minors) in very seductive poses; those people felt that the ads shouldn't be on the streets or in any kind of magazine. However, before censoring something as pornographic, we have to determine if it is really pornographic or simply a use of sensuality to sell a product. In order to be able to make any judgment of that, we need first to determine what child pornography is. By reading and by discussing with other people what constitutes child pornography, I have concluded that child pornography is any material that focuses on the sexuality of a child, that has the intention to be pornographic, and that humiliates those who view the material. Calvin Klein ads may be in poor taste, but they are not child pornography because they don't contain the elements of child pornography.

2   The first part of the definition states that child pornography is any material that focuses on the sexuality of a child, that is, material which drives the attention of the viewer to the sexual organs of the child and shows sexual activities. For example, a picture that shows a ten-year-old girl nude, and in which the camera takes a close-up of her sexual organs, can be defined as child pornography because it focuses on the sexual organs of the girl. On the other hand, a work of art in which a girl is nude but which drives the attention of the viewer not to her sexuality but to something else, is not child pornography. Edvuard Munch's "Puberty" for instance, portrays nudity, but it emphasizes the girl's suffering, so it is not pornography. Although no one can deny that the models in CK ads are posed in sensual positions, no sexual activity is portrayed, and no sexual organ is shown. A young girl in one of the ads, for instance, is pushing her jeans down as if to take them off, she is looking at the viewer in a challenging way, and her tiny T-shirt is barely covering her stomach; but while the picture is sexually suggestive, it does not depict sexual acts or focus on sexual organs. In another ad, a girl dressed in the same sort of tiny T-shirt is lying sideways on a bench, her jeans pulled down on her hips and an inch or two of her stomach showing. The picture could suggest the idea that she is not an innocent girl, and it undoubtedly focuses on her sensuality; but it doesn't amount to child pornography because it does not focus on her sexual organs or portray any sexual activity. Moreover, to me the girl looks like one of those teenagers that you see every day, walking on the street, wearing her jeans on her hips, and showing off her underwear. What is shown in the CK ads is not far away from the way many teens dress nowadays. Of course, sensuality is explicit in the ads and not on the streets, but judging something as pornographic because it is sensual is not legitimate.

3   Another important part of the definition of child pornography is the intention of the material. A pornographic item has as its main objective the provocation of sexual arousal; pornography provokes sexual desire. A picture of a ten-year-old

girl who is bare and who is opening her legs in front of the camera is certainly material for a hard-core pornographic magazine because the purpose of the picture is to arouse other people sexually. Determining the intention to be pornographic is of course difficult at times because not all material that focuses on the sexuality of a child is intended for pornographic purposes. To use an obvious example, many medical reports contain pictures that emphasize the sexual organs of children, but the intention of those pictures is educational. Nevertheless, for something sexually explicit to be considered pornographic, it must have the intention of arousing sexual desire. Otherwise, it could be considered a scientific or an artistic work.

Calvin Klein ads are not meant to be pornographic; they are   4
meant to sell products. In order to sell their products, the CK ads try to identify the models in the ads with adolescents because adolescents are beginning to use their sexuality to attract their peers. The models in the ads look very sensual, as if they can seduce anyone, so that insecure adolescents will think that "maybe if I wear Calvin Klein jeans, I'll be as seductive as that girl and maybe some boy will finally look at me." Adolescents identify with the models and therefore buy CK jeans: it's that simple. And it works. As Alan Millstein, editor of the Fashion Network report, said in a recent issue of *Time*, CK jeans are "flying out of the stores" as a result of the ads. You can see the phenomenon yourself the next time you go to a mall and see a group of teenagers all looking alike: with the same jeans, the same hairstyle, the same shoes. And it's not just any kind of jeans; they have to be produced by Guess? or Calvin Klein. In short, for better or for worse, the sensuality used in CK ads is just the expression of the patterns of behavior and beliefs of many American adolescents. The ads are intended to sell jeans—it's that simple.

Finally, in cases of child pornography, humiliation is typi-   5
cally present; pornography degrades and exploits a person. Although pornography includes humiliation, not all humiliating material is pornographic. For example, imagine a picture of a prostitute working on the streets; the picture is humiliating because it shows the exploitation of human beings, but it is not pornographic because it does not focus on the sexuality of the prostitute and because its intention is not pornographic. On the other hand, a young boy or girl in a porno movie is being exploited because, undoubtedly, the movie is showing a relationship of unequal power between a weak child and a strong adult who can manipulate the actions of the child.

In Calvin Klein ads, no humiliation is present because they   6
are not being degraded or exploited. The pictures do not imply

a relationship of power and submission between the person who took the picture and the persons depicted. Instead, as Calvin Klein himself affirmed in a statement published in the *New York Times* on August 28, the ads intend to show "the strength of character and independence" of the young people photographed. In other words, the ads try to demonstrate that adolescents can take care of themselves and make the right decisions (even, apparently, in the case of buying jeans). The ads I looked at while preparing this essay showed teenagers with confident faces and self-assured poses.

7   In spite of Calvin Klein's personal defense, many people persist in believing that the ads are instances of child pornography because young models are being posed seductively and suggestively; the ads seem to be sexualizing children. However, sexuality and sensuality are things natural to adolescence, not things unnatural. Whether people like it or not, it is normal and natural for a teenager to explore his or her sensuality. I'm not saying that showing the sexual parts of a teenager with the intention to arouse someone is not pornographic; it is. Nor am I saying that showing a picture of an eight-year-old in a sensual way is natural. It isn't. But the Calvin Klein ads are showing adolescents who really are using sensuality as a way to attract their peers, and, more important, the ads are intended to be commercial, not pornographic.

8   The only serious mistake that I can see in the ads is that they address a topic that is still taboo in our society, one that we continue to avoid confronting because it's easier to cheat ourselves into believing that adolescents are far away from being sexually active. Why is our society afraid to confront the sexuality of adolescents?

9   Will these ads cause adolescents to be more sexually active? I doubt it. It seems to me that the ads, more than playing with the sensuality of the models, are dealing with the social value of teenagers in our society. Although the main question around the Calvin Klein ads was whether or not they were pornographic, to me what needs to get the attention of the community is the social mores that the ads reflect. The ads seem to me to show us our adolescents—how they use things to attract people—things like cars, hairstyles, and clothing. It appears that we must have things in order to live and to be respected; we must have things in order to seem attractive or interesting human beings. Calvin Klein ads show how empty our culture is, how we value superficial things and attitudes. In that sense, the ads are discouraging indeed; frustrating indeed.

10   But they aren't pornographic.

David Grad
SOUND OFF ON NAPSTER

In August 2000, Yahoo! Internet Life *magazine published a roundtable discussion about the merits of Napster, the technology for downloading music through the Internet for free. The discussion was arranged and edited by David Grad, who makes a career of arranging discussions of substantive issues. He also writes for many Internet publications and creates a weekly* Yahoo! Internet Life *Digital Music Newsletter. Participants in the exchange that follows include the recording artists Chuck D, John Flansburgh, Aimee Mann, Todd Rundgren, and Alanis Morissette; Ian Clarke (creator of Freenet); Shawn Fanning (who created Napster); Marc Geiger, Hilary Rosen, and Danny Goldberg (all CEOs of recording companies); and Richard Metzger (a "Creator of Disinformation").*

As Marvin Gaye once asked, "What's goin' on?" 1

On any given day, millions of consumers defy both artists 2
and record companies as they feverishly consume the industry's products for free. It's estimated that in 1999 there were one billion unauthorized downloads of copyrighted music. Piracy or progress? It all depends on whom you ask.

When Shawn Fanning created NAPSTER as a way for him 3
and his friends to share MP3 files, he had no idea he had opened a Pandora's box. Since its arrival in cyberspace last year, the file-swapping program has been besieged with lawsuits. At the same time it has helped foster a marketplace philosophy that "music should be free." When Metallica and Dr. Dre took legal aim at Napster, alleging that the program facilitates piracy, a full-blown war erupted, pitting artists against

fans, the established recording industry against new-media startups, and artists against one another.

4   To get an idea of what life after the revolution will sound like, we gathered some major players in this world (see below) and asked for their assessment of the volatile present and the uncertain future. In some cases, our roundtable members were torn between what they saw as the potentials of technology and the legal and moral issues involved. Singer-songwriter Aimee Mann thinks Napster might turn out to be a valuable service that works as a radio station, but she doesn't feel that it could effectively protect the rights of artists. There were also some uneasy alliances. Rock icon Todd Rundgren, no fan of the Recording Industry Association of America (RIAA) or big labels, found himself basically agreeing with RIAA President Hilary Rosen in his opposition to Napster. Although Fanning was unable to comment on many of the discussion points because of existing lawsuits against his company, he remains hopeful that this war will end with many winners. Taking rebellious positions against the record labels were Chuck D, DIS-INFORMATION's Richard Metzger, and Ian Clarke, the 23-year old creator of FREENET, a U.K.-based file-sharing program that goes beyond Napster to allow for the swapping of any kind of digital information, including software.

5   Our roundtable about the state of music in the summer of 2000 was put together over the course of weeks and reveals a group of people who share a common passion for the issues, though their opinions differ. But they all seemed to agree on one thing: Music will never be the same.

6   Y-LIFE: Amid the heated debate over digital piracy, file sharing, and artists' rights, one key question begs to be answered: Whose music is it anyway?

7   CHUCK D: You'd like to say that the music is the artist's, but it isn't, because the copyrights and the masters are controlled by the company—usually by a former lawyer or accountant who happened to luck into a position of governing art. The record companies have used technology as an excuse, but their red tape and political angles have made it difficult for artistry to exist in the first place.

8   GEIGER: It's like a painting you own that nobody sees—a song that's exclusively owned by a label or an artist and not also by a consumer is music that's not being heard. If you define success for an artist, it's really having your music owned by as many people as possible. If someone said their music was illegally downloaded gazillions of times, that's a measure of success, not failure. When people sing along with a song at a

concert, it has become the public's music, right? With music that's successful, you want to have the special bond between creator and consumer—a shared ownership.

GOLDBERG: It's not rational to think that being the fan gives you ownership and control over the copyright with the people that created it. In the '60s there was a lot of rhetoric about how everything should be free. I was a hippie, and there were a lot of things I liked about it. But I remember these radical hippies who were saying, "Music should belong to the people" to Jerry Garcia, and he said, "Where were the people when I was practicing my guitar?" 9

MANN: Good for Jerry. Where are the people when I'm spending six hours riding in a van trying to look for a rest stop? It's unfair to obtain somebody's music for free. It's work. People are entitled to make a living. 10

MORISSETTE: I don't think that a lot of people who are getting the music for free are thinking about whom it's affecting. There have been these proverbial injustices by record companies against artists, so maybe people feel that they're helping the artist out by not paying record companies their 85 percent. But they're not only taking away the 85 percent from the record companies, they're taking away the small percentage that's given to the artist. 11

METZGER: I find the figures indicating that most people will listen to but not archive MP3s to be really revealing. The music industry used to sticker albums with the message that "home taping is killing music," and we all know now that was utter nonsense. A few months back, I scoured the Web for MP3s of Lou Reed concerts from the early '70s, and soon after I found myself buying the remainder of his '70s catalog that I didn't already have on CD. Who lost out in this transaction? Nobody. Who gained? Everybody, not the least being me, the music consumer and born-again Lou Reed fan. 12

CHUCK D: File sharing and downloadable distribution is the new radio. It's a fantastic way for art to get exposed. This new realm can actually introduce artists into the marketplace, and this new technology and format could allow a global expansion of their art. The fans will always be willing to support art financially if it's fair, and I don't think it has been fair over the last 20 years. 13

ROSEN: Though most people don't realize it, only about 15 percent of all releases sell enough copies to make a profit, and those record sales support the other 85 percent, including those from new and emerging artists. Sales of recordings don't just support the musical artist. Piracy cheats producers, composers, sound engineers, studio musicians, publishers, 14 and vocalists out of their share of royalties, on which they generally depend for their livelihoods.

CHUCK D: [But] now there's going to be more money in the music marketplace than ever before, because of the global expansion of the Internet and the fact that everybody is interconnected. The problem for artists who feel like they have something to lose and the corporations that spawned them is that there are going to be a hell of lot of hands in the pot.

GLASER: From the standpoint of justice and fairness, products like Napster aren't just preventing The Man from ripping us off, they're hurting the legitimate interests of artists, and not just fat-cat artists—they're quite undiscriminating in that way. That kind of product is not the right basis for the long-term vitality of music.

RUNDGREN: Napster is the most transparently illegal thing that I've ever seen on the Web. This is a hypocrisy that the Web has fostered, this idea that everything is free. There's so much hypocrisy behind this Napster thing. I think what really drove it was profound ignorance of the rights of people who write a song or book or anything else.

FANNING: When I developed Napster at school, I was not trying to start a revolution, as people have said. It was just a small project that solved a reliability issue with existing technology. There were Web-based search engines at the time, there were a lot of things that were trying to do what Napster does so well now, so it just seemed like a next step. There was a demand for a service like Napster. That would explain why it has grown faster than any Internet company in history in terms of users. It's something that's extremely valuable to the consumer, the artist, and the industry.

RUNDGREN: [But] the problem with Napster is that it unilaterally declares that all intellectual property has to be given away for free. It makes no distinction about whether you're screwing over some company or whether you're screwing over some poor guy trying to survive off his songwriting and playing skills. I want the right to decide whether to give my stuff away or not.

CLARKE: What is property? If you possess something, and I want to possess it, I must deprive you of it. Information isn't like that. You can have a piece of information—for example, a piece of music—and you can listen to it and enjoy it. I can then copy it from you, or you can share it with me. The quality of the music you have isn't depreciated in any way. What's currently happening in terms of piracy is an inevitable consequence of communications technology.

GOLDBERG: The fact that you can physically do something does not mean that it is right, moral, or will become the status quo. It seems pretty unlikely that copyright of intellectual property is going to disappear from the world economy because, obviously, it wouldn't just apply to music. It would apply to the entire television business, the entire movie business, publishing, software. . . .

CHUCK D: Technology will always be technology and force the climate to change. Intellectual property copyright laws that came into place in the 20th century might not fit in the 21st century, just like they didn't fit in the 19th century because that technology hadn't been invented yet. 22

GOLDBERG: I think it is in the self-interest of people who own music to make it free on a regular basis: We do free downloads from every album, and we beg radio to play our music for free, because that's how you market your product. But at the same time that it's legal to copy something for limited use, if somebody takes a Stephen King novel and makes 25,000 photocopies of it for sale by mail order—that's still illegal. 23

CLARKE: Censorship is the attempt to prevent people from communicating, and under that definition, copyright is censorship. The real issue is that information can be treated like property, that information is property, and that's the idea being challenged by these technologies. 24

FLANSBURGH: In the 21st century, that might end up being a widely held view. But all we have to go on as models are the 19th and 20th centuries. Twentieth-century popular music in the U.S., with a very simple structure of paying songwriters, resulted in the most fruitful period of songwriting and music creation that has ever been. 25

CLARKE: Copyright law is unenforceable, period. The only question is whether there is an incentive for people to exploit that unenforceability. People can use Freenet now and use it to distribute copyrighted material, and there is no way to punish them for it. 26

Y-LIFE: The perception with the Napster lawsuit has been that of a small, grassroots company, supported by the fans, being attacked by the recording establishment. Is that fair? 27

MANN: Listen, commerce built on the honor system is a big f— king dream. That's not going to happen. Try to consider how it is for the artists. This is what we do; this is what we have to sell. We write music and we play music and we record music. I don't have a big giant record deal or a movie deal. I don't make money on the road; I lose money on the road. A *Newsweek* article said, "It's the kids versus the suits." Well, it's not really that—it's kids versus the damn musicians, the people you supposedly like, whose music you listen to. 28

FLANSBURGH: At the core of the problem is that people can't relate to the practical realities of a working musician. I was 29 talking to the other guitarist after a show and we were wondering how many people there probably thought we were millionaires—which is certainly not the case. If I wanted to make a better living, less hard, I could do it with any middle-class job. I could sell real estate and make the same amount of dough.

30   MANN: That's the mythology of being a musician, where things are made to look so glamorous. That's why I irritate a lot of people, because I talk about the problems of being in the music business and on major labels. People just don't want to hear it, because it blows the vibe. They want to believe in the mythology. It's easy to think that people like me are really wealthy and have it made, and what would it matter if they downloaded my record for free. Well, it matters a lot.

31   MORISSETTE: Napster presents huge problems for the artists. It raises the question—which is positive—of where and how artists are compensated. But I don't agree with the model they've set up. The artist should be the person who's ultimately in a position to decide when, where, and how something should be shared with whomever they choose to share it with.

32   Y-LIFE: Can't programs like Napster actually help expand a musician's reach and introduce people to music they might not otherwise hear?

33   FANNING: The potential that Napster has to expose people to new material is amazing. If you have obscure tastes and you don't feel that many people like a particular song, suddenly you have the capability of meeting another person who is into it and being exposed to other material that they're interested in.

34   MANN: It's possible that Napster works mainly as a radio station, so people can hear music before they buy it. Many is the record I've bought based on hearing part of one song played on the radio, and the rest of the record was terrible. I think that's a legitimate concern, but I don't know what kind of provision you can make to ensure that somebody actually purchases the music.

35   CHUCK D: Everybody thought the cassette recorder and radio would be threats to the market, and that proved to be wrong. So with this new technology, everybody's saying the same thing, and all it's doing is leading the masses back to the store. I think what you will see in the cases of Dre and Metallica is some of their biggest sales ever.

36   GOLDBERG: In a year where you had a billion illegal downloads, record sales increased 6.5 percent, and they particularly grew in the U.S., which has more Internet use than any other country. Record sales also increased among the youngest sector of the audience—the demographic most

likely to do unauthorized downloading. I don't know what conclusion can be drawn from this, but it's crazy not to admit it's happening. In the short term, the involvement of people online with music has actually caused an increase in the paid music business.

Y-LIFE: So how do we deal with piracy? What do you think of 37 the Metallica and Dre lawsuits?

FLANSBURGH: One thing that is unfortunate about Metallica be- 38 ing the spokesman for the musicians' side of things is that their example is so singularly unusual. It's sort of like the Mighty Thor representing you at the U.N. They are internationally rich, and, more important, their music is constantly being pushed on audiences. So much of their stuff is promotionally omnipresent. It confuses the basic issue.

MANN: I'm probably the kind of person that people would go to 39 Napster for; one is less likely to be able to find my record in a big, obvious display in Tower Records. You can't turn on the radio and hear it four times a day. So you search for it on Napster. Well, I sell a tiny fraction of the records that anybody on a major label can sell.

METZGER: This whole Metallica farce will be seen one day as 40 *the* textbook example of how to set an antagonistic agenda with the public. It's the dumbest thing they could have done, and it's gonna come back and bite Metallica in the ass, hard. What fools they are if they think throwing a few college kids in jail for trading unauthorized Metallica tracks on Napster is gonna change things. Even if venture capital won't invest in any Napster-type companies, dozens of underground Napster-type permutations will pop up.

GEIGER: I don't know if it's jail time we're talking about here. 41 You don't go to jail for a cable box violation. That's a scare tactic. But a $500 or $1,000 fine, that would make you say, "Forget it, I'll just pay." I think the key word is deterrent. But at present, I don't think anything is right, based on the fact that the majors are not making their music available, and that's really the big issue.

RUNDGREN: That could be the justification for any kind of steal- 42 ing. Just because somebody won't give me something, I have a right to steal it? This is just profound ignorance fostered by the notion that everything can be gotten for free if you use the Internet.

Y-LIFE: But at this point, Napster has registered 10 million 43 users since August 1999. At least 13 million Americans have downloaded music for free on the Net. Is it too late to put the cat back in the bag?

ROSEN: This isn't about policing the Internet or trying to put all 44 of the cats back in the bag. Our efforts to protect copyrighted materials are aimed at finding a fair business model for artists, record labels, and online music services. There is a big difference between a consumer making a copy, or download, for his or her own personal use, and that same consumer making the file available on Napster, where it can be freely downloaded by thousands of people. This isn't a consumer rights issue.

45 GLASER: For every product the RIAA initiates a lawsuit against, they should also stimulate a program within the member labels to make that same capability available on a commercial basis. You don't like the way MP3 is doing Beam-it? Great! Sue them over it, and the same day get your members to announce commercial terms under which they will make the same feature available. You don't like what Napster is doing in terms of facilitating illegal sharing? Fine! The day you sue, announce a program to make that same capability is available to consumers on a reasonable economic basis. That is the only way to combat piracy: Show people what the legal valid alternatives are, and the vast majority of them will follow that path.

46 METZGER: Music has been around for 40,000 years and the music industry for about 80 years. Whenever you hear someone talking about MP3 and Napster, and they remark that the majors are here to stay, what history are they basing this prognosis on? In the digital age, if you can no longer hold it, there's no need to produce it, wrap cellophane around, ship it, and stock it on shelves. What value does the record industry offer to musicians, as opposed to teenage pop acts? Not much as far as I can tell.

47 Y-LIFE: What's the solution?

48 GEIGER: I think we're in the most unstable period in the history of the music business. This is all about extremes. We're in the inflection point, so enjoy the ride. Forrester Research said there would be three stages—the age of piracy, the age of promotion, and the age of commerce, and I think until you come out on the other end of the age of commerce, nothing is stabilized. It's going to settle out one day with a new set of rules, and the one thing that I'm sure about is that it will work for consumers in the end.

49 ROSEN: The seminal asset is the artist. We're all going to experience many new opportunities online. But one premise should remain our mantra: The artists and those who invest in their creativity should be able to determine their own fate.

50 CHUCK D: Over the last 20 years, labels have ripped off both artists and the public. With the advent of the CD, something they're making for as little 89 cents, they found it beneficial to be in cahoots with retail outlets and force consumers to

spend $17 on something that shouldn't cost that much. Right now, with this new technology, the consumer has gotten to it first. Now, for the first time, the audience is a participant. That's why the big corporations are screaming and trying to say it's on the artists' behalf. The artists were never a part of the equation in the first place.

MORISSETTE: It's a matter of the Internet, record companies, and artists coming together and not taking the stance that has been taken thus far—that one side will win and another will lose. So we need to find a way, whether it's through the artists' own Web pages or other sites, to access the music easily and still protect it. That I support and am excited about. The introduction of new technology is genius. The main reason why record companies exist is to help artists distribute art that they couldn't distribute through the back of a bus. So there is a way that everyone can synergize and help each other.   51

MANN: I don't know, I think the poor musicians will get poorer. I don't have a whole lot of hope that the average Napster user will care about that. I'm sure there are exceptions; I just hope there are *a lot* of exceptions. But the Net giveth and the Net taketh away. People like the idea of downloading music, that they own it, and that's the end of it. What can you do, except appeal to people's consciences?   52

Y-LIFE: A recent study by Webnoize shows that among college students who use Napster, over 50 percent would pay $15 a month for the service. Do you see this type of subscription model as a possibility?   53

METZGER: If the industry as a whole would get together and come up with a subscription-based, Napster-style database with everything, perhaps administered by ASCAP or BMI, maybe even in conjunction with Napster, which would cost $20 a month or whatever, and the most popular downloaded songs on this giant Web jukebox would get the most money with prorated micropayments—Shania Twain and Backstreet Boys would still make more money than Captain Beefheart, sadly—I can maybe see the industry survive, at least a little while longer. But the almost comic bungling that they've shown so far leads me to believe the industry's days are numbered.   54

GOLDBERG: If things are going to be digitally delivered, the people who own this stuff count. I think the record companies are going to become major players in e-commerce. They have to find out what consumers want, and very few people have lines fast enough to express preferences right now.   55

ROSEN: The recording industry understands the needs of consumers. We want to provide the best-quality product   56 possible and are as excited about the possibilities offered by the Internet as the rest. [But] online piracy is a very real threat, one that everyone who uses a computer or listens to music should be concerned about. Record companies lose. Creative artists lose. But, most important, consumers lose. Investments in new music require that people believe that their efforts are worthwhile. Piracy takes away their incentive.

57　CLARKE: If you can get people to pay for something, and they're willing to do that voluntarily, then they're going to do that. If people think they're being treated unfairly, and there are alternatives such as Freenet, then they will go to the alternative.

58　RUNDGREN: The labels should put everything they have on servers and start working out aggregate music-delivery deals. Record labels have to start thinking about getting out of the inventory business. We want to leave all the duplication to the audiences themselves.

60　Y-LIFE: Why haven't the labels already done that?

61　CHUCK D: The industry has always prided itself on keeping technology out of the hands of the people. They were previously approached on MP3 and the advantages of file sharing. The major record companies refused and rejected these new options. The current situation arose because people said, "Hey, this is something I want for me, and I can't get it the old way." Necessity is always the reason for something like this.

62　FLANSBURGH: The problem is that the major labels don't feel comfortable putting their stuff in a format where piracy is so widespread. They aren't that naïve—after all, these people aren't high *all* the time.

62　GLASER: The major labels are big, hide-bound organizations that can't move as quickly as individual artists want to or an Internet startup might want to. That's why there's a mismatch between how fast the market is moving and how fast the major labels are willing to respond.

63　ROSEN: It was clear that just a few years ago the marriage of the technology industry and the creative community was very rocky. The tech people all said that artists needed to get with the times. On the creative side, we got smarter about how business models would have to change.

64　FANNING: Fear stems from ignorance, and when a new technology comes out there is some fear, some fighting, and ultimately they learn how to incorporate the technology into their model, and things are settled peacefully. I think we're at the end of the fighting period and in the settlement period where people are beginning to realize the potential of this technology.

Ruben Bolling

TOM THE DANCING BUG PRESENTS

"Tom the Dancing Bug" cartoons are distributed to many publications by the Universal Press Syndicate. This one was produced in 2000.

Paul Winston

COPYING THIS ARTICLE
IS STRICTLY FORBIDDEN

Paul Winston writes frequently for a variety of Internet publications. The following argument appeared in September 2000, in a magazine called Business Insurance *(and at www.businessinsurance.com).*

1   There is a legal battle being waged whose outcome could dramatically affect how business is done in the new millennium.

2   You may have heard of this dispute, involving a software program called Napster, and figured it had little to do with you because: a) You don't listen to Metallica, and b) You couldn't download a music file from the Internet even if you wanted to. I believe, however, that the Napster dispute has the potential to destroy current copyright protections for any material—including this column—and wreak havoc on free market economies.

3   Napster is a program that enables computer users to copy and exchange digital music files, resulting in a vast, automated exchange where files are freely traded. Essentially, Napster allows your computer to search the files on other computers using its software and download copies of whatever you like. If you want to find a particular song by Metallica, for example, you put your query online, and the software matches you with people who have these selections, just as people are perusing your hard drive and wondering whether to download your Toto music library. It's an automated process, so you can enter your search parameters, go away, and come back to find the job has been completed.

4   I mention Metallica because that band has taken the lead in trying to shut down Napster, charging that this free exchange of its music is copyright infringement and theft. Contrary to the warm fuzzy feelings that Metallica invokes, the band does what it does for the money, and it has no interest in giving its work away for free. While many other artists share Metallica's view, some do not; they see the free exchange of their music as an excellent way to gain recognition and interest. Often, though, these Napster supporters are bands that are not now making any money on their music anyway, and as soon as people start paying for their CDs, they'll likely change their minds and start to vote Republican.

5   The issue, as I see it, boils down to one of choice: Whether an original literary or artistic work is freely copied and

shared should be up to the person or entity that created it in the first place.

If Metallica says no, that should be its right, and violators   6
should be prosecuted. If Ned's Garage Band from Pocatello, Idaho, wants its musical message to spread as widely as possible, it should be free to use Napster, MP3 or whatever other technology exists to share its songs of potato love.

Current U.S. copyright statutes clearly protect the ability of   7
the originator of material to control the copying, publishing and sale of that work. So it is amazing to me that the courts hearing the Napster dispute are even contemplating any argument that would contravene that right, which long existed under common law before it was the subject of legislation. While a trial court moved recently to block Napster Inc., creator of the software, a federal appeals court that will hear arguments next month has stayed that move.

If courts ultimately rule that copyrights do not block the ex-   8
change and copying of music or published material, not only will a lot of musicians find their revenue streams dry up but so too will any business that relies on intellectual property as an asset or source of income.

Book publishers, broadcasters, newspapers and software de-   9
velopers are among those that would be especially hard hit. If people were free to copy, print and exchange books, instead of buying them, pretty soon authors and publishers would have to find other lines of work to feed themselves. Where would Harry Potter be in this brave new world? And what about Amazon.com, let alone the corner bookstore?

Technology is the source of this new battle over ownership of   10
the right to distribute information. Technology has enabled images, sounds and words to be broken down into a digital code. With the spread of personal computers and the growth of the Internet, it has become quite easy to share these perfect copies with millions of others.

Not only does Web technology make this possible but it also   11
has conditioned us to expect to receive free information. As early companies sought to stake out a place on the Internet and lure visitors to their sites, they often offered free information. Book publishers offered free excerpts. Music companies offered free electronic singles. News organizations put all their information online for free.

I believe that the resulting mindset—that we are entitled to   12
whatever we find on the Web—is at least partly responsible for the belief by some individuals that copyrights aren't worth the pixels used to display them.

If this view that all information should be free prevails, even-   13
tually there will be nothing worthwhile for those pixels to

display. The vast majority of companies and individuals will likely conclude, despite lip service to such noble concepts as art for art's sake and media's duty to serve the masses, that if no one is willing to pay for their efforts, then why should they bother?

Steve Smith

NAPSTER = BETAMAX

Steve Smith wrote the following essay on the Napster contro-versy in September 2000. It appeared in Twice *magazine (and at twice.com).* Twice—*which stands for* This Week In Consumer Electronics—*is a semiweekly business newspaper devoted to the electronics industry. It is directed not to con-sumers but to those who operate independent and chain retail electronics operations.*

1   Maybe my coffee didn't kick in early enough last Wednesday morning. Or maybe I'm just a 20th century kind of guy . . . you know, the law is the law, I've felt that there's no such thing as a free lunch . . . and there aren't legal grounds to provide some-one else's copyrighted digital music free on the Internet.

2   While I'm no apologist for Hollywood, the recording indus-try or their phalanx of lawyers, I also don't care for the fast and loose bromides coming from Napster, MP3.com and their lawyers. Before reading a story on Napster's legal strategy in the Wall Street Journal last week by reporter Lee Gomes, I rather naively told my colleagues at TWICE that if the website wins, recording artists will be hurt.

3   I was correctly "reminded" (read "beaten to a pulp") by my col-leagues that if Napster loses this case copyright holders will go after all forms of digital home recording. The result will be that the amount of digital audio and video programming available on the market will be limited by copyright holders. And such new technologies as recordable DVD, TiVo, Replay Networks, HD—VCRs, etc., etc., etc., will also be in legal jeopardy.

4   In his story, Gomes reports that Napster is using the 1984 Sony Betamax decision, as well as the 1992 Audio Home Recording Act, which gives consumers certain rights to make personal copies of music on digital audio tape, as part of its

defense, which seems to be right on the money. But almost two weeks ago the U.S. Copyright Office rejected Napster's defense. I guess that's why we have a court system.

One of the "friends of the court" in this case is the Consumer   5
Electronics Association, which is supporting Napster's position. CEA president Gary Shapiro delivered a speech at The Media Institute in late July that addressed the entire issue.

While he made many excellent points, I think a key one that   6
hasn't been discussed in depth is the length of copyrights in this country. "What began as a term of a few years," said Shapiro, "has expanded into a century [95 years in the case of works for hire], thanks to the unopposed force of the copyright lobby. Indeed, the Disney Company pushed extension of copyright term past Congress without any serious discussion of the constitutional implications."

(Disney's position is understandable. Can you imagine what   7
would happen to Disney's stock if Mickey, Minnie, Donald and the rest went into public domain? Disney's position is also hypocritical, as one industry source pointed out, "I guess it's OK for them to make movies about Peter Pan, Pinocchio and Grimm's fairy tales that are now in the public domain.")

Shapiro said that the founding fathers "insisted" that copy-   8
rights and patents be a "limited term . . . because a copyright is a monopoly." He also added that today's copyright term is "five times the patent term—it must be shortened." That's where the battle line is. Copyright law was out of step when it was extended in the past century, and it is certainly outmoded in the new one.

Hollywood won't go bankrupt. Remember, it fought its   9
movie stars appearing on radio in the '30s and '40s, saw television as a major threat in the '50s and '60s, grudgingly accepted cable in the '70s, and attacked the VCR in the '80s. The record companies have been "giving away" their product on radio since the '20s. With every technological step, media companies have made more money than ever before. And so have performing artists. They should all kiss the feet of the electronics and computer industries for all they've done to improve their businesses.

Yes, there will be plenty of pirated software out there in the   10
future as the digital age expands. There's plenty of pirated software out there now. But should we throw out the proverbial baby with the bathwater? The time has come to straighten out copyright law for the 21st century and have media companies develop for themselves new business models that will work in the digital age.

ON CIVIL DISOBEDIENCE

■

Henry David Thoreau
CIVIL DISOBEDIENCE

*Henry David Thoreau (1817–1862) is best known for his clas-
sic* Walden *(1854), an autobiographical, satiric, spiritual, scientific, and naturalistic "self-help book" based on his two
years' stay at Walden Pond, near Boston. A friend of Ralph
Waldo Emerson and other transcendentalists, Thoreau expressed his idealism in a number of concrete ways, for example, in his opposition to slavery and the Mexican War. His refusal to pay taxes to support the Mexican War inspired his
essay "Civil Disobedience" (1849). First delivered as a lecture
in 1848, "Civil Disobedience" influenced the thinking of
Mahatma Gandhi and Martin Luther King Jr.*

1   I heartily accept the motto,—"That government is best which
governs least"; and I should like to see it acted up to more
rapidly and systematically. Carried out, it finally amounts to
this, which also I believe,—"That government is best which
governs not at all"; and when men are prepared for it, that will
be the kind of government which they will have. Government
is at best but an expedient; but most governments are usually,
and all governments are sometimes, inexpedient. The objections which have been brought against a standing army, and
they are many and weighty, and deserve to prevail, may also at
last be brought against a standing government. The standing
army is only an arm of the standing government. The government itself, which is only the mode which the people have chosen to execute their will, is equally liable to be abused and per-
verted before the people can act through it. Witness the present
Mexican war, the work of comparatively a few individuals

using the standing government as their tool; for, in the outset, the people would not have consented to this measure.

This American government—what is it but a tradition, 2 though a recent one, endeavoring to transmit itself unimpaired to posterity, but each instant losing some of its integrity? It has not the vitality and force of a single living man; for a single man can bend it to his will. It is a sort of wooden gun to the people themselves. But it is not the less necessary for this; for the people must have some complicated machinery or other, and hear its din, to satisfy that idea of government which they have. Governments show thus how successfully men can be imposed on, even impose on themselves, for their own advantage. It is excellent, we must all allow. Yet this government never of itself furthered any enterprise, but by the alacrity with which it got out of its way. *It* does not keep the country free. *It* does not settle the West. *It* does not educate. The character inherent in the American people has done all that has been accomplished; and it would have done somewhat more, if the government had not sometimes got in its way. For government is an expedient by which men would fain succeed in letting one another alone; and, as has been said, when it is most expedient, the governed are most let alone by it. Trade and commerce, if they were not made of India-rubber, would never manage to bounce over the obstacles which legislators are continually putting in their way; and, if one were to judge these men wholly by the effects of their actions and not partly by their intentions, they would deserve to be classed and punished with those mischievous persons who put obstructions on the railroads.

But, to speak practically and as a citizen, unlike those who 3 call themselves no-government men, I ask for, not at once no government, but *at once* a better government. Let every man make known what kind of government would command his respect, and that will be one step toward obtaining it.

After all, the practical reason why, when the power is once in 4 the hands of people, a majority are permitted, and for a long period continue, to rule is not because they are most likely to be in the right, nor because this seems fairest to the minority, but because they are physically the strongest. But a government in which the majority rule in all cases cannot be based on justice, even as far as men understand it. Can there not be a government in which majorities do not virtually decide right and wrong, but conscience?—in which majorities decide only those questions to which the rule of expediency is applicable? Must the citizen ever for a moment, or in the least degree, resign his conscience to the legislator? Why has every man a conscience, then? I think that we should be men first, and subjects afterward. It is not desirable to cultivate a respect for the law, so much as for the right. The only obligation which I have a right to assume is to do at any time what I think right. It is truly enough said, that a corporation has no conscience; but a corporation of conscientious men is a corporation *with* a conscience. Law never made men a whit more just; and, by means of their respect for it, even the well-disposed are daily made the agents of injustice. A common and natural result of an undue respect for law is, that you may see a file of soldiers, colonel, captain, corporal, privates, powder-monkeys, and all, marching in admirable order over hill and dale to the wars, against their will, ay, against their common sense and consciences, which makes it very steep marching indeed, and produces a palpitation of the heart. They have no doubt that it is a damnable business in which they are concerned; they are all peaceably inclined. Now, what are they? Men at all? or small movable forts and magazines, at the service of some unscrupulous man in power? Visit the Navy-Yard, and behold a marine, such a man as an American government can make, or such as it can make a man with its black arts,—a mere shadow and reminiscence of humanity, a man laid out alive and standing, and already, as one may say, buried under arms with funeral accompaniments, though it may be,—

> "Not a drum was heard, not a funeral note,
>   As his corse to the rampart we hurried;
> Not a soldier discharged his farewell shot
>   O'er the grave where our hero we buried."[1]

5   The mass of men serve the state thus, not as men mainly, but as machines, with their bodies. They are the standing army, and the militia, jailers, constables, posse comitatus, etc. In most cases there is no free exercise whatever of the judgment or of the moral sense; but they put themselves on a level with wood and earth and stones; and wooden men can perhaps be manufactured that will serve the purpose as well. Such command no more respect than men of straw or a lump of dirt. They have the same sort of worth only as horses and dogs. Yet such as these even are commonly esteemed good citizens. Others—as most legislators, politicians, lawyers, ministers, and office-holders—serve the state chiefly with their heads; and, as they rarely make any moral distinctions, they are as likely to serve the Devil, without *intending* it, as God. A very

---

[1]From "Burial of St. John Moore at Corunna" by Charles Wolfe (1817).

few, as heroes, patriots, martyrs, reformers in the great sense, and *men*, serve the state with their consciences also, and so necessarily resist it for the most part; and they are commonly treated as enemies by it. A wise man will only be useful as a man, and will not submit to be "clay," and "stop a hole to keep the wind away," but leave that office to his dust at least:—

> "I am too high-born to be propertied,
> To be a secondary at control,
> Or useful serving-man and instrument
> To any sovereign state throughout the world."[2]

He who gives himself entirely to his fellow-men appears to them useless and selfish; but he who gives himself partially to them is pronounced a benefactor and philanthropist.   6

How does it become a man to behave toward this American government to-day? I answer, that he cannot without disgrace be associated with it. I cannot for an instant recognize that political organization as *my* government which is the *slave's* government also.   7

All men recognize the right of revolution; that is, the right to refuse allegiance to, and to resist, the government, when its tyranny or its inefficiency are great and unendurable. But almost all say that such is not the case now. But such was the case, they think, in the Revolution of '75. If one were to tell me that this was a bad government because it taxed certain foreign commodities brought to its ports, it is most probable that I should not make an ado about it, for I can do without them. All machines have their friction; and possibly this does enough good to counterbalance the evil. At any rate, it is a great evil to make a stir about it. But when the friction comes to have its machine, and oppression and robbery are organized, I say, let us not have such a machine any longer. In other words, when a sixth of the population of a nation which has undertaken to be the refuge of liberty are slaves, and a whole country is unjustly overrun and conquered by a foreign army, and subjected to military law, I think that it is not too soon for honest men to rebel and revolutionize. What makes this duty the more urgent is the fact that the country so overrun is not our own, but ours is the invading army.   8

Paley,[3] a common authority with many on moral questions, in his chapter on the "Duty of Submission to Civil Government," resolves all civil obligation into expediency; and he proceeds to   9

---

[2]The line before the qotation is from *Hamlet* V. i. 236–37; the quotation is from Shakespeare's *King John* V. ii 79–82.

[3]William Paley (1743–1805), English theologian.

say, "that so long as the interest of the whole society requires it, that is, so long as the established government cannot be resisted or changed without public inconveniency, it is the will of God that the established government be obeyed, and no longer. . . . This principle being admitted, the justice of every particular case of resistance is reduced to a computation of the quantity of the danger and grievance on the one side, and of the probability and expense of redressing it on the other." Of this, he says, every man shall judge for himself. But Paley appears never to have contemplated those cases to which the rule of expediency does not apply, in which a people, as well as an individual, must do justice, cost what it may. If I have unjustly wrested a plank from a drowning man, I must restore it to him though I drown myself. This, according to Paley, would be inconvenient. But he that would save his life, in such a case, shall lose it. This people must cease to hold slaves, and to make war on Mexico, though it cost them their existence as a people.

10   In their practice, nations agree with Paley; but does any one think that Massachusetts does exactly what is right at the present crisis?

> "A drab of state, a cloth-o'-silver slut,
> To have her train borne up, and her soul trail in the dirt."

Practically speaking the opponents to a reform in Massachusetts are not a hundred thousand politicians at the South, but a hundred thousand merchants and farmers here, who are more interested in commerce and agriculture than they are in humanity, and are not prepared to do justice to the slave and to Mexico, *cost what it may.* I quarrel not with far-off foes, but with those who, near at home, coöperate with, and do the bidding of, those far away, and without whom the latter would be harmless. We are accustomed to say, that the mass of men are unprepared; but improvement is slow, because the few are not materially wiser or better than the many. It is not so important that many should be as good as you, as that there be some absolute goodness somewhere; for that will leaven the whole lump. There are thousands who are *in opinion* opposed to slavery and to the war, who yet in effect do nothing to put an end to them; who, esteeming themselves children of Washington and Franklin, sit down with their hands in their pockets, and say that they know not what to do, and do nothing; who even postpone the question of freedom to the question of free-trade, and quietly read the prices-current along with the latest advices from Mexico, after dinner, and, it may be, fall asleep over them both. What is the price-current of an honest man and patriot to-day? They hesitate, and they regret, and sometimes they petition; but they do nothing in earnest and with effect. They will wait, well disposed, for others to remedy the evil, that they may no longer have it to regret. At most, they give only a cheap vote, and a feeble countenance and Godspeed, to the right, as it goes by them. There are nine hundred and ninety-nine patrons of virtue to one virtuous man. But it is easier to deal with the real possessor of a thing than with the temporary guardian of it.

All voting is a sort of gaming, like checkers or backgammon,   11
with a slight moral tinge to it, a playing with right and wrong, with moral questions; and betting naturally accompanies it. The character of the voters is not staked. I cast my vote, perchance, as I think right; but I am not vitally concerned that that right should prevail. I am willing to leave it to the majority. Its obligation, therefore, never exceeds that of expediency. Even voting *for the right* is *doing* nothing for it. It is only expressing to men feebly your desire that it should prevail. A wise man will not leave the right to the mercy of chance, nor wish it to prevail through the power of the majority. There is but little virtue in the action of masses of men. When the majority shall at length vote for the abolition of slavery, it will be because they are indifferent to slavery, or because there is but little slavery left to be abolished by their vote. *They* will then be the only slaves. Only *his* vote can hasten the abolition of slavery who asserts his own freedom by his vote.

I hear of a convention to be held at Baltimore, or elsewhere,   12
for the selection of a candidate for the Presidency, made up chiefly of editors, and men who are politicians by profession; but I think, what is it to any independent, intelligent, and respectable man what decision they may come to? Shall we not have the advantage of his wisdom and honesty, nevertheless? Can we not count upon some independent votes? Are there not many individuals in the country who do not attend conventions? But no: I find that the respectable man, so called, has immediately drifted from his position, and despairs of his country, when his country has more reason to despair of him. He forthwith adopts one of the candidates thus selected as the only *available* one, thus proving that he is himself *available* for any purposes of the demagogue. His vote is of no more worth than that of any unprincipled foreigner or hireling native, who may have been bought. O for a man who is a *man*, and, as my neighbor says, has a bone in his back which you cannot pass your hand through! Our statistics are at fault: the population has been returned too large. How many *men* are there to a square thousand miles in this country? Hardly one. Does not

America offer any inducement for men to settle here? The American has dwindled into an Odd Fellow,—one who may be known by the development of his organ of gregariousness, and a manifest lack of intellect and cheerful self-reliance; whose first and chief concern, on coming into the world, is to see that the Almshouses are in good repair; and, before yet he has lawfully donned the virile garb, to collect a fund for the support of the widows and orphans that may be; who, in short, ventures to live only by the aid of the Mutual Insurance company, which has promised to bury him decently.

13   It is not a man's duty, as a matter of course, to devote himself to the eradication of any, even the most enormous wrong; he may still properly have other concerns to engage him; but it is his duty, at least, to wash his hands of it, and, if he gives it no thought longer, not to give it practically his support. If I devote myself to other pursuits and contemplations, I must first see, at least, that I do not pursue them sitting upon another man's shoulders. I must get off him first, that he may pursue his contemplations too. See what gross inconsistency is tolerated. I have heard some of my townsmen say, "I should like to have them order me out to help put down an insurrection of the slaves, or to march to Mexico;—see if I would go"; and yet these very men have each, directly by their allegiance, and so indirectly, at least, by their money, furnished a substitute. The soldier is applauded who refuses to serve in an unjust war by those who do not refuse to sustain the unjust government which makes the war; is applauded by those whose own act and authority he disregards and sets at naught; as if the state were penitent to that degree that it hired one to scourge it while it sinned, but not to that degree that it left off sinning for a moment. Thus, under the name of Order and Civil Government, we are all made at last to pay homage to and support our own meanness. After the first blush of sin comes its indifference; and from immoral it becomes, as it were, *un*moral, and not quite unnecessary to that life which we have made.

14   The broadest and most prevalent error requires the most disinterested virtue to sustain it. The slight reproach to which the virtue of patriotism is commonly liable, the noble are most likely to incur. Those who, while they disapprove of the character and measures of a government, yield to it their allegiance and support are undoubtedly its most conscientious supporters, and so frequently the most serious obstacles to reform. Some are petitioning the state to dissolve the Union, to disregard the requisitions of the President. Why do they not dissolve it themselves,—the union between themselves and the state,—and refuse to pay their quota into its treasury? Do not they stand in the same relation to the state that the state does to the

Union? And have not the same reasons prevented the state from resisting the Union which have prevented them from resisting the state?

How can a man be satisfied to entertain an opinion merely, and enjoy *it?* Is there any enjoyment in it, if his opinion is that he is aggrieved? If you are cheated out of a single dollar by your neighbor, you do not rest satisfied with knowing that you are cheated, or with saying that you are cheated, or even with petitioning him to pay you your due; but you take effectual steps at once to obtain the full amount, and see that you are never cheated again. Action from principle, the perception and the performance of right, changes things and relations; it is essentially revolutionary, and does not consist wholly with anything which was. It not only divides states and churches, it divides families; ay, it divides the *individual,* separating the diabolical in him from the divine. 15

Unjust laws exist: shall we be content to obey them, or shall we endeavor to amend them, and obey them until we have succeeded, or shall we transgress them at once? Men generally, under such a government as this, think that they ought to wait until they have persuaded the majority to alter them. They think that, if they should resist, the remedy would be worse than the evil. But it is the fault of the government itself that the remedy *is* worse than the evil. *It* makes it worse. Why is it not more apt to anticipate and provide for reform? Why does it not cherish its wise minority? Why does it cry and resist before it is hurt? Why does it not encourage its citizens to be on the alert to point out its faults, and *do* better than it would have them? Why does it always crucify Christ, and excommunicate Copernicus and Luther, and pronounce Washington and Franklin rebels? 16

One would think, that a deliberate and practical denial of its authority was the only offense never contemplated by government; else, why has it not assigned its definite, its suitable and proportionate penalty? If a man who has no property refuses but once to earn nine shillings for the state, he is put in prison for a period unlimited by any law that I know, and determined only by the discretion of those who place him there; but if he should steal ninety times nine shillings from the state, he is soon permitted to go at large again. 17

If the injustice is part of the necessary friction of the machine of government, let it go, let it go; perchance it will wear smooth,—certainly the machine will wear out. If the injustice has a spring, or a pulley, or a rope, or a crank, exclusively for itself, then perhaps you may consider whether the remedy will not be worse than the evil; but if it is of such a nature that it requires you to be the agent of injustice to another, then, I say, 18 break the law. Let your life be a counter friction to stop the machine. What I have to do is to see, at any rate, that I do not lend myself to the wrong which I condemn.

19   As for adopting the ways which the state has provided for remedying the evil, I know not of such ways. They take too much time, and a man's life will be gone. I have other affairs to attend to. I came into this world, not chiefly to make this a good place to live in, but to live in it, be it good or bad. A man has not everything to do, but something; and because he cannot do *everything*, it is not necessary that he should do *something* wrong. It is not my business to be petitioning the Governor or the Legislature any more than it is theirs to petition me; and if they should not hear my petition, what should I do then? But in this case the state has provided no way; its very Constitution is the evil. This may seem to be harsh and stubborn and unconciliatory; but it is to treat with the utmost kindness and consideration the only spirit that can appreciate or deserves it. So is all change for the better, like birth and death, which convulse the body.

20   I do not hesitate to say, that those who call themselves Abolitionists should at once effectually withdraw their support, both in person and property, from the government of Massachusetts, and not wait till they constitute a majority of one, before they suffer the right to prevail through them. I think that it is enough if they have God on their side, without waiting for that other one. Moreover, any man more right than his neighbors constitutes a majority of one already.

21   I meet this American government, or its representative, the state government, directly, and face to face, once a year—no more—in the person of its tax-gatherer; this is the only mode in which a man situated as I am necessarily meets it; and it then says distinctly, Recognize me; and the simplest, the most effectual, and, in the present posture of affairs, the indispensablest mode of treating with it on this head, of expressing your little satisfaction with and love for it, is to deny it then. My civil neighbor, the tax-gatherer, is the very man I have to deal with,—for it is, after all, with men and not with parchment that I quarrel,—and he has voluntarily chosen to be an agent of the government. How shall he ever know well what he is and does as an officer of the government, or as a man, until he is obliged to consider whether he shall treat me, his neighbor, for whom he has respect, as a neighbor and well-disposed man, or as a maniac and disturber of the peace, and see if he can get over this obstruction to his neighborliness without a ruder and more impetuous thought or speech corresponding with his action. I know this well, that if one thousand, if one hundred, if ten men whom I could name,—if ten

honest men only,—ay, if *one* HONEST man, in this State of Massachusetts, *ceasing to hold slaves*, were actually to withdraw from this copartnership, and be locked up in the county jail therefor, it would be the abolition of slavery in America. For it matters not how small the beginning may seem to be; what is once well done is done forever. But we love better to talk about it: that we say is our mission. Reform keeps many scores of newspapers in its service, but not one man. If my esteemed neighbor, the State's ambassador, who will devote his days to the settlement of the question of human rights in the Council Chamber, instead of being threatened with the prisons of Carolina, were to sit down the prisoner of Massachusetts, that State which is so anxious to foist the sin of slavery upon her sister,—though at present she can discover only an act of inhospitality to be the ground of a quarrel with her—the Legislature would not wholly waive the subject the following winter.

22

Under a government which imprisons any unjustly, the true place for a just man is also a prison. The proper place today, the only place which Massachusetts has provided for her freer and less desponding spirits, is in her prisons, to be put out and locked out of the State by her own act, as they have already put themselves out by their principles. It is there that the fugitive slave, and the Mexican prisoner on parole, and the Indian come to plead the wrongs of his race should find them; on that separate, but more free and honorable ground, where the State places those who are not *with* her, but *against* her,—the only house in a slave State in which a free man can abide with honor. If any think that their influence would be lost there, and their voices no longer afflict the ear of the State, that they would not be as an enemy within its walls, they do not know by how much truth is stronger than error, nor how much more eloquently and effectively he can combat injustice who has experienced a little in his own person. Cast your whole vote, not a strip of paper merely, but your whole influence. A minority is powerless while it conforms to the majority; it is not even a minority then; but it is irresistible when it clogs by its whole weight. If the alternative is to keep all just men in prison, or give up war and slavery, the State will not hesitate which to choose. If a thousand men were not to pay their tax-bills this year, that would not be a violent and bloody measure, as it would be to pay them, and enable the State to commit violence and shed innocent blood. This is, in fact, the definition of a peaceable revolution, if any such is possible. If the tax-gatherer, or any other public officer, asks me, as one has done, "But what shall I do?" my answer is, "If you really wish to do anything, resign your office." When the subject has refused allegiance, and the officer has resigned his office, then the revolution is accomplished. But even suppose blood should flow. Is there not a sort of blood shed when the conscience is wounded? Through this wound a man's real manhood and immortality flow out, and he bleeds to an everlasting death. I see this blood flowing now.

23   I have contemplated the imprisonment of the offender, rather than the seizure of his goods,—though both will serve the same purpose,—because they who assert the purest right, and consequently are most dangerous to a corrupt State, commonly have not spent much time in accumulating property. To such the State renders comparatively small service, and a slight tax is wont to appear exorbitant, particularly if they are obliged to earn it by special labor with their hands. If there were one who lived wholly without the use of money, the State itself would hesitate to demand it of him. But the rich man— not to make any invidious comparison—is always sold to the institution which makes him rich. Absolutely speaking, the more money, the less virtue; for money comes between a man and his objects, and obtains them for him; and it was certainly no great virtue to obtain it. It puts to rest many questions which he would otherwise be taxed to answer; while the only new question which it puts is the hard but superfluous one, how to spend it. Thus his moral ground is taken from under his feet. The opportunities of living are diminished in proportion as what are called the "means" are increased. The best thing a man can do for his culture when he is rich is to endeavor to carry out those schemes which he entertained when he was poor. Christ answered the Herodians according to their condition. "Show me the tribute-money," said he;—and one took a penny out of his pocket;—if you use money which has the image of Caesar on it, and which he has made current and valuable, that is, *if you are men of the State,* and gladly enjoy the advantages of Caesar's government, then pay him back some of his own when he demands it. "Render therefore to Caesar that which is Caesar's, and to God those things which are God's,"—leaving them no wiser than before as to which was which; for they did not wish to know.

24   When I converse with the freest of my neighbors, I perceive that, whatever they may say about the magnitude and seriousness of the question, and their regard for the public tranquillity, the long and the short of the matter is, that they cannot spare the protection of the existing government, and they dread the consequences to their property and families of disobedience to it. For my own part, I should not like to think that I ever rely on the protection of the State. But, if I deny the authority of the State when it presents its tax-bill, it will soon

take and waste all my property, and so harass me and my children without end. This is hard. This makes it impossible for a man to live honestly, and at the same time comfortably, in outward respects. It will not be worth the while to accumulate property; that would be sure to go again. You must hire or squat somewhere, and raise but a small crop, and eat that soon. You must live within yourself, and depend upon yourself always tucked up and ready for a start, and not have many affairs. A man may grow rich in Turkey even, if he will be in all respects a good subject of the Turkish government. Confucius said: "If a state is governed by the principles of reason, poverty and misery are subjects of shame; if a state is not governed by the principles of reason, riches and honors are the subjects of shame." No: until I want the protection of Massachusetts to be extended to me in some distant Southern port, where my liberty is endangered, or until I am bent solely on building up an estate at home by peaceful enterprise, I can afford to refuse allegiance to Massachusetts, and her right to my property and life. It costs me less in every sense to incur the penalty of disobedience to the State than it would to obey. I should feel as if I were worth less in that case.

Some years ago, the State met me in behalf of the Church, 25 and commanded me to pay a certain sum toward the support of a clergyman whose preaching my father attended, but never I myself. "Pay," it said, "or be locked up in the jail." I declined to pay. But, unfortunately, another man saw fit to pay it. I did not see why the schoolmaster should be taxed to support the priest, and not the priest the schoolmaster; for I was not the State's schoolmaster, but I supported myself by voluntary subscription. I did not see why the lyceum should not present its tax-bill, and have the State to back its demand, as well as the Church. However, at the request of the selectmen, I condescended to make some such statement as this in writing:—"Know all men by these presents, that I, Henry Thoreau, do not wish to be regarded as a member of any incorporated society which I have not joined." This I gave to the town clerk; and he has it. The State, having thus learned that I did not wish to be regarded as a member of that church, has never made a like demand on me since; though it said that it must adhere to its original presumption that time. If I had known how to name them, I should then have signed off in detail from all the societies which I never signed on to; but I did not know where to find a complete list.

I have paid no poll-tax[4] for six years. I was put into jail once 26 on this account, for one night; and, as I stood considering the

---

[4]Tax assessed against a person (not property); payment was frequently prerequisite for voting.

walls of solid stone, two or three feet thick, the door of wood and iron, a foot thick, and the iron grating which strained the light, I could not help being struck with the foolishness of that institution which treated me as if I were mere flesh and blood and bones, to be locked up. I wondered that it should have concluded at length that this was the best use it could put me to, and had never thought to avail itself of my services in some way. I saw that, if there was a wall of stone between me and my townsmen, there was still a more difficult one to climb or break through before they could get to be as free as I was. I did not for a moment feel confined, and the walls seemed a great waste of stone and mortar. I felt as if I alone of all my townsmen had paid my tax. They plainly did not know how to treat me, but behaved like persons who are underbred. In every threat and in every compliment there was a blunder; for they thought that my chief desire was to stand the other side of that stone wall. I could not but smile to see how industriously they locked the door on my meditations, which followed them out again without let or hindrance, and *they* were really all that was dangerous. As they could not reach me, they had resolved to punish my body; just as boys, if they cannot come at some person against whom they have a spite, will abuse his dog. I saw that the State was half-witted, that it was timid as a lone woman with her silver spoons, and that it did not know its friends from its foes, and I lost all my remaining respect for it, and pitied it.

27   Thus the State never intentionally confronts a man's sense, intellectual or moral, but only his body, his senses. It is not armed with superior wit or honesty, but with superior physical strength. I was not born to be forced. I will breathe after my own fashion. Let us see who is the strongest. What force has a multitude? They only can force me who obey a higher law than I. They force me to become like themselves. I do not hear of *men* being *forced* to live this way or that by masses of men. What sort of life were that to live? When I meet a government which says to me, "Your money or your life," why should I be in haste to give it my money? It may be in a great strait, and not know what to do: I cannot help that. It must help itself; do as I do. It is not worth the while to snivel about it. I am not responsible for the successful working of the machinery of society. I am not the son of the engineer. I perceive that, when an acorn and a chestnut fall side by side, the one does not remain inert to make way for the other, but both obey their own laws, and spring and grow and flourish as best they can, till one, perchance, overshadows and destroys the other. If a plant cannot live according to its nature, it dies; and so a man.

The night in prison was novel and interesting enough. The 28
prisoners in their shirt-sleeves were enjoying a chat and the
evening air in the doorway, when I entered. But the jailer said,
"Come, boys, it is time to lock up;" and so they dispersed, and I
heard the sound of their steps returning into the hollow apartments. My room-mate was introduced to me by the jailer as "a
first-rate fellow and a clever man." When the door was locked,
he showed me where to hang my hat, and how he managed
matters there. The rooms were whitewashed once a month;
and this one, at least, was the whitest, most simply furnished,
and probably the neatest apartment in the town. He naturally
wanted to know where I came from, and what brought me
there; and, when I had told him, I asked him in my turn how
he came there, presuming him to be an honest man, of course;
and, as the world goes, I believe he was. "Why," said he, "they
accuse me of burning a barn; but I never did it." As near as I
could discover, he had probably gone to bed in a barn when
drunk, and smoked his pipe there; and so a barn was burnt. He
had the reputation of being a clever man, had been there some
three months waiting for his trial to come on, and would have
to wait as much longer; but he was quite domesticated and
contented, since he got his board for nothing, and thought that
he was well treated.

He occupied one window, and I the other; and I saw that if 29
one stayed there long, his principal business would be to look
out the window. I had soon read all the tracts that were left
there, and examined where former prisoners had broken out,
and where a grate had been sawed off, and heard the history of
the various occupants of that room; for I found that even here
there was a history and a gossip which never circulated beyond
the walls of the jail. Probably this is the only house in the town
where verses are composed, which are afterward printed in a
circular form, but not published. I was shown quite a long list
of verses which were composed by some young men who had
been detected in an attempt to escape, who avenged themselves by singing them.

I pumped my fellow-prisoner as dry as I could, for fear I 30
should never see him again; but at length he showed me which
was my bed, and left me to blow out the lamp.

It was like traveling into a far country, such as I had never 31
expected to behold, to lie there for one night. It seemed to me
that I never had heard the town-clock strike before, nor the
evening sounds of the village; for we slept with the windows
open, which were inside the grating. It was to see my native village in the light of the Middle Ages, and our Concord was
turned into a Rhine stream, and visions of knights and castles

passed before me. They were the voices of old burghers that I heard in the streets. I was an involuntary spectator and auditor of whatever was done and said in the kitchen of the adjacent village-inn,—a wholly new and rare experience to me. It was a closer view of my native town. I was fairly inside of it. I never had seen its institutions before. This is one of its peculiar institutions; for it is a shire town. I began to comprehend what its inhabitants were about.

32   In the morning, our breakfasts were put through the hole in the door, in small oblong-square tin pans, made to fit, and holding a pint of chocolate, with brown bread, and an iron spoon. When they called for the vessels again, I was green enough to return what bread I had left; but my comrade seized it, and said that I should lay that up for lunch or dinner. Soon after he was let out to work at haying in a neighboring field, whither he went every day, and would not be back till noon; so he bade me good-day, saying that he doubted if he should see me again.

33   When I came out of prison—for some one interfered, and paid that tax,—I did not perceive that great changes had taken place on the common, such as he observed who went in a youth and emerged a tottering and gray-headed man; and yet a change had to my eyes come over the scene,—the town, and State, and country,—greater than any that mere time could effect. I saw yet more distinctly the State in which I lived. I saw to what extent the people among whom I lived could be trusted as good neighbors and friends; that their friendship was for summer weather only; that they did not greatly propose to do right; that they were a distinct race from me by their prejudices and superstitions, as the Chinamen and Malays are; that in their sacrifices to humanity they ran no risks, not even to their property; that after all they were not so noble but they treated the thief as he had treated them, and hoped, by a certain outward observance and a few prayers, and by walking in a particular straight though useless path from time to time, to save their souls. This may be to judge my neighbors harshly; for I believe that many of them are not aware that they have such an institution as the jail in their village.

34   It was formerly the custom in our village, when a poor debtor came out of jail, for his acquaintances to salute him, looking through their fingers, which were crossed to represent the grating of a jail window, "How do ye do?" My neighbors did not thus salute me, but first looked at me, and then at one another, as if I had returned from a long journey. I was put into jail as I was going to the shoemaker's to get a shoe which was mended. When I was let out the next morning, I proceeded to finish my errand, and, having put on my mended shoe, joined a huckleberry party, who were impatient to put themselves under my conduct;

and in half an hour,—for the horse was soon tackled,—was in the midst of a huckleberry field, on one of our highest hills, two miles off, and then the State was nowhere to be seen.

This is the whole history of "My Prisons."   35

Mahatma Gandhi
LETTER TO LORD IRWIN

Mahatma Gandhi (Mahatma means "of great soul") was born in India in 1869, studied law in London, and in 1893 went to South Africa, where he opposed discriminatory legislation against Indians, was exposed to the writing of Henry David Thoreau, and carried on a famous correspondence with the Russian novelist Leo Tolstoy concerning civil disobedience. In 1914 he returned to India, and about 1920 began a lifetime of committed support for India's independence from England—notably through the practice and encouragement of nonviolent resistance (satyagraha). After a decade of sporadic civil disobedience and periodic imprisonments, Gandhi in 1930 prepared a Declaration of Independence for India and soon after led a remarkable (and famous) 200-mile march to the sea to collect salt in symbolic defiance of the English government's monopoly on that product; by the end of the year, more than 100,000 people were jailed in the campaign. India of course did finally achieve independence, in 1947. The following year, while trying to calm tensions between Hindus and Moslems, Gandhi was assassinated.

The following letter was sent by Gandhi to the British viceroy in India, Lord Irwin, in March 1930, just ten days before the salt march was to begin. It was sent from Satyagraha Ashram, a community established to practice Gandhi's method of nonviolent resistance.

Satyagraha Ashram, Sabarmati,
March 2, 1930

Dear Friend,

Before embarking on civil disobedience and taking the risk I   1
have dreaded to take all these years, I would fain approach you and find a way out.

2   My personal faith is absolutely clear. I cannot intentionally hurt anything that lives, much less fellow human beings, even though they may do the greatest wrong to me and mine. Whilst, therefore, I hold the British rule to be a curse, I do not intend harm to a single Englishman or to any legitimate interest he may have in India.

3   I must not be misunderstood. Though I hold the British rule in India to be a curse, I do not, therefore, consider Englishmen in general to be worse than any other people on earth. I have the privilege of claiming many Englishmen as dearest friends. Indeed much that I have learnt of the evil of British rule is due to the writings of frank and courageous Englishmen who have not hesitated to tell the unpalatable truth about that rule.

4   And why do I regard the British rule as a curse?

5   It has impoverished the dumb millions by a system of progressive exploitation and by a ruinously expensive military and civil administration which the country can never afford.

6   It has reduced us politically to serfdom. It has sapped the foundations of our culture. And, by the policy of cruel disarmament, it has degraded us spiritually. Lacking the inward strength, we have been reduced, by all but universal disarmament, to a state bordering on cowardly helplessness.

7   In common with many of my countrymen, I had hugged the fond hope that the proposed Round Table Conference might furnish a solution. But, when you said plainly that you could not give any assurance that you or the British Cabinet would pledge yourselves to support a scheme of full Dominion Status, the Round Table Conference could not possibly furnish the solution for which vocal India is consciously, and the dumb millions are unconsciously, thirsting.

8   It seems as clear as daylight that responsible British statesmen do not contemplate any alteration in British policy that might adversely affect Britain's commerce with India or require an impartial and close scrutiny of Britain's transactions with India. If nothing is done to end the process of exploitation India must be bled with an ever increasing speed. The Finance Member regards as a settled fact the 1/6 ratio which by a stroke of the pen drains India of a few crores.[1] And when a serious attempt is being made through a civil form of direct action, to unsettle this fact, among many others, even you cannot help appealing to the wealthy landed classes to help you to crush that attempt in the name of an order that grinds India to atoms.

9   Unless those who work in the name of the nation understand and keep before all concerned the motive that lies behind the

[1] In Indian currency, a crore is equivalent to ten million rupees.

craving for independence, there is every danger of independence coming to us so changed as to be of no value to those toiling voiceless millions for whom it is sought and for whom it is worth taking. It is for that reason that I have been recently telling the public what independence should really mean.

Let me put before you some of the salient points.   10

The terrific pressure of land revenue, which furnishes a large   11
part of the total, must undergo considerable modification in an independent India. Even the much vaunted permanent settlement benefits the few rich zamindars,[2] not the ryots.[3] The ryot has remained as helpless as ever. He is a mere tenant at will. Not only, then, has the land revenue to be considerably reduced, but the whole revenue system has to be so revised as to make the ryot's good its primary concern. But the British system seems to be designed to crush the very life out of him. Even the salt he must use to live is so taxed as to make the burden fall heaviest on him, if only because of the heartless impartiality of its incidence. The tax shows itself still more burdensome on the poor man when it is remembered that salt is the one thing he must eat more than the rich man both individually and collectively.

The iniquities sampled above are maintained in order to   12
carry on a foreign administration, demonstrably the most expensive in the world. Take your own salary. It is over Rs. 21,000 per month, besides many other indirect additions. The British Prime Minister gets £5,000 per year, i.e., over Rs. 5,400 per month at the present rate of exchange. You are getting over Rs. 700 per day against India's average income of less than annas 2 per day. The Prime Minister gets Rs. 180 per day against Great Britain's average income of nearly Rs. 2 per day. Thus you are getting much over five thousand times India's average income. The British Prime Minister is getting only ninety times Britain's average income. On bended knees I ask you to ponder over this phenomenon. I have taken a personal illustration to drive home a painful truth. I have too great a regard for you as a man to wish to hurt your feelings. I know that you do not need the salary you get. Probably the whole of your salary goes for charity. But a system that provides for such an arrangement deserves to be summarily scrapped.

If India is to live as a nation, if the slow death by starvation   13
of her people is to stop, some remedy must be found for immediate relief. The proposed Conference is certainly not the rem-

---

[2]A zamindar is a landowner.
[3]A ryot is a tenant farmer.

edy. It is not a matter of carrying conviction by argument. The matter resolves itself into one of matching forces. Conviction or no conviction, Great Britain would defend her Indian commerce and interests by all the forces at her command. India must consequently evolve force enough to free herself from that embrace of death.

14   It is common cause that, however disorganized and, for the time being, insignificant it may be, the party of violence is gaining ground and making itself felt. Its end is the same as mine. But I am convinced that it cannot bring the desired relief to the dumb millions. And the conviction is growing deeper and deeper in me that nothing but unadulterated non-violence can check the organized violence of the British Government. Many think that non-violence is not an active force. My experience, limited though it undoubtedly is, shows that non-violence can be an intensely active force. It is my purpose to set in motion that force as well against the organized violent force of the British rule as [against] the unorganized violent force of the growing party of violence. To sit still would be to give rein to both the forces above mentioned. Having an unquestioning and immovable faith in the efficacy of non-violence as I know it, it would be sinful on my part to wait any longer.

15   This non-violence will be expressed through civil disobedience, for the moment confined to the inmates of the Satyagraha Ashram, but ultimately designed to cover all those who choose to join the movement with its obvious limitations.

16   I know that in embarking on non-violence I shall be running what might fairly be termed a mad risk. But the victories of truth have never been won without risks, often of the gravest character. Conversion of a nation that has consciously or unconsciously preyed upon another, far more numerous, far more ancient and no less cultured than itself, is worth any amount of risk.

17   I have deliberately used the word "conversion." For my ambition is no less than to convert the British people through non-violence, and thus make them see the wrong they have done to India. I do not seek to harm your people. I want to serve them even as I want to serve my own. I believe that I have always served them. I served them up to 1919 blindly. But when my eyes were opened and I conceived non-cooperation, the object still was to serve them. I employed the same weapon that I have in all humility successfully used against the dearest members of my family. If I have equal love for your people with mine it will not long remain hidden. It will be acknowledged by them even as the members of my family acknowledged it after they had tried me for several years. If the people

join me as I expect they will, the sufferings they will undergo, unless the British nation sooner retraces its steps, will be enough to melt the stoniest hearts.

The plan through civil disobedience will be to combat such 18 evils as I have sampled out. If we want to sever the British connection it is because of such evils. When they are removed the path becomes easy. Then the way to friendly negotiation will be open. If the British commerce with India is purified of greed, you will have no difficulty in recognizing our independence. I respectfully invite you then to pave the way for immediate removal of those evils, and thus open a way for a real conference between equals, interested only in promoting the common good of mankind through voluntary fellowship and in arranging terms of mutual help and commerce equally suited to both. You have unnecessarily laid stress upon the communal problems that unhappily affect this land. Important though they undoubtedly are for the consideration of any scheme of government, they have little bearing on the greater problems which are above communities and which affect them all equally. But if you cannot see your way to deal with these evils and my letter makes no appeal to your heart, on the 11th day of this month, I shall proceed with such co-workers of the Ashram as I can take, to disregard the provisions of the salt laws. I regard this tax to be the most iniquitous of all from the poor man's standpoint. As the independence movement is essentially for the poorest in the land the beginning will be made with this evil. The wonder is that we have submitted to the cruel monopoly for so long. It is, I know, open to you to frustrate my design by arresting me. I hope that there will be tens of thousands ready, in a disciplined manner, to take up the work after me, and, in the act of disobeying the Salt Act to lay themselves open to the penalties of a law that should never have disfigured the Statute-book.

I have no desire to cause you unnecessary embarrassment, 19 or any at all, so far as I can help. If you think that there is any substance in my letter, and if you will care to discuss matters with me, and if to that end you would like me to postpone publication of this letter, I shall gladly refrain on receipt of a telegram to that effect soon after this reaches you. You will, however, do me the favour not to deflect me from my course unless you can see your way to conform to the substance of this letter.

This letter is not in any way intended as a threat but is a 20 simple and sacred duty peremptory on a civil resister. Therefore I am having it specially delivered by a young English friend who believes in the Indian cause and is a full believer in non-violence and whom Providence seems to have sent to me, as it were, for the very purpose.

> I remain,
> Your sincere friend,
> M. K. Gandhi

Martin Luther King Jr.

Born in Atlanta and educated at Morehouse College, Crozer Theological Seminary (near Philadelphia), and Boston University, Martin Luther King Jr. (1929–1968) was the most visible leader of the civil rights movement of the 1960s. An ordained minister with a doctorate in theology from Boston University, he worked especially in the South and through nonviolent means to overturn segregation statutes, to increase the number of African American voters, and to support other civil rights initiatives. Reverend King won the Nobel Peace Prize in 1964. When he was assassinated in 1968, all America mourned.

On April 12, 1963, in order to have himself arrested on a symbolic day (Good Friday), Reverend Martin Luther King Jr. disobeyed a court injunction forbidding demonstrations in Birmingham, Alabama. (See the photo on the next page.) That same day, eight leading white Birmingham clergymen (Christian and Jewish) published a letter in the Birmingham News *calling for the end of protests and exhorting protesters to work through the courts for the redress of their grievances. On the morning after his arrest, while held in solitary confinement, King began his response to these clergymen—his famous "Letter from Birmingham Jail." Begun in the margins of newspapers and on scraps of paper and finished by the following Tuesday, the letter was widely distributed and later became a central chapter in King's* Why We Can't Wait *(1964).*

PUBLIC STATEMENT
BY EIGHT ALABAMA
CLERGYMEN

April 12, 1963

We the undersigned clergymen are among those who, in 1
January, issued "An Appeal for Law and Order and Common
Sense," in dealing with racial problems in Alabama. We expressed understanding that honest convictions in racial matters
could properly be pursued in the courts, but urged that decisions
of those courts should in the meantime be peacefully obeyed.

Since that time there had been some evidence of increased 2
forbearance and a willingness to face facts. Responsible citizens have undertaken to work on various problems which
cause racial friction and unrest. In Birmingham, recent public

events had given indication that we all have opportunity for a new constructive and realistic approach to racial problems.

3 However, we are now confronted by a series of demonstrations by some of our Negro citizens, directed and led in part by outsiders. We recognize the natural impatience of people who feel that their hopes are slow in being realized. But we are convinced that these demonstrations are unwise and untimely.

4 We agree rather with certain local Negro leadership which has called for honest and open negotiation of racial issues in our area. And we believe this kind of facing of issues can best be accomplished by citizens of our own metropolitan area, white and Negro, meeting with their knowledge and experience of the local situation. All of us need to face that responsibility and find proper channels for its accomplishment.

5 Just as we formerly pointed out that "hatred and violence have no sanction in our religious and political traditions," we also point out that such actions as incite to hatred and violence, however technically peaceful those actions may be, have not contributed to the resolution of our local problems. We do not believe that these days of new hope are days when extreme measures are justified in Birmingham.

6 We commend the community as a whole, and the local news media and law enforcement officials in particular, on the calm manner in which these demonstrations have been handled. We urge the public to continue to show restraint should the demonstrations continue, and the law enforcement officials to remain calm and continue to protect our city from violence.

7 We further strongly urge our own Negro community to withdraw support from these demonstrations, and to unite locally in working peacefully for a better Birmingham. When rights are consistently denied, a cause should be pressed in the courts and in negotiations among local leaders, and not in the streets. We appeal to both our white and Negro citizenry to observe the principles of law and order and common sense. Signed by:

> C. C. J. Carpenter, D.D., LL.D.,
> *Bishop of Alabama*
> Joseph A. Durick, D.D.,
> *Auxiliary Bishop, Diocese of Mobile, Birmingham*
> *Rabbi* Milton L. Grafman,
> *Temple Emanu-El, Birmingham, Alabama*
> *Bishop* Paul Hardin,
> *Bishop of the Alabama-West Florida Conference of the Methodist Church*
> *Bishop* Nolan B. Harmon,
> *Bishop of the North Alabama Conference of the Methodist Church*

George M. Murray, D.D., LL.D.,
Bishop Coadjutor, Episcopal Diocese of Alabama
Edward V. Ramage,
*Moderator, Synod of the Alabama Presbyterian Church
    in the United States*
Earl Stallings,
Pastor, First Baptist Church, Birmingham, Alabama

LETTER FROM
BIRMINGHAM JAIL

April 16, 1963

My Dear Fellow Clergymen:

1 While confined here in the Birmingham city jail, I came across your recent statement calling my present activities "unwise and untimely." Seldom do I pause to answer criticism of my work and ideas. If I sought to answer all the criticisms that cross my desk, my secretaries would have little time for anything other than such correspondence in the course of the day, and I would have no time for constructive work. But since I feel that you are men of genuine good will and that your criticisms are sincerely set forth, I want to try to answer your statement in what I hope will be patient and reasonable terms.

2 I think I should indicate why I am here in Birmingham, since you have been influenced by the view which argues against "outsiders coming in." I have the honor of serving as president of the Southern Christian Leadership Conference, an organization operating in every southern state, with headquarters in Atlanta, Georgia. We have some eighty-five affiliated organizations across the South, and one of them is the Alabama Christian Movement for Human Rights. Frequently we share staff, educational and financial resources with our affiliates. Several months ago the affiliate here in Birmingham asked us to be on call to engage in a nonviolent direct-action program if such were deemed necessary. We readily consented, and when the hour came we lived up to our promise. So I, along with several members of my staff, am here because I was invited here. I am here because I have organizational ties here.

3 But more basically, I am in Birmingham because injustice is here. Just as the prophets of the eighth century B.C. left their villages and carried their "thus saith the Lord" far beyond the

boundaries of their home towns, and just as the Apostle Paul left his village of Tarsus and carried the gospel of Jesus Christ to the far corners of the Greco-Roman world, so am I compelled to carry the gospel of freedom beyond my own home town. Like Paul, I must constantly respond to the Macedonian call for aid.

4   Moreover, I am cognizant of the interrelatedness of all communities and states. I cannot sit idly by in Atlanta and not be concerned about what happens in Birmingham. Injustice anywhere is a threat to justice everywhere. We are caught in an inescapable network of mutuality, tied in a single garment of destiny. Whatever affects one directly, affects all indirectly. Never again can we afford to live with the narrow, provincial "outside agitator" idea. Anyone who lives inside the United States can never be considered an outsider anywhere within its bounds.

5   You deplore the demonstrations taking place in Birmingham. But your statement, I am sorry to say, fails to express a similar concern for the conditions that brought about the demonstrations. I am sure that none of you would want to rest content with the superficial kind of social analysis that deals merely with effects and does not grapple with underlying causes. It is unfortunate that demonstrations are taking place in Birmingham, but it is even more unfortunate that the city's white power structure left the Negro community with no alternative.

6   In any nonviolent campaign there are four basic steps: collection of the facts to determine whether injustices exist; negotiation; self-purification; and direct action. We have gone through all these steps in Birmingham. There can be no gainsaying the fact that racial injustice engulfs this community. Birmingham is probably the most thoroughly segregated city in the United States. Its ugly record of brutality is widely known. Negroes have experienced grossly unjust treatment in the courts. There have been more unsolved bombings of Negro homes and churches in Birmingham than in any other city in the nation. These are the hard, brutal facts of the case. On the basis of these conditions, Negro leaders sought to negotiate with the city fathers. But the latter consistently refused to engage in good-faith negotiation.

7   Then, last September, came the opportunity to talk with leaders of Birmingham's economic community. In the course of the negotiations, certain promises were made by the merchants—for example, to remove the stores' humiliating racial signs. On the basis of these promises, the Reverend Fred Shuttlesworth and the leaders of the Alabama Christian Movement for Human Rights agreed to a moratorium on all demonstrations. As the weeks and months went by, we realized that we were the victims of a broken promise. A few signs, briefly removed, returned; the others remained.

As in so many past experiences, our hopes had been blasted, 8
and the shadow of deep disappointment settled upon us. We had
no alternative except to prepare for direct action, whereby we
would present our very bodies as a means of laying our case before the conscience of the local and the national community.
Mindful of the difficulties involved, we decided to undertake a
process of self-purification. We began a series of workshops on
nonviolence, and we repeatedly asked ourselves: "Are you able
to accept blows without retaliating?" "Are you able to endure
the ordeal of jail?" We decided to schedule our direct-action program for the Easter season, realizing that except for Christmas,
this is the main shopping period of the year. Knowing that a
strong economic-withdrawal program would be the by-product
of direct action, we felt that this would be the best time to bring
pressure to bear on the merchants for the needed change.

Then it occurred to us that Birmingham's mayoral election 9
was coming up in March, and we speedily decided to postpone
action until after election day. When we discovered that the
Commissioner of Public Safety, Eugene "Bull" Connor, had
piled up enough votes to be in the run-off, we decided again to
postpone action until the day after the run-off so that the
demonstrations could not be used to cloud the issues. Like
many others, we waited to see Mr. Connor defeated, and to this
end we endured postponement after postponement. Having
aided in this community need, we felt that our direct action
program could be delayed no longer.

You may well ask: "Why direct action? Why sit-ins, marches 10
and so forth? Isn't negotiation a better path?" You are quite
right in calling for negotiation. Indeed, this is the very purpose
of direct action. Nonviolent direct action seeks to create such a
crisis and foster such a tension that a community which has
constantly refused to negotiate is forced to confront the issue.
It seeks so to dramatize the issue that it can no longer be ignored. My citing the creation of tension as part of the work of
the nonviolent-resister may sound rather shocking. But I must
confess that I am not afraid of the word "tension." I have
earnestly opposed violent tension, but there is a type of constructive, nonviolent tension which is necessary for growth.
Just as Socrates felt that it was necessary to create a tension in
the mind so that individuals could rise from the bondage of
myths and half-truths to the unfettered realm of creative analysis and objective appraisal, so must we see the need for nonviolent gadflies to create the kind of tension in society that will
help men rise from the dark depths of prejudice and racism to
the majestic heights of understanding and brotherhood.

The purpose of our direct-action program is to create a situ- 11
ation so crisis-packed that it will inevitably open the door to

negotiation. I therefore concur with you in your call for negotiation. Too long has our beloved Southland been bogged down in a tragic effort to live in monologue rather than dialogue.

12   One of the basic points in your statement is that the action that I and my associates have taken in Birmingham is untimely. Some have asked: "Why didn't you give the new city administration time to act?" The only answer that I can give to this query is that the new Birmingham administration must be prodded about as much as the outgoing one, before it will act. We are sadly mistaken if we feel that the election of Albert Boutwell as mayor will bring the millennium to Birmingham. While Mr. Boutwell is a much more gentle person than Mr. Connor, they are both segregationists, dedicated to maintenance of the status quo. I have hope that Mr. Boutwell will be reasonable enough to see the futility of massive resistance to desegregation. But he will not see this without pressure from devotees of civil rights. My friends, I must say to you that we have not made a single gain in civil rights without determined legal and nonviolent pressure. Lamentably, it is an historical fact that privileged groups seldom give up their privileges voluntarily. Individuals may see the moral light and voluntarily give up their unjust posture; but, as Reinhold Niebuhr has reminded us, groups tend to be more immoral than individuals.

13   We know through painful experience that freedom is never voluntarily given by the oppressor; it must be demanded by the oppressed. Frankly, I have yet to engage in a direct-action campaign that was "well timed" in the view of those who have not suffered unduly from the disease of segregation. For years now I have heard the word "Wait!" It rings in the ear of every Negro with piercing familiarity. This "Wait" has almost always meant "Never." We must come to see, with one of our distinguished jurists, that "justice too long delayed is justice denied."

14   We have waited for more than 340 years for our constitutional and God-given rights. The nations of Asia and Africa are moving with jetlike speed toward gaining political independence, but we still creep at horse-and-buggy pace toward gaining a cup of coffee at a lunch counter. Perhaps it is easy for those who have never felt the stinging darts of segregation to say, "Wait." But when you have seen vicious mobs lynch your mothers and fathers at will and drown your sisters and brothers at whim; when you have seen hate-filled policemen curse, kick and even kill your black brothers and sisters; when you see the vast majority of your twenty million Negro brothers smothering in an airtight cage of poverty in the midst of an affluent society; when you suddenly find your tongue twisted and your speech stammering as you seek to explain to your six-year-old daughter why she can't go to the public amusement

park that has just been advertised on television, and see tears welling up in her eyes when she is told that Funtown is closed to colored children, and see ominous clouds of inferiority beginning to form in her little mental sky, and see her beginning to distort her personality by developing an unconscious bitterness toward white people; when you have to concoct an answer for a five-year-old son who is asking: "Daddy, why do white people treat colored people so mean?"; when you take a cross-country drive and find it necessary to sleep night after night in the uncomfortable corners of your automobile because no motel will accept you; when you are humiliated day in and day out by nagging signs reading "white" and "colored"; when your first name becomes "nigger," your middle name becomes "boy" (however old you are) and your last name becomes "John," and your wife and mother are never given the respected title "Mrs."; when you are harried by day and haunted by night by the fact that you are a Negro, living constantly at tiptoe stance, never quite knowing what to expect next, and are plagued with inner fears and outer resentments; when you are forever fighting a degenerating sense of "nobodiness"—then you will understand why we find it difficult to wait. There comes a time when the cup of endurance runs over, and men are no longer willing to be plunged into the abyss of despair. I hope, sirs, you can understand our legitimate and unavoidable impatience.

You express a great deal of anxiety over our willingness to   15
break laws. This is certainly a legitimate concern. Since we so diligently urge people to obey the Supreme Court's decision of 1954 outlawing segregation in the public schools, at first glance it may seem rather paradoxical for us consciously to break laws. One may well ask: "How can you advocate breaking some laws and obeying others?" The answer lies in the fact that there are two types of laws: just and unjust. I would be the first to advocate obeying just laws. One has not only a legal but a moral responsibility to obey just laws. Conversely, one has a moral responsibility to disobey unjust laws. I would agree with St. Augustine that "an unjust law is no law at all."

Now, what is the difference between the two? How does one   16
determine whether a law is just or unjust? A just law is a man-made code that squares with the moral law or the law of God. An unjust law is a code that is out of harmony with the moral law. To put it in the terms of St. Thomas Aquinas: An unjust law is a human law that is not rooted in eternal law and natural law. Any law that uplifts human personality is just. Any law that degrades human personality is unjust. All segregation statutes are unjust because segregation distorts the soul and damages the personality. It gives the segregator a false sense of superiority and the segregated a false sense of inferiority.

Segregation, to use the terminology of the Jewish philosopher Martin Buber, substitutes an "I–it" relationship for an "I–thou" relationship and ends up relegating persons to the status of things. Hence segregation is not only politically, economically and sociologically unsound, it is morally wrong and sinful. Paul Tillich has said that sin is separation. Is not segregation an existential expression of man's tragic separation, his awful estrangement, his terrible sinfulness? Thus it is that I can urge men to obey the 1954 decision of the Supreme Court, for it is morally right; and I can urge them to disobey segregation ordinances, for they are morally wrong.

17   Let us consider a more concrete example of just and unjust laws. An unjust law is a code that a numerical or power majority group compels a minority group to obey but does not make binding on itself. This is *difference* made legal. By the same token, a just law is a code that a majority compels a minority to follow and that it is willing to follow itself. This is *sameness* made legal.

18   Let me give another explanation. A law is unjust if it is inflicted on a minority that, as a result of being denied the right to vote, had no part in enacting or devising the law. Who can say that the legislature of Alabama which set up that state's segregation laws was democratically elected? Throughout Alabama all sorts of devious methods are used to prevent Negroes from becoming registered voters, and there are some counties in which, even though Negroes constitute a majority of the population, not a single Negro is registered. Can any law enacted under such circumstances be considered democratically structured?"

19   Sometimes a law is just on its face and unjust in its application. For instance, I have been arrested on a charge of parading without a permit. Now, there is nothing wrong in having an ordinance which requires a permit for a parade. But such an ordinance becomes unjust when it is used to maintain segregation and to deny citizens the First-Amendment privilege of peaceful assembly and protest.

20   I hope you are able to see the distinction I am trying to point out. In no sense do I advocate evading or defying the law, as would the rabid segregationist. That would lead to anarchy. One who breaks an unjust law must do so openly, lovingly, and with a willingness to accept the penalty. I submit that an individual who breaks a law that conscience tells him is unjust, and who willingly accepts the penalty of imprisonment in order to arouse the conscience of the community over its injustice, is in reality expressing the highest respect for law.

21   Of course, there is nothing new about this kind of civil disobedience. It was evidenced sublimely in the refusal of

Shadrach, Meshach and Abednego to obey the laws of Nebuchadnezzar, on the ground that a higher moral law was at stake. It was practiced superbly by the early Christians, who were willing to face hungry lions and the excruciating pain of chopping blocks rather than submit to certain unjust laws of the Roman Empire. To a degree, academic freedom is a reality today because Socrates practiced civil disobedience. In our own nation, the Boston Tea Party represented a massive act of civil disobedience.

We should never forget that everything Adolf Hitler did in Germany was "legal" and everything the Hungarian freedom fighters did in Hungary was "illegal." It was "illegal" to aid and comfort a Jew in Hitler's Germany. Even so, I am sure that, had I lived in Germany at the time, I would have aided and comforted my Jewish brothers. If today I lived in a Communist country where certain principles dear to the Christian faith are suppressed, I would openly advocate disobeying that country's antireligious laws.

I must make two honest confessions to you, my Christian and Jewish brothers. First, I must confess that over the past few years I have been gravely disappointed with the white moderate. I have almost reached the regrettable conclusion that the Negro's great stumbling block in his stride toward freedom is not the White Citizen's Counciler or the Ku Klux Klanner, but the white moderate, who is more devoted to "order" than to justice; who prefers a negative peace which is the absence of tension to a positive peace which is the presence of justice; who constantly says: "I agree with you in the goal you seek, but I cannot agree with your methods of direct action"; who paternalistically believes he can set the timetable for another man's freedom; who lives by a mythical concept of time and who constantly advises the Negro to wait for a "more convenient season." Shallow understanding from people of good will is more frustrating than absolute misunderstanding from people of ill will. Lukewarm acceptance is much more bewildering than outright rejection.

I had hoped that the white moderate would understand that law and order exist for the purpose of establishing justice and that when they fail in this purpose they become the dangerously structured dams that block the flow of social progress. I had hoped that the white moderate would understand that the present tension in the South is a necessary phase of the transition from an obnoxious negative peace, in which the Negro passively accepted his unjust plight, to a substantive and positive peace, in which all men will respect the dignity and worth of human personality. Actually, we who engage in nonviolent direct action are not the creators of tension. We merely bring to the surface the hidden tension that is already alive. We bring it out in the open, where it can be seen and dealt with. Like a boil that can never be cured so long as it is covered up but must be opened with all its ugliness to the natural medicines of air and light, injustice must be exposed, with all the tension its exposure creates, to the light of human conscience and the air of national opinion before it can be cured.

25   In your statement you assert that our actions, even though peaceful, must be condemned because they precipitate violence. But is this a logical assertion? Isn't this like condemning a robbed man because his possession of money precipitated the evil act of robbery? Isn't this like condemning Socrates because his unswerving commitment to truth and his philosophical inquiries precipitated the act by the misguided populace in which they made him drink hemlock? Isn't this like condemning Jesus because his unique God-consciousness and never-ceasing devotion to God's will precipitated the evil act of crucifixion? We must come to see that, as the federal courts have consistently affirmed, it is wrong to urge an individual to cease his efforts to gain his basic constitutional rights because the quest may precipitate violence. Society must protect the robbed and punish the robber.

26   I had also hoped that the white moderate would reject the myth concerning time in relation to the struggle for freedom. I have just received a letter from a white brother in Texas. He writes: "All Christians know that the colored people will receive equal rights eventually, but it is possible that you are in too great a religious hurry. It has taken Christianity almost two thousand years to accomplish what it has. The teachings of Christ take time to come to earth." Such an attitude stems from a tragic misconception of time, from the strangely irrational notion that there is something in the very flow of time that will inevitably cure all ills. Actually, time itself is neutral; it can be used either destructively or constructively. More and more I feel that the people of ill will have used time much more effectively than have the people of good will. We will have to repent in this generation not merely for the hateful words and actions of the bad people but for the appalling silence of the good people. Human progress never rolls in on wheels of inevitability; it comes through the tireless efforts of men willing to be co-workers with God, and without this hard work, time itself becomes an ally of the forces of social stagnation. We must use time creatively, in the knowledge that time is always ripe to do right. Now is the time to make real the promise of democracy and transform our pending national elegy into a creative psalm of brotherhood. Now is the time to

lift our national policy from the quicksand of racial injustice to the solid rock of human dignity.

You speak of our activity in Birmingham as extreme. At first 27 I was rather disappointed that fellow clergymen would see my nonviolent efforts as those of an extremist. I began thinking about the fact that I stand in the middle of two opposing forces in the Negro community. One is a force of complacency, made up in part of Negroes who, as a result of long years of oppression, are so drained of self-respect and a sense of "somebodiness" that they have adjusted to segregation; and in part of a few middle-class Negroes who, because of a degree of academic and economic security and because in some ways they profit by segregation, have become insensitive to the problems of the masses. The other force is one of bitterness and hatred, and it comes perilously close to advocating violence. It is expressed in the various black nationalist groups that are springing up across the nation, the largest and best-known being Elijah Muhammad's Muslim movement. Nourished by the Negro's frustration over the continued existence of racial discrimination, this movement is made up of people who have lost faith in America, who have absolutely repudiated Christianity, and who have concluded that the white man is an incorrigible "devil."

I have tried to stand between these two forces, saying that we 28 need emulate neither the "do-nothingism" of the complacent nor the hatred and despair of the black nationalist. For there is the more excellent way of love and nonviolent protest. I am grateful to God that, through the influence of the Negro church, the way of nonviolence became an integral part of our struggle.

If this philosophy had not emerged, by now many streets of 29 the South would, I am convinced, be flowing with blood. And I am further convinced that if our white brothers dismiss as "rabble-rousers" and "outside agitators" those of us who employ nonviolent direct action, and if they refuse to support our nonviolent efforts, millions of Negroes will, out of frustration and despair, seek solace and security in black-nationalist ideologies—a development that would inevitably lead to a frightening racial nightmare.

Oppressed people cannot remain oppressed forever. The 30 yearning for freedom eventually manifests itself, and that is what has happened to the American Negro. Something within has reminded him of his birthright of freedom, and something without has reminded him that it can be gained. Consciously or unconsciously, he has been caught up by the *Zeitgeist,* and with his black brothers of Africa and his brown and yellow brothers of Asia, South America and the Caribbean, the United States Negro is moving with a sense of great urgency toward the promised land of racial justice. If one recognizes this vital urge that has engulfed the Negro community, one should readily understand why public demonstrations are taking place. The Negro has many pent-up resentments and latent frustrations, and he must release them. So let him march; let him make prayer pilgrimages to the city hall; let him go on freedom rides—and try to understand why he must do so. If his repressed emotions are not released in nonviolent ways, they will seek expression through violence; this is not a threat but a fact of history. So I have not said to my people: "Get rid of your discontent." Rather, I have tried to say that this normal and healthy discontent can be channeled into the creative outlet of nonviolent direct action. And now this approach is being termed extremist.

31   But though I was initially disappointed at being categorized as an extremist, as I continued to think about the matter I gradually gained a measure of satisfaction from the label. Was not Jesus an extremist for love: "Love your enemies, bless them that curse you, do good to them that hate you, and pray for them which despitefully use you, and persecute you." Was not Amos an extremist for justice: "Let justice roll down like waters and righteousness like an ever-flowing stream." Was not Paul an extremist for the Christian gospel: "I bear in my body the marks of the Lord Jesus." Was not Martin Luther an extremist: "Here I stand; I cannot do otherwise, so help me God." And John Bunyan: "I will stay in jail to the end of my days before I make a butchery of my conscience." And Abraham Lincoln: "This nation cannot survive half slave and half free." And Thomas Jefferson: "We hold these truths to be self-evident, that all men are created equal . . . " So the question is not whether we will be extremists, but what kind of extremists we will be. Will we be extremists for hate or for love? Will we be extremists for the preservation of injustice or for the extension of justice? In that dramatic scene on Calvary's hill three men were crucified. We must never forget that all three were crucified for the same crime—the crime of extremism. Two were extremists for immorality, and thus fell below their environment. The other, Jesus Christ, was an extremist for love, truth and goodness, and thereby rose above his environment. Perhaps the South, the nation and the world are in dire need of creative extremists.

32   I had hoped that the white moderate would see this need. Perhaps I was too optimistic; perhaps I expected too much. I suppose I should have realized that few members of the oppressor race can understand the deep groans and passionate yearnings of the oppressed race, and still fewer have the vision to see that injustice must be rooted out by strong, persistent and determined action. I am thankful, however, that some of

our white brothers in the South have grasped the meaning of this social revolution and committed themselves to it. They are still all too few in quantity, but they are big in quality. Some—such as Ralph McGill, Lillian Smith, Harry Golden, James McBride Dabbs, Ann Braden and Sarah Patton Boyle—have written about our struggle in eloquent and prophetic terms. Others have marched with us down nameless streets of the South. They have languished in filthy, roach-infested jails, suffering the abuse and brutality of policemen who view them as "dirty nigger-lovers." Unlike so many of their moderate brothers and sisters, they have recognized the urgency of the moment and sensed the need for powerful "action" antidotes to combat the disease of segregation.

Let me take note of my other major disappointment. I have been so greatly disappointed with the white church and its leadership. Of course, there are some notable exceptions. I am not unmindful of the fact that each of you has taken some significant stands on this issue. I commend you, Reverend Stallings, for your Christian stand on this past Sunday, in welcoming Negroes to your worship service on a nonsegregated basis. I commend the Catholic leaders of this state for integrating Spring Hill College several years ago. 33

But despite these notable exceptions, I must honestly reiterate that I have been disappointed with the church. I do not say this as one of those negative critics who can always find something wrong with the church. I say this as a minister of the gospel, who loves the church; who was nurtured in its bosom; who has been sustained by its spiritual blessings and who will remain true to it as long as the cord of life shall lengthen. 34

When I was suddenly catapulted into the leadership of the bus protest in Montgomery, Alabama, a few years ago, I felt we would be supported by the white church. I felt that the white ministers, priests and rabbis of the South would be among our strongest allies. Instead, some have been outright opponents, refusing to understand the freedom movement and misrepresenting its leaders; all too many others have been more cautious than courageous and have remained silent behind the anesthetizing security of stained-glass windows. 35

In spite of my shattered dreams, I came to Birmingham with the hope that the white religious leadership of this community would see the justice of our cause and, with deep moral concern, would serve as the channel through which our just grievances could reach the power structure. I had hoped that each of you would understand. But again I have been disappointed. 36

I have heard numerous southern religious leaders admonish their worshipers to comply with a desegregation decision because it is the law, but I have longed to hear white ministers 37 declare: "Follow this decree because integration is morally right and because the Negro is your brother." In the midst of blatant injustices inflicted upon the Negro, I have watched white churchmen stand on the sideline and mouth pious irrelevancies and sanctimonious trivialities. In the midst of a mighty struggle to rid our nation of racial and economic injustice, I have heard many ministers say: "Those are social issues, with which the gospel has no real concern." And I have watched many churches commit themselves to a completely otherworldly religion which makes a strange, un-Biblical distortion between body and soul, between the sacred and the secular.

38   I have traveled the length and breadth of Alabama, Mississippi and all the other southern states. On sweltering summer days and crisp autumn mornings I have looked at the South's beautiful churches with their lofty spires pointing heavenward. I have beheld the impressive outlines of her massive religious-education buildings. Over and over I have found myself asking: "What kind of people worship here? Who is their God? Where were their voices when the lips of Governor Barnett dripped with words of interposition and nullification? Where were they when Governor Wallace gave a clarion call for defiance and hatred? Where were their voices of support when bruised and weary Negro men and women decided to rise from the dark dungeons of complacency to the bright hills of creative protest?"

39   Yes, these questions are still in my mind. In deep disappointment I have wept over the laxity of the church. But be assured that my tears have been tears of love. There can be no deep disappointment where there is not deep love. Yes, I love the church. How could I do otherwise? I am in the rather unique position of being the son, the grandson and the great-grandson of preachers. Yes, I see the church as the body of Christ. But, oh! How we have blemished and scarred that body through social neglect and through fear of being non-conformists.

40   There was a time when the church was very powerful—in the time when the early Christians rejoiced at being deemed worthy to suffer for what they believed. In those days the church was not merely a thermometer that recorded the ideas and principles of popular opinion; it was a thermostat that transformed the mores of society. Whenever the early Christians entered a town, the people in power became disturbed and immediately sought to convict the Christians for being "disturbers of the peace" and "outside agitators." But the Christians pressed on, in the conviction that they were "a colony of heaven," called to obey God rather than man. Small in number, they were big in commitment. They were too God-intoxicated to be "astronomically intimidated." By their effort

and example they brought an end to such ancient evils as infanticide and gladiatorial contests.

Things are different now. So often the contemporary church   41
is a weak, ineffectual voice with an uncertain sound. So often
it is an arch-defender of the status quo. Far from being disturbed by the presence of the church, the power structure of
the average community is consoled by the church's silent—and
often even vocal—sanction of things as they are.

But the judgment of God is upon the church as never before.   42
If today's church does not recapture the sacrificial spirit of the
early church, it will lose its authenticity, forfeit the loyalty of
millions, and be dismissed as an irrelevant social club with no
meaning for the twentieth century. Every day I meet young
people whose disappointment with the church has turned into
outright disgust.

Perhaps I have once again been too optimistic. Is organized   43
religion too inextricably bound to the status quo to save our
nation and the world? Perhaps I must turn my faith to the inner spiritual church, the church within the church, as the true
ekklesia and the hope of the world. But again I am thankful to
God that some noble souls from the ranks of organized religion have broken loose from the paralyzing chains of conformity and joined us as active partners in the struggle for freedom. They have left their secure congregations and walked the
streets of Albany, Georgia, with us. They have gone down the
highways of the South on tortuous rides for freedom. Yes, they
have gone to jail with us. Some have been dismissed from their
churches, have lost the support of their bishops and fellow
ministers. But they have acted in the faith that right defeated is
stronger than evil triumphant. Their witness has been the spiritual salt that has preserved the true meaning of the gospel in
these troubled times. They have carved a tunnel of hope
through the dark mountain of disappointment.

I hope the church as a whole will meet the challenge of this   44
decisive hour. But even if the church does not come to the aid of
justice, I have no despair about the future. I have no fear about
the outcome of our struggle in Birmingham, even if our motives
are at present misunderstood. We will reach the goal of freedom
in Birmingham and all over the nation, because the goal of
America is freedom. Abused and scorned though we may be,
our destiny is tied up with America's destiny. Before the pilgrims landed at Plymouth, we were here. Before the pen of
Jefferson etched the majestic words of the Declaration of
Independence across the pages of history, we were here. For
more than two centuries our forebears labored in this country
without wages; they made cotton king; they built the homes of
their masters while suffering gross injustice and shameful hu-

miliation—and yet out of a bottomless vitality they continued to thrive and develop. If the inexpressible cruelties of slavery could not stop us, the opposition we now face will surely fail. We will win our freedom because the sacred heritage of our nation and the eternal will of God are embodied in our echoing demands.

45   Before closing I feel impelled to mention one other point in your statement that has troubled me profoundly. You warmly commended the Birmingham police force for keeping "order" and "preventing violence." I doubt that you would have so warmly commended the police force if you had seen its dogs sinking their teeth into unarmed, nonviolent Negroes. I doubt that you would so quickly commend the policemen if you were to observe their ugly and inhumane treatment of Negroes here in the city jail; if you were to watch them push and curse old Negro women and young Negro girls; if you were to see them slap and kick old Negro men and young boys; if you were to observe them, as they did on two occasions, refuse to give us food because we wanted to sing our grace together. I cannot join you in your praise of the Birmingham Police Department.

46   It is true that the police have exercised a degree of discipline in handling the demonstrators. In this sense they have conducted themselves rather "nonviolently" in public. But for what purpose? To preserve the evil system of segregation. Over the past few years I have consistently preached that nonviolence demands that the means we use must be as pure as the ends we seek. I have tried to make clear that it is wrong to use immoral means to attain moral ends. But now I must affirm that it is just as wrong, or perhaps even more so, to use moral means to preserve immoral ends. Perhaps Mr. Connor and his policemen have been rather nonviolent in public, as was Chief Pritchett in Albany, Georgia, but they have used the moral means of nonviolence to maintain the immoral end of racial injustice. As T. S. Eliot has said: "The last temptation is the greatest treason: To do the right deed for the wrong reason."

47   I wish you had commended the Negro sit-inners and demonstrators of Birmingham for their sublime courage, their willingness to suffer and their amazing discipline in the midst of great provocation. One day the South will recognize its real heroes. They will be the James Merediths, with the noble sense of purpose that enables them to face jeering and hostile mobs, and with the agonizing loneliness that characterizes the life of the pioneer. They will be old, oppressed, battered Negro women, symbolized in a seventy-two-year-old woman in Montgomery, Alabama, who rose up with a sense of dignity and with her people decided not to ride segregated buses, and

who responded with ungrammatical profundity to one who inquired about her weariness: "My feets is tired, but my soul is at
rest." They will be the young high school and college students,
the young ministers of the gospel and a host of their elders,
courageously and nonviolently sitting in at lunch counters and
willingly going to jail for conscience sake. One day the South
will know that when these disinherited children of God sat
down at lunch counters, they were in reality standing up for
what is best in the American dream and for the most sacred
values in our Judaeo-Christian heritage, thereby bringing our
nation back to those great wells of democracy which were dug
deep by the founding fathers in their formulation of the
Constitution and the Declaration of Independence.

Never before have I written so long a letter. I'm afraid it is   48
much too long to take your precious time. I can assure you that
it would have been much shorter if I had been writing from a
comfortable desk, but what else can one do when he is alone in
a narrow jail cell, other than write long letters, think long
thoughts and pray long prayers?

Malcolm X

MESSAGE
TO THE GRASS ROOTS

The life of Malcolm X is well known because of Alex Haley's
The Autobiography of Malcolm X *and Spike Lee's adoring
1993 film* Malcolm X. *Born in 1925 into challenging circumstances, the victim of a tortured childhood that created his
seething alienation, and drawn first to a life of petty crime,
Malcolm X in prison was converted to Islam and thereafter became a leader in the Black Muslims and the black nationalist
movement of the early 1960s. A spellbinding, charismatic
speaker who was assassinated in 1965 (only months after returning from a pilgrimage to Africa and the Near East and re-
nouncing his separatist agenda), Malcolm X was a foil to his
contemporary, Martin Luther King Jr. The following speech
was delivered on November 10, 1963 (six months after King
wrote his "Letter from Birmingham Jail," two weeks before*

*President Kennedy was assassinated, and less than a year be-
fore the passage of the Civil Rights Act of 1964), to an all-black
audience gathered in Detroit for a Northern Negro Leadership
Conference; it was also broadcast over the radio. The speech
reveals the terms of Malcolm X's differences with King: the two
disagreed about the wisdom of segregation versus integration
and about whether nonviolent resistance or violent revenge is
the better means of countering racism.*

1   We want to have just an off-the-cuff chat between you and me,
us. We want to talk right down to earth in a language that
everybody here can easily understand. We all agree tonight, all
of the speakers have agreed, that America has a very serious
problem. Not only does America have a very serious problem,
but our people have a very serious problem. America's problem
is us. We're her problem. The only reason she has a problem is
she doesn't want us here. And every time you look at yourself,
be you black, brown, red or yellow, a so-called Negro, you represent a person who poses such a serious problem for America
because you're not wanted. Once you face this as a fact, then
you can start plotting a course that will make you appear intelligent, instead of unintelligent.

2   What you and I need to do is learn to forget our differences.
When we come together, we don't come together as Baptists or
Methodists. You don't catch hell because you're a Baptist, and
you don't catch hell because you're a Methodist. You don't
catch hell because you're a Methodist or Baptist, you don't
catch hell because you're a Democrat or a Republican, you
don't catch hell because you're a Mason or an Elk, and you
sure don't catch hell because you're an American; because if
you were an American, you wouldn't catch hell. You catch hell
because you're a black man. You catch hell, all of us catch hell,
for the same reason.

3   So we're all black people, so-called Negroes, second-class citizens, ex-slaves. You're nothing but an ex-slave. You don't like to
be told that. But what else are you? You are ex-slaves. You didn't
come here on the "Mayflower." You came here on a slave ship.
In chains, like a horse, or a cow, or a chicken. And you were
brought here by the people who came here on the "Mayflower,"
you were brought here by the so-called Pilgrims, or Founding
Fathers. They were the ones who brought you here.

4   We have a common enemy. We have this in common: We
have a common oppressor, a common exploiter, and a common
discriminator. But once we all realize that we have a common
enemy, then we unite—on the basis of what we have in common. And what we have foremost in common is that enemy—

the white man. He's an enemy to all of us. I know some of you all think that some of them aren't enemies. Time will tell.

In Bandung back in, I think, 1954, was the first unity meeting in centuries of black people. And once you study what happened at the Bandung conference, and the results of the Bandung conference, it actually serves as a model for the same procedure you and I can use to get our problems solved. At Bandung all the nations came together, the dark nations from Africa and Asia. Some of them were Buddhists, some of them were Muslims, some of them were Christians, some were Confucianists, some were atheists. Despite their religious differences, they came together. Some were communists, some were socialists, some were capitalists—despite their economic and political differences, they came together. All of them were black, brown, red or yellow.

The number-one thing that was not allowed to attend the Bandung conference was the white man. He couldn't come. Once they excluded the white man, they found that they could get together. Once they kept him out, everybody else fell right in and fell in line. This is the thing that you and I have to understand. And these people who came together didn't have nuclear weapons, they didn't have jet planes, they didn't have all of the heavy armaments that the white man has. But they had unity.

They were able to submerge their little petty differences and agree on one thing: That there one African came from Kenya and was being colonized by the Englishman, and another African came from the Congo and was being colonized by the Belgian, and another African came from Guinea and was being colonized by the French, and another came from Angola and was being colonized by the Portuguese. When they came to the Bandung conference, they looked at the Portuguese, and at the Frenchman, and at the Englishman, and at the Dutchman, and learned or realized the one thing that all of them had in common—they were all from Europe, they were all Europeans, blond, blue-eyed and white skins. They began to recognize who their enemy was. The same man that was colonizing our people in Kenya was colonizing our people in the Congo. The same one in the Congo was colonizing our people in South Africa, and in Southern Rhodesia, and in Burma, and in India, and in Afghanistan, and in Pakistan. They realized all over the world where the dark man was being oppressed, he was being oppressed by the white man; where the dark man was being exploited, he was being exploited by the white man. So they got together on this basis—that they had a common enemy.

And when you and I here in Detroit and in Michigan and in America who have been awakened today look around us, we too realize here in America we all have a common enemy, whether he's in Georgia or Michigan, whether he's in California or New York. He's the same man—blue eyes and blond hair and pale skin—the same man. So what we have to do is what they did. They agreed to stop quarreling among themselves. Any little spat that they had, they'd settle it among themselves, go into a huddle—don't let the enemy know that you've got a disagreement.

9   Instead of airing our differences in public, we have to realize we're all the same family. And when you have a family squabble, you don't get out on the sidewalk. If you do, everybody calls you uncouth, unrefined, uncivilized, savage. If you don't make it at home, you settle it at home; you get in the closet, argue it out behind closed doors, and then when you come out on the street, you pose a common front, a united front. And this is what we need to do in the community, and in the city, and in the state. We need to stop airing our differences in front of the white man, put the white man out of our meetings, and then sit down and talk shop with each other. That's what we've got to do.

10   I would like to make a few comments concerning the difference between the black revolution and the Negro revolution. Are they both the same? And if they're not, what is the difference? What is the difference between a black revolution and a Negro revolution? First, what is a revolution? Sometimes I'm inclined to believe that many of our people are using this word "revolution" loosely, without taking careful consideration of what this word actually means, and what its historic characteristics are. When you study the historic nature of revolutions, the motive of a revolution, the objective of a revolution, the result of a revolution, and the methods used in a revolution, you may change words. You may devise another program, you may change your goal and you may change your mind.

11   Look at the American Revolution in 1776. That revolution was for what? For land. Why did they want land? Independence. How was it carried out? Bloodshed. Number one, it was based on land, the basis of independence. And the only way they could get it was bloodshed. The French Revolution—what was it based on? The landless against the landlord. What was it for? Land. How did they get it? Bloodshed. Was no love lost, was no compromise, was no negotiation. I'm telling you—you don't know what a revolution is. Because when you find out what it is, you'll get back in the alley, you'll get out of the way.

12   The Russian Revolution—what was it based on? Land; the landless against the landlord. How did they bring it about? Bloodshed. You haven't got a revolution that doesn't involve

bloodshed. And you're afraid to bleed. I said, you're afraid to bleed.

As long as the white man sent you to Korea, you bled. He   13
sent you to Germany, you bled. He sent you to the South
Pacific to fight the Japanese, you bled. You bleed for white
people, but when it comes to seeing your own churches being
bombed and little black girls murdered, you haven't got any
blood. You bleed when the white man says bleed; you bite
when the white man says bite; and you bark when the white
man says bark. I hate to say this about us, but it's true. How
are you going to be nonviolent in Mississippi, as violent as you
were in Korea? How can you justify being nonviolent in
Mississippi and Alabama, when your churches are being
bombed, and your little girls are being murdered, and at the
same time you are going to get violent with Hitler, and Tojo,
and somebody else you don't even know?

If violence is wrong in America, violence is wrong abroad. If   14
it is wrong to be violent defending black women and black
children and black babies and black men, then it is wrong for
America to draft us and make us violent abroad in defense of
her. And if it is right for America to draft us, and teach us how
to be violent in defense of her, then it is right for you and me to
do whatever is necessary to defend our own people right here
in this country.

The Chinese Revolution—they wanted land. They threw the   15
British out, along with the Uncle Tom Chinese. Yes, they did.
They set a good example. When I was in prison, I read an article—don't be shocked when I say that I was in prison. You're
still in prison. That's what America means: prison. When I was
in prison, I read an article in *Life* magazine showing a little
Chinese girl, nine years old; her father was on his hands and
knees and she was pulling the trigger because he was an Uncle
Tom Chinaman. When they had the revolution over there, they
took a whole generation of Uncle Toms and just wiped them
out. And within ten years that little girl became a full-grown
woman. No more Toms in China. And today it's one of the
toughest, roughest, most feared countries on this earth—by the
white man. Because there are no Uncle Toms over there.

Of all our studies, history is best qualified to reward our re-   16
search. And when you see that you've got problems, all you
have to do is examine the historic method used all over the
world by others who have problems similar to yours. Once you
see how they got theirs straight, then you know how you can
get yours straight. There's been a revolution, a black revolution, going on in Africa. In Kenya, the Mau Mau were revolutionary; they were the ones who brought the word "Uhuru" to

the fore. The Mau Mau, they were revolutionary, they believed in scorched earth, they knocked everything aside that got in their way, and their revolution also was based on land, a desire for land. In Algeria, the northern part of Africa, a revolution took place. The Algerians were revolutionists, they wanted land. France offered to let them be integrated into France. They told France, to hell with France, they wanted some land, not some France. And they engaged in a bloody battle.

17   So I cite these various revolutions, brothers and sisters, to show you that you don't have a peaceful revolution. You don't have a turn-the-other-cheek revolution. There's no such thing as a nonviolent revolution. The only kind of revolution that is nonviolent is the Negro revolution. The only revolution in which the goal is loving your enemy is the Negro revolution. It's the only revolution in which the goal is a desegregated lunch counter, a desegregated theater, a desegregated park, and a desegregated public toilet; you can sit down next to white folks—on the toilet. That's no revolution. Revolution is based on land. Land is the basis of all independence. Land is the basis of freedom, justice, and equality.

18   The white man knows what a revolution is. He knows that the black revolution is world-wide in scope and in nature. The black revolution is sweeping Asia, is sweeping Africa, is rearing its head in Latin America. The Cuban Revolution—that's a revolution. They overturned the system. Revolution is in Asia, revolution is in Africa, and the white man is screaming because he sees revolution in Latin America. How do you think he'll react to you when you learn what a real revolution is? You don't know what a revolution is. If you did, you wouldn't use that word.

19   Revolution is bloody, revolution is hostile, revolution knows no compromise, revolution overturns and destroys everything that gets in its way. And you, sitting around here like a knot on the wall, saying, "I'm going to love these folks no matter how much they hate me." No, you need a revolution. Whoever heard of a revolution where they lock arms, as Rev. Cleage was pointing out beautifully, singing "We Shall Overcome"? You don't do that in a revolution. You don't do any singing, you're too busy swinging. It's based on land. A revolutionary wants land so he can set up his own nation, an independent nation. These Negroes aren't asking for any nation—they're trying to crawl back on the plantation.

20   When you want a nation, that's called nationalism. When the white man became involved in a revolution in this country against England, what was it for? He wanted this land so he could set up another white nation. That's white nationalism.

The American Revolution was white nationalism. The French Revolution was white nationalism. The Russian Revolution too—yes, it was—white nationalism. You don't think so? Why do you think Khrushchev and Mao can't get their heads together? White nationalism. All the revolutions that are going on in Asia and Africa today are based on what?—black nationalism. A revolutionary is a black nationalist. He wants a nation. I was reading some beautiful words by Rev. Cleage, pointing out why he couldn't get together with someone else in the city because all of them were afraid of being identified with black nationalism. If you're afraid of black nationalism, you're afraid of revolution. And if you love revolution, you love black nationalism.

21 To understand this, you have to go back to what the young brother here referred to as the house Negro and the field Negro back during slavery. There were two kinds of slaves, the house Negro and the field Negro. The house Negroes—they lived in the house with master, they dressed pretty good, they ate good because they ate his food—what he left. They lived in the attic or the basement, but still they lived near the master; and they loved the master more than the master loved himself. They would give their life to save the master's house—quicker than the master would. If the master said, "We got a good house here," the house Negro would say, "Yeah, we got a good house here." Whenever the master said "we," he said "we." That's how you can tell a house Negro.

22 If the master's house caught on fire, the house Negro would fight harder to put the blaze out than the master would. If the master got sick, the house Negro would say, "What's the matter, boss, *we* sick?" *We* sick! He identified himself with his master, more than his master identified with himself. And if you came to the house Negro and said, "Let's run away, let's escape, let's separate," the house Negro would look at you and say, "Man, you crazy. What you mean, separate? Where is there a better house than this? Where can I wear better clothes than this? Where can I eat better food than this?" That was that house Negro. In those days he was called a "house nigger." And that's what we call them today, because we've still got some house niggers running around here.

23 This modern house Negro loves his master. He wants to live near him. He'll pay three times as much as the house is worth just to live near his master, and then brag about "I'm the only Negro out here." "I'm the only one on my job." "I'm the only one in this school." You're nothing but a house Negro. And if someone comes to you right now and says, "Let's separate," you say the same thing that the house Negro

said on the plantation. "What you mean, separate? From America, this good white man? Where you going to get a better job than you get here?" I mean, this is what you say. "I ain't left nothing in Africa," that's what you say. Why, you left your mind in Africa.

24   On that same plantation, there was the field Negro. The field Negroes—those were the masses. There were always more Negroes in the field than there were Negroes in the house. The Negro in the field caught hell. He ate leftovers. In the house they ate high up on the hog. The Negro in the field didn't get anything but what was left of the insides of the hog. They call it "chitt'lings" nowadays. In those days they called them what they were—guts. That's what you were—gut-eaters. And some of you are still gut-eaters.

25   The field Negro was beaten from morning to night; he lived in a shack, in a hut; he wore old, castoff clothes. He hated his master. I say he hated his master. He was intelligent. That house Negro loved his master, but that field Negro—remember, they were in the majority, and they hated the master. When the house caught on fire, he didn't try to put it out; that field Negro prayed for a wind, for a breeze. When the master got sick, the field Negro prayed that he'd die. If someone came to the field Negro and said, "Let's separate, let's run," he didn't say "Where we going?" He'd say, "Any place is better than here." You've got field Negroes in America today. I'm a field Negro. The masses are the field Negroes. When they see this man's house on fire, you don't hear the little Negroes talking about "*our* government is in trouble." They say, "*The* government is in trouble." Imagine a Negro: "*Our* government"! I even heard one say "*our* astronauts." They won't even let him near the plant—and "*our* astronauts"! "*Our* Navy"—that's a Negro that is out of his mind, a Negro that is out of his mind.

26   Just as the slavemaster of that day used Tom, the house Negro, to keep the field Negroes in check, the same old slave-master today has Negroes who are nothing but modern Uncle Toms, twentieth-century Uncle Toms, to keep you and me in check, to keep us under control, keep us passive and peaceful and nonviolent. That's Tom making you nonviolent. It's like when you go to the dentist, and the man's going to take your tooth. You're going to fight him when he starts pulling. So he squirts some stuff in your jaw called novocaine, to make you think they're not doing anything to you. So you sit there and because you've got all of that novocaine in your jaw, you suffer—peacefully. Blood running all down your jaw, and you don't know what's happening. Because someone has taught you to suffer—peacefully.

The white man does the same thing to you in the street, 27
when he wants to put knots on your head and take advantage
of you and not have to be afraid of your fighting back. To keep
you from fighting back, he gets these old religious Uncle Toms
to teach you and me, just like novocaine, to suffer peacefully.
Don't stop suffering—just suffer peacefully. As Rev. Cleage
pointed out, they say you should let your blood flow in the
streets. This is a shame. You know he's a Christian preacher. If
it's a shame to him, you know what it is to me.

There is nothing in our book, the Koran, that teaches us to 28
suffer peacefully. Our religion teaches us to be intelligent. Be
peaceful, be courteous, obey the law, respect everyone; but if
someone puts his hand on you, send him to the cemetery. That's
a good religion. In fact, that's that old-time religion. That's the
one that Ma and Pa used to talk about: an eye for an eye, and a
tooth for a tooth, and a head for a head, and a life for a life.
That's a good religion. And nobody resents that kind of religion
being taught but a wolf, who intends to make you his meal.

This is the way it is with the white man in America. He's a 29
wolf—and you're sheep. Any time a shepherd, a pastor, teaches
you and me not to run from the white man and, at the same
time, teaches us not to fight the white man, he's a traitor to you
and me. Don't lay down a life all by itself. No, preserve your
life, it's the best thing you've got. And if you've got to give it up,
let it be even-steven.

The slavemaster took Tom and dressed him well, fed him 30
well and even gave him a little education—a *little* education;
gave him a long coat and a top hat and made all the other
slaves look up to him. Then he used Tom to control them. The
same strategy that was used in those days is used today, by the
same white man. He takes a Negro, a so-called Negro, and
makes him prominent, builds him up, publicizes him, makes
him a celebrity. And then he becomes a spokesman for
Negroes—and a Negro leader.

I would like to mention just one other thing quickly, and that 31
is the method that the white man uses, how the white man
uses the "big guns," or Negro leaders, against the Negro revolution. They are not a part of the Negro revolution. They are used
against the Negro revolution.

When Martin Luther King failed to desegregate Albany, 32
Georgia, the civil-rights struggle in America reached its low
point. King became bankrupt almost, as a leader. The
Southern Christian Leadership Conference was in financial
trouble; and it was in trouble, period, with the people when
they failed to desegregate Albany, Georgia. Other Negro civil-
rights leaders of so-called national stature became fallen idols.

As they became fallen idols, began to lose their prestige and influence, local Negro leaders began to stir up the masses. In Cambridge, Maryland, Gloria Richardson; in Danville, Virginia, and other parts of the country, local leaders began to stir up our people at the grass-roots level. This was never done by these Negroes of national stature. They control you, but they have never incited you or excited you. They control you, they contain you, they have kept you on the plantation.

33   As soon as King failed in Birmingham, Negroes took to the streets. King went out to California to a big rally and raised I don't know how many thousands of dollars. He came to Detroit and had a march and raised some more thousands of dollars. And recall, right after that Roy Wilkins attacked King. He accused King and CORE [Congress Of Racial Equality] of starting trouble everywhere and then making the NAACP [National Association for the Advancement of Colored People] get them out of jail and spend a lot of money; they accused King and CORE of raising all the money and not paying it back. This happened; I've got it in documented evidence in the newspaper. Roy started attacking King, and King started attacking Roy, and Farmer started attacking both of them. And as these Negroes of national stature began to attack each other, they began to lose their control of the Negro masses.

34   The Negroes were out there in the streets. They were talking about how they were going to march on Washington. Right at that time Birmingham had exploded, and the Negroes in Birmingham—remember, they also exploded. They began to stab the crackers in the back and bust them up 'side their head—yes, they did. That's when Kennedy sent in the troops, down in Birmingham. After that, Kennedy got on the television and said "this is a moral issue." That's when he said he was going to put out a civil-rights bill. And when he mentioned civil-rights bill and the Southern crackers started talking about how they were going to boycott or filibuster it, then the Negroes started talking—about what? That they were going to march on Washington, march on the Senate, march on the White House, march on the Congress, and tie it up, bring it to a halt, not let the government proceed. They even said they were going out to the airport and lay down on the runway and not let any airplanes land. I'm telling you what they said. That was revolution. That was revolution. That was the black revolution.

35   It was the grass roots out there in the street. It scared the white man to death, scared the white power structure in Washington, D.C., to death; I was there. When they found out that this black steamroller was going to come down on the capital, they called in Wilkins, they called in Randolph, they called

in these national Negro leaders that you respect and told them, "Call it off." Kennedy said, "Look, you all are letting this thing go too far." And Old Tom said, "Boss, I can't stop it, because I didn't start it." I'm telling you what they said. They said, "I'm not even in it, much less at the head of it." They said, "These Negroes are doing things on their own. They're running ahead of us." And that old shrewd fox, he said, "If you all aren't in it, I'll put you in it. I'll put you at the head of it. I'll endorse it. I'll welcome it. I'll help it. I'll join it."

A matter of hours went by. They had a meeting at the Carlyle   36
Hotel in New York City. The Carlyle Hotel is owned by the Kennedy family; that's the hotel Kennedy spent the night at, two nights ago; it belongs to his family. A philanthropic society headed by a white man named Stephen Currier called all the top civil-rights leaders together at the Carlyle Hotel. And he told them, "By you all fighting each other, you are destroying the civil-rights movement. And since you're fighting over money from white liberals, let us set up what is known as the Council for United Civil Rights Leadership. Let's form this council, and all the civil-rights organizations will belong to it, and we'll use it for fund-raising purposes." Let me show you how tricky the white man is. As soon as they got it formed, they elected Whitney Young as its chairman, and who do you think became the co-chairman? Stephen Currier, the white man, a millionaire. Powell was talking about it down at Cobo Hall today. This is what he was talking about. Powell knows it happened. Randolph knows it happened. Wilkins knows it happened. King knows it happened. Every one of that Big Six— they know it happened.

Once they formed it, with the white man over it, he promised   37
them and gave them $800,000 to split up among the Big Six; and told them that after the march was over they'd give them $700,000 more. A million and a half dollars—split up between leaders that you have been following, going to jail for, crying crocodile tears for. And they're nothing but Frank James and Jesse James and the what-do-you-call-'em brothers.

As soon as they got the setup organized, the white man made   38
available to them top public-relations experts; opened the news media across the country at their disposal, which then began to project these Big Six as the leaders of the march. Originally they weren't even in the march. You were talking this march talk on Hastings Street, you were talking march talk on Lenox Avenue, and on Fillmore Street, and on Central Avenue, and 32nd Street and 63rd Street. That's where the march talk was being talked. But the white man put the Big Six at the head of it; made them the march. They became the march. They took it

over. And the first move they made after they took it over, they invited Walter Reuther, a white man; they invited a priest, a rabbi, and an old white preacher, yes, an old white preacher. The same white element that put Kennedy into power—labor, the Catholics, the Jews, and liberal Protestants; the same clique that put Kennedy in power, joined the march on Washington.

39   It's just like when you've got some coffee that's too black, which means it's too strong. What do you do? You integrate it with cream, you make it weak. But if you pour too much cream in it, you won't even know you ever had coffee. It used to be hot, it becomes cool. It used to be strong, it becomes weak. It used to wake you up, now it puts you to sleep. This is what they did with the march on Washington. They joined it. They didn't integrate it, they infiltrated it. They joined it, became a part of it, took it over. And as they took it over, it lost its militancy. It ceased to be angry, it ceased to be hot, it ceased to be uncompromising. Why, it even ceased to be a march. It became a picnic, a circus. Nothing but a circus, with clowns and all. You had one right here in Detroit—I saw it on television— with clowns leading it, white clowns and black clowns. I know you don't like what I'm saying, but I'm going to tell you anyway. Because I can prove what I'm saying. If you think I'm telling you wrong, you bring me Martin Luther King and A. Philip Randolph and James Farmer and those other three, and see if they'll deny it over a microphone.

40   No, it was a sellout. It was a takeover. When James Baldwin came in from Paris, they wouldn't let him talk, because they couldn't make him go by the script. Burt Lancaster read the speech that Baldwin was supposed to make; they wouldn't let Baldwin get up there, because they know Baldwin is liable to say anything. They controlled it so tight, they told those Negroes what time to hit town, how to come, where to stop, what signs to carry, what song to sing, what speech they could make, and what speech they couldn't make; and then told them to get out of town by sundown. And every one of those Toms was out of town by sundown. Now I know you don't like my saying this. But I can back it up. It was a circus, a performance that beat anything Hollywood could ever do, the performance of the year. Reuther and those other three devils should get an Academy Award for the best actors because they acted like they really loved Negroes and fooled a whole lot of Negroes. And the six Negro leaders should get an award too, for the best supporting cast.

Gwendolyn Brooks
THE MOTHER

Gwendolyn Brooks (1917–2000), who lived in Chicago, was one of the most important American poets of the last century. In her many books of poetry she often concentrated on the struggle of the individual against difficult circumstances, as in the following poem. "The Mother" first appeared in Brooks's first book, A Street in Bronzeville *(1945), which takes the reader on a trip through the various facets of an African American community; most recently it was reprinted in her 1991 book* Blacks.

Abortions will not let you forget.　　　　　　　　　　　1
You remember the children you got that you did not get,
The damp small pulps with a little or with no hair,
The singers and workers that never handled the air.
You will never neglect or beat　　　　　　　　　　　　5
Them, or silence or buy with a sweet.
You will never wind up the sucking-thumb
Or scuttle off ghosts that come.
You will never leave them, controlling your luscious sigh,
Return for a snack of them, with gobbling mother-eye.　10

I have heard in the voices of the wind the voices of my
　　dim killed children.
I have contracted. I have eased
My dim dears at the breasts they could never suck.
I have said, Sweets, if I sinned, if I seized　　　　　　15
Your luck
And your lives from your unfinished reach,
If I stole your births and your names,

Your straight baby tears and your games,
Your stilted or lovely loves, your tumults, your marriages,
20   aches, and your deaths,
If I poisoned the beginnings of your breaths,
Believe that even in my deliberateness I was not
deliberate.
Though why should I whine,
25   Whine that the crime was other than mine?—
Since anyhow you are dead.
Or rather, or instead,
You were never made.
But that too, I am afraid,
30   Is faulty: oh, what shall I say, how is the truth to be said?
You were born, you had body, you died.
It is just that you never giggled or planned or cried.

Believe me, I loved you all.
Believe me, I knew you, though faintly, and I loved, I
35   loved you
All.

Sallie Tisdale

WE DO
ABORTIONS HERE

A registered nurse and writer, Tisdale (born 1957) has pub-
lished two books about the nursing profession, The Sorcerer's
Apprentice: Medical Miracles and Other Disasters *(1986)*
and Harvest Moon: Portrait of a Nursing Home *(1987), as*
well as Lot's Wife: Salt and the Human Condition *(1988).*
(She has also published a book on the issue of pornography,
Talk Dirty to Me, *and she writes frequently for* Tricycle, *a Zen*
Buddhist publication.) In the following essay, published in
1987 in Harper's *magazine (a prestigious forum for discus-*
sions of American culture and politics), Tisdale describes her
experiences as a nurse in an abortion clinic. Does her essay
take a position on the abortion question?

We do abortions here; that is all we do. There are weary, grim   1
moments when I think I cannot bear another basin of bloody remains, utter another kind phrase of reassurance. So I leave the
procedure room in the back and reach for a new chart. Soon I
am talking to an eighteen-year-old woman pregnant for the
fourth time. I push up her sleeve to check her blood pressure
and find row upon row of needle marks, neat and parallel and
discolored. She has been so hungry for her drug for so long that
she has taken to using the loose skin of her upper arms; her el-
bows are already a permanent ruin of bruises. She is surprised
to find herself nearly four months pregnant. I suspect she is often surprised, in a mild way, by the blows she is dealt. I prepare
myself for another basin, another brief and chafing loss.

"How can you stand it?" Even the clients ask. They see the   2
machine, the strange instruments, the blood, the final stroke
that wipes away the promise of pregnancy. Sometimes I see
that too: I watch a woman's swollen abdomen sink to softness
in a few stuttering moments and my own belly flip-flops with
sorrow. But all it takes for me to catch my breath is another interview, one more story that sounds so much like the last one.
There is a numbing sameness lurking in this job: the same
questions, the same answers, even the same trembling tone in
the voices. The worst is the sameness of human failure, of inadequacy in the face of each day's dull demands.

In describing this work, I find it difficult to explain how   3
much I enjoy it most of the time. We laugh a lot here, as
friends and as professional peers. It's nice to be with women all
day. I like the sudden, transient bonds I forge with some
clients: moments when I am in my strength, remembering
weakness, and a woman in weakness reaches out for my
strength. What I offer is not power, but solidness, offered almost eagerly. Certain clients waken in me every tender urge I
have—others make me wince and bite my tongue. Both challenge me to find a balance. It is a sweet brutality we practice
here, a stark and loving dispassion.

I look at abortion as if I am standing on a cliff with a tele-   4
scope, gazing at some great vista. I can sweep the horizon with
both eyes, survey the scene in all its distance and size. Or I can
put my eye to the lens and focus on the small details, suddenly so
close. In abortion the absolute must always be tempered by the
contextual, because both are real, both valid, both hard. How
can we do this? How can we refuse? Each abortion is a measure
of our failure to protect, to nourish our own. Each basin I empty
is a promise—but a promise broken a long time ago.

I grew up on the great promise of birth control. Like many   5
women my age, I took the pill as soon as I was sexually active.

To risk pregnancy when it was so easy to avoid seemed stupid, and my contraceptive success, as it were, was part of the promise of social enlightenment. But birth control fails, far more frequently than laboratory trials predict. Many of our clients take the pill; its failure to protect them is a shocking realization. We have clients who have been sterilized, whose husbands have had vasectomies; each one is a statistical misfit, fine print come to life. The anger and shame of these women I hold in one hand, and the basin in the other. The distance between the two, the length I pace and try to measure, is the size of an abortion.

6   The procedure is disarmingly simple. Women are surprised, as though the mystery of conception, a dark and hidden genesis, requires an elaborate finale. In the first trimester of pregnancy, it's a mere few minutes of vacuuming, a neat tidying up. I give a woman a small yellow Valium, and when it has begun to relax her, I lead her into the back, into bareness, the stirrups. The doctor reaches in her, opening the narrow tunnel to the uterus with a succession of slim, smooth bars of steel. He inserts a plastic tube and hooks it to a hose on the machine. The woman is framed against white paper that crackles as she moves, the light bright in her eyes. Then the machine rumbles low and loud in the small windowless room; the doctor moves the tube back and forth with an efficient rhythm, and the long tail of it fills with blood that spurts and stumbles along into a jar. He is usually finished in a few minutes. They are long minutes for the woman; her uterus frequently reacts to its abrupt emptying with a powerful, unceasing cramp, which cuts off the blood vessels and enfolds the irritated, bleeding tissue.

7   I am learning to recognize the shadows that cross the faces of the women I hold. While the doctor works between her spread legs, the paper drape hiding his intent expression, I stand beside the table. I hold the woman's hands in mine, resting them just below her ribs. I watch her eyes, finger her necklace, stroke her hair. I ask about her job, her family; in a haze she answers me; we chatter, faces close, eyes meeting and sliding apart.

8   I watch the shadows that creep up unnoticed and suddenly darken her face as she screws up her features and pushes a tear out each side to slide down her cheeks. I have learned to anticipate the quiver of chin, the rapid intake of breath, and the surprising sobs that rise soon after the machine starts to drum. I know this is when the cramp deepens, and the tears are partly the tears that follow pain—the sharp, childish crying when one bumps one's head on a cabinet door. But a well of woe seems to open beneath many women when they hear that thumping sound. The anticipation of the moment has finally come to

fruit; the moment has arrived when the loss is no longer an imagined one. It has come true.

I am struck with the sameness and I am struck every day by   9
the variety here—how this commonplace dilemma can so display the differences of women. A twenty-one-year-old woman, unemployed, uneducated, without family, in the fifth month of her fifth pregnancy. A forty-two-year-old mother of teenagers, shocked by her condition, refusing to tell her husband. A twenty-three-year-old mother of two having her seventh abortion, and many women in their thirties having their first. Some are stoic, some hysterical, a few giggle uncontrollably, many cry.

I talk to a sixteen-year-old uneducated girl who was raped.   10
She has gonorrhea. She describes blinding headaches, attacks of breathlessness, nausea. "Sometimes I feel like two different people," she tells me with a calm smile, "and I talk to myself."

I pull out my plastic models. She listens patiently for a time,   11
and then holds her hands wide in front of her stomach.

"When's the baby going to go up into my stomach?" she asks.   12
I blink. "What do you mean?"   13
"Well," she says, still smiling, "when women get so big, isn't   14
the baby in your stomach? Doesn't it hatch out of an egg there?"

My first question in an interview is always the same. As I   15
walk down the hall with the woman, as we get settled in chairs and I glance through her files, I am trying to gauge her, to get a sense of the words, and the tone, I should use. With some I joke, with others I chat, sometimes fall into a brisk, business-line patter. But I ask every woman, "Are you sure you want to have an abortion?" Most nod with grim knowing smiles. "Oh, yes," they sigh. Some seek forgiveness, offer excuses. Occasionally a woman will flinch and say, "Please don't use that word."

Later I describe the procedure to come, using care with my   16
language. I don't say "pain" any more than I would say "baby." So many are afraid to ask how much it will hurt. "My sister told me—" I hear. "A friend of mine said—" and the dire expectations unravel. I prick the index finger of a woman for a drop of blood to test, and as the tiny lancet approaches the skin she averts her eyes, holding her trembling hand out to me and jumping at my touch.

It is when I am holding a plastic uterus in one hand, a suc-   17
tion tube in the other, moving them together in imitation of the scrubbing to come, that women ask the most secret question. I am speaking in a matter-of-fact voice about "the tissue" and "the contents" when the woman suddenly catches my eye and asks, "How big is the baby now?" These words suggest a quiet need for a definition of the boundaries being drawn. It isn't so

odd, after all, that she feels relief when I describe the growing bud's bulbous shape, its miniature nature. Again I gauge, and sometimes lie a little, weaseling around its infantile features until its clinging power slackens.

18   But when I look in the basin, among the curdlike blood clots, I see an elfin thorax, attenuated, its pencilline ribs all in parallel rows with tiny knobs of spine rounding upwards. The translucent arm and hand swim beside.

19   A sleepy-eyed girl, just fourteen, watched me with a slight and goofy smile all through her abortion. "Does it have little feet and little fingers and all?" she'd asked earlier. When the suction was over she sat up woozily at the end of the table and murmured, "Can I see it?" I shook my head firmly.

20   "It's not allowed," I told her sternly, because I knew she didn't really want to see what was left. She accepted this statement of authority, and a shadow of confused relief crossed her plain, pale face.

21   Privately, even grudgingly, my colleagues might admit the power of abortion to provoke emotion. But they seem to prefer the broad view and disdain the telescope. Abortion is a matter of choice, privacy, control. Its uncertainty lies in specific cases: retarded women and girls too young to give consent for surgery, women who are ill or hostile or psychotic. Such common dilemmas are met with both compassion and impatience; they slow things down. We are too busy to chew over ethics. One person might discuss certain concerns, behind closed doors, or describe a particularly disturbing dream. But generally there is to be no ambivalence.

22   Every day I take calls from women who are annoyed that we cannot see them, cannot do their abortion today, this morning, now. They argue the price, demand that we stay after hours to accommodate their job or class schedule. Abortion is so routine that one expects it to be like a manicure: quick, cheap, and painless.

23   Still, I've cultivated a certain disregard. It isn't negligence, but I don't always pay attention. I couldn't be here if I tried to judge each case on its merits; after all, we do over a hundred abortions a week. At some point each individual in this line of work draws a boundary and adheres to it. For one physician the boundary is a particular week of gestation; for another, it is a certain number of repeated abortions. But these boundaries can be fluid too: one physician overruled his own limit to abort a mature but severely malformed fetus. For me, the limit is allowing my clients to carry their own burden, shoulder the responsibility themselves. I shoulder the burden of trying not to judge them.

This city has several "crisis pregnancy centers" advertised in   24
the Yellow Pages. They are small offices staffed by volunteers,
and they offer free pregnancy testing, glossy photos of dead fetuses, and movies. I had a client recently whose mother is active
in the antiabortion movement. The young woman went to the
local crisis center and was told that the doctor would make her
touch the dismembered baby, that the pain would be the most
horrible she could imagine, and that she might, after an abortion, never be able to have children. All lies. They called her at
home and at work, over and over and over, but she had been wise
enough to give a false name. She came to us a fugitive. We who
do abortions are marked, by some, as impure. It's dirty work.

When a delivery man comes to the sliding glass window by   25
the reception desk and tilts a box toward me, I hesitate. I read
the packing slip, assess the shape and weight of the box in the
light of its supposed contents. We request familiar faces. The
doors are carefully locked; I have learned to half glance around
at bags and boxes, looking for a telltale sign. I register with security when I arrive, and I am careful not to bang a door. We
are a little on edge here.

Concern about size and shape seem to be natural, and so is   26
the relief that follows. We make the powerful assumption that
the fetus is different from us, and even when we admit the similarities, it is too simplistic to be seduced by form alone. But
the form is enormously potent—humanoid, powerless, palm-
sized, and pure, it evokes an almost fierce tenderness when
viewed simply as what it appears to be. But appearance, and
even potential, aren't enough. The fetus, in becoming itself, can
ruin others: its utter dependence has a sinister side. When I am
struck in the moment by the contents in the basin, I am careful
to remember the context, to note the tearful teenager and the
woman sighing with something more than relief. One kind of
question, though, I find considerably trickier.

"Can you tell what it is?" I am asked, and this means gender.   27
This question is asked by couples, not women alone. Always
couples would abort a girl and keep a boy. I have been asked
about twins, and even if I could tell what race the father was.

An eighteen-year-old woman with three daughters brought   28
her husband to the interview. He glared first at me, then at his
wife, as he sank lower and lower in the chair, picking his teeth
with a toothpick. He interrupted a conversation with his wife
to ask if I could tell whether the baby would be a boy or a girl.
I told him I could not.

"Good," he replied in a slow and strangely malevolent voice,   29
"'cause if it was a boy I'd wring her neck."

30   In a literal sense, abortion exists because we are able to ask such questions, able to assign a value to the fetus which can shift with changing circumstances. If the human bond to a child were as primitive and unflinchingly narrow as that of other animals, there would be no abortion. There would be no abortion because there would be nothing more important than caring for the young and perpetuating the species, no reason for sex but to make babies. I sense this sometimes, this word-less organic duty, when I do ultrasounds.

31   We do ultrasound, a sound-wave test that paints a faint, gray picture of the fetus, whenever we're uncertain of gestation. Age is measured by the width of the skull and confirmed by the length of the femur or thighbone; we speak of a pregnancy as being a certain "femur length" in weeks. The usual concern is whether a pregnancy is within the legal limit for an abortion. Women this far along have bellies which swell out round and tight like trim muscles. When they lie flat, the mound rises softly above the hips, pressing the umbilicus upward.

32   It takes practice to read an ultrasound picture, which is grainy and etched as though in strokes of charcoal. But suddenly a rapid rhythmic motion appears—the beating heart. Nearby is a soft oval, scratched with lines—the skull. The leg is harder to find, and then suddenly the fetus moves, bobbing in the surf. The skull turns away, an arm slides across the screen, the torso rolls. I know the weight of a baby's head on my shoulder, the whisper of lips on ears, the delicate curve of a fragile spine in my hand. I know how heavy and correct a newborn cradled feels. The creature I watch in secret requires nothing from me but to be left alone, and that is precisely what won't be done.

33   These inadvertently made beings are caught in a twisting web of motive and desire. They are at least inconvenient, sometimes quite literally dangerous in the womb, but most often they fall somewhere in between—consequences never quite believed in come to roost. Their virtue rises and falls outside their own nature: they become only what we make them. A fetus created by accident is the most absolute kind of surprise. Whether the blame lies in a failed IUD, a slipped condom, or a false impression of safety, that fetus is a thing whose creation has been actively worked against. Its existence is an error. I think this is why so few women, even late in pregnancy, will consider giving a baby up for adoption. To do so means making the fetus real—imagining it as something whole and outside oneself. The decision to terminate a pregnancy is sometimes so difficult and confounding that it creates an enormous demand for immediate action. The decision is rejection; the

pregnancy has become something to be rid of, a condition to be ended. It is a burden, a weight, a thing separate.

Women have abortions because they are too old, and too   34
young, too poor, and too rich, too stupid, and too smart. I see women who berate themselves with violent emotions for their first and only abortion, and others who return three times, five times, hauling two or three children, who cannot remember to take a pill or where they put the diaphragm. We talk glibly about choice. But the choice for what? I see all the broken promises in lives lived like a series of impromptu obstacles. There are the sweet, light promises of love and intimacy, the glittering promise of education and progress, the warm promise of safe families, long years of innocence and community. And there is the promise of freedom: freedom from failure, from faithlessness. Freedom from biology. The early feminist defense of abortion asked many questions, but the one I remember is this: is biology destiny? And the answer is yes, sometimes it is. Women who have the fewest choices of all exercise their right to abortion the most.

Oh, the ignorance. I take a woman to the back room and ask   35
her to undress; a few minutes later I return and find her positioned discreetly behind a drape, still wearing underpants. "Do I have to take these off too?" she asks, a little shocked. Some swear they have not had sex. Many do not know what a uterus is, how sperm and egg meet, how sex makes babies. Some late seekers do not believe themselves pregnant; they believe themselves *impregnable.* I was chastised when I began this job for referring to some clients as girls: it is a feminist heresy. They come so young, snapping gum, sockless and sneakered, and their shakily applied eyeliner smears when they cry. I call them girls with maternal benignity. I cannot imagine them as mothers.

   36

The doctor seats himself between the woman's thighs and reaches into the dilated opening of a five-month pregnant uterus. Quickly he grabs and crushes the fetus in several places, and the room is filled with a low clatter and snap of forceps, the click of the tanaculum,[1] and a pulling, sucking sound. The paper crinkles as the drugged and sleepy woman shifts, the nurse's low, honey-brown voice explains each step in delicate words.   37

I have fetus dreams, we all do here: dreams of abortions one after the other; of buckets of blood splashed on the walls; trees full of crawling fetuses. I dreamed that two men grabbed me

---

[1]A type of sharp forceps used on bleeding arteries.

and began to drag me away: "Let's do an abortion," they said with a sickening leer, and I began to scream, plunged into a vision of sucking, scraping pain, of being spread and torn by impartial instruments that do only what they are bidden. I woke from this dream barely able to breathe and thought of kitchen tables and coat hangers, knitting needles striped with blood, and women all alone clutching a pillow in their teeth to keep the screams from piercing the apartment-house walls. Abortion is the narrowest edge between kindness and cruelty. Done as well as it can be, it is still violence—merciful violence, like putting a suffering animal to death.

38   Maggie, one of the nurses, received a call at midnight not long ago. It was a woman in her twentieth week of pregnancy; the necessarily gradual process of cervical dilation begun the day before had stimulated labor, as it sometimes does. Maggie and one of the doctors met the woman at the office in the night. Maggie helped her onto the table, and as she lay down the fetus was delivered into Maggie's hands. When Maggie told me about it the next day, she cupped her hands into a small bowl—"It was just like a little kitten," she said softly, wonderingly. "Everything was still attached."

39   At the end of the day I clean out the suction jars, pouring blood into the sink, splashing the sides with flecks of tissue. From the sink rises a rich and humid smell, hot, earthy, and moldering; it is the smell of something recently alive beginning to decay. I take care of the plastic tub on the floor, filled with pieces too big to be trusted to the trash. The law defines the contents of the bucket I hold protectively against my chest as "tissue." Some would say my complicity in filling that bucket gives me no right to call it anything else. I slip the tissue gently into a bag and place it in the freezer, to be burned at another time. Abortion requires of me an entirely new set of assumptions. It requires a willingness to live with conflict, fearlessness, and grief. As I close the freezer door, I imagine a world where this won't be necessary, and then return to the world where it is.

Mary Meehan
A PRO-LIFE VIEW
FROM THE LEFT

Mary Meehan has written many articles on various topics for respected newspapers and periodicals such as The Nation, The Washington Monthly, *and* The Washington Post. *In 1980, she contributed the following article to* The Progressive, *a monthly magazine that, true to its name, takes a liberal stance toward current public issues.*

The abortion issue, more than most, illustrates the occasional tendency of the Left to become so enthusiastic over what is called a "reform" that it forgets to think the issue through. It is ironic that so many on the Left have done on abortion what conservatives and Cold War liberals did on Vietnam: They marched off in the wrong direction, to fight the wrong war, against the wrong people. 1

Some of us who went through the anti-war struggles of the 1960s and early 1970s are now active in the right-to-life movement. We do not enjoy opposing our old friends on the abortion issue, but we feel that we have no choice. We are moved by what pro-life feminists call the "consistency thing"—the belief that respect for human life demands opposition to abortion, capital punishment, euthanasia, and war. We don't think we have either the luxury or the right to choose some types of killing and say that they are all right, while others are not. A human life is a human life; and if equality means anything, it means that society may not value some human lives over others. 2

Until the last decade, people on the Left and Right generally agreed on one rule: We all protected the young. This was not merely agreement on an ethical question: It was also an expression of instinct, so deep and ancient that it scarcely required explanation. 3

Protection of the young included protection of the unborn, for abortion was forbidden by state laws throughout the United States. Those laws reflected an ethical consensus, not based solely on religious tradition but also on scientific evidence that human life begins at conception. The prohibition of abortion in the ancient Hippocratic Oath is well known. Less familiar to many is the Oath of Geneva, formulated by the World Medical Association in 1948, which included these 4 words: "I will maintain the utmost respect for human life from the time of conception." A Declaration of the Rights of the Child, adopted by the United Nations General Assembly in 1959, declared that "the child, by reason of his physical and mental immaturity, needs special safeguards and care, including appropriate legal protection, before as well as after birth."

5   It is not my purpose to explain why courts and parliaments in many nations rejected this tradition over the past few decades, though I suspect their action was largely a surrender to technical achievement—if such inventions as suction aspirators can be called technical achievements. But it is important to ask why the Left in the United States generally accepted legalized abortion.

6   One factor was the popular civil-libertarian rationale for freedom of choice in abortion. Many feminists presented it as a right of women to control their own bodies. When the objection was raised that abortion ruins *another person's* body, they respond that a) it is not a body, just a "blob of protoplasm" (thereby displaying ignorance of biology); or b) it is not really a "person" until it is born. When it was suggested that this is a wholly arbitrary decision, unsupported by any biological evidence, they said, "Well, that's your point of view. This is a matter of individual conscience, and in a pluralistic society people must be free to follow their consciences."

7   Unfortunately, many liberals and radicals accepted this view without further question. Perhaps many did not know that an eight-week-old fetus has a fully human form. They did not ask whether American slaveholders before the Civil War were right in viewing blacks as less than human and as private property; or whether the Nazis were correct in viewing mental patients, Jews, and Gypsies as less than human and therefore subject to the final solution.

8   Class issues provided another rationale. In the late 1960s, liberals were troubled by evidence that rich women could obtain abortions regardless of the law, by going to careful society doctors or to countries where abortion was legal. Why, they asked, should poor women be barred from something the wealthy could have? One might turn this argument on its head by asking why rich children should be denied protection that poor children have.

9   But pro-life activists did not want abortion to be a class issue one way or the other; they wanted to end abortion everywhere, for all classes. And many people who had experienced poverty did not think providing legal abortion was any favor to poor

women. Thus, in 1972, when a Presidential commission on population growth recommended legalized abortion, partly to remove discrimination against poor women, several commission members dissented.

One was Graciela Olivarez, a Chicana who was active in civil 10 rights and anti-poverty work. Olivarez, who later was named to head the Federal Government's Community Services Administration, had known poverty in her youth in the Southwest. With a touch of bitterness, she said in her dissent, "The poor cry out for justice and equality and we respond with legalized abortion." Olivarez noted that blacks and Chicanos had often been unwanted by white society. She added, "I believe that in a society that permits the life of even one individual (born or unborn) to be dependent on whether that life is 'wanted' or not, all its citizens stand in danger." Later she told the press, "We do not have equal opportunities. Abortion is a cruel way out."

Many liberals were also persuaded by a church/state argu- 11 ment that followed roughly this line: "Opposition to abortion is a religious viewpoint, particularly a Catholic viewpoint. The Catholics have no business imposing their religious views on the rest of us." It is true that opposition to abortion is a religious position for many people. Orthodox Jews, Mormons, and many of the fundamentalist Protestant groups also oppose abortion. (So did the mainstream Protestant churches until recent years.) But many people are against abortion for reasons that are independent of religious authority or belief. Many would still be against abortion if they lost their faith; others are opposed to it after they *have* lost their faith, or if they never had any faith. Only if their non-religious grounds for opposition can be proven baseless could legal prohibition of abortion fairly be called an establishment of religion. The pro-abortion forces concentrate heavily on religious arguments against abortion and generally ignore the secular arguments—possibly because they cannot answer them.

Still another, more emotional reason is that so many conser- 12 vatives oppose abortion. Many liberals have difficulty accepting the idea that Jesse Helms can be right about *anything*. I do not quite understand this attitude. Just by the law of averages, he has to be right about something, sometime. Standing at the March for Life rally at the U.S. Capitol last year, and hearing Senator Helms say that "We reject the philosophy that life should be only for the planned, the perfect, or the privileged," I thought he was making a good civil-rights statement.

If much of the leadership of the pro-life movement is right- 13 wing, that is due largely to the default of the Left. We "little people" who marched against the war and now march against abortion would like to see leaders of the Left speaking out on behalf of the unborn. But we see only a few, such as Dick Gregory, Mark Hatfield, Jesse Jackson, Richard Neuhaus, Mary Rose Oakar. Most of the others either avoid the issue or support abortion. We are dismayed by their inconsistency. And we are not impressed by arguments that we should work and vote for them because they are good on such issues as food stamps and medical care.

14   Although many liberals and radicals accepted legalized abortion, there are signs of uneasiness about it. Tell someone who supports it that you have many problems with the issue, and she is likely to say, quickly, "Oh, I don't think I could ever have one myself, but. . . ." or "I'm really not pro-*abortion;* I'm pro-*choice*" or "I'm *personally* opposed to it, but. . . ."

15   Why are they personally opposed to it if there is nothing wrong with it?

16   Perhaps such uneasiness is a sign that many on the Left are ready to take another look at the abortion issue. In the hope of contributing toward a new perspective, I offer the following points:

17   *First,* it is out of character for the Left to neglect the weak and helpless. The traditional mark of the Left has been its protection of the underdog, the weak, and the poor. The unborn child is the most helpless form of humanity, even more in need of protection than the poor tenant farmer or the mental patient or the boat people on the high seas. The basic instinct of the Left is to aid those who cannot aid themselves—and that instinct is absolutely sound. It is what keeps the human proposition going.

18   *Second,* the right to life underlies and sustains *every other* right we have. It is, as Thomas Jefferson and his friends said, self-evident. Logically, as well as in our Declaration of Independence, it comes before the right to liberty and the right to property. The right to exist, to be free from assault by others, is the basis of equality. Without it, the other rights are meaningless, and life becomes a sort of warfare in which force decides everything. There is no equality, because one person's convenience takes precedence over another's life, provided only that the first person has more power. If we do not protect this right for everyone, it is not guaranteed for everyone, because anyone can become weak and vulnerable to assault.

19   *Third,* abortion is a civil-rights issue. Dick Gregory and many other blacks view abortion as a type of genocide. Confirmation of this comes in the experience of pro-life activists who find open bigotry when they speak with white voters about public funding of abortion. Many white voters believe abortion is a

solution for the welfare problem and a way to slow the growth of the black population. I worked two years ago for a liberal, pro-life candidate who was appalled by the number of anti-black comments he found when discussing the issue. And Representative Robert Dornan of California, a conservative pro-life leader, once told his colleagues in the House, "I have heard many rock-ribbed Republicans brag about how fiscally conservative they are and then tell me that I was an idiot on the abortion issue." When he asked why, said Dornan, they whispered, "Because we have to hold them down, we have to stop the population growth." Dornan elaborated: "To them, population growth means blacks, Puerto Ricans, or other Latins," or anyone who "should not be having more than a po-lite one or two 'burdens on society.'"

Fourth, abortion exploits women. Many women are pres-   20
sured by spouses, lovers, or parents into having abortions they do not want. Sometimes the coercion is subtle, as when a hus-band complains of financial problems. Sometimes it is open and crude, as when a boyfriend threatens to end the affair un-less the woman has an abortion, or when parents order a mi-nor child to have an abortion. Pro-life activists who do "clinic counseling" (standing outside abortion clinics, trying to speak to each woman who enters, urging her to have the child) report that many women who enter clinics alone are willing to talk and to listen. Some change their minds and decide against abortion. But a woman who is accompanied by someone else often does not have the chance to talk, because the husband or boyfriend or parent is so hostile to the pro-life worker.

Juli Loesch, a feminist/pacifist writer, notes that feminists   21
want to have men participate more in the care of children, but abortion allows a man to shift total responsibility to the woman: "He can *buy* his way out of accountability by making 'The Offer' for 'The Procedure.'" She adds that the man's sexual role "then implies—exactly nothing: no relationship. How quickly a 'woman's right to choose' comes to serve a 'man's right to use.'" And Daphne de Jong, a New Zealand feminist, says, "If women must submit to abortion to preserve their lifestyle or career, their economic or social status, they are pan-dering to a system devised and run by men for male conve-nience." She adds, "Of all the things which are done to women to fit them into a society dominated by men, abortion is the most violent invasion of their physical and psychic integrity. It is a deeper and more destructive assault than rape. . . ."

Loesch, de Jong, Olivarez, and other pro-life feminists be-   22
lieve men should bear a much greater share of the burdens of child-rearing than they do at present. And de Jong makes a

radical point when she says, "Accepting short-term solutions like abortion only delays the implementation of real reforms like decent maternity and paternity leaves, job protection, high-quality child care, community responsibility for dependent people of all ages, and recognition of the economic contribution of childminders." Olivarez and others have also called for the development of safer and more effective contraceptives for both men and women. In her 1972 dissent, Olivarez noted with irony that "medical science has developed four different ways for killing a fetus, but has not yet developed a safe-for-all-to-use contraceptive."

23   *Fifth*, abortion is an escape from an obligation that is owed to another. Doris Gordon, Coordinator of Libertarians for Life, puts it this way: "Unborn children don't cause women to become pregnant but parents cause their children to be in the womb, and as a result, they need parental care. As a general principle, if we are the cause of another's need for care, as when we cause an accident, we acquire an obligation to that person as a result. . . . We have no right to kill in order to terminate any obligation."

24   *Sixth*, abortion brutalizes those who perform it, undergo it, pay for it, profit from it, and allow it to happen. Too many of us look the other way because we do not want to think about abortion. A part of reality is blocked out because one does not want to see broken bodies coming home, or going to an incinerator, in those awful plastic bags. People deny their own humanity when they refuse to identify with, or even acknowledge, the pain of others.

25   With some it is worse: They are making money from the misery of others, from exploited women and dead children.

Anna Quindlen

ABORTION IS TOO COMPLEX TO FEEL ALL ONE WAY ABOUT

Anna Quindlen (born 1955) for a number of years wrote a widely praised, syndicated column for The New York Times *and many other newspapers. She won a Pulitzer Prize for commentary in 1992. Her work has been collected in several books, including* Thinking Out Loud: On the Personal, the Political, the Public, and the Private *(1993). The following essay appeared in* The New York Times *in 1986. (For another essay by Quindlen, see page 499.)*

It was always the look on their faces that told me first. I was the freshman dormitory counselor and they were the freshmen at a women's college where everyone was smart. One of them could come into my room, a golden girl, a valedictorian, an 800 verbal score on the SATs, and her eyes would be empty, seeing only a busted future, the devastation of her life as she knew it. She had failed biology, messed up the math; she was pregnant. 1

That was when I became pro-choice. 2

It was the look in his eyes that I will always remember, too. 3
They were as black as the bottom of a well, and in them for a few minutes I thought I saw myself the way I had always wished to be—clear, simple, elemental, at peace. My child looked at me and I looked back at him in the delivery room, and I realized that out of a sea of infinite possibilities it had come down to this: a specific person born on the hottest day of the year, conceived on a Christmas Eve, made by his father and me miraculously from scratch.

Once I believed that there was a little blob of formless proto- 4
plasm in there and a gynecologist went after it with a surgical instrument, and that was that. Then I got pregnant myself—eagerly, intentionally, by the right man, at the right time—and I began to doubt. My abdomen still flat, my stomach roiling with morning sickness, I felt not that I had protoplasm inside but instead a complete human being in miniature to whom I could talk, sing, make promises. Neither of these views was accurate; instead, I think, the reality is something in the middle. And there is where I find myself now, in the middle, hating the idea of abortions, hating the idea of having them outlawed.

5   For I know it is the right thing in some times and places. I remember sitting in a shabby clinic far uptown with one of those freshman, only three months after the Supreme Court had made what we were doing possible, and watching with wonder as the lovely first love she had had with a nice boy unraveled over the space of an hour as they waited for her to be called, degenerated into sniping and silences. I remember a year or two later seeing them pass on campus and not even acknowledge one another because their conjoining had caused them so much pain, and I shuddered to think of them married, with a small psyche in their unready and unwilling hands.

6   I've met 14-year-olds who were pregnant and said they could not have abortions because of their religion, and I see in their eyes the shadows of 22-year-olds I've talked to who lost their kids to foster care because they hit them or used drugs or simply had no money for food and shelter. I read not long ago about a teenager who said she meant to have an abortion but she spent the money on clothes instead; now she has a baby who turns out to be a lot more trouble than a toy. The people who hand out those execrable little pictures of dismembered fetuses at abortion clinics seem to forget the extraordinary pain children may endure after they are born when they are unwanted, even hated or simply tolerated.

7   I believe that in a contest between the living and the almost living, the latter must, if necessary, give way to the will of the former. That is what the fetus is to me, the almost living. Yet these questions began to plague me—and, I've discovered, a good many other women—after I became pregnant. But they became even more acute after I had my second child, mainly because he is so different from his brother. On two random nights 18 months apart the same two people managed to conceive, and on one occasion the tumult within turned itself into a curly-haired brunet with merry black eyes who walked and talked late and loved the whole world, and on another it became a blond with hazel Asian eyes and a pug nose who tried to conquer the world almost as soon as he entered it.

8   If we were to have an abortion next time for some reason or another, which infinite possibility becomes, not a reality, but a nullity? The girl with the blue eyes? The improbable redhead? The natural athlete? The thinker? My husband, ever at the heart of the matter, put it another way. Knowing that he is finding two children somewhat more overwhelming than he expected, I asked if he would want me to have an abortion if I accidentally became pregnant again right away. "And waste a perfectly good human being?" he said.

Coming to this quandary has been difficult for me. In fact, I 9
believe the issue of abortion is difficult for all thoughtful people.
I don't know anyone who has had an abortion who has not been
haunted by it. If there is one thing I find intolerable about most
of the so-called right-to-lifers, it is that they try to portray abortion rights as something that feminists thought up on a slow
Saturday over a light lunch. That is nonsense. I also know that
some people who support abortion rights are most comfortable
with a monolithic position because it seems the strongest front
against the smug and sometimes violent opposition.

But I don't feel all one way about abortion anymore, and I 10
don't think it serves a just cause to pretend that many of us do.
For years I believed that a woman's right to choose was absolute, but now I wonder. Do I, with a stable home and marriage and sufficient stamina and money, have the right to
choose abortion because a pregnancy is inconvenient right
now? Legally I do have that right; legally I want always to have
that right. It is the morality of exercising it under those circumstances that makes me wonder.

Technology has foiled us. The second trimester has become a 11
time of resurrection; a fetus at six months can be one woman's
late abortion, another's premature, viable child. Photographers
now have film of embryos the size of a grape, oddly human,
flexing their fingers, sucking their thumbs. Women have am-
niocentesis to find out whether they are carrying a child with
birth defects that they may choose to abort. Before the procedure, they must have a sonogram, one of those fuzzy black-
and-white photos like a love song heard through static on the
radio, which shows someone is in there.

I have taped on my VCR a public-television program in 12
which somehow, inexplicably, a film is shown of a fetus in
utero scratching its face, seemingly putting up a tiny hand to
shield itself from the camera's eye. It would make a potent
weapon in the arsenal of the antiabortionists. I grow sentimental about it as it floats in the salt water, part fish, part human
being. It is almost living, but not quite. It has almost turned my
heart around, but not quite turned my head.

Mike Royko

A POX ON BOTH
YOUR HOUSES

*Royko (1922–1997), a syndicated columnist associated with
the* Chicago Tribune—*and with Chicago in general, since he
worked as a reporter for several Chicago newspapers for many
years—wrote the following commentary in July 1992, a few
days after the Supreme Court upheld both* Roe v. Wade *and
most parts of a controversial Pennsylvania law requiring
women desiring an abortion to wait 24 hours, to receive written material on the medical procedure, and, if they are minors,
to inform their parents. Mike Royko won a Pulitzer Prize for
social commentary.*

1   "Why are all those women so mad?" asked Slats Grobnik, gesturing at the TV set. "The old man stop for a few after work?"

2   No, it is far more serious than that. They are an anti-
abortion group, furious because the Supreme Court has upheld the right of women to get abortions.

3   The TV switched to another angry group of women.

4   "Now what's this bunch mad about? They're yelling louder
than the others."

5   They are a pro-abortion group, and they are furious because
the Supreme Court has upheld a few restrictions.

6   "Like what?"

7   A 24-hour waiting period. Parental consent for teen-agers.
And women being told what their options are, such as adoption, and what kind of medical and financial help is available if
she has the baby.

8   "Wait a minute, I don't get it."

9   Get what?

10   "I can see how the anti-abortion crowd would be mad because abortions are still legal, right?"

11   That's what the court said.

12   "Then if they're legal, what's the other side got to beef about?"

13   They don't like any kind of restrictions. They feel it is a
threat to their control over their own bodies.

14   "Waiting 24 hours? Nowadays, you got to wait 24 hours for
everything. It takes longer than that to get a tooth drilled or
your car tuned up. So what's the big rush? And what's wrong
with telling some girl about financial help or that there are
people who want to adopt kids?"

They believe that is not society's business to intrude on their 15
right to control their own bodies.

"Hey, when the draft board told me I was gonna go fight in 16
Korea, that was messing with my right to control my body, because I guarantee you, I didn't want my body being shot up by
no Chinese commies. So I wind up putting in two years with
society, by way of the government, telling my body where it's
going to go and what it's going to do. If I want to stick a needle
in my arm and shoot up with dope, that's illegal. Even though
that arm is part of my body right?"

Correct. 17

"See, that's what bothers me about this abortion fight. These 18
people don't always make sense."

Which side? 19

"Both sides. They're not always, what'ya call it, consistent?" 20

In what way? 21

"Well, the one side says they are pro-life. Now, does that 22
mean that they're against frying someone in the electric chair?"

I would doubt that. 23

"That's what I thought, because I know a few of the pro-life 24
ladies and they want to hang 'em high. And were they against us
dropping bombs and killing women and children in Iraq because
we wanted to put this rich emir back on his throne in Kuwait?"

I would guess that they were part of the mainstream of public 25
opinion that delighted in the triumphs of our heroic video war.

"That's what I think. So when they say they're pro-life, it all 26
depends on what life, right?"

Yes, the unborn. 27

"And don't get me wrong. I don't have any trouble with that. 28
Especially when I read that there's been 26 million abortions in
the last 19 years. You know what that works out to on my
pocket calculator?"

Lots. 29

"Yeah, more than 26,000 a week. About 3,700 a day. About 30
156 an hour. Almost three a minute. Think about it. Every 20
or 30 seconds, there's an abortion. Are there really that many
people whose lives are gonna be ruined if they have a kid? I'm
supposed to believe that it's a disaster if they gotta wait 24
hours? Or if someone talks to them about adoption?"

But it is a question of choice, which is why they call them- 31
selves pro-choice.

"They don't sound like they're in favor of a choice if they're 32
in a flap because they don't want some young girl to wait 24
hours or to listen to what somebody's got to say about her options. Another thing—how do they feel about frying John Gacy,
that serial killer who buried his victims under his house?"

33   What does he have to do with it?

34   "Well, I noticed something. Some women I know who are in favor of abortion are against the death penalty, and that don't make sense to me. How can you be in favor of killing some harmless little thing in a woman's tummy but you get all weepy when they pull the switch on some ax murderer? I don't see how you can be for one and not the other."

35   Well, maybe they believe that the decision as to whether John Gacy is executed should be made by his mother.

36   "Yeah, I guess that makes sense, kind of a pro-choice thing."

37   Right. So, where do you stand?

38   "On what?"

39   Abortion. Are you for it or against it?

40   "Forget it. If I say I'm against, then they'll say I'm in favor of killing women, right?"

41   It wouldn't surprise me.

42   "And if I'm for it, they'll say I'm a baby-killer, right?"

43   Almost a certainty.

44   "So you're not gonna corner me. There's one thing I'm sure of, though. We got to check on the diets of American women."

45   What do their diets have to do with it?

46   "If there's been 26 million abortions over the last 19 years, they should try eating more brain foods."

Jim McCloskey and *Mike Luckovich*

EDITORIAL CARTOONS
ON ABORTION

Nearly every American is shocked whenever a physician or other health-care worker is injured or murdered by antiabortion fanatics. Late in 1993, the murder of a Florida physician motivated the two editorial cartoons on the next page. The first, by Jim McCloskey of the Creators Syndicate, Incorporated, appeared in a number of newspapers; the second, by Mike Luckovich, appeared in the Atlanta Constitution. *The two illustrate how differing assumptions can lead to differing responses to the same incident.*

GAY, LESBIAN, AND BISEXUAL RIGHTS

■
———————————●———————————

Michael Cunningham
TAKING THE CENSUS
OF QUEER NATION

Michael Cunningham is a member of the gay rights group Act
Up. *A writer of fiction and nonfiction, he contributed the following essay to* Mother Jones *in the summer of 1992.* Mother
Jones, *published bimonthly, is a liberal, irreverent magazine of
commentary on current affairs. (Some of the names of people
in this essay—the ones identified by first name only—have
been changed.)*

1   Tim and I were walking home late from St. Vincent's Hospital
in New York City, where we'd been sitting with what remained
of a friend named John. We went every night, although John
had been unconscious for nearly a week. We hoped that if we
held his hand and spoke to him something might still register.
Doctors suspect that hearing is the last sense to go. You should
talk to the dying.

2   As Tim and I walked home through the streets of the West
Village, we talked about John's funeral. "Definitely something
glamorous," Tim said. "He'd hate anything morbid."

3   I agreed. When he was healthy, John had dyed his hair
platinum. He'd worn baggy shorts and purple high tops.
Lamentation wasn't his style.

4   On the corner where we parted, I looked closely at Tim's
face. He was deeply pale, putty-colored, and his eyes looked
unnaturally large in his skull. He had AIDS too. He was still
working full-time and keeping two hospital vigils.

5   "What are you eating?" I asked. "You look like you've lost
weight."

He waved my question away. "I'm eating all the right things," he said. "I'm taking perfect care of myself. Give it a rest, Mom." 6

We said good-night, and he turned down Fourth Street, a scrawny, determined figure in oversized hoop earrings. I watched him for a moment, thinking about the workings of ordinary courage. 7

I'd just made it home and into bed when the phone rang. It was Tim. 8

"Hi," he said. "Guess where I'm calling from? St. Vincent's." 9

"Shit," I said. "Did John die right after we left?" 10

"No, it's not John," he said. His voice carried a thin, slightly blurred tone of good cheer, as if he'd been drugged. "It's me. I got beaten up. About five minutes after I left you. By three guys." 11

I went to get him with another friend of his, an English journalist named Karen. Tim was woozy and slightly manic from painkillers, and his fair hair was swathed in bandages. Karen asked him if he'd gotten a good look at the men who beat him. 12

"You know, I don't exactly remember them," he said in a chipper voice. "I know they were yelling 'faggot' at me. And I think I yelled back. Something like, 'You got it, sweethearts— who wants to be first?' Then I was in the emergency room, being stitched up. Poof. There one minute, here the next." 13

Karen and I got him back to his apartment and put him to bed. We sat with him until he fell asleep. Karen whispered, "He looks about fifteen, doesn't he?" He did look preternaturally young and wan, his blue-veined eyelids translucent, the bandage white around his head. He was a cheerful, domestically inclined boy from Indiana. He adored his friends, had a cat named Aretha, and always fell asleep before it was time to go out to the clubs. Someone had hit his frail, compromised body with a two-by-four. Someone, somewhere in the city, was congratulating himself at that moment. Someone was laughing and popping a beer. 14

To calm myself I laid my hand, gently, on Tim's scrawny chest. I felt the steady effort of his breathing. After a moment, Karen put her hand on top of mine. "This makes me crazy," I said to her. "This makes me want to hurt people." I was furious at myself for failing to watch out for Tim. And I was angry at Tim. Why did he have to talk back to those morons? 15

Karen shook her head disapprovingly, and I was suddenly, fiercely angry at her as well. Because she and her girlfriend are staunchly opposed to violence in any form. Because she refuses to have anything to do with activist groups like ACT UP (the AIDS Coalition to Unleash Power) or Queer Nation, the radical gay-rights organization spawned by ACT UP to strike back at all the people who'd beat up an innocent gay kid like Tim. 16

Because several weeks earlier, as we passed a series of posters announcing the homosexuality of some very big—and very closeted—Hollywood stars, she hissed: "The fascists who force other people to come out are doing us more harm than good."

17   If you're straight, it may be hard to understand the need for an obstreperous, in-your-face organization like Queer Nation. It may be hard to imagine the intricate combination of rage and terror that constitutes the gay zeitgeist of 1992. There's a virus ticking its way through the arteries of people we love. That would be enough to make us crazy, right there. But what's driven some of us around the bend is the fact that, even as our friends keep dying, the hatred of homosexuals flourishes.

18   Gay-bashing is up all over the country. Homophobia is thriving like mosquitoes in August, and it comes as often as not in relatively subtle, nonviolent packages. Take Magic Johnson, for instance. Shortly after announcing he was HIV-positive, he inspired wild applause on the Arsenio Hall show when he said, "I'm nowhere near homosexual." People cheered. If you're a person of color, try to imagine a celebrity telling an appreciative audience, "I thank God I'm white!" If you're Jewish, imagine the same audience clapping and whistling when a celebrity announces, "No way am I a Jew."

19   If you're gay and you're not angry, you're just not paying attention.

20   I myself belong to ACT UP. I've helped engineer an on-screen takeover of the *MacNeil/Lehrer Newshour* (you'd be surprised at how easy it is to get into a television studio). I've chained myself to the White House gates. I've committed these and other acts of civil disobedience in the company of people I consider heroes. I confess up front to deep affection and respect for Queer Nation, which was launched just over two years ago by a band of ACT UP members from New York City who wanted to concentrate on gay issues outside the realm of AIDS.

21   Queer Nation is a peculiar mix of outrage and wackiness—you could call it the illegitimate child of Huey Newton and Lucy Ricardo. Male and female members go en masse to straight bars and hockey games, where they kiss their lovers passionately. They stage impromptu fashion shows in suburban shopping malls, featuring men in tutus and women in Harley-Davidson gear.

22   The name itself started as a joke of sorts. "Queer Nation" was a temporary moniker, offered in jest. Once the founding members got used to it, though, they didn't mind the idea of throwing a word like "queer" back in the faces of those who'd been spitting it at them for decades. They decided they could repossess the insult; they could cauterize it by taking it on them-

selves. Besides, the word emphasizes difference. Members aren't trying to say to the straight world, "Accept us, because we're just like you." That was the old tactic, which is now known disparagingly as assimilationism. Queer Nation's official tag line is "We're here. We're queer. Get used to it."

By the time it was a year old, Queer Nation existed in over 23 sixty cities, from New York and San Francisco to Indianapolis and Shreveport. Now, just past its second anniversary, no one's quite sure how many chapters there are. The rise has been swift but chaotic, and established chapters have burned out nearly as quickly as new ones have appeared. Since I started writing this article, the Eugene and Houston chapters have taken off while the San Francisco chapter has dissolved.

Like ACT UP, Queer Nation is ferociously democratic and 24 decentralized. Its founders were determined not to emulate what they called the "hierarchical, patriarchal" pecking order by which most groups—from the Young Republicans to the Crips and the Bloods—are run. At every chapter, anyone who shows up at a meeting is instantaneously a full member. Some chapters are run by consensus; some simply function as a forum for people who want to recruit others for demonstrations. The prevailing aim—you could call it an obsession—is to exclude no one.

It would be easy to play up Queer Nation's kind intentions 25 and zany antics. But members can also be loudly confrontational. They've irritated a lot of people, including other lesbians and gay men. Gay opposition is wildly various, but I can offer a quintessential scenario. Say your parents are visiting from Michigan, and you've finally decided to come out to them. You're a relatively ordinary citizen with a nine-to-five job. In a quiet restaurant, over coffee, you say it: "Listen, I guess you may have suspected this. I don't want to keep secrets from you anymore. I'm gay." Your mother cries and tells you she loves you anyway. She says it with a certain forced conviction, which doesn't quite ring true. Your father is murderously silent. This is the hardest thing you've ever done. As you leave the restaurant, your mother is sniffling and your father is glacial. You're searching for something else to say, some way to make them understand that you haven't suddenly transformed yourself into an alien. As you struggle for the right words, you walk out of the restaurant into a band of men and women carrying QUEER POWER signs. They're blowing whistles. Some wear nose rings and combat boots. Two of the men have on dresses, and one sports a Nancy Sinatra wig. As they pass, somebody slaps a Day-Glo sticker on your father's seersucker jacket. The sticker says GO GIRL.

26   Opposition to Queer Nation's tactics doesn't end with questions of style or demeanor. Last September, gay riots exploded in Los Angeles and San Francisco after California governor Pete Wilson vetoed AB 101, a bill that would have outlawed job discrimination on the basis of sexual orientation. After his veto, Queer Nationals and other gay activists hurled police barricades through windows. They set fires in the streets. And some of them threatened to expose gay members of Wilson's staff, further igniting the ongoing debate about outing, tactics, and propriety.

27   Gay activists face a fundamental question familiar to feminists and civil-rights leaders, among others. Do we play by the rules, court public sympathy, and push steadily but politely for recognition? Or do we make ourselves so unpleasant that yielding to our demands finally becomes easier than ignoring us? I myself favor the noisier alternatives. I believe the AIDS epidemic has taught us that nobody will listen unless we scream. But still, I'm plagued by doubts. At ACT UP meetings, when members talk about planning a new action that will "show our anger," I find myself asking, What exactly do we expect people to do with our anger once we've shown it to them? As I set out to visit Queer Nation chapters around the country, that question was on my mind. And on my first stop, in Atlanta, Georgia, a woman named Cheryl Summerville was pondering it too.

28   Cheryl Summerville may have been the best-behaved lesbian in the world. She lived outside Atlanta with her lover, Sandra Riley, in a house the two women helped build themselves. She and Riley were raising Summerville's son from a long-dissolved marriage and were thinking of having a child of their own. Summerville had a decent job as a cook at the local Cracker Barrel, one of a chain of country-style restaurants.

29   But in February of 1991, the associate manager of the restaurant, Marilee Gonzalez, called Summerville into her office. Gonzalez, who had been friendly with Summerville, told her in a nervous but formal tone that Cracker Barrel had decided to reexamine its policy about gay and lesbian employees. She asked, "Are you a lesbian?"

30   Summerville answered: "Marilee, you know I am. You going to fire me for that?"

31   That day, Summerville received a pink slip on the orders of Cracker Barrel district manager Jody Waller. The restaurant's general manager filed a separation notice with the Georgia Department of Labor, on which he wrote: "This employee is being terminated due to violation of company policy. The employee is gay."

Waller was complying with a memo sent to the managers of   32
all outlets by Cracker Barrel's main office in Lebanon,
Tennessee. The memo said, in part: "It is inconsistent with our
concept and values, and is perceived to be inconsistent with
those of our customer base, to continue to employ individuals
in our operating units whose sexual preferences fail to demonstrate normal heterosexual values which have been the foundation of families in our society."

In all, eighteen lesbians and gay men were fired from   33
Cracker Barrel's outlets. Some managers called the employees
they suspected into their offices and formally asked if they
were homosexual. Others just convened staff meetings and announced that certain employees were being terminated in ac-
cordance with company policy.

Summerville simply didn't get it at first. In every respect but   34
one, she'd always been a model of conventional good behavior.
She'd received a "personal achievement award," given by
Cracker Barrel to outstanding staff members, and was up for
another. She'd helped build a house with her own hands,
adored her parents and son, earned a living through hard
work. Her single transgression was to love another woman
and, even in that, she'd been modest and forthright. She hadn't
concealed her love for Sandra Riley, nor had she flaunted it.
Now she was out of work, for failing to display normal values.

At first, Summerville assumed she could take Cracker Barrel   35
to court. But only a few states and about sixty cities and counties have barred discrimination on the basis of sexual preference in both public and private employment. Atlanta isn't
among them. When Summerville learned she had no legal recourse, she called ACT UP for help, but was told that it worked
only on issues relating directly to AIDS. She was referred to the
Atlanta chapter of Queer Nation.

Summerville was not a political person. She wasn't tortured   36
by ideals or abstractions—she just wanted to live an uncomplicated life. The idea of speaking to a group that called itself
Queer Nation gave her a kind of vertigo. "It took me a week to
get up the nerve," she says. She and Sandra Riley made a dry
run in their car past the Five Points Community Center, where
the group's next meeting was to take place. The center looked
ordinary enough. But still.

On the night of the meeting, she and Riley were so nervous   37
they arrived twenty minutes early. As the members started
drifting in, Summerville was surprised to find that they looked
like everybody else. "I didn't expect just normal-looking people," she says. "I thought we were in the wrong place. They
were wearing just jeans and T-shirts. One of 'em came in in a
suit, and I sure as hell didn't expect that."

38   Despite this, Summerville and Riley stood out, even among the conservatively dressed men. They are ample women, and they dress along suburban lines. Sandra Riley favors ruffles. She carries a pocketbook. "To start with, they ignored us," Summerville recalls. "They probably thought we'd stumbled into the wrong place or something."

39   But after the meeting was called to order, the first item of business was the firings at Cracker Barrel. "Somebody asked, 'What are we going to do about this?'" Summerville remembers. "And I said: 'Hey it was me. I'm one of 'em.'" Everyone turned to look at the short, stocky woman in a sweatshirt and jeans. "I want to know what we can do about it," she said.

40   The first demonstration against Cracker Barrel was held in a rainstorm. Thirty-plus people marched in front of the restaurant with signs, urging customers to stay away until the chain reversed its policy. It was, generally, a humiliating experience. "It was just kind of nasty," Summerville says. "It was pouring, and a few of us slipped in the mud. People laughed at us."

41   Before the picket lines started, members had been rebuffed when they tried to meet with the Cracker Barrel management to present their complaints. Soon after, the central office sent a memo to all Cracker Barrel outlets, claiming that its "recent position on the employment of homosexuals in a limited number of stores may have been a well-intentioned over-reaction to the perceived values of our customers and their comfort levels with these individuals."

42   If the firings themselves didn't qualify as national news, Cracker Barrel's subsequent change of heart apparently did. The controversy was reported in *The New York Times,* the *Wall Street Journal,* and the *Atlanta Journal & Constitution,* which also ran an editorial excoriating Cracker Barrel and asking how any discrimination could have possibly been "well-intentioned."

43   While it withdrew its chainwide policy about the discharge of homosexuals, Cracker Barrel turned down Queer Nation's demand that individual outlets be specifically forbidden from practicing sexual discrimination in hiring. It also refused to re-hire the fired employees, and balked at Queer Nation's request for a written apology.

44   In March of last year, Queer Nation started staging sit-ins aimed at cutting Cracker Barrel's profits. The idea was simple: members filled as many tables as possible, ordered the bare minimum, and sat there for two or three hours. When they ordered their coffees or Cokes, the protesters at each table gave their waitress a five-dollar tip wrapped in a note that said: "We realize that you are not the source of the discriminatory policy

of Cracker Barrel. We in no way want to penalize you or make your life more difficult. On the contrary, we want to assure that YOU are not the next victim of renegade bigotry at Cracker Barrel."

Every few weeks, Queer Nation hit a different Cracker Barrel 45 outlet, always on Sunday, after church. Last June, I went to the ninth Cracker Barrel sit-in with Lynn Cothren, a thin blond man wearing madras shorts and love beads. Cothren, a founding member of Queer Nation/Atlanta, is something of an anomaly. In an organization that eschews the very idea of leaders, he boldly proclaimed himself chair of the Atlanta chapter. The demonstrations against Cracker Barrel were largely his idea.

Nearly 120 people had gathered in a parking lot next to the 46 Cracker Barrel in Union City, about ten miles outside Atlanta. They were a living monument to the notion that, aside from some fundamental appetites, human beings have very little in common. There were women in plaid flannel shirts, and women with rouge and pink lipstick. There were middle-aged men in sweat suits, bodybuilders, and reedy, acne-scarred boys who still carried the mortified auras of their adolescent torments.

Everyone was nervous. Most of the protesters had picketed 47 or participated in sit-ins before, but none had ever been arrested for civil disobedience. Although the towers and spires of Atlanta were visible on the horizon, Union City was a conservative town. No one was sure what would happen or how any of us would be treated when taken to jail.

Cheryl Summerville and Sandra Riley stood close together, 48 holding hands in the parking lot. Neither had slept the night before. Riley, a large woman with long hair and a lovely, innocent face, looked as if she might cry at any moment. But when Summerville told her that she thought she should change her mind, Riley said: "What am I going to do while you're in jail? Sit outside worrying about you? No thanks." To be arrested, Riley wore heels and a blue flowered dress. She carried a white pocketbook.

After we all assembled, we filed into the restaurant. To 49 reach the dining room we passed through a gift shop that sold penny candy, stars-and-stripes decals, and plaster cherry pies with lattice crusts. The restaurant proper featured turn-of-the-century memorabilia screwed to its walls—farm implements and brown photographs of families. Hard shadowless light caromed off its acoustic ceiling.

I sat at a table with a fiftyish woman named Marty. She'd 50 come with her gay son and his lover and a young lesbian named Elizabeth, who'd been cut off by her family. Marty introduced her as "my adopted daughter." When I asked Marty how she felt about her son being gay, she drawled, "I've known he was gay since he was in the fourth grade, so I've had plenty of time to get used to it." When I asked if she'd rather he was straight, she said, "Well, he's a hell of a lot happier than one of his brothers, who's married with two kids."

51   A cheerful waitress brought us menus, and we told her we were just having coffee. We gave her her five-dollar tip up front, wrapped in the note explaining what we were doing there. She smiled graciously, and pocketed the tip and the note without reading it. Slowly the restaurant filled with protesters. I drifted through, asking the few remaining nonmembers for reactions. A beige-faced woman in a biscuit-colored jumpsuit said: "I don't carry on about my sexuality in public. I don't know why you all have to carry on about yours." At another table, a man with a beard said: "Cracker Barrel was right to fire those people. What with AIDS and all, I don't want 'em touching food my kids are gonna eat."

52   Most of the waitresses didn't appear to mind. Some even seemed to be having a good time. An older woman swept through the room periodically, filling coffee cups, and when she got to us she said to Marty: "Honey, I'm cuttin' you off. You're starting to shake the whole table."

53   I went to Cothren's table and asked him what, exactly, he thought this protest was accomplishing. He looked at me as if he couldn't believe I would ask such a question. "We're putting direct pressure on them," he said. "We're cutting into their business."

54   "But so far," I said, "you've gotten only one minor concession. Obviously, their fundamental attitude hasn't changed. None of the people who were fired have their jobs back."

55   "We're going to win," Cothren answered in an impatient tone, as if I simply didn't understand the righteousness of Queer Nation's cause or the immensity of his will.

56   An hour passed before Jody Waller, the district manager, appeared with two cops and began working his way through the restaurant, table by table. Waller was a trim man with glasses and a receding hairline, wearing a tie and a navy blazer. At each table he announced: "I'm asking you to leave now. If you don't leave, you'll be arrested. Do you understand?"

57   Eighteen people chose to stay and be arrested. The rest of us went to the jail house to wait until they were released. We marched in an orderly circle before the jail, which was located in a town that seemed to consist only of the jail, a post office, and several unprosperous-looking antique stores. We carried signs that said THERE'S BIGOTRY IN MY BISCUIT and CRACKER BARREL SERVES HATE. We displayed the signs to ourselves and

to an occasional passing car. In two hours, not a single person walked by on the street.

At the end of two hours, several demonstrators were re- 58 leased. We gathered around them expectantly, and they told us they'd been treated with surprising respect. A court date had been set for mid-August, when a judge would rule on Cracker Barrel's trespassing charge. Summerville and Riley stood close together, talking happily to their friends. Riley's white shoes were unsmudged.

We started back to our cars, planning to meet at a bar in 59 Atlanta for a celebratory beer. But as we were dispersing, a battered pickup truck roared toward us from down the street. As it screamed past, a gang of shirtless teenage boys yelled, "Faggots." They all wore their hair below their shoulders, a minor cosmetic freedom won by others before they were born. They turned around and passed us a second time, still hollering insults.

They left a chill in the air. Any one of them could have been Jody Waller's wild son, testing his limits before he grew up and 60 got his own job managing a Cracker Barrel. Cothren didn't hesitate. He turned and marched back into the jail—a skinny, wrathful twenty-eight-year-old man in Bermuda shorts—to demand that his pot-bellied jailers track down the boys and arrest them for verbal assault.

As I traveled around the country visiting other chapters of 61 Queer Nation, I kept thinking, God, these people are young. If furious exuberance is the organization's most salient feature, youth is a close second. I've just turned thirty-nine, and in my travels I met only a handful of women and men my age or older. More often, I found myself among people who could literally have been my sons or daughters. The media liaison from the now-defunct San Francisco chapter tried to reassure me that the group's reputation for youth was exaggerated, saying proudly, "Some of us are in our late twenties and even our early thirties."

Youth, with its energy and its bottomless outrage, may ac- 62 count for that fact that Queer Nation demonstrations are sometimes ignited by events that seem less than urgent. When the residents of Gay Court, in a suburban community east of San Francisco, petitioned to change the name of their street to High Eagle Road, a band of protesters from Queer Nation showed up with banners and bullhorns. In New York City, I went with about twenty activists to stage a "kiss-in" in a straight bar, where the patrons frankly couldn't have cared less. Looking for drama, I asked a straight-looking guy in a crewneck sweater what he thought about all this. "All *what*?" he asked.

63   "Those people over there," I said. "The ones who are kissing. The ones with the stickers that say 'Queer.'"

64   He looked calmly at a pair of tattooed men who were kissing passionately among a bevy of big-haired secretaries sipping margaritas. He shrugged. "Guess it means they're queer," he replied.

65   Youth, combined with Queer Nation's adamantly non-hierarchical structure, may also partially account for the fact that the group is often disorganized nearly to the point of incoherence. In preparing to write this article, I made dozens of calls across the country and learned repeatedly that the person whose name I'd been given had left town for a few months, or moved away entirely, or fought with other members and quit. Members conceive passionate devotions and then burn out. They leave Queer Nation over philosophical differences, or because their grades are suffering, or because they've fallen in love with other members who don't return their affections.

66   When I called a contact person in Shreveport, Louisiana, his mother answered the phone and told me, cordially, that her son had gone to live with his lover. When I reached him at his lover's house, he said that Queer Nation/Shreveport consisted entirely of himself and another man occasionally distributing literature on safer sex.

67   I had planned to attend a demonstration being held by Queer Nation of Lincoln, Nebraska. Together with Queer Nation/Iowa City, members were going to Iowa State University in Ames, where a heterosexual supremacist group—consisting of about a dozen people committed to fighting the very concept of gay rights—was campaigning for formal recognition by the university. Queer Nation was going to parade in front of the group leader's house, kissing and holding hands. I was looking forward to the demonstration. I'd made plane reservations. But when I called about some last-minute details, I learned that the action had been called off because a main organizer had set fire to another member's house.

68   I did go to Salt Lake City, because I'd heard Queer Nation was thriving there and because the woman I'd first contacted continued to answer her phone over a period of several months. Still, I arrived too late. By the time my plane landed, the group was in disarray. A splinter group had formed. Members were writing vicious lampoons of one another in the chapter's newsletter.

69   I admit it. I was beginning to feel a certain despair.

70   I also visited Queer Nation/San Francisco, which several months after I left degenerated into internecine battles and then disbanded entirely. In January of 1991, it was among the largest chapters in the country, attracting as many as four hundred to

its weekly meetings. It carried out one of Queer Nation's most notorious protests, when bands of Queer Nationals did everything possible to disrupt the filming of *Basic Instinct,* a thriller about murderous lesbians and bisexual women.

By autumn, its numbers had dropped to the low twenties. Last December, the few remaining members agreed to dissolve the group. Some members there even call Queer Nation/San Francisco a "fad that fizzled out." Others say that it was done in by racism and sexism among the members themselves. 71

Tensions had flourished from the beginning. Soon after the San Francisco chapter was established, bands of women and people of color started LABIA (Lesbians and Bi-Women in Action) and United Colors. These organizations-within-the-organization were called "focus groups" and were meant to concentrate on issues that might escape the attention of the larger body. 72

As ever-increasing numbers packed themselves into the dour ochre-and-brown auditorium of San Francisco's Women's Building, members of LABIA and United Colors consistently felt that certain white men dominated. At one meeting last winter, several members came to the floor and asked the group at large to contribute a hundred dollars to a march. They were turned down—no big deal. But after the meeting, a group of white male members started arguing about the march with a group of women. The argument grew so heated that the women left, with the men following them down the street, still shouting their opinions. The men's raucous voices brought faces to apartment windows; a passerby asked the women if they needed help. 73

Later, the men claimed they'd only been carrying on an impassioned discourse. The women said they'd been terrorized. This was one of a number of incidents in which some of the white men told one version of a story and the women or people of color told another. Several months later, when a band of men from Queer Nation plastered stickers on the home of a lesbian city supervisor, LABIA pulled out altogether, claiming that the male "terrorism" could no longer be countenanced. 74

Christine Carraher, one of the founding members of the bisexual focus group UBIQUITOUS, explains: "There's a wide gulf between a lot of lesbians and gay men. Sometimes I think it's worse than the one that exists between straight men and women." 75

"Some of these guys believe feminists are doing to men what Big Nurse did to the warders in *One Flew Over the Cuckoo's Nest,*" said a male member of the group. 76

As these tensions built, a big, noisy, politically savvy New Yorker named Mitchell Halberstadt started showing up at 77 meetings and shouting other members out of the room. Halberstadt is a classic New York activist, all bombast and aggression. When he arrived in San Francisco, he brought his swagger to a group that employed two "vibes watchers" at every meeting to make sure no one felt intimidated, and permitted members to stop the meeting and discuss their grievances every time they felt personally insulted. But now, if women or people of color stopped a meeting to complain of a racist or sexist remark, they were often shouted down by Halberstadt and several other men. Because there was no formalized code of behavior for the meetings, and no decision could be made without consensus, the abusive tirades had to be tolerated. More and more people left.

78   At a meeting in early November, there was another confrontation. When one of the few female members started to walk out of the room, Halberstadt barred the door, screaming, "How dare you try to leave!" Frank Herron, a physically imposing man, told Halberstadt he was out of line and that he would do anything to stop him from threatening the others. And so the group that had pledged itself to banding together against homophobia was about to begin slugging it out over racism and sexism.

79   In an attempt to recover some sense of equilibrium, the members who stayed on—down to about twenty-five—held a special session in late November to discuss ways in which the general meetings could be better managed. At the session, John Woods of United Colors and a white member named Allen Carson proposed that the group agree to a ban on all sexist and racist language, although they did not offer a specific list of forbidden terms. Halberstadt blocked the proposal and later claimed: "My politics are antiauthoritarian. [This is] a power grab by wannabe bureaucrats."

80   Soon after that session, the handful of remaining members called a "hiatus" until March, at which time they would regroup and see what, if anything, they could get to rise from the ashes.

81   When I accepted the assignment to write about Queer Nation a year ago, I was full of zeal. I confess to ending my story in a state of confusion. I had expected to write a story about heroism, and I did, in fact, meet heroic people everywhere I went. I'd prefer to write only about their strength and solidarity. I don't like reporting about the squabbles, the naiveté, the self-destructive tendencies. I likewise don't quite know what to make of the fact that, of the chapters I visited, the only one that's holding together effectively—the group in Atlanta—is the only one with an old-fashioned leader. (Cheryl Summerville is now the chapter's cochair.) It's also the only one

embroiled in a battle with a clear-cut villain, which may help account for its strength. Fighting homophobia, sexism, and racism, is, for most of us, a little like battling crabgrass. It's everywhere, so intricately stitched into the lawn that you can't quite tell where to begin.

My misgivings about Queer Nation stem mainly from its ten-   82
dency toward self-destruction, and this criticism is shared by other lesbians and gay men. Becky Moorman, publisher of *The Bridge*, a lesbian and gay magazine based in Utah, says: "The [lesbian and gay] community's really divided about what Queer Nation is doing. Their protests aren't focused. They need to decide who they're speaking to and what they're trying to say." Anthony Christiansen, an openly gay Ph.D. candidate in Columbia University's clinical-psychology program, adds: "Queer Nation focuses so much on our difference [from het-erosexuals], they lose track of our connectedness. There are millions of complex situations out there—being gay isn't as cut-and-dried as they'd like to make out."

That may be the heart of the problem. We are probably the   83
most diverse of all persecuted groups. A Martian field biologist sent to earth to capture two homosexual specimens could eas-ily bring back a twenty-three-year-old white guy with an MBA from Yale and a sixty-five-year-old black lesbian separatist from Detroit. Queer Nation, fostered by people who've been unfairly excluded, is determined to be utterly inclusive. That's turning out to mean equal voice not only for women and men of all colors but also for the foolish, the prejudiced, and the outright deluded.

Perhaps Queer Nation is simply an early, flawed step toward   84
a new kind of lesbian and gay militancy. Frank Herron of San Francisco insists that the city's chapter hasn't been a failure: "It's spawned a dozen groups doing different things. We've drawn a lot of people into activism." Herron sees the future of gay activism as a welter of small groups modeled on revolu-tionary cells. "Twelve people can reach a decision more easily than five hundred can," he says. "If these twelve need help, they work with another group of twelve. I don't know if we'll ever have a cohesive national gay activist organization."

Meanwhile, it's difficult not to feel panicky, because, as we   85
argue over structure and focus, as we bicker among ourselves, our people are being attacked in increasing numbers. Since I was in Atlanta, Cheryl Summerville and Sandra Riley have be-come more famous and, simultaneously, more widely despised. After Summerville appeared on the Oprah Winfrey show in January, her sixteen-year-old son was so tormented by his classmates that she and Riley chose to move him to another school. There have been hate letters and threats. Riley has

closed her sewing and alterations business so that she can be home when the boy gets back from school.

86   And as we struggle to set a coherent agenda, our people continue to die. My friend Tim, for one, died while I was working on this story. It was sudden, if that term can be applied to someone who'd had AIDS for almost three years. He was comparatively well and then he caught pneumonia and then he died. His parents, who hadn't spoken to him in years, didn't want his ashes. Karen is keeping them in a box in her apartment until we decide what to do with them. Another friend has taken Aretha, Tim's cat.

87   Just before Tim died, I found myself sitting with Karen at his bedside. He was unconscious, breathing noisily and steadily on a respirator. As Karen and I sat watching him, I told her I was struggling to write an article about Queer Nation. She shrugged dismissively. "A bunch of thugs," she said.

88   "Right," I said. "That's right. And you've got a better idea, haven't you?" My voice was loud enough to surprise me.

89   "Honey, calm down," she said with a nervous smile.

90   "You've got a much better solution," I said. "It's very effective to be discreet in public and send a little money to the Gay Men's Health Crisis and write features about the ten best espresso bars in lower Manhattan. Thank you for your contribution."

91   A nurse put her head through the curtains and asked if everything was all right. We told her not to worry, to get on with her other business.

92   "You don't need to scream at me," Karen said quietly after the nurse had gone.

93   "I know," I said.

94   "I'm not the one you're really angry at."

95   "I know. Let's not talk about it, okay?"

96   Of course, she was right. But I couldn't calm myself. Later, after Tim died, I was able to see how stupid I'd been. How quickly I'd self-destructed. Karen had been there for me to scream at, and, even more important, she understood what I was screaming about. A man like Jody Waller, standing smugly with two cops behind him, doesn't get the point. There's no outward evidence that he suspects he's doing anything wrong.

97   Karen and I will never be friends. Now that Tim is gone, there's no reason for us to know each other. But during Tim's last days, she and I managed to act like compatriots. We had to. There was a funeral to plan, and, if we didn't do it, nobody would.

98   It's hard to know what to do sometimes. I wish I felt more certain about how to proceed. I wish I'd walked Tim home that night after we left St. Vincent's. I keep thinking I could have protected him.

Bruce Bawer
NOTES ON STONEWALL

Bruce Bawer (born 1956 in New York City) is a professional writer with a background in literary studies. In addition to several books on one or another literary matter (his most recent is Prophets and Professors), *he has published a book of poems and a volume of film criticism. Bawer's 1993 book* A Place at the Table: The Gay Individual in American Society *was for several months the number-one best-seller in gay bookstores. A former director of the National Book Critics Circle, Bawer reviews books frequently for the* New York Times Book Review *and the* Washington Post Book World *and has also*

published essays and reviews in The American Scholar, The
Nation, The Hudson Review, Newsweek, *and* The Advocate.
"Notes on Stonewall" appeared in The New Republic, *a respected magazine on public affairs that once had a liberal
slant but now occupies a middle position editorially.*

1   Twenty-five years ago, in the early morning hours of June 28,
1969, several patrons at the Stonewall bar in Greenwich
Village, many of them flamboyant drag queens and prostitutes,
refused to go quietly when police carried out a routine raid on
the place. Their refusal escalated into five days of rioting by
hundreds of people. Though it wasn't the first time anyone had
contested the right of the state to punish citizens just for being
gay, that rioting marked a pivotal moment because news of it
spread in every direction and sparked the imaginations of
countless gay men and lesbians around the world. It made
them examine, and reject, the silence, shame and reflexive
compliance with prejudice to which most of them had simply
never conceived a realistic alternative.

2   There is something wondrous about Stonewall, and it is this:
that a mere handful of late-night bar patrons, many of them
confused, lonely individuals living at the margins of society,
started something that made a lot of lesbians and gay men do
some very serious thinking of a sort they had never quite done
before—thinking that led to action and to a movement. It was
the beginning of a revolution in attitudes toward homosexuality. How odd it is to think that those changes could all be
traced back to a drunken riot at a Greenwich Village bar on a
June night in 1969. But they can. And that's why Stonewall deserves to be commemorated.

3   Today, however, Stonewall is not only commemorated but
mythologized. Many gay men and lesbians routinely speak of
it as if it was a sacred event that lies beyond the reach of objective discourse. They talk as if there was no gay rights activism at all before Stonewall, or else they mock pre-Stonewall
activists as Uncle Toms. They recite the name "Stonewall" itself with the same reverence that American politicians reserve
for the names of Washington and Lincoln. And indeed the
word is perfectly suited to the myth, conjuring as it does an
image of a huge, solid barrier separating the dark ages prior to
the day that Judy Garland died from the out-loud-and-proud
present. Every year, on what has long since become an all-
purpose gay holiday—a combination of Independence Day,
May Day, Mardi Gras and, since the advent of HIV, Memorial
Day as well—millions ritualistically revisit the raucous, defiant
marginality of Stonewall in marches around the world. This

year in New York, on the twenty-fifth anniversary, the ritual will reach a climax. For many, Stonewall has already become a Platonic model of gay activism—and, indeed, a touchstone of gay identity.

A few weeks ago, in a sermon about an entirely different sub-   4
ject, the rector of the Episcopal church I belong to in New York used the phrase "the politics of nostalgia." The phrase has stuck in my mind, for it seems to me that both sides of the gay rights struggle are trapped in what may well be characterized as a politics of nostalgia. Many of those who resist acceptance of homosexuality and reject equal rights for gay men and les-bians know on some level that they are wrong, but they cling to old thinking because a change, however just, seems to them a drastic departure from the comfortable world of "don't ask, don't tell." Some gay people, likewise, cling to what might be called the Stonewall sensibility, reacting defensively and vio-lently, as if to some horrendous blasphemy or betrayal, even to the hint that perhaps the time has come to move in some way beyond that sensibility. Such people often declare proudly that they have been "in the trenches" for twenty-five years, which is to say that in a way they have been reliving Stonewall every day since June 1969.

Yet every day *can't* be Stonewall—or shouldn't. And in fact the   5
time *has* come to move beyond the Stonewall sensibility. For, thanks largely to developments that can trace their inspiration to that barroom raid, some things *have* changed since 1969. Levels of tolerance have risen; gay rights laws have been passed; in the last quarter-century, and especially recently, gay Americans have come out of the closet in increasing numbers. As a result, it has become clear to more and more heterosexuals that gay America is as diverse as straight America—that many of the people who were at the Stonewall bar on that night twenty-five years ago represent an anachronistic politics that largely has ceased to have salience for gay America today. To say this is not to condemn people who consider themselves mem-bers of that fringe or to read them out of the gay community. It is simply to say that for gay America to continue to be defined largely by its fringe is a lie, and that this lie, like all lies about homosexuality, needs to be countered vigorously. The Stonewall sensibility—like the Stonewall myth—has to be abandoned.

On May 6 *The New York Times* described the arguments   6
among gay leaders about the planning of Stonewall 25, the forthcoming New York event that will culminate in a march on the United Nations. Some of these leaders worried that Stonewall 25 wouldn't focus enough on the fact that many of the Stonewall heroes were transvestite and transsexual

hustlers. One woman wanted, in her words, to "radicalize" Stonewall 25. "Stonewall," she told the *Times*, "was a rebellion of transgender people, and this event has the potential to reduce our whole culture to an Ikea ad."

7   It is strange to read the words of those who speak, on the one hand, as if Stonewall, in and of itself, achieved something once and for all time that gay Americans are now free to celebrate, and, on the other, as if the kind of growing acceptance that is represented by the depiction of a middle-class gay couple in a furniture commercial on network t.v. is bad news, a threat to a Stonewall-born concept of gay identity as forever marginal. It would almost seem as if those leaders don't realize that Stonewall was only part of a long, complex process that is still proceeding, and that the best way to honor it is to build upon it by directing that process as wisely and responsibly as we can.

8   In the May 3 issue of the gay magazine *The Advocate*, activist Torie Osborn wrote that thirty-nine gay leaders, whom she described as "our community's best and brightest," had gathered recently to discuss the state of the movement and "retool [it] to match the changing times." The group, she wrote, "had a collective 750 years of experience in gay rights or other political work." But even as she wrote of seeking "common ground" and "common vision" among the gay leaders, Osborn reaffirmed the linking of gay rights to "other progressive movements with which many of us identify."

9   In other words, she embraced the standard post-Stonewall practice of indiscriminately linking the movement for gay equal rights with any left-wing cause to which any gay leader might happen to have a personal allegiance. That practice dates back to 1969, when radical activists, gay and straight, were quick to use the gay rights movement as a way to prosecute their own unrelated revolutionary agendas. Such linkages have been a disaster for the gay rights movement; not only do they falsely imply that most gay people sympathize with those so-called progressive movements, but they also serve to reinforce the idea of homosexuality itself as a "progressive" phenomenon, as something that is essentially political in nature. Osborn wrote further that she and the other gay leaders at the summit "talked about separating strategic thinking into two discrete areas: our short-term political fights and the long-term cultural war against systematic homophobia." And she added that "we have virtually no helpful objective data or clear strategy on the long-term war, which grapples with deep-seated sexphobia as well as heterosexism." Her conclusion (my emphasis): *We need to start working on this problem.*

10   With all due respect to Osborn and her fellow gay leaders, it seems to me more than a bit astonishing that in spite of their

collective 750 years of experience, at least some of them only now have begun to realize that homosexuals should be giving thought to something other than short-term political conflicts. At the same time, those leaders still can't quite understand the long-term challenge as anything other than, in Osborn's words, a "war." Nor can they see that achieving real and lasting equality is a matter not of changing right-wingers into left-wingers, or of emancipating Americans from "sex-phobia," but of liberating people from their discomfort with homosexuality, their automatic tendency to think of homosexuals in terms of sex and their often bizarre notions of who gay people are, what gay people value and how gay people live.

Perhaps, at the threshold of the second generation of the   11
post-Stonewall gay rights movement, it behooves us to recall that, as I've noted, there *was* at least some species of gay activism prior to Stonewall. Years before those patrons at the Stonewall bar hurled garbage, beer bottles, feces and four-letter words at the policemen who had come to arrest them, a few small groups of men in business suits and women in dresses staged sober, orderly marches at which they carried signs that announced their own homosexuality and that respectfully demanded an end to anti-homosexual prejudice. Those people were even more radical than the rioters at Stonewall, and— dare I say it?—perhaps even more brave, given how few they were, how premeditated their protests and how much some of them had to lose by publicly identifying themselves as gay. They were heroes, too; they won a few legal battles and they might have won more. Sure, Stonewall was, without question, an important step—indeed, the biggest single step the gay rights movement has taken. But that's all it was: a step, the first big one in a long, difficult journey. It was a reaction to intolerance, and it set us on the road to tolerance. The next road leads to acceptance—acceptance not only of gay people by straight people, but an easier acceptance by young gay people of their own sexuality. It's a different road—and, in a way, a harder one.

First-generation post-Stonewall gay activists saw themselves   12
as street combatants in a political war. Second generation activists would better see themselves as participants in an educational program of which the expressly political work is only a part. Getting America to accept homosexuality will first be a matter of education. The job is not to shout at straight Americans, "We're here, we're queer, get used to it." The job is to do the hard, painstaking work of *getting* straight Americans used to it. This isn't dramatic work; nor is it work that provides a quick emotional release. Rather, it requires discipline, commitment, responsibility.

13   In some sense, of course, most straight Americans *are* used to the idea of people being gay. The first generation of the post-Stonewall gay rights movement has accomplished that. At the same time, it has brought us to a place where many straight Americans are sick and tired of the very word "gay." They've heard it a million times, yet they don't understand it nearly well enough. They still feel uncomfortable, confused, threatened. They feel that the private lives of homosexuals have been pushed "in their faces," but they don't really *know* about those private lives.

14   And why should they be expected to? Yes, at Gay Pride Day marches, some gay men and lesbians, like the Stonewall rioters, have exposed America to images of raw sexuality—images that variously amuse, titillate, shock and offend while revealing nothing important about who most of those people really are. Why, then, do some people do such things? Perhaps because they've been conditioned to think that on that gay high holy day, the definitively gay thing to do is to be as defiant as those heroes twenty-five years ago. Perhaps they do it because they can more easily grasp the concept of enjoying one day per year of delicious anarchy than of devoting 365 days per year to a somewhat more disciplined and strategically sensible demonstration designed to advance the causes of respect, dignity and equality.

15   And perhaps they do it because, frankly, it is relatively easy to do. Just as standing up at a White House press conference and yelling at the president can take less courage than coming out to your parents or neighbors or employers, so taking off your pants or your bra for a Gay Pride Day march in the company of hundreds of thousands of known allies can be easier than taking down your defenses for a frank conversation with a group of colleagues at an office lunch about how it was to grow up gay. For an insecure gay man or lesbian, moreover, explaining can feel awfully close to apologizing, and can open one up to charges of collaboration with the enemy by those who join the author Paul Monette in seeing America as the "Christian Reich" and themselves as members of the queer equivalent of the French resistance.

16   As a friend said to me recently, building acceptance of homosexuals is like teaching a language. When gays speak about themselves, they are speaking one language; when most straight people speak about gays, they are speaking another. Most heterosexuals look at gay lives the way I look at a page of German. I may be able to pick out a few familiar words, but I feel awkward when I use them, and if I try to put together a sentence I'm likely to find myself saying something I don't

mean at all, perhaps even something offensive or hurtful. There's only one way to get past that feeling of confusion: tireless, meticulous dedication to study. You can't learn a foreign language overnight, and you can't teach it by screaming it at people. You teach it word by word, until, bit by bit, they feel comfortable speaking it and can find their way around the country where it's spoken. That's the job of the second generation of post-Stonewall gay activism: to teach those who don't accept us the language of who gay people are and where gay people live. Indeed, to the extent that professional homophobes have stalled progress in the movement toward legal and social parity for gay men and lesbians, it is not because those homophobes are so crafty, and certainly not because they are right. It is because they have spoken to straight America in its own language and addressed its concerns, whereas gay Americans, more often than not, out of an understandable fear and defensive self-righteousness, haven't.

Some reviewers in the gay press read the title of my book, *A*   17
Place at the Table: The Gay Individual in American Society, as a sign that I, personally, long to sit at a dinner table with people like Pat Buchanan and Jerry Falwell—that this book is my attempt to indicate to them that I'm a nice, well-mannered gay man and that I, along with the other nice, well-mannered gay men, should be allowed at the table while the "bad," ill-mannered gays are excluded. Some other gay press reviewers have understood that I don't mean that at all, and that I feel everyone should be welcome at the American table, but they have angrily rejected the idea: "Why," one critic wrote, "should *I* want to sit at that table?" A writer for the gay magazine *Out* dismissed the book in one line: "Bruce Bawer has written a book about the gay individual in American society entitled *A Place at the Table.* Some will prefer take-out."

What these reactions signify to me is a powerful tendency   18
among some homosexuals to recoil reflexively from the vision of an America where gays live as full and open members of society, with all the rights, responsibilities and opportunities of heterosexuals. Many gay people, indeed, have a deep, unarticulated fear of that metaphorical place at the table. This is understandable: gay people, as a rule, are so used to minimizing their exposure to homophobia, by living either in the closet or on the margins of society, that for someone—even a fellow gay person—to come along and invoke an image of gay America sitting openly at a table with straight America can seem, to them, like a hostile act. This sense of threat—this devotion to the margin—may help explain the gay-activist rancor toward the movie *Philadelphia.* But most gay men and lesbians were

happy to see a movie that showed homosexuality as part of the mainstream, just as most are pleased by the new tendency to depict gay life, in everything from Ikea ads to movies like *Four Weddings and a Funeral* in a matter-of-fact way, as an integrated part of society.

19   Am I attacking radicalism? No. I'm saying that the word "radical" must be defined anew by each generation. In the late twentieth century, when radicalism has often been viewed as a fashion choice, it's easy to lose sight of what real radicalism is. It's not a matter of striking a defiant pose and maintaining that pose over a period of years; it's not a matter of signing on to a certain philosophy or program and adhering to it inflexibly for the rest of your life. And it's not always a matter of manning barricades or crouching in trenches. It's a matter of honest inquiry, of waking up every morning and looking at the social circumstances in which you find yourself and having the vision to perceive what needs to be done and the courage to follow up on that vision, wherever it may take you. It's a matter of going to the *root* of the problem, wherever that root may lie.

20   And going to the root of this particular problem means going to the root of prejudice. It means probing the ignorance and fear that are responsible for the success of anti-gay crusaders. It means seriously addressing those opponents' arguments against gay rights, in which they combine a defense of morality and "family values" with attacks on homosexuality as anti-God, anti-American and anti-family. Too often, the first generation of the post-Stonewall gay movement has responded to such rhetoric by actually saying and doing things that have only reinforced the homophobes' characterization of homosexuality. The second generation of the movement would do well to respond not by attacking the American values and ridiculing the religious faith that these people claim as a basis for their prejudice, but by making it clear just how brutal, how un-American and how anti-religious their arguments and their prejudice are.

21   And there are a *lot* of untruths out there to overcome. More and more people understand that homosexuals are no more likely to be child molesters than heterosexuals are, but there remains on the part of many people a lingering discomfort about such notions, and anti-gay crusaders exploit that discomfort with ambiguous, dishonest rhetoric suggesting that homosexuals are (to quote a recent statement published in *The Wall Street Journal* by a group of religious figures calling itself the Ramsey Colloquium) a threat to the "vulnerabilities of the young." That's a lie. But how can homosexuals help

heterosexuals understand it's a lie so long as some gay political leaders, in the best Stonewall tradition, feel more comfortable condemning the Log Cabin Republicans than they do
condemning the North American Man-Boy Love Association?

Likewise, more and more people understand that homosexu-   22
als' lives are no more about sex than their lives are, but there are
many who still *don't* understand that, and the anti-gay crusaders exploit their ignorance by saying (again in the words of
the Ramsey Colloquium) that gay people "define" themselves by
their "desires alone," that they seek "liberation from constraint,"
from obligations to the larger society and especially to the
young, and from all human dignity. *That's* a lie. But how can
gays help straights understand it's a lie so long as a few marchers
on Gay Pride Day feel the best way to represent all gay men and
lesbians is to walk down the avenue in their underwear?

Anti-gay propagandists shrewdly exploit the fact that we live   23
in times when there's ample reason for concern about children.
American children today grow up in an often uncivil and
crime-ridden society, and with a pop culture that is at best
value-neutral and at worst aggressive and ugly. Altogether too
many of those kids grow up inured to the sight of beggars
sleeping on the sidewalk, of condoms and hypodermic needles
in the gutter, of pornographic magazines on display at street-
corner kiosks. Anti-gay propagandists routinely link homosexuality to these phenomena, seeing homosexual orientation,
and gay people's openness about it, and gay people's desire for
equal rights and equal respect, as yet more signs of the decline
of morals, of the family, of social cohesion and stability and of
civilization generally.

One of Stonewall's legacies is that gay leaders have too often   24
accepted this characterization of the conflict and see any attempt to correct it as "sex-negative." The second generation of
post-Stonewall gay activism has to make it clear that that's not
the way the sides break down at all, and that when it comes to
children, the real interests of parents and of gay people (many
of whom are themselves parents, of course) are not unalterably
opposed, but are, in fact, perfectly congruent. Gay adults care
about children, too; and they know from experience something
that straight parents can only strive to understand—namely,
what it's like to grow up gay.

Homosexuals, of course, are *not* a threat to the family;   25
among the things that threaten the family are parents' profound ignorance about homosexuality and their reluctance to
face the truth about it. In the second generation of the post-
Stonewall gay rights movement, gay adults must view it as an
obligation to ensure that parents understand that truth—and

understand, too, that according equal rights to homosexuals and equal recognition to same-sex relationships (and creating an atmosphere in which gay men and lesbians can live openly without fear of losing their jobs or homes or lives) would not threaten the institution of the family but would actually strengthen millions of American families.

26   It is ironic that, to a large extent, what perpetuates Stonewall-style antagonism between gay and straight are not our differences, really, but traits that we all share as human beings. We all, for instance, fear the unknown. To most straight people, homosexuality is an immense unknown; to gay people, a society that would regard sexual orientation indifferently and grant homosexuals real equality is also an immense unknown. But it is also our humanity that makes most of us long to know and live with the truth, even in the wake of a lifetime of lies. The greatest tribute we can pay to the memory of Stonewall is to work in our own homes and workplaces to dismantle, lie by lie, the wall of lies that has divided the families of America for too long.

John Berresford
Rights
and Responsibilities,
Not Freebies
and Frolics

John Berresford does most of his writing as part of his job as an antitrust lawyer for the Federal Communications Commission in Washington, but he did find time to contribute the following article to The Washington Post *in June 1995. The* Post *is a politically moderate newspaper with a national as well as local readership, rather like* The New York Times.

1   I am gay and have been in the gay rights movement since I came out in 1981. I am also a conservative, a libertarian.

2   Sad to say, the gay rights movement has always been seen as being on the political left, as one more whining interest group claiming entitlement to all sorts of special treatment from the

government. Or we are seen as having a simply fabulous time cavorting at Gay Pride parades and throwing condoms at Catholic services. Whether as crybabies or as Dionysian celebrants, we always appear outside the mainstream.

I cringe at both images. Most gay men and women do not go   3
around demanding government favors or living a hedonistic "gay lifestyle." But just enough of us act out these images, or tolerate them, that they become real in the public mind. Middle America feels uncomfortable about this, at the very least. Our right-wing enemies love it, because it gives them someone to hate and someone to use as a foil for attracting mainstream support to their own causes. By accepting, and in some cases cultivating, these images, we lose friends and help our enemies.

As a conservative, I wish such images would evaporate. If   4
there was ever a time when they made sense, on grounds of either truthfulness or usefulness, it ended when the Republicans took control of Congress. The waiting line for government benefits now leads nowhere, and public frolics now gain nothing but disapproval.

What can government give gays? Merely the form, not the   5
substance, of what we need and want. What we are really after is not merely legal rights but acceptance into the mainstream of American life—and acceptance is granted or withheld by the mainstream majority at its pleasure. If we want to be accepted, we must be welcomed. Lord knows it's easier to change the votes of a few legislators than the hearts and minds of millions of our fellow citizens. But politicians are weathervanes, they are not the wind.

So we should end some of our present practices: 6

We should loudly reject all "compensatory" agendas: hiring   7
quotas, affirmative action and group reparations—all of which I've heard advocated for "when we get our rights." The people who benefit most from such programs are the bureaucrats who administer them and the members of the "victim" groups with the best political connections.

We should stop pressing for "domestic partners" legislation.   8
It creates a special class of rights for a small class of people. The real beneficiaries would be the lawyers who would litigate the differences and similarities between domestic partnership and marriage.

We should not hate Jesse Helms, Pat Robertson and their al-   9
lies. Leave the hating to them. They will eventually destroy themselves, as Joe McCarthy and other haters did.

We should stop feeling sorry for ourselves. We may be vic-   10
tims, but frankly no one cares. This country's wellsprings of

liberal guilt began running dry about 20 years ago, and by now they are flat empty.

11 Finally, we should stop seeing AIDS as anybody else's problem. The sad fact is that every gay man who got AIDS by sex got it from another gay man, and by doing something he chose to do. People with AIDS deserve sympathy, but it is the sympathy one extends to a chain smoker who comes down with lung cancer. It is not the same kind of sympathy one feels for someone who was struck by lightning or run down by a drunk driver.

12 But that's enough on the negative side. What positive actions can we take?

13 For starters, each of us should come out whenever it is reasonably safe. The best way to explode the myths about us is for each of us to become known as just another human being with the same needs, goals and drives as other human beings—except in a single respect that poses no threat to anyone else.

14 Our legislative goal should be for civil rights legislation with disclaimers of any quotas, guidelines, reparations or government-imposed and group-based remedies. It should emphasize private lawsuits for damages rather than enforcement of a bureaucracy.

15 In the legislatures, we should also lobby for the right to marry. Domestic-partners legislation makes us an officially sanctioned class of oddities and freaks. By seeking marriage, we demonstrate our wish to be part of the great American middle-class way of life.

16 Among ourselves, we must be willing to talk about morals, to impose them on ourselves and to do so conspicuously. As long as our primary image is one of gleeful promiscuity—an image promoted not only by our enemies but also by our own magazines and our own bars—we will be ostracized. Until we start imposing honesty, fidelity and emotion on our lives—in other words, until we are willing to talk about moral standards—we will make little real progress in social acceptance.

17 In a curious way, AIDS itself may be helping us find social acceptance. This terrible disease has brought to a screeching halt—at least in my generation of gay men—the manic boozing, drugging, and screwing of the '70s and '80s. It has forced us to attend more to friendships, stability and the consequences of our action. It has opened us to human suffering; one friend told me that caring for someone with AIDS was the first unselfish thing he had done in his adult life. AIDS has enabled us to show, to ourselves and to the mainstream, that we too are capable of great suffering, compassion, work and sacrifice. By our work with each other, we have shown mainstream society what we have to offer it, and how much it loses and wastes by excluding us.

The common theme of all this is simply facing the facts, 18
working to bring out the best in ourselves and offering something admirable to the mainstream. All these views put me in
odd company politically. But if you had to agree about everything with everyone else in an organization before you could
join it, we'd have 260 million political parties in this country.
Conservatives are the people I happen to agree with most of
the time. At least they are attempting to deal with the moral issues of our time (such as welfare dependency and violence) on
a moral plane, and not as something for which the only remedy is another government program and more spending.

After I come out to them, I find that most conservatives are 19
perfectly tolerant (and not as cloyingly condescending as my
liberal straight friends). The Helmses and Robertsons are in
the minority. And it eventually dawns on the conservatives that
if they want to keep the support of gays like me, they had better keep at least a distance between themselves and the haters.

Finally, moving in conservative circles permits me to ask my 20
conservative friends where this country would be without
those great gays—Whittaker Chambers, J. Edgar Hoover, Walt
Whitman and Cardinal Spellman. It's a polite way to remind
them that we have been in their midst and doing good deeds
from the beginning.

My liberal friends tend to employ three styles of attack on my 21
views. The first is ad hominem: How can you talk about morality when we all know that once you did this or that randy deed?
My answer is that (a) the fact that your first response is to attack
the messenger (me) shows that you can't repel the message; and
(b) I had my adolescence like everyone else, and it's over.

My liberal friends' second attack is some variation on "Do 22
you mean that you're against all attempts to right the wrongs
that have been done to us?" My answer is that I am as much in
favor of basic civil rights for gays as they are. Where we differ
is in the need for group-based remedies and in perceiving ourselves as victims whose main recourse should be coercion by
the government.

The third attack from my liberal friends is usually some 23
form of "Well, you have a good point, but. . . ." At that, I know
I've made some progress.

I have a feeling there are many more conservative gays than 24
there seem to be. The time is ripe for us to leave the plantation
of liberal government and start acting like what we are—a
group of adults who want to live lives as normal and as healthy
as everyone else in the mainstream. If we do, I think we will be
on the path to my dream—an America in which being gay is no
more remarkable than being left-handed.

Dan Chaon

TRANSFORMATIONS

Dan Chaon, born in Nebraska, lives in Cleveland, Ohio, and teaches at Oberlin College. He has published a number of short stories; the one reprinted here appeared in 1991 in Story, *a prestigious quarterly that prints only short fiction. Since then he has published* Fitting Ends and Other Stories *(1995) and* Among the Missing *(2001). The latter was nominated for the National Book Award.*

1   The first time I saw my brother Corky in women's clothes, I was eleven and he was fourteen. He came out of my parents' bedroom in my mother's good dress, the one with bird of paradise flowers patterned on it, and her high heels and lipstick. I thought he was kidding. He chased after me, talking in a Southern accent, and I ran off laughing. Corky was always pretending to be someone else, dressing up in clothes he'd bought at the Catholic rummage house or found in the garage, imitating the mannerisms of his math teacher, or Uncle Evan, who drove semi trucks and stuttered, or some disc jockey on the radio. I didn't realize then, not for years and years actually, that he was gay and all.

2   He is still your brother, my father told me when he showed me the picture. This was the second time I'd seen Corky in women's clothes. In the photo, he was wearing a big red wig, a blue-jean skirt, pumps, and a blouse with fringe. He looked like a country singer. My father asked me: "Do you know who this is?" All I said was, Yes, and, It figures.

3   My father shook his head at me. He liked to pretend that he didn't care what Corky was, just so long as he was happy. That was the official line. But I'd seen the kind of cloudy distance that came into his eyes when he talked to Corky on the phone. I'd noticed him, once, studying an old Polaroid of the three of us, pheasant hunting, examining it as if looking for clues. I'd seen his expression when one of his buddies from the electrician's union asked: "So how's that boy of yours doing back East?" My father shifted from foot to foot. "Oh, fine, fine," he said quickly, and looked down.

4   But he looked me sternly in the eyes. "He is still your brother," he said. He folded his thick hands, staring glumly at the glossy black-and-white photo.

5   "My sister, you mean," I said.

He frowned. "You're getting pretty smart-mouthed," he said.   6
He laid the photo on the kitchen table between us, like some important document I was supposed to sign. "He does this as entertainment," my father said. The words "CABARET BERLINER, New York," were printed on the bottom of the picture.

"I'll bet," I said.   7

My brother worked at a bar in New York City. We'd known   8
that. We also knew he was gay. He'd told my parents over the phone after he'd been away a year. I wasn't sure how they reacted at first, though they seemed calm by the time they got around to telling me. Corky had come to a decision, my father said, and my mother nodded grimly. For a long time afterward, my father wouldn't refer to it at all except as "your brother's decision," though he also pointed out to me that the words "fag" and "queer" were worse than swearing as far as he was concerned.

Corky was going to college in New York at the time, but he   9
dropped out shortly after to audition for plays and work in bars at night. He hadn't been home since he told them. Instead, he sent clippings, pictures, lists of productions he was trying out for. "One thing about Corky," my father pointed out to me as he looked through the packets Corky sent. "At least he knows what he wants, and he's not afraid to go after it."

It was my senior year in high school, and my father thought   10
I had no ambition. Maybe that was true. In any case, I wasn't like Corky had been when he was in high school. His senior year, there was always something about him taped to the refrigerator—a certificate of merit, or a clipping from the local paper about a scholarship he'd won. He pinned the acceptance letters from colleges in neat rows on a bulletin board in our room, as if they were rare butterflies.

That was why I was surprised when he called to say he was   11
taking some time off to attend my high school graduation. I went to the Catholic school as Corky had, but there was no chance of me ending up valedictorian like him. For a while maybe people wondered whether I'd be a teacher's pet like Corky, and they even sometimes called me by his name. But it didn't take them long to find out that I wasn't going to leave any brilliant reputation in my wake. My father always said that I didn't "apply myself" like Corky did. Out of ninety-six seniors I was ranked forty-ninth. I would just be a vague, doughy face in the middle of the third row. There was no great cause for celebration. I hadn't found a job or a college to attend in the fall. But at least my parents had a son who could give them grandchildren, they could appreciate that. And as for that fat, mustached drama teacher, Sister Vincent, who continually

remembered Corky's beautiful singing voice and his performance in *South Pacific*, well, I wished she could see his new
song and dance at Cabaret Berliner.

12   Corky came home two days before graduation. My mother
and father and I went to pick him up at Stapleton Airport in
Denver. The whole way there, I worried. I couldn't help but
imagine Corky appearing to us in a feather boa and an evening
gown or something, trotting down the ramp to meet us with a
big lipstick grin. I told myself I was being low-minded and
ugly, but that image of him kept popping into my mind. My
face felt hot.

13   Meanwhile, my parents acted like everything was wonderful. The full moon reflected off the early May snow that still
lay on the fields, and my father kept howling like a wolf. It
seemed to amuse my mother, because she chuckled every time
he did it, and laughed aloud when he grabbed her around the
waist and growled.

14   I was sitting in the back seat, watching the car drift toward
the center of the road while they horsed around. "I hope we
wreck," I said.

15   The three of us stood there in the waiting area, watching the
planes land. We didn't recognize Corky when he approached
us, but at least he was wearing normal clothes. He'd dyed his
hair bright red—it was shoulder-length, tied in a ponytail.
When he was close enough, I noticed the little crease in his ear-
lobe that meant it was pierced, but he didn't have an earring.
He hugged my mother, kissing her lightly. Then he turned and
kissed my father. My father always kissed us on the lips, and
wasn't even afraid to do it in public. He puckered up like a cartoon character, and it would've been funny if he wasn't so
earnest about it. Here he was, this big, middle-aged construction worker, smacking lips with his son. He didn't even hesitate
knowing Corky was gay, though I looked around to see if people were staring.

16   When my brother turned to me, I stuck out my hand. I didn't
want him kissing on me. "So," he said, and squeezed my palm,
hard. "The graduate!"

17   I shrugged. "Yeah, well," I said. "I'm just glad it's over."

18   He kept holding my hand till I pulled back a little. He
grinned. "Congratulations," he said.

19   "Congratulations to you, too," I said, though I didn't know why.

20   As we drove back to Mineral, I watched my brother suspi-
ciously. Ever since we were little he'd always been the center of
things, and I doubted that he'd come all that way just to con-

gratulate me. I kept expecting him to take over at any minute. I remembered how, when we were young, we had a place behind the house, an old shed we'd furnished with lawn chairs and cinder blocks and such. This became the plantation from *Gone with the Wind*—Corky was Rhett and Scarlett, I was the slaves; or a rocket—Corky was the captain and the alien invaders, I was the crew that got killed. Once, when I was eleven and he was fifteen, and he was going to play the lead in *South Pacific,* he got me all excited about trying out for the part of his little Polynesian son. He gave me the music and then made fun of me, standing by the bedroom door and warbling like an old chicken.

Maybe, I thought, Corky had changed. It had been a long time since I'd really spoken to him. It had been several years since I'd seen him, and I seldom felt like talking to him on the phone. Even when my father *did* put me on the line, I couldn't think of what to say. "What's new," Corky would ask, and I'd shrug: "Nothing." Maybe he'd become a totally different person, and I hadn't known. 21

But I couldn't tell. He was so motionless as we drove that he hardly seemed real. He just stared, like some stone idol, out toward the passing telephone poles and fields and the grasshopper oil wells nodding against the moonlit sky. His hands remained in his lap, except once, when he suddenly touched his hair with his fingertips as if adjusting a hat. When my parents asked him a question he leaned forward, smiling politely. "What? What did you say?" 22

It was late, nearly one in the morning, when we got home. Corky went to the bedroom to unpack—our old room, my room now—and when I came in he was already stretched out on the upper bunk. It used to be that I slept in the bottom and he slept in the top, but since he'd left I'd been using the lower bunk to store papers and laundry and stuff. He looked down at me and smiled. 23

"That's my bed," I told him. 24

He sat up and his bare feet dangled over the edge, swinging lightly. He was wearing silky-looking pajamas. We'd always just slept in our underwear, and I imagined that this was what he wore when he lay down next to another man. "That's rich," he said. "You know, all these years I wanted that bottom bunk. I suppose you always wanted the top." 25

"I didn't care one way or another," I said. I began to take handfuls of dirty laundry from the bottom bunk and put them on the floor. "You can sleep there if you want." 26

He nodded and lay back. "It's been a long time since I've heard any news from you." 27

28   "Yeah, well," I said. "My life isn't that exciting."

29   "You've really changed the room around," he said. He gestured to a poster of a model in a white bikini who was holding a six-pack of beer. "She's sexy," he said.

30   "Yeah," I said. "I guess."

31   He looked from the poster to me, his lips puckered out a little. "So," he said at last. "Do you have a girlfriend, Todd?"

32   "Yes," I said. "Sort of." I didn't. I had friends that were girls, and one of them I took to most of the dances. But I wasn't like some of the guys in school, who'd been going steady with one girl since eighth grade. All the girls I liked had either paired off or weren't interested. The furtive gropes and kisses after dances hadn't amounted to much. I was afraid that even if I got a girl to do more, I'd be clumsy, and I couldn't stand the thought of her laughing, maybe telling her friends. "You know," I told Corky. "I date around and stuff."

33   "Good for you," he said. He pulled his feet up onto the bed the way a fish would flip its tail. Then he laughed. I could feel my ears warming.

34   "What's so funny?" I said.

35   "Nothing," he said. "Just the way you said it." He deepened his voice to a macho swagger. "'I date around and stuff.'" He laughed again. "You used to be such a little high-voiced thing."

36   "Hm," I said. He leaned back and I turned off the light. I moved over near the closet, where it was darkest, so I could undress without him seeing me. The hangers made wind-chime sounds as I brushed them.

37   "It's so weird, being home," he said. His voice floated from the top bunk as I took off my shirt. I decided to sleep in my jeans. I didn't have any pajamas. "You can't believe how strange it is."

38   "Well, nothing has changed," I said. I groped across the dim room to my bed. I could see the lump where he was lying, a shadow bending toward me.

39   "No," he said, "no." And then, slowly: "So did you see the picture I sent?" The house was still. I could hear water whispering through the pipes in the walls; I could hear him breathing.

40   "I saw it." I tried to make my voice noncommittal. I sighed deeply, like I was already almost asleep.

41   He didn't say anything for a long time, and I thought he might have drifted off. When he spoke out of the dark, finally, his voice sounded odd, twittery, not like him, and it made my neck prickle. "Sometimes," he said, "I'm glad I sent it and other times not." I didn't say anything. "Todd?" he whispered.

42   I waited. I recalled the way we used to lie in our bunks when we were little and tell each other jokes and make up songs. I

remembered how I would go to sleep to the sound of his murmuring, crooning. "What," I whispered back finally.

"How did Mom and Dad react?" 43

"How should I know?" I mumbled. "They don't tell me anything." 44

"What did they say?" 45

"What did you expect them to say?" 46

"I don't know," he said. "It's hard to explain." 47

But I didn't want him to explain. I didn't want to keep picturing him in that outfit, swishing and singing, maybe kissing a member of his audience, leaving a bright wing of lipstick on his forehead. "They didn't say much of anything," I told him. "They don't care what you do in your personal life." 48

"Do you?" 49

"Why should I?" I whispered. I rolled over, pretending to be asleep. 50

When I woke, my brother was already up. I could hear him talking in the kitchen, and the sound of eggs cracking on a skillet. I went to the bathroom to shower and when I came back to dress, I couldn't help but notice Corky's suitcase. It was expensive-looking, dark strips of leather bound around brick-red cloth. Through the walls I could hear the vague whisper of conversation and I bent down, running my hands along the sides, finding the zipper. 51

Most of the things had been taken out. He'd put them in dresser drawers my mother had cleared out for him. But there was a compartment along one side, and when I opened it, I found what I figured I'd find. It gave me a fluttery feeling in my stomach: a skirt, a flowered blouse, pantyhose, a box of make-up with the colors arranged chromatically. Beneath that were more photos—Corky gripping a fireman's pole, his leg sliding along it, his eyes looking seductively away; being lifted by a group of men in tuxedos, his head flung back, his arms open wide, jeweled necklaces in his clenched fists. There were two clippings of advertisements for Cabaret Berliner: a drawing of a man's hairy leg with a high heel on his foot, and underneath, in small letters, the words: Corky Petersen with Sister Mary Josephine—After Tea Dance Party. Another had a photo of Corky in his cowgirl outfit. I wondered if he was planning to show us a sample of his act. I closed the suitcase quickly. 52

They didn't look up when I came into the kitchen. They were sitting at the table, eating toast and scrambled eggs. Corky was telling my father that New York City was in a state of collapse and had been ever since Reagan took office. He said the homeless filled the streets, that a bag lady had died on his doorstep. 53

My father kept nodding very seriously, frowning, "Mm-hmm," as if he were talking to a grownup. He never spoke to me that way. Then Corky began to tell about the semis that parked outside his apartment at night, and how his whole place filled up with diesel fumes. He was afraid to light a cigarette. In the middle of this, he looked up and saw me standing there. "Well, hello, Sleeping Beauty," he said, and cocked his hand on his hip.

54   I glared at him. "Mornin'," I said in my deepest voice. I slid into the chair at the far end of the table.

55   "You hungry, punkin?" my mother asked brightly.

56   I looked sternly at her. I wanted to tell them that my name was Todd, not Sleeping Beauty or pumpkin. But all I said was, No. Then I looked at Corky. "So how come you live in New York if you don't like it?"

57   Corky shrugged. "Frankly," he said, "there's no other place I could stand." Then he leaned toward my father and lowered his voice. "I'll tell you what's really scary," he said. "This AIDS thing. Out here, I'm sure no one realizes, but it's really terrifying."

58   My father blushed and we were all silent. "Well," my father said, and cleared his throat. "I hope you're being careful." He picked at his eggs.

59   "Careful?" Corky said. He gave a short laugh. "I can't even tell you. The other night I was out with this guy." He stopped. All of us were sitting stiffly, and my father had a pinched look on his face. He touched his eyelids, as if to clear away the image of Corky and this man, this lover.

60   "Well, anyway," Corky said. "He didn't even want to kiss. He goes: 'I don't know you well enough yet.'" He took a bite of toast, nervously, then looked over at me and winked. I kept my face expressionless. He winked again. "So, Todd." He said my name as if it were some ridiculously cheerful exclamation, like "gee whiz," or "wowee," the kind of thing he used to say with mocking relish when he was in high school. "Tomorrow's the big day!" he said. "Graduation. Commencement. The beginning of a new life."

61   "Right," I said. I didn't like to think about it that way. I couldn't imagine myself working a regular job forty hours a week, or leaving home for college or the service; it seemed amazing to me that Corky lived alone, and paid his own bills, got up in the morning without my mother waking him.

62   "Yes, Toddy," my mother said quickly. "We haven't seen you in your cap and gown."

63   "Yeah, and you're not going to either," I said.

64   "What's the matter," my father said. I could see how it was going to go. They'd do anything to escape more information about Corky's sex life. "Are you ashamed of your cap and gown?"

"I just don't want to put it on, that's all," I said. "What's the 65
big deal?"

"Oh, come on, Todd," my brother said. He grinned. I shook 66
my head at all of them. It figured—even with all of them looking at me, the focus was still on Corky underneath.

"I feel like a dancing dog," I said. I pushed away from the table. 67

When I went into my bedroom, I just stood there for a 68
minute, staring at Corky's suitcase, then to the window. The
morning was warm and clear. Outside, the grass was a sickly
yellow-green in the patches that appeared where the snow had
drawn back. It made me think of a horror movie I'd seen where
the smooth, pale skin of a dead woman peeled away to reveal a
monster's face. At last, I went to the closet and took the box
out. The cap and gown were still wrapped in plastic, and I tore
it away roughly. I slid the gown over my head, the silky cloth
slick against my bare arms, my neck. I fit the cap over my hair,
and it fit snugly. It made me think of a wig. The tassel dangled
in front of my nose.

When I came into the kitchen my brother began to hum a 69
jazzy "Pomp and Circumstance," snapping his fingers. The
gown billowed around me, the cap tilted against my line of vision, and I shambled forward, trying to imagine how Clint
Eastwood would walk in a cap and gown.

"You look real nice," my father nodded. 70

"Stand up straight," my mother said. 71

It would have been nice to say that I was going out that night 72
with a group of friends to some party out on somebody's farm
where everyone was singing and carrying on around a keg an
older brother had bought. Some of my classmates were doing
that, but not *my* friends. Jeanine's grandparents were coming
in from California that night, Craig's family was taking him out
to dinner, Lisa and Jeff, both of them too straight for their own
good, were going to a special Mass or wake or whatever it was
for graduating seniors. I remember Corky and the other seniors who were in plays had a formal dinner for themselves.
They'd sent out calligraphied invitations, and dressed up in
coats and ties. At the party, they'd put parts of Corky's valedictorian speech to the music of *My Fair Lady*. He'd come home
late, singing in a Cockney accent at the top of his lungs.

And what did I do? I sat around. Corky was busy providing 73
the entertainment. As I sat after breakfast and read a horror
book, my brother helped with the dishes and told my mother
about Jacek, a Yugoslavian man he'd dated, a man who made
independent films and had done a video for a rock group.
Actually, Corky didn't say they'd dated. That was only to be

guessed from the careful description he'd given. My mother drew various dishes out of the soapy water, nodding as if she didn't quite understand what it all meant.

74   After lunch, we went for a drive. Corky seemed excited. He wanted to drive by Rattlesnake Knob, he said, and take pictures to show his friends in New York. I pictured him joking about it at some cocktail party, showing his photos to a group of lithe, smirking gay men, as they stood before the huge picture window of some penthouse, surrounding Corky, looking at the pictures and then to the city lights that blurred to dazzles, to the Statue of Liberty with the moon hanging over her head. "How quaint," they'd murmur.

75   The four of us squeezed into the cab of the pickup, with Corky and me in the middle. We drove out toward the hills, and when we passed the rock house, Corky made us stop.

76   The house stood in the middle of a field. It had been built by pioneers and the sod roof had long since collapsed. The rest of it had been built of pumice rock they'd gathered from the hills, and from the smattering of trees they'd found by the creek and cut down. It was still recognizable as a house, there was still the frame of the doors and windows, though the wood was mostly rotten and even the stone walls were crumbling. My father used to take us out here when we were little, and tell us about pioneers. Corky wanted to take a picture.

77   He got out of the truck and strode purposefully through the ditch to the fence. We followed after. He stretched the lines of barbed wire apart so he could squeeze through, then paused on the other side and looked closely at the wire. "Hey, Dad," he said, as we came to the edge of the fence. "Look at the strands of this wire. It's really intricate. Is that rare?"

78   My father bent over to look with Corky, so their foreheads nearly touched, so they looked like mirror images of one another, leaning over, hands on their knees. "No," my father said. "No, not rare. Just old." He sighed, straightening up. It used to be that, wherever we went, my father would be pointing things out, explaining things. As we'd drive up into the hills, my father would tell us how the trickle of creek we'd passed a mile back had made them; over millions of years a valley was created with hills on either side. I remember imagining the gray hills with their jagged lace of pumice cliffs, rising up on either side, pushing slowly out of the flat prairie like mushrooms. He taught us trivia that seemed amazing then—how to tell a rattlesnake from a bullsnake; types of barbed wire. Maybe he was remembering the same thing, because he just stood there, touching his fingers to his eyelids, as Corky clicked his camera at the rusty barbed wire.

"So," my brother said to me as we walked across the pasture to   79
the rock house. "Am I going to get to meet one of these girlfriends
of yours? Is one of them going to stop by the house tomorrow?"

"I don't know," I said. My parents looked at me. They didn't   80
say anything, but it still made me feel like a failure. They
knew I didn't have a girlfriend. Even in the one thing I had
over Corky I was a flop. Corky stopped in front of the rock
house, which was surrounded by tall dry weeds, and put his
hands on his hips. He looked over his shoulder at me, and I
sighed. My parents glanced at me, and I stared down at the
sod. "They're not really girlfriends," I said. "They're just friend
friends."

When I looked up, my eyes met Corky's. I couldn't tell what   81
he was thinking. "Hey," he said. "Why don't you all stand in
front of the place? That'll make a nice shot."

We arranged ourselves—my father stood behind my mother   82
and me and pulled us close to him so he could hide his pot
belly. He and Corky were the tall ones in the family, and I'd inherited my mother's shortness. We pressed together. "Smile,"
Corky called, and stepped back. I set my lips into one of those
smiles I knew was crooked and silly, but I couldn't stop it.
"That's great," Corky said. He aimed the camera at us. "It's one
of those pictures you'll keep forever, you know?" We separated
from our cluster. Corky took another picture.

As we walked back to the car, Corky put his arm around my   83
shoulders. I stiffened, but I didn't shrug him off. "I think just
plain friends are the best kind," he said.

"Yeah, right," I said. He tilted his head as if a cool breeze   84
were blowing.

"I sing this song in my show called 'We're Only Friends.' It's   85
really great. I've got this sort of Dietrich look, and the tune is a
30s German thing, you know." He began to sing softly, his voice
raspy, deep, but strikingly like a woman's. His voice carried,
wafting in the open air.

I didn't know what he was trying to prove. Maybe he was   86
trying to get us used to the idea. Maybe he was just needling
my parents. Maybe he was showing off. Whatever he thought,
the Subject kept coming into our conversations. He had given
a man my mother's recipe for fried chicken. He used "Blue
Moon," my father's favorite song, as the closing number for
his show. He kept at it, through dinner, after, as we were
watching TV, tossing little bits out for our consideration. My
father had gotten a glazed look, as if he could hear someone
far away calling his name. My mother looked more and more
bewildered.

87   As for me, I found myself thinking about the clothes I'd seen in his suitcase. I wondered if and when he was planning to put them on.

88   When he came into the bedroom late that night I was lying on the bottom bunk, reading my book. "Corky," I said. He was bent down, searching through his suitcase. "Do you—" I cleared my throat. I watched him collect a toothbrush and dental floss from his bag. "I mean you normally wear normal clothes, don't you?"

89   He looked up at me, not smiling. "I only dress for my act, if that's what you mean."

90   I nodded. I took a deep breath. "How come you packed women's clothes?"

91   His eyes narrowed. I remembered how he used to have his secret drawers, a scrapbook full of old clippings and things, the way he'd come in and found me looking through it. "Keep out of my stuff, you pig!" he'd shouted, and started punching me.

92   "What do you mean?" he said softly. He was looking me up and down, appraising me, and I watched him set the items in his hand back into the bag. He unzipped the compartment and pulled out the make-up kit, the photos. "This stuff?" he said fiercely. For a minute, I shrank back, as if he were my older brother again and I'd ruined another game. He stared at me, and then suddenly shook his head. "Todd," he said, as if remembering some other brother that wasn't me. "I thought maybe someone might have wanted to see my show." He shook his head. "People pay money to see it." He put the blouse to his face. "Here," he said, and threw it at me, hitting the book I was still holding in my hand. "Smell it."

93   It must have been the look on my face that made him laugh. I held it and sniffed the air. I had dark thoughts about what I was supposed to smell.

94   "Old Spice," he said. "For the manly man." It was my father's brand. "It's a joke," he said. He picked out the bunch of pictures and clippings and walked over to the bunks with them. He put them on top of the blouse. "If you want to look at this stuff, you can," he said. "I'm going to brush my teeth."

95   Before he got to the door, he turned. "What did you think?" he said. "I came home for the sole purpose of ruining your graduation by running around in drag?"

96   I looked down at the pictures of him. "Why *did* you come home?" I said.

97   He put his back to me. "Because I was stupid," he said.

98   At my graduation party, my relatives drank and gave me money. Commencement was as long and dull as the past four years of high school had been. In her speech, the valedictorian

kept referring to the future as a train, and I imagined myself
standing on the railroad tracks, watching it bear down on me.

The party made it even worse. There I was, in the middle of   99
the living room, holding a paper plate—melting ice cream, a
slice of chocolate cake—dabbing the frosting from the base of
the little wax graduate that had been in the center of the cake,
that my mother had insisted I take as a memento. After the
first time, when my uncle Evan had come up to me and
handed me an envelope, and asked me what my plans were,
and I tried to tell him I had a lot of options I was considering, I
gave up. The next time, when my aunt Susan handed me a card
and asked me the same question, I just shrugged.

Which of them had futures that were so wonderful? I   100
watched my great-aunt Birdie, already drunk even before
noon. She'd been married twice and now was living with some
man in Denver. Or my cousin David, who'd just gone bankrupt.
Or Grandpa Mitch, who a few months before had a heart attack, who had to crawl from the bedroom, down the hall to the
phone. "Oh, he looks so thin, so pale," they whispered behind
his back. "He shouldn't be in that old house alone." Soon, he'd
be in a rest home. My parents sat on the couch near my grandfather, looking nervously at Corky. It was sickening. They'd
spent the better part of their lives raising us, and look what
that got them.

Corky was across the room, sitting on a folding chair with   101
his legs crossed. He was right on the edge of the kitchen; people had to walk past him to get to the food and the beer. I
watched my relatives move slowly by, their eyes fixed on him.
They asked him how life was treating him in the Big Apple,
and tightened their smiles.

I stirred my ice cream and cake together. Even I couldn't   102
help staring at him. Aunt Birdie came weaving up to me, fid-
dling with the tab on her beer. A napkin was stuck to her shoe,
dragging behind her as she sidled up to me. "Congratulations,
precious," she said, and pushed her lips to my forehead, leaning against me for support. "What's in your future?" she asked,
and pushed a crumpled bill into my jacket pocket. I shook my
head. "Nothing." Corky had lit another cigarette and was saying: "That sounds an awful lot like a play I auditioned for."
Aunt Birdie kissed me on the eyelid, and I slid away from her
grasp. I decided I needed to go outside for a while.

It was cold. I leaned against the side of the house and   103
bunched my jacket together at the neck, staring out past the
yard to the driveway, which was crowded with my relative's ve-
hicles. I breathed slowly. For a minute I'd imagined I might
spin out of control. I might have broken free of Aunt Birdie,

lisping and sashaying, cooing: "My new play I auditioned for. Oh, how wonderful I am." I might have told everyone, in a loud voice, what hypocrites my parents were: "We're so proud of our Corky! How nice it is to have a son who's so glamorous and successful."

104   Corky came out a few moments later. He exhaled smoke as he poked his head out the door. "Todd," he said. "You're missing your party." He kept his body inside the house, so it looked like his head was disembodied, moving along the doorframe. He bent so he could look at me upside down. It was an old game from childhood. We used to practice miming around the edges of the doors, so from the other side it looked like we were floating, or being lifted by an invisible force. "Todd," he said, in a Donald Duck voice. "Why so glum, Todd?" His head vanished then, like a puppet yanked from a stage. He came out of the house, and stood beside me.

105   In the house, someone had turned on music, my father's Patsy Cline tape. It drifted mournfully in the stillness, wisping through the walls.

106   I sighed. "Did you ever," I said at last, "wonder what was going to happen to you?"

107   There was a flicker in his eyes, as if he'd forgotten something important. His smile wavered. "No," he said.

108   I considered this. Probably, he'd always known. "Well," I said. "What do you think will happen to me, then? Because I wonder. I wonder a lot."

109   He stared at me for a long time, and then put another cigarette to his lips. "You'll probably be miserable," he said. "Like everybody else." Our eyes met, and then we both looked down. His words hung there, with both of us considering them—as if he'd dropped a bowl at my feet, and we were both looking at the shards of broken glass. In the house, I could hear my father laughing.

110   "Thanks a lot," I said stiffly. "Sorry I asked."

111   He shrugged, and pulled a folded bill out of his pocket. He pushed it into my hand. "Maybe I will go squeeze into that dress," he whispered.

112   "Don't," I said through my teeth. I looked at the piece of paper in my hand. A hundred-dollar bill. "I can't take this," I said. "That's too much."

113   He lifted his eyebrows, and I watched him put it back in his pocket. His hand slid out of his pocket holding a nickel, which he flipped toward me. I fumbled, caught it. "There," he said.

114   "Very funny," I said. He dragged deeply on his cigarette.

115   We stared at each other. "Go ahead," my brother whispered. Smoke curled around his face as he breathed, and he pushed

his hands through his dyed hair, loosening his ponytail. "I know you're dying to. Say 'faggot.' Say 'cocksucker.'" He smirked at me. But then as I watched, it seemed that some awful transformation was coming over his face. It was trembling and contorting like there was something beneath it trying to escape. For a second I imagined that he must be seeing something terrifying, a dark shape lunging at us, and I turned quickly. But there was only the empty yard.

"Say it," he whispered. "Say it."   116

Peter J. Gomes
HOMOPHOBIC?
READ YOUR BIBLE

Peter J. Gomes (born 1942) is an American Baptist minister. Widely respected as one of the most distinguished preachers in the nation, he has served since 1970 in the Memorial Church at Harvard University. Since 1974 he has been Plummer Professor of Christian Morals at Harvard Divinity School as well. He wrote the following piece for the New York Times *in 1992.*

Opposition to gays' civil rights has become one of the most visible symbols of American civic conflict this year, and religion has become the weapon of choice. The army of the discontented, eager for clear villains and simple solutions and ready for a crusade in which political self-interest and social anxiety can be cloaked in morality, has found hatred of homosexuality to be the last respectable prejudice of the century.   1

Ballot initiatives in Oregon and Maine would deny homosexuals the protection of civil rights laws. The Pentagon has steadfastly refused to allow gays into the armed forces. Vice President Dan Quayle is crusading for "traditional family values." And Pat Buchanan, who is scheduled to speak at the Republican National Convention this evening, regards homosexuality as a litmus test of moral purity.   2

Nothing has illuminated this crusade more effectively than a work of fiction, "The Drowning of Stephan Jones," by Bette Greene. Preparing for her novel, Ms. Greene interviewed more than 400 young men incarcerated for gay-bashing, and   3 scrutinized their case studies. In an interview published in *The Boston Globe* this spring, she said she found that the gay-bashers generally saw nothing wrong in what they did, and, more often than not, said their religious leaders and traditions sanctioned their behavior. One convicted teen-age gay-basher told her that the pastor of his church had said, "Homosexuals represent the devil, Satan," and that the Rev. Jerry Falwell had echoed that charge.

4   Christians opposed to political and social equality for homosexuals nearly always appeal to the moral injunctions of the Bible, claiming that Scripture is very clear on the matter and citing verses that support their opinion. They accuse others of perverting and distorting texts contrary to their "clear" meaning. They do not, however, necessarily see quite as clear a meaning in biblical passages on economic conduct, the burdens of wealth, and the sin of greed.

5   Nine biblical citations are customarily invoked as relating to homosexuality. Four (Deuteronomy 23:17, I Kings 14:24, I Kings 22:46, and II Kings 23:7) simply forbid prostitution, by men and women.

6   Two others (Leviticus 18:19–23 and Leviticus 20:10–16) are part of what biblical scholars call the Holiness Code. The code explicitly bans homosexual acts. But it also prohibits eating raw meat, planting two different kinds of seed in the same field, and wearing garments with two different kinds of yarn. Tattoos, adultery, and sexual intercourse during a woman's menstrual period are similarly outlawed.

7   There is no mention of homosexuality in the four Gospels of the New Testament. The moral teachings of Jesus are not concerned with the subject.

8   Three references from St. Paul are frequently cited (Romans 1:26–2:1, I Corinthians 6:9–11, and I Timothy 1:10). But St. Paul was concerned with homosexuality only because in Greco-Roman culture it represented a secular sensuality that was contrary to his Jewish-Christian spiritual idealism. He was against lust and sensuality in anyone, including heterosexuals. To say that homosexuality is bad because homosexuals are tempted to do morally doubtful things is to say that heterosexuality is bad because heterosexuals are likewise tempted. For St. Paul, anyone who puts his or her interest ahead of God's is condemned, a verdict that falls equally upon everyone.

9   And lest we forget Sodom and Gomorrah, recall that the story is not about sexual perversion and homosexual practice. It is about inhospitality, according to Luke 10:10–13, and failure to care for the poor, according to Ezekiel 16:49–50: "Behold, this was the iniquity of thy sister Sodom, pride, fullness of

bread, and abundance of idleness was in her and in her daughters, neither did she strengthen the hand of the poor and needy." To suggest that Sodom and Gomorrah is about homosexual sex is an analysis of about as much worth as suggesting that the story of Jonah and the whale is a treatise on fishing.

Part of the problem is a question of interpretation. Fundamentalists and literalists, the storm troopers of the religious right, are terrified that Scripture, "wrongly interpreted," may separate them from their values. That fear stems from their own recognition that their "values" are not derived from Scripture, as they publicly claim. 10

Indeed, it is through the lens of their own prejudices that they "read" Scripture and cloak their own views in its authority. We all interpret Scripture: Make no mistake. And no one truly is a literalist, despite the pious temptation. The questions are, By what principle of interpretation do we proceed, and by what means do we reconcile "what it meant then" to "what it means now"? 11

These matters are far too important to be left to scholars and seminarians alone. Our ability to judge ourselves and others rests on our ability to interpret Scripture intelligently. The right use of the Bible, an exercise as old as the church itself, means that we confront our prejudices rather than merely confirm them. 12

For Christians, the principle by which Scripture is read is nothing less than an appreciation of the work and will of God as revealed in that of Jesus. To recover a liberating and inclusive Christ is to be freed from the semantic bondage that makes us curators of a dead culture rather than creatures of a new creation. 13

Religious fundamentalism is dangerous because it cannot accept ambiguity and diversity and is therefore inherently intolerant. Such intolerance, in the name of virtue, is ruthless and uses political power to destroy what it cannot convert. 14

It is dangerous, especially in America, because it is antidemocratic and is suspicious of "the other," in whatever form that "other" might appear. To maintain itself, fundamentalism must always define "the other" as deviant. 15

But the chief reason that fundamentalism is dangerous is that, at the hands of the Rev. Pat Robertson, the Rev. Jerry Falwell, and hundreds of lesser-known but equally worrisome clerics, preachers, and pundits, it uses Scripture and the Christian practice to encourage ordinarily good people to act upon their fears rather than their virtues. 16

Fortunately, those who speak for the religious right do not speak for all American Christians, and the Bible is not theirs 17

alone to interpret. The same Bible that the advocates of slavery used to protect their wicked self-interests is the Bible that in-
18   spired slaves to revolt and their liberators to action.

The same Bible that the predecessors of Mr. Falwell and Mr. Robertson used to keep white churches white is the source of the inspiration of the Rev. Martin Luther King, Jr., and the
19   social reformation of the 1960's.

The same Bible that antifeminists use to keep women silent in the churches is the Bible that preaches liberation to captives and says that in Christ there is neither male nor female,
20   slave nor free.

And the same Bible that on the basis of an archaic social code of ancient Israel and a tortured reading of Paul is used to condemn all homosexuals and homosexual behavior includes metaphors of redemption, renewal, inclusion, and love—principles that invite homosexuals to accept their freedom and responsibility in Christ and demands that their fellow Christians
21   accept them as well.

The political piety of the fundamentalist religious right must not be exercised at the expense of our precious freedoms. And in this summer of our discontent, one of the most precious freedoms for which we must all fight is freedom from this last prejudice.

Mike Ritter
GAYS IN THE MILITARY

Mike Ritter's nationally syndicated cartoons appear in many magazines and newspapers, including those in his home city of Phoenix. They are also published on the Internet. The following cartoon was a response to the controversy over gays in the military that developed during the first term of President Clinton.

VI

CRIME AND PUNISHMENT

Introduction

You've heard all the statistics.

According to the Department of Justice, a violent crime occurs somewhere in the United States every twenty seconds. A murder occurs every half hour (about 22,000 in 2000). Someone is raped every six minutes. Over fifteen million arrests were made in 2000, over a million of them for drug abuse violations. Many more Americans are in prison, per capita, than citizens in any other "developed" nation. The point is this: Although crime rates have been dropping for the past decade, crime has become an inescapable fact of life in the United States. And what to do about it has become a perennial issue, as the selections in this part demonstrate.

The first set of readings, a sort of transition from the previous part on civil liberties and civil rights, discusses the question of gun control. Should the ownership and possession of firearms be restricted? An absolute "no" is the answer of those who wish to protect citizens' right to bear arms. They cite for support the Second Amendment to our Constitution: "A well regulated militia being necessary to the security of a free state, the right of the people to keep and bear arms shall not be infringed." On the other hand, a number of people (some of them included in this book) contend that the right to purchase and keep guns is not absolute, that we already restrict in certain reasonable ways "the right to bear arms" (e.g., you can't own rocket launchers or a tank; you can't own guns if you're a minor or a convicted felon or mentally incompetent), and that the Supreme Court has consistently ruled gun control laws to be constitutional. Faced with certain abuses—shocking assassinations; 25,000 shooting deaths each year—proponents of gun control simply argue for additional reasonable restrictions, particularly on the handguns that are so available in our society and so commonly employed in the conduct of violent crime. Just what is it about Americans and guns, anyway? Why do they figure so prominently in our society? Can anything be done about it? Should anything be done about it? Do guns cause crime, or are people responsible?

That brings up the question posed by the second set of readings in this part of *Conversations:* Should we continue the practice of capital punishment in the United States?

From the mid-1960s to 1977 no executions were carried out in the United States as the nation debated the abuses in the application of capital punishment and the wisdom of carrying out such punishment at all; indeed, capital punishment has been outlawed in a great many nations and condemned by the Roman Catholic Church. The Pope made his opposition to the death penalty a public focus of his visit to the United States in 1999, and the execution of born-again Karla Faye Tucker in 1998 made many conservative Christians denounce capital punishment. But in 1976, the Supreme Court by a 5–4 vote decided that capital punishment is constitutional under certain circumstances. Executions inevitably followed, and so the debate about capital punishment has been renewed: Is capital punishment an expression of justice, "an eye for an eye"? Is it a useful deterrent to other would-be murderers? Or does it feed one of our basest instincts—for revenge? Is the death penalty cruel and unusual punishment? Is it unfairly applied to minority criminals, especially for crimes against majority members? If so, is this an argument for abolition, or for improving our system of justice?

Part Six concludes with a discussion of whether illegal drugs should be regulated or made legal. In the face of persistent and debilitating drug use, some have proposed legalization—not because they see drugs as less than a menace, but because they trust in other measures than law to fight it. Those who would legalize drugs propose that we approach drug abuse as an economic and medical problem rather than as a legal one. Legalizers (or "decriminalizers") wish to minimize the effects of illegal drugs by eliminating black market profits; legalization would drive down drug prices, the argument goes, and therefore reduce secondary crime motivated by the need to finance the drug habit. Legalizers would regulate drugs and tax drug producers, as liquor is regulated and taxed; the revenues could be used for education and drug prevention campaigns, and for treatment of drug addicts. Those who would legalize drugs argue by analogy to the prohibition of alcohol in the 1920s, a prohibition that made average citizens into criminals, made gangsters and rumrunners into millionaires, and reduced respect for law throughout the land. But those against legalization also point to Prohibition—to the end of Prohibition in 1930, when alcohol use skyrocketed. They argue that legalizing drugs would result in an inevitable

684 Crime and Punishment

spread in the use of cocaine and heroin, and an inevitable
increase in cocaine babies, child abuse, wrecked automobiles and airplanes, and wrecked lives. And they contend
that it is against the American grain to legalize immoral
acts, no matter how often the acts are being committed.

In any case, what to do about drugs—and what to do
about crime and criminals in general—will continue to engage our national attention.

SHOULD GUNS
BE REGULATED?

■

Leonard Kriegel

A LOADED QUESTION:
WHAT IS IT ABOUT
AMERICANS AND GUNS?

Leonard Kriegel (born 1933), a writer of fiction and essays, contributed the following piece to Harper's *magazine, a publication featuring contributions on U.S. politics and culture, in mid-1992. The article itself will tell you more about him.*

I have fired a gun only once in my life, hardly experience   1
enough to qualify one as an expert on firearms. As limited as
my exposure to guns has been, however, my failure to broaden
that experience had nothing at all to do with moral disapproval
or with the kind of righteous indignation that views an eight-
year-old boy playing cops and robbers with a cap pistol as a
preview of the life of a serial killer. None of us can speak with
surety about alternative lives, but had circumstances been different I suspect I not only would have hunted but very probably would have enjoyed it. I might even have gone in for target
shooting, a "sport" increasingly popular in New York City,
where I live (like bowling, it is practiced indoors in alleys). To
be truthful, I have my doubts that target shooting would really
have appealed to me. But in a country in which grown men feel
passionately about a game as visibly ludicrous as golf, anything is possible.

The single shot I fired didn't leave me with a traumatic ha-   2
tred of or distaste for guns. Quite the opposite. I liked not only
the sense of incipient skill firing that shot gave me but also the
knowledge that a true marksman, like a good hitter in baseball,

had to practice—and practice with a real gun. Boys on the cusp of adolescence are not usually disciplined, but they do pay attention to the demands of skill. Because I immediately recognized how difficult it would be for me to practice marksmanship, I was brought face to face with the fact that my career as a hunter was over even before it had started.

3   Like my aborted prospects as a major league ballplayer, my short but happy life as a hunter could be laid at the metaphorical feet of the polio virus which left me crippled at the age of eleven. Yet the one thing that continues to amaze me as I look back to that gray February afternoon when I discovered the temptation of being a shooter and hunter is that I did not shoot one or the other of the two most visible targets—myself or my friend Jackie, the boy who owned the .22.

4   Each of us managed to fire one shot that afternoon. And when we returned to the ward in which we lived along with twenty other crippled boys between the ages of nine and thirteen, we regaled our peers with a story unashamedly embellished in the telling. As the afternoon chill faded and the narrow winter light in which we had hunted drifted toward darkness, Jackie managed to hide the .22 from ward nurses and doctors on the prowl. What neither of us attempted to hide from the other boys was our brief baptism in the world of guns.

5   Like me, Jackie was a Bronx boy, as ignorant about guns as I was. Both of us had been taken down with polio in the summer of '44. We had each lost the use of our legs. We were currently in wheelchairs. And we had each already spent a year and a half in the aptly named New York State Reconstruction Home, a state hospital for long-term physical rehabilitation. Neither of us had ever fired anything more lethal than a Daisy air rifle, popularly known as a BB gun—and even that, in my case at least, had been fired under adult supervision. But Jackie and I were also American claimants, our imaginations molded as much by Hollywood westerns as by New York streets. At twelve, I was a true Jeffersonian who looked upon the ownership of a six-shooter as every American's "natural" right.

6   To this day I don't know how Jackie got hold of that .22. He refused to tell me. And I still don't know how he got rid of it after our wheelchair hunt in the woods. For months afterward I would try to get him to promise that he and I would go hunting again, but, as if our afternoon hunt had enabled him to come to terms with his own illusions about the future (something that would take me many more years), Jackie simply shook his head and said, "That's over." I begged, wheedled, cajoled,

threatened. Jackie remained obdurate. A single shot for a single hunt. It would have to be sufficient.

I never did find out whether or not I hit the raccoon. On the 7 ride back to the ward, Jackie claimed I had. After he fired his shot, he dropped from his wheelchair and slid backward on his rump to the abandoned water pipe off the side of the dirt road into which the raccoon had leaped at the slashing crack of the .22. His hand came down on something red—a bloodstain, he excitedly suggested, as he lifted himself into his wheelchair and we turned to push ourselves back to the ward. It looked like a rust stain to me, but I didn't protest. I was quite willing to take whatever credit I could. That was around an hour after the two of us, fresh from lunch, had pushed our wheelchairs across the hospital grounds, turning west at the old road that cut through the woods and led to another state home, this one ministering to the retarded. The .22, which lay on Jackie's lap, had bounced and jostled as we maneuvered our wheelchairs across that rutted road in search of an animal—any animal would do—to shoot. The early February sky hung above us like a charcoal drawing, striations of gray slate shadings feeding our nervous expectation.

It was Jackie who first spotted the raccoon. Excited, he 8 handed the .22 to me, a gesture spurred, I then thought, by friendship. Now I wonder whether his generosity wasn't simply self-protection. Until that moment, the .22 lying across Jackie's dead legs had been an abstraction, as much an imitation gun as the "weapons" boys in New York City constructed out of the wood frames and wood slats of fruit and vegetable crates, nails, and rubber bands—cutting up pieces of discarded linoleum and stiff cardboard to use as ammunition. I remember the feel of the .22 across my own lifeless legs, the weight of it surprisingly light, as I stared at the raccoon who eyed us curiously from in front of the broken pipe. Then I picked up the gun, aimed, and squeezed the trigger, startled not so much by the noise nor by the slight pull, but by the fact that I had actually fired at something. The sound of the shot was crisp and clean. I felt as if I had done something significant.

Jackie took the gun from me. "Okay," he said eagerly. "My 9 turn now." The raccoon was nowhere in sight, but he aimed in the direction of the water pipe into which it had disappeared and squeezed the trigger. I heard the crack again, a freedom of music now, perhaps because we two boys had suddenly been bound to each other and had escaped, for this single winter afternoon moment, the necessary but mundane courage which dominates the everyday lives of crippled children. "Okay," I heard him cry out happily, "we're goddamn killers now."

10   A formidable enough hail and farewell to shooting. And certainly better than being shot at. God knows what happened to that raccoon. Probably nothing; but for me, firing that single shot was both the beginning and the end of my life as a marksman. The raccoon may have been wounded, as Jackie claimed. Perhaps it had crawled away, bleeding, to die somewhere in the woods. I doubt it. And I certainly hope I didn't hit it, although in February 1946, six months before I returned to the city and to life among the "normals," I would have taken its death as a symbolic triumph. For that was a time I needed any triumph I could find, no matter how minor. Back then it seemed natural to begin an uncertain future with a kill—even if one sensed, as I did, that my career as a hunter was already over. The future was hinting at certain demands it would make. And I was just beginning to bend into myself, to protect my inner man from being crushed by the knowledge of all I would never be able to do. Hunting would be just another deferred dream.

11   But guns were not a dream. Guns were real, definitive, stamped on the imagination of their functional beauty. A gun was not a phallic symbol; a gun didn't offer me revenge on polio; a gun would not bring to life dead legs or endow deferred dreams with substance. I am as willing as the next man to quarantine reality within psychology. But if a rose is no more than a rose, then tell me why a gun can't simply be a gun? Guns are not monuments to fear and aspiration any more than flowers are.

12   I was already fascinated by the way guns looked. I was even more fascinated by what they did and by what made people use them. Like any other twelve-year-old boy, I was absorbed by talk about guns. Six months after the end of the Second World War, boys in our ward were still engrossed by the way talking about guns entangled us in the dense underbrush of the national psyche. And no one in that ward was more immersed in weaponry than I. On the verge of adolescence, forced to seek and find adventure in my own imagination, I was captivated by guns.

13   It was a fascination that would never altogether die. A few weeks ago I found myself nostalgically drifting through the arms and armor galleries of the Metropolitan Museum of Art. Years ago I had often taken my young sons there. A good part of my pleasure now derived from memories pinned to the leisurely innocence of those earlier visits. As I wandered among those rich cabinets displaying ornate pistols and rifles whose carved wood stocks were embossed with gold and silver and ivory and brass, I was struck by how incredibly lovely many of these weapons were. It was almost impossible to con-

ceive of them as serving the function they had been designed to serve. These were not machines designed to kill and maim. Created with an eye to beauty, their sense of decorative purpose was as singular as a well-designed eighteenth-century silver drinking cup. These guns in their solid display cases evoked a sense of the disciplined craftsmanship to which a man might dedicate his life.

Flintlocks, wheel locks, a magnificent pair of ivory pistols 14 owned by Catherine the Great—all of them as beckoning to the touch of fingers, had they not been securely locked behind glass doors, as one of those small nineteenth-century engraved cameos that seem to force time itself to surrender its pleasures. I gazed longingly at a seventeenth-century wheel lock carbine, coveting it the way I might covet a drinking cup by Cellini or a small bronze horse and rider by Bologna. Its beautifully carved wooden stock had been inlaid with ivory, brass, silver, and mother-of-pearl, its pride of artisanship embossed with the name of its creator, Caspar Spät. I smiled with pleasure. Then I wandered through the galleries until I found myself in front of a case displaying eighteenth-century American flintlock rifles, all expressing the democratic spirit one finds in Louis Sullivan's buildings or Whitman's poetry or New York City playgrounds built by the WPA during the Great Depression. Their polished woods were balanced by ornately carved stag-antler powder horns, which hung like Christmas decorations beneath them. To the right was another display case devoted to long-barreled Colt revolvers; beyond that, a splendidly engraved 1894 Winchester rifle and a series of Smith & Wesson revolvers, all of them decorated by Tiffany.

And yet they were weapons, designed ultimately to do what 15 weapons have always done—destroy. Only in those childlike posters of the 1970s did flower stems grow out of the barrel of a gun. People who shoot, like people who cook, understandably choose the best tools available. And if it is easier to hit a target with an Uzi than a homemade zip gun, chances are those who want to hit the target will feel few qualms about choosing the Uzi.

Nonetheless, these galleries are a remarkable testimony to 16 the functional beauty of guns. Nor am I the only person who has been touched by their beauty. The problem is to define where the killing ceases and the beauty begins. At what point does a young boy's sense of adventure transform itself into the terror of blood and destruction and pain and death? I remember my sons' excitement when they toured these splendid galleries with me. (Yes, doctor, I did permit them to enjoy guns. And neither became a serial killer.) These weapons helped bring us together, bound father and sons, just as going to base-ball games or viewing old Chaplin movies had.

17   Geography may not be the sole father of morality, but one would have to be remarkably naive to ignore its claims alto-gether. As I write this, I can see on the table in front of me a newspaper headlining the most recent killings inflicted on New York City's anarchic populace. Firearms now rule street and schoolyard, even as the rhetoric of politicians demanding strict gun control escalates—along with the body count.

18   And yet I recognize that one man's fear and suffering is an-other man's freedom and pleasure. Here is the true morality of geography. Like it or not, we see the world against a landscape of accommodation. Guns may be displayed behind glass cases in that magnificent museum, but in the splendid park in which that museum has been set down like a crowning jewel, guns have been known to create not art but terror. Functional beauty, it turns out, does not alter purpose.

19   I have a friend who has lived his entire life in small towns in Maine. My friend is both a hunter and a connoisseur of guns. City streets and guns may be a volatile mix, but the Maine woods and guns apparently aren't. Rifles and pistols hang on my friend's living room wall like old family portraits. They are lived with as comfortably as a family heirloom. My friend speaks knowingly of their shape, describes each weapon lov-ingly, as if it possessed its own substance. He is both literate and civilized, but he would never deny that these guns are more than a possession to him. They are an altar before which he bends the knee, a right of ownership he considers invio-lable, even sacrosanct. And yet my friend is not a violent man.

20   I, too, am not a violent man. But I am a New Yorker. And like most people who live in this city, I make certain assumptions about the value of the very indignities one faces by choosing to live here. If I didn't, I probably couldn't remain in New York. For with all of the problems it forces one to face, the moral ge-ography of New York also breeds a determination not to give in to the daily indignities the city imposes.

21   During the summer of 1977, I lived within a different moral geography. I was teaching a graduate seminar on Manhood and American Culture at the University of New Mexico in Albuquerque, tracing the evolution of the American man from Ben Franklin's sturdy, middle-class acolyte to the rugged John Wayne of *Stagecoach*. Enchanted by the New Mexico land-scape, I would frequently drive off to explore the small towns and brilliant canyons in whose silences ghosts still lingered. One day a friend volunteered to drive with me into the Manzano Mountains. I had announced my desire to look at the

ruins of a seventeenth-century mission fort at Gran Quivira, while he wanted me to meet a man who had, by himself, built a house in those haunting, lovely mountains.

Tension between Anglos and Hispanics was strong in New   22
Mexico in the summer of 1977. Even a stranger could feel a palpable, almost physical, struggle for political and cultural hegemony. Coming from a New York in which the growing separation of black and white was already threatening to transform everyday life into a racial battlefield, I did not feel particularly intimidated by this. Instead of black and white, New Mexico's ethnic and racial warfare would be between Anglo, Hispanic, and Indian. Mountainair, where we were to visit my friend's friend, was considered an Anglo town. Chilili, some miles up the road, was Hispanic.

My friend's friend had built his house on the outskirts of   23
Mountainair, with a magnificent view of ponderosa pine. He was a man in his early sixties and had come to New Mexico from Virginia soon after World War II to take a job as a technical writer in a nuclear research laboratory in Albuquerque. Before the war he had done graduate work in literature at the University of Virginia, but the demands of fatherhood had decided him against finishing his doctorate. Like so many Americans before him, he had taken wife and young children to start over in the West.

In the warmth and generosity of his hospitality, however, he   24
remained a true Southerner. As we sat and talked and laughed in a huge sun-drenched living room that opened onto that magnificent view of the mountains and pines and long New Mexico sky, I could not help but feel that here was the very best of this nation—a man secure in himself, a man of liberal sympathies and a broad understanding of human behavior and a love of children and grandchildren and wife, a man who spoke perceptively of Jane Austen's novels and spoke sadly of the savage threat of drugs (his oldest son, a veteran of the war in Vietnam, was living with him, along with wife and three-year-old daughter, trying to purge the heroin addiction that threatened to wreck his life).

I remember him happily holding forth on Jane Austen's   25
Persuasion when his body suddenly seemed to freeze in mid-sentence. I could hear a motor in the distance. Without another word, he turned and crossed the room. Twin double-barreled shotguns hung on the wall above the fireplace. He took one, his right hand scooping shells from a canvas bag hanging from a thong looped around a horseshoe nail banged shoulder-high into the wall. His son, the ex-Marine, grabbed the other gun and scooped shells from the same bag. Through

the glassed-in cathedral living room leading to the porch, I watched the two of them stand side by side, shotguns pointed at a pickup truck already out of range. "Those bastards!" I heard my host snarl.

26   "We'll get 'em yet, Pop," his son said. "I swear it."

27   After we left to drive on to the ruins of Gran Quivira, I asked the friend who had accompanied me to explain what had happened. "A pickup truck from Chilili. Hispanics driving up the mountain to cut trees. It's illegal. But they do it anyway."

28   "Do the trees belong to your friend?"

29   "Not his trees. Not his mountain." Then he shrugged.

30   "But it's his gun."

31   I angrily cast my eyes at the man and find myself staring into the twin barrels of a shotgun loosely held but pointed directly at me. It is that same summer in Albuquerque, three weeks later, and I am sitting in the driver's seat of my car, my ten-year-old son, Bruce, directly behind me. Alongside him is the eleven-year-old daughter of the man who had invited me to teach at the University of New Mexico. I have just backed my car away from a gasoline pump to allow another car to move out of the garage into the road. As the other car came out of the gas station, the man with the shotgun adroitly cut me off and maneuvered his rust-pocked yellow pickup ahead of me in line before I could get back to the gas pump.

32   My first reaction is irritation with my car, as if the steel and chrome were sentient and responsible. It is the same ugly gold 1971 Buick in which, five summers earlier, I had driven through a Spanish landscape remarkably similar to the New Mexico in which I now find myself. Bruce had been with me then, too, along with his older brother and mother. But it is not the Buick that attracts men with guns. Nor is it that mythical violence of American life in which European intellectuals believe so fervently. In Spain we had been stopped at a roadblock, a sand-bagged machine gun aimed by one of Franco's troops perusing traffic like a farmer counting chickens in a henhouse. The soldiers had asked for passports, scowled at the children, examined the Buick as if it were an armored tank, inspecting glove compartment and trunk and wedging their hands into the spaces between seat and back. At the hotel restaurant at which we stopped for lunch twenty minutes later, we learned that two *guardia civil* had been ambushed and killed by Basque guerrillas. During Franco's last years, such acts grew more and more frequent. Spain was filled with guns and soldiers. One was always aware of the presence of soldiers patrolling the vacation beaches of the Costa del Sol—and particularly aware of their guns.

As I am aware of the shotgun now. And as I am growing   33
aware of that same enraged sense of humiliation and helplessness that seized me as those Spanish soldiers examined car
and sons and wife, their guns casually pointed at all I loved
most in the world, these other lives that made my life significantly mine. "Guns don't kill, people do!" Offer that mind-
deadening cliché to a man at a roadblock watching the faces of
soldiers for whom the power of a gun is simply that it permits
them to feel contempt for those without guns. Tell that to a
man sitting in a car with two young children, contemplating
doing what he knows he cannot do because the gun is in another man's hands. Both in Spain and in this New Mexico that
Spain had planted in the New World like a genetic acorn
breeding prerogatives of power, guns endowed men with a way
to settle all questions of responsibility.

The man with the shotgun says nothing. He simply holds the   34
weapon in his beefy hand, its muzzle casually pointed in my
direction. I toy with the notion of getting out of the car and
confronting him. I am angry, enraged. I don't want to give in to
his rude power. Only my son and my colleague's daughter are
in the back of the car. Defensively, I turn to look at them. My
colleague's daughter is wide-eyed and frightened. Bruce is
equally frightened, but his eyes are on me. I am his father and
he expects me to do something, to say something, to alter the
balance of expectation and reality. Our car was on line for gas
first. To a ten-year-old, justice is a simple arithmetic.

To that ten-year-old's father it is not necessarily more com-   35
plex. I could tell myself that it was insane to tell a man pointing a shotgun at me and these two children that he has broken
the rules. Chances are he wouldn't have fired, would probably
have responded with a shrug of the shoulders no more threatening than a confession of ignorance.

Obviously, none of this mattered. My growing sense of hu-   36
miliation and rage had nothing to do with having to wait an extra minute or two while the station attendant filled the tank of
the pickup. I was in no particular rush. I was simply returning
home from a day-long excursion to a state park, where my son
and his new friend had crawled through caves and climbed
rocks splashed by a warm spring. But I was facing a man with
a shotgun, a man who understood that people with guns define
options for themselves.

The man with the gun decides whether or not to shoot, just as   37
he chooses where to point his gun. It is not political power that
stems from the barrel of a gun, as Maoists used to proclaim so
ritualistically. It is individual power, the ability to impose one's
presence on the world, simply because guns always do what

language only sometimes does: Guns command! Guns command attention, guns command discipline, guns command fear.

38   And guns bestow rights and prerogatives, even to those who have read Jane Austen and engaged the world in their own comedy of manners. There is a conditional nature to all rights. And there are obligations that should not be shunted aside. Guns are many things, some symbolic, some all too real. But in real life they are always personal and rarely playful. They measure not capacity but the obligation the bearer of the gun has to believe that power belongs not to the gun but to him. And yet were I to tell this to my friend in Maine—that sophisticated, literate, humane man—I suspect he would turn to me and say, "That's right. There's always got to be somebody's finger on the trigger."

39   A confession, then: I may be as fascinated by guns as my gun-owning and gun-loving friend in Maine, but were it up to me, I would rid America of its guns. I would be less verbally self-righteous about gun control than I was in the past, for I think I have begun to understand those who, like my friend in Maine, have arguments of their own in defense of guns. They are formidable arguments. Their fear matches mine, and I assume that their anguish over the safety of their children is also equal to mine. I, too, know the statistics. I can repeat, as easily as he can, that in Switzerland, where an armed citizenry is the norm, the homicide rate is far lower than in many countries that carefully control the distribution of guns to their populace. Laws are simply words on paper—unless they embody what a population wants.

40   There is no logic with which I can convince my gun-owning friend in Maine. But there are images I wish I could get him to focus on. Like me, he is a writer. Only I write about cities, and my friend writes about the Maine woods. He is knowledgeable about animals and rocks and trees and silence, and I am knowledgeable about stubs of grass growing between cracks in a concrete sidewalk and the pitch and pull of conflicting voices demanding recognition. I wish I could explain to him the precise configuration of that double-barreled shotgun pointing at me and those two children. Maybe then I could convince him that truth is not merely a matter of geography. Yes, guns don't kill and people do—but in the America he and I share, those people usually kill with guns.

41   Four years after that incident at the gas station, I was sitting with Bruce in a brasserie in Paris. It was a sunny July afternoon and we were eating lunch at a small outside table, the walls of the magisterial Invalides beckoning to us from across the street. Bruce was fourteen, and fifteen minutes earlier he

had returned from his first trip alone on the Paris Metro. Suddenly a man approached, eyes menacing and bloodshot. He was short and thick, his body seemingly caked by the muscularity of a beaten-down club fighter or an unemployed stevedore. He stared at us, eyes filled with the rage of the insane. Then he flexed his muscles as if he were on exhibit as a circus strong man, cried out something—a sound I remember as a cross between gargling and choking—and disappeared just as suddenly down the street.

The incident still haunts me. The French, I suspect, are as violent as they like to claim we Americans are. But in Paris it is difficult for a man filled with rage and craziness to get hold of a gun. Not impossible, mind you, just difficult. Somewhere along the line, the French have learned not that guns don't kill and people do but that people with guns can kill. And they know what we have yet to acknowledge—that when the Furies dance in the head it's best to keep the weapons in display cases in the museum. For that, at least, I wish my friend in Maine could learn to be grateful. As I was, eating lunch with my son in Paris. 42

Roy Innis

GUN CONTROL SPROUTS FROM RACIST SOIL

Roy Innis was born in the Virgin Islands in 1934. As a youth he moved with his family to New York City, and he has continued to make his home there. He contributed the following article to the Wall Street Journal *in November 1991 while he was serving as the national chairman of the Congress of Racial Equality.*

What irony. Most black leaders (as distinct from rank-and-file blacks) are supporters, at least in public, of the gun control— really, prohibition—movement. Do they realize that America's gun-control movement sprouted from the soil of Roger B. Taney, the racist chief justice who wrote the infamous *Dred Scott* decision of 1857? 1

In the early part of the 19th century, Dred Scott, a black slave, had been taken by his owner from Missouri, a slave 2 state, to Illinois, a free state. From there he was taken into the Wisconsin territory, free territory above the 36° 30' latitude of the Missouri Compromise. After living in free territory for a while, he returned with his owner to Missouri.

3   When his owner died in 1846, Scott sued in the state courts of Missouri for his freedom, on the ground that he had lived in free territory. He won his case, but it was reversed in the Missouri Supreme Court. Scott appealed to the federal courts, since the person he was actually suing, John Sanford, the executor of the estate that owned Scott, lived in New York.

4   It was in that setting that Chief Justice Taney made his infamous rulings:

> 1. That black people, whether free or slave, were not citizens of the U.S.; therefore, they had no standing in court.
> 2. Scott was denied freedom.
> 3. The Missouri Compromise was ruled unconstitutional.

5   Well known to most students of race relations is the former attorney general and secretary of the Treasury's pre-civil war dictum that black people "being of an inferior order" had "no right which any white man was bound to respect." Much less known are his equally racist pronouncements denying black people, whether slave or free, specific constitutional protections enjoyed by whites.

6   In *Dred Scott* Chief Justice Taney, writing for the court's majority, stated that if blacks were "entitled to the privileges and immunities of citizens, . . . it would give persons of the negro race, who were recognized as citizens in any one state of the union, the right . . . to keep and carry arms wherever they went. And all of this would be done in the face of the subject race of the same color, both free and slaves, and inevitably producing discontent and insubordination among them, and endangering the peace and safety of the state. . . ."

7   Although much of Justice Taney's overly racist legal reasoning was repudiated by events that followed—such as the Civil War and Reconstruction—the subliminal effects were felt throughout that era. In the post-Reconstruction period, when the pendulum swung back to overt racism, Justice Taney's philosophy resurfaced. It was during this period that racial paranoia about black men with guns intensified. It was potent enough to cause the infringement on the Second Amendment to the Constitution's "right . . . to keep and bear arms."

8   Under natural law, a freeman's right to obtain and maintain the implements of self-defense has always been sacred. This right was restricted or prohibited for serfs, peasants and

slaves. Gun control was never an issue in America until after   9
the Civil War when black slaves were freed.

It was this change in the status of the black man, from slave
to freeman, that caused racist elements in the country (North
and South) to agitate for restrictions on guns—ignoring long
established customs and understanding of the Second
Amendment. The specter of a black man with rights of a freeman, bearing arms, was too much for the early heirs of Roger
Taney to bear.

The 14th and 15th Amendments to the Constitution, along   10
with the various Reconstruction civil rights acts, prevented
gun prohibitionists from making laws that were explicitly
racist and that would overtly deny black people the right to
bear arms. The end of Reconstruction signaled the return of
Taneyism—overtly among the masses and covertly on the
Supreme Court. Gun-control legislation of the late 19th and
early 20th centuries, enacted at the state and local levels, was
implicitly racist in conception. And in operation, those laws in-
vidiously targeted blacks.

With the influx of large numbers of Irish, Italian and Jewish   11
immigrants into the country, gun laws now also targeted
whites from the underprivileged classes of immigrants.
Eventually these oppressive gun laws were extended to affect
all but a privileged few. Throughout the history of New York
state's Sullivan law, enacted at the start of the 20th century,
mainly the rich and powerful have had easy access to licenses
to carry handguns. Some of the notables who have received
that privilege include Eleanor Roosevelt, John Lindsay, Donald
Trump, Arthur Sulzberger, Joan Rivers and disk jockey
Howard Stern.

Of the 27,000 handgun carry permits in New York City, fewer   12
than 2% are issued to blacks—who live and work in high-crime
areas and really are in need of protection.

And what of the origins of the National Rifle Association,   13
which is wrongly viewed as a racist organization by the black
supporters of gun prohibition? It was inspired and organized
by Union Army officers after the Civil War.

Elizabeth Swazey
WOMEN AND HANDGUNS

Elizabeth Swazey, an attorney, a certified firearms instructor, and the former director of the National Rifle Association's group on women's issues, used to write a column every other month for American Rifleman *magazine (a publication of the NRA that is devoted to articles of various kinds on various kinds of firearms). The following such column appeared in 1992.*

1   James Michael Barnes failed to appear in court on March 8, 1991. He was dead.

2   According to New Jersey *Courier-Post* staff reporters Alan Guenther and Renee Winkler, by February 1990 the relationship between Amy Gardiner and James Michael Barnes had broken off. On February 9, he appeared on Gardiner's doorstep to return some of her things. Instead, he raped her. He even photographed the event. Barnes pled guilty to assault and was sentenced to two years probation. He also was ordered to stay away from Gardiner and her relatives.

3   He didn't. According to court documents, Barnes broke into Gardiner's home, stole from her, left a hot iron on her carpet and smeared her walls and furniture with feces.

4   During this period, Barnes was charged with robbing and intimidating another ex-girlfriend. Bail was set at $50,000 cash. Barnes stayed in jail until January 17. On that date, prosecutors sought to have his opportunity for bail revoked on grounds he was a threat to Gardiner. But the judge actually *reduced* Barnes' bail to $25,000. Barnes posted the 10% required and was free that afternoon.

5   Free to look for Amy Gardiner.

6   But in the meantime, Gardiner had done three things. She had filed harassment charges against Barnes; she had changed her address; and she had purchased a shotgun. Two weeks later at 9:30 in the evening, Gardiner's doorbell rang. She was alone and didn't answer the door. Soon the telephone rang. When she answered, the caller hung up. Sensing danger, Gardiner went to the bedroom to get the shotgun. Barnes, armed with a revolver and a disturbed mind, kicked in the front door and stormed into the bedroom, threatening to kill her. Gardiner fired once. Barnes died. The terror was over. But at what cost?

7   Taking the life of another human being, *no matter how justified,* carries a heavy burden. Why New Jersey Superior Court

Judge Joseph F. Green, Jr., allowed Barnes to buy temporary freedom for $2,500 is beyond me. Is that the price he places on a woman's suffering, on the white-hot fear she felt that night, alone, with a madman trying to kill her?

Amy Gardiner could be any of us, *You, Your wife, daughter or* 8 *friend.* According to the Dept. of Justice, three of four American women will face crime in their lifetimes. And, as has been held in another case, ". . . a government and its agents are under no general duty to provide public services, such as police protection, to any particular individual citizen. . . ." *Warren v. District of Columbia,* 444 A.2d 1 (D.C.App.181).

Or, put another way, "[T]here is no constitutional right to 9 be protected by the state against being murdered by criminals or madmen." *Bowers v. DeVito,* 686 F.2d 616, at 618 (7th Cir. 1982).

Amy Gardiner faced a criminal madman. Thankfully, the in- 10 nocent life prevailed. And while it is human nature to avoid thinking about unpleasant topics, we must recognize that *any one of us* could be violently attacked. Until our criminal justice system becomes a victims' justice system—and NRA is helping turn the tide through our *CrimeStrike* program—violent criminals like James Michael Barnes will continue to be routinely set free. We need to decide, in advance, how to respond if you, I or a loved one is threatened.

Owning a gun, and whether to use it in lawful self-defense, 11 are *deeply personal choices* that each individual must make. For those who decide in favor of gun ownership, NRA can help. We offer introductory Personal Protection Seminars for women across the country, and the intensive Personal Protection Program to men and women nationwide through a network of certified instructors. Information about both is available by simply calling (800) 368-5714 or (202) 828-6224.

Handgun Control, Inc. (HCI) doesn't want women to have 12 this choice. The group's Chairman Emeritus Pete Shields advises women faced with criminal attack to "give them what they want." But what James Michael Barnes wanted was for Amy Gardiner *to be dead.*

Sometimes HCI softens its message by expressing "concern" 13 that if a woman tried to use a gun in self-defense, it would be taken away and used against her. Why doesn't HCI Chair Sarah Brady ever say this about men? Amy Gardiner faced an armed attacker and prevailed. And the most recent National Crime Survey by the Bureau of Justice Statistics found that in *less than 1%* of cases did criminals manage to turn guns against their owners.

14   HCI says one of its principal political goals this year is to conduct a "public information campaign" about "the extremist nature of the gun lobby and alert women . . . that they've been targeted as a new market. . . ."

15   So the lines are drawn: NRA says defend your right to defend yourself. HCI says give criminals what they want. Now who's extreme?

*Below is the Web site for an organization known as Women
Against Gun Control (WAGC). The site mounts on argument
in support of the right to bear arms, but what are the specific
visual elements on the Web site that contribute to that argu-
ment? A stringer running across the top reads "The Second
Amendment is the Equal Rights Amendment." And the far
right-hand margin includes two scrolls: one with the names
Rosie O'Donnell, Janet Reno, Diane Feinstein, and Hillary
Clinton, and a motto reading "Let's Blow Holes in Their
Arguments"; and one with a picture of a burglar and a motto
reading "If women are disarmed, a rapist will never hear STOP
OR I'LL SHOOT!"*

National Rifle Association
DONT EDIT THE BILL
OF RIGHTS

The ad printed on these two pages, developed and paid for by the National Rifle Association Institute for Legislative Action, appeared in USA Today *and many other newspapers in December 1991—on the 200th anniversary of the ratification of the Bill of Rights.*

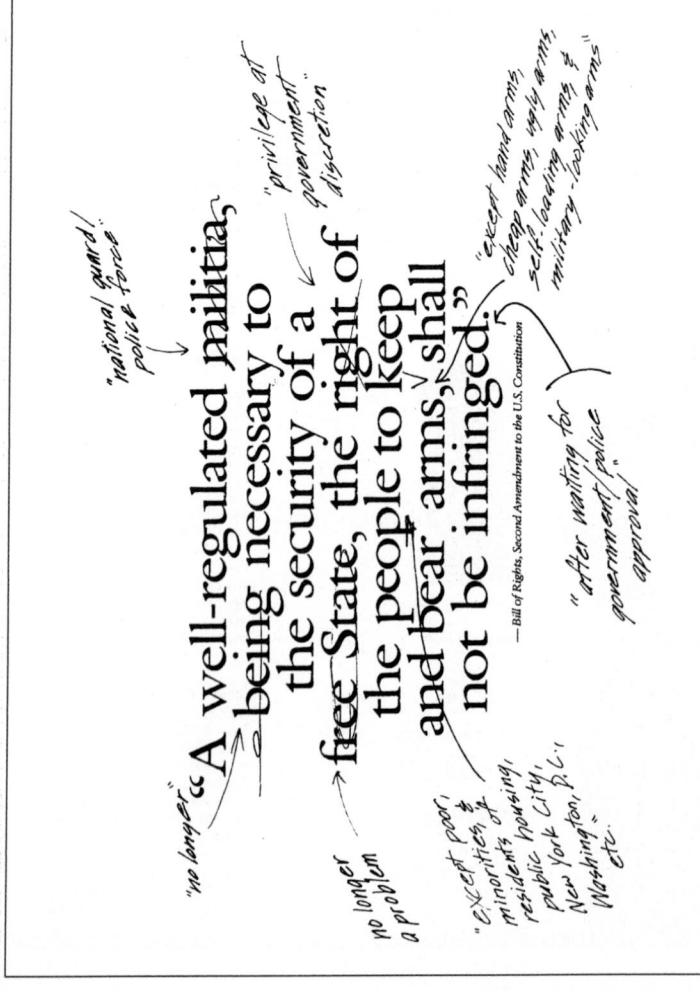

Before anyone edits the Bill of Rights, the authors would like a word with you:

"No free man shall ever be debarred the use of arms."

THOMAS JEFFERSON

"Arms in the hands of citizens may be used at individual discretion... in private self-defense."

JOHN ADAMS

"[The Constitution preserves] the advantage of being armed which Americans possess over the people of almost every other nation... [where] the governments are afraid to trust the people with arms."

JAMES MADISON

"... arms discourage and keep the invader and plunderer in awe, and preserve order in the world as well as property... Horrid mischief would ensue were [the law-abiding] deprived of the use of them."

THOMAS PAINE

"Laws that forbid the carrying of arms... disarm only those who are neither inclined nor determined to commit crimes... Such laws make things worse for the assaulted and better for the assailants; they serve rather to encourage than to prevent homicides, for an unarmed man may be attacked with greater confidence than an armed man."

THOMAS JEFFERSON, quoting Cesare Beccaria

"A militia, when properly formed, are in fact the people themselves... and include all men capable of bearing arms... To preserve liberty it is essential that the whole body of the people always possess arms and be taught alike... how to use them."

RICHARD HENRY LEE

"The Constitution shall never be construed to prevent the people of the United States who are peaceable citizens from keeping their own arms."

SAMUEL ADAMS

"I ask, sir, what is the militia? It is the whole people... To disarm the people... is the best and most effectual way to enslave them..."

GEORGE MASON

A message on celebration of the 200th Anniversary of the Ratification of the Bill of Rights, December 15, 1791. Paid for by the National Rifle Association Institute for Legislative Action. For more information, call 202-828-6100.

Paul Lawton
CONSTITUTIONAL LAW
AND THE SECOND
AMENDMENT

Paul Lawton was a student at the University of Texas at Austin when he wrote the following essay for a writing course there. He's now pursuing a career in journalism.

In the end more than they wanted freedom, they wanted security. When the Athenians finally wanted not to give to society but for society to give to them, when the freedom they wished for was freedom from responsibility, then Athens ceased to be free.

—Edward Gibbon (1737–1794)

1   In 1994 Congress passed an outright ban on nineteen different types of assault weapons under the Schumer amendment to the Clinton Crime Bill. Representative John Dingell (D–MI) remarked when the bill passed that the ban was "obnoxious, offensive and contrary to the rights of all Americans." This, however, did not stop the representative from voting for the Crime Bill, in which the ban was contained. His reasoning was that he considered the remainder of the bill to be "smart and tough" (*Washington Times*, 8/26/94). While the representative seemed to have "voted his conscience" on the bill, one wonders if this ban circumvented the Second Amendment to satisfy the American public's need for safer streets.

2   The push against the assault weapons was extremely popular last year, and lawmakers were quick to jump on the bandwagon against weapons that are designed to "kill humans." Many argued that the weapons had no useful purpose for hunting and that the weapons were also impractical for defending the homestead. But even so, the federal government is supposed to amend the Constitution before they do something that is strictly prohibited by its own guidelines. For instance, to circumvent the First Amendment's right to burn the American flag, the bill would need, under Article Five of the Constitution, a two-thirds approval in both houses. The bill would then need to be approved by three-fourths of the state

legislatures before burning the flag could not be considered protected speech under the First Amendment.

There is nothing inherently wrong or evil with this amend-   3
ment process. Indeed, Chief Justice John Marshall wrote in the nineteenth century that the Constitution was "intended to endure for ages to come, and, consequently, to be adapted to the various crises of human affairs." Marshall presented the very modern idea that the Constitution is meant to be amended to fit the various needs of future generations. Thus, many people gripped with fear from violent crime in America would probably express a wish to ban weapons whose sole purpose is the taking of human life.

However, many groups including the para-militaries which   4
have recently been labeled as promoters of hate, have espoused the view that assault weapons are covered under the Second Amendment and cannot, without amendment, be legally banned by the federal government. The pro-gun control movement has argued quite the opposite, that the Second Amendment does not guarantee, in fact, an individual right and only refers to a state militia's right to bear arms.

In order to understand what the pro-gun control move-   5
ment believes about the Second Amendment's application to individual rights, it is important to look at the actual text of the amendment:

> A well-regulated Militia, being necessary for the security of a
> free State, the right of the people to keep and bear Arms,
> shall not be infringed.

One can clearly see the confusion that the word "Militia"   6
brings into the meaning of the amendment. Thus, the Pro-Gun Control Movement, along with the American Bar Association, the ACLU, and texts such as Tribe's *American Constitutional Law,* have enunciated that the Second Amendment only applies to state militias and makes no reference to an individual right.

From this interpretation, it has been assumed that, since the   7
right to bear arms is not an individual right, the extent to which citizens may keep weapons can be limited by the federal government. To many so-called experts, the federal government was thus within its legal limits to ban assault weapons. However, by taking a close look at the actual language of the Second Amendment and the legal precedent set by the Supreme Court of the United States, it becomes obvious that the 102nd Congress passed a law that was entirely unconstitutional and the very antithesis of what the past and current interpretation of the amendment should allow.

8   The language of the Second Amendment can most clearly be linked to the generation of the idea that only the militia has the right to "keep and bear arms." However, Roy Copperud, a leading legal expert who is impartial to the gun control debate, was recently interviewed on the possible interpretations of the amendment. Copperud concluded that the structure of the sentence indicates that existence of the right to keep arms is assumed and that "the thrust of the sentence is that the right shall be preserved inviolate for the sake of ensuring a militia." He also concluded that the language of the amendment, although still acceptable in modern times, could be rewritten as, "Since a well-regulated militia is necessary to the security of a free state, the right of the people to keep and bear arms shall not be abridged" (Schulman, Second Amendment Foundation). This clearly shows that the meaning of the sentence is that all citizens need weapons to protect the state and that the federal government should realize this fact and not interfere with the natural right of the people to protect themselves and their society.

9   The intent and belief in an armed populace is clearly present in the Founding Father's rhetoric. Thomas Jefferson wrote that "the strongest reason for the people to retain the right to keep and bear arms is, as a last resort, to protect themselves against tyranny in government." This Lockonian philosophy that man has a natural justified right for self-protection was present in many of the leaders of the time and reflects itself in the language of the Bill of Rights and consequently the Second Amendment.

10   This clearly shows that the language of the amendment does not coincide with the contemporary interpretation of the amendment. However, this is not the *coup de grace* of the pro-gun control argument. Rather it presents only half a case in a constitutional interpretation. The second half of the case is the Supreme Court's judicial precedent on the Second Amendment.

11   Judicial precedent is important because the Court is not able to go back in time and ask the original framers what they meant and how far the federal government can go before it is infringing on the rights of the people. Thus, the Court looks at its own past decisions to help decide if a law is in fact unconstitutional. Unfortunately for the pro-gun control movement, the judicial precedent of the Court does not indicate a strong agreement with the assault weapon ban of 1994.

12   Perhaps the first case the court talked about concerning the right to bear arms is the 1856 *Scott* v. *Sandford* case, most commonly referred to as the Dred Scott decision. Though the final decision was remarkably barbaric, the rhetoric used by the judges to defend their decision shows an opinion of the court that affirms the belief that the right to arms is a natural right

of free men. In the opinion, the judges ruled that one of the criteria for Scott to be free would be the right of free speech and the right "to keep and carry arms wherever . . . [he] went" (LEXIS, 60 U.S. 393).

The next case, which dealt specifically with the Second   13
Amendment, was *United States* v. *Cruikshank* in 1876 where the court recognized that the right to keep and bear arms "is not a right granted by the Constitution . . . [but n]either is it in any manner dependent upon that instrument for its existence" (LEXIS).

But perhaps the most stunning indictment against the   14
Assault Weapons Ban comes from *United States* v. *Miller* in 1939. Here the court devised a test to discern if a weapon is applicable under the Second Amendment clause. The weapon in question was a sawed-off shotgun and the court ruled that:

> In the absence of any evidence tending to show that possession or use of a "shotgun having a barrel of less than eighteen inches in length" at this time has some reasonable relationship to the preservation or efficiency of a well-regulated militia, we cannot say that the Second Amendment guarantees the right to keep and bear such an instrument. Certainly it is not within judicial note that this weapon is any part of the ordinary military equipment or that its use could contribute to the common defense.

Thus, the court ruled that the weapon must be of military use to   15
be protected under the Second Amendment, which clearly destroys the pro-gun opinion that assault weapons can be banned because they are neither hunting nor self-protection firearms. Here the Court ruled the opposite to be true. Only weapons used for military purpose are protected (153 U.S. 535).

The Court also issued an opinion in Miller that the militia   16
mentioned in the Second Amendment consists of "all males physically capable of acting in concert for the common defense." They further elaborated on the duties of this civilian militia by saying that "when called for service these men . . . [are] expected to appear bearing arms supplied by themselves and of the kind in common use at the time" (307 U.S. 174). More precisely, contrary to Miller, the Court declared that the people mentioned in the Second Amendment included all citizens of the United States and not just young males. The 1990 *United States* v. *Verdugo-Urquirdez* decision further clarified that the Second Amendment applies to all citizens and legal aliens in the United States (110 S. Ct. 3039).

17   Thus, the court decisions render a view of the Second
Amendment that cannot possibly allow for the prohibition of
any weapon that might be used for war. Since the Bill of Rights
is the final say on whether the government has overstepped its
boundaries, it becomes clear that the 1994 U.S. Congress overstepped its boundaries into the rights of its rulers. It seems in-
comprehensible that this bill would pass when a scant fourteen
years ago the Subcommittee on the Constitution of the
Committee on the Judiciary remarked that "The conclusion is
thus inescapable that the history, concept, and wording of the
Second Amendment to the Constitution of the United States,
as well as its interpretation by every major commentator and
court in the first half-century after its ratification, indicates
that what is protected is an individual right of a private citizen
to own and carry firearms in a peaceful manner." This careless
disregard for both the limitations and rules of the Constitution
certainly should make the federal government suspect to the
American people. For in the end, the rights guaranteed in the
amendments are the only protection against a tyrannical government the people have. Any attempt to erode these liberties
should be inquired about to the fullest extent. Any attempt to
circumvent this process should be considered inexcusable.

Robert Goldwin

Gun Control
Is Constitutional

*Goldwin is a scholar affiliated with the American Enterprise
Institute, a conservative research institute. He contributed
the following to the* Wall Street Journal, *the conservative
business-news daily, in December 1991. The letters published
after it and responding to it appeared a few weeks later in the
same newspaper.*

1   Congress has been dismayingly inconsistent in its voting on
gun-control legislation this year, first passing the Brady Bill,
then moving in the opposite direction by defeating a provision
to ban certain assault weapons and ammunition. But in one respect members of Congress are consistent: they demand respect for our "constitutional right to own a gun." They cite the

Constitution's Second Amendment and argue it prohibits effective national regulation of the private ownership of guns.

But there are strong grounds for arguing that the Second   2
Amendment is no barrier to gun-control legislation. In my opinion, it even provides a solid constitutional basis for effective national legislation to regulate guns and gun owners.

The best clues to the meaning of the key words and phrases   3
are in debates in the First Congress of the United States. The Members of that Congress were the authors of the Second Amendment. A constitutional amendment calling for the prohibition of standing armies in time of peace was proposed by six state ratifying conventions. Virginia's version, later copied by New York and North Carolina, brought together three elements in one article—affirmation of a right to bear arms, reliance on state militia, and opposition to a standing army.

"That the people have a right to keep and bear arms; that a   4
well regulated militia, composed of the body of the people trained to arms, is the proper, natural, and safe defense of a free state; that standing armies, in times of peace, are dangerous to liberty, and therefore ought to be avoided. . . ."

The purpose was to limit the power of the new Congress to   5
establish a standing army, and instead to rely on state militias under the command of governors. The Constitution was ratified without adopting any of the scores of proposed amendments. But in several states ratification came only with solemn pledges that amendments would follow.

Soon after the First Congress met, James Madison, elected   6
as a congressman from Virginia on the basis of such a pledge, proposed a number of amendments resembling yet different from articles proposed by states. These eventually became the Bill of Rights. In the version of the arms amendment he presented, Madison dropped mention of a standing army and added a conscientious objector clause.

"The right of the people to keep and bear arms shall not be   7
infringed, a well armed and well regulated militia being the best security of a free country, but no person religiously scrupulous of bearing arms shall be compelled to render military service in person."

In this version, "bearing arms" must mean "to render mili-   8
tary service," or why else would there have to be an exemption for religious reasons? What right must not be infringed? The right of the people to serve in the militia.

This militia amendment was referred to a congressional   9
committee and came out of committee in this form:

"A well regulated militia, composed of the body of the peo-   10
ple, being the best security of a free state, the right of the people

to keep and bear arms shall not be infringed; but no person religiously scrupulous shall be compelled to bear arms."

11   Two significant changes had been made: first, the phrase "to render military service in person" was replaced by the phrase, "to bear arms," again indicating that they are two ways to say the same thing; second, an explanation was added that the "militia" is "composed of the body of the people."

12   The House then debated this new version in committee of the whole and, surprisingly, considering the subsequent history of the provision, never once did any member mention the private uses of arms, for self-protection, or hunting, or any other personal purpose. The debate focused exclusively on the conscientious objector provision. Eventually the committee's version was narrowly approved. The Senate in turn gave it its final form: briefer, unfortunately more elliptical, and with the exemption for conscientious objectors deleted:

13   "A well-regulated militia, being necessary to the security of a free state, the right of the people to keep and bear arms, shall not be infringed."

14   Certain explanations were lost or buried in this legislative process: that the right to bear arms meant the right to serve in the militia; that just about everybody was included in the militia; and that the amendment as a whole sought to minimize if not eliminate reliance on a standing army by emphasizing the role of the state militia, which would require that everyone be ready to be called to serve.

15   But what about the private right "to keep and bear arms," to own a gun for self-defense and hunting? Isn't that clearly protected by the amendment? Didn't just about everyone own a gun in 1791? Wouldn't that "right" go without saying? Yes, of course, it would go without saying, especially then when there were no organized police forces and when hunting was essential to the food supply.

16   But such facts tell us almost nothing relevant to our question. Almost everyone also owned a dog for the same purposes. The Constitution nevertheless says nothing about the undeniable right to own a dog. There are uncountable numbers of rights not enumerated in the Constitution. These rights are neither denied nor disparaged by not being raised to the explicit constitutional level. All of them are constitutionally subject to regulation.

17   The right to bear arms protected in the Second Amendment has to do directly with "a well-regulated militia." More evidence of the connection can be found in the Militia Act of 1792.

18   "Every free able-bodied white male citizen" (it was 1792, after all) was required by the act to "enroll" in the militia for

training and active service in case of need. When reporting for service, every militiaman was required to provide a prescribed rifle or musket, and ammunition.

Here we see the link of the private and public aspects of 19 bearing arms. The expectation was that every man would have his own firearms. But the aspect that was raised to the level of constitutional concern was the public interest in those arms.

What does this mean for the question of gun control today? 20 Well, for example, it means that Congress has the constitutional power to enact a Militia Act of 1992, to require every person who owns a gun or aspires to own one to "enroll" in the militia. In plain 1990s English, if you want to own a gun, sign up with the National Guard.

Requiring every gun owner to register with the National 21 Guard (as we require 18-year-olds to register with the Selective Service) would provide the information about gunowners sought by the Brady and Staggers bills, and much more. Standards could be set for purchase or ownership of guns, and penalties could be established.

Restoring a 200-year-old understanding of the Constitution 22 may be difficult, but there isn't time to dawdle. Americans now own more than 200 million guns, and opinion polls show Americans want gun control. Why not avail ourselves of the Second Amendment remedy? Call in the militia, which is, after all, "composed of the body of the people."

RESPONSES TO ROBERT GOLDWIN: LETTERS TO THE EDITOR OF THE *WALL STREET JOURNAL*

In his "Gun Control Is Constitutional" the American Enterprise 1 Institute's Robert A. Goldwin's principal concern, it seems, is to deny that the right to keep and bear arms precludes the power to regulate gun ownership and use. Few would disagree. Even activities protected by the First Amendment may be regulated when they threaten the rights of others.

But Mr. Goldwin also writes that "The right to bear arms 2 protected in the Second Amendment has to do directly with 'a well regulated militia'"; thus, arguably, he continues, "if you want to own a gun, sign up with the National Guard." Clearly, this goes well beyond regulating to protect the rights of others. This would condition the "right" to keep and bear arms on joining the National Guard.

3 Mr. Goldwin's mistake stems from his having confused a necessary with a sufficient condition. The Second Amendment, in its language and its history, makes plain that the need for a well-regulated militia is a *sufficient* condition for the right to keep and bear arms. Yet Mr. Goldwin treats it as a *necessary* condition, which enables him to conclude that Congress could deny an individual the right to own a gun if he did not join the National Guard.

4 Mr. Goodwin makes this mistake, in turn, because he has misread Madison's original version of the Second Amendment, which exempted conscientious objectors from military service. Thus he says that "In this version, 'bearing arms' must mean 'to render military service,' or why else would there have to be an exemption for religious reasons? What right must not be infringed? The right of the people to serve in the militia."

5 Plainly, any conscientious objector provision would arise not from a *right* but from a *duty* to serve in the militia. Yet Mr. Goldwin believes the amendment means, as he later says, "that the right to bear arms meant the right to serve in the militia." Thus does he reduce the first of these rights to the second, when clearly it is much broader.

Roger Pilon
Senior Fellow and Director
Center for Constitutional Studies
CATO Institute

1 The militia is not the National Guard but rather the people of the original states. In Ohio, we have an Ohio militia that is not a part of the National Guard. The fear of standing armies and the control these armed men gave a central government was foremost in the Framers' minds when writing the Bill of Rights. Thomas Jefferson moved to prevent this type of power in a few people's hands by the Second Amendment. He stated, "No free man shall ever be debarred the use of arms."

2 The addition in the early drafts of a conscientious-objector clause was added for the preservation of religious freedoms, which the Colonists had not had in England. It is unfortunate today's "scholars" seem to spend their time picking apart history and the great thoughts of the visionary men who formed this country.

In my personal celebration of this 200-year-old document, I 3
have pledged the following: I will give up my freedom of
speech when they cut out my tongue; I will give up my right to
worship when they have slain my God and myself; I will assemble with the people of my choice even when they are im-
prisoned, and I will give up my rifle when they pry my cold
dead fingers from around it.

Samuel R. Bush III

Let those who want guns join the National Guard, says Mr. 1
Goldwin. Ah, the sanctimonious arrogance of it. What gives
Mr. Goldwin the right to deny mine when I abide by the laws?

He stresses the differences between the world of 1791 and 2
today to suit his prejudice. He studiously ignores other major
differences between 1791 and today.

In 1791, punishment was swifter and surer. Plea bargaining 3
was not epidemic; judges did not provide revolving doors on
prisons. There was no army of drug dealers and junkies prey-
ing on the public. If anything, the reasons for citizens to own
weapons for self-defense are more compelling today than they
were in 1791.

Let Mr. Goldwin show us how he would make us safer in our 4
homes and we might understand his wish to strip away our
only sure defense.

Carl Roessler

Mr. Goldwin suggests gun control via enlistment in the 1
National Guard. Swell idea. Updating the right to bear arms
from 1791 to 1991, when I report for service, I'll bring, as required, a few items consistent with the current infantryman's
inventory: a Barett Light .50 semiautomatic sniper rifle, so I
can reach out and touch people half a mile away; a Squad
Automatic Weapon firing 5.56mm rounds at the rate of a
whole lot per second out of 30-round clips or hundred-round
belts; a 40mm grenade launcher . . . but you get the idea. Then,
as a thoroughly modern, well-regulated militiaman, I'll take
my weapons home, just as did Morgan's riflemen, and the musket bearers of Lexington and Concord, and the Colonial light
artillerists.

Andrew L. Isaac

Daniel Polsby

THE FALSE PROMISE
OF GUN CONTROL

The following essay appeared in March 1994 in The Atlantic
Monthly, *a venerable, mildly left-of-center monthly magazine
that carries book and movie reviews, original poetry and fiction, and commentary on current events and issues. Daniel
Polsby (born 1945), a full-time professor of law at
Northwestern University for over two decades, is now on the
faculty of George Mason University. He teaches courses in
criminal law and regularly writes on constitutional, criminal,
and family law for academic publications.*

1 During the 1960s and 1970s the robbery rate in the United
States increased sixfold, and the murder rate doubled; the rate
of handgun ownership nearly doubled in that period as well.
Handguns and criminal violence grew together apace, and national opinion leaders did not fail to remark on the coincidence.

2 It has become a bipartisan article of faith that more handguns cause more violence. Such was the unequivocal conclusion of the National Commission on the Causes and Prevention
of Violence in 1969, and such is now the editorial opinion of
virtually every influential newspaper and magazine, from *The
Washington Post* to *The Economist* to the *Chicago Tribune*.
Members of the House and Senate who have not dared to confront the gun lobby concede the connection privately. Even if
the National Rifle Association can produce blizzards of angry
calls and letters to the Capitol virtually overnight, House members one by one have been going public, often after some new
firearms atrocity at a fast-food restaurant or the like. And last
November they passed the Brady bill.

3 Alas, however well accepted, the conventional wisdom about
guns and violence is mistaken. Guns don't increase national
rates of crime and violence—but the continued proliferation of
gun-control laws almost certainly does. Current rates of crime
and violence are a bit below the peaks of the late 1970s, but because of a slight oncoming bulge in the risk population of
males aged fifteen to thirty-four, the crime rate will soon
worsen. The rising generation of criminals will have no more
difficulty than their elders did in obtaining the tools of their
trade. Growing violence will lead to calls for laws still more se-

vere. Each fresh round of legislation will be followed by renewed frustration.

Gun-control laws don't work. What is worse, they act per- 4 versely. While legitimate users of firearms encounter intense regulation, scrutiny, and bureaucratic control, illicit markets easily adapt to whatever difficulties a free society throws in their way. Also, efforts to curtail the supply of firearms inflict collateral damage on freedom and privacy interests that have long been considered central to American public life. Thanks to the seemingly never-ending war on drugs and long experience attempting to suppress prostitution and pornography, we know a great deal about how illicit markets function and how costly to the public attempts to control them can be. It is essential that we make use of this experience in coming to grips with gun control.

The thousands of gun-control laws in the United States are 5 of two general types. The older kind sought to regulate how, where, and by whom firearms could be carried. More recent laws have sought to make it more costly to buy, sell, or use firearms (or certain classes of firearms, such as assault rifles, Saturday-night specials, and so on) by imposing fees, special taxes, or surtaxes on them. The Brady bill is of both types: it has a background-check provision, and its five-day waiting period amounts to a "time tax" on acquiring handguns. All such laws can be called scarcity-inducing, because they seek to raise the cost of buying firearms, as figured in terms of money, time, nuisance, or stigmatization.

Despite the mounting number of scarcity-inducing laws, no 6 one is very satisfied with them. Hobbyists want to get rid of them, and gun-control proponents don't think they go nearly far enough. Everyone seems to agree that gun-control laws have some effect on the distribution of firearms. But it has not been the dramatic and measurable effect their proponents desired.

Opponents of gun control have traditionally wrapped their 7 arguments in the Second Amendment to the Constitution. Indeed, most modern scholarship affirms that so far as the drafters of the Bill of Rights were concerned, the right to bear arms was to be enjoyed by everyone, not just a militia, and that one of the principal justifications for an armed populace was to secure the tranquillity and good order of the community. But most people are not dedicated antiquitarians, and would not be impressed by the argument "I admit that my behavior is very dangerous to public safety, but the Second Amendment says I have a right to do it anyway." That would be a case for repealing the Second Amendment, not respecting it.

Fighting the Demand Curve

8   Everyone knows that possessing a handgun makes it easier to intimidate, wound, or kill someone. But the implication of this point for social policy has not been so well understood. It is easy to count the bodies of those who have been killed or wounded with guns, but not easy to count the people who have avoided harm because they had access to weapons. Think about uniformed police officers, who carry handguns in plain view not in order to kill people but simply to daunt potential attackers. And it works. Criminals generally do not single out police officers for opportunistic attack. Though officers can expect to draw their guns from time to time, few even in big-city departments will actually fire a shot (except in target practice) in the course of a year. This observation points to an important truth: people who are armed make comparatively unattractive victims. A criminal might not know if any one civilian is armed, but if it becomes known that a large number of civilians do carry weapons, criminals will become warier.

9   Which weapons laws are the right kinds can be decided only after considering two related questions. First, what is the connection between civilian possession of firearms and social violence? Second, how can we expect gun-control laws to alter people's behavior? Most recent scholarship raises serious questions about the "weapons increase violence" hypothesis. The second question is emphasized here, because it is routinely overlooked and often mocked when noticed; yet it is crucial. Rational gun control requires understanding not only the relationship between weapons and violence but also the relationship between laws and people's behavior. Some things are very hard to accomplish with laws. The purpose of a law and its likely effects are not always the same thing. Many statutes are notorious for the way in which their unintended effects have swamped their intended ones.

10   In order to predict who will comply with gun-control laws, we should remember that guns are economic goods that are traded in markets. Consumers' interest in them varies. For religious, moral, aesthetic, or practical reasons, some people would refuse to buy firearms at any price. Other people willingly pay very high prices for them.

11   Handguns, so often the subject of gun-control laws, are desirable for one purpose—to allow a person tactically to dominate a hostile transaction with another person. The value of a weapon to a given person is a function of two factors: how much he or she wants to dominate a confrontation if one oc-

curs, and how likely it is that he or she will actually be in a situation calling for a gun.

Dominating a transaction simply means getting what one wants without being hurt. Where people differ is in how likely it is that they will be involved in a situation in which a gun will be valuable. Someone who *intends* to engage in a transaction involving a gun—a criminal, for example—is obviously in the best possible position to predict that likelihood. Criminals should therefore be willing to pay more for a weapon than most other people would. Professors, politicians, and newspaper editors are, as a group, at very low risk of being involved in such transactions, and they thus systematically underrate the value of defensive handguns. (Correlative, perhaps, is their uncritical readiness to accept studies that debunk the utility of firearms for self-defense.) The class of people we wish to deprive of guns, then, is the very class with the most inelastic demand for them—criminals—whereas the people most likely to comply with gun-control laws don't value guns in the first place. 12

Do Guns Drive Up Crime Rates?

Which premise is true—that guns increase crime or that the fear of crime causes people to obtain guns? Most of the country's major newspapers apparently take this problem to have been solved by an article published by Arthur Kellermann and several associates in the October 7, 1993, *New England Journal of Medicine*. Kellermann is an emergency-room physician who has published a number of influential papers that he believes discredit the thesis that private ownership of firearms is a useful means of self-protection. (An indication of his wide influence is that within two months the study received almost 100 mentions in publications and broadcast transcripts indexed in the Nexis data base.) For this study Kellermann and his associates identified fifteen behavioral and fifteen environmental variables that applied to a 388-member set of homicide victims, found a "matching" control group of 388 non-homicide victims, and then ascertained how the two groups differed in gun ownership. In interviews Kellermann made clear his belief that owning a handgun markedly increases a person's risk of being murdered. 13

But the study does not prove that point at all. Indeed, as Kellermann explicitly conceded in the text of the article, the causal arrow may very well point in the other direction: the threat of being killed may make people more likely to arm 14 themselves. Many people at risk of being killed, especially people involved in the drug trade or other illegal ventures, might well rationally buy a gun as a precaution, and be willing to pay a price driven up by gun-control laws. Crime, after all, is a dangerous business. Peter Reuter and Mark Kleiman, drug-policy researchers, calculated in 1987 that the average crack dealer's risk of being killed was far greater than his risk of being sent to prison. (Their data cannot, however, support the implication that ownership of a firearm causes or exacerbates the risk of being killed.)

15   Defending the validity of his work, Kellermann has emphasized that the link between lung cancer and smoking was initially established by studies methodologically no different from his. Gary Kleck, a criminology professor at Florida State University, has pointed out the flaw in this comparison. No one ever thought that lung cancer causes smoking, so when the association between the two was established the direction of the causal arrow was not in doubt. Kleck wrote that it is as though Kellermann, trying to discover how diabetics differ from other people, found that they are much more likely to possess insulin than nondiabetics, and concluded that insulin is a risk factor for diabetes.

16   *The New York Times,* the *Los Angeles Times, The Washington Post, The Boston Globe,* and the *Chicago Tribune* all gave prominent coverage to Kellermann's study as soon as it appeared, but none saw fit to discuss the study's limitations. A few, in order to introduce a hint of balance, mentioned that the NRA, or some member of its staff, disagreed with the study. But readers had no way of knowing that Kellermann himself had registered a disclaimer in his text. "It is possible," he conceded, "that reverse causation accounted for some of the association we observed between gun ownership and homicide." Indeed, the point is stronger than that: "reverse causation" may account for *most* of the association between gun ownership and homicide. Kellermann's data simply do not allow one to draw any conclusion.

17   If firearms increased violence and crime, then rates of spousal homicide would have skyrocketed, because the stock of privately owned handguns has increased rapidly since the mid-1960s. But according to an authoritative study of spousal homicide in the *American Journal of Public Health,* by James Mercy and Linda Saltzman, rates of spousal homicide in the years 1976 to 1985 fell. If firearms increased violence and crime, the crime rate should have increased throughout the 1980s, while the national stock of privately owned handguns increased by more than a million units in every year of the decade. It did not. Nor should the rates of violence and crime

in Switzerland, New Zealand, and Israel be as low as they are, since the number of firearms per civilian household is comparable to that in the United States. Conversely, gun-controlled Mexico and South Africa should be islands of peace instead of having murder rates more than twice as high as those here. The determinants of crime and law-abidingness are, of course, complex matters, which are not fully understood and certainly not explicable in terms of a country's laws. But gun-control enthusiasts, who have made capital out of the low murder rate in England, which is largely disarmed, simply ignore the counterexamples that don't fit their theory.

If firearms increased violence and crime, Florida's murder   18
rate should not have been falling since the introduction, seven years ago, of a law that makes it easier for ordinary citizens to get permits to carry concealed handguns. Yet the murder rate has remained the same or fallen every year since the law was enacted, and it is now lower than the national murder rate (which has been rising). As of last November 183,561 permits had been issued, and only seventeen of the permits had been revoked because the holder was involved in a firearms offense. It would be precipitate to claim that the new law has "caused" the murder rate to subside. Yet here is a situation that doesn't fit the hypothesis that weapons increase violence.

If firearms increased violence and crime, programs of in-   19
duced scarcity would suppress violence and crime. But—another anomaly—they don't. Why not? A theorem, which we could call the futility theorem, explains why gun-control laws must either be ineffectual or in the long term actually provoke more violence and crime. Any theorem depends on both observable fact and assumption. An assumption that can be made with confidence is that the higher the number of victims a criminal assumes to be armed, the higher will be the risk—the price—of assaulting them. By definition, gun-control laws should make weapons scarcer and thus more expensive. By our prior reasoning about demand among various types of consumers, after the laws are enacted criminals should be better armed, compared with noncriminals, than they were before. Of course, plenty of noncriminals will remain armed. But even if many noncriminals will pay as high a price as criminals will to obtain firearms, a larger number will not.

Criminals will thus still take the same gamble they already   20
take in assaulting a victim who might or might not be armed. But they may appreciate that the laws have given them a freer field, and that crime still pays—pays even better, in fact, than before. What will happen to the rate of violence? Only a relatively few gun-mediated transactions—currently, five percent

of armed robberies committed with firearms—result in someone's actually being shot (the statistics are not broken down into encounters between armed assailants and unarmed victims, and encounters in which both parties are armed). It seems reasonable to fear that if the number of such transactions were to increase because criminals thought they faced fewer deterrents, there would be a corresponding increase in shootings. Conversely, if gun-mediated transactions declined— if criminals initiated fewer of them because they feared encountering an armed victim or an armed good Samaritan—the number of shootings would go down. The magnitude of these effects is, admittedly, uncertain. Yet it is hard to doubt the general tendency of a change in the law that imposes legal burdens on buying guns. The futility theorem suggests that gun-control laws, if effective at all, would unfavorably affect the rate of violent crime.

21   The futility theorem provides a lens through which to see much of the debate. It is undeniable that gun-control laws work—to an extent. Consider, for example, California's background-check law, which in the past two years has prevented about 12,000 people with a criminal record or a history of mental illness or drug abuse from buying handguns. In the same period Illinois's background-check law prevented the delivery of firearms to more than 2,000 people. Surely some of these people simply turned to an illegal market, but just as surely not all of them did. The laws of large numbers allow us to say that among the foiled thousands, some potential killers were prevented from getting a gun. We do not know whether the number is large or small but it is implausible to think it is zero. And, as gun-control proponents are inclined to say, "If only one life is saved . . ."

22   The hypothesis that firearms increase violence does predict that if we can slow down the diffusion of guns, there will be less violence; one life, or more, *will* be saved. But the futility theorem asks that we look not simply at the gross number of bad actors prevented from getting guns but at the effect the law has on *all* the people who want to buy a gun. Suppose we succeed in piling tax burdens on the acquisition of firearms. We can safely assume that a number of people who might use guns to kill will be sufficiently discouraged not to buy them. But we cannot assume this about people who feel that they must have guns in order to survive financially and physically. A few lives might indeed be saved. But the overall rate of violent crime might not go down at all. And if guns are owned predominantly by people who have good reason to think they will use them, the rate might even go up.

Are there empirical studies that can serve to help us choose   23
between the futility theorem and the hypothesis that guns increase violence? Unfortunately, no: the best studies of the effects of gun-control laws are quite inconclusive. Our statistical
tools are too weak to allow us to identify an effect clearly
enough to persuade an open-minded skeptic. But it is precisely
when we are dealing with undetectable statistical effects that
we have to be certain we are using the best models available of
human behavior.

Sealing the Border

Handguns are not legally for sale in the city of Chicago, and   24
have not been since April of 1982. Rifles, shotguns, and ammunition are available, but only to people who possess an Illinois
Firearm Owner's Identification card. It takes up to a month to
get this card, which involves a background check. Even if one
has a FOID card there is a waiting period for the delivery of a
gun. In few places in America is it as difficult to get a firearm
legally as in the city of Chicago.

Yet there are hundreds of thousands of unregistered guns in   25
the city, and new ones arriving all the time. It is not difficult to
get handguns—even legally. Chicago residents with FOID cards
merely go to gun shops in the suburbs. Trying to establish a
city as an island of prohibition in a sea of legal firearms seems
an impossible project.

Is a state large enough to be an effective island, then?   26
Suppose Illinois adopted Chicago's handgun ban. Same problem again. Some people could just get guns elsewhere: Indiana
actually borders the city, and Wisconsin is only forty miles away.
Though federal law prohibits the sale of handguns in one state
to residents of another, thousands of Chicagoans with summer
homes in other states could buy handguns there. And, of course,
a black market would serve the needs of other customers.

When would the island be large enough to sustain a   27
weapons-free environment? In the United States people and
cargoes move across state lines without supervision or hindrance. Local shortages of goods are always transient, no matter whether the shortage is induced by natural disasters, pro-
hibitory laws, or something else.

Even if many states outlawed sales of handguns, then, they   28
would continue to be available, albeit at a somewhat higher
price, reflecting the increased legal risk of selling them. Mindful
of the way markets work to undermine their efforts, gun-
control proponents press for federal regulation of firearms,

because they believe that only Congress wields the authority to frustrate the interstate movement of firearms.

29   Why, though, would one think that federal policing of illegal firearms would be better than local policing? The logic of that argument is far from clear. Cities, after all, are comparatively small places. Washington, D.C., for example, has an area of less than 45,000 acres. Yet local officers have had little luck repressing the illegal firearms trade there. Why should federal officers do any better watching the United States' 12,000 miles of coastline and millions of square miles of interior? Criminals should be able to frustrate federal police forces just as well as they can local ones. Ten years of increasingly stringent federal efforts to abate cocaine trafficking, for example, have not succeeded in raising the street price of the drug.

30   Consider the most drastic proposal currently in play, that of Senator John Chafee, of Rhode Island, who would ban the manufacture, sale, and home possession of handguns within the United States. This proposal goes far beyond even the Chicago law, because existing weapons would have to be surrendered. Handguns would become contraband, and selling counterfeit, stolen, and contraband goods is big business in the United States. The objective of law enforcement is to raise the costs of engaging in crime and so force criminals to take expensive precautions against becoming entangled with the legal system. Crimes of a given type will, in theory, decline as soon as the direct and indirect costs of engaging in them rise to the point at which criminals seek more profitable opportunities in other (not necessarily legal) lines of work.

31   In firearms regulation, translating theory into practice will continue to be difficult, at least if the objective is to lessen the practical availability of firearms to people who might abuse them. On the demand side, for defending oneself against predation there is no substitute for a firearm. Criminals, at least, can switch to varieties of law-breaking in which a gun confers little or no advantage (burglary, smash-and-grab), but people who are afraid of confrontations with criminals, whether rationally or (as an accountant might reckon it) irrationally, will be very highly motivated to acquire firearms. Long after the marijuana and cocaine wars of this century have been forgotten, people's demand for personal security and for the tools they believe provide it will remain strong.

32   On the supply side, firearms transactions can be consummated behind closed doors. Firearms buyers, unlike those who use drugs, pornography, or prostitution, need not recurrently expose themselves to legal jeopardy. One trip to the marketplace is enough to arm oneself for life. This could justify a con-

sumer's taking even greater precautions to avoid apprehension, which would translate into even steeper enforcement costs for the police.

Don Kates Jr., a San Francisco lawyer and a much-published 33 student of this problem, has pointed out that during the wars in Southeast and Southwest Asia local artisans were able to produce, from scratch, serviceable pot-metal counterfeits of AK-47 infantry rifles and similar weapons in makeshift backyard foundries. Although inferior weapons cannot discharge thousands of rounds without misfiring, they are more than deadly enough for light to medium service, especially by criminals and people defending themselves and their property, who ordinarily use firearms by threatening with them, not by firing them. And the skills necessary to make them are certainly as widespread in America as in the villages of Pakistan or Vietnam. Effective policing of such a cottage industry is unthinkable. Indeed, as Charles Chandler has pointed out, crude but effective firearms have been manufactured in prisons—highly supervised environments, compared with the outside world.

Seeing that local firearms restrictions are easily defeated, 34 gun-control proponents have latched onto national controls as a way of finally making gun control something more than a gesture. But the same forces that have defeated local regulation will defeat further national regulation. Imposing higher costs on weapons ownership will, of course, slow down the weapons trade to some extent. But planning to slow it down in such a way as to drive down crime and violence, or to prevent motivated purchasers from finding ample supplies of guns and ammunition, is an escape from reality. And like many another such, it entails a morning after.

Administering Prohibition

Assume for the sake of argument that to a reasonable degree of 35 criminological certainty, guns are every bit the public-health hazard they are said to be. It follows, and many journalists and a few public officials have already said, that we ought to treat guns the same way we do smallpox viruses or other critical vectors of morbidity and mortality—namely, isolate them from potential hosts and destroy them as speedily as possible. Clearly, firearms have at least one characteristic that distinguishes them from smallpox viruses: nobody wants to keep smallpox viruses in the nightstand drawer. Amazingly enough, gun-control literature seems never to have explored the problem of getting weapons away from people who very much want to keep them in the nightstand drawer.

36   Our existing gun-control laws are not uniformly permissive and, indeed, in certain places are tough even by international standards. Advocacy groups seldom stress the considerable differences among American jurisdictions, and media reports regularly assert that firearms are readily available to anybody anywhere in the country. This is not the case. For example, handgun restrictions in Chicago and the District of Columbia are much less flexible than the ones in the United Kingdom. Several hundred thousand British subjects may legally buy and possess sidearms, and anyone who joins a target-shooting club is eligible to do so. But in Chicago and the District of Columbia, excepting peace officers and the like, only grandfathered registrants may legally possess handguns. Of course, tens or hundreds of thousands of people in both those cities—nobody can be sure how many—do in fact possess them illegally.

37   Although there is, undoubtedly, illegal handgun ownership in the United Kingdom, especially in Northern Ireland (where considerations of personal security and public safety are decidedly unlike those elsewhere in the British Isles), it is probable that Americans and Britons differ in their disposition to obey gun-control laws: there is reputed to be a marked national disparity in compliance behavior. This difference, if it exists, may have something to do with the comparatively marginal value of firearms to British consumers. Even before it had strict firearms regulation, Britain had very low rates of crimes involving guns; British criminals, unlike their American counterparts, prefer burglary (a crime of stealth) to robbery (a crime of intimidation).

38   Unless people are prepared to surrender their guns voluntarily, how can the U.S. government confiscate an appreciable fraction of our country's nearly 200 million privately owned firearms? We know that it is possible to set up weapons-free zones in certain locations—commercial airports and many courthouses and, lately, some troubled big-city high schools and housing projects. The sacrifices of privacy and convenience, and the costs of paying guards, have been thought worth the (perceived) gain in security. No doubt it would be possible, though it would probably not be easy, to make weapons-free zones of shopping centers, department stores, movie theaters, ball parks. But it is not obvious how one would cordon off the whole of an open society.

39   Voluntary programs have been ineffectual. From time to time community-action groups or police departments have sponsored "turn in your gun" days, which are nearly always disappointing. Sometimes the government offers to buy guns

at some price. This approach has been endorsed by Senator Chafee and the *Los Angeles Times*. Jonathan Alter, of *Newsweek,* has suggested a variation on this theme: youngsters could exchange their guns for a handshake with Michael Jordan or some other sports hero. If the price offered exceeds that at which a gun can be bought on the street, one can expect to see plans of this kind yield some sort of harvest—as indeed they have. But it is implausible that these schemes will actually result in a less-dangerous population. Government programs to buy up surplus cheese cause more cheese to be produced without affecting the availability of cheese to people who want to buy it. So it is with guns.

One could extend the concept of intermittent roadblocks of the sort approved by the Supreme Court for discouraging drunk driving. Metal detectors could be positioned on every street corner, or ambulatory metal-detector squads could check people randomly, or hidden magnetometers could be installed around towns, to detect concealed weapons. As for firearms kept in homes (about half of American households), warrant-less searches might be rationalized on the well-established theory that probable cause is not required when authorities are trying to correct dangers to public safety rather than searching for evidence of a crime.   40

In a recent "town hall" meeting in California, President Bill Clinton used the word "sweeps," which he did not define, to describe how he would confiscate firearms if it were up to him. During the past few years the Chicago Housing Authority chairman, Vincent Lane, has ordered "sweeps" of several gang-ridden public-housing projects, meaning warrantless searches of people's homes by uniformed police officers looking for contraband. Lane's ostensible premise was that possession of firearms by tenants constituted a lease violation that, as a conscientious landlord, he was obliged to do something about. The same logic could justify any administrative search. City health inspectors in Chicago were recently authorized to conduct warrantless searches for lead hazards in residential paint. Why not lead hazards in residential closets and nightstands? Someone has probably already thought of it.   41

Ignoring the Ultimate Sources of Crime and Violence

The American experience with prohibition has been that black marketeers—often professional criminals—move in to profit when legal markets are closed down or disturbed. In order to combat them, new laws and law-enforcement techniques are   42 developed, which are circumvented almost as soon as they are put in place. New and yet more stringent laws are enacted, and greater sacrifices of civil liberties and privacy demanded and submitted to. But in this case the problem, crime and violence, will not go away, because guns and ammunition (which, of course, won't go away either) do not cause it. One cannot expect people to quit seeking new weapons as long as the tactical advantages of weapons are seen to outweigh the costs imposed by prohibition. Nor can one expect large numbers of people to surrender firearms they already own. The only way to make people give up their guns is to create a world in which guns are perceived as having little value. This world will come into being when criminals choose not to use guns because the penalties for being caught with them are too great, and when ordinary citizens don't think they need firearms because they aren't afraid of criminals anymore.

43   Neither of these eventualities seems very likely without substantial departures in law-enforcement policy. Politicians' nostrums—increasing the punishment for crime, slapping a few more death-penalty provisions into the code—are taken seriously by few students of the crime problem. The existing penalties for predatory crimes are quite severe enough. The problem is that they are rarely meted out in the real world. The penalties formally published by the code are in practice steeply discounted, and criminals recognize that the judicial and penal systems cannot function without bargaining in the vast majority of cases.

44   This problem is not obviously one that legislation could solve. Constitutional ideas about due process of law make the imposition of punishments extraordinarily expensive and difficult. Like the tax laws, the criminal laws are basically voluntary affairs. Our system isn't geared to a world of wholesale disobedience. Recalibrating the system simply by increasing its overall harshness would probably offend and then shock the public long before any of its benefits were felt.

45   To illustrate, consider the prospect of getting serious about carrying out the death penalty. In recent years executions have been running at one or two dozen a year. As the late Supreme Court Justice Potter Stewart observed, those selected to die constitute a "capriciously selected random handful" taken from a much larger number of men and women who, just as deserving of death, receive prison sentences. It is not easy to be exact about that much larger number. But as an educated guess, taking into account only the most serious murders—the ones that were either premeditated or committed in the course of a dangerous felony—there are perhaps 5,000 prisoners a

year who could plausibly be executed in the United States: say, 100,000 executions in the next twenty years. It is hard to think that the death penalty, if imposed on this scale, would not noticeably change the behavior of potential criminals. But what else in national life or citizens' character would have to change in order to make that many executions acceptable? Since 1930 executions in the United States have never exceeded 200 a year. At any such modest rate of imposition, rational criminals should consider the prospect of receiving the death penalty effectively nil. On the best current evidence, indeed, they do. Documentation of the deterrent effect of the death penalty, as compared with that of long prison sentences, has been notoriously hard to produce.

The problem is not simply that criminals pay little attention 46 to the punishments in the books. Nor is it even that they also know that for the majority of crimes, their chances of being arrested are small. The most important reason for criminal behavior is this: the income that offenders can earn in the world of crime, as compared with the world of work, all too often makes crime appear to be the better choice.

Thus the crime bill that Bill Clinton introduced last year, 47 which provides for more prisons and police officers, should be of only very limited help. More prisons means that fewer violent offenders will have to be released early in order to make space for new arrivals; perhaps fewer plea bargains will have to be struck—all to the good. Yet a moment's reflection should make clear that one more criminal locked up does not necessarily mean one less criminal on the street. The situation is very like one that conservationists and hunters have always understood. Populations of game animals readily recover from hunting seasons but not from loss of habitat. Mean streets, when there are few legitimate entry-level opportunities for young men, are a criminal habitat so to speak, in the social ecology of modern American cities. Cull however much one will, the habitat will be reoccupied promptly after its previous occupant is sent away. So social science has found.

Similarly, whereas increasing the number of police officers 48 cannot hurt, and may well increase people's subjective feelings of security, there is little evidence to suggest that doing so will diminish the rate of crime. Police forces are basically reactive institutions. At any realistically sustainable level of staffing they must remain so. Suppose 100,000 officers were added to police rosters nationwide, as proposed in the current crime bill. This would amount to an overall personnel increase of about 18 percent, which would be parceled out according to the iron laws of democratic politics—distributed throughout states and congressional districts—rather than being sent to the areas that most need relief. Such an increase, though unprecedented in magnitude, is far short of what would be needed to pacify some of our country's worst urban precincts.

49   There is a challenge here that is quite beyond being met with tough talk. Most public officials can see the mismatch between their tax base and the social entropies they are being asked to repair. There simply isn't enough money; existing public resources, as they are now employed, cannot possibly solve the crime problem. But mayors and senators and police chiefs must not say so out loud: too-disquieting implications would follow. For if the authorities are incapable of restoring public safety and personal security under the existing ground rules, then obviously the ground rules must change, to give private initiative greater scope. Self-help is the last refuge of nonscoundrels.

50   Communities must, in short, organize more effectively to protect themselves against predators. No doubt this means encouraging properly qualified private citizens to possess and carry firearms legally. It is not morally tenable—nor, for that matter, is it even practical—to insist that police officers, few of whom are at a risk remotely as great as are the residents of many city neighborhoods, retain a monopoly on legal firearms. It is needless to fear giving honest men and women the training and equipment to make it possible for them to take back their own streets.

51   Over the long run, however, there is no substitute for addressing the root causes of crime—bad education and lack of job opportunities and the disintegration of families. Root causes are much out of fashion nowadays as explanations of criminal behavior, but fashionable or not, they are fundamental. *The root cause of crime is that for certain people, predation is a rational occupational choice.* Conventional crime-control measures, which by stiffening punishments or raising the probability of arrest aim to make crime pay less, cannot consistently affect the behavior of people who believe that their alternatives to crime will pay virtually nothing. Young men who did not learn basic literacy and numeracy skills before dropping out of their wretched public schools may not have been worth hiring at the minimum wage set by George Bush, let alone at the higher, indexed minimum wage that has recently been under discussion by the Clinton Administration. Most independent studies of the effects of raising minimum wages show a similar pattern of excluding the most vulnerable. This displacement, in turn, makes young men free, in the nihilistic, nothing-to-lose sense, to dedicate their lives to crime. Their legitimate opportunities, always precarious in a society where

race and class still matter, often diminish to the point of being for all intents and purposes absent.

Unfortunately, many progressive policies work out in the same way as increases in the minimum wage—as taxes on employment. One example is the Administration's pending proposal to make employer-paid health insurance mandatory and universal. Whatever the undoubted benefits of the plan, a payroll tax is needed to make it work. Another example: in recent years the use of the "wrongful discharge" tort and other legal innovations has swept through the courts of more than half the states, bringing to an end the era of "employment at will," when employees (other than civil servants) without formal contracts—more than three quarters of the work force—could be fired for good reason, bad reason, or no reason at all. Most commentators celebrated the loss of the at-will rule. How could one object to a new legal tenet that prohibited only arbitrary and oppressive behavior by employers? 52

But the costs of the rule are not negligible, only hidden. At-will employment meant that companies could get out of the relationship as easily as employees could. In a world where dismissals are expensive rather than cheap, and involve lawyers and the threat of lawsuits, rational employers must become more fastidious about whom they hire. By raising the costs of ending the relationship, one automatically raises the threshold of entry. The burdens of the rule fall unequally. Worst hit are entry-level applicants who have little or no employment history to show that they would be worth their pay. 53

Many other tax or regulatory schemes, in the words of Professor Walter Williams, of George Mason University, amount to sawing off the bottom rungs of the ladder of economic opportunity. By suppressing job creation and further diminishing legal employment opportunities for young men on the margin of the work force, such schemes amount to an indirect but unequivocal subsidy to crime. 54

The solution to the problem of crime lies in improving the chances of young men. Easier said than done, to be sure. No one has yet proposed a convincing program for checking all the dislocating forces that government assistance can set in motion. One relatively straightforward change would be reform of the educational system. Nothing guarantees prudent behavior like a sense of the future, and with average skills in reading, writing, and math, young people can realistically look forward to constructive employment and the straight life that steady work makes possible. 55

But firearms are nowhere near the root of the problem of violence. As long as people come in unlike sizes, shapes, ages, 56 and temperaments, as long as they diverge in their taste for risk and their willingness and capacity to prey on other people or to defend themselves from predation, and above all as long as some people have little or nothing to lose by spending their lives in crime, dispositions to violence will persist.

57   This is what makes the case for the right to bear arms, not the Second Amendment. It is foolish to let anything ride on hopes for effective gun control. As long as crime pays as well as it does, we will have plenty of it, and honest folk must choose between being victims and defending themselves.

———————■———————

George Orwell

A HANGING

Born Eric Arthur Blair in India in 1903, educated in England, and a member of the Imperial Police in Burma for five years, George Orwell was England's most prominent political writer in the decade before his death in 1950. A socialist but no communist, he wrote numerous books of fiction and nonfiction, but he is best remembered for Animal Farm *(1945) and* 1984 *(1948)—novels that contributed to our culture terms such as* doublespeak *and* Big Brother. *His fictional description of "A Hanging" appeared in* Shooting an Elephant and Other Essays *(1950); it was first published in 1931.*

It was in Burma, a sodden morning of the rains. A sickly light, like yellow tinfoil, was slanting over the high walls into the jail yard. We were waiting outside the condemned cells, a row of sheds fronted with double bars, like small animal cages. Each cell measured about ten feet by ten and was quite bare within except for a plank bed and a pot for drinking water. In some of them brown, silent men were squatting at the inner bars, with their blankets draped round them. These were the condemned men, due to be hanged within the next week or two.

One prisoner had been brought out of his cell. He was a Hindu, a puny wisp of a man, with a shaven head and vague liquid eyes. He had a thick, sprouting mustache, absurdly too big for his body, rather like the mustache of a comic man on the films. Six tall Indian warders were guarding him and getting him ready for the gallows. Two of them stood by with rifles and fixed bayonets, while the others handcuffed him, passed a chain through his handcuffs and fixed it to their belts, and lashed his arms tight to his sides. They crowded very close

1

2

about him, with their hands always on him in a careful, caress-
ing grip, as though all the while feeling him to make sure he
was there. It was like men handling a fish which is still alive
and may jump back into the water. But he stood quite unresist-
ing, yielding his arms limply to the ropes, as though he hardly
noticed what was happening.

3   Eight o'clock struck and a bugle call, desolately thin in the
wet air, floated from the distant barracks. The superintendent
of the jail, who was standing apart from the rest of us, moodily
prodding the gravel with his stick, raised his head at the sound.
He was an army doctor, with a gray toothbrush mustache and
a gruff voice. "For God's sake, hurry up, Francis," he said irrita-
bly. "The man ought to have been dead by this time. Aren't you
ready yet?"

4   Francis, the head jailer, a fat Dravidian in a white drill suit
and gold spectacles, waved his black hand. "Yes sir, yes sir," he
bubbled. "All iss satisfactorily prepared. The hangman iss waiting. We shall proceed."

5   "Well, quick march, then. The prisoners can't get their breakfast till this job's over."

6   We set out for the gallows. Two warders marched on either
side of the prisoner, with their rifles at the slope; two others
marched close against him, gripping him by arm and shoulder,
as though at once pushing and supporting him. The rest of us,
magistrates and the like, followed behind. Suddenly, when we
had gone ten yards, the procession stopped short without any
order or warning. A dreadful thing had happened—a dog,
come goodness knows whence, had appeared in the yard. It
came bounding among us with a loud volley of barks and leapt
round us wagging its whole body, wild with glee at finding so
many human beings together. It was a large woolly dog, half
Airedale, half pariah. For a moment it pranced around us, and
then, before anyone could stop it, it had made a dash for the
prisoner, and jumping up tried to lick his face. Everybody
stood aghast, too taken aback even to grab the dog.

7   "Who let that bloody brute in here?" said the superintendent
angrily. "Catch it, someone!"

8   A warder detached from the escort charged clumsily after
the dog, but it danced and gamboled just out of his reach, taking everything as part of the game. A young Eurasian jailer
picked up a handful of gravel and tried to stone the dog away,
but it dodged the stones and came after us again. Its yaps
echoed from the jail walls. The prisoner, in the grasp of the two
warders, looked on incuriously, as though this was another for-
mality of the hanging. It was several minutes before someone
managed to catch the dog. Then we put my handkerchief

through its collar and moved off once more, with the dog still straining and whimpering.

It was about forty yards to the gallows. I watched the bare 9 brown back of the prisoner marching in front of me. He walked clumsily with his bound arms, but quite steadily, with that bobbing gait of the Indian who never straightens his knees. At each step his muscles slid neatly into place, the lock of hair on his scalp danced up and down, his feet printed themselves on the wet gravel. And once, in spite of the men who gripped him by each shoulder, he stepped lightly aside to avoid a puddle on the path.

It is curious; but till that moment I had never realized what 10 it means to destroy a healthy, conscious man. When I saw the prisoner step aside to avoid the puddle, I saw the mystery, the unspeakable wrongness, of cutting a life short when it is in full tide. This man was not dying, he was alive just as we are alive. All the organs of his body were working—bowels digesting food, skin renewing itself, nails growing, tissues forming—all toiling away in solemn foolery. His nails would still be growing when he stood on the drop, when he was falling through the air with a tenth-of-a-second to live. His eyes saw the yellow gravel and the gray walls, and his brain still remembered, foresaw, reasoned—even about puddles. He and we were a party of men walking together, seeing, hearing, feeling, understanding the same world; and in two minutes, with a sudden snap, one of us would be gone—one mind less, one world less.

The gallows stood in a small yard, separate from the main 11 grounds of the prison, and overgrown with tall prickly weeds. It was a brick erection like three sides of a shed, with planking on top, and above that two beams and a crossbar with the rope dangling. The hangman, a gray-haired convict in the white uniform of the prison, was waiting beside his machine. He greeted us with a servile crouch as we entered. At a word from Francis the two warders, gripping the prisoner more closely than ever, half led, half pushed him to the gallows and helped him clumsily up the ladder. Then the hangman climbed up and fixed the rope round the prisoner's neck.

We stood waiting, five yards away. The warders had formed 12 in a rough circle round the gallows. And then, when the noose was fixed, the prisoner began crying out to his god. It was a high, reiterated cry of "Ram! Ram! Ram! Ram!" not urgent and fearful like a prayer or cry for help, but steady, rhythmical, almost like the tolling of a bell. The dog answered the sound with a whine. The hangman, still standing on the gallows, produced a small cotton bag like a flour bag and drew it down over the prisoner's face. But the sound, muffled by the cloth, still persisted, over and over again: "Ram! Ram! Ram! Ram! Ram!"

13   The hangman climbed down and stood ready, holding the lever. Minutes seemed to pass. The steady, muffled crying from the prisoner went on and on, "Ram! Ram! Ram!" never faltering for an instant. The superintendent, his head on his chest, was slowly poking the ground with his stick; perhaps he was counting the cries, allowing the prisoner a fixed number—fifty, perhaps, or a hundred. Everyone had changed color. The Indians had gone gray like bad coffee, and one or two of the bayonets were wavering. We looked at the lashed, hooded man on the drop, and listened to his cries—each cry another second of life; the same thought was in all our minds; oh, kill him quickly, get it over, stop that abominable noise!

14   Suddenly the superintendent made up his mind. Throwing up his head he made a swift motion with his stick. "Chalo!" he shouted almost fiercely.

15   There was a clanking noise, and then dead silence. The prisoner had vanished, and the rope was twisting on itself. I let go of the dog, and it galloped immediately to the back of the gallows; but when it got there it stopped short, barked, and then retreated into a corner of the yard, where it stood among the weeds, looking timorously out at us. We went round the gallows to inspect the prisoner's body. He was dangling with his toes pointed straight downwards, very slowly revolving, as dead as a stone.

16   The superintendent reached out with his stick and poked the bare brown body; it oscillated slightly. "*He's* all right," said the superintendent. He backed out from under the gallows, and blew out a deep breath. The moody look had gone out of his face quite suddenly. He glanced at his wristwatch. "Eight minutes past eight. Well, that's all for this morning, thank God."

17   The warders unfixed bayonets and marched away. The dog, sobered and conscious of having misbehaved itself, slipped after them. We walked out of the gallows yard, past the condemned cells with their waiting prisoners, into the big central yard of the prison. The convicts, under the command of warders armed with lathis, were already receiving their breakfast. They squatted in long rows, each man holding a tin pannikin, while two warders with buckets marched around ladling out rice; it seemed quite a homely, jolly scene, after the hanging. An enormous relief had come upon us now that the job was done. One felt an impulse to sing, to break into a run, to snigger. All at once everyone began chattering gaily.

18   The Eurasian boy walking beside me nodded towards the way we had come, with a knowing smile: "Do you know sir, our

friend (he meant the dead man) when he heard his appeal had been dismissed, he pissed on the floor of his cell. From fright. Kindly take one of my cigarettes, sir. Do you not admire my new silver case, sir? From the boxwallah, two rupees eight annas. Classy European style."

Several people laughed—at what, nobody seemed certain. 19

Francis was walking by the superintendent, talking garru- 20
lously: "Well, sir, all has passed off with the utmost satisfactoriness. It was all finished—flick! Like that. It iss not always so—oah, no! I have known cases where the doctor was obliged to go beneath the gallows and pull the prisoner's legs to ensure decease. Most disagreeable!"

"Wriggling about, eh? That's bad," said the superintendent. 21

"Ach, sir, it iss worse when they become refractory! One 22
man, I recall, clung to the bars of hiss cage when we went to take him out. You will scarcely credit, sir, that it took six warders to dislodge him, three pulling at each leg. We reasoned with him, 'My dear fellow,' we said, 'think of all the pain and trouble you are causing to us!' But no, he would not listen! Ach, he was very troublesome!"

I found that I was laughing quite loudly. Everyone was 23
laughing. Even the superintendent grinned in a tolerant way. "You'd better all come out and have a drink," he said quite genially. "I've got a bottle of whiskey in the car. We could do with it."

We went through the big double gates of the prison into the 24
road. "Pulling at his legs!" exclaimed a Burmese magistrate suddenly, and burst into a loud chuckling. We all began laughing again. At that moment Francis' anecdote seemed extraordinarily funny. We all had a drink together, native and European alike, quite amicably. The dead man was a hundred yards away.

Edward I. Koch
DEATH AND JUSTICE

Outspoken and controversial, Edward I. Koch (born 1924) served as the Democratic mayor of New York City from 1978 to 1989. He has always been eager to engage in public debate on controversial issues in his three books, in his hundreds of speeches, and in his published articles. In 1985, he contributed the following essay to The New Republic, *an influential public affairs magazine generally considered middle-of-the-road in its outlook.*

1   Last December a man named Robert Lee Willie, who had been convicted of raping and murdering an 18-year-old woman, was executed in the Louisiana state prison. In a statement issued several minutes before his death, Mr. Willie said: "Killing people is wrong. . . . It makes no difference whether it's citizens, countries, or governments. Killing is wrong." Two weeks later in South Carolina, an admitted killer named Joseph Carl Shaw was put to death for murdering two teenagers. In an appeal to the governor for clemency, Mr. Shaw wrote: "Killing is wrong when I did it. Killing is wrong when you do it. I hope you have the courage and moral strength to stop the killing."

2   It is a curiosity of modern life that we find ourselves being lectured on morality by cold-blooded killers. Mr. Willie previously had been convicted of aggravated rape, aggravated kidnapping, and the murders of a Louisiana deputy and a man from Missouri. Mr. Shaw committed another murder a week before the two for which he was executed, and admitted mutilating the body of the 14-year-old girl he killed. I can't help wondering what prompted these murderers to speak out against killing as they entered the death-house door. Did their newfound reverence for life stem from the realization that they were about to lose their own?

3   Life is indeed precious, and I believe the death penalty helps to affirm this fact. Had the death penalty been a real possibility in the minds of these murderers, they might well have stayed their hand. They might have shown moral awareness before their victims died, and not after. Consider the tragic death of Rosa Velez, who happened to be home when a man named Luis Vera burglarized her apartment in Brooklyn. "Yeah, I shot her," Vera admitted. "She knew me, and I knew I wouldn't go to the chair."

During my 22 years in public service, I have heard the pros 4
and cons of capital punishment expressed with special intensity. As a district leader, councilman, congressman, and mayor,
I have represented constituencies generally thought of as liberal. Because I support the death penalty for heinous crimes of
murder, I have sometimes been the subject of emotional and
outraged attacks by voters who find my position reprehensible
or worse. I have listened to their ideas. I have weighed their objections carefully. I still support the death penalty. The reasons
I maintain my position can be best understood by examining
the arguments most frequently heard in opposition.

1. *The death penalty is "barbaric."* Sometimes opponents of 5
capital punishment horrify with tales of lingering death on the
gallows, of faulty electric chairs, or of agony in the gas chamber. Partly in response to such protests, several states such as
North Carolina and Texas switched to execution by lethal injection. The condemned person is put to death painlessly, without ropes, voltage, bullets, or gas. Did this answer the objections of death penalty opponents? Of course not. On June 22,
1984, *The New York Times* published an editorial that sarcastically attacked the new "hygienic" method of death by injection,
and stated that "execution can never be made humane through
science." So it's not the method that really troubles opponents.
It's the death itself they consider barbaric.

Admittedly, capital punishment is not a pleasant topic. 6
However, one does not have to like the death penalty in order
to support it any more than one must like radical surgery, radiation, or chemotherapy in order to find necessary these attempts at curing cancer. Ultimately we may learn how to cure
cancer with a simple pill. Unfortunately, that day has not yet
arrived. Today we are faced with the choice of letting the cancer spread or trying to cure it with the methods available,
methods that one day will almost certainly be considered barbaric. But to give up and do nothing would be far more barbaric and would certainly delay the discovery of an eventual
cure. The analogy between cancer and murder is imperfect, because murder is not the "disease" we are trying to cure. The
disease is injustice. We may not like the death penalty, but it
must be available to punish crimes of cold-blooded murder,
cases in which any other form of punishment would be inadequate and, therefore, unjust. If we create a society in which injustice is not tolerated, incidents of murder—the most flagrant
form of injustice—will diminish.

2. *No other major democracy uses the death penalty.* No 7
other major democracy—in fact, few other countries of any

description—are plagued by a murder rate such as that in the United States. Fewer and fewer Americans can remember the days when unlocked doors were the norm and murder was a rare and terrible offense. In America the murder rate climbed 122 percent between 1963 and 1980. During that same period, the murder rate in New York City increased by almost 400 percent, and the statistics are even worse in many other cities. A study at M.I.T. showed that based on 1970 homicide rates a person who lived in a large American city ran a greater risk of being murdered than an American soldier in World War II ran of being killed in combat. It is not surprising that the laws of each country differ according to differing conditions and traditions. If other countries had our murder problem, the cry for capital punishment would be just as loud as it is here. And I daresay that any other major democracy where 75 percent of the people supported the death penalty would soon enact it into law.

8   3. *An innocent person might be executed by mistake.* Consider the work of Adam Bedau, one of the most implacable foes of capital punishment in this country. According to Mr. Bedau, it is "false sentimentality to argue that the death penalty should be abolished because of the abstract possibility that an innocent person might be executed." He cites a study of the 7,000 executions in this country from 1893 to 1971, and concludes that the record fails to show that such cases occur. The main point, however, is this. If government functioned only when the possibility of error didn't exist, government wouldn't function at all. Human life deserves special protection, and one of the best ways to guarantee that protection is to assure that convicted murderers do not kill again. Only the death penalty can accomplish this end. In a recent case in New Jersey, a man named Richard Biegenwald was freed from prison after serving 18 years formurder; since his release he has been convicted of committing four murders. A prisoner named Lemuel Smith, who, while serving four life sentences for murder (plus two life sentences for kidnapping and robbery) in New York's Green Haven Prison, lured a woman corrections officer into the chaplain's office and strangled her. He then mutilated and dismembered her body. An additional life sentence for Smith is meaningless. Because New York has no death penalty statute, Smith has effectively been given a license to kill.

9   But the problem of multiple murder is not confined to the nation's penitentiaries. In 1981, 91 police officers were killed in the line of duty in this country. Seven percent of those arrested in the cases that have been solved had a previous arrest for murder. In New York City in 1976 and 1977, 85 persons arrested for homicide had a previous arrest for murder. Six of

these individuals had two previous arrests for murder, and one had four previous murder arrests. During those two years the New York police were arresting for murder persons with a previous arrest for murder on the average of one every 8.5 days. This is not surprising when we learn that in 1975, for example, the median time served in Massachusetts for homicide was less than two-and-a-half years. In 1976 a study sponsored by the Twentieth Century Fund found that the average time served in the United States for first-degree murder is ten years. The median time served may be considerably lower.

4. *Capital punishment cheapens the value of human life.* On the contrary, it can be easily demonstrated that the death penalty strengthens the value of human life. If the penalty for rape were lowered, clearly it would signal a lessened regard for the victims' suffering, humiliation, and personal integrity. It would cheapen their horrible experience, and expose them to an increased danger of recurrence. When we lower the penalty for murder, it signals a lessened regard for the value of the victim's life. Some critics of capital punishment, such as columnist Jimmy Breslin, have suggested that a life sentence is actually a harsher penalty for murder than death. This is sophistic nonsense. A few killers may decide not to appeal a death sentence, but the overwhelming majority make every effort to stay alive. It is by exacting the highest penalty for the taking of human life that we affirm the highest value of human life.

5. *The death penalty is applied in a discriminatory manner.* This factor no longer seems to be the problem it once was. The appeals process for a condemned prisoner is lengthy and painstaking. Every effort is made to see that the verdict and sentence were fairly arrived at. However, assertions of discrimination are not an argument for ending the death penalty but for extending it. It is not justice to exclude everyone from the penalty of the law if a few are found to be so favored. Justice requires that the law be applied equally to all.

6. *Thou Shalt Not Kill.* The Bible is our greatest source of moral inspiration. Opponents of the death penalty frequently cite the sixth of the Ten Commandments in an attempt to prove that capital punishment is divinely proscribed. In the original Hebrew, however, the Sixth Commandment reads, "Thou Shalt Not Commit Murder," and the Torah specifies capital punishment for a variety of offenses. The biblical viewpoint has been upheld by philosophers throughout history. The greatest thinkers of the 19th century—Kant, Locke, Hobbes, Rousseau, Montesquieu, and Mill—agreed that natural law properly authorizes the sovereign to take life in order to vindicate justice.

Only Jeremy Bentham was ambivalent. Washington, Jefferson, and Franklin endorsed it. Abraham Lincoln authorized executions for deserters in wartime. Alexis de Tocqueville, who expressed profound respect for American institutions, believed that the death penalty was indispensable to the support of social order. The United States Constitution, widely admired as one of the seminal achievements in the history of humanity, condemns cruel and inhuman punishment, but does not condemn capital punishment.

13   7. *The death penalty is state-sanctioned murder.* This is the defense with which Messrs. Willie and Shaw hoped to soften the resolve of those who sentenced them to death. By saying in effect, "You're no better than I am," the murderer seeks to bring his accusers down to his own level. It is also a popular argument among opponents of capital punishment, but a transparently false one. Simply put, the state has rights that the private individual does not. In a democracy, those rights are given to the state by the electorate. The execution of a lawfully condemned killer is no more an act of murder than is legal imprisonment an act of kidnapping. If an individual forces a neighbor to pay him money under threat of punishment, it's called extortion. If the state does it, it's called taxation. Rights and responsibilities surrendered by the individual are what give the state its power to govern. This contract is the foundation of civilization itself.

14   Everyone wants his or her rights, and will defend them jealously. Not everyone, however, wants responsibilities, especially the painful responsibilities that come with law enforcement. Twenty-one years ago a woman named Kitty Genovese was assaulted and murdered on a street in New York. Dozens of neighbors heard her cries for help but did nothing to assist her. They didn't even call the police. In such a climate the criminal understandably grows bolder. In the presence of moral cowardice, he lectures us on our supposed failings and tries to equate his crimes with our quest for justice.

15   The death of anyone—even a convicted killer—diminishes us all. But we are diminished even more by a justice system that fails to function. It is an illusion to let ourselves believe that doing away with capital punishment removes the murderer's deed from our conscience. The rights of society are paramount. When we protect guilty lives, we give up innocent lives in exchange. When opponents of capital punishment say to the state: "I will not let you kill in my name," they are also saying to murderers: "You can kill in your *own* name as long as I have an excuse for not getting involved."

16   It is hard to imagine anything worse than being murdered while neighbors do nothing. But something worse exists. When

those same neighbors shrink back from justly punishing the murderer, the victim dies twice.

Jacob Weisberg

THIS IS YOUR DEATH

The following account appeared in The New Republic *in July 1991.* The New Republic *is a weekly magazine of opinion about various public issues; it is considered to be middle-of-the-road in its general slant on things. In what way is Weisberg's article a contribution to the national discussion on the death penalty? Is Weisberg's own position on the death penalty apparent here?*

Thanks to the decision of a California district judge last week, the American public has been spared the spectacle of criminals being executed on television. But the lawsuit, filed by KQED, the public television station in San Francisco, still served a useful function. It reminded people not only that the United States remains the only advanced democracy that executes criminals, but that it is the only country in the world with a grotesque array of execution techniques worth televising. A century ago Americans knew full well what it meant for the state to hang someone from the end of a rope. Today, thanks to the century-long search for a more "humane" method, we know little about the range of practices that would be featured on the execution channel. 1

Of the five means of execution still extant in the United States, the oldest is hanging, which was nearly universal before 1900. The gallows was last used in Kansas in 1965 and remains an option in Delaware, Montana, and Washington State. If a hanging were ever televised, viewers would see the blindfolded prisoner standing on a trap door with a rope fastened around his neck, the knot under his left ear. So long as he is hooded, it is impossible to know for how long after the trap door opens the victim suffers, or at what point he loses consciousness. But according to Harold Hillman, a British physiologist who has studied executions, the dangling person feels cervical pain, and probably suffers from an acute headache as well, a result of the rope closing off the veins of the neck. 2

In the opinion of Dr. Cornelius Rosse, the chairman of the Department of Anatomy at the University of Washington School of Medicine, the belief that fracture of the spinal cord 3 causes instantaneous death is wrong in all but a small fraction of cases. The actual cause of death is strangulation or suffocation. In medical terms, the weight of the prisoner's body causes tearing of the cervical muscles, skin, and blood vessels. The upper cervical vertebrae are dislocated, and the spinal cord is separated from the brain, which causes death.

4   Clinton Duffy, the warden at San Quentin from 1942 to 1954, who participated in sixty hangings, described his first thus:

> The man hit bottom and I observed that he was fighting by pulling on the straps, wheezing, whistling, trying to get air, that blood was oozing through the black cap. I observed also that he urinated, defecated, and droppings fell on the floor, and the stench was terrible. I also saw witnesses pass out and have to be carried from the witness room. Some of them threw up.

It took ten minutes for the condemned man to die. When he was taken down and the cap removed, "big hunks of flesh were torn off" the side of his face where the noose had been, "his eyes were popped," and his tongue was "swollen and hanging from his mouth." His face had also turned purple. The annals of Walla Walla State Penitentiary in Washington, which was seeking to hire an executioner in 1988 when Charles Campbell obtained a stay of execution, are filled with horror stories: prisoners partially decapitated by overlong drops, or pleading with hangmen to take them up and drop them again.

5   Almost as rare as hanging—but still around—is the firing squad. Gary Gilmore, who was shot in Utah in 1977, was the last to die by this method, which remains an option only there and in Idaho. Gilmore was bound to a chair with leather straps across his waist and head, and in front of an oval-shaped canvas wall. A black hood was pulled over his head. A doctor then located his heart with a stethoscope and pinned a circular white cloth target over it. Five shooters armed with .30-caliber rifles loaded with single rounds (one of them blank to spare the conscience of the executioners) stood in an enclosure twenty feet away. Each man aimed his rifle through a slot in the canvas and fired.

6   Though shooting through the head at close range causes nearly instantaneous death, a prisoner subjected to a firing squad dies as a result of blood loss caused by rupture of the heart or a large blood vessel, or tearing of the lungs. The person shot loses consciousness when shock causes a fall in the support of blood to the brain. If the shooters miss, by accident

or intention, the prisoner bleeds to death slowly, as Elisio J. Mares did in Utah in 1951. It took Gilmore two minutes to die.

It was to mitigate the barbarism of these primitive methods 7 that New York introduced the electric chair in 1890 as a humane alternative. Eighty-three people have been electrocuted since the Supreme Court reinstated capital punishment in 1976, making the method the most common one now in use. It is probably the most gruesome to watch. After being led into the death chamber, the prisoner is strapped to the chair with belts that cross his chest, groin, legs, and arms. Two copper electrodes are then attached: one to his leg, a patch of which will have been shaved bare to reduce resistance to electricity, and another to his shaved head. The electrodes are either soaked in brine or treated with gel (Electro-Creme) to increase conductivity and reduce burning. The prisoner will also be wearing a diaper.

The executioner gives a first jolt of between 500 and 2,000 8 volts, which lasts for thirty seconds. Smoke usually comes out of the prisoner's leg and head. A doctor then examines him. If he's not dead, another jolt is applied. A third and fourth are given if needed to finish the job. It took five jolts to kill Ethel Rosenberg. In the grisly description of Justice Brennan:

> . . . the prisoner's eyeballs sometimes pop out and rest on [his] cheeks. The prisoner often defecates, urinates, and vomits blood and drool. The body turns bright red as its temperature rises, and the prisoner's flesh swells and his skin stretches to the point of breaking. Sometimes the prisoner catches on fire, particularly if [he] perspires excessively. Witnesses hear a loud and sustained sound like bacon frying, and the sickly sweet smell of burning flesh permeates the chamber.

An electrocuted corpse is hot enough to blister if touched. Thus autopsy must be delayed while internal organs cool. According to Robert H. Kirschner, the deputy chief medical examiner of Cook County, Illinois, "The brain appears cooked in most cases."

There is some debate about what the electrocuted prisoner 9 experiences before he dies, but most doctors I spoke to believe that he feels himself being burned to death and suffocating, since the shock causes respiratory paralysis as well as cardiac arrest. According to Hillman, "It must feel very similar to the medieval trial by ordeal of being dropped in boiling oil." Because the energy of the shock paralyzes the prisoner's muscles, he cannot cry out. "My mouth tasted like cold peanut butter. I felt a burning in my head and my left leg, and I jumped against the straps," Willie Francis, a 17-year-old who survived an attempted execution in 1946, is reported to have said. Francis was successfully executed a year later.

10   Though all methods of execution can be botched, electrocutions go wrong frequently and dramatically, in part because the equipment is old and hard to repair. At least five have gone awry since 1983. If the electrical current is too weak, the prisoner roasts to death slowly. An instance of this was the May 4, 1990, killing of Jesse Joseph Tafero in Florida. According to witnesses, when the executioner flipped the switch, flames and smoke came out of Tafero's head, which was covered by a mask and cap. Twelve-inch blue and orange flames sprouted from both sides of the mask. The power was stopped, and Tafero took several deep breaths. The superintendent ordered the executioner to halt the current, then try it again. And again.

11   The affidavits presented for an internal inquiry into what went wrong describe the bureaucratization of the death penalty brilliantly. In the words of one of the officials:

> . . . while working in the Death Chamber, proceeding with the execution as scheduled, I received an indication from Mr. Barton to close my electric breaker. I then told the executioner to close his electric breaker. When the executioner completed the circuit, I noticed unusual fire and smoke coming from the inmate's headpiece. After several seconds, I received an indication to open the electrical breaker to stop the electrical flow. At this time, I noticed the body move as if to be gasping for air. After several seconds, I received the indication to close the breaker the second time, which I did. Again, I noticed the unusual fire and smoke coming from the headpiece. After several seconds, I received the third indication to close the breaker, and again, the fire and smoke came from the headpiece . . .

And so on. Apparently a synthetic sponge, soaked in brine, had been substituted for the natural one applied to Tafero's head. This reduced the flow of electricity to as little as one hundred volts, and ended up torturing the prisoner to death. According to the state prison medical director, Frank Kligo, who attended, it was "less than aesthetically attractive."

12   Advanced technology does not always make the death penalty less painful to undergo or more pleasant to watch. The gas chamber, which was invented by an army medical corps officer after World War I, was first introduced as a humane alternative to the electric chair in 1924 in Nevada. The original

idea, which proved impracticable, was to surprise the prisoner by gassing him in his cell without prior warning. Seven states, including California, still use the gas chamber. The most recent fatality was Leo Edwards, a 36-year-old who was killed in Jackson County, Mississippi, in 1989.

Had KQED won its suit, millions of viewers would have joined 13 a dozen live witnesses in seeing Robert Alton Harris, who murdered two teenage boys in San Diego in 1978, led into a green, octagonal room in the basement of San Quentin Penitentiary. Inside the chamber are two identical metal chairs with perforated seats, marked "A" and "B." The twin chairs were last used in a double execution in 1962. If Harris's execution goes ahead this year or next, two orderlies will fasten him into chair A, attaching straps across his upper and lower legs, arms, groin, and chest. They will also affix a long stethoscope to Harris's chest so that a doctor on the outside can pronounce death.

Beneath the chair is a bowl filled with sulfuric acid mixed 14 with distilled water, with a pound of sodium cyanide pellets suspended in a gauze bag just above. After the door is sealed, and when the warden gives the signal, an executioner in a separate room flicks a lever that releases the cyanide into the liquid. This causes a chemical reaction that releases hydrogen cyanide gas, which rises through the holes in the chair. Like most death row prisoners, Harris is likely to have been reduced to a state of passive acquiescence by his years on death row, and will probably follow the advice of the warden to breathe deeply as soon as he smells rotten eggs. As long as he holds his breath nothing will happen. But as soon as he inhales, according to the testimony of Duffy, the former warden, Harris will lose consciousness in a few seconds. "At first there is evidence of extreme horror, pain, and strangling. The eyes pop. The skin turns purple and the victim begins to drool. It is a horrible sight," he testified.

In medical terms, victims of cyanide gas die from hypoxia, 15 which means the cut-off of oxygen to the brain. The initial result of this is spasms, as in an epileptic seizure. Because of the straps, however, involuntary body movements are restrained. Seconds after he first inhales, Harris will feel himself unable to breathe, but will not lose consciousness immediately. "The person is unquestionably experiencing pain and extreme anxiety," according to Dr. Richard Traystman of Johns Hopkins. "The pain begins immediately and is felt in the arms, shoulders, back, and chest. The sensation is similar to the pain felt by a person during a heart attack, where essentially the heart is being deprived of oxygen." Traystman adds: "We would not use asphyxiation, by cyanide gas or by any other substance, in our laboratory to kill animals that have been used in experiments."

16 Harris will stop wriggling after ten or twelve minutes, and the doctor will pronounce him dead. An exhaust fan then sucks the poison air out of the chamber. Next the corpse is sprayed with ammonia, which neutralizes traces of the cyanide that may remain. After about half an hour, orderlies enter the chamber, wearing gas masks and rubber gloves. Their training manual advises them to ruffle the victim's hair to release any trapped cyanide gas before removing him.

17 Thanks to these grotesqueries, states are increasingly turning to lethal injection. This method was imagined for decades (by Ronald Reagan, among others, when he was governor of California in 1973), but was technically invented in 1977 by Dr. Stanley Deutsch, who at the time chaired the Anesthesiology Department at Oklahoma University Medical School. In response to a call by an Oklahoma state senator for a cheaper alternative to repairing -the state's derelict electric chair, Deutsch described a way to administer drugs through an intravenous drip so as to cause death rapidly and without pain. "Having been anesthetized on several occasions with ultra short-acting barbiturates and having administered these drugs for approximately 20 years, I can assure you that this is a rapid, pleasant way of producing unconsciousness," Deutsch wrote to state senator Bill Dawson in February 1977. The method was promptly adopted in Oklahoma, and is now either the exclusive method or an option in half of the thirty-six states with death penalty laws. It is becoming the method of choice around the country because it is easier on both the witnesses and the prisoner.

18 A recent injectee was Lawrence Lee Buxton, who was killed in Huntsville, Texas, on February 26. Buxton was strapped to a hospital gurney, built with an extension panel for his left arm. Technicians stuck a catheter needle into Buxton's arm. Long tubes connected the needle through a hole in a cement block wall to several intravenous drips. The first, which was started immediately, dispensed harmless saline solution. Then, at the warden's signal, a curtain went up, which permitted the witnesses—reporters and friends of the soon-to-be deceased—to view the scene. Unlike some prisoners, Buxton did not have a long wait before the warden received a call from the governor's office, giving the final go-ahead.

19 According to Lawrence Egbert, an anesthesiologist at the University of Texas in Dallas who has campaigned against lethal injection as a perversion of medical practice, the first drug administered was sodium thiopental, a common barbitu-

rate used as an anesthetic, which puts patients quickly to sleep. A normal dose for a long operation is 1,000 milligrams; Buxton got twice that. As soon as he lost consciousness, the executioner administered pavulon, another common muscle relaxant used in heart surgery. The dose was 100 milligrams, ten times the usual, which stops the prisoner's breathing. This would have killed him in about ten minutes; to speed the process, an equal dose of potassium chloride was subsequently administered. This is another drug commonly used in bypass surgery that relaxes the heart and stops it pumping. It works in about ten seconds. All witnesses heard was the prisoner take a deep breath, then a gurgling noise as his tongue dropped back in his mouth. Watt Espy, who has compiled a list of 17,718 executions in America, from the early period of drownings, burnings, sawings-in-half, pressings-to-death, and even the crucifixions of two mutinous Continental Army soldiers, compares lethal injection to the way a devoted owner treats "a faithful dog he's loved and cherished."

The only physical pain, if the killing is done correctly, "is the 20 pain of the initial prick of the needle," according to Traystman. There are, however, some potential hitches. Since doctors are precluded by medical ethics from participating in executions, except to pronounce death, the injections are often performed by incompetent or inexperienced technicians. If a death worker injects the drugs into muscle instead of a vein, or if the needle becomes clogged, extreme pain can result. This is what happened when James Autry was killed in 1984 in Texas. *Newsweek* reported that he "took at least ten minutes to die and throughout much of that time was conscious, moving about, and complaining of pain." Many prisoners have damaged veins from injecting drugs intravenously, and technicians sometimes struggle to find a serviceable one. When Texas executed Stephen Morin, a former heroin addict, orderlies prodded his arms with catheters for forty-one minutes. Being strapped to a table for a lengthy period while waiting to die is a form of psychological torture arguably worse than most physical kinds. This is demonstrated by the fact that mock executions, which cause no physical pain, are a common method of torture around the world. The agony comes not from the prospect of pain, but from the expectation of death.

Televised executions would mark the reversal of the process 21 described in Louis P. Masur's *Rites of Execution* and Robert Johnson's *Death Work*, whereby executions have been removed further and further from the community that compels them. Through the eighteenth century, executions were atavistic spectacles performed in full public view. In the nineteenth they were moved inside the prison yard and witnessed by only a few. In the twentieth century, executions moved deep inside the bowels of prisons, where they were performed ever more quickly and quietly to attract minimal notice. American death penalty opponents in the 1800s supported the abolition of public executions as a way-station to ending all executions. They thought that eliminating the grossest manifestations of public barbarism would inevitably lead to the end of capital punishment as an institution. The reform had the opposite effect, however. Invisible executions shocked the sensibilities of fewer people, and dampened the momentum of the reform movement.

22   Those abolitionists who now support televising executions have absorbed this historical lesson. They want to bring back the equivalent of public executions in order to shock the public into opposing all executions. They hope to accomplish with pictures what Arthur Koestler did with words in his 1955 tract *Reflections on Hanging,* the publication of which led to the abolition of the rope in Great Britain in 1969.

23   But advances in the art of killing may have deprived them of that tactic. The prospect of televised executions is likely to accelerate the trend away from grisly methods and toward ever more hermetic ways of dispatching wrongdoers. Had the KQED suit been successful, Henry Schwarzschild, a retired ACLU death penalty expert, speculates that California would have responded by quickly joining the national trend toward lethal injection.

24   Michael Kroll of the Death Penalty Information Center objects to televising executions for exactly this reason. He argues that a video camera would capture only a "very antiseptic moment at the end of a very septic process." With the advent of death by the needle, execution itself is becoming so denatured and mechanistic as to be unshocking even to most live witnesses. This throws death penalty opponents back upon a less vivid, but more compelling case: that it is punishing people with death, not the manner in which they are killed, that is the true issue here; that capital punishment is to be opposed not simply because it is cruel, but because it is wrong.

Anecdotal

words of the <u>American Medical Association</u>, "It is clear that addiction is not simply the product of a failure of individual willpower. . . . It is properly viewed as a disease, and one that physicians can help many individuals control and overcome."

The nature of addiction is very important to the argument in 3 favor of decriminalization. The sad truth is that heroin and morphine addiction is, for most users, a lifetime affliction that is impervious to any punishment that the criminal-justice system could reasonably mete out.

Given the nature of addiction—whether to narcotics or co- 4 caine—and the very large number of Americans using drugs (the National Institute on Drug Abuse estimates that one in six working Americans has a substance abuse problem), laws restricting their possession and sale have had predictable consequences—most of them bad.

Crimes Committed by Addicts

Addicts commit crimes in order to pay for their drug habits. 5 According to the Justice Department, 90 percent of those who voluntarily seek treatment are turned away. In other words, on any given day, nine out of every ten addicts have no legal way to *statistical* satisfy their addiction. And, failing to secure help, an untreated addict will commit a crime every other day to maintain his habit.

Whether one relies on studies, or on simple observation, it is 6 indisputable that drug users are committing vast amounts of crime. Baltimore, the city with which I am most familiar, is no exception. According to James A. Inciardi, of the Division of Criminal Justice at the University of Delaware, a 1983 study of addicts in Baltimore showed that ". . . there were high rates of criminality among heroin users during those periods that they were addicted and markedly lower rates during times of nonaddiction." The study also showed that addicts committed crimes on a persistent day-to-day basis and over a long period of time. And the trends are getting worse. Thus, while the total number of arrests in Baltimore remained almost unchanged between 1983 and 1987, there was an approximately 40 percent increase in the number of drug-related arrests.

On the other hand, statistics recently compiled by the 7 Maryland Drug and Alcohol Abuse Administration indicate that crime rates go down among addicts when treatment is available. Thus, for example, of the 6,910 Baltimore residents admitted to drug-abuse treatment in fiscal 1987, 4,386 or 63 percent had been arrested one or more times in the 24-month period prior to admission to treatment, whereas of the 6,698 Baltimore residents who were discharged from drug treatment in fiscal 1987, 6,152 or 91.8 percent were not arrested during the time of their treatment. These statistics tend to support the view that one way to greatly reduce drug-related crime is to assure addicts legal access to methadone or other drugs.

Overload of the Criminal-Justice System

8   We cannot prosecute our way out of the drug problem. There are several reasons for this, but the most basic reason is that the criminal-justice system cannot—without sacrificing our civil liberties—handle the sheer volume of drug-related cases.

9   Nationwide last year, over 750,000 people were arrested for violating drug laws. Most of these arrests were for possession. In Baltimore, there were 13,037 drug-related arrests in 1987. Between January 1, 1988 and July 1, 1988, there were 7,981 drug-related arrests. Those numbers are large, but they hardly reflect the annual total number of drug violations committed in Baltimore. Should we, therefore, try to arrest still more? Yes—as long as the laws are on the books. But as a practical matter, we don't have any place to put the drug offenders we are now arresting. The population in the Baltimore City Jail is currently 2,900 inmates, even though its inmate capacity is only 2,700. This shortage of prison space has led to severe overcrowding, and Baltimore is now under court order to reduce its jail population.

10   Will more prisons help? Not in any significant way. We simply cannot build enough of them to hold all of America's drug offenders—which number in the millions. And even if we could, the cost would far exceed what American taxpayers would be willing to pay.

11   Decriminalization is the single most effective step we could take to reduce prison overcrowding. And with less crowded prisons, there will be less pressure on prosecutors to plea bargain and far greater chance that non-drug criminals will go to jail—and stay in jail.

12   The unvarnished truth is that in our effort to prosecute and imprison our way out of the drug war, we have allowed the drug lords to put us exactly where they want us: wasting enormous resources—both in money and in personnel—attacking the fringes of the problem (the drug users and small-time pushers), while the heart of the problem—the traffickers and their profits—goes unsolved.

Failed Supply-Side Policies

Not only can we not prosecute our way out of our drug morass,   13
we cannot interdict our way out of it either. Lately, there have
been calls for stepped-up border patrols, increased use of the
military and greater pressure on foreign governments.

Assuming these measures would reduce the supply of illegal   14
drugs, that reduction would not alleviate the chaos in our
cities. According to statistics recently cited by the American
Medical Association, Latin American countries produced be-   *Anecdotal*
tween 162,000 and 211,400 metric tons of cocaine in 1987.
That is five times the amount needed to supply the US market.
Moreover, we are probably only interdicting 10 to 15 percent of
the cocaine entering this country. Thus, even if we quadrupled
the amount of cocaine we interdict, the world supply of cocaine would still far outstrip US demand.

If the drug laws in the US simply didn't achieve their intent,   15
perhaps there would be insufficient reason to get rid of them.
But these laws are doing more than not working—they are vio-   *logical*
lating Hippocrates' famous admonition: First, do no harm.

The legal prohibition of narcotics, cocaine and marijuana   16
demonstrably increases the price of those drugs. For example,
an importer can purchase a kilogram of heroin for $10,000. By
the time that kilogram passes through the hands of several mid-
dlemen, its street value can reach $1,000,000. Such profits can't
help but attract major criminal entrepreneurs willing to take
any risk to keep their product coming to the American market.

Victimization of Children

Perhaps the most tragic victims of our drug laws are children.   17
Many, for example, have been killed as innocent bystanders in
gun battles among traffickers. Furthermore, while it is true
that drug prohibition probably does keep some children from
experimenting with drugs, almost any child who wants drugs
can get them. Keeping drugs outlawed has not kept them out
of children's hands.

Recent statistics in both Maryland and Baltimore prove the   18
point: In a 1986–87 survey of Maryland adolescents, 13 percent
of eighth graders, 18.5 percent of tenth graders and 22.3 percent of twelfth graders report that they are currently using
drugs. In Baltimore, the percentages are 16.6, 16.5 and 20.3,   *statistical*
respectively. It should be noted that these numbers exclude alcohol and tobacco, and that current use means at least once a

month. It should also be noted that these numbers show a decrease from earlier surveys in 1982 and 1984. Nevertheless, the fact remains that drugs are being widely used by students. Moreover, these numbers do not include the many young people who have left school or who failed to report their drug use.

19   A related problem is that many children, especially those living in the inner city, are frequently barraged with the message that selling drugs is an easy road to riches. In Baltimore, as in many other cities, small children are acting as lookouts and runners for drug pushers, just as they did for bootleggers during Prohibition. Decriminalization and the destruction of the black market would end this most invidious form of child labor.

20   As for education, decriminalization will not end the *Just Say No* and similar education campaigns. On the contrary, more money will be available for such programs. Decriminalization will, however, end the competing message of "easy money" that the drug dealers use to entice children. Furthermore, decriminalization will free up valuable criminal-justice resources that can be used to find, prosecute and punish those who sell drugs to children.

21   This said, if there has been one problem with the current drug-reform debate, it has been the tendency to focus on narrow problems and narrow solutions. That is, we talk about the number of people arrested, the number of tons of drugs entering our ports, the number of available treatment centers, and so on, but there is a bigger picture out there. We, as a nation, have not done nearly enough to battle the social and economic problems that make drug abuse an easy escape for the despairing, and drug trafficking an easy answer to a lack of education and joblessness.

22   Adolescents who take drugs are making a not-so-subtle statement about their confidence in the future. Children without hope are children who will take drugs. We need to give these children more than simple slogans. We need to give them a brighter tomorrow, a sense of purpose, a chance at economic opportunity. It is on that battlefield that the real war against drugs must be fought.

Spread of AIDS

23   The 1980s have brought another major public health problem that is being made still worse because of our drug laws: AIDS. Contaminated intravenous drug needles are now the principal means of transmission for the HIV infection. The users of drug needles infect not only those with whom they share needles, but also their sex partners and their unborn children.

One way to effectively slow this means of transmission   24
would be to allow addicts to exchange their dirty needles for
clean ones. However, in a political climate where all illicit drug
use is condemned, and where possession of a syringe can be a
criminal offense, few jurisdictions have been willing to initiate
a needle exchange program. This is a graphic example, along
with our failure to give illegal drugs to cancer patients with intractable pain, of our blind pursuit of an irrational policy.

The Mixed Message of Tobacco and Alcohol

The case for the decriminalization of drugs becomes even   25
stronger when illegal drugs are looked at in the context of legal
drugs.

It is estimated that over 350,000 people will die this year   26
from tobacco-related diseases. Last year the number was
equally large. And it will be again next year. Why do millions of
people continue to engage in an activity which has been
proven to cause cancer and heart disease? The answer is that
smoking is more than just a bad habit. It is an addiction. In
1988, Surgeon General C. Everett Koop called nicotine as addictive as heroin and cocaine. And yet, with the exception of
taxes and labeling, cigarettes are sold without restriction.

By every standard we apply to illicit drugs, tobacco should   27
be a controlled substance. But it is not, and for good reason.
Given that millions of people continue to smoke—many of
whom would quit if they could—making cigarettes illegal
would be an open invitation to a new black market.

The certain occurrence of a costly and dangerous illegal to-   28
bacco trade (if tobacco were outlawed) is well understood by
Congress, the Bush Administration and the criminal-justice
community. No rationally thinking person would want to bring
such a catastrophe down upon the US—even if it would prevent some people from smoking.

Like tobacco, alcohol is a drug that kills thousands of   29
Americans every year. It plays a part in more than half of all
automobile fatalities and is also frequently involved in sui-
cides, non-automobile accidents, domestic disputes and crimes
of violence. Millions of Americans are alcoholic, and alcohol
costs the nation billions of dollars in health care and lost productivity. So why not ban alcohol? Because, as almost every
American knows, we already tried that. Prohibition turned out
to be one of the worst social experiments this country has ever
undertaken.

I will not review the sorry history of Prohibition except to   30
make two important points. The first is that in repealing

Prohibition, we made significant mistakes that should not be repeated in the event that drug use is decriminalized. Specifically, when alcohol was again made legal in 1934, we made no significant effort to educate people as to its dangers. There were no (and still are no) *Just Say No* campaigns against alcohol. We allowed alcohol to be advertised and have associated it with happiness, success and social acceptability. We have also been far too lenient with drunk drivers.

31   The second point is that, notwithstanding claims to the contrary by critics of decriminalization, there are marked parallels between the era of Prohibition and our current policy of making drugs illegal, and important lessons to be learned from our attempts to ban the use and sale of alcohol.

32   During Prohibition, the government tried to keep alcohol out of the hands of millions of people who refused to give it up. As a result, our cities were overrun by criminal syndicates enriching themselves with the profits of bootleg liquor and terrorizing anyone who got in their way. We then looked to the criminal-justice system to solve the crime problems that Prohibition created. But the criminal-justice system—outmanned, outgunned and often corrupted by enormous black market profits—was incapable of stopping the massive crime wave that Prohibition brought, just as it was incapable of stopping people from drinking.

33   As a person now publicly identified with the movement to reform our drug laws through the use of some form of decriminalization, I consider it very important to say that I am not soft on either drug use or drug dealers. I am a soldier in the war against drugs. As Maryland's State Attorney, I spent years prosecuting and jailing drug traffickers, and had one of the highest rates of incarceration for drug convictions in the country. And if I were still State's Attorney, I would be enforcing the law as vigorously as ever. My experience as a prosecutor did not in any way alter my passionate dislike for drug dealers, it simply convinced me that the present system doesn't work and cannot be made to work.

34   During the Revolutionary War, the British insisted on wearing red coats and marching in formation. They looked very pretty. They also lost. A good general does not pursue a strategy in the face of overwhelming evidence of failure. Instead, a good general changes from a losing strategy to one that exploits his enemy's weakness, while exposing his own troops to only as much danger as is required to win. The drug war can be beaten and the public health of the US can be improved if we are willing to substitute common sense for rhetoric, myth and blind persistence, and to put the war

in the hands of the Surgeon General, not the Attorney General.

William Bennett

SHOULD DRUGS BE LEGALIZED?

Prominent Republican leader William Bennett (born 1943) studied and played football (and the guitar for a rock group) at Williams College. Later he earned a doctorate in philosophy at the University of Texas and a law degree at Harvard, and taught at the University of Southern Mississippi, Boston University, and the University of Wisconsin. He joined the Reagan administration as chair of the National Endowment for the Humanities in 1981 and became Secretary of Education in 1985; in 1988, he was appointed as the nation's "drug czar"—in charge of waging President Bush's "war on drugs." He published the following argument in 1990 in Reader's Digest. *Note, too, the exchange between Bennett and Milton Friedman that is reprinted after this selection.*

Since I took command of the war on drugs, I have learned 1 from former Secretary of State George Schultz that our concept of fighting drugs is "flawed." The only thing to do, he says, is to "make it possible for addicts to buy drugs at some regulated place." Conservative commentator William F. Buckley, Jr., suggests I should be "fatalistic" about the flood of cocaine from South America and simply "let it in." Syndicated columnist Mike Royko contends it would be easier to sweep junkies out of the gutters "than to fight a hopeless war" against the narcotics that send them there. Labeling our efforts "bankrupt," federal judge Robert W. Sweet opts for legalization, saying, "If our society can learn to stop using butter, it should be able to cut down on cocaine."

Flawed, fatalistic, hopeless, bankrupt! I never realized surrender was so fashionable until I assumed this post.

Though most Americans are overwhelmingly determined to 3 go toe-to-toe with the foreign drug lords and neighborhood pushers, a small minority believe that enforcing drug laws imposes greater costs on society than do drugs themselves. Like addicts seeking immediate euphoria, the legalizers want peace at any price, even though it means the inevitable proliferation of a practice that degrades, impoverishes and kills.

4   I am acutely aware of the burdens drug enforcement places upon us. It consumes economic resources we would like to use elsewhere. It is sometimes frustrating, thankless and often dangerous. But the consequences of *not* enforcing drug laws would be far more costly. Those consequences involve the intrinsically destructive nature of drugs and the toll they exact from our society in hundreds of thousands of lost and broken lives ... human potential never realized ... time stolen from families and jobs ... precious spiritual and economic resources squandered.

5   That is precisely why virtually every civilized society has found it necessary to exert some form of control over mind-altering substances and why this war is so important. Americans feel up to their hips in drugs now. They would be up to their necks under legalization.

6   Even limited experiments in drug legalization have shown that when drugs are more widely available, addiction skyrockets. In 1975 Italy liberalized its drug law and now has one of the highest heroin-related death rates in Western Europe. In Alaska, where marijuana was decriminalized in 1975, the easy atmosphere has increased usage of the drug, particularly among children. Nor does it stop there. Some Alaskan schoolchildren now tout "coca puffs," marijuana cigarettes laced with cocaine.

7   Many legalizers concede that drug legalization might increase use, but they shrug off the matter. "It may well be that there would be more addicts, and I would regret that result," says Nobel laureate economist Milton Friedman. The late Harvard Medical School psychiatry professor Norman Zinberg, a longtime proponent of "responsible" drug use, admitted that "use of now illicit drugs would certainly increase. Also, casualties probably would increase."

8   In fact, Dr. Herbert D. Kleber of Yale University, my deputy in charge of demand reduction, predicts legalization might cause "a five-to-sixfold increase" in cocaine use. But legalizers regard this as a necessary price for the "benefits" of legalization. What benefits?

9   1. *Legalization will take the profit out of drugs.* The result supposedly will be the end of criminal drug pushers and the big foreign drug wholesalers, who will turn to other enterprises because nobody will need to make furtive and dangerous trips to his local pusher.

But what, exactly, would the brave new world of legalized 10
drugs look like? Buckley stresses that "adults get to buy the
stuff at carefully regulated stores." (Would you want one in
your neighborhood?) Others, like Friedman, suggest we sell the
drugs at "ordinary retail outlets."

Former City University of New York sociologist Georgette 11
Bennett assures us that "brand-name competition will be prohibited" and that strict quality control and proper labeling will
be overseen by the Food and Drug Administration. In a touching egalitarian note, she adds that "free drugs will be provided
at government clinics" for addicts too poor to buy them.

Almost all the legalizers point out that the price of drugs will 12
fall, even though the drugs will be heavily taxed. Buckley, for
example, argues that somehow federal drugstores will keep the
price "low enough to discourage a black market but high
enough to accumulate a surplus to be used for drug education."

Supposedly, drug sales will generate huge amounts of rev- 13
enue, which will then be used to tell the public not to use drugs
and to treat those who don't listen.

In reality, this tax would only allow government to *share* the 14
drug profits now garnered by criminals. Legalizers would have
to tax drugs heavily in order to pay for drug education and
treatment programs. Criminals could undercut the official
price and still make huge profits. What alternative would the
government have? Cut the price until it was within the lunch-
money budget of the average sixth-grade student?

2. *Legalization will eliminate the black market.* Wrong. And not 15
just because the regulated prices could be undercut. Many legalizers admit that drugs such as crack or PCP are simply too dangerous to allow the shelter of the law. Thus criminals will provide
what the government will not. "As long as drugs that people very
much want remain illegal, a black market will exist," says legalization advocate David Boaz of the libertarian Cato Institute.

Look at crack. In powdered form, cocaine was an expensive 16
indulgence. But street chemists found that a better and far less
expensive—and far more dangerous—high could be achieved
by mixing cocaine with baking soda and heating it. Crack was
born, and "cheap" coke invaded low-income communities with
furious speed.

An ounce of powdered cocaine might sell on the street for 17
$1200. That same ounce can produce 370 vials of crack at $10
each. Ten bucks seems like a cheap hit, but crack's intense ten-
to 15-minute high is followed by an unbearable depression.
The user wants more crack, thus starting a rapid and costly descent into addiction.

18   If government drugstores do not stock crack, addicts will find it in the clandestine market or simply bake it themselves from their legally purchased cocaine.

19   Currently crack is being laced with insecticides and animal tranquilizers to heighten its effect. Emergency rooms are now warned to expect victims of "sandwiches" and "moon rocks," life-threatening smokable mixtures of heroin and crack. Unless the government is prepared to sell these deadly variations of dangerous drugs, it will perpetuate a criminal black market by default.

20   And what about children and teen-agers? They would obviously be barred from drug purchases, just as they are prohibited from buying beer and liquor. But pushers will continue to cater to these young customers with the old, favorite come-ons—a couple of free fixes to get them hooked. And what good will anti-drug education be when these youngsters observe their older brothers and sisters, parents and friends lighting up and shooting up with government permission?

21   Legalization will give us the worst of both worlds: millions of *new* drug users and a thriving criminal black market.

22   3. *Legalization will dramatically reduce crime.* "It is the high price of drugs that leads addicts to robbery, murder and other crimes," says Ira Glasser, executive director of the American Civil Liberties Union. A study by the Cato Institute concludes: "Most, if not all, 'drug-related murders' are the result of drug prohibition."

23   But researchers tell us that many drug-related felonies are committed by people involved in crime *before* they started taking drugs. The drugs, so routinely available in criminal circles, make the criminals more violent and unpredictable.

24   Certainly there are some kill-for-a-fix crimes, but does any rational person believe that a cut-rate price for drugs at a government outlet will stop such psychopathic behavior? The fact is that under the influence of drugs, normal people do not act normally, and abnormal people behave in chilling and horrible ways. DEA agents told me about a teen-age addict in Manhattan who was smoking crack when he sexually abused and caused permanent internal injuries to his one-month-old daughter.

25   Children are among the most frequent victims of violent, drug-related crimes that have nothing to do with the cost of acquiring the drugs. In Philadelphia in 1987 more than half the child-abuse fatalities involved at least one parent who was a heavy drug user. Seventy-three percent of the child-abuse deaths in New York City in 1987 involved parental drug use.

26   In my travels to the ramparts of the drug war, I have seen nothing to support the legalizers' argument that lower drug

prices would reduce crime. Virtually everywhere I have gone, police and DEA agents have told me that crime rates are highest where crack is cheapest.

4. *Drug use should be legal since users only harm themselves.* 27 Those who believe this should stand beside the medical examiner as he counts the 36 bullet wounds in the shattered corpse of a three-year-old who happened to get in the way of his mother's drug-crazed boyfriend. They should visit the babies abandoned by cocaine-addicted mothers—infants who already carry the ravages of addiction in their own tiny bodies. They should console the devastated relatives of the nun who worked in a homeless shelter and was stabbed to death by a crack addict enraged that she would not stake him to a fix.

Do drug addicts only harm themselves? Here is a former co- 28 caine addict describing the compulsion that quickly draws even the most "responsible" user into irresponsible behavior: "Everything is about getting high, and any means necessary to get there becomes rational. If it means stealing something from somebody close to you, lying to your family, borrowing money from people you know you can't pay back, writing checks you know you can't cover, you do all those things— things that are totally against everything you have ever believed in."

Society pays for this behavior, and not just in bigger insur- 29 ance premiums, losses from accidents and poor job performance. We pay in the loss of a priceless social currency as families are destroyed, trust between friends is betrayed and promising careers are never fulfilled. I cannot imagine sanctioning behavior that would increase that toll.

I find no merit in the legalizers' case. The simple fact is that 30 drug use is wrong. And the moral argument, in the end, is the most compelling argument. A citizen in a drug-induced haze, whether on his back-yard deck or on a mattress in a ghetto crack house, is not what the founding fathers meant by the "pursuit of happiness." Despite the legalizers' argument that drug use is a matter of "personal freedom," our nation's notion of liberty is rooted in the ideal of a self-reliant citizenry. Helpless wrecks in treatment centers, men chained by their noses to cocaine—these people are slaves.

Imagine if, in the darkest days of 1940, Winston Churchill 31 had rallied the West by saying, "This war looks hopeless, and besides, it will cost too much. Hitler can't be *that* bad. Let's surrender and see what happens." That is essentially what we hear from the legalizers.

This war *can* be won. I am heartened by indications that ed- 32 ucation and public revulsion are having an effect on drug use.

The National Institute on Drug Abuse's latest survey of current users shows a 37-percent *decrease* in drug consumption since 1985. Cocaine is down 50 percent; marijuana use among young people is at its lowest rate since 1972. In my travels I've been encouraged by signs that Americans are fighting back.

33   I am under no illusion that such developments, however hopeful, mean the war is over. We need to involve more citizens in the fight, increase pressure on drug criminals and build on antidrug programs that have proved to work. This will not be easy. But the moral and social costs of surrender are simply too great to contemplate.

Milton Friedman

PROHIBITION
AND DRUGS

When he was on the faculty of the University of Chicago, Milton Friedman won the Nobel Prize for his "monetarist" school of economics, one that stresses stable growth in the supply of money and credit in an economy. A conservative who influenced the policies of Ronald Reagan and George Bush, he enjoys writing about a range of public issues. Recently a senior research fellow at the Hoover Institute at Stanford University and now retired, he wrote the two following essays on the legalization of drugs—one for Newsweek *(1972) and one for the* Wall Street Journal *(1989).*

The Wall Street Journal *article, which contains a reference in paragraph five to the* Newsweek *essay, is an "open letter" to William Bennett, the nation's "drug czar" (i.e., director of the Office of National Drug Policy) under former President Bush. Bennett is the author of the previous essay in this section as well as the response to Milton Friedman that is reprinted after Friedman's two essays. Friedman's own counter-response follows that, on page 770.*

1   "The reign of tears is over. The slums will soon be only a memory. We will turn our prisons into factories and our jails into storehouses and corncribs. Men will walk upright now, women will smile, and the children will laugh. Hell will be forever for rent."

That is how Billy Sunday, the noted evangelist and leading   2
crusader against Demon Rum, greeted the onset of Prohibition
in early 1920. We know now how tragically his hopes were
doomed. New prisons and jails had to be built to house the
criminals spawned by converting the drinking of spirits into a
crime against the state. Prohibition undermined respect for the
law, corrupted the minions of the law, created a decadent
moral climate—but did not stop the consumption of alcohol.

Despite this tragic object lesson, we seem bent on repeating   3
precisely the same mistake in the handling of drugs.

Ethics and Expediency

On ethical grounds, do we have the right to use the machinery   4
of government to prevent an individual from becoming an alcoholic or a drug addict? For children, almost everyone would
answer at least a qualified yes. But for responsible adults, I, for
one, would answer no. Reason with the potential addict, yes.
Tell him the consequences, yes. Pray for and with him, yes. But
I believe that we have no right to use force, directly or indirectly, to prevent a fellow man from committing suicide, let
alone from drinking alcohol or taking drugs.

I readily grant that the ethical issue is difficult and that men   5
of goodwill may well disagree. Fortunately, we need not resolve
the ethical issue to agree on policy. *Prohibition is an attempted
cure that makes matters worse—for both the addict and the rest
of us.* Hence, even if you regard present policy toward drugs as
ethically justified, considerations of expediency make that policy most unwise.

Consider first the addict. Legalizing drugs might increase the   6
number of addicts, but it is not clear that it would. Forbidden
fruit is attractive, particularly to the young. More important,
many drug addicts are deliberately made by pushers, who give
likely prospects their first few doses free. It pays the pusher to
do so because, once hooked, the addict is a captive customer. If
drugs were legally available, any possible profit from such inhumane activity would disappear, since the addict could buy
from the cheapest source.

Whatever happens to the number of addicts, the individual   7
addict would clearly be far better off if drugs were legal. Today,
drugs are both incredibly expensive and highly uncertain in
quality. Addicts are driven to associate with criminals to get
the drugs, become criminals themselves to finance the habit,
and risk constant danger of death and disease.

8   *Consider next the rest of us.* Here the situation is crystal-clear. The harm to us from the addiction of others arises almost wholly from the fact that drugs are illegal. A recent committee of the American Bar Association estimated that addicts commit one-third to one-half of all street crime in the U.S. Legalize drugs, and street crime would drop dramatically.

9   Moreover, addicts and pushers are not the only ones corrupted. Immense sums are at stake. It is inevitable that some relatively low-paid police and other government officials—and some high-paid ones as well—will succumb to the temptation to pick up easy money.

Law and Order

10   Legalizing drugs would simultaneously reduce the amount of crime and raise the quality of law enforcement. Can you conceive of any other measure that would accomplish so much to promote law and order?

11   But, you may say, must we accept defeat? Why not simply end the drug traffic? That is where experience under Prohibition is most relevant. We cannot end the drug traffic. We may be able to cut off opium from Turkey—but there are innumerable other places where the opium poppy grows. With French cooperation, we may be able to make Marseilles an unhealthy place to manufacture heroin—but there are innumerable other places where the simple manufacturing operations involved can be carried out. So long as large sums of money are involved—and they are bound to be if drugs are illegal—it is literally hopeless to expect to end the traffic or even to reduce seriously its scope.

12   In drugs, as in other areas, persuasion and example are likely to be far more effective than the use of force to shape others in our image.

Milton Friedman

AN OPEN LETTER
TO BILL BENNETT

Dear Bill:

In Oliver Cromwell's eloquent words, "I beseech you, in the 1
bowels of Christ, think it possible you may be mistaken" about
the course you and President Bush urge us to adopt to fight
drugs. The path you propose of more police, more jails, use of
the military in foreign countries, harsh penalties for drug
users, and a whole panoply of repressive measures can only
make a bad situation worse. The drug war cannot be won by
those tactics without undermining the human liberty and individual freedom that you and I cherish.

You are not mistaken in believing that drugs are a scourge 2
that is devastating our society. You are not mistaken in believing that drugs are tearing asunder our social fabric, ruining the
lives of many young people, and imposing heavy costs on some
of the most disadvantaged among us. You are not mistaken in
believing that the majority of the public share your concerns.
In short, you are not mistaken in the end you seek to achieve.

Your mistake is failing to recognize that the very measures 3
you favor are a major source of the evils you deplore. Of course
the problem is demand, but it is not only demand, it is demand
that must operate through repressed and illegal channels.
Illegality creates obscene profits that finance the murderous
tactics of the drug lords; illegality leads to the corruption of
law enforcement officials; illegality monopolizes the efforts of
honest law forces so that they are starved for resources to fight
the simpler crimes of robbery, theft and assault.

Drugs are a tragedy for addicts. But criminalizing their use 4
converts that tragedy into a disaster for society, for users and
non-users alike. Our experience with the prohibition of drugs
is a replay of our experience with the prohibition of alcoholic beverages.

I append excerpts from a column that I wrote in 1972 on 5
"Prohibition and Drugs." The major problem then was heroin
from Marseilles; today, it is cocaine from Latin America. Today,
also, the problem is far more serious than it was 17 years ago:
more addicts, more innocent victims; more drug pushers, more
law enforcement officials; more money spent to enforce prohibition, more money spent to circumvent prohibition.

6   Had drugs been decriminalized 17 years ago, "crack" would never have been invented (it was invented because the high cost of illegal drugs made it profitable to provide a cheaper version) and there would today be far fewer addicts. The lives of thousands, perhaps hundreds of thousands of innocent victims would have been saved, and not only in the U.S. The ghettos of our major cities would not be drug-and-crime-infested no-man's lands. Fewer people would be in jails, and fewer jails would have been built.

7   Colombia, Bolivia and Peru would not be suffering from narco-terror, and we would not be distorting our foreign policy because of narco-terror. Hell would not, in the words with which Billy Sunday welcomed Prohibition, "be forever for rent," but it would be a lot emptier.

8   Decriminalizing drugs is even more urgent now than in 1972, but we must recognize that the harm done in the interim cannot be wiped out, certainly not immediately. Postponing decriminalization will only make matters worse, and make the problem appear even more intractable.

9   Alcohol and tobacco cause many more deaths in users than do drugs. Decriminalization would not prevent us from treating drugs as we now treat alcohol and tobacco: prohibiting sales of drugs to minors, outlawing the advertising of drugs and similar measures. Such measures could be enforced, while outright prohibition cannot be. Moreover, if even a small fraction of the money we now spend on trying to enforce drug prohibition were devoted to treatment and rehabilitation, in an atmosphere of compassion not punishment, the reduction in drug usage and in the harm done to the users could be dramatic.

10   This plea comes from the bottom of my heart. Every friend of freedom, and I know you are one, must be as revolted as I am by the prospect of turning the United States into an armed camp, by the vision of jails filled with casual drug users and of an army of enforcers empowered to invade the liberty of citizens on slight evidence. A country in which shooting down unidentified planes "on suspicion" can be seriously considered as a drug-war tactic is not the kind of United States that either you or I want to hand on to future generations.

William Bennett

A RESPONSE
TO MILTON FRIEDMAN

Dear Milton:

There was little, if anything, new in your open letter to me 1
calling for the legalization of drugs (*The Wall Street Journal*,
Sept. 7). As your 1972 article made clear, the legalization argument is an old and familiar one, which has recently been revived by a small number of journalists and academics who insist that the only solution to the drug problem is no solution at
all. What surprises me is that you would continue to advocate
so unrealistic a proposal without pausing to consider seriously
its consequences.

If the argument for drug legalization has one virtue it is its 2
sheer simplicity. Eliminate laws against drugs, and street crime
will disappear. Take the profit out of the black market through
decriminalization and regulation, and poor neighborhoods will
no longer be victimized by drug dealers. Cut back on drug enforcement, and use the money to wage a public health campaign against drugs, as we do with tobacco and alcohol.

Counting Costs

The basic premise of all these propositions is that using our 3
nation's laws to fight drugs is too costly. To be sure, our attempts to reduce drug use do carry with them enormous costs.
But the question that must be asked—and which is totally ignored by the legalization advocates—is, what are the costs of
not enforcing laws against drugs?

In my judgment, and in the judgment of virtually every seri- 4
ous scholar in this field, the potential costs of legalizing drugs
would be so large as to make it a public policy disaster.

Of course, no one, including you, can say with certainty 5
what would happen in the U.S. if drugs were suddenly to become a readily purchased product. We do know, however, that
wherever drugs have been cheaper and more easily obtained,
drug use—and addiction—has skyrocketed. In opium and cocaine producing countries, addiction is rampant among the
peasants involved in drug production.

6   Professor James Q. Wilson tells us that during the years in which heroin could be legally prescribed by doctors in Britain, the number of addicts increased forty-fold. And after the repeal of Prohibition—an analogy favored but misunderstood by legalization advocates—consumption of alcohol soared by 350%.

7   Could we afford such dramatic increases in drug use? I doubt it. Already the toll of drug use on American society—measured in lost productivity, in rising health insurance costs, in hospitals flooded with drug overdose emergencies, in drug caused accidents, and in premature death—is surely more than we would like to bear.

8   You seem to believe that by spending just a little more money on treatment and rehabilitation, the costs of increased addiction can be avoided. That hope betrays a basic misunderstanding of the problems facing drug treatment. Most addicts don't suddenly decide to get help. They remain addicts either because treatment isn't available or because they don't seek it out. The National Drug Control Strategy announced by President Bush on Sept. 5 goes a long way in making sure that more treatment slots are available. But the simple fact remains that many drug users won't enter treatment until they are forced to—often by the very criminal justice system you think is the source of the problem.

9   As for the connection between drugs and crime, your unswerving commitment to a legalization solution prevents you from appreciating the complexity of the drug market. Contrary to your claim, most addicts do not turn to crime to support their habit. Research shows that many of them were involved in criminal activity before they turned to drugs. Many former addicts who have received treatment continue to commit crimes during their recovery. And even if drugs were legal, what evidence do you have that the habitual drug user wouldn't continue to rob and steal to get money for clothes, food or shelter? Drug addicts always want more drugs than they can afford, and no legalization scheme has yet come up with a way of satisfying that appetite.

10   The National Drug Control Strategy emphasizes the importance of reclaiming the streets and neighborhoods where drugs have wrought havoc because, I admit, the price of having drug laws is having criminals who will try to subvert them. Your proposal might conceivably reduce the amount of gang- and dealer-related crime, but it is fanciful to suggest that it would make crime vanish. Unless you are willing to distribute drugs freely and widely, there will always be a black market to undercut the regulated one. And as for the potential addicts, for the

school children and for the pregnant mothers, all of whom would find drugs more accessible and legally condoned, your proposal would offer nothing at all.

So I advocate a larger criminal justice system to take drug 11 users off the streets and deter new users from becoming more deeply involved in so hazardous an activity. You suggest that such policies would turn the country "into an armed camp." Try telling that to the public housing tenants who enthusiastically support plans to enhance security in their buildings, or to the residents who applaud police when a local crack house is razed. They recognize that drug use is a threat to the individual liberty and domestic tranquility guaranteed by the Constitution.

I remain an ardent defender of our nation's laws against ille- 12 gal drug use and our attempts to enforce them because I believe drug use is wrong. A true friend of freedom understands that government has a responsibility to craft and uphold laws that help educate citizens about right and wrong. That, at any rate, was the Founders' view of our system of government.

Liberal Ridicule

Today this view is much ridiculed by liberal elites and entirely 13 neglected by you. So while I cannot doubt the sincerity of your opinion on drug legalization, I find it difficult to respect. The moral cost of legalizing drugs is great, but it is a cost that apparently lies outside the narrow scope of libertarian policy prescriptions.

I do not have a simple solution to the drug problem. I doubt 14 that one exists. But I am committed to fighting the problem on several fronts through imaginative policies and hard work over a long period of time. As in the past, some of these efforts will work and some won't. Your response, however, is to surrender and see what happens. To my mind that is irresponsible and reckless public policy. At a time when national intolerance for drug use is rapidly increasing, the legalization argument is a political anachronism. Its recent resurgence is, I trust, only a temporary distraction from the genuine debate on national drug policy.

Milton Friedman

A RESPONSE
TO WILLIAM BENNETT

1   William Bennett is entirely right (editorial page, Sept. 19) that "there was little, if anything, new in" my open letter to him— just as there is little, if anything, new in his proposed program to rid this nation of the scourge of drugs. That is why I am so disturbed by that program. It flies in the face of decades of experience. More police, more jails, more-stringent penalties, increased efforts at interception, increased publicity about the evils of drugs—all this has been accompanied by more, not fewer, drug addicts; more, not fewer, crimes and murders; more, not less, corruption; more, not fewer, innocent victims.

2   Like Mr. Bennett, his predecessors were "committed to fighting the problem on several fronts through imaginative policies and hard work over a long period of time." What evidence convinces him that the same policies on a larger scale will end the drug scourge? He offers none in his response to me, only assertion and the conjecture that legalizing drugs would produce "a public policy disaster"—as if that is not exactly what we already have.

3   Legalizing drugs is not equivalent to surrender in the fight against drug addiction. On the contrary, I believe that legalizing drugs is a precondition for an effective fight. We might then have a real chance to prevent sales to minors; get drugs out of the schools and playgrounds; save crack babies and reduce their number; launch an effective educational campaign on the personal costs of drug use—not necessarily conducted, I might add, by government; punish drug users guilty of harming others while "under the influence"; and encourage large numbers of addicts to volunteer for treatment and rehabilitation when they could do so without confessing to criminal actions. Some habitual drug users would, as he says, "continue to rob and steal to get money for clothes, food or shelter." No doubt also there will be "a black market to undercut the regulated one"— as there now is bootleg liquor thanks to high taxes on alcoholic beverages. But these would be on a far smaller scale than at present. Perfection is not for this world. Pursuing the unattainable best can prevent achievement of the attainable good.

4   As Mr. Bennett recognizes, the victims of drugs fall into two classes: those who choose to use drugs and innocent victims— who in one way or another include almost all the rest of us.

Legalization would drastically reduce the number of innocent victims. That is a virtual certainty. The number of self-chosen victims might increase, but it is pure conjecture that the number would, as he asserts, skyrocket. In any event, while both groups of victims are to be pitied, the innocent victims surely have a far greater claim on our sympathy than the self-chosen victims—or else the concept of personal responsibility has been emptied of all content.

A particular class of innocent victims generally overlooked is foreigners. By what right do we impose our values on the residents of Colombia? Or, by our actions undermine the very foundations of their society and condemn hundreds, perhaps thousands, of Colombians to violent death? All because the U.S. government is unable to enforce its own laws on its own citizens. I regard such actions as indefensible, entirely aside from the distortions they introduce into our foreign policy. 5

Finally, he and I interpret the "Founders' view of our system of government" very differently. To him, they believed "that government has a responsibility to . . . help educate citizens about right and wrong." To me, that is a totalitarian view opening the road to thought control and would have been utterly unacceptable to the Founders. I do not believe, and neither did they, that it is the responsibility of government to tell free citizens what is right and wrong. That is something for them to decide for themselves. Government is a means to enable each of us to pursue our own vision in our own way so long as we do not interfere with the right of others to do the same. In the words of the Declaration of Independence, "all Men are . . . endowed by their Creator with certain unalienable Rights, that among these are Life, Liberty, and the pursuit of Happiness. That to secure these Rights Governments are instituted among Men, deriving their just powers from the consent of the Governed." In my view, Justice Louis Brandeis was a "true friend of freedom" when he wrote, "Experience should teach us to be most on our guard to protect liberty when the government's purposes are beneficial. Men born to freedom are naturally alert to repel invasions of their liberty by evil-minded rulers. The greater dangers to liberty lurk in insidious encroachment by men of zeal, well meaning, but without understanding." 6

Milton Friedman
Hoover Institution
Stanford, California

Common Sense for Drug Policy
WANTED: DRUG CZAR

The ad below was produced by Common Sense for Drug Policy, a public interest group based in Washington, D.C., and distributed widely. Do you think the presentation is effective? Does the appearance as a kind of "wanted poster" work for or against its message?

WANTED:
"Drug Czar"
Director of Office of National Drug Control Policy

Responsible for $20 billion budget. Cabinet position reports directly to the President.

Experienced in field of public health. Understands that most users are not addicts and are otherwise responsible citizens; and that drug abuse is a health problem that is not effectively treated by incarceration.

Integrity to objectively analyze and publicly endorse peer reviewed scientific evidence regardless of political pressures. Examples are marijuana as a safe and effective treatment of certain serious illnesses and funding syringe exchanges to combat the rapid spread of HIV/AIDS.

Courage to speak out against drug war ideologues, racists, political opportunists and entrenched interests such as the prison-industrial complex and the drug testing industry. Willingness to resist demonizing illegal drug users, many of whom are good parents, good workers, and good citizens.

Honesty to publicly acknowledge that some illegal drugs, such as marijuana and Ecstasy, are safer than some legal drugs like alcohol and tobacco.

Receptive to studying new approaches pioneered in Australia, Canada, Holland and Switzerland and in the states of Arizona, California, Hawaii, Maine and Nevada that expand drug treatment, reduce the spread of disease, allow access to medicine and decrease reliance on law enforcement.

Understands basic economic principles of supply and demand. Will avoid unjustified intervention in sovereign countries in the Quixotic effort to stem supply. Will replace current prohibition of relatively benign marijuana and Ecstasy with regulations and taxes similar to those for alcohol and tobacco.

$125,000 per year, excellent benefits.
Opportunity to make a real difference.
Apply with resume to President of the United States
The White House

American Public Health Association, Mohammad N. Akhter, MD, MPH, Executive Director;
Common Sense for Drug Policy, Kevin B. Zeese, President;
National Black Police Association, Ronald Hampton, Executive Director;
United Methodist Church, General Board of Church and Society, The Rev. Dr. Thomas White Wolf Fassett.

For information contact **Common Sense for Drug Policy,**
Kevin B. Zeese, President, 3220 N Street NW #141, Washington, DC 20007

Charles Van Deventer

I'M PROOF: THE WAR ON DRUGS IS WORKING

Charles Van Deventer, who now lives and works in Los Angeles, tells you a lot about himself in the following personal testimony about the war on drugs, published in Newsweek *in July 2001.*

In the ongoing debate about the effectiveness of the war on 1 drugs, I've never heard a politician, scientist, filmmaker or journalist tell my story. That's odd, because I believe my experience with illegal drugs is by far the most common. I'm a former casual drug user who thinks illegal drugs should remain illegal.

I'm not exactly anybody's poster boy for the war on drugs. 2 I've experienced very little hardship because of drugs. I've never been to prison or a 12-step program. None of my friends died using drugs. I used illicit hard-core drugs during half of my 20s and then quit before I hit rock bottom. Why? The same reason most people do: because the stigma of illegal-drug use is too great.

At the height of my drug use I was a 24-year-old advertising 3 copywriter living in Manhattan. I had friends who were artists, grad students, lawyers and waitresses. If we didn't think we were too cool to do so, I'm sure we would have compared ourselves to "Friends."

Together we'd spend what little disposable income we had to 4 buy ecstasy and coke and Special K and more. Sometimes it was fun. Sometimes it wasn't. More than anything, we felt the invincibility you feel only when you're young and looking forward to your future.

I can remember giggling for hours and dancing until dawn. 5 I can remember the rush of adrenaline when guys in down jackets would make eye contact and say, "Hey, homeboy, what you need?" I can also remember a particular Monday morning after a weekend of taking ecstasy and acid together. I was reading a newspaper article about Rebecca Lobo's last game at U Conn. I started crying. Crying! At the sports page! I knew the drugs were hurting me mentally. I had to be more careful.

There is some logic to the argument that since drugs are 6 easy to obtain, making them legal will enable the government to focus on treating addicts. But drugs aren't nearly as easy to buy as the media and lawmakers want you to believe. Drugs are easy to get only if you're willing to do just about anything to get them. If you're just doing it for fun, it's harder to score. No one I knew was really willing to get arrested.

Sometimes my friends and I would sit for hours nursing drinks at a bar while we got the courage to make a deal in some other bar or on the street. Most nights we'd just go home a little drunk, our window of opportunity closed for that evening. The next morning we'd wake up with a hangover and still have money left for brunch and laundry.

7   There were a lot of nights when we actually did it. We'd buy from the first dealer we saw. I'd say about a third of the time the drugs wouldn't work. We didn't have the guts to ask for our money back. We certainly didn't have another $30 each to try again. This was fun for us. It was part of the game.

8   The drug culture crept into my life in predictable ways. My ads started to look a lot like the fliers I saw for raves. My circle of friends got tighter and tighter until we excluded anyone who wasn't cool enough to understand the thrill of losing one's mind. Instead of expanding my horizons, drugs made them narrower and narrower. If I'd had a reliable source, I'd have done drugs all the time. I considered them a lifestyle choice, like identifying with a political party or driving a particular brand of car. I wasn't an addict yet—but I was close.

9   And that's the thing: while addictive tendencies may very well be genetic, becoming an actual drug addict happens over time. Quickly for some, slower for others. The more barriers there are—be they the cops or the hassle or the fear of dying—the less likely you are to get addicted.

10   A couple of times I almost got arrested trying to buy drugs on the street. Or maybe I didn't. Was that bicycle cop really following me? Was the rumor about undercover cops patrolling the East Village true? Drugs can make you paranoid, so I suppose I'll never know. But I felt I was in danger of getting arrested, and that was enough. I wouldn't make eye contact when I walked by the drug dealers on my block. By the age of 27, I wasn't feeling invincible anymore.

11   Around this time the whole drug thing had begun to wear off anyway. I started dating a woman who didn't like drugs. One of my friends lost his job; another got married. According to the anti-drug pamphlets I've read, I went from being a "recre-

ational" drug user to an "occasional" one. I haven't had the occasion in years.

My experience lacks the drama of addiction. No one will ever   12
win an Academy Award telling it, or get elected trying to stop
it, or make money treating it. But it is much more common
than you may like to believe. The road to addiction was just
bumpy enough that I chose not to go down it. In this sense, we
are winning the war on drugs just by fighting them.

SCIENCE
AND SOCIETY

Introduction

No one doubts that science and technology have become central enterprises in our culture. Some scientists would like to have it otherwise, actually; they would like to insulate science as much as possible from social pressures. But that would be impossible: Not only is it impossible to keep scientific developments in medicine, genetic engineering, evolutionary biology, supercolliders, space exploration, and environmental science away from public scrutiny, it is also not in our interest to do so. For ultimately science and technology are themselves social creations, carried out through very human means for human purposes; that has already been made quite clear in the discussion of race in Part Three of this book and in the controversies over abortion and gay rights in Part Five. To try to dehumanize science and technology is to diminish them. Nevertheless, as science and technology become more central to our society, it is inevitable that conflicts between science and technology (on the one hand) and society (on the other) will become more important and more complicated. The scientific enterprise will inevitably involve ethical and rhetorical dimensions.

The first readings in this part establish that very clearly. When in February 1997 the English scientist Ian Wilmut announced that he had successfully cloned a ewe called Dolly, people around the world began to debate the wisdom of permitting research that could lead to the cloning of human beings. With thoughts of Frankenstein no doubt in the back of their cultural memories, many people wondered whether cloning would lead to all sorts of monstrous developments—to the birth of all kinds of unimagined mutations. Others argued that cloning humans would be immoral on the grounds that it would be unfair and demeaning to cloned individuals, that it could change for the worse our fundamental notions of what it means to be human or motivate people to try to produce a master race, that it would amount to testing things on human beings, and that it would usurp the prerogative of God in creating human life. On the other hand, a number of people felt that cloning could have many good consequences—for example, it might offer a way for infertile couples to conceive a child, or permit the development of replacement body parts (such as skin that could benefit burn victims), or lead to improvements in the treatment of certain genetic diseases. Supporters tend to be less convinced that cloning would be immoral: wouldn't cloned human beings have the rights of any other human being?

Where do you stand on the issue? Is cloning moral? Would a ban on cloning be an unfortunate restriction on the human drive to know? Do the ethical concerns outweigh the possible benefits that might be derived from cloning technologies? Will the benign motives of those who would seek cloning be overwhelmed by those who would exploit the technology for personal gain? The first section of this part of *Conversations* takes up these and related questions in a way that will stimulate your own thinking.

The second section takes up the vexing question of AIDS: How should we fight this terrible, worldwide epidemic that has already claimed many millions of people throughout the world? (In 2000, more than 20 million people had contracted the disease.) First recognized in the United States in the early 1980s, AIDS (or acquired immunodeficiency syndrome) seems to be caused by the human immunodeficiency virus—HIV—that is spread through sexual contact, through the reuse of infected needles (especially by drug users), through childbirth (when the mother is infected), or through the transfusion of contaminated blood. Since the causes of the AIDS epidemic are well understood, the question arises: How should we fight it? Should citizens reconsider the sexual mores that have become conventional in the past few decades? Should health-care workers or other citizens have to undergo regular testing for HIV? Should laws be passed requiring HIV carriers to inform their sexual partners that they carry the virus? Can health-care workers be required to treat AIDS patients? Will ingrained cultural practices need to be modified if AIDS is to be checked? This section mirrors a debate about a public health issue that is on everyone's mind these days.

The third section takes up one of the most important subjects of our time, the environment. As population expands and natural areas are threatened by development, Americans are weighing the relative merits of environmental protection and economic exploitation. Is the relationship between people and the environment inevitably adversarial? Is nature inevitably at odds with the technological? Do we have a custodial responsibility to nature that derives from morality and from our long-term prospects for self-preservation? Rachel Carson's *Silent Spring* made environmentalism a political issue in the early 1960s, so that President Richard Nixon created the Environmental Protection Agency in 1973. But long before that, in the nineteenth century, Americans were drawn to the green world, were sanctifying it in their art and literature, and were beginning to think about preservation. But even as some Americans were revering the land as a special landscape that sustained them morally and spiritually, pioneers moving westward were subduing it for their own economic purposes, in the process spoiling rivers and air and virgin forests—and native peoples—in the name of development. Are science and technology friends or foes of the environment? What is a suitable balance between resource development and resource protection? To what extent should we devote scarce resources to the protection of little-known species? How can poorer nations develop economically without environmental repercussions? Questions like these are debated every day, especially since organized environmental groups are legion—Earth First, the Sierra Club, the Nature Conservancy—and so *Conversations* includes an exchange about "the meaning of wilderness."

This part and this book end appropriately with a look at one of the most important political and social developments of our times: the computer. Many people are convinced that computer technology has been an unqualified blessing for our society—that its use in speeding up routine operations and making information available with breathtaking ease is one of the great technological improvements of our day. They look forward to further applications of computer technology that we cannot begin to imagine, and they envision a more democratic society emerging from computer technology. But others aren't so sure, especially when it comes to Internet communications. What happens to our sense of community in the Computer Age? What happens to political institutions in the United States? Is the Internet making the fruits of technology available to more people, or is it simply offering even more advantages to the wealthy at the expense of the poor? And what of the other cultural effects of the computer: Will it smooth over differences? Will it fragment us into semiautonomous collections of special interest groups? How can we ensure that all Americans have access to the benefits of computers? What should the government's role be in promoting the "information highway"?

The advances brought by science and technology solve many human problems, but with these advances come a number of perplexing ethical dilemmas. This is the lesson of this final part of *Conversations,* and this is the challenge to all citizens, whether or not they are scientists, at the beginning of a new century.

┌─────────────────────────────────────┐
│   │
│   **SHOULD RESEARCH**   │
│   **ON CLONING**   │
│   **BE PERMITTED?**   │
│   │
│   ■   │
│   │
└─────────────────────────────────────┘

Virginia Morell

A CLONE OF ONE'S OWN

Discover *magazine—a science-oriented publication owned by Disney that seeks a broad readership—published the following essay in May 1998.*

1   Last February, when Brigitte Boisselier, a French chemist, heard that Scottish scientists had produced Dolly, a sheep cloned from an adult cell, she was one of the few researchers whom the news did not surprise. A member of a fringe religious organization called the Raelian Movement, Boisselier had expected such a development: the group's leader, Rael, had predicted it 23 years before. It seems that Rael, a former French sports journalist, received the news of the impending discovery from extraterrestrials. They send him such announcements periodically, since he's half E.T. himself. According to a Raelian fact sheet (which could also serve as a script for The X-Files), his mother was transported aboard a UFO, where she was inseminated by one of these otherworldly beings. In 1946, Rael was born "from this union," and 27 years later he began receiving messages from the distant paternal side of his family. Most of these celebrate science and technology, predicting a future when we Earthlings will "rationally understand [our] origins" and begin making synthetic people. Cloning human beings, apparently, is one of the steps we must take on this path.

2   "Rael told us this would happen," says Boisselier, "so when we heard the news we weren't shocked; we were organized." Indeed, so organized that one month later—even as medical

ethicists, politicians, and pundits debated whether the technique should ever be applied to humans, and President Clinton asked for a moratorium on such research—the Raelians launched a company called Valiant Venture Ltd., the world's first human cloning firm. Advertised on the Web, Valiant Venture offers a service called Clonaid to help parents who want to have a child cloned from one of them. Boisselier signed on as the firm's scientific director and is now busy overseeing experiments that she believes will lead to the first cloned human in a mere two years.

"We need to do many experiments first with other species to 3 be sure that it can be done without causing any damage," says Boisselier. "And we also need to raise more funds." Nevertheless, the company, now 14 months old, is making "good progress." As of late February, it had a list of more than 100 people (Raelians and nonbelievers) who would like to be cloned or to have someone they love cloned—for a minimum fee of $200,000. Boisselier claims that her firm's research is advancing, although she would not say where the studies are taking place or who is doing them, making it impossible to verify her claims. But because the procedure can be performed in a relatively simple, inexpensive laboratory, as other scientists have noted, there is also no reason to doubt that the Raelians are doing exactly what they say: taking the first experimental steps to produce a human clone. "We've subcontracted the work to labs where it's legal to do this," Boisselier explains, noting that human cloning is banned in France. "To say that human cloning is forbidden won't stop the science," she says. "It's important that society knows that this is possible, that it can be— and will be—done . . . In a few years, I expect there'll be a lot of cloned people, that it will be done everywhere in the world. This is what happens with technological advances."

Boisselier's outspoken enthusiasm for producing human 4 clones is rare among scientists. Since Dolly's appearance, only one other researcher—Richard Seed, a Chicago physicist turned biologist—has jumped publicly into human cloning. He held a press conference in early January to say that he intends to open up shop as soon as he raises the funds. Like Boisselier, he has a list of people who want to be cloned (although his is shorter, only four candidates), and he also thinks human cloning can be a reality in a rather short time and with only a few million dollars for start-up costs. But most other researchers are far more cautious, especially since they have yet to clone an adult of any of our closest relatives, other primates. These researchers regard announcements like Seed's and Boisselier's as not only premature but off the wall. More than one referred to Seed as a kook, an oddball simply out to make a name for himself. Seed's announcement that human cloning was part of God's "plan for humankind [to] become one with God" did not help that image.

5   For all their faith in science and their apparently more rigorous approach to cloning, Boisselier and the Raelians are obviously far outside the mainstream. Their offer also plays on the fears of parents, says Mark Sauer, a reproductive endocrinologist at Columbia, since they propose to store the cells of living children. These cells could be used later to produce a clone of the child should the child die. "That's exploitation of the worst kind," says Sauer. "It plays on every parent's fears. And then what about a child who's produced that way? Will he or she be burdened by the memories of the first child?" Sauer adds that he suspects "in time, it will be possible to use adult cells to clone someone." But because of the many unanswered questions—both technical and ethical—human cloning "has not been endorsed by anyone, and certainly not by those of us working in reproductive medicine. It's premature to make these kinds of announcements and may lead to unwanted legislation." Indeed, as of late February, California had already banned human cloning, 24 other states were considering such laws, and eight bills were being weighed in Congress. Or cloning may be regulated by the Food and Drug Administration, which has asserted its right to do so.

6   Yet because cloning offers a way around certain reproductive problems—primarily by giving an infertile or homosexual couple a chance to have a biological child—most researchers agree that one day it's likely to be an option at many fertility clinics. Human cloning, as horrific as the idea sounds to some, will happen, they say, perhaps not as soon as Boisselier and Seed estimate but far sooner than one would have guessed before Dolly trotted onto the world's stage. "It's no longer in the realm of science fiction," says Lee Silver, a Princeton geneticist and the author of *Remaking Eden*, a book about cloning and other reproductive technologies. "The technological breakthrough has already happened, although the details of how to do this with human cells still need to be worked out. Once they're refined, it'll be just a matter of time."

7   Those refinements are already taking place. In January, scientists from a Massachusetts firm, Advanced Cell Technology, showed off three cloned calves, Charlie, George, and Albert, which were apparently produced via a more sophisticated (and patentable) technique than the one used to produce Dolly. At human fertility clinics, researchers are pursuing studies of human eggs that could lay the groundwork for cloning, although

that is not the purported intent. And the National Institutes of Health has funded two projects to clone rhesus monkeys, although only embryonic and fetal cells, not those from adults, will be used. Still, these types of studies bring human cloning closer to reality.

Good old-fashioned curiosity is pushing the field as well. "Ethics aside, I have to say as a scientist I find the technological problems fascinating," says David Ledbetter, a human geneticist at the University of Chicago, voicing a sentiment others in human reproductive biology share. "Why is this difficult to do? What will it take to make it work? How do you make a clone?" As Ledbetter's queries suggest, making a human clone is not simply a matter of following a recipe. The journal article announcing Dolly's birth didn't spell out a formula for cloning mammals; in fact, it didn't identify the actual cell that supplied Dolly's genetic material. Yet even without that key piece of information, Dolly's appearance was utterly astounding, since most biologists believed that it was impossible to produce a cloned mammal using any adult cell. "That's what everyone thought," says Don Wolf, a senior scientist at the Oregon Regional Primate Research Center in Beaverton, who's overseeing the rhesus monkey cloning project. "But Ian Wilmut [the Scottish scientist who led the Dolly project] came up with a clever innovation, a neat trick that proved us all wrong." 8

Before Dolly, researchers thought that adult cells could not be induced to produce a clone because they are already differentiated. As a fertilized egg develops into an adult, it divides into two, then four, then eight identical cells. Soon, however, the cells begin to specialize, becoming bone or skin, nerve or tissue. These differentiated cells all share the same DNA—the blueprint of the body—but they follow different parts of the instructions it contains. "In a sense, they're programmed," says Wolf, and as they age, it becomes more and more difficult to reprogram them, to make them switch functions. That's exactly what the Scottish team did when they produced Dolly: they took the genetic material from a differentiated adult cell and made it behave like the genetic material in a newly fertilized egg. Their success, however, does not mean that it is now easy to reprogram a human adult cell. If anything, notes Wolf, researchers suspect that every species is unique in its requirements for setting its cellular clock back to zero. Low-key and soft-spoken, Wolf stepped into the cloning spotlight last year, when the primate center announced that he had produced two monkeys, called Neti (an acronym for "nuclear embryo transfer infant") and Ditto, using a technique similar to the one used to make Dolly. Despite Ditto's name and stories in the 9 press, the monkeys are not identical copies of each other; they are only brother and sister. They were cloned using cells taken from two different embryos that shared an egg donor and a sperm donor. Still, their existence demonstrates that the formerly unthinkable is doable—and with primates.

10   Further, Wolf suspects he could produce clones from adult monkey cells as well, although, he is quick to add, he's not attempting to do so. "I have no desire to compete with the Richard Seeds of this world," says Wolf. "Nor do I want to see a knee-jerk reaction from our legislators that bans everything we're trying to do, particularly with techniques that have such tremendous potential for biomedical research." Already Congress has made research on human embryos off-limits to anyone receiving federal grants. Those who do not comply will have their labs shut down. It's safer, Wolf and others say, simply to avoid the subject.

11   Wolf retired from the primate center in 1996; he came back only after receiving the two NIH grants to produce a series of cloned monkeys for medical research and is now setting up his new lab. When complete, it will occupy three rooms in one of the center's squat beige buildings. In one, two researchers dressed in lab coats are peering through their microscopes at petri dishes filled with pinkish masses of monkey tissue. Somewhere in the gelatinous mix are the eggs, each about five-thousandths of an inch across. The researchers' task is to pluck out the good ones gently with a thin glass tube called a micropipette, then place these in a fresh dish for later use. Judging from the back and neck stretches the duo indulge in during a break, their efforts require almost as much concentration as trying to induce a spoon to bend. "This is going to be the main place of activity, Room 003," says Wolf, pausing briefly to check on his group's progress, then leading the way outside, where tall pines and firs tower overhead.

12   Wolf moves through the lushly landscaped grounds to a nondescript conference room, where he pulls up a chair and begins explaining the enormous boon genetically identical monkeys will be to medical researchers trying, for example, to develop an AIDS vaccine. "They'd be an ideal model system," says Wolf, since they'd have identical immune systems, eliminating an important potential cause of confusion when scientists test such a vaccine or other treatment.

13   The center already raises rhesus monkeys for medical research; most are used in experiments here and some are sold to other medical research institutions. While awaiting their fate, the monkeys live in grassy two-acre enclosures where they pick at the grass, climb tree stumps, play, and mate, keep-

ing an eye out for their feeders. From a distance and to the uninitiated, they all look so much alike they could easily be clones. When mature, Neti and Ditto will join one of these troops. For the time being, they're kept with other young monkeys in a smaller yet roomy cage, although no one seems sure which cage they're in or if they're even in the same one. Since their brief moment of celebrity, they've been treated like any other adolescent monkeys at the center, and since they apparently look like the other adolescents, they are no longer singled out for show.

To make Neti and Ditto, Wolf followed a procedure that has   14
frequently been used in the cattle industry for producing prized breeds. It is not, however, easily done; even in cattle, only 1 to 4 percent of such pregnancies yield offspring. In light of that low percentage, Wolf's first efforts represented "a tremendous success," says Dee Schramm, a reproductive physiologist at the Wisconsin Regional Primate Research Center in Madison. From 52 transplanted embryos, Wolf produced two healthy monkeys. "Yes, that's encouraging," Wolf acknowledges, "but you really can't draw any conclusions or expectations from what we did. After all, we've only done it twice." Still, the success has encouraged Schramm and his colleague David Watkins to attempt to clone rhesus monkeys themselves. They, too, have a grant for work using fetal and embryonic cells. They also plan to produce monkey embryos from adult cells, to study the differences in embryonic development among clones produced from different sorts of cells. However, they won't implant embryos produced from adults into female monkeys; only clones made from fetal and embryonic cells will be carried to term. Schramm says he hopes to have "several pairs of identical monkeys over the next two years." The work is so slow and tedious, he adds, that "I don't foresee any monkey cloning factories."

That's because it's tricky to reprogram any differentiated cell,   15
whether embryonic or adult. To turn a cell's clock back to zero, researchers like Wolf and Schramm use a technique called nuclear transfer technology. This is the basic method that produced Dolly, Neti and Ditto, and the three identical calves. In all three cases, the scientists removed an egg's nucleus (that is, its DNA, the genetic material that makes each individual unique) and replaced it with the nucleus from another cell. For Dolly, the nuclear material came from an adult cell; that of Neti and Ditto came from two separate embryos; and the calves' was derived from the cells of a single fetus. In all cases the cuckooed eggs were then persuaded to grow and divide normally.

16   That's the straightforward part of the formula. In between
lies a minefield of potential problems, many unique to whatever species is being cloned. "We're not following a recipe,"
says Wolf. The conditions under which the embryos grow vary
widely: each animal has its own required temperature, for example. And an embryo's cells begin to differentiate at different
moments for different species. Sheep, calves, monkeys, and humans all reach the eight-cell stage before they start differentiating, but mice begin when the embryo consists of only two cells,
which is why no one is cloning them. "There's also a lot of variation among mammalian species just in the size and nature of
the egg," Wolf adds. In some mammals, such as pigs, eggs are
dark in color, making it hard to tell if they are viable. While
that's not a problem for manipulating rhesus monkey or human eggs, where any discoloration means the egg is dead, simply getting the eggs is. "You can get buckets of eggs from
slaughterhouses" for livestock species, explains Schramm. "But
every egg you get from a monkey is worth its weight in gold."

17   In the case of Neti and Ditto, eggs were first harvested from
several rhesus females whose ovaries had been stimulated with
hormones. "You give them hormone shots twice a day for eight
days," says Schramm, and "then, if you're lucky, maybe you get
20 eggs. Out of these, 16 may be mature. And from these 16,
perhaps 12 will be fertilized." The eggs are fertilized by placing
them in a dish with the male monkeys' sperm, and the resulting cells are grown in a nutrient broth under what Wolf terms
"well-defined conditions; this is something we know a lot
about from human infertility studies and that can be applied
to our monkeys." Each embryo is allowed to grow for three
days, dividing into eight cells. At this stage, all the cells are
still identical to one another and largely unprogrammed.
"Theoretically, you could produce a complete individual from
each of these cells," says Wolf, giving you eight identical monkeys. But only theoretically, because most do not survive the
coming manipulations.

18   In the next step, the cells, called blastomeres, are carefully
teased apart; they constitute the donor nuclei. "Each one," explains Wolf, "is really one-eighth of an embryo," but that one-
eighth contains the key ingredient: the nuclear DNA, all that's
apparently needed to get the process ticking again.

19   You might expect that geneticists could divide each embryo
into eight blastomeres, wait for each blastomere to grow into
an eight-cell embryo, and repeat the process indefinitely. But
that's not possible, says Wolf, because the embryo's cells begin
differentiating into limbs and organs after a certain amount of
time has passed since its development began, regardless of

how many cells it has. An embryo grown from a blastomere will have only an eighth as many cells to work with as an entire embryo; if you divided it again, it would have only a sixty-fourth as many cells. "As development proceeds, when time for it to differentiate arrives, it doesn't have enough cells for the job," says Wolf, and even a blastomere will be less viable than an entire embryo. Because the cues to develop come from the cell's cytoplasm—the material that fills the cell—rather than the nucleus, the blastomere's clock can be reset by transferring its genetic material to a new egg full of fresh cytoplasm.

Using micropipettes, the scientists remove and discard the 20 nuclear DNA from another batch of rhesus monkey eggs. That leaves the cytoplast—that is, the egg's membrane and the material that once surrounded its chromosomes. A donor cell, one of the blastomeres, is then placed next to the chromosome-free egg in a petri dish. "In normal fertilization, an egg is in a quiescent state at the time it is ovulated," says Wolf. "The sperm triggers the egg to be activated, and the cytoplasm starts the program of events that will lead to development. But here, we aren't giving the cytoplast any sperm, so we must artificially stimulate" the two cells with a chemical treatment. A pulse of electricity then causes the two cells to fuse, and a "reconstituted" embryo is formed. The order of these two steps, however, was reversed when the Massachusetts researchers at Advanced Cell Technology cloned their calves; and the chemical treatment was apparently bypassed altogether when Dolly was made. "It could be species differences, or it could be artifacts of the lab," says Wolf. "It's too early to say.

"Once we have the embryo, we can treat it as we do any 21 other," he continues. "Most often we freeze them until we have a monkey ready for an implant." That's the other big hurdle—making sure that the recipient monkey is at the right point in her cycle for the embryo to take. Prospective recipients are monitored for several weeks beforehand. To do the actual transfer, a veterinarian surgically places the embryo into the monkey's oviduct. "Women have short, straight cervixes," explains Wolf, "so surgery isn't required" when embryos are transplanted at fertility clinics. "But a monkey's cervix is tortuous, and the only way we can implant the embryos is surgically, although we're trying to come up with other methods."

At the end of all this labor, only eight twins can be produced, 22 and that's assuming that every transfer succeeds, which is "pie in the sky," says Wolf. "It's not the optimal method, although we used it to make Neti and Ditto." But Wolf wants a series of clones, and for this, he says, "we need a lot of identical nuclei." He expects to retrieve these donor nuclei from the cells of fetal monkeys, such as their embryonic stem cells (undifferentiated precursors for other cell types) or fibroblasts (the cells that form the body's connective tissue, which are commonly grown in labs). Both kinds can be propagated in large numbers in test tubes, making it possible, he says, "to produce a clone size that is infinite in number." In other words, he expects to turn out identical monkeys, like a copying machine with a jammed "on" switch. "We don't know yet if we can do this; that's what we're working on now."

23 And in fact, this same technique—growing a line of fetal cells for subsequent nuclear transfer—enabled researchers at Advanced Cell Technology to produce the identical calves. "It's a very efficient method for us already," says Steven Stice, the firm's chief scientific officer. "We're producing more viable embryos than we have cows to put them in." (Oddly, the company has had no luck cloning a pig. "They are very different from cattle," says Stice. "Every step has to be reevaluated. We're not sure what we're doing wrong.")

24 Scientists first began trying to clone animals using adult cells in 1938, when the German embryologist Hans Spemann proposed making a clone by removing an egg's nucleus and replacing it with the nucleus from another cell. Those efforts failed until the 1970s, when frogs were finally cloned via the nuclear transfer method. None of the cloned frogs, however, made it past the tadpole stage. And that's where the idea of adult cloning stayed until Dolly arrived.

25 "It couldn't be done; that was what everyone said," explains Wolf, "which is why this was such a revolutionary discovery." The Scottish team "found a way to reprogram that adult cell." They did so by starving the adult cells, thus inactivating them. Wilmut began with a vial of frozen cells taken from the udder of a six-year-old sheep. His team thawed them and placed them in a growth serum with only minimal nutrients for five days. "That's the trick that made all the difference," says Wolf. The adult cells were then fused with 277 different eggs. Out of all these attempts, only one lamb was born: Dolly. "That tells you that something was desperately wrong with the other 276," says Steen Willadsen, an embryologist at St. Barnabas Medical Center in Livingston, New Jersey.

26 Because of this low success rate, "we're a long ways off from getting adult cloning to work on a regular basis even in domestic animals," adds Lawrence Layman, a reproductive endocrinologist at the University of Chicago. "It'd be highly unethical at this stage to try it in humans," since the probability of miscarriages and birth defects is high. Stice agrees: "It'd be complete folly. We've used hundreds of thousands of eggs in cattle

over the last ten years to achieve these results. To start at ground zero now with humans would be morally wrong and misguided."

Some researchers worry too that damage from aging DNA   27 may be passed on to the cloned infant. "It's going to be very instructive, watching Dolly age," says Julian Leakey, a biochemist at the National Center for Toxicological Research in Jefferson, Arkansas. "If she goes through puberty, she may be okay." But she might also have acquired some random genetic mutation that could lead to problems early in life. "That's the potential danger of cloning adults," says Leakey, "which is why it would be useful to do controlled tests in short-lived mammals, such as rodents, first. Then you could work out the odds of using aged tissue versus young tissue for cloning."

There are other unanswered questions. It's not clear which   28 cells were used to make Dolly. "They don't know which cell from the udder worked, or why it worked," says Ledbetter. "That's a big gap, and it means we don't have any idea if every cell type will work or only certain ones." Some researchers even question that it was an adult cell at all: the udder cells were taken from a pregnant sheep, and fetal cells are known to circulate in a mother's body. Nor do researchers know if the serum starvation trick will work with other species.

Despite the difficulties, says Willadsen, "the technique will   29 be—is being—perfected" . . . somewhere. And once that happens, it's only a matter of time before we see the first cloned humans—individuals who are a physical copy, or twin, of their mother or father, but separated by at least a generation. "When that first cloned child is born, not only will no one know that he or she is different," says Lee Silver, "no one will know that he or she is a clone. People will probably say things like, 'Oh, you look so much like your mother [if she was the nucleus donor],' and she'll smile. But no one will know, at least not until the kid is 16 and decides to sell her story to the tabloids for a million dollars."

From studying twins that were separated at birth and raised   30 in different families, researchers surmise that such clones will also be likely to share intellectual abilities and personality traits with their sole biological parent. Clones may thus follow in the footsteps of their parent but only in a very general way. "They will be separated by an entire generation," notes Sandra Scarr, a professor emerita of psychology at the University of Virginia in Charlottesville. "And as we all know, the cultural and social circumstances of the next generation are never the same as those of the preceding one. It's those social attitudes that shape a person's view of the world, including everything from how you view the stock market to the excesses of war. So the clones may be similar in intellect and personality, but their content will be different." Identical twins reared in the same house, she notes, listen to the same bedtime stories, eat at the family table together, attend the same schools, have the same friends and teachers. The clone and its parent, however, will share none of these experiences. "And these are the kinds of things that influence how one expresses one's genetic potential."

31   "People think it's going to be a robot or automaton," says Thomas Bouchard, who's led the long-term twin studies at the University of Minnesota. "Nothing could be further from the truth. They'll be their own persons, and that's why the idea of cloning doesn't bother me in the least. It's nonsense to be afraid of it." Yet because of this culturally ingrained idea of what a clone is, some ethicists are concerned that the parent of a clone may try to exert excessive control over the child. "Parents already control their children to an extraordinary degree," says Lori Andrews, a professor at the Kent College of Law. "Will these clones be held in some kind of genetic bondage to their parent? They might put undue pressure on the child to grow up in a certain way, so that it really doesn't have its own identity."

32   Other researchers question how similar the clones will be, even physically. "We already know from studying monkeys and children that there's considerable variation at birth," says Christopher Coe, a psychologist at the University of Wisconsin in Madison. Coe intends to explore this variation with the cloned rhesus monkeys that his colleagues Watkins and Schramm are attempting to produce. Since the cloned embryos will be implanted in different mothers, they'll "give us the best opportunity we've ever had to clarify what we mean by nature versus nurture," says Coe. "It's the project I've dreamed about since graduate school, 20 years ago." For instance, how different will a cloned monkey that's implanted in an older mother be from one that's grown in a younger mother? "To what degree do in utero influences affect the development of the baby?" asks Coe. "And how much do the mother's actions, what she eats, and whether or not she's dominant or submissive, influence her baby's growth? The prenatal environment plays a far bigger role in shaping a baby than most people realize." The cloned monkeys, he believes, will probably look alike (although they could also differ in such things as their weight at birth) but will nevertheless "be quite different."

33   Other research on human twins also suggests that such things as how early the cells divide into twins and where the twins are placed in the uterus affect how "identical" they are

after birth. "I think that's the real question: Just how different will these cloned babies be at birth, despite being genetically identical to their parent?" adds Coe. In an effort to establish the cloned monkeys' individuality, he will be measuring everything from their birth weight to how quickly they hold up their heads and how long they nurse.

Then too there's the question of the influence of the mito- 34 chondrial DNA. Not all of a cell's DNA is found in the nucleus; the mitochondria, tiny organs a cell uses to transform food into energy, have their own DNA. Although the donor egg will receive a new nucleus, it will retain its mitochondrial DNA, which may well be different from the donor's. "It's only a small amount of genetic variation, but it's there," says Silver, though, he adds, "there is nothing in the mitochondrial DNA that matters in making us different from each other."

In short, cloning yourself will not roll the clock back. It will 35 not produce your soul mate and may not even give you your complete identical twin. What it will do is give you a baby that is more biologically related to you than anyone else. And that, says Silver, is why cloning will happen and few people will harshly judge those with infertility problems who choose it as a way to reproduce. "It's instinctive, I think, to want to have a biological child. That's what cloning offers—a chance for some people to have what they thought they never could have: a child of their own."

Charles Krauthammer

OF (HEADLESS)
MICE . . . AND MEN

Charles Krauthammer is a cultural commentator whose views appear in many magazines. He especially frequently contributes to the Washington Post, *to* New Republic, *and to* Time *magazine, where the following essay was published in January 1998.*

Last year Dolly the cloned sheep was received with wonder, tit- 1 ters and some vague apprehension. Last week the announcement by a Chicago physicist that he is assembling a team to produce the first human clone occasioned yet another wave of Brave New World anxiety. But the scariest news of all—and largely overlooked—comes from two obscure labs, at the University of Texas and at the University of Bath. During the past four years, one group created headless mice; the other, headless tadpoles.

2   For sheer Frankenstein wattage, the purposeful creation of these animal monsters has no equal. Take the mice. Researchers found the gene that tells the embryo to produce the head. They deleted it. They did this in a thousand mice embryos, four of which were born. I use the term loosely. Having no way to breathe, the mice died instantly.

3   Why then create them? The Texas researchers want to learn how genes determine embryo development. But you don't have to be a genius to see the true utility of manufacturing headless creatures: for their organs—fully formed, perfectly useful, ripe for plundering.

4   Why should you be panicked? Because humans are next. "It would almost certainly be possible to produce human bodies without a forebrain," Princeton biologist Lee Silver told the *London Sunday Times.* "These human bodies without any semblance of consciousness would not be considered persons, and thus it would be perfectly legal to keep them 'alive' as a future source of organs."

5   "Alive." Never have a pair of quotation marks loomed so ominously. Take the mouse-frog technology, apply it to humans, combine it with cloning, and you are become a god: with a single cell taken from, say, your finger, you produce a headless replica of yourself, a mutant twin, arguably lifeless, that becomes your own personal, precisely tissue-matched organ farm.

6   There are, of course, technical hurdles along the way. Suppressing the equivalent "head" gene in man. Incubating tiny infant organs to grow into larger ones that adults could use. And creating artificial wombs (as per Aldous Huxley), given that it might be difficult to recruit sane women to carry headless fetuses to their birth/death.

7   It won't be long, however, before these technical barriers are breached. The ethical barriers are already cracking. Lewis Wolpert, professor of biology at University College, London, finds producing headless humans "personally distasteful" but, given the shortage of organs, does not think distaste is sufficient reason not to go ahead with something that would save lives. And Professor Silver not only sees "nothing wrong, philosophically or rationally," with producing headless humans for organ harvesting; he wants to convince a skeptical public that it is perfectly O.K.

8   When prominent scientists are prepared to acquiesce in—or indeed encourage—the deliberate creation of deformed and

dying quasi-human life, you know we are facing a bioethical abyss. Human beings are ends, not means. There is no grosser corruption of biotechnology than creating a human mutant and disemboweling it at our pleasure for spare parts.

The prospect of headless human clones should put the whole debate about "normal" cloning in a new light. Normal cloning is less a treatment for infertility than a treatment for vanity. It is a way to produce an exact genetic replica of yourself that will walk the earth years after you're gone. 9

But there is a problem with a clone. It is not really you. It is but a twin, a perfect John Doe Jr., but still a junior. With its own independent consciousness, it is, alas, just a facsimile of you. 10

The headless clone solves the facsimile problem. It is a gate-way to the ultimate vanity: immortality. If you create a real clone, you cannot transfer your consciousness into it to truly live on. But if you create a headless clone of just your body, you have created a ready source of replacement parts to keep you—your consciousness—going indefinitely. 11

Which is why one form of cloning will inevitably lead to the other. Cloning is the technology of narcissism, and nothing satisfies narcissism like immortality. Headlessness will be cloning's crowning achievement. 12

The time to put a stop to this is now. Dolly moved President Clinton to create a commission that recommended a tempo-rary ban on human cloning. But with physicist Richard Seed threatening to clone humans, and with headless animals al-ready here, we are past the time for toothless commissions and meaningless bans. 13

Clinton banned federal funding of human-cloning research, of which there is none anyway. He then proposed a five-year ban on cloning. This is not enough. Congress should ban hu-man cloning now. Totally. And regarding one particular form, it should be draconian: the deliberate creation of headless hu-mans must be made a crime, indeed a capital crime. If we flinch in the face of this high-tech barbarity, we'll deserve to live in the hell it heralds. 14

Virginia Postrel
FATALIST ATTRACTION

*In the summer of 1998, Virginia Postrel posted the following
essay on cloning to* Reason Online, *an Internet site that is
dedicated to encouraging intelligent exchanges on important
public issues. (Its motto is, "The best minds, the most important issues.")*

1   Twenty years ago, the bookstore in which I was working closed
for a few hours while we all went to the funeral of one of our colleagues. Herbie was a delightful guy, well liked by everyone. He
died in his 20s—a ripe old age back then for someone with cystic
fibrosis. In keeping with the family's wishes, we all contributed
money in his memory to support research on the disease. In
those days, the best hope was that scientists would develop a
prenatal test that would identify fetuses likely to have C.F., allowing them to be aborted. The thought made us uncomfortable. "Would you really want Herbie never to be?" said my boss.

2   But science has a way of surprising us. Two decades later,
abortion is no longer the answer proposed for cystic fibrosis.
Gene therapy—the kind of audacious high-tech tool that
generates countless references to *Brave New World* and
Frankenstein—promises not to stamp out future Herbies but
to cure them.

3   This spring I thought of Herbie for the first time in years. It
was amid the brouhaha over cloning, as bioethicists galore
were popping up on TV to demand that scientists justify their
unnatural activities and Pat Buchanan was declaring that
"mankind's got to control science, not the other way around."

4   It wasn't the technophobic fulminations of the anti-cloning
pundits that brought back Herbie's memory, however. It was a
letter from my husband's college roommate and his wife. Their
16-month-old son had been diagnosed with cystic fibrosis. He
was doing fine now, they wrote, and they were optimistic about
the progress of research on the disease.

5   There are no Herbies on *Crossfire*, and no babies with deadly
diseases. There are only nature and technology, science and society, "ethics" and ambition. Our public debate about biotechnology is loud and impassioned but, most of all, abstract.
Cowed by an intellectual culture that treats progress as a myth,
widespread choice as an indulgence, and science as the source
of atom bombs, even biotech's defenders rarely state their case
in stark, personal terms. Its opponents, meanwhile, act as

though medical advances are an evil, thrust upon us by scheming scientists. Hence Buchanan talks of "science" as distinct from "mankind" and ubiquitous Boston University bioethicist George Annas declares, "I want to put the burden of proof on scientists to show us why society needs this before society permits them to go ahead and [do] it."

That isn't, however, how medical science works. True, there 6 are research biologists studying life for its own sake. But the advances that get bioethicists exercised spring not from pure science but from consumer demand: "Society" may not ask for them, but individual people do.

Living in a center of medical research, I am always struck by 7 the people who appear on the local news, having just undergone this or that unprecedented medical procedure. They are all so ordinary, so down-to-earth. They are almost always middle-class, traditional families, people with big medical problems that require unusual solutions. They are not the Faustian, hedonistic yuppies you'd imagine from the way the pundits talk.

And it is the ambitions of such ordinary people, with yearn- 8 ings as old as humanity—for children, for health, for a long and healthy life for their loved ones—of which the experts so profoundly disapprove. As we race toward what Greg Benford aptly calls "the biological century," we will hear plenty of warnings that we should not play God or fool Mother Nature. We will hear the natural equated with the good, and fatalism lauded as maturity. That is a sentiment about which both green romantics and pious conservatives agree. And it deserves far more scrutiny than it usually gets.

Nobody wants to stand around and point a finger at this 9 woman [who had a baby at 63] and say, "You're immoral." But generalize the practice and ask yourself, "What does it really mean that we won't accept the life cycle or life course?" Leon Kass, the neocons' favorite bioethicist, told *The New York Times*, "That's one of the big problems of the contemporary scene. You've got all kinds of people who make a living and support themselves but who psychologically are not grown up. We have a culture of functional immaturity."

It sounds so profound, so wise, to denounce "functional im- 10 maturity" and set oneself up as a grown-up in a society of brats. But what exactly does it mean in this context? Kass can't possibly think that 63-year-olds will start flocking to fertility clinics—that was the quirky action of one determined woman. He is worried about something far more fundamental: our unwillingness to put up with whatever nature hands out, to accept our fates, to act our ages. "The good news," says Annas of human cloning, "is I think *finally we have a technology that we can all agree shouldn't be used."* (Emphasis added.) Lots of biotech is bad, he implies, but it's so damned hard to get people to admit it.

11   When confronted with such sentiments, we should remember just what Mother Nature looks like unmodified. Few biotechnophobes are as honest as British philosopher John Gray, who in a 1993 appeal for greens and conservatives to unite, wrote of "macabre high-tech medicine involving organ transplantation" and urged that we treat death as "a friend to be welcomed." Suffering is the human condition, he suggested: We should just lie back and accept it. "For millennia," he said, "people have been born, have suffered pain and illness, and have died, without those occurrences being understood as treatable diseases."

12   Gray's historical perspective is quite correct. In the good old days, rich men did not need divorce to dump their first wives for trophies. Childbirth and disease did the trick. In traditional societies, divorce, abandonment, annulment, concubinage, and polygamy—not high-tech medicine—were the cures for infertility. Until the 20th century, C.F. didn't need a separate diagnosis, since it was just one cause of infant mortality among many. Insulin treatment for diabetes (highly unnatural) didn't exist until the 1920s. My own grandmother saw her father, brother, and youngest sister die before she was in middle age. In 1964 a rubella epidemic left a cohort of American newborns deaf.

13   These days, we in rich countries have the wonderful luxury of rejecting even relatively minor ailments, from menstrual cramps to migraines, as unnecessary and treatable. "People had always suffered from allergies. . . . But compared to the other health problems people faced before the middle of the twentieth century, the sneezing, itching, and skin eruptions had for the most part been looked at as a nuisance," writes biologist Edward Golub. "In the modern world, however, they became serious impediments to living a full life, and the discovery that a whole class of compounds called antihistamines could control the symptoms of allergy meant that allergic individuals could lead close to normal lives. The same story can be told for high blood pressure, depression, and a large number of chronic conditions."

14   Treating chronic conditions is, if anything, more nature-defiant than attacking infectious diseases. A woman doesn't have to have a baby when she's 63 to refuse to "accept the life cycle or life course." She can just take estrogen. And, sure enough, there is a steady drumbeat of criticism against such unnatural measures, as there is against such psychologically

active drugs as Prozac. We should, say the critics, just take what nature gives us.

In large part, this attitude stems from a naive notion of 15 health as the natural state of the body. In fact, disease and death are natural; the cures are artificial. And as we rocket toward the biological century, we will increasingly realize that a bodily state may not be a "disease," but just something we wish to change. Arceli Keh was not sick because her ovaries no longer generated eggs; she was simply past menopause. To say she should be able to defy her natural clock (while admitting that mid-60s parenthood may not be the world's greatest idea) doesn't mean declaring menopause a disease. Nor does taking estrogen, any more than taking birth control pills, mean fertility is a sickness.

"The cloned human would be an attack on the dignity and 16 integrity of every single person on this earth," says German Research Minister Juergen Ruettgers, demanding a worldwide ban, lest such subhumans pollute the planet. (The Germans want to outlaw even the cloning of human cells for medical research.) Human cloning is an issue, but it is not *the* issue in these debates. They are really about whether centralized powers will wrest hold of scientists' freedom of inquiry and patients' freedom to choose—whether one set of experts will decide what is natural and proper for all of us—and whether, in fact, nature should be our standard of value.

Ruettgers is wildly overreacting and, in the process, attack- 17 ing the humanity of people yet unborn. As Ron Bailey has noted, human cloning is not that scary, unless you're afraid of identical twins, nor does it pose unprecedented ethical problems. No one has come up with a terribly plausible scenario of when human cloning might occur. Yet judging from the history of other medical technologies, the chances are good that if such a clone were created, the parents involved would be ordinary human beings with reasons both quite rare and extremely sympathetic. We should not let the arrogant likes of Ruettgers block their future hopes.

John Kilner

STOP CLONING AROUND

When the cloning controversy erupted in the spring of 1997, John Kilner was director of the Center for Bioethics and Human Dignity in Bannockburn, Illinois (near Chicago). He contributed the following article later that year to Christianity Today, *an evangelical Christian publication with a conservative editorial position. Kilner has written many articles and books on topics related to medical ethics. He later developed the argument presented here into a longer essay in a book he coedited called* The Reproductive Revolution *(1999).*

1   Cigar, the champion racehorse, is a dud as a stud. Attempts to impregnate numerous mares have failed. But his handlers are not discouraged. They think they might try to have Cigar cloned.

2   If a sheep and a monkey can be cloned—and possibly a race-horse—can human clones be far behind? The process is novel, though the concept is not.

3   We have long known that virtually every cell of the body contains a person's complete genetic code. The exception is sperm or egg cells, each of which contains half the genetic material until the sperm fertilizes the egg and a new human being with a complete genetic code begins growing.

4   We have now learned that the partial genetic material in an unfertilized egg cell may be replaced by the complete genetic material from a cell taken from an adult. With a full genetic code, the egg cell behaves as if it has been fertilized. At least, that is how Dolly, the sheep cloned in Scotland, came to be. Hence, producing genetic copies of human beings now seems more likely.

5   We have been anticipating this possibility in humans for decades and have been playing with it in our imaginations. The movie *The Boys from Brazil* was about an attempt to clone Adolf Hitler. And in Aldous Huxley's novel *Brave New World*, clones were produced to fulfill undesirable social roles. More recently the movie *Multiplicity* portrayed a harried man who jumped at the chance to have himself copied—the better to tend to his office work, his home chores, and his family rela-tionships. It all seems so attractive, at first glance, in our hec-tic, achievement-crazed society.

The Costs of Clones

But how do we achieve this technologically blissful state? 6
Multiplicity is silent on this matter, implying that technique is
best left to scientists, as if the rest of us are interested only in
the outcome. But the experiments of Nazi Germany and the resulting Nuremberg Trials and Code taught us long ago that
there is some knowledge that we must not pursue if it requires
the use of immoral means.

The research necessary to develop human cloning will cause 7
the deaths of human beings. Such deaths make the cost unac-
ceptably high. In the process used to clone sheep, there were
277 failed attempts—including the deaths of several defective
clones. In the monkey-cloning process, a living embryo was intentionally destroyed by taking the genetic material from the
embryo's eight cells and inserting it into eight egg cells whose
partial genetic material had been removed. Human embryos
and human infants would likewise be lost as the technique is
adapted to our own race.

Goal Rush

Yet, as we press toward this new mark, we must ask: Is the pro- 8
duction of human clones even a worthwhile goal? As movies
and novels suggest, and godly wisdom confirms, human
cloning is something neither to fool around with nor to attempt.

Cloning typically involves genetically copying some living 9
thing for a particular purpose—a wheat plant that yields much
grain, a cow that provides excellent milk. Such utilitarian approaches may be fine for cows and corn, but human beings,
made in the image of God, have a God-given dignity that prevents us from regarding other people merely as means to fulfill
our desires. We must not, for instance, produce clones with low
intelligence (or low ambition) to provide menial labor, or produce clones to provide transplantable organs (their identical genetic code would minimize organ rejection). We should not
even clone a child who dies tragically in order to remove the parents' grief, as if the clone could actually be the child who died.

All people are special creations of God who should be loved 10
and respected as such. We must not demean them by fundamentally subordinating their interests to those of others.

There is a host of problems with human cloning that we 11
have yet to address. Who are the parents of a clone produced
in a laboratory? The donor of the genetic material? The donor
of the egg into which the material is transferred? The scientist

who manipulates cells from anonymous donors? Who will provide the necessary love and care for this embryo, fetus, and then child especially when mistakes are made and it would be easier simply to discard it?

12 The problems become legion when having children is removed from the context of marriage and even from responsible parenthood. For instance, Hope College's Allen Verhey asks whether parenting is properly considered making children to match a specific design, as is clearly the case with cloning, or whether parenting is properly regarded as a disposition to be hospitable to children as given." Clearly, from a biblical perspective, it is the latter.

13 Further, the Bible portrays children as the fruit of a one-flesh love relationship, and for good reason. It is a context in which children flourish—in which their full humanity, material and nonmaterial, is respected and nourished. Those who provide them with physical (genetic) life also care for their ongoing physical as well as nonphysical needs.

14 As Valparaiso University's Gilbert Meilaender told *Christianity Today,* this further separation of procreating from marriage is bad for children. "The child inevitably becomes a product," says ethicist Meilaender, someone who is made, not begotten.

15 "To beget a child is to give birth to one who is like us, equal in dignity, for whom we care, but whose being we do not simply control. To 'make' a child is to create a product whose destiny we may well think we can shape. Hence, the 'begotten, not made' language of the creed is relevant also to our understanding of the child and of the relation between the generations.

16 "If our purpose is to clone people as possible sources of perfectly matching organs," says Meilaender, "that clearly shows how we could come to regard the clone as a being we control— as simply an ensemble of parts or organs."

Xeroxing Michael

17 It is all too easy to lose sight of the fact that people are more than just physical beings, Meilaender's ensembles of organs. What most excites many people about cloning is the possibility of duplicate Michael Jordans, Mother Teresas, or Colin Powells. However, were clones of any of these heroes to begin growing today, those clones would not turn out to be our heroes, for our heroes are not who they are simply because of their DNA. They, like us, were shaped by genetics and environment alike, with the spiritual capacity to evaluate, disregard, and at times to overcome either or both. Each clone would be

subject to a unique set of environmental influences, and our loving God would surely accord each a unique personal relationship with him.

The problem with cloning is not the mere fact that technology is involved. Technology can help us do better what God has for us to do. The problem arises when we use technology for purposes that conflict with God's. And, as C. S. Lewis argued, technology never merely represents human mastery over nature; it also involves the power of some people over other people. This is as true in the genetic revolution as it was in the Industrial Revolution. When human cloning becomes technically possible, who will control who clones whom and for what ends? Like nuclear weaponry, the power to clone in the "wrong hands" could have devastating consequences. 18

There is wisdom in President Clinton's immediate move to forestall human cloning research until public debate and expert testimony have been digested and policies formulated. But there is even greater wisdom in never setting foot on the path that leads from brave new sheep to made-to-order organ donors, industrial drones, and vanity children. 19

Kenan Malik

THE MORAL CLONE

In May 2001, Kenan Malik, author of Man, Beast, and Zombie *and* The Meaning of Race: Race, History, and Culture in Western Society, *published the following essay in* Prospect *magazine, a British publication on public issues and contemporary culture.*

The Pope condemns their work as "abhorrent." Jeremy Rifkin warns that they are striking a "Faustian bargain" which could pave the way to a "commercial eugenics civilisation." The object of this hostility is two doctors, the US-based Panayiotis Zavos and the Italian Severino Antinori, who, in March, declared their intention of helping infertile couples conceive through the use of cloning techniques. 1

From Aldous Huxley's picture of human production lines in *Brave New World* to Michael Marshall Smith's description in his novel *Spares* of farms where the rich keep clones of themselves so that their organs can be "harvested" for transplants, 2 cloning has been a metaphor for the creation of an immoral, inhuman world. The birth in February 1997 of Dolly the sheep transformed such visions from the realms of science fiction to science fact. It seemed only a matter of time before humans could also be duplicated, a prospect greeted with almost universal condemnation. Even Ian Wilmut, Dolly's creator, believes that we should "reject this proposed use of cloning."

3   I want to argue that the current debate about cloning turns the ethical issues on their head. There are no reasons to regard the cloning of humans as unethical. There is, on the other hand, something deeply immoral about a campaign that seeks to block the advancement, not just of reproductive technology, but also of other medical techniques based on cloning methods which could save countless lives.

4   There are three main objections to cloning: that it undermines human dignity and personal identity; that it uses people as objects; and that it is unnatural. Opponents argue that it is immoral to create exact copies of people. According to the bioethicist Leon Kass, "the cloned individual will be saddled with a genotype that has already lived. He will not be fully a surprise to the world." Others worry that unethical governments, or even corporations, may institute a programme to create production line people, perhaps even a race of Adolf Hitlers.

5   Such arguments misunderstand both the character of cloning and the nature of human beings. To clone an organism—whether Dolly or Adolf Hitler—scientists take an egg and remove its nucleus, the part that includes, among other things, the bulk of the DNA. Next, they remove the nucleus from a cell belonging to the adult that is to be cloned and insert it into the egg. The reconstructed egg is stimulated, either electrically or chemically, to trick it into behaving like a fertilised egg. If this is successful, the egg divides and becomes an embryo, which is then transferred into the uterus of a surrogate mother. Pregnancy then follows its normal course.

6   Any human child conceived in this fashion will be the genetic twin of the person who is the cell donor. But to have the same genome is not to be the same person. Genes play an important part in shaping who we are but they are not the only influence on us.

7   If having the same genome means being the same person, then all naturally-born identical twins would be exact duplicates of each other. This is not the case. Identical twins differ in everything from their fingerprints to their personalities. Children conceived with the aid of cloning technology will be even more different from their genetic parents than are most natural twins from each other. Most naturally conceived

identical twins grow up in roughly the same environment. Cloned children, on the other hand, will be born into a different family from their "twin," have different parents and siblings, and have different experiences from the day they are born. In other words they will be nothing like their parent whose genome they inherit.

Children conceived though cloning will be indistinguishable 8 from children conceived naturally, whether these happen to be identical twins or not. Each will be a unique human being with a unique identity and an unpredictable future.

What of the argument that cloning turns human beings into 9 means, not ends? Cloned children, critics say, will simply be the means for their parents' self-aggrandisement. This may well be true, but it is also true for many children born in conventional ways. Twenty years ago opponents of the then-nascent in vitro fertilisation (IVF) technology also argued that "test-tube" babies were being treated as objects. Anyone who has witnessed the emotional and financial commitment that couples have to invest in IVF treatment will recognise, however, that such children are very much wanted and treasured by their parents. The same will be true for any cloned child.

Faced with the implausibility of most of their arguments, op- 10 ponents of cloning generally fall back on the claim that cloning is repugnant because it is unnatural. "From time immemorial," Jeremy Rifkin says, "we have thought of the birth of our progeny as a gift bestowed by God or a beneficent nature." According to Rifkin, "the coming together of sperm and egg represents a moment of surrender to forces outside of our control."

Cloning is certainly unnatural. But then so is virtually every 11 human activity. The whole point of any medical intervention from taking an aspirin to heart surgery is to ensure that humans are not at the mercy of "forces outside our control." If we were to look upon human conception as simply a "gift from God," then contraception, abortion and IVF would all have to be ruled immoral. Cloning is no more unnatural than IVF. If we are happy to accept the latter (as most people are), then why should we not accept the former too?

There is only one argument against human cloning that has 12 any substance. Many experts believe that it is precipitous to attempt to clone human beings today because the procedure is insufficiently safe. It remains difficult to get reconstructed eggs to develop into embryos and many of these embryos show abnormalities. In the case of Dolly, for instance, Ian Wilmut began with 277 reconstructed eggs, of which 29 developed into embryos. Of these 29 embryos only one resulted in a pregnancy that went to term. Given such problems, the consensus among most scientists is that Zavos and Antinori are being hasty in their plans to clone humans. Cloning techniques have yet to be fine-tuned and the risk of conceiving deformed children is too great. The question of safety, however, is not an ethical one. Ethical injunctions are absolute: under no circumstances should we attempt to clone a human. Safety considerations are relative: when the technology has become more refined, we can proceed.

13   By preventing cloning research, opponents are preventing the development of new treatments that draw upon cloning techniques, and hence are allowing many people to suffer unnecessarily. A case in point is the controversy over "therapeutic cloning." Therapeutic cloning is a means of growing human tissue that fuses the techniques that helped create Dolly with another new medical technology: the ability to grow embryonic stem (ES) cells.

14   The cells of an adult human are highly specialised; under normal circumstances a liver cell will always stay a liver cell, and a skin cell can never become anything else. Stem cells, however, are cells that can develop into any kind of tissue: liver, skin, nerve, heart. The best source of such stem cells are tiny embryos, a few days old. If we could take the nucleus of, say, a healthy cell from a patient with Parkinson's disease and fuse it with an enucleated stem cell, we could grow brain tissue that could potentially replace the patient's damaged cells. Because such tissue would be genetically identical to that of the patient, there would be no problem of tissue rejection. Such a technique could help patients with problems from Parkinson's and Alzheimer's to diabetes, leukaemia and even heart disease.

15   Therapeutic cloning is a way of growing human tissues, it has nothing to do with creating new human beings. The embryo is a pin-prick of about two dozen cells; because it could potentially be a human life does not mean that it *is* one. Anyone who objects to therapeutic cloning must logically object not only to all forms of abortion but to IVF too, which produces spare embryos in pursuit of a successful pregnancy.

16   According to the *Telegraph*, "The difference between therapeutic cloning, to create 'spare part' organs, and reproductive cloning, to create babies, is only one of purpose—a secondary distinction." In both cases "the embryo is treated as a disposable object, deprived of any humanity." The same "fundamental moral objections," the *Telegraph* claims, "apply to all human cloning."

17   As a result of such arguments, most European states still ban research into therapeutic cloning. Britain finally licensed certain forms of cloning research last year, but only in very lim-

ited cases. In the US, the Bush administration is expected to ban federal funding for any form of ES-cell research. In a special report on therapeutic cloning, the journal *Nature* asked recently why it was that only a dozen or so research teams are pursuing work in such a promising area. A large part of the answer, it concluded, was the degree of political restriction.

Opponents of cloning like to present the debate as one between an immoral science, hell-bent on progress at any cost, and those who seek to place scientific advancement within a moral framework. But what is moral about allowing unnecessary suffering? Theologians and Luddites are using norms drawn from dogmatic and reactionary visions of life to prevent the alleviation of human suffering.   18

Scott Adams
DILBERT

Scott Adams (born 1957 in the Catskill Mountains of New York) moved to California to obtain an MBA in 1986, and to begin a career in finance in the San Francisco Bay Area. But after working in a bank at a series of jobs that he describes (on his web page) as "humiliating," he began poking fun at the stresses of workplace culture in a cartoon series that he named "Dilbert." In 1989, he began syndicating his cartoons nationwide, and they remain tremendously popular despite—or because of—their anti-establishment message. The cartoon below suggests that cloning may have implications that go beyond the obvious ones. What might some of those implications be?

Hanna Rosin
THE HOMECOMING

Hanna Rosin published the following account of AIDS in the African American community in the June 5, 1995, issue of The New Republic, *a middle-of-the-road magazine of political and cultural affairs. (The essay reprinted after this one, by Ann Louise Bardach, was in the same issue.)*

1   A middle-aged black man named Otis is about to reveal his most intimate secret to a perfect stranger. He checks to make sure nobody's lurking around the corner (lst and M, southeast Washington, D.C., a block full of prostitutes and addicts). He hears a dealer hawking "face" (heroin), and waits, tugging anxiously at his faded blue sweatshirt, until the man skulks away. Then he leans over to this stranger, an outreach worker from the local AIDS clinic, and whispers that he has, "Well, you know, the disease."

2   Otis says he found out he was HIV-positive in 1986, during a wave of infections that alerted AIDS researchers they had been wrong about the virus. At first, they predicted it would shift away from white gay men to terrorize the broad population, mutating into an equal-opportunity killer. Instead, it found people like Otis—poor, addicted and black. Blacks, 12 percent of the population, account for one-third of all AIDS cases. Three out of five new AIDS victims now are black, up from one in five in 1986. Black women are now fifteen times more likely to have AIDS than white women, and their children, eighteen times more likely. By now, AIDS should be familiar, yet Otis can't bring himself to mention it by name.

3   Otis's story helps explain how HIV has been able to make such inroads in poor black America. He found out he was positive by

a fluke. When he was in prison on possession charges, nurses from the National Institutes of Health offered $15 to anyone who would agree to be tested, and Otis volunteered because he needed the money. (It took the nurse fifteen tries to find a live vein.) He's not sure where he got the virus—either from his girl-friend, whose husband was a junkie (now dead), or from his cousin, who once stole his works and lent them to a "small, skinny guy who had that look, you know, like he was a homo."

Each time Otis tells the truth, he becomes a pariah. He says   4
his wife left him when people found out he was positive and started calling her a "diseased bitch." His 14-year-old niece, visiting from Georgia with her son, "freaked when she found out, started screaming, 'He's been using the same bathroom, he touched my baby.'" When he confided in his minister, the man pointed at him the next day in church and preached about the sins of bad living. Otis won't go to an AIDS clinic, even for a prescription: "Nope. No way in hell. That's, you know . . . a homo place, and your mama or your cousin or anybody could see you go in and then you're branded for life." What about medicine? "Somebody told me it makes your hair fall out," he says defensively. Only once does Otis let down his defenses, when he talks about the night he went to a support group at a local church. Most of the people were in advanced stages, looked sickly and could barely move, and "it tore me down. I thought, 'This is my future.'"

Wayne Greaves has been chief of Howard University's AIDS   5
clinic since before it existed, when nine patients with a mys-tery disease were crammed into a corner of the hospital. A wiry, wound-up man, he is as apt to lash out at his no-show pa-tients as at "bigots" at the NIH. Three years ago he co-authored a study that is perhaps the best clue to the virus's surge among blacks, although it remains buried in the *Journal of AIDS*. Greaves and two colleagues reviewed autopsy reports of sev-enty HIV-positive inner-city patients. What they found sur-prised even Greaves: about half had been diagnosed *after death*, even though most showed obvious symptoms of AIDS-related diseases. The shame around AIDS in black America makes prevention almost impossible and treatment widely re-fused, and it keeps infection on an increasingly upward curve. "There are some people who would rather not know," Greaves says angrily. "A lot, actually, would rather not know."

One reason they'd rather not know is the uneasiness in the   6
community about open homosexuality, still closely associated with the disease. "There's an enormous hidden population," says Frank Oldham, former director of Washington's Agency for HIV/AIDS, "a huge number of bisexual men who don't

identify as gay. It's fascinating: they go to church, to the park with their families, then at night you'll see them cruising the gay bars." Many see nothing wrong with this way of living. "Open homosexuality is viewed as something imposed on us by the gay white culture," explains Alonzo Fair, from a group called URBAN, which has widely polled Washington's blacks about AIDS. "The black community has always accepted homosexuality. There is always a gay person in church or who lives down the street or a cousin, and that's perfectly fine. It's only when that person defines himself as gay, you know, adopts the gay white culture, like doing the rainbow flag thing, that the community reacts negatively. For a black man, family comes first."

7   This devotion to family can end up destroying it. Men who do risky things but don't consider themselves at risk are the virus's welcome mat into the black home. Black men are twice as likely as white men to be bisexual, according to a recent study of 65,000 HIV-positive men published in *American Journal of Public Health*. Black drug users, who sometimes double as male prostitutes, are four times as likely. This makes black America vulnerable to the kind of heterosexual breakout that white America has so far avoided and that is the norm in other parts of the world. Half the black bisexual men in the study were married when they died. It's likely their wives didn't know: in a California AIDS study, only one-fifth of the black women responding were aware that their partners were bisexual. As a result, AIDS is now the leading killer of young black women.

8   Race itself does not affect one's chances of contracting HIV, as in, say, sickle-cell anemia. But inner-city ills do. For example, one-quarter of all black men in their 20s, and 15 percent of adult males, rotate through prison. Among inmates, unprotected anal sex is common. Prison is thus a place where the virus can spread to men who may have sex with men while in jail and with women when they get out. In 1990, doctors at Riker's Island conducted what is called a blind seroprevalence test. They took the name tags off blood samples used in mandatory syphilis tests and checked them for HIV. A quarter of both male and female samples tested positive, a result since replicated in other big city prisons. A study of long-term inmates in the Florida jail system found that 20 percent had contracted HIV while in prison. The confessionals in *Angoli,* the best of the prison magazines, tell all. One Louisiana inmate who tested positive in 1989 admitted that he and his cellmate did "every unsafe thing you could do." Another, who knew he was positive yet still had sex with other inmates, mused,

"Maybe I shouldn't do it no more . . . but if the guy is willing to go for it. . . . We all have to die sooner or later."

At the same time, suspicion and mistrust of mainstream 9 medical institutions make it harder to mount an effective, communal response. It's easy to see this phenomenon at work in east Washington, D.C., not far from Otis's block, at a place called Paradise Manor. Here, identical new swing sets perch on every trimmed lawn, and each tidy brick housing complex bears a name like Harmony, Freedom or Justice. Occupying four units of Miracle is the Abundant Life Clinic, a center for alternative therapies specializing in AIDS and run by Dr. Abdul Alim Muhammed, health minister for the Nation of Islam. Walk inside and the waiting room exudes none of the menacing air you find at Nation rallies; to the background accompaniment of a Whitney Houston tape, the staff chats flirtatiously, the women tossing back their brightly patterned veils. If not for the blown-up portrait of Louis Farrakhan and the Lyndon LaRouche pamphlets ("WHO OWNS HENRY KISSINGER?"), you might mistake this for any other AIDS clinic.

Muhammed sweeps into the room, tall and striking in his 10 crisp white lab coat and mint-striped shirt, and greets me cheerfully. He has reason to be upbeat. Mayor Marion Barry has appointed him co-director of the AIDS transition team, elevating him to unofficial AIDS czar for the black community in Washington, D.C. Add that to an award in 1993 from then-Mayor Sharon Pratt Kelly and $500,000 in federal grants over the last two years, and he's the most prominent black anti-AIDS figure in the capital. We move into his office and he takes a seat behind his glass-topped desk. In this sterile, pleasant room, it's hard to picture him as he was a year ago, fulminating to a Baltimore crowd about AIDS being "the perfect genocidal weapon" manufactured by the white government against black people, issuing death threats to Baltimore Mayor Kurt Schmoke.

Muhammed's latest initiative is convincing Mayor Barry to 11 divert a $2 million grant from the city's largest AIDS clinic, run by, as he sees it, white homosexuals, to his own. With that money, he'll be closer to achieving his mission to "save the world." This mission includes widespread mandatory testing, followed by treatment with his miracle drug, Kemron. The drug was discovered by Joseph Cummins, a white veterinarian in Amarillo, Texas, the only white man whose photo will ever grace the walls of the Abundant Life Clinic. In 1989, Cummins trekked to the Kenyan Medical Research Institute with his discovery, a protein-like drug called alpha interferon, which is used to treat a rare form of leukemia. There, doctors fed their patients wafers laced with low doses of the drug. After three months of a study with no control group, the doctors breathlessly announced a miracle. Ninety-nine of 101 patients bounded back to health, they claimed. "Fifty AIDS victims have already been cured!" cheered Kenyan President Daniel Arap Moi. On the other side of the world, his euphoria provided an occasion for New York's *Amsterdam News* to blast the "racist white press" for "cabalistically ignoring this amazing discovery."

12   It was hardly ignored. In 1991, the World Health Organization conducted a study of 150 patients in Zambia and concluded that Kemron produced no benefits. In an effort to settle the question, the National Institutes of Health in 1992 reviewed thirteen clinical trials from around the world. Their study concluded that alpha interferon "is not recommended for persons of HIV infection" and that patients using it should immediately switch to other drugs.

13   The news failed to squelch interest in Kemron. In March 1992, Farrakhan announced that the Abundant Life Clinic would market the drug aggressively in the United States. Ads ran every week in *The Final Call*, the group's paper, and the marketing campaign proved a smashing success. Thousands of patients, by the NIH's estimate, most of whom were poor and without insurance, shelled out money for the miracle drug. And at a premium: the Nation sells Kemron for $150 to $250 for a one-month supply, depending on the brand, and charges a $1,000 initiation fee. Other vendors price the drug at $65 for a thirty-day supply. It's clearly a profitable business.

14   At its worst, the story of Kemron is about the Nation's shameless manipulation of scared proselytes. There is also, however, a less scandalous, if ultimately more disturbing point here: so widespread are fears of government institutions and white doctors among African Americans, that they will take any alternative over conventional medical treatment.

15   One study attempted to quantify these fears. In 1990, researchers from the Southern Christian Leadership Conference (SCLC) handed out surveys to 1,000 black churchgoers in five cities: Atlanta, Charlotte, Detroit, Kansas City and Tuscaloosa. More than one-third agreed that AIDS was a form of genocide against blacks; another third were unsure. And more than a third believed HIV was produced in a germ-warfare lab, a theory shared by 40 percent of black college students enrolled in Washington, D.C.

16   Consider these musings on the origin of the virus, solicited from passersby in one random inner-city block in Albany one

afternoon last December. They are set to a Public Enemy soundtrack in *HIV and Genocide: Responding to African American Community Concerns,* a New York State Health Department training video: "It came from Vietnam. It started with chemical warfare, and then the government put it out into the population." "It was an experiment, OK. It was an experiment and then someone spread it on one group of people, onto one nationality. I'm not saying I'm prejudiced because I'm not. But that's my opinion, and everyone has a right to an opinion." "I don't know if it was the government or some secret organization outside the government but I believe the government had a hand into it or the secret organization had a hand into it." "I think first it was some kind of laboratory experiment. Then they perpetrated it on people of color in Africa and Haiti and places that the powers that be think of as throwaway people. Now people like me—and I don't consider myself a throwaway person—now I have the virus."

"If it looks like a duck, and walks like a duck, well then?" says Ron Simmons, director of Us Helping Us: People Into Living, the only group in Washington, D.C., founded by gay black men to support their own. Bundled in a black hooded sweatshirt, surrounded by photos of black men in zebra-print thongs and a stern portrait of Malcolm X, he puts his feet up on his desk and expounds on the origin of the HIV virus. "My thinking is they're killing black and brown folks, and the reason they gave it to white folks first is because it was too soon after the Atlanta child murders in '78, and there would have been riots." 17

Under the Centers for Disease Control and Prevention's new community initiative, Simmons's group was recently awarded a $50,000 federal grant. It will use the money to expand an already-thriving network of support groups for black men through which group leaders promote a philosophy of holistic healing: herbs, vitamins, Chinese teas, breathing exercises and absolutely no AZT, or any other of the standard chemical drugs. Simmons says he never tells members not to take AZT; he just guides them toward an "informed decision": "One thing about corporate medicine is they find a way to make money off you until you're in your grave," he jeers, holding up a copy of his bible, *Poison by Prescription: The AZT Story.* "Black folks have what I call a healthy paranoia. After all, they did it once, so they can do it again." 18

"They" is the U.S. government—specifically, the Public Health Service. What they did was the Tuskegee Syphilis Study, a forty-year experiment on untreated syphilis in 400 black sharecroppers in Alabama which followed them to "end point," 19 or death. Researchers carried on with the experiment until 1972, twenty years after penicillin became the standard treatment for the disease, and could have been used to cure the men under study.

20   Long considered this country's worst large-scale violation of medical ethics, Tuskegee has become the parable by which many blacks understand their relationship to public health services. From Los Angeles to Atlanta, groups such as Us Helping Us preach the virtues of healthy paranoia. "Tuskegee has taken on a life of its own as a disaster myth," says Stephen Thomas, a professor at Emory University who conducted the SCLC conspiracy study and has since polled 6,000 blacks around the country. "It has transcended being a historical event and turned into an urban legend, a personification of medical abuses and racism."

21   The result has been a lot of refused treatment. Dr. Joe Timpone, director of D.C. General Hospital's AIDS Unit, estimates that about one-fifth of his 800 black patients will not take AZT. It's hard enough, he complains, to persuade people with no money for bus fare or a babysitter, who miss an average of half their appointments, to stick to a regimen of bimonthly visits and fifteen pills a day. Add in chronic suspicion and his job becomes "almost impossible." A study by the AIDS Research Consortium in Atlanta found that 80 percent of women who should have been taking AZT or other antiretroviral drugs weren't. "If an AIDS vaccine came out tomorrow," warns Thomas, "a significant number of blacks would not take it."

22   Not even if it were free. Wayne Greaves from Howard University spends his days convincing people to enroll in clinical trials, studies of experimental medicine, where patients receive free care and medication. Most of his efforts are fruitless. "Even here, where we are mostly black, they won't come near us. We go out and recruit, and they say, 'Yeah, yeah, the money's coming from the NIH, right, so who are you trying to kid?'" Mary Lynn, the outreach worker for the program, who hikes around Washington seeing hundreds of people a week, says that around 70 percent ask about Tuskegee. "They're completely convinced they'll be used as guinea pigs for some evil agenda."

23   In adults, AZT only slows HIV's progression; it doesn't cure anyone. But in the case of babies born HIV-positive, the drug actually can be a cure. In February 1994, a joint French-American study found that giving AZT to a pregnant woman and her infant child dramatically reduces the baby's chances of contracting the virus from 25.5 percent to 8.3 percent—"by far the most important and helpful news to come out of the epidemic," says Elaine Abrams, director of Harlem Hospital's

AIDS Pediatric Clinic. But the news would be better if women who heard it believed it. "They just say no," says Abrams, almost all of whose 200 patients are black. "Plenty of women refuse to get tested, to have their infants tested or to take medicine. Maybe they're afraid, or they see a healthy-looking baby in their arms and it all doesn't make sense." In a recent focus group on maternal transmission of HIV, conducted by the New York State Health Department, two groups of pregnant women split evenly by race, with black mothers-to-be refusing to "take that poison," as one put it.

Black clergy, the community's natural leaders, only feed the 24 paranoia. When a clean-needles program was first proposed in New York City in 1989, Calvin O. Butts of the Abyssinian Baptist Church decreed he was "not in favor of cooperating with the devil," meaning those who might perpetuate addiction. Leading the national charge was Reverend Graylan Ellis-Hagler, who now presides over the Plymouth Congregational Church in Washington. "First, the white establishment pushes drugs into the community," he told the *Atlantic* in 1993. "They cripple the community politically and economically with the drugs. They send the males to jail. Then someone hands us needles to maintain the dependency."

Religious opposition killed needle-exchange programs in 25 every city except New York, which squeezed through a trial program in 1991. The result is the only unqualified success story in the prevention war. In a city where half of intravenous drug users test positive, the program cut infection rates by 50 to 75 percent, according to a study of its 2,500 participants. Now, Ellis-Hagler is willing to relent, he says, "because there aren't strong enough feelings from the community to create a hysteria," although he still finds the program "a pitiful last resort, and racist." It may be too late. By now, momentum has died down. Washington, for example, has only enough money for a tiny pilot program inconveniently located in a downtown federal building.

The vacuum has been filled by a kind of generic sermoniz- 26 ing, drained of any urgency. Ten years ago, ministers routinely refused to preside over funerals of people who died of AIDS, and funeral homes refused to bury them. That kind of disgust has mostly been replaced by evasive homilies, expressed by a scattered few, such as Washington's Reverend Pervis "Fireball" McKenna, who takes pride in insisting, "I preach against all sin and that's one of them. I'm with the Bible on sin, and all of it is against God, period, whether it be homosexuals or whatever." In milder forms, ministers presiding over funerals will say "this person was a sinner, but he renounced that world at the end of his life," or they won't mention how the person died.

27   A typical example is the Metropolitan Baptist Church, a favorite of Washington, D.C.'s, black gay community. On a recent Sunday, the pews were packed with men in crisp wool suits and women in white gloves with straightened hair, their well-behaved children in tow. The choir, 100 strong, seemed to be the refuge for many of the single, and some obviously gay men. The imposing Reverend H. Beecher Hicks Jr., draped in purple velvet vestments, presided. In his trembling baritone, he admonished his flock of "black bourgeoisie" to remember their roots, to exercise compassion outside the church walls.

28   The church has had an AIDS ministry for two years and its director has been instructed never to use the word "gay," says a former adviser. Mostly it educates congregation members that it's OK to shake hands with the HIV-positive, to "love the sinner but not the sin," says Hicks. Its mission is the same as the dozens of other help ministries run by the church. "I don't make a lot out of it," explains Hicks. "It's like Alcoholics Anonymous, Narcotics Anonymous, like people who are depressed or divorced. We find a way to meet everyone's personal needs, and don't lift one up over the other."

29   As of January, some 84,568 young African Americans had died of AIDS.

Ann Louise Bardach
THE WHITE CLOUD

Ann Louise Bardach is a writer who contributes to Vanity Fair *and other magazines that examine contemporary culture. The following essay appeared in* The New Republic *in June 1995, in the same issue as the previous item by Hanna Rosin.*

1   Freddie Rodriguez is discouraged. He has just come from his afternoon's activity of trying to stop men from having unprotected sex in Miami's Alice Wainwright Park, a popular gay cruising spot. Rodriguez, 29, is a slim, handsome Cuban-American with a pale, worried face who works for Health Crisis Network. "I take a bag of condoms to the park with me and I try talking to people before they duck in the bushes and

have sex," he explains. "I tell them how dangerous it is. Sometimes I beg them to use a condom. Sometimes they listen to me. Today, no one was interested." Most of the men, he says, are Latinos and range in age from 16 to 60. Many are married and would never describe themselves as gay. "Discrimination is not really the issue here. Most Latinos do not identify themselves as gay, so they're not discriminated against," he says, his voice drifting off. "Ours is a culture of denial."

To understand why the second wave of AIDS is hitting 2 Latinos particularly hard, one would do well to start in Miami. Once a mecca for retirees, South Beach today is a frenzy of dance and sex clubs, for hetero- and homosexual alike. "We have the highest rate of heterosexual transmission in the country, the second-highest number of babies born with AIDS and we are number one nationwide for teen HIV cases," says Randi Jenson, reeling off a litany that clearly exhausts him. Jenson supervises the Miami Beach HIV/AIDS Project and sits on the board of the Gay, Lesbian and Bisexual Community Center. "And we have the highest rate of bisexuality in the country." When I ask how he knows this, he says, "Trust me on this one, *we know.* . . . The numbers to watch for in the future will be Hispanic women—the wives and girlfriends."

Already, AIDS is the leading cause of death in Miami and 3 Fort Lauderdale for women ages 25 to 44, four times greater than the national average. According to the Centers for Disease Control and Prevention (CDC), AIDS cases among Hispanics have been steadily rising. But any foray into the Latino subculture shows that the numbers do not tell the whole story, and may not even tell half. CDC literature notes that "it is believed that AIDS-related cases and deaths for Latinos are understated by at least 30 percent. Many Hispanics do not and cannot access HIV testing and health care." Abetted by widespread shame about homosexuality, a fear of governmental and medical institutions (particularly among undocumented immigrants) and cultural denial as deep as Havana Harbor, AIDS is moving silently and insistently through Hispanic America. It is the stealth virus.

"No one knows how many Latino HIV cases are out there," 4 Damian Pardo, an affable Cuban-American, who is president of the board of Health Crisis Network, tells me over lunch in Coral Gables. "All we know is that the numbers are not accurate—that the actual cases are far higher. Everyone in the community lies about HIV." Everyone, according to Pardo, means the families, the lovers, the priests, the doctors and the patients. "The Hispanic community in South Florida is far more affluent than blacks. More often than not, people see their own family doctor who simply signs a falsified death certificate. It's a conspiracy of silence and everyone is complicitous."

5   Freddie Rodriguez—smart, affluent, urbane—didn't learn that Luis, his Nicaraguan lover, was HIV-positive until it was too late to do anything about it. "He was my first boyfriend. He would get sick at times but he refused to take a blood test. He said that it was impossible for him to be HIV-positive. I believed him. One day, he disappeared. Didn't come home, didn't go to work—just disappeared." Frantic, Rodriguez called the police and started phoning hospitals. Finally, Luis turned up at Jackson Memorial Hospital. He had been discovered unconscious and rushed to intensive care. When Rodriguez arrived at the hospital, he learned that his lover was in the AIDS wing. Even then, Luis insisted it was a mistake. Two weeks later, he was dead. "I had to tell Luis's family that he was gay," Rodriguez says, "that I was his boyfriend and that he had died of AIDS. They knew nothing. He lived a completely secret life."

6   Although Rodriguez was enraged by his lover's cowardice, he understood his dilemma all too well. He remembered how hard it was to tell his own family. "When I was 22, I finally told my parents that I was gay. My mother screamed and ran out of the room. My father raised his hands in front of his eyes and told me, 'Freddie do you see what's in front of me? It's a big, white cloud. I do not hear anything, see anything and I cannot remember anything because it is all in this big white cloud.' And then he left the room." One of Rodriguez's later boyfriends, this one Peruvian, was also HIV-positive, but far more duplicitous. "He flat out lied to me when I asked him. He knew, but he only told me after we broke up, *after* we had unsafe sex," says Rodriguez, who remains HIV-negative. "Part of the *machismo* ethic," Rodriguez explains, "is not wearing a condom."

7   Miami's Body Positive, which provides psychological and non-clinical services to AIDS patients, is housed in a pink concrete bubble off Miami's Biscayne Boulevard. The building and much of its funding are provided by founder Doris Feinberg, who lost both her sons to AIDS during the late 1980s. The gay Cuban-American star of MTV's "The Real World," Pedro Zamora, worked here for the last five years of his life and started its P.O.P. program—Peer Outreach for Persons Who Are Positive. Ernie Lopez, a 26-year-old Nicaraguan who has been Body Positive's director for the last five years, estimates that 40 percent of the center's clients are Latino, in a Miami population that is 70 percent Hispanic. On the day I visit, I see mostly black men at the facility. Lopez warns me not to be fooled. "The Latino numbers are as high as the blacks, but they are not registered," he says. "Latinos want anonymity. They

come in very late—when they are desperate and their disease is very progressed. Often it's too late to help them."

"Soy completo," is what they often say in Cuba, meaning, 8 "I'm a total human being." It is the preferred euphemism for bisexuality and in the *machista* politics of Latino culture, bisexuality is a huge step up from being gay. It is this cultural construct that prevents many Latin men from acknowledging that they could be vulnerable to HIV, because it is this cultural construct that tells them they are not gay. Why worry about AIDS if only gay men get AIDS? "To be bisexual is a code," says Ernesto Pujol, a pioneer in Latino AIDS education. "It means, 'I sleep with men but I still have power.' I think there is a legitimate group of bisexuals, but for many bisexuality is a codified and covered homosexuality." Self-definitions can get even more complex. "I'm not gay," a well-known intellectual told me in Havana last year. "How could I be gay? My boyfriend is married and has a family."

Without putting too fine a point on it, what defines a gay 9 man in some segments of the Latino world is whether he's on the top or the bottom during intercourse. "The salient property of the *maricon*," my Cuban friend adds, "is his passivity. If you're a 'top,'—*el bugaron*—you're not a faggot." Moreover, there are also many heterosexual Latino men who do not regard sex with another man as a homosexual act. "A lot of heterosexual Latinos—say, after a few drinks—will fuck a transvestite as a surrogate woman," says Pujol, "and that is culturally acceptable—absolutely acceptable." Hence the potential for HIV transmission is far greater than in the mainstream Anglo world.

According to Pujol, "only Latinos in the States are interested 10 in other gay men. They have borrowed the American liberated gay model. In Latin America, the hunt is for 'straight' men. Look at the transvestites on Cristina's (the Spanish-language equivalent of "Oprah") talk show. Their boyfriends are always some macho hunk from the *bodega*." Chino, a Cuban gay now living in Montreal, typifies the cultural divide. "I don't understand it here," he says scornfully. "It's like girls going out with girls."

"If you come out," says Jorge B., a Cuban artist in Miami 11 Beach, "you lose your sex appeal to 'straight' men" (straight in this context meaning married men who have sex with other men). The Hispanic preference for "straight men" is so popular that bathhouses such as Club Bodycenter in Coral Gables are said to cater to a clientele of older married men who often pick up young lovers after work before joining their families for dinner. Some men will not risk going to a gay bar, says Freddie Rodriguez. "They go to public restrooms where they can't be identified." While many gay Hispanics do eventually "come out," they do so at a huge price—a shattering loss of esteem within their family and community. "The priest who did Mass at my grandfather's funeral denied communion to me and my brother," recalls Pardo. "He knew from my mother's confession that we were gay."

12   Latino attitudes here are, of course, largely imported, their cultural fingerprints lifted straight out of Havana, Lima or Guatemala City. Consider Chiapas, Mexico, where gay men were routinely arrested throughout the 1980s; many of their bodies were later found dumped in a mass grave. Or Ecuador, where it is against the law to be a homosexual, and effeminate behavior or dress can be grounds for arrest. Or Peru, where the Shining Path has targeted gays for assassination. Or Colombia, where death squads do the same, characteristically mutilating their victims' genitals.

13   While Latino hostility to homosexuals in the United States tends to be less dramatic, it can also be virulent, particularly when cradled in reactionary politics. In Miami, right-wing Spanish-language stations daily blast their enemies as "communists, traitors and Castro puppets." But the epithet reserved for the most despised is "homosexual" or "*maricon*." When Nelson Mandela visited Miami in 1990, he was denounced daily as a "*marijuanero maricon*"—a pot-smoking faggot—for having supported Fidel Castro.

14   On the other side of the country, AIDS Project Los Angeles is the second-largest health provider for AIDS patients in the United States (after Gay Men's Health Crisis in New York). It's a sparkling facility with a food bank, a dental program and all manner of support services. Housed in the David Geffen Building at the corner of Fountain and Vine, it is well-provided for by a generous Hollywood community. Currently, AIDS Project Los Angeles attends to the needs of more than 4,500 clients, 60 percent of whom are gay men. Roughly one-fourth of the total are Latinos, and the majority of those are Mexican. Thirty-two-year-old Troy Fernandez is one of the project's senior aides on public policy. Born in Yonkers and of Puerto Rican descent, Fernandez is a caramel-colored black man with long dreadlocks streaming down his back. Dressed in crisp white jeans, he's as slim and elegant as a fountain pen. He's also HIV-positive—part of the second wave.

15   Although Fernandez "did the downtown dance scene and Fire Island," in his 20s, he didn't go to the bathhouses, and he was never on the front line of the party scene. Even when the political equation of the gay revolution—"the more promiscuous, the

more liberated"—still had currency, Fernandez was warier than his peers. By 1981, friends of his had started to die of the mysterious illness then known as the gay plague. Fernandez got himself checked out as soon as HIV testing became available, and came up negative year after year while he continued to practice safe sex. Then he moved to Los Angeles and met Rodrigo.

Rodrigo was a well-educated Mexican-American, a high-level insurance executive, a Republican conservative and "completely closeted." Among Rodrigo's tightly knit family, only one of his brothers—also gay—knew his secret. When Fernandez asked his partner if he was HIV-positive, he said no. He'd never been tested, but he knew he wasn't. He also insisted he was monogamous. "It's all about what risks you are willing to take," says Fernandez slowly. "I understand why people stop practicing safe sex. One is always renegotiating the risk factors at some level. You see, you want to believe that your lover is telling you the truth." 16

In 1990, Rodrigo got sick. By then Fernandez had become suspicious, and pressed his partner to be tested. "I told him he had to do it for my sake," he says, "if nothing else." When Rodrigo learned he was positive "it was a double whammy," says Fernandez. "He had to admit that he was sick and dying and worse—he had to admit that he was gay." Within the year, Fernandez learned that he, too, had the virus. Remembering, he lets loose a long sigh. "I don't have an answer for why I took a chance. I knew better, but it only takes one time." Fernandez surmises on the basis of personal anecdotal experience that as many as "90 percent [of gay] Latinos are closeted. Many may have self-identified but tell no one else." He bases his estimate on the number of married men who come into AIDS Project Los Angeles. "They always say they need the information for their brother or brother-in-law." 17

Rarely visible in the statistics are the wives and girlfriends of these men—the group that experts predict will soar to the top of the AIDS charts by the end of the decade. Currently, blacks and Latinas make up 77 percent of all AIDS cases among women; the number of Latina cases is seven times higher than that of Anglo women. Researchers have long known that the "receptive partner," is at greater risk of contracting not only HIV but all sexually transmitted diseases. For reasons generally unknown, women tend to get sicker sooner and die faster. Moreover, for many Latinas striving to be good Catholic wives in a culture where church and family are the co-pillars of the community, contracting HIV is an unfathomable betrayal and an irredeemable disgrace. 18

19   Ernesto Pujol remembers a Salvadoran housewife in her mid-50s, then living in Brooklyn. "She had just tested positive. She was crying. She was so bitter—so angry at her husband and the waste of her life. She had bought the whole Latina martyrdom of being the faithful wife." The husband was a drunk who had battered her, belittled her, and who would finally kill her. Still, she maintained that her husband had been infected by female prostitutes—and never looked at the evidence that he had had sex with men. "None of the women I worked with ever admitted that their spouses were gay or bisexual," says Pujol. "They would say, 'He drinks, you know.' They would rather blame prostitutes than consider the culturally unacceptable possibility of other men."

20   Wanda Santiago, 36, has lived much of her life as a pariah. A Puerto Rican lesbian, born and raised in Brooklyn, Santiago learned in 1989 that she was HIV-positive. At 13, she started doing drugs when her family moved to a rough neighborhood in Williamsburg. At 16, she was pregnant and married and drinking. After three years, her husband left. "I knew I was gay since I was 8," she says, "but I thought getting married would cure me." In 1978, Santiago came out and turned the care of her young son over to her mother.

21   Santiago suspects she contracted HIV during her romance with an Ecuadoran woman who was stationed with the Navy in Virginia. "I was crazy about her," says Santiago, who lived with the woman for three years. "Every now and then, she would bring a man to our bed," says Santiago. "It could have been one of them, or maybe I got it from a needle." A few years after her relationship hit the skids, Santiago sobered up for good, but by then she was feeling tired all the time. "For a week after I tested positive, I refused to believe it," she says. "Total denial."

22   Until 1991, Santiago worked for the Health & Rehabilitation Service screening Latinas with sexually transmitted diseases for HIV. "A lot of them refused to be tested," she says. "If they did test positive, they wouldn't believe it. The fear overwhelmed them. They would say, 'Don't talk about it,' 'I don't have it' and 'Don't tell my husband.' Many were in denial about their husbands screwing around. They thought they would get blamed for getting the disease. It's much worse in Hispanic culture than it is for whites or blacks because Hispanics won't even talk about it. A lot of the women were afraid to use condoms because they would get beat up by their husbands. See, if you're infected by a man, you're a whore. If you're infected by drugs, then you deserve it. But it's OK for a man to have HIV because it's OK for a man to whore around."

Mary Lou Duran has been working with the community in   23
East Los Angeles for twenty-one years, the last three and a half
of them as a case manager for the HIV patients at Altamed
Services. Her clients are women: primarily Mexican-American
or Central American refugees, both legal and undocumented,
ranging in age from 17 to 56, and including "several grand-
mothers." A few of the older women may have gotten the virus
from blood transfusions during surgery in Mexico, before the
availability of HIV testing. But the overwhelming majority
were infected by spouses or lovers. "One woman, from
Guatemala, died in October," Duran says. "She had a very aggressive virus and died in less than three and a half years. She
got it from a boyfriend and left a child behind. I feel the majority of the women I see are innocent victims—wives and girlfriends who have no idea what is going on." Duran then relates
a more personal experience: "In my own family, there have
been three deaths—three nephews who were gay. But my family says, 'No one has died of AIDS.' They call it cancer. We can't
comfort each other because we can't discuss it. 'They weren't
gay,' they say, and 'They didn't have AIDS.'"

By coincidence, one of Duran's ailing nephews ran into her at   24
a clinic where she was working. "He was shocked to see me," she
remembers. "He was sick—very progressed by the time he came
in for help." They chatted briefly, awkwardly. It was her only
personal contact with the tragedy in her family. "I have always
been a community worker and my family has come to me when
they have a need of sorts, but never while I do this work. They
have never asked for my help. They have no interest or curiosity
in my work. They never ask any questions. Nothing is ever said.
The entire community is in denial. They just don't believe it is
happening. They think that AIDS is about gay white males."

When not manning the AIDS project, Troy Fernandez makes   25
the rounds of Hollywood bathhouses, doing what amounts to
"interventions"—foisting condoms on men before they have
sex. "The culture of the bathhouses has changed," he says, his
voice brightening. "Some people sit around and talk. Sure, it's
still mainly sex but there's some talk." Fernandez doesn't believe closing the bathhouses serves any purpose. "If you close
the Hollywood Spa or the Compound, people will simply go to
Plummer Park or the restroom at the Beverly Center. My
friends in New York say the bathrooms at Juilliard are very
busy these days. Face it, we are not going to stop people from
having sex."

What then are the prospects of halting the second wave?   26
Fernandez is initially speechless, and it takes a few minutes for

him to get pumped up again. "We should get real that what we're doing is not working." He sings the praises of another program he's involved in—*Saber es Poder* (Knowledge is Power), which enables him and others to go into heavily Hispanic schools and talk to kids in grades seven through twelve. "But I can't say 'dick' to a kid in a school program without losing funding," he complains. "The truth is, Joycelyn Elders was right. We have to start talking to kids when they're young, not when it's too late or the second wave will keep rolling along and then the third wave and then the fourth wave."

27   As for Ernesto Pujol, he says he will never forget Carla, a soft-spoken, graceful Puerto Rican he met during his days running the Brooklyn AIDS unit of New York's Crisis Intervention Services. Happily married to a Brazilian man, Carla was at work on her doctorate. "The entire family got sick about the same time," says Pujol. "Her husband, she and their 2-year-old daughter. He died first, then the baby. I remember the day in the hospital that she told her family that she had AIDS and of course they became hysterical. It was very sad. She was a devout Catholic and AIDS caused her a great crisis of faith—like a slap in the face. As a couple, they had everything going for them—white upper-middle-class Latinos who could pass, educated and charming. Her husband had told her that he got it from an old girlfriend who was an addict but I suspected that he had had prior bisexual behavior. She chose to believe what her husband told her and I wasn't about to take that away from her. He was a very terrific, wonderful guy who was also working on his doctorate. But he was haunted by his past—and HIV is a past that won't ever let go of you."

AIDS PUBLIC
EDUCATION ADS

The ads on the following pages were developed as a part of AIDS-education campaigns. The first, from the United States Department of Health and Human Services, began appearing about 1990. The second, a product of the American Red Cross targeted at the Hispanic American community, began appearing in 1988.

Talk About AIDS

How About Dinner, A Movie, And A Talk About AIDS?

Marie: *That's not exactly my idea of a great date.*

Why?

Marie: *Because it's kind of depressing.*

When you think about AIDS and being single, what's the first thing that comes to mind?

Marie: *Be careful!*

AIDS scares you?

Marie: *Sure. But, it's something I have to think about.*

When you say you think about it, what do you mean?

Marie: *I ask myself questions I never thought about before.*

Do you ask guys?

Marie: *I'm starting to.*

How is that working out?

Marie: *Actually, not so bad.*

AMERICA
RESPONDS
TO AIDS
1-800-342-AIDS
1-800-AIDS-TTY

U.S. DEPARTMENT OF HEALTH AND HUMAN SERVICES • PUBLIC HEALTH SERVICE • CENTERS FOR DISEASE CONTROL   CDC

¿Qué les espera en el futuro?

¡Protéjalos! Infórmese acerca del SIDA. Llame a la Cruz Roja en su comunidad.

Con nuestro agradecimiento a la Cruz Roja Colombiana, Seccional Caldas

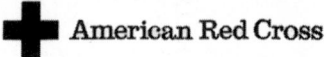 American Red Cross

Jesse Green
FLIRTING WITH SUICIDE

Jesse Green often contributes articles to the Sunday New York Times Magazine, *which carried the following item in September 1996.*

Mark Ebenhoch has on his "command" voice: the voice of fearless authority he learned during twelve years in the Marines. A fearless voice hardly seems appropriate now, in my hotel room, talking about sex; he wants to get rid of it but it keeps reemerging. If he had the money, he'd also get rid of the tattoos: the one on the left arm that reads "U.S.M.C. and damn proud" and the one on his chest, the so-called meat patch with his social security number and blood type: B-positive. Which could be his catch phrase. Be positive. 1

So he talks about what has brought him to this state—he is H.I.V. negative but wonders how long he can hold on—as if he were announcing a baseball game. "Heck, I'd been such a good boy, followed my church upbringing, wouldn't cuss, even in the corps. I was celibate for 13 years instead of being gay! So then, last year when I finally came out, I came out flying like a bat out of hell. Wednesday, Friday, Saturday I'd go to this bar called Friends, which was outside a military base that was notorious for gay bashings. I'd walk in and it was a really friendly atmosphere, so I sat down and ordered a beer. Once, this guy, not even my type really, sat down next to me. He was military, which I could tell from his haircut, and it didn't take that long, a drink or two and a couple cigarettes, before he said, 'Do you want to go do something?' And it was like, O.K., let's go. 2

"He followed me home in the car and there was this incredible anticipation, with his headlights in the rearview mirror. *I wonder what he's like . . . I wonder what we're going to do.* And I'd show him the house and offer him something to drink but then the first time somebody swings that first kiss, you can just forget it. And by now, I've had four or five beers. I don't have any rubbers and stuff. In California the bars give you the condoms free; not in North Carolina, where I was living then. And no one brings it up. It's not thought about. Well, for a split second but I say to myself: I know this is a marine, I know he gets checked every six months and he's probably the safest bet in the world. And *this* one was married. 3

"It was like I was finally inside the candy store I'd been looking at forever. I wasn't about to deny myself now. So during 4 that time, those two or three months, I guess I had over 20 partners. A lot of the time I was drunk, though, so I can't say for sure. Sometimes you'd go home with somebody you might not really want because of loneliness, and in that position I sure wouldn't mention safe sex. I'd always wait for them to say something about it." He nods his head sharply, as if dismissing an underling. "But no one did."

5   That no one mentioned safe sex to Mark Ebenhoch does not mean no one knew what it was. Gay men have had more than a decade to get the message—and for the most part, have. In the years after AIDS was first reported, in 1981, the gay community, largely on its own, masterminded what may be the most intensive public health intervention ever. Armed with explicit fliers and scary ads urging the use of condoms for every sexual contact—and, later, with subtler messages trying to promote this new behavior as fun—educators undertook the complete reorganization of gay mating habits. By some measures, the effort was amazingly successful: a 1994 New York City study showed that gay men's average number of unsafe-sex contacts dropped from more than 11 per year in 1980 to 1 per year in 1991. But by other measures, as Mark Ebenhoch's story and a thousand others like it demonstrate, the effort faded. Which leads to a question of perspective: Are the cemeteries half full or half empty?

6   Getting people to change their private behavior for the public good, or even for their own well-being, has been a chronic national problem. Recent reports—much politicized this election season—show that drug use by teen-agers, after a period of steady decline, more than doubled between 1992 and 1995. Highly visible efforts to combat the problem of "children having children" haven't worked either: 4 out of 10 American women become pregnant by the time they reach age 20—almost a million teenagers a year. Indeed, despite decades of effort, there is no clear consensus on what kinds of interventions even make a difference. Prescriptive, authoritarian campaigns like Just Say No may be effective in certain already-motivated populations, but they virtually repel those who most need addressing. And even if successful interventions are found, they tend to stop working long before anyone is willing to give them up.

7   An examination of AIDS prevention efforts in the gay community shows why. For a while, the safe-sex posters and fliers worked well, at least while it was still believed that the disease might disappear momentarily. The optimism engendered by the early statistics led some AIDS organizations to conclude that their educational mission was complete; San Francisco's

Stop AIDS Project disbanded in 1987. But when it became clear that no cure was imminent, and that the changes adopted for a finite emergency would have to be sustained over a lifetime instead, the gay community was caught short. By 1991, it was common knowledge that men who had been safe for at least six years were slipping more and more often, and that many men who had never been safe saw no point in starting now.

The Stop AIDS Project reconstituted itself in 1990, but the   8
renewal of prevention efforts there and elsewhere took place in a much grimmer context. It was by then evident that black and Latino men (whose infection rates were much higher than those of white men) had never been adequately reached, and that young homosexuals especially were on the brink of disaster. According to a 1991 study, more than half of the nation's 20-year-old gay men will contract H.I.V. during their lifetime, if current trends continue. But even among the population of older, white gay men who most successfully absorbed the original prevention message, things began to look less golden. Though the annual rate of new infections in San Francisco had decreased from well over 10 percent in the early 80's to 1.4 percent in 1990, that rate has nearly doubled in just the last six years. Perversely, even the good news about a new class of drugs called protease inhibitors—which have reduced blood levels of H.I.V. in some patients to undetectable levels—has backfired: many gay men are now talking about AIDS as a manageable disease, and using this premature hope as an excuse for returning to the unsafe practices of the past.

Despite these reversals, the one-note educational strategy of   9
the prevention organizations has barely changed since 1985. That strategy basically boils down to normative, hand-slapping variations on Just Say No, which are almost interchangeable with similar preachments about driving drunk, smoking cigarettes and motorcycling without a helmet. "These things can become jokes very quickly," says Lloyd Johnston, who as program director at the University of Michigan's Institute for Social Research has studied adolescent drug use for 25 years. "Remember the fried egg campaign? *This is your brain. This is your brain on drugs.* It was only a slogan, and the best you can say for a slogan is that it may work for a little while. This one did. It definitely spoke to kids, at least for a time; then it lost its persuasive power and maybe even became negative. In a way, the more successful these things are, the shorter their shelf life."

Aside from the paternalism of such campaigns, Johnston   10
blames their eventual failure on a phenomenon he calls "generational forgetting." Improvement in one decade means that young people in the next see fewer examples, either first hand

or in the media, of the consequences of risky behavior. At the same time, that improvement allows public health officials to let down their guard, and government agencies to cut back financing. With less negative and positive reinforcement, the cycle starts again. "Which is a strong parallel to AIDS," says Johnston. "At the beginning of the epidemic many young gay men knew about or cared for people who were dying; they felt that tragedy and pain personally. Now we have a new generation replacing them who haven't gone through it. The most convincing prevention message in any field is direct experience—but it's also the most costly."

11   How cost is measured is the crux of the problem. Our current notions of public health are based on old, even ancient, models. Developed to contain everything from the plague to polio, classical interventions targeted more cohesive and tractable societies, and made less intrusive demands. *Cover your mouth and nose when sneezing.* But how do you "do public health" (as public health people like to say) in a democracy? How do you weigh individual liberty against statistical risk? And what happens when the behavior in question isn't a sneeze but part of a person's deepest core of identity? What if it's something he profoundly enjoys and does not *want* to give up?

12   When a natural drive like sex gets tangled in unintended and even tragic results, public health is at its worst. "Moralistic slogans and intervention programs based unrealistically on no-sex vows do *not* reduce teen pregnancy or sexual activity," says Gloria Feldt, president of the Planned Parenthood Federation of America. "In fact, there have been studies that show they may actually *increase* the desire of teenagers to experiment: to find out what it is they've been told to say no to. And then because they haven't been given the tools with which to experiment safely—and because they've been told that they are bad people if they prepare—the likelihood of pregnancy only goes up. Basically such programs don't work," she concludes, "because ignorance is *not* bliss."

13   This is a phrase I've also heard from a Berkeley psychologist named Walt Odets, but Odets goes even further. Suggesting that coercive messages like "a condom every time" are unjustifiably broad, he has condemned AIDS prevention efforts as at best counterproductive and at worst dishonest—"not only withholding information from gay men but lying to them." In response to the huge stir such proclamations have caused in the AIDS community, Odets has dug in his heels; the question of whether prevention efforts have succeeded or failed is to him almost obscene. Indeed, though you can look at studies of gay men and make a credible case for either proposition,

looking at gay men themselves, you cannot. Many of those who show up in the data as H.I.V.-negative are struggling in ways statistical analysis won't pick up until it's too late; some consider themselves *statistics to be*. Such men exist in an illogical limbo: they are not sick but don't feel safe and, despite years of posters and pamphlets, can barely tell the difference.

A living rebuke to the status quo in AIDS education, these 14 men were largely ignored until Odets started asking a series of contrarian questions: *Have some prevention campaigns actually increased the likelihood of transmission? Are risk-elimination strategies for gay men actually homophobic?* For the last few years, Odets has insisted on a re-evaluation of the entire effort—a call to arms with implications for all public health campaigns. In a recent book, in impromptu jeremiads and in a series of withering articles (one of them called "The Fatal Mistakes of AIDS Education"), he has argued that prevention organizations have failed even the basic requirements of a sustainable initiative: to identify appropriate target audiences, provide them with accurate information and respect their right to weigh risk against benefit according to their own values. In doing so, he concludes, the groups have been guilty of ignoring the deepest root of gay men's unsafety: the psychological root, what they *feel*.

That Odets has been vilified for such conclusions is, in a 15 way, just another sign of the brittleness of the gay community after 15 years of AIDS. But public health interventions are generally most necessary in exactly those communities most sensitive to criticism. In the gay community, that sensitivity has often resulted in the sacrifice of candor to political correctness. Until 1995, for instance, there was not a single AIDS prevention program for gay men in the country specifically targeted to those who were uninfected—the only logical audience—for fear of offending infected men *by suggesting their condition was something to avoid*. And it is still taboo in AIDS circles to broach the subject of promiscuity. At one gay men's support group I attended, a 20-year-old who described himself as promiscuous was hissed into rewording his own experience: "All right, *slutty*," he said, to applause.

Promiscuity is famously defined as any amount of sex 16 greater than what you are having. Admittedly, it's an unhelpful word. And yet, *promiscuous* is how many gay men describe at least a part of their life. Some of them mean a kind of innocent, adolescent freedom, but what others really mean is *compulsive* sex—sex that cannot be credibly taken as political liberation or personal ecstasy because it does not bring joy, cannot be controlled and is used, exactly like alcohol or drugs, to assuage a nonsexual need. Either way, these words are important in understanding AIDS, despite the inability of the AIDS establishment to utter them. Which is why, at a time when public health interventions of all kinds seemed to be failing, I set out to talk to H.I.V.-negative men who were having problems with unsafe sex: the ones who were floridly unsafe, the ones who slipped now and then, the ones who were so scared of being unsafe that they had no sex at all. I was hoping they would be able to answer the question that has bothered me since 1991: Why are gay men—ordinary gay men, who appear to function normally and enjoy the pleasures of life—systematically killing themselves?

17   "I do fit the bill and am interested," came the E-mail response from Mark Ebenhoch—though at this point I still knew him only by his handle, Nailinch9. Sitting at my computer, I had posted messages on various electronic bulletin boards, explaining that I was looking for H.I.V.-negative gay men willing to talk about their unsafe sexual experiences. I did wonder what kind of person would respond to such an inquiry, but Nailinch9 addressed this problem at once. "My reasons are simple," he wrote. "If there is a way to prevent this type of behavior and share it maybe someone else would miss the selfish hell I've put myself through."

18   I had, through more traditional methods, spoken to many men who also seemed to fit the bill, but most of them insisted on anonymity. Some said they were ashamed of the way they were endangering themselves and did not wish friends or family to know the difficult truths of their lives. Others—many others—were tormented about what even *constituted* unsafe sex. Over the last few years they had slowly come to accept the idea that unprotected anal sex was virtually the only way they might contract AIDS; Gay Men's Health Crisis, in New York, had reviewed dozens of scientific papers and found only four reports of "individuals presumed to have been infected by H.I.V. through oral sex" in the United States as of 1995. Then, in June, a report about oral transmission of an AIDS-like virus in six rhesus monkeys implied that the common wisdom was false. And though all of the major AIDS organizations dismissed that conclusion, the men I spoke to were left so confused that they could barely make rational decisions about safety at all.

19   Mark Ebenhoch was not confused. Though he knew better, he had been unsafe at least several dozen times since his first adult sexual experience with a male, last year. He was forthcoming about the other things in his life that may have influenced him.

Alarmingly, he seemed to match, point by point, each of the predictors of risk that AIDS educators have identified, combining in one short story the factors I had been hearing about singly from dozens of other men. For my purposes he was, in a way, *too* good. For his own purposes he was not good enough.

And goodness had much to do with it. Mark was born into a chaotic family that zigzagged between Ohio, Florida, Arizona and California; his mother, he says, was constantly getting married—"like Elizabeth Taylor without the money." His father left when Mark was 9, after which Mark shut down emotionally and devoted himself to fabricating a demeanor of perfect obedience and normalcy. If this was at the expense of real feelings, so be it; feelings tended to get in the way. At 10, his mother has told him, he was molested by a man assigned to be a big brother. Mark remembers nothing of the incident except being forced to wear a tiny blue-and-white swimsuit. "Which was agony," he says. "I was extremely bashful and had very low self-esteem. At 13 I still looked 9. Even now. . . ."   20

Even now, at 36, only the slightly toughened skin of a marine and the weary cast of his gray blue eyes contradict the general impression of extreme youth. When I meet him in person, on a scorching April Los Angeles day, he's wearing a white mesh tank top, skimpy white corduroy shorts and strange, ill-fitting, orange-tinted sunglasses. He is thin—too thin—and pool-boy blond. Despite the gold hoop in his ear and the pink-triangle ring on his left pinky, he comes off a little blank: edging sometimes toward gruffness, sometimes toward warmth, but always watchful, as if on patrol.   21

What stability Mark has had in his life has come from the U.S.M.C.: "the most homophobic, macho service, which was part of what attracted me to it." After joining directly from high school in 1977, he spent 12 of the next 18 years among "Uncle Sam's Misguided Children," either as a reservist or on active duty, including a stint as a Stinger antiaircraft gunner in the gulf war. Between enlistments he took various jobs—purchasing agent, mechanic, long-haul trucker—before ending up in Hollywood as an assistant military adviser on such films as "Platoon," "Forrest Gump" and, most recently, "Sergeant Bilko." Throughout it all he was celibate and lonely, though in his command voice there is no trace of sadness. "So when I finally decided to come out, it felt like a Niagra Falls of relief. It's not like I didn't know about AIDS. We had an AIDS-awareness class every six months in the corps. And, as a senior sergeant, when I knew the men were going out, I'd say, 'You know what's out there, you know what to do, just do it.' But when it came time for *me* to be safe, no one was there to say anything. Even   22 if they had, I doubt I'd have listened. I was on a euphoric mission. 'I am going to experiment,' I said 'and see what it's all about.' *I want I want I want!*

23   "Maybe I'm an extreme case," he continues, "but I've met plenty of people like me. Go down Santa Monica Boulevard and look in the bars: it's lost people. And people like us don't pay any attention to the posters and ads. Don't they get it? It's *hard* to be safe. Think of the situation if you're looking to meet someone. You have to put away a lot of alcohol in the first place, just to get up the nerve, and then your reasoning is off. Last time, I was so toasted, I remember the room spinning. Lucky I passed out so nothing happened. But you can't blame it all on alcohol either. It's something within you that makes you go on these binges. You remember what it feels like when somebody wants you: you're a god. And then it's over and you're a heel again. Alcohol is a tool to free yourself to destroy yourself if you already want to. And no poster is going to solve that."

24   If Mark Ebenhoch exemplifies many of the co-factors for H.I.V. risk—recent emergence from the closet, lack of financial and domestic stability, alcohol use, depression, compulsiveness, a history of sexual abuse—he is not necessarily typical. Most of the men I spoke to fell into more definable single categories of risk. One group, consisting mainly of men over 40, seemed to be pushed toward unsafety by the accumulated grief of 15 years' devastation. Many suffer from survivor guilt, marked by depression, isolation and sometimes even a subconscious desire to seek communion with their lost friends by courting the same fate. These men are often ridiculed as whiners, which reinforces their isolation. A letter last October to The Bay Area Reporter in San Francisco, responding to an article about the emergence of H.I.V.-negative support groups, sarcastically suggested the formation of similar groups for men who felt neglected because they didn't have *breast cancer*. Such men were invited to seek further information by writing "Victims-Are-Us" in the "PoorMe Building" at "4 Crybaby Lane."

25   Young men get more sympathy, if not more actual support. Several expressed to me the feeling that they would get AIDS no matter what they did; why even try to be safe? For them, ghoulish as it sounds, contracting the disease seemed almost like a rite of initiation into the gay community. Others were just too ecstatic about coming out of the closet to think about the consequences of their new-found freedoms. These young men, like young men of every stripe, felt themselves to be immortal or at any rate not subject to the biological facts that govern other lives. A 21-year-old named Danny O'Toole told me

that "practically everyone" he knows has a lot of unsafe sex and that they justify it with all sorts of magical thoughts. "They seem to believe that just being in a relationship protects them from risk" he said, "even if the partner is H.I.V.-positive. And others don't even bother to ask, thinking: 'If he isn't concerned, why should I be?'"

Older men in "serodiscordant" couples, in which one partner   26
is H.I.V.-positive and the other is not, sometimes don't want to face reality, either. They may already feel separated from one another by the difference in their status, and condoms seem to underline that. When *both* partners are uninfected, though there is of course no risk of transmission, fears about unsafety may arise anyway, in the form of questions about fidelity. One man I spoke to, who said he sometimes had sex outside of his long-term relationship, was afraid to tell his lover that they should consider using condoms. And another man, who was in a monogamous relationship, told me that, despite everything, he sometimes feared he was putting himself at risk. He had somehow acquired the belief that, whatever they might say and promise, gay men (like all men) were inherently untrustworthy.

It's not hard to see where he got that idea. The unwavering   27
focus of safe-sex campaigns on external condom use—no matter what you think you know about your partner—has led Danny O'Toole, for instance, to a bleak conclusion: If you can't trust, you can't love, so why even bother having a relationship? And while celibacy is certainly a way of remaining uninfected, it isn't a very happy outcome of safe-sex education. Still for some, it's better than trusting the inconstant compass of self-preservation; a man need not be delusional, suicidal, alcoholic or self-loathing to slip once and make a fatal error. He need only be human.

"It's about love, finally, or what you think is love," Mark says.   28
Several days after our first meeting, he is telling me about the most unsafe of his unsafe encounters. Like all gay men I have spoken to, but unlike any prevention poster, he sees his behavior in an emotional context. "I'd made a decision to come out publicly. So the night before, New Year's Eve, I'm at this bar, and there's this one very good-looking individual about my age or so—preppy, brown hair and just cute, period. At 2 in the morning I make my attack, bum a cigarette. Alcohol wasn't a factor for me but *he* was sloshed. And he was into amyl nitrate, which I'd never been introduced to until I went home with him. So this went on for an entire weekend. Never thought about precautions. If we would have had to go through the whole nine yards of talking about it, you would have lost everything.

This wild, instinctive, spontaneous, split-second fun would just . . . die. It's too much work. I mean, if you have to plan for three weeks to go on a camping trip for one day, that one day isn't worth it, right? Why even go?"

29   Mark isn't alone in his complaint. Most gay men (and straight men, for that matter) agree that condoms interfere not only with physical sensation but with the spiritual sensation of union. They may also make sex more real than one's romantic illusions can tolerate; just tearing the foil package makes some people feel they are admitting the specter of death into their bedrooms.

30   "Thinking back on it, I should have definitely said something. But at the time I thought: it doesn't make any difference *now* whether I try to be safe or not. Especially because I was falling in love. And, of course, *that's* when I begin to find out that he was a very unhappy person, extremely promiscuous all over the world. And that's when I finally go, *Oh, my god.* I replayed the events over and over, looking to find out how many instances there could have been of transmission: were there any cuts or injuries? It stopped all of my sexual activity—for a while."

31   I ask Mark if he's heard of a strategy called "negotiated safety," which is now a widely accepted approach to AIDS prevention for gay men in Australia, Canada and Great Britain. Instead of pushing "a condom every time," public health officials ask gay men to talk about risks with their partners and to tailor their condom use to the individual circumstances.

32   Mark responds acidly, as if I haven't understood his point. "Things are happening so fast you're just not thinking about that, I'm sorry. If the world was a perfect place, yeah, but not everybody is going to be perfect."

33   It is not the answer I wanted, and Mark knows it. He looks rather forlornly around my hotel room. "A teacher in North Carolina who just bought a brand new condo, yes, he's going to have negotiated safety or whatever. But where are the rest of us supposed to learn how to love right? Maybe I did it wrong, but I wanted to experience happiness. Isn't that what we all want? Someone who's there for you, even if just for a moment?"

34   Strangely, I'm reminded of the dilemma of poor, teen-age girls, for whom sex and even pregnancy may be a way of repairing, if only temporarily, a damaged sense of self-esteem. No wonder campaigns aimed at holding such girls to a vow of chastity, or that simply throw birth control at them, have so little chance of working; they are as misdirected as the safe-sex campaigns that have so far failed to reach Mark. Still, I make a little campaign of my own. "But don't you want to be safe," I ask, "so that you can try for that nice life you describe?"

"I can say that I would like to: that's the kind of answer you   35
give yourself," Mark answers flatly. "But I don't know what I'm
going to feel like next week after I get four or five rejections."

As the lilt of enthusiasm slowly fades, Mark's voice begins to   36
resemble, in its sheer bewilderment, other voices I've been
hearing. Listening to them individually, I had been able to
think of unsafe sex as an individual problem; listening to them
all combined in Mark's encompassing story, I begin to think of
it as a problem of community. Not just the *AIDS* community,
with its effective or ineffective messages, but the *gay* community, such as it is, which so fears the imposition of external values that it can barely promote any of its own.

"I regret a lot of things I did," he adds quietly. "But I regret   37
that I have to be gay in a world that bashes you or gives you
AIDS. I don't think I have it now, but I probably will eventually.
And if I do, it'll be from hooking up with the wrong person, a
lonely person, a person who doesn't feel he has any reason to
care—someone like me."

A month earlier, Mark had rolled up his sleeve for an H.I.V.   38
test; to his surprise, he was still O.K. Still, it can take six
months for the antibodies to show up, so he was only slightly
relieved. "I'll get tested again in June," he says. "And then
we'll see."

"What the hell is this?" Walt Odets exclaims. A trim, hand-   39
some man with pale blue eyes and graying temples, Odets reminds me of Warren Beatty—but on speed. Right now, he's
looking at an AIDS prevention poster that features photographs of various enthusiastic people with this legend: "Can't
be afraid . . . We have control." He almost blows up. "They
waste millions of dollars on this and they have no idea what to
say. 'We have control'? What does that mean? 'Can't be afraid'?
Why not? Men *are* afraid, they *don't* have control. These messages are a complete denial of what is actually happening in
men's lives!"

If Odets is a bit edgy, it's partly because he has never been in   40
a sex club before. Indeed, he has only come to this one, in a
bleak industrial San Francisco neighborhood on a Friday night
in February, to accompany his friend Ed Wolf, who works for
San Francisco's AIDS Health Project. Wolf spends two
evenings a month here, offering free, anonymous H.I.V. testing
and counseling to patrons; the club's owner has set him up in
an unused space on the second floor, formerly a nursery
school. Downstairs, though I am expecting a scene that would
shame a Bosch etching of hell, the club seems anything but
decadent. Rather, there is a frank acceptance of the mechanical

nature of the enterprise. Explicit safe-sex warnings abound, and monitors, who strictly prohibit anal contact of any kind, lend the place a kind of kindergarten propriety. I guess it's true, as many people have said, that AIDS is happening more in bedrooms than in bathhouses: more for the hope of love than for the always-reneged-upon promise of lust. Still, for all the constant palaver about the joys of anonymous sex, there is no joy here tonight. The customers—inside and especially in the long line outside—look anything but liberated; they seem grim, determined, ground down by grief.

41   No one has yet come upstairs for testing, and while Wolf sets out his fliers and forms, Odets paces the room, checking the Mickey Mouse clock. Wolf, though he works for one of the organizations whose efforts Odets once criticized, agrees with much of what his friend says and has the equanimity to tolerate the rest. "But the others," he whispers confidentially, "they *hate* him. You don't know!" In fact, I do: Odets has made such a pest of himself in San Francisco that none of the major AIDS organizations there will work with him. Instead he has consulted on projects for Gay Men's Health Crisis, 3,000 miles away in New York.

42   It isn't hard to see why Walt Whitman Odets (named for the poet) rankles. Raised in Manhattan, he is anything but the laid-back Californian, and his habits, especially for a man whose mission is risk reduction, seem immoderate. At 49, he smokes, drinks, scarfs down eggs and bacon and rhapsodizes about his days flying planes and driving motorcycles. He is a daredevil, I come to realize, both physically and intellectually. But that doesn't mean he's wrong.

43   "Most prevention efforts have been based on risk-elimination rather than risk reduction," he tells me during another of our many talks over the course of a year. "But the question is whether one *ever* eliminates risk for things that are valuable. As a society, we do all kinds of things that may or may not be in the interest of our long-term health because we consider them important. We *weigh* the risks against the value. If you say to a man, 'In order not to get H.I.V. you are never going to have sex again without a condom,' his response would be that that seemed impossible. But there's a difference between going out with a guy you've never met whose status you don't ask about, and a friend you've known 10 years who tells you he's negative. Education has refused to allow gay men even to *think* about that difference. It's like telling people that if they want to be safe drivers, they must always drive 35 miles per hour without regard to when, where, or road conditions. Which any sane person will instantly reject."

As it happens, this conversation is taking place in a cubicle 44
at a Mercedes dealership; Odets is waiting for his car to be ser-
viced while a $175,000 black convertible revolves on a platform
behind us. The lone sign on the wall seems to be a relevant
warning: *The State of California does not provide for a cooling-
off period. All contracts are final.*

But Odets is oblivious to his context. "We don't say to hetero- 45
sexuals: 'A condom every time' for the rest of their lives. We expect them to enter relationships and dispense with condoms
when their H.I.V.-negative status is confirmed. It's a very old
story, telling gay men how to have sex; publicly they're complying, privately they're doing something else. We're the only
country in the Western world that is continuing to even *discuss*
the issue of oral sex in gay men. Oral sex *can* transmit H.I.V.,
but the risk is comparable to everyday, ordinary risk in modern
life, like driving a well-maintained car at moderate speeds on
the superhighway with a lap belt and shoulder belt on. Not to
acknowledge the low risk is to deny the value of sex between
men. Of course, the educators don't mean any harm, and God
knows they've been working longer than I have. They want to
err conservatively, which is understandable. But if erring conservatively means giving instructions that we know will not be
followed, is that the best approach to education?"

"How *would* you word the message?" I ask. 46

"'As a sexually active adult there are many occasions during 47
which you will probably have to use a condom to avoid transmission of H.I.V. and there are many others where you won't.'
That sounds like something a person could conceive of doing
for 60 years."

"So why have prevention agencies avoided saying just that?" 48

"Partly, it's because education is still based on the feeling that 49
we need an absolutely reduced task for gay men," Odets says.
"A single clear message—which is patronizing. And partly, it's
because the campaigns are constructed from an advertising
point of view, like soft drinks. They show a poster to a focus
group and ask: 'Do you like this?' If no, they don't use it. Well,
why don't they like it? Is it because it's addressing something
difficult and true? You have to create anxiety; the anxiety is
justly motivated. Instead we seem to produce comfy campaigns
that leave people with a false sense of resolution and calm."

Like Odets, I have found some of these campaigns, particu- 50
larly the ones that try to eroticize safer sex, coercive or coy. But
I have to admit that I have been comforted by others. San
Francisco's famous "Be Here for the Cure" series, which Odets
has excoriated as dangerous, was beautiful and popular.
Looking back on it now, though, I do wonder whom it was

aimed at. Did it mean to tell men who were already infected that they should try not to die? Or uninfected men not to worry if they *did* contract AIDS? Odets has pointed out that the two groups need different kinds of support, and that you can't help protect H.I.V.-negative men unless you acknowledge that it is a disaster to become H.I.V.-positive. "You have to understand that we were working in an environment in which there was a real fear of offending H.I.V.-positive people," says Bill Hayes, who led the team that created the campaign. "But maybe we were overreacting. My own boyfriend, who has AIDS, doesn't feel the need to have his self-esteem supported by ad campaigns."

51   The unwillingness to distinguish between the two populations has produced what Odets calls a unique confusion in the gay community between the normally distinct categories of *carrier* and *public*. "H.I.V.-negative men should not be thinking of themselves as carriers, or as destined to get H.I.V. just because they're gay. By helping them think that way we make it more likely that this will come true. But," he adds darkly, "this confusion is part of a much larger mental health problem. Partly it's a matter of the identification gay men already have with being dirty and defective."

52   Odets has often been criticized for drawing conclusions from his experience with patients in his private practice: 25 privileged psychotics, they're sometimes called. (In reality, there are only 20, none psychotic.) Be that as it may, the H.I.V.-negative men I spoke to about their unsafe-sex adventures all echoed at least some part of Odets's thesis. They feel their dilemmas to be essentially psychological. Some of the AIDS prevention organizations, on the other hand, suffer from what has to be called an anti-psychological prejudice: a disbelief, almost, in the power of the subconscious. Understandably eager to ingratiate themselves with the mainstream medical establishment on which they depend for funds, they have gravitated toward purely "medical" interventions. But what this fails to acknowledge is that people are strange. They react not only to rational thoughts but also to illogical feelings, and do what appear to be insupportable, destructive things.

53   "The truth is that the community is rife with self-hatred," says Odets, displaying the genius for provocation that has got him into so much trouble. "There is no question you can ask that doesn't eventually go back to that. It's not necessarily conscious; its a diffuse feeling about oneself. Which is why gay men have the profound need to be liked and do good; if I criticize the AIDS prevention programs they feel as if I'm saying that we *haven't* done good, that we've failed again. The first

failure, of course, is being homosexual. There's not a gay man alive who doesn't feel he's failed his family. And then we all got caught by a sexual epidemic, and we've beat a hasty retreat and been apologizing ever since."

Americans have difficulty discussing *any* kind of sex frankly, 54 which may be why our teen pregnancy rate is double the rate of Canada, for instance. But anal sex, which for many gay men is the defining act of gayness, is virtually unmentionable—despite being common among heterosexuals too. Odets would see this prudishness as another factor in gay men's self-loathing, another way they are "mangled" by a hateful society.

It's a strong word, and he uses it often; does Odets himself 55 feel *mangled?*

"My father"—the playwright Clifford Odets—"was open and 56 comfortable about homosexuality; but when he died. . . ." Odets pauses for perhaps the first time; he was 16 when his father died, still yearning for public approval. "I felt unprotected from the rest of the world's disdain."

Only a few days after returning from Los Angeles, I receive a 57 series of breathless E-mails from Mark Ebenhoch. "I did something now that I'm in seriously deep" the first one begins. Feeling rather like the parent of an adolescent boy, I brace myself for the rest of the message. As it turns out, my fears are justified for what Mark has done is the most dangerous thing I can imagine. He has fallen in love.

"I left you on Tuesday and I went to Apache Territory, the 58 bar, to kinda think about what we discussed. As I was trying to get picked up by this guy I had been getting to know, B. had been watching me the whole time . . . until I couldn't take it anymore and went over to say hi. That's where it all started.

"We did nothing sexually on Tuesday. And Wednesday we 59 went to the mountains . . . and the rest of the night was very very sweet. We were safe but. . . ." And here Mark goes on to explain that his new friend has full-blown AIDS.

If any hardness lingered in my heart toward men who risk 60 their lives for sex, Mark has finally worn it down to a core of helplessness. It would be easy to dismiss him as atypical; most gay men do not appear to be as childlike, as impractical, as self-destructive as he is. But of course Mark doesn't *appear* that way either, thanks to the command voice and the other forms of camouflage he has perfected over the years. It's only when you get to know him that you see how far his life has come from what he meant it to be. And then you wonder how many other people are masking beneath a facade of daily competence a willingness to flirt with disaster. In this main trait,

Mark is exactly like most gay men I spoke to about unsafe sex: he refuels himself over and over not so much from a love of life itself as from an apparently bottomless reservoir of hope for the companionship that makes life worth it.

61   "I hope I can hold on," one of the E-mails concludes. "I don't know where to go from here. Someday maybe it all will become clear. Thanks for the worry but I'll survive (always have somehow) Mark."

62   The flier advertising the workshop was not like any I'd seen before. In it, three men, average-looking and fully dressed, sit around a table; one of them is thinking to himself: "If I tell my friends that I've had unsafe sex, they don't know what to do." Below the picture, the text describes a three-session workshop for H.I.V.-negative gay men or gay men who haven't tested. Such men are invited to come talk about "testing, partying, and the sex you are having, what it means to you and what it may cost you."

63   It did not surprise me to learn that G.M.H.C. flier was, in part, the result of a collaboration with Walt Odets. The tag line, "Staying negative—it's not automatic," had the open-ended quality I'd so often heard him endorse. What did surprise me was how effective it was. Some two dozen men showed up at the sessions I attended, on Tuesday nights in mid-July, visibly relieved to be talking to one another in a noncommercial, nonsexual atmosphere. Usually safe, they were worried about the times they'd slipped, or about slipping in the future. Most agreed that residual feelings of shame over their homosexuality enhanced their risk, that they were confused and anxious about the safety of oral sex; that they wanted to be in long-term relationships, and that the gay "community"—at least as it was most evident to them in the form of bars and phone-sex ads—was not helping them in their struggle to stay safe.

64   G.M.H.C., which began its programs for H.I.V.-negative men in the spring of 1995, considers them highly successful, as do I. Still, only a few other organizations have followed their lead. For many in the prevention business, profound questions remain about the validity of Odets's approach.

65   "It's a tricky issue," said David Nimmons, who with Richard Elovich helped develop the G.M.H.C. program. "Walt has argued very persuasively against lumping H.I.V.-negative and H.I.V.-positive men together, and I obviously agree. But that's not to say there isn't a common interest in keeping as many men uninfected as possible. Here's something uncanny: Men who test positive are likely to be more consistently adherent, as a group, to safe-sex practices than negative men. That's a hard act to explain if you follow the model of self-interest which is

what most of AIDS prevention has been based on. On the other hand, men who *should* have the motivation of self-interest—H.I.V.-negative men—increasingly say that things are getting in the way of their following out that self-interest. It makes you want to look at other things, like altruism and communal continuity, that cut across the serochasm."

It is something of a surprise to hear a discussion of spiritual 66 motivation from the head of the largest AIDS-prevention education program in the world; Nimmons (who has recently left G.M.H.C.) supervised a staff of 51 people and an annual budget of about $3.9 million. But, unlike many others in the field, Nimmons accepts the psychological nature of the epidemic. On the other hand, Nimmons would not go so far as Odets in targeting gay men's low self-esteem. "Low compared to what?" he asks. "Compared to women who are anorexic and bulimic because they need to fit an externally determined mold? Ours is a culture that instills self-loathing in *everyone*, particularly in minority groups. It's part of what keeps the power structure intact. I don't want to gainsay that it's there, but are all *your* friends shriveled in self-doubt? We don't have any more mental illness or psychopathology than anyone else.

"Now I don't want to be a cheerleader either. Mental health 67 and community health are intrinsic to effective long-term prevention. We've been looking obsessively at monads and gonads: at people as individuals, not in communities, at sexual acts instead of sexual values. That's where we have to go next. And we have to go there regardless of AIDS itself."

Regardless of AIDS itself. As I think about this phrase, I real- 68 ize that what Odets (if not Nimmons) has been suggesting all along is that there is an epidemic beneath the epidemic we know about. Beneath and beyond. It predates AIDS and will probably outlast it and comes not from a virus but a vacancy. Like most minorities in America, gay men grow up feeling different, but uniquely they grow up both different and *alone*. They are unlike, and often cannot speak to, the families that raise them. Odets puts it plainly: "Gay adolescents are subjected to developmental abuses that make adult relationships harder. Society has a lot of nerve subjecting them to this kind of abuse and then, when they come out the other end of the tube mangled at 25, to accuse them of depravity."

If, as Odets says, gay men feel inordinately bad about them- 69 selves, many work doubly hard to make up for it by developing their capacities for empathy, decency and loyalty. The epidemic has accelerated this process, or intensified its substations: lo, we were actors, waiters, lawyers; now we're lay epidemiologists and social workers. We were pansies and perverts;

now we're heroes on the 6 o'clock news. We are finally, if temporarily, accredited Americans, and part of the reason AIDS organizations have so entrenched themselves against the new realities is that hard-won halos are not easily discarded. But halos cannot ameliorate the underlying problem, which stems from how homosexuals are hated. And while other groups are hated, too, the tragedy for gay men has been that the thing that makes them different (indeed, perhaps the *only* thing) is the thing that has bound them inextricably to the worst public health disaster of our era.

70   The problem, finally, isn't sex but love—and the 6 o'clock news doesn't want to talk about that. And while no one seriously argues that it is the job of public health to make gay men happy, ignoring the role that homophobia plays in the psychology of AIDS (or, for that matter, ignoring the role that joblessness plays in the psychology of drug addiction) means ignoring an element of disease at least as powerful as biology. If we care about public health, there is little choice but to care about people's feelings too. As Thomas Delbanco, a professor of medicine at Harvard Medical School, points out, you can find tons of papers analyzing the public health benefits of universal sigmoidoscopy to detect colon cancer—"but try to find one that tells you the best way to get a man or a woman to bare his or her bottom on a periodic basis to a large tube."

71   Delbanco, who was trained in an era when doctors were gods but now sees himself as a "hopefully expert adviser" to his patients, thinks it's time for prevention organizations to make the same kinds of attitude adjustment. It will not be easy. Public health has contented itself with maintaining *quantity* of life assuming that *quality* of life will (or ought to) take care of itself. If AIDS teaches us anything, it's that the formula works the other way around. At the same time, we seem to get the prevention we deserve. Politicians want quick fixes because they're cheaper and catchier than long-term solutions. (When prevention works, it's invisible of course: you can't see it because it *prevents* something.) And we abet those politicians by clamoring, albeit fitfully, for war instead of change. Democracy be damned—we want drug czars, AIDS czars—as if behavior driven by feelings could be corralled by an attack of the cavalry.

72   In a country that has outgrown its ability to promote strong norms, or finds the very idea of norms too normative, public health must find new methods of intervening in dangerous private behavior. What would that intervention look like? Instead of Just Say No, drug prevention might include nuanced discussions about the relative risks of marijuana and harder drugs,

just as Odets wants gay men to distinguish between different kinds of sex. Instead of promoting vows of chastity, pregnancy prevention programs might ask a girl to envision the kind of life she wants before weighing how a baby could enhance, or ruin it. What all such programs would rely on is candor: complete information, delivered in plain language, respectful of individual values—which seems obvious until you realize it's rarely done. And the bitterest pill in prevention today is that the programs already exist. Largely unfinanced or ignored, they sit even now in bookcases and file drawers, waiting for political winds to shift while the epidemics rage.

Mark Ebenhoch's command voice, which hasn't worked any 73 better for him than it has for AIDS educators, is almost completely gone now. Even over the phone, when I speak to him in mid-July, I can hear the change. His affair with B. has ended unhappily and, he adds, almost as an afterthought, he has some news we have both been fearing: he is finally H.I.V.-positive himself. A psychiatrist has put him on antidepressants. "Sometimes I think that if I had gotten help three years ago— emotional help, psychiatric help—I most likely wouldn't be positive now. I'd have had a clearer head. But really, it was my own fault. There's no other way around it."

As a person with H.I.V., Mark is suddenly eligible for the 74 whole range of benefits provided by AIDS organizations—including the free counseling that might have helped him earlier. And the Veterans Administration provides him with a handsome monthly disability check. In a way, becoming positive has been a windfall; could Mark be forgiven a bit of cynicism? In a world where financing for AIDS research keeps increasing but agencies that serve gay youths go begging for pennies, should we be surprised if gay men wonder whether the disease is more important than they are? For AIDS will someday end. And when the promise of the protease inhibitors is fulfilled, when the vaccine arrives in our elementary schools, will anyone turn as feverish a light on what *else* is destroying gay men? Will anyone see it as their responsibility to help assuage the damage inflicted, and replayed night after night, upon boys whose only real desire was to be liked, to be loved, to be good?

But somehow Mark *isn't* cynical. "I have an upbeat attitude," 75 he says. "With the news about the new drug treatments, I'm cautiously optimistic. And I'm letting go of a lot of things. Because of the medication I'm on I cannot drink alcohol; and I quit smoking cigarettes. I've completely stopped the promiscuity, too. I want to live well. I'm eating better. Believe it or not, I have a date tonight, not a pickup but a real date. With a guy I met through the Internet. I went into the Gay and Lesbian Bulletin Board—where I met you—and looked in the personals under H.I.V.-positive. And I found a guy that was rather interesting. We're going to go out and have coffee and something to eat, and talk. And that's it. I want to find somebody who will"— he searches for the word he wants—"*belong* to me. And that means somebody H.I.V.-positive now.

76   "In a way it's a relief," he says, echoing a sentiment I have heard too frequently from newly infected men. "I don't have to wonder anymore. That awful waiting is gone. So now, if I do find someone, the relationship can be 100 percent real with nothing in the way. That's what I want: 100 percent natural, wholesome and real. Maybe now that I'm H.I.V.-positive, I can finally have my life."

John Muir

SAVE THE HETCH HETCHY VALLEY!

The famous nineteenth-century naturalist John Muir, founder of the Sierra Club, wrote the following appeal a century ago. It was an effort—an unsuccessful effort, as it turned out—to block the construction of a dam in the Yosemite National Park area that was designed to provide water to the San Francisco area. Muir spent his life hiking through the American West and recording what he saw in a way that persuaded people to preserve outstanding wilderness areas. Two of his best known books are The Mountains of California *(1894) and* Our National Parks *(1901). You will hear more about him when you read William Cronon's "The Trouble with Wilderness" later in this segment.*

Yosemite is so wonderful that we are apt to regard it as an exceptional creation, the only valley of its kind in the world; but Nature is not so poor as to have only one of anything. Several other yosemites have been discovered in the Sierra that occupy the same relative positions on the Range and were formed by the same forces in the same kind of granite. One of these, the Hetch Hetchy Valley, is in the Yosemite National Park about twenty miles from Yosemite and is easily accessible to all sorts of travelers by a road and trail that leaves the Big Oak Flat road at Bronson Meadows a few miles below Crane Flat, and to mountaineers by way of Yosemite Creek basin and the head of the middle fork of the Tuolumne.

It is said to have been discovered by Joseph Screech, a hunter, in 1850, a year before the discovery of the great

Yosemite. After my first visit to it in the autumn of 1871, I have always called it the "Tuolumne Yosemite," for it is a wonderfully exact counterpart of the Merced Yosemite, not only in its sublime rocks and waterfalls but in the gardens, groves and meadows of its flowery park-like floor. The floor of Yosemite is about 4000 feet above the sea; the Hetch Hetchy floor about 3700 feet. And as the Merced River flows through Yosemite, so does the Tuolumne through Hetch Hetchy. The walls of both are of gray granite, rise abruptly from the floor, are sculptured in the same style and in both every rock is a glacier monument.

3   Standing boldly out from the south wall is a strikingly picturesque rock called by the Indians, Kolana, the outermost of a group 2300 feet high, corresponding with the Cathedral Rocks of Yosemite both in relative position and form. On the opposite side of the Valley, facing Kolana, there is a counterpart of the El Capitan that rises sheer and plain to a height of 1800 feet, and over its massive brow flows a stream which makes the most graceful fall I have ever seen. From the edge of the cliff to the top of an earthquake talus it is perfectly free in the air for a thousand feet before it is broken into cascades among talus boulders. It is in all its glory in June, when the snow is melting fast, but fades and vanishes toward the end of summer. The only fall I know with which it may fairly be compared is the Yosemite Bridal Veil; but it excels even that favorite fall both in height and airy-fairy beauty and behavior. Lowlanders are apt to suppose that mountain streams in their wild career over cliffs lose control of themselves and tumble in a noisy chaos of mist and spray. On the contrary, on no part of their travels are they more harmonious and self-controlled. Imagine yourself in Hetch Hetchy on a sunny day in June, standing waist-deep in grass and flowers (as I have often stood), while the great pines sway dreamily with scarcely perceptible motion. Looking northward across the Valley you see a plain, gray granite cliff rising abruptly out of the gardens and groves to a height of 1800 feet, and in front of it Tueeulala's silvery scarf burning with irised sun-fire. In the first white outburst at the head there is abundance of visible energy, but it is speedily hushed and concealed in divine repose, and its tranquil progress to the base of the cliff is like that of a downy feather in a still room. Now observe the fineness and marvelous distinctness of the various sun-illumined fabrics into which the water is woven; they sift and float from form to form down the face of that grand gray rock in so leisurely and unconfused a manner that you can examine their texture, and patterns and tones of color as you would a piece of embroidery held in the hand. Toward the top of the fall you see groups of booming, comet-like

masses, their solid, white heads separate, their tails like combed silk interlacing among delicate gray and purple shadows, ever forming and dissolving, worn out by friction in their rush through the air. Most of these vanish a few hundred feet below the summit, changing to varied forms of cloud-like drapery. Near the bottom the width of the fall has increased from about twenty-five feet to a hundred feet. Here it is composed of yet finer tissues, and is still without a trace of disorder—air, water and sunlight woven into stuff that spirits might wear.

So fine a fall might well seem sufficient to glorify any valley; but here, as in Yosemite, Nature seems in nowise moderate, for a short distance to the eastward of Tueeulala booms and thunders the great Hetch Hetchy Fall, Wapama, so near that you have both of them in full view from the same standpoint. It is the counterpart of the Yosemite Fall, but has a much greater volume of water, is about 1700 feet in height, and appears to be nearly vertical, though considerably inclined, and is dashed into huge outbounding bosses of foam on projecting shelves and knobs. No two falls could be more unlike—Tueeulala out in the open sunshine descending like thistledown; Wapama in a jagged, shadowy gorge roaring and thundering, pounding its way like an earthquake avalanche.

Besides this glorious pair there is a broad, massive fall on the main river a short distance above the head of the Valley. Its position is something like that of the Vernal in Yosemite, and its roar as it plunges into a surging trout-pool may be heard a long way, though it is only about twenty feet high. On Rancheria Creek, a large stream, corresponding in position with the Yosemite Tenaya Creek, there is a chain of cascades joined here and there with swift flashing plumes like the one between the Vernal and Nevada Falls, making magnificent shows as they go their glacier-sculptured way, sliding, leaping, hurrahing, covered with crisp clashing spray made glorious with sifting sunshine. And besides all these a few small streams come over the walls at wide intervals, leaping from ledge to ledge with bird-like song and watering many a hidden cliff-garden and fernery, but they are too unshowy to be noticed in so grand a place.

The correspondence between the Hetch Hetchy walls in their trends, sculpture, physical structure, and general arrangement of the main rock-masses and those of the Yosemite Valley has excited the wondering admiration of every observer. We have seen that the El Capitan and Cathedral rocks occupy the same relative positions in both valleys; so also do their Yosemite points and North Domes. Again, that part of the Yosemite north wall immediately to the east of the

Yosemite Fall has two horizontal benches, about 500 and 1500 feet above the floor, timbered with golden-cup oak. Two benches similarly situated and timbered occur on the same relative portion of the Hetch Hetchy north wall, to the east of Wapama Fall, and on no other. The Yosemite is bounded at the head by the great Half Dome. Hetch Hetchy is bounded in the same way, though its head rock is incomparably less wonderful and sublime in form.

7   The floor of the Valley is about three and a half miles long, and from a fourth to half a mile wide. The lower portion is mostly a level meadow about a mile long, with the trees restricted to the sides and the river banks, and partially separated from the main, upper, forested portion by a low bar of glacier-polished granite across which the river breaks in rapids.

8   The principal trees are the yellow and sugar pines, digger pine, incense cedar, Douglas spruce, silver fir, the California and golden-cup oaks, balsam cottonwood, Nuttall's flowering dogwood, alder, maple, laurel, tumion, etc. The most abundant and influential are the great yellow or silver pines like those of Yosemite, the tallest over two hundred feet in height, and the oaks assembled in magnificent groves with massive rugged trunks four to six feet in diameter, and broad, shady, wide-spreading heads. The shrubs forming conspicuous flowery clumps and tangles are manzanita, azalea, spiræa, brier-rose, several species of ceanothus, calycanthus, philadelphus, wild cherry, etc.; with abundance of showy and fragrant herbaceous plants growing about them or out in the open in beds by themselves—lilies, Mariposa tulips, brodiaeas, orchids, iris, spraguea, draperia, collomia, collinsia, castilleja, nemophila, larkspur, columbine, goldenrods, sunflowers, mints of many species, honeysuckle, etc. Many fine ferns dwell here also, especially the beautiful and interesting rock-ferns—pellaea, and cheilanthes of several species—fringing and rosetting dry rock-piles and ledges; woodwardia and asplenium on damp spots with fronds six or seven feet high; the delicate maidenhair in mossy nooks by the falls, and the sturdy, broad-shouldered pteris covering nearly all the dry ground beneath the oaks and pines.

9   It appears, therefore, that Hetch Hetchy Valley, far from being a plain, common, rock-bound meadow, as many who have not seen it seem to suppose, is a grand landscape garden, one of Nature's rarest and most precious mountain temples. As in Yosemite, the sublime rocks of its walls seem to glow with life, whether leaning back in repose or standing erect in thoughtful attitudes, giving welcome to storms and calms alike, their brows in the sky, their feet set in the groves and gay flowery meadows, while birds, bees, and butterflies help the river and

waterfalls to stir all the air into music—things frail and fleeting and types of permanence meeting here and blending, just as they do in Yosemite, to draw her lovers into close and confiding communion with her.

Sad to say, this most precious and sublime feature of the Yosemite National Park, one of the greatest of all our natural resources for the uplifting joy and peace and health of the people, is in danger of being dammed and made into a reservoir to help supply San Francisco with water and light, thus flooding it from wall to wall and burying its gardens and groves one or two hundred feet deep. This grossly destructive commercial scheme has long been planned and urged (though water as pure and abundant can be got from outside of the people's park, in a dozen different places), because of the comparative cheapness of the dam and of the territory which it is sought to divert from the great uses to which it was dedicated in the Act of 1890 establishing the Yosemite National Park.

The making of gardens and parks goes on with civilization all over the world, and they increase both in size and number as their value is recognized. Everybody needs beauty as well as bread, places to play in and pray in, where Nature may heal and cheer and give strength to body and soul alike. This natural beauty-hunger is made manifest in the little window-sill gardens of the poor, though perhaps only a geranium slip in a broken cup, as well as in the carefully tended rose and lily gardens of the rich, the thousands of spacious city parks and botanical gardens, and in our magnificent National Parks—the Yellowstone, Yosemite, Sequoia, etc.—Nature's sublime wonderlands, the admiration and joy of the world. Nevertheless, like anything else worth while, from the very beginning, however well guarded, they have always been subject to attack by despoiling gainseekers and mischief-makers of every degree from Satan to Senators, eagerly trying to make everything immediately and selfishly commercial, with schemes disguised in smug-smiling philanthropy, industriously, sham-piously crying, "Conservation, conservation, panutilization," that man and beast may be fed and the dear Nation made great. Thus long ago a few enterprising merchants utilized the Jerusalem temple as a place of business instead of a place of prayer, changing money, buying and selling cattle and sheep and doves; and earlier still, the first forest reservation, including only one tree, was likewise despoiled. Ever since the establishment of the Yosemite National Park, strife has been going on around its borders and I suppose this will go on as part of the universal battle between right and wrong, however much its boundaries may be shorn, or its wild beauty destroyed.

12   The first application to the Government by the San Francisco Supervisors for the commercial use of Lake Eleanor and the Hetch Hetchy Valley was made in 1903, and on December 22nd of that year it was denied by the Secretary of the Interior, Mr. Hitchcock, who truthfully said:

> Presumably the Yosemite National Park was created such by law because of the natural objects of varying degrees of scenic importance located within its boundaries, inclusive alike of its beautiful small lakes, like Eleanor, and its majestic wonders, like Hetch Hetchy and Yosemite Valley. It is the aggregation of such natural scenic features that makes the Yosemite Park a wonderland which the Congress of the United States sought by law to reserve for all coming time as nearly as practicable in the condition fashioned by the hand of the Creator—a worthy object of national pride and a source of healthful pleasure and rest for the thousands of people who may annually sojourn there during the heated months.

13   In 1907 when Mr. Garfield became Secretary of the Interior the application was renewed and granted; but under his successor, Mr. Fisher, the matter has been referred to a Commission, which as this volume goes to press still has it under consideration.

14   The most delightful and wonderful camp-grounds in the Park are its three great valleys—Yosemite, Hetch Hetchy, and Upper Tuolumne; and they are also the most important places with reference to their positions relative to the other great features—the Merced and Tuolumne Cañons, and the High Sierra peaks and glaciers, etc., at the head of the rivers. The main part of the Tuolumne Valley is a spacious flowery lawn four or five miles long, surrounded by magnificent snowy mountains, slightly separated from other beautiful meadows, which together make a series about twelve miles in length, the highest reaching to the feet of Mount Dana, Mount Gibbs, Mount Lyell and Mount McClure. It is about 8500 feet above the sea, and forms the grand central High Sierra camp-ground from which excursions are made to the noble mountains, domes, glaciers, etc.; across the Range to the Mono Lake and volcanoes and down the Tuolumne Cañon to Hetch Hetchy. Should Hetch Hetchy be submerged for a reservoir, as proposed, not only would it be utterly destroyed, but the sublime cañon way to the heart of the High Sierra would be hopelessly blocked and the great camping-ground, as the watershed of a city drinking system, virtually would be closed to the public. So far as I have

learned, few of all the thousands who have seen the Park and seek rest and peace in it are in favor of this outrageous scheme.

One of my later visits to the Valley was made in the autumn   15
of 1907 with the late William Keith, the artist. The leaf-colors were then ripe, and the great god-like rocks in repose seemed to glow with life. The artist, under their spell, wandered day after day along the river and through the groves and gardens, studying the wonderful scenery; and, after making about forty sketches, declared with enthusiasm that although its walls were less sublime in height, in picturesque beauty and charm Hetch Hetchy surpassed even Yosemite.

That any one would try to destroy such a place seems incred-   16
ible; but sad experience shows that there are people good enough and bad enough for anything. The proponents of the dam scheme bring forward a lot of bad arguments to prove that the only righteous thing to do with the people's parks is to destroy them bit by bit as they are able. Their arguments are curiously like those of the devil, devised for the destruction of the first garden—so much of the very best Eden fruit going to waste; so much of the best Tuolumne water and Tuolumne scenery going to waste. Few of their statements are even partly true, and all are misleading.

Thus, Hetch Hetchy, they say, is a "low-lying meadow." On   17
the contrary, it is a high-lying natural landscape garden, as the photographic illustrations show.

"It is a common minor feature, like thousands of others." On the contrary it is a very uncommon feature; after Yosemite, the rarest and in many ways the most important in the National Park.

"Damming and submerging it 175 feet deep would enhance   18
its beauty by forming a crystal-clear lake." Landscape gardens, places of recreation and worship, are never made beautiful by destroying and burying them. The beautiful sham lake, forsooth, would be only an eyesore, a dismal blot on the landscape, like many others to be seen in the Sierra. For, instead of keeping it at the same level all the year, allowing Nature centuries of time to make new shores, it would, of course, be full only a month or two in the spring, when the snow is melting fast; then it would be gradually drained, exposing the slimy sides of the basin and shallower parts of the bottom, with the gathered drift and waste, death and decay of the upper basins, caught here instead of being swept on to decent natural burial along the banks of the river or in the sea. Thus the Hetch Hetchy dam-lake would be only a rough imitation of a natural lake for a few of the spring months, an open sepulcher for the others.

19   "Hetch Hetchy water is the purest of all to be found in the Sierra, unpolluted, and forever unpollutable." On the contrary, excepting that of the Merced below Yosemite, it is less pure than that of most of the other Sierra streams, because of the sewerage of camp-grounds draining into it, especially of the Big Tuolumne Meadows camp-ground, occupied by hundreds of tourists and mountaineers, with their animals, for months every summer, soon to be followed by thousands from all the world.

20   These temple destroyers, devotees of ravaging commercialism, seem to have a perfect contempt for Nature, and, instead of lifting their eyes to the God of the mountains, lift them to the Almighty Dollar.

21   Dam Hetch Hetchy! As well dam for water-tanks the people's cathedrals and churches, for no holier temple has ever been consecrated by the heart of man.

Wallace Stegner

A WILDERNESS LETTER

Wallace Stegner (1909–93) was an important novelist in the United States after World War II. He wrote more than thirty books, including Angle of Repose, *which won the Pulitzer Prize, and* The Spectator Bird, *which won the National Book Award in 1976. Stegner was also a committed conservationist, and his books often feature American Western themes and settings. As a creative writing teacher at Stanford, he taught Edward Abbey and Wendell Barry. In 1960 he wrote the following letter, a famous argument for the spiritual values found in the wild; it helped persuade Congress to create the National Wilderness Preservation System in 1964.*

Los Altos, Calif.
Dec. 3, 1960

David E. Pesonen
Wildland Research Center
Agricultural Experiment Station
243 Mulford Hall
University of California
Berkeley 4, Calif.

Dear Mr. Pesonen:

I believe that you are working on the wilderness portion of 1
the Outdoor Recreation Resources Review Commission's report. If I may, I should like to urge some arguments for wilderness preservation that involve recreation, as it is ordinarily
conceived, hardly at all. Hunting, fishing, hiking, mountain-
climbing, camping, photography, and the enjoyment of natural
scenery will all, surely, figure in your report. So will the wilderness as a genetic reserve, a scientific yardstick by which we
may measure the world in its natural balance against the world
in its man-made imbalance. What I want to speak for is not so
much the wilderness uses, valuable as those are, but the
wilderness *idea,* which is a resource in itself. Being an intangible and spiritual resource, it will seem mystical to the practi-
cal-minded—but then anything that cannot be moved by a
bulldozer is likely to seem mystical to them.

I want to speak for the wilderness idea as something that has 2
helped form our character and that has certainly shaped our
history as a people. It has no more to do with recreation than
churches have to do with recreation, or than the strenuousness
and optimism and expansiveness of what historians call the
"American Dream" have to do with recreation. Nevertheless,
since it is only in this recreation survey that the values of wilderness are being compiled, I hope you will permit me to insert this
idea between the leaves, as it were, of the recreation report.

Something will have gone out of us as a people if we ever let 3
the remaining wilderness be destroyed; if we permit the last
virgin forests to be turned into comic books and plastic cigarette cases; if we drive the few remaining members of the wild
species into zoos or to extinction; if we pollute the last clear air
and dirty the last clean streams and push our paved roads
through the last of the silence, so that never again will
Americans be free in their own country from the noise, the exhausts, the stinks of human and automotive waste. And so that
never again can we have the chance to see ourselves single,

separate, vertical, and individual in the world, part of the environment of trees and rocks and soil, brother to the other animals, part of the natural world and competent to belong in it. Without any remaining wilderness we are committed wholly, without chance for even momentary reflection and rest, to a headlong drive into our technological termite-life, the Brave New World of a completely man-controlled environment. We need wilderness preserved—as much of it as is still left, and as many kinds—because it was the challenge against which our character as a people was formed. The reminder and the reassurance that it is still there is good for our spiritual health even if we never once in ten years set foot in it. It is good for us when we are young, because of the incomparable sanity it can bring briefly, as vacation and rest, into our insane lives. It is important to us when we are old simply because it is there—important, that is, simply as idea.

4   We are a wild species, as Darwin pointed out. Nobody ever tamed or domesticated or scientifically bred us. But for at least three millennia we have been engaged in a cumulative and ambitious race to modify and gain control of our environment, and in the process we have come close to domesticating ourselves. Not many people are likely, any more, to look upon what we call "progress" as an unmixed blessing. Just as surely as it has brought us increased comfort and more material goods, it has brought us spiritual losses, and it threatens now to become the Frankenstein that will destroy us. One means of sanity is to retain a hold on the natural world, to remain, insofar as we can, good animals. Americans still have that chance, more than many peoples; for while we were demonstrating ourselves the most efficient and ruthless environment-busters in history, and slashing and burning and cutting our way through a wilderness continent, the wilderness was working on us. It remains in us as surely as Indian names remain on the land. If the abstract dream of human liberty and human dignity became, in America, something more than an abstract dream, mark it down at least partially to the fact that we were in subtle ways subdued by what we conquered.

5   The Connecticut Yankee, sending likely candidates from King Arthur's unjust kingdom to his Man Factory for rehabilitation, was over-optimistic, as he later admitted. These things cannot be forced, they have to grow. To make such a man, such a democrat, such a believer in human individual dignity, as Mark Twain himself, the frontier was necessary, Hannibal and the Mississippi and Virginia City, and reaching out from those the wilderness; the wilderness as opportunity and as idea, the thing that has helped to make an American different

from and, until we forget it in the roar of our industrial cities, more fortunate than other men. For an American, insofar as he is new and different at all, is a civilized man who has renewed himself in the wild. The American experience has been the confrontation by old peoples and cultures of a world as new as if it had just risen from the sea. That gave us our hope and our excitement, and the hope and excitement can be passed on to newer Americans, Americans who never saw any phase of the frontier. But only so long as we keep the remainder of our wild as a reserve and a promise—a sort of wilderness bank.

As a novelist, I may perhaps be forgiven for taking literature 6 as a reflection, indirect but profoundly true, of our national consciousness. And our literature, as perhaps you are aware, is sick, embittered, losing its mind, losing its faith. Our novelists are the declared enemies of their society. There has hardly been a serious or important novel in this century that did not repudiate in part or in whole American technological culture for its commercialism, its vulgarity, and the way in which it has dirtied a clean continent and a clean dream. I do not expect that the preservation of our remaining wilderness is going to cure this condition. But the mere example that we can as a nation apply some other criteria than commercial and exploitative considerations would be heartening to many Americans, novelists or otherwise. We need to demonstrate our acceptance of the natural world, including ourselves; we need the spiritual refreshment that being natural can produce. And one of the best places for us to get that is in the wilderness where the fun houses, the bulldozers, and the pavements of our civilization are shut out.

Sherwood Anderson, in a letter to Waldo Frank in the 1920s, 7 said it better than I can. "Is it not likely that when the country was new and men were often alone in the fields and the forest they got a sense of bigness outside themselves that has now in some way been lost. . . . Mystery whispered in the grass, played in the branches of trees overhead, was caught up and blown across the American line in clouds of dust at evening on the prairies. . . . I am old enough to remember tales that strengthen my belief in a deep semi-religious influence that was formerly at work among our people. The flavor of it hangs over the best work of Mark Twain. . . . I can remember old fellows in my home town speaking feelingly of an evening spent on the big empty plains. It had taken the shrillness out of them. They had learned the trick of quiet. . . ."

We could learn it too, even yet; even our children and 8 grandchildren could learn it. But only if we save, for just such absolutely nonrecreational, impractical, and mystical uses as this, all the wild that still remains to us.

9   It seems to me significant that the distinct downturn in our literature from hope to bitterness took place almost at the precise time when the frontier officially came to an end, in 1890, and when the American way of life had begun to turn strongly urban and industrial. The more urban it has become, and the more frantic with technological change, the sicker and more embittered our literature, and I believe our people, have become. For myself, I grew up on the empty plains of Saskatchewan and Montana and in the mountains of Utah, and I put a very high valuation on what those places gave me. And if I had not been able periodically to renew myself in the mountains and deserts of western America I would be very nearly bughouse. Even when I can't get to the back country, the thought of the colored deserts of southern Utah, or the reassurance that there are still stretches of prairie where the world can be instantaneously perceived as disk and bowl, and where the little but intensely important human being is exposed to the five directions and the thirty-six winds, is a positive consolation. The idea alone can sustain me. But as the wilderness areas are progressively exploited or "improved," as the jeeps and bulldozers of uranium prospectors scar up the deserts and the roads are cut into the alpine timberlands, and as the remnants of the unspoiled and natural world are progressively eroded, every such loss is a little death in me. In us.

10   I am not moved by the argument that those wilderness areas which have already been exposed to grazing or mining are already deflowered, and so might as well be "harvested." For mining I cannot say much good except that its operations are generally short-lived. The extractable wealth is taken and the shafts, the tailings, and the ruins left, and in a dry country such as the American West the wounds men make in the earth do not quickly heal. Still, they are only wounds; they aren't absolutely mortal. Better a wounded wilderness than none at all. And as for grazing, if it is strictly controlled so that it does not destroy the ground cover, damage the ecology, or compete with the wildlife it is in itself nothing that need conflict with the wilderness feeling or the validity of the wilderness experience. I have known enough range cattle to recognize them as wild animals; and the people who herd them have, in the wilderness context, the dignity of rareness; they belong on the frontier, moreover, and have a look of rightness. The invasion they make on the virgin country is a sort of invasion that is as old as Neolithic man, and they can, in moderation, even emphasize a man's feeling of belonging to the natural world. Under surveil-

lance, they can belong; under control, they need not deface or mar. I do not believe that in wilderness areas where grazing has never been permitted, it should be permitted; but I do not believe either that an otherwise untouched wilderness should be eliminated from the preservation plan because of limited existing uses such as grazing which are in consonance with the frontier condition and image.

Let me say something on the subject of the kinds of wilder- 11 ness worth preserving. Most of those areas contemplated are in the national forests and in high mountain country. For all the usual recreational purposes, the alpine and forest wilderness are obviously the most important, both as genetic banks and as beauty spots. But for the spiritual renewal, the recognition of identity, the birth of awe, other kinds will serve every bit as well. Perhaps, because they are less friendly to life, more abstractly nonhuman, they will serve even better. On our Saskatchewan prairie, the nearest neighbor was four miles away, and at night we saw only two lights on all the dark rounding earth. The earth was full of animals—field mice, ground squirrels, weasels, ferrets, badgers, coyotes, burrowing owls, snakes. I knew them as my little brothers, as fellow creatures, and I have never been able to look upon animals in any other way since. The sky in that country came clear down to the ground on every side, and it was full of great weathers, and clouds, and winds, and hawks. I hope I learned something from knowing intimately the creatures of the earth; I hope I learned something from looking a long way, from looking up, from being much alone. A prairie like that, one big enough to carry the eye clear to the sinking, rounding horizon, can be as lonely and grand and simple in its forms as the sea. It is as good a place as any for the wilderness experience to happen; the vanishing prairie is as worth preserving for the wilderness idea as the alpine forests.

So are great reaches of our western deserts, scarred some- 12 what by prospectors but otherwise open, beautiful, waiting, close to whatever God you want to see in them. Just as a sample, let me suggest the Robbers' Roost country in Wayne County, Utah, near the Capitol Reef National Monument. In that desert climate the dozer and jeep tracks will not soon melt back into the earth, but the country has a way of making the scars insignificant. It is a lovely and terrible wilderness, such a wilderness as Christ and the prophets went out into: harshly and beautifully colored, broken and worn until its bones are exposed, its great sky without a smudge of taint from Technocracy, and in hidden corners and pockets under its cliffs the sudden poetry of springs. Save a piece of country like that intact, and it does not matter in the slightest that only a few people every year will go into it. That is precisely its value. Roads would be a desecration, crowds would ruin it. But those who haven't the strength or youth to go into it and live can simply sit and look. They can look two hundred miles, clear into Colorado: and looking down over the cliffs and canyons of the San Rafael Swell and the Robbers' Roost they can also look as deeply into themselves as anywhere I know. And if they can't even get to the places on the Aquarius Plateau where the present roads will carry them, they can simply contemplate the *idea*, take pleasure in the fact that such a timeless and uncontrolled part of earth is still there.

These are some of the things wilderness can do for us. That is   13 the reason we need to put into effect, for its preservation, some other principle than the principles of exploitation or "usefulness" or even recreation. We simply need that wild country available to us, even if we never do more than drive to its edge and look in. For it can be a means of reassuring ourselves of our sanity as creatures, a part of the geography of hope.

Very sincerely yours,

Wallace Stegner

Greenpeace is an international organization famous for its activist approach to environmental protection. Its members militantly work to protect environmental resources and (in the tradition of Wallace Stegner) to maintain wilderness areas in their natural states. The screenshot on page 861 of the Greenpeace Web site during 2002 reveals its values and tactics: against a green backdrop, Greenpeace posts a current story and various updates (for members and visitors) of its activities around the world.

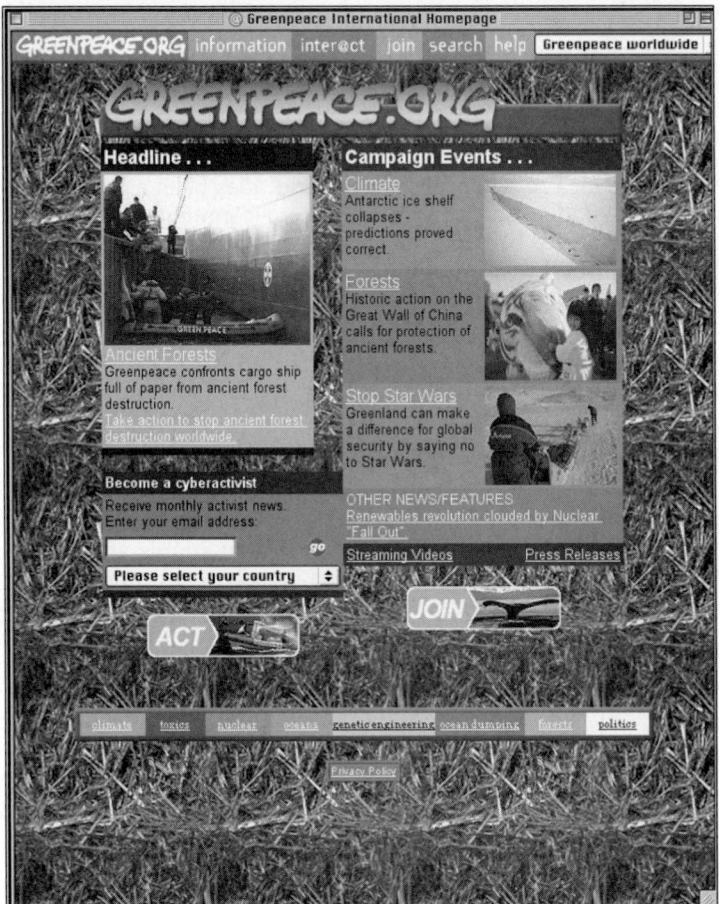

William Cronon

THE TROUBLE
WITH WILDERNESS

*William Cronon is a professor of history, geography, and envi-
ronmental studies at the University of Wisconsin, Madison. He
is the author of many books, including* Changes in the Land:
Indians, Colonists, and the Ecology of New England *(1983)
and* Nature's Metropolis: Chicago and the Great West *(1991).
*The following essay is an excerpt from a piece that appeared in
his* Uncommon Ground: Toward Reinventing Nature *(1995).
Published in the inaugural issue of* Environmental History, *a
magazine designed for academics, in January 1996, it inspired
many responses—including the one published after it in this
book by Samuel P. Hays.*

The Time Has Come to Rethink Wilderness

1   This will seem a heretical claim to many environmentalists, since the idea of wilderness has for decades been a fundamental tenet—indeed, a passion—of the environmental movement, especially in the United States. For many Americans wilderness stands as the last remaining place where civilization, that all too human disease, has not fully infected the earth. It is an island in the polluted sea of urban-industrial modernity, the one place we can turn for escape from our own too-muchness. Seen in this way, wilderness presents itself as the best antidote to our human selves, a refuge we must somehow recover if we hope to save the planet. As Henry David Thoreau once famously declared, "In Wildness is the preservation of the World."[1]

2   But is it? The more one knows of its peculiar history, the more one realizes that wilderness is not quite what it seems. Far from being the one place on earth that stands apart from humanity, it is quite profoundly a human creation—indeed, the creation of very particular human cultures at very particular moments in human history. It is not a pristine sanctuary where the last remnant of an untouched, endangered, but still transcendent nature can for at least a little while longer be encountered without the contaminating taint of civilization. Instead, it is a product of that civilization, and could hardly be contaminated by the very stuff of which it is made. Wilderness hides its unnaturalness behind a mask that is all the more beguiling because it seems so natural. As we gaze into the mirror it holds up for us, we too easily imagine that what we behold is Nature when in fact we see the reflection of our own unexamined longings and desires. For this reason, we mistake ourselves when we suppose that wilderness can be the solution to our culture's problematic relationships with the nonhuman world, for wilderness is itself no small part of the problem.

3   To assert the unnaturalness of so natural a place will no doubt seem absurd or even perverse to many readers, so let me hasten to add that the nonhuman world we encounter in wilderness is far from being merely our own invention. I celebrate with others who love wilderness the beauty and power of the things it contains. Each of us who has spent time there can conjure images and sensations that seem all the more hauntingly real for having engraved themselves so indelibly on our memories. Such memories may be uniquely our own, but they are also familiar enough be to be instantly recognizable to others. Remember this? The torrents of mist shoot out from the base of a great waterfall in the depths of a Sierra canyon, the tiny droplets cooling your face as you listen to the roar of

the water and gaze up toward the sky through a rainbow that hovers just out of reach. Remember this too: looking out across a desert canyon in the evening air, the only sound a lone raven calling in the distance, the rock walls dropping away into a chasm so deep that its bottom all but vanishes as you squint into the amber light of the setting sun. And this: the moment beside the trail as you sit on a sandstone ledge, your boots damp with the morning dew while you take in the rich smell of the pines, and the small red fox—or maybe for you it was a raccoon or a coyote or a deer—that suddenly ambles across your path, stopping for a long moment to gaze in your direction with cautious indifference before continuing on its way. Remember the feelings of such moments, and you will know as well as I do that you were in the presence of something irreducibly nonhuman, something profoundly Other than yourself. Wilderness is made of that too.

And yet: what brought each of us to the places where such 4
memories became possible is entirely a cultural invention. Go back 250 years in American and European history, and you do not find nearly so many people wandering around remote corners of the planet looking for what today we would call "the wilderness experience." As late as the eighteenth century, the most common usage of the word "wilderness" in the English language referred to landscapes that generally carried adjectives far different from the ones they attract today. To be a wilderness then was to be "deserted," "savage," "desolate," "barren"—in short, a "waste," the word's nearest synonym. Its connotations were anything but positive, and the emotion one was most likely to feel in its presence was "bewilderment" or terror.[2]

Many of the word's strongest associations then were biblical, 5
for it is used over and over again in the King James Version to refer to places on the margins of civilization where it is all too easy to lose oneself in moral confusion and despair. The wilderness was where Moses had wandered with his people for forty years, and where they had nearly abandoned their God to worship a golden idol.[3] "For Pharaoh will say of the Children of Israel," we read in Exodus, "They are entangled in the land, the wilderness hath shut them in."[4] The wilderness was where Christ had struggled with the devil and endured his temptations: "And immediately the Spirit driveth him into the wilderness. And he was there in the wilderness for forty days tempted of Satan; and was with the wild beasts; and the angels ministered unto him."[5] The "delicious Paradise" of John Milton's Eden was surrounded by "a steep wilderness, whose hairy sides / Access denied" to all who sought entry.[6] When Adam and Eve were driven from that garden, the world they entered was

a wilderness that only their labor and pain could redeem. Wilderness, in short, was a place to which one came only against one's will, and always in fear and trembling. Whatever value it might have arose solely from the possibility that it might be "reclaimed" and turned toward human ends— planted as a garden, say, or a city upon a hill.[7] In its raw state, it had little or nothing to offer civilized men and women.

6   But by the end of the nineteenth century, all this had changed. The wastelands that had once seemed worthless had for some people come to seem almost beyond price. That Thoreau in 1862 could declare wildness to be the preservation of the world suggests the sea change that was going on. Wilderness had once been the antithesis of all that was orderly and good—it had been the darkness, one might say, on the far side of the garden wall—and yet now it was frequently likened to Eden itself. When John Muir arrived in the Sierra Nevada in 1869, he would declare, "No description of Heaven that I have ever heard or read of seems half so fine."[8] He was hardly alone in expressing such emotions. One by one, various corners of the American map came to be designated as sites whose wild beauty was so spectacular that a growing number of citizens had to visit and see them for themselves. Niagara Falls was the first to undergo this transformation, but it was soon followed by the Catskills, the Adirondacks, Yosemite, Yellowstone, and others. Yosemite was deeded by the U.S. government to the state of California in 1864 as the nation's first wildland park, and Yellowstone became the first true national park in 1872.[9]

7   By the first decade of the twentieth century, in the single most famous episode in American conservation history, a national debate had exploded over whether the city of San Francisco should be permitted to augment its water supply by damming the Tuolumne River in Hetch Hetchy valley, well within the boundaries of Yosemite National Park. The dam was eventually built, but what today seems no less significant is that so many people fought to prevent its completion. Even as the fight was being lost, Hetch Hetchy became the battle cry of an emerging movement to preserve wilderness. Fifty years earlier, such opposition would have been unthinkable. Few would have questioned the merits of "reclaiming" a wasteland like this in order to put it to human use. Now the defenders of Hetch Hetchy attracted widespread national attention by portraying such an act not as improvement or progress but as desecration and vandalism. Lest one doubt that the old biblical metaphors had been turned completely on their heads, listen to John Muir attack the dam's defenders. "Their arguments," he wrote, "are curiously like those of the devil, devised for the

destruction of the first garden—so much of the very best Eden fruit going to waste; so much of the best Tuolumne water and Tuolumne scenery going to waste."[10] For Muir and the growing number of Americans who shared his views, Satan's home had become God's own temple.

The sources of this rather astonishing transformation were 8 many, but for the purposes of this essay they can be gathered under two broad headings: the sublime and the frontier. Of the two, the sublime is the older and more pervasive cultural construct, being one of the most important expressions of that broad transatlantic movement we today label as romanticism; the frontier is more peculiarly American, though it too had its European antecedents and parallels. The two converged to remake wilderness in their own image, freighting it with moral values and cultural symbols that it carries to this day. Indeed, it is not too much to say that the modern environmental movement is itself a grandchild of romanticism and post-frontier ideology, which is why it is no accident that so much environmentalist discourse takes its bearings from the wilderness these intellectual movements helped create. Although wilderness may today seem to be just one environmental concern among many, it in fact serves as the foundation for a long list of other such concerns that on their face seem quite remote from it. That is why its influence is so pervasive and, potentially, so insidious.

To gain such remarkable influence, the concept of wilder- 9 ness had to become loaded with some of the deepest core values of the culture that created and idealized it: it had to become sacred. This possibility had been present in wilderness even in the days when it had been a place of spiritual danger and moral temptation. If Satan was there, then so was Christ, who had found angels as well as wild beasts during His sojourn in the desert. In the wilderness the boundaries between human and nonhuman, between natural and supernatural, had always seemed less certain than elsewhere. This was why the early Christian saints and mystics had often emulated Christ's desert retreat as they sought to experience for themselves the visions and spiritual testing He had endured. One might meet devils and run the risk of losing one's soul in such a place, but one might also meet God. For some that possibility was worth almost any price.

By the eighteenth century this sense of the wilderness as a 10 landscape where the supernatural lay just beneath the surface was expressed in the doctrine of the *sublime*, a word whose modern usage has been so watered down by commercial hype and tourist advertising that it retains only a dim echo of its former power.[11] In the theories of Edmund Burke, Immanuel Kant, William Gilpin, and others, sublime landscapes were those rare places on earth where one had more chance than elsewhere to glimpse the face of God.[12] Romantics had a clear notion of where one could be most sure of having this experience. Although God might, of course, choose to show Himself anywhere, He would most often be found in those vast, powerful landscapes where one could not help feeling insignificant and being reminded of one's own mortality. Where were these sublime places? The eighteenth century catalog of their locations feels very familiar, for we still see and value landscapes as it taught us to do. God was on the mountaintop, in the chasm, in the waterfall, in the thunder-cloud, in the rainbow, in the sunset. One has only to think of the sites that Americans chose for their first national parks—Yellowstone, Yosemite, Grand Canyon, Rainier, Zion—to realize that virtually all of them fit one or more of these categories. Less sublime landscapes simply did not appear worthy of such protection; not until the 1940s, for instance, would the first swamp be honored, in Everglades National Park, and to this day there is no national park in the grasslands.[13]

11   Among the best proofs that one had entered a sublime landscape was the emotion it evoked. For the early romantic writers and artists who first began to celebrate it, the sublime was far from being a pleasurable experience. The classic description is that of William Wordsworth as he recounted climbing the Alps and crossing the Simplon Pass in his autobiographical poem *The Prelude*. There, surrounded by crags and waterfalls, the poet felt himself literally to be in the presence of the divine—and experienced an emotion remarkably close to terror:

The immeasurable height
Of woods decaying, never to be decayed,
The stationary blasts of waterfalls,
And in the narrow rent at every turn
Winds thwarting winds, bewildered and forlorn,
The torrents shooting from the clear blue sky,
The rocks that muttered close upon our ears,
Black drizzling crags that spake by the way-side
As if a voice were in them, the sick sight
And giddy prospect of the raving stream,
The unfettered clouds and region of the Heavens,
Tumult and peace, the darkness and the light—
Were all like workings of one mind, the features
Of the same face, blossoms upon one tree;

> Characters of the great Apocalypse,
> The types and symbols of Eternity,
> Of first, and last, and midst, and without end.[14]

This was no casual stroll in the mountains, no simple sojourn in the gentle lap of nonhuman nature. What Wordsworth described was nothing less than a religious experience, akin to that of the Old Testament prophets as they conversed with their wrathful God. The symbols he detected in this wilderness landscape were more supernatural than natural, and they inspired more awe and dismay than joy or pleasure. No mere mortal was meant to linger long in such a place, so it was with considerable relief that Wordsworth and his companion made their way back down from the peaks to the sheltering valleys.

Lest you suspect that this view of the sublime was limited to   12
timid Europeans who lacked the American know-how for feeling at home in the wilderness, remember Henry David Thoreau's 1846 climb of Mount Katahdin, in Maine. Although Thoreau is regarded by many today as one of the great American celebrators of wilderness, his emotions about Katahdin were no less ambivalent than Wordsworth's about the Alps.

> It was vast, Titanic; and such as man never inhabits. Some part of the beholder, even some vital part, seems to escape through the loose grating of his ribs as he ascends. He is more lone than you can imagine. . . . Vast, Titanic, inhuman Nature has got him at disadvantage, caught him alone, and pilfers him of some of his divine faculty. She does not smile on him as in the plains. She seems to say sternly, why came ye here before your time? This ground is not prepared for you. Is it not enough that I smile in the valleys? I have never made this soil for thy feet, this air for thy breathing, these rocks for thy neighbors. I cannot pity nor fondle thee here, but forever relentlessly drive thee hence to where I *am* kind. Why seek me where I have not called thee, and then complain because you find me but a stepmother?[15]

This is surely not the way a modern backpacker or nature lover would describe Maine's most famous mountain, but that is because Thoreau's description owes as much to Wordsworth and other romantic contemporaries as to the rocks and clouds of Katahdin itself. His words took the physical mountain on which he stood and transmuted it into an icon of the sublime: a symbol of God's presence on earth. The power and the glory of that icon were such that only a prophet might gaze on it for long. In effect, romantics like Thoreau joined Moses and the children of Israel in Exodus when "they looked toward the wilderness, and behold, the glory of the Lord appeared in the cloud."[16]

13   But even as it came to embody the awesome power of the sublime, wilderness was also being tamed—not just by those who were building settlements in its midst but also by those who most celebrated its inhuman beauty. By the second half of the nineteenth century, the terrible awe that Wordsworth and Thoreau regarded as the appropriately pious stance to adopt in the presence of their mountaintop God was giving way to a much more comfortable, almost sentimental demeanor. As more and more tourists sought out the wilderness as a spectacle to be looked at and enjoyed for its great beauty, the sublime in effect became domesticated. The wilderness was still sacred, but the religious sentiments it evoked were more those of a pleasant parish church than those of a grand cathedral or a harsh desert retreat. The writer who best captures this late romantic sense of a domesticated sublime is undoubtedly John Muir, whose descriptions of Yosemite and the Sierra Nevada reflect none of the anxiety or terror one finds in earlier writers. Here he is, for instance, sketching on North Dome in Yosemite Valley:

> No pain here, no dull empty hours, no fear of the past, no fear of the future. These blessed mountains are so compactly filled with God's beauty, no petty personal hope or experience has room to be. Drinking this champagne water is pure pleasure, so is breathing the living air, and every movement of limbs is pleasure, while the body seems to feel beauty when exposed to it as it feels the campfire or sunshine, entering not by the eyes alone, but equally through all one's flesh like radiant heat, making a passionate ecstatic pleasure glow not explainable.

14   The emotions Muir describes in Yosemite could hardly be more different from Thoreau's on Katahdin or Wordsworth's on the Simplon Pass. Yet all three men are participating in the same cultural tradition and contributing to the same myth: the mountain as cathedral. The three may differ in the way they choose to express their piety—Wordsworth favoring an awe-filled bewilderment, Thoreau a stern loneliness, Muir a welcome ecstasy—but they agree completely about the church in

which they prefer to worship. Muir's closing words on North Dome diverge from his older contemporaries only in mood, not in their ultimate content:

> Perched like a fly on this Yosemite dome, I gaze and sketch and bask, oftentimes settling down into dumb administration without definite hope of ever learning much, yet with the longing, unresting effort that lies at the door of hope, humbly prostrate before the vast display of God's power, and eager to offer self-denial and renunciation with eternal toil to learn any lesson in the divine manuscript.[17]

Muir's "divine manuscript" and Wordsworth's "Characters of the great Apocalypse" were in fact pages from the same holy book. The sublime wilderness had ceased to be a place of satanic temptation and become instead a sacred temple, much as it continues to be for those who love it today.

But the romantic sublime was not the only cultural movement 15 that helped transform wilderness into a sacred American icon during the nineteenth century. No less important was the powerful romantic attraction of primitivism, dating back at least to Rousseau—the belief that the best antidote to the ills of an overly refined and civilized modern world was a return to simpler, more primitive living. In the United States, this was embodied most strikingly in the national myth of the frontier. The historian Frederick Jackson Turner wrote in 1893 the classic academic statement of this myth, but it had been part of American cultural traditions for well over a century. As Turner described the process, easterners and European immigrants, in moving to the wild unsettled lands of the frontier, shed the trappings of civilization, rediscovered their primitive racial energies, reinvented direct democratic institutions, and thereby reinfused themselves with a vigor, an independence, and a creativity that were the source of American democracy and national character. Seen in this way, wild country became a place not just of religious redemption but of national renewal, the quintessential location for experiencing what it meant to be an American.

One of Turner's most provocative claims was that by the 16 1890s the frontier was passing away. Never again would "such gifts of free land offer themselves" to the American people. "The frontier has gone," he declared, "and with its going has closed the first period of American history."[18] Built into the frontier myth from its very beginning was the notion that this crucible of American identity was temporary and would pass away. Those who have celebrated the frontier have almost always looked backward as they did so, mourning an older, simpler, truer world that is about to disappear forever. That world and all of its attractions, Turner said, depended on free land—on wilderness. Thus, in the myth of the vanishing frontier lay the seeds of wilderness preservation in the United States, for if wild land had been so crucial in the making of the nation, then surely one must save its last remnants as monuments to the American past—and as an insurance policy to protect its future. It is no accident that the movement to set aside national parks and wilderness areas began to gain real momentum at precisely the time that laments about the passing frontier reached their peak. To protect wilderness was in a very real sense to protect the nation's most sacred myth of origin.

17   Among the core elements of the frontier myth was the powerful sense among certain groups of Americans that wilderness was the last bastion of rugged individualism. Turner tended to stress communitarian themes when writing frontier history, asserting that Americans in primitive conditions had been forced to band together with their neighbors to form communities and democratic institutions. For other writers, however, frontier democracy for communities was less compelling than frontier freedom for individuals.[19] By fleeing to the outer margins of settled land and society—so the story ran—an individual could escape the confining strictures of civilized life. The mood among writers who celebrated frontier individualism was almost always nostalgic; they lamented not just a lost ways of life but the passing of the heroic men who had embodied that life. Thus Owen Wister in the introduction to his classic 1902 novel *The Virginian* could write of "a vanished world" in which "the horseman, the cow-puncher, the last romantic figure upon our soil" rode only "in his historic yesterday" and would "never come again." For Wister, the cowboy was a man who gave his word and kept it ("Wall Street would have found him behind the times"), who did not talk lewdly to women ("Newport would have thought him old-fashioned"), who worked and played hard, and whose "ungoverned hours did not unman him."[20] Theodore Roosevelt wrote with much the same nostalgic fervor about the "fine, manly qualities" of the "wild rough-rider of the plains." No one could be more heroically masculine, thought Roosevelt, or more at home in the western wilderness:

There he passes his days, there he does his life-work, there, when he meets death, he faces it as he has faced many other evils, with quiet, uncomplaining fortitude. Brave, hospitable, hardy, and adventurous, he is the grim pioneer of our race; he prepares the way for the civilization from before whose face he must himself disappear. Hard and dangerous though his existence is, it has yet a wild attraction that strongly draws to it his bold, free spirit.[21]

This nostalgia for a passing frontier way of life inevitably   18
implied ambivalence, if not downright hostility, toward modernity and all that it represented. If one saw the wild lands of the frontier as freer, truer, and more natural than other, more modern places, then one was also inclined to see the cities and factories of urban-industrial civilization as confining, false, and artificial. Owen Wister looked at the post-frontier "transition" that had followed "the horseman of the plains," and did not like what he saw: "a shapeless state, a condition of men and manners as unlovely as is that moment in the year when winter is gone and spring not come, and the face of Nature is ugly."[22] In the eyes of writers who shared Wister's distaste for modernity, civilization contaminated its inhabitants and absorbed them into the faceless, collective, contemptible life of the crowd. For all of its troubles and dangers, and despite the fact that it must pass away, the frontier had been a better place. If civilization was to be redeemed, it would be by men like the Virginian who could retain their frontier virtues even as they made the transition to post-frontier life.

The mythic frontier individualist was almost always mascu-   19
line in gender: here, in the wilderness, a man could be a real man, the rugged individual he was meant to be before civilization sapped his energy and threatened his masculinity. Wister's contemptuous remarks about Wall Street and Newport suggest what he and many others of his generation believed—that the comforts and seductions of civilized life were especially insidious for men, who all too easily became emasculated by the femininizing tendencies of civilization. More often than not, men who felt this way came, like Wister and Roosevelt, from elite class backgrounds. The curious result was that frontier nostalgia became an important vehicle for expressing a peculiarly bourgeois form of antimodernism. The very men who most benefited from urban-industrial capitalism were among those who believed they must escape its debilitating effects. If the frontier was passing, then men who had the means to do so should preserve for themselves some remnant of its wild landscape so that they might enjoy the regeneration and renewal

that came from sleeping under the stars, participating in blood sports, and living off the land. The frontier might be gone, but the frontier experience could still be had if only wilderness were preserved.

20   Thus the decades following the Civil War saw more and more of the nation's wealthiest citizens seeking out wilderness for themselves. The elite passion for wild land took many forms: enormous estates in the Adirondacks and elsewhere (disingenuously called "camps" despite their many servants and amenities), cattle ranches for would-be rough riders on the Great Plains, guided big-game hunting trips in the Rockies, and luxurious resort hotels wherever railroads pushed their way into sublime landscapes. Wilderness suddenly emerged as the landscape of choice for elite tourists, who brought with them strikingly urban ideas of the countryside through which they traveled. For them, wild land was not a site for productive labor and not a permanent home; rather, it was a place of recreation. One went to the wilderness not as a producer but as a consumer, hiring guides and other backcountry residents who could serve as romantic surrogates for the rough riders and hunters of the frontier if one was willing to overlook their new status as employees and servants of the rich.

21   In just this way, wilderness came to embody the national frontier myth, standing for the wild freedom of America's past and seeming to represent a highly attractive natural alternative to the ugly artificiality of modern civilization. The irony, of course, was that in the process wilderness came to reflect the very civilization its devotees sought to escape. Ever since the nineteenth century, celebrating wilderness has been an activity mainly for well-to-do city folks. Country people generally know far too much about working the land to regard *un*worked land as their ideal. In contrast, elite urban tourists and wealthy sportsmen projected their leisure-time frontier fantasies onto the American landscape and so created wilderness in their own image.

22   There were other ironies as well. The movement to set aside national parks and wilderness areas followed hard on the heels of the final Indian wars, in which the prior human inhabitants of these areas were rounded up and moved onto reservations. The myth of the wilderness as "virgin," uninhabited land had always been especially cruel when seen from the perspective of the Indians who had once called that land home. Now they were forced to move elsewhere, with the result that tourists could safely enjoy the illusion that they were seeing their nation in its pristine, original state, in the new morning of God's own creation.[23] Among the things that most marked the new

national parks as reflecting a post-frontier consciousness was the relative absence of human violence within their boundaries. The actual frontier had often been a place of conflict, in which invaders and invaded fought for control of land and resources. Once set aside within the fixed and carefully policed boundaries of the modern bureaucratic state, the wilderness lost its savage image and became safe: a place more of reverie than of revulsion or fear. Meanwhile, its original inhabitants were kept out by dint of force, their earlier uses of the land redefined as inappropriate or even illegal. To this day, for instance, the Blackfeet continue to be accused of "poaching" on the lands of Glacier National Park that originally belonged to them and that were ceded by treaty only with the proviso that they be permitted to hunt there.[24]

23   The removal of Indians to create an "uninhabited wilderness"—uninhabited as never before in the human history of the place—reminds us just how invented, just how constructed, the American wilderness really is. To return to my opening argument: there is nothing natural about the concept of wilderness. It is entirely a creation of the culture that holds it dear, a product of the very history it seeks to deny. Indeed, one of the most striking proofs of the cultural invention of wilderness is its thoroughgoing erasure of the history from which it sprang. In virtually all of its manifestations, wilderness represents a flight from history. Seen as the original garden, it is a place outside of time, from which human beings had to be ejected before the fallen world history could properly begin. Seen as the frontier, it is a savage world at the dawn of civilization, whose transformation represents the very beginning of the national historical epic. Seen as the bold landscape of frontier heroism, it is the place of youth and childhood, into which men escape by abandoning their pasts and entering a world of freedom where the constraints of civilization fade into memory. Seen as the sacred sublime, it is the home of a God who transcends history by standing as the One who remains untouched and unchanged by time's arrow. No matter what the angle from which we regard it, wilderness offers us the illusion that we can escape the cares and troubles of the world in which our past has ensnared us.[25]

24   This escape from history is one reason why the language we use to talk about wilderness is often permeated with spiritual and religious values that reflect human ideals far more than the material world of physical nature. Wilderness fulfills the old romantic project of secularizing Judeo-Christian values so as to make a new cathedral not in some pretty human building but in God's own creation, Nature itself. Many environmental-

ists who reject traditional notions of the Godhead and who regard themselves as agnostics or even atheists nonetheless express feelings tantamount to religious awe when in the presence of wilderness—a fact that testifies to the success of the romantic project. Those who have no difficulty seeing God as the expression of our human dreams and desires nonetheless have trouble recognizing that in a secular age Nature can offer precisely the same sort of mirror.

25   Thus it is that wilderness serves as the unexamined foundation on which so many of the quasi-religious values of modern environmentalism rest. The critique of modernity that is one of environmentalism's most important contributions to the moral and political discourse of our time more often than not appeals, explicitly or implicitly, to wilderness as the standard against which to measure the failings of our human world. Wilderness is the natural, unfallen antithesis of an unnatural civilization that has lost its soul. It is a place of freedom in which we can recover the true selves we have lost to the corrupting influences of our artificial lives. Most of all, it is the ultimate landscape of authenticity. Combining the sacred grandeur of the sublime with the primitive simplicity of the frontier, it is the place where we can see the world as it really is, and so know ourselves as we really are—or ought to be.

26   But the trouble with wilderness is that it quietly expresses and reproduces the very values its devotees seek to reject. The flight from history that is very nearly the core of wilderness represents the false hope of an escape from responsibility, the illusion that we can somehow wipe clean the slate of our past and return to the tabula rasa that supposedly existed before we began to leave our marks on the world. The dream of an unworked natural landscape is very much the fantasy of people who have never themselves had to work the land to make a living—urban folk for whom food comes from a supermarket or a restaurant instead of a field, and for whom the wooden houses in which they live and work apparently have no meaningful connection to the forests in which trees grow and die. Only people whose relation to the land was already alienated could hold up wilderness as a model for human life in nature, for the romantic ideology of wilderness leaves precisely nowhere for human beings actually to make their living from the land.

27   This, then, is the central paradox: wilderness embodies a dualistic vision in which the human is entirely outside the natural. If we allow ourselves to believe that nature, to be true, must also be wild, then our very presence in nature represents its fall. The place where we are is the place where nature is not. If this is so—if by definition wilderness leaves no place for hu-

man beings, save perhaps as contemplative sojourners enjoying their leisurely reverie in God's natural cathedral—then also
by definition it can offer no solution to the environmental and
other problems that confront us. To the extent that we celebrate wilderness as the measure with which we judge civilization, we reproduce the dualism that sets humanity and nature
at opposite poles. We thereby leave ourselves little hope of discovering what an ethical, sustainable, *honorable* human place
in nature might actually look like.

Worse: to the extent that we live in an urban-industrial civi-   28
lization but at the same time pretend to ourselves that our *real*
home is in the wilderness, to just that extent we give ourselves
permission to evade responsibility for the lives we actually
lead. We inhabit civilization while holding some part of ourselves—what we imagine to be the most precious part—aloof
from its entanglements. We work our nine-to-five jobs in its institutions, we eat its food, we drive its cars (not least to reach
the wilderness), we benefit from the intricate and all too invisible networks with which it shelters us, all the while pretending
that these things are not an essential part of who we are. By
imagining that our true home is in the wilderness, we forgive
ourselves the homes we actually inhabit. In its flight from history, in its siren song of escape, in its reproduction of the dangerous dualism that sets human beings outside of nature—in
all of these ways, wilderness poses a serious threat to responsible environmentalism at the end of the twentieth century.

By now I hope it is clear that my criticism in this essay is not   29
directed at wild nature per se, or even at efforts to set aside
large tracts of wild land, but rather at the specific habits of
thinking that flow from this complex cultural construction
called wilderness. It is not the things we label as wilderness
that are the problem—for nonhuman nature and large tracts of
the natural world *do* deserve protection—but rather what we
ourselves mean when we use the label. Lest one doubt how
pervasive these habits of thought actually are in contemporary
environmentalism, let me list some of the places where wilderness serves as the ideological underpinning for environmental
concerns that might otherwise seem quite remote from it.
Defenders of biological diversity, for instance, although sometimes appealing to more utilitarian concerns, often point to
"untouched" ecosystems as the best and richest repositories of
the undiscovered species we must certainly try to protect.
Although at first blush an apparently more "scientific" concept
than wilderness, biological diversity in fact invokes many of
the same sacred values, which is why organizations like the
Nature Conservancy have been so quick to employ it as an al-

ternative to the seemingly fuzzier and more problematic concept of wilderness. There is a paradox here, of course. To the extent that biological diversity (indeed, even wilderness itself) is likely to survive in the future only by the most vigilant and self-conscious management of the ecosystems that sustain it, the ideology of wilderness is potentially in direct conflict with the very thing it encourages us to protect.[26]

30 The most striking instances of this have revolved around "endangered species," which serve as vulnerable symbols of biological diversity while at the same time standing as surrogates for wilderness itself. The terms of the Endangered Species Act in the United States have often meant that those hoping to defend pristine wilderness have had to rely on a single endangered species like the spotted owl to gain legal standing for their case—thereby making the full power of the sacred land inhere in a single numinous organism whose habitat then becomes the object of intense debate about appropriate management and use.[27] The ease with which anti-environmental forces like the wise-use movement have attacked such single-species preservation efforts suggests the vulnerability of strategies like these.

31 Perhaps partly because our own conflicts over such places and organisms have become so messy, the convergence of wilderness values with concerns about biological diversity and endangered species has helped produce a deep fascination for remote ecosystems, where it is easier to imagine that nature might somehow be "left alone" to flourish by its own pristine devices. The classic example is the tropical rain forest, which since the 1970s has become the most powerful modern icon of unfallen, sacred land—a veritable Garden of Eden—for many Americans and Europeans. And yet protecting the rain forest in the eyes of First World environmentalists all too often means protecting it from the people who live there. Those who seek to preserve such "wilderness" from the activities of native peoples run the risk of reproducing the same tragedy—being forceably removed from an ancient home—that befell American Indians. Third World countries face massive environmental problems and deep social conflicts, but these are not likely to be solved by a cultural myth that encourages us to "preserve" peopleless landscapes that have not existed in such places for millennia. At its worst, as environmentalists are beginning to realize, exporting American notions of wilderness in this way can become an unthinking and self-defeating form of cultural imperialism.[28]

32 Perhaps the most suggestive example of the way that wilderness thinking can underpin other environmental concerns has

emerged in the recent debate about "global change." In 1989 the journalist Bill McKibben published a book entitled *The End of Nature*, in which he argued that the prospect of global climate change as a result of unintentional human manipulation of the atmosphere means that nature as we once knew it no longer exists.[29] Whereas earlier generations inhabited a natural world that remained more or less unaffected by their actions, our own generation is uniquely different. We and our children will henceforth live in a biosphere completely altered by our own activity, a planet in which the human and the natural can no longer be distinguished, because the one has overwhelmed the other. In McKibben's view, nature has died, and we are responsible for killing it. "The planet," he declares, "is utterly different now."[30]

But such a perspective is possible only if we accept the 33 wilderness premise that nature, to be natural, must also be pristine—remote from humanity and untouched by our common past. In fact, everything we know about environmental history suggests that people have been manipulating the natural world on various scales for as long as we have a record of their passing. Moreover, we have unassailable evidence that many of the environmental changes we now face also occurred quite apart from human intervention at one time or another in the earth's past.[31] The point is not that our current problems are trivial, or that our devastating effects on the earth's ecosystems should be accepted as inevitable or "natural." It is rather that we seem unlikely to make much progress in solving these problems if we hold up to ourselves as the mirror of nature a wilderness we ourselves cannot inhabit.

To do so is merely to take to a logical extreme the paradox 34 that was built into wilderness from the beginning: if nature dies because we enter it, then the only way to save nature is to kill ourselves. The absurdity of this proposition flows from the underlying dualism it expresses. Not only does it ascribe greater power to humanity that we in fact possess—physical and biological nature will surely survive in some form or another long after we ourselves have gone the way of all flesh—but in the end it offers us little more than a self-defeating counsel of despair. The tautology gives us no way out: if wild nature is the only thing worth saving, and if our mere presence destroys it, then the sole solution to our own unnaturalness, the only way to protect sacred wilderness from profane humanity, would seem to be suicide. It is not a proposition that seems likely to produce very positive or practical results.

And yet radical environmentalists and deep ecologists all too 35 frequently come close to accepting this premise as a first principle. When they express, for instance, the popular notion that our environmental problems began with the invention of agriculture, they push the human fall from natural grace so far back into the past that all of civilized history becomes a tale of ecological declension. Earth First! founder Dave Foreman captures the familiar parable succinctly when he writes,

> Before agriculture was midwifed in the Middle East, humans were in the wilderness. We had no concept of "wilderness" because everything was wilderness and *we were a part of it.* But with irrigation ditches, crop surpluses, and permanent villages, we became *apart from* the natural world. . . . Between the wilderness that created us and the civilization created by us grew an ever-widening rift.[32]

In this view the farm becomes the first and most important battlefield in the long war against wild nature, and all else follows in its wake. From such a starting place, it is hard not to reach the conclusion that the only way human beings can hope to live naturally on earth is to follow the hunter-gatherers back into a wilderness Eden and abandon virtually everything that civilization has given us. It may indeed turn out that civilization will end in ecological collapse or nuclear disaster, whereupon one might expect to find any human survivors returning to a way of life closer to that celebrated by Foreman and his followers. For most of us, though, such a debacle would be cause for regret, a sign that humanity had failed to fulfill its own promise and failed to honor its own highest values—including those of the deep ecologists.

36   In offering wilderness as the ultimate hunter-gatherer alternative to civilization, Foreman reproduces an extreme but still easily recognizable version of the myth of frontier primitivism. When he writes of his fellow Earth Firsters that "we believe we must return to being animal, to glorying in our sweat, hormones, tears, and blood" and that "we struggle against the modern compulsion to become dull, passionless androids," he is following in the footsteps of Owen Wister.[33] Although his arguments give primacy to defending biodiversity and the autonomy of wild nature, his prose becomes most passionate when he speaks of preserving "the wilderness experience." His own ideal "Big Outside" bears an uncanny resemblance to that of the frontier myth: wide open spaces and virgin land with no trails, no signs, no facilities, no maps, no guides, no rescues, no modern equipment. Tellingly, it is a land where hardy travelers can support themselves by hunting with "primitive weapons

(bow and arrow, atlatl, knife, sharp rock)."[34] Foreman claims that "the primary value of wilderness is not as a proving ground for young Huck Finns and Annie Oakleys," but his heart is with Huck and Annie all the same. He admits that "preserving a quality wilderness experience for the human visitor, letting her or him flex Paleolithic muscles or seek visions, remains a tremendously important secondary purpose."[35] Just so does Teddy Roosevelt's rough rider live on in the greener garb of a new age.

However much one may be attracted to such a vision, it en- 37 tails problematic consequences. For one, it makes wilderness the locus for an epic struggle between malign civilization and benign nature, compared with which all other social, political, and moral concerns seem trivial. Foreman writes, "The preservation of wildness and native diversity is *the* most important issue. Issues directly affecting only humans pale in comparison."[36] Presumably so do any environmental problems whose victims are mainly people, for such problems usually surface in landscapes that have already "fallen" and are no longer wild. This would seem to exclude from the radical environmentalist agenda problems of occupational health and safety in industrial settings, problems of toxic waste exposure on "unnatural" urban and agricultural sites, problems of poor children poisoned by lead exposure in the inner city, problems of famine and poverty and human suffering in the "overpopulated" places of the earth—problems, in short, of environmental justice. If we set too high a stock on wilderness, too many other corners of the earth become less than natural and too many other people become less than human, thereby giving us permission not to care much about their suffering or their fate.

It is no accident that these supposedly inconsequential envi- 38 ronmental problems affect mainly poor people, for the long affiliation between wilderness and wealth means that the only poor people who count when wilderness is *the* issue are hunter-gatherers, who presumably do not consider themselves to be poor in the first place. The dualism at the heart of wilderness encourages its advocates to conceive of its protection as a crude conflict between the "human" and the "nonhuman"—or, more often, between those who value the nonhuman and those who do not. This in turn tempts one to ignore crucial differences *among* humans and the complex cultural and historical reasons why different peoples may feel very differently about the meaning of wilderness.

Why, for instance, is the "wilderness experience" so often 39 conceived as a form of recreation best enjoyed by those whose class privileges give them the time and resources to leave their jobs behind and "get away from it all"? Why does the protection of wilderness so often seem to pit urban recreationists against rural people who actually earn their living from the land (excepting those who sell goods and services to the tourists themselves)? Why in the debates about pristine natural areas are "primitive" peoples idealized, even sentimentalized, until the moment they do something unprimitive, modern, and unnatural, and thereby fall from environmental grace? What are the consequences of a wilderness ideology that devalues productive labor and the very concrete knowledge that comes from working the land with one's own hands?[37] All of these questions imply conflicts among different groups of people, conflicts that are obscured behind the deceptive clarity of "human" vs. "nonhuman." If in answering these knotty questions we resort to so simplistic an opposition, we are almost certain to ignore the very subtleties and complexities we need to understand.

40   But the most troubling cultural baggage that accompanies the celebration of wilderness has less to do with remote rain forests and peoples than with the ways we think about ourselves—we American environmentalists who quite rightly worry about the future of the earth and the threats we pose to the natural world. Idealizing a distant wilderness too often means not idealizing the environment in which we actually live, the landscape that for better or worse we call home. Most of our most serious environmental problems start right here, at home, and if we are to solve those problems, we need an environmental ethic that will tell us as much about *using* nature as about *not* using it. The wilderness dualism tends to cast any use as *ab*-use, and thereby denies us a middle ground in which responsible use and non-use might attain some kind of balanced, sustainable relationship. My own belief is that only by exploring this middle ground will we learn ways of imagining a better world for all of us: humans and nonhumans, rich people and poor, women and men, First Worlders *and* Third Worlders, white folks and people of color, consumers and producers—a world better for humanity in all of its diversity and for all the rest of nature too. The middle ground is where we actually live. It is where we—all of us, in our different places and ways—make our homes.

41   That is why, when I think of the times I myself have come closest to experiencing what I might call the sacred in nature, I often find myself remembering wild places much closer to home. I think, for instance, of a small pond near my house where water bubbles up from limestone springs to feed a series of pools that rarely freeze in winter and so play home to water-

fowl that stay here for the protective warmth even on the coldest of winter days, gliding silently through streaming mists as the snow falls from gray February skies. I think of a November evening long ago when I found myself on a Wisconsin hilltop in rain and dense fog, only to have the setting sun break through the clouds to cast an otherworldly golden light on the misty farms and woodlands below, a scene so unexpected and joyous that I lingered past dusk so as not to miss any part of the gift that had come my way. And I think perhaps most especially of the blown-out, bankrupt farm in the sand country of central Wisconsin where Aldo Leopold and his family tried one of the first American experiments in ecological restoration, turning ravaged and infertile soil into carefully tended ground where the human and the nonhuman could exist side by side in relative harmony. What I celebrate about such places is not *just* their wildness, though that certainly is among their most important qualities; what I celebrate even more is that they remind us of the wildness in our own backyards, of the nature that is all around us if only we have eyes to see it.

Indeed, my principal objection to wilderness is that it may   42
teach us to be dismissive or even contemptuous of such humble places and experiences. Without our quite realizing it, wilderness tends to privilege some parts of nature at the expense of others. Most of us, I suspect, still follow the conventions of the romantic sublime in finding the mountaintop more glorious than the plains, the ancient forest nobler than the grasslands, the mighty canyon more inspiring than the humble marsh. Even John Muir, in arguing against those who sought to dam his beloved Hetch Hetchy valley in the Sierra Nevada, argued for alternative dam sites in the gentler valleys of the foothills—a preference that had nothing to do with nature and everything with the cultural traditions of the sublime.[38] Just as problematically, our frontier traditions have encouraged Americans to define "true" wilderness as requiring very large tracts of roadless land—what Dave Foreman calls "The Big Outside." Leaving aside the legitimate empirical question in conservation biology of how large a tract of land must be before a given species can reproduce on it, the emphasis on big wilderness reflects a romantic frontier belief that one hasn't really gotten away from civilization unless one can go for days at a time without encountering another human being. By teaching us to fetishize sublime places and wide open country, these peculiarly American ways of thinking about wilderness encourage us to adopt too high a standard for what counts as "natural." If it isn't hundreds of square miles big, if it doesn't give us God's-eye views or grand vistas, if it doesn't permit

us the illusion that we are alone on the planet, then it really is-
n't natural. It's too small, too plain, or too crowded to be *authentically* wild.

43   In critiquing wilderness as I have done in this essay, I'm
forced to confront my own deep ambivalence about its meaning for modern environmentalism. On the one hand, one of my
own most important environmental ethics is that people
should always be conscious that they are part of the natural
world, inextricably tied to the ecological systems that sustain
their lives. Any way of looking at nature that encourages us to
believe we are separate from nature—as wilderness tends to
do—is likely to reinforce environmentally irresponsible behavior. On the other hand, I also think it no less crucial for us to
recognize and honor nonhuman nature as a world we did not
create, a world with its own independent, nonhuman reasons
for being as it is. The autonomy of nonhuman nature seems to
me an indispensable corrective to human arrogance. Any way
of looking at nature that helps us remember—as wilderness
also tends to do—that the interests of people are not necessarily identical to those of every other creature or of the earth itself is likely to foster *responsible* behavior. To the extent that
wilderness has served as an important vehicle for articulating
deep moral values regarding our obligations and responsibilities to the nonhuman world, I would not want to jettison the
contributions it has made to our culture's ways of thinking
about nature.

44   If the core problem of wilderness is that it distances us too
much from the very things it teaches us to value, then the question we must ask is what it can tell us about *home*, the place
where we actually live. How can we take the positive values we
associate with wilderness and bring them closer to home? I
think the answer to this question will come by broadening our
sense of the otherness that wilderness seeks to define and protect. In reminding us of the world we did not make, wilderness
can teach profound feelings of humility and respect as we confront our fellow beings and the earth itself. Feelings like these
argue for the importance of self-awareness and self-criticism
as we exercise our own ability to transform the world around
us, helping us set responsible limits to human mastery—which
without such limits too easily becomes human hubris.
Wilderness is the place where, symbolically at least, we try to
withhold our power to dominate.

Wallace Stegner once wrote of

the special human mark, the special record of human passage, that distinguishes man from all other species. It is rare

enough among men, impossible to any other form of life. *It is simply the deliberate and chosen refusal to make any marks at all....* We are the most dangerous species of life on the planet, and every other species, even the earth itself, has cause to fear our power to exterminate. But we are also the only species which, when it chooses to do so, will go to great effort to save what it might destroy.[39]

The myth of wilderness, which Stegner knowingly reproduces in these remarks, is that we can somehow leave nature untouched by our passage. By now it should be clear that this for the most part is an illusion. But Stegner's deeper message then becomes all the more compelling. If living in history means that we cannot help leaving marks on a fallen world, then the dilemma we face is to decide what kinds of marks we wish to leave. It is just here that our cultural traditions of wilderness remain so important. In the broadest sense, wilderness teaches us to ask whether the Other must always bend to our will, and, if not, under what circumstances it should be allowed to flourish without our intervention. This is surely a question worth asking about everything we do, and not just about the natural world.

When we visit a wilderness area, we find ourselves surrounded by plants and animals and physical landscapes whose otherness compels our attention. In forcing us to acknowledge that they are not of our making, that they have little or no need of our continued existence, they recall for us a creation far greater than our own. In the wilderness, we need no reminder that a tree has its own reasons for being, quite apart from us. The same is less true in the gardens we plant and tend ourselves: there it is far easier to forget the otherness of the tree.[40] Indeed, one could almost measure wilderness by the extent to which our recognition of its otherness requires a conscious, willed act on our part. The romantic legacy means that wilderness is more a state of mind than a fact of nature, and the state of mind that today most defines wilderness is *wonder*. The striking power of the wild is that wonder in the face of it requires no act of will, but forces itself upon us—as an expression of the nonhuman world experienced through the lens of our cultural history—as proof that ours is not the only presence in the universe. 45

Wilderness gets us into trouble only if we imagine that this experience of wonder and otherness is limited to the remote corners of the planet, or that it somehow depends on pristine landscapes we ourselves do not inhabit. Nothing could be more misleading. The tree in the garden is in reality no less other, no less worthy of our wonder and respect, than the tree 46 in an ancient forest that has never known an ax or a saw—even though the tree in the forest reflects a more intricate web of ecological relationships. The tree in the garden could easily have sprung from the same seed as the tree in the forest, and we can claim only its location and perhaps its form as our own. Both trees stand apart from us; both share our common world. The special power of the tree in the wilderness is to remind us of this fact. It can teach us to recognize the wildness we did not see in the tree we planted in our own backyard. By seeing the otherness in that which is most unfamiliar, we can learn to see it too in that which at first seemed merely ordinary. If wilderness can do this—if it can help us perceive and respect a nature we had forgotten to recognize as natural— then it will become part of the solution to our environmental dilemmas rather than part of the problem.

47   This will only happen, however, if we abandon the dualism that sees the tree in the garden as artificial—completely fallen and unnatural—and the tree in the wilderness as natural— completely pristine and wild. Both trees in some ultimate sense are wild; both in a practical sense now depend on our management and care. We are responsible for both, even though we can claim credit for neither. Our challenge is to stop thinking of such things according to a set of bipolar moral scales in which the human and the nonhuman, the unnatural and the natural, the fallen and the unfallen, serve as our conceptual map for understanding and valuing the world. Instead, we need to embrace the full continuum of a natural landscape that is also cultural, in which the city, the suburb, the pastoral, and the wild each has its proper place, which we permit ourselves to celebrate without needlessly denigrating the others. We need to honor the Other within and the Other next door as much as we do the exotic Other that lives far away—a lesson that applies as much to people as it does to (other) natural things. In particular, we need to discover a common middle ground in which all of these things, from the city to the wilderness, can somehow be encompassed in the word "home." Home, after all, is the place where finally we make our living. It is the place for which we take responsibility, the place we try to sustain so we can pass on what is best in it (and in ourselves) to our children.[41]

48   The task of making a home in nature is what Wendell Berry has called "the forever unfinished lifework of our species." "The only thing we have to preserve nature with," he writes, "is culture; the only thing we have to preserve wildness with is domesticity."[42] Calling a place home inevitably means that we will *use* the nature we find in it, for there can be no escape from manip-

ulating and working and even killing some parts of nature to make our home. But if we acknowledge the autonomy and otherness of the things and creatures around us—an autonomy our culture has taught us to label with the word "wild"—then we will at least think carefully about the uses to which we put them, and even ask if we should use them at all. Just so can we still join Thoreau in declaring that "in Wildness is the preservation of the World," for *wildness* (as opposed to wilderness) can be found anywhere: in the seemingly tame fields and woodlots of Massachusetts, in the cracks of a Manhattan sidewalk, even in the cells of our own bodies. As Gary Snyder has wisely said, "A person with a clear heart and open mind can experience the wilderness anywhere on earth. It is a quality of one's own consciousness. The planet is a wild place and always will be."[43] To think ourselves capable of causing "the end of nature" is an act of great hubris, for it means forgetting the wildness that dwells everywhere within and around us.

Learning to honor the wild—learning to remember and acknowledge the autonomy of the other—means striving for critical self-consciousness in all of our actions. It means the deep reflection and respect must accompany each act of use, and means too that we must always consider the possibility of nonuse. It means looking at the part of nature we intend to turn toward our own ends and asking whether we can use it again and again and again—sustainably—without its being diminished in the process. In means never imagining that we can flee into a mythical wilderness to escape history and the obligation to take responsibility for our own actions that history inescapably entails. Most of all, it means practicing remembrance and gratitude, for thanksgiving is the simplest and most basic of ways for us to recollect the nature, the culture, and the history that have come together to make the world as we know it. If wildness can stop being (just) out there and start being (also) in here, if it can start being as humane as it is natural, then perhaps we can get on with the unending task of struggling to live rightly in the world—not just in the garden, not just in the wilderness, but in the home that encompasses them both.

49

Notes

1. Henry David Thoreau, "Walking," *The Works of Thoreau*, ed. Henry S. Canby (Boston, Massachusetts: Houghton Mifflin, 1937), p. 672.
2. *Oxford English Dictionary*, s.v. "wilderness"; see also Roderick Nash, *Wilderness and the American Mind*, 3rd ed. (New Haven, Connecticut: Yale Univ. Press, 1982), pp. 1–22; and Max

Oelschlaeger, *The Idea of Wilderness: From Prehistory to the Age of Ecology* (New Haven, Connecticut: Yale Univ. Press, 1991).
3. Exodus 32:1–35, KJV.
4. Exodus 14:3, KJV.
5. Mark 1:12–13, KJV; see also Matthew 4:1–11; Luke 4:1–13.
6. John Milton, "Paradise Lost," *John Milton: Complete Poems and Major Prose*, ed. Merritt Y. Hughes (New York: Odyssey Press, 1957), pp. 280–81, lines 131–42.
7. I have discussed this theme at length in "Landscapes of Abundance and Scarcity," in Clyde Milner et al., eds., *Oxford History of the American West* (New York: Oxford Univ. Press, 1994), pp. 603–37. The classic work on the Puritan "city on a hill" in colonial New England is Perry Miller, *Errand into the Wilderness* (Cambridge, Massachusetts: Harvard Univ. Press, 1956).
8. John Muir, *My First Summer in the Sierra* (1911), reprinted in *John Muir: The Eight Wilderness Discovery Books* (London, England: Diadem; Seattle, Washington: Mountaineers, 1992), p. 211.
9. Alfred Runte, *National Parks: The American Experience*, 2nd ed. (Lincoln: Univ. of Nebraska Press, 1987).
10. John Muir, *The Yosemite* (1912), reprinted in *John Muir: Eight Wilderness Discovery Books*, p. 715.
11. Scholarly work on the sublime is extensive. Among the most important studies are Samuel Monk, *The Sublime: A Study of Critical Theories in XVII-Century England* (New York: Modern Language Association, 1935); Basil Willey, *The Eighteenth-Century Background: Studies on the Idea of Nature in the Thought of the Period* (London, England: Chattus and Windus, 1949); Marjorie Hope Nicolson, *Mountain Gloom and Mountain Glory: The Development of the Aesthetics of the Infinite* (Ithaca, New York: Cornell Univ. Press, 1959); Thomas Weiskel, *The Romantic Sublime: Studies in the Structure and Psychology of Transcendence* (Baltimore, Maryland: Johns Hopkins Univ. Press, 1976); Barbara Novak, *Nature and Culture: American Landscape Painting, 1825–1875* (New York: Oxford Univ. Press, 1980).
12. The classic works are Immanuel Kant, *Observations on the Feeling of the Beautiful and Sublime* (1764), trans. John T. Goldthwait (Berkeley: Univ. of California Press, 1960); Edmund Burke, *A Philosophical Enquiry into the Origin of Our Ideas of the Sublime and Beautiful*, ed. James T. Boulton (1958; Notre Dame, Indiana: Univ. of Notre Dame Press, 1968); William Gilpin, *Three Essays: On Picturesque Beauty; on Picturesque Travel; and on Sketching Landscape* (London, England, 1803).
13. See Ann Vileisis, "From Wastelands to Wetlands" (unpublished senior essay, Yale Univ., 1989); Runte, *National Parks*.

14. William Wordsworth, "The Prelude," bk. 6, in Thomas Hutchinson, ed., *The Poetical Works of Wordsworth* (London, England: Oxford Univ. Press, 1936), p. 536.

15. Henry David Thoreau, *The Maine Woods* (1864), in *Henry David Thoreau* (New York: Library of America, 1985), pp. 640–41.

16. Exodus 16:10, KJV.

17. John Muir, *My First Summer in the Sierra*, p. 238. Part of the difference between these descriptions may reflect the landscapes the three authors were describing. In his essay, "Reinventing Common Nature: Yosemite and Mount Rushmore—A Meandering Tale of a Double Nature," Kenneth Olwig notes that early American travelers experienced Yosemite as much through the aesthetic tropes of the pastoral as through those of the sublime. The ease with which Muir celebrated the gentle divinity of the Sierra Nevada had much to do with the pastoral qualities of the landscape he described. See Olwig, "Reinventing Common Nature: Yosemite and Mount Rushmore—A Meandering Tale of a Double Nature," *Uncommon Ground: Toward Reinventing Nature*, ed. William Cronon (New York: W. W. Norton & Co., 1995), pp. 379–408.

18. Frederick Jackson Turner, *The Frontier in American History* (New York: Henry Holt, 1920), pp. 37–38.

19. Richard Slotkin has made this observation the linchpin of his comparison between Turner and Theodore Roosevelt. See Slotkin, *Gunfighter Nation: The Myth of the Frontier in Twentieth-Century America* (New York: Atheneum, 1992), pp. 29–62.

20. Owen Wister, *The Virginian: A Horseman of the Plains* (New York: Macmillan, 1902), pp. viii–ix.

21. Theodore Roosevelt, *Ranch Life and the Hunting Trail* (1888; New York: Century, 1899), p. 100.

22. Wister, *Virginian*, p. x.

23. On the many problems with this view, see William M. Denevan, "The Pristine Myth: The Landscape of the Americas in 1492," *Annals of the Association of American Geographers* 82 (1992): 369–85.

24. Louis Warren, "The Hunter's Game: Poachers, Conservationists, and Twentieth-Century America" (Ph.D. diss., Yale University, 1994).

25. Wilderness also lies at the foundation of the Clementsian ecological concept of the climax. See Michael Barbour, "Ecological Fragmentation in the Fifties" in Cronon, *Uncommon Ground*, pp. 233–55, and William Cronon, "Introduction: In Search of Nature," in Cronon, *Uncommon Ground*, pp. 23–56.

26. On the many paradoxes of having to manage wilderness in order to maintain the appearance of an unmanaged landscape, see John C. Hendee et al., *Wilderness Management*, USDA Forest Service Miscellaneous Publication No. 1365 (Washington, D.C.: Government Printing Office, 1978).

27. See James Proctor, "Whose Nature?: The Contested Moral Terrain of Ancient Forests," in Cronon, *Uncommon Ground*, pp. 269–97.

28. See Candace Slater, "Amazonia as Edenic Narrative," in Cronon, *Uncommon Ground*, pp. 114–31. This argument has been powerfully made by Ramachandra Guha, "Radical American Environmentalism: A Third World Critique," *Environmental Ethics* 11 (1989): 71–83.

29. Bill McKibben, *The End of Nature* (New York: Random House, 1989).

30. McKibben, *The End of Nature*, p. 49.

31. Even comparable extinction rates have occurred before, though we surely would not want to emulate the Cretaceous-Tertiary boundary extinctions as a model for responsible manipulation of the biosphere!

32. Dave Foreman, *Confessions of an Eco-Warrior* (New York: Harmony Books, 1991), p. 69 (italics in original). For a sampling of other writings by followers of deep ecology and/or Earth First!, see Michael Tobias, ed., *Deep Ecology* (San Diego, California: Avant Books, 1984); Bill Devall and George Sessions, *Deep Ecology: Living as if Nature Mattered* (Salt Lake City, Utah: Gibbs Smith, 1985); Michael Tobias, *After Eden: History, Ecology, and Conscience* (San Diego, California: Avant Books, 1985); Dave Foreman and Bill Haywood, eds., *Ecodefense: A Field Guide to Monkey Wrenching*, 2nd ed. (Tucson, Arizona: Ned Ludd Books, 1987); Bill Devall, *Simple in Means, Rich in Ends: Practicing Deep Ecology* (Salt Lake City, Utah: Gibbs Smith, 1988); Steve Chase, ed., *Defending the Earth: A Dialogue between Murray Bookchin & Dave Foreman* (Boston, Massachusetts: South End Press, 1991); John Davis, ed., *The Earth First! Reader: Ten Years of Radical Environmentalism* (Salt Lake City, Utah: Gibbs Smith, 1991); Bill Devall, *Living Richly in an Age of Limits: Using Deep Ecology for an Abundant Life* (Salt Lake City, Utah: Gibbs Smith, 1993); Michael E. Zimmerman et al., eds., *Environmental Philosophy: From Animal Rights to Radical Ecology* (Englewood Cliffs, New Jersey: Prentice-Hall, 1993). A useful survey of the different factions of radical environmentalism can be found in Carolyn Merchant, *Radical Ecology: The Search for a Livable World* (New York: Routledge, 1992). For a very interesting critique of this literature (first published in the anarchist newspaper *Fifth Estate*), see George Bradford, *How Deep is Deep Ecology?* (Ojai, California: Times Change Press, 1989).

33. Foreman, *Confessions of an Eco-Warrior*, p. 34.

34. Foreman, *Confessions of an Eco-Warrior*, p. 65. See also Dave Foreman and Howie Wolke, *The Big Outside: A Descriptive Inventory of the Big Wilderness Areas of the U.S.* (Tucson, Arizona: Ned Ludd Books, 1989).

35. Foreman, *Confessions of an Eco-Warrior*, p. 63.

36. Foreman, *Confessions of an Eco-Warrior*, p. 27.
37. See Richard White, "'Are You an Environmentalist or Do You Work for a Living?': Work and Nature," in Cronon, *Uncommon Ground*, pp. 171–85. Compare its analysis of environmental knowledge through work with Jennifer Price's analysis of environmental knowledge through consumption. It is not much of an exaggeration to say that the wilderness experience is essentially consumerist in its impulses.
38. Compare with Muir, *Yosemite*, in *John Muir: Eight Wilderness Discovery Books*, p. 714.
39. Wallace Stegner, ed., *This Is Dinosaur: Echo Park Country and Its Magic Rivers* (New York: Knopf, 1955), p. 17 (italics in original).
40. Katherine Hayles helped me see the importance of this argument.
41. Analogous arguments can be found in John Brinckerhoff Jackson, "Beyond Wilderness," *A Sense of Place, a Sense of Time* (New Haven, Connecticut: Yale Univ. Press, 1994), pp. 71–91, and in the wonderful collection of essays by Michael Pollan, *Second Nature: A Gardener's Education* (New York: Atlantic Monthly Press, 1991).
42. Wendell Berry, *Home Economics* (San Francisco, California: North Point, 1987), pp. 138, 143.
43. Gary Snyder, quoted in *New York Times*, "Week in Review," 18 September 1994, p. 6.

Samuel P. Hays

RESPONSE

TO WILLIAM CRONON

Samuel P. Hays taught history at the University of Pittsburgh before his retirement. He has published two groundbreaking books on environmental history, Conservation and the Gospel of Efficiency: The Progressive Conservation Movement, 1890–1920 *(1959) and* Beauty, Health, and Permanence: Environmental Politics in the United States, 1955–1985 *(1987; written with his wife, Barbara). He has also written dozens of articles related to environmental history and the "meanings" attached to wilderness. His response here is to the preceding essay in this book; it appeared in 1996 in the magazine* Environmental History.

1   Bill Cronon's "trouble with wilderness" is ostensibly an assessment of the role the wilderness idea plays for environmentalists in the United States. But his "trouble" is far less with that
wilderness idea and more with his own. He is wrestling with a
wilderness idea that is confined to a few writers rather than
with wilderness devotees who actually do it. Hence his account
is well off the mark.

2   For this rejoinder, I draw on two sources of evidence, quite
different from Cronon's. First is my own experience in the eastern wilderness movement running through the decade of the
1970s. I was one of a considerable number of easterners who
thought that there was wilderness in the East. We studied
USGS topographic maps; identified large, roadless sections;
scouted them out; drew up proposals for their protection as
wilderness areas; and presented the plans to our congressional
delegations. Henry David Thoreau, John Muir, and Roderick
Nash were never mentioned. We had no thought of preserving
"virgin" forest, since almost all of it was cut-over. It was the
Forest Service who argued that none of it was wilderness because it wasn't "pristine." We retorted that it wasn't how it
came to be that was important but what it looked like now, and
we quoted that provision of the 1964 act that spoke of wilderness as a place where "human intrusion is relatively unnotice-
able." What's more, we thought of it all as part of our own
"backyard," not as something far away and remote.

3   At about the same time I decided to find out about the
wilderness movement in the country as a whole, joined several
dozen organizations (western as well as eastern) to obtain
their newsletters and documents, and proceeded to build an
archive of wilderness activity. I found out that it wasn't much
different "out there." People became interested in large roadless areas they knew about; they wrote about their "backyard;"
they didn't try to persuade others to read "major thinkers" to
get their support but, just like we did, to expose them to it
through slide shows and directly by taking them there. The dynamics of human engagement with wilderness was the same:
people living in an urbanized society who felt that wilderness
areas would enhance the quality of their life while enjoying
modern material standards of urban living. As I observe it, the
dynamics of Bureau of Land Management wilderness, today's
political "hot spot," are much the same.

4   This is perhaps enough to make the reader understand why I
view Bill Cronon's problem as that he hasn't looked much at
the wilderness movement. He has read a few writers who have
much to say about wilderness philosophy, but he has not followed those active in the fray and the more day-to-day and

down-to-earth ideas and actions wilderness advocates carried out. Most of those advocates have long been "going forward" to the "right nature"; Cronon just has not noticed.

To make several arguments in rebuttal to Cronon about the values involved in wilderness action: 5

First, most wilderness engagement does not look toward some remote area, but toward the area of one's personal experience—my backyard. People near the candidate areas undertook wilderness action, saying simply, "we have some, too, right here." This created tension between old and new advocates. The Sierra Club, for example, tried to keep Oregon wilderness confined to the Cascades. But others argued that the Coast Range and eastern Oregon had some lively candidates. They were brought together by the Oregon Natural Resources Council that outmaneuvered the Sierra Club with its more restricted view.

Second, wilderness advocates did not point toward a "more natural" past for the temporal significance of what they were doing; instead they pointed to the future. What appealed to people most was they hoped to save something they valued for those who would come later. When economists got to work to try to identify the values people placed on wilderness through contingent valuation, the idea of "return" was not among them. Instead, people spoke of "bequest value." Wilderness advocates only thought of going forward to the world of their grandchildren. 6

Third, the main human engagement with wilderness has long been outdoor recreation, not the romanticizing of nature, and still is. Wide-ranging outdoor recreation interest grew rapidly after World War II. Wilderness guidebooks included information about distances and landmarks along the way, not about stages of forest biological change. Most units in the wilderness system were "rocks and ice" above the tree line rather than forested areas. If I am not mistaken the French Pete area in the Oregon Cascades was the first fully forested watershed to be designated wilderness, and thus the first area to have a biological content that was taken seriously. Because we had no rocks and ice, easterners helped to bring "biological nature" into the wilderness movement and even urged the Sierra Club to adopt that view of the wilderness. 7

Fourth, wilderness proposals are usually thought of not in terms of perpetuating some "original" or "pristine" condition but as efforts to "save" wilderness areas from development. "Land saving" is the watchword of almost all "nature" programs. We enjoy wilderness today because our forebears bypassed it as "The Lands that Nobody Wanted." We now turn the past action of neglect into the present and deliberate action 8 of "saving" for the future. The experience of rapid destruction of nature and restricting development now and in the future define the world of wilderness action.

9   Fifth, wilderness was not thought of as an attempt to create a role for humans amid nature, but to create a role for nature amid humans. Most wilderness advocates were urbanized people who thought of wilderness as part of an urbanized society. The great majority of wilderness advocates enjoyed modern amenities of life and thought of wilderness as another such. Keep the cities and their benefits, yes, but let's add some nature to all that in order to enhance the "good life."

10   Cronon's wilderness is a world of abstracted ideas, real enough to those who participate in it, but divorced from the values and ideas inherent in wilderness action. The evidence for such values is abundant but it takes a bit of work to get it, far more time and effort than that required by the more attractive task of emphasizing ideas of "major thinkers" whose writings libraries have close at hand.

11   Human attempts to bring nature into their urbanized environment have been many and far-reaching: the conservation commissions of New England, dating from the mid-1960s; federal urban open space programs of the same era; land conservancies and land trusts, now numbering more than 1,000; wild and scenic rivers and trails, programs, augmented today with the ever popular rails-to-trails; wetlands; new tropical breeding bird habitats and the currently popular "Partners in Flight;" natural area programs in almost every state; nongame programs; endangered species habitats; "Watchable Wildlife Programs;" biodiversity reserves; eastern "old growth;" state and local land-buying referenda that have increased state park acreage since 1970 by 16 percent. In all of these Cronon's wilderness idea has played a mighty limited role. However, all of these programs have one theme in common: make sure that nature will play an ever greater role in a society where urbanization is proceeding at a rapid pace.

12   Cronon succumbs to the temptation to bring in peripheral issues that are useful in advancing the polemical argument, but they actually distort history. One is the notion that wilderness is an "elitist" playground. Participation in wilderness recreation is actually middle class. Users are primarily local and daytime, and in terms of occupation and income are a cross-section of the area population. Cronon also seeks to enhance his argument by absorbing into it both biodiversity and endangered species issues. However, the recreation content of wilderness and the ecological content of biodiversity differ markedly, come from different sources, have different mean-

ings, and it has been a bit of a wrench for the first to accept the second. Further, while some endangered species require large, intact forest habitats, most do not; they include suburban and rural habitats, streams and riparian areas, highway berms, barrens, wetlands, small woodlands, and a host of areas hardly associated with wilderness.

Cronon argues that the wilderness idea diverts environmen-   13
talists from the real world of environmental affairs; he appeals to the environmental justice movement's political ideology to make the case for neglect. But the blinders in this case belong to Cronon. Almost every sector of the diverse environmental community thinks that it is "neglected"; this leads to a wide range of intra-environmental disputes. Cronon's "right nature" groups are well divorced as a whole from those groups preoc-cupied with urban pollution issues. By the same token, groups preoccupied with pollution issues are divorced from groups engaging in "land saving." Both groups ignore issues of popu-lation and limits. It is one thing to use the accompanying polemics to organize history; it is another to examine these in-tra-environmental relationships as a subject for historical analysis. Despite divergence the organizations act as if they are part of the same piece and their activities, even land saving and opposition to hazardous waste siting, frequently cross the boundaries of specialization and dispute.

Cronon's essay reflects the temptation for historians to draw   14
into their historical analyses both personal moral struggles and the ideology of contemporary debate. This tendency is more than risky. Transfer of the accompanying polemics into environmental history not only invites bad history but also the risk that it will obscure the abundant opportunities ahead in pursuing the field of environmental history.

With a degree of clear thinking and vigilance historians can   15
avoid these dangers, and bring an historical analysis shaped by an independent historical perspective to both personal and po-litical dimensions of environmental affairs. In this case, such vigilance requires that we not be diverted into the wilderness thickets into which Cronon's "Trouble" so temptingly invites us.

John Perry Barlow

IS THERE A THERE
IN CYBERSPACE?

John Perry Barlow ran a cattle ranch in Wyoming for seventeen years while writing songs for The Grateful Dead. *Forced to sell his ranch in 1988, he began writing and speaking about computer-mediated communication. He is a cofounder of the Electronic Frontier Foundation and is on the board of directors of WELL (Whole Earth 'Lectronic Link). Barlow frequently discusses Internet issues in interviews and in his own writing. The following essay appeared in the March/April 1995 issue of the* Utne Reader, *a left-of-center magazine that publishes articles on issues of public interest, including several of the others in this section of* Conversations.

1   I am often asked how I went from pushing cows around a remote Wyoming ranch to my present occupation (which *The Wall Street Journal* recently described as "cyber-space cadet"). I haven't got a short answer, but I suppose I came to the virtual world looking for community.

2   Unlike most modern Americans, I grew up in an actual place, an entirely nonintentional community called Pinedale, Wyoming. As I struggled for nearly a generation to keep my ranch in the family, I was motivated by the belief that such places were the spiritual home of humanity. But I knew their future was not promising.

3   At the dawn of the 20th century, over 40 percent of the American workforce lived off the land. The majority of us lived in towns like Pinedale. Now fewer than 1 percent of us

extract a living from the soil. We just became too productive for our own good.

Of course, the population followed the jobs. Farming and 4 ranching communities are now home to a demographically insignificant percentage of Americans, the vast majority of whom live not in ranch houses but in more or less identical split-level "ranch homes" in more or less identical suburban "communities." Generica.

In my view, these are neither communities nor homes. I be- 5 lieve the combination of television and suburban population patterns is simply toxic to the soul. I see much evidence in contemporary America to support this view.

Meanwhile, back at the ranch, doom impended. And, as I 6 watched community in Pinedale growing ill from the same economic forces that were killing my family's ranch, the Bar Cross, satellite dishes brought the cultural infection of television. I started looking around for evidence that community in America would not perish altogether.

I took some heart in the mysterious nomadic City of the 7 Deadheads, the virtually physical town that follows the Grateful Dead around the country. The Deadheads lacked place, touching down briefly wherever the band happened to be playing, and they lacked continuity in time, since they had to suffer a new diaspora every time the band moved on or went home. But they had many of the other necessary elements of community, including a culture, a religion of sorts (which, though it lacked dogma, had most of the other, more nurturing aspects of spiritual practice), a sense of necessity, and, most importantly, shared adversity.

I wanted to know more about the flavor of their interaction, 8 what they thought and felt, but since I wrote Dead songs (including "Estimated Prophet" and "Cassidy"), I was a minor icon to the Deadheads, and was thus inhibited, in some socially Heisenbergian way, from getting a clear view of what really went on among them.

Then, in 1987, I heard about a "place" where Deadheads 9 gathered where I could move among them without distorting too much the field of observation. Better, this was a place I could visit without leaving Wyoming. It was a shared computer in Sausalito, California, called the Whole Earth 'Lectronic Link, or WELL. After a lot of struggling with modems, serial cables, init strings, and other computer arcana that seemed utterly out of phase with such notions as Deadheads and small towns, I found myself looking at the glowing yellow word "Login:" beyond which lay my future.

10   "Inside" the WELL were Deadheads in community. There were thousands of them there, gossiping, complaining (mostly about the Grateful Dead), comforting and harassing each other, bartering, engaging in religion (or at least exchanging their totemic set lists), beginning and ending love affairs, praying for one another's sick kids. There was, it seemed, everything one might find going on in a small town, save dragging Main Street and making out on the back roads.

11   I was delighted. I felt I had found the new locale of human community—never mind that the whole thing was being conducted in mere words by minds from whom the bodies had been amputated. Never mind that all these people were deaf, dumb, and blind as paramecia or that their town had neither seasons nor sunsets nor smells.

12   Surely all these deficiencies would be remedied by richer, faster communications media. The featureless log-in handles would gradually acquire video faces (and thus expressions), shaded 3-D body puppets (and thus body language). This "space," which I recognized at once to be a primitive form of the cyberspace William Gibson predicted in his sci-fi novel *Neuromancer,* was still without apparent dimensions or vistas. But virtual reality would change all that in time.

13   Meanwhile, the commons, or something like it, had been rediscovered. Once again, people from the 'burbs had a place where they could encounter their friends as my fellow Pinedalians did at the post office and the Wrangler Cafe. They had a place where their hearts could remain as the companies they worked for shuffled their bodies around America. They could put down roots that could not be ripped out by forces of economic history. They had a collective stake. They had a community.

14   It is seven years now since I discovered the WELL. In that time, I cofounded an organization, the Electronic Frontier Foundation, dedicated to protecting its interests and those of other virtual communities like it from raids by physical government. I've spent countless hours typing away at its residents, and I've watched the larger context that contains it, the Internet, grow at such an explosive rate that, by 2004, every human on the planet will have an e-mail address unless the growth curve flattens (which it will).

15   My enthusiasm for virtuality has cooled. In fact, unless one counts interaction with the rather too large society of those with whom I exchange electronic mail, I don't spend much time engaging in virtual community at all. Many of the near-term benefits I anticipated from it seem to remain as far in the future as they did when I first logged in. Perhaps they always will.

Pinedale works, more or less, as it is, but a lot is still missing 16
from the communities of cyberspace, whether they be places
like the WELL, the fractious newsgroups of USENET, the
silent "auditoriums" of America Online, or even enclaves on
the promising World Wide Web.

What is missing? Well, to quote Ranjit Makkuni of Xerox 17
Corporation's Palo Alto Research Center, "the *prāna* is missing," *prāna* being the Hindu term for both breath and spirit. I
think he is right about this and that perhaps the central question of the virtual age is whether or not *prāna* can somehow be
made to fit through any disembodied medium.

Prāna is, to my mind, the literally vital element in the holy 18
and unseen ecology of relationship, the dense mesh of invisible
life, on whose surface carbon-based life floats like a thin film.
It is at the heart of the fundamental and profound difference
between information and experience. Jaron Lanier has said
that "information is alienated experience," and, that being
true, *prāna* is part of what is removed when you create such
easily transmissible replicas of experience as, say, the evening
news.

Obviously a great many other, less spiritual, things are also 19
missing entirely, like body language, sex, death, tone of voice,
clothing, beauty (or homeliness), weather, violence, vegetation,
wildlife, pets, architecture, music, smells, sunlight, and that ol'
harvest moon. In short, most of the things that make my life
real to me.

Present, but in far less abundance than in the physical 20
world, which I call "meat space," are women, children, old
people, poor people, and the genuinely blind. Also mostly
missing are the illiterate and the continent of Africa. There is
not much human diversity in cyberspace, which is popu-
lated, as near as I can tell, by white males under 50 with
plenty of computer terminal time, great typing skills, high
math SATS, strongly held opinions on just about everything,
and an excruciating face-to-face shyness, especially with the
opposite sex.

But diversity is as essential to healthy community as it is to 21
healthy ecosystems (which are, in my view, different from
communities only in unimportant aspects).

I believe that the principal reason for the almost universal 22
failure of the intentional communities of the '60s and '70s was
a lack of diversity in their members. It was a rare commune
with any old people in it, or people who were fundamentally
out of philosophical agreement with the majority.

Indeed, it is the usual problem when we try to build some- 23
thing that can only be grown. Natural systems, such as human

communities, are simply too complex to design by the engineering principles we insist on applying to them. Like Dr. Frankenstein, Western civilization is now finding its rational skills inadequate to the task of creating and caring for life. We would do better to return to a kind of agricultural mind-set in which we humbly try to re-create the conditions from which life has sprung before. And leave the rest to God.

24   Given that it has been built so far almost entirely by people with engineering degrees, it is not so surprising that cyberspace has the kind of overdesigned quality that leaves out all kinds of elements nature would have provided invisibly.

25   Also missing from both the communes of the '60s and from cyberspace are a couple of elements that I believe are very important, if not essential, to the formation and preservation of real community: an absence of alternatives and a sense of genuine adversity, generally shared. What about these?

26   It is hard to argue that anyone would find losing a modem literally hard to survive, while many have remained in small towns, have tolerated their intolerances and created entertainment to enliven their culturally arid lives simply because it seemed there was no choice but to stay. There are many investments—spiritual, material, and temporal—one is willing to put into a home one cannot leave. Communities are often the beneficiaries of these involuntary investments.

27   But when the going gets rough in cyberspace, it is even easier to move than it is in the 'burbs, where, given the fact that the average American moves some 12 times in his or her life, moving appears to be pretty easy. You can not only find another bulletin board service (BBS) or newsgroup to hang out in, you can, with very little effort, start your own.

28   And then there is the bond of joint suffering. Most community is a cultural stockade erected against a common enemy that can take many forms. In Pinedale, we bore together, with an understanding needing little expression, the fact that Upper Green River Valley is the coldest spot, as measured by annual mean temperature, in the lower 48 states. We knew that if somebody was stopped on the road most winter nights, he would probably die there, so the fact that we might loathe him was not sufficient reason to drive on past his broken pickup.

29   By the same token, the Deadheads have the Drug Enforcement Administration, which strives to give them 20-year prison terms without parole for distributing the fairly harmless sacrament of their faith. They have an additional bond in the fact that when their Microbuses die, as they often do, no one but another Deadhead is likely to stop to help them.

But what are the shared adversities of cyberspace? Lousy   30
user interfaces? The flames of harsh invective? Dumb jokes?
Surely these can all be survived without the sanctuary provided by fellow sufferers.

One is always free to yank the jack, as I have mostly done.   31
For me, the physical world offers far more opportunity for
prāna-rich connections with my fellow creatures. Even for
someone whose body is in a state of perpetual motion, I feel I
can generally find more community among the still-embodied.

Finally, there is that shyness factor. Not only are we trying to   32
build community here among people who have never experienced any in my sense of the term, we are trying to build community among people who, in their lives, have rarely used the
word *we* in a heartfelt way. It is a vast club, and many of the
members—following Groucho Marx—wouldn't want to join a
club that would have them.

And yet . . .   33

How quickly physical community continues to deteriorate.   34
Even Pinedale, which seems to have survived the plague of
ranch failures, feels increasingly cut off from itself. Many of
the ranches are now owned by corporate types who fly their
Gulfstreams in to fish and are rarely around during the many
months when the creeks are frozen over and neighbors are
needed. They have kept the ranches alive financially, but they
actively discourage their managers from the interdependence
my former colleagues and I require. They keep agriculture on
life support, still alive but lacking a functional heart.

And the town has been inundated with suburbanites who flee   35
here, bringing all their terrors and suspicions with them. They
spend their evenings as they did in Orange County, watching
television or socializing in hermetic little enclaves of fundamentalist Christianity that seem to separate them from us and
even, given their sectarian animosities, from one another. The
town remains. The community is largely a wraith of nostalgia.

So where else can we look for the connection we need to pre-   36
vent our plunging further into the condition of separateness
Nietzsche called sin? What is there to do but to dive further
into the bramble bush of information that, in its broadcast
forms, has done so much to tear us apart?

Cyberspace, for all its current deficiencies and failed   37
promises, is not without some very real solace already.

Some months ago, the great love of my life, a vivid young   38
woman with whom I intended to spend the rest of it, dropped
dead of undiagnosed viral cardiomyopathy two days short of
her 30th birthday. I felt as if my own heart had been as shred-
ded as hers.

39   We had lived together in New York City. Except for my daughters, no one from Pinedale had met her. I needed a community to wrap around myself against colder winds than fortune had ever blown at me before. And without looking, I found I had one in the virtual world.

40   On the WELL, there was a topic announcing her death in one of the conferences to which I posted the eulogy I had read over her before burying her in her own small town of Nanaimo, British Columbia. It seemed to strike a chord among the disembodied living on the Net. People copied it and sent it to one another. Over the next several months I received almost a megabyte of electronic mail from all over the planet, mostly from folks whose faces I have never seen and probably never will.

41   They told me of their own tragedies and what they had done to survive them. As humans have since words were first uttered, we shared the second most common human experience, death, with an openheartedness that would have caused grave uneasiness in physical America, where the whole topic is so cloaked in denial as to be considered obscene. Those strangers, who had no arms to put around my shoulders, no eyes to weep with mine, nevertheless saw me through. As neighbors do.

42   I have no idea how far we will plunge into this strange place. Unlike previous frontiers, this one has no end. It is so dissatisfying in so many ways that I suspect we will be more restless in our search for home here than in all our previous explorations. And that is one reason why I think we may find it after all. If home is where the heart is, then there is already some part of home to be found in cyberspace.

43   So . . . does virtual community work or not? Should we all go off to cyberspace or should we resist it as a demonic form of symbolic abstraction? Does it supplant the real or is there, in it, reality itself?

44   Like so many true things, this one doesn't resolve itself to a black or a white. Nor is it gray. It is, along with the rest of life, black/white. Both/neither. I'm not being equivocal or wishy-washy here. We have to get over our Manichean sense that everything is either good or bad, and the border of cyberspace seems to me a good place to leave that old set of filters.

45   But really it doesn't matter. We are going there whether we want to or not. In five years, everyone who is reading these words will have an e-mail address, other than the determined Luddites who also eschew the telephone and electricity.

46   When we are all together in cyberspace we will see what the human spirit, and the basic desire to connect, can create there. I am convinced that the result will be more benign if we go

there open-minded, open-hearted, and excited with the adventure than if we are dragged into exile.

And we must remember that going to cyberspace, unlike previous great emigrations to the frontier, hardly requires us to leave where we have been. Many will find, as I have, a much richer appreciation of physical reality for having spent so much time in virtuality.   47

Despite its current (and perhaps in some areas permanent) insufficiencies, we should go to cyberspace with hope. Groundless hope, like unconditional love, may be the only kind that counts.   48

M. Kadi

WELCOME TO CYBERIA

M. Kadi is a pseudonym for the author, who works as a consultant in the computer industry in the San Francisco Bay Area of California but who wishes to write about computer issues anonymously. She contributed this essay to the Winter/Spring 1994–95 issue of H2SO4, *which, as its name implies, is an inexpensively produced, avant garde, irreverent, small-circulation magazine based in San Francisco that publishes literary and political commentaries, both serious and not-so-serious, and tries to bring together both academic and nonacademic writers and readers. It publishes works from many political and cultural perspectives. The essay published here also appeared in truncated form in the* Utne Reader *(which often republishes items from the alternative press) along with several other selections in this section of* Conversations, *by Barlow and Rheingold.*

Computer networking offers the soundest basis for world peace that has yet been presented. Peace must be created on the bulwark of understanding. International computer networks will knit together the peoples of the world in bonds of mutual respect; its possibilities are vast, indeed.

—*Scientific American,* June 1994

Cyberspace is a new medium. Every night on Prodigy, CompuServe, GEnie and thousands of smaller computer bulletin boards, people by the hundreds of thousands are logging on to a great computer-mediated gabfest, an interactive debate that allows them to leap over barriers of time, place, sex and social status.

—Time Magazine

The Internet is really about the rise of not merely a new technology, but a new culture—a global culture where time, space, borders and even personal identity are radically redefined.

—OnLine Access Magazine

1   Computer bulletin board services offer up the glories of e-mail, the thought provocation of Newsgroups, the sharing of ideas implicit in public posting, and the interaction of real-time chats. The fabulous, wonderful limitless world of Communication is just waiting for you to log on. Sure. Yeah. Right.

2   I confess, I am a dedicated cyber-junkie. It's fun. It's interesting. It takes me places where I've never been before. I sign on once a day, twice a day, three times a day, more and more; I read, I post, I live. Writing an article on the ever-expanding, ever-entertaining, ever-present world of online existence would have been easy for me. But it would have been familiar, perhaps dull and it might have been a lie. The world does not need another article on the miracle of online reality; what we need, what I need, what this whole delirious, inter-connected, global-community of a world needs, is a little reality check.

3   To some extent the following scenario will be misleading. There *are* flat rate online services (Netcom for one) which offer significant connectivity for a measly 17 dollars a month. But I'm interested in the activities and behavior of the private service users who will soon comprise a vast majority of online citizens. Furthermore, let's face facts. The U.S. government by and large foots the bill for the Internet, through maintaining the structural (hardware) backbone, including, among other things, funding to major universities. As surely as the Department of Defense started this whole thing, AT&T or Ted Turner is going to end up running it, so I don't think it's too unrealistic to take a look at the Net as it exists in its commercial form in order to expose some of the realities lurking behind the regurgitated media rhetoric and the religious fanaticism of net junkies.

4   The average person, J. Individual, has an income. How much of J. Individual's income is going to be spent on computer connectivity? Does $120 a month sound reasonable?

Well, you may find that a bit too steep for your pocketbook, but the brutal fact is that $120 is a "reasonable" monthly amount. The major on-line services have a monthly service charge of approximately $15. Fifteen dollars to join the global community, communicate with a diverse group of people, and access the world's largest repository of knowledge since the Alexandrian library doesn't seem unreasonable, does it? But don't overlook the average per-hour connection rate of $3 (which can skyrocket upwards of $10, depending on your modem speed and service). You might think that you are a crack whiz with your communications software—that you are rigorous and stringent and never, ever respond to e-mail or a forum while you're on-line—but let me tell you that no one is capable of logging on efficiently every time. Thirty hours per month is a realistic estimate.

In case you think 30 hours a month is an outrageous estimate, think of it in terms of television. (OK, so you don't own a television, well, goody-for-you—imagine that you do!) 30 hours, is, quite obviously, one hour a day. That's not so much. 30 hours a month in front of a television is simply the evening news plus a weekly Seinfeld/Frazier [sic] hour. 30 hours a month is less time than the average car-phone owner spends on the phone while commuting. Even a conscientious geek, logging on for e-mail and the up-to-the-minute news that only the net services can provide is probably going to spend 30 hours a month online. And, let's be truthful here, 30 hours a month ignores shareware downloads, computer illiteracy, real-time chatting, interactive game playing and any serious forum following, which by nature entail a significant amount of scrolling and/or downloading time.

If you are really and truly going to use the net services to connect with the global community, the hourly charges are going to add up pretty quickly. Take out a piece of paper, pretend you're writing a check, and print out "One hundred and twenty dollars—" and tell me again, how diverse is the on-line community?

That scenario aside, let's pretend that you're single, that you don't have children, that you rarely leave the house, that you don't have a TV and that money is not an issue. Meaning, pretend for a moment that you have as much time and as much money to spend online as you damn-well want. What do you actually do online?

Well, you download some cool shareware, you post technical questions in the computer user group forums, you check your stocks, you read the news and maybe some reviews—Hey, you've already passed that 30 hour limit! But, of course, since "computer networks make it easy to reach out and touch

strangers who share a particular obsession or concern," you are participating in the online forums, discussion groups, and conferences.

9   Let's review the structure of forums. For the purposes of this essay, we will examine the smallest of the major user-friendly commercial services—America OnLine (AOL). There is no precise statistic available (at least none that the company will reveal—you have to do the research by HAND!!!) on exactly how many subject-specific discussion areas (folders) exist on AOL. Any online service is going to have zillions of posts pertaining to computer usage (e.g., the computer games area of AOL breaks into five hundred separate topics with over 100,000 individual posts), so let's look at a less popular area: the "Lifestyles and Interests" department.

10   For starters, there are 57 initial categories within the Lifestyles and Interests area. One of these categories is Ham Radio. Ham Radio? How can there possibly be 5,909 separate, individual posts about Ham Radio? 5,865 postings in the Biking (and that's just bicycles, not motorcycles) category. Genealogy—22,525 posts. The Gay and Lesbian category is slightly more substantial—36,333 posts. There are five separate categories for political and issue discussion. The big catch-all topic area, The Exchange, has over 100,000 posts. Basically, service wide (on the smallest service, remember) there are over a million posts.

11   So, you want to communicate with other people, join the online revolution, but obviously you can't wade through everything that's being discussed—you need to decide which topics interest you, which folders to browse. Within The Exchange alone (one of 57 subdivisions within one of another 50 higher divisions) there are 1,492 separate topic-specific folders—each containing a rough average of 50 posts, but with many containing close to 400 . . .

12   So there you are, J. Individual, ready to start interacting with folks, sharing stories and communicating. You have narrowed yourself into a single folder, three tiers down in the AOL hierarchy, and now you must choose between nearly fifteen hundred folders. Of course, once you choose a few of these folders, you will then have to read all the posts in order to catch up, be current, and not merely repeat a previous post.

13   A polite post is no more than two paragraphs long (a screenful of text which obviously has a number of intellectually negative implications). Let's say you choose ten folders (out of 1,500). Each folder contains an average of 50 posts. Five hundred posts, at, say, one paragraph each, and you're now looking at the equivalent of a two hundred page book.

Enough with the stats. Let me back up a minute and present   14
you with some very disturbing, but rational, assumptions. J.
Individual wants to join the online revolution to connect and
communicate. But, J. Individual is not going to read all one
million posts on AOL. (After all, J. Individual has a second online service.) Exercising choice is J. Individual's god-given right
as an American, and, by gosh, J. Individual is going to make
some decisions. So J. is going to ignore all the support
groups—after all, J. is a normal, well-adjusted person and all of
J.'s friends are normal, well-adjusted people; what does J. need
to know about alcoholism or incest victims? J. Individual is
white. So J. Individual is going to ignore all the multicultural
folders. J. couldn't give a hoot about gender issues and does not
want to discuss religion or philosophy. Ultimately, J. Individual
does not engage in topics that do not interest J. Individual. So
who is J. meeting? Why, people who are *just like* J.

J. Individual has now joined the electronic community.   15
Surfed the Net. Found some friends. *Tuned in, turned on, and
geeked out.* Traveled the Information Highway and, just a few
miles down that great democratic expressway, J. Individual has
settled into an electronic suburb.

Are any of us so very different? It's my time and my money   16
and I am not going to waste any of it reading posts by disgrun-
tled Robert-Bly drum-beating men's-movement boys who think
that they should have some say over, for instance, whether or
not I choose to carry a child to term simply because a condom
broke. I know where I stand. I'm an adult. I know what's up
and I am not going to waste my money arguing with a bunch
of neanderthals.

Oh yeah; I am so connected, so enlightened, so open to the   17
opposing viewpoint. I'm out there, meeting all kinds of people
from different economic backgrounds (who have $120 a
month to burn), from all religions (yeah, right, like anyone actually discusses religion anymore from a user standpoint),
from all kinds of different ethnic backgrounds and with all
kinds of sexual orientations (as if any of this ever comes up
outside of the appropriate topic folder).

People are drawn to topics and folders that interest them   18
and therefore people will only meet people who are interested
in the same topics in the same folders. Rarely does anyone venture into a random folder just to see what others (the Other?)
are talking about.

Basically, between the monetary constraints and the sheer   19
number of topics and individual posts, the great Information
Highway is not a place where you will enter an "amazing web
of new people, places, and ideas." One does not encounter

people from "all walks of life" because there are too many people and too many folders. Diversity might be out there (and personally I don't think it is), but the simple fact is that the average person will not encounter it because with one brain, one job, one partner, one family, and one life, no one has the time!

20 Just in case these arguments based on time and money aren't completely convincing, let me bring up a historical reference. Please take another look at the opening quote of this essay, from *Scientific American*. It was featured in their 50 Years Ago Today column. Where you read "computer networking," the quote originally contained the word *television*. Amusing, isn't it?

21 Finally, for me, there is a subtle and terrible irony lurking within the Net: the Net, despite its speed, its exchange, ultimately reeks of stasis. In negating physical distance, the immediacy of electronic transfers devalues movement and the journey. In one minute a thought is in my head, and the next minute it is typed out, sent, read, and in your head. The exchange may be present, but the journey is imperceptible. The Infobahn hype would have us believe that this phenomenon is a fast-paced dynamic exchange, but the feeling, when you've been at it long enough, is that this exchange of ideas lacks movement. Lacking movement and the journey, to me it loses all value.

22 Maybe this is prejudice. Words are not wine, they do not necessarily require age to improve them. Furthermore, I have always hated the concept that Art comes only out of struggle and suffering. So, to say that e-mail words are weaker somehow because of the nature, or lack, of their journey, is to romanticize the struggle. I suppose I am anthropomorphising text too much—but I somehow sense that one works harder to endow one's handwritten words with a certain strength, a certain soul, simply because those things are necessary in order to survive a journey. The ease of the e-mail journey means that your words don't need to be as well-prepared, or as well-equipped.

23 Electronic missives lack time, space, embodiment and history (in the sense of a collection of experiences). Lacking all these things, an electronic missive is almost in complete opposition to my existence and I can't help but wonder what, if anything, I am communicating.

Howard Rheingold

THE VIRTUAL
COMMUNITY

This essay, excerpted from Rheingold's book The Virtual
Community *(1993), first appeared in the* Utne Reader *with
several other essays reprinted in this section of* Conversations.

In the summer of 1986, my then-2-year-old daughter picked up   1
a tick. There was this blood-bloated *thing* sucking on our
baby's scalp, and we weren't quite sure how to go about getting
it off. My wife, Judy, called the pediatrician. It was 11 o'clock in
the evening. I logged onto the WELL, the big Bay Area infonet,
and contacted the Parenting conference (a conference is an online conversation about a specific subject). I got my answer online within minutes from a fellow with the improbable but genuine name of Flash Gordon, M.D. I had removed the tick by the
time Judy got the callback from the pediatrician's office.

What amazed me wasn't just the speed with which we ob-   2
tained precisely the information we needed to know, right
when we needed to know it. It was also the immense inner
sense of security that comes with discovering that real people—most of them parents, some of them nurses, doctors, and
midwives—are available, around the clock, if you need them.
There is a magic protective circle around the atmosphere of
the Parenting conference. We're talking about our sons and
daughters in this forum, not about our computers or our opinions about philosophy, and many of us feel that this tacit understanding sanctifies the virtual space.

The atmosphere of this particular conference—the attitudes   3
people exhibit to each other in the tone of what they say in public—is part of what continues to attract me. People who never
have much to contribute in political debate, technical argument, or intellectual gamesmanship turn out to have a lot to say
about raising children. People you knew as fierce, even nasty,
intellectual opponents in other contexts give you emotional
support on a deeper level, parent to parent, within the boundaries of this small but warmly human corner of cyberspace.

In most cases, people who talk about a shared interest don't   4
disclose enough about themselves as whole individuals on-line
to inspire real trust in others. But in the case of the subcom-
munity called the Parenting conference, a few dozen of us,
scattered across the country, few of whom rarely if ever saw

the others face to face, have a few years of minor crises to knit us together and prepare us for serious business when it comes our way. Another several dozen read the conference regularly but contribute only when they have something important to add. Hundreds more read the conference every week without comment, except when something extraordinary happens.

5 Jay Allison and his family live in Massachusetts. He and his wife are public-radio producers. I've never met them face to face, although I feel I know something powerful and intimate about the Allisons and have strong emotional ties to them. What follows are some of Jay's postings on the WELL:

6 *"Woods Hole. Midnight. I am sitting in the dark of my daughter's room. Her monitor lights blink at me. The lights used to blink too brightly so I covered them with bits of bandage adhesive and now they flash faintly underneath, a persistent red and green, Lillie's heart and lungs.*

7 *"Above the monitor is her portable suction unit. In the glow of the flashlight I'm writing by, it looks like the plastic guts of a science-class human model, the tubes coiled around the power supply, the reservoir, the pump.*

8 *"Tina is upstairs trying to get some sleep. A baby monitor links our bedroom to Lillie's. It links our sleep to Lillie's too, and because our souls are linked to hers, we do not sleep well.*

9 *"I am naked. My stomach is full of beer. The flashlight rests on it, and the beam rises and falls with my breath. My daughter breathes through a white plastic tube inserted into a hole in her throat. She's 14 months old."*

10 Sitting in front of our computers with our hearts racing and tears in our eyes, in Tokyo and Sacramento and Austin, we read about Lillie's croup, her tracheostomy, the days and nights at Massachusetts General Hospital, and now the vigil over Lillie's breathing and the watchful attention to the mechanical apparatus that kept her alive. It went on for days. Weeks. Lillie recovered, and relieved our anxieties about her vocal capabilities after all that time with a hole in her throat by saying the most extraordinary things, duly reported on-line by Jay.

11 Later, writing in *Whole Earth Review,* Jay described the experience:

12 *"Before this time, my computer screen had never been a place to go for solace. Far from it. But there it was. Those nights sitting up late with my daughter, I'd go to my computer, dial up the WELL, and ramble. I wrote about what was happening that night or that year. I didn't know anyone I was "talking" to. I had never laid eyes on them. At 3:00 A.M. my "real" friends were asleep, so I turned to this foreign, invisible community for support. The WELL was always awake.*

"Any difficulty is harder to bear in isolation. There is nothing   13
to measure against, to lean against. Typing out my journal en-
tries into the computer and over the phone lines, I found fellow-
ship and comfort in this unlikely medium."

Many people are alarmed by the very idea of a virtual com-   14
munity, fearing that it is another step in the wrong direction,
substituting more technological ersatz for yet another natural
resource or human freedom. These critics often voice their
sadness at what people have been reduced to doing in a civilization that worships technology, decrying the circumstances
that lead some people into such pathetically disconnected lives
that they prefer to find their companions on the other side of a
computer screen. There is a seed of truth in this fear, for communities at some point require more than words on a screen if
they are to be other than ersatz.

Yet some people—many people—who don't do well in spon-   15
taneous spoken interaction turn out to have valuable contributions to make in a conversation in which they have time to
think about what to say. These people, who might constitute a
significant proportion of the population, can find written communication more authentic than the face-to-face kind. Who is
to say that this preference for informal written text is somehow
less authentically human than opting for audible speech?
Those who critique computer-mediated communication because some people use it obsessively hit an important target,
but miss a great deal more when they don't take into consideration people who use the medium for genuine human interaction. Those who find virtual communities cold places point at
the limits of the technology, its most dangerous pitfalls, and we
need to pay attention to those boundaries. But these critiques
don't tell us how the Allisons, my own family, and many others
could have found the community of support and information
we found in the WELL when we needed it. And those of us
who do find communion in cyberspace might do well to pay attention to the way the medium we love can be abused.

Although dramatic incidents are what bring people together   16
and stick in their memories, most of what goes on in the
Parenting conference and most virtual communities is informal conversation and downright chitchat. The model of the
WELL and other social clusters in cyberspace as "places"
emerges naturally whenever people who use this medium discuss its nature. In 1987, Stewart Brand quoted me in his book
The Media Lab about what tempted me to log onto the WELL
as often as I did: "There's always another mind there. It's like
having the corner bar, complete with old buddies and delightful

newcomers and new tools waiting to take home and fresh graffiti and letters, except instead of putting on my coat, shutting down the computer, and walking down to the corner, I just invoke my telecom program and there they are. It's a place."

17   I've changed my mind about a lot of aspects of the WELL over the years, but the sense of place is still as strong as ever. As Ray Oldenburg proposes in his 1989 book *The Great Good Place*, there are three essential places in people's lives: the place we live, the place we work, and the place we gather for conviviality. Although the casual conversation that takes place in cafés, beauty shops, pubs, and town squares is universally considered to be trivial, idle talk, Oldenburg makes the case that such places are where communities can come into being and continue to hold together. These are the unacknowledged agoras of modern life. When the automobilecentric, suburban, fast-food, shopping-mall way of life eliminated many of these "third places" from traditional towns and cities around the world, the social fabric of existing communities started shredding.

18   Oldenburg puts a name and a conceptual framework on a phenomenon that every virtual community member knows instinctively, the power of informal public life:

19   *"Third places exist on neutral ground and serve to level their guests to a condition of social equality. Within these places, conversation is the primary activity and the major vehicle for the display and appreciation of human personality and individuality. Third places are taken for granted and most have a low profile. Since the formal institutions of society make stronger claims on the individual, third places are normally open in the off hours, as well as at other times. The character of a third place is determined most of all by its regular clientele and is marked by a playful mood, which contrasts with people's more serious involvement in other spheres. Though a radically different kind of setting for a home, the third place is remarkably similar to a good home in the psychological comfort and support that it extends.*

20   *"Such are the characteristics of third places that appear to be universal and essential to a vital informal public life. . . .*

21   *"The problem of place in America manifests itself in a sorely deficient informal public life. The structure of shared experience beyond that offered by family, job, and passive consumerism is small and dwindling. The essential group experience is being replaced by the exaggerated self-consciousness of individuals. American lifestyles, for all the material acquisition and the seeking after comforts and pleasures, are plagued by boredom, loneliness, alienation, and a high price tag. . . .*

22   *"Unlike many frontiers, that of the informal public life does not remain benign as it awaits development. It does not become*

easier to tame as technology evolves, as governmental bureaus and agencies multiply, or as population grows. It does not yield to the mere passage of time and a policy of letting the chips fall where they may as development proceeds in other areas of urban life. To the contrary, neglect of the informal public life can make a jungle of what had been a garden while, at the same time, diminishing the ability of people to cultivate it."

It might not be the same kind of place that Oldenburg had in mind, but many of his descriptions of third places could also describe the WELL. Perhaps cyberspace is one of the informal public places where people can rebuild the aspects of community that were lost when the malt shop became a mall. Or perhaps cyberspace is precisely the *wrong* place to look for the rebirth of community, offering not a tool for conviviality but a life-denying simulacrum of real passion and true commitment to one another. In either case, we need to find out soon.   23

Because we cannot see one another in cyberspace, gender, age, national origin, and physical appearance are not apparent unless a person wants to make such characteristics public. People whose physical handicaps make it difficult to form new friendships find that virtual communities treat them as they always wanted to be treated—as thinkers and transmitters of ideas and feeling beings, not carnal vessels with a certain appearance and way of walking and talking (or not walking and not talking).   24

One of the few things that enthusiastic members of virtual communities in places like Japan, England, France, and the United States all agree on is that expanding their circle of friends is one of the most important advantages of computer conferencing. It is a way to *meet* people, whether or not you feel the need to affiliate with them on a community level. It's a way of both making contact with and maintaining a distance from others. The way you meet people in cyberspace puts a different spin on affiliation: In traditional kinds of communities, we are accustomed to meeting people, then getting to know them; in virtual communities, you can get to know people and *then* choose to meet them. Affiliation also can be far more ephemeral in cyberspace because you can get to know people you might never meet on the physical plane.   25

How does anybody find friends? In the traditional community, we search through our pool of neighbors and professional colleagues, of acquaintances and acquaintances of acquaintances, in order to find people who share our values and interests. We then exchange information about one another, disclose and discuss our mutual interests, and sometimes we   26 become friends. In a virtual community we can go directly to the place where our favorite subjects are being discussed, then get acquainted with people who share our passions or who use words in a way we find attractive. In this sense, the topic is the address: You can't simply pick up a phone and ask to be connected with someone who wants to talk about Islamic art or California wine, or someone with a 3-year-old daughter or a 40-year-old Hudson; you can, however, join a computer conference on any of those topics, then open a public or private correspondence with the previously unknown people you find there. Your chances of making friends are increased by several orders of magnitude over the old methods of finding a peer group.

27   You can be fooled about people in cyberspace, behind the cloak of words. But that can be said about telephones or face-to-face communication as well; computer-mediated communications provide new ways to fool people, and the most obvious identity swindles will die out only when enough people learn to use the medium critically. In some ways, the medium will, by its nature, be forever biased toward certain kinds of obfuscation. It will also be a place where people often end up revealing themselves far more intimately than they would be inclined to do without the intermediation of screens and pseudonyms.

28   Point of view, along with identity, is one of the great variables in cyberspace. Different people in cyberspace look at their virtual communities through differently shaped keyholes. In traditional communities, people have a strongly shared mental model of the sense of place—the room or village or city where their interactions occur. In virtual communities, the sense of place requires an individual act of imagination. The different mental models people have of the electronic agora complicate the question of why people seem to want to build societies mediated by computer screens. A question like that leads inexorably to the old fundamental questions of what forces hold any society together. The roots of these questions extend farther than the social upheavals triggered by modern communications technologies.

29   When we say "society," we usually mean citizens of cities in entities known as nations. We take those categories for granted. But the mass-psychological transition we made to thinking of ourselves as part of modern society and nation-states is historically recent. Could people make the transition from the close collective social groups, the villages and small towns of premodern and precapitalist Europe, to a new form of social solidarity known as society that transcended and encompassed all previous kinds of human association? Ferdinand Tönnies, one of the founders of sociology, called the

premodern kind of social group *gemeinschaft*, which is closer to the English word *community*, and the new kind of social group he called *gesellschaft*, which can be translated roughly as *society*. All the questions about community in cyberspace point to a similar kind of transition, for which we have no technical names, that might be taking place now.

Sociology student Marc Smith, who has been using the 30 WELL and the Net as the laboratory for his fieldwork, pointed me to Benedict Anderson's *Imagined Communities*, a study of nation-building that focuses on the ideological labor involved. Anderson points out that nations and, by extension, communities are imagined in the sense that a given nation exists by virtue of a common acceptance in the minds of the population that it exists. Nations must exist in the minds of their citizens in order to exist at all. "Virtual communities require an act of imagination," Smith points out, extending Anderson's line of thinking to cyberspace, "and what must be imagined is the idea of the community itself."

Stephen Doheny-Farina

IMMERSIVE VIRTUALISTS
AND WIRED
COMMUNITARIANS

Stephen Doheny-Farina teaches courses in technical writing, electronic communications, and the rhetoric of the Internet at Clarkson College in upstate New York. The following article is a chapter from his 1996 book (Yale University Press) entitled The Wired Neighborhood, *which is an extended meditation on the meanings that the Internet holds for contemporary culture, especially for our notions of community.*

Many of the loudest voices of the net tell us that a revolution is 1 going on, and that revolutions mean change, and that this change can be painful for some, but that overall the revolution is good. Notice the emphases, for example, in the following excerpt from National Public Radio's *All Things Considered*, a segment from February 3, 1994, entitled "Pile-Ups Could Be

Problem for Information Highway." The real problem, this interview tells us, is the difficulty in getting everyone online. But once online, let the good times roll:

2   NOAH ADAMS, HOST: The traffic report for the information network, the Internet highway, is smooth going, but there's a pileup at the America Online ramp causing congestion. The computer on-line services offer bulletin boards and magazine articles, research, and shopping along with access to Internet, the vast grid of computer systems. The on-line services have become very popular, and America Online is the fastest growing. The membership more than doubled last year. But lately the service has often been slow, and sometimes subscribers simply aren't able to log on. Computer analyst Fred Davis joins us from KQED.

3   After some discussion:

4   ADAMS: Is it possible that this [electronic communication via Internet] is just a fad, just a fashionable thing to do, you're sort of browsing around and next year we'll be doing something else?

4   DAVIS: No, this is a major change in the way that humans communicate. And it's bringing people closer together all over the world. People are having international romances over the Information Superhighway, Internet, fax machines, and so forth. It just brings us all closer together, and it's addictive. Once you get the feel of creating a community based on your interests rather than arbitrary geography, it's a really exciting and compelling thing for humans to do.

6   ADAMS: So we better figure out how to do it.

The net pulls you in—but (apparently) in a good way. It brings people closer together, enabling us to create vibrant communities while overcoming the caprice of geography. It entices us with the promise of romance, love, and (safe) sex. Everybody will get online and communicate with everyone else.

7   According to this view the old regime is crumbling. The mass media as we know it is dead. Newspapers don't give us news, because in the time frame of the net what newspapers print is old news before ink meets paper. Book publishing is dead when anyone's words can reach millions of potential readers moments after the final draft is finished. The music industry withers away when any musician can make high-quality digital recordings at home and distribute them to the world via the net. Television networks are inconsequential when everyone has the power to produce programming for everyone else.

Governments as we know them are increasingly powerless because nations become irrelevant when communication technologies make borders as porous as air. Power goes to those
who can control the flow of information. But when all information, all music, all art, all words, all images, all ideas are
digitized, then everyone can access, alter, create, and transmit
anything, anywhere, anytime. Welcome to the spectacle. Enter
the teeming, buzzing cacophony of cyberspace. The revolution
is here. The kings are dead. Long live us all—all virtual citizens
in the egalitarian, electronic democracy that is the net.

And we participate in this electronic parlor as children of the   8
convergence: that moment when the bandwidth widens, when
all communication technologies blend seamlessly and transparently into a single, inevitable *pan*media—the melding of
telecommunications, computers and computer networks, cellular, cable, and satellite data transmission, television, radio,
and print media, and while we're at it, virtual reality technology, biotechnology, artificial intelligence, and nanotechnology,
turning every one of us into the liberated, mind-expanded, and
globally connected cyborgian citizens of the global community.
Says William Mitchell in *City of Bits:* "By this point in the evolution of miniature electronic products, you will have acquired
a collection of interchangeable, snap-in organs connected by
exonerves. Where these electronic organs interface to your sen-
sory receptors and your muscles, there will be continuous bit-
spits across the carbon/silicon gap. And where they bridge to
the external digital world, your nervous system will plug into
the worldwide digital net. You will have become a modular, re-
configurable, infinitely extensible cyborg."[1]

This vision represents the manifestation of our will to virtu-   9
ality. If we are to achieve these dreams of the simulacrum, we
must know that the virtual can sustain us—that the virtual is
life and community. That is, as the virtualization of human relations continues, we come to see its product as life-giving and
life-affirming. We recognize that we can live not only a life on
the net but a rich and nurturing life on the net (this vision also
incorporates the counter-position: we cannot live much of a
life off the net). If we accept consciously or unconsciously that
the net is life, we accept that it is natural and organic. It is the
fertile ground on which we can grow a life with others in our
virtual communities.

What is living and what is not is up for grabs in this elec-   10
tronic circus. First of all, you don't have to look hard to find
tiny manifestations of the science fiction dreams of the human-
like machine. If you start examining any number of magazines
about science and technology, you can't swing a dead (computer)

mouse without hitting an article about something new in biotechnology and artificial intelligence. Scientists at DuPont, for example, are creating silicon devices that simulate brain functions in increasingly complex ways. As these silicon-based machines evolve, they will work more like organic brains and less like standard digital computers. They will have different capabilities, just as digital machines have capabilities that organic brains don't have. "They will be less like the idiots that digital boxes are now," says Michael Gruber, "utterly dependent on flawless programming, and more like dogs: trainable, but with an inherent set of instincts and abilities, herding our processes and reactions and systems like a border collie runs a flock of sheep." At the Mobile Robot Lab at the Massachusetts Institute of Technology, Rodney Brooks and his team have developed a variety of robots that operate not by a preprogrammed plan but by adapting their capabilities to their surroundings. They read the environment and react accordingly. In short, they learn.[2]

11   But these machines with seemingly lifelike intelligences pale in comparison to the sophisticated cyborgian organism, the complex human-machine hybrid, already operating within our midst. It has been given different names—I refer to it as the net, while others call it the medianet (Kroker and Weinstein), information (Barlow), the datasphere (Douglas Rushkoff)—but these names refer to the same vast, amorphous, ever changing, immortal being with an unambiguous social agenda: free the individual. Whereas the robotic devices I described may be able to perform tasks that empower humans in a variety of ways, the net—according to many technotopists—is an organic, political entity. It votes libertarian every time.

12   This libertarian life force can best be illustrated by first examining the Internet. In its current form the Internet is designed to operate as a decentralized network, with multiple pathways along which information can flow. The genesis of this system is described in Howard Rheingold's brief history of the original core of the Internet, the U.S. Defense Department's ARPANET, which was designed so that if any part of the network was disabled (in a nuclear attack), the rest of the network could function and all network traffic could simply be rerouted. There would be no central command. This decentralized web appears organic to observers like Rheingold: "Information can take so many alternative routes when one of the nodes of the network is removed that the Net is almost immortally flexible. It is this flexibility that CMC telecom pioneer John Gilmore referred to when he said, 'The Net interprets censorship as damage and routes around it.' "[3]

The Internet thus appears immortal. If you choke off one tendril, information can react and reach its destination via another route.

The question here is one of agency: Who or what can initiate 13 and carry out actions? I considered this question after reading an article by John Perry Barlow in *Wired* magazine—a lengthy piece that attempted to redefine intellectual property in the digital age. I liked Barlow's argument because its premise was that a unit of information is not an objective entity with a fixed meaning that can be transferred from one decoder to another; rather, meaning-making is a collaborative process of negotiation in which participants interpret and construct the meanings of the unit of information in a myriad of ways. Information is a verb, not a noun.[4] What I did not like was that Barlow, while arguing that information is an action and not an entity, still spoke of information as an objective thing throughout the article.

I wrote him a note via e-mail (which he later forwarded to 14 the magazine and which was printed in the June 1994 issue). I told him that I agreed with his overall position but thought that his piece suffered from a "debilitating metaphor":

> Throughout your argument you objectify information while you simultaneously try to undermine that objectification. That is, you argue effectively that information is not a thing but a process/relationship/verb; however, you cast information as a thing throughout the piece.
>
> I think the danger in how you characterize information is this: Many people are utterly convinced that information is a thing—a commodity that can be transferred—and they base their actions on this flimsy foundation. . . . While you argue against the concept of information transfer, you actually argue against yourself by continually casting information as an agent, not an action. Information doesn't want to be free, informers do. The meanings are rhetorical in nature: They are negotiated, they are constantly constructed and reconstructed during their interactions among participants in the communicative acts. By saying things like "information wants to change" etc., you give agency to the code—even though your purpose is just the opposite.[5]

My point is simply that the only agents in communication are humans. Things don't communicate; individuals interpret things and give them meaning.

15   Barlow's response reveals a very different position. He wrote:

> It's a problem of my personal semantics. I call a lot of non-thingish things things, like, to use a big one, this Thing Called Love. Language, or at least English, is limited in its ability to describe the nonspecific action or state of being.
>
> Actually, since I believe information is a life form, there are many cases where information may be seen to act upon . . . uh . . . things.[6]

Ah, so information does indeed want to be free. In Barlow's view, the "thing" has agency, and the net is an organic entity pulsating with information that seeks its own expression and cannot be censored.

16   But that's not all. According to Douglas Rushkoff, the net is not only alive but has a variety of agendas. Rushkoff describes the datasphere, an entity like Kroker and Weinstein's medianet, which encompasses all electronic communication networks from the vestiges of the traditional mass media to the distributed connectivity of the Internet and of facsimile and telephony technologies. You can recognize the datasphere as the life force it is, according to Rushkoff, if you've grown up after its ascendancy in the past two or three decades. Those who have "don't just receive and digest media. They manipulate it. They play with it. The media is not a mirror—it is an 'other.' They are in a living relationship with it."[7] And this relationship makes possible a symbiotic effort to liberate people and ideas in the face of the monolithic controls over public expression throughout the world.

17   While most people (those older than about age thirty) who are critical of mass-communication technologies argue that these technologies are used by centers of power to further the status quo, younger people who share the life force with the net, states Rushkoff, have appropriated its reach to unleash "media viruses" to fight the power: "Those who grew up after the development of the datasphere see the media very differently. More than a set of tools, the media is an entity unto itself that must be reckoned with on its own terms. The initiators of media viruses depend on a very optimistic vision of how the web of media nodes can serve to foster new cultural growth. Rather than stunting our natural development by amputating our limbs and numbing our senses, the media can accelerate evolution. The activists . . . believe the media can extend the human, or even the planetary spirit."[8]

Citing the work of Noam Chomsky and others, Rushkoff argues that the datasphere is breaking the hold of the public relations era, the era of one-way mass communication. In the PR era, a few messages came from a few sources, and those messages were geared to maintain the current power structure. Now the datasphere enables interactivity; it fragments information providers. Viruses within the datasphere challenge authority and provide voice to individuals. And those in opposition, those like myself, do not understand the symbiosis of humans and the datasphere. As long as we don't look at the new communication technologies as part of our nature, we can never see them as anything but the enemy of the natural. In Rushkoff's view our relationship with the net is part of what makes us human; it is our natural world. Our place is in any number of virtual communities of interest. The new geography—unbound by the nasty, dull, exclusionary necessities of physical space—is an unending and liberating virtual landscape where we can take social relations and collectives to a new level.[9]

Some technotopists who believe this argument will admit that virtuality alone cannot sustain a culture, society, or community. But what they do seem to argue is that the foundation for culture, society, or community is our symbiosis with virtualizing technologies. In *The Virtual Community,* for example, Howard Rheingold tells stories about people who develop emotional attachments by communicating electronically with each other in the parenting forum on the WELL, a computer conferencing system. Some of the most compelling stories involve people who became acquainted online and who go to great lengths to support each other in times of crisis—just as neighbors should in the ideal neighborhood. Rheingold uses these stories to anticipate his critics:

> Many people are alarmed by the very idea of a virtual community, fearing that it is another step in the wrong direction, substituting more technological ersatz for yet another natural resource or human freedom. These critics often voice their sadness at what people have been reduced to doing in a civilization that worships technology, decrying the circumstances that lead some people into such pathetically disconnected lives that they prefer to find their companions on the other side of a computer screen. There is a seed of truth in this fear, for virtual communities require more than words on a screen at some point if they intend to be other than ersatz.[10]

18

19

20   His tales of online relationships blossoming into offline human interaction and support apparently validate the foundation that is the online community. But if you read Rheingold's stories carefully, you begin to realize that nearly all the participants share a geographic place—a diverse place, undoubtedly, but a place nonetheless: the Bay Area around San Francisco. It is out of this foundation that so-called virtual relationships can grow into something that may not capture but may at least approach real community. It is out of the face-to-face WELL picnics at a public park that simple text on a screen begins to develop into something more than just the image of community.

21   Rheingold and Rushkoff see the net as a means for social empowerment. I share their goal but fear that both place their faith in a shadow whose images are so lifelike that they appear real. I fear that the continual virtualization of community reveals that geophysical community is dying. As we invest ourselves in the simulation, the simulated phenomena disappear.[11]

22   The technotopists imbue the net, medianet, datasphere— whatever you want to call it—with agency. They believe that interacting with it is sustaining. They are convinced that it is possible to live within it. Humans lose agency, they say, and the medianet gains it.

23   I agree that the media virus enables a counterculture. The question is, counter to what? The culture is wholly maintained within the datasphere; nothing else exists. The counterculture that the media virus represents is thus not radical. To place your faith in the empowerment of the datasphere is a quintessentially conservative act: don't worry, be happy; surrender to the power of the datasphere. The most radical and most difficult act would be to resist that power.

24   But resistance is difficult, because social forces push us to lead virtualized lives. Many of the proponents of virtualization seem to fall into one of two camps. In one camp are those futurists and technotopian visionaries who argue that our destiny is to move from the material world to virtuality, that to examine our evolution is to see the movement away from the body and toward the intellect. To these people, being online is an end in itself; virtuality ultimately must become immersive, thereby making virtual community our goal.

25   Far less grandiose in vision are those of the other camp, who see the continuing virtualization of everyday life as a way to improve our material lives. Virtuality is a tool to help us solve social, psychological, economic, and environmental problems. To these people, our offline lives define our selves, and our goal is to participate in healthy geophysical communities.

If we speak of a healthy community, we cannot be speaking of a community that is merely human. We are talking about a neighborhood of humans in a place, plus the place itself: its soil, its water, its air, and all the families and tribes of the nonhuman creatures that belong to it. If the place is well preserved, if its entire membership, natural and human, is present in it, and if the human economy is in practical harmony with the nature of the place, then the community is healthy.... A healthy community is sustainable; it is, within reasonable limits, self-sufficient and, within reasonable limits, self-determined—that is, free of tyranny.[12]

It is not unusual to read analyses of our post-industrial, information-infused, media- and image-saturated, transitionary times telling us that traditional communities are irrelevant, endangered, or impotent in the face of sweeping economic and social change.[13] One such vision, put forth by Peter Drucker, represents a commonly held view of the present and near future. In a broad analysis of what he describes as the most pervasive cultural change in history—the rise of the "knowledge society"—Drucker makes it clear that the "old community" is dead. Unfortunately, the social needs fulfilled by those old communities remain.[14]   26

The knowledge society is one in which the driving economic force is the development and application of new knowledge. In such an economy—one fueled by education and technology—the most important resource is not cheap labor, natural resources, or political will; it is the ability to develop and maintain a culture of learning. Unlike industrial economies, a knowledge society will be able to survive global competition only by providing its members with lifelong education so that they may create and use knowledge productively. "The acquisition and distribution of formal knowledge may come to occupy the place in the politics of the knowledge society which the acquisition and distribution of property and income have occupied in our politics over the two or three centuries that we have come to call the Age of Capitalism" (66). There will be less and less need for individuals to obtain prescribed schooling during a set period (for example, from ages seven to twenty-one). Instead, in order to succeed, individuals will become lifelong students.   27

Such a scenario depicts communication technologies as the response to a need for knowledge. New communication technologies, remember, can deliver anything, anywhere, anytime (or so we are told). Because knowledge will be widely available,   28 competition among knowledge creators, distributors, and users will increase dramatically. "The knowledge society will inevitably become far more competitive than any society we have yet known—for the simple reason that with knowledge being universally accessible, there will be no excuses for nonperformance. There will be no 'poor' countries. There will only be ignorant countries" (68). And the same applies for entities smaller than countries. Industries, corporations, and individuals will all succeed or fail based on their ability to manipulate knowledge.

29   At the same time, one of the prerequisites for success in this hypercompetitive environment is constant change, the condition for continual social transience:

> People no longer stay where they were born, either in terms of geography or in terms of social position and status. By definition, a knowledge society is a society of mobility. And all of the social functions of the old communities, whether performed well or poorly (and most were performed very poorly indeed), presupposed that the individual and the family would stay put. But the essence of a knowledge society is mobility in terms of where one lives, mobility in terms of what one does, mobility in terms of one's affiliations. People no longer have roots. People no longer have a neighborhood that controls what their home is like, what they do, and, indeed, what their problems are allowed to be. (74)

30   The old community may be gone, but our need for the kinds of protection and healing available in the old community has not disappeared. The problems that beset individuals and families—crime, domestic violence, substance abuse, divorce, and so on—will persist and, in an increasingly competitive society like the knowledge meritocracy Drucker describes, will probably intensify. The public sector will not be able to deal with those problems; witness the failures of the welfare state. Nor is the private sector appropriately equipped to handle the "social tasks" of the knowledge society: "In fact, practically all these tasks—whether education or health care; the anomies and diseases of a developed and, especially, a rich society, such as alcohol and drug abuse; or the problems of incompetence and irresponsibility such as those of the underclass in the American city—lie outside the employing institution" (72).

31   The answer, according to Drucker, lies in the middle ground between the public and private sector. The services and opportunities of the "social sector" must fill the void. "The old communities—family, village, parish, and so on—have all but

disappeared in the knowledge society," says Drucker. "Their place has largely been taken by the new unit of social integration, the organization. Where community was fate, organization is voluntary membership. Where community claimed the entire person, organization is a means to a person's end, a tool" (76). The social sector consists primarily of volunteer-based, nonprofit enterprises, from churches to charitable organizations. Through such organizations, individuals can both help and be helped, in a reciprocal spiral that, in Drucker's view, can "create citizenship" and re-create *a sense* of community. That is, only through the social sector—a salve to the socially dysfunctional—can individuals take part in the process of maintaining a community. "Modern society and modern policy have become so big and complex that citizenship—that is, responsible participation—is no longer possible. All we can do as citizens is to vote once every few years and to pay taxes all the time" (76). Unless, of course, we become engaged in the work of the social sector.

I urge you to feel as sad about this vision as I do. Have we   32
devolved so far that the only way to participate in healing social wounds, creating social connections, and maintaining social bonds is by joining bureaucracies and institutions? No matter how benevolent or socially and spiritually conscious, they are still bureaucracies and institutions. Where is the future of interpersonal bonding unmediated by systems? Where is the future of random, unexpected, unintended, but inevitable community-building of individuals of unlike mind and appearances?

I'm afraid Drucker's social sector—even in its most efficient   33
and grand state—is a paltry substitute for what is lost when geophysical community disappears. The organizations in a social sector unbound by community may serve as important nodes in a social service network, but they are like nodes without the connecting strands. However closely linked one organization is to another, they still float in the ether, islands of service and good intentions. Factor into this mix the pull of the net away from geographic ties and toward the virtual, and you have at best a surrogate community atop the spindly legs of procedural bureaucracies.

So while Drucker correctly recognizes the inadequacy of a   34
society built on the twin towers of the public and private sectors, I disagree that a third support can be constructed to fill the void. Instead, the private and public sectors must be encompassed by the normal functionings of placed communities.

What we are left with is a politics of opposition between, on   35
one hand, proponents of individual freedom and, on the other,

bureaucracies that regulate individual actions. The missing middle ground cannot arise without a collectivity of individuals committed to inhabiting a place and to enduring and working with each other to improve the condition of everyone in that place. "We have largely lost the sense that our capacity to live well in a place might depend upon our ability to relate to neighbors (especially neighbors with a different life-style) on the basis of shared habits of behavior" (79). We have come to accept that committing to a place is an expression of personal choice and personal taste. Or, quite often, it is forced on us either by our need to find work or by our need to live with or near another person.

36   I have a couple of friends who want to move away from northern New York. Our north country is a vast stretch of farms, rolling hills, and rivers dropping out of the Adirondacks to the south and flowing into the great St. Lawrence River to the north. It is poor, cold, and, to many observers, desolate. My friends tell me that it can no longer sustain them. One is unhappy with her job and says, like many who talk about leaving, that she wants to live somewhere warmer. My other friend, however, loves the cold and the snow but wants to move east of the big lake, Champlain, and settle in Vermont. He believes that his business—often on the brink of bankruptcy here—has a better chance over there. But that is only part of the issue. Everything, he tells me, is better over there: the economy, the social life, the environment. People take better care of their homes and their businesses. They care more about their culture; they are less provincial; they aren't always suspicious of change and have achieved a balance between accepting the progressive and holding on to traditions. Vermont, he says, is more attuned to individual initiative. Simply put, there's just a different ethic over there.

37   I listen to these complaints and say, "Well, yeah, you're right. Life in the north country can be difficult . . . " At this point I can't really think of much to say besides "but I want to stay." I'll admit I came here to take a job—but I also came here because I thought it might be a place to commit to. I'm willing to inhabit a place with faults, a place that is difficult to live in, a place where I cannot satisfy all my wants and needs. I am willing to do this for the sake of becoming part of a community.

38   My friend who wants to move to Vermont wants to commit to that place. That is good. I have been in his position; I've given up on a place and moved away from people I was close to. Nonetheless, I am disheartened when I hear him talk about moving. It is such a long process to develop a friendship; I in-

vest so much time and effort, and the older I get, the harder it is to stay in touch with remote friends and family members. No amount of telephone conversations and e-mail can re-create the experience of sharing daily life. So when I hear people close to me talk of leaving, part of me wants to dispense with them immediately and go nurture other local relationships. Of course, I cannot do this; one doesn't eliminate emotional ties so coldly. No, I act as if I believe that after my friends or family members move, we can maintain our relationships by keeping in touch via technology. But we cannot really maintain those relationships, because over time the foundation for our relationship, the social and geographic ties of a common place, fades.

Sometimes I find myself assessing others on the basis of their interests in staying here. This is probably a foolish criterion. "The longing to become an inhabitant rather than a drifter," says Scott Russell Sanders, "sets me against the current of my culture, which nudges everyone into motion. Newton taught us that a body at rest tends to stay at rest, unless acted on by an outside force. We are acted on ceaselessly by outside forces—advertising, movies, magazines, speeches—and also by the inner force of biology."[15]

I find myself in the maddening position of recognizing the ever-increasing artificial mediation of the natural world while remaining committed to breaking down that mediation to regain a sense of the here and now. I'm seeking what Albert Borgmann describes in *Crossing the Postmodern Divide* as postmodern realism, the necessary response to our hypermediated condition: "Having left modernism behind us, we now have to decide whether to proceed on the endless and joyless plain of hypermodernism or to cross over to another and more real world. For this country in particular, the latter task comes to settling down in the land that has come to be ours, to give up the restless search for a hyperreal elsewhere, and to come to terms with nature and tradition in a patient and vigorous way." As we are on the brink of surrendering to the most powerful mediation engines of all, we must resist the lure of the hyperreal. And if we must become wired, we must turn that telepresence toward, as Borgmann describes it, the "focal realities" of the local places we inhabit.[16]

One day I received an e-mail message directed to all the members of an electronic forum—a "list"—devoted to discussing community computer networks. The writer described a murder that had occurred in her community: a child had been shot and killed by another child. She wondered what those of us interested in community networks had to say about that. Two responses follow.

39

40

41

From: MILTON LOPES <MLOPES@UGA.CC.UGA.EDU>
Subject: Re: A shooting in the community . . . or how do we
stop the hemorrhage
X-To: "Communet: Community and Civic Network Discussion
List" communet@elk.uvm.edu

42 Teenage violence is a subject that needs to be discussed on a
national forum. It involves no less than our future as a nation.
If this is not the place to discuss it, where is the place? I recently facilitated a community meeting following the senseless
shooting of two students by a fellow student who they had earlier been harassing. The community was in an uproar.
Attending were school officials, police officers, community
leaders, parents, and youth. The youth made more sense than
any of the other groups. They simply called for teachers who
cared, parents who spent some time with them, complete families, the teaching of and practice of morals, in the marketplace, at home, in school, in government. They looked at us
adults, and found us long on verbiage, but short on example. I
have facilitated other meetings in which adult posturing was
simply no answer to the pleas of the children. We have abandoned the basic principles which for most of us were taught by
our elders. We are too busy consuming, and selling, and living
for the moment. Listen to the children. I hope your grief finds
resonance with this entire list.

Milton E. Lopes
From: Tres English <tenglish@WEST.CSCWC.PIMA.EDU>
Subject: Making more time (Was: A shooting in the commu-
nity . . .)

[After quoting from the preceding message, English added the
following.]

43 I have concluded that the real reason for this accelerating
breakup of our society are those things which physically break
us up on a day-to-day, moment-to-moment basis. That is the
road system, TV, financial system, etc. that have the effect of
requiring us to spend more and more *time* separated from
family and neighbors.
   It is not quality time that matters. It is simply time.
   I have a question for participants in this list.
   How can we structure a community computer network so
that we are able to recreate more stable geographic communities where people have more time to spend with each other,
both as families and as neighborhoods?

I don't think there is a solution to kids killing each other, and all the rest, unless we can recreate the foundations of a stable society—the continuing, unplanned interactions between the same people for a long period of time.

> Tres English.
> Tenglish@west.cscwc.pima.edu

A community is bound by place, which always includes complex social and environmental necessities. It is not something you can easily join. You can't subscribe to a community as you subscribe to a discussion group on the net. It must be lived. It is entwined, contradictory, and involves all our senses. It involves the "continuing, unplanned interactions between the same people for a long period of time." Unfortunately, communities across the nation are being undermined and destroyed by a variety of forces. Global computer networks like the Internet, for example, represent a step in the continual virtualization of human relations. The hope that the incredible powers of global computer networks can create new virtual communities, more useful and healthier than the old geographic ones, is thus misplaced. The net seduces us and further removes us from our localities—unless we take charge of it with specific, community-based, local agendas. These agendas are currently under development in many communities through the community network movement. If we do not, as communities, as a society, support this movement, we risk the further disappearance of local communities within globalized virtual collectives of alienated and entertained individuals.

Notes

1. Mitchell, William J., *City of Bits: Space, Place, and the Infobahn* (Cambridge: MIT Press, 1995), 29–30. For another extensive discussion of our cyborgian destiny see Stone, Allucquere Rosanne, *The War of Desire and Technology at the Close of the Mechanical Age* (Cambridge: MIT Press, 1995).
2. Gruber, Michael, "Neurobotics," *Wired* 2.10 (October 1994): 111; on Brooks and his team see Freedman, David H., "Bringing Up RoboBaby," *Wired* 2.12 (December 1994): 74. (December 1994): 74.
3. Rheingold, Howard, *The Virtual Community: Homesteading on the Electronic Frontier* (Reading, Mass.: Addison-Wesley, 1993), 7.
4. Barlow, John Perry, "The Economy of Ideas," *Wired* 2.03 (March 1994): 84; Doheny-Farina, Stephen, letter to "Rants and Raves," *Wired* 2.06 (June 1994): 22.

5. I make this argument in detail in Doheny-Farina, Stephen, *Rhetoric, Innovation, Technology: Case Studies of Technical Communication in Technology Transfers* (Cambridge: MIT Press, 1992).

6. Barlow, John Perry, response to Stephen Doheny-Farina, "Rants and Raves," *Wired* 2.06 (June 1994): 22.

7. Rushkoff, Douglas, *Media Virus* (New York: Ballantine Books, 1994), 31.

8. Rushkoff, 21.

9. Rushkoff, 218. Rushkoff points out that critics like Kroker were born too early to understand the medianet. "Kroker's brilliant but misguided analysis is typical of his generation of philosophers who, growing up before the advent of mass media, have only the tools to observe media but not the language or translation skills to partake in it.... the inferences he draws totally ignore the nature of the new and growing relationship between our lives and our media. As long as we view media, or technology for that matter, as something separate from ourselves—something unnatural—we will always see it as the enemy to the natural unfolding of our culture."

10. Rheingold, 23.

11. Baudrillard, Jean, "Simulacra and Simulations," in *Selected Writings*, ed. Mark Poster (Stanford: Stanford University Press, 1988), 166–184. Virtual community is like Disneyland, and placed communities, like America: "Disneyland is there to conceal the fact that it is the 'real' country, all of 'real' America, which *is* Disneyland.... Disneyland is presented as imaginary in order to make us believe that the rest is real, when in fact all of Los Angeles and the America surrounding it are no longer real, but of the order of the hyperreal and of simulation. It is no longer a question of a false representation of reality ... but of concealing the fact that the real is no longer real" (172).

12. Berry, Wendell, *Sex, Economy, Freedom, and Community* (New York: Pantheon Books, 1993), 14–15.

13. For example, the 150th anniversary issue of the *Economist* (January 1994).

14. Drucker, Peter, "The Age of Social Transformation," *Atlantic Monthly* 274, no. 5 (November 1994): 53–80. All quotations in the following discussion of Drucker's views are from this article.

15. Sanders, Scott Russell, *Staying Put: Making a Home in a Restless World* (Boston: Beacon Press, 1993), 117.

16. Borgmann, Albert, *Crossing the Postmodern Divide* (Chicago: University of Chicago Press, 1992), 126.

David Horsey

BROKEN PROMISES OF THE COMPUTER AGE

David Horsey is an editorial cartoonist for the Seattle Post-Intelligencer. *He produced this cartoon in November 1997; it was published not only in Seattle but also in many other newspapers across the country.*

PART I

Page 1: Doug Menuez/Getty Images.

Page 19: Bob Daemmrich/The Image Works.

PART II

PART V

PART VI

PART VII